KU-450-372

Leeds Metropolitan University
17 0271029 6

BUSINESS MARKETING MANAGEMENT

a strategic view of industrial and organizational markets

SIXTH EDITION

BUSINESS MARKETING MANAGEMENT

a strategic view of industrial and organizational markets

SIXTH EDITION

MICHAEL D. HUTT
Arizona State University

THOMAS W. SPEH
Miami University

THE DRYDEN PRESS
Harcourt Brace College Publishers

Fort Worth Philadelphia San Diego New York Orlando Austin San Antonio
Toronto Montreal London Sydney Tokyo

Publisher: George Provol
Acquisitions Editor: Bill Schoof
Product Manager: Lisé Johnson
Developmental Editor: Traci Keller
Project Editor: Jim Patterson
Art Director: Burl Dean Sloan
Production Manager: Lois West
Electronic Publishing Coordinator: Kathi Embry

ISBN: 0-03-020633-2
Library of Congress Catalog Card Number: 97-65088

Cover Illustration: Robert Neubecker

Address for orders:
The Dryden Press
6277 Sea Harbor Drive
Orlando, FL 32887-6777
1-800-782-4479

Address for editorial correspondence:
The Dryden Press
301 Commerce Street, Suite 3700
Fort Worth, TX 76102

Website address:
http://www.hbcollege.com

Printed in the United States of America

9 0 1 2 3 4 5 **016** 9 8 7 6 5

To Rita
and
To Michele, Scott, Michael, and Betsy

THE DRYDEN PRESS SERIES IN MARKETING

Assael
Marketing

Avila, Williams, Ingram, and LaForge
The Professional Selling Skills Workbook

Bateson
Managing Services Marketing: Text and Readings
Third Edition

Blackwell, Blackwell, and Talarzyk
Contemporary Cases in Consumer Behavior
Fourth Edition

Boone and Kurtz
Contemporary Marketing Wired
Ninth Edition

Churchill
Basic Marketing Research
Third Edition

Churchill
Marketing Research: Methodological Foundations
Sixth Edition

Czinkota and Ronkainen
Global Marketing

Czinkota and Ronkainen
International Marketing
Fifth Edition

Czinkota and Ronkainen
International Marketing Strategy: Environmental Assessment and Entry Strategies

Dickson
Marketing Management
Second Edition

Engel, Blackwell, and Miniard
Consumer Behavior
Eighth Edition

Futrell
Sales Management: Teamwork, Leadership, and Technology
Fifth Edition

Grover
Theory & Simulation of Market-Focused Management

Ghosh
Retail Management
Second Edition

Hassan and Blackwell
Global Marketing: Managerial Dimensions and Cases

Hoffman/Bateson
Essentials of Services Marketing

Hutt and Speh
Business Marketing Management: A Strategic View of Industrial and Organizational Markets
Sixth Edition

Ingram, LaForge, and Schwepker
Sales Management: Analysis and Decision Making
Third Edition

Lewison
Marketing Management: An Overview

Lindgren and Shimp
Marketing: An Interactive Learning System

Krugman, Reid, Dunn, and Barban
Advertising: Its Role in Modern Marketing
Eighth Edition

Oberhaus, Ratliffe, and Stauble
Professional Selling: A Relationship Process
Second Edition

Parente, Vanden Bergh, Barban, and Marra
Advertising Campaign Strategy: A Guide to Marketing Communication Plans

Rosenbloom
Marketing Channels: A Management View
Fifth Edition

Sandburg
Discovering Your Marketing Career CD-ROM

Schaffer
Applying Marketing Principles Software

Schellinck and Maddox
Marketing Research: A Computer-Assisted Approach

Schnaars
MICROSIM

Schuster and Copeland
Global Business: Planning for Sales and Negotiations

Shimp
Advertising, Promotion, and Supplemental Aspects of Integrated Marketing Communications
Fourth Edition

Talarzyk
Cases and Exercises in Marketing

Terpstra and Sarathy
International Marketing
Seventh Edition

Weitz and Wensley
Readings in Strategic Marketing Analysis, Planning, and Implementation

Zikmund
Exploring Marketing Research
Sixth Edition

Harcourt Brace College Outline Series

Peterson
Principles of Marketing

Preface

Special challenges and opportunities confront the marketer who intends to serve the needs of organizations rather than households. Commercial enterprises, institutions, and all levels of government constitute a lucrative and complex market worthy of separate analysis. A growing number of collegiate schools of business in the United States, Canada, and Europe have added industrial or business marketing to their curricula. In addition, a large and growing network of scholars in the United States and Europe is actively engaged in research to advance theory and practice in the business marketing field. Both the breadth and quality of this research has increased markedly during the past decade.

The rising importance of the field can be demonstrated by several factors. First, because more than half of all business school graduates enter firms that compete in business markets, a comprehensive treatment of business marketing management appears to be particularly appropriate. The business marketing course provides an ideal platform to deepen a student's knowledge of the competitive realities of the global marketplace, relationship management, cross-functional decision-making processes, supply chain management, product quality, and related areas. Such core content areas strike a responsive chord with corporate recruiters and squarely address key educational priorities established by the American Assembly of Collegiate Schools of Business (AACSB). Second, the business marketing course provides a perfect vehicle for examining the special features of high-technology markets and for isolating the unique challenges that confront the marketing strategist in this arena. High-tech markets represent a rapidly growing and dynamic sector of the world economy and a fiercely competitive global battleground, but yet, often receive only modest attention in the traditional marketing curriculum. Third, the Institute for the Study of Business Markets (ISBM) at Pennsylvania State University has provided important impetus to research in the area. ISBM has become a major information resource for researchers and practitioners and has assumed an active role in stimulating and supporting research on substantive business marketing issues.

Three objectives guided the development of this edition:

1. *To highlight the similarities between consumer goods and business-to-business marketing and to explore the points of departure in depth.* Particular attention is given to market analysis, organizational buying behavior, relationship management, and the ensuing adjustments required in the marketing strategy elements used to reach organizational customers.

2. *To present a managerial rather than a descriptive treatment of business marketing.* Whereas some descriptive material is required to convey the dynamic nature of the business marketing environment, the relevance of the material is linked to business marketing management decision making.

3. *To integrate the growing body of literature into an operational treatment of business marketing management.* In this text, relevant work is drawn from organizational buying behavior, procurement, organizational behavior, logistics, strategic management, and the behavioral sciences, as well as from specialized studies of business marketing strategy components.

The book is structured to provide a complete and timely treatment of business marketing while minimizing the degree of overlap with other courses in the marketing curriculum. A basic marketing principles course (or relevant managerial experience) provides the needed background for this text.

New To This Edition

Although the basic objectives, approach, and style of the first five editions have been maintained, several changes and additions have been made that reflect both the growing body of literature and the emerging trends in business marketing practice. Specifically, the following distinctive features are incorporated into the sixth edition:

- A streamlined and richly illustrated discussion of organizational buying behavior
- A new chapter, "Relationship Strategies for Business Markets"
- A timely treatment of strategy formulation in high-technology industries
- New coverage of the technology adoption life cycle and marketing strategies for high-technology products
- New and expanded coverage of supply chain management; strategic alliances; target costing; product quality and value; and Internet strategies
- Extensive coverage of new product and service development for business markets
- An operational treatment of the marketing control process that integrates the central themes of the volume
- Contemporary business marketing strategies and challenges illustrated with three types of vignettes: "Inside Business Marketing," "Ethical Business Marketing," and—new to this edition— "Managing in the 21st Century."

Organization of the Sixth Edition

The needs and interests of the reader provided the focus in the development of this volume. The authors' goal is to present a clear, timely, and interesting examination of business marketing management. To this end, each chapter provides an overview, highlights key concepts, and includes several carefully chosen examples of contemporary business marketing practice as well as a cogent summary and a set of provocative discussion questions.

The book is divided into six parts with a total of 18 chapters. Part I introduces the distinguishing features of the business marketing environment. Careful examination is given to each of the major types of customers that constitute the business market. Organizational buying behavior and relationship management establish the theme of Part II, in which the many forces encircling the organizational buying process are explored in depth. This edition has been thoroughly updated to incorporate the substantial amount of research that has been conducted in this area since the fifth edition was published.

After this important background is established for understanding buyer–seller relationships, Part III centers on the intelligence function and on the techniques that can be employed in assessing market opportunities. Chapter–length attention is given to the topics of business marketing intelligence, market segmentation, and market potential and sales forecasting. This edition also provides expanded treatment of international market analysis.

Part IV centers on the planning process and on designing marketing strategy for business markets. Recent work drawn from the strategic management and strategic marketing areas provides the foundation for this section. This edition provides expanded treatment to the challenges and enticing opportunities that confront the strategist in high-technology industries. Special emphasis is given to competitive analysis and to the interfacing of marketing with other key functional areas such as manufacturing, research and development, and customer service. This functionally integrated planning perspective serves as a focal point in the analysis of the strategy development process. Here at the core of the volume, a separate chapter provides an integrated treatment of strategy formulation for the international market arena. Next, each component of the marketing mix is examined from a business marketing perspective. Adding further depth to this core section are the chapters on managing product innovation and managing services for business markets.

Part V examines techniques for evaluating business marketing strategy and performance. It provides a compact treatment of marketing control systems and presents an organizing framework for marketing profitability analysis. Special attention is given to the critical area of strategy implementation in the business marketing environment. Part VI includes a collection of cases tailored to the business marketing environment.

Cases

Part VI includes 17 cases, 8 of which are new to this edition. These cases, of varying lengths, isolate one or more business marketing problems. Included among the new selections for this edition are two cases that raise provocative issues and illustrate the best practices of leading-edge firms: Hewlett-Packard and PeopleSoft. Other cases new to this edition provide students with a variety of business marketing strategy applications. A *Case Planning Guide*, which keys the cases to relevant text chapters, provides an organizing structure for Part VI.

Teaching Package

A comprehensive and thoroughly updated *Instructor's Manual, Test Bank, and Transparency Masters* are available to include suggestions for course design and support materials for teaching each chapter. Guidelines are provided for end-of-chapter discussion questions, and suggestions are provided for case use and analysis. The *Instructor's Manual* for the sixth edition also provides a list of candidate readings especially suited to the business marketing course and a series of cooperative learning exercises to spark in-class involvement and discussion. Several hundred objective test questions are found in the manual, and a comprehensive set of essay questions is included to allow instructors to tailor exams to their particular needs. A total of 62 transparency masters are available.

A *computerized test bank* for DOS, Macintosh, and Windows is also available with this edition.

A new marketing business-to-business web site on the Internet enhances the way business-to-business marketing can be taught. The web site will provide the latest information about "what's new" and "what's cool" in marketing business-to-business. Links to other related sites and much more are planned for the site.

The Dryden Press will provide complimentary supplements or supplement packages to those adopters qualified under our adoption policy. Please contact your local sales representative to learn how you may qualify. If as an adopter or potential user you receive supplements you do not need, please return them to your sales representative or send them to:

Attn: Returns Department
Troy Warehouse
465 South Lincoln Drive
Troy, MO 63379

Acknowledgments

The development of a textbook draws upon the contributions of many individuals. First, we would like to thank our students and former students at Arizona State University, Miami University, the University of Alabama, and the University of Vermont. They provided important input and feedback when selected concepts or chapters were class-tested. We would also like to thank our colleagues at each of these institutions for their assistance and support.

Second, we express our gratitude to several distinguished colleagues who carefully reviewed the manuscript at various stages of development and provided incisive comments and valuable suggestions that improved the sixth edition. They include: Jon M. Hawes, *University of Akron;* J. David Lichtenthal, *Baruch College;* Richard E. Plank, *Western Michigan University;* and Elizabeth Wilson Woodside, *Louisiana State University.*

We would also like to express our continuing appreciation to others who provided important suggestions that helped shape earlier editions: Paul F. Anderson,

Pennsylvania State University; Joseph A. Bellizzi, *Arizona State University–West Campus*; Paul D. Boughton, *Saint Louis University*; Michael R. Czinkota, *Georgetown University*; S. Altan Erdem, *University of Houston–Clear Lake*; Srinath Gopalakrishna, *University of Missouri, Columbia*; Paris A. Gunther, *University of Cincinnati*; Jon M. Hawes, *University of Akron*; Jay L. Laughlin, *Kansas State University*; Gary L. Lilien, *Pennsylvania State University*; Lindsay N. Meredith, *Simon Fraser University*; Bernard A. Rausch, *Illinois Institute of Technology*; David A. Reid, *The University of Toledo*; Paul A. Roobol, *Western Michigan University*; James F. Wolter, *Grand Valley State University*; Lauren K. Wright, *California State University–Chico*; and John M. Zerio, *American Graduate School of International Management*.

Third, we would like to thank the Institute for the Study of Business Markets at Pennsylvania State University for giving us access to their rich working paper series.

A number of business marketing practitioners, including several participants in past management development seminars, provided valuable suggestions and interesting examples. We are especially indebted to Jeffrey A. Coopersmith, *Directel, Inc.*; Gerry Daley, *The Black-Clawson Company, Shartle-Pandia Division*; Patrick W. Fitzgerald, *Cincinnati Electric Equipment Company*; Rod O'Connor, *Motorola, Inc., Government Electronics Group*; Edward Sauer, *Industrial Product Division, Procter & Gamble*; and Cap Stubbs, *Raychem Corporation*.

The talented staff of The Dryden Press displayed a high level of enthusiasm and deserves special praise for their contributions in shaping this edition. In particular, Bill Schoof provided valuable advice and direction for this edition. In turn, our developmental editor, Traci Keller, kept us on schedule and added spirit to the process; and our project editor, Jim Patterson, provided a steady hand and superb production assistance. We also want to extend our thanks to others at Dryden who contributed their special talents to this edition, including Burl Sloan, art director; Lois West, production manager; Lisé Johnson, product manager; and electronic publishing coordinator Kathi Embry.

Finally, but most importantly, our overriding debt is to our wives, Rita and Michele, whose encouragement, understanding, and expertise were vital to the completion of this edition. Their involvement and dedication are deeply appreciated.

Michael D. Hutt
Thomas W. Speh
September 1997

About the Authors

Michael D. Hutt, (Ph.D., Michigan State University) is the Earl and Gladys Davis Distinguished Professor of Marketing at Arizona State University. He has also held faculty positions at Miami University (Ohio) and the University of Vermont.

Dr. Hutt's teaching and research interests are concentrated in the areas of business-to-business marketing and strategic marketing. His current research centers on the cross-functional role that marketing managers assume in the formation of strategy. Dr. Hutt's research has been published in the *Journal of Marketing*, *Journal of Marketing Research*, *Sloan Management Review*, *Journal of Retailing*, *Journal of the Academy of Marketing Science*, and other scholarly journals. He is also the co-author of *Macro Marketing* (John Wiley & Sons).

Assuming a variety of leadership roles for American Marketing Association programs, he recently co-chaired the 1996 Faculty Consortium on Strategic Marketing Management. He is a member of the editorial review boards of the *Journal of Marketing*, *Journal of Business-to-Business Marketing*, *Journal of Business & Industrial Marketing*, *Journal of Strategic Marketing*, and the *Journal of Business Research*. Dr. Hutt has consulted on marketing strategy issues for firms such as Motorola, Lucent Technologies, Arvin Industries, ADT, and Black-Clawson, and for the food industry's Public Policy Subcommittee on the Universal Product Code.

Thomas W. Speh, Ph.D., is the James Evans Rees Distinguished Professor of Distribution and Director of the Warehousing Research Center at Miami University (Ohio). Prior to his tenure at Miami, Dr. Speh taught at the University of Alabama.

Dr. Speh has been a regular participant in professional marketing and logistics meetings and has published articles in a number of academic and professional journals, including the *Journal of Marketing, Journal of the Academy of Marketing Sciences, Journal of Business Logistics, Journal of Retailing, Journal of Purchasing and Materials Management, I.C.C. Practitioner's Journal, and Industrial Marketing Management*. He was the recipient of the Beta Gamma Sigma Distinguished Faculty award for excellence in teaching at Miami University's School of Business and of the Miami University Alumni Association's Effective Educator award.

Dr. Speh has been active in both the Warehousing Education and Research Council (WERC) and the Council of Logistics Management (CLM). He has served as president of WERC and as a member of the executive committee for both WERC and CLM. Dr. Speh has been a consultant on strategy issues to such organizations as Xerox, Procter & Gamble, Burlington Northern Railroad, Sara Lee, J. M. Smucker Co., and Millenium Petrochemicals, Inc.

Case Contributors

Erin Anderson, *University of Pennsylvania (The Wharton School)*
Jan Willem Bol, *Miami University (Ohio)*
Eric Cannell, *University of Illinois, Champaign-Urbana*
Andrew D. Dyer, *Georgetown University*
D. Michael Fields, *Southwest Missouri State University*
Gary L. Frankwick, *Oklahoma State University*
John B. Gifford, *Miami University (Ohio)*
Michael Gilbertson, *Augustine Medical, Inc.*
Peter G. Goulet, *University of Northern Iowa*
H. Michael Hayes, *University of Colorado at Denver*
Neil C. Herndon, Jr., *Southwest Missouri State University*
Michael D. Hutt, *Arizona State University*
Roger A. Kerin, *Southern Methodist University (Edwin L. Cox School of Business)*
Charles Manz, *Arizona State University*
David C. Munn, *ITSMA, Lexington, Massachusetts*
Richard C. Munn, *ITSMA, Lexington, Massachusetts*
Lester A. Neidell, *University of Tulsa*
James E. Nelson, *University of Colorado, Boulder*
Stuart U. Rich, *University of Oregon*
William Rudelius, *University of Minnesota*
Frank Shipper, *Salisbury State University*
N. Craig Smith, *Georgetown University*
Alan J. Stenger, *Pennsylvania State University*
Brian Wansink, *University of Pennsylvania (The Wharton School)*

Contents in Brief

Contents

BUSINESS MARKETING MANAGEMENT

a strategic view of industrial and organizational markets

SIXTH EDITION

Part I

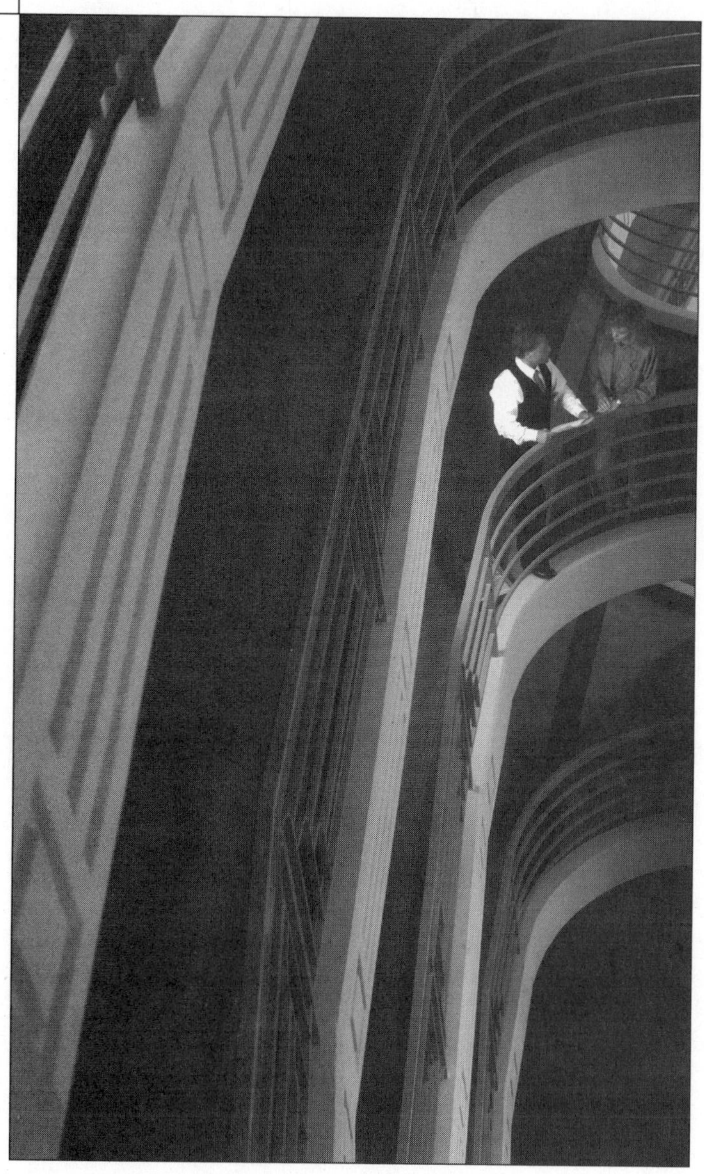

The Environment of Business Marketing

Chapter 1

A Business Marketing Perspective

The business market poses special challenges and significant opportunities for the marketing manager. This chapter introduces the complex forces that are unique to the business marketing environment. After reading this chapter, you will understand

1. the dynamic nature of the business marketing environment as well as the basic similarities and differences between consumer-goods and business marketing
2. the underlying factors that influence the demand for industrial goods
3. the nature of buyer-seller relationships in the supply chain for a product
4. the types of customers in this important market.
5. the basic characteristics of industrial products and services.

Business Marketing

Business marketers serve the largest market of all: The dollar volume of transactions in the industrial or business market significantly exceeds that of the ultimate consumer market. In the business market, a single customer can account for an enormous level of purchasing activity. For example, the General Motors purchasing department spends more than $70 billion annually on industrial products and services—more than the gross domestic products of Ireland, Portugal, Turkey, or Greece. The 1,350 professional buyers at General Motors each spend more than $40 million annually. Others, such as General Electric (G.E.), Du Pont, and International Business Machines (IBM), spend more than $60 million per day on purchases to support their operations.[1] Indeed, all formal organizations—large or small, public or private, profit or not-for-profit—participate in the exchange of industrial products and services, thus constituting the business market.

[1]Anne Millen Porter and Elena Epatko Murphy, "Hey, Big Spender . . . The 100 Largest Industrial Buyers," *Purchasing* 119 (9 November 1995): pp. 31-42.

Business markets are "markets for products and services, local to international, bought by businesses, government bodies, and institutions (such as hospitals) for incorporation (for example, ingredient materials or components), for consumption (for example, process materials, office supplies, consulting services), for use (for example, installations or equipment), or for resale.... The only markets not of direct interest are those dealing with products or services which are principally directed at personal use or consumption such as packaged grocery products, home appliances, or consumer banking."[2] The factors that distinguish business marketing from consumer marketing are the nature of the customer and how that customer uses the product. In business marketing, the customers are organizations (businesses, governments, institutions).

Business firms buy industrial goods to form or facilitate the production process or use as components for other goods and services. Government agencies and private institutions buy industrial goods to maintain and deliver services to their own market: the public. Industrial or business marketing (the terms can be used interchangeably) accounts for more than half the economic activity in the United States, Canada, and most other nations. More than 50 percent of all business school graduates join firms that compete directly in the business market. The heightened interest in high technology markets—and the sheer size of the business market—has spawned increased emphasis on business marketing management in universities and corporate executive training programs.[3]

This book explores the special opportunities and challenges that the business market presents and identifies the new requirements for managing the marketing function in this vital sector of the global economy. The following questions establish the theme of this first chapter: What are the similarities and differences between consumer-goods marketing and business marketing? What customers constitute the business market? How can the multitude of industrial goods be classified into manageable categories? What forces influence the behavior of business market demand?

Business Marketing Management

Many large firms that produce goods such as steel, production equipment, or computer-memory chips cater exclusively to business market customers and never directly interact with their ultimate consumers. Other firms participate in both the consumer-goods and the business markets. The introduction of laser printers and personal computers brought Hewlett-Packard, historically a business-to-business marketer, into the consumer market. Conversely, lagging consumer markets prompted Sony Corporation to expand to the business market by introducing office automation products. Both companies had to reorient their marketing strategies dramatically because of the significant differences between the buying behavior exhibited in the consumer versus the business markets.

---

[2] Prospectus for the Institute for the Study of Business Markets, College of Business Administration, the Pennsylvania State University.

[3] B. G. Yovovich, *New Marketing Imperatives: Innovation Strategies for Today's Marketing Challenges* (Englewood Cliffs, N.J.: Prentice-Hall, 1995), pp. 229-237.

Products like cellular phones, office furniture, personal computers, and software are purchased in both the consumer and the business markets. What distinguishes business marketing from consumer-goods marketing is the *intended use of the product* and the *intended consumer.* Sometimes the products are identical, but a fundamentally different marketing approach is needed to reach the organizational buyer.

BUSINESS MARKETS VERSUS CONSUMER-GOODS MARKETS

The basic task of management cuts across both consumer-goods and business marketing. Marketers serving both sectors can benefit by rooting their organizational plan in a *market orientation,* which requires superior proficiency in understanding and satisfying customers.[4] Such market-driven firms demonstrate

- a set of values and beliefs that places the customers' interests first;[5]
- the ability to generate, disseminate, and productively use superior information about customers and competitors;[6]
- and the coordinated use of interfunctional resources (for example, research and development, manufacturing).[7]

Distinctive Capabilities

A close examination of a market-driven firm will reveal two particularly important capabilities: market sensing and customer linking.[8] First, the **market-sensing capability** concerns how well the organization is equipped to continuously sense changes in its market and to anticipate customer responses to marketing programs. Market-driven firms spot market changes and react well in advance of their competitors (for example, Coca-Cola in the consumer-goods market and 3M in the business market). Second, the **customer-linking capability** comprises the particular skills, abilities, and processes that an organization has developed to create and manage close customer relationships.

Consumer-goods firms, such as Procter and Gamble, demonstrate these capabilities in working with powerful retailers like Wal-Mart. Here, multifunctional teams in both organizations work together by sharing delivery and product movement information and by jointly planning promotional activity and product changes. While evident in manufacturer-reseller relations in the consumer-goods market,

---

[4]George S. Day, "The Capabilities of Market-Driven Organizations," *Journal of Marketing* 58 (October 1994): pp. 37-52.
[5]Rohit Deshpande, John U. Farley, and Frederick E. Webster Jr., "Corporate Culture, Customer Orientation, and Innovativeness in Japanese Firms: A Quadrad Analysis," *Journal of Marketing* 57 (January 1993): pp. 23-37.
[6]Ajay K. Kohli and Bernard J. Jaworski, "Market Orientation: The Construct, Research Propositions, and Managerial Implications," *Journal of Marketing* 54 (April 1990): pp. 1-18.
[7]John C. Narver and Stanley F. Slater, "The Effect of a Market Orientation on Business Profitability," *Journal of Marketing* 54 (October 1990): pp. 20-35.
[8]Day, "Capabilities of Market-Driven Organizations," pp. 37-52.

strong customer-linking capabilities are *crucial* in the business market where close buyer-seller relationships prevail.

Partnering for Increased Value

A business marketer becomes a preferred supplier to major industrial customers such as Xerox, Texas Instruments, or Motorola by working closely as a partner, developing an intimate knowledge of the customer's operations, and contributing unique value to that customer's business. Business marketing programs increasingly involve a customized blend of tangible products, service support, and ongoing information services both before and after the sale. Market-driven firms place a high priority on customer-linking capabilities and closely align product decisions—as well as delivery, handling, service, and other supply-chain activities—with the customer's operations. For a firm like Motorola to deliver maximum value to its customers, it must receive maximum value from its suppliers. For instance, Motorola's Paging Products Group could not have achieved its 60 percent global market share without the cost, quality, technology, and other advances contributed by its suppliers.[9]

Creating the Value Proposition[10]

Business marketing strategy must be based on an assessment of the company, the competitor, and the customer. A successful strategy focuses on identifying those opportunities in which the firm can deliver superior value to customers based on its distinctive competencies. From this perspective, marketing can be best understood as the process of defining, developing, and delivering value.

Market-driven firms attempt to match their resources, skills, and capabilities with particular customer needs that are not being adequately served. By understanding customer needs, marketing managers can define value from the customer's perspective and convert that information into requirements for creating satisfied customers. In turn, a firm's capabilities and skills determine the degree to which the company can meet these requirements and provide greater value than its competitors.

Given many strategic paths, the **value proposition** signals the chosen direction by specifying how the organization proposes to deliver superior value to customers. The value proposition is an important organizing force in the firm because it directs all employees to focus on customer requirements, and it provides the means for the firm to position its offerings in the minds of customers.

MARKETING'S CROSS-FUNCTIONAL RELATIONSHIPS

Rather than operating in isolation from other functional areas, the successful business marketing manager is an integrator—one who understands the capabilities of

[9]Jordan D. Lewis, *The Connected Corporation: How Leading Companies Win through Customer-Supplier Alliances* (New York: The Free Press, 1995), p. 3.

[10]Frederick E. Webster Jr., *Market-Driven Management: Using the New Marketing Concept to Create a Customer-Oriented Company* (New York: John Wiley & Sons, Inc., 1994), p. 60.

manufacturing, research and development (R&D), and customer service and who applies these strengths in developing marketing strategies that are responsive to customer needs.[11] Close and tightly integrated cross-functional relationships underlie the strategy success stories of firms such as Hewlett-Packard and 3M. As firms adopt leaner and more agile structures and emphasize cross-functional teams, the business marketing manager assumes an important and challenging role in strategy formation.

Business marketing success depends to a large degree on such functional areas in the firm as engineering, R&D, manufacturing, and technical service. Planning in the industrial setting thus requires more functional interdependence and a closer relationship to total corporate strategy than planning in the consumer-goods sector. B. Charles Ames points out that "changes in marketing strategy are more likely to involve capital commitments for new equipment, shifts in development activities, or departures from traditional engineering and manufacturing approaches, any one of which would have companywide implications."[12] All business marketing decisions—product, price, promotion, and distribution—are affected, directly or indirectly, by other functional areas. In turn, business decisions in R&D and in manufacturing and procurement, as well as adjustments in the overall corporate strategy, are influenced by marketing considerations. Business marketing planning must be coordinated and synchronized with corresponding planning efforts in R&D, procurement, finance, production, and other areas (see Figure 1.1).

Business marketing and consumer-goods marketing are different. A common body of knowledge, principles, and theory applies to both consumer and business marketing, but because their buyers and markets function quite differently, they merit separate attention. Consumer and business marketing differ in the nature of markets, market demand, buyer behavior, buyer-seller relationships, environmental influences (economic, political, legal), and market strategy. Yet, the potential payoffs are high for the firm that can successfully penetrate the business market.

BUSINESS MARKET DEMAND

The nature of the demand for industrial products poses unique challenges—and opportunities—for the marketing manager.

Derived Demand

Demand for industrial products is derived from ultimate consumer demand. Customers in the business market, such as commercial firms, governments, and not-for-profit institutions, buy goods and services in order to produce other goods and services for their own customers. For example, Compaq Computer spends more than 50 percent of each sales dollar

---

[11] Michael D. Hutt, "Cross-Functional Working Relationships in Marketing," *Journal of the Academy of Marketing Science* 23 (fall 1995): pp. 351-357.

[12] B. Charles Ames, "Trappings vs. Substance in Industrial Marketing," *Harvard Business Review* 48 (July/August 1996): pp. 95-96.

Figure 1.1 Business Marketing Planning: A Functionally Integrated Perspective

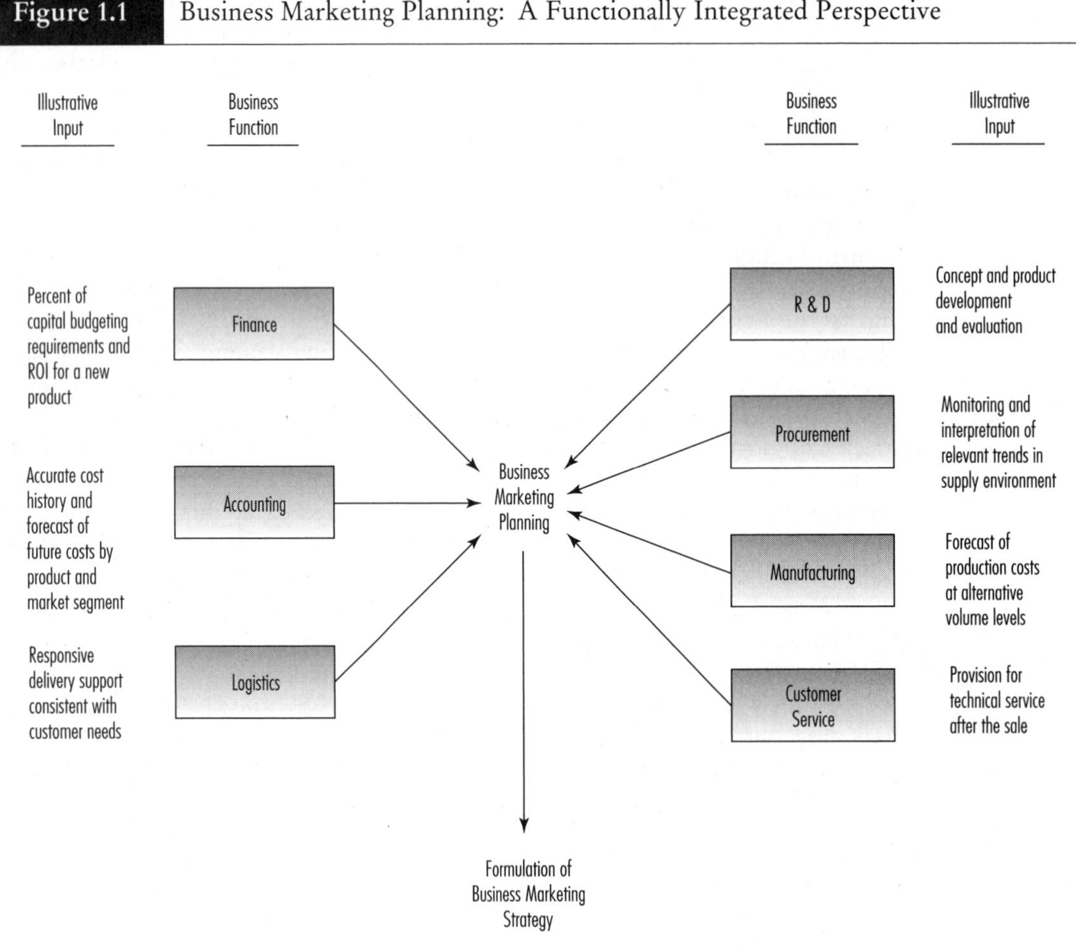

on purchased materials.[13] Most of the parts and components embodied in the computer are designed by Compaq engineers, then produced to their specifications by other firms—a carefully chosen set of industrial suppliers. The order size that each of these suppliers receives from Compaq depends on how well Compaq's computers are selling. As this example illustrates, demand for an industrial product is derived from the buying organization's customers (computer buyers), not from the buying organization itself (Compaq Computer).

The Anatomy of an Automobile[14]

Consider the materials and components that constitute Chrysler's LH automobile. Some of the components are manufactured by Chrysler, but the finished product reflects the

[13]Porter and Murphy, "Hey, Big Spenders," p. 32.
[14]Ernest Raia, "The Extended Enterprise," *Purchasing* 107 (4 March 1993): pp. 48-51.

Managing in the 21st Century

THE BOUNDARYLESS ORGANIZATION

Jack Welch, the CEO of General Electric Company, uses the term "boundaryless" to describe everything G.E. stands for: "A boundaryless manager should embody speed, simplicity, and self-confidence; serve customers with devotion, act with integrity; serve as an active agent of unceasing change; and more, much more."

Most of all, boundarylessness represents an emphasis on cooperation across all the artificial barriers that can divide organizational members with common interests. To explain, Welch uses the three dimensions of a house:

- The *horizontal* barriers are the walls that divide groups of individuals into isolated compartments by functional area, product line, or geographic location. Why shouldn't Marketing talk to R&D, or Tokyo to Milwaukee?
- The *vertical* barriers are the layers (floors and ceilings) that come with the hierarchy. When differences in rank obstruct open communication, the mission of the organization is stifled.
- The *external* barriers are the outside walls. Beyond them are found many groups with whom close relationships are essential, such as customers, suppliers, and alliance partners.

Succeeding in complex businesses requires teamwork on a grand scale, and G.E. has demonstrated that cooperation is an essential characteristic of organizational success. Jack Welch's vision aptly depicts the challenging environment in which the business marketing manager operates.

Source: Noel M. Tichy and Stratford Sherman, *Control Your Destiny or Someone Else Will* (New York: Doubleday, 1993), pp. 234-235; and Betsy Morris, "Roberto Goizueta and Jack Welch: The Wealth Builders," Fortune, (December 11, 1995), pp. 80-102.

efforts of 200 suppliers or business marketers who deal directly with Chrysler. These suppliers, portrayed in Figure 1.2, worked in a close partnership with Chrysler as the LH sedan was developed from scratch in 39 months. In fact, they were each given their own key to the automaker's new billion dollar technology center in Auburn Hills, Michigan!

The Extended Enterprise. The LH sedan features one of the largest windshields ever made for a passenger car, covering an area of 15 square feet. Guardian Industries was the chosen supplier because the firm had developed a proprietary process that could bend the glass into the required shape without creating optical distortion. Guardian invested $35 million in a new plant to make the LH windshields and supplies all the glass for Chrysler's new series of small cars. Other suppliers invested in facilities to improve their ability to provide just-in-time deliveries to Chrysler. For example, Textron built a plant dedicated to producing interior trim parts for the LH sedan and located a new design facility near the Chrysler Technology Center.[15]

[15]Jeffrey H. Dyer, "How Chrysler Created an American Keiretsu," *Harvard Business Review* 74 (July/August 1996): pp. 42-56.

Figure 1.2 Anatomy of an Automobile: Suppliers for the Chrysler LH

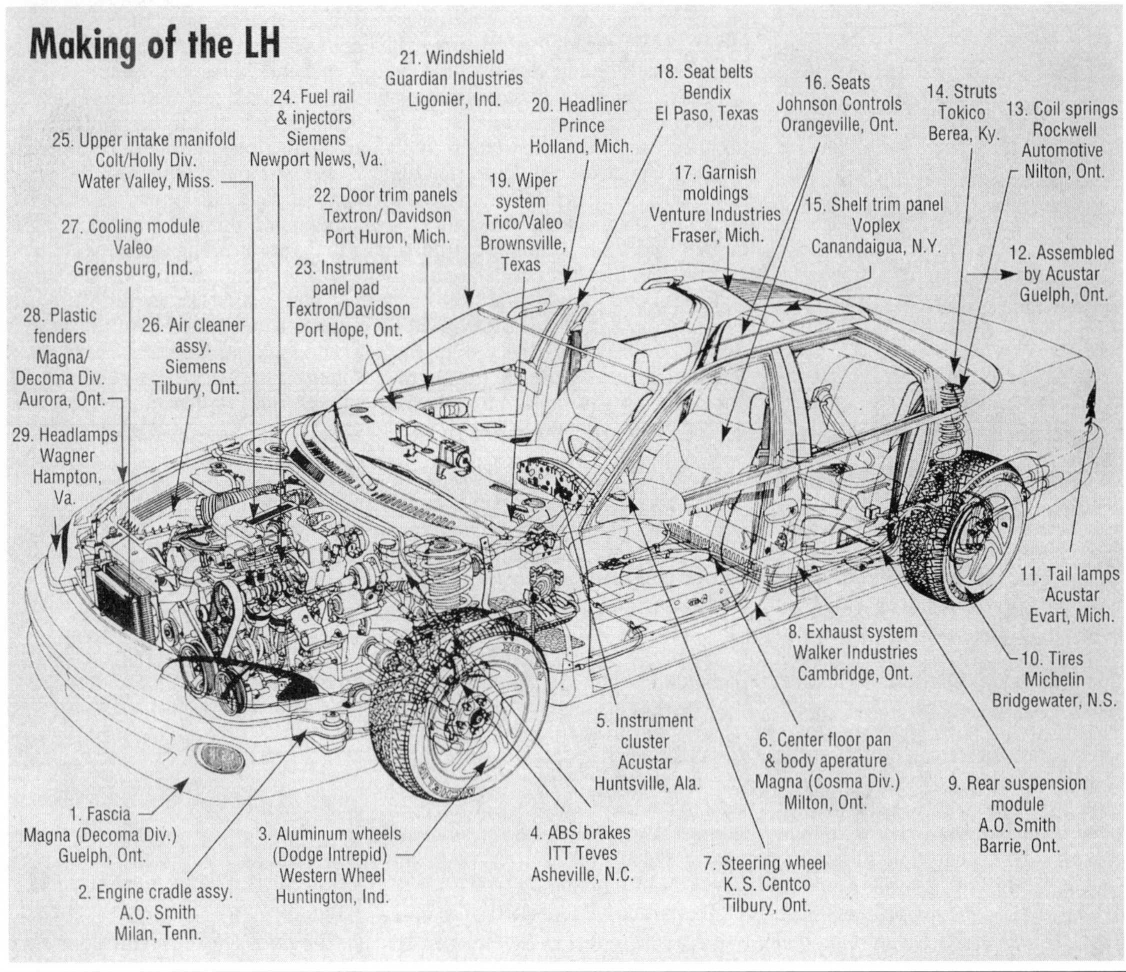

Source: Ernest Raia, "The Extended Enterprise," *Purchasing* 114 (4 March 1993), p. 49.

In purchasing an LH sedan, the customer is stimulating the demand for a diverse array of products produced by business marketing firms—such as tires from Michelin, tail lamps from Acustar, seats from Johnson Controls, seat belts from Bendix, and coil springs from Rockwell Automotive. Such suppliers represent the **extended enterprise** of Chrysler and dramatically influence the quality and reliability of the automobile.

Monitoring Demand

Because demand is derived, the business marketing manager must carefully monitor demand patterns and changing buying preferences in the final consumer markets, often on a worldwide basis. If auto producers forecast that sales will climb or fall next year,

When Japanese researchers realized that the frequency of a noise was as important to customers as its loudness, they tried to "tune" the car to create a pleasing sound.

Source: Drawing by Elwood H. Smith; reprinted with permission.

the business marketer must make corresponding changes in the forecast for this segment of the market. Any changes in styling, design, or composition dictated by automobile buyers, competitive pressure, economic conditions, or government agencies may create opportunities for some business marketers—and problems for others.

Environmental Forces Influence Demand

In monitoring and forecasting demand, the business marketer must be alert to factors in the competitive, economic, political, and legal environment that directly or indirectly influence demand. A mild recession cuts deeply into some segments of the business market while leaving other segments unscathed. Rising interest rates alter the purchasing plans of both home buyers and commercial enterprises contemplating expansion. Federal legislation requiring improvements in gas mileage increases demand for lightweight materials like aluminum. Two decades ago, steel accounted for 10 percent of the purchase price of an automobile, compared to just 2.5 percent of the price today.[16] Ecological concerns, which render some industrial products and processes obsolete, create challenging replacement opportunities. For example, Baxter International, a manufacturer of medical products, assists hospitals—its main customers—in establishing environmental programs and has redesigned products and packaging to meet customers' waste reduction goals.[17] Foreign markets that offer

[16]Louis Uchitelle, "Three Major Steel Companies Raising Prices by 3% to 5%," *New York Times,* 2 August 1996, sec. C, p. 4.

[17]Weld F. Royal, "It's Not Easy Being Green," *Sales & Marketing Management* 147 (July 1995): pp. 84-90.

lucrative potential to some business marketers, such as software producers, may pose a serious challenge to other domestic producers, such as the steel industry. Constant surveillance of these and other environmental forces is fundamental to accurate demand analysis in the business market.

Stimulating Demand

Some business marketers must not only monitor final consumer markets, but also develop a marketing program that reaches the ultimate consumer directly. Aluminum producers use television and magazine ads to point out the convenience and recycling opportunities that aluminum containers offer to the consumer—because the ultimate consumer influences aluminum demand by purchasing soft drinks in aluminum, rather than plastic, containers. Over 4 billion pounds of aluminum are used annually in the production of beverage containers. Similarly, Boeing promotes the convenience of air travel in a media campaign targeted to the consumer market to create a favorable environment for longer-term demand for its planes; Du Pont advertises to ultimate consumers to stimulate the sales of carpeting that incorporates their product.

Price Sensitivity

Demand elasticity refers to the responsiveness of the quantity demanded to a change in price. Demand is elastic when a given percentage change in price brings about an even larger percentage change in the quantity demanded. Inelasticity results when demand is insensitive to price—for example, when the percentage change in demand is less than the percentage change in price. Consider the demand for electronic components that is stimulated by companies making digital cameras. As long as final consumers continue to purchase these cameras and are generally insensitive to price, manufacturers of the equipment are relatively insensitive to the price of electronic components. At the opposite end of the spectrum, if consumers are price sensitive when purchasing soup and other canned grocery products, manufacturers of soup will be price sensitive when purchasing metal cans. Thus, the derived demand indicates that the demand for metal cans is price elastic.

Final consumer demand has a pervasive impact on the demand for products in the business market. By being sensitive to trends in the consumer market, the business marketer can often identify both impending problems and opportunities for growth and diversification.

A Global Market Perspective

According to Michael E. Porter, "In international markets, innovations that yield competitive advantage anticipate both domestic and foreign needs."[18] Indeed, the relevant unit of analysis in an increasing number of industries today is not the domestic but the worldwide market position. The accelerating demand for industrial goods in the international market and the dramatic rise in competition—from Western Europe, Japan, the

---

[18]Michael E. Porter, "The Competitive Advantage of Nations," *Harvard Business Review* 68 (March/April, 1990): p. 74.

Pacific Rim (with Korea, Taiwan, Hong Kong, and Singapore becoming active players), and nearby industrialized countries (notably India and Brazil)—necessitate a global perspective on competition. Meanwhile, Eastern Europe will likely evolve into an important customer and source of world industrial competition in the years ahead.

James Brian Quinn astutely observes that "improved telecommunications, air transport, financial services, storage, and cargo-handling technologies mean that virtually all manufacturers (regardless of size) must consider supply sources, markets, and competition on a worldwide scale—or lose their competitive positions."[19] A thorough competitive assessment must involve an analysis of formidable competitors in distant markets.

A global orientation is especially important to business marketers competing in rapidly changing industries like telecommunications and electronics or, at the other end of the continuum, in basic commodity industries such as steel and forest products. Japanese steelmakers are formidable competitors and enjoy cost and quality advantages over their major U. S. counterparts. In turn, many U.S.-based industrial firms such as Intel, Boeing, and Motorola have moved to establish a position of strength for selected products in Japan. For example, Motorola is the worldwide market leader in the rapidly growing cellular telephone industry and Intel is the dominant force in the microprocessor industry.

John F. Welch Jr., chairman and CEO of G.E., spawned a strategic redirection that has provided G.E. with world market-share leadership in nearly all of its major businesses. He offers this challenging profile for competing successfully in the global market:

> *The winners ... will be those who can develop a culture that allows them to move faster, communicate more clearly, and involve everyone in a focused effort to serve ever more demanding customers. To move toward that winning culture, we've got to create what we call a "boundaryless" company. We no longer have the time to climb over barriers between functions like engineering and marketing.... Geographic barriers must evaporate. Our people must be as comfortable in Delhi and Seoul as they are in Louisville or Schenectady. The lines between the company and its vendors must be blurred into a smooth, fluid process with no other objective than satisfying the customer and winning in the marketplace.*[20]

Business and Consumer Marketing: A Contrast

Many consumer-goods companies with a strong reputation in the consumer market decide to capitalize on perceived opportunities in the business market. The move is often prompted by a maturing product line, a desire to diversify operations, or the

[19]James Brian Quinn, *Intelligent Enterprise: A Knowledge and Service Based Paradigm for Industry* (New York: The Free Press, 1992), pp. 220-221.

[20]"Today's Leaders Look to Tomorrow," *Fortune,* 26 March 1990, p. 30; see also Betsy Morris, "Robert Goizueta and Jack Welch: The Wealth Builders," *Fortune,* 11 December 1995, pp. 80-102.

strategic opportunity to profitably apply R&D or production strength in a rapidly growing business market. Procter and Gamble Company (P&G), departing from its packaged consumer-goods tradition, is using its expertise in oils, fats, and pulps to diversify into fast-growing industries.

The J. M. Smucker Company operates successfully in both the consumer and the business markets. Smucker, drawing upon its consumer product base (jellies and preserves), produces filling mixes used by manufacturers of yogurt and dessert items. Marketing strawberry preserves to ultimate consumers differs significantly from marketing a strawberry filling to a manufacturer of yogurt. Key differences are highlighted in the following illustration.

SMUCKER: A CONSUMER AND BUSINESS MARKETER

Smucker reaches the consumer market with a line of products sold through a range of retail outlets. New products are carefully developed, tested, targeted, priced, and promoted for particular segments of the market. To secure distribution, the firm employs food brokers who call on both wholesale- and retail-buying units. The company's own sales force reaches selected larger accounts. Achieving a desired degree of market exposure and shelf space in key retail-food outlets is essential to any marketer of consumer food products. Promotional plans for the line include media advertising, coupons, special offers, and incentives for retailers. Pricing decisions must reflect the nature of demand, costs, and the behavior of competitors. In sum, the marketer must manage each component of the marketing mix: product, price, promotion, and distribution.

The marketing mix takes on a different form in the business market. Attention centers on manufacturers that potentially could use Smucker products to produce other goods; the Smucker product will lose its identity as it is blended into yogurt, cakes, or cookies. Once Smucker has listed all the potential users of its product (for example, large food processors, bakeries, yogurt producers), the business marketing manager attempts to identify meaningful market segments that Smucker can profitably serve. A specific marketing strategy is developed for each market segment.

When a potential organizational consumer is identified, the company's sales force calls directly on the account. The salesperson *may* begin by contacting a company president but, at first, generally spends a great deal of time with the R&D director or the product development group leader. The salesperson is thus challenged to identify the **key buying influentials**—those who will have power in the buying process. Senior-level Smucker executives may also assist in the selling process.

Armed with product specifications (for example, desired taste, color, calories), the salesperson returns to the R&D department at Smucker to develop samples. Several months may pass before a mixture is finally approved. Next, attention turns to price, and the salesperson's contact point shifts to the purchasing department. Because large quantities (truckloads or drums rather than jars) are involved, a few cents per pound can be significant to both parties. Quality and service are also vitally important.

Once a transaction is culminated, the product is shipped directly from the Smucker warehouse to the manufacturer's plant. The salesperson follows up frequently with the purchasing agent, the plant manager, and other executives. Product movement and delivery information is openly shared and close working relationships develop between managers at Smucker and key decision makers in the buying organization. How much business can Smucker expect from this account? The performance of the new consumer product in the marketplace will determine this: The demand for industrial goods is, as noted, derived from ultimate consumer demand. Note also the importance of (1) developing a close and continuing working relationship with business market customers, and (2) understanding the requirements of the total range of buying influentials in the target company.

DISTINGUISHING CHARACTERISTICS

The foregoing illustration spotlights some of the features that differentiate business marketing strategy from consumer-goods marketing strategy. The business marketer emphasizes personal selling rather than advertising (TV, newspaper) to reach potential buyers. Only a small portion of the business marketer's promotional budget is likely to be invested in advertising, most commonly through trade journals or direct mail. This advertising, however, often establishes the foundation for a successful sales call. The industrial salesperson must understand the technical aspects of the organization's requirements and how those requirements can be satisfied, as well as knowing who influences the buying decision and why.

The business marketer's product also includes an important service component. The organizational consumer evaluates the quality of the physical entity and the quality of the attached services. Attention centers on the total package of benefits the consumer will receive. Price negotiation is frequently an important part of the industrial buying/selling process. Products made to particular quality or design specifications must be individually priced. Business marketers generally find that direct distribution to larger customers strengthens relationships between buyer and seller. Smaller accounts can be profitably served through intermediaries—manufacturers' representatives or industrial distributors.

As the Smucker example has illustrated, business marketing strategies differ from consumer-goods marketing strategies in the relative emphasis given to certain elements of the marketing mix. It is important to note that the example also highlights fundamental differences between the buyers in each market. In an organization, a variety of individuals influence the purchase decision. Several major questions confront Smucker's business marketing manager: Who are key participants in the purchasing process? What is their relative importance? What criteria does each apply to the decision? Thus, the business marketer must understand the *process* that an organization follows in purchasing a product and identify which organizational members have roles in this process. Depending on the complexity of the purchase, this process may span many weeks or months and may involve the participation of several members of the organization. The business marketer who becomes involved in the purchase process early may have the greatest chance for success.

Table 1.1 Relationship View: A Business Marketing Imperative

Transactional View	Relationship View
Purpose of marketing is to make a sale	Purpose of marketing is to create a customer
Sale is result and the measure of success	Sale is beginning of relationship; profit is measure of success
Business is defined by its products and factories	Business is defined by its customer relationships
Price is determined by competitive market forces; price is an input	Price is determined by negotiation and joint decision making; price is an outcome
Communications are aimed at aggregates of customers	Communications are targeted and tailored to individuals
Marketer is valued for its products and prices	Marketer is valued for its present and future problem-solving capability
Objective: to make the next sale; find the next customer	Objective: to satisfy the customer you have by delivering superior value

Source: Presentation by Frederick E. Webster Jr. at Special Session on "Relationship Marketing," at the 1993 American Marketing Association Educators' Conference (August), Boston, Massachusetts.

A RELATIONSHIP EMPHASIS

Relationships in the business market are often close and enduring. Rather than constituting the end result, a sale signals the beginning of a relationship. By convincing a large food processor such as General Foods to use its product, Smucker initiates a potential long-term business relationship. More than ringing up a sale, Smucker creates a customer! To maintain that relationship, the business marketer must satisfy the customer by providing superior value. Table 1.1 contrasts the traditional transactional view with the relationship view. The relationship view provides an important foundation for understanding buyer-seller relations in the business market. Relationship strategy issues are considered throughout this volume.

THE SUPPLY CHAIN

Figure 1.3 further illuminates the importance of a relationship perspective in business marketing by considering the chain of suppliers involved in the creation of an automobile. Consider Honda and Ford. At its Marysville, Ohio, auto assembly plant, Honda spends more than $5 billion annually for materials and components from some 300 North American suppliers.[21] These expenditures by the 300-member purchasing staff at Honda of America represent 80 percent of the firm's annual sales. Similarly, Ford relies on a vast supplier network, including firms such as TRW and Johnson

[21]Kevin R. Fitzgerald, "For Superb Supplier Development: Honda Wins!" *Purchasing* 118 (21 September 1995): pp. 32-40.

Figure 1.3 The Supply Chain

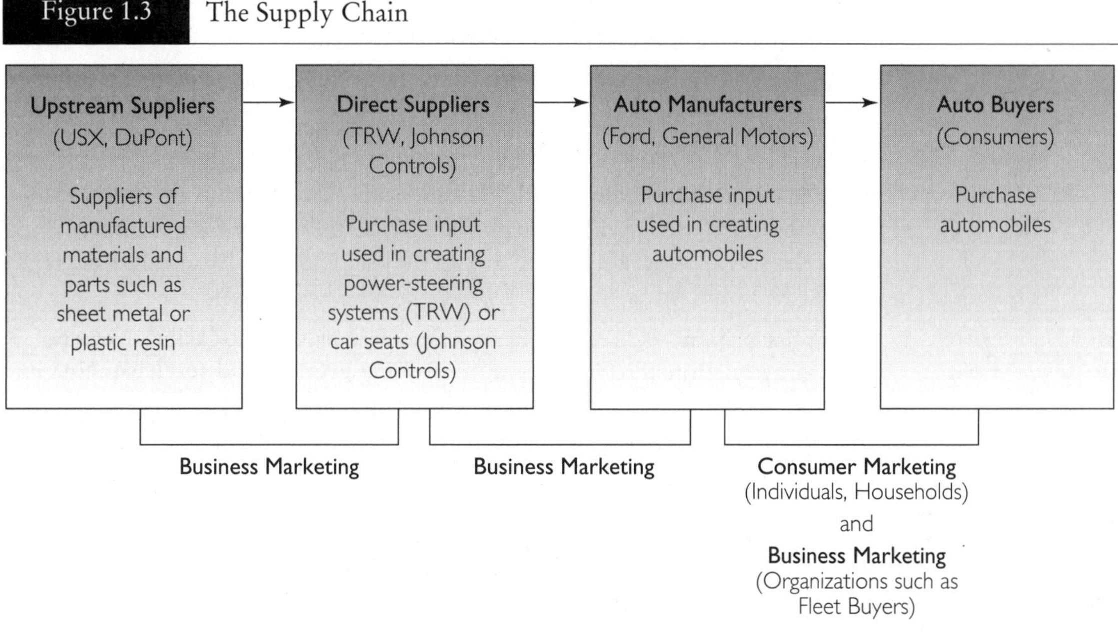

Controls, to contribute half of the more than 10,000 parts of a typical Ford car. The relationships between these auto producers and their suppliers fall squarely into the business marketing domain. Similarly, business marketers such as TRW rely on a whole host of others farther back on the supply chain for raw materials, components, and other support. Each organization in this chain is involved in the creation of a product, marketing processes (including delivery), and support and service after the sale. In performing these value-creating activities, each also affects the quality level of the Honda or Ford product. Michael Porter and Victor Millar observe that "to gain competitive advantage over its rivals, a company must either perform these activities at a lower cost or perform them in a way that leads to differentiation and a premium price (more value)."[22]

PROCUREMENT TRENDS AND THE SUPPLY CHAIN

The search for improved quality and superior performance have spawned a significant shift in the purchasing practices of automakers such as Chrysler and Honda, as well as those of other leading-edge firms like Compaq and Motorola. To develop profitable relationships with organizational customers, business marketers must be attuned to these changes. Rather than relying on competitive bidding and dealing at arms-length

[22]Michael E. Porter and Victor E. Millar, "How Information Gives You Competitive Advantage," *Harvard Business Review* 63 (July/August 1985): pp. 149-160; see also Michael E. Porter, *Competitive Advantage* (New York: The Free Press, 1985).

with a large number of suppliers, a new approach to purchasing has been adopted in many industries. This approach is characterized by:[23]

- longer-term and closer relationships with fewer suppliers (for example, over the past decade, the number of suppliers utilized by Motorola, Chrysler, and Ford have been reduced by 60 percent or more)
- closer interactions among multiple functions—manufacturing, engineering, and logistics as well as sales and purchasing—on both the buying and selling sides (for example, through computer links with its suppliers, Motorola can change specifications and delivery schedules)
- supplier proximity to allow just-in-time delivery and to facilitate closer working relationships targeted at improving product and service quality along the supply chain (for example, Johnson Controls, a producer of auto seats and trim, operates ten plants near its major customers, which include Ford, Toyota, and General Motors[24]

MANAGING RELATIONSHIPS IN THE SUPPLY CHAIN

The trends in procurement place a premium on the supply-chain management capabilities of the business marketer. Chrysler spends 90 percent of its purchasing dollars with 150 suppliers. Thomas Stallkamp, Chrysler's vice president of procurement and supply, notes that once they decide on a supplier for a component or material, "the supplier will have the business forever, providing the supplier continues to meet quality, cost, technology and delivery requirements."[25] Of particular importance to Chrysler is the quality of engineering support that it receives from suppliers. Chrysler actively seeks supplier partners that will contribute fresh ideas and innovative technology to attract buyers of future Chrysler products.

To effectively initiate and sustain a profitable relationship with a customer like Chrysler, the business marketer must carefully manage the multiple linkages that define the relationship. Given these new marketing requirements, Frank V. Cespedes emphasizes the importance of "concurrent marketing" among the groups that are most central to customer contact efforts: product, sales, and service units.[26] In his view, recent market developments place more emphasis on the firm's ability to

- generate timely market knowledge by segment and by individual account;
- customize product service packages for diverse customer groups; and
- capitalize on local field knowledge from sales and service units to inform product strategy in real time.

---

[23]Frank V. Cespedes, *Concurrent Marketing: Integrating Products, Sales, and Service* (Boston: Harvard Business School Press, 1995), pp. 14-18.
[24]James B. Treece, "U. S. Parts Makers Just Won't Say Uncle," *Business Week,* 10 August 1987, pp. 76-78.
[25]"Chrysler Pushes Quality Down the Supply Chain," *Purchasing* 118 (13 July 1995): p. 126.
[26]Cespedes, *Concurrent Marketing,* chap. 2.

Developing and nurturing close, long-term relationships is an important goal for the business marketer. Built on trust and demonstrated performance, such strategic partnerships require open lines of communication between multiple layers of the buying and selling organizations. Given the rising importance of long-term, strategic relationships with both customers and suppliers, organizations are increasingly emphasizing relationship management skills. Since these skills reside in people rather than in organizational structures, roles, or tasks, marketing personnel with these skills will become valuable assets to the organization.[27]

Time and the Supply Chain[28]

The ways that leading companies manage time in the supply chain—in new product development and introduction, production, and sales and distribution—are the most powerful new sources of competitive advantage. According to George Stalk Jr. and Thomas M. Hout, "Time as a source of competitive advantage is relevant whenever customers have to wait to receive the value that they have decided they want." Successful time-based competitors are able to conceive, develop, and introduce new products and services much faster than their competitors, without sacrificing product quality or marketability. In the automobile industry, for example, firms such as Honda, Ford, Toyota, and Chrysler assume active leadership roles in managing time in their respective supply chains. Other successful time-based competitors include Compaq, Motorola, Canon, Intel, Sony, Merck, and Microsoft.

Rapid product development provides a firm with a number of competitive advantages. First, the quick product developer enjoys market advantages by incorporating more current technology into the product. If both Honda and General Motors are designing an auto for the 2000 model year, but Honda needs only two years to design the model while GM requires three, Honda has an edge. It can use 1998-available technology, whereas GM's designs use 1997 technology. Second, the fast product developer can introduce a product before customer preferences change—and then counter with a responsive offering when they do. Third, faster development times cut costs by reducing overhead and by using engineering and production resources more efficiently.[29]

How to Get Faster

To compress time and enjoy these competitive advantages, supply-chain leaders can take three steps. First, they can provide each company in the chain with more complete and timely information concerning orders, new products, and special needs. To illustrate, accurate demand-based information saves time and money by reducing uncertainty and the amount of inventory that each member of the supply chain must hold. Performance can also be improved by on-line systems that transmit quality and

---

[27]Frederick E. Webster Jr., "The Changing Role of Marketing in the Corporation," Journal of Marketing, 56 (October 1992), p. 14.

[28]George Stalk Jr. and Thomas M. Hout, *Competing against Time: How Time-based Competition Is Reshaping Global Markets* (New York: The Free Press, 1990).

[29]Rebecca Blumenstein, "Big Three Pare Design Time for New Autos," *The Wall Street Journal,* 9 August 1996, sec. A, p. 3.

delivery data to supply-chain members on a real-time basis. Second, supply-chain leaders shorten work cycles by removing the obstacles to compression that one company often unknowingly imposes on another. For example, a supplier may make engineering improvements in a power steering system and then alert the automobile manufacturer. The manufacturer in turn makes design changes in the car to accommodate the improved system. Earlier collaboration on these changes could have resulted in their new products being available in automobile showrooms months sooner. Chrysler attributes much of its success in speeding product development to early supplier involvement. Third, supply-chain leaders can compress time by synchronizing lead times and capacities among the levels of the supply chain to coordinate work flow. The goal here is to manage the chain so that each member can count on its suppliers to provide needed materials on a consistent schedule, regardless of which version of the final product is being made by the chain (for example, Honda Accord or Honda Civic).

The quest for quality and the search for competitive advantage have spawned a quiet revolution in the business market. Business market customers are reducing the size of their supplier lists, forming strategic partnerships with "quality" suppliers, and emphasizing long-term contracts and speed to an unprecedented degree. Understanding the needs of business market customers is vital in this challenging environment.

Business Market Customers

Business market customers can be broadly classified into three categories: (1) commercial enterprises, (2) governmental organizations, and (3) institutions. Each will be explored in Chapter 2. However, the supply-chain concept provides a solid foundation for introducing the commercial customers that constitute the business market.

COMMERCIAL ENTERPRISES AS CONSUMERS

Commercial enterprises can also be divided into three categories: (1) users, (2) original equipment manufacturers (OEMs), and (3) dealers and distributors.

Users

Users purchase industrial products or services to produce other goods or services that are, in turn, sold in the business or consumer markets. User customers purchase goods—such as computers, photocopiers, or automated manufacturing systems—to set up or support the manufacturing process. When purchasing machine tools from G.E., an auto manufacturer is a user. These machine tools do not become part of the automobile but instead help to produce it.

Original Equipment Manufacturers (OEMs)

The OEM purchases industrial goods to incorporate into other products sold in the business or ultimate consumer market. For example, Intel Corporation produces the

INSIDE BUSINESS MARKETING

YOU CAN'T SHRINK TO GREATNESS

Whether CEOs (chief executive officers) call it cost cutting or downsizing or restructuring or reengineering, many U. S. firms have been actively pursuing strategies to reduce their size with fewer employees and fewer operating units. Given slow revenue growth, rising expenses, and short time frames within which to improve profitability, cost cutting provides an obvious solution to immediate bottom-line problems. Indeed, many firms have reduced their costs in strategic ways by simplifying and improving business processes and by shifting resources to more promising business opportunities.

Dwight L. Gertz and João P. A. Baptista of Mercer Management Consulting argue that "the strategy of shrinkage is running its course for many companies . . . because there's always the question of what comes next." Their research suggests that those companies that outperform their rivals in a particular industry—firms such as Hewlett-Packard and Dell Computer—share a set of common traits:

- They focus selectively on better-chosen customers, learn all they can about those customers and their needs, and serve those needs with intense dedication.
- They become exceptionally proficient at rapidly developing large numbers of new products that offer superior value to customers.
- They find and develop the most effective ways to link customer segments with their products and services.

Properly executed, these strategies provide a pathway to profitable growth in many industries.

Source: Dwight L. Gertz and João P. A. Baptista, *Grow to Be Great: Breaking the Downsizing Cycle* (New York: The Free Press, 1995), pp. 1-21.

microprocessors that constitute the heart of Compaq's personal computer. In purchasing these microprocessors, Compaq would be classified as an OEM.

Dealers and Distributors

Dealers and distributors include those commercial enterprises that purchase industrial goods for resale (in basically the same form) to users and OEMs. The distributor accumulates, stores, and sells a large assortment of goods to industrial users, assuming title of the goods purchased. Handling billions of dollars worth of transactions each year, industrial distributors are growing in size and sophistication. The strategic role assumed by distributors in the business market is examined in detail in Chapter 13.

Overlap of Categories

The three categories of commercial enterprises are not mutually exclusive. Their classification is based on the intended purpose that the product serves for the customer. Ford is a user when purchasing a machine tool for the manufacturing process, but the same company is an OEM when purchasing radios to be incorporated into the ultimate consumer product.

A marketer must have a good understanding of the diverse organizational consumers in the business market. Properly classifying commercial customers as users, OEMs, or dealers or distributors is an important first step to a sharpened understanding of the buying criteria that a particular commercial customer uses in evaluating an industrial product.

Understanding Buying Motivations

Consider the different types of commercial customers that purchase a particular industrial product such as electrical timing mechanisms. Each class of commercial customer views the product differently because each purchases the product for a different reason.

A food processing firm such as Pillsbury buys electrical timers for use in a high-speed canning system. For this customer, quality, reliability, and prompt and predictable delivery are critical. Whirlpool, an OEM that incorporates the industrial product directly into consumer appliances, is concerned with the impact of the timers on the quality and dependability of the final consumer product. Since the timers will be needed in large quantities, the appliance manufacturer is also concerned about the producer's production capacity and delivery reliability. Finally, an industrial distributor is most interested in matching the capability of the timing mechanisms to the needs of customers (users and OEMs) in a specific geographical market.

Classifying Goods for the Business Market[30]

Having classified the customers that constitute the business market, we must now ask what type of goods they require, and how each type is marketed. One useful method of classifying industrial goods is to ask the following question: How does the industrial good or service enter the production process, and how does it enter the cost structure of the firm? The answer enables the marketer to identify those who are influential in the organizational buying process and to understand how to design an effective business marketing strategy. In general, industrial goods can be divided into three broad categories: entering goods, foundation goods, and facilitating goods (see Figure 1.4).

ENTERING GOODS

Entering goods are those that become part of the finished product. This category of goods consists of raw materials and manufactured materials and parts. Their cost is an expense item that is assigned to the manufacturing process.

---

[30]Data on the dollar purchases of particular products by selected customers are drawn from Porter and Murphy, "Hey Big Spenders," pp. 31-42.

Figure 1.4 Classifying Goods for the Business Market

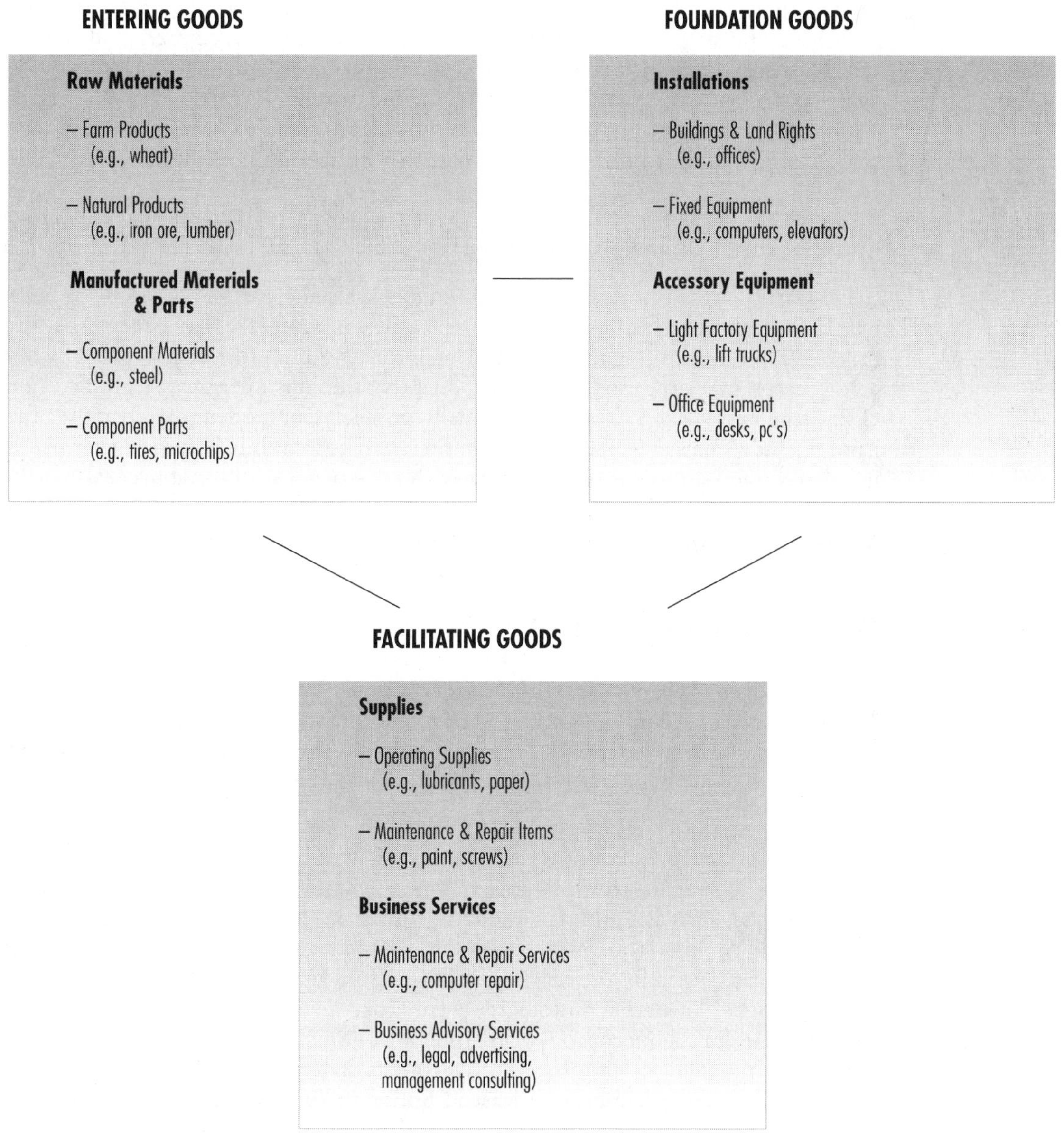

ENTERING GOODS

Raw Materials

– Farm Products
(e.g., wheat)

– Natural Products
(e.g., iron ore, lumber)

Manufactured Materials & Parts

– Component Materials
(e.g., steel)

– Component Parts
(e.g., tires, microchips)

FOUNDATION GOODS

Installations

– Buildings & Land Rights
(e.g., offices)

– Fixed Equipment
(e.g., computers, elevators)

Accessory Equipment

– Light Factory Equipment
(e.g., lift trucks)

– Office Equipment
(e.g., desks, pc's)

FACILITATING GOODS

Supplies

– Operating Supplies
(e.g., lubricants, paper)

– Maintenance & Repair Items
(e.g., paint, screws)

Business Services

– Maintenance & Repair Services
(e.g., computer repair)

– Business Advisory Services
(e.g., legal, advertising, management consulting)

Source: Adapted from Philip Kotler, *Marketing Management: Analysis, Planning, and Control,* 4th ed. (Englewood Cliffs, N.J.: Prentice-Hall, 1980), p. 172, with permission of Prentice-Hall, Inc.

Raw Materials

Observe in Figure 1.4 that raw materials include both farm products and natural products. Raw materials are processed only to the level required for economical handling and transport; they basically enter the production process of the buying organization in their natural state. AT&T purchases substantial quantities of copper, gold, and silver to be used in making telephone and communication equipment. McDonald's uses over 700 million pounds of potatoes each year and dictates the fortunes of many farmers in that segment of agriculture. In fact, when attempting to introduce a raspberry sorbet, McDonald's found, to its surprise, that not enough raspberries were being grown![31]

Manufactured Materials and Parts

In contrast to raw materials, manufactured materials and parts undergo more initial processing. Component materials such as textiles or sheet steel have been processed before reaching a clothing manufacturer or automaker but must be processed further before becoming part of the finished product that the consumer buys. Both Ford and G.E. spend more than $900 million annually on steel. Component parts, on the other hand, include small motors, motorcycle tires, and automobile batteries; they can be installed directly into another product with little or no additional processing. For example, Black & Decker spends $100 million each year on plastic parts and Sun Microsystems spends more than $200 million on displays and monitors.

FOUNDATION GOODS

The distinguishing characteristic of foundation goods is that they are **capital items.** As capital goods are used up or worn out, a portion of their original cost is assigned to the production process as a depreciation expense. Foundation goods include installations and accessory equipment.

Installations

Installations include the major long-term investment items that underlie the manufacturing process, such as **buildings and land rights** and **fixed equipment.** Large computers and machine tools are examples of fixed equipment. The demand for installations is shaped by the economic climate (for example, favorable interest rates) but is driven by the market outlook for a firm's products. In the face of strong worldwide demand for its microprocessors, Intel is building new plants, expanding existing ones, and making significant investments in capital equipment. A typical semiconductor chip plant costs at least $1 billion to build, with equipment accounting for $600 million of the cost, while the land and building account for the rest.[32]

---

[31]Quinn, *Intelligent Enterprise,* p. 20.

[32]Dean Takahashi, "Makers of Chip Equipment Beginning to Share the Pain," *The Wall Street Journal,* 14 August 1996, sec. B, p. 6.

Accessory Equipment

Accessory equipment is generally less expensive and short-lived compared to installations, and is not considered part of the fixed plant. This equipment can be found in the plant as well as in the office. Portable drills, personal computers, and fax machines illustrate this category.

FACILITATING GOODS

Facilitating goods are the supplies and services (see Figure 1.4) that support organizational operations. Because these goods do not enter the production process or become part of the finished product, their costs are handled as **expense items.**

Supplies

Virtually every organization requires **operating supplies,** such as typing paper or business forms, and **maintenance and repair items,** such as paint and cleaning materials. These items generally reach a broad cross-section of industrial users. In fact, they are very similar to the kinds of supplies that consumers might purchase at a hardware or discount store.

Services

As competitive pressure forces firms to reduce the size of the management staff and focus on their core competencies, many firms are shifting selected service functions to outside suppliers. This opens up opportunities for firms who provide such services as computer support, payroll processing, logistics, food operations, and equipment maintenance. These specialists possess a level of expertise or efficiency that organizations can profitably tap. The motivating force for outsourcing by an organization is improved productivity, as the ad by GE Information Services illustrates (see Figure 1.5). Business services include **maintenance and repair support** (for example, machine repair) and **advisory support** (for example, management consulting or information management). Like supplies, services are considered expense items.

In the business market, services have experienced dramatic growth in such areas as computer support and training, temporary staffing, management consulting, and equipment leasing. For example, the market for computer services and software is growing twice as fast as the market for traditional computer hardware. This is creating strong demand for the services of firms such as Andersen Consulting and Computer Associates that offer problem-solving skills in the areas of information processing and management. The Internet also provides a path to the services market. For instance, Ernst & Young offers small businesses an opportunity to query the firm's consultants electronically in exchange for a flat-fee annual subscription of $6,000.[33]

---

[33]Thomas E. Weber, "Ernst & Young's Consulting Services to Be Sold on Internet for Annual Fee," *The Wall Street Journal,* 5 August 1996, sec. B, p. 7.

Figure 1.5 A Business Marketing Ad That Encourages Outsourcing to Improve Productivity

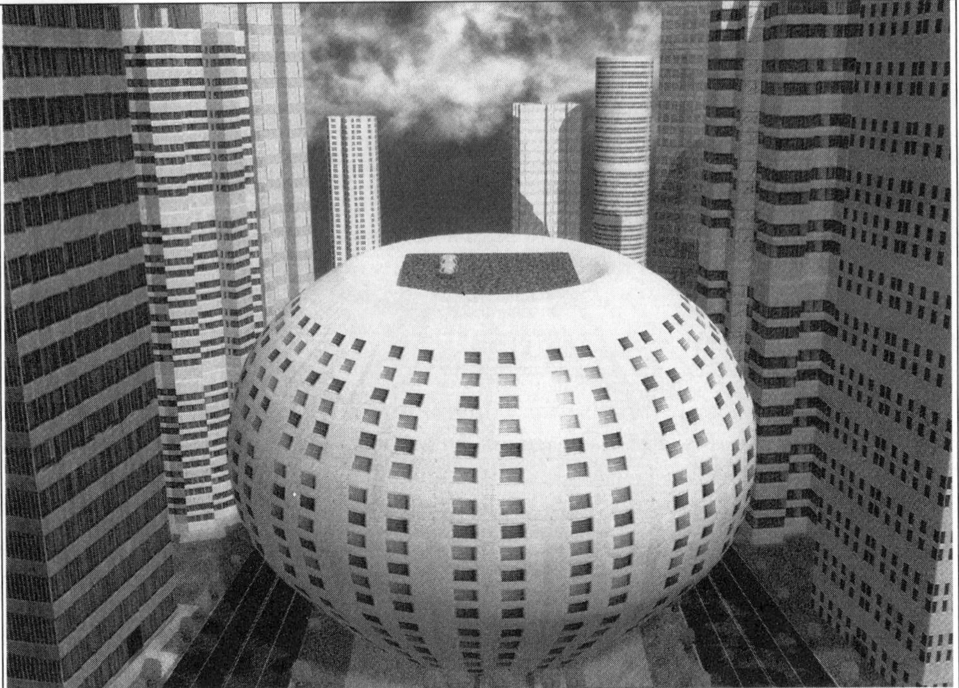

The days of the bloated business are over.

Ballooning costs. Bulging warehouses. Is your business growing in the wrong places? Let GE Information Services relieve some of the pressure.

We help you reduce swollen inventories and take the bulk out of your business, so you can be faster in your markets, more responsive to your customers and more attractive to your shareholders. We enabled a major electronics manufacturer to cut supplier cycle times from 6 days to 1 and slash warehouse space requirements by 50%. Another client has increased salesforce productivity, allowing salespeople to double the amount of "face time" they can spend with clients and prospects.

GE Information Services works with thousands of the world's best known businesses to help reduce costs and improve profitability. Our Business Productivity Solutions[SM] can help you expand where you really want to—in your marketplace.

Productivity. It's All We Do.[SM]

GE Information Services

For more information, please call 1-800-560-GEIS, or write GE Information Services, MC07F3, 401 N. Washington St., Rockville, MD 20850. Find us on the Internet at http://www.geis.com.

Source: Courtesy GE Information Services.

Business Marketing Strategy

Marketing pattern differences reveal the significance of a goods classification system. A marketing strategy appropriate for one category of goods may be entirely unsuitable for another. Often, entirely different promotional, pricing, and distribution strategies are required. The physical nature of the industrial good and its intended use by the organizational customer dictate to an important degree the requirements of the marketing program.

ILLUSTRATION: MANUFACTURED MATERIALS AND PARTS

Recall that manufactured materials and parts enter the buying organization's own product. Whether a part is standardized or customized will often dictate the nature of marketing strategy. For custom-made parts, personal selling activities assume an important role in marketing strategy. The salesperson must link the engineering departments of the buying and selling firms. Though the product is the critical factor in making a sale, once the account is sold, reliable delivery and responsive customer service become primary. Standardized parts are typically purchased in larger quantities on a contractual basis, and the marketing strategy centers on providing a competitive price, reliable delivery, and supporting services. Frequently, industrial distributors are used to achieve responsive delivery service to smaller accounts.

Personal selling is pivotal for many customized materials and parts; advertising is more important for many standardized items. The salesperson must call not only on purchasing agents but also on other key buying influentials (engineers and production managers) who develop product specifications. Careful management of the buyer-seller relationship is crucial to the salesperson's role. Sometimes component marketers will utilize manufacturers' representatives: intermediaries who are independent salespersons representing a variety of suppliers of noncompeting products. The manufacturers' representative is paid a commission on sales and provides a cost-effective way to secure a quality selling effort in markets where demand is low. Advertising supplements personal selling activities. The basic advertising appeals focus on product quality, delivery reliability, price, and service. Many producers of component parts and materials attempt to gain a differential advantage based on their ability to design unique parts for specific applications and also to provide the parts on a timely basis to meet production requirements.

To illustrate, Intel produces microprocessors that are used in diverse applications: automobiles, aircraft, communication equipment, and computers. Often, such sophisticated components are not visible to the prospective buyer or user. Observe in Figure 1.6 how Compaq's advertising is geared toward enhancing the visibility of the "Intel Inside" trademark.

For manufactured materials and parts, the marketer's challenge is to locate and accurately define the unique needs of diverse customers, uncover key buying influences, and adjust the marketing program to serve these customers profitably.

Figure 1.6 A Business Marketing Ad That Highlights the "Hidden" Intel Components for Prospective Buyers

A COMPAQ WITH A 100MHz PENTIUM® PROCESSOR FOR $1,899?

IT'S HERE.

Introducing the Compaq® Armada 1120, the new notebook that can really keep up with you — whether you're on the road, or back in the office. That's because its powerful 100MHz Pentium® processor means high-level performance for Windows® 95 (conveniently preinstalled), and your other demanding business software.

The Armada also comes standard with an 810MB hard drive, and 8MB RAM memory expandable to 24MB. Plus a tilting, full-function keyboard and 10.4" CSTN color display.

Best of all, the Armada 1120 comes with the quality and reliability you'll only find in a Compaq PC. So call today to order. (After all, at this low price they're likely to move even faster than you do.)

COMPAQ ARMADA 1120 ◈ $1,899*

- 100MHz Pentium® Processor
- 8MB RAM expandable to 24MB
- 810MB Hard Drive
- 10.4" CSTN Color Display (also available in CTFT)
- 3.5" 1.44MB Diskette Drive
- Two PCMCIA Type II Slots (or one Type III)
- Tilting, Full-Function Keyboard
- Enhanced NiMH Battery
- Windows 95, MS-Works, and Astound CSE Software Preinstalled
- 1-Year Worldwide Limited Warranty†

TO ORDER CALL:

1-800-888-5952
M-F 7-7 Sat. 9-3 CST. Ask for our free catalog

1-800-308-7774
For your nearest Compaq Authorized Reseller

Source: Courtesy Compaq Computer Corporation.

ILLUSTRATION: INSTALLATIONS

Installations were classified earlier as foundation goods because they are capital assets that affect the buyer's scale of operations. Here the product itself is the central force in marketing strategy, and direct manufacturer-to-user channels of distribution are the norm. Less costly, more standardized installations such as lathes may be sold through marketing intermediaries.

Once again, personal selling is the dominant promotional tool. The salesperson works closely with prospective organizational buyers. Negotiations can span several months and involve the top executives in the buying organization, especially for buildings or custom-made equipment. Multiple buying influences complicate the selling task, as each executive may apply slightly different criteria to the decision process. Trade advertising and direct mail advertising supplement and reinforce personal selling.

Buying motives center on economic factors (such as the projected performance of the capital asset) and emotional factors (such as industry leadership). A buyer may be quite willing to select a higher-priced installation if the projected return on investment supports the decision. For example, a packaging machine that saves the using organization one gram of plastic per unit produced would yield substantial cost savings over its productive life and would be preferred over lower-priced alternatives that did not offer such savings. In summary, the focal points for the marketing of installations include a strong personal selling effort, effective engineering and product design support, and the capability to offer a product that provides a higher return on investment than its competition. Initial price, distribution, and advertising play lesser roles.

ILLUSTRATION: SUPPLIES

The final illustration centers on a facilitating good: supplies. Again we find different marketing patterns. Most supply items reach a horizontal market of organizational customers from many different industries. Although some large users are serviced directly, a wide variety of marketing intermediaries are required to cover this broad and diverse market adequately.

The purchasing agent plays the dominant role in the choice of suppliers and evaluates alternative suppliers on dependability, breadth of assortment, convenience, and price. While always searching for value, the purchasing agent lacks the time to carefully evaluate all available alternatives whenever a purchase requirement surfaces. Thus, dependable sources have the edge.

For supplies, the marketer's promotional mix includes catalog listings, advertising, and, to a lesser extent, personal selling. Advertising is directed to resellers (industrial distributors) and final users. Personal selling is less important for supplies than it is for other categories of goods with a high unit value, such as installations. Thus, personal selling efforts may be confined to resellers and large users of supplies. The degree of emphasis given to personal selling depends on the size of the company, the length of the firm's product line, and the amount of potential demand concentrated in large accounts or in particular geographic areas. For example, a large industrial firm that produces a wide assortment of supply items is better equipped to develop a direct sales force than are smaller firms with narrow product lines.

In general, then, the marketing strategy for supplies centers on developing the proper assortments of products to match the needs of diverse groups of customers. The selection of an effective group of industrial distributors is often fundamental to the marketing strategy. Price may be critical in the marketing strategy, since many supply items are undifferentiated. By providing the proper product assortment, timely and reliable delivery, and competitive prices, an industrial marketer of supply items may be able to develop a long-term contractual relationship with a customer.

The focus and direction of marketing strategy change from one category of industrial goods to another. Yet in every case, the marketer's ultimate concern must be how potential organizational customers view a particular product. Views may be quite different from customer to customer; potential buyers have varying levels of experience with specific products, in addition to having distinct organizational objectives and requirements. The successful business marketer recognizes unique organizational needs and satisfies them.

A Look Ahead

The chief components of the business marketing management process are shown in Figure 1.7. Business marketing strategy is formulated within the boundaries established by the corporate mission and objectives. A corporation determining its mission must define its business and purpose, assess environmental trends, and evaluate its strengths and weaknesses. Corporate objectives provide guidelines within which specific marketing objectives are formed. Business marketing planning must be coordinated and synchronized with corresponding planning efforts in R&D, procurement, finance, production, customer service, and other areas. Clearly, strategic plans emerge out of a bargaining process among functional areas. Managing conflict, promoting cooperation, and developing coordinated strategies are all fundamental to the business marketer's interdisciplinary role.

The business marketing management framework (Figure 1.7) provides an overview of the five major parts of this volume. This chapter introduced some of the features that distinguish industrial from consumer-goods marketing. The remaining chapter in Part I scrutinizes the nature of business market organizations and the major types of industrial customers: commercial enterprises, governmental units, and institutions.

Organizational buying behavior constitutes the theme of Part II, which first examines the organizational buying process and the myriad forces that affect the organizational decision maker. Special attention is also given to particular strategies that business marketers can follow in developing relationships with business market customers. Part III turns to the measurement of business market opportunities, demonstrating specific techniques for evaluating the relative attractiveness of alternative sectors of the market and for selecting target segments.

Part IV centers on designing business marketing strategy. Each component of the marketing mix is treated from a business marketing perspective. Special attention is also given to the marketing of services. Formulation of the business marketing mix (see Figure 1.7) requires careful coordination with such functional areas in the firm as R&D and production. The processes of monitoring and controlling the marketing program are analyzed in Part V. A central theme is how business marketing management seeks to minimize the discrepancy between expected and actual results in target markets by planning for and acquiring relevant and timely marketing information.

Figure 1.7 A Framework for Business Marketing Management

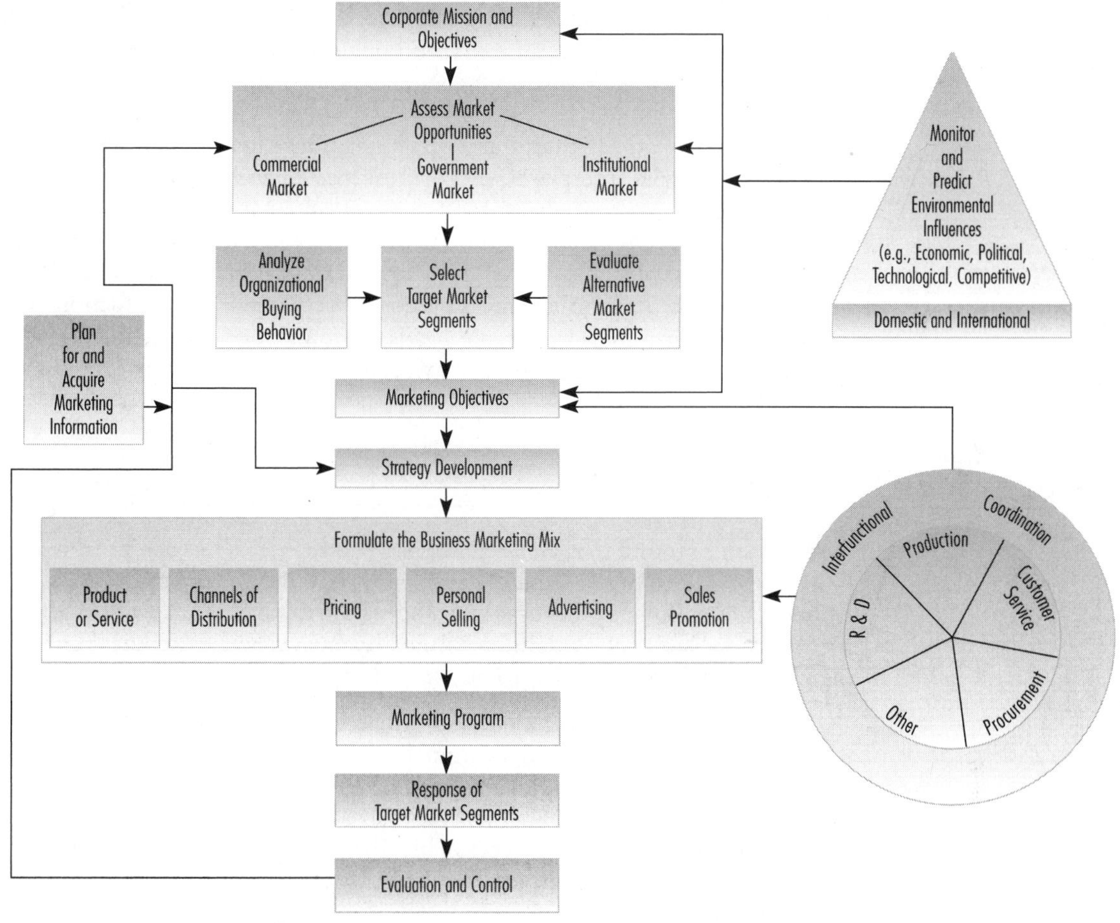

Summary

The business market offers significant opportunities and special challenges for the marketing manager. Market-driven firms in the business market demonstrate superior skills in understanding and satisfying customers. They also possess strong market-sensing and customer-linking capabilities. Although a common body of knowledge and theory spans all of marketing, important differences exist between consumer and business marketing, among them the nature of markets, demand patterns, buyer behavior, and buyer-seller relationships.

The dramatic rise in competition on a worldwide basis requires a global perspective of markets. To secure a competitive advantage in this challenging environment, business market customers are developing closer, more collaborative ties with fewer suppliers than they have used in the past, and are demanding quality and speed from their suppliers to an unprecedented degree. These important trends in procurement place a premium on the supply-chain management capabilities of the business marketer. Business marketing programs increasingly involve a customized blend of tangible products, service support, and ongoing information services both before and after the sale. Relationship management constitutes the heart of business marketing.

The diverse organizations that make up the business market can be broadly divided into (1) commercial enterprises, (2) governmental organizations, and (3) institutions. Because purchases made by these organizational consumers are linked to goods and services that they generate in turn, derived demand is an important and often volatile force in the business market. Industrial goods can be classified into three categories, based on how the product enters the cost structure and the production process of the buying organization: (1) entering goods, (2) foundation goods, and (3) facilitating goods. Specific categories of goods may require unique marketing programs.

Discussion Questions

1. A recent study found that General Motors had higher costs than Ford or Chrysler because it produced more auto parts itself instead of buying them from outside suppliers. What factors might contribute to this cost disparity? What decision rules might be applied by an automaker in determining what to make versus what to buy from suppliers?
2. Du Pont, one of the largest industrial producers of chemicals and synthetic fibers, spends millions of dollars annually on advertising its products to final consumers. For example, Du Pont invested more than one million dollars in a TV advertising blitz that emphasized the comfort of jeans made of Du Pont's stretch polyester-cotton blend. Since Du Pont does not produce jeans or market them to final consumers, why are large expenditures made on consumer advertising?
3. What are the chief differences between consumer-goods marketing and business marketing? Use the following matrix as a guide in organizing your response:

	Consumer-Goods Marketing	**Business Marketing**
Customers	__________	__________
Buying Behavior	__________	__________
Buyer/Seller Relationship	__________	__________
Product	__________	__________
Price	__________	__________
Promotion	__________	__________
Channels	__________	__________

4. Explain how a company such as G.E. might be classified by some business marketers as a user customer but by others as an OEM customer.

5. Spending a day in the life of a marketing manager would demonstrate the critical importance of relationship management skills as that manager interacts with employees of other functional areas and, indeed, with representatives from both customer and supplier organizations. Explore the strategic significance of such relationships.

6. Consumer products are frequently classified as convenience, shopping, or specialty goods. This classification system is based on how consumers shop for particular products. Would this classification scheme apply equally well in the business marketing environment?

7. Evaluate this statement: "The ways that leading companies manage time in the supply chain—in new product development, in production, in sales and distribution—are the most powerful new sources of competitive advantage."

8. Evaluate this statement: "The demand for major equipment (a foundation good) is likely to be less responsive to shifts in price than that for materials, supplies, and components." Do you agree or disagree? Support your position.

9. Many firms are shifting selected service functions to outside suppliers. For example, Lucent Technologies, the Bell Labs equipment company, recently outsourced its information management function to IBM. What factors would prompt such a decision and what criteria would a customer, like Lucent Technologies, emphasize in choosing a supplier?

Chapter 2

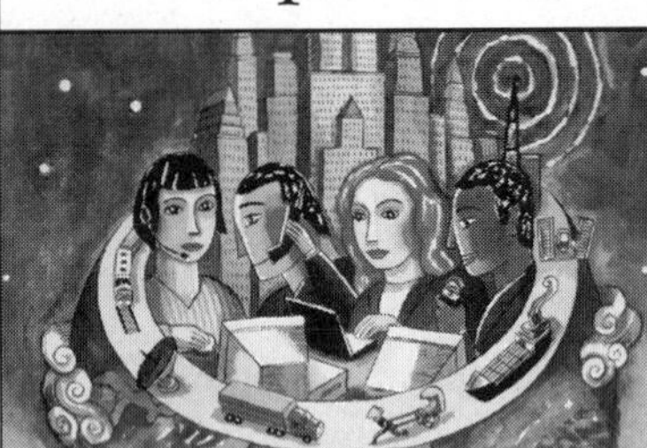

The Business Market: Perspectives on the Organizational Buyer

The business marketer requires an understanding of the needs of a diverse mix of organizational buyers drawn from three broad sectors of the business market—commercial enterprises, government (all levels), and institutions—as well as from an expanding array of international buyers. After reading this chapter, you will understand

1. the nature and central characteristics of each of these market sectors.
2. how the purchasing function is organized in each of these components of the business market.
3. the importance and distinguishing characteristics of international organizational buyers.
4. the need to design a unique marketing program for each sector of the business market.

The vast business market is characterized by tremendous diversity. Many goods commonly viewed as final consumer products generate significant demand in the business market. For example, all-vegetable deep-frying oil is a common grocery item that also enjoys a huge market in the business marketing arena. In fact, estimates place the total business market usage of deep-frying oil at somewhere close to 400 million gallons annually. Deep-frying oil is bought by *commercial firms*—manufacturers of food products (frozen foods, breaded fish, and so forth), fast-food restaurant chains, airline meal-preparation contractors, hotel restaurant operators, and business firms that furnish food for their employees; *institutions*—schools, hospitals, and universities (educational institutions, including schools, colleges and universities, sell more than $17 billion of food annually, whereas health-care institutions exceed $23 billion in annual food sales); and *governments*—federal, state, and local (the U. S. Army is the single largest food-service organization in the world, and various officer and NCO clubs serve nearly $1 billion in food each year). The magnitude of the food-service market and its importance to manufacturers of deep-frying oil is illustrated by its projected sales volume in 1996: $314 billion![1]

The channels of distribution as well as the product characteristics and packaging configurations for deep-frying oils reflect the diversity of the business marketer's customers and of their requirements. For commercial firms in the food-processing industry, purchases of deep-frying oil are made directly from the manufacturer. A processor of frozen fish who is a significant user of deep-frying oil will buy standard grade oil in railroad-car quantities. Some large food processors utilize fryers that have the capacity for 1,000 pounds of oil.

In the restaurant market, oil is purchased directly from the manufacturer through the restaurant chain's own wholesaling company or through food-service distributors (wholesalers). Most company-owned Burger King franchises purchase deep-frying oil through Burger King's own subsidiary distributor, whereas the independent franchisees are free to buy from any manufacturer or distributor. For many school districts, on the other hand, deep-frying oil is purchased in much smaller quantities from a distributor. Universities, depending on the size of their food-service operation, will either purchase directly from the manufacturer (like the University of Texas, which runs a sizable food-service operation) or a food-service distributor (that also supplies hundreds of additional grocery and food-service products). Military purchases are made through a formal bidding process and usually provide the oil supplier with a six-month to one-year contract for supplying a stipulated quantity of oil. However, in some instances, the chef at a particular officers' club will specify that only a certain brand of deep-frying oil should be purchased. In this case, the bidding process is circumvented.

Requirements for product quality are as diverse as the types of buyers in the food-service market. For a small, elegant restaurant, how long the deep-frying oil lasts and its effect on the taste of the food will be critical factors, so the highest-quality oil will be purchased. A school district will be responsive to cost and concentrate on finding the lowest-priced oil. The Marriott Corporation, which operates a major in-flight meal-preparation business for the airlines, will pay close attention to product availability (that is, delivery service) as well as cost and quality.

Each of the three business market sectors—commercial firms, institutions, and governments—have identifiable and unique characteristics that must be understood by the business marketer. A significant first step in creating successful marketing strategy is to isolate the unique dimensions of each of the major sectors of the business market. How much market potential does each sector represent? Who makes the purchasing decision? The answers provide a foundation upon which the marketing manager can formulate marketing programs that respond to the specific needs and characteristics of each business market sector.

---

[1]Michael Bartlett, "Restaurants and Institutions' 1996 Annual Forecasts," *Restaurants and Institutions,* 1 January 1996, p. 18.

Commercial Enterprises: Unique Characteristics

Commercial enterprises include manufacturers, construction companies, service firms (for example, hotels), transportation companies, selected professional groups (for example, dentists), and resellers (wholesalers and retailers purchasing equipment and supplies for use in their operations). Manufacturers are the most important commercial customers, spending more than $1.5 trillion on materials each year.

DISTRIBUTION BY SIZE

A startling fact about the study of manufacturers is that there are so few of them. Available evidence suggests that there are approximately 387,000 manufacturing firms in the United States.[2] And though only 36,000 manufacturing firms (9.3 percent) employ more than 100 workers each, this handful of firms ships more than 75 percent of all products manufactured in the United States. Clearly, these large buyers can be very important to the business marketer. Because each large firm has such vast sales potential, the business marketer will often tailor a marketing strategy for each customer. Smaller manufacturing firms also constitute an important segment for the business marketer. In fact, almost two-thirds of all manufacturers in the United States employ fewer than 20 people.[3] Because the organizational buyer in smaller firms has different needs and often a different orientation, the astute marketer will adjust the marketing program to the particular needs of this market segment.

GEOGRAPHICAL CONCENTRATION

Distribution of industrial firms by size is not the only form of concentration important to the business marketer: Manufacturers are also concentrated geographically (see Figure 2.1). Primary areas of industrial concentration include the Midwest (Ohio, Indiana, Illinois, and Michigan) and the Middle Atlantic states (New Jersey, Pennsylvania, and New York). However, significant industrial growth and concentration have occurred in the Southeast and Southwest during the past two decades. In the 1970s eight Southwestern states (Arizona, California, Colorado, Nevada, New Mexico, Oklahoma, Texas, and Utah) accounted for 15.7 percent of all shipments by manufacturers; by the 1990s their share had risen to 21.1 percent.[4] Four states—California, New York, Ohio, and Illinois—employ almost five million people in manufacturing,

---

[2]U.S. Department of Commerce, Bureau of the Census, *Statistical Abstract of the United States, Report #859, Establishments, Employees and Payroll: 1992* (Washington, D.C., 1992).

[3]U.S. Department of Commerce, Bureau of the Census, *Annual Survey of Manufacturers, Statistics for Industry Groups* (Washington, D.C., 1994), p. 3-5.

[4]U.S. Department of Commerce, Bureau of the Census, *Annual Survey of Manufacturers, Geographic Area Statistics* (Washington, D.C., 1992), pp. 3-5 to 3-11.

Figure 2.1 Geographic Concentration of Manufacturing in the United States: Percentage of U.S. Manufacturing Employment

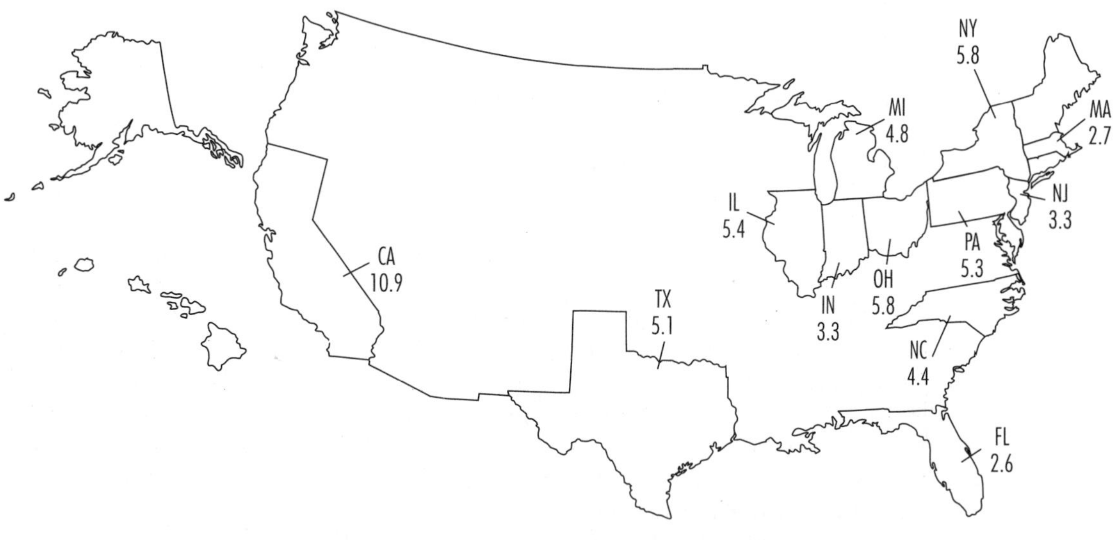

Source: U.S. Department of Commerce, Bureau of the Census, *1991 Annual Survey of Manufacturers, Geographic Area Statistics* (Washington, D.C., 1992), pp. 3-5 to 3-11.

representing 28 percent of the nation's jobs in manufacturing.[5] Most large metropolitan areas are lucrative business markets. Geographical concentration of industry, however, means only that a large potential volume exists in a given area; the requirements of each buyer may still vary significantly.

Geographic concentration has some important implications for the formulation of marketing strategy. First, firms can concentrate their marketing efforts in areas of high market potential and make effective use of a full-time personal sales force in these markets. Second, distribution centers in large-volume areas can ensure rapid delivery to a large proportion of customers. Finally, firms may not be able to tie their salespeople to specific geographic areas because many large buying organizations entrust to one individual the responsibility for purchasing certain products and materials for the entire company.

For example, the Kroger Company, a huge supermarket chain, has centralized purchasing in Cincinnati for store supplies and fixtures. Thus, everything from paper bags to display cases are purchased in Cincinnati for distribution to individual stores. A paper-bag salesperson whose territory includes all retail stores in Tennessee and

[5]U.S. Department of Commerce, Bureau of the Census, *Census of Manufacturers, Report MC92-SUM* (Washington, D.C., October 1994), p. 1.

Arkansas cannot be very effective against a competitor who maintains a sales office in Cincinnati. The marketer requires an understanding of how a potential buyer's purchasing organization is structured.

THE PURCHASING ORGANIZATION

Every firm, regardless of its organizational characteristics, must procure the materials, supplies, equipment, and services necessary to operate the business successfully. On average, more than half of every dollar earned from sales of manufactured products is spent on materials, supplies, and equipment needed to produce the goods.[6] The 100 largest industrial firms (from a purchasing standpoint) annually spend almost $600 billion on a wide array of goods and services.[7] Ford was the largest buyer, followed by General Motors and Chrysler Corporation. The magnitude of expenditures by large corporations is staggering—in one year Chrysler spent $1.5 billion on seats alone, while McDonnell Douglas doled out $850 million for jet engines and Hewlett-Packard spent $1.04 billion on semiconductors.[8] How goods and services are purchased depends on such factors as the nature of the business, the size of the firm, and the volume, variety, and technical complexity of items purchased. Rarely do individual departments within a corporation do their own buying. Procurement is usually administered by an individual whose title is manager of purchasing, purchasing agent, director of purchasing, or materials manager.

Purchasing in Large Firms

In large firms purchasing has become quite specialized, with the work typically divided into five categories:

1. *Management.* Purchasing management tasks emphasize the development of policies, procedures, controls, and mechanics for coordinating purchasing operations with operations of other departments.
2. *Buying.* Buying includes developing specifications and requirements, reviewing requisitions, conducting informal research, investigating vendors, interviewing salespeople, studying costs and prices, and negotiating.
3. *Follow-up and expediting.* Order follow-up and expediting involves vendor liaison work such as reviewing the status of orders, writing letters, telephoning and faxing vendors, and occasionally visiting vendors' plants.
4. *Special research work.* Any well-developed purchasing operation has an unending number of projects and studies requiring specialized knowledge

[6]Stuart Heinritz, Paul U. Farrell, Larry Giunipero, and Michael Kolchin, *Purchasing, Principles, and Applications* (Englewood Cliffs, N.J.: Prentice-Hall, 1991), p. 4.
[7]Anne Millen Porter, "The 100 Largest Buyers," *Purchasing* 119 (November 1995): pp. 34-42.
[8]Ernest Raia, "Top 100: 1992," *Purchasing* 113 (19 November 1992): p. 49.

and uninterrupted effort, including economic and market studies, special cost studies, vendor investigations, and systems studies.

5. *Clerical.* Every department must write orders and maintain not only working files but also catalog and library materials and records for commodities, vendors, and prices.[9]

The purchasing manager is responsible for administering the purchasing process and, on occasion, may be involved in the negotiations of a small number of important contracts.

The day-to-day purchasing function is carried out by buyers, each of whom is responsible for a specific group of products. Organizing the purchasing function in this way permits buyers to acquire a high level of technical expertise on a limited number of items. As products and materials become more sophisticated, buyers must become more knowledgeable about material characteristics, manufacturing processes, and design specifications. In some cases, the salesperson requires enough knowledge of competing products to respond effectively to a buyer's probing questions.

The typical purchasing department is organized by type of product to be procured. If the firm is large, buyers will not report directly to the purchasing manager but to an intermediate-level manager, usually with the title of purchasing agent or buying department manager. The buyers will be specialized by type of product and will concentrate all their attention on buying just a few items in their assigned product category. Frequently, a sizable group will be employed to conduct research, evaluate materials, and perform cost studies.

Purchasing on the Internet

Exponential growth of the World Wide Web in the 1990s has stimulated the rapid expansion of purchasing activities over the Internet. Using the Internet, buyers are able to scan the Web to find new suppliers, check on current suppliers, and track business trends that affect their industry, and in some cases, place an order.[10] Importantly, research on potential suppliers and communicating with suppliers are some of the most frequent applications on the Internet. Though applications are somewhat limited, some firms are actually ordering low-value, frequently ordered products through the Internet. Purchasing's use of the Internet is expected to grow quickly once security problems with sensitive pricing and payment data are solved. A key requirement will be the development of encryption software that assures secure transactions. Incentives for using the Internet to transmit purchase orders are significant: It is estimated that purchase orders processed over the Internet would cost only $5, compared to the current average purchase-order cost of $100.[11] The Inside Business Marketing

[9]Donald W. Dobler, David N. Burt, and Lamar Lee Jr., *Purchasing and Materials Management* (New York: McGraw-Hill, 1990), p. 99.
[10]"Where Exactly Is the Internet?" *Purchasing* 120 (15 February 1996): p. 5.
[11]"Buyers Find Sources on the Internet," *Purchasing* 119 (14 December 1995): p. 82.

box on page 41 illustrates how buyers may use the Internet to find suppliers and supplier information.

The Marketer's Role

The nature and size of the purchasing department will have an important bearing on the formulation of marketing strategy. Considering the large number of small companies in the United States, most purchasing departments are one- or two-person operations. The purchasing agent may report to the president, general manager, controller, or production manager. The purchasing agent in the small firm may lack detailed knowledge and expertise. In this case, the industrial salesperson should be viewed as an extension of the customer's purchasing department, acting as a consultant and providing assistance wherever required.

When dealing with the large corporation, in which specialized buyers assigned to limited product categories have achieved sophistication in purchasing, the salesperson must be able to respond to specific questions about product quality, performance, and costs. Purchasing units in large organizations are likely to use computer technology that significantly expands their ability to gather, process, and store information on the attributes and the performance history of alternative suppliers.

Some large corporations that have geographically dispersed manufacturing facilities, with relatively similar requirements for supplies and materials, coordinate a significant volume of their purchases through a centralized procurement unit. Mead Corporation's Dayton, Ohio, headquarters directs the flow of equipment and materials to plant locations in Tennessee, Michigan, Wisconsin, and other locations. In response to centralized purchasing, many business marketers have developed a national accounts sales force, assigning one or more salespersons the responsibility of meeting the needs of a single large customer with sizable sales potential. (The strategic implications of centralized buying and national accounts selling are explored in Chapter 3.) Sales personnel and marketing managers who can effectively adapt to the purchasing conditions in each market segment are generally the leading marketers in their industry.

MATERIALS MANAGEMENT: INTEGRATING PURCHASING INTO THE BUSINESS OPERATION

Many manufacturers have adopted a more broad-based and integrated approach to the organization of purchasing activities. Under this organizational concept, referred to as **materials management,** an individual manager oversees all activities principally concerned with the flow of materials into an organization (including determination of manufacturing requirements; production scheduling; and the procurement, storage, and disbursement of materials).[12] Table 2.1 describes the array of tasks typically

---

[12]Michael R. Leenders and Harold E. Fearon, *Purchasing and Materials Management* (Homewood, Ill.: Richard D. Irwin, Inc., 1993), p. 5.

THE ORGANIZATION'S RESPONSIBLITY

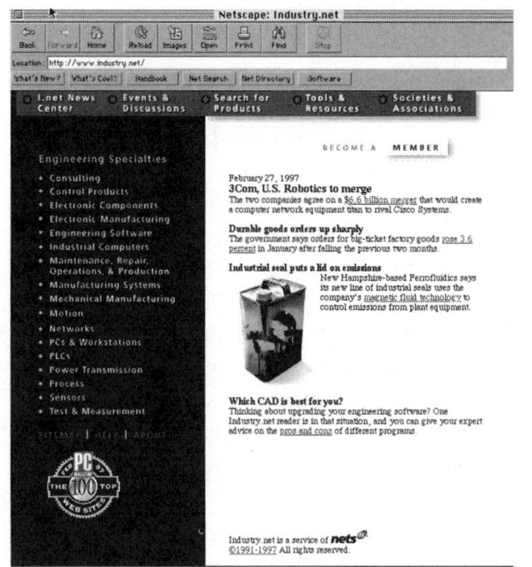

I. Find the Industry Net home page. Industry Net provides information on suppliers of various products.

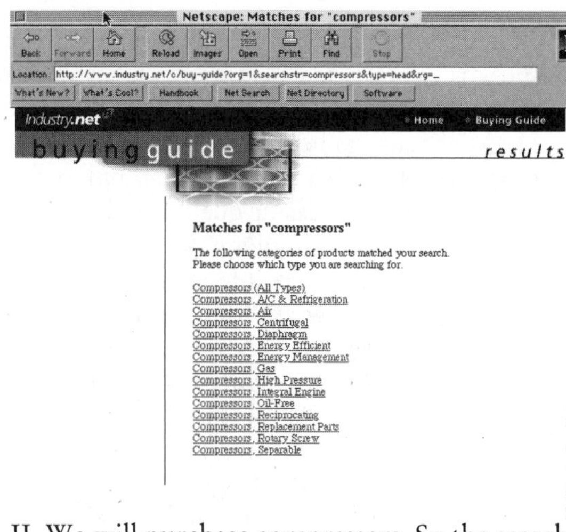

II. We will purchase compressors. So the search shows that we must select the type of compressor.

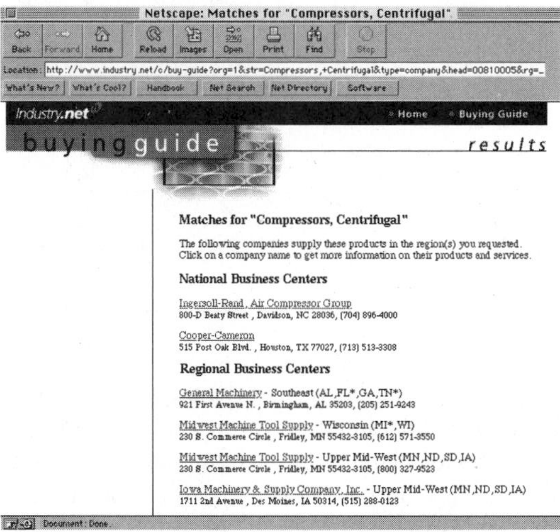

III. The search next takes us to our choice, "Centrifugal Compressors" Business Centers and specific firms selling this product are listed.

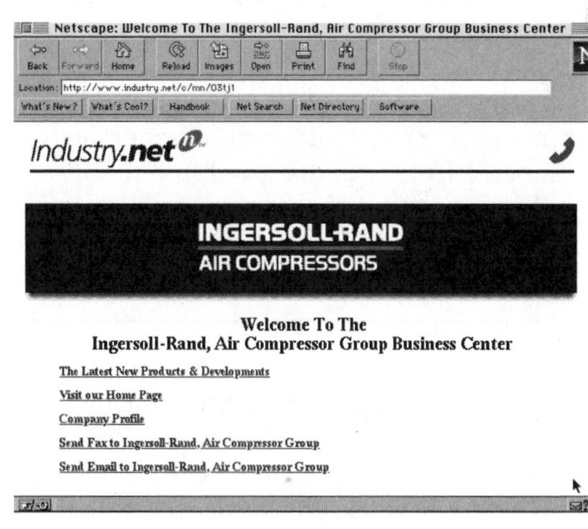

IV. We select Ingersoll-Rand for further investigation. Ingersoll's web site will provide information on the company, new products, and how to communicate with them.

HONDA OF AMERICA: WORLD-CLASS SUPPLIER RELATIONSHIPS

Honda of America Manufacturing, Inc. (HAM) views their suppliers as a key strategic element to the success of their business. HAM's focus has been to develop world class suppliers who will adopt Honda's approach to reducing costs, increasing quality, and developing leading-edge technology.

Honda goes to great lengths to help suppliers understand that they seek a long-term, mutually-beneficial relationship and that Honda will commit resources to **help** suppliers reach the desired level of performance. Suppliers are an essential ingredient to the "Honda Team," and as one Honda senior vice president states: "If suppliers aren't an integral part of our thinking and activity, we will surely fail."

Interaction between Honda and its suppliers is continuous: frequently, the 800 HAM personnel who work with suppliers will reside at the supplier's plant for months at a time; suppliers involved in new model design may spend months at the Honda development centers in Marysville, Ohio, and in Japan. Honda's involvement with suppliers is comprehensive, ranging from examining and fine-tuning supplier manufacturing processes, to encouraging suppliers to develop quality circles, and to becoming politically involved in issues that affect business. Some suppliers find this approach threatening at first, but most adjust to it and end up benefiting a great deal. The president of a major supplier raves about Honda:

> *"There's no question that once Honda determines they want to work with you, they truly are committed to you as a valued team member. After our initial visits to Honda, we concluded that we wanted to be like them. We have adopted many of their approaches for our company."*

The significance of Honda's approach to their suppliers is best explained by that same vice president:

> *"If you are not committed to Honda's process, it can be intimidating; but with Honda, the long-term partnership is there. It's truly successful for both parties."*

Source: Adapted from "For Supplier Development—Honda Wins," *Purchasing* 119 (21 September 1995), pp. 32–40.

included under the materials management umbrella. Note that the purchasing function is only one element of the entire materials management process. By giving the materials manager overall authority, the activities of various departments can be coordinated in order to ensure that the total cost of materials to the organization is minimized. Without this central authority, savings in one function, such as purchasing, may add cost in another, such as inventory control.

Materials management has made purchasing personnel aware of the need to evaluate every element in the flow of purchased materials—including net delivered price, inventory control, traffic, receiving, and production control. The result places an

Table 2.1 Tasks of Materials Management

1. *Production planning:* To prepare the master production plan in support of the sales levels projected in the marketing plan.
2. *Requirements planning:* To translate planned production levels into materials requirements to establish the base for ordering.
3. *Scheduling:* To develop complete and detailed work schedules to determine production sequences and dates.
4. *Purchasing planning:* To establish materials budgets, ordering cycles, quantities, and dates as well as due dates for incoming materials.
5. *Order placement:* To execute purchasing plan by placing purchase orders with approved vendors and responding to emergency requests.
6. *Expediting:* To follow up on orders placed and shipments en route to make sure that materials are received on time.
7. *Traffic:* To select modes of transportation and carriers and to audit freight bills.
8. *Materials handling and storage:* To receive, inspect, move, store, and protect all incoming materials.
9. *Shipping:* To select, pack, and ship the finished product to the customer.
10. *Inventory control:* To manage inventory levels to minimize investment while avoiding stockouts.

Source: Eberhard E. Scherring, *Purchasing Management* (Englewood Cliffs, N.J.: Prentice-Hall, 1989), p. 85.

extremely heavy burden on the business marketing strategist. Marketing managers must coordinate all activities that affect the materials management function of their customers—including sales management, credit, traffic, expediting, warehousing, and production—and must be able to secure the necessary distribution support from their own logistics department.

Just-in-Time Systems

A strategy of purchasing, production, and inventory practiced in many industries is referred to as **just in time** or **JIT.** The essence of the concept is to deliver defect-free parts and materials to the production process just at the moment they are needed. John Flanagan and James Morgan succinctly capture the essence of JIT:

> *JIT is not just a system for keeping track of orders and schedules. It is a discipline that calls for continuous re-examination of how manufacturers go about*

> *making what they make—making the production cycle more and more functional, making it tighter from order to shipment—including interactions with suppliers. In short, it is a discipline that attacks waste at every level.*[13]

The JIT concept was originally introduced by the Toyota Motor Company nearly 40 years ago and it has now taken hold in many manufacturing industries globally. In the United States, industries from automobiles to apparel have adopted the JIT concept. In the apparel industry's just-in-time inventory system, the distribution capability of fabric suppliers is critical. Suppliers that can synchronize their own production, inventory, and distribution systems with those of the apparel maker have the best chance of winning sizable, long-term contracts. The advent of the materials management concept and the associated JIT philosophy has stimulated a more systematic approach to business marketing strategy and a closer working relationship between buyers and sellers.

Just-in-time systems link purchasing, procurement, manufacturing, and logistics in such a way that the storage, movement, inspection, and production of all materials needed for the manufacturing of a given product are clearly specified. Inherent to such a system is a precise sequencing and scheduling of when these activities are to be completed. The goals of JIT are to minimize parts and materials inventories, improve product quality, maximize production efficiency, and provide optimal levels of customer service. At the core of any JIT system is the idea that parts and materials inventories are to be avoided; the goal is simply to eliminate inventory. General Motor's Buick facility in Flint, Michigan, was able to do just that with the implementation of a JIT system: Inventory on hand and in transit was reduced from $48 million to $25 million. Other companies have reported inventory savings of up to 70 percent with the implementation of JIT systems.[14]

Supply-Chain Management

A strategy very much related to JIT that is gaining wider acceptance in the business-to-business market is the practice of **supply-chain management (SCM).** SCM is a technique for linking a manufacturer's operations with those of all its strategic suppliers and its key intermediaries and customers. It seeks to integrate the relationships and operations of both immediate, first-tier suppliers and those several tiers back in the supply chain. A buyer following an SCM strategy will reach several tiers back in the supply chain to assist second, third, and fourth tier suppliers in meeting JIT requirements like quality, delivery, and the providing of timely information. The goal of SCM is to improve timing and costs in manufacturing and delivery through strong vendor relationships.[15]

Implementation of a supply-chain management system often results in working with fewer vendors. Streamlining the vendor base enables the buyer to more

---

[13]John Flanagan and James P. Morgan, *Just-in-Time for the '90s* (Washington, D.C.: DREF, 1989), p. 19.
[14]Heinritz et al., *Purchasing, Principles, and Applications*, p. 309.
[15]Rick Mullin, "Managing the Outsourced Enterprise," *Journal of Business Strategy* (July/August 1996): p. 32.

Managing in the 21st Century

TRENDS RESHAPING THE PURCHASING FUNCTION

A variety of forces are reshaping how organizations will buy materials, parts, and services in the future. Business marketers have an urgent need to monitor these forces because they are reshaping the way organizations buy products and services. Some of the most significant forces transforming the purchasing process include:

1. *Information technology.* Increasingly, Electronic Data Interchange (EDI) is used to link buyers and sellers through their computer systems. EDI permits direct transmission of orders and data between vendors and customers, greatly reducing time, paperwork, and administrative effort. EDI is becoming the preferred way of doing business for both small and large organizations. The Internet will be increasingly used as a tool for researching suppliers, finding product information, and placing orders.

2. *Quality.* Purchasing personnel will continually upgrade their skills in evaluating quality and will assume "ownership" for the quality of supplier performance in all areas. In short, the quality of incoming parts and components is taken as a given.

3. *Fewer suppliers.* Significant advantages will continue to accrue to buyers who are able to pare the supplier base to a select few vendors who are able to meet all requirements effectively. Partnership relations with vendors will be the norm.

4. *Worldwide sourcing.* Information and transportation technology have made global sourcing a reality in many industries. For purchasing, the supplier choice is expanded, but the complexities of dealing with new or different cultures and legal requirements are challenging.

5. *Flexible manufacturing.* "Fragmented production," or the ability to produce goods efficiently in small production runs is becoming the norm. Purchasing will be challenged to deal with the contracting, timing, and inventory decisions involved in flexible manufacturing systems.

6. *Focus on relationships.* More firms will seek long-term relationships with their suppliers as a way to enhance quality and lower costs. A "supply chain" perspective increasingly will be adopted: buyers will form relationships with firms that are one or more tiers behind them in the supply chain. Buyers will be amenable to signing long-term contracts with vendors who will willingly "invest" resources in programs for their customers.

7. *Total cost of ownership (TOC).* Buyers will emphasize the total cost of ownership (TOC) that is associated with buying a vendor's product. TOC looks at many parameters associated with a vendor and its products, many of which are not directly related to the purchase price. Some of the key parameters include the cost to order and ship, special handling costs, costs generated from the impact on the buyer's manufacturing process, and the cost of defects. The focus will be to critically examine *all* costs incurred as a result of doing business with a particular vendor.

Business marketers will be challenged to develop and evolve their tactics and strategies to respond to the evolution of the purchasing function as these trends take hold.

Sources: This material is based on Stuart Heinritz, Paul U. Farrell, Larry Giunipero, and Michael Kolchin, *Purchasing, Principles, and Applications* (Englewood Cliffs, NJ: Prentice-Hall, Inc., 1991), pp. 28–30; Joseph R. Carter and Ram Narasimhan, "A Comparison of North American and European Future Purchasing Trends," *International Journal of Purchasing and Materials Management,* 32 (spring 1996), pp. 12–22; Thomas J. Wall, The ABCs of EDI," supplement to *Sales and Marketing Management,* 148 (January/February 1996), p. 31; "Supplier Integration: A New Level of Supply Chain Management," *Purchasing,* 120 (January 11, 1996), p. 110.

effectively and efficiently manage the entire supply chain. In addition, the supply-chain approach seeks to achieve unified operations among *all* suppliers in the chain. Integration and uniformity is achieved through information sharing, joint planning, shared technology, joint problem solving, and shared benefits. Many experts feel that the advent of supply-chain management will create a higher order of competition—in which supply chains compete against other supply chains rather than individual firms competing against one another.[16]

Close Buyer-Seller Relationships

Companies that adopt the JIT and SCM approaches typically change the way they do business with their suppliers. According to Michael Leenders and Harold Fearon, buyers using the JIT concept must "deal with suppliers of high and consistent quality and with reliable delivery. These imply that concentrating purchases with fewer nearby suppliers may be necessary. Substantial supplier training and cooperation is required to assist in the design and operation of an effective JIT system."[17] Thus, JIT manufacturers often reduce the number of suppliers and enter into multiyear contracts with this smaller group of suppliers.

Allied-Signal, an aerospace and automotive materials firm, feels its competitive success in the 1990s is tied to its ability to respond quickly to the marketplace. As a result, the company will reduce its supplier base from 9,500 to 3,500, and the remaining suppliers will have to show how they will be able to (1) meet exacting quality standards; (2) reduce prices by 10–15 percent; and (3) cut lead times by 30 percent.[18] In return for these single-source, multiyear agreements, suppliers will be expected to deliver high-quality, defect-free materials on a just-in-time basis. The net impact of JIT is that customers and suppliers are communicating more freely, sharing what was once considered proprietary information, and nurturing a close buyer-seller relationship. For JIT manufacturers the trend is definitely in the direction of a reduced supplier base, with single sourcing of many components. Customers that adopt the SCM approach look for ways to reconcile differences in the operating styles and coordination processes of their suppliers. Vendors will be encouraged to meld their operating methods with several other vendors as well as with the customer. These efforts will bind the suppliers and customer into an effective operating "system."

Many buyers today look at the relationship with their vendors as partnerships. Such relationships are often referred to as "strategic alliances," and they involve an enlightened view of the buyer-seller interaction. In these situations, buyers and sellers share sensitive business information, agree to work in a single-source mode, and work to totally integrate their operations so that the buyer's delivery and production requirements are met. General Electric seeks out partnership arrangements with suppliers, but finds that "the most difficult task is convincing top management that multiple sourcing isn't necessary in running a business." A key challenge

---

[16]Robert Monczka and James P. Morgan, "Supplier Integration: A New Level of Supply Chain Management," *Purchasing* 120 (11 January 1996): p. 110.

[17]Leenders and Fearon, *Purchasing and Materials Management*, p. 219.

[18]Joe Mullich, "Allied Signal Puts Emphasis on Speed," *Business Marketing* 78 (April 1993): p. 16.

in managing the relationship with suppliers is to move beyond the urge to "beat the vendor up over cost."[19] Buyers need to focus on evaluating long-term total costs associated with dealing with a particular supplier. As the adoption of JIT systems and the SCM approach accelerates and global competitive pressures increase, the need to develop effective buyer-seller partnerships will be magnified. Such partnerships may prove to be the ingredient that ensures the long-term survival of both buyer and seller.

JIT: Strategy Implications

The implications of JIT and SCM to business marketers are far reaching and perhaps severe. In those industries where these approaches are being adopted, the ability to respond to exacting requirements is fundamental for survival. The ability to deliver defect-free components exactly when they are required provides the edge needed in this new competitive environment. In addition, suppliers are called upon to be a part of the customer's new product design process, as well as to work with their own suppliers to reduce cost and enhance quality. The business marketer wishing to participate in JIT programs and leading-edge supply chains must focus careful attention on developing a quality-management program that ensures that products meet quality standards before they leave the plant. In addition, manufacturing flexibility, delivery capabilities, and responsiveness to customers' requirements are critical elements in forging long-term relationships with customers. Information will play a pivotal role: Supplier data on costs and pricing, supplier input to product design, and the electronic (computer) linkage of all suppliers and the ultimate customer are all features of the buyer-seller relationship that are becoming more important. Some business marketers have been slow to respond to this new environment. If the business marketer can become an effective component of the customer's supply chain, the impact is significant: a possible single-source position in a long-term relationship in which the supplier is viewed as an extension of the customer's company. Importantly, a core component of marketing strategy will be how effectively the business marketer can manage its own supply network in a manner that elevates the performance of its customer's supply chain. Business marketers that are not part of an integrated supply chain will find it difficult to compete in the future.

Governments: Unique Characteristics

Like commercial enterprises, institutions and government purchasers are also enhancing the effectiveness of the purchasing function through the use of materials management and other methods. As indicated in Chapter 1, the federal government is the largest consumer in the United States; its buying procedures are highly

---

[19]Rick Mullin, "Managing the Outsourced Enterprise," p. 30.

Table 2.2 Types of Governmental Units

Type of Unit		Number of Units
U.S. government		1
State government		50
Local government		86,692
County	3,043	
Municipalities	19,296	
Towns & Townships	16,666	
School districts	14,556	
Special districts	33,131	
Total		86,743

Source: U.S. Department of Commerce, Bureau of the Census, *Statistical Abstract of the United States* (Washington, D.C., 1995), p. 297.

specialized and often very confusing. To compete effectively in the government market, the business marketer must develop a thorough comprehension of this complex buying process. A first step is to understand the variety of governmental units and their characteristics.

There are 86,743 governmental units in the United States (see Table 2.2). Note that a vast majority of these governmental units are local, providing the business marketer with a widely dispersed market. However, there is some market concentration; 10 states account for 49 percent of all governmental units in the United States.[20] The numbers in Table 2.2 are somewhat misleading, indicating the ratio of state and federal units to local units as 1 to 1,700. In reality, many functional areas within state government (education, state police, highway) and agencies within the federal government (defense, space, interior, transportation, postal service) are responsible for a sizable procurement volume. Thus, within federal and state governments, hundreds of people, agencies, and functional areas have direct and indirect influence on the purchasing process.

It is estimated that federal, state, and local government expenditures for current operations were $1,323.8 billion in 1994, with the federal government accounting for $500 billion of the total expenditure and state and local governments accounting for the other 823 billion.[21] Clearly, governmental units rival the commercial sector in terms of total market potential.

[20]U.S. Department of Commerce, Bureau of the Census, *Statistical Abstract of the United States* (Washington, D.C., 1995), p. 297.
[21]Ibid., p. 356.

INFLUENCES ON GOVERNMENT BUYING

Another level of complexity is added to the governmental purchasing process by the array of influences on this process. In federal, state, and large city procurement, buyers report to and are influenced by dozens of interested parties who specify, legislate, evaluate, and use the goods and services. Clearly, the range of outside influences extends far beyond the originating agency.

UNDERSTANDING GOVERNMENT CONTRACTS

Government purchasing is also affected by goals and programs that have broad social overtones, including compliance, set-asides, and minority subcontracting. The **compliance program** requires that government contractors maintain affirmative action programs for minorities, women, and the handicapped. Firms failing to do so are barred from holding government contracts. In the **set-aside program,** a certain percentage of a given government contract is "set aside" for small or minority businesses; no others can participate in that proportion of the contract. The **minority subcontracting program** may require that major contractors subcontract a certain percentage of the total contract to minority firms. For example, Ohio law requires that 7 percent of all subcontractors on state construction projects be minorities. The potential government contractor must understand these programs and how they apply to the firm.

Most government procurement, at any level, is based on laws that establish contractual guidelines.[22] The federal government has set forth certain general contract provisions as part of the federal procurement regulations. These provisions include stipulations regarding product inspection, payment methods, actions as a result of default, and disputes, among many others.

Without a clear comprehension of the procurement laws, the vendor is in an unfavorable position during the negotiation phase. The vendor particularly needs to explore the advantages and disadvantages of the two basic types of contracts:

1. *Fixed-price contracts.* A firm price is agreed to before the contract is awarded, and full payment is made when the product or service is delivered as agreed.

2. *Cost-reimbursement contracts.* The vendor is reimbursed for allowable costs incurred in performance of the contract and is sometimes allowed a certain number of dollars above cost as profit.

Each type of contract has built-in incentives to control costs or to cover future contingencies.

---

[22]Harold E. Fearon, Donald W. Dobler, and Kenneth H. Killen, *The Purchasing Handbook* (New York: McGraw-Hill, 1992), pp. 821, 836.

Generally, the fixed-price contract provides the greatest profit potential, but it also poses greater risks if unforeseen expenses are incurred, if inflation increases dramatically, or if conditions change. For example, inflation and unanticipated development problems resulted in a $60 million loss for a defense contractor producing the first 20 fighter planes for the Navy. However, if the seller can reduce costs significantly during the contract, profits may exceed those estimated when the contract was negotiated. Cost-reimbursement contracts are carefully administered by the government because of the minimal incentives for contractor efficiency. Contracts of this type are usually employed for government projects involving considerable developmental work for which it is difficult to estimate efforts and expenses.

To overcome the inefficiencies of both the cost-reimbursement contract (which often leads to cost overruns) and the fixed-price contract (which can discourage firms from bidding because project costs are uncertain), the government often employs incentive contracts. The incentive contract rewards firms when their actual costs on a project are below target costs, and it imposes a penalty when they exceed target costs.

TELLING VENDORS HOW TO SELL: USEFUL PUBLICATIONS

Unlike most customers, governments often go to great lengths to explain to potential vendors exactly how to do business with them. For example, the federal government makes available such publications as *Doing Business with the General Services Administration, Selling to the Military,* and *Selling to the U.S. Air Force.* Government agencies also hold periodic seminars to orient businesses to the buying procedures used by the agency. The objective is to encourage firms to seek government business.

PURCHASING ORGANIZATIONS AND PROCEDURES: GOVERNMENT

Government and commercial purchasing are organized similarly. However, governments tend to emphasize clerical functions because of the detailed procedures the law requires. Although the federal government is the largest single industrial purchaser, it does not operate like a single company but like a combination of several large companies with overlapping responsibilities and thousands of small independent units.[23] The federal government has more than 15,000 purchasing authorities (departments, agencies, and so on). Figure 2.2 provides an example of the diversity of government buying. Every government agency possesses some degree of buying influence or authority. Federal government procurement is divided into two categories: defense and nondefense.

[23]Ibid., p. 838.

Figure 2.2 The Diversity of Federal Government Procurement

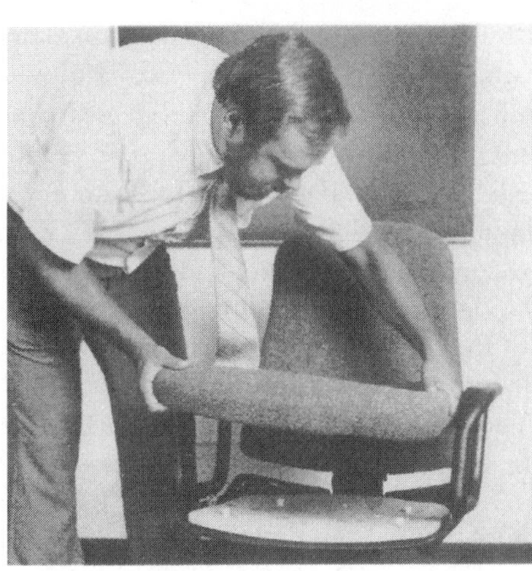

Source: U.S. General Services Administration, *Doing Business with the Federal Government* (Washington, D.C., 1993).

Defense Procurement

The Department of Defense (DOD) spends a large proportion of the federal government's total procurement budget. The DOD's procurement operation is said to be the largest business enterprise in the world, with 170,000 employees who sign 56,000 contracts daily for close to $190 billion in annual expenditures.[24] The end of the cold war signals a new era for the DOD: It must achieve the mission more efficiently and effectively with a smaller force.

Each DOD military division—Army, Navy, and Air Force—is responsible for its own major purchases. However, the Defense Logistics Agency (DLA) procures billions of dollars worth of supplies used in common by all branches. The DLA's budget for procurement was more than $10 billion in 1994.[25] The purposes of the DLA are to obtain favorable prices through volume purchasing and to reduce duplication of purchasing within the military. Defense-related items may also be procured by other government agencies, such as the General Services Administration (GSA). In fact, the DOD is the GSA's largest customer. Under current agreements between the GSA and the DOD, the military purchases through the GSA many items such as cars, desks, office machines, and hand tools.[26] Also, many supplies for military-base operations are procured locally.

Because of the many abuses in defense procurement, the Competition in Contracting Act was passed in 1984.[27] The act requires either competitive bids or justification of sole sourcing. Potential suppliers are required to follow detailed DOD rules and regulations in preparation of their bids. In addition, a sole-source relationship will be carefully reviewed and evaluated as to its conformance with applicable laws.

Nondefense Procurement

Nondefense procurement is administered by a wide variety of agencies, including cabinet departments (for example, Health and Human Services, Commerce), commissions (for example, the Federal Trade Commission), the executive branch (for example, the Bureau of the Budget), federal agencies (for example, the Federal Aviation Agency), and federal administrations (for example, the GSA). The Department of Commerce centralizes the procurement of supplies and equipment for its Washington office and all local offices. The Department of the Interior, on the other hand, instructs each area and district office of the Mining Enforcement and Safety Administration to purchase mine-safety equipment and clothing locally.

Like the DLA, the GSA centralizes the procurement of many general-use items (for example, office furniture, pens, light bulbs) for all civilian government agencies. The Federal Supply Service of the GSA is like the purchasing department of a large diversified corporation because it provides a consolidated purchasing, storing, and distribution network for the federal government. The Federal Supply Service purchases many items commonly used by other government agencies, including office supplies, small tools, paint, paper, furniture, maintenance supplies, and duplicating

---

24 Heinritz et al., *Purchasing, Principles, and Applications*, p. 455.

25 Leslie Kaufman, "The Top Government Purchasers: Defense Logistics Agency–Supply Budget Bucks Downward Trend," *Government Executive* 26 (August 1994): p. 113.

26 U.S. General Services Administration, "Doing Business with the GSA" (Washington, D.C., 1996).

27 Dobler et al., *Purchasing and Materials Management*, p. 688.

Ethical Business Marketing

GLOBALIZATION REQUIRES NEW GROUND RULES

The practice of "sourcing"—using cheap foreign labor to make goods that are sold to domestic buyers—has moved up the political agenda, increasing the pressure on companies to be more accountable for the labor and human rights records of their overseas suppliers. Some well-known firms have taken a strong stand by publishing definitive policies regarding the use of foreign labor. All companies that use "sourcing" will need to consider the cost of setting and maintaining standards against the impact on corporate image of being perceived as a bad-or-uncaring player. The heart of the issue regarding "sourcing" is the link between the plight of domestic and overseas workers, and some firms have introduced codes of conduct that set standards for working conditions in foreign manufacturing facilities.

A shining example is the approach taken by Levi Strauss & Co. Levi Strauss operates in many countries and diverse cultures. Special care is taken in selecting contractors in those countries where goods are produced to ensure that products are being made in a manner that is consistent with the company's values and reputation. The company has adopted a set of global sourcing guidelines that establish the standards contractors must meet to ensure that practices are compatible with corporate values. For instance, the guidelines ban the use of child and prison labor, stipulate environmental requirements, and establish that working hours can not exceed 60 hours per week, with at least one day off in seven.

Source: Adapted from: Robert D. Hass, "Ethics in the Trenches." *Across the Board* 31 (May 1994). pp. 12–13 and Ken Cottrill, "Global Codes of Conduct," *Journal of Business Strategy* 17 (May/June 1996), pp. 55–59.

equipment. In some cases, the GSA operates retail-like stores, where any federal buyer can go to purchase equipment and supplies. The GSA has enormous purchasing power, buying more than $14 billion of products and services annually.[28]

Under the Federal Supply Schedule Program, departments within the government may purchase specified items from an approved supplier at an agreed-upon price. This program provides federal agencies with the sources of products such as furniture, appliances, office equipment, laboratory equipment, and the like. Once a supplier has bid and been approved, the schedule may involve an indefinite-quantity contract for a term of one to three years. The schedule permits agencies to place orders directly with suppliers.

An important aspect of the GSA's procurement activities is the operation of its Business Service Centers (BSC), through which businesses may obtain advice from trained counselors, information on contract opportunities throughout the federal government, and step-by-step help with contracting procedures. The BSCs are located in 11 major cities across the nation.

[28]Jack Sweeny, "GSA Contracts to Include Services," *Computer Reseller News,* 8 April 1996, p. 113.

The GSA is moving rapidly to adopt electronic procurement and payment procedures through a recently developed Federal Acquisition Computer Network (FACNET). FACNET will enable suppliers to obtain information on proposed procurements, submit responses to solicitations, query special databases, and receive awards on a government-wide basis over the Internet.[29] In addition, the GSA maintains an extensive home page on the Internet that provides information on many facets of doing business with them.[30]

FEDERAL BUYING

The president may set the procurement process in motion when he signs a congressional appropriation bill, or an accountant in the General Accounting Office may initiate the process by requesting a new desktop computer. It should be understood that the federal government buys almost everything. In fact, it would be difficult to name a product or service that is not listed at least occasionally in the federal government's publication, *Commerce Business Daily* (*CBD*). The *CBD* is published every Monday through Saturday by the Department of Commerce. It lists all government procurement proposals, subcontracting leads, contract awards, and sales of surplus property. It is important to note that a proposed procurement action appears in the *CBD* only once. A potential supplier has at least 30 days prior to bid opening in which to respond. By law, all intended procurement actions of $10,000 or more, both civilian and military, are published in the *CBD*. Copies of the *CBD* are available at various government field offices as well as local public libraries.

Once a procurement need is documented and publicly announced, the government will follow one of two general procurement strategies: formal advertising (also known as open bid) or negotiated contract.

Formal Advertising

Formal advertising means the government will solicit bids from appropriate suppliers; usually, the lowest bidder is awarded the contract. This strategy is followed when the product is standardized and the specifications straightforward. The interested supplier must gain a place on a bidder's list (or monitor the *CBD* on a daily basis—which suggests that a more effective approach is to get on the bidder's list by filing the necessary forms available from the GSA Business Service Centers). Then, each time the government requests bids for a particular product, the supplier receives an invitation to bid. The invitation to bid specifies the item and the quantity to be purchased, provides detailed technical specifications, and stipulates delivery schedules, warranties required, packing requirements, and other purchasing details. The bidding firm bases its bid on its own cost structure and on the anticipation of competitive bid levels.

---

[29]Office of Enterprise Development, GSA, "Doing Business with the GSA" (Washington, D.C., 1996).
[30]The GSA's Internet address is http://www.gsa.gov

Procurement personnel review each bid for conformance to specifications. For example, one company was disqualified on a $70 million contract for base PBX systems. Although the firm complained that there was no functional need for digital technology in the systems, they were automatically disqualified for not meeting the mandatory bid specifications for a fully digital PBX system. Thus, a critical aspect of marketing strategy for the firm soliciting government business is to develop procedures that ensure all specifications are carefully met. Bid price is obviously another essential strategic dimension in doing business with the government. Contracts are generally awarded to the lowest bidder; however, the government agency may select the next-to-lowest bidder if it can document that the lowest bidder would not responsibly fulfill the contract.

Formal advertising is expensive and time-consuming for all parties, generating a substantial volume of paperwork. However, the process does allow free and open competition. In addition, the government has fairly good assurance that there is no collusion and that it has obtained the lowest possible price.

Negotiated Contract Buying

A negotiated contract is used to purchase products and services that cannot be differentiated on the basis of price alone (such as complex scientific equipment or R&D projects) or when there are few suppliers. There may be some competition, because the contracting office can conduct negotiations with several suppliers simultaneously.

Obviously, negotiation is a much more flexible procurement procedure; the government buyers may exercise considerable personal judgment. Procurement is based on the more subjective factors of performance and quality as well as on price. The procurement decision for the government is much like that of the large corporation: Which is the best possible product at the lowest price, and will the product be delivered on time? Usually, extensive personal selling by the potential contractor is required to convince the government that the firm can perform. The selling effort should include negotiating favorable terms and reasonable payment dates as well as investigating future contracts for which the company may want to bid.

In an effort to streamline government negotiation and buying procedures, some agencies are changing competitive source-selection rules. For example, one new approach is to allow oral proposals.[31] Using this method, each bidding team is called into a conference room and given a set amount of time to convince observers why it can do the best job on a contract. This speeds up the process of negotiation and bidding, and allows for an effective exchange of information. It also challenges the business marketer to carefully craft the presentation and to effectively deliver it to the government procurement team.

Selling to the government is involved, time consuming, and paper generating. Government markets are among the most sophisticated and complex environments within which the business marketer operates.

---

[31]"Federal Acquisition Guide: Bidding Farewell to Old Ways," *Government Executive* 28 (February 1996): p. 5A.

FEDERAL VERSUS COMMERCIAL BUYING

As this chapter has illustrated, there are numerous characteristics that differentiate the federal acquisition process from the commercial buying process. For example, much of the initiative for a major system acquisition originates with the buyer in the case of the defense purchase. In addition, rigid standards (some defined by law) apply to cost, product specifications, completion dates, and technical procedures. As a result, a marketer positioned to sell to the government has a much different marketing strategy focus than does a firm that concentrates on the commercial sector.

The government seller emphasizes (1) understanding the complex rules and standards that must be met; (2) developing a system to keep informed of each agency's procurement plans; (3) generating a strategy for product development and R&D that facilitates the firm's response to government product needs; (4) developing a communications strategy that focuses on how technology meets agency objectives; and (5) generating a negotiation strategy to secure favorable terms regarding payment, contract completion, and cost overruns due to changes in product specifications.

The Institutional Market: Unique Characteristics

The institutional market constitutes the third important market component. Institutional buyers make up a sizable market—in 1993, total expenditures on public elementary and secondary schools alone exceeded $437 billion, and national health expenditures exceeded $884 billion.[32] Schools and health-care facilities are important factors in the institutional market, which also includes penal institutions, colleges and universities, libraries, foundations, art galleries, and clinics. On one hand, institutional purchasers are similar to governments in that the purchasing process is often constrained by political considerations and dictated by law. In fact, many institutions are administered by government units—schools, for example. On the other hand, other institutions are privately operated and managed like corporations; they may even have a broader range of purchase requirements than their large corporate counterparts. Like the commercial enterprise, institutions are ever cognizant of the value of efficient purchasing. If a university can save $100,000 through purchasing efficiencies, and its endowment earns 10 percent, the $100,000 savings is equivalent to an endowment gift of $1 million. Because the institutional market is similar to the other markets, its characteristics will be presented very briefly.

INSTITUTIONAL BUYERS: PURCHASING PROCEDURES

Diversity is the key element in the institutional market. For example, the institutional marketing manager must first be ready to respond to a school purchasing agent

[32]U.S. Department of Commerce, Bureau of the Census, *Statistical Abstract of the United States: 1995* (115th ed.), U.S. Department of the Census (Washington, D.C., 1995), pp. 109, 150.

who buys in great quantity for an entire city's school system through a formal bidding procedure, and then be ready to respond to a former pharmacist who has been elevated to purchasing agent for a small rural hospital.

Health-care institutions provide a good example of the diversity of this market. Some small hospitals delegate responsibility for food purchasing to the chief dietitian. Although many of these hospitals have purchasing agents, the agent cannot place an order unless it has been approved by the dietitian. In larger hospitals, decisions may be made by committees composed of a business manager, purchasing agent, dietitian, and cook. In still other cases, hospitals may belong to buying groups consisting of many local hospitals, or meal preparation may be contracted out. In an effort to contain costs, large hospitals have adopted a materials management type of purchasing organization for purchase, storage, movement, and distribution of goods and equipment. Because of these varied purchasing environments, successful institutional marketers usually maintain a separate marketing manager, staff, and sales force in order to tailor marketing efforts to each situation.

For many institutions, once the budget for a department has been established, the department will attempt to spend up to that budget limit. Thus, institutions may buy simply because there are unused funds in the budget. A business marketer should carefully evaluate the budgetary status of potential customers in the institutional segment of the market.

Because many institutions face strong budgetary pressures, they often look to outsource segments of their operations. School districts may look to third-party contractors to purchase food and supplies and to manage their meal service operations. For example, in Los Angeles, Marriott Corporation manages food service operations at the city's charter schools, while in Chicago, three different contract companies each operate 10 food preparation departments.[33] Many universities have turned over operation of their bookstores, beverage contracts, and management of their student unions to outside contractors. Business marketers must carefully analyze and understand the operational strategy of their institutional customers. Frequently, extensive sales and marketing attention will have to be focused on the third-party contract operators.

Multiple Buying Influences

The institutional market offers some unique applications for the concept of multiple buying influences (discussed in Chapter 1). Many institutions are staffed with professionals—doctors, professors, researchers, and others. In most cases, depending on size, the institution will employ a purchasing agent and, in large institutions, a sizable purchasing department or materials management department. There is great potential for conflict between those responsible for the purchasing function and the professional staff for whom the purchasing department is buying. The purchasing department is in constant contact with suppliers and can challenge restrictive

[33]Susie Stephenson, "Schools," *Restaurants and Institutions* 106 (1 August 1996): pp. 60–64.

specifications, can secure information on market availability, and can arrange for product demonstrations from several major suppliers. However, many staff professionals resent losing their authority to buy from whom they wish. Business marketing and sales personnel, in formulating their marketing and personal selling approaches, must understand these conflicts and be able to respond to them. Often, the salesperson must carefully cultivate the professional staff in terms of product benefits and service while developing a delivery timetable, maintenance contract, and price schedule to satisfy the purchasing department.

Group Purchasing

An important factor in institutional purchasing is group purchasing. Hospitals, schools, and universities may join cooperative purchasing associations to obtain quantity discounts. Universities affiliated with the Education and Institutional Purchasing Cooperative enjoy favorable contracts established by the Cooperative and can purchase a wide array of products directly from vendors at the low negotiated prices. The Cooperative spends more than $100 million on goods annually. Cooperative buying allows institutions to enjoy lower prices, improved quality (through improved testing and vendor selection), reduced administrative cost, standardization, better records, and greater competition.[34]

Hospital group purchasing represents a significant market exceeding $1 billion. Group purchasing has become widely accepted: More than one-third of public sector hospitals in the United States are members of some type of affiliated group. Health-care providers at all levels are involved in buying groups—HPG, a buying group for hospices, affords its members the opportunity to buy from drug manufacturers at the "institutional" price, rather than at retail prices.[35] Most hospital group purchasing is done at the regional level through hospital associations. However, for-profit hospital chains, which are a growing factor in the health-care field, also engage in a form of group buying. Humana, a chain of more than 100 hospitals, buys from its central headquarters for all units in the chain. It is obviously a significant customer for health-care suppliers.

Group purchasing poses special challenges for the business marketer. The marketer must be in a position to develop not only strategies for dealing with individual institutions but also unique strategies for the special requirements of cooperative purchasing groups and large hospital chains. The buying centers—individual institution versus cooperative purchasing group—may vary considerably in composition, criteria, and level of expertise. For the purchasing groups, discount pricing will assume special importance. Vendors who sell through purchasing groups must also have distribution systems that effectively deliver products to individual group members. And even though vendors have a contract with a large cooperative association, they must

---

[34]Michael R. Leenders, Harold E. Fearon, and Wilbur B. England, *Purchasing and Materials Management* (Homewood, Ill.: Richard D. Irwin, 1989), p. 535.

[35]Judy Chi, "Hospices Getting Discounts via Buying Group," *Drug Topics* 140 (8 April 1996): pp. 52–53.

Managing in the 21st Century

GENERAL ELECTRIC'S PURCHASING MOVES TO THE INTERNET

General Electric is representative of many companies who are using the Internet for a variety of purchasing activities. GE's Internet purchasing process is implemented through an arrangement called the *Trading Process Network* (TPN), which matches GE buyers throughout the country with a wide array of suppliers. The TPN allows suppliers to download GE's Request for Proposals and communicate with GE managers; it also provides diagrams of parts specifications for potential suppliers to review on-screen.

The importance of the electronic approach at GE is underscored by the $1 billion worth of goods purchased through the Internet in 1996. Within a few years, GE expects to purchase 50 percent of its requirements through the Internet. The Internet allows GE to reduce purchasing cost and expand the base of suppliers from whom they buy. An added advantage is the ability to combine orders from several GE divisions, enabling the company to request price concessions from vendors and to achieve higher volume discounts.

Tim Smart, "E-sourcing: A Cheaper Way of Doing Business," *Business Week* (August 5, 1996), pp. 82–83.

still be prepared to respond individually to each institution that places an order against the contract.

Professional Purchasing on the Rise

Many institutions, particularly health-care facilities, are faced with a severe cash squeeze and have come to recognize the importance of sound management practices in accomplishing their mission (education, health care). As a result, institutions are rapidly adopting purchasing policies and procedures that have proven successful in industry. Business marketers will be increasingly challenged in the institutional market to respond effectively to professional purchasing personnel who are as skilled in their jobs as are those in commercial firms.

Institutional Purchasing Practices

In many respects the purchasing practices of large institutions are similar to those of large commercial firms. However, there are some important distinctions between institutional and commercial purchasing. The policies regarding cooperative buying, preference to local vendors, and the delegation of purchasing responsibility for food, pharmaceuticals, and a variety of other items are of particular importance. It is just these characteristics that the business marketer must understand in order to carefully develop a sales and communication strategy for this prospective institutional customer.

The International Marketplace for Industrial Goods and Services

A complete picture of the business market must include a horizon that stretches beyond the boundaries of the United States. Probably the most significant business trend during the past 10 years has been the development of a truly global economy. Many speculate that 75 percent of the world economy will be fully integrated within the next few years.[36] While economies in Europe and the United States remain in a slow growth mode, spectacular growth is being recorded in other areas. In the first half of the 1990s, gross domestic product (GDP) rose in China by an average of 12.2 percent, in Thailand by 8.9 percent, in Malaysia by 8.6 percent, and in Taiwan by 6.5 percent.[37]

Business marketers from machine-tool makers to paper mills are finding that they can no longer limit their marketing activities to the confines of the United States and still assure their long-term profitability. The demand for many industrial products is growing more rapidly in many foreign countries than in the United States. Countries like Germany, Japan, Korea, and Brazil offer large and growing markets for most industrial products. In addition, many U.S. manufacturers are producing components, subassemblies, and even finished products offshore in a desire to reduce labor costs. Thus, the demand for industrial products by many U.S. firms may have its roots in a foreign country.

A significant trend having a major impact on industrial marketers is the escalation of **international sourcing.** A. T. Kearney, Inc., reports that 80 percent of *Fortune* 1000 firms use international sourcing for components—a 50 percent increase from five years earlier.[38] U.S. firms look to offshore sources for a variety of reasons, including cost, quality, technology, continuity of supply, and competition.[39] Domestic suppliers of industrial parts, components, and materials will be challenged to develop new techniques and strategies to remain competitive with many of their offshore rivals.

United States companies are dramatically expanding their participation in the global market. An understanding of international markets for industrial products will be a core requirement for the successful business marketing manager of the future. John F. Welch Jr., chief executive officer at G.E., notes: "You can't be a world-class competitor with a domestic headset. You've got to think of selling not in 50 states, but in 50 nations. You have to think of sourcing not in one state or one country, but in 50 countries."[40]

What makes the international marketing job different from marketing to domestic industrial customers? A number of factors must be considered by the U.S. marketer when attempting to penetrate international markets, and these factors center on

---

[36]Victor H. Pooler, *Global Purchasing, Reach for the World* (New York: Von Nostrand Reinhold, 1992), p. 1.

[37]David Smith, "All Aboard the Orient Express," *Management Today,* April 1996, pp. 46-49.

[38]A. T. Kearney, Inc., in "Boardroom Reports," 15 June 1990, p. 5.

[39]Leenders and Fearon, *Purchasing and Materials Management*, p. 497.

[40]Mark Potts and Peter Behr, *The Leading Edge* (New York: McGraw-Hill, 1987), p. 21.

the differences both in the buying process and in the environment in which the transactions take place.

CULTURAL DIFFERENCES AFFECT PURCHASING BEHAVIOR

Ingrained sociocultural patterns, biases, customs, and attitudes—in short, the cultural underpinnings of a country and its people—have a pervasive impact on how buying decisions are made. These manifestations of culture vary dramatically from country to country. Business marketers must closely examine such cultural differences when formulating strategies for each of their international markets. For example, Japanese culture affects the decision-making process within the typical Japanese company. Decisions are usually made by consensus rather than by upper-management decree. Thus the decision process is very slow and deliberate, and the responsible party is a group rather than an individual. In this type of decision-making climate, patience and low-pressure selling tactics are the keys to success.

Chinese buyers also tend to differ in their view of the buyer-seller relationship. Trade experts say the Chinese highly value interpersonal relationships and prefer to do business with friends, which often means getting to know potential suppliers in nonwork settings. Thus, negotiations with Chinese buyers usually include considerable "social time," such as banquets, recreation, sightseeing trips, and tea. Clearly, the business marketer must understand these important cultural impacts on purchase behavior.

PRODUCT USE AND APPLICATION MAY VARY BY COUNTRY

Due to the physical characteristics of the people, the state of economic development, geographic considerations, and a host of additional factors, product designs may need to be altered from area to area or from country to country. Some firms gain a competitive advantage by tailoring their products to individual countries. Hyster, a U.S. producer of forklift trucks, carefully adjusts its product offerings to specific countries in which it competes. In Spain, for example, there is a greater need for smaller trucks because of the large food and wine industries; whereas in Germany, with its large automobile industry, the demand is for heavier trucks. Similarly, General Electric Medical Systems designs products specifically for the Japanese market. Their computer-tomography scanners are smaller than similar domestic scanners because Japanese hospitals are smaller than most U.S. facilities and because the product is scaled to the Japanese patient's smaller size.

On the other hand, other companies secure a competitive advantage by standardizing the product design and exploiting similarities across countries. Boeing (aircraft), Canon (copiers), and Caterpillar (heavy equipment) pursue this strategy. Other elements of the marketing program (for example, marketing communications and service strategies) may be customized to meet the unique needs of buyers in each country.

Remanufacturing—the process in which worn-out products are restored to like-new condition—can also assume a role in many developing markets. This strategy responds to the needs of some potential customers, especially in Third World markets, who simply cannot afford new products. Many capital-equipment items sold in South American countries, for instance, are remanufactured. Remanufactured items are particularly well suited for these markets because they are often only 40–65 percent of the cost of a new item, and their production is based on unskilled labor as opposed to skilled labor and capital equipment.[41]

BUYING PROCEDURES AND POLICIES ARE DIFFERENT

The process of purchasing, including the formal procedures, negotiations, personnel, and bureaucracy, may show marked differences from one country to another. As indicated earlier, decision making is often a group process in many Asian countries. Frequently, these buyers will go to extraordinary lengths to avoid individual action on any decision. Because of the group decision-making process, purchasing decisions are made over a rather long time horizon. The business marketer must be patient and resist the temptation to short-circuit the process.

In some purchase contracts negotiated with foreign buyers, the seller will be required to buy a given quantity of some product manufactured in the foreign country or to accept some of its revenue in the form of goods. The seller must then find a market for these items. Such arrangements are referred to as **countertrade.** As an example, Combustion Engineering negotiated a deal with a Brazilian company (government operated) for $20 million of offshore drilling equipment. In return, Combustion was required to spend $5 million on shoes from Brazil. Of the world's 171 countries, 141 demand countertrade in some or all of their purchases.[42] The ability and willingness to accept countertrade is a significant marketing tool that is correlated to success in many foreign markets. Countertrade is particularly important in countries with "soft currencies" (currencies that cannot be converted to other currencies) and may be the only way to effect a transaction.

Success in the international business market rests on an understanding of the customer and of the surrounding market forces. Although similarities exist in the business marketing process across countries, the marketing strategy must be targeted to the culture, product usage, and buying procedures of the foreign buyers.

---

[41]Diane McConocha and Thomas W. Speh, "Remarketing: Commercialization of Remanufacturing Technology," *Journal of Business and Industrial Marketing* 6 (winter/spring 1991): pp. 23–37.

[42]Fearon, Dobler, and Killen, *The Purchasing Handbook*, p. 194.

Figure 2.3 A Market-Centered Organization

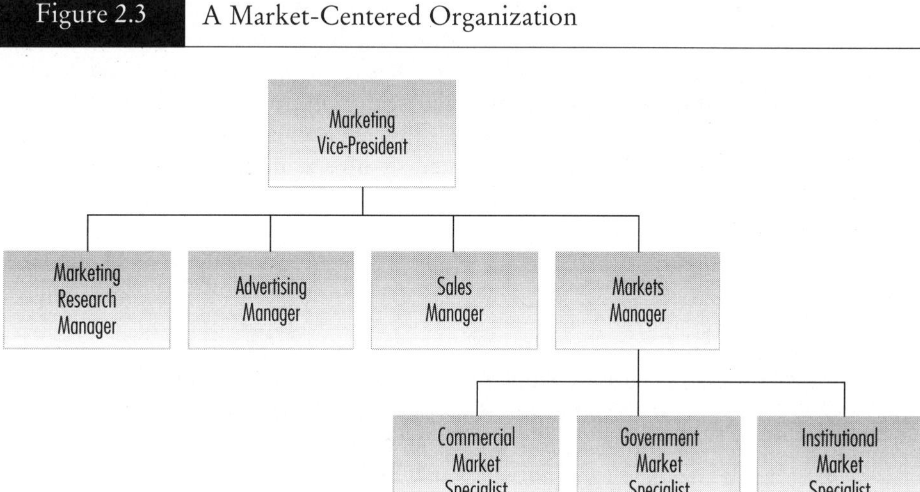

Source: Ernest Raia, "The Extended Enterprise," *Purchasing* 114 (4 March 1993): p. 49.

Dealing with Diversity: A Market-Centered Organization

Because each sector of the business market is unique, many firms have built market specialization into the marketing organization. To illustrate, the industrial products area of the J. M. Smucker Company is organized around market sectors. The institutional, military, and industrial markets are each managed by different individuals, each thoroughly knowledgeable about one particular market. Other companies, such as the Dow Chemical Company, have designed the marketing function to capitalize on their position in the global market. Relying on cross-functional teams located in each geographical area, five product vice presidents manage Dow's global product strategies. Dow's geographical diversity allows the firm to capitalize on local country opportunities. For example, Dow Latin America launched a herbicide for pasture applications in Colombia, whereas Dow Europe was the first to introduce a broad-spectrum herbicide for cereal grains.[43] Mack Hanan refers to such structures as market centered.[44] He contends that the most effective way to satisfy the needs of distinct customer groups is to build the firm's divisions around major customer markets.

One form of a market-centered organizational scheme is illustrated in Figure 2.3. Observe that a market manager supervises and coordinates the activities of three

---

[43]Thomas H. Naylor, *The Corporate Strategy* (New York: Basic Books, 1986), pp. 221–223.
[44]Mack Hanan, "Reorganize Your Company around Its Markets," *Harvard Business Review* 52 (November/December 1974): pp. 63–74.

market specialists. Each market specialist examines the buying processes, the product preferences, and the similarities and differences between customers in one sector of the business market. Such an analysis enables the market specialist to further categorize customers within a particular sector into meaningful market segments and to design specialized marketing programs for each segment. A market-centered organization provides the business marketer with a structure for dealing effectively with diversity in the industrial market.

Summary

A large market awaits the business marketing manager. The market can be divided into three major components: commercial enterprises, governments (federal, state, and local), and institutions. Recently, business marketers have seen their market horizons broadened to a global level. The marketer requires an understanding of the unique characteristics and the structure of the purchasing function in each sector.

Commercial enterprises include manufacturers, construction companies, service firms, transportation companies, selected professional groups, and resellers. Of these, manufacturers account for the largest dollar volume of purchases. Furthermore, although the majority of manufacturing firms are small, buying power is concentrated in the hands of relatively few large manufacturing establishments, which are also concentrated geographically. Commercial enterprises, such as service establishments and transportation or utility companies, are more widely dispersed. Often, the purchasing process is administered by a purchasing manager or purchasing agent. In larger firms, the purchasing function has become quite specialized, placing heavy demands on the industrial salesperson who must match the expertise of potential buyers. In smaller organizations, one person may be responsible for all buying activities. The materials management concept, along with just-in-time systems and the supply-chain management approach, require the careful coordination of a vendor's total marketing and distribution operations.

Many marketers find dealing with the government sector of the industrial market frustrating. However, government is the largest consumer in the United States. The diligent marketer who acquires an understanding of the procurement laws and of the varying contracts employed by the government can find a lucrative market. Federal buying follows two general procurement strategies: formal advertising or negotiated contract. The formal advertising approach, frequently followed for standardized products, involves the solicitation of bids from appropriate suppliers. Negotiated contracts are employed for unique requirements and are typified by discussion and bargaining throughout all phases of the contract.

International buyers represent a large and growing market for most industrial products and services; however, culture, product use, and buying procedures may be radically different from country to country. Each of these elements has a far-reaching and significant impact on the purchasing process.

Diversity is the characteristic that typifies the institutional market. Institutional buyers are somewhere between commercial enterprise and government buyers in terms of their characteristics, orientations, and purchasing processes. Cooperative purchasing—a unique aspect of this segment—necessitates a special strategic response by potential suppliers. Many business marketers have found that a market-centered organization provides the specialization required to meet the needs of each sector of the market.

Discussion Questions

1. Research suggests that an increasing number of buying organizations have adopted the materials management concept. Describe this concept and outline the managerial implications that it raises for the business marketer.
2. Compare and contrast the two general procurement strategies employed by the federal government: (1) formal advertising and (2) negotiated contract.
3. Institutional buyers fall somewhere between commercial enterprises and government buyers in terms of their characteristics, orientation, and purchasing process. Explain.
4. Evaluate the wisdom of this personal selling strategy: The approach that is appropriate for large purchasing departments is equally effective in small purchasing departments.
5. Explain how the decision-making process that a university might employ in selecting a new computer would differ from that of a commercial enterprise. Who would be the key participants in the process in each setting?
6. Fearing red tape and mounds of paperwork, Tom Bronson, president of B&E Electric, has always avoided the government market. A recent discussion with a colleague, however, has rekindled Tom's interest in this business market sector. What steps should B&E Electric take to learn more about this market?
7. Discuss the likely future role of the Internet in the purchasing of industrial products.
8. Discuss the key factors that a U.S. marketing manager would have to address when developing a strategy to compete in South America and Asia.
9. Why have some industrial firms moved away from product-centered organizations and toward market-centered organizations?

Part II

The Organizational Buying Process

Organizational Buying Behavior

The organizational buyer is influenced by a wide array of forces inside and outside the organization. Knowledge of these forces provides the marketer with a foundation on which to build responsive business marketing strategies. After reading this chapter, you will understand

1. the decision process that organizational buyers apply as they confront differing buying situations and the resulting strategy implications for the business marketer.
2. the individual, group, organizational, and environmental variables that influence organizational buying decisions.
3. a model of organizational buying behavior that integrates these important influences.
4. how a knowledge of organizational buying characteristics enables the marketer to make more informed decisions about product design, pricing, and promotion.

Market-driven business firms continuously sense and act on trends in their markets. In designing a new line of forklifts for the business market, Clark Equipment Co. is giving an unprecedented level of attention to driver comfort and engine noise level.[1] Why? As companies have cut middle management layers and simplified decision making, the composition of the buying decision group has changed. Actual equipment operators have become far more important in making the final decision. Users spend a considerable portion of their workday operating the equipment and often receive financial incentives that are tied to their performance. This means that driver comfort

[1]B. G. Yovovich, *New Marketing Imperatives: Innovative Strategies for Today's Marketing Challenges* (Englewood Cliffs, N.J.: Prentice-Hall, 1995), pp. 4–5.

and equipment reliability (minimal equipment downtime) are now more critical criteria in the buying decision.

Understanding the dynamics of organizational buying behavior is crucial for identifying profitable segments of the organizational market, for locating buying influences within these segments, and for reaching these organizational buyers efficiently and effectively with an offering that responds to their needs. Each decision the business marketer makes is based on a probable response of organizational buyers. This chapter explores the key stages of the organizational buying process and isolates the salient characteristics of different purchasing situations. Next, attention will turn to the myriad forces that influence organizational buying behavior. Knowledge of how organizational buying decisions are made provides the business marketer with a solid foundation for building responsive marketing strategies.

The Organizational Buying Process

Organizational buying behavior is a process rather than an isolated act or event. Tracing the history of a procurement decision in an organization uncovers critical decision points and evolving information requirements. In fact, organizational buying involves several stages, each of which yields a decision. Likewise, the composition of the decision-making unit can vary from one stage to the next as organizational members enter and leave the procurement process.

Table 3.1 presents a model of the eight-stage sequence of activities in the organizational buying process.[2] Recognition of a problem or of a potential opportunity triggers the purchasing process. For example, the firm's manufacturing equipment becomes outmoded or a salesperson initiates consideration of a product by demonstrating opportunities for improving the organization's performance. During the procurement process, many small or incremental decisions are made that ultimately translate into the final selection of a supplier. To illustrate, a quality-control engineer might unknowingly establish specifications for a new production system that only supplier A can meet. This type of decision early in the buying process will dramatically influence the favorable evaluation and ultimate selection of supplier A.

Some research suggests that the eight stages in the model of the procurement process may not progress sequentially and may vary with the complexity of the purchasing situation. However, the model provides important insights into the organizational buying process. Certain stages may be completed concurrently; the process may be reoriented at any point by a redefinition of the basic problem; or the process may be discontinued by a change in the external environment or in upper-management thinking. The organizational buying process is shaped by a

[2]The discussion in this section is based on Patrick J. Robinson, Charles W. Faris, and Yoram Wind, *Industrial Buying and Creative Marketing* (Boston: Allyn and Bacon, Inc., 1967), pp. 12–18; see also Gopalakrishnan R. Iyer, "Strategic Decision Making in Industrial Procurement: Implications for Buying Decision Approaches and Buyer-Seller Relationships," *Journal of Business & Industrial Marketing* 11, no. 3/4 (1996): pp. 80–93.

Table 3.1 The Buygrid Framework for Industrial Buying Situations

Buying Stages	Buying Situations		
	New Task	Modified Rebuy	Straight Rebuy
1. Anticipation or recognition of a problem (need) and a general solution			
2. Determination of characteristics and quantity of needed item			
3. Description of characteristics and quantity of needed item			
4. Search for and qualification of potential sources			
5. Acquisition and analysis of proposals			
6. Evaluation of proposals and selection of supplier(s)			
7. Selection of an order routine			
8. Performance feedback and evaluation			

Note: The most complex buying situations occur in the upper left portion of the buygrid framework and involve the largest number of decision makers and buying influences.

Source: From the Marketing Science Institute Series, *Industrial Buying and Creative Marketing*, by Patrick J. Robinson, Charles W. Faris, and Yoram Wind. Copyright 1967 by Allyn and Bacon, Inc., Boston. Reprinted with permission.

host of internal and external forces such as changes in economic or competitive conditions or a basic shift in organizational priorities.

Organizations that have significant experience in purchasing a particular product will approach the decision quite differently than first-time buyers. Therefore attention must center on buying situations rather than on products. Three types of buying situations have been delineated: (1) new task, (2) modified rebuy, and (3) straight rebuy.[3] As illustrated in Table 3.1, each type of buying situation must be related to the eight-stage buying process.

NEW TASK

In the **new-task** buying situation, the problem or need is perceived by organizational decision makers as totally different from previous experiences; therefore a significant amount of information is required for decision makers to explore alternative ways of solving the problem and to search for alternative suppliers.

[3]Robinson, Faris, and Wind, *Industrial Buying and Creative Marketing*, chap. 1; see also Erin Anderson, Wujin Chu, and Barton Weitz, "Industrial Purchasing: An Empirical Exploration of the Buyclass Framework," *Journal of Marketing* 51 (July 1987): pp. 71–86; and Morry Ghingold, "Testing the 'Buygrid' Buying Process Model," *Journal of Purchasing and Materials Management* 22 (winter 1986): pp. 30–36.

When confronting a new-task buying situation, organizational buyers operate in a stage of decision making referred to as **extensive problem solving.**[4] The buying influentials and decision makers lack well-defined criteria for comparing alternative products and suppliers, but they also lack strong predispositions toward a particular solution.

Buying Decision Approaches[5]

Two distinct buying decision approaches are used: judgmental new task and strategic new task. The greatest level of uncertainty confronts firms in **judgmental new task** situations because of the technical complexity of the product, the difficulty of evaluating the alternatives, or the unpredictable aspects of dealing with a new supplier. Consider purchasers of a special type of injection molding machine who are uncertain about the model or brand to choose, the suitable level of quality, and the appropriate price to pay. For such purchases, the buying activities include a moderate amount of information search and a moderate use of formal tools in evaluating key aspects of the buying decision.

Even more effort is invested in all buying activities for **strategic new task** decisions. These purchasing decisions are of extreme importance to the firm—strategically and financially. If the buyer perceives that a rapid pace of technological change surrounds the decision, search effort is increased, but is concentrated in a shorter time period.[6] Long-range planning drives the decision process. To illustrate, a large health insurance company placed a $600,000 order for workstation furniture. The long-term impact on the work environment shaped the six-month decision process and involved the active participation of personnel from several departments.

Strategy Guidelines

The business marketer confronting a new-task buying situation can gain a differential advantage by participating actively in the initial stages of the procurement process. The marketer should gather information on the problems facing the buying organization, isolate specific requirements, and offer proposals to meet the requirements. Ideas that lead to new products often originate not with the marketer but with the customer.

Marketers who are presently supplying other items to the organization ("in" suppliers) have an edge over other firms; they can see problems unfolding and are familiar with the "personality" and behavior patterns of the organization. The successful business marketer carefully monitors the changing needs of organizations and is prepared to assist new-task buyers.

---

[4]The levels of decision making discussed in this section are drawn from John A. Howard and Jagdish N. Sheth, *The Theory of Buyer Behavior* (New York: John Wiley and Sons, 1969), chap. 2.

[5]The discussion of buying decision approaches in this section is drawn from Michele D. Bunn, "Taxonomy of Buying Decision Approaches," *Journal of Marketing* 57 (January 1993): pp. 38–56.

[6]Allen M. Weiss and Jan B. Heide, "The Nature of Organizational Search in High Technology Markets," *Journal of Marketing Research* 30 (May 1993): pp. 230–233.

STRAIGHT REBUY

When there is a continuing or recurring requirement, buyers have substantial experience in dealing with the need, and they require little or no new information. Evaluation of new alternative solutions is unnecessary and unlikely to yield appreciable improvements. Thus, a **straight rebuy** approach is appropriate.

Routinized response behavior is the decision process organizational buyers employ in the straight rebuy. Organizational buyers have well-developed choice criteria to apply to the purchase decision. The criteria have been refined over time as the buyers have developed predispositions toward the offerings of one or a few carefully screened suppliers.

Buying Decision Approaches

Research suggests that organizational buyers employ two buying decision approaches: causal and routine low priority. **Causal purchases** involve no information search or analysis and the product or service is of minor importance to the firm. The focus is simply in transmitting the order. In contrast, **routine low priority** decisions are somewhat more important to the firm and involve a moderate amount of analysis. Describing the purchase of $5,000 worth of cable to be used as component material, a buyer aptly describes this decision process approach:

> *On repeat buys, we may look at other sources or alternate methods of manufacturing, etc. to make sure no new technical advancements are available in the marketplace. But, generally, a repeat buy is repurchased from the supplier originally selected, especially for low dollar items.*

Strategy Guidelines

The purchasing department handles straight rebuy situations by routinely selecting a supplier from a list (formal or informal) of acceptable vendors and then placing an order. The marketing task appropriate in this situation depends on whether the marketer is an "in" supplier (on the list) or an "out" supplier (not among the chosen few). An "in" supplier must reinforce the buyer-seller relationship, meet the buying organization's expectations, and be alert and responsive to the changing needs of the organization.

The "out" supplier faces a number of obstacles and must convince the organization that significant benefits can be derived from breaking the routine. This can be difficult because organizational buyers perceive risk in shifting from the known to the unknown. The organizational spotlight shines directly on them if an untested supplier falters. Testing, evaluations, and approvals may be viewed by buyers as costly, time-consuming, and unnecessary.

The marketing effort of the "out" supplier rests on an understanding of the basic buying needs of the organization: information gathering is essential. The marketer must convince organizational buyers that their purchasing requirements have changed or that the requirements should be interpreted differently. The objective is to persuade decision makers to reexamine alternative solutions and revise the preferred list to include the new supplier.

MODIFIED REBUY

In the **modified rebuy** situation, organizational decision makers feel that significant benefits may be derived from a reevaluation of alternatives. The buyers have experience in satisfying the continuing or recurring requirement, but they believe it worthwhile to seek additional information, and perhaps to consider alternative solutions.

Several factors may trigger such a reassessment. Internal forces include the search for quality improvements or cost reductions. A marketer offering cost, quality, or service improvements can be an external precipitating force. The modified rebuy situation is most likely to occur when the firm is displeased with the performance of present suppliers (for example, poor delivery service).

Limited problem solving best describes the decision-making process for the modified rebuy. Decision makers have well-defined criteria, but are uncertain about which suppliers can best fit their needs.

Buying Decision Approaches

Two buying decision approaches typify this buying class category. Both give strong emphasis to the strategic objectives and long-term needs of the firm. The **simple modified rebuy** involves a narrow set of choice alternatives and encompasses a moderate amount of both information search and analysis. Buyers concentrate on the long-term relationship potential of suppliers.

The **complex modified rebuy** involves a large set of choice alternatives and is characterized by little uncertainty. The range of choice enhances the negotiating strength of the buyer. The importance of the decision motivates buyers to actively search for information, apply sophisticated analysis techniques, and carefully consider long-term needs. This decision situation is particularly well-suited to a competitive bidding process. For example, one publisher purchased $2.5 million worth of computer stock paper and spread the order among several suppliers chosen in a competitive bidding process.

Strategy Guidelines

In a modified rebuy, the direction of the marketing effort depends on whether the marketer is an "in" or an "out" supplier. An "in" supplier should make every effort to understand and satisfy the procurement need and to move decision makers into a straight rebuy. The buying organization perceives potential payoffs from a reexamination of alternatives. The "in" supplier should ask why, and act immediately to remedy any customer problems. The marketer may be out of touch with the buying organization's requirements.

The goal of the "out" supplier should be to hold the organization in modified rebuy status long enough for the buyer to evaluate an alternative offering. Knowing the factors that led decision makers to reexamine alternatives could be pivotal. A particularly effective strategy for an "out" supplier is to offer performance guarantees as part of the proposal.[7] To illustrate, the following guarantee prompted International Circuit Technology, a manufacturer of printed circuit boards, to change to a new supplier for plating chemicals: "Your plating costs will be no more than *x* cents per square foot or we will make up the difference."[8] Given the nature of the production process, plating costs can be easily monitored by comparing the square footage of circuit boards moving down the plating line with the cost of plating chemicals for the period. Pleased with the performance, International Circuit Technology now routinely reorders from this new supplier.

Strategy Implications

Although past research provides some useful guidelines, great care must be exercised in forecasting the likely composition of the buying center for a particular purchasing situation.[9] The business marketer should attempt to identify purchasing patterns that apply to the firm. For example, the classes of industrial goods introduced in Chapter 1 (such as foundation goods versus facilitating goods) involve varying degrees of technical complexity and financial risk for the buying organization.

The business marketer must therefore view the procurement problem or need from the perspective of the buying organization. How far has the organization progressed with the specific purchasing problem? How does the organization define the task at hand? How important is the purchase to the organization? The answers will direct and form the business marketer's response and also provide insight into the composition of the decision-making unit. Again, each type of buying situation could represent a different market segment that requires a specialized marketing strategy. Xerox, for example, deploys some sales teams that concentrate on servicing and penetrating existing customers, and others that specialize in obtaining new customers.

Forces Shaping Organizational Buying Behavior

The eight-stage model of the organizational buying process provides the foundation for exploring the myriad forces that influence a particular buying decision by an organization. Observe in Figure 3.1 how organizational buying behavior is influenced by environmental forces (for example, the growth rate of

---

[7]Christopher P. Puto, Wesley E. Patton III, and Ronald H. King, "Risk Handling Strategies in Industrial Vendor Selection Decisions," *Journal of Marketing* 49 (winter 1985): pp. 89–98.

[8]Somerby Dowst, "CEO Report: Wanted: Suppliers Adept at Turning Corners," *Purchasing* 101 (29 January 1987): pp. 71–72.

[9]Donald W. Jackson Jr., Janet E. Keith, and Richard K. Burdick, "Purchasing Agents' Perceptions of Industrial Buying Center Influence," *Journal of Marketing* 48 (fall 1984): pp. 75–83.

Figure 3.1 Forces Influencing Organizational Buying Behavior

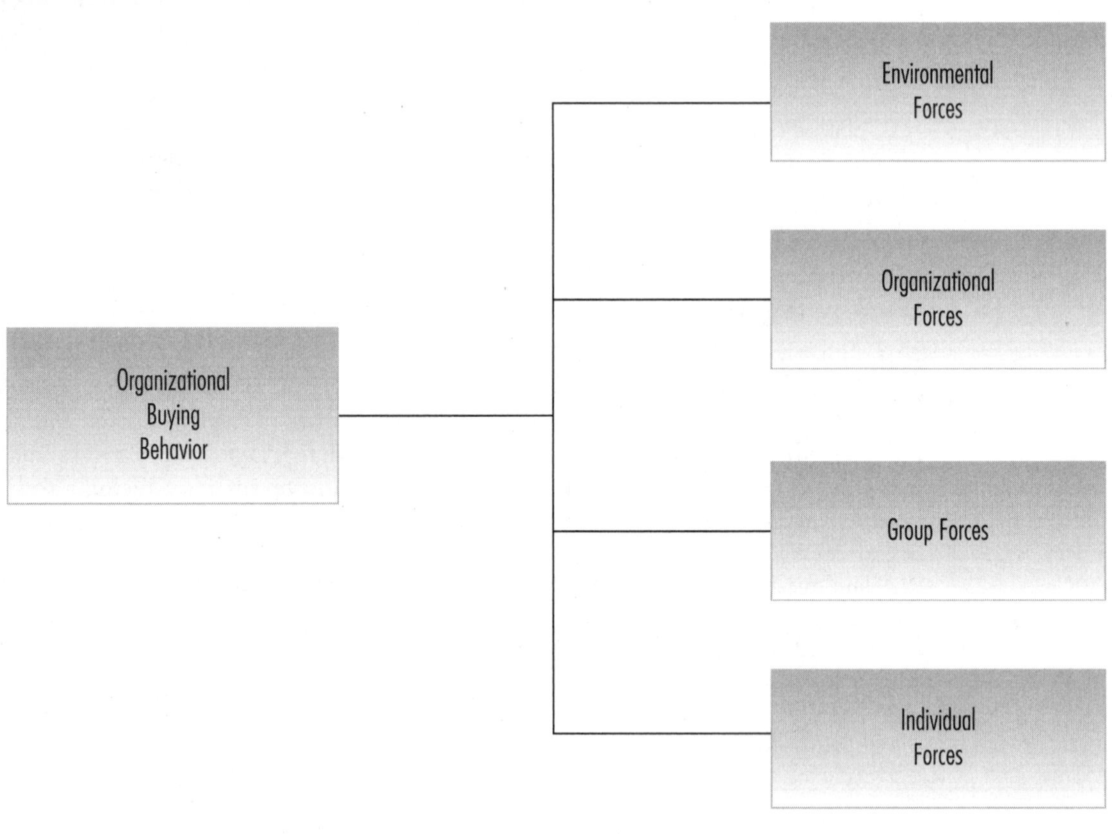

the economy); organizational forces (for example, the size of the buying organization); group forces (for example, composition and roles of members); and individual forces (for example, personal preferences).

ENVIRONMENTAL FORCES

A projected change in business conditions, a technological development, or a new piece of legislation can drastically alter organizational buying plans. Among the types of environmental forces that shape organizational buying behavior are economic, political, legal, and technological influences. Collectively, such environmental influences define the boundaries within which buyer-seller relationships develop in the business market.

Economic Influences

The general condition of the economy is reflected in economic growth, employment, price stability, income, and the availability of resources, money, and credit. Because of the derived nature of industrial demand, the marketer must also be sensitive to the strength of demand in the ultimate consumer market. The demand for many industrial products fluctuates more widely than the general economy. Firms that operate on a global scale must be sensitive to the economic conditions that prevail across regions. For example, as the U.S. economy moves out of a recession, the European economy may continue to sputter. A wealth of political and economic forces dictate the vitality and growth of an economy.

The economic environment influences an organization's ability and, to a degree, its willingness to buy. However, shifts in general economic conditions do not affect all sectors of the market evenly. For example, a rise in interest rates may damage the housing industry (including lumber, cement, and insulation) but may have minimal effects on industries such as paper, hospital supplies, office products, and soft drinks. Marketers that serve broad sectors of the organizational market must be particularly sensitive to the differential impact of selective economic shifts on buying behavior.

Political and Legal Influences

The political environment includes tariffs and trade agreements with other countries, government funding of selected programs, and government attitudes toward business and social service activities. For example, by gradually eliminating tariffs on computers and other products, the North American Free Trade Agreement (NAFTA) is creating a significant opportunity for some U. S. and Canadian marketers in Mexico.

The legal environment includes forces at the federal, state, and local levels that specify the boundaries of the buyer-seller relationship. The impact of governmental influences is illustrated in the debate that surrounds the proposal that automobiles must average 40 miles per gallon by the year 2000. To achieve this goal, virtually every part of the automobile will have to be redesigned. This in turn will increase demand for machine tools, aluminum, lightweight steel, plastic, and related materials. Similarly, health care reform proposals have spawned significant changes in the way in which hospitals and health maintenance organizations (HMOs) operate and in the procedures that they use to buy pharmaceutical products and medical supplies.

Technological Influences

Rapidly changing technology can restructure an industry and dramatically alter organizational buying plans. The technological environment defines the availability of goods and services to the buying organization and, in turn, the quality of goods and services that the organization can provide to its consumers.

The rate of technological change in an industry influences the composition of the decision-making unit in the buying organization. As the pace of technological change increases, the importance of the purchasing manager in the buying process declines. Technical and engineering personnel tend to be more important to organizational buying processes in which the rate of technological change is great. Recent research also suggests that buyers who perceive the pace of technological change to be more rapid will (1) conduct more intense search efforts and (2) spend less time on their overall search processes.[10] Allen Weiss and Jan Heide suggest that "In cost-benefit terms, a fast pace of change implies that distinct benefits are associated with search effort, yet costs are associated with prolonging the process" because the acquired information is "time sensitive."[11]

In the face of rapidly changing technology, buying organizations often use technological procedures to help them forecast the periods in which major changes in technology might occur. The marketer must also actively monitor signs of technological change and be prepared to adapt marketing strategy to deal with new technological environments. Because the most recent wave of technological change is as dramatic as any in history, the implications for organizational decision making are profound and involve changing definitions of industries, new sources of competition, changing product life cycles, and the increased globalization of markets.[12]

Environmental Uncertainty

As the information needs of buying groups grow in response to higher environmental uncertainty (for example, changes in company leadership, or in economic conditions), more people participate in making buying decisions. Research also indicates that the influence of the purchasing agent increases with the level of environmental uncertainty. Why? Robert Spekman and Louis Stern respond that as a firm's external environment becomes more unstable, the information processing function of the purchasing agent "becomes central to a firm's ability to effectively gather, analyze, and act on relevant environmental information,"[13] and purchasing agents thus become more influential.[14] This research highlights the importance of monitoring key environmental trends and tracing their impact on the organizational buying process.

---

[10]Allen M. Weiss and Jan B. Heide, "The Nature of Organizational Search in High Technology Markets," *Journal of Marketing Research* 30 (May 1993): pp. 220–233; see also Jan B. Heide and Allen M. Weiss, "Vendor Consideration and Switching Behavior for Buyers in High-Technology Markets," *Journal of Marketing* 59 (July 1995): pp. 30–43.

[11]Weiss and Heide, "The Nature of Organizational Search," p. 221.

[12]Noel Capon and Rashi Glazer, "Marketing and Technology: A Strategic Coalignment," *Journal of Marketing* 51 (July 1987): pp. 1–14; see also Rashi Glazer, "Marketing in an Information-Intensive Environment: Strategic Implications of Knowledge as an Asset," *Journal of Marketing* 55 (October 1991): pp. 1–19.

[13]Robert E. Spekman and Louis W. Stern, "Environmental Uncertainty and Buying Group Structure: An Empirical Investigation," *Journal of Marketing* 43 (spring 1979): p. 56.

[14]Robert E. Spekman, "Information and Influence: An Exploratory Investigation of the Boundary Role Person's Basis of Power," *Academy of Management Journal* 22 (March 1979): pp. 104–117.

ORGANIZATIONAL FORCES

An understanding of the buying organization is based on the strategic priorities of the firm, the role that purchasing occupies in the executive hierarchy, and the competitive challenges that the firm confronts.

Strategic Priorities

Organizational buying decisions are made to facilitate organizational activities and to support the firm's mission and strategies. A business marketer who understands the strategic priorities and concerns that occupy key decision makers is better equipped to respond to customer needs. For example, IBM centers attention on how its information technology and assorted services can improve the efficiency of a retailer's operations or advance the customer service levels of a hotel chain. Alternatively, a supplier to Hewlett-Packard will strike a responsive chord with executives by offering a new component part that will increase the performance or lower the cost of its ink-jet printers. To provide such customer solutions, the business marketer requires an intimate understanding of the opportunities and threats that the customer confronts.

Strategic Role of Purchasing

In many firms, purchasing strategy is becoming more closely tied to corporate strategy. To illustrate, purchasing (sourcing) executives at Motorola have a clear understanding of the firm's objectives, markets, and competitive strategies.

> *Ask the Paging Products Group's strategic sourcing director Neil MacIver what he knows about its markets, and he is fast to respond: "We know where we are strong and where we are not; we know why we are selling and why not. We go over the numbers in daily meetings. It is inherent in the nature of our jobs that we have to know this."* [15]

Compared to traditional buyers, recent research suggests that more strategically oriented purchasing managers are (1) more receptive to information and draw it from a wide variety of sources; (2) more sensitive to the importance of longer-term supplier relationships, questions of price in relation to performance, and broader environmental issues; and (3) more focused on the competencies of suppliers in evaluating alternative firms.[16] Moreover, these purchasing managers are evaluated on performance dimensions that are more tightly linked to strategic performance.

---

[15] Jordan D. Lewis, *The Connected Corporation: How Leading Companies Win through Customer-Supplier Alliances* (New York: The Free Press, 1995), p. 202.

[16] Robert E. Spekman, David W. Stewart, and Wesley J. Johnston, "An Empirical Investigation of the Organizational Buyer's Strategic and Tactical Roles," *Journal of Business-to-Business Marketing* 2, no. 4 (1995): pp. 37–63.

Table 3.2 Selected Trends in Purchasing Strategy

Trend	*Description*
Suppliers will become increasingly important to success in achieving corporate goals and objectives.	Organizations are focusing on core competencies and relying on suppliers as a source for product and process technology to continuously upgrade performance.
New purchasing performance measurements will emphasize purchasing effectiveness rather than purchasing efficiency.	This reflects a shift away from a tactical perspective (for example, cost savings) to a more strategic orientation (for example, cycle time for developing new products).
Purchasing will assume increasing responsibility for tasks that are strategic in scope.	Illustrative tasks include (1) economic forecasting, (2) conducting make-or-buy analyses, and (3) global purchasing.
Continual emphasis will be placed on electronic data interchange (EDI)systems with suppliers.	This provides a mechanism for synchronizing activities with suppliers, sharing information, and reducing costs in the supply chain.

Source: Adapted from Robert M. Moncka and Robert J. Trent, *Purchasing and Sourcing Strategy: Trends and Implications* (Tempe, Ariz.: Center for Advanced Purchasing Studies, 1995), pp. 69–71.

Strategic Trends in Purchasing

Given rising competitive pressures, purchasing managers are forging close relationships with those suppliers that can give their firms a competitive advantage in quality, cost, technology development, speed of response, or other critical performance areas (see Table 3.2). Increasingly, electronic data interchange (EDI) systems are being used to synchronize the activities of the buying organization with those of the selling organization. As purchasing assumes a more strategic role in the firm, the business marketer must understand the competitive realities of the customer's business and develop a **value proposition**—products, services, ideas—that advances the performance goals of the customer organization. For example, Motorola's Paging Products Group is keenly interested in working with suppliers who can contribute technology or component parts that enhance the value of the firm's product for customers and that strengthen its competitive position.

ORGANIZATIONAL POSITIONING OF PURCHASING

An organization that centralizes procurement decisions will approach purchasing differently than will a company where purchasing decisions are made at individual user locations. When purchasing is centralized, a separate organizational unit is given authority for purchases at a regional, divisional, or headquarters level. For example, Mead Corporation's centralized purchasing function directs the purchase of common materials used by Mead plants across the United States. Boeing, AT&T, 3M, Hewlett-Packard, and Xerox are among other corporations that emphasize centralized procurement. A marketer who is sensitive to organizational influences can more accurately map the decision-making process, isolate buying influentials, identify salient buying criteria, and target marketing strategy for both centralized as well as decentralized organizations.[17]

Centralization of Procurement: Contributing Factors

Why is there a trend toward centralizing purchasing? Several factors contribute to this trend. First, through centralization, purchasing strategy can be better integrated with corporate strategy. For example, the corporate procurement group at Compaq Computer Corporation was established to manage the purchase of strategic commodities, such as microprocessors and memory, on a worldwide basis. The centralized group maintains a close working relationship with 50 strategic suppliers who are fundamental to Compaq's success in the personal computer market.[18]

Second, an organization with multiple plant locations can often achieve cost savings by pooling common requirements. Before the procurement function was centralized at General Motors, 106 buying locations spent more than $10 million annually on nearly 24 million pairs of work gloves, buying over 200 styles from 90 sources. The cost savings generated from pooling the requirements for this item alone are substantial.

Third, the nature of the supply environment also can determine whether purchasing is centralized. If the supply environment is dominated by a few large sellers, centralized buying may be particularly useful in securing favorable terms and proper service. If the supply industry consists of many small firms, each covering limited geographical areas, decentralized purchasing may achieve better support.

Finally, the location of purchasing in the organization often hinges on the location of key buying influences. If engineering plays an active role in the purchasing process, the purchasing function must be in close organizational and physical proximity.

Centralization versus Decentralization

Centralized and decentralized procurement differ substantially.[19] Centralization leads to specialization. Purchasing specialists for selected items develop comprehensive knowledge of supply and demand conditions, vendor options, supplier cost factors, and other information relevant to the supply environment. This knowledge, and the

---

[17]E. Raymond Corey, *The Organizational Context of Industrial Buyer Behavior* (Cambridge, Mass.: Marketing Science Institute, 1978), pp. 99–112.

[18]James Carbone, "Compaq Uses World Class Suppliers to Stay #1," *Purchasing* 118 (17 August 1995): pp. 34–39.

[19]Joseph A. Bellizzi and Joseph J. Belonax, "Centralized and Decentralized Buying Influences," *Industrial Marketing Management* 11 (April 1982): pp. 111–115; Arch G. Woodside and David M. Samuel, "Observation of Centralized Corporate Procurement," *Industrial Marketing Management* 10 (July 1981): pp. 191–205; and E. Raymond Corey, *The Organizational Context of Industrial Buying Behavior*, pp. 6–12.

significant volume of business that specialists control, enhances their buying strength and supplier options.

The priority given to selected buying criteria is also influenced by centralization or decentralization. By identifying the buyer's organizational domain, the marketer can generally identify the purchasing manager's objectives. Centralized purchasing units place more weight on strategic considerations such as long-term supply availability and the development of a healthy supplier complex. Decentralized buyers may emphasize more tactical concerns such as short-term cost efficiency and profit considerations. Organizational buying behavior is greatly influenced by the monitoring system that measures the performance of the unit.

Personal selling skills and the brand preferences of users influence purchasing decisions more at user locations than at centralized buying locations. At user locations, E. Raymond Corey points out that "engineers and other technical personnel, in particular, are prone to be specific in their preferences, while nonspecialized, nontechnical buyers have neither the technical expertise nor the status to challenge them"[20] as can purchasing specialists at central locations. Differing priorities between central buyers and local users often lead to conflict in the buying organization. In stimulating demand at the user level, the marketer should assess the potential for conflict and attempt to develop a strategy that can resolve any differences between the two organizational units.

The organization of the marketer's selling strategy should parallel the organization of the purchasing function of key accounts. To avoid disjointed selling activities and internal conflict in the sales organization, and to serve the special needs of important customers, many business marketers have developed national account management programs to establish a close working relationship that, according to Benson Shapiro and Rowland Moriarty, "cuts across multiple levels, functions, and operating units in both the buying and selling organizations."[21] For example, the chief executive officers (CEOs) of each of the 50 major suppliers to Compaq Computer Corporation communicate regularly with Compaq's president and CEO. There is also frequent communication between Compaq and its suppliers at all corporate levels.[22] Thus, the trend toward the centralization of the procurement function on the buying side has been matched by the development of national account management programs on the selling side.

GROUP FORCES

Multiple buying influences and group forces are critical in organizational buying decisions. The organizational buying process typically involves a complex set of smaller

---

[20]Corey, *The Organizational Context*, p. 13.

[21]Benson P. Shapiro and Rowland T. Moriarty, *National Account Management: Emerging Insights* (Cambridge, Mass.: Marketing Science Institute, 1982), p. 8; see also Michael D. Hutt, Wesley J. Johnston, and John R. Ronchetto Jr., "Selling Centers and Buying Centers: Formulating Strategic Exchange Patterns," *Journal of Personal Selling and Sales Management* 5 (May 1985): pp. 33–40.

[22]Carbone, "Compaq Uses World Class Suppliers," p. 34.

INSIDE BUSINESS MARKETING

A HANDWRITTEN NOTE SEALS A MULTIBILLION-DOLLAR ORDER FOR BOEING

Boeing had spent millions of dollars in the design of its 777 airplane, and Boeing management had to decide whether sufficient market interest existed to justify the enormous cost of moving from the drawing board to the factory. Actually, Boeing needed a commitment from a large customer to buy a sufficient number of the new planes to make the investment worthwhile.

United Airlines was considering the Boeing 777 along with two direct competitors: the Airbus-330 and the McDonnel Douglas-11. During a long weekend of negotiations in Chicago, teams from each of the competing manufacturers made presentations to United's top management team. After the initial presentations, senior executives at United were divided. Jim Guyette, executive vice president, strongly favored Boeing, but the chief financial officer felt that Airbus would be the best choice. In preparing for a meeting with Stephen Wolf, chairman of the board of United, Jim Guyette wanted something personal from Boeing to bolster his case. So he penned a handwritten note that said something like, "We agree to work together to deliver a service-ready plane." After obtaining signatures from the Boeing executives, Guyette used the note to convince the United chairman of Boeing's new dedication to customers and serving United Airlines well in the years ahead. After this meeting, United ordered thirty-four 777s —at a cost of roughly $120 million each—and took an option on another thirty-four planes.

Source: Karl Sabbagh, *21st Century Jet: The Making and Marketing of the Boeing 777* (New York: Scribner, 1996), pp. 47–55.

---

decisions made or influenced by several individuals. The degree of involvement of group members in the procurement process varies from routine rebuys, in which the purchasing agent simply takes into account the preferences of others, to complex new-task buying situations, in which a group plays an active role throughout the decision process.

The industrial salesperson must address three questions.

- Which organizational members take part in the buying process?
- What is each member's relative influence in the decision?
- What criteria are important to each member in evaluating prospective suppliers?

The salesperson who can correctly answer these questions is ideally prepared to meet the needs of a buying organization and has a high probability of becoming the chosen supplier.

The Buying Center

The concept of the buying center provides rich insights into the role of group forces in organizational buying behavior.[23] The **buying center** consists of those individuals who participate in the purchasing decision and who share the goals and risks arising from the decision. The size of the buying center varies, but an average buying center will include more than 4 persons per purchase; the number of people involved in all stages of one purchase may be as many as 20.[24]

The composition of the buying center may change from one purchasing situation to another and is not prescribed by the organizational chart. A buying group evolves during the purchasing process in response to the information requirements of the specific purchase situation. Because organizational buying is a *process* rather than an isolated act, different individuals are important to the process at different times.[25] A design engineer may exert significant influence early in the purchasing process when product specifications are being established; others may assume a more dominant role in later phases. A salesperson must define the buying situation and the information requirements from the organization's perspective in order to anticipate the size and composition of the buying center. Again, the composition of the buying center evolves during the purchasing process, varies from firm to firm, and varies from one purchasing situation to another.

Isolating the Buying Situation. Defining the buying situation and determining whether the firm is in the early or later stages of the procurement decision-making process are important first steps in defining the buying center. The buying center for a new-task buying situation in the not-for-profit market is presented in Table 3.3. The product, intensive-care monitoring systems, is a complex and costly purchase. Buying center members are drawn from five functional areas, each participating to varying degrees in the decision process. A marketer who concentrated exclusively on the purchasing function would be overlooking key buying influentials.

Erin Anderson and her colleagues queried a large sample of sales managers concerning the patterns of organizational buying behavior that their salespeople confront on a daily basis. Sales forces that frequently encounter new-task buying situations generally observe that:

> *The buying center is large, slow to decide, uncertain about its needs and the appropriateness of the possible solutions, more concerned about finding a good*

---

[23]For a comprehensive review of buying center research, see Wesley J. Johnston and Jeffrey E. Lewin, "Organizational Buying Behavior: Toward an Integrative Framework," *Journal of Business Research* 35 (January 1996): pp. 1–15; and J. David Lichtenthal, "Group Decision Making in Organizational Buying: A Role Structure Approach," in *Advances in Business Marketing*, vol. 3, ed. Arch G. Woodside (Greenwich, Conn.: JAI Press, 1988), pp. 119–157.

[24]For example, see Robert D. McWilliams, Earl Naumann, and Stan Scott, "Determining Buying Center Size," *Industrial Marketing Management* 21 (February 1992): pp. 43–49.

[25]Arch G. Woodside, "Conclusions on Mapping How Industry Buys," in *Advances in Business Marketing and Purchasing*, vol. 5, ed. Arch G. Woodside (Greenwich, Conn.: JAI Press, 1992), pp. 283–300; see also Gary L. Lilien and M. Anthony Wong, "Exploratory Investigation of the Structure of the Buying Center in the Metalworking Industry," *Journal of Marketing Research* 21 (February 1984): pp. 1–11.

Table 3.3 The Involvement of Buying Center Participant at Different Stages of the Procurement Process

	Stages of Procurement Process for a Medical Equipment Purchase			
Buying Center Participants	**Identification of need**	**Establishment of Objectives**	**Identification and Evaluation of Buying Alternatives**	**Selection of Suppliers**
Physicians	High	High	High	High
Nursing	Low	High	High	Low
Administration	Moderate	Moderate	Moderate	High
Engineering	Low	Moderate	Moderate	Low
Purchasing	Low	Low	Low	Moderate

Source: Adapted by permission of the publisher from Gene R. Laczniak, "An Empirical Study of Hospital Buying," *Industrial Marketing Management* 8 (January 1979), p. 61. Copyright © 1979 by Elsevier Science Publishing Co., Inc.

solution than getting a low price or assured supply, more willing to entertain proposals from "out" suppliers and less willing to favor "in" suppliers, more influenced by technical personnel, [and] less influenced by purchasing agents."[26]

By contrast, Anderson and her colleagues found that sales forces facing more routine purchase situations (that is, straight and modified rebuys) frequently observe buying centers that are "small, quick to decide, confident in their appraisals of the problem and possible solutions, concerned about price and supply, satisfied with 'in' suppliers, and more influenced by purchasing agents."[27]

Predicting Composition

A marketer can also predict the composition of the buying center by projecting the impact of the industrial product on various functional areas in the buying organization. If the procurement decision will affect the marketability of a firm's product (for example, product design, price), the marketing department will be active in the decision process. Engineering will be influential in decisions about new capital equipment, materials, and components; setting specifications; defining product performance requirements; and qualifying potential vendors. Manufacturing executives will be included in the buying center for procurement decisions that affect the production mechanism (for example, the acquisition of materials or parts used in

[26]Anderson, Chu, and Weitz, "Industrial Purchasing," p. 82.
[27]Ibid.

Ethical Business Marketing

GIFTS FROM SUPPLIERS: FORD'S POLICY

What policies do firms set on accepting gifts from suppliers? Here's the policy at Ford. While soliciting gifts and favors is never permissible, if there is a legitimate business purpose it's all right to accept gifts and favors that are freely offered by suppliers, dealers, and others with whom Ford does business, subject to these important limitations:

- The gift must be of nominal value and must involve no more than normal sales promotion or publicity.
- Social amenities must be appropriate and limited, and must never give the appearance of impropriety.
- Any discounts on goods or services offered to you by a supplier must be made generally available and cannot be for your benefit only.
- You may never accept cash or gift certificates or gifts of food or alcohol.
- You may not borrow money, except from qualified financial institutions on generally available terms.

Source: Ford Motor Company, *Standards of Corporate Conduct*, 1996, p. 6.

production). When procurement decisions involve a substantial economic commitment or impinge on strategic or policy matters, top management will have considerable influence.

Buying Center Influence

Members of the buying center assume different roles throughout the procurement process. Frederick Webster Jr. and Yoram Wind have given the following labels to each of these roles: users, influencers, buyers, deciders, and gatekeepers.[28]

As the role name implies, **users** are the personnel who will be using the product in question. Users may have anywhere from inconsequential to extremely important influence on the purchase decision. In some cases, the users initiate the purchase action by requesting the product. They may even develop the product specifications.

Gatekeepers control information to be reviewed by other members of the buying center. The control of information may be accomplished by disseminating printed information, such as advertisements, or by controlling which salesperson will speak to which individuals in the buying center. To illustrate, the purchasing agent

[28]Frederick E. Webster Jr. and Yoram Wind, *Organizational Buying Behavior* (Englewood Cliffs, N.J.: Prentice-Hall, 1972), p. 77. For a review of buying role research, see J. David Lichtenthal, "Group Decision Making in Organizational Buying," pp. 119–157.

might perform this screening role by opening the gate to the buying center for some sales personnel and closing it to others.

Influencers affect the purchasing decision by supplying information for the evaluation of alternatives or by setting buying specifications. Typically, those in technical departments, such as engineering, quality control, and R&D, are significant influences on the purchase decision. Sometimes, individuals outside the buying organization can assume this role. For high-tech purchases, technical consultants often assume an influential role in the decision process and broaden the set of alternatives being considered.[29]

Deciders are the individuals who actually make the buying decision, whether or not they have the formal authority to do so. The identity of the decider is the most difficult role to determine: *buyers* may have formal authority to buy, but the president of the firm may actually make the decision. A decider could be a design engineer who develops a set of specifications that only one vendor can meet.

The **buyer** has formal authority to select a supplier and implement all procedures connected with securing the product. The power of the buyer is often usurped by more powerful members of the organization. The buyer's role is often assumed by the purchasing agent, who executes the administrative functions associated with a purchase order.

One person could assume all roles in a purchase situation or separate individuals could assume different buying roles. To illustrate, as users, personnel from marketing, accounting, purchasing, and production may all have a stake in which information technology system is selected. Thus, the buying center can be a very complex organizational phenomenon.

Identifying Patterns of Influence. Key influencers are frequently located outside the purchasing department. To illustrate, the typical capital equipment purchase involves an average of four departments, three levels of the management hierarchy (for example, manager, regional manager, vice president), and seven different individuals.[30] In purchasing component parts, personnel from production and engineering are often most influential in the decision. It is interesting to note that a comparative study of organizational buying behavior found striking similarities across four countries (the United States, the United Kingdom, Australia, and Canada) with regard to the involvement of various departments in the procurement process.[31]

---

[29]Philip L. Dawes and Paul G. Patterson, "The Use of Technical Consultancy Services by Firms Making High-Technology Purchasing Decisions," in *Twenty-First Annual Conference of the European Marketing Academy,* ed. Klaus G. Grunert and Dorthe Fuglede (Aarhus, Denmark: The Aarhus School of Business), pp. 261–275.

[30]Wesley J. Johnston and Thomas V. Bonoma, "The Buying Center: Structure and Interaction Patterns," *Journal of Marketing* 45 (summer 1981): pp. 143–156; see also Gary L. Lilien and M. Anthony Wong, "An Exploratory Investigation of the Structure of the Buying Center in the Metalworking Industry," *Journal of Marketing Research* 21 (February 1984): pp. 1–11.

[31]Peter Banting, David Ford, Andrew Gross, and George Holmes, "Similarities in Industrial Procurement across Four Countries," *Industrial Marketing Management* 14 (May 1985): pp. 133–144.

Table 3.4 Clues for Identifying Powerful Buying Center Members

- *Isolate the personal stakeholders.* Those individuals who have an important personal stake in the decision will exert more influence than other members of the buying center. For example, the selection of production equipment for a new plant will spawn the active involvement of manufacturing executives.
- *Follow the information flow.* Influential members of the buying center are central to the information flow that surrounds the buying decision. Other organizational members will direct information to them.
- *Identify the experts.* Expert power is an important determinant of influence in the buying center. Those buying center members who possess the most knowledge—and ask the most probing questions to the salesperson—are often influential.
- *Trace the connections to the top.* Powerful buying center members often have direct access to the top-management team. This direct link to valuable information and resources enhances the status and influence of the buying center members.
- *Understand purchasing's role.* Purchasing is dominant in repetitive buying situations by virtue of technical expertise, knowledge of the dynamics of the supplying industry, and close working relationships with individual suppliers.

Source: Adapted from John R. Ronchetto, Michael D. Hutt, and Peter H. Reingen, "Embedded Influence Patterns in Organizational Buying Systems," *Journal of Marketing* 53 (October 1989), pp. 51–62.

Past research provides some valuable clues for identifying powerful buying center members (see Table 3.4).[32] To illustrate, individuals who have an important personal stake in the decision, possess expert knowledge concerning the choice at hand, and/or are central to the flow of decision-related information tend to assume an active and influential role in the buying center. Purchasing managers assume a dominant role in repetitive buying situations.

Based on their buying center research, Donald W. Jackson Jr. and his colleagues provide these strategy recommendations:

> *Marketing efforts will depend upon which individuals of the buying center are more influential for a given decision. Since engineering and manufacturing are more influential in product selection decisions, they may have to be sold on product characteristics. On the other hand, since purchasing is most influential in supplier selection decisions, they may have to be sold on company characteristics.*[33]

---

[32]John R. Ronchetto, Michael D. Hutt, and Peter H. Reingen, "Embedded Influence Patterns in Organizational Buying Systems," *Journal of Marketing* 53 (October 1989): pp. 51–62; see also Ajay Kohli, "Determinants of Influence in Organizational Buying: A Contingency Approach," *Journal of Marketing* 53 (July 1989): pp. 50–65; and Daniel H. McQuiston and Peter R. Dickson, "The Effect of Perceived Personal Consequences on Participation and Influence in Organizational Buying," *Journal of Business Research* 23 (September 1991): pp. 159–177.

[33]Jackson, Keith, and Burdick, "Purchasing Agents' Perceptions of Industrial Buying Center Influence," pp. 75–83.

INDIVIDUAL FORCES

Individuals, not organizations, make buying decisions. Each member of the buying center has a unique personality, a particular set of learned experiences, a specified organizational function, and a perception of how best to achieve both personal and organizational goals. Importantly, research confirms that organizational members who perceive that they have an important personal stake in the buying decision will participate more forcefully in the decision process than their colleagues.[34] To understand the organizational buyer, the marketer should be aware of individual perceptions of the buying situation.

Differing Evaluative Criteria

Evaluative criteria are specifications that organizational buyers use to compare alternative industrial products and services; however, these may conflict. Industrial product users generally value prompt delivery and efficient servicing; engineering values product quality, standardization, and testing; and purchasing assigns the most importance to maximum price advantage and economy in shipping and forwarding.[35]

Product perceptions and evaluative criteria differ among organizational decision makers as a result of differences in educational backgrounds, source and type of information exposure, interpretation and retention of relevant information (perceptual distortion), and level of satisfaction with past purchases.[36] Engineers have an educational background different from that of plant managers or purchasing agents; they are exposed to different journals, attend different conferences, and possess different professional goals and values. A sales presentation that is effective with purchasing may be entirely off the mark with engineering.

Understanding the Reward and Measurement Systems.[37] What factors motivate individual decision makers during the organizational buying process? Two types of rewards motivate them:

1. *Intrinsic rewards:* Rewards that are attained on a personal basis (for example, feelings of accomplishment or self-worth)
2. *Extrinsic rewards:* Rewards that are distributed by the organization (for example, salary increases or promotions)

---

[34]McQuiston and Dickson, "The Effect of Perceived Personal Consequences on Participation and Influence in Organizational Buying," pp. 159–177.

[35]Jagdish N. Sheth, "A Model of Industrial Buyer Behavior," *Journal of Marketing* 37 (October 1973): p. 51; see also Sheth, "Organizational Buying Behavior: Past Performance and Future Expectations," *The Journal of Business & Industrial Marketing* 11, no. 3/4 (1996): pp. 7–24.

[36]Sheth, "A Model of Industrial Buyer Behavior," pp. 52–54.

[37]Paul F. Anderson and Terry M. Chambers, "A Reward/Measurement Model of Organizational Buying Behavior," *Journal of Marketing* 49 (spring 1985): pp. 7–23; see also Terry M. Chambers, Paul F. Anderson, and B. J. Dunlap, "Preferences, Intentions, and Behavior of Organizational Buyers under Different Reward Conditions," *Journal of Business Research* 14 (December 1986): pp. 533–547.

In an experimental setting, research demonstrates that purchasing managers prefer and choose those vendors that will allow them to attain maximum extrinsic rewards. Thus, the attributes individuals emphasize in evaluating alternative industrial suppliers are likely to reflect the reward and measurement systems of their primary work group. Also, individual expectations about the offerings of alternative suppliers will differ. Purchasing managers have been rewarded for one set of behaviors, such as reducing the cost of materials, whereas engineers have been rewarded for another, such as improving the quality of products. This difference will lead to conflicting advocacy positions within the buying group. How is this conflict resolved?

Recent research suggests that the more the informal and formal reward systems emphasize the local performance of departments, rather than their combined performance in meeting organizational goals, the more likely there is to be interdepartmental conflict in the buying process.[38] In such situations, the salesperson can develop strategies to manage conflict in the decision-making process. For example, the salesperson could create situations in which the parties in conflict might be encouraged to confront the conflict and move toward problem solving. A product demonstration, where both departments are invited to participate, could be part of such a strategy.

Responsive Marketing Strategy. A marketer who is sensitive to differences in the product perceptions and evaluative criteria of individual buying center members is well equipped to prepare responsive marketing strategy. To illustrate, a research study examined the industrial adoption of solar air-conditioning systems and identified the criteria of importance to key decision makers.[39] Buying center participants for this purchase typically include production engineers, heating and air-conditioning (HVAC) consultants, and top managers. The study revealed that marketing communications directed at production engineers should center on operating costs and energy savings; HVAC consultants should be addressed concerning noise level and initial cost of the system; and top managers are most interested in whether the technology is state-of-the-art. Knowledge of the criteria that key buying center participants employ is of significant operational value to the marketer when designing new products and when developing and targeting advertising and personal selling presentations.

Information Processing

Volumes of information flow into every organization through direct mail advertising, the Internet, journal advertising, trade news, word of mouth, and personal sales

---

[38]Donald W. Barclay, "Interdepartmental Conflict in Organizational Buying: The Impact of Organizational Context," *Journal of Marketing Research* 28 (May 1991): pp. 145–159. For related research, see R. Venkatesh, Ajay K. Kohli, and Gerald Zaltman, "Influence Strategies in Buying Centers," *Journal of Marketing* 59 (October 1995): pp. 71–82; and Mark A. Farrell and Bill Schroder, "Influence Strategies in Organizational Buying Decisions," *Industrial Marketing Management* 25 (July 1996): pp. 293–303.

[39]Jean-Marie Choffray and Gary L. Lilien, "Assessing Response to Industrial Marketing Strategy," *Journal of Marketing* 42 (April 1978): pp. 20–31.

presentations. What an individual organizational buyer chooses to pay attention to, comprehend, and retain has an important bearing on procurement decisions.

Selective Processes. Information processing is generally encompassed in the broader term **cognition**, which U. Neisser defines as "all the processes by which the sensory input is transformed, reduced, elaborated, stored, recovered, and used."[40] Important to an individual's cognitive structure are the processes of selective exposure, attention, perception, and retention.

1. *Selective exposure.* Individuals tend to accept communication messages that are consistent with their existing attitudes and beliefs. For this reason, a purchasing agent chooses to talk to some salespersons and not to others.
2. *Selective attention.* Individuals filter or screen incoming stimuli in order to admit only certain ones to cognition. Thus, an organizational buyer will be more likely to notice a trade advertisement that is consistent with his or her needs and values.
3. *Selective perception.* Individuals tend to interpret stimuli in terms of their existing attitudes and beliefs. This explains why organizational buyers may modify or distort a salesperson's message in order to make it more consistent with their predispositions toward the company.
4. *Selective retention.* Individuals tend to store in memory only information pertinent to their own needs and dispositions. An organizational buyer may retain information concerning a particular brand because it matches his or her criteria.

Each of these selective processes influences the way an individual decision maker will respond to marketing stimuli. Because the procurement process often spans several months and because the marketer's contact with the buying organization is infrequent, marketing communications must be carefully designed and targeted.[41] Poorly conceived messages will be "tuned out" or immediately forgotten by key decision makers. Those messages that are deemed important to achieving goals are retained.

Risk-Reduction Strategies

Individuals are motivated by a strong desire to reduce the level of risk in purchase decisions. The perceived risk concept includes two components: (1) uncertainty about the outcome of a decision, and (2) the magnitude of consequences associated with

---

[40]U. Neisser, *Cognitive Psychology* (New York: Appleton, 1966), p. 4.

[41]See, for example, Brent M. Wren and James T. Simpson, "A Dyadic Model of Relationships in Organizational Buying: A Synthesis of Research Results," *Journal of Business & Industrial Marketing* 11, no. 3/4 (1996): pp. 68–79.

INSIDE BUSINESS MARKETING

BEST PRACTICES FOR CUSTOMER SATISFACTION IN BUSINESS MARKETING FIRMS

Keeping current customers satisfied is just as important as attracting new ones. Firms that have a reputation for delivering high levels of customer satisfaction do things differently than their competitors. The CEOs and presidents of these firms are obsessed with customers. In turn, employees throughout these organizations understand the link between their jobs (the particular tasks they perform) and customer satisfaction. All the divisions of these firms embrace customer satisfaction as a goal, but particular units are given the freedom to customize customer service performance measures to meet their own needs.

These leading-edge firms collect several kinds of customer satisfaction data. They capture overall trends with periodic surveys; they trace particular transactions and secure customer feedback on what could be improved; and they ask customers to rate the quality of the product, the service, and the interaction. Most importantly, these firms actively use the quantitative and qualitative data to inform decision making and to motivate employee performance. Customer satisfaction performance charts are prominently displayed on company walls. Compensation for managers at all organizational levels is tied to customer satisfaction measurements. Organizations that feature the best practices for customer satisfaction comprise managers who are focused on continuous improvement in the processes that create a satisfied customer.

Source: Abbie Griffin, Greg Gleason, Rick Preiss, and Dave Shevenaugh, "Best Practices for Customer Satisfaction in Manufacturing Firms," *Sloan Management Review* 36 (winter 1995), pp. 87–90.

making the wrong choice. Research highlights the importance of perceived risk and the purchase type in shaping the structure of the decision-making unit.[42] Individual decision making is likely to occur in organizational buying for straight rebuys and for modified rebuy situations when the perceived risk is low. In these situations, the purchasing agent may initiate action.[43] Modified rebuys of higher risk and new tasks seem to spawn a group structure.

In confronting "risky" purchase decisions, how do organizational buyers behave? As the risk associated with an organizational purchase decision increases:[44]

- The buying center will become larger and will comprise members with high levels of organizational status and authority.

[42]Elizabeth J. Wilson, Gary L. Lilien, and David T. Wilson, "Developing and Testing a Contingency Paradigm of Group Choice in Organizational Buying," *Journal of Marketing Research* 28 (November 1991): pp. 452–466.

[43]Sheth, "A Model of Industrial Buyer Behavior," p. 54; see also W.E. Patton III, Charles P. Puto, and Ronald H. King, "Which Buying Decisions Are Made by Individuals and Not by Groups?" *Industrial Marketing Management* 15 (May 1986): pp. 129–138.

[44]Johnston and Lewin, "Organizational Buying Behavior: Toward an Integrative Framework," pp. 8–10. See also Puto, Patton, and King, "Risk Handling Strategies in Industrial Vendor Selection Decisions," pp. 89–95.

- The information search will be active and a wide variety of information sources will be consulted to guide and support an important purchase decision. As the decision process unfolds, personal information sources (for example, discussions with managers at other organizations that have made similar purchases) become more important.
- Buying center participants will be motivated to invest greater effort and to deliberate more carefully throughout the purchase process.
- Sellers who have a proven track record with the firm will be favored. The choice of a familiar supplier helps reduce the perceived risk associated with a purchase.

Rather than price, product quality and after-sale service are typically most important to organizational buyers when they confront "risky" decisions. When introducing new products, entering new markets, or approaching new customers, the marketing strategist should evaluate the impact of alternative strategies on perceived risk.

The Organizational Buying Process: Major Elements

The behavior of organizational buyers is influenced by environmental, organizational, group, and individual factors. Each of these spheres of influence has been discussed in an organizational buying context, with particular attention to how the industrial marketer should interpret these forces and, more important, factor them directly into marketing strategy planning. A model of the organizational buying process is presented in Figure 3.2, which serves to reinforce and integrate the key areas discussed so far in this chapter.[45]

This framework focuses on the relationship between an organization's buying center and the three major stages in the individual purchase decision process:

1. The screening of alternatives that do not meet organizational requirements
2. The formation of decision participants' preferences
3. The formation of organizational preferences

Observe that individual members of the buying center use various evaluative criteria and are exposed to various sources of information, which influence the industrial brands that are included in the buyer's **evoked set of alternatives**—the alternative

[45]Choffray and Lilien, "Assessing the Response to Industrial Marketing Strategy," pp. 20–31. Other models of organizational buying behavior include Webster and Wind, *Organizational Buying Behavior*, pp.28–37; and Sheth, "A Model of Industrial Buyer Behavior," pp. 50–56. For a comprehensive review, see Sheth, "Organizational Buying Behavior," pp. 7–24; and Johnston and Lewin, "Organizational Buying Behavior," pp. 1–15.

Figure 3.2 Major Elements of Organizational Buying Behavior

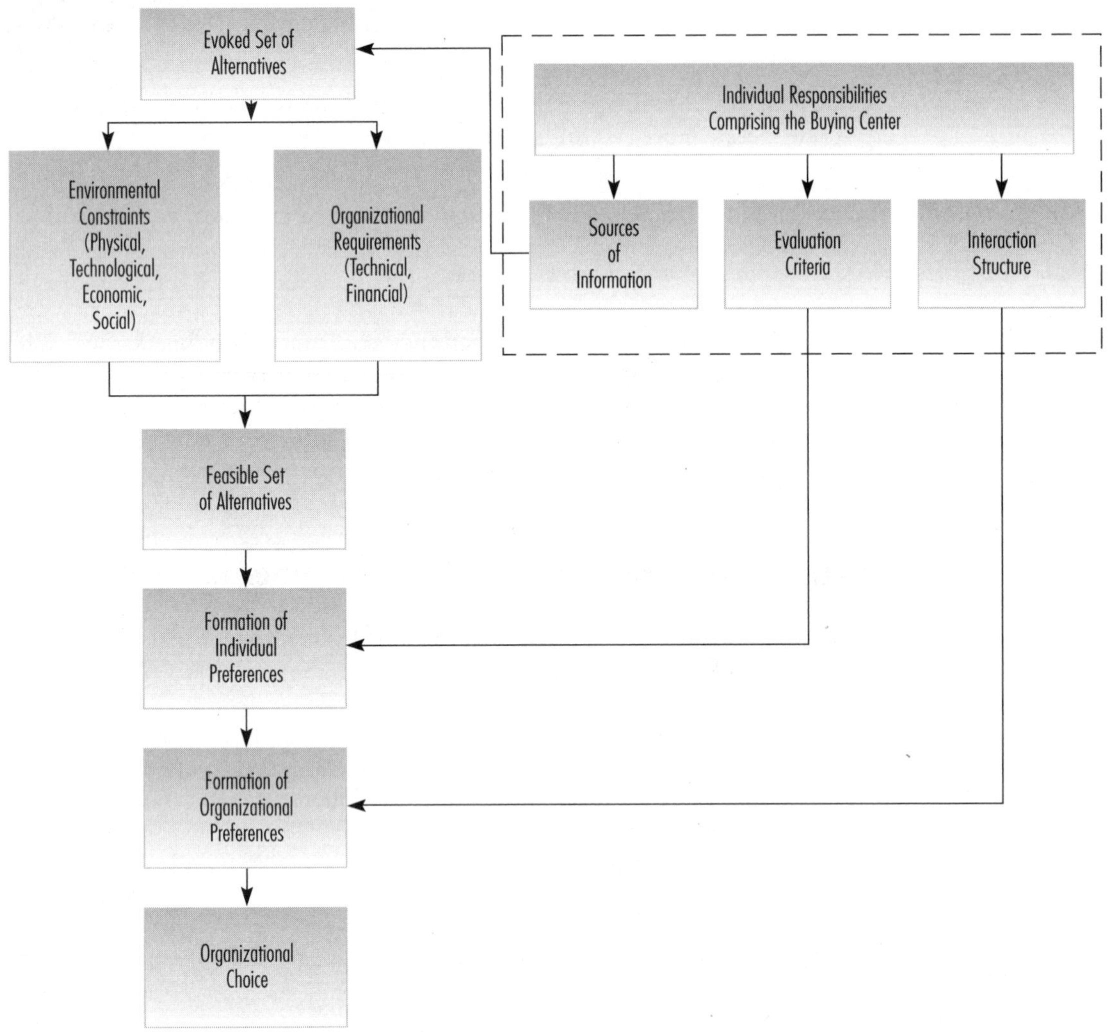

Source: Jean-Marie Choffray and Gary L. Lilien, "Assessing Response to Industrial Marketing Strategy," *Journal of Marketing* 42 (April 1978), p. 22. Reprinted by permission of the American Marketing Association.

brands that a buyer calls to mind when a need arises and that represent only a few of the many brands available.[46]

[46]Howard and Sheth, *The Theory of Buyer Behavior*, p. 26; see also Ronald P. LeBlanc, "Environmental Impact on Purchase Decision Structure," *Journal of Purchasing and Materials Management* 17 (spring 1981): pp. 30–36; and Lowell E. Crow, Richard W. Olshavsky, and John O. Summers, "Industrial Buyers' Choice Strategies: A Protocol Analysis," *Journal of Marketing Research* 17 (February 1980): pp. 34–44.

Environmental constraints and organizational requirements influence the procurement process by limiting the number of product alternatives that satisfy organizational needs. For example, capital equipment alternatives that exceed a particular cost (initial or operating) may be eliminated from further consideration. The remaining brands become the **feasible set of alternatives** for the organization, from which individual preferences are defined. The **interaction structure** of the members of the buying center, who have differing criteria and responsibilities, leads to the formation of organizational preferences and ultimately to organizational choice.

An understanding of the organizational buying process enables the marketer to play an active rather than a passive role in stimulating market response. The marketer who identifies organizational screening requirements and the salient evaluative criteria of individual buying center members can make more informed product design, pricing, and promotional decisions.

Summary

Knowledge of the process that organizational buyers follow in making purchasing decisions is fundamental to responsive marketing strategy. As a buying organization moves from the problem recognition phase, in which a procurement need is defined, to later phases, in which suppliers are screened and ultimately chosen, the marketer can play an active role. In fact, the astute marketer often triggers initial awareness of the problem and aids the organization in effectively solving that problem. Incremental decisions made throughout the buying process narrow the field of acceptable suppliers and dramatically influence the ultimate outcome.

The nature of the buying process depends on the organization's level of experience with similar procurement problems. It is thus crucial to know how the organization defines the buying situation: as a new task, a modified rebuy, or a straight rebuy. Each buying situation requires a unique problem-solving approach, involves unique buying influentials, and demands a unique marketing response.

A myriad of forces—which can be classified as environmental, organizational, group, and individual—influence organizational buying behavior. First, environmental forces define the boundaries within which industrial buyers and sellers interact, such as the general business conditions or the rate of technological change. Second, organizational forces dictate the link between buying activities and the strategic priorities of the firm and the position that the purchasing function occupies in the organizational structure. Third, the relevant unit of analysis for the marketing strategist is the buying center. The composition of this group evolves during the buying process, varies from firm to firm, and changes from one purchasing situation to another. Fourth, the marketer must ultimately concentrate attention on individual members of the buying center. Each has a particular set of experiences and a unique personal and organizational frame of reference to bring to bear on the buying decision. The marketer who is sensitive to individual differences is best equipped to develop responsive marketing communications that will be remembered by the organizational buyer.

Unraveling the complex forces that encircle the organizational buying process is indeed difficult. This chapter offers a framework that enables the marketing manager to begin this task by asking the right questions. The answers will provide the basis for effective and efficient business marketing strategy.

Discussion Questions

1. What strategic advantage does the marketer gain by reaching the buying organization at the early rather than the late stages of the purchase decision process?

2. Jim Jackson, an industrial salesperson for Pittsburgh Machine Tool, will call on two accounts this afternoon. The first will be a buying organization that Jim has been servicing for the past three years. The second call, however, poses more of a challenge. This buying organization has been dealing with a prime competitor of Pittsburgh Machine Tool for five years. Jim, who has a good rapport with the purchasing and engineering departments, feels that the time may be right to penetrate this account. Recently, Jim learned that the purchasing manager was extremely unhappy with the poor delivery service provided by the firm's existing supplier. Define the buying situations confronting Jim and outline the appropriate strategy that he should follow in each case.

3. Mike Weber, the purchasing agent for Smith Manufacturing, views the purchase of widgets as a routine buying decision. What factors might lead him to alter this position? More important, what factors will determine whether a particular supplier, such as Albany Widget, will be considered by Mike?

4. Harley-Davidson, the U.S. motorcycle producer, recently purchased some sophisticated manufacturing equipment to enhance its position in a very competitive market. First, what environmental forces might have been important in spawning this capital investment? Second, which functional units were likely to have been represented in the buying center?

5. Compaq Computer Corporation centralizes its procurement decisions at the headquarters level. Discuss how it would approach purchasing differently than a competitor that decentralizes purchasing across various plant locations.

6. The Kraus Toy Company recently decided to develop a new electronic game. Can an electrical parts supplier predict the likely composition of the buying center at Kraus Toy? What steps could an industrial salesperson take to influence the composition of the buying center?

7. Explain how the composition of the buying center evolves during the purchasing process and how it varies from one firm to another, as well as from one purchasing situation to another. What steps can a salesperson take to identify the influential members of the buying center?

8. Carol Brooks, purchasing manager for Apex Manufacturing Co., read *The Wall Street Journal* this morning and carefully studied, clipped, and saved a full-page ad by the Allen-Bradley Company. Ralph Thornton, the production manager at Apex, read several articles from the same paper but could not recall seeing this particular ad or, for that matter, any ads. How could this occur?

9. Millions of notebook computers are purchased each year by organizations. Identify several evaluative criteria that purchasing managers might use in choosing a particular brand. In your view, which criteria would be most decisive in the buying decision?

10. The levels of risk associated with organizational purchases range on a continuum from low to high. Discuss how the buying process for a risky purchase differs from the process that is triggered for a routine purchase.

Chapter 4

Relationship Strategies for Business Markets

A well-developed ability to create and sustain successful working relationships with customers and alliance partners gives business marketing firms a significant competitive advantage. After reading this chapter, you will understand

1. the formal evaluation systems and analytical approaches that organizational buyers employ when measuring value and evaluating supplier relationships.
2. the patterns of buyer-seller relationships in the business market.
3. a procedure for designing effective relationship marketing strategies.
4. the critical determinants of success in managing strategic alliances.

On providing superior value to customers, Gary Tooker, vice chairman and CEO of Motorola, aptly describes the competitive challenge:

> *Fame is a fleeting thing. When the alarm rings tomorrow morning, you'd better get up and understand that your customers expect more from you than they did the day before. You'd better find ways to be better.*[1]

A business marketer who wishes to find a place on Motorola's preferred list of suppliers must be prepared to help the firm provide more value to its demanding customers. To this end, the marketer must provide exceptional performance in quality, delivery, and, over time, cost competitiveness. The supplier must also understand how Motorola measures value and how these value expectations can be met or surpassed in the supplier's product and service offering. Building and maintaining lasting customer relationships

[1]Jordan D. Lewis, *The Connected Organization: How Leading Companies Win through Customer-Supplier Alliances* (New York: The Free Press, 1995), p. 289.

requires careful attention to detail, meeting promises, and swiftly responding to new requirements.

The new era of business marketing is built upon effective relationship management. Many business marketing firms create what might be called a "collaborative advantage" by demonstrating special skills in managing relationships with key customers or by jointly developing innovative strategies with alliance partners.[2] These firms have learned how to be good partners and these superior relationship skills are a valuable asset in the business market. (See Figure 4.1 for an illustration.) This chapter explores the types of relationships that characterize the business market. What approaches do organizational customers use in gauging the value of a supplier's products and services? What strategies can business marketers employ to build profitable relationships with customers? What are the special challenges and opportunities that emerge when two firms collaborate in a strategic alliance?

How Customers Measure Value and Evaluate Performance

Organizational customers are interested in the total capabilities of a supplier and how these capabilities might assist them in improving *their* competitive position—now and in the future. To develop profitable relationships with organizational customers, the business marketer requires an understanding of the tools that organizational buyers use to measure value. Value propositions developed by the business marketer must be based on skills and resources that provide value as perceived by customers.

MEASURING VALUE

The accurate measurement of value is crucial to the purchasing function. The principles and tools of value analysis aid the professional buyer in approaching this task. **Value analysis** is a method of weighing the comparative value of materials, components, and manufacturing processes from the standpoint of their purpose, relative merit, and cost in order to uncover ways of improving products, lowering costs, or both. For example, ideas from suppliers enable Chrysler to reduce costs by $1 billion annually. When Allied Signal reduced the complexity of its antilock braking systems, Chrysler's annual costs were cut by $744,000![3] Note that rather straightforward design and manufacturing alternatives can produce spectacular cost savings. Value is achieved when the proper function is secured for the proper cost. Because functions can be accomplished in a number of different ways, the most cost-efficient way of

---

[2]Rosabeth Moss Kanter, "Collaborative Advantage," *Harvard Business Review* 72 (July/August 1994): pp. 96–108.

[3] "Chrysler Expects $1 Billion in Cost Reduction from Suppliers," *Purchasing* 119 (11 April 1996): pp. 49–50.

Figure 4.1 A Business Marketing Ad That Focuses on Relationship Management

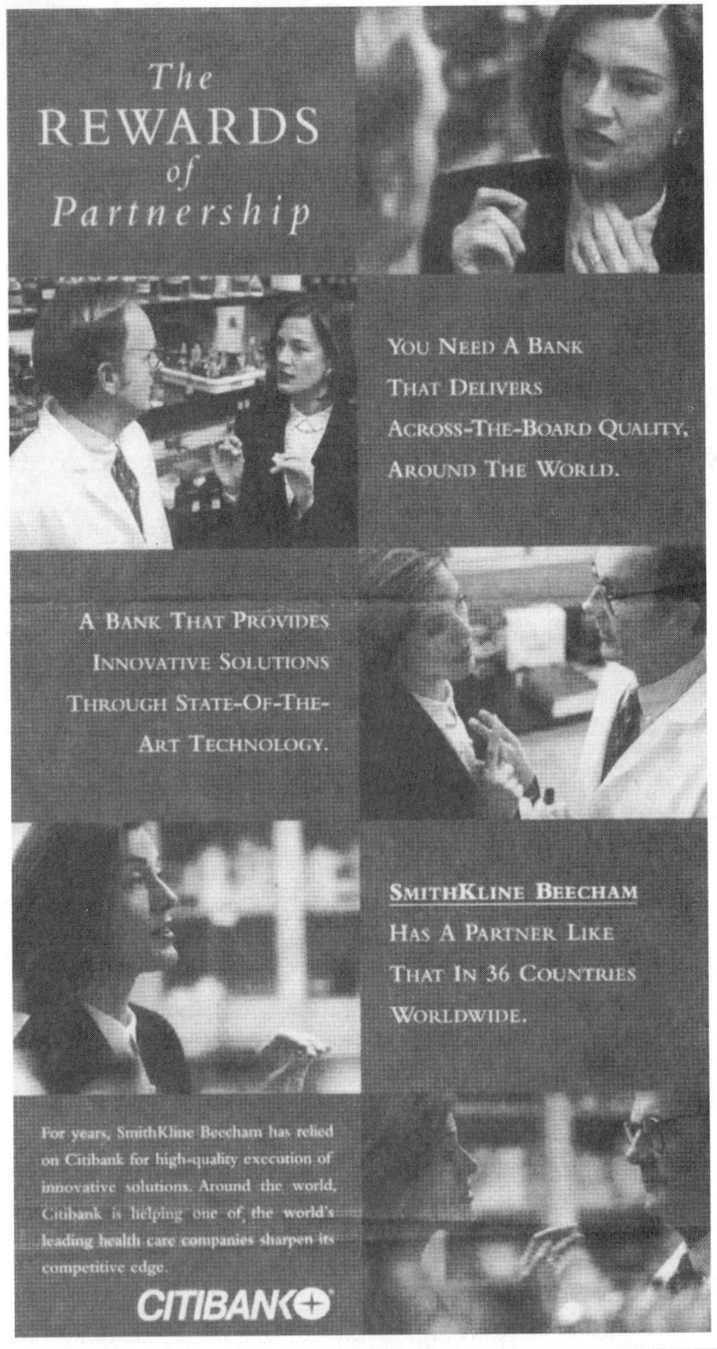

Source: Citibank, N. A.

fully accomplishing a function establishes its value. The value-in-use concept reflects this philosophy.

Value in Use[4]

Value-in-use (VIU) is defined as a product's economic value to the user relative to a specific alternative in a particular application. Thus, VIU centers on a specific usage situation and constitutes the price that would equalize the overall costs and benefits of using one product rather than another. Consider the following example.

A chemical plant uses 200 O-rings to seal valves carrying corrosive materials. These O-rings cost $5.00 each and must be changed during regular maintenance every two months. A purchasing agent located a supplier of a new product that performs the same function while offering twice the corrosive resisting power and twice the useful life (four months versus two months). The value-in-use of the new product can be determined by performing the following calculations:

(1) Annual cost of existing product:

$$200 \text{ (rings)} \times \$5 \text{ per ring} \times 6 \text{ changes per year} = \$6{,}000$$

(2) Value-in-use of new product:

$$200 \text{ (rings)} \times 3 \text{ changes per year} \times \text{VIU} = \$6{,}000$$
$$\text{VIU} = \$10$$

The purchasing agent could pay $10 per unit and receive the same benefits as the existing alternative. Often, other benefits and costs must be considered in VIU calculations.

Suppose that the cost of a plant shutdown is $5,000 and the new product allows a longer period between shutdowns—4 months versus 2 months. When these costs are considered, the value-in-use of the new alternative increases dramatically:

(3) Annual cost of existing product when shutdown cost is considered:

Equipment cost +	Shutdown cost	= Annual cost of existing product
(200 × 6 × $5)	+ ($5,000 × 6 plant shutdowns)=	$36,000

(4) Value-in-use of new product when shutdown cost is considered:

$$(200 \times 3 \times \text{VIU}) + (\$5{,}000 \times 3 \text{ plant shutdowns}) = \$36{,}000$$
$$\text{VIU} = \$35$$

Target Costing

The target costing approach has a simple logic: determining what price the end customers (for example, auto buyers) are willing to pay for a product and then working

[4]Material in this section provided by Gary L. Lilien, Research Director, Institute for the Study of Business Markets, The Pennsylvania State University. See also Valerie Kijewski and Eunsang Yoon, "Market-Based Pricing: Beyond Price-Performance Curves," *Industrial Marketing Management* 19 (February 1990): pp. 11–19.

backward to calculate the allowable costs for systems and components. Leading Japanese electronics and vehicle manufacturers have used this technique to their advantage, and companies have adopted the approach in the United States and Europe.

According to Robin Cooper and W. Bruce Chew, target costing requires managers "to make a series of decisions that include defining the product that customers want, ascertaining the economics required for profitability, allocating targets to components, and identifying the gap between target costs and initial projections of manufacturing costs."[5] To use target costing, a buying organization must work closely with its suppliers—particularly during the design process, but also when cost targets are being established.

Chrysler used target costing for its successful LH model. Corporate purchasing gave the project team a prequalified list of suppliers considered to have the best engineering and manufacturing capabilities. The team then selected suppliers and worked with them to design the components and set cost targets.[6]

Value Tools: The Marketer's Role

Prudent business marketers are eager to understand customer needs better, to provide the exact level of product design and performance required, and to demonstrate the value-in-use of their products and services. Such a strategy is especially timely given the striking majority of purchasing managers who actively encourage supplier participation in value analysis.[7] Many business marketers routinely conduct value-in-use studies to document the incremental savings and the superior value a customer gains by using the firm's products and services. For firms that employ target costing, a supplier is chosen before the component or system is even designed. The business marketer must be prepared to demonstrate the total capabilities of the firm and to meet cost targets at desired quality levels.

EVALUATING SUPPLIER PERFORMANCE

Once a contract is awarded to a supplier, the evaluation process takes a different form. Actual performance must be evaluated. Buyers rate supplier performance in assessing the quality of past decisions, in making future vendor selections—and as a negotiating tool to gain leverage in buyer-seller relationships. The specific method and the scope of the rating system vary by industry and firm.[8] Three common rating systems include the categorical plan, the weighted-point plan, and the cost-ratio plan.

---

[5]Robin Cooper and W. Bruce Chew, "Control Tomorrow's Costs through Today's Designs," *Harvard Business Review* 74 (January/February 1996): p. 94.

[6]Jeffrey H. Dyer, "How Chrysler Created an American Keiretsu," *Harvard Business Review* 74 (July/August 1996): pp. 51–52.

[7]James Carbone, "Value Analysis: For Some More Important Than Ever," *Purchasing* 119 (20 June 1996): pp. 33–34.

[8]For example, see Larry C. Giunipero and Daniel J. Brewer, "Performance Based Evaluation Systems," *International Journal of Purchasing and Materials Management* 29 (winter 1993): pp. 35–41; see also James Carbone, "How AT&T Gets Six-Sigma Quality," *Purchasing* 118 (12 January 1995): pp. 52–53.

INSIDE BUSINESS MARKETING

ISO 9000: The International Quality Standard

Located in Geneva, Switzerland, the International Standards Organization (ISO) was created to promote the development of a series of product and service standards that would be recognized by 89 member nations, including the United States. Products produced by companies that have attained ISO 9000 certification flow freely across national boundaries and are no longer subjected to individual national standards. ISO 9000 identifies the basic attributes of a manufacturer's quality management program and specifies procedures and approaches to ensure that products and services are produced in accordance with the process standards specified by the firm. For certification, an independent audit organization verifies that (1) procedures are in place to measure quality, (2) a review process has been established to monitor quality, and (3) qualified personnel are available to implement these policies.

Many organizational buyers in Europe use ISO 9000 certification as a screening device for identifying potential suppliers. Because of its growing acceptance as a standard of quality assurance, ISO 9000 has also been adopted by many industries in the United States, including the auto industry. Note that ISO 9000 standards are not product standards (for example, the Good Housekeeping Seal of Approval)—they only ensure that a quality system is employed by the supplier.

Source: Wade Ferguson, "Impact of the ISO 9000 Series Standards on Industrial Marketing," *Industrial Marketing Management* 25 (July 1996): pp. 305–310.

Categorical Plan

Under the categorical plan, supplier performance is evaluated by several departments that maintain informal records on each major vendor, perhaps including purchasing, engineering, quality control, receiving, and inspection. For every major supplier, each department develops a list of significant performance factors. At a regularly scheduled meeting (usually monthly), each major supplier is tested against each set of criteria and given an overall group evaluation. Suppliers are then categorized as preferred, neutral, or unsatisfactory. Ease of administration is the chief advantage of this highly subjective method.

The Weighted-Point Plan

In the weighted-point plan, the buying organization weights each performance factor according to its relative importance. Quality might be given a weight of 40; service, 30; and price, 30. This system alerts the business marketer to the nature and importance of the evaluative criteria used by a particular organization. The marketer's total offering can then be adjusted to fit the organization's needs more precisely.

Observe in Figure 4.2 how Chrysler Corporation "grades" suppliers of electronic components. Under this program, suppliers can be awarded a total of 100 points, including up to 40 points for quality, 25 points for pricing, 25 points for delivery,

Figure 4.2 How Chrysler Grades Suppliers

SUPPLIER RATING CHART:

Supplier Name: ____________ Commodity: ____________

Shipping Location: ____________ Annual Sales Dollars: ____________

Quality 40%	**5 Excellent**	**4 Good**	**3 Satisfactory**	**2 Fair**	**1 Poor**	**0 N/A**
Supplier defect rates						
SQA program conformance						
Sample approval performance						
Responsiveness to quality problems						
Overall rating						
Delivery 25%						
Avoidance of late or overshipments						
Ability to expand production capacity						
Engineering sample delivery performance						
Response to fluctuating supply demands						
Overall delivery rating						
Price 25%						
Price competitiveness						
Absorption of economic price increases						
Submission of cost savings plans						
Payment terms						
Overall price rating						
Technology 10%						
State-of-the-art component technology						
Sharing research development capability						
Capable and willing to provide circuit design services						
Responsiveness to engineering problems						
Overall technology rating						

Buyer: ____________ Date: ____________

Comments: ____________

Source: Courtesy Chrysler Corporation.

and 10 points for technical assistance. Note that a number of dimensions are evaluated for each performance factor. For example, the quality rating is determined by the following factors:

- The supplier's defect rate

- Conformance to a statistical quality audit (SQA) of the supplier's manufacturing plant in which purchasing and engineering inspect manufacturing processes and controls
- The performance of samples provided by the supplier
- The responisveness of the supplier to quality problems

Working with other departments, such as engineering and production control, purchasing calculates a performance score for each supplier. In the pricing area, Chrysler is giving increased attention to the cost savings plans submitted by the supplier.[9] Detailed records are kept of the number of proposals each supplier makes and the dollar savings that they generate. By focusing on continual improvement, suppliers can improve their profitability and increase the amount of sales they generate from Chrysler. Those scoring 91 points or higher make the preferred supplier list. It is important to note that only 300 of Chrysler's 1,000 electronics suppliers achieve this distinction, and they receive more than 80 percent of the firm's $350 million annual budget for electronic components. Suppliers scoring 83 to 90 points continue to be used, but to a lesser degree than preferred suppliers. Those scoring 70 to 83 points are placed in a marginal category and risk being eliminated from the supplier roster unless they work with Chrysler to improve. Suppliers scoring less than 70 points are usually dropped automatically.

The weighted-point plan is more objective and flexible than the categorical method. The buying organization can adjust the weights of various performance factors to meet particular needs. Likewise, the method forces the organizational buyer to define the key attributes of a supplier.

Cost-Ratio Plan

The cost-ratio method draws upon standard cost analysis. Under this plan, the buying organization evaluates quality, delivery, and service, assigning a minus (-) weight for favorable performance on a factor and a plus (+) weight for unfavorable performance. (That's right—a minus for good performance, a plus for bad performance. You will soon see why.) The weights for each performance factor are derived from standard cost calculations. For the delivery rating, the standard cost base might include the expense of factory downtime and rescheduling caused by a delinquent shipment as well as telephone follow-ups and associated costs. A penalty rating of +0.02 might be assigned for a shipment received one week late and a stronger penalty of +0.05 might be assigned for a shipment delayed three weeks. Similar weights, based on standard costs, are designated for quality and service and then combined into one final composite rating for each supplier. This composite rating is used to calculate an "adjusted price" for each major supplier. As an example, supplier X will be evaluated using this approach.

Illustration: The Cost-Ratio Method. Assume that supplier X bids $80 and has a quality cost ratio of +1 percent, a delivery cost ratio of +5 percent, and a service cost ratio

[9]Dyer, "How Chrysler Created an American Keiretsu," pp. 52–56; see also Lisa M. Ellram, "A Structured Method for Applying Purchasing Cost Management Tools," *International Journal of Purchasing and Materials Management* 32 (winter 1996): pp. 11–19.

of -1 percent. The three cost ratios sum to +5 percent. Thus, the adjusted price for supplier X is $80 + (0.05 × 80) = $84. The organizational buyer would select the vendor offering the most economical total package rather than the supplier with the lowest bid price. Poor delivery performance clearly damaged the position of supplier X. A competing supplier offering solid delivery performance and competitive quality and service would be selected even at a slightly higher bid price.

A computerized cost accounting system is needed to provide the cost estimates that form the core of the cost-ratio plan. While the method has generated widespread interest, many firms find the weighted-point plan simpler and more flexible. The quality of each method—categorical, weighted-point, and cost-ratio—depends on the accuracy and appropriateness of the underlying assumptions of the evaluator.

VENDOR ANALYSIS: IMPLICATIONS FOR THE MARKETER

Business marketers must be sensitive to the evaluation criteria of organizational buyers and to how these criteria are weighted. Many criteria may be factored into a buyer's ultimate decision: quality, service, price, company image, and capability. Buyers' perceptions are also critical. When products are perceived as highly standardized, price assumes more importance. On the other hand, when products are perceived as unique, other criteria may dominate. The price of a product cannot be separated from the attached bundle of services and other intangible values.

Economic criteria assume significant importance in many industrial buying decisions,[10] especially the anticipated costs associated with buying, storing, and using the product. By contrast, product performance criteria evaluate the extent to which the product is likely to maximize performance. Economic criteria are important in the purchase of standard products of simple construction with standard applications. Performance criteria are more important in the evaluation of complex products or novel applications. The marketer who secures a new account must be prepared to pass frequent performance tests.

To this point, the discussion has centered on the systems that organizational buyers use in evaluating suppliers. Attention now turns to the critical issue of managing buyer-seller relationships in the business market.

Relationship Management

The forces of global competition have reshaped the nature of managerial work and have spawned new ways of structuring organizations and buyer-seller relationships. The new organizational forms emphasize partnerships with other firms (for example, General Electric's emphasis on strategic alliances); teamwork among members of the organization with team members drawn from two or more supplier firms (for

[10]Donald R. Lehmann and John O'Shaughnessy, "Decision Criteria Used in Buying Different Categories of Products," *Journal of Purchasing and Materials Management* 18 (spring 1982): pp. 9–14.

HOW SUPPLIER PARTNERSHIPS REVIVED CHRYSLER

Partnerships with suppliers have helped Chrysler to significantly improve performance and strengthen its competitive position. By working closely with suppliers, Chrysler has attained the following objectives:

1. *Shortened the product development cycle.* Rather than devoting 12 to 18 months to sending out bids for quotations, analyzing bids, negotiating contracts, and bringing suppliers on board, Chrysler now involves suppliers at the conceptual stage of product development. The firm has reduced the time it takes to develop a new vehicle by more than 40 percent.

2. *Reduced the overall costs of vehicle development.* By giving partners greater responsibility for design and manufacturing, the costs of designing and engineering a new vehicle have declined. By developing products more quickly and by tapping the expertise of suppliers, the investment in tools (such as dies and molds) has been reduced. In the past, investments in these tools had to be made much earlier in the development process and costly changes were often required.

3. *Reduced procurement (transaction) costs.* Chrysler reduced the number of overall suppliers it uses and reduced the size of its purchasing staff by 30 percent. By eliminating the competitive bidding system and by working with a streamlined list of suppliers, negotiating and contracting costs drop.

4. *Increased market share and profitability.* Chrysler's profit-per-vehicle rose from $250 in the mid-1980s to more than $2,000 in the mid-1990s as its share of the U. S. car and truck market exceeded 14.5 percent—a 25-year high for Chrysler in the U. S. market.

Source: Jeffrey H. Dyer, "How Chrysler Created an American Keiretsu," *Harvard Business Review* 74 (July/August 1996), pp. 46–47.

example, new product teams at Motorola and Chrysler); sharing of responsibility for developing converging technologies (for example, work processing projects by Xerox and Microsoft); and less reliance on formal contracting, competitive bidding, and managerial control systems.

TYPES OF RELATIONSHIPS[11]

A business marketer may begin a relationship with General Electric (G.E.) as a supplier (one of many), move to a preferred supplier status as a G.E. partner (one

[11]This section is largely based on Frederick E. Webster Jr., "The Changing Role of Marketing in the Corporation," *Journal of Marketing* 56 (October 1992): pp. 1–17, except when others are cited.

Figure 4.3 The Spectrum of Buyer-Seller Relationships

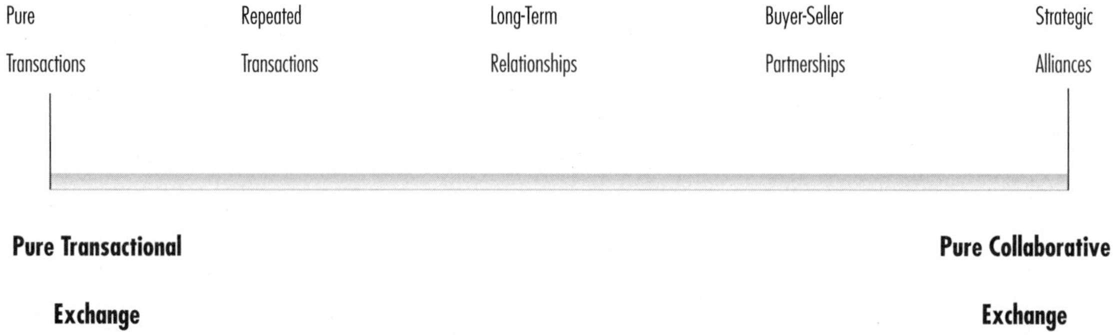

Source: Adapted with modifications from Frederick E. Webster Jr., "The Changing Role of Marketing in the Corporation," *Journal of Marketing* 56 (October 1992): p. 5.

of a few), and ultimately join forces with the firm in a strategic alliance. Observe in Figure 4.3 that several types of marketing relationships are positioned on a continuum with pure transactions and strategic alliances serving as the end points. Pure **transactional exchange** centers on the timely exchange of basic products for highly competitive market prices. Moving across the continuum, relationships become closer or more collaborative. Pure **collaborative exchange,** according to James Anderson and James Narus, involves "a process where a customer and supplier firm form strong and extensive social, economic, service, and technical ties over time, with the intent of lowering total costs and/or increasing value, thereby achieving mutual benefit."[12] An understanding of the unique characteristics of each relationship type provides a foundation for developing responsive business marketing strategies.

Pure Transactions

Pure transactions are rare in the business market but provide a useful starting point for exploring types of relationships. Frederick Webster defines a **pure transaction** as "a one-time exchange of value between two parties with no prior or subsequent interaction. Price, established in the competitive marketplace, contains all the information

[12]James C. Anderson and James A Narus, "Partnering as a Focused Market Strategy," *California Management Review* 33 (spring 1991): p. 96. See also Ven Srivam, Robert Krapfel, and Robert Spekman, "Antecedents to Buyer-Seller Collaboration: An Analysis from the Buyer's Perspective," *Journal of Business Research* (December 1992): pp. 303–320.

necessary for both parties to conclude the exchange."[13] The output of one producer is indistinguishable from the output of another.

Repeated Transactions

The frequent purchase of some industrial components, maintenance, and operating supplies reflects the success of marketers in achieving product differentiation and creating preference and loyalty. Repeat purchase and loyalty move the level of exchange beyond a pure transaction. When a meaningful and close buyer-seller relationship does not exist, the presence of trust and credibility signal the potential for developing a long-term relationship.

Long-Term Relationships

This relationship type involves relatively long-term contractual commitments, but the relationship is managed in an arms-length and adversarial manner. Here the buyer is pitted against the seller in a battle centered on low price. Frederick Webster Jr. recounts the use of this approach in the automobile industry:

> *The automobile manufacturers for decades had depended on thousands of vendors, with many vendors for each item, in a system that was fundamentally and intentionally adversarial. . . . The largest share of the business usually went to the vendor with the lowest price, though several others were given smaller shares to keep them involved, to keep pressure on the low price supplier, and to provide alternative sources of supply in the event of delivery or quality problems.*[14]

Over the past decade, competitive forces in the global marketplace have transformed buyer-seller relationships not only in the automobile industry, but also in the telecommunications, office equipment, computer, and other industries as well.

Buyer-Seller Partnerships

Firms that emphasize partnerships with suppliers have reduced the size of their supplier list and rely on one or a few suppliers for a particular part. The chosen suppliers promise to deliver defect-free parts on a precise timetable, often within minutes of their use in a just-in-time production system.

Prices are not determined solely by market forces, but instead are an outcome of a negotiation process based on mutual dependence in which quality, delivery, and technical support assume importance. Early supplier involvement in new product development initiatives and an open exchange of information are important features of the buyer-seller partnership.

---

[13]Webster, "The Changing Role of Marketing in the Corporation," p. 6.
[14]Ibid., p. 7.

Figure 4.4a A Traditional Bow-Tie Relationship

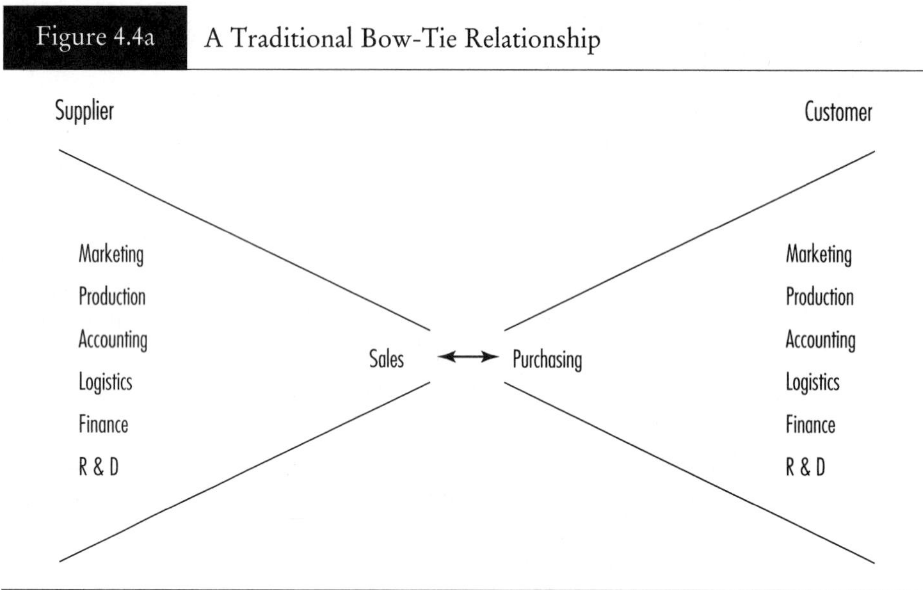

Figure 4.4b Interactive Cross-Functional Teams

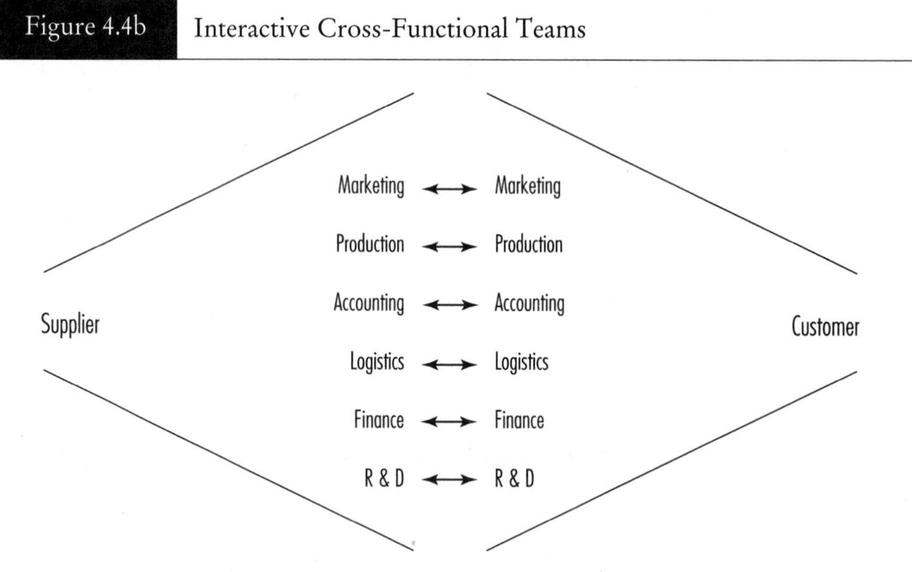

Source: Presentation by Wal-Mart and Procter & Gamble at the American Marketing Association Educators' Conference, August 1994.

Figure 4.4a depicts the traditional "bow-tie" relationship in which the purchasing agent and the salesperson assume the primary roles in the exchange process. For long-term relationships or buyer-seller partnerships, however, the boundaries between the firms become more transparent. Interactive, cross-functional teams now openly exchange ideas for improving efficiency and effectiveness (see Figure 4.4b). The goal is to create new value together.

Strategic Alliances

In some cases, the partnership between a supplier and a customer moves to the next stage and becomes a strategic alliance. What distinguishes a **strategic alliance** from other forms of interfirm cooperation is the intent to move each of the partners toward the attainment of some long-term, *strategic* goal.

Some alliances are formed between suppliers and customers to ensure a smooth flow of materials and components into the customer's manufacturing processes. Intel, for example, has formed such alliances with selected suppliers. In a similar arrangement, Canon supplies laser engines to Hewlett-Packard for its successful line of printers. Other alliances are formed to develop a new product, to gain access to a particular market, or to combine expertise in the development of convergent technologies. All involve the commitment of capital and management resources to the shared objective of strengthening the partners' competitive standing. (Further attention is given to strategic alliances later in this chapter.)

Commitment and Trust[15]

Relationship marketing centers on all marketing activities directed toward establishing, developing, and maintaining successful exchanges with customers, alliance partners, and other constituents. What factors contribute to the success or failure of specific relationship marketing efforts? Does success hinge on the relative power of the partners? Robert M. Morgan and Shelby D. Hunt offer these incisive thoughts:

> *The presence of relationship commitment and trust is central to successful relationship marketing, not power and its ability to "condition others." Commitment and trust are "key" because they encourage marketers to (1) work at preserving relationship investments by cooperating with exchange partners, (2) resist attractive short-term alternatives in favor of the expected long-term benefits of staying with existing partners, and (3) view potentially high-risk actions as being prudent because of the belief that their partners will not act opportunistically.*[16]

Relationship commitment involves the belief by a partner that an ongoing relationship is so important that it deserves maximum efforts to maintain it. In turn,

---

[15]This section is based on Robert M. Morgan and Shelby D. Hunt, "The Commitment-Trust Theory of Relationship Marketing," *Journal of Marketing* 58 (July 1994): pp. 20–38. See also F. Robert Dwyer, Paul H. Schurr, and Sejo Oh, "Developing Buyer-Seller Relationships," *Journal of Marketing* 51 (April 1987): pp. 11–27.

[16]Morgan and Hunt, "The Commitment-Trust Theory of Relationship Marketing," p. 22.

Figure 4.5 The Account Behavior Spectrum

Short Time Horizon ⟵	⟶ **Long Time Horizon**
Typified by always-a-share customers	Typified by lost-for-good customers
Lower switching costs	High switching costs
Smaller investment actions	Substantial investment actions, especially in procedures and lasting assets
Lower perceived exposure	High perceived exposure
Focus on a product or on a person	Focus on a technology or on a vendor
Lower importance	Higher importance: strategic, operational, and personal
Transaction Marketing Transactional Exchange	**Relationship Marketing Collaborative Exchange**

Source: Adapted with modifications from Barbara Bund Jackson, *Winning and Keeping Industrial Customers* (Lexington, Mass.: Lexington Books, 1985), p. 168. Reprinted by permission of the publisher. Copyright D. C. Heath and Company.

trust exists when one party has confidence in a partner's reliability and integrity. Commitment and trust are linked directly to the success of relationship marketing strategies.

The Account Behavior Spectrum[17]

Knowledge of the different forms that relationships take in the business market provides a foundation for developing specific relationship marketing strategies for a particular customer. Barbara Bund Jackson suggests that business marketers should assess "the time horizon within which a customer makes a commitment to a supplier and also the actual pattern the relationship follows over time." Figure 4.5 highlights the typical characteristics of customers at the end points of the account behavior spectrum: always-a-share customers (transactional exchange) and lost-for-good customers (collaborative exchange).

LOST-FOR-GOOD CUSTOMERS

The **lost-for-good customer** makes a series of purchases over time, faces high costs in switching to a new supplier, and views the commitment to a particular supplier as

[17]This section is based on Barbara Bund Jackson, "Build Customer Relationships That Last," *Harvard Business Review* 63 (November/December 1985): pp. 120–128; and Jackson, *Winning and Keeping Industrial Customers* (Lexington, Mass.: Lexington Books, 1985).

relatively permanent. Once won, this type of account is likely to remain loyal to a particular supplier for a long time. If lost, however, it is often "lost for good." This behavior fits some purchasers of computers, office automation systems, communications equipment, and heavy construction equipment. For example, Ford recently decided that it needed a single supplier of office systems to improve communication in its North American operations. Business marketers attempting to secure the Ford account recognize that if they are unsuccessful, years may pass before Ford will consider a totally new system. For the winning bidder, a long, prosperous relationship can be nurtured. Once won, this type of buyer is an asset; once lost, it is lost for good. Switching costs are especially important to lost-for-good customers.

Switching Costs

In considering possible changes from one selling firm to another, organizational buyers consider two **switching costs**: investments and risk of exposure. First, organizational buyers invest in their relationships with suppliers in many ways, as Barbara Bund Jackson states: "They invest *money*; they invest in *people*, as in training employees to run new equipment; they invest in *lasting assets*, such as equipment itself; and they invest in changing basic business *procedures* like inventory handling."[18] Because of these past investments, buyers may be hesitant to incur the disruptions and switching costs that result when new suppliers are selected.

Risk of exposure provides a second major category of switching costs. Attention centers on the risks to organizational buyers of making the wrong choice. Customers perceive more risk exposure when they purchase products important to their operations, when they buy from less established suppliers, and when they buy technically complex products.

Strategy Guidelines

Relationship marketing, targeted on strong and lasting commitments, is especially appropriate for lost-for-good accounts. Business marketers can sensibly invest resources in order to secure commitments and to aid customers with long-range planning. Given the long time horizon and the considerable stakes involved, customers are concerned both with marketers' long-term capabilities and with their immediate performance. Because the customers perceive significant risk, they demand competence and commitment from the selling organization and are easily frightened by even a hint of supplier inadequacy.

In purchasing computer workstations, research confirms that switching costs and concerns for product compatibility limit a buyer's consideration set.[19] This suggests that existing suppliers should promote product-specific learning within the buying organization to further strengthen the relationship. The study furthermore

[18]Jackson, "Build Customer Relationships That Last," p. 125.

[19]Jan B. Heide and Allen M. Weiss, "Vendor Consideration and Switching Behavior for Buyers in High Technology Markets," *Journal of Marketing* 59 (July 1995): pp. 30–43.

suggests that the concentration of decision-making authority also limits the buyer's consideration set. By advocating standard qualification procedures for suppliers to be employed across the organization, existing suppliers could strengthen their position with the customer.

ALWAYS-A-SHARE CUSTOMERS

The **always-a-share customer** (see Figure 4.5) purchases repeatedly from some product category, displays less loyalty or commitment to a particular supplier, and can easily switch part or all of the purchases from one vendor to another. Because of low switching costs, these customers may share their patronage over time with multiple vendors and adopt a short time horizon in their commitments with suppliers. This behavior fits some buyers of commodity chemicals, computer terminals, and shipping services. A business marketer who offers an immediate, attractive combination of product, price, technical support, and other benefits has a chance of winning business from always-a-share customers. Thus, **transaction marketing**—marketing that emphasizes the individual sale—is most appropriate for the always-a-share buyer.

INTERMEDIATE CUSTOMERS

The behavior of many customers in the business market corresponds to an intermediate point in the account behavior spectrum, somewhere between pure transactional exchange and pure collaborative exchange. The particular position that a customer occupies depends on a host of factors: the characteristics of the product category, the customer's pattern of product usage, and the actions taken by both the supplier and the customer. For example, purchasers of a commodity such as carbon steel generally fit the always-a-share model. However, a steel user who adopts a just-in-time production system requires close cooperation and scheduling with suppliers. The customer's usage pattern and the supplier's investment in adapting to the buyer's special requirements can create behavior that corresponds more to the lost-for-good model.

Relationship Marketing Strategies

Business marketers often have a portfolio of customers who span the account behavior spectrum: Some emphasize low price and a transaction perspective while others place a premium on substantial service and desire a more collaborative relationship. Indeed, some customers fall somewhat in the middle of the account spectrum and represent accounts that might be effectively upgraded to a level that adds value to the relationship for both parties. To develop responsive and profitable relationship marketing strategies, special attention must be given to four areas: (1) selecting accounts, (2) developing account-specific product offerings, (3) implementing relationship strategies, and (4) evaluating relationship strategy outcomes.[20]

ACCOUNT SELECTION

Account selection requires a clear understanding of customer needs, a tight grasp on the costs that will be incurred in serving different groups of customers, and an accurate forecast of potential profit opportunities. The choice of potential accounts to target is facilitated by an understanding of how different customers define value. **Value,** as defined by James Anderson and James Narus, refers to "the economic, technical, service, and social benefits received by a customer firm in exchange for the price paid for a product offering."[21] By gauging the value of their offerings to different groups of customers, business marketers are better equipped to target accounts and to determine how to provide enhanced value to particular customers.

The account selection process should also consider profit potential. Because the product is critical to their operations, some customers place a high value on supporting services (for example, technical advice and training) and are willing to pay a premium price for this support. Other customers do not value service support and are extremely price sensitive in making product selection decisions. Frank Cespedes asserts that

> *Account selection, therefore, must be explicit about which demands the seller can meet and leverage in dealings with other customers. Otherwise, the seller risks overserving unprofitable accounts and wasting resources that might be allocated to other customer groups.*[22]

DEVELOPING ACCOUNT-SPECIFIC PRODUCT OFFERINGS

To develop customer-specific product offerings, the business marketer should next examine the nature of buyer-seller relationships that characterize the industry. The strategies pursued by competing firms in an industry fall into a range referred to as the **industry bandwidth** of working relationships. Business marketers either attempt to span the bandwidth with a portfolio of relationship marketing strategies or concentrate on a single strategy, thereby having a narrower range of relationships than the industry bandwidth.

---

[20]This section draws on Anderson and Narus, "Partnering as a Focused Market Strategy," pp. 95–113.
[21]Ibid., p. 98.
[22]Frank V. Cespedes, *Concurrent Marketing: Integrating Product, Sales, and Service* (Boston: Harvard Business School Press, 1995), p. 193.

Figure 4.6 Transactional and Collaborative Working Relationships

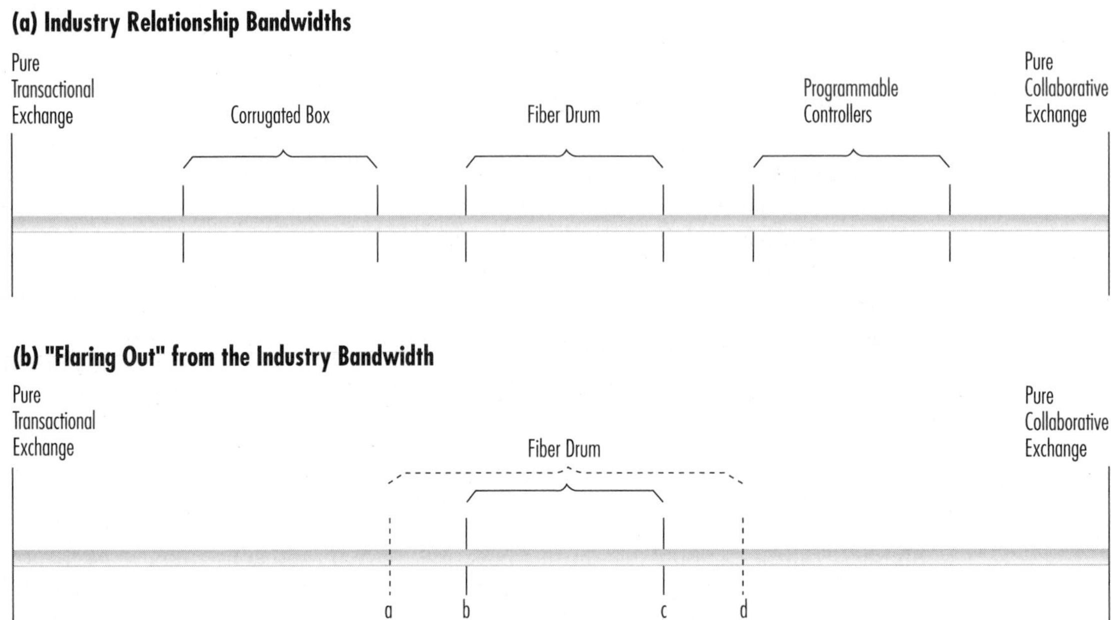

Source: Adapted from James C. Anderson and James A. Narus, "Partnering as a Focused Marketing Strategy," *California Management Review* 33 (spring 1991), p. 97. Copyright © 1991 by the Regents of the University of California. Reprinted by permission of the Regents.

Observe in Figure 4.6 how three different industries (corrugated box, fiber drum, and programmable controllers) are positioned on the relationship continuum. Because of the complexity and dynamic nature of the underlying technology, collaborative relations characterize the programmable controller industry. Here the core product can be augmented by a range of services such as the codesign of unique manufacturing systems, installation, training, and maintenance agreements. By contrast, collaborative relations in the fiber drum industry tend to be more focused and center on helping customers adapt their operational procedures (for example, lifting and stacking) to accommodate fiber drums. Because many buyers view the product as a commodity, long-term supply agreements and just-in-time inventory programs represent the only vehicle for collaboration in the corrugated box industry.

By diagnosing the spectrum of relationship strategies followed by competitors in an industry, a business marketer can tailor strategies that more closely respond both to customers who desire a collaborative emphasis as well as to those who seek a transaction emphasis. The strategy involves *flaring out* from the industry bandwidth in the collaborative as well as in the transactional direction (see Figure 4.6b).

Flaring Out by Unbundling

An unbundling strategy can be pursued to reach those customers who desire a greater transaction emphasis. Here related services are unbundled to yield the core product (**a** in Figure 4.6b), which meets the basic price, quality, and availability requirements of customers. For each service that is unbundled, the price is lowered. Augmented services, such as technical assistance and delivery, are each offered, but in a menu fashion, on an incremental price basis. Importantly, the price increments for the entire set of unbundled services should be greater than the price premium sought for the collaborative offering. This reflects the efficiencies involved in providing the complete bundle of services to a collaborative account. This pricing policy is market oriented in that it allows customer firms to choose the product and relationship offering that *they perceive* to provide the greatest value.

Flaring Out with Augmentation

At the other extreme, the collaborative offering (**d** in Figure 4.6b) becomes the augmented product enriched with those features valued by the customer firm. Augmented features might include coordinated cost-reduction programs, technical assistance, delivery schedule guarantees, and cooperative advertising. Because collaborative efforts are designed to add value or reduce the costs of exchange between partnering firms, a price premium should be received for the collaborative offering.

Creating Flexible Service Offerings[23]

Business marketers can gain a competitive edge by creating a portfolio of service offerings and then drawing on this portfolio to provide customized solutions for groups of customers or even individual customers. First, an offering should be created that includes the bare-bones-minimum number of services that are valued by all customers in a particular segment of the market. Microsoft Corporation refers to these offerings as "naked solutions." Second, optional services are created that add value to customers by reducing costs or improving the performance of their operations. To meet the needs of particular customers, optional services can then be "custom wrapped" with the core offering to create added value in the relationship.

Baxter International uses flexible service offerings to meet the needs of its hospital customers. For those transactional customers who do business with Baxter on an order-by-order basis, the core offering is emphasized. However, a more elaborate set of services provides the focus of Baxter's strategy with strategic customers—those

---

[23]This section is based on James C. Anderson and James A. Narus, "Capturing the Value of Supplementary Services," *Harvard Business Review* 73 (January/February 1995): pp. 75–83.

who have made contractual commitments toward a long-term relationship with the firm. These services create value for the hospitals because they are designed to help them improve their efficiency and financial performance.

IMPLEMENTING RELATIONSHIP STRATEGIES

The sales force assumes a central relationship management role in the business market. Technical service and customer service personnel also assume implementation roles that are important and visible within buying organizations. Successful relationship strategies are shaped by an effective organization and deployment of the personal selling effort and close coordination with supporting units, such as logistics and technical service. Some firms divide the sales organization into units that each serve a distinct relationship category such as transactional accounts or strategic accounts. For example, the sales force for Motorola's Semiconductor Group comprises three units: a *strategic market* sales force responsible for 60 partnership accounts, a *geographic* sales force responsible for the thousands of transactional accounts that buy Motorola products, and a *distributor* sales force that serves the needs of resellers of the firm's products.

The strategic market sales force consists of teams of sales representatives, application engineers, quality engineers, and others that are assigned to particular partnership accounts. In contrast, members of the geographic sales force act individually and perform traditional selling tasks. Through a careful screening process, promising transaction accounts are periodically upgraded to partnerships. Finally, the distributor sales force serves channel members that carry Motorola products and assists them in maintaining sound working relationships with this segment of Motorola's customer base.

EVALUATING RELATIONSHIP STRATEGY OUTCOMES

Some relationship-building efforts will fail because the expectations of the parties do not mesh—for example, when the business marketer follows a relationship approach and the customer responds in a transaction mode.[24] By isolating customer needs and the associated costs of augmented service features, the marketer is better equipped to profitably match the appropriate product offering to the needs of a particular customer.

The goal of a relationship is to enable the buyer and seller to maximize joint value. This points to the need for a formal evaluation of relationship outcomes. For example, Motorola sales executives work closely with their partnership accounts to establish mutually defined goals. After an appropriate period, partnerships that do not meet these goals are downgraded and shifted from the strategic market sales force to the geographic sales force.

---

[24]Frederick E. Webster Jr., *Market-Driven Management: Using the New Marketing Concept to Create a Customer-Oriented Company* (New York: John Wiley & Sons, 1994), pp. 166–171.

Monitoring Relationships

An array of factors can damage relationships and business marketers should be particularly sensitive to the signs of stress. Customer requirements may change as a result of changes in the market that the customer organization serves, new competitors in that market, new technology, or continual pressures for cost reduction. For example, under pressure from its competitors, Ford has asked suppliers to cut costs 5 percent per year through 1999.[25] Some suppliers viewed the request as heavy-handed, while others were more constructive. A marketing manager at a leading microcontroller company noted that "Ford's way is cooperative and collaborative." Business marketers must be alert to the changing requirements of customers and be sensitive to the competitive forces that drive buying decisions in customer organizations.

Demonstrating Commitment

Relationships with customers can also be damaged by product quality problems, late deliveries, or inadequate service support. Each can pose a serious threat to the relationship and signal a lack of commitment on the part of the marketer. In turn, the customer's definition of value changes over the course of the relationship. As Frederick E. Webster Jr. notes,

> *If quality is defined as meeting and exceeding customer expectations, and if the customer's expectations keep increasing as the company improves its performance and competitors make promises of superior value, continuous improvement is an inevitable requirement for survival in the customer relationship.*[26]

Business marketers should also continually update the value of their product and relationship offering. Attention here should center on particular new services that might be incorporated into the offering as well as on existing service elements that might be unbundled or curtailed. Working relationships with customer firms are among the most important marketing assets of the firm. They deserve delicate care and continual nurturing!

Strategic Alliances

Not only do business marketing managers form close relationships with customers, they also develop close bonds with other firms. The traditional management assumption that "good fences make good corporations" has given way to a new philosophy: Firms are stretching their formal boundaries by creating strong ties with other firms.[27]

---

[25]"Ford to Suppliers: Cut Costs 5%/Year," *Purchasing* 118 (1 June 1995): p. 43.

[26]Webster, *Market-Driven Management*, p. 169.

[27]Rosabeth Moss Kanter, "Becoming PALS: Pooling, Allying, and Linking across Companies," *The Academy of Management Executive* 3 (August 1989): p. 183.

Managing in the 21st Century

WORLD-CLASS LEADERS

Many contemporary leaders of organizations have succeeded by focusing on the needs of their own firm and by being the best advocate for their own interest group. Leaders of the future will have to do much more in a borderless world comprising organizations that are removing boundaries. Future leaders will demonstrate a special ability to bring together individuals from diverse functions, disciplines, and organizations to find a common purpose in goals that improve the entire industry and expand the offerings for everyone. Innovative ideas challenge boundaries, create tension, and present new opportunities. Leaders of the future must be *integrators* who see beyond obvious differences in functions and organizations, *diplomats* who can resolve the inevitable "us" versus "them" conflicts, *cross-fertilizers* who can transfer the best from one place to another, and *deep thinkers* who can conceptualize new possibilities.

Source: Rosabeth Moss Kanter, "World-Class Leaders: The Power of Partnering," in *The Leader of the Future: New Visions, Strategies, and Practices,* ed. Frances Hesselbein, Marshall Goldsmith, and Richard Beckhard (San Francisco: Jossey-Bass, 1996), pp. 89–98.

Strategic alliances are assuming an increasingly prominent role in the strategy of leading business firms. **Strategic alliances,** according to George Day, involve "a formal long-run linkage, funded with direct co-investments by two or more companies, that pool complementary capabilities and resources to achieve generally agreed objectives."[28] In contrast, a **joint venture** involves the formation of a separate independent organization by the venture partners.

The driving force behind the formation of a strategic alliance is the desire of one firm to leverage its core competencies by linking them with others who have complementary expertise, thereby expanding the product and geographic scope of the organization. Examples of strategic alliances include the partnerships between AT&T and American Express (unified credit card and calling card), between Microsoft and Xerox (integrated office products), among IBM, Siemens, and Toshiba (memory chips), and among Hitachi, Sony, and Motorola (multimedia workstations and home entertainment systems).

BENEFITS OF STRATEGIC ALLIANCES

G.E. has more than 100 strategic partnerships, and its statement of operating objectives points to still more:

[28]George S. Day, *Market Driven Strategy: Processes for Creating Value* (New York: The Free Press, 1990), p. 272.

> *To achieve a #1 or #2 global product-market position requires participation in each major market of the world. This requires several different forms of participation: trading technology for market access; trading market access for technology; and trading market access for market access. This "share to gain" becomes a way of life.*[29]

Jack Welch, chief executive officer of G.E., notes that "Alliances are a big part of this game [of global competition]. . . . The least attractive way to win on a global basis is to think you can take on the world all by yourself."[30]

Partners to an alliance seek such benefits as (1) access to markets or to technology (a motivating force for G.E.); (2) economies of scale that might be gained by combining manufacturing, R&D, or marketing activities; (3) faster entry of new products to markets (for example, when partners with established channels of distribution in different countries swap new products); and (4) sharing of risk.[31] Simply put, there is a tremendous cost—and risk—in a firm's creating its own distribution channels, logistical network, manufacturing plant, and R&D function in every key market in the world. Also, it takes time to develop relationships with channel members and customers and to develop the skills of employees. Alliances provide another option.

ALLIANCE MANAGEMENT CHALLENGES

The value or competitive advantage created by an alliance rests on the joint efforts of the parties. Although offering significant benefits, alliances often fall short of expectations or dissolve. Managing an alliance involves special challenges.

Negotiating the Contract

The alliance contract provides an outline of broad areas of cooperation. While often a lengthy document, the contract cannot begin to cover all the issues and surprises that will spring up once the alliance relationship is initiated. Often, alliance agreements are broadly negotiated by senior executives who turn the final details and day-to-day management of the alliance over to middle managers. The implementation of alliance strategy can be hampered as managers flesh out the details with their counterparts in the partner firm. Painful negotiations often create tension between the parties before things are even under way. A marketing manager who heads an alliance team at a high-tech firm isolated one source of friction that is common in negotiations:

---

[29]General Electric Company, *Operating Objectives to Meet Challenges of the '90s* (Fairfield, Conn.: General Electric Company, 14 March 1988).

[30]Michael Y. Yoshino and U. Srinivasa Rangan, *Strategic Alliances: An Entrepreneurial Approach to Globalization* (Boston: Harvard Business School Press, 1995), p. 3.

[31]Kenichi Ohmae, "The Global Logic of Strategic Alliances," *Harvard Business Review* 67 (March/April 1989): pp. 143–154.

The thing that took the most time was the question: "What happens when we divorce?" It took us a year to negotiate this thing. Three months to cut the deal and nine months to protect each other's corporate assets when we divide. That's what killed the trust.[32]

Protecting Core Assets

Many firms are involved in multiple alliances—which can provide an added source of tension to a relationship. Indeed, the partner firm may be a rival or involved in other alliance relationships with competitors. Here the business marketer may find it particularly difficult to strike a balance between trusting one's partner on one hand and protecting the firm's strategic interests and assets on the other. An alliance manager aptly describes the problem:

We are involved in half a dozen alliances. Some are with rivals and some are not. Our plans call for different levels of information to different alliances. Sometimes I have meetings with different managers from partner firms. It's so hard to keep in mind what can be and cannot be disclosed to different partners. . . . One slip could cause damage.[33]

Linking Systems and Structures

The basic idea behind an alliance is to create added value by effectively linking the core competencies of one firm with those of another. Sometimes things do not work together smoothly. The partner firms may have incompatible systems and decision structures that delay decision making, create inefficiencies, and frustrate alliance personnel, as expressed by one manager:

Our alliance team is empowered to make decisions—even those that involve significant resources. At the partner firm, they always have to go check with senior executives—follow the channels.

DETERMINANTS OF ALLIANCE SUCCESS

Successful alliances involve a collaborative relationship in which the parties create new value together, rather than an exchange relationship ("you get something back for what you put in"). Rosabeth Moss Kanter emphasizes that "Alliances cannot be controlled by formal systems but require a dense web of interpersonal connections and internal infrastructures that enhance learning."[34]

---

[32]Edwin R. Stafford, Beth A. Walker, and Michael D. Hutt, "Managing Alliance Relationships," working paper, Arizona State University, 1996.
[33]Yoshino and Rangan, *Strategic Alliances*, p. 111.
[34]Kanter, "Collaborative Advantage," p. 97.

Figure 4.7 Close and Important Alliance Connections

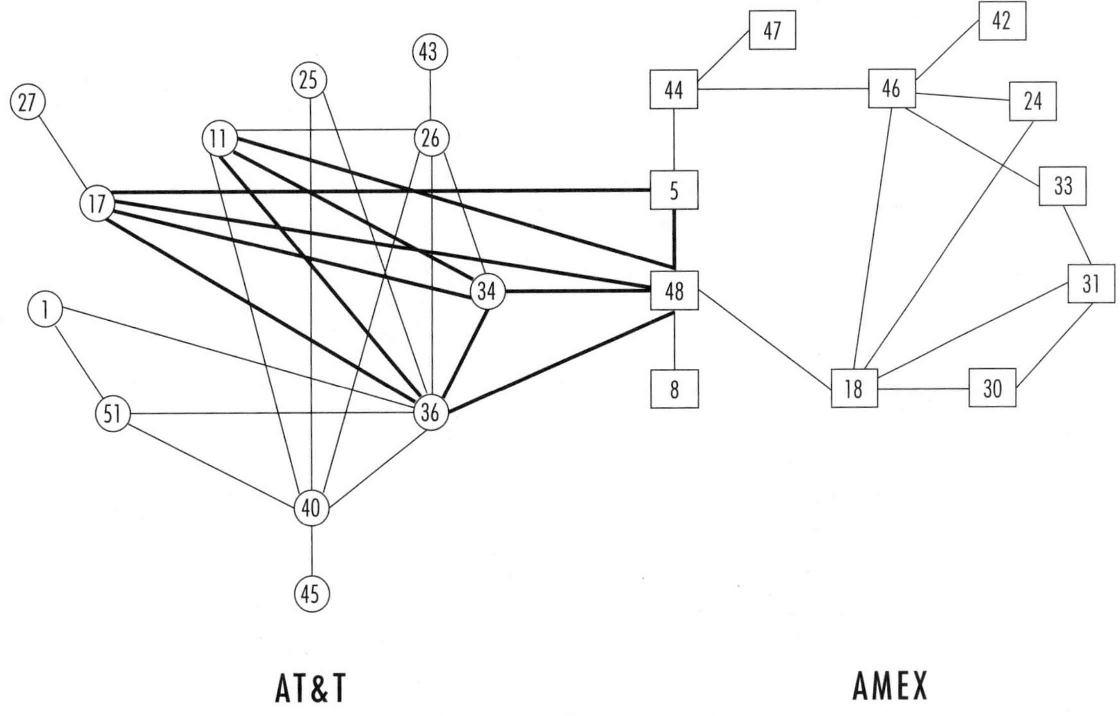

Edwin R. Stafford, Beth A. Walker, and Michael D. Hutt, "Managing Alliance Relationships," working paper, Arizona State University, 1996.

Developing a Shared Understanding

Observe the interpersonal connections that unite managers in the AT&T–American Express alliance that markets a cobranded credit and calling card targeted to the business market (see Figure 4.7). The lines connect alliance personnel who have *frequent* and *important* communications and who consider the working relationship to be close. These are the circuits through which alliance information flows, decisions are made, and conflicts are resolved. Fundamental to the success of the alliance are the working relationships (those connected by dark lines in Figure 4.7) that span organizational boundaries and unite the partnering firms. As close, working relationships develop among the alliance participants, psychological contracts, based on trust and shared goals, replace the formal alliance agreement. **Psychological contracts** consist of unwritten and largely nonverbalized sets of congruent expectations and assumptions held by the parties to the alliance about each other's prerogatives and obligations.[35] By promoting openness and flexibility, these interpersonal bonds can speed alliance progress—decisions can be made quickly, unexpected events can be more readily handled, learning is enhanced, and new possibilities for joint action emerge.

[35]Peter Smith Ring and Andrew H. Van de Ven, "Developmental Processes of Cooperative Interorganizational Processes" *Academy of Management Review* 19 (January 1992): pp. 90–118.

Integrating Points of Contact

Firms that are adept at managing strategic alliances use a flexible approach, letting their alliances evolve in form as conditions change over time; they invest adequate resources and management attention in these relationships, and they integrate the organizations so that the appropriate points of contact and communication are managed. Successful alliances achieve five levels of integration:[36]

1. *strategic integration*, which entails continuing contact among senior executives to define broad goals or discuss changes in each company;
2. *tactical integration*, which brings middle managers together to plan joint activities, to transfer knowledge, or to isolate organizational or system changes that will improve interfirm connections;
3. *operational integration*, which provides the information, resources, or personnel that managers require to carry out the day-to-day work of the alliance;
4. *interpersonal integration*, which builds a necessary foundation for personnel in both organizations to know one another personally, learn together, and create new value; and
5. *cultural integration*, which requires managers involved in the alliance to have the communication skills and cultural awareness to bridge the differences.

Even though significant problems may threaten strategic alliances, a firm that can assemble and manage a portfolio of successful partnerships can secure a competitive advantage in the global market. Indeed, some firms have mastered the art of developing and sustaining successful partnerships. For example, Corning Glass Works is involved in successful partnerships with Dow Chemical, Owens-Illinois, and Eastman Kodak, as well as with partners in France, Great Britain, Australia, West Germany, and China, among others.

Summary

Relationships, rather than simple transactions, provide the central focus in business marketing. By demonstrating superior skills in managing relationships with key customers as well as with alliance partners, business marketing firms can create a collaborative advantage.

To develop profitable relationships with customers, business marketers must first understand the tools that organizational buyers use to measure the value of a supplier's product offering. A central task of the purchasing function is to weigh the comparative value of materials, components, and processes in relation to their purpose, relative merit,

[36]Kanter, "Collaborative Advantage," pp. 105–107.

and cost. Business marketers must be prepared to demonstrate the superior value-in-use a customer gains by using the firm's products and services. Some organizational buyers use target costing—they determine what price *their* customers will pay for a new product and then work backward to set precise cost targets for the components and materials that they will procure.

Organizational customers use formal rating systems to evaluate the performance of suppliers. Such systems key on supplier attributes that are important to the buying organization, such as quality, service, delivery, and price. Specific vendor rating systems range from the easily administered categorical plan to the complex cost-ratio method. Many firms have devised their own weighted-point plans.

Valuable insights into relationship marketing can be secured by examining the time horizon within which a customer makes a commitment to a supplier. Switching costs, the level of perceived risk, and the importance of the purchase provide benchmarks for defining the likely pattern a relationship will follow. The relationship marketing process involves four stages: (1) selecting customer accounts, (2) developing account-specific offerings, (3) implementing relationship strategies, and (4) evaluating relationship strategy outcomes.

The driving force behind the formation of a strategic alliance is the desire of one firm to leverage its core competencies by linking them with another firm that has complementary expertise, thereby creating joint value and new market opportunities. Firms adept at managing strategic alliances are proactive in creating the conditions for mutually-beneficial relationships.

Discussion Questions

1. The Boeing 777 was the first commercial jet devised by Boeing's "design-build team" that included suppliers and airline managers. Suppliers such as Rockwell International and Honeywell were tied into the process via computer links. When the first 777 came off the assembly line, parts snapped together so precisely that its nose-to-tail measurement was off less than 23/1000 of an inch from design goals. A senior purchasing executive at Boeing commented that progress was achieved not simply because of the computer links but because of the mutual respect and trust among those who pulled the plans together. What criteria would be important to Boeing in evaluating suppliers? In building a relationship, who would likely be involved on the selling side and on the buying side?

2. IBM was recently awarded a $200 million contract by Ford to supply new office automation systems. Digital Equipment Corporation and Wang Laboratories, Inc. lost out on the contract but a Ford official noted, "we're not locked in—we'll go elsewhere if IBM products don't measure up." In your view, what emotional and rational buying motives might have entered into this decision? After losing the first round, what strategies might Digital Equipment Corporation and Wang Laboratories employ when pursuing the Ford account in the future?

3. Some consulting organizations persuasively argue that by properly incorporating suppliers into their product development process, firms can cut their bills for purchased parts and materials by as much as 30 percent. Explore how a buyer-seller partnership might create these cost savings.

4. Describe the process that Kodak would follow in using target costing for a new camera. Since the suppliers that will contribute components to the camera must be selected before the camera is even designed, what criteria would Kodak emphasize in selecting suppliers?

5. Motorola and Hewlett-Packard compete in some markets, are respectively customer and supplier for each other in various markets, share suppliers in several markets, often have the same customers, and have alliances in yet other markets. What steps can be taken by the firms to achieve joint goals, minimize conflicts, and protect their core assets?

6. Discuss the switching costs that Southwest Airlines would incur if they began to phase out their Boeing fleet of airliners with replacements from Airbus Industrie. What steps could Airbus take to reduce these switching costs? How might Boeing counter to strengthen its relationship to Southwest?

7. Describe how an office supply firm may have a *core* offering of products and services for a small manufacturer and an *augmented* offering for a university.

8. Knowing how to be a good partner is an asset in the business market. Describe the characteristics of a successful strategic alliance and outline the steps that alliance partners can take to increase the odds that alliance goals will be achieved.

Part III

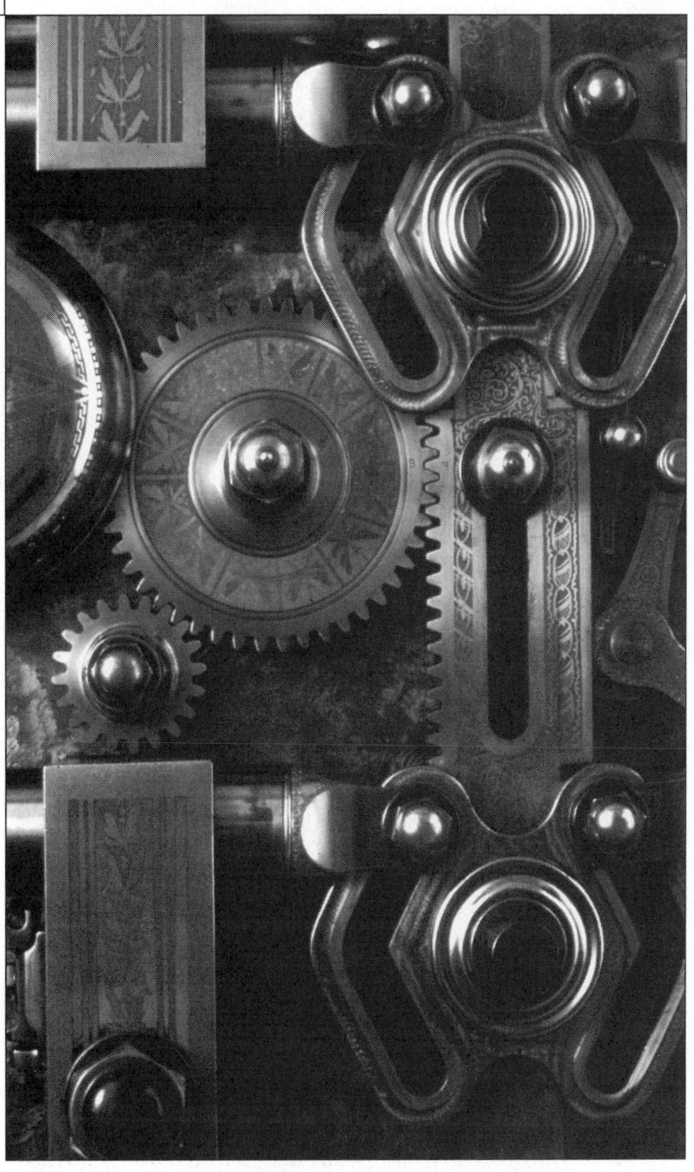

Assessing Market Opportunities

Chapter 5

Business Marketing Intelligence

The cornerstone of creative and effective marketing strategies is good information. Information about the customers, the competitors, and the environment, gathered continuously and organized to support decision making, enables the business marketing manager to base decisions on the realities of the marketplace rather than on hunch and intuition. The result is improved marketing performance. The system for capturing the necessary information for business marketing decision making is the marketing intelligence system. After reading this chapter, you will understand

1. the components of, and requirements for, an effective marketing intelligence system.
2. the need to develop the information base as a decision support system to ensure maximum managerial relevance.
3. how to use key secondary sources of information for business market planning.
4. the nature and function of marketing research in the business marketing environment

Marketing intelligence is a systematic process for generating the information needed to effectively manage business marketing strategy. Marketing strategy decisions will be based on information about market potential, customer requirements, industry and market trends, present and future competitive behavior, expected sales, market-segment size and requirements, and sales and profit performance for customers, products, and territories. Marketing intelligence activities are thus focused on developing the research methodologies, data sources, and processing capabilities necessary to evoke this information in a form that supports marketing strategy development.

This chapter explores the strategic role of information in business marketing management. First, the key components of a marketing intelligence system are delineated. Particular attention is devoted to the decision support system, which is the core of the marketing intelligence function in the industrial firm. Next, the secondary sources of information available to the business marketer are described and evaluated. Finally, the role and the unique characteristics of marketing research in the business market environment are analyzed.

The Role of Information: A Case Illustration

The value of marketing intelligence in the marketing decision process is illustrated by the case of a new industrial firm trying to compete in a very competitive market situation.

DCW+, Inc., is a national third-party logistics company comprising 11 independent regional member firms that provide warehousing, transportation, and logistics management services to their clients. Essentially, DCW+ is a marketing and sales organization that offers clients a national network of distribution through the facilities and logistics management capabilities of its 11 member companies. The firm was founded and began operations in 1995, and faced the severe challenge of a new company trying to enter a growing, but highly competitive, market.

Several basic questions had to be answered by the firm as it began to formulate its marketing strategy:

- Had the outsourcing of logistics activities—warehousing, transportation, and inventory management—reached its peak, or would the trend continue? If so, how long would it last?
- How should the market for third-party logistics services be segmented?
- Which segments offer the most promise in terms of size and growth prospects?
- Who are the important competitors in each segment? What are their strengths and weaknesses?
- Can specific target accounts in each segment be identified? Can the key decision makers within those accounts be identified? Which accounts offer the greatest potential?

To answer these questions and to forge a strategy to enter the market, DCW+ needed to develop a marketing intelligence system. The firm began by searching published materials that focused on outsourcing, and followed this with an analysis of the different types of needs that existed for third-party logistics services (using information in various articles in trade and professional journals and magazines). The analysis of secondary data—information supplied by an outside source—indicated that the market for third-party logistics services was growing rapidly and was expected to double in revenue during the next five years. An extensive review of industry reports, summaries of presentations at conferences and seminars, trade articles, and newspaper articles suggested that several distinct market segments could be identified on the basis of the type of industry, logistics requirements, size of firm, and type of firm (wholesale, retail, and so on).

Internal databases also helped define the market and its dimensions. In total, the 11 member firms served more than 900 current customers, and significant effort was expended to create a database of these customers to identify the potential for providing them with a national distribution network. The database was set up to capture such elements as current revenue, type of service currently provided, number of warehouses provided by the member firm versus the total number of warehouses in the customer's logistics system, and various other company-specific information. By analyzing the database, DCW+ could identify which accounts offered the greatest opportunity for additional business. The company also searched the trade press for articles about each of the high-potential clients. This secondary data, along with the firm's internal database, enabled DCW+ to identify and prioritize those current customers that offered the highest probability of additional revenue.

To examine other noncustomer target markets, DCW+ commissioned a marketing research study. The study was composed of two elements: (1) a mailing list and (2) a survey of firms on the mailing list. For each market segment, the firm purchased a CD-ROM containing a list of all the firms in the segment along with relevant descriptive data on the firms. Once the specific target firms were identified, DCW+ sent questionnaires that focused on the respondents' logistics structures, systems, and problems. The analysis of the survey then enabled DCW+ to select and prioritize specific target accounts in each market segment. Based on the information gathered in the survey and the actual sales results of each target firm, DCW+ is in the process of developing a model to predict which target accounts are the best prospects. In the future, data will be collected and fed into the model to develop a "score" based on the values of the input variables. Higher scores indicate higher probabilities of success with a particular account.

The combined data sources—internal, external, and market research surveys—along with the business models are important components of the DCW+ marketing intelligence system. The information provided by the system enabled the company to develop a database about trends in the industry, track potential accounts, and analyze the viability of different market segments. As a result, the company was well positioned to create effective marketing strategy and tactics to target those accounts with the highest sales potential.

As this example suggests, marketing intelligence is a multifaceted function that is the primary driving force behind many decisions made by business marketing managers. Valuable marketing information must be created systematically—data from a variety of sources must be transformed into information that will support executive decision making. As Irwin Gross points out,

> *We are in the age of information. Suddenly, new means for collecting and disseminating information are bringing costs down and easing availability. Business marketers must make a commitment to information as a necessary part of doing business. Market research and intelligence can no longer be treated as a sporadic and optional activity.*[1]

[1]Irwin Gross, "Why All of Industry Needs Research," *Business Marketing* 72 (April 1987): p. 114.

In fact, computerizing the sales operation is a mainstream concern in an overwhelming proportion of larger companies: A survey of 300 sales executives at 100 large companies showed that more than 80 percent are involved in sales force automation (SFA).[2] The portable PC is becoming a staple asset for supporting daily sales-related activities. SFA provides access to order status information; customer profiles; decision support tools for analysis across customers, products, and areas; and the integration of functions such as credit, order fulfillment, inventory control, and customer service. These sales force data systems become a key ingredient in the firm's total intelligence system.

Maintaining an effective marketing intelligence system is the hallmark of a market-oriented business marketer. Those firms that are best at being customer-driven are distinguished by their skill at anticipating market opportunities and responding to those opportunities before their competitors. George Day points out that firms that have an effective "market learning process" are noted for their ability to (1) assess the market with an open mind, (2) disseminate market information broadly within the firm, (3) use frameworks and information models that allow everyone to focus on key points and interpret the data in a common manner, and (4) develop a way for the organization to remember what has been learned.[3] As these important characteristics suggest, the prudent business marketing manager will develop an intelligence system that provides the information necessary for continuous examination of the market as well as for effective strategic decision making.

Business Marketing Intelligence Defined

Business marketing intelligence refers to the broad spectrum of information required to make decisions and to manage business marketing strategy effectively. The manager for the marketing intelligence system is responsible for designing and implementing systems and procedures to gather, record, analyze, and interpret all forms of pertinent marketing information. A comprehensive business marketing intelligence system might include the following components:

1. *Formal marketing research studies.*
   Marketing research may be conducted to determine buyer intentions, analyze primary demand, evaluate competitive behavior and performance, monitor the economic and industry environment, evaluate customer satisfaction, measure market share, analyze advertising effectiveness, determine price elasticity, evaluate distributor performance and satisfaction, or determine buying-center composition and behavior.

[2]Thayer C. Taylor, "SFA: The Newest Orthodoxy," *Sales and Marketing Management* 145 (February 1993): p. 26.

[3]George S. Day, "Continuous Learning about Markets," *California Management Review* 36 (summer 1994): pp. 9–31.

2. *Market potential and sales forecasting.*
   The intelligence system must assemble data to determine market potentials and sales forecasts as well as appropriate methodologies.

3. *Financial and accounting performance analysis.*
   The intelligence system must coordinate the marketing needs with financial and accounting functions. The system should generate periodic reports on revenues, costs, and profits by customer, distributor, product, and territory. These results are compared with objectives set forth in the marketing plan.

4. *New product research.*
   In many business markets, especially in high-technology industries, success hinges on effective allocation of R&D expenditures. The intelligence function develops procedures for generating new product ideas; monitoring customers, intermediaries, and competitors for new product ideas; testing the concepts of new products; test marketing; and evaluating the performance of new products.

5. *Secondary data files.*
   The sources of published information are diverse and include departments of federal and state governments, local governments, universities, institutes, trade associations, consulting firms, and private research organizations. The marketing intelligence function is responsible for determining which secondary data is relevant and then collecting, analyzing, and disseminating it regularly to the appropriate decision makers.

Marketing intelligence is clearly a broad and complex function whose effectiveness will dramatically affect the quality of industrial marketing decisions. Key components of the business marketing intelligence system—including the decision support system described in the following section—are sketched in Figure 5.1.

COMPONENTS OF A DECISION SUPPORT SYSTEM

The heart of the marketing intelligence function is what John D. C. Little refers to as a decision support system (DSS): a coordinated collection of data, systems, tools, and techniques with the necessary software and computer hardware through which an organization gathers and interprets relevant information from the business and the environment and turns it into information that can be acted upon.[4] A DSS includes the following components:

[4]John D. C. Little, Lakshmi Mohan, and Antoine Hatoun, "Using Decision Support Systems," *Industrial Marketing* 67 (March 1982): p. 50. This section is based on portions of this article.

Figure 5.1 A Business Marketing Intelligence System

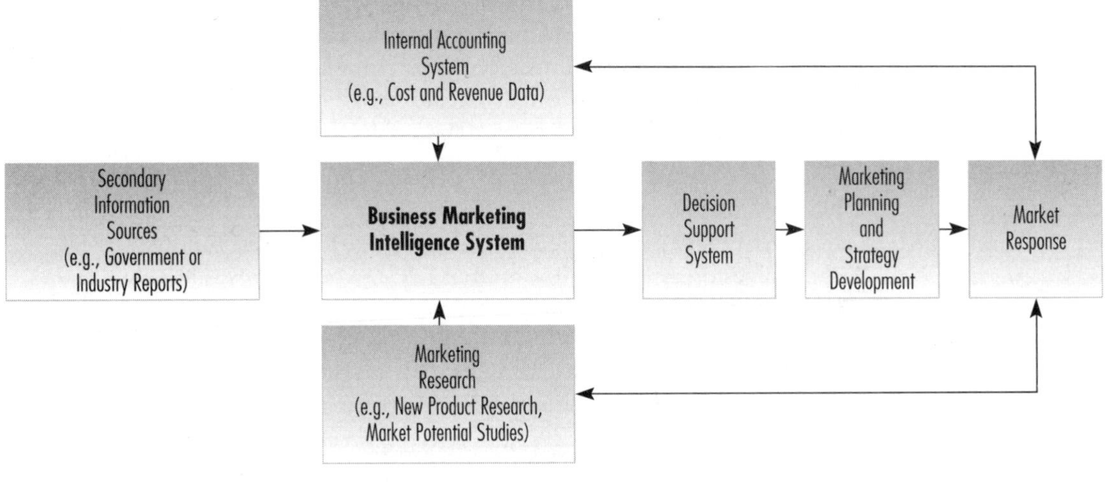

1. *Database.*
   The intelligence function develops and coordinates the flow of information from the multitude of external and internal sources. The primary task is to capture the data so that it can be used with the other components of the DSS to make decisions. A critical objective is to centralize all data in proper form and in sufficient detail so that it is accessible for decision making.

2. *Decision models.*
   A model may be nothing more sophisticated than a rule of thumb—for example, "for each 1 percent decline in territorial market share, trade promotion advertising should be increased by 5 percent." Or models may be complicated computer-driven mathematical equations. In any case, models are quantitative or qualitative conceptualizations of how a system operates. The model expresses perceptions as to what data and variables are important and how the variables are related.

3. *Statistics and manipulation.*
   This aspect of the DSS produces meaningful information by relating the data to the models. The typical operation involves segregating numbers into groups, aggregating them, taking ratios, ranking them, plotting, making tables, and so forth. General managerial models (for example, pro forma profit and loss statements, budgeting statements, and forecasting statements) and more complex models (for example, marketing mix planning, product portfolio analysis, and new product tracking) are aspects of data analysis performed in the statistical manipulation process.

4. *Display.*
The display function is the interface between the business marketing manager and the DSS. Much of the communication is achieved through interactive computing. The widespread use of CRTs, PCs, and microcomputer links to mainframe systems enhances the manager's ability to interact with the DSS. It is vital that information be able to flow back and forth between computer and decision maker because business decisions often require that the manager backtrack and experiment with different scenarios before choosing one course of action.[5]

As John Little points out, business marketing is a fertile area for a DSS because the markets are complex and typically heterogeneous, the impact of technological change is significant, and the pricing and sales force decisions are critical.[6] An effective DSS is especially relevant in the industrial sphere; many industrial firms find they have an overload of reports and data and a significant lack of effective information.

REQUIRED DECISION SUPPORT SYSTEM ATTRIBUTES

To be effective, the DSS must incorporate four important attributes: managerial capability, analysis, flexibility, and usability. First, the system should be able to provide managers with reports tailored to specific needs and market situations. Systems that impose a common format on all users and that emphasize standardized rather than customized reports fail to meet the marketing manager's needs. Second, the system must be analytical rather than simply generate reports. In addition to capturing historical information, the DSS should allow the evaluation of scenarios (for example, "what would happen if . . ."). The DSS should allow the manager to forecast the response of the market to alternative marketing strategies under a range of competitive and business environment situations. Third, the system must possess the flexibility and speed to adapt quickly to changes in information requirements. Fourth, usability implies that the system is "user friendly"; that is, it is easy to incorporate it into the daily operation of business. The networking of PCs and their links to large mainframes couples the power of a large database with the flexibility of the PC, and the net result is more effective applications of the DSS.

One *Fortune* 500 company built a PC-based decision support tool that enables sales offices to access and query corporate marketing databases.[7] A sales office can use different modules for business review reporting, market planning, and general information.

Enhanced technology, sophisticated software, development of the Internet, and computer networking are dramatically enhancing the application of the DSS to marketing problems and strategic planning. Firms are linking their DSS through all of

---

[5]John F. Towey, "Information Please," *Management Accounting* (February 1989): p. 53.
[6]Little, Mohan, and Hatoun, "Using Decision Support Systems," p. 52.
[7]Thayer C. Taylor, "Making the Most of Technology," *Sales and Marketing Management* 145 (July 1993): p. 24.

Managing in the 21st Century

INFORMATION NETWORKS: THE NEXT STAGE FOR THE AUTOMATED SALES FORCE

Current efforts in sales force automation (SFA) have focused on the field sales representative's need to reduce administrative time and improve responsiveness to customers. The next wave of enhancing the information system for managing selling efforts will come through shared access to data, and it will greatly enhance the sales and marketing managers' effectiveness. Computer networking holds the key to enabling computers and managers to share data. These networks are supported by one computer designated as the network server—it manages the network. Each salesperson or manager is hooked on line to the network through the server.

The benefits of networked SFA systems are considerable:

1. *Better customer information.* The sales manager is able to evaluate data from all sales representatives, thereby identifying purchasing patterns and spotting industry, geographic, and product trends.
2. *Reduced costs.* Administrative costs are reduced because many administrative tasks can be built into the network system. Examples include order placement and generation of routine correspondence.
3. *Customer continuity.* If a sales representative leaves, the manager retains all critical client data in the network, including client history, correspondence, scheduled meetings, and future sales calls.
4. *Better reporting.* The SFA system reduces reporting burdens by automatically entering repetitive information into the system. The network then consolidates sales representatives' reports and produces a more comprehensive management report.
5. *Companywide integration.* A key feature of a networked SFA system is the ability to integrate sales department functions with other elements of the overall corporate intelligence system.
6. *Improved communication.* Almost all corporate communication can be delivered faster, more accurately, and more comprehensively over a network e-mail system.

Clearly, networks lift SFA systems onto a higher plateau of benefits and make a major impact on overall marketing efficiency and effectiveness.

Source: Adapted from George W. Colombo, "The Next Generation," *Sales and Marketing Management* 145 (June 1993): pp. 67–69.

their offices worldwide as well as linking other members of the supply chain with one another. One large manufacturer now inputs data about its distribution system into the DSS to ensure that orders are promptly received by its supply chain partners.[8] Some strategic DSSs attempt to optimize the entire supply chain, including making decisions about the best geographic location for plants and distribution centers.[9] The

[8]Robert L. Scheier, "Timing Is Everything," *Computerworld.* 5 August 1996, p. 63.
[9]Kevin Parker, "Demand Management and Beyond," *Manufacturing Systems,* June 1996, pp. 2a–14a.

Internet and corporate intranets are rapidly becoming the primary vehicles to provide enterprisewide decision support. In dozens of worldwide offices, 3M Corporation provides employees with strategic information while centrally managing its data warehouse.

Data Warehouses

A key result of the enhanced sophistication of computing software and the development of networked PCs has been the creation of the **data warehouse.** A data warehouse is a collection of data to support management decisions. A significant value of the ideal data warehouse is its ability to support ad hoc queries from users who may not know exactly what specific data they are seeking.[10] DSS tools enable users to access specific information from the data warehouse and to perform important, even strategic, analysis of that information.

A data warehouse works by extracting data in bulk from operational and transaction-based databases—such as sales volumes, production quantities, or inventory levels—and transporting it to a data warehouse at specified intervals.[11] Data can also be derived from sources such as demographic and business databases. Managers then access the data warehouse in a number of ways, most often by pulling data from the warehouse into the manager's own analysis software (such as a spreadsheet). Increasingly, data warehouses are being accessed through company intranets, and, in many instances, corporate data warehouses are being made commercially accessible to outside companies and individuals through the Internet. CompuCom, a reseller of PC products, found that offering their data warehouse to customers on their Web site has resulted in fewer calls to the company's call center, instantaneous customer service, and an enhancement of the company's image as a technology leader.[12] Business marketers that have designed an exceptional data warehouse will enable decision makers to (1) obtain access to key data quickly, (2) analyze the data without having programming skills, and (3) manipulate the data in any manner to suit the nature of the analysis process.[13]

MANIPULATING DATA

A DSS is the core of the intelligence function in the industrial firm. The working DSS permits data aggregation at any level desired. For example, sales data can be stored by customer, product, and territory so that management can easily manipulate and evaluate infinite sets of data—including total sales, sales by top customers, sales by territory, sales by large territories, or sales by product to specified customers in selected territories. In this way, the intelligence system is totally responsive to the level

[10]Teri Robinson, "A Front-line Hope for a Back-end Tool," *Software Magazine*, July 1996, pp. S6–S10.
[11]Ian Cobb, "Data Warehousing: The Latest Fad?" *Management Accounting* 74 (June 1996): p. 46.
[12]Tom Smith, "Intranet Impact (Part I)—Opening the Doors to the Data Warehouse," *Communications Week*, 15 July 1996, p. 78.
[13]Lisa Modisette, "Accessing a Warehouse of Information (Part I)," *Cellular Business*, January 1996, p. 72.

of analysis required for a specific business marketing decision. A focal point for any market intelligence system is the broad spectrum of secondary information available.

Secondary Information Sources

Whether developed through painstaking market research studies or gleaned from existing publications, information exists to support business decisions. Secondary information gathered and published by government agencies, trade associations, trade publications, and independent research firms provides a valuable and often inexpensive start to building knowledge of the market. Of the many external sources of business information, secondary data is the principal source of information about a company's competitive and external environment. Sources of secondary data abound; the real issue is to understand where to look for useful data in the face of so many possibilities.[14] The Standard Industrial Classification (SIC) system is a vital source, because the vast majority of secondary information is reported on the basis of SIC codes.

THE STANDARD INDUSTRIAL CLASSIFICATION SYSTEM

In order to develop meaningful data on U.S. businesses, the federal government has segmented all business activity into fairly homogeneous categories. Each category is assigned a code—its Standard Industrial Classification code. The SIC system facilitates the collection, tabulation, and analysis of a wide variety of economic data. The *Standard Industrial Classification Manual,* published by the Office of Management and Budget and distributed through the U.S. Government Printing Office, describes the SIC fully.

The purpose of the SIC system is to identify groups of business firms that produce the same type of product. Every plant and business establishment in the United States is assigned a code that reflects the primary product produced at that location. The SIC coding system works in the following way:

First, the nation's economic activity is divided into ten *basic industries,* each of which is given a two-digit classification code. For example, codes 01–09 represent agriculture, 19–39 manufacturing, 70–89 services, and so on. Next, *major groups* are developed within each basic industry. Each major group has a specific two-digit code. Thus, manufacturing has 20 two-digit codes, each representing a major group such as SIC 34, which represents fabricated metal products.

Major groups are then further subdivided into three-digit *industry groups.* There are more than 150 industry groups, including SIC 342, which represents hand tools and hardware. The next level of detail, four-digit codes, are specific industries. The SIC contains over 450 specific industries, of which SIC 3423, hand and edge tools, is an example.

---

[14]William E. Cox Jr., *Industrial Marketing Research* (New York: John Wiley and Sons, 1979), p. 30.

The SIC system extends to additional levels of detail in some cases. *Product classes* are defined by five-digit codes; the SIC contains 1,300 of these. Finally, *products* are assigned seven-digit codes; this subdivision contains 10,000 segments.

A NEW SET OF CLASSIFICATION CODES

Beginning in 1997, a new system for classifying business will be employed to replace the Standard Industrial Classification code.[15] This new set of codes, called the North American Industrial Classification System (NAICS), is a result of the North American Free Trade Agreement (NAFTA); it provides for standardization among Canada, Mexico, and the United States in the way that economic data are reported. As a consequence of the common classification language, it will be easier to make comparisons in international trade, industrial production, labor costs, and other statistics.[16]

The 1997 economic census is the first to use the NAIC System, although a limited amount of data will continue to be published according to the old SIC system during the transition to the new approach. Detailed conversion tables will indicate how the new classification system affects each industry and identify where discontinuities in the time series of data occur. The switch to the new system will present challenges to business marketers who have used data compiled under the old SIC system. Questions arise as to maintaining time series integrity, converting to the new system from the old, and understanding the classification criteria so that the correct code can be identified.[17]

Figure 5.2 illustrates the basic elements of the NAIC system; as it indicates, the more digits, the finer the classification. Note that the hierarchic structure of NAICS allows industry data to be summarized at several levels of detail. Additional classifications extend the mining and manufacturing industries into thousands of product categories.

The process of classifying economic activity in economies as vast and diverse as those in the United States, Canada, and Mexico is a tremendous undertaking. The industry classification codes are invaluable tools with which business marketers can collect and analyze data about their markets from a variety of sources, knowing that the data are developed from a common base.

USING CLASSIFICATION CODES

Industrial firms are segmented by the products they produce and by the production processes they employ. Each classification group should be relatively homogeneous in terms of raw materials required, components used, manufacturing processes

[15]U.S. Census Bureau, "1997 Economic Census: What's New?" *The Official Statistics*, http://www.census.gov.pub.epcd/www.ec97new.html (World Wide Web site; cited 27 September 1996).

[16]Jennifer Boettcher, "NAFTA Prompts a New Code System for Industry—the Death of SIC and the Birth of NAICS," *Database* 19 (April/May 1996): pp. 42–45.

[17]Ibid., p. 45.

Figure 5.2 North American Industrial Classification System

A. NAICS Codes with Corresponding Economic Sectors

NAICS Codes	Economic Sector
11	Agriculture, forestry, and fishing
21	Mining
22	Utilities
23	Construction
31–33	Manufacturing
43	Wholesale trade
44–45	Retail trade
47–48	Transportation
51	Information
52	Finance and insurance
53	Real estate and rental and leasing
56	Professional and technical services
57	Management and support services
61	Education services
62	Health and social assistance
71	Arts, entertainment, and recreation
72	Food services, drinking places, and accommodations
81	Other services, except public administration
93	Public administration
98	Estates and trusts
99	Nonclassifiable

B. Examples of Different NAICS Summarization Levels

NAICS Level	NAICS Code	Example 1	NAICS Code	Example 2
Sector	31–33	Manufacturing	51	Information
Subsector	334	Computer and electronic product manufacturing	513	Broadcasting and telecommunications
Industry group	3346	Manufacturing and reproduction of magnetic and optical media	5133	Telecommunications
Industry	33461	Manufacturing and reproduction of magnetic and optical media	51332	Wireless telecommunications carriers, except satellite
U.S. industry	334611	Reproduction of software	513321	Paging

employed, and problems faced. As a result, the codes are often excellent bases on which to segment markets. If the manager understands the needs and requirements of a few firms within a classification category, requirements can be projected for all firms within that category. For example, most firms manufacturing truck trailers (*old* SIC 3715) will need to purchase components such as wheels, tires, sheet steel, grease, oil, plastic parts, and electric parts. Their requirements will be similar, and potential suppliers can evaluate the total market through a detailed analysis of a few SIC 3715 companies. Suppose a supplier of steel wheels determines through a sales analysis of present customers that SIC 3715 firms spend eight cents per dollar of their final shipments on wheels. A market estimate of total wheel sales to SIC 3715 firms for 1999 could be developed by estimating total shipment costs by SIC 3715 companies in 1999 and multiplying them by $0.08. If the estimate of 1999 SIC 3715 shipments is $2,718 million in trailers, potential wheel sales would be $2,718 million times $0.08, or $217.4 million.

Identifying New Customers

The classification codes are useful for identifying new customers. The marketing manager can study a four-digit industry to evaluate whether these firms could use the marketer's product or service. Although this analysis provides only rough estimates, it is helpful in eliminating industries that are not potential product users. Classification code groups that show promise of possible use can be singled out for evaluation in depth.

Segmentation

Because each sector identified by a classification code is relatively homogeneous in terms of problems and processes, segmentation on the basis of the classification codes is often effective. An understanding of the classification system is particularly relevant for gathering market information because so many government agencies, trade associations, and private research firms collect data on the basis of these codes.

PUBLISHED SOURCES OF BUSINESS MARKETING DATA

Marketing decisions are only as good as the data used to generate them. The breadth of data available to the business marketing manager provides both an opportunity and a challenge. The opportunity arises from the wealth of available industrial market data. Government at all levels, trade associations, trade publications, and private research companies publish a great deal of economic data on a national, state, and county basis. Most of this data is collected by classification code (SIC or NAICS), allowing for industry-by-industry (and sometimes product-by-product) analysis.

The challenge is to develop familiarity with secondary data sources, to understand the nature of the data in these sources, and to comprehend how the data can enhance business marketing. Many of the secondary data sources can be used to define target segments in the organizational market, estimate market potential, forecast sales, evaluate competitors, and provide an understanding of market needs.

Federal Government Data Sources

Federal data are industry oriented; the basic unit of analysis is a particular four-digit NAICS category. For this reason, federal data sources are often the cornerstone for the determination of market and sales potentials by industry.

Every five years, the Bureau of Census gathers detailed information about the nation's economy and publishes economic summary reports of industries and geographic areas from the national to the local level. One report on manufacturing, for example, provides comprehensive statistics about manufacturing establishments, activities, and production. Some of the more important data shown in the manufacturing sector report includes number of employees, value added by manufacturing, cost of materials, and capital expenditures. The data are summarized by four-digit NAICS industries. Prior to 1997, the Census Bureau treated each sector of the economy (for example, manufacturing, transportation, retailing, wholesaling, and so on) separately. Starting with the economic census of 1997, however, the bureau will issue one printed summary report for each major sector in the U.S. economy, featuring general statistics by industry for the nation and each state. More detailed data are available on CD-ROM and on the Internet.

The economic census makes it possible to investigate, by geographic region, the size and scope of potential customer industries. The primary difficulty is the timeliness of the data—the census data are published only every five years. In addition, publication can follow data collection by one to three years. However, some of this data is available on the Internet, which helps to speed its accessibility. Table 5.1 suggests how the data contained in the economic census can be used in a variety of ways to answer strategic and tactical questions.

The Census Bureau publishes *A Guide to the 1997 Economic Census and Related Statistics* (available primarily on the Internet; see Table 5.1), which describes the scope, coverage, classifications, data items, and publications for the economic census and for related surveys that provide monthly, quarterly, and annual data.

Other Data Sources

The federal government primarily collects statistics on industry; however, states, local governments, and private industrial directories provide data on individual firms. State and local governments publish annual directories of businesses within their jurisdictions. The directories generally include company name, address, SIC/NAICS code, products produced, sales volume, and number of employees. The directories enable the marketing manager to evaluate market potential firm by firm for well-defined geographic areas. For example, by combining information from industrial directories with sales data from internal sources, a business marketer can create a customer and

Table 5.1 How Economic Census Data Is Used

• Calculate market share

A restaurant supply wholesaler calculated that it had roughly an 11 percent market share—its own sales divided by state totals for similar businesses—in its primary sales region in the northern mountain states. The wholesaler used that figure as a target when it expanded into Arizona and New Mexico.

• Locate business markets

A firm that had developed software to manage quality control operations listed industries most likely to use its product, then ranked the top industries based on census figures for added value and growth. The firm customized software to appeal to those top prospects. Census data on CD-ROM also made it easy to find areas where large plants in the target industries were located.

A diskette duplication service used the numbers of businesses by ZIP code on CD-ROM to assess the completeness and coverage of its direct mail list of service and retail businesses. For industries where its coverage was poor, the firm purchased commercial mailing lists or advertising space in appropriate trade periodicals.

• Locate distributors or resellers

An electrical supplies wholesaler consulted census of construction industries reports to determine receipts of electrical contractors by state and to examine trends in industry expenditures for materials and supplies.

• Design sales territories and set sales quotas

An insurance company used counts of establishments and sales by business type to redesign sales territories and set quotas and incentive levels for agents. By comparing census figures to their own records on customers, company executives identified which kinds of businesses were better prospects than others.

• Enhance business-opportunity presentations to banks or venture capitalists

A small manufacturer of solar water-heater panels sought to attract new investors. It changed its prospectus to prominently feature the use of its product in growing industries, with census data to back it up.

• Maintain local tax base

A community action corporation in western Pennsylvania used census of manufacturers data on the steel industry and its customers to determine the feasibility of local efforts to reopen a closed steel plant. Census figures helped convince them that this was not a good investment, despite local enthusiasm for the project.

• Assist local businesses

A state economic development agency identified industries with the most export activity using an exports from manufacturing plants report. The agency gave those industries top priority as it launched a program to assist companies in finding trade leads.

• Public policy and statistics

Federal and state agencies look to economic census data to gauge the effectiveness of programs such as minority contracting guidelines, trade policies, and job retraining.

The Federal Emergency Management Agency uses the ZIP code CD-ROM to inventory manufacturing locations by industry and size. They estimate potential losses to productive capacity that might result from a major flood or other disaster.

Note: Send your comments regarding the economic census via e-mail to econ@census.gov

Source: Adapted from the Bureau of the Census, "How People Use Economic Census Data," *The Official Statistics,* http:\\www.census.gov\epcd\www\ec97uses.html (World Wide Web site; cited 27 September 1996).

prospect profile for each NAICS segment. This information would serve as a road map to guide sales and promotion efforts.

Private industrial directories and research companies, such as Dun & Bradstreet or Standard & Poor's, maintain up-to-date files on industrial firms. For example, *Dun's Market Identifiers,* which provides current information on sales volume, products, employees, and location for more than 3.5 million firms, enables a manager to quickly obtain information on an individual company.

The Information Access Company (IAC) offers another good example of the type of information available on line. IAC produces a family of 21 on-line databases that include comprehensive coverage of news and information on companies, industries, products, markets, and technologies. IAC's databases feature specialized coverage of such subjects as marketing, computers, management, health, law, and scholarly research. The IAC family of files can be accessed through 15 on-line services, including CompuServe, DIALOG, LEXIS/NEXIS, ESA (European Space Agency), and GBI (German Business Information).

Trade associations often provide industry statistics that are not found in government sources (for example, average age of capital equipment in the industry). Trade publications also report industry-oriented data. *Iron Age* conducts an annual census of the metalworking industry, which includes data on plants and employees. Research firms and business press publishers often publish research studies that focus on purchasing and reading habits in various industries. These studies are often valuable in helping business marketers select appropriate magazines for their advertising messages. One such study, "Purchase Influence in American Business," was conducted by a professional market research firm that surveyed more than 5,000 top-level managers to assess their influence on the purchase of more than 32 categories of products and services as well as to determine the business publications they read.[18] The results can help managers select which publication will be most effective for specific types of product advertising.

International Data Sources

The United Nations is the primary source for international industrial data. The Statistical Office of the United Nations in New York publishes a vast array of statistics and reports. The annual two-volume *Yearbook of Industrial Statistics* includes reports of country and regional trends in business activity, statistics for more than 500 industrial products, and import and export data for a variety of commodities. Private research companies are also important resources of international business data. Dun & Bradstreet publishes *Principal International Business,* which provides information on almost 50,000 large companies in 133 countries, arranged both geographically and by classification code number. Predicasts produces *Globalbase*, which abstracts 800 newspapers, business journals, and trade publications concentrated in Western Europe—and its coverage is expanding to include Scandinavia and the Pacific Rim.[19] *Dun's Market Identifiers* can search a global file that includes 1.7 million locations in more than 300,000 corporate families. The rapid ascent of Japan in world markets has spawned a variety of statistical publications on Japan alone. *Japan Company Handbook* supplies sales, financial data, and company outlook for more than 1,000 Japanese firms. As business marketing becomes global,

[18]Sue Kapp, "Studies Help Direct Ad Dollars," *Business Marketing* 74 (June 1989): p. 34.
[19]Mick O'Leary, "Globalbase Reaches New Global Markets," *Information Today*, June 1994, pp. 11–12.

the marketing manager must be able to adapt the marketing intelligence system to capture secondary data worldwide.

DEVELOPING A DATABASE FROM SECONDARY SOURCES

In creating a bank of secondary data for decision making, business marketers are increasingly turning to on-line computer database searching. The business marketer pays a fee to an information service and, through a personal computer and some communications software, gains access to the desired database. The periodical and publication base is scanned and the required information is downloaded from the database to the user's personal computer. On-line database searching dramatically reduces the time-consuming and costly process of a library search or of gathering the raw data firsthand.

The Internet has greatly expanded the business marketer's ability to create a unique and customized database. A wide array of search engines exist that allow a researcher to tap into information provided by almost every imaginable organization—including the U.S. Census Bureau, trade associations, and individual companies. The Internet provides a "virtual library" right in the researcher's office. Many of the database services in the following discussion can be accessed via the Internet.

A wide variety of on-line database services exist, ranging from "supermarket" services such as DIALOG, NEXIS, and CompuServe, which store hundreds of different databases from a wide array of independent sources, to specialized vendors such as INVESTEXT, which offers the complete text of financial analyses on publicly held firms. Selection of the appropriate database is made difficult by the fact that more than 5,000 computer databases are currently available.[20] In addition, many databases offer similar, and in many cases, identical files. For instance, DIALOG and NEXIS both offer Dun & Bradstreet reports, newswires, and Predicasts, a database of full-text articles from over 600 newsletters.

The information provided by the databases can be reported in three different formats: (1) a simple listing of the articles in bibliographic form, (2) a summary of each article, and (3) the complete text of each article. (Most databases make all these options available.) Business marketing managers can use these databases to customize analyses for specific problems. The types of reports include bibliographies on almost any business topic; time series data on production, consumption, imports, and exports of products and services; financial data on specific companies; and performance trends for industries. Figure 5.3 provides an example of the *Management Contents* database. Database searching offers two important advantages for generating secondary information: (1) expediency—extensive library search time is totally eliminated; and (2) custom-designed analyses—all available databases can be scanned at the same time, or the search can be limited to specific topics, industries, companies, or countries. Using databases can be expensive: DIALOG charges $10–12 per hour for connect time only, while searches cost $60–120 per hour; NEXIS charges a $50 monthly subscription fee, connect time is $39 per hour, and a search in one file ranges from $3 to $40.[21]

---

[20] "Everything You Always Wanted to Know—By PC," *Business Week,* 1 October 1990, p. 176.

[21] Christel Beard and Betsy Wiesendanger, "The Marketer's Guide to On-line Databases," *Sales and Marketing Management* 145 (January 1993): p. 38.

Figure 5.3 Sample Record from the *Management Contents* Database

0423752

Management Contents

How benchmarking can improve business reengineering. (includes related article) Richman, Theodor; Koontz, Charles; Planning Review (a publication of the Planning Forum) v21 Nov-Dec, 1993, p26(3)

Many programs involving improvement processes have been characterized by benchmarking and reengineering practices. Benchmarking is a process by which operating targets and productivity programs are determined with exemplary industry practices as a basis. Reengineering, on the other hand, is defined by structural and cultural change in an organization, with the goal of achieving increased productivity. Although some managers have opted to implement both strategies separately, an alternative method is to incorporate both processes into a single approach in managing change. Among the benefits derived from employing a business process, reengineering approaches are the delineation of specific reengineering goals, the provision of concise examples of best industry practices and implementation methods, and the identification of new business possibilities.

Most databases are available on line or on CD-ROM. The Internet is an effective tool for locating databases and providing extensive information about them. Many database companies offer site license programs that enable users to load information from the database onto their internal systems and distribute this information to a group of users at a corporate site.

Selecting the appropriate database and vendor is an important and sometimes difficult task. The user must first consider a number of factors—including the type of information needed, the format of the information, how current the information must be, and the depth and breadth of the desired data. Choosing the wrong database can easily lead the user to a dead end and waste company resources. To learn more about on-line databases, the manager may consult a variety of references. For example, *The Directory of On-line Databases* provides useful guidance in the selection and use of different databases.[22]

The development of a secondary database is one aspect of the marketing intelligence function. An equally important, and often more difficult, aspect is the market research function: the gathering of primary information.

Business Marketing Research

Business marketing research is defined as the systematic gathering, recording, and analysis of information and opportunities relating to the marketing of industrial goods and services. It typically includes sales and market potential analysis, sales

[22]The *Directory of Online Databases* (Detroit: Gale Research Inc.), published quarterly. *The Directory of Online Databases* is also available online, together with the *Directory of Portable Database,* as the *Cuadra Directory of Databases.* The file is available online through the Data-Star (File CUAD), ORBIT (File CUAD), and Questal (File CUADRA) services. The file is reloaded quarterly.

Managing in the 21st Century

THE INFORMATION EXPLOSION

The databases described here provide an excellent window into the future of the almost instantaneous availability of massive amounts of secondary information. Information Access Company (IAC) is just one of hundreds of firms who specialize in on-line and CD-ROM business-related databases. The company's lineup of products offers an impressive information library for most business-to-business marketers. The IAC "Family of Files" include the following different types of databases.

Multi-Industry Databases

IAC INDUSTRY EXPRESS

IAC[SM] Industry Express combines a rolling 30 days of content from leading trade and business publications in four IAC databases: PROMT, Trade & Industry Database, Newsletter Database, and Computer Database. The database releases each article, which includes 100 percent of its original text, at or near the time of the periodical's publication.

PROMT

Since its introduction on line in 1973, **PROMT** remains the most widely used business database in the world, and the benchmark by which all other business databases are judged.

International in scope and outlook, PROMT covers 65 industries—offering substantive information about companies, the products and technologies they develop, and the markets in which they compete. PROMT is ideal for first-stop or retrospective searching, and its precise hierarchical coding lets you focus as broadly or narrowly as your search requires. PROMT is essential for any business marketer conducting strategic planning, research and development, or competitive analysis.

TRADE & INDUSTRY DATABASE

Trade & Industry (T&I) Database complements PROMT with a focus on market and industry trends, management concerns and challenges, legislative and regulatory decisions, global economic conditions, product reviews, biographies, and corporate profiles. T&I contains 75 percent of the original text, and uses Predicasts Product Codes in addition to its own detailed subject term indexing.

NEWSLETTER DATABASE

Newsletter Database is a virtual library of more than 600 full text newsletters—a source of expert opinion, insightful analysis, and inside information on industries and business activities spanning five continents.

COMPANY INTELLIGENCE

Company Intelligence (CI) is the only database that combines company directory-style information with the latest news—quick snapshots of more than 200,000 private and public international companies. The news section includes references from up to ten recent stories drawn from as many as 4,000 sources.

GLOBALBASE

Globalbase is international in focus with a concentration on Europe and the Pacific Rim. To the mix of domestic and overseas intelligence available in other IAC databases, Globalbase adds an unusual collection of 1,000 hard-to-find trade journals and newspapers published in more than 50 countries.

(continued)

Managing in the 21st Century

THE INFORMATION EXPLOSION *(continued)*

Specialized Industry Databases

COMPUTER DATABASE

Computer Database provides extensive coverage of leading business and consumer publications in the computer, telecommunications, and electronics industries. This database is regarded for its excellent product evaluations and focus on user techniques and applications.

AEROSPACE/DEFENSE MARKETS & TECHNOLOGY

Aerospace/Defense Markets & Technology (A/DM&T) is the leading database for worldwide aerospace and defense industry information, featuring coverage of products and technologies that have significant commercial applications across a variety of industries.

Marketing and Consumer Databases

MARKETING AND ADVERTISING REFERENCE SERVICE

Marketing and Advertising Reference Service (MARS) focuses on the marketing activities of consumer products and services companies.

MAGAZINE DATABASE

Magazine Database is the on-line barometer of popular culture, focusing on consumer behavior and lifestyles, media trends, political opinion, and leisure activities.

News Databases

NEWSEARCH

Newsearch (available only on DIALOG) provides current news and awareness from nine IAC databases, containing the most recent two through six weeks of information on business, politics, law, and health. It is updated daily.

NATIONAL NEWSPAPER INDEX

The **National Newspaper Index (NNI),** ideal for fact checking and background research, contains comprehensive indexing of the *New York Times, Los Angeles Times, Wall Street Journal, Washington Post, Christian Science Monitor,* and *PR Newswire.*

forecasting, market surveys, experiments, observational studies, competitive analyses, and benchmarking. Formalized marketing research often provides the data used in planning and control. Business marketing research usually undertakes primary data studies—surveys, observation, or experiments—when conclusive research is needed or secondary data is too limited for the decision at hand. In 1995, business marketers spent $2.4 billion on proprietary market research performed by external marketing research companies.[23]

[23]Charles Waltner, "Technology Advances Drive Thirst for Data," *Advertising Age's Business Marketing,* June 1996, p. 513.

The terms *marketing research* and *marketing intelligence* are frequently confused by students and managers alike. Marketing research is more narrow in scope; it is but one component of the industrial marketing intelligence system. Marketing research is generally undertaken for unique projects with specific objectives. Marketing intelligence is an ongoing function designed to provide continuous information for decision making. One aspect of marketing intelligence is the design and implementation of marketing research projects to create an information base for making individual decisions. What are the distinguishing characteristics of business marketing research?

Marketing research involves certain basic elements that apply generally. In any context, the research study must be planned, a data-gathering instrument designed, and a sampling plan created. The data must then be gathered, processed, analyzed, and reported. However, because of the environment of the business market and the nature of organizational buying, business marketing research differs from consumer-goods research. Some of the more relevant differences follow.

1. *Business marketing research relies more heavily on exploratory studies, secondary data, and expert judgment data in industrial research.* Because of demand concentration, market information tends to be concentrated among a few knowledgeable people, who may be surveyed when time and cost constrain large sample designs. The wealth of government and trade association data by SIC categories provides a valuable secondary database for many business marketing decisions.

2. *Business marketing research places more emphasis on surveys as opposed to experimental and observational primary data methods.* Experimental and observational studies are not as effective in business as in consumer-goods markets.

3. *Personal interviewing is stressed in business marketing research.* Usually, specific respondents can be identified in the business market (although they are sometimes difficult to reach), and the target population is smaller and more concentrated. Thus, specific individuals in the buying center can be singled out for in-depth interviews.

4. *Business marketing research is concerned with the determination of market size and potential, as opposed to the consumer research concern for psychological market segmentation.*[24] Market attractiveness provides the foundation for the business marketing planning process.

5. *Business marketing researchers typically work with smaller samples (because of the smaller universe and concentration of buyers).*[25] Small samples offer the ability to use in-depth interviewing, but sometimes preclude making generalizations from the research findings.

[24]The first four items are based on Wiliam E. Cox Jr. and Luis V. Dominguiz, "The Key Issues and Procedures of Industrial Marketing Research," *Industrial Marketing Management* 8 (January 1979): pp. 81–93.

[25]Rohit Deshpande and Gerald Zaltman, "A Comparison of Factors Affecting the Use of Marketing Information in Consumer and Industrial Firms," *Journal of Marketing Research* 24 (February 1987): p. 114.

6. *Surveys in business marketing frequently encounter problems different from those of surveys in consumer research; as a consequence, the survey process is often quite different.* In industrial studies, accesibility to respondents is very limited and they are often preoccupied with other priorities.

Finally, business marketing research places increasing emphasis on systematic studies of the organizational buying process. Significant advances have been made over the past ten years, but refined marketing research approaches will be required to enable the business marketer to comprehend more fully the buying center in target organizations.

Some experts observe that business marketers are increasingly using many of the sophisticated research tools utilized by consumer-goods firms. Focus groups, psychological probing techniques, conjoint or trade-off analysis, and quantitative modeling are some of the tools finding application in business marketing settings.[26] This increasing use of sophisticated consumer-research tools is explained by heightened levels of competition and the resulting need to improve understanding of business customer needs and attitudes.

THE TASKS OF BUSINESS MARKETING RESEARCH

Ronald Paul reports on the usage of various kinds of marketing research by business marketers.[27] Paul indicates that industrial companies use research heavily in the areas of forecasting, business trends, potential, competitive studies, market share, market characteristics, sales analysis, and sales quota determination. (Many of these topics will be discussed later in the text.) Clearly, an effective marketing research department is a valuable asset in developing and controlling the business marketing program.

RESEARCH METHODS

Although business marketers rely heavily on secondary data, primary data is often collected to gain firsthand knowledge of customer attitudes, motivations, and buying intentions. All types of marketing research include the following basic methods for gathering primary data:

1. *Surveys.* Interviewers question people who are believed to possess the information desired.
2. *Observation.* People and behavior are viewed and the information is recorded without asking questions.

---

[26]Tom Eisenhart, "Advanced Research Finds a New Market," *Business Marketing* 74 (March 1989): p. 51.
[27]Ronald Paul, "Research Alternatives for Industrial Marketers," in *Marketing Handbook*, vol. 1, ed. Edwin E. Bobrow and Mark D. Bobrow (Homewood, Ill: Dow-Jones Irwin, 1985), p. 209.

3. *Experimentation.* Researchers set up a controlled situation in which the outcome of some test is evaluated and in which one or more factors are varied to measure cause-and-effect relationships.

Surveys are the most common data-gathering method in business marketing research, because they can provide the type of information business marketers seek.

Though not a frequently used approach, some business marketers effectively use the observation method. Steelcase, the office furniture manufacturer, for example, believes that in some instances the best information is often gleaned through detached observation, by viewing customers from a vantage point further removed than the typical survey or interview approach provides.[28] Studying customers under normal, natural conditions affords a unique understanding of customers and their behavior. Steelcase used just such a method recently when it designed a new product specifically for work teams. During the design stage, the company decided it could learn the most by seeing firsthand how teams actually operate. It set up video cameras at various companies and exhaustively analyzed the tapes, looking for patterns of behavior and motion. As a result, Steelcase created modular office units that could be arranged around a common space where a team works, fostering synergy, while also allowing a person to work alone when necessary[29] (see Figure 5.4). The firm felt that typical market data would not have been as effective in the design process as knowing how people actually work.

FOCUS OF SURVEY RESEARCH

Survey techniques are effective for gathering primary data of the following types:

- Awareness and knowledge
- Attitudes and opinions
- Intentions
- Motivations
- Demographic characteristics
- Behavior

As this list suggests, the purpose of the survey is to understand the buying behavior of present and potential industrial customers in order to formulate appropriate marketing strategy. The survey method may be the only way to gather specific data concerning attitudes, motivations, and behavior—this material is usually not available in secondary sources. Survey data can also be pivotal in evaluating performance and adjusting market strategies.

---

[28]Justin Martin, "Ignore Your Customer," *Fortune*, 1 May 1995, p. 126.
[29]Ibid., p. 126.

Figure 5.4 Steelcase Advertisement Describing Observation Research to Create Work Environments

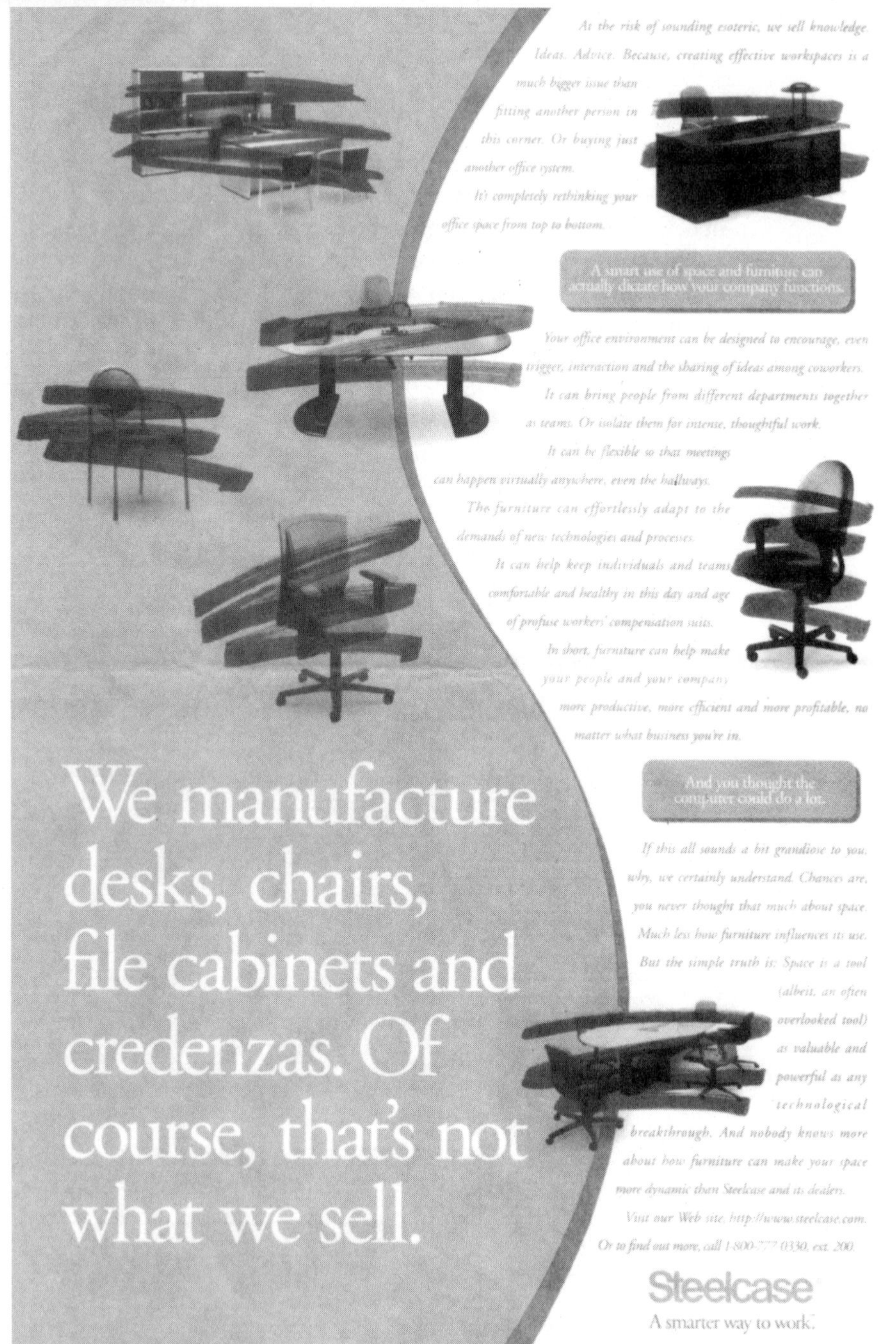

Source: Courtesy Steelcase Inc.

SURVEY METHODS IN BUSINESS MARKETING

Three methods of contact with respondents prevail in business marketing: (1) personal interview, (2) telephone, and (3) mail.

Personal Interviews

Because business marketing research often uses relatively small samples and because much of the information involves in-depth questioning and probing, personal interviewing is the dominant survey approach. Generally, the greater the complexity of the information sought, the more effective is personal interviewing. When technical data, graphs, and illustrations are required, personal interviews are the only choice.

Personal interviewing usually produces high response rates because the interviewer can locate and secure the attention of the correct respondent. In addition, more information can generally be elicited through personal interviews. But personal interviewing is the most expensive and time-consuming form of survey research, and the expense may limit its application. The cost per completed interview is estimated to range from $150 to $400.[30]

A research technique that is being increasingly applied to business marketing research problems is the **focus group interview.**[31] A focus group consists of between 6 and 12 people interviewed in an informal group setting. Open-ended questions are used to stimulate group interaction, and a moderator will lead the discussion much like a therapist does in group therapy. Sessions may last up to three hours and are often videotaped so that different managers can evaluate them.

Business marketing focus groups can be effective in uncovering issues, defining the range of opinions on the issue, testing advertising concepts, exploring product needs, and evaluating service perceptions. Standard Register, a business form manufacturer, used a series of focus groups comprising business form buyers to determine buyers' priorities. Before using the focus groups, the firm believed they "were great service people"; however, the focus groups indicated that, although service was the buyers' first priority, Standard Register "had little in terms of service that made them stand out from the crowd."[32] The company quickly created a new customer service management position and initiated a strategy to enhance responsiveness to customers. Generally, focus groups enable researchers to probe issues in greater depth than they could in structured questionnaires. The information can be gathered and analyzed quickly at a relatively low cost. The process is also flexible: The questioning can change direction instantly, and new areas can be explored. Importantly, the data from the focus group session is highly subjective and most experts suggest results should be substantiated through additional quantitative studies.

---

[30]Vincent P. Barabba, "The Market Research Encyclopedia," *Harvard Business Review* 68, no. 1 (January/February 1990): p. 106.

[31]B.G. Yovovich, "Focusing on Consumers Needs and Motivations," *Business Marketing* 76 (March 1991): p. 41.

[32]Sue Kapp, "Customer Service is Ex-Fighter Jock's Latest Mission," *Business Marketing* 75 (August 1990): p. 19.

Telephone Surveys

Telephone interviewing is useful in business marketing research, particularly for evaluating advertising recall, assessing corporate image, and measuring company and brand awareness. If prior contact has been made with respondents who share a vocabulary of technical terms, telephone surveys are a cost-effective way to obtain primary information. For telephone surveys to be effective, the researcher must be able to reach the correct respondent. Telephone interviews are clearly the fastest method for gathering information. They are generally less expensive than personal interviews, averaging from $20 to $90 per completed interview.[33] Their major drawbacks include (1) the limitations on the amount and kind of information that can be gathered and (2) the inability to detect and control interviewer bias. Telephone interviewers often have difficulty gaining access to the respondent, as secretaries are adept at screening calls. Nevertheless, some firms find telephone surveys effective when advice or opinions are required to make a particular decision rapidly. In this case, a broad listing of firms can be maintained from which a sample can be quickly drawn.

Mail Surveys

Mail surveys are restricted in terms of the amount and the complexity of information that can be gathered. The quality and quantity of data resulting from a mail survey depend on the respondent's interest in the topic and on the degree of difficulty of the questions. The most severe problem associated with industrial mail surveys is nonresponse, particularly from large firms. The nonresponse problem has two facets: (1) the original respondent simply fails to return the survey, or (2) the survey is returned by someone other than the original respondent. The latter is often difficult to detect, but does reduce the validity of the survey. Generally, response rates to industrial mail surveys tend to be lower than for consumer surveys. This is a continuing problem and one that business marketing researchers must address.

Mail surveys take more time to construct and administer than do telephone surveys, but they are not as demanding as personal interviews. Because of the impersonal nature of the contact and the complexity of the subject matter, the wording and structure of the questionnaire are extremely critical. To secure meaningful response rates, follow-up mailings are frequently required. As one might expect, mail surveys are generally the least expensive survey method, costing between $5 and $10 per completed survey.[34]

Table 5.2 uses six criteria to compare the three survey techniques. The inherent trade-offs among the three survey methods must be evaluated in light of the type of information sought, the time and research funds available, and the levels of reliability required. Only then can the appropriate method be selected.

---

[33]Barabba, "The Market Research Encyclopedia," p. 106.
[34]Ibid.

Table 5.2 A Comparison of Business Marketing Survey Methods

	Criteria					
Approach	**Cost**	**Information Quality**	**Information Quantity**	**Nonresponse Problem**	**Response Rate (without Incentives)**	**Interviewer Bias**
Personal interview	Highest cost per respondent	Can elicit in-depth, complex information	Extensive	Few problems, as a result of face-to-face contact	70–90%	Hard to detect and control
Telephone	Second-highest cost	Complex if prior contact established	Moderate	Difficult to ensure that contact is made with correct respondent	20–85%	Hard to detect and control
Mail	Least cost	Moderately complex	Moderate	Difficult to control who responds and how many will respond	10–85%	Can be controlled by rigorous pretesting

Source: Adapted from Vincent P. Barabba, "The Market Research Encyclopedia," *Harvard Business Review* 68 (January/February 1990), p. 106.

Benchmarking

Benchmarking is a relatively new form of research that often relies on interviews and direct interaction with "benchmarking partners" to gather data. The American Productivity & Quality Center defines benchmarking as "the process of continuously comparing and measuring an organization against business leaders anywhere in the world to gain information that will help the organization take action to improve its performance."[35]

The process of benchmarking typically comprises four steps: (1) understanding and analyzing your own company's procedures and performance in a given process (such as generating sales leads or designing incentive programs); (2) looking at other departments and companies to determine who really is the best at a given process; (3) collecting and sharing information on the process through surveys, site visits, and consultants; and (4) analyzing the data to see what portions of other companies' methods might work for you.[36]

Benchmarking can be used to evaluate any aspect of a firm's marketing and sales operations. Texas Instrument's defense and electronics group uses the technique to

[35]Betsy Wiesendanger, "Benchmarking for Beginners," *Sales and Marketing Management* 144 (November 1992): p. 60.

[36]Ibid.

develop standards for calling on key customers; Hewlett-Packard has applied benchmarking to improve inventory turnover. Potential benchmarking partners do not need to work in the same industry; effective marketing processes can be found in almost any industry setting. Many industrial firms have found exceptional customer service procedures in such varying places as medical clinics and veterinary offices. The focus of benchmarking studies can be on almost anything, but must include an analysis of critical success factors—those things that have a high correlation with satisfying the customer and, therefore, with the success of the company. Critical success factors might include a knowledgeable and responsive sales force, on-time delivery, building strategic alliances with suppliers and partners, or having a responsive repair service capability.

Effective benchmarking depends on locating the right partners and gaining their cooperation to participate in the process. Suppliers and customers are often good sources for finding partners. Secondary library resources may also be used to locate firms who are exceptionally effective at the critical success processes. It is important to carefully plan the design of the study as benchmarking can be costly. One survey of over 80 firms revealed that the full cost, on average, of a total benchmarking project was $68,000.[37]

ORGANIZING FOR RESEARCH

The research function can be centralized, decentralized, or contracted out to specialized business marketing research companies. For maximum impact, research findings must be effectively integrated into the decision-making process. The organizational placement of the research function will have a definite effect on whether this goal is accomplished. Deciding how to organize the marketing research function requires consideration of several delicate organizational issues. Generally, marketing research should be free from the influence of those whom its work affects, should have a location that is conducive to maximum operational efficiency, and should have the wholehearted support of the executive to whom it reports.[38]

Two-Tier Research Staff

Large industrial firms often have both a centralized corporate marketing research unit and smaller-scale divisional marketing research units. The central research unit usually has a full-time staff whose major functions are to gather broad-gauged data on the economy and the industry and to conduct studies for product line alternatives, new product opportunities, and acquisitions. The centralized research staff may significantly contribute to the development of marketing plans and strategy. In general, centralized

[37]Ibid, p. 63.

[38]*Marketing, Business and Commercial Research in Industry*, Studies in Business Policy, no. 27 (New York: National Industrial Conference Board, 1955), p.7, as reported in H. Robert Dodge, *Industrial Marketing* (New York: McGraw-Hill, 1970), p. 117.

research activities affect more than one group or division by preparing economic forecasts, planning support, and researching management science and information systems.[39] Divisional research activities usually affect performance areas by focusing on such topics as product sales rates, advertising effectiveness, and market share.

Management Support

Regardless of how the business marketing research function is organized, the research unit requires the support of top management. The central research department should report to a high-level executive or even to the president to ensure that (1) marketing research information will be used properly in the decision-making process, and (2) the marketing research function will be given a fair hearing during the corporate budgeting process. The contribution of marketing research can be realized to its fullest extent when top management recognizes its role in the development and control of business marketing strategy.

UTILIZING "OUTSIDE" RESEARCH SPECIALISTS

Many types of business marketing research require specialized skills. Studies on organizational buying behavior, company image evaluations, or strategic adjustments required by environmental conditions may dictate outside assistance. The range of alternatives is wide—from free advice provided by advertising agencies to expensive special-purpose studies conducted by management consultants or market research specialists. Some consulting and marketing organizations specialize in the business marketing field.[40] The purpose and scope of the needed research and the funds available determine which form of outside assistance is most appropriate.

An important mode of industrial research is the multiclient study. For instance, a market research firm might propose to study the market for specialty steel products. The research firm circulates a written proposal to firms that might benefit from such a study. If enough firms are willing to participate, the cost of the research is shared among them. A company such as Du Pont receives hundreds of such proposals every year.

Business marketing research provides the data necessary to evaluate performance and to plan future marketing strategies. The business marketing research process uses techniques and tools different from those employed in the consumer-goods market. However, sound research methods are equally necessary. The organization of the marketing research function will depend on the size, nature, and role of research in the industrial firm. However, for research to be effective, top management must understand that research plays a vital role in business marketing management.

---

[39]William P. Hall, "Marketing Research for Industrial Products," *Industrial Marketing Management* 4 (1975): p. 211.

[40]For example, see Hall, "Marketing Research for Industrial Products," p. 211.

Ethical Business Marketing

COMPETITIVE INFORMATION COLLECTION: PRINCIPLES FOR CONSULTANTS

Regarding the ethical principles of competitive intelligence gathering, a *Fortune* 500 manufacturer has said,

> There are boundaries to legal and ethical information collection conduct beyond which the efforts of the Company or its consultants must not go. The Company's policy is firm that we must not be involved in industrial espionage or theft of trade secrets.

The manufacturer has documented the following specific examples regarding its information collection policy.

1. Information appearing in the press or otherwise generally available may be assembled and distributed, as may legal documents open to public inspection such as patent applications, recorded deeds, SIC reports, and the like. Copies of competitive publications such as annual reports and public relations releases may be secured and utilized.
2. Photographs of competitive plants may be taken from public highways or sidewalks, but activities that hold competitors of others to unforeseeable standards of self-protection should be avoided. Thus, aerial photography is not to be used because it is not the kind of public exposure that a competitor would normally expect to have to defend against.
3. In the course of obtaining information, consultants should not expressly or impliedly represent that their status is merely that of the general public. For example, the consultant should not participate in public plant tours or visit the vicinity of competitive plants for the purpose of overhearing the conversations of the plant employees.
4. If consultants receive information that they believe might be confidential or proprietary or in conflict with other obligations, they must not provide the information to the Company or otherwise utilize it on behalf of the Company until the Company has had an opportunity to evaluate the manner in which the information was obtained and the propriety of its receiving the data.

Source: Based on a *Fortune* 500 company's policy on competitive information collection.

USING RESEARCH IN THE BUSINESS MARKETING PROCESS

For most business marketers, information will be the pivotal asset necessary to develop an understanding of the customer and for creating effective marketing strategies. Customer information supplied from primary research studies is necessary to assure that the firm is (1) developing products that effectively meet customer needs and (2) marketing those products in ways that achieve a positive response from target customers. James Bondra claims that *the advent of the "totally wired" corporation has been delayed by marketing's slow embrace of information technology. Marketing has important responsibilities for positioning the business, developing company strategy, and building cross-functional relationships. In many industrial companies, marketing has done none of these things.*[41]

Business marketing firms must be prepared to become *information-driven* firms in the future. According to a recent article in *Advertising Age*, such preparation would begin with three important directives:[42]

1. Begin to treat customer information as an important company asset and to invest in its development.
2. Develop tools that enable the calculation of customer value and the return on investment of marketing activities.
3. Create a plan that will guide the evolution of the company to become information driven.

Besides its critical role in creating a wide array of customer information, market research activities will be used in several other important ways.

Market Potential and Sales Forecasting

The marketing intelligence function is responsible for maintaining the database used to estimate market potential and to forecast sales, as well as for developing the appropriate methodologies and models for generating these estimates. Because these estimation procedures are so important, they will be discussed in greater detail in Chapter 7.

New Product Research

Much of the research activity associated with new products is undertaken through formal market research studies. An important component of this type of research is the formulation of systematic procedures to gather new product ideas from customers, intermediaries, sales personnel, competitors, and management. Without formal systems, many new product concepts will go unrecognized, and significant opportunities for sales growth will be lost. (Many of the issues associated with new product research will be treated in Chapter 11, Managing Innovation and New Industrial Product Development.)

---

[41]James C. Bondra, "Marketing's Role in Cross-Functional Information Management," *Industrial Marketing Management* 25 (May 1996): pp. 187–195.

[42]"Arm Your Company for the Info-Driven Marketing Future," *Advertising Age*, 23 October 1995, p. 29.

Marketing Control

The success of marketing strategy partially depends on the ability of the marketing manager to understand the requirements of target customers and to develop a marketing mix that will meet those requirements effectively. Equally important is the system whereby the manager evaluates actual against planned performance and objectives: the **marketing control system.** Although the control process is vital in evaluating past performance, it is even more important to the future. Information generated by the marketing control system is an essential element in revising existing marketing strategies, formulating new strategies, and allocating funds to specific programs. The requirements of an effective control system are strict—data must be continuously gathered on the appropriate performance measures. Central to the business marketing intelligence system are (1) systems and procedures for generating the required performance information, and (2) readily accessible information banks for continuously evaluating performance. Because the marketing control aspects of the intelligence system are substantial and significant, marketing control will be examined in detail in Chapter 18.

Competitor Intelligence

Current approaches to developing business and marketing strategy focus to a significant extent on creating a **competitive strategy**—a strategy based on an analysis of the firm's industry, a prediction of the industry's future evolution, an understanding of competitors, and an analysis of the firm's position relative to those competitors.[43] Thus, a core application of marketing research techniques in the business-to-business environment is the collection of accurate and reliable information about competitors. These types of competitive analyses are finding increasing application. A Conference Board study found that 67 percent of surveyed companies planned to increase their competitive intelligence activities, while almost none indicated they would cut back.[44]

Competitive intelligence is a structured approach, and a resulting data set, that develops detailed information about competitors' characteristics, activities, costs, and strategies. The aim of the competitive intelligence system is to create a database on competitors that will facilitate the company's development of its marketing strategy. The competitive database makes it possible to quickly identify threats and opportunities, respond rapidly to changes in competitors' strategies, and improve the overall effectiveness of the planning process. The Conference Board study cited earlier indicated that pricing, strategy, and sales data, in that order, are the most useful types of competitive information.[45]

All survey research methods can be utilized to develop competitive intelligence, and creative approaches will often be required. In one instance, a researcher trying to

---

[43]Kathleen Behof, "The Right Way to Snoop on the Competition," *Sales and Marketing Management* 139 (May 1986): p. 48.

[44]"Marketers Turn to Competitive Intelligence," *Business Marketing* 73 (December 1988): p. 23.

[45]Ibid., p. 24.

discover whether a competitor would open a plant in a particular city visited every country club in the city to inquire about new membership applications. The researcher discovered that the competitor's executives had applied and thereby confirmed the new plant location.[46] Secondary information sources are also used in competitive information gathering, particularly of federal, state, and local government data. Secondary sources, however, have distinct limitations in competitive intelligence because of timeliness and lack of focus on specific issues and current concerns. Primary research—interviews, focus groups, surveys, trade show intelligence, and field observations—will be required, and, in most cases, will be the major ingredient in building a competitor database.

Sources of competitive intelligence abound—including the sales force, annual reports, industry directories, customers, suppliers, and on-line databases. However, effective competitive intelligence depends not only on the information, but on how the information is used. To be effective, a competitive intelligence system must consider the following applications:

1. *Specific objectives.* To avoid wasted efforts and an overwhelming quantity of data, the manager must carefully determine the exact information to be gathered.
2. *How the data will be used.* Data requirements to plan an ad campaign will be much different from those to develop a manufacturing strategy.
3. *Data gathering approach.* It is important to evaluate the best way to administer the competitive intelligence program. Data can be collected in a number of ways: as part of every marketing manager's job; by the sales force; by a trained competitive intelligence staff; by the marketing research department; or by an outside research firm. If the program is to be permanent or is to become part of strategic planning, then some type of internal process will be required.
4. *Integration into strategic planning.* A system will be required to ensure that the competitive intelligence is provided to managers on a periodic basis for use in the planning process. Monthly computer reports, a competitive intelligence newsletter, or regular competitive intelligence meetings are different approaches for making sure the information is used on an ongoing basis.

THE COST OF PRIMARY RESEARCH

The substantial cost of collecting primary data must be balanced against its probable value to management. Managers must always take risks because of incomplete information; they cannot afford the luxury of sophisticated research every time a decision must be made. The cost of primary research can be more easily justified as the financial

[46]Michael E. Porter, *Competitive Strategy* (New York: The Free Press, 1980), p. xiv.

risk of a decision increases. If the level of risk is low, the cost of gathering more information may be greater than the financial loss associated with a poor decision. Primary research should be used when the manager believes that the risk can be greatly reduced at a reasonable cost.

Summary

A key aspect of marketing strategy formulation is the development of an information base that facilitates decision making, monitors the environment, and simplifies performance evaluation; the marketing intelligence system accomplishes these objectives. The marketing intelligence system is composed of models, information-gathering procedures, and analysis and marketing research techniques to provide a continuous information flow. This function includes marketing research studies, sales forecasting, market potential estimation, control systems, and secondary data files.

The intelligence system is designed to provide management with a decision support system—data, models, manipulation, and displays that make information accessible for the decision-making process. Gathering and evaluating secondary data is another important dimension of marketing intelligence. The amount of secondary data available to the business marketing manager is staggering; many business marketers are turning to on-line computer searches of secondary data as a means to gather, disseminate, and use such data more effectively.

Marketing research refers to the techniques and procedures for gathering primary data for decision making. Business marketing research is unique because of the nature of the business market and of the organizational buying process. Much primary research in the industrial setting involves surveys—personal, mail, or telephone. Benchmarking has become an important research tool for evaluating marketing performance in a variety of critical areas. Gathering the necessary data to control marketing activities also falls within the domain of the intelligence system. For marketing research to contribute to the marketing strategy process, top management support is critical.

Finally, sales forecasting and market potential estimates require significant data and extensive knowledge of market segments. Specific techniques for segmenting the business market constitute the theme of the next chapter.

Discussion Questions

1. Describe the key components of a business marketing intelligence system and the role that each component assumes in managing the marketing function in an industrial firm.

2. Some experts contend that business marketing is an especially fertile area for the application of a decision support system. First, describe the features of the business market that lend themselves to a DSS. Next, describe the attributes that a DSS should possess to aid the marketing manager.

3. How has the Internet enhanced the marketing manager's ability to develop databases to be used for analysis purposes?
4. Describe the NAICS and how it would be used by a business marketing manager.
5. What information can the business marketer draw from the economic census? How can this information be used in the process of formulating strategy?
6. The Alberg Machine Tool Company would like to evaluate the relative attractiveness of particular international markets. Suggest some international data sources that the firm might consult.
7. How would you organize a benchmarking study of a company's market research department? What types of firms would be good benchmarking partners?
8. Houston Electronics recently introduced a new component that appears to have significant potential among manufacturers of personal computers. The firm would like to use a business marketing research study to identify the composition of the buying centers for this product. Develop a research design.
9. Formulate a business marketing research problem that would lend itself to a telephone survey.
10. The marketing research function can be centralized at the corporate level or decentralized at the divisional level. Likewise, the marketing research function can be found in research and development or may be fully integrated into the marketing department. What factors must be considered in positioning the marketing research function in the corporate structure of the industrial firm?

Chapter 6

Segmenting the Business Market

The business marketing manager serves a market comprising many different types of organizational customers with varying needs. Only when this aggregate market is broken down into meaningful categories can the business marketing strategist readily and profitably respond to unique needs. After reading this chapter, you will understand

1. the benefits of and requirements for segmenting the business market
2. the potential bases for segmenting the business market
3. a procedure for evaluating and selecting market segments
4. the role of market segmentation in the development of business marketing strategy

A strategist at Hewlett-Packard notes:

> *Knowing customers' needs is not enough. . . . We need to know what new products, features, and services will surprise and delight them. We need to understand their world so well that we can bring new technology to problems that customers may not yet truly realize they have.*[1]

High-growth companies like Hewlett-Packard succeed by

- selecting a well-defined group of potentially profitable customers;

[1]David E. Schnedler, "Use Strategic Market Models to Predict Customer Behavior," *Sloan Management Review* 37 (spring 1996): p. 92.

- developing a distinctive value proposition (product and/or service offering) that meets these customers' needs better than their competitors; and
- focusing marketing resources on acquiring, developing, and retaining profitable customers.[2]

The business market consists of three broad sectors—commerical enterprises, institutions, and government. Whether marketers elect to operate in one or all of these sectors, they will encounter diversity in organizations, purchasing structures, and decision-making styles. Each sector has many segments; each segment may have unique needs and require a unique marketing strategy. The business marketer who recognizes the needs of the various segments of the market is best equipped to isolate profitable market opportunities and to respond with an effective marketing program.

The goal of this chapter is to demonstrate how the manager can select and evaluate segments of the business market. First, the benefits of and the requirements for successful market segmentation are delineated. Second, specific bases upon which the business market can be segmented are explored and evaluated. This section demonstrates the application of key buyer behavior concepts (examined in Chapter 4) and secondary information sources (discussed in Chapter 5) to market segmentation decisions. Third, a framework is provided for evaluating and selecting market segments. Procedures for assessing the costs and benefits of entering alternative market segments and for implementing a segmentation strategy are emphasized.

Business Market Segmentation: Requirements and Benefits

Yoram Wind and Richard N. Cardozo define a **market segment** as "a group of present or potential customers with some common characteristic which is relevant in explaining (and predicting) their response to a supplier's marketing stimuli."[3] In the business market, a select group of customers often accounts for a disproportionate share of a firm's sales and profit. An extensive survey of business-to-business firms found that the top 20 percent of customers contributed a median 75 percent of sales volume to these firms and that 50 percent of a typical firm's sales came from just 10 percent of its customers.[4] What about profit? When the costs of serving particular customers are isolated, many firms are surprised to learn that a large portion of their

[2] Dwight L. Gertz and João P. A. Baptista, *Grow to Be Great: Breaking the Downsizing Cycle* (New York: The Free Press, 1995), p. 54.

[3] Yoram Wind and Richard N. Cardozo, "Industrial Market Segmentation," *Industrial Marketing Management* 3 (March 1974): p. 155; see also Peter R. Dickson and James L. Ginter, "Market Segmentation, Product Differentiation, and Marketing Strategy," *Journal of Marketing* 51 (April 1987): pp. 1–10.

current customer base contributes little to profitability. Such patterns demonstrate the importance of choosing market segments wisely.

REQUIREMENTS

A business marketer has four criteria for evaluating the desirability of potential market segments:

1. *Measurability*. Marketers evaluate the degree to which information on the particular buyer characteristics exists or can be obtained.
2. *Accessibility*. Marketers evaluate the degree to which the firm can effectively focus its marketing efforts on chosen segments.
3. *Substantiality*. Marketers evaluate the degree to which the segments are large or profitable enough to be worth considering for separate marketing cultivation.
4. *Compatibility*. Marketers evaluate the degree to which the firm's marketing and business strengths match the present and expected competitive and technological state of the market.

Thus, the art of market segmentation involves identifying groups of consumers that are sufficiently large, and sufficiently unique, to justify a separate marketing strategy. The competitive environment of the market segment is a factor that must be analyzed.

EVALUATING THE COMPETITIVE ENVIRONMENT[5]

In selecting a market segment, the business marketer is also choosing a competitive environment. In extremely dynamic industries, such as the computer or telecommunications industries, Richard A. D'Aveni emphasizes that "market stability is threatened by short product life cycles, short product design cycles, new technologies, frequent entry by unexpected outsiders, repositioning by incumbents, and radical redefinitions of market boundaries as diverse industries emerge."[6] **Competitive analysis** is the process by which a firm attempts to define the boundaries of its industry,

[4]Frank V. Cespedes, *Concurrent Marketing: Integrating Product, Sales, and Service* (Boston: Harvard Business School Press, 1995), pp. 186–188; and William A. O'Connel and William Keenan Jr., "The Shape of Things to Come," *Sales & Marketing Management* 148 (January 1996): pp. 37–45.

[5]Shaker A. Zahra and Sherry S. Chaples, "Blind Spots in Competitive Analysis," *Academy of Management Executive* 7 (May 1993): 7–27.

[6]Richard A. D'Aveni with Robert Gunther, *Hypercompetitive Rivalries: Competing in Highly Dynamic Environments* (New York: The Free Press, 1995), p. 2

identify competitors, and determine the strengths and weaknesses of its rivals—while anticipating their actions. Fundamental to this process is a focus on the strategic intent of current and potential competitors. Here attention is directed to competitors' core competencies and how they can be leveraged in the pursuit of new applications, especially in divergent industries. **Core competence** is the blend of individual technologies and production skills that underlie a firm's myriad product lines. For example, Canon has leveraged its core competencies in fine optics and microelectronics into an impressive range of products: electronic cameras, jet printers, laser fax machines, and color copiers.[7] By examining core competencies, a clearer portrait is provided of Canon's strategic intent across diverse market sectors.

In considering the core competencies of competitors, scenarios of industry change and competitor entry and exit should also be examined. Which firms (current and potential) find this segment attractive? How do we match up with each? When, where, and how will they enter? This line of inquiry requires testing one's assumptions about the industry boundaries by probing suppliers' and customers' perceptions of substitutes and industry newcomers.

Business marketing strategists can secure additional insights by examining the particular actions (moves and countermoves) of competitors and by evaluating what they did versus what they could have done. The particular response chosen may reveal how a competitor sees its strengths. In turn, a speedy, visible, and forceful move signals a competitor's strong commitment to a particular market segment.

A Balanced View[8]

A **competitor-centered** analysis emphasizes a direct comparison of a firm's products, services, coverage, sales force capabilities, and related factors with those of target competitors. By contrast, a **customer-oriented** approach relies on customer assessments of competing firms and the array of offerings to arrive at conclusions about the strength of a firm's competitive advantage. Rather than relying on one perspective, a balanced approach works best. Competitor-centered firms often restrict attention to a few target competitors and become overly concerned with comparisons of relative costs and operating variables. For example, the chief executive officer of Compaq Computers admitted to overlooking new competitors because he was almost exclusively focused on IBM. But customer-oriented firms can go awry by relying so heavily on customer sources of information that they may overlook new competitive factors. To illustrate, by using a direct sales channel to customers through phone ordering, the success of Dell Computer surprised many of its rivals. These rivals overlooked the large number of sophisticated computer buyers who preferred to buy direct from a firm like Dell.

---

[7]C. K. Prahalad and Gary Hamel, "The Core Competence of the Corporation," *Harvard Business Review* 69 (May/June 1990): pp. 79–91.

[8]George S. Day, "Continuous Learning about Markets," *California Management Review* 36 (summer 1994): pp. 9–31.

EVALUATING THE TECHNOLOGICAL ENVIRONMENT

The business marketing strategist must also carefully assess the technological environment in which the firm elects to compete. To illustrate, 3M's extensive growth during several decades was based on its R&D skills in three critical related technologies: abrasives, adhesives, and coating-banding. As the firm began to add new core technologies, particularly through acquisitions, 3M entered new business areas that were less connected to its core competencies. Success became harder to achieve. Today, businesses based on 3M's traditional core technologies continue to generate an average return on assets about 50 percent higher than the return generated by the new business areas.[9]

Three features of the technological environment are especially relevant: (1) **product technology** (the set of ideas embodied in the product or service); (2) **process technology** (the set of ideas or steps involved in the production of a product or service); and (3) **management technology** (the management procedures associated with selling the product or service and with administering the business).[10] Changes occurring in any of these areas can lead to less market-segment stability, shifts in traditional product market boundaries, and new sources of competition. To illustrate, technological change is blurring traditional boundaries in the computer, telecommunications, and financial services industries. Michael Porter observes that

> *Technology strategy must reinforce the competitive advantage a firm is seeking to achieve and sustain. . . . A firm must know its relative strengths in key technologies, as well as make a realistic assessment of its ability to keep up with technological change. Considerations of pride should not obscure such an assessment or a firm will squander resources in an area in which it has little hope of contributing to its competitive advantage.*[11]

MAKING A COMMITMENT

Business market segments must be selected with care because of the close working relationship between buyer and seller after the sale. To serve a segment, significant resource commitments may be necessary to provide the level of field sales and customer service support that customers expect.[12] Although producers of consumer goods such as toothpaste can shift from one demographic or lifestyle segment to another relatively quickly, industrial firms may have to realign their entire marketing strategy (for example, retrain salespersons) and alter the manufacturing process to meet the needs of a new market segment. Posttransaction service commitments to

---

[9]James Brian Quinn, *Intelligent Enterprise: A Knowledge and Service Based Paradigm for Industry* (New York: The Free Press, 1992), pp. 216–217.

[10]Noel Capon and Rashi Glazer, "Marketing and Technology: A Strategic Coalignment," *Journal of Marketing* 51 (July 1987): pp. 1–14.

[11]Michael E. Porter, "Technology and Competitive Advantage," *Journal of Business Strategy* 5 (winter 1985): p. 78; see also Robert A. Burgelman and Andrew S. Grove, "Strategic Dissonance," *California Management Review* 38 (winter 1996): pp. 8–25.

[12]Cespedes, *Concurrent Marketing*, pp. 50–57.

Managing in the 21st Century

STRATEGY IS REVOLUTION

"You can either surrender the future to revolutionary challenges or revolutionize the way your company creates strategy. What is required is not a little tweak to the traditional planning process, but a new philosophical foundation: strategy *is* revolution; everything else is tactics." Gary Hamel, who advanced this bold and intriguing position, offers several paths to industry revolution. For example, a would-be revolutionary might begin completing the following steps:

1. **Reconceiving a product or service.** In every industry, *X* units of dollars buy *Y* units of value. A firm can *radically improve the value equation* as Hewlett-Packard has done in the printer business.
2. **Redefining market space.** Revolutionary strategies go beyond the served market and focus on the total imaginable market (for example, personal communication devices targeted to business-to-business customers and individuals on a global basis).
3. **Redrawing industry boundaries.** Firms can gain a competitive advantage by compressing the supply chain. For example, Xerox plans to reinvent the way organizations distribute printed materials such as catalogs and user manuals. Why not transmit the information digitally, printing it close to where it is needed?

Source: Gary Hamel, "Strategy as Revolution," *Harvard Business Review*, 74 (July/August 1996): pp. 70-73.

the new segment may continue for years. Thus, the decision to enter a particular market segment carries with it significant long-term resource commitments for the business marketer. Such decisions are not easily reversed.

BENEFITS

If the requirements for effective segmentation are met, several benefits accrue to the firm. First, the mere attempt to segment the organizational market forces the marketer to become more attuned to the unique needs of customer segments. Although beneficial to firms of any size, market segmentation is crucial to the low market share firm. Often, segments are identified that are being neglected or inadequately served by competitors. R. G. Hammermesh, M. J. Anderson Jr., and J. E. Harris point out that "To be successful, a low market share company must compete in the segments where its own strengths will be most highly valued and where its large competitors will be most unlikely to compete."[13]

[13]R. G. Hammermesh, M. J. Anderson Jr., and J. E. Harris, "Strategies for Low Market Share Businesses," *Harvard Business Review* 56 (May/June 1978): p. 98.

Second, knowledge of the needs of particular market segments helps the business marketer focus product development efforts, develop profitable pricing strategies, select appropriate channels of distribution, develop and target advertising messages, and train and deploy the sales force. Thus, market segmentation provides the foundation for efficient and effective business marketing strategies.

Third, market segmentation provides the business marketer with guidelines that are of significant value in allocating marketing resources. Industrial firms often serve multiple market segments and must continually monitor the relative attractiveness and performance of these segments. Research by Mercer Management Consulting indicates that, for many companies, nearly one-third of their market segments generate no profit and 30 to 50 percent of marketing and customer service costs are wasted on efforts to acquire and retain customers in these segments.[14] Ultimately, the costs, revenues, and profits accruing to the firm must be evaluated segment by segment—and even account by account. As market or competitive conditions change, corresponding adjustments may be required in the firm's market segmentation strategy. Thus, market segmentation provides a basic unit of analysis for marketing planning and control.

Bases for Segmenting Business Markets

Whereas the consumer-goods marketer is interested in securing meaningful profiles of individuals (demographics, lifestyle, benefits sought), the business marketer profiles organizations (size, end use) and organizational buyers (decision style, criteria). Thus, the business or organizational market can be segmented on several bases, broadly classified into two major categories: macrosegmentation and microsegmentation.

Macrosegmentation centers on the characteristics of the buying organization and the buying situation, thus dividing the market by such organizational characteristics as size, geographic location, SIC or NAICS category, and organizational structure. In contrast, **microsegmentation** requires a higher degree of market knowledge, focusing on the characteristics of decision-making units within each macrosegment—including buying decision criteria, perceived importance of the purchase, and attitudes toward vendors. Yoram Wind and Richard Cardozo recommend a two-stage approach to business market segmentation: (1) identify meaningful macrosegments, and then (2) divide the macrosegments into microsegments[15] (see Figure 6.1).

In evaluating alternative bases for segmentation, the marketer is attempting to identify good predictors of differences in buyer behavior. Once such differences

[14]Gertz and Baptista, *Grow to Be Great*, p. 55.

[15]Wind and Cardozo, "Industrial Market Segmentation," p. 155; see also Richard N. Cardozo, "Analyzing Industrial Markets," in *Handbook of Modern Marketing*, ed. Victor P. Buell (New York: McGraw-Hill,1986), pp. 11-1 to 11-11.

Figure 6.1 A Hierarchy of Business Market Segmentation

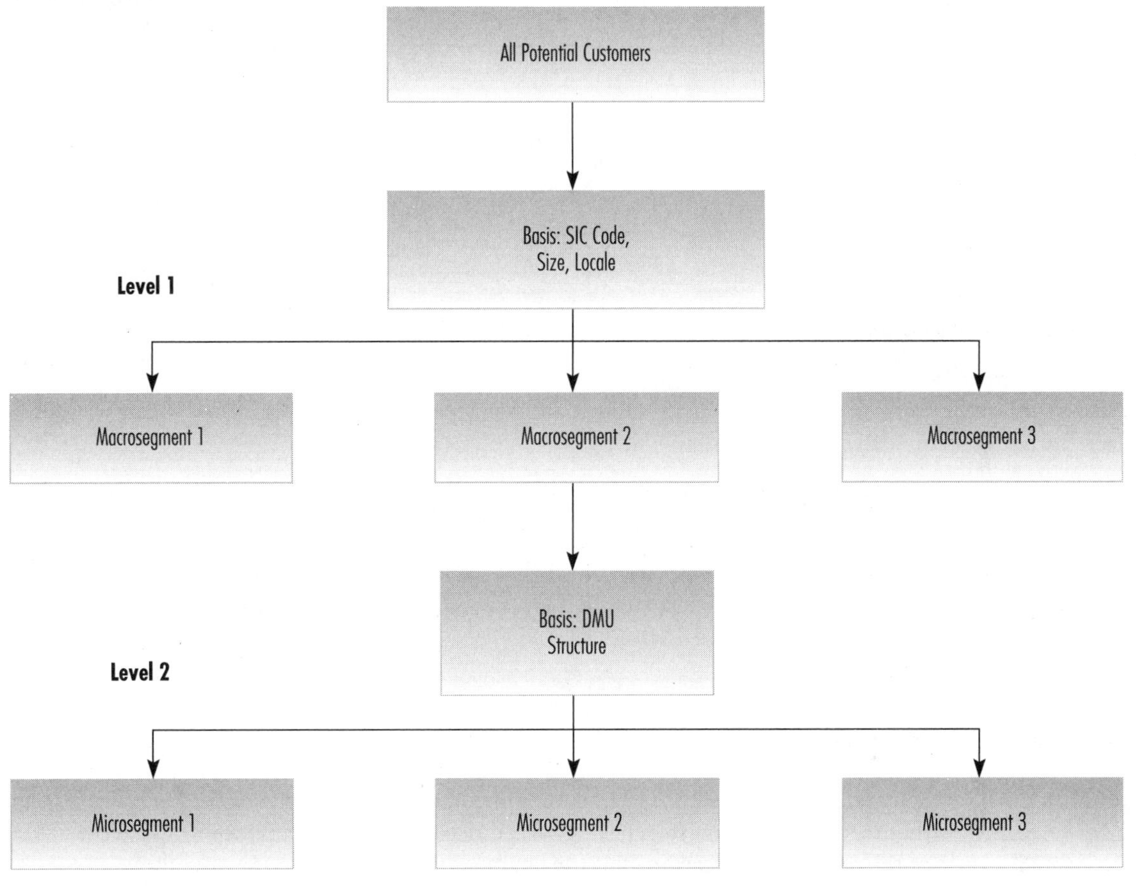

Source: Exhibit 9-11 (page 311) from *Decision Making Marketing: A Model-Building Approach* by Gary L. Lilien and Philip Kotler. Copyright 1983 by Harper & Row Publishers, Inc. Reprinted by permission of the publisher.

are recognized, the marketer can approach target segments with appropriate marketing strategy. Secondary sources of information (see Chapter 5), coupled with data in a firm's information system, can be used to divide the market into macrolevel segments. The concentration of the business market allows some marketers to monitor the purchasing patterns of each customer. For example, a firm that sells industrial products to paper manufacturers is dealing with hundreds of potential buying organizations in the United States and Canadian markets; a paper manufacturer selling to ultimate consumers is dealing with millions of potential customers. Such market concentration, coupled with rapidly advancing marketing intelligence systems, makes it easier for the business marketer to monitor the purchasing patterns of individual organizations.

Table 6.1 Selected Macrolevel Bases of Segmentation

Variables	Illustrative Breakdowns
Characteristics of Buying Organizations	
Size (the scale of operations of the organization)	Small, medium, large; based on sales or number of employees
Geographical location	New England, Middle Atlantic, South Atlantic, East North Central, etc.
Usage rate	Nonuser, light user, moderate user, heavy user
Structure of procurement	Centralized, decentralized
Product/Service Application	
SIC or NAICS category	Varies by product or service
End market served	Varies by product or service
Value in use	High, low
Characteristics of Purchasing Situation	
Type of buying situation	New task, modified, rebuy, straight rebuy
Stage in purchase decision process	Early stages, late stages

MACROLEVEL BASES

Selected macrolevel bases of segmentation are presented in Table 6.1. Recall that these are concerned with general characteristics of the buying organization, the nature of the product application, and the characteristics of the buying situation.

Macrolevel Characteristics of Buying Organizations

The marketer may find it useful to partition the market by size of potential buying organizations. Large buying organizations may possess unique requirements and respond to marketing stimuli that are different from those responded to by smaller firms. The influence of presidents, vice presidents, and owners declines with an increase in corporate size; the influence of other participants, such as purchasing managers, increases.[16] Alternatively, the marketer may recognize regional variations and adopt geographical units as the basis for differentiating marketing strategies.

[16]Joseph A. Bellizzi, "Organizational Size and Buying Influences," *Industrial Marketing Management* 10 (February 1981): pp. 17–21; see also Lowell E. Crow and Jay D. Lindquist, "Impact of Organizational and Buyer Characteristics on the Buying Center," *Industrial Marketing Management* 14 (February 1985): pp. 49–58.

Usage rate constitutes another macrolevel variable. Buyers are classified on a continuum ranging from nonuser to heavy user. Heavy users may have different needs than moderate or light users. For example, heavy users may place more value on technical or delivery support services than their counterparts. Likewise, an opportunity may exist to convert moderate users into heavy users through adjustments in the product or service mix.

The structure of the procurement function constitutes a final macrolevel characteristic of buying organizations. Firms with a centralized purchasing function behave differently than do those with decentralized procurement (see Chapter 3). The structure of the purchasing function influences the degree of buyer specialization, the criteria emphasized, and the composition of the buying center. Centralized buyers place significant weight on long-term supply availability and the development of a healthy supplier complex. Decentralized buyers emphasize short-term cost efficiency.[17] Thus, the position of procurement in the organizational hierarchy provides a base for categorizing organizations and for isolating specific needs and marketing requirements. Many business marketers develop a national accounts sales team to meet the special requirements of large centralized procurement units.

Product/Service Application

Because a specific industrial good is often used in different ways, the marketer can divide the market on the basis of specific end-use applications. Consider IBM (see Figure 6.2). The ad for its Internet service features the benefits of the technology in one industry application (brokerage services) and its potential for others. The SIC system and related information sources described in the previous chapter are especially valuable when segmenting the market on the basis of end use. To illustrate, the manufacturer of a component such as springs may reach industries incorporating the product into machine tools, bicycles, surgical devices, office equipment, telephones, and missile systems. Similarly, Intel's microchips are used in household appliances, retail terminals, toys, and aircraft as well as in computers. By isolating the specialized needs of each user group, the firm is better equipped to differentiate customer requirements and to evaluate emerging opportunities.

Value in Use

Strategic insights are also provided by exploring the value in use of various customer applications.[18] Recall our discussion of value analysis in Chapter 4. **Value in**

---

[17]E. Raymond Corey, *The Organizational Context of Industrial Buyer Behavior* (Cambridge, Mass.: Marketing Science Institute, 1978), pp. 6–12; see also Robert M. Monczka and Robert J. Trent, *Purchasing and Sourcing Strategy: Trends and Implications* (Tempe, Ariz.: Center for Advanced Purchasing Studies, 1995).

[18]For example, see Horst O. Bender, "Industrial Conversion Framework: A New Tool to Assess Business Markets," in *A Strategic Approach to Business Marketing*, ed. Robert E. Spekman and David T. Wilson (Chicago: American Marketing Association, 1985), pp. 17–29.

Figure 6.2 An Ad Featuring the Benefits of a Technology in One Industry Application—and Its Potential for Others

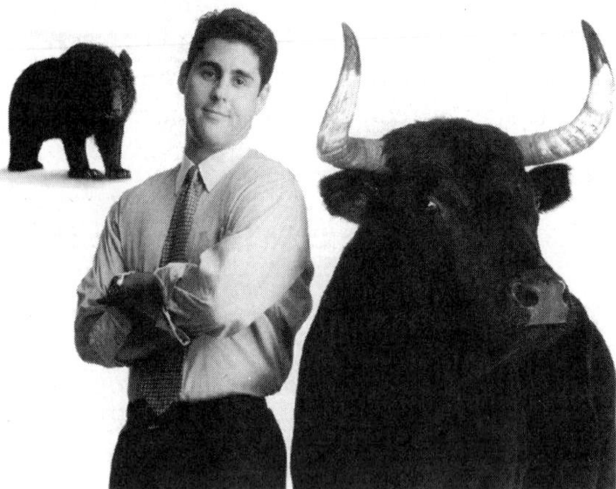

Source: Courtesy International Business Machines.

use is a product's economic value to the user relative to a specific alternative in a particular application. The economic value of an offering frequently varies by customer application. Milliken & Company, the textile manufacturer, has built one of its businesses by becoming a major supplier of towels to industrial laundries. These customers pay Milliken a 10 percent premium over equivalent towels offered by competitors.[19] Why? Milliken provides added value, such as a computerized routing program that improves the efficiency and effectiveness of the industrial laundries' pick-up and delivery function.

The segmentation strategy adopted by a manufacturer of precision motors further illuminates the value-in-use concept.[20] The firm found that its customers

[19]Philip Kotler, "Marketing's New Paradigm: What's Really Happening Out There," *Planning Review* 20 (September/October 1992): pp. 50–52.

[20]Robert A. Garda, "How to Carve Niches for Growth in Industrial Markets," *Management Review* 70 (August 1981): pp. 15–22.

differed in the motor speed required in their applications and that a new, low-priced machine introduced by a dominant competitor wore out quickly when used in high- and medium-speed applications. The marketer concentrated on this vulnerable segment, demonstrating the superior life cycle cost advantages of the firm's products. A long-term program was also initiated to develop a competitively priced product and service offering for customers in the low-speed segment.

Purchasing Situation

A final macrolevel base for segmenting the organizational market is the purchasing situation. First-time buyers have perceptions and information needs that differ from those of repeat buyers. Therefore, buying organizations are classified as being in the early or late stages of the procurement process, or alternatively, as *new-task*, *straight rebuy*, or *modified rebuy* organizations (see Chapter 3). The position of the firm in the procurement decision process or its location on the buying situation continuum dictates marketing strategy.

These examples illustrate those macrolevel bases of segmentation that business marketers can apply to the organizational market. Other macrolevel bases may more precisely fit a specific situation. A key benefit of segmentation is that it forces the manager to search for bases that explain similarities and differences among buying organizations.

ILLUSTRATION: MACROSEGMENTATION[21]

An industrial firm with an innovative technical product sought to become the leader in a market that comprised many small- and medium-sized firms. Based on the purchase decision process, three segments were identified:

1. **First Time Prospects:** Customers who see a possible need for the product and have started to evaluate alternative suppliers—but who have not yet purchased the product.
2. **Novices:** Customers who have purchased the product for the first time within the past three months.
3. **Sophisticates:** Experienced customers who have either purchased the product before and are now ready to rebuy, or who have recently repurchased.

---

[21]Thomas S. Robertson and Howard Barich, "A Successful Approach to Segmenting Industrial Markets," *Planning Review* 20 (November/December 1992): pp. 4–11.

Table 6.2 What Buyers of Industrial Products Look For

First-Time Prospects	Novices	Sophisticates
Dominant theme		
"Take care of me."	"Help me make it work."	"Talk technology to me."
Benefits sought		
A sales rep who knows and understands my business	Easy-to-read manuals	Compatibility with existing systems
An honest sales rep	Technical support hot lines	Products customized to customer needs
A vendor who has been in business for some time	A high level of training	Track record of vendor
A sales rep who can communicate in an understandable manner	Sales reps who are knowledgeable	Maintenance speed in fixing problems
A trial period		Post-sales support and technical support
A high level of training		
What's less important		
Sales rep's knowledge of products and services	An honest sales rep	Training
	A sales rep who knows and understands my business	Trial
		Easy-to-read manuals
		A sales rep who can communicate in an understandable manner

Source: Adapted from Thomas S. Robertson and Howard Barich, "A Successful Approach to Segmenting Industrial Markets," *Planning Review* 20 (November/December 1992), p. 7.

Observe from Table 6.2 that, for this particular industrial market, the three segments value different benefits. For example, novices seek easy-to-read manuals and technical support hot lines whereas sophisticates want system compatibility and products customized to their needs. The business marketer responded by developing sharply focused marketing strategies for each macrosegment.

MICROLEVEL BASES

Having identified macrosegments, the marketer often finds it useful to divide each macrosegment into smaller microsegments on the basis of the similarities and differences between decision-making units.[22] Often, several microsegments—each with

[22]Wind and Cardozo, "Industrial Market Segmentation," p. 155.

Table 6.3 Selected Microlevel Bases of Segmentation

Variables	Illustrative Breakdowns
Key criteria	Quality, delivery, supplier reputation
Decision-specific conflict	High . . . low
Purchasing strategies	Optimizer, satisficer
Structure of decision-making unit	Major decision participants (for example, purchasing manager and plant manager)
Importance of purchase	High importance . . . low importance
Attitude toward vendors	Favorable . . . unfavorable
Organizational innovativeness	Innovator . . . follower
Personal characteristics	
Demographics	Age, educational background
Decision style	Normative, conservative, mixed mode
Risk	Risk taker, risk avoider
Confidence	High . . . low
Job responsibility	Purchasing, production, engineering

unique requirements and unique responses to marketing stimuli—are buried in macrosegments. To isolate them effectively, the marketer must move beyond secondary sources of information by soliciting input from the sales force or by conducting a special market segmentation study. Selected microbases of segmentation appear in Table 6.3.

Key Criteria

For some industrial goods, the marketer can divide the market according to which criteria are assigned the most importance in the purchase decision.[23] Criteria include product quality, prompt and reliable delivery, technical support, price, and supply continuity. The marketer also might divide the market based on supplier profiles that appear to be preferred by decision makers (for example, high quality, prompt delivery, premium price versus standard quality, less-prompt delivery, low price).

[23]David E. Schnedler, "Use Strategic Models to Predict Customer Behavior," pp. 85–92; and Kenneth E. Mast and John M. Hawes, "Perceptual Differences between Buyers and Engineers," *Journal of Purchasing and Materials Management* 22 (spring 1986): pp. 2–6; Donald W. Jackson Jr., Richard K. Burdick, and Janet E. Keith, "Purchasing Agents' Perceived Importance of Marketing Mix Components in Different Industrial Purchase Situations," *Journal of Business Research* 13 (August 1985): pp. 361–373; and Donald R. Lehmann and John O'Shaughnessy, "Decision Criteria Used in Buying Different Categories of Products," *Journal of Purchasing and Materials Management* 18 (spring 1982): pp. 9–14.

Illustration: Price versus Service [24]

Signode Corporation produces and markets a line of steel strappings used for packaging a range of products, including steel and many manufactured items. Facing stiff price competition and a declining market share, management wanted to move beyond traditional macrolevel segmentation to understand how Signode's 174 national accounts viewed price versus service tradeoffs. Four segments were uncovered:

1. **Programmed buyers** (sales = \$6.6 million): Customers who were not particularly price or service sensitive and who made purchases in a routinized fashion. Product is not central to their operation.
2. **Relationship buyers** (sales = \$31 million): Knowledgeable customers who valued partnership with Signode and did not push for price or service concessions. Product is moderately important to the firm's operations.
3. **Transaction buyers** (sales = \$24 million): Large and very knowledgeable customers who actively considered the price versus service tradeoffs, but often placed price over service. Product is very important to their operations.
4. **Bargain hunters** (sales = \$23 million): Large-volume buyers who were very sensitive to any changes in price or service. Product is very important to their operations.

The study enabled Signode to sharpen its strategies in this mature business market and to gain a clearer understanding of the cost of serving the various segments. Particularly troubling to management was the bargain hunter segment. These customers demanded the lowest prices and the highest levels of service, and had the highest propensity to switch. Management decided to use price cuts only as a defense against cuts made by competitors. Attention was directed instead at ways to add service value to this and other segments.

Fast-Cycle Strategies

Service responsiveness is assuming an increasingly important role in many industrial buying decisions. Business market customers can be surprisingly sensitive to time and are often willing to pay a premium price for responsiveness. George Stalk Jr. and Thomas M. Hout note that "If the customers who are the most sensitive to responsiveness and choice can be locked-up, a time-based competitor secures an almost unassailable and profitable advantage."[25] For example, Atlas Corporation developed a commanding position in the industrial door market by providing customized

[24]V. Kasturi Rangan, Rowland T. Moriarty, and Gordon S. Swartz, "Segmenting Customers in Mature Industrial Markets," *Journal of Marketing* 56 (October 1992): pp. 72–82.

[25]George Stalk Jr. and Thomas M. Hout, *Competing Against Time: How Time-based Competition Is Re-Shaping Global Markets* (New York: The Free Press, 1990), p. 102.

products in just four weeks, much faster than the industry average of 12 to 15 weeks. Atlas compressed time by building just-in-time factories and, most important, by automating its entire order entry, engineering, pricing, and scheduling processes. Nearly all incoming orders can be priced and scheduled while the caller is still on the telephone. The faster information, decisions, and materials can flow through an organization, the faster the firm can respond to customer orders or adjust to shifts in market demand and competitive conditions. **Fast-cycle companies** manage both the cycle of industrial activities throughout the organization and the cycle time of the entire delivery system—the number of days it takes to develop a new product or to ship a customer's order.

The marketer can benefit by examining the criteria employed by decision-making units in various sectors of the business market—commercial, governmental, and institutional. As organizations in each sector undergo restructuring efforts, the buying criteria employed by key decision makers also change. For example, the cost pressures and reform efforts in the health-care industry are changing the way in which hospitals buy medical equipment and pharmaceuticals. To reduce administrative costs and enhance bargaining power, hospitals are following the lead of commercial enterprises by streamlining their operations. Also, they are forming buying groups, centralizing the purchasing function, and insisting on lower prices and better service. Reform efforts are likewise moving government buyers to search for more efficient purchasing procedures and for better value from vendors. Those marketers that respond in this challenging environment will be rewarded.

Purchasing Strategies

Microsegments can be classified according to the purchasing strategy employed by buying organizations. Richard Cardozo has identified two purchasing profiles as satisficers and optimizers.[26]

Satisficers approach a given purchasing requirement by contacting familiar suppliers and placing the order with the first supplier to satisfy product and delivery requirements. **Optimizers** consider numerous suppliers, familiar and unfamiliar, solicit bids, and examine all alternative proposals carefully before selecting a supplier.

These purchasing strategies have numerous implications. A supplier entering the market would have a higher probability of penetrating a decision-making unit made up of optimizers than of penetrating a unit consisting of satisficers who rely on familiar suppliers.

Identifying different purchasing patterns can help the marketer understand differing responses to marketing stimuli. A business marketer who serves the institutional food market, for example, encounters both satisficers and optimizers. Large universities review and test menu alternatives carefully, consult with student committees, and analyze the price-per-unit-cooked before selecting a supplier (optimizers). Restaurants

[26]Richard N. Cardozo, "Situational Segmentation of Industrial Markets," *European Journal of Marketing* 14, no. 5/6 (1980): pp. 264–276.

and company cafeterias may follow a different pattern. The restaurant manager, consulting with the chef, selects a supplier that provides the required product quality and delivery (satisficer). Remember that satisficing and optimizing are only two of many purchasing strategies of organizational buyers.

Structure of the Decision-Making Unit

The structure of the decision-making unit, or buying center, likewise provides a means of dividing the business market into subsets of customers by isolating the patterns of involvement in the purchasing process of particular decision participants (for example, engineering versus top management). For the medical equipment market, Du Pont initiated a formal positioning study among hospital administrators, radiology department administrators, and technical managers in order to identify the firm's relative standing and the specific needs (criteria) for each level of buying influence within each segment.[27] The growing importance of buying groups, multihospital chains, and nonhospital health-care delivery systems pointed to the need for a more refined segmentation approach.

The study indicates that the medical equipment market can be segmented on the basis of the type of institution and the responsibilities of the decision makers and decision influencers in those institutions. The structure of the decision-making unit and the decision criteria used vary across the following three segments:

- groups selecting a single supplier that must be used by all member hospitals, such as investor-owned hospital chains
- groups selecting a small set of suppliers from which individual hospitals may select needed products
- private group practices and the nonhospital segment

Based on the study, Du Pont's salespersons can tailor their presentations to the decision-making dynamics of each segment. In turn, advertising messages can be more precisely targeted. Such an analysis enables the marketer to identify meaningful microsegments and respond with finely tuned marketing communications.

Importance of Purchase

Classifying organizational customers on the basis of the perceived importance of a particular product is especially appropriate when the product is applied in various ways by various customers. Buyer perceptions differ according to the impact of the product on the total mission of the firm. A large commercial enterprise may consider the purchase of an office machine routine; the same purchase for a small manufacturing concern is "an event."

Attitudes toward Vendors

The attitudes of decision-making units toward the vendors in a particular product class provide another means of microsegmentation. An analysis of how various clusters of

---

[27]Gary L. Coles and James D. Culley, "Not All Prospects Are Created Equal," *Business Marketing* 71 (May 1986): pp. 52–57.

buyers view alternative sources of supply often uncovers opportunities in the form of vulnerable segments being either neglected or not fully satisfied by competitors.

Organizational Innovativeness

Some organizations are more innovative and willing to purchase new industrial products than others. A study of the adoption of new medical equipment among hospitals found that psychographic variables can improve a marketer's ability to predict the adoption of new products.[28] These include such factors as an organization's level of change resistance or desire to excel. When psychographic variables are combined with organizational demographic variables (for example, size), accuracy in predicting organizational innovativeness increases.

Because products will diffuse more rapidly in some segments than in others, microsegmentation on the basis of organizational innovativeness enables the marketer to identify segments that should be targeted first when new products are introduced. The accuracy of new product forecasting is also improved when diffusion patterns are estimated segment by segment.[29]

Personal Characteristics

Some microsegmentation possibilities deal with the personal characteristics of decision makers: demographics (age, education), personality, decision style, risk preference or risk avoidance, confidence, job responsibilities, and so forth. Although some interesting studies have shown the viability of segmentation on the basis of individual characteristics, further research is needed to explore its potential as a firm base for microsegmentation.[30]

ILLUSTRATION: MICROSEGMENTATION[31]

Hewlett-Packard had one offering in the minicomputer market (the HP 3000) and planned to introduce another (the HP 9000). The managers of the existing product feared that the new offering would cannibalize the market demand that they had spent years developing. By contrast, the managers of the new offering wanted to pursue growth, regardless of the consequences for the HP 3000 business. To resolve the issue, a segmentation study was commissioned by the group marketing manager as part of a thorough strategic assessment.

---

[28]Thomas S. Robertson and Yoram Wind, "Organizational Psychographics and Innovativeness," *Journal of Consumer Research* 7 (June 1980): pp. 24–31; see also Robertson and Hubert Gatignon, "Competitive Effects on Technology Diffusion," *Journal of Marketing* 50 (July 1986): pp. 1–12.

[29]Yoram Wind, Thomas S. Robertson, and Cynthia Fraser, "Industrial Product Diffusion by Market Segment," *Industrial Marketing Management* 11 (February 1982): pp. 1–8.

[30]For example, see David T. Wilson, "Industrial Buyers' Decision-Making Styles," *Journal of Marketing Research* 8 (November 1971): p. 433.

[31]Schnedler, "Use Strategic Models to Predict Customer Behavior," pp. 85–92. For other segmentation studies, see Mark J. Bennion Jr., "Segmentation and Positioning in a Basic Industry," *Industrial Market Management* 16 (February 1987): pp. 9–18; Arch G. Woodside and Elizabeth J. Wilson, "Combining Macro and Micro Industrial Market Segmentation," in *Advances in Business Marketing,* ed. Arch G. Woodside (Greenwich, Conn.: JAI Press, 1986), pp. 241–257; and Peter Doyle and John Saunders, "Market Segmentation and Positioning in Specialized Industrial Markets," *Journal of Marketing* 49 (spring 1985): pp. 24–32.

Figure 6.3 Microsegments for the Minicomputer Market

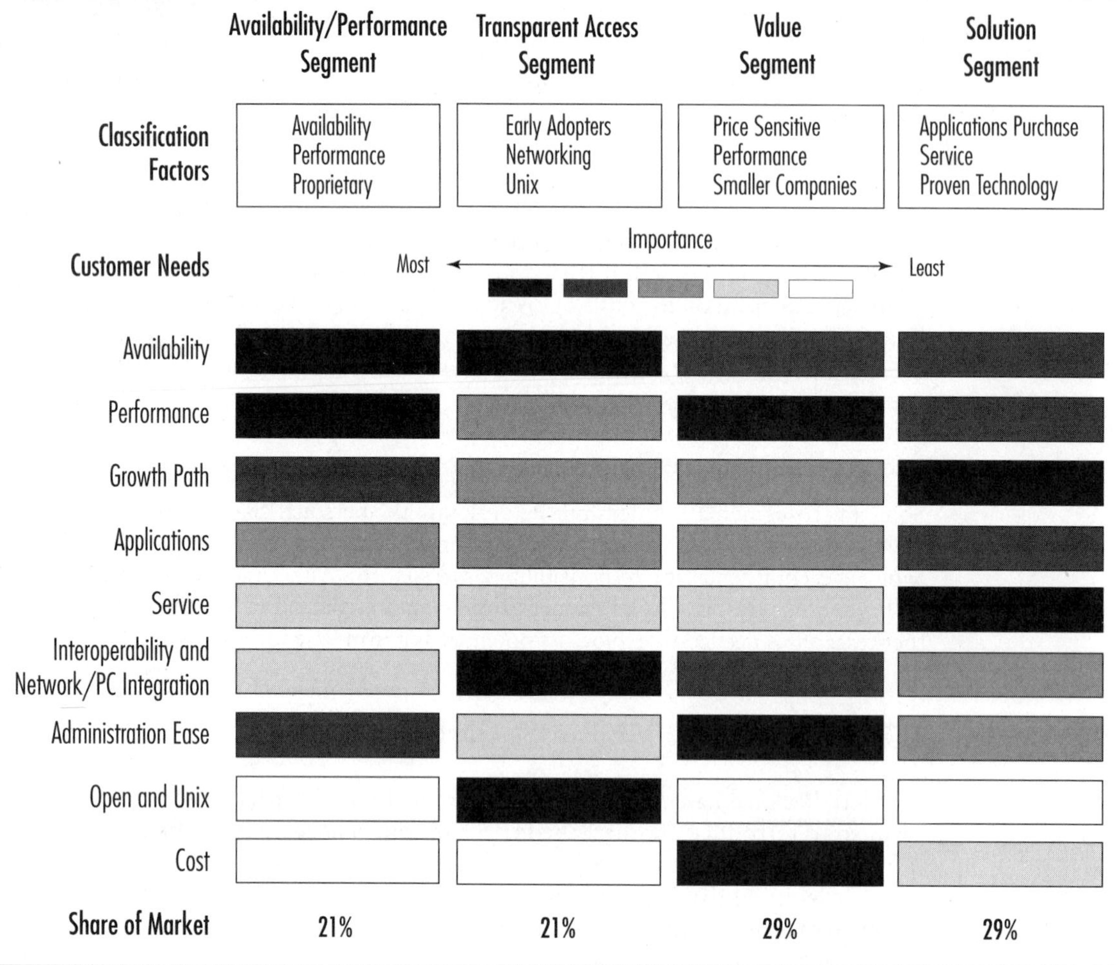

Source: David E. Schnedler, "Use Strategic Market Models to Predict Customer Behavior," *Sloan Management Review* 37 (spring 1996): p. 92. Reprinted by permission of the publisher.

The segmentation study provided evidence that the two products could be successfully differentiated. In Figure 6.3, observe the four segments of the minicomputer market and how customer needs vary across segments. Hewlett-Packard strategists believe that the HP 3000 (the existing offering) provides a solid fit for the *availability/performance* or the *solutions* segment. In turn, the HP 9000 could be targeted to the *transparent access* or the *value* segment. Once the segmentation strategy was formulated, salespersons were better equipped to propose solutions to the information technology needs of their customers.

A Model for Segmenting the Organizational Market

Macrosegmentation centers on characteristics of buying *organizations* (for example, size), product application (for example, end market served), and characteristics of the purchasing situation (for example, stage in the purchase decision process). Microsegmentation concentrates on characteristics of organizational decision-making *units*—for instance, choice criteria assigned the most importance in the purchase decision.

IDENTIFYING MARKET SEGMENTS

The model in Figure 6.4 combines these macrosegment bases and outlines the steps required for effective segmentation. This approach to organizational market segmentation begins with an analysis of key characteristics of the organization and of the buying situation (macrodimensions)[32] in order to identify, evaluate, and select meaningful macrosegments. Note that the segmentation task is complete at this stage if *each* of the selected macrosegments exhibits a *distinct* response to the firm's marketing stimuli. Because the information needed for macrosegmentation can often be drawn from secondary information sources, the research investment is low.

The cost of research increases, however, when microlevel segmentation is required. A marketing research study is often needed to identify characteristics of decision-making units, as the Hewlett-Packard case illustrated. At this level, chosen macrosegments are divided into microsegments on the basis of similarities and differences between the decision-making units in order to identify small groups of buying organizations that each exhibit a distinct response to the firm's marketing strategy. Observe in Figure 6.4 that the desirability of a particular target segment depends upon the costs and benefits of reaching that segment. The costs are associated with marketing strategy adjustments such as modifying the product, providing special service support, altering personal selling or advertising strategies, or entering new channels of distribution. The benefits include the short- and long-term opportunities that would accrue to the firm for tapping this segment. The marketer must evaluate the potential profitability of alternative segments before investing in separate marketing strategies. This requires a process of evaluation that makes explicit the near-term potential and the longer-term resource commitments necessary to effectively serve customers in a segment.

EVALUATING MARKET SEGMENTS

To evaluate the relative attractiveness of alternative market segments, the business marketer must assess company, competitive, and market factors. For the global marketer,

[32]Wind and Cardozo, "Industrial Market Segmentation," pp. 153–166; see also John Morton, "How to Spot the Really Important Prospects," *Business Marketing* 75 (January 1990): pp. 62–67.

Figure 6.4 An Approach to Segmentation of Business Markets

Identify macrosegments based on organizational characteristics (e.g., size, SIC)
Select a set of "acceptable" macrosegments based on corporate objectives and resources
Evaluate each selected segment (i.e., does this segment exhibit a distinct response to our firm's marketing program?)
If yes, select the desired target macrosegment based on the costs and benefits associated with reaching the segment
Stop if macrosegment = target segment
If no, identify within each macrosegment the relevant microsegments based on key decision-making unit characteristics (e.g., purchasing strategy)
Select the desired target microsegment based on the costs and benefits associated with reaching the segment
Identify the complete profile of the segment based on macrolevel and microlevel characteristics

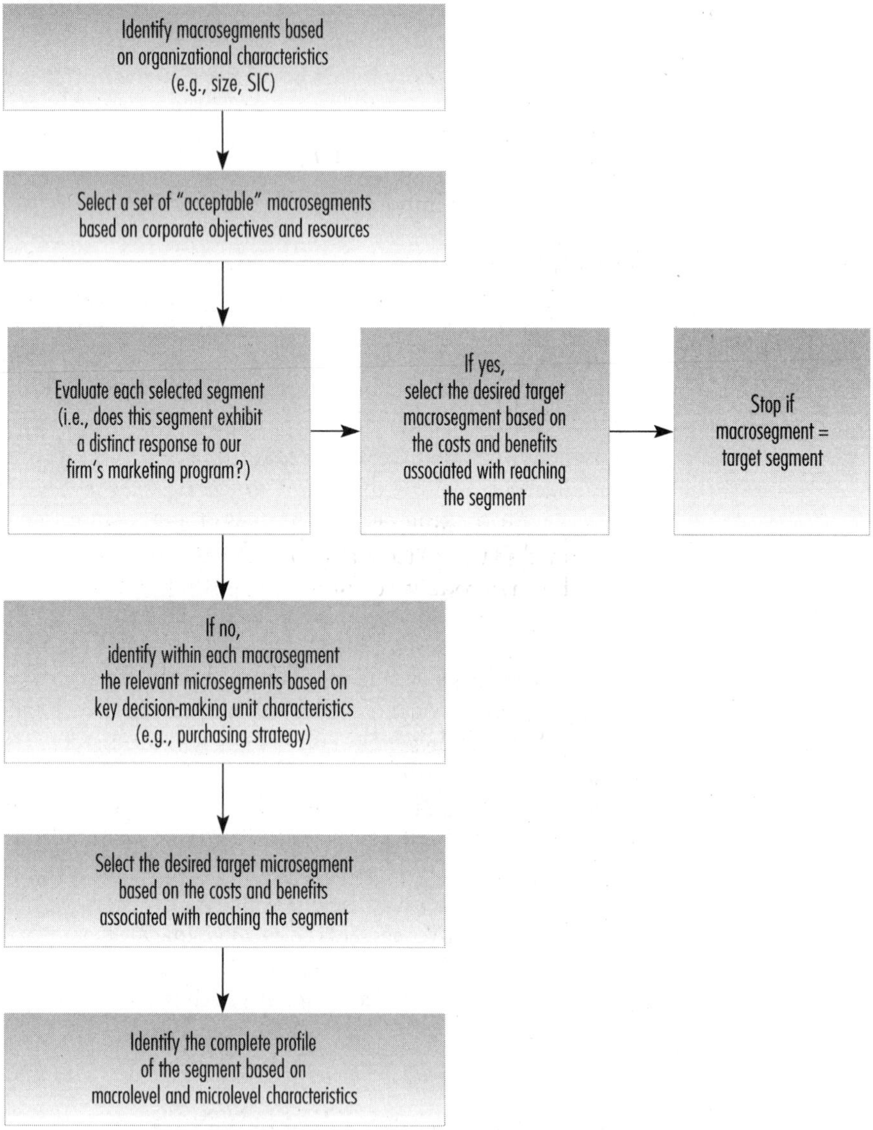

Source: Adapted by permission of the publisher from Yoram Wind and Richard Cardozo, "Industrial Market Segmentation," *Industrial Marketing Management* 3 (March 1974): p. 156. Copyright 1974 by Elsevier Science Publishing Co., Inc.

this analysis extends to the selection of prospective target countries and to an assessment of possible segments within these countries. Franklin Root notes that *the scope of segmentation is greater in large-country markets than in small-country markets; in high-income, technologically sophisticated markets than in low-income, low-technology markets; and for highly differentiated products than for standard or commodity-like products. But segmentation may be profitable in any heterogeneous market.*[33]

Segment Positioning by Country[34]

Figure 6.5 illustrates the importance of evaluating market opportunities and business strengths segment by segment within each target country. This framework includes four components:

- Part A assesses the opportunities and threats offered by alternative market segments in a given country.
- Part B analyzes business strengths and weaknesses. Note that this phase involves a situation analysis and marketing audit by country.
- Part C evaluates alternative market segment candidates and positioning strategies for each segment. S_1P_3 represents the heavy-user segment that is satisfied with a particular product offering and that is motivated to purchase by the product performance.
- Part D evaluates market opportunities in relation to company strengths. Observe that S_1P_3, the heavy user/satisfied segment, provides an attractive market opportunity (high) that matches the company's strength (high). The industrial firm has the manufacturing, R&D, and marketing skills required to satisfy the needs of the market segment. By following this procedure, the most attractive target markets can be identified.

This approach recognizes the interdependence of marketing and other business functions, enables the business marketing manager to link company strengths directly to market segment needs, and establishes a foundation for assessing both the risks and expected returns of alternative marketing strategies in an international market context.

---

[33]Franklin R. Root, *Entry Strategies for International Markets* (Lexington, Mass.: Lexington Books, 1987), p. 176; see also Subhash C. Jain, "Standardization of International Marketing Strategy: Some Research Hypotheses," *Journal of Marketing* 53 (January 1989): pp. 70–79; and Saeed Samiee and Kendall Roth, "The Influence of Global Marketing Standardization in Performance," *Journal of Marketing* 56 (April 1992): pp. 1–17.

[34]The following discussion is based on Yoram Wind and Thomas S. Robertson, "Marketing Strategy: New Directions for Theory and Research," *Journal of Marketing* 47 (spring 1983): pp. 16–22. See also Imad B. Baalbaki and Naresh K. Malhotra, "Marketing Management Bases for International Market Segmentation: An Alternate Look at the Standardization Customization Debate," *International Marketing Review* 10, no. 1 (1993): pp. 19–43.

Figure 6.5 Market Opportunities and Business Strength Analysis by Segment Positioning

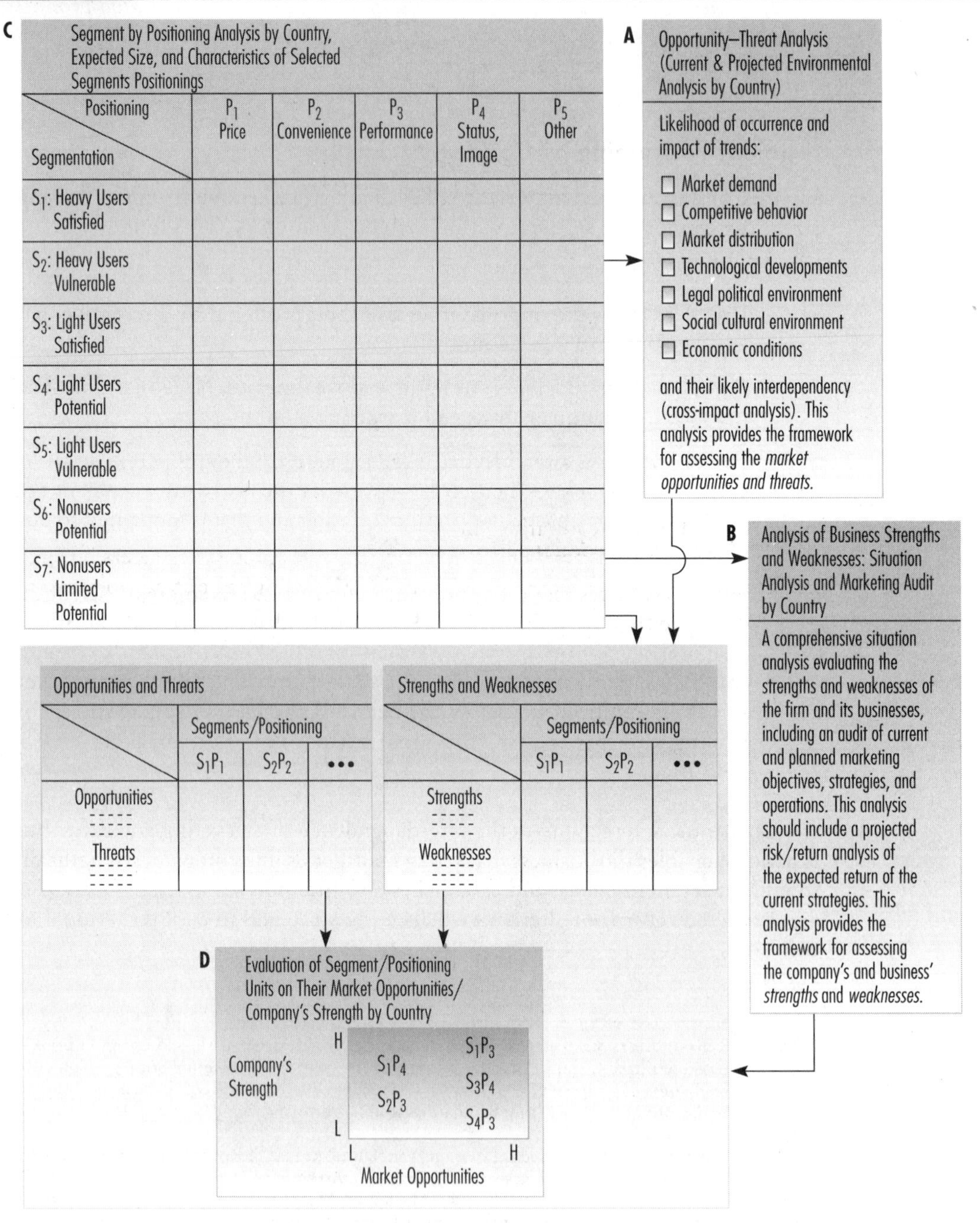

Source: Yoram Wind and Thomas S. Robertson, "Marketing Strategy: New Directions for Theory and Research," *Journal of Marketing* 47 (spring 1983): p. 18. Reprinted by permission of the American Marketing Association.

Implementing a Segmentation Strategy

A well-developed segmentation plan will fail without careful attention to how the plan will be implemented. The successful implementation of a segmentation strategy requires attention to the following issues:

- How should the sales force be organized?
- What special technical or customer service requirements will organizations in the new segment have? Who will provide these services?
- Which media outlets can be used to target advertising at the new segment?
- Will adjustments be required in the logistical network in order to meet particular inventory requirements?
- What adaptations will be needed to serve selected international market segments?

The astute business marketing strategist must plan, coordinate, and monitor implementation details. Frank Cespedes points out that "As a firm's offering becomes a product-service-information mix that must be customized for diverse segments, organizational interdependencies increase"[35] and marketing managers, in particular, are involved in more cross-functional tasks. Managing the critical points of contact with the customer is fundamental to the marketing manager's role in the firm.

Summary

The business market contains a complex mix of customers with diverse needs and objectives. The marketing strategist who analyzes the aggregate market and identifies neglected or inadequately served groups of buyers (segments) is ideally prepared for a market assault. Specific marketing strategy adjustments can be made to fit the unique needs of each target segment. Of course, such differentiated marketing strategies are feasible only when the target segments are measurable, accessible, compatible, and large enough to justify separate attention.

Procedurally, business market segmentation involves categorizing actual or potential buying organizations into mutually exclusive clusters (segments), each of which exhibits a relatively homogeneous response to marketing strategy variables. To accomplish this task, the business marketer can draw upon two types of segmentation bases: macrolevel and microlevel. Macrodimensions are the key characteristics of buying organizations and of the purchasing situation. The SIC and NAICS, together with other secondary sources of information, are valuable in macrolevel segmentation. Microlevel bases of segmentation center on key characteristics of the decision-making unit and require a higher level of market knowledge.

[35] Cespedes, *Concurrent Marketing*, p. 271.

This chapter outlined a systematic approach for the business marketer to apply when identifying and selecting target segments. Before a final decision is made, the marketer must weigh the costs and benefits of a segmented marketing strategy. The market potential of possible target segments must be calculated, and a careful assessment must be made of company versus competitive strengths. Techniques for measuring market potential (opportunity) provide the theme for the next chapter.

Discussion Questions

1. Automatic Data Processing, Inc. (ADP) handles payroll and tax filing processing for more than 300,000 customers. In other words, firms outsource these functions to ADP. Suggest possible segmentation bases that ADP might employ in this service market. What criteria would be important to organizational buyers in making the decision to turn payroll processing over to an outside firm?
2. AT&T, Microsoft, Dow Jones, and Hewlett-Packard are all involved in the information business, and all offer equipment and services that enable consumers to access information in an efficient manner. What implications does this raise for competitive analysis and for market segmentation?
3. Firms use their information systems to track what existing customers buy, where they buy, and how they buy. A leading management expert suggests that equal attention should be given to noncustomers because they generally outnumber customers. Evaluate this position.
4. Two years ago, Jackson Machine Tool selected four SIC categories as key market segments. A unique marketing strategy was then developed for each segment. In retrospect, Jackson management wonder whether they have been appealing to the right segments of the market. Again this year, sales were up slightly, profits were down rather sharply. They need your help. Outline the approach that you would follow in evaluating the appropriateness of their segmentation.
5. Peter Drucker persuasively argues that traditional accounting systems do not capture the true benefits of automated manufacturing equipment. According to Drucker, such approaches emphasize the costs of *doing* something, whereas the main benefit of automation lies in eliminating—or at least minimizing—the cost of *not doing* something (for example, not producing defective parts that become scrap). Explain how a producer of automated equipment might employ a value-in-use segmentation strategy.
6. A recent *Wall Street Journal* article noted that "segment" is the new buzzword for PC retailers. First, suggest possible macro- and microsegments that a PC retailer might wish to consider and describe the process that you would follow in evaluating their relative attractiveness. Second, suggest marketing strategies that the retailer could follow in reaching them.

7. Explain why entry into a particular market segment by an industrial firm such as Du Pont often entails a greater commitment than a comparable decision made by a consumer-products company like General Foods.
8. Sara Lee Corporation derives more than $1.5 billion of sales each year from the institutional market (for example, hospitals, schools, restaurants). Explain how a firm such as Sara Lee or General Mills might apply the concept of market segmentation to the institutional market.
9. What personal selling strategy would be most appropriate when dealing with an organizational buyer who is an optimizer? A satisficer?
10. Some firms follow a single-stage segmentation approach, using macrodimensions; others use both macrodimensions and microdimensions. As a business marketing manager, what factors would you consider in making a choice between the two methods?

Chapter 7

Organizational Demand Analysis

The business marketer confronts the difficult task of predicting the market response of organizational customers. The efficiency and effectiveness of the marketing program rests on the manager's ability to isolate and measure organizational demand patterns and forecast specific levels of sales. Accurate projections of market potential and future sales are among the most significant and challenging dimensions of organizational demand analysis. After reading this chapter, you will understand

1. the importance of organizational demand analysis to business marketing management.
2. the role of market potential analysis and sales forecasting in the planning and control process.
3. specific techniques to effectively measure market potential and develop a sales forecast.

To implement business marketing strategy successfully, the business marketing manager must estimate the potential market for the firm's products. Accurate estimates of potential business enable the manager to allocate scarce resources to the customer segments, products, and territories that offer the greatest return. Estimates of market potential also provide the manager with a standard that can be used to assess the firm's performance in the product and market situations targeted. As one management expert suggests, "Without a forecast of total market demand, decisions on investment, marketing support, and other resource allocations will be based on hidden, unconscious assumptions about industrywide requirements, and they'll often be wrong."[1]

Sales forecasting is likewise vital to marketing management. The sales forecast reflects management's estimate of the probable level of company sales, taking into

[1]F. William Barnett, "Four Steps to Forecast Total Market Demand," *Harvard Business Review* 66 (July/August 1988): p. 28.

account both potential business and the level and type of marketing effort demanded. Virtually every decision made by the marketer is based on a forecast, formal or informal.

Organizational demand analysis is composed of sales forecasting and market potential analysis, and this chapter explores its role in the planning and control process. First, the nature and purpose of both the market potential estimate and the sales forecast are examined and contrasted. Once the groundwork is established, several methods of measuring market potential are described, illustrated, and evaluated. The chapter concludes with an examination of the salient dimensions of sales forecasting, along with selected sales forecasting techniques.

Organizational Demand Analysis

The business marketing manager must analyze organizational demand from two perspectives. First, what is the highest possible level of market demand that may accrue to all producers in this industry in a particular time period? The answer constitutes the market potential for a product. Market potential is influenced by the level of industry marketing effort and the assumed conditions in the external environment. Second, what level of sales can the firm reasonably expect to achieve, given a particular level and type of marketing effort and a particular set of environmental conditions? The answer constitutes the firm's sales forecast. Note that the forecast depends on the level of the firm's marketing effort. Thus, the marketing plan must be developed before the sales forecast. This section examines the significance of both components of organizational demand analysis for business marketing management.

THE ROLE OF MARKET POTENTIAL IN PLANNING AND CONTROL

Market potential is the maximum possible sales of all sellers of a given product in a defined market during a specified time period.[2] Maximum sales opportunities for a product of an individual company is referred to as **sales potential,** which is the maximum share of market potential an individual company might expect for a specific product or product line.[3]

An example will clarify the nature of potentials. Assume that manufacturers of aircraft engines and parts generated shipments of $9 billion this year. What level of market potential would be expected for the industry next year? Based on commercial airline activity, total volume for the industry next year might be projected to increase by 20 percent. Thus, the aircraft-engine industry has a market potential of $10.8 billion ($9 billion × 1.20). Of this, the aircraft-engine division of General Electric in

[2]William E. Cox Jr. and George N. Havens, "Determination of Sales Potentials and Performance for an Industrial Goods Manufacturer," *Journal of Marketing Research* 14 (November 1977): p. 574.

[3]Francis E. Hummer. *Market and Sales Potentials* (New York: The Ronald Press Company, 1961), p. 8.

Cincinnati might expect to obtain 14 percent, based on current market share, anticipated marketing efforts, production capacity, and other factors. General Electric's sales potential is therefore $1.51 billion for next year ($10.8 billion × 0.14).

Potential Represents Opportunity

In most instances, market potentials exceed total market demand, and sales potentials exceed actual company sales volume. Market potential is just that—an opportunity to sell. In the example of aircraft engines and parts, market potential may not be converted to demand for a number of reasons: The government may reduce aircraft defense spending, commercial airlines may postpone aircraft orders if passenger airline travel declines, or a strike against major aircraft manufacturers could reduce their production of jet engines. Similarly, sales potentials are ideals based on an assumed set of circumstances: past market performance; a certain level of competitive activity; and a variety of events, both favorable and unfavorable to the firm. Clearly, a change in competitors' actions, a decline in the general economy, or a reduction in the level and effectiveness of marketing may cause actual sales to fall short of sales potential.

Potentials: Planning and Control by Segment

The primary application of market and sales potential information is clearly in the planning and control of marketing strategy by market segment. Recall from Chapter 6 that *segments* refer to homogeneous units—customers, products, territories, or channels—for which marketing efforts are tailored. Once sales potentials are determined for each segment, the manager can allocate expenditures on the basis of potential sales volume. There is little benefit in spending huge sums of money on advertising and personal selling in segments where the market opportunity is low. Of course, expenditures would have to be based on both potential and the level of competition. Actual sales in each segment can also be compared with potential sales, taking into account the level of competition, in order to evaluate the effectiveness of the marketing program.

Consider the experience of a Cleveland manufacturer of quick-connective couplings for power transmission systems. For more than 20 years, one of its large distributors had been increasing its sales volume. In fact, this distributor was considered one of the firm's top producers. The firm then analyzed the sales potentials for each of its 31 distributors. The large distributor ranked thirty-first in terms of volume relative to potential, actualizing only 15.4 percent of potential. A later evaluation revealed that the distributor's sales personnel did not know the most effective way to sell couplings to its large accounts.

Life-Cycle Potential

Market potential is crucial for go/no-go decisions on new industrial products. The "size of market" has been shown to be a significant screening factor for launching new industrial products. David Kendall and Michael French propose the concept of "life-cycle market potential" as an effective way of analyzing the market size for new industrial products.[4] They suggest that life-cycle market potential is "the greatest number of product adoptions that will eventually occur in a particular market over the product life-cycle, given expected environmental conditions and expected aggregate effects of marketing actions by the industry." The life-cycle measure is useful because it provides realistic boundaries for total sales over the product's life and it is possible to make reasonable estimates of its value. Life-cycle market potential is measured by estimating total annual sales of the generic product class (based on the number of customers and their usage of the product) and scaling down this estimate based on concept tests with potential customers (for example, a market share estimate is multiplied by the estimate of total product class sales). Total sales over the life cycle can then be calculated by estimating repeat purchases and length of time until saturation. This total life-cycle potential then serves as a benchmark to help decide whether the new product should be introduced.

As this discussion demonstrates, market and sales potentials are pivotal in the marketing planning and control process. Therefore, great care must be taken to determine market and sales potential estimates. The business marketing manager must thoroughly understand the various techniques for developing potentials accurately.

THE ROLE OF THE SALES FORECAST

The second component of organizational demand analysis, sales forecasting, likewise poses a significant challenge. The sales forecast answers the question: What level of sales do we expect next year, given a particular level and type of marketing effort? Once potentials have been determined, the business marketing manager can allocate resources to the various elements of the marketing mix. Only after the marketing strategy is developed can expected sales be forecasted. Many firms are tempted to use the forecast as a tool for deciding the level of marketing expenditures. One recent study (which sampled 900 firms) found that slightly more than 25 percent of the respondent firms set their advertising budgets after the sales forecast was developed.[5] Small companies whose budgeting and forecasting decisions were fragmented made up the majority of the firms in this group. Clearly, marketing strategy is a determinant of the level of sales and not vice versa. Figure 7.1. illustrates the position of market potential estimates and the sales forecast in the planning process

The sales forecast represents the firm's best estimate of the sales revenue expected to be generated by a given marketing strategy. The forecast will usually be less than sales potential. The firm may find that it is uneconomical to try to capture all available business. Strong competitors within certain segments may preclude the achievement of total potential sales. Like sales potential data, the sales forecast is an aid in the allocation of resources and in the measurement of performance.

---

[4]David L. Kendall and Michael T. French, "Forecasting the Potential for New Industrial Products," *Industrial Marketing Management* 20, no. 3 (August 1990): p. 177.

[5]Douglas C. West, "Advertising Budgeting and Sales Forecasting: The Timing Relationship," *International Journal of Advertising* 14, no. 1 (1995): pp. 65–77.

Figure 7.1 The Relationship between Potential and the Forecast

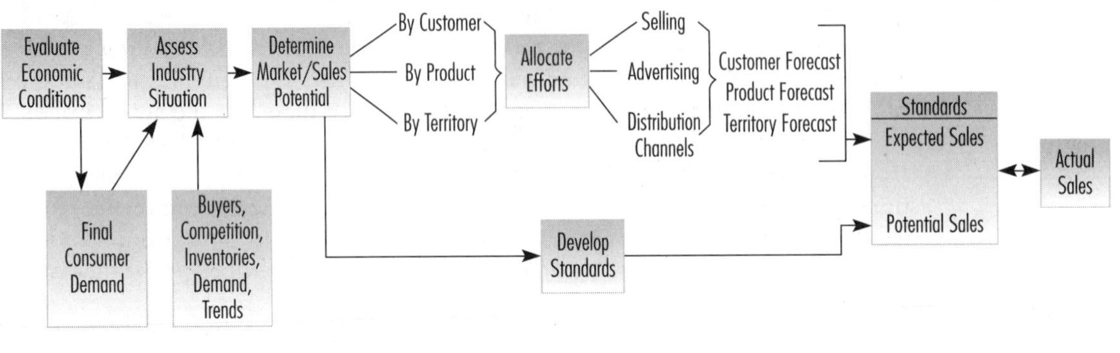

APPLYING MARKET POTENTIAL AND THE SALES FORECAST

Market potential estimates and sales forecasts complement each other in the marketing planning process. Market potential data are usually vital to sales forecasting: Market potential provides direction as to which opportunities the firm should pursue, and the sales forecast is generated once the level of resources to be applied to each opportunity has been decided. Market potential estimates are used to determine where the firm's attention should be focused, the total and relative levels of expenditure to apply to each opportunity, and the benchmarks for evaluating performance. The sales forecast, in contrast, typically provides direction for making short-run, tactical decisions.

Thus, estimates of actual sales over the next year guide management in planning production, estimating purchasing requirements, setting inventory levels, scheduling transportation and the warehouse work force, estimating working capital requirements, and planning short-term expenditures on promotion and advertising. Two- to five-year projections of sales (based on the analysis of market potential) help guide decision making about plant and warehouse facilities and capital requirements and about channel strategy and structure. In summary, market potential provides guidelines for the general direction the firm will take (in terms of markets and product opportunities) and for budget allocations to those opportunities. The sales forecast directs the timing of short-range tactical expenditures and long-term capital spending.

Supply Chain Links

Sales forecasts are critical to the smooth operation of the entire supply chain.[6] Sales forecast data is used to distribute inventory, manage stock levels, and schedule

[6]Rosemary Smart, "Forecasting: A Vision of the Future Driving the Supply Chain of Today," *Logistics Focus* 3 (October 1995): pp. 15–16.

resources for all the members of a supply chain that provide materials, components, and services to a manufacturer. Accurate forecasts go hand in hand with good business practices and effective management policies in directing the entire supply chain process. Specific tools are available to develop accurate estimates of market potential; the business marketer must understand the purposes of alternative techniques as well as their values and limitations.

Determining Market and Sales Potentials

The secondary data available, whether the product is new or established, the number of potential customers, and the extent of internal company information all play a role in estimating potentials. Estimating market potential requires analysis of variables that relate to, or cause, aggregate demand for the product. It is crucial to find the best measures of the underlying variables so that potential can be measured accurately. This section will examine statistical series methods and survey methods of measuring market and sales potentials.

STATISTICAL SERIES METHODS

Statistical series methods presume a continuing close correlation between the level of product demand and some statistical set (called a statistical series), such as the number of production workers or the value added by manufacturing. Assuming the connection is logical—that is, there is a sound underlying relationship between the two items—then product demand can be projected indirectly by projecting the statistical series. First, the manager must identify specific industries that either use or could use the firm's product. Second, a measure of economic activity is determined for each actual and potential consumer industry. The measure of economic activity is assumed to represent the relative sales volume of each industry. For example, the number of production workers is frequently used as the statistical series representing potential demand. Presumably, the larger the work force in an industry, the greater the potential need for a given industrial product, whether it is a component or capital equipment. Other statistical series used include value added, capital-equipment expenditures, materials consumed, total value of shipments, and total employees and payrolls.

The rationale behind using the single series method is that many industrial products have a variety of applications in a multitude of consuming industries. It would be impractical, if not impossible, to estimate directly all the potential applications of the product as well as the total quantities involved. To make the task of estimating market potential manageable, the analyst turns to information that is easily available—a statistical series. The analyst relates one of these series to the demand for the firm's product. Consider aluminum cans. Secondary data reveal that in a given year, the malt beverage industry spent \$2.2 billion on aluminum cans with total shipments amounting to \$12 billion. Thus, a relationship between demand for cans and total dollar shipments (the statistical series) can be established. For every dollar of malt beverage sales, 18 cents in aluminum cans will be used ($2.2 billion/$12 billion = $0.18 per dollar of beverages). Potential for next year could be estimated either for a given region (by determining estimated malt beverage sales in the region for next year) or for another segment of the malt beverage industry (for example, by estimating light beer sales for next year). Past relationships between demand for a product and a statistical series provide a reasonably firm basis for evaluating market potential in various market segments and regions.

Single Series Method

The single series method calculates market potential on the basis of secondary data reflecting the relative buying power of industrial markets. To use this procedure, management must have adequate knowledge of the SIC or NAICS groups that are potential users of a product. Let us consider how this approach may be used to analyze absolute market potential (dollars or units).

Estimates of absolute market potential for the entire United States, various geographic areas, or specific NAICS groups can be determined with a statistical series using the following approach:

1. Select a statistical series that appears to be related to demand for the product.
2. For each target NAICS industry, determine the relationship of the series to the demand for the product whose potential is being estimated.
3. Forecast the statistical series and its relationship to demand for the desired time frame.
4. Determine market potential by relating demand to future values of the statistical series.

Selecting a Statistical Series

To determine market potential using a statistical series, the analyst must first evaluate which statistical series is best related to the demand for the product. The demand for some products may be highly correlated to the number of production workers—uniforms, hand soap, and some office products are good examples. In other cases, value added or the value of shipments is better correlated to demand. For example, due to the high level of automation in the industry, the demand for metal cans by the beverage industry is more closely related to the value of beverage shipments than to the number of industry production workers.

Important criteria in selecting a statistical series are twofold: (1) data on the series must be available and (2) future estimates of the series should be easier to predict than product demand would be. Many of the statistical series reported by the Department of Commerce in the economic census can be forecasted for one to three years with reasonable accuracy. Private research firms (such as Predicasts and Standard &

Table 7.1 Usage Factor for Ball Bearings

Industry	1997 Bearing Sales to the Industry (in Millions of Dollars)	1997 Value of Using Industry Shipments (in Millions of Dollars)	Demand Factor (Bearings per Dollar of Shipments)
Motor vehicles	$1,680	$75,271	$0.022
Trucks and Trailers	39	2,767	0.014

Note: Industry values are hypothetical.

Poor's), as well as some on-line data services, develop predictions on many of the series for various industries. In addition, *The U.S. Industrial Outlook,* published by the Department of Commerce, makes short- and long-term projections of employment, sales, and capital spending for a vast array of industries. Thus, if an industrial firm determines that consuming industries could use four units of a product per $1,000 of the consuming industry's output, an estimate of market potential for 1999 could be made by consulting a reference source that forecasts 1999 sales of the consuming industry. Market potential would equal four units multiplied by the estimated 1999 sales (in thousands of dollars) of the consuming industry.

Determining the Relationship between Demand and Statistical Series

Once the series has been selected, data on the series must be collected and related to demand in order to develop what might be termed a "demand" or a "usage" factor—that is, the quantity of the product demanded per unit of the statistical series.

One approach is to use the economic census to develop the database for the statistical series, and then relate this to prior levels of demand for the product—either by NAICS code or by geographic region. Assume we wish to estimate market potential for ball bearings in 1999, and that motor vehicles and truck trailers are the primary target markets. The statistical series is value of shipments. To determine the usage or demand factor, we relate past ball bearing demand to the value of shipments in the motor vehicle and truck trailer industry (Table 7.1).

Sales of bearings to the target industries would be gleaned from trade sources, whereas the statistical series, value of shipments, could be found in the economic census. Thus, in motor vehicles, 2.2 cents worth of bearings were purchased for each dollar of shipments. An estimate of market potential in 1999 would be developed by multiplying 0.022 by the projected value of shipments to be made by the motor vehicle industry in that year.

Suppose a manufacturer of plastic resins wants to analyze market potential in four industries with which the firm has never dealt. There is no published data. A short survey of firms in each industry group could be implemented to assess resin purchases and some other statistical series such as production workers. The results would be tallied for each industry group, and a usage factor of resin (pounds) per production worker calculated for each. The result could then be used to forecast market potential in each industry by estimating total production workers in the relevant year and multiplying that by the usage or demand factor. The validity of this approach depends on how well the firms in the sample represent the target industries.

The "Materials Consumed" section of the economic census shows the quantity and value of materials, containers, and supplies consumed by specific industries (see Table 7.2). A marketer of paper containers could determine from this section that firms in the confectionery industry would use 3.3 cents worth of paper containers for each dollar of shipments by the candy products industry ($343 million in paper containers for $10.3 billion in shipments). Unfortunately, the level of detail for each industry varies. For some industries, specific components and raw materials are not detailed, only total materials consumed. In the case of candy products, individual types of paper containers are not indicated. Thus, the manager must use caution in using this type of information

Table 7.2 Candy Products-Materials Consumed

Materials Consumed	**Quantity**	**Dollar Value (in Millions)**
Sugar (tons)	1,047,100	$462
Sugar subtitutes (tons)	49,200	46
Cocoa powder (tons)	11,100	10
Chocolate coatings (tons)	171,200	223
Unsweetened chocolate (tons)	35,500	80
Nutmeats (million pounds)	186	196
Milk	-	212
Corn syrup (million pounds)	1,166	146
High fructose corn syrup (million pounds)	162	28
Crystalline fructose (million pounds)	3	1
Cocoa butter (tons)	30,600	98
Flavors (tons)	-	108
Fat and oils	197,400	95
Paper containers and packaging	-	343
Metal cans	-	12
Glass	-	7
Other materials	-	398
Materials, containers, suppliers, NSK	-	308

Note: Total shipments of candy products in 1992 amounted to $10.2 billion.

Source: Bureau of the Census, *Census of Manufactures, Industry Series 2061-2068*, (Washington, D.C.: U.S. Department of Commerce, 1992), p. 32.

Understanding Limitations

Estimating a demand or usage factor this way must take into account the limitations of the approach. The analysis is based on averages; an average consumption of a given component per dollar of output or per production worker is computed. The average may or may not hold true for a particular target industry. Product usage may vary considerably from firm to firm, even in the same industry category. Further, the demand factor is based on historical relationships that may change dramatically; that is, the industry may use more or less of the product as a result of technological change, manufacturing system reconfigurations, or changes in final consumer demand. Nevertheless, carefully derived estimates of the relationship between demand and a statistical series can be powerful tools for measuring market potential.

Forecasting the Statistical Series

Once the relationship of the demand to the series has been documented (the demand or usage factor has been determined), management will estimate future values of the series in one of two ways: by independently forecasting expected values, using their own estimated growth rates; or by relying on forecasts made by government, trade associations, or private research firms. The goal is to project the series forward so that future market potential can be assessed by multiplying the demand factor by the estimated future value of the series.

Future values of the usage factor must also be estimated. The demand or usage factor expresses the relationship between the demand and the series in terms such as "dollar of product per dollar of consuming industry sales" or "pounds of product per production worker." If we are estimating market potential two years into the future, we must ask whether usage of the product per unit of output in the consuming industry will change during that period. Management may want to adjust the demand or usage factor to reflect predicted changes in product usage among the targeted industries. An analysis of production processes, technology, competitive actions, and final consumer demand may be required to adjust the usage factor properly. A good example is found in the plastics industry: The move to lighten automobiles in order to enhance gas mileage would indicate a substantial increase in the "pounds of plastic per automobile" usage factor over the next five years. Similarly, in the beverage industry, aluminum cans are increasingly replacing glass containers, but the pounds of aluminum used per dollar of beverage output may also be declining because lighter and lighter aluminum material is being used in the cans.

Determining Market Potential

The final step is the easiest one: The demand or usage factor is multiplied by the forecasted value of the statistical series. Once this stage has been reached, the difficult data and estimation problems have been resolved, and the calculation is routine. Management must be sure that potential is calculated for all relevant market segments. For planning and control purposes, market potential estimates may be required for various customer segments, industry groups, territories, and distribution channels. A comprehensive example is shown in Table 7.3.

Table 7.3 Estimating Market Potential with a Statistical Series[a]

Problem: Estimate market potential for metal cans in three industries for the State of California for 1999.

Product: Metal cans

Market: Region: California
Industries: Processed fruits and vegetables; Malt beverages; Bottled and canned soft drinks

Step 1: Select statistical series: Value of shipments, 1992

Step 2: Determine the relationship of the demand and the statistical series (usage or demand factor)

Consuming Industries	Total U.S. Metal Cans Consumed, 1992[b] (in Millions)	Total U.S. Value of Shipments, 1992[b] (in Millions)	Usage Factor (Dollars of Cans/ Dollars of Shipments)
Processed fruits and vegetables (F&V)	$1,221	$15,066	$0.0810
Malt beverages (MB)	2,815	17,340	0.1623
Soft drinks (SD)	3,343	25,417	0.1315

Step 3: Forecast the series for the desired time frame

A. Estimate the value of shipments in California, 1999

Industry	Value of Shipments by California Industries, 1992[c] (in Millions)	Projected Annual Growth Rate[d]	Computation	Estimated Value of Shipments by California Industries, 1999 (in Millions)
F&V	$4,234	1.0%	$\$4,234 \times (1.01)^7$	$4,539
MB	896	0.7	$896 \times (1.007)^7$	960
SD	2,879	2.0	$2,879 \times (1.02)^7$	3,087

B. Adjust usage factor

Industry	Usage Factor	Estimated Usage Change,[e] 1999	Adjusted Usage Factor
F&V	0.0810	(5.0)%	0.0770
MB	0.1623	0	0.1623
SD	0.1315	2.0	0.1341

In summary, the effectiveness of the single series method of estimating market potential depends on the following: how well the demand or usage factor represents underlying demand, the quality of the data used, the ability to estimate future values of the series and usage factors, and the extent of distortion caused by using averages and gross estimates. This approach is well suited to industrial products that are commonly used. For new products, unique items, and rarely used components, this approach is not appropriate because the data are insufficient. Modifications to the series and considerable management judgment are required to estimate potential. One way to develop better estimates is to use more than one statistical series.

Table 7.3 (continued)

Step 4: Determine market potential

Industry	Adjusted Usage Factor	Estimated Value of Shipments by California Industries, 1999 (in Millions)		Market Potential for California Industries, 1999 (in Millions)
F&V	0.0770	$4,539		$350
MB	0.1623	960		156
SD	0.1341	3,087		414
			Total	920

[a]A similar approach encompassing four steps—defining the market, dividing the market into segments, forecasting the "demand drivers" in each segment, and conducting sensitivity analyses—is presented in F. William Barnett, "Four Steps to Forecast Total Market Demand," *Harvard Business Review* 66 (July/August 1988): pp. 28–38.

[b]Bureau of the Census, 1992 *Census of Manufactures, Industry Series 2033, 2082, 2086,* U.S. Department of Commerce, pp. 32, 36, and 38.

[c]Bureau of the Census, 1992 *Census of Manufactures, Industry Series,* p. 21.

[d]*U.S. Industrial Outlook* (Washington, D.C.: U.S. Department of Commerce, International Trade Division, 1990), pp. 34–7, 34–24, and 34–39.

[e]Metal can usage forecasted to decline in foods, remain stable in beer, and increase in the soft drink industry by 1999. *U.S. Industrial Outlook* (1990) pp. 11-1, 11-2.

Multiple Statistical Series Method

Because the demand for a product depends on a host of factors, using one variable to estimate demand is frequently insufficient. Business marketers often use sophisticated statistical techniques to measure the combined influence of a number of series on market potential. Those factors most closely associated with industry demand are given the highest weight or relative influence.

For example, a manufacturer of industrial cranes believes that product sales are related to the number of production workers and to customer expenditures on new plant and equipment (P&E). Data for these variables are secured from government sources. Analyzing the data using statistical regression yields an equation that relates crane sales to the number of production workers and to plant and equipment expenditures. The regression equation indicates the nature of the relationship between a dependent variable (industry sales) and the independent variables (expenditures = x_1 and workers = x_2). The resulting equation might look like this:

$$\text{Potential crane sales} = 7{,}920 + (0.2363 \times \text{P\&E expenditures}) - (1.024 \times \text{production workers})$$

In this case, crane sales increase directly with plant and equipment expenditures, but sales decrease as the size of the work force expands (probably because there is less automation in plants with a large labor force).

Once the crane supplier determines the amount of P&E expenditures and the number of production workers in any given market, total potential can be calculated. If Ohio has 9,000 production workers in user industries, and new P&E expenditures are estimated at $16 million, total potential crane sales in Ohio are

$$\begin{aligned} \text{Potential} &= 7{,}920 + (0.2363 \times \$16 \text{ million}) - (1.024 \times 9{,}000) \\ &= \$3{,}779{,}504 \end{aligned}$$

As with the single series method, great care must be taken in selecting the appropriate series. It may be necessary to experiment with several series to see which combination produces the best estimates. Sales potential estimates for prior years can be compared to actual sales in those years to evaluate which combination is most predictive.

MARKET SURVEYS

To avoid the problems inherent in historical statistical data, firms can use market surveys to gather primary information on future buyer intentions. Surveys are also used to generate data to be used with the statistical series. (The techniques and procedures for conducting industrial market surveys were treated in Chapter 5.) For current applications, it is important to note the use of survey results when estimating market and sales potentials, and when determining the demand or usage factor to be used in the single statistical series approach.

The survey method is particularly useful for estimating market potential of new products. Surveys can provide information about whether specific plants are in the market for a new product, about the extent of their needs, and about the likelihood of purchase. Surveys are useful in determining the potential product use by specific industry groups, the plants in each industry that have the greatest potential, and the relative importance of each industry group to total sales. Recall from Chapter 6 that a product's economic value to a user (value in use) can vary by market segment. Surveys can be profitably used to determine the value in use for various customers or market segments. Surveys have also been utilized to evaluate the purchase potential of individual firms.

A complete enumeration of the market can sometimes be made, and the potential volumes for each prospective customer can be summed to arrive at a total market potential. A complete census of the market is warranted when (1) the markets are very concentrated, (2) there is direct sales contact, (3) orders have a relatively high value, and (4) the unit volume is low.[7] The difficulty is collecting data for all potential users of the product. Typically, the sales force is assigned the task of collecting information. Developing information on existing customers is routine, but it becomes more difficult to solicit information from the user who is not a customer. Salespeople often experience difficulties in reaching the individual in a noncustomer firm who has the information they need. They may also be reluctant to allocate a significant amount of time to collecting the data. However, in some industries, buyers are eager to share their annual raw material and component requirements with vendors in order to facilitate vendor

[7]William E. Cox Jr., *Industrial Marketing Research* (New York: John Wiley and Sons, 1979), p. 158.

planning and therefore assure a continuity of supply. The automobile industry, for example, provides steel suppliers with detailed estimates of its requirements for steel.

Uses and Limitations

The survey method is appropriate in estimating the market potential for new products, especially in providing estimates based on objective facts and opinions rather than on executive judgment. In addition, the survey can target specific industries that represent the greatest market potential for new or existing products. Its limitation is the one associated with any survey—the research method used. Nonrepresentative samples and nonresponse bias can distort findings, the wrong person in the respondent companies may fill out the questionnaire, and a small sample size may make sophisticated statistical analysis impossible. A particularly difficult problem is assessing whom to contact. The researcher must invest considerable effort to find the best source of data. It is the responsibility of the marketing manager to resolve the data collection problems and to ensure that the survey design will generate valid results.

EVALUATING MARKET POTENTIAL ESTIMATES

Estimating market potential involves considerable art—applying sound judgment to the method and its requirements. An important consideration is the quality of the data used to derive the market potential estimate. Information that is dated or invalid for the situation will not produce viable estimates of demand, regardless of the sophistication and precision of the methodology used.

The Essential Dimensions of Sales Forecasting

Selection of a sales forecasting technique depends on many factors, including the period for which the forecast is desired, the purpose of the forecast, the availability of data, the level of technical expertise possessed by the company, the accuracy desired, the nature of the product, and the extent of the product line. Evaluations of each factor suggest the limits within which the firm must work in terms of forecasting methods.

GENERAL APPROACHES TO FORECASTING

A company uses forecasting to plan and attempt to influence its future: The forecast is a major component of the decision-making process.[8] Because all budgets in a company ultimately depend on how many units will be sold, the sales forecast often determines

[8]Paul A. Herbig, John Milewicz, and James E. Golden, "The Do's and Don'ts of Sales Forecasting," *Industrial Marketing Management* 22 (February 1993): p. 49.

companywide commitments for everything from raw materials and labor to capital equipment and advertising.[9] Various types of forecasts are often required because estimates of future sales are applied to so many activities. A forecast to determine inventory commitments for the next month has to be more precise than one used to set sales quotas, which may differ from expected sales due to their motivational value. A five-year forecast of growth in the machine-tool industry will require a very detailed and sophisticated model incorporating numerous economic variables, whereas a six-month projection of number 28 ball bearing sales may simply require the extrapolation of a trend line. Some firms use *early warning systems* to alert them about changes in market demand for their products.[10] Early warning systems are designed to sample the market in advance of a selling season or period to detect major shifts in demand. The data generated from this early "forecast" are then used to plan operations, production, and the delivery schedule for materials and supplies. The forecasting process may use either a *top-down* or *bottom-up* approach—or a combination of the two.

Top-Down Forecasting

In the **top-down** approach, estimates of the general economy and the industry first give managers a picture of the environmental conditions under which they will be operating. These estimates include evaluations of all economic and industry variables that would influence sales of their products. The database necessary to develop these forecasts might include economic indicators such as GNP, unemployment, capital expenditures, price indexes, industrial production, and housing starts. A model (that is, a mathematical equation) is created to link the economic indicators to either industry or product sales. For example, Interroyal, a major supplier of commercial and institutional furniture, uses a forecasting model in which current GNP, construction starts 18 months earlier, and current P&E expenditures are linked to expected sales of metal office furniture.

The top-down approach will often include **econometrics,** which refers to large, multivariable, computer-based models of the U.S. economy. Such models attempt to forecast changes in total U.S. economic activity or in specific industries by the use of complex equations that may number more than 1,000 for a single model. Econometric models are available from commercial, university, and bank sources. Chase Econometric Associates, for example, provides clients with a monthly report of more than 200 economic indicators plus current quarter data and data for the next ten quarters.

A drawback of the top-down approach is the gross level at which the forecasts are made. In some cases, the forecasts are too general to be useful. Some experts believe that the top-down approach limits the value of a forecast in developing strategy and may limit the forecast's overall credibility.[11]

---

[9]Geoffrey Lancaster and Robert Lomas, "A Managerial Guide to Forecasting," *International Journal of Physical Distribution and Materials Management* 16 (1986): p. 6.

[10]Paul V. Tiplitz, "Do You Need an Early Warning System?" *Journal of Business Forecasting Methods and Systems* 14 (spring 1995): pp. 8–10.

[11]Barbara G. Cohen, "A New Approach to Strategic Forecasting," *The Journal of Business Strategy* 9 (September/October 1988): p. 38.

Bottom-Up Forecasting

Whereas the top-down approach begins with a macrolevel view of the economy and industry and is initiated by upper management, the **bottom-up** method of sales forecasting originates with the sales force and marketing personnel. The logic behind the bottom-up approach is that sales personnel possess a good understanding of the market in terms of customer requirements, inventory situations, and general market trends. Salespeople can also procure economic data from corporate staff so that their projections will be based not only on historical sales data and customer needs but also on economic and industry data.

The bottom-up approach works well when sales are limited to a well-defined industry. Jet aircraft manufacturers are a good example. A firm supplying gaskets for jets knows that there are long lead times in the production of engines and a limited number of producers. Thus, salespeople know almost exactly what will be built in the next one to three years, and by whom. Specific estimates of the gaskets required can be made, so there is little need for an all-encompassing macroeconomic forecast. Although some firms believe salespeople are not realistic enough to create a reliable forecast, they still use sales force input because of its motivational value. One firm asks all 120 salespeople to develop forecasts for their territory that they "can not only live with, but that they could guarantee."[12]

Combination Approach

Rarely are the top-down or the bottom-up procedures used exclusively. The more common approach is to use both, with the marketing executive being responsible for coordinating the estimates. For example, Miracle Adhesives, a marketer of adhesives, sealant, and coatings, develops a sales forecast by polling their territory salespeople in order to estimate sales for the coming year (based on a review of customers and prospects); these forecasts are then reviewed by the divisional sales manager in light of historical sales trends, market trends, economic conditions, and scheduled marketing programs. The final forecast is derived by adjusting the sales force estimates on the basis of the broader economic data.

THE FORECASTING TIME FRAME

Sales forecasts may be prepared on a day-to-day basis for inventory control, or an estimate of sales ten years into the future may be needed to plan additional plant and warehouse capacity. The methodologies selected for each of these forecasts would probably differ; each forecasting method is suited for a specific forecasting time frame. In fact, the time horizon for which forecasts are prepared can often serve as a substitute for most of the criteria used to evaluate forecasting techniques. Time horizons reflect such characteristics

---

[12]William Keenan Jr., "Numbers Racket," *Sales and Marketing Management* 147 (May 1995): pp. 64–76.

as the value of accuracy in forecasting, the cost of various methodologies, the timeliness of their results, and the types of data patterns involved in the sales data.[13]

Although the forecasting time frame may range from a year to ten or fifteen years, four basic time frames are common.[14]

1. *Immediate term.*
   Forecasts for this period range from daily to monthly. The purpose is to support operating decisions on such things as delivery scheduling and inventory.
2. *Short term.*
   Short-term forecasts range from one to six months. The time frame may overlap with the immediate and intermediate terms. Short-term forecasts are necessary for planning merchandising and promotion, production scheduling, and cash requirements. The seasonal sales pattern is generally of most interest here.
3. *Intermediate term.*
   This time frame generally ranges from six months to two years. Intermediate-term forecasts are used to set promotional levels, assess sales personnel needs, and set capital requirements. Seasonal, cyclical, and turning points in the sales data are emphasized. Some experts suggest that a sales forecast should span at least five quarters to mitigate the contrived conditions caused by the cyclical calendar year.[15]
4. *Long term.*
   Long-term forecasts extend beyond two years to estimate trends and rates of sales growth for broad product lines. The results are used to make major strategic decisions, including product line changes, capital requirements, distribution channels, and plant expansion.

Forecasting Methods

As discussed, the sales forecast may be highly mathematical or informally based on sales force estimates. Two primary approaches to sales forecasting are recognized: (1) qualitative and (2) quantitative, which includes time series and causal analysis. Each category contains a variety of techniques; David Georgoff and Robert Murdick maintain that effective forecasting requires an understanding that

---

[13]Spyros Makridakis and Steven Wheelwright, "Forecasting: Issues and Challenges for Marketing Management," *Journal of Marketing* 41 (October 1977): p. 30.

[14]Adapted from Robert A. Lomas and Geoffrey A. Lancaster, "Sales Forecasting for the Smaller Organization," *Industrial Marketing Management* 20 (February 1978): p. 37.

[15]Angelo Guadagno, "Mastering the 'Magic' of Sales Forecasting," *American Salesman* 40 (November 1995): pp. 16–23.

FORECAST ACCURACY DEPENDS ON . . .

Time Horizons. The longer the time frame, the more likely patterns and relationships will change, thus invalidating the forecast.

Technological Change. A fast pace of technological change will undermine basic patterns and relationships, resulting in forecasting inaccuracies.

Barriers to Entry. Ease of entrance and exit to market or industry enables new competitors to drastically change established patterns, or disrupt a forecast.

Elasticity of Demand. Products with inelastic demand usually can be forecasted more accurately because they typically are required by the user, and purchases cannot be delayed or eliminated.

Expenditures. Dollars can be invested in the forecasting process to increase its accuracy (for example, better data, more sophisticated techniques), but there is a limit. At some point, the value of marginal changes in accuracy are offset by the additional expenditures on the forecasting techniques.

Source: Adapted from Paul A. Herbig, John Milewicz, and James E. Golden, "The Do's and Don'ts of Sales Forecasting," *Industrial Marketing Management 22* (February 1993): pp. 51, 52.

while each technique has strengths and weaknesses, every forecasting situation is limited by constraints like time, funds, competencies, or data. Balancing the advantages and disadvantages of techniques with regard to a situation's limitations and requirements is a formidable but important management task.[16]

QUALITATIVE TECHNIQUES

Qualitative techniques, which are also referred to as *management judgment* or *subjective* techniques, rely on informed judgment and rating schemes. The sales force, top-level executives, or distributors may be called upon to use their knowledge of the economy, the market, and the customers to create qualitative estimates of demand. Techniques for qualitative analysis include the executive judgment method, the sales force composite method, and the Delphi method.

The effectiveness of qualitative approaches depends on the close relationships between customers and suppliers that are typical in the industrial market. Qualitative techniques work well for such items as heavy capital equipment or for situations in which the nature of the forecast does not lend itself to mathematical analysis. These techniques are also suitable for new product or new technology forecasts in which historical data are scarce or nonexistent.[17] An important advantage of qualitative

[16]David M. Georgoff and Robert G. Murdick, "Manager's Guide to Forecasting," *Harvard Business Review* 64 (January/February 1986): p. 111.

[17]A. Michael Segalo, *The IBM/PC Guide to Sales Forecasting* (Wayne, Pa.: Banbury, 1985), p. 21.

approaches is that users of the forecast are brought into the forecasting process. The effect is usually an increased understanding of the procedure and a higher level of commitment to the resultant forecast.

Executive Judgment

In a large sample of business firms, the executive judgment method enjoys a high level of usage.[18] The judgment method, which combines and averages top executives' estimates of future sales, is popular because it is easy to apply and to understand. Typically, executives from a variety of departments, such as sales, marketing, production, finance, and purchasing, are brought together to apply their collective expertise, experience, and opinions to the forecast.

The primary limitation of the approach is that it does not systematically analyze cause-and-effect relationships. Further, because there is no established formula for deriving estimates, new executives may have difficulty making reasonable forecasts. The resulting forecasts are only as good as the opinions of the executives. The accuracy of the executive judgment approach is also difficult to assess in a way that allows meaningful comparison with alternative techniques.[19]

The executives' "ballpark" estimates for the intermediate and the long-run time frames are often used in conjunction with forecasts developed quantitatively. However, when historical data are limited or unavailable, the executive judgment approach may be the only alternative. Mark Moriarty and Arthur Adams suggest that executive judgment methods produce accurate forecasts when (1) forecasts are made frequently and repetitively, (2) the environment is stable, and (3) the linkage between decision, action, and feedback is short.[20] Business marketers should examine their forecasting situation in light of these factors in order to assess the viability of the executive judgment technique.

Sales Force Composite

The rationale behind the sales force composite approach is that salespeople can effectively estimate future sales volume because they know the customers, the market, and the competition. In addition, participating in the forecasting process gives sales personnel an understanding of how forecasts are derived and a heightened incentive to achieve the desired level of sales. The composite forecast is developed by combining the sales estimates from all salespeople.

Few companies rely solely on sales force estimates, but usually adjust or combine the estimates with forecasts developed either by top management or by quantitative methods. The advantage of the sales force composite method is the ability

---

[18]Nada Sanders, "Forecasting Practices in U.S. Corporations: Survey Results," *Interfaces* 24 (March/April 1994): pp. 92–100.

[19]Makridakis and Wheelwright, "Forecasting: Issues and Challenges," p. 31.

[20]Mark M. Moriarty and Arthur J. Adams, "Management Judgment Forecasts, Composite Forecasting Models and Conditional Efficiency," *Journal of Marketing Research* 21 (August 1984): p. 248.

to draw on sales force knowledge about markets and customers. This advantage is particularly important for the business market in which buyer-seller relationships are close and enduring. The salesperson is often the best source of information about customer purchasing plans and inventory levels. The method can also be executed relatively easily at minimal cost. An added benefit is that the process of creating a forecast forces a sales representative to carefully review these accounts in terms of future sales.[21]

The problems of sales force composites are similar to those associated with the executive judgment approach: They do not involve systematic analysis of cause and effect, and they rely on informed judgment and opinions. Some sales personnel may overestimate sales in order to look good or underestimate them in order to generate a lower quota. All estimates must be carefully reviewed by management.

To improve the quality of sales force composite estimates, salespeople should be provided with information about major factors that might affect their forecasts, such as economic conditions, political considerations, manufacturing constraints, customer profitability, changes in corporate policy, and so on.[22] Salespeople can provide extremely valuable information for forecasting. When good historical data are not available, the salesperson's experience and judgment become the primary input for forecasting. Sales force estimates are relatively accurate for immediate and short-term projections, but they are not very effective for long-range projections.

Delphi Method

In the Delphi approach to forecasting, the opinions of a panel of experts on future sales are converted into an informed consensus through a highly structured feedback mechanism.[23] As in the executive judgment technique, management officials are used as the panel, but each estimator remains anonymous. On the first round, written opinions about the likelihood of some future event are sought (for example, sales volume, competitive reaction, or technological breakthroughs). The responses to this first questionnaire are used to produce a second. The objective is to provide feedback to the group so that first-round estimates and information available to some of the experts are made available to the entire group.

After each round of questioning, the analyst who administers the process will assemble, clarify, and consolidate information for dissemination in the succeeding round. Throughout the process, panel members are asked to reevaluate their estimates based on the new information from the group. Opinions are kept anonymous, eliminating both "me too" estimates and the need to defend a position. After continued reevaluation, the goal is to achieve a consensus. The number of experts will vary from six to hundreds, depending on how the process is organized and its purpose. The number of rounds of questionnaires will depend on how rapidly the group reaches consensus.

---

[21] Stewart A. Washburn, "Don't Let Sales Forecasting Spook You," *Sales and Marketing Management* 140 (September 1988): p. 118.

[22] Herbig, Milewicz, and Golden, "The Do's and Don'ts of Sales Forecasting," p. 54.

[23] Raymond E. Willis, *A Guide to Forecasting for Planners and Managers* (Englewood Cliffs, N.J.: Prentice-Hall, 1987), p. 343.

Delphi Application

The Delphi technique is usually applied to long-range forecasting. The technique is particularly well suited to (1) new product forecasts, (2) estimation of future events for which historical data are limited, or (3) situations that are not suited to quantitative analysis. When the market for a new product is not well defined and the product concept is unique, the Delphi technique can produce some broad-gauged estimates.

The Delphi technique suffers from the same problems as any other qualitative approach, but it may be the only way to develop certain types of estimates. However, there are some shortcomings specific to the approach. Assembling a panel of truly independent experts is extremely difficult. Officials in the same firm or individuals in the same profession tend to read the same literature, have similar training and background, and share the same attitudes on the phenomena under study. Some experts refuse to modify their views in light of feedback, thereby negating the consensus-forming process.

Qualitative forecasting is important in the forecasting process. The techniques can be applied to develop ballpark estimates when the uniqueness of the product, the unavailability of data, and the nature of the situation preclude application of quantitative techniques. The accuracy of qualitative forecasts is difficult to measure due to the lack of standardization. Typically, qualitative estimates will be merged with those developed quantitatively. Table 7.4 summarizes the qualitative approaches.

QUANTITATIVE TECHNIQUES

Quantitative forecasting, also referred to as *systematic* or *objective* forecasting, offers two primary methodologies: (1) time series and (2) regression or causal. **Time series** techniques use historical data ordered in time to project the trend and growth rate of sales. The rationale behind time series analysis is that the past pattern of sales will apply to the future. However, to discover the underlying pattern of sales, the analyst must first understand all of the possible patterns that may affect the sales series. Thus, a time series of sales may include trend, seasonal, cyclical, and irregular patterns. Once the effect of each has been isolated, the analyst can then project the expected future of each pattern. Time series methods are well suited to short-range forecasting because the assumption that the future will be like the past is more reasonable over the short run than over the long run.[24]

Regression or **causal** analysis, on the other hand, uses an opposite approach, identifying factors that have affected sales in the past and implementing them in a mathematical model.[25] A sale is expressed mathematically as a function of the items that affect it. Recall the earlier discussion of market potential in which a regression equation was used to project potential based on production workers and on new equipment expenditures. A forecast is derived by projecting values for each of the factors in the model,

---

[24]Spyros Makridakis, "A Survey of Time Series," *International Statistics Review* 44, no. 1 (1976): p. 63.
[25]Segalo, *Sales Forecasting*, p. 27.

Table 7.4 Summary of Qualitative Forecasting Techniques

Technique	Approach	Application
Executive judgment	Combining and averaging top executives' estimates of future sales	Ballpark estimates; new product sales estimates; intermediate and long-term time frames
Sales force composite	Combining and averaging individual salespersons' estimates of future sales	Effective when intimate knowledge of customer plans is important; useful for short and intermediate terms
Delphi method	Consensus of opinion on expected future sales volume is obtained by providing each panelist with the projections of all other panelists on preceding rounds. Panelists modify estimates until a consensus is achieved.	Appropriate for long-term forecasting; effective for projecting sales of new products or forecasting technological advances

inserting these values into the regression equation, and solving for expected sales. Typically, causal models are more reliable for intermediate than for long-range forecasts because the magnitude of each factor affecting sales must first be estimated for some future time, which becomes difficult when estimating farther into the future.

A recent study on forecasting methods suggests that the choice of methodology be based on the underlying behavior of the market rather than the time horizon of the forecast.[26] This research indicates that when markets are sensitive to changes in market and environmental variables, causal methods work best whether the forecast is short or long range; time series approaches are more effective when the market exhibits no sensitivity to market and/or environmental changes.

Time Series Analysis

A **time series** is nothing more than a set of chronologically ordered data points. Company sales reported monthly for the past five years are an example. A time series is composed of measurable patterns, and the objective of the analysis is to identify these patterns so that they may be projected. A time series has four components:

- T = Trend
- C = Cycle
- S = Seasonal
- I = Irregular

Figure 7.2 depicts the T, C, and S components of a time series.

[26]Robert J. Thomas, "Method and Situational Factors in Sales Forecast Accuracy," *Journal of Forecasting* 12 (January 1993): p. 75.

Figure 7.2 Trend, Cycle, and Seasonal Components of a Time Series

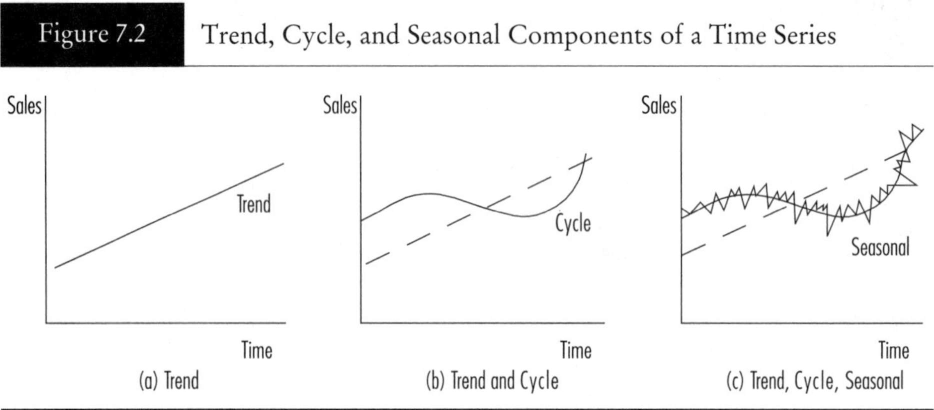

The **trend** indicates the long-term general direction of the data. The trend may be a straight line of the form $y = a + bx$ (see Figure 7.2a); or a curve, $y = ab^x$; or $y = bx + cx^2$. The **cycle** represents the intermediate term with regular upswings and downswings of the data around the trend. For example, the industrial chemical industry in England shows a fairly regular rise and fall in demand over four- or five-year periods. The cycle variations are shown in Figure 7.2b. The cycle may originate from business cycle movements in the economy as a whole, from business conditions within an industry, from consumer spending fluctuations in finished goods markets, from inventory swings in industry, or from a succession of new product introductions. The cycle is extremely difficult to estimate because reversals need not occur at fixed intervals, and, as a result, the pattern may lack any regularity.

The **seasonal** pattern (depicted in Figure 7.2c) represents regular, recurring movements within the year. Data expressed daily, weekly, monthly, and quarterly may show seasonal patterns, which depend on such factors as seasonality of final consumption, end-of-period inventory adjustments, tax dates, business vacations, pipeline inventory adjustments, and scheduling of special promotions.

The **irregular** component in a time series reflects short-term random movements in the data that do not conform to a pattern related to the calendar. Many factors contribute to such random swings in sales patterns (for example, strikes, competitive actions). Generally, the assumption is that these short-term random effects will average out over a year.

When forecasting future sales volumes, actual sales can be expressed as a combination of all four time series elements:

$$\text{Actual sales} = \text{trend} \times \text{seasonal} \times \text{cycle} \times \text{irregular}$$

To develop a forecast, the analyst must determine each pattern and then extrapolate all four into the future. This requires a significant amount of historical sales information. Once a forecast of each pattern is developed, the sales forecast is assembled by combining the estimates for each pattern.

Ethical Business Marketing

THE WRONG WAY TO USE FORECASTING

Sophisticated forecasting approaches, combined with the power of the computer and the ready availability of powerful databases, provide the potential for dramatically enhancing the decision support systems used by business marketers. That potential, however, may go unrealized. In fact, important questions are being raised about the way forecasts are generated and used in the decision-making process. Unrealistic forecasts and the manipulation of computer models are practices that some firms have employed to sway decisions toward some predetermined outcome or to influence viability of a product or brand. In short, it appears that the politics of model building and forecasting deserve as much attention as the technical aspects and objective procedures associated with creating sales and business forecasts.

In some cases, motives other than predicting future sales often politicize the forecasting and modeling process, to the detriment of managerial decision quality. In essence, some firms routinely manipulate elements of the forecasting process. A recent study examined the different ways that forecast results are manipulated or distorted:

1. **Management requests staff revisions.** For example, after reviewing the forecast, a senior manager requests staff to adjust revenue projections to a more favorable level.

2. **Managers make their own revisions.** For instance, a senior manager personally adjusts the forecast developed by the staff.

3. **Management requests "backcasts."** Here a senior manager predetermines an "appropriate" level of revenue, then requests the staff to generate a forecast to support this level.

4. **Incorrect techniques and assumptions are used.** For example, improper assumptions about industry growth are purposely used in forecasts and models.

5. **Management ignores the forecast.** The forecast produced by a model is dismissed by senior management as being "inaccurate."

6. **The forecast model is incomplete.** Politically sensitive variables are purposely excluded from the computer model.

Interestingly, the study found that the most common manipulation of the forecast process or output was related to adjusting revenue projections to more favorable levels—45 percent of respondents indicated this behavior regularly occurs. The study indicated that highly-manipulative firms were characterized by poor training for both management and staff in forecasting techniques, ineffective control systems, high interdivisional politics, and the perception that senior management exhibits "elitist" attitudes. In addition, "highly manipulative" environments are associated with a perception that ethical behavior is not encouraged in the firm.

Because the manipulation of forecast output is unethical and counterproductive, and also leads to negative long-term effects, top management should be encouraged to carefully review the forecast process in their firm. The study's results suggest some solutions: better training for the managers, specification of company codes of conduct, institution of more formalized forecasting procedures that include workable control systems, and programs that will foster positive attitudes among senior managers toward their subordinates.

Source: Based upon Craig S. Galbraith and Gregory B. Merrill, "The Politics of Forecasting: Managing the Truth," *California Management Review* 38 (winter 1996): pp. 29–43.

Regression or Causal Techniques

Causal techniques have as their objective the determination of a relationship between sales and a variable presumed to be related to sales; knowledge of the causal variable can be used to determine expected future sales volumes. The method requires a significant amount of historical data to establish a valid relationship. The model mathematically expresses the causal relationship, and the mathematical formula is usually referred to as a regression equation.

A critical aspect of regression analysis is to identify the economic variable(s) to which past sales are related. For forecasting purposes, the *Survey of Current Business* is particularly helpful because it contains monthly, quarterly, and annual figures for hundreds of economic variables. The forecaster can test an array of economic variables from the *Survey* to find the variable(s) with the best relationship to past sales.

As with the statistical series approach, two general rules should be followed in evaluating economic series. First, the economic series (variable) should be logically related to company sales.[27] Forecasters are often tempted to break this rule because they can easily "try out" any number of variables; a variable may be found to be highly correlated to past sales, but with no logical connection. Such spurious relationships are not effective for forecasting future sales because they are usually accidental and may not hold true. Second, it should be easier to forecast the economic variable than to project the sales level. The causal approach develops a sales forecast by establishing the relationship of sales to some other economic variable. Knowledge of this relationship is then used to estimate sales by determining future values of the economic variable and the corresponding sales level. If the variable is one for which future projections are either not available or of questionable validity, sales may as well be estimated directly.

To create a sales forecast with causal analysis, the analyst must first determine the mathematical relationship between sales and the causal variable. This relationship is then expressed in the form of a linear equation: $y = a + bx$, where a and b are the coefficients that express the relationship and x represents the causal variable from which estimates are made. Sales are then forecast by inserting estimated future values of x into the equation.

Use of Regression Techniques

Causal models are the most sophisticated forecasting tools. A study found that only 17 percent of firms regularly use regression techniques for forecasting and that 24 percent have never tried them.[28] Regression models are useful to industrial firms projecting final consumer demand for items of which their products become a part. For example, American Can projects motor oil sales based on a regression model that integrates auto registrations, average miles driven per car, average crankcase size, and

---

[27]Frank H. Eby and William J. O'Neill, *The Management of Sales Forecasting* (Lexington, Mass.: Lexington Books, 1977), p. 145.

[28]Douglas J. Dalrymple, "Sales Forecasting Methods and Accuracy," *Business Horizons* 18 (December 1975): p. 70.

average interval between oil changes as causal variables. Finally, an important dimension in forecasting is the ability to predict a turning point in the sales series. To the extent that turning points in causal variables can be foreseen, turns in company sales can be predicted.

Limitations

Although causal methods have measurable levels of accuracy, there are some important caveats and limitations. First, as already discussed, the fact that sales and some causal variables are correlated (associated) does not mean that the independent variable (x) caused sales. The independent variable should be logically related to sales.

Second, because both x and y have the same trend pattern, one may be, in effect, correlating only trends, whereas the other components (for example, cyclical and seasonal) are not highly correlated.[29] Thus, regression equations whose variables are highly correlated may be unsuitable for short-range projections in which cyclical and seasonal factors are important.

Third, regression methods require considerable historical data for equations to be valid and reliable, but the data required to establish stable relationships may not be available. Caution must always be used in extrapolating relationships into the future. The equation relates what *has* happened; economic and industry factors may change in the future, making past relationships invalid.

The last, and probably the most crucial, limitation associated with causal methods is the problem of determining future values of independent or causal variables. As we have discussed, before the regression equation can be used to project future sales levels, future values of the independent variables must be determined. Thus, as Spyros Makridakis points out, "what is actually done is to shift the burden of forecasting from that of directly predicting some factor of interest (sales) to another one which attempts to estimate several independent variables before it can forecast."[30] In the final analysis, the quality of the sales forecast generated by regression models will depend on the forecaster's ability to generate valid and reliable estimates of the independent variables.

USING SEVERAL FORECASTING TECHNIQUES

Recent research on forecasting techniques indicates that improvements in forecasting accuracy can be achieved by combining the results of several forecasting methods.[31] The results of combined forecasts greatly surpass most individual projections, techniques,

---

[29]Paul E. Green and Donald S. Tull, *Research for Marketing Decisions,* 3d ed. (Englewood Cliffs, N.J.: Prentice-Hall, 1975), p. 669.

[30]Makridakis, "A Survey of Time Series," p. 62.

[31]See, for example, Essam Mahmaud, "Accuracy in Forecasting, a Survey," *Journal of Forecasting* 3 (April/June 1984): p. 139; and Spyros Makridakis and Robert L. Winkler, "Averages of Forecasts: Some Empirical Results," *Management Science* 29 (September 1983): p. 987.

and analyses by experts.[32] Mark Moriarty and Arthur Adams suggest that managers should use a composite forecasting model that includes both systematic (quantitative) and judgmental (qualitative) factors.[33] In fact, they suggest that a composite forecast be created to provide a standard of comparison in evaluating the results provided by any single forecasting approach. Each forecasting approach relies on varying data to derive sales estimates. By considering a broader range of factors that affect sales, the combined approach provides a more accurate forecast. Rather than searching for the single "best" forecasting technique, business marketers should direct increased attention to the composite forecasting approach.

Besides using several forecasting techniques, firms need to examine several other facets of forecasting in an effort to improve forecast results. Robert Fildes and Robert Hastings found that providing training about sophisticated forecasting techniques, spending more time on improving input data, and making forecasters accountable for their performance are important ways to enhance forecasting efforts.[34]

One study (discussed earlier) concluded that when quantitative methods are used, judgmental adjustments are frequently made. Additional research suggests that managers must carefully decide which quantitative forecasts they select for modification through judgmental approaches.[35] When judgmental appraisal fails to identify poor forecasts, the full benefits of revision are unlikely to be achieved.[36] The results of this investigation indicated the managers were indeed effective in selecting the poorer forecasts for judgmental revision and they tended to select forecasts that were underestimated rather than overestimated. Thus, not only did managers typically improve upon forecasts made by a quantitative model, they revised the poorer forecasts. The result is better and more consistent forecasts.

Forecasts developed by interfunctional teams of managers appear to be gaining favor among business marketers. A study of forecasting approaches determined that team-based forecasts appear to be more accurate than other approaches for industry-level and long-range forecasts.[37] Respondents express higher satisfaction levels when a team collectively develops the forecast. These results suggest the necessity for interfunctional development of strategic forecasts.

ROLE OF THE COMPUTER IN SALES FORECASTING

Computers enable the business marketing manager to improve sales forecasting because they can store vast quantities of data, test and compare various forecasting

[32]Georgoff and Murdick, "Manager's Guide to Forecasting," p. 119.

[33]Moriarty and Adams, "Management Judgment Forecasts," p. 248.

[34]Robert Fildes and Robert Hastings, "The Organization and Improvement of Market Forecasting," *I.E.E.C. Engineering Management Review* (fall 1995): pp. 42–43.

[35]Sanders, "Forecasting Practices in U.S. Corporations," pp. 92–100.

[36]Brian P. Mathews and A. Diamantopoulous, "Judgmental Revision of Sales Forecasts: Effectiveness of Forecast Selection," *Journal of Forecasting* 9 (July/September 1990): p. 412.

[37]Kenneth B. Kahn, "The Impact of Team-based Forecasting," *Journal of Business Forecasting* 13 (summer 1994): pp. 18–21.

methodologies, and evaluate the reliability of the forecast. Modern microcomputers and the availability of commercial database services make it possible to perform complex modeling, economic analyses, and market forecasting on an almost-routine basis.[38] The computer is not limited to the quantitative forecasting techniques. It can be useful, for example, in the sales force composite approach by maintaining data files for the sales force and by aggregating the forecasts of individuals.

Managers may use the computer in sales forecasting by developing their own forecasting programs or by purchasing existing software.[39] For example, the *Sales & Market Forecasting Tool Kit* can help the user develop bottom-up forecasts or top-down estimates.[40] Bottom-up estimates are derived by polling customers or by using historical data; the "chain method" develops an estimate for the entire market, and then helps the user estimate market share. A final segment of this model helps analyze how factors like competition, advertising, promotion, and price can affect sales. Most computer hardware manufacturers offer extensive libraries of software applicable to forecasting problems. Independent computer service organizations, including time-sharing firms, have canned programs that will effectively handle most of the popular time series and regression techniques. Many general purpose software packages also include sales forecasting procedures.

Some firms develop their own forecasting software. MK Electric, a large British firm, has created a "demand planning" model that takes into account historical sales, current activity, market intelligence, and promotional activity to provide a timely and more accurate sales forecast.[41] This forecasting software is credited with dramatic improvement in customer service along with a reduction in total inventory cost of 10 million pounds.

Although the computer is a powerful tool for forecasting purposes, management must realize that it is only that—a tool. Computer-generated forecasts are only as good as the data and the techniques on which they are grounded. An inappropriate technique does not generate a valid forecast merely because the computer was used to create the forecast. As Gordon Bolt suggests, "Computer forecasts must be 'humanized' by being subjected to human intelligence and judgment."[42] Computers do not replace judgment; in fact they may necessitate higher levels of management judgment in selecting forecasting techniques, inputting correct data, and interpreting computer output.

Typically, PC-based programs develop forecasts through either expert systems or automatic forecasting.[43] The expert systems method utilizes a set of decision rules appropriate to the particular forecasting situation and helps the user decide on the

[38]Craig S. Galbraith and Gregory B. Merrill, "The Politics of Forecasting: Managing the Truth," *California Management Review* 38 (winter 1996): pp. 29–43.

[39]Eby and O'Neill, *The Management of Sales Forecasting,* p. 61.

[40]Dennis James, "Forecast Your Success," *Success,* July/August 1993, p. 44.

[41]Roy Holder, "Demand Planning: A Step Closer to the Truth," *Works Management* 49 (April 1996): pp. 32–34.

[42]Gordon J. Bolt, *Market and Sales Forecasting Manual* (Englewood Cliffs, N.J.: Prentice-Hall, 1982), p. 270.

[43]Marvin Bryan, "Programs Make Forecasting Accessible," *PC Week,* 24 April 1989, p. 100.

appropriate approach. Automatic forecasting, on the other hand, typically utilizes a fixed decision sequence to complete the forecast without user intervention. These techniques enable managers with limited statistical backgrounds to develop effective quantitative sales estimates. Regression techniques and time series analysis are the common forecasting techniques included in the PC-based models.

TECHNIQUE SELECTION

Recognizing that all forecasts are subject to error, management must decide on the degree of error that can be tolerated when seeking a forecasting technique.[44] Ultimately, the technique selected should make the "best" use of available data. The selection of a forecasting technique is based on a variety of criteria; choosing the appropriate approach is a demanding task and requires an understanding of the strengths and weaknesses of the available alternatives. The task is an important one because, by using the best available forecasting approach, more accurate predictions for the future can be made. Business marketers who can better anticipate the future gain an important competitive advantage and enhance the efficiency and effectiveness of their operations.

Summary

Estimating market potential and forecasting sales are the two most significant dimensions of organizational demand analysis. Each is fundamental to marketing planning and control. Knowledge of market potential enables the marketer to isolate market opportunity and efficiently allocate marketing resources to product and customer segments that offer the highest return. Measures of market potential also provide a standard against which the manager can monitor performance. Similarly, the sales forecast—the firm's best estimate of expected sales with a particular marketing plan—forces the manager to ask the right questions and to consider various strategies before allocating resources.

The methods for developing estimates of market potential fall into two categories: (1) statistical series methods and (2) market surveys. The marketer must know the strengths and weaknesses of each and understand their appropriateness to a particular marketing environment.

Sales forecasts are developed for various periods, ranging from the immediate (daily or weekly) to the long-term time frame (two or more years), depending on their purpose.

The forecasting techniques available to the business marketer are (1) qualitative and (2) quantitative. Qualitative techniques rely on informed judgments of future

[44]Lancaster and Lomas, "A Managerial Guide to Forecasting," p. 3.

sales and include the executive judgment, the sales force composite, and the Delphi methods. By contrast, quantitative techniques have more complex data requirements and include time series and causal approaches. The time series method uses chronological historical data to project the future trend and growth rate of sales. Causal methods, on the other hand, seek to identify factors that have affected sales in the past and to incorporate these factors into a mathematical model. The computer is a valuable tool, facilitating the forecasting process for all methods.

The essence of good forecasting is to combine effectively the forecasts provided by various methods. The process of sales forecasting is challenging and requires a good working knowledge of the available alternatives described in this chapter.

Discussion Questions

1. Explain how the use of the sales forecast differs from that of an estimate of market potential.
2. What is the underlying logic of statistical series methods used in measuring market potential?
3. What statistical series are provided in the *Economic Census*?
4. Distinguish between single and multiple statistical series methods for estimating market potential.
5. Why are market surveys favored over statistical series methods in measuring the market potential for new industrial products?
6. How could a business marketing manager use NAICS information to determine demand potential in the Boston market? Be very specific—this manager is totally unfamiliar with the NAICS system.
7. The business marketing manager must develop not one but many forecasts over several time frames. Explain.
8. Compare and contrast the sales force composite and the Delphi methods of developing a sales forecast.
9. Although qualitative forecasting techniques are important in the sales forecasting process in many industrial firms, the marketing manager must understand the limitations of these approaches. Outline these limitations.
10. As alternative methods for sales forecasting, what is the underlying logic of (1) time series and (2) regression or causal methods?
11. What are the limitations that must be understood before applying and interpreting the sales forecasting results generated by causal methods?
12. What role does a computer have in facilitating the sales forecasting process?

13. What are the features of the business market that support the use of qualitative forecasting approaches? What benefits does the business market analyst gain by combining these qualitative approaches with quantitative forecasting methods?

Exercises

1. The McConocha Company manufactures ink for use in all types of printing operations. The Midwest sales manager is confronted with the need to develop sales quotas for five salespersons located in Pennsylvania, Ohio, Michigan, Indiana, and Illinois. The sales quotas are to be based on the market potential for printing ink in each state; preliminary analysis suggests that SIC 2711 (newspapers), SIC 2721 (periodicals), SIC 2732 (book printing), and SIC 2751 (letterpress commercial printing) are the primary ink-using industries. Historical sales records suggest that the cost of printing ink constitutes about 0.1 percent of the sales dollar for the using industries. Using the old SIC system, the 1992 *Census of Manufactures,* or the 1992 *Survey of Business,* determine

   a. The total market potential for each SIC industry for the entire five-state area

   b. The total market potential for each state

   c. The relative market potential for each state

   What cautions should the McConocha sales manager use when applying market potential data to the formulation of sales quotas?

2. The Bol Company manufactures electronic controls for sale to book publishing companies. A primary market is New York State, where past sales volumes have not satisfied management expectations. Last year the firm had sales of $8.2 million to book publishers in New York State, while total U.S. sales to book publishers reached $58.4 million. The following data is gleaned from company and other published sources to evaluate the firm's performance in New York:

Number of Customers in New York State	Total Sales Made by New York State Book Publishers	Total U.S. Sales of All Book Publishers
142	$2.2 billion	$10 billion

   How well did the company perform last year on the basis of sales volume in New York State? Explain your answer.

3. The Stearns Company requires an estimate of total dollar market potential for the purpose of allocating advertising expenditures to the East Coast market. A small-scale study of a sample of customers in each of the firm's SIC groups provides the following data on "valve purchases per dollar of value added":

SIC	Value Purchases/Dollar of Value Added	Total Value Added: East Coast
2992	$.11	$21,100
3291	.08	5,600
3541	.07	48,500
3559	.05	28,400
3662	.12	12,500
3679	.10	17,000

Determine the total dollar market potential for the East Coast market.

Part IV

Formulating Business Marketing Strategy

Chapter 8

Business Marketing Planning: Strategic Perspectives

To this point, the textbook has examined the techniques available to the business marketing manager for segmenting the business market, forecasting market potential, and forecasting sales. Moreover, you have developed an understanding of relationship marketing, organizational buying behavior, and the unique characteristics and strategic role of the business marketing intelligence system. All of this provides a perspective that is fundamentally important to the business marketing planner. After reading this chapter, you will understand

1. the dimensions that characterize market-driven organizations and the importance of this orientation to competitive advantage.
2. the sources of competitive advantage and how they can be converted into superior positions of advantage in the business market.
3. marketing's strategic role in corporate strategy development.
4. the special challenges that confront the strategist in high-technology markets.
5. the multifunctional nature of business marketing decision making.

For more than a decade, companies have scrambled to restructure, downsize, and reengineer. One strategy expert suggests that these efforts to improve efficiency did very little to generate distinctive competitive advantages. Today at one firm after another—from J. M. Smucker Company to IBM to Hewlett-Packard to United Parcel Service—strategy provides the central focus in the quest for higher top-line revenue and increased profits.[1]

[1]John A. Byrne, "Strategic Planning: After a Decade of Gritty Downsizing, Big Thinkers Are Back in Vogue," *Business Week*, August 26, 1996, p. 48.

Regis McKenna summarizes the new role of the marketer in business strategy:

> *In a time of exploding choice and unpredictable change, marketing—the new marketing—is the answer.... The marketer must be the integrator, both internally—synthesizing technological capability with marketing needs—and externally to bring the customer into the company as a participant in the development and adaptation of goods and services. It is a fundamental shift in the role and purpose of marketing: from manipulation of the customer to genuine customer involvement, from telling and selling to communicating and sharing knowledge; from last-in-line function to corporate-credibility champion.*[2]

To meet the challenges brought on by growing domestic and global competition, industrial firms are increasingly recognizing the vital role that the marketing function assumes in the development and implementation of successful business strategies. Effective business strategies share many common characteristics, but at a minimum, they are responsive to market needs, they exploit the special competencies of the organization, and they employ valid assumptions about environmental trends and competitive behavior. Above all, they must offer a realistic basis for securing and sustaining a competitive advantage. This chapter examines the nature and critical importance of strategy development in the business marketing firm.

First, the characteristics that define market-driven organizations are examined, while exploring the meaning and strategic value of this orientation. The sources of competitive advantage are then identified, along with the levers a firm can use to convert these sources into superior positions of advantage in the business market. Finally, the role that the marketing function assumes in corporate strategy development is presented, with a functionally integrated perspective of business marketing planning. This discussion provides a foundation for exploring business marketing strategy on a global scale—the theme of the next chapter.

Market-Driven Organizations[3]

Leading-edge organizations stay close to the customer and ahead of competition. Peter Drucker notes that "the single most important thing to remember about any enterprise is that there are no results inside its walls. The result of a business is a satisfied customer.... [I]nside an enterprise there are only cost centers. Results exist only on the outside."[4] A market-driven organization displays a deep and enduring

[2]Regis McKenna, *Relationship Marketing: Successful Strategies for the Age of the Customer* (Reading, Mass: Addison-Wesley, 1991), p. 4.

[3]The discussion in this section draws on George S. Day, *Market Driven Strategy: Processes for Creating Value* (New York: The Free Press, 1990), chap. 14; and Subra Balakrishnan, "Benefits of Customer and Competitive Orientations in Industrial Markets," *Industrial Marketing Management* 25 (July 1996): pp. 257–269; see also Ajay K. Kohli and Bernard J. Jaworski, "Market Orientation: The Construct, Research Propositions, and Managerial Implications," *Journal of Marketing* 54 (April 1990): pp. 1–18.

[4]Peter F. Drucker, "Management and the World's Work," *Harvard Business Review* 66 (September/October 1988): pp. 65–76.

commitment to the principle that the purpose of a business is to attract and satisfy customers at a profit.

George Day suggests that a market-driven organization has a three-level focus that includes

- *commitment to a set of processes, beliefs, and values that permeate all aspects and activities, that are*
- *guided by a deep and shared understanding of consumers' needs and behavior, and competitors' capabilities and intentions, for the purpose of*
- *achieving superior performance by satisfying customers better than the competitors.*[5]

CAPABILITIES OF MARKET-DRIVEN ORGANIZATIONS

Market-driven organizations demonstrate superior market-sensing and customer-linking capabilities.[6]

Market-Sensing as a Distinctive Capability

Market-driven firms are centered on customers—they take an outside-in view of strategy and demonstrate an ability to sense market trends ahead of their competitors. Whereas all organizations scan the environment to spot trends, opportunities, and threats, market-driven organizations approach these activities in a more systematic manner. In market-driven firms, market monitoring is frequent and intensive, customer contact employees actively feed market information to management, knowledge of existing and emerging market segments is extensive, and market information systems make it easy for managers across functions to retrieve comprehensive and timely information (see Table 8.1).

Customer-Linking as a Distinctive Capability

Market-driven firms demonstrate customer-linking capabilities—they possess special skills for creating and managing close customer relationships. Because of the resource commitments required, special attention is given to the choice of which customers to serve collaboratively (see Chapter 4). Successful collaboration requires a close partnership and joint problem solving. There is also a heightened need for cross-functional coordination and information sharing to work collaboratively with customers. For example, field sales and services units need a deep understanding of their

---

[5]Day, *Market-Driven Strategy,* p. 358.

[6]This section is based on George S. Day, "The Capabilities of Market-Driven Organizations," *Journal of Marketing* 58 (October 1994): pp. 37–52.

Table 8.1 Assessing Market-Sensing Capabilities

1. How extensively does the business explore and understand its customers and channel partners?						
Limited to publicly available information and informal sales force feedback	❑	❑	❑	❑	❑	Strong commitment to thoroughly understanding the market as basis for strategic decisions
2. Extent of market monitoring?						
Seldom done beyond tracking sales and market share	❑	❑	❑	❑	❑	Frequent and extensive—including post-transaction follow-ups, customer satisfaction, and quality monitoring
3. Willingness of customer contact employees to feed market information to management?						
Poor—no incentives or mechanisms are available	❑	❑	❑	❑	❑	Excellent—there is a continuous flow of information about customer needs and competitors' activity
4. Knowledge of market segments?						
Limited—based on available data and industry classification	❑	❑	❑	❑	❑	Extensive—considerable investments are made in identifying need-based segments and tracking emerging segment opportunities
5. Knowledge of competitors?						
Limited to readily available data on direct competition	❑	❑	❑	❑	❑	Thorough insights into all those with an opportunity to serve the customer
6. Adequacy of market information systems?						
Incompatible databases and software difficulties make it impossible to extract information	❑	❑	❑	❑	❑	Systems make it easy for all managers to retrieve comprehensive and timely information
7. Role of the market research function?						
Limited to sales analysis and occasional negotiations with outside data suppliers	❑	❑	❑	❑	❑	Widely recognized for expertise in undertaking market studies and developing useful strategy recommendations
8. Sharing of lessons about market behavior and activity between functions and countries?						
Minimal	❑	❑	❑	❑	❑	Excellent—there is ongoing sharing at several levels

Source: Adapted from George S. Day, "Continuous Learning about Markets," *California Management Review* 36 (summer 1994): pp. 25–26.

customers' business processes in order to analyze and optimize the value-in-use components of the exchange. In addition, notes Frank Cespedes, "since the buyer is not only purchasing a product but also organizational prowess, field sales and service personnel require more familiarity with their own company's business processes across a variety of functional areas."[7] Market-driven firms develop the appropriate structural linkages (for example, teams or liaison units), information systems (for example, joint databases), and management processes (for example, career paths and training programs) to achieve a collaborative advantage and to deliver value and satisfaction to their most important customers.[8]

DIMENSIONS OF MARKET-DRIVEN MANAGEMENT

In a market-driven organization, this orientation is achieved and sustained by making appropriate moves along four interlocking dimensions: (1) shared beliefs and values, (2) organizational structures and systems, (3) strategy development processes, and (4) supporting programs (see Figure 8.1).

1. *Shared beliefs and values.* All decisions within market-driven organizations begin with the customer and the associated opportunities for advantage. Firms such as Federal Express, Intel, and 3M exhibit these values. Providing superior quality and service on the customer's own terms is a basic value that permeates the entire organization and is continually supported and reinforced by the actions of senior managers. In turn, there is attention to service at every level of value creation in the company. Included here are internal activities that encourage production line employees to appreciate that the customer they must satisfy is the next person on the assembly line.

2. *Organization structure and systems.* Market-driven organizations employ an organization structure that mirrors the segmentation plan of the firm, so that responsibilities for serving each primary market segment are clearly defined. Moreover, the employees closest to the customers are given the power and authority to meet customer needs. Federal Express, with over 40,000 employees in more than three hundred cities worldwide, involves a maximum of only five organizational layers between its nonmanagement employees and its chief operating officer or chief executive officer. Incentive systems emphasize the need to go "to the limit" to insure customer satisfaction.[9]

---

[7]Frank V. Cespedes, *Concurrent Marketing: Integrating Product, Sales, and Service* (Boston, Mass.: Harvard Business School Press, 1995), pp. 267–270.

[8]Ibid., chap. 10.

[9]James Brian Quinn, *Intelligent Enterprise: A Knowledge and Service Based Paradigm for Industry* (New York: The Free Press, 1992), p. 136.

Figure 8.1 Dimensions of Market-Driven Management

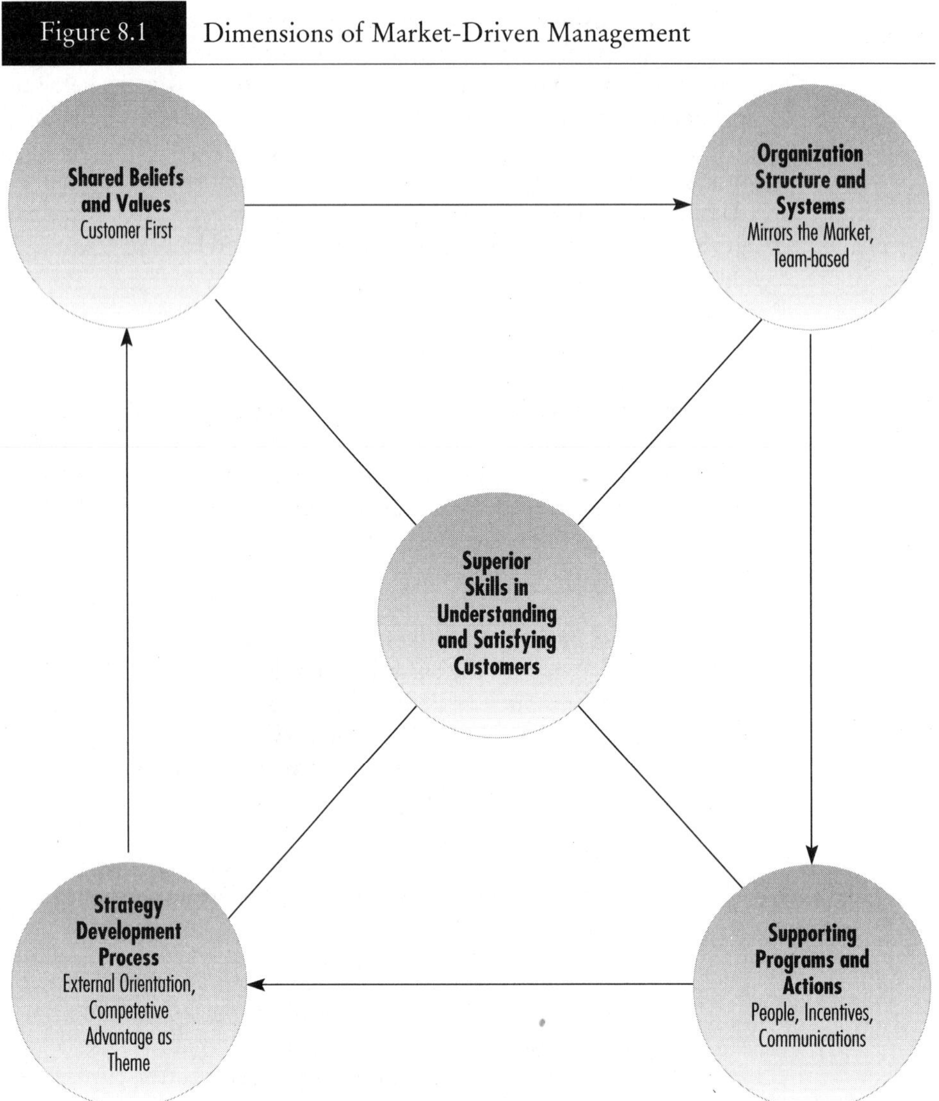

Source: George S. Day, *Market Driven Strategy: Processes for Creating Value* (New York: The Free Press, 1990), p. 358. Reprinted with permission of The Free Press, a division of Simon & Schuster. Copyright © 1990 by George S. Day.

3. *Strategy development.* Rather than rely on rigid systems geared to the preparation of annual budgets, market-driven firms operate with planning systems that are adaptive, participative, and well grounded in appropriate market information. Adaptive planning is facilitated by the astute blending of information from top-down and bottom-up sources, and is directed to helping the organization learn how to cope with a changing

environment. Learning takes place in a participative context, largely occurring in multifunctional teams where operating managers debate, resolve strategic issues, and select strategic options.

4. *Supporting programs and actions.* A customer-first orientation is deeply ingrained in a market-driven firm and is particularly apparent in each "moment of truth" for the organization—the point of contact between the customer and the organization. At Intel, teams are constantly formed and re-formed around challenging and ambitious projects. Using variants of this system to manage its technological resources, Intel has become a consistent leader in semiconductor innovation.[10] At 3M, employees are encouraged to champion new products that provide solutions to customer problems, such as its Post-it Software Notes (see Figure 8.2).

George Day emphasizes the benefits of a customer-first orientation:

> *When everyone understands the importance of putting the customer first, while staying ahead of the competition, they have a reason for doing their jobs. Then "quality" becomes an understood dedication rather than an imposed dictum, "fast response" a meaningful innovation rather than a mechanical metric, "market share" an earned result rather than a warlike target....*[11]

Assessing Competitive Advantage[12]

Competitive advantage can be examined from the vantage point of competitors or of customers. A competitor-based assessment targets this question: How do our capabilities and offerings compare with those of competitors? Here the focus is on identifying areas where the firm has relative superiority in skills and resources. In contrast, a customer-oriented assessment involves a detailed analysis of customer benefits by segment to identify those actions a company might take to improve performance.

George Day and Robin Wensley point out that:

> *A competitor-centered perspective leads to a preoccupation with costs and controllable activities that can be compared directly with corresponding activities of close rivals. Customer-focused approaches have the advantage of examining the full range of competitive choices in light of the customers' needs and perceptions of superiority, but lack an obvious connection to activities and variables that are controlled by management.*[13]

---

[10]Richard Brandt, "Tiny Transistors and Cold Pizza," *Business Week.* 29 March 1993, pp. 94–95.
[11]Day, *Market-Driven Strategy,* p. 375.
[12]The discussion in this section draws on George S. Day and Robin Wensley, "Assessing Advantage: A Framework for Diagnosing Competitive Superiority," *Journal of Marketing* 52 (April 1988): pp. 1–20. See also Stanley F. Slater, "The Challenges of Sustaining Competitive Advantage," *Industrial Marketing Management* 25 (January 1996): pp. 47–58.
[13]Ibid., Day and Wensley, p. 2.

Figure 8.2 3M Ad Emphasizing Its Position as an Innovation Leader

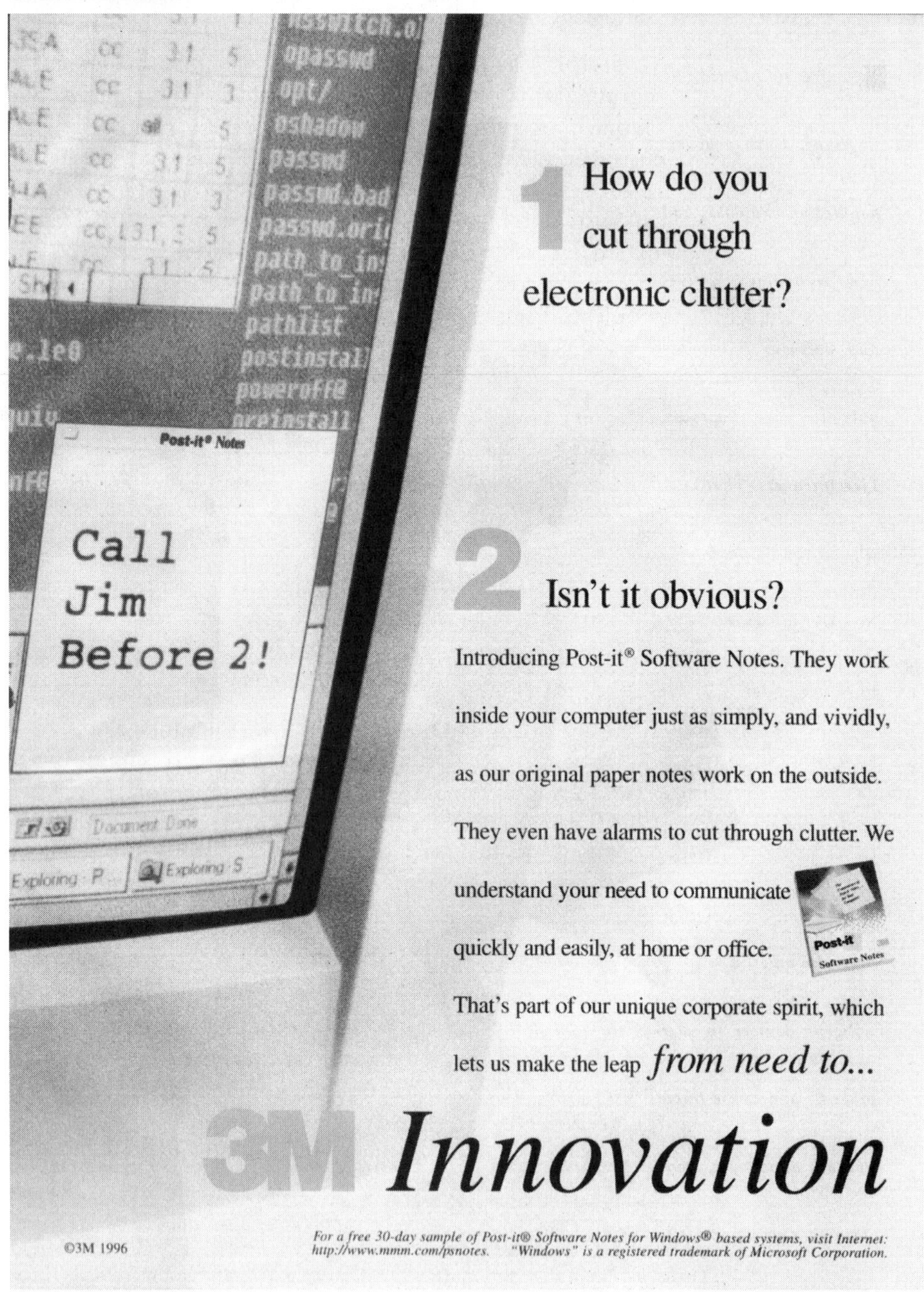

Source: Courtesy of 3M Company.

Figure 8.3 The Elements of Competitive Advantage

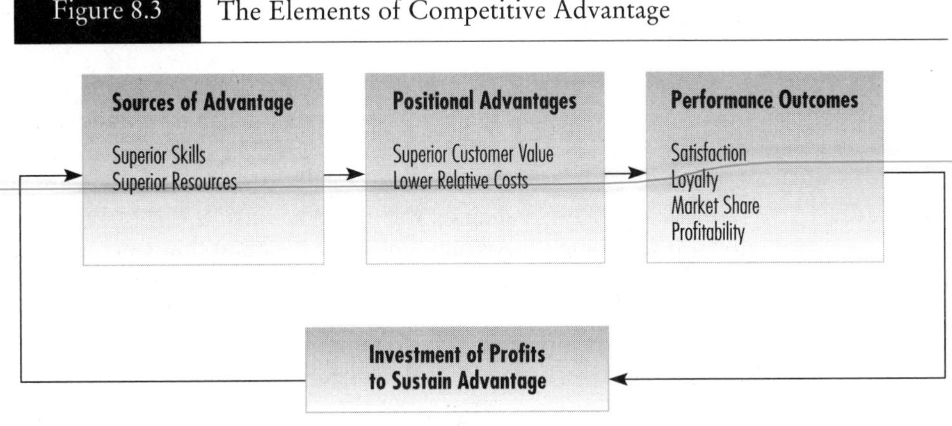

Source: George S. Day and Robin Wensley, "Assessing Advantage: A Framework for Diagnosing Competitive Superiority," *Journal of Marketing* 52 (April 1988): p. 3. Reprinted with permission of the American Marketing Association.

Observe that a balance of these perspectives is provided in Figure 8.3. Positions of advantage are based on the provision of superior customer value or on the achievement of lower relative costs and the resulting profitability and market share performance. Importantly, positional and performance superiority are derived from relative superiority in the skills and resources that a firm has to deploy. In turn, these skills and resources are an outgrowth of past investments made to enhance a firm's competitive position. To maintain a position of advantage, the firm must erect barriers that make imitation by competitors more difficult. Because these barriers to imitation are continually eroding, the firm must make a continuing stream of investments to sustain or improve the advantage.

SOURCES OF ADVANTAGE

A business marketing firm gains a competitive advantage through its superior skills and resources. **Superior skills** are the distinctive capabilities of key personnel that set them apart from the personnel of competing firms. Some of the benefits of superior skills emerge from the ability to perform individual functions more effectively than other firms. To illustrate, superior engineering may lead to greater reliability in the finished product. Other skills result from the systems and organizational structures that enable a company to adapt faster and more responsively to changing market requirements.

James Brian Quinn emphasizes the importance of a sharp strategic focus:

Each company should focus its strategic investments and management attention on those core competencies—usually intellectual or service activities—

> *where it can achieve and maintain "best in world" status, i.e., a significant long-term competitive advantage.*[14]

To illustrate, Boeing cannot possibly design and manufacture more than a small portion of the many components and subsystems that are embodied in its planes. While producing some systems where it has special expertise, Boeing concentrates on the core competencies of aircraft design, relationships with its worldwide customers, aircraft assembly, and managing the massive logistics systems necessary to support its global procurement program. Experts speculate that Boeing could use its systems expertise and knowledge of air travel to penetrate markets such as air-traffic control and reservation systems.[15]

Superior resources are more tangible requirements for advantage that enable a firm to exercise its capabilities. Included among superior resources are the following elements:

- Number of salespersons and service representatives by territory, region, and market
- Expenditures on advertising and promotional support
- Distribution coverage (number of industrial distributors who carry the firm's products)
- Scale of manufacturing facilities and the availability of automated assembly lines
- Expenditures on R&D

Often, competitor analysis centers on making direct comparisons and ranking key competitors on each skill or resource dimension. Benchmarking goes much further.

BENCHMARKING

To define and nurture core competencies, benchmarking provides a valuable tool that goes beyond a mere analysis of competitors. Benchmarking involves identifying the best practices employed by organizations worldwide, learning about them, and implementing them in the firm. While competitive analysis is limited to firms that produce similar products or services, benchmarking involves a function-against-function comparison using firms drawn from diverse industries. Any excellent company that has the same type of operation, customer group, or information can be used. For example, in addition to examining direct competitors, Xerox benchmarked L. L. Bean for distribution procedures, Procter & Gamble for marketing, Deere

---

[14]Quinn, *Intelligent Enterprise,* p. 32.

[15]Andy Reinhardt and Seanna Browder, "Booming Boeing," *Business Week,* 30 September 1996, pp. 118–125.

Managing in the 21st Century

CHIEF LEARNING OFFICERS

A growing number of U.S. corporations such as U.S. West, General Electric (G.E.), Monsanto, Hewlett-Packard, and Coca-Cola have created a new senior executive position. The titles vary from chief learning officer to chief knowledge officer to director of knowledge management. While the title varies, the task is the same: to gather the knowledge from a corporation's far-flung divisions and to apply that knowledge where it will do the most good.

For example, Steven Kerr, who assumes this role at G.E., identifies best practices in one of the firm's divisions and applies this knowledge to improve the performance of another division. Alternatively, Richard Baumbusch, the learning officer at U.S. West, accompanied repair crews on service calls in Arizona to study what affected their performance. He found that service employees tended to be more productive when they received regular feedback from supervisors. He measured performance improvements and applied the lessons learned throughout the company, which employs more than 50,000 people in 14 states.

Organizations that develop a capacity for learning will gain a competitive advantage. Likewise, leaders who ask, listen, learn, and apply that knowledge will have a significant edge over their slower and less proactive competitors.

Leah Beth Ward, "In the Executive Alphabet, You Call Them CLO's," *The New York Times*, 12 February 1996, p. C12.

Company for central computer operations, and Florida Power & Light for its quality process. Valuable insights were likewise gathered from the other firms and measurable goals were established for each function.[16] A senior executive at Motorola, a firm that embraces benchmarking, notes: "The further away from our industry we reach for comparisons, the happier we are. We are seeking competitive superiority, after all, not just competitive parity."[17]

POSITIONS OF ADVANTAGE

What we see in the market—from the perspective of customers or competitors—is the positional advantage of a business. This can be achieved by providing the lowest delivered cost or by providing superior customer value.

[16]Robert C. Camp, "Competitive Benchmarking: Xerox's Powerful Quality Tool," in *Making Total Quality Happen*, ed. Frank Caropreso (New York: The Conference Board, 1990), pp. 35–37. For a related treatment, see David A. Garvin, "Leveraging Processes for Strategic Advantage," *Harvard Business Review* 73 (September/October 1995): pp. 75–90.

[17]A. Steven Walleck, J. David O'Halloran, and Charles A. Leader, "Benchmarking World-Class Performance," *The McKinsey Quarterly*, no. 1 (1991): p. 10.

Lowest Delivered Cost Position

An overall cost advantage is obtained by performing most activities at a lower cost than competitors while offering a comparable product. To illustrate, NUCOR has achieved a low-cost position in the steel industry by making extensive use of scrap metal rather than iron ore and by producing all of its steel using the efficient continuous-casting method. To succeed, a cost strategy must offer an acceptable level of value to customers. If the low-cost position is achieved by providing marginal quality or eliminating desired features, the price discount demanded by customers will more than offset the cost advantage.

Value Superiority

George Day and Robin Wensley explain value superiority in the following way:

> *A business is differentiated when some value-adding activities are performed in a way that leads to perceived superiority along dimensions that are valued by customers. For these activities to be profitable, the customer must be willing to pay a premium for the benefits and the premium must exceed the added costs of superior performance.*[18]

Dwight Gertz and João Baptista elaborate:

> *A company's product or service is competitively superior if, at price equality with competing products, target segments always choose it. Thus, value is defined in terms of customer choice in a competitive context.*[19]

There are many ways for a firm to differentiate products and service.

- Provide superior service or technical assistance competence through speed, responsiveness to complex orders, or ability to solve special customer problems
- Provide superior quality that reduces customer costs or improves their performance
- Offer innovative product features that employ new technologies
- Gain broad distribution coverage

CONVERTING SKILLS AND RESOURCES INTO SUPERIOR POSITIONS

Michael Porter proposes that the drivers of positional advantage are those particular skills and resources that have the greatest impact on reducing costs or creating value to customers.[20] There are two principal types: cost drivers and drivers of differentiation.

---

[18]Day and Wensley, "Assessing Advantage," pp. 3–4.

[19]Dwight L. Gertz and João P. A. Baptista, *Grow to Be Great: Breaking the Downsizing Cycle* (New York: The Free Press, 1995), p. 128.

[20]Michael E. Porter, *Competitive Advantage: Creating and Sustaining Superior Performance* (New York: The Free Press, 1985).

Drivers of Cost Differences

Cost drivers represent the structural determinants of each activity (for example, production) that are largely under a company's control. The principal driver, **economies of scale,** reflects increased efficiency due to size. Large plants cost less per unit to build and operate than smaller plants. Scale effects also apply to many other cost elements such as sales, distribution, research and development, and purchasing.

Learning is a second driver of costs and represents efficiency improvements that result from practice and the exercise of skill and ingenuity in repetitive activities. To illustrate, personnel at Intel learned how to improve the performance of a piece of production equipment and thereby reduced the cost of producing an advanced microchip.

A third cost driver is the extent of **linkages** of activities within a firm. The cost of one activity (for example, inventory) may depend on how another activity is performed (for example, production). To illustrate, closer coordination between purchasing and production may reduce inventory carrying costs. Other drivers of cost that may be important include the rate of capacity utilization, the degree of vertical integration, and the sharing of activities across several business units (for example, a common sales force).

Differentiation

Drivers of differentiation represent the possible underlying reasons why one firm outperforms another on attributes important to customers. Three principal drivers are policy choices, linkages, and timing:

1. **Policy choices** concern what activities to perform and how aggressively to perform them. These include product or service features and performance, level of promotion, and the skills and experience of personnel employed in the activity.
2. **Linkages** among key activities such as coordination between the firm and suppliers can speed product development, while linkages between sales and service can improve the effectiveness of order handling.
3. **Timing** of entry provides first-mover advantages in a market.

Other drivers of differentiation include location, synergy from sharing a sales force or other activity with another division of the firm, or economies derived from large-scale operations that permit broader market coverage or more responsive service through a number of locations. When activated by an effective strategy, the drivers of differentiation correspond to the sources of advantage that reside in the superior skills or resources of the firm.

Marketing's Strategic Role

Many firms—like Johnson and Johnson, Motorola, and Dow Chemical—have numerous divisions, product lines, products, and brands. Policies established at the corporate level provide the framework for strategy development in each business division to ensure survival and growth of the entire enterprise. In turn, corporate and divisional policies establish the boundaries within which individual product or market managers develop strategy.

THE HIERARCHY OF STRATEGIES

Three major levels of strategy dominate most large multiproduct organizations: (1) corporate strategy, (2) business-level strategy, and (3) functional strategy.[21]

Corporate strategy defines the businesses in which a company will compete, preferably in a manner that utilizes resources to convert distinctive competence into competitive advantage. Essential questions at this level include: What are our core competencies? What businesses are we in? What businesses should we be in? How should we allocate resources across these businesses to achieve our overall organizational goals and objectives? At this level of strategy, the role of marketing is to (1) assess market attractiveness and the competitive effectiveness of the firm, (2) promote a customer orientation to the various constituencies in management decision making, and (3) formulate the firm's overall value proposition (as a reflection of its distinctive competencies, in terms reflecting customer needs) and to articulate it to the market and to the organization at large. According to Frederick Webster Jr., "At the corporate level, marketing managers have a critical role to play as advocates, for the customer and for a set of values and beliefs that put the customer first in the firm's decision making...."[22]

Business-level strategy centers on how a firm will compete in a given industry and will position itself against its competitors. The focus of competition is not between corporations; rather, it is between their individual business units. A **strategic business unit (SBU)** is a single business or collection of businesses that has a distinct mission, a responsible manager, and its own competitors, and that is relatively independent of other business units. The 3M Corporation has defined 20 strategic business units, each of which develops a plan describing how its particular mix of products will be managed to secure a competitive advantage consistent with the level of investment and risk that management is willing to accept. An SBU could be one or more divisions of the industrial firm, a product line within one division, or, on occasion, a single product. Strategic business units may share resources such as a sales force with other business units in order to achieve economies of scale. An SBU may serve one or many product-market units.

For each business unit within the corporate portfolio, the following essential questions must be answered: How can we compete most effectively for the product-market served by the business unit? What distinctive skills can give the business unit

---

[21]This discussion draws on Frederick E. Webster Jr., "The Changing Role of Marketing in the Corporation," *Journal of Marketing* 56 (October 1992): pp. 1–17.

[22]Ibid., p. 11.

a competitive advantage? Similarly, the CEO at G.E., Jack Welch, asks his operating executives to crisply answer the following questions:[23]

- Describe the global competitive environment in which you operate.
- In the last three years, what have your competitors done?
- In the same period, what have you done to them in the marketplace?
- How might they attack you in the future?
- What are your plans to leapfrog them?

The marketing function contributes to the planning process at this level by providing a detailed and complete analysis of customers and competitors and the firm's distinctive skills and resources for competing in particular market segments.

Functional strategy centers on how resources allocated to the various functional areas can be used most efficiently and effectively to support the business-level strategy. The primary focus of marketing strategy at this level is to allocate and coordinate marketing resources and activities to achieve the firm's objective within a specific product market.

STRATEGY FORMULATION AND THE HIERARCHY[24]

The interplay among the three levels of the strategy hierarchy can be illustrated by examining the collective action perspective of strategy formulation.[25] This approach applies to strategic decisions that (1) cut across functional areas, (2) involve issues related to the organization's long-term objectives, or (3) involve the allocation of resources across business units or product markets. Included here are decisions regarding the direction of corporate strategy, the application of a core technology, or the choice of an alliance partner.

Observe in Figure 8.4 that strategic decision processes often involve the active participation of several functional interest groups who hold markedly different beliefs concerning the appropriateness of particular strategies or corporate goals. Strategic decisions represent the outcome of a bargaining process among functional interest groups (including marketing), each of whom may interpret the proposed strategy in an entirely different light.

---

[23]Noel M. Tichy and Stratford Sherman, *Control Your Destiny or Someone Else Will* (New York: Doubleday, 1993), p. 26.

[24]Gary L. Frankwick, James C. Ward, Michael D. Hutt, and Peter H. Reingen, "Evolving Patterns of Organizational Beliefs in the Formation of Marketing Strategy," *Journal of Marketing* 58 (April 1994): pp. 96–110; see also Michael D. Hutt, Beth A. Walker, and Gary L. Frankwick, "Hurdle the Cross-Functional Barriers to Strategic Change," *Sloan Management Review* 36 (spring 1995): pp. 22–30.

[25]Orville C. Walker Jr., Robert W. Ruekert, and Kenneth J. Roering, "Picking Proper Paradigms: Alternative Perspectives on Organizational Behavior and Their Implications for Marketing Management Research," in *Review of Marketing*, ed. Michael J. Houston (Chicago: American Marketing Association, 1987), pp. 3–36.

Figure 8.4 A Collective Action Perspective of the Strategy Formulation Process

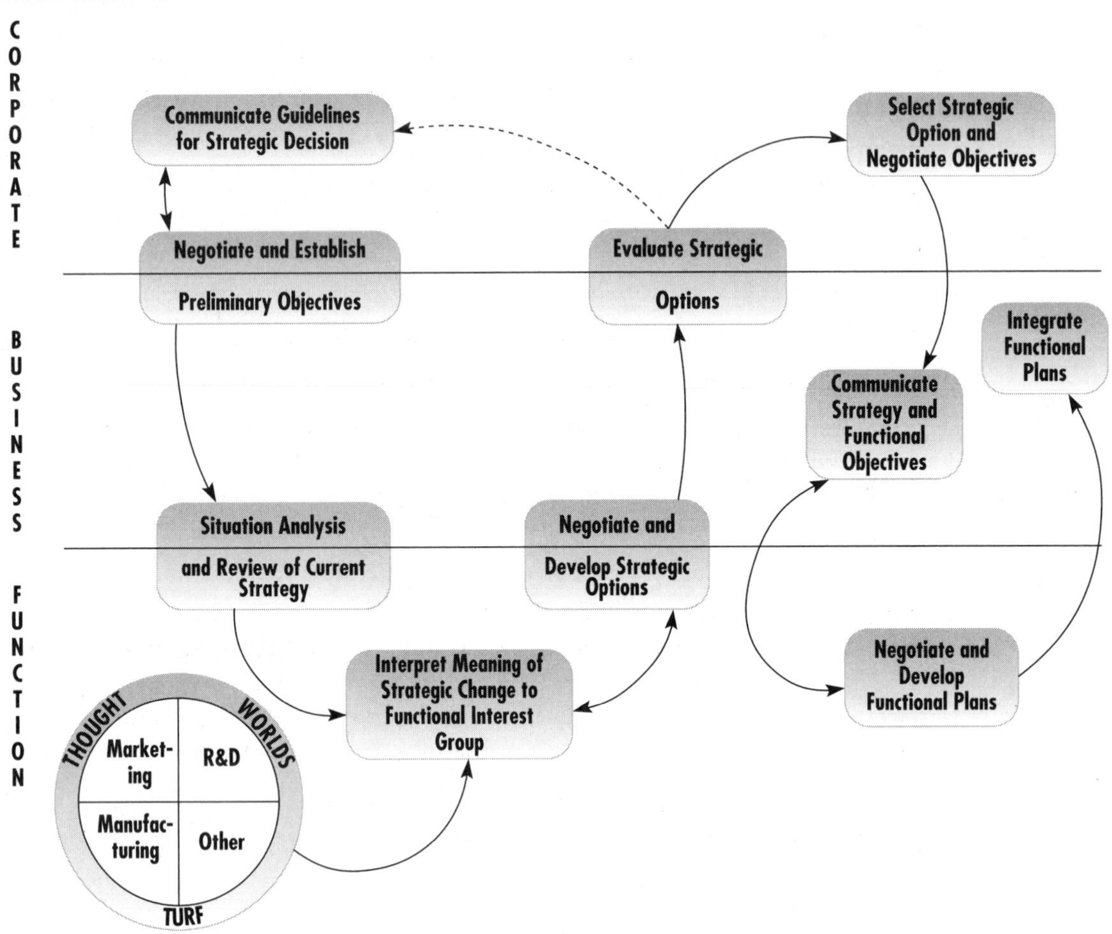

Source: Gary L. Frankwick, James C. Ward, Michael D. Hutt, and Peter H. Reingen, "Evolving Patterns of Organizational Beliefs in the Formation of Strategy," *Journal of Marketing* 58 (April 1994): p. 98. Reprinted with permission from *Journal of Marketing*, published by the American Marketing Association.

Turf Issues and Thought-World Views

Two forces contribute to the conflict that often divides participants in the strategy formulation process. First, different meanings assigned to a proposed strategy are often motivated by deeper differences in what might be called "organizational subcultures." Subcultures exist in an organization when one subunit shares different values, beliefs, and goals than another subunit, resulting in different **thought worlds.** For example, marketing managers are concerned with market opportunities and competitors, while R&D managers view technical sophistication and innovation as means to organizational success. Second, functional managers are likely to resist those strategic changes that threaten their **turf.** To the extent that the subunit domain defines the individual's identity and connotes prestige and power, the organizational member may be quite reluctant to see the domain altered by a strategic decision.

Negotiated Outcomes

Collective decisions emerge from a process of negotiation and compromise among partisan participants. The differences in goals, thought worlds, and self-interests across participants lead to conflicts concerning what actions should be taken. Choices must be negotiated with each interest group attempting to achieve its own ends. The ultimate outcomes of collective decisions tend to unfold in an incremental manner and depend more on the partisan values and influence of the various interest groups than on rational analysis. A study of highly contested strategic decision in a *Fortune* 500 company illustrates the tension that may exist between marketing and R&D.

Two marketing executives describe how the decision was ultimately resolved.[26] According to the marketing manager:

> *[Marketing] did an extremely effective job of stepping right in the middle of it and strangling it.... What has happened is by laying out the market unit concerns and again, refocusing on the fact that we are market-based, basically what Marketing did was force the R&D team into submission where they no longer have the autonomy they once had to go about making decisions—they now get input. And whether it's formal or informal, they definitely get the buy-in of marketing before they move forward on what they're doing now.*

According to the vice president of marketing:

> *Before I felt it was technology driving the process. Now I feel that technology is partnering with the marketplace. And the reason I feel that way is because we have [marketing people] in place that are working closely with how the technology develops.*

Figure 8.5 illustrates how Oracle Systems promotes its software as a tool for coordinating activities across functional areas and business units.

Implications for Marketing Managers

In advocating a particular strategic course, marketing managers must be sensitive to the likely response that an initiative may arouse in other functional interest groups. To build pockets of commitment and trust, managers should develop and use a communication network that includes organizational members who have a major stake in the decision. These personal networks can be used by marketing managers to understand the interests of other stakeholders, communicate their own interests clearly and sensitively, and thus diffuse the anxiety of others concerning threats to their turf.

---

[26]Frankwick, Ward, Hutt, and Reingen, "Evolving Patterns of Organizational Beliefs," pp. 107–108.

Figure 8.5 The Challenge of Achieving Cross-Functional Coordination

"Only Oracle Applications provide the flexibility we need to integrate 22 business units in 120 locations across 27 countries."

Dr. Keith Turnbull, Executive Vice President

Alcoa

Alcoa, the world's largest manufacturer of aluminum and related products, operates 22 independent business units spanning 27 countries. They needed applications that each business unit could rapidly adapt while still sharing common business process and data. Alcoa chose Oracle Applications.

Market Management
Supply Chain Management
Human Resources
Manufacturing
Projects
Finance
Applied Technology

Oracle is the world's fastest-growing supplier of open business applications, with more manufacturing and financial application sites running than anyone else.

Oracle Applications automate your entire enterprise with over 30 integrated software modules for finance, supply chain management, manufacturing, project systems, human resources and market management.

Do your business applications provide the flexibility you need to manage your business? If not, call Oracle at 1-800-633-1057, ext. 10060 today. Or find us on the Web at http://www.oracle.com/applications

Source: Courtesy of Oracle Systems Corporation.

Creating Strategy in High-Technology Industries

Forecasting the future and charting a strategic course are especially difficult in high-technology industries. Compaq Computer, a leader in the personal computer (PC) market, grew from zero to $1 billion in sales volume in less than five years. Hewlett-Packard's PC printer business became a $10 billion enterprise in less than a decade, and, over a 15-year stretch, Microsoft has grown from a specialized software company to the richest and most powerful software company in the world.[27] The winds of change continue. Firms such as Oracle Corporation and Sony are committing hundreds of millions of dollars to designing simple information appliances to access the Internet.[28] Sony, for example, will offer consumers a variety of easy-to-use appliances, including Web-browsing video games and digital televisions that double as Internet cruisers. Under such chaotic conditions, how can senior executives make informed strategic decisions in high-technology industries?

DYNAMIC FORCES

In dynamic industries, strategic actions will eventually begin to lead or lag behind the strategic intent that was carefully orchestrated by the firm's top management team. Consider the transformation of the computer industry[29] (see Figure 8.6). In 1980, a firm such as Digital Equipment Company (DEC) competed in this industry with its own vertical block of semiconductor chips, computer operating systems, and application software that was then sold as a package by the DEC sales force. The development of the microprocessor signaled a change in the industry. By combining what before had been many chips into a single chip, the microprocessor could be used to produce all types of personal computers. Moreover, the microprocessor provided the basic building block for the industry and fueled the efficient mass production of personal computers for home and office users. Over time, a new horizontal computer industry emerged with a new competitive order. Some firms like DEC, which had prospered in the old vertical computer industry, suffered while some new entrants, such as Dell Computer and Compaq Computer, thrived.

MAJOR TURNING POINTS[30]

Defined by top management, **strategic intent** represents an ambitious target that a firm is pursuing over the coming decade and emphasizes the distinctive competencies that must

---

[27]Geoffrey A. Moore, *Inside the Tornado: Marketing Strategies from Silicon Valley's Cutting Edge* (New York: Harper Business, 1995), pp. 3–4.

[28]Ira Sager, "The Race is on to Simplify," *Business Week*, 24 June 1996, p. 74.

[29]Andrew S. Grove, *Only the Paranoid Survive: How to Exploit the Crisis Points That Challenge Every Company and Career* (New York: Currency by Doubleday, 1996), pp. 39–52.

[30]The following discussion is based on: Robert A. Burgelman and Andrew S. Grove, "Strategic Dissonance," *California Management Review* 38 (winter 1996): pp. 8–28.

INSIDE BUSINESS MARKETING

HEWLETT-PACKARD'S STRATEGY IN THE PRINTER MARKET: ATTACK!

Developed by Hewlett-Packard (H-P) engineers, inkjet technology had compelling advantages over laser printers for the mass market: It was less expensive; it was more easily adaptable for color printing; and no other firm had perfected it. At a two-day retreat at a lodge on Oregon's Mount Hood in 1989, a group of marketing managers and engineers came up with a new positioning strategy for the inkjet printer business. Rather than positioning the inkjet as a low-cost alternative to H-P's laser printers, the group concluded that they should go after the Japanese-dominated dot-matrix market. H-P teams began to study Seiko Epson Corporation—the market share leader in the dot-matrix printer business. They surveyed Epson's customers, studied its marketing strategies and public financial data, and tore apart its printers for ideas in design and manufacturing. They found that Epson used price cuts as a tactical weapon to ward off challengers; consumers liked the reliability of Epson machines; and Epson printers were designed to be manufactured easily. H-P responded by tripling its warranty to three years and redesigning its printers for ease of manufacturing.

H-P quickly gained a lead in the marketplace. When Japanese printer makers tried to move into the inkjet market, they found that H-P had a lock on many important patents.(H-P has 50 patents that cover how ink travels through the printer head.) Continuous improvements in manufacturing and economies of scale enabled H-P to undercut the prices of competitors. For example, before NEC Corporation could introduce its low-priced monochrome inkjet printer, H-P introduced an improved color version and slashed prices on its popular black-and-white model by 40 percent over six months. NEC withdrew its new, overpriced entry a few months after the introduction.

H-P invested in a laboratory breakthrough and then kept market share by enforcing rules that their Japanese competitors have used for years: Go for mass markets, cut costs, sustain a rapid pace in unleashing product variations and price cuts, and target the enemy.

Source: Stephen Kreider Yoder, "Shoving Back: How H-P Used Tactics of the Japanese to Beat Them at Their Game," *The Wall Street Journal,* 8 September 1994, pp. A1, A6.

be developed to achieve this desired competitive position.[31] As industry dynamics begin to change, some organizational members will see danger ahead and will begin to question the firm's current strategic intent. Often, middle managers and salespersons, who are closest to the customer and openly exposed to the competitive threat, sense the changes first. For example, Intel Corporation's core business in the 1970s and early 1980s was dynamic random access memory (DRAM) products. Middle managers at Intel had already begun to devote more resources to microprocessors *before* top management had made the decision to transform itself from a memory company to a microprocessor company.

[31]Gary Hamel and C. K. Prahalad, "Strategic Intent," *Harvard Business Review* 67 (May/June 1989): pp. 63–76.

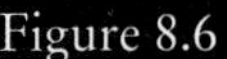

The Transformation of the Computer Industry

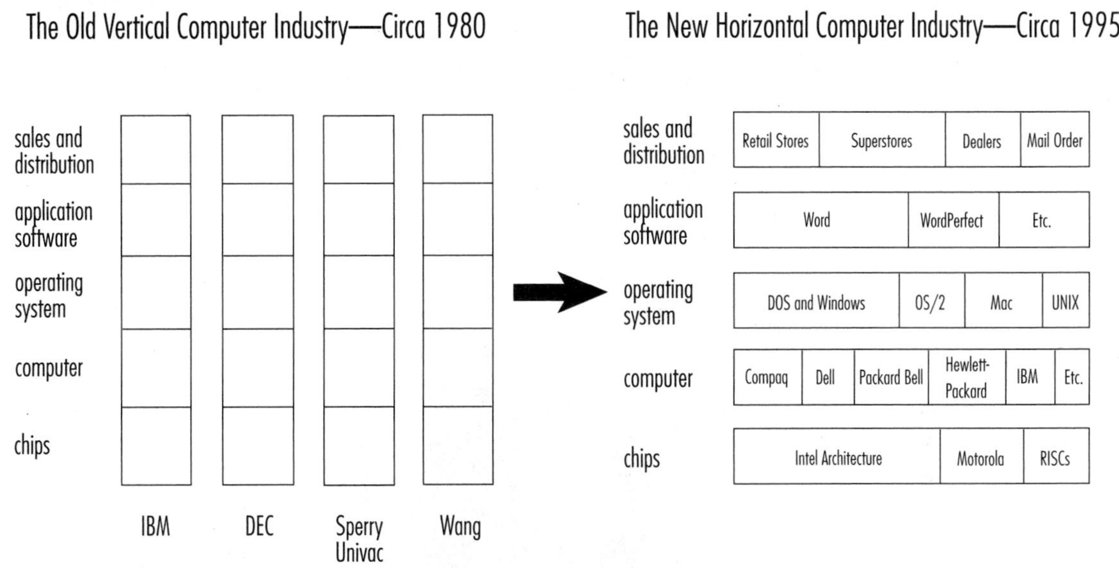

Source: Andrew S. Grove, *Only the Paranoid Survive: How to Exploit the Crisis Points That Challenge Every Company and Career* (New York: Currency by Doubleday, 1996), p. 44. Copyright © 1996 by Andrew S. Grove. Used by permission of Doubleday, a division of Bantam Doubleday Dell Publishing Group, Inc.

Strategic dissonance exists when there is a growing divergence between what the company puts forth as its strategy and the particular actions taken by its managers. As the Intel example illustrates, strategic dissonance often signals that the firm had reached a **strategic inflection point** in its development—a major crossroad for the firm. Robert Burgelman and Andrew Grove define a strategic inflection point as "the giving way of one type of industry dynamics to another; the change of one winning strategy into another; the replacement of an existing technological regime by a new one."[32]

Valley of Death

By altering their profitable growth paths, these changes create a "valley of death" for the existing firms in the industry. Witness the changing fortunes in the computer industry as it was transformed from a vertical industry into a horizontal one (see Figure 8.7). Firms that can successfully develop a new strategic intent that capitalizes on the new industry conditions can traverse the valley of death and enjoy a new era of profitable growth (like that of Intel Corporation). However, those firms that are

---

[32]Burgelman and Grove, "Strategic Dissonance," p. 10.

Figure 8.7 The Transformation Process in a High-Tech Company

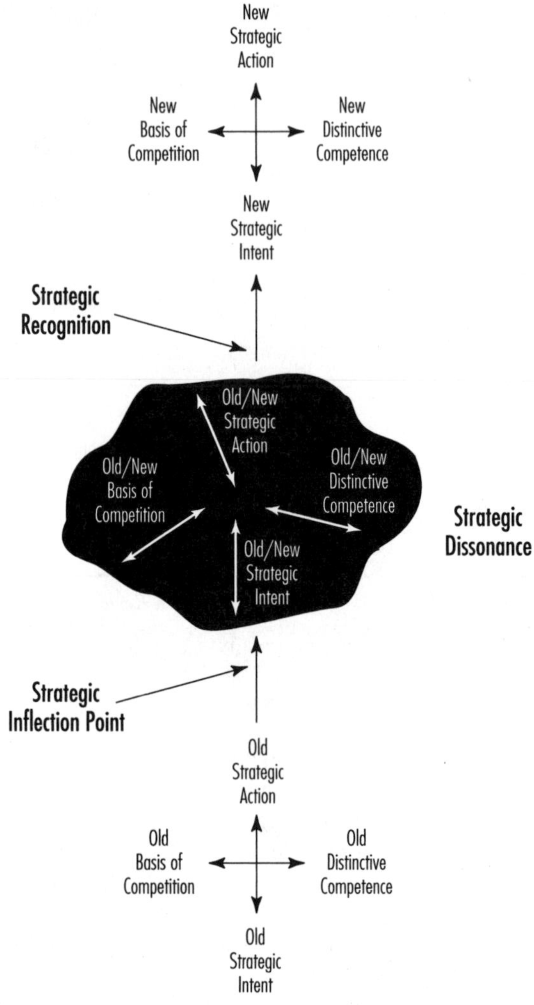

Source: From Robert A. Burgelman and Andrew S. Grove, "Strategic Dissonance," *California Management Review* 38 (winter 1996): p. 18. Copyright © 1996 by the Regents of the University of California. Reprinted from the California Management Review, vol. 38, no. 2. By permission of the Regents.

unable to adapt to the new industry conditions will survive with severely limited performance prospects—or they will die.

STRATEGIC RECOGNITION

How can top management know when an event signals a strategic inflection point in an industry? Andrew Grove, president and CEO of Intel Corporation, notes:

> *Most strategic inflection points, instead of coming in with a bang, approach on little cat feet. They are often not clear until you can look at the events in retrospect. Later, when you ask yourself when you first had an inkling that you were facing a strategic inflection point, your recollections are about a trivial sign hinting that the competitive dynamics had changed.*[33]

Strategic Signals

Business marketers should ask the following questions to explore whether a change in industry conditions signals a strategic inflection point:[34]

1. *Are your key competitors about to change?* When divergent views exist within the firm about the field of competitors that you confront, or the importance of selected competitors seems to be shifting, significant changes may be underway in the industry.
2. *Are key complementors to your product about to change?* **Complementors** are firms that provide supporting products or services, such as software and Internet access in the computer industry. The entry of new complementors may signal that industry dynamics are changing.
3. *Are alarms being sounded by managers and salespersons at the boundary of your organization?* Those closest to the market are often the first to sense important changes in customer behavior or competitive action.

Top Management's Role

By focusing on what they can control, middle managers will often try to adjust their own work to respond to strategic change. Managing such strategic dissonance requires **strategic recognition:** the capacity of top management to appreciate the strategic importance of managerial initiatives after they have been launched but before definitive environmental feedback is available. The role for top management, then, is to recognize the gap between the firm's stated strategy and the actions of its managers, explore the possibility that this may be a strategic inflection point, and openly examine how the gap can be closed by defining a new strategic intent.

FORMULATING NEW STRATEGIC INTENT

Traversing the dark valley associated with a strategic inflection point requires top management to develop a mental image of what the industry will look like and

---

[33]Grove, *Only the Paranoid Survive,* p. 107.
[34]Ibid., pp. 107–108.

what the company's strategy should look like on the other side (see Figure 8.7). To develop a clear strategic course, a balance is required between bottom-up and top-down strategic dialogues. Broad debate among technical, marketing, and strategic points of view must draw upon representatives from different levels in the organization.

Culture Is the Key

Two attributes of an organization's culture can aid a firm in transforming itself and adapting to new industry conditions. First, employees should actively contribute to the debate that surrounds the decision. For example, Intel Corporation's culture actively encourages vigorous debate among employees to thoroughly explore the issues and emphasizes a process that is indifferent to rank. The focus is on finding what is best for the company as opposed to what is best for a particular division or functional area. Intel refers to this mechanism as **constructive confrontation.** New Intel employees are taught how this feature of the culture has been vital to shaping the firm's success.

Second, the strategic processes of the firm should encourage debate but yield clear decisions that are accepted by the entire organization. Often, executives will accelerate decision making by using a two-step process, called **consensus with qualification.**[35] Executives will discuss an issue and attempt to gain a consensus. However, if consensus appears unlikely, the key manager and the most relevant functional head get together and make the choice, guided by the input of the rest of the group. By taking a realistic view of conflict, consensus with qualification speeds decision making. Kathleen Eisenhardt explains why:

> *Most people want a voice in the decision-making process, but are willing to accept that their opinions may not prevail. Consensus with qualification goes one better by giving them added influence when the choice particularly affects their part of the organization.*[36]

Hewlett-Packard: A Learning Organization

Organizations that encourage open debate of strategic issues and that can rally broad organizational support behind the chosen course demonstrate the attributes of a powerful, adaptive learning organization. Take Hewlett-Packard (H-P) for example. The firm has been able to successfully move through several transformations—from instruments to computers, from minicomputer-based technology to microprocessor-based technology. Recently, H-P transformed itself again by becoming the global leader in desktop printing. H-P demonstrates a culture that is ready for a strategic inflection point.

---

[35]Kathleen M. Eisenhardt, "Speed and Strategic Choice: How Managers Accelerate Decision Making," *California Management Review* 32 (spring 1990): pp. 49–56.

[36]Ibid., p. 50.

Marketing's Cross-Functional Relationships

The creation of a boundaryless organization is an important value that underlies G.E.'s current organizational style. To achieve this goal, CEO Jack Welch emphasizes the importance of eliminating artificial barriers—removing the horizontal barriers that divide functional areas, the vertical barriers that come from the formal hierarchy, and the external barriers that prevent close relationships with customers, suppliers, and alliance partners.[37] The restructuring of organizations, the reengineering of business processes, and the search for quicker, more efficient responses to changing customer needs and competitive realities are important strategic priorities in business practice. As firms adopt leaner and more agile structures and emphasize cross-functional teams, the business marketing manager assumes an important and challenging role in strategy formulation.

All business marketing decisions—product, price, promotion, or distribution—are affected, directly or indirectly, by other functional areas. In turn, business decisions in research and development and in manufacturing and procurement, as well as adjustments in the overall corporate strategy, are influenced by marketing considerations. Business marketing planning must be coordinated and synchronized with corresponding planning efforts in R&D, procurement, finance, manufacturing, and other areas.

CROSS-FUNCTIONAL CONNECTIONS

Effective business marketing managers develop close working relationships with their colleagues in manufacturing, R&D, logistics, and other functions. They understand the critical role that each function assumes in the design and execution of strategy and, in turn, what each functional area requires from marketing.

Table 8.2 explores the interrelationships between marketing and four business functions. Observe the significant role that each assumes in the development and implementation of marketing strategy. For example, new product development is the focus of the marketing–R&D interface, from idea generation to performance evaluation of the finished product. The importance of nurturing an effective marketing–R&D interface is reinforced by the sizable investments R&D commands in industrial firms. Motorola, Boeing, and G.E. each spend more than $1 billion annually and IBM more than $5 billion on R&D investments.[38] Successful new product developments depend heavily on marketing research for product features desired by target market segments and for how potential organizational buyers view trade-offs among product attributes. If marketing fails to provide adequate market and competitive information, R&D personnel will be in the precarious position of determining the direction of new product development without the benefit of market knowledge. A successful relationship between marketing and R&D requires that each understands the strengths, weaknesses, and potential contributions of the other. For instance, a promising new product spawned by R&D may fail because the firm lacks the marketing strengths required to penetrate a particular market segment.

---

[37]Tichy and Sherman, *Control Your Destiny or Someone Else Will,* p. 235.

[38]"In the Labs, The Fight to Spend Less, Get More," *Business Week,* 28 June 1993, pp. 102–104.

Table 8.2 Formulating Business Marketing Strategy: Vital Cross-Functional Connections

Function	Contribution to Strategy	Support Required from Marketing
Manufacturing	• Determines the volume, variety, and quality of products that can be marketed • Influences the speed with which the business marketer can respond to changing market or competitive needs	• Accurate and timely sales forecast
R&D	• Provides critical technical direction in new product development process • Remains abreast of competitive technology	• Data on market and competitive trends • Marketing research on product features desired by target segments
Logistics	• Provides on-time accurate shipments to customers • Develops timely order tracking and status reports	• Accurate and timely sales forecasts • Delivery service requirements by customer or segment
Technical service	• Implements post-sale activities such as installation and training • Serves as troubleshooter for customer problems	• Account-specific goals and plans • Promises made to the customer during the selling process

Once a new product is developed and manufactured, the logistics and technical services functions assume special significance in strategy implementation. Two factors assigned particular importance by customers are (1) the speed and reliability of delivery service and (2) the quality and availability of technical service after the sale (see Chapter 4). Close coordination between marketing and both of these vital service functions is required to provide the service level that organizational customers expect.

FUNCTIONALLY INTEGRATED PLANNING: THE MARKETING STRATEGY CENTER[39]

Rather than operating in isolation from other functional areas, the successful business marketing manager is an integrator—one who understands the capabilities of

[39]Michael D. Hutt and Thomas W. Speh, "The Marketing Strategy Center: Diagnosing the Industrial Marketer's Interdisciplinary Role," *Journal of Marketing* 48 (fall 1984): pp. 53–61; see also Jeen-Su Lim and David A. Reid, "Vital Cross-Functional Linkages with Marketing," *Industrial Marketing Management* 22 (February 1993): pp. 159–165.

manufacturing, R&D, and customer service and who capitalizes on their strengths in developing marketing strategies that are responsive to customer needs. **Responsibility charting** constitutes an approach that can be used to classify decision-making roles and to highlight the multifunctional nature of business marketing decision making. The structure of a responsibility chart is provided in Table 8.3. The decision areas (rows) illustrated in the matrix might, for example, relate to a planned product line expansion. The various functional areas that may assume particular roles in this decision process head the columns of the matrix. The alternative roles that can be assumed by participants in the decision-making process are defined in the following list.[40]

1. *Responsible* (R): The manager takes initiative for analyzing the situation, developing alternatives, and assuring consultation with others and then makes the initial recommendation. Upon approval of decision, the role ends.
2. *Approve* (A): The manager accepts or vetoes a decision before it is implemented, or chooses from alternatives developed by the participants assuming a "responsible" role.
3. *Consult* (C): The manager is consulted or asked for substantive input prior to the approval of the decision but does not possess veto power.
4. *Implement* (M): The manager is accountable for the implementation of the decision, including notification of other relevant participants concerning the decision.
5. *Inform* (I): Although not necessarily consulted before the decision is approved, the manager is informed of the decision once it is made.

Representatives of a particular functional area may, of course, assume more than one role in the decision-making process. The technical service manager may be consulted during the new product development process and may also be held accountable for implementing service support strategy. Likewise, the marketing manager may be responsible for and approve many of the decisions related to the product line expansion. For other actions, several decision makers may participate. To illustrate, the business unit manager, after consulting R&D, may approve (accept or veto) a decision for which the marketing manager is responsible.

The members of the organization who become involved in the business marketing decision-making process constitute the marketing strategy center. The composition or functional area representation of the strategy center evolves during the marketing strategy development process, varies from firm to firm, and varies from one strategy situation to another. Likewise, the composition of the marketing strategy center is not strictly prescribed by the organizational chart. The needs of a particular strategy situation, especially the information requirements, significantly influence the composition of the strategy center. Thus, the marketing strategy center shares certain parallels with the buying center (see Chapter 3).

---

[40]Joseph E. McCann and Thomas N. Gilmore, "Diagnosing Organizational Decision Making Through Responsibility Charting," *Sloan Management Review* 25 (winter 1983): pp. 3–15.

Table 8.3 Interfunctional Involvement in Marketing Decision Making: An Illustrative Responsibility Chart

	Organizational Function						
Decision Area	**Marketing**	**Manufacturing**	**R&D**	**Logistics**	**Technical Service**	**Strategic Business Unit Manager**	**Corporate Level Planner**
PRODUCT							
Design specifications							
Performance characteristics							
Reliability							
PRICE							
List price							
Discount structure							
TECHNICAL SERVICE SUPPORT							
Customer training							
Repair							
PHYSICAL DISTRIBUTION							
Inventory level							
Customer service level							
SALES FORCE							
Training							
ADVERTISING							
Message development							
CHANNEL							
Selection							

Note: Decision role vocabulary: R = responsible; A = approve; C = consult; M = implement; I = inform; X = no role in decision

Managing Strategic Interdependencies

A central challenge for the business marketer in the strategy center is to minimize interdepartmental conflict while fostering shared appreciation of the interdependencies with other functional units. Individual strategy center participants are motivated by both personal and organizational goals. Company objectives are interpreted by these individuals in relation to their level in the hierarchy and the department they represent. Various functional units operate under unique reward systems and reflect unique orientations or thought worlds. For example, marketing managers are evaluated on the basis of sales, profits, or market share; production managers on the basis of manufacturing efficiency and cost-effectiveness. In turn, R&D managers may be oriented toward long-term objectives; customer service managers may emphasize more immediate ones. Strategic plans emerge out of a bargaining process among functional areas. Managing conflict, promoting cooperation, and developing coordinated strategies are all fundamental to the business marketer's interdisciplinary role. By understanding the concerns and orientations of personnel from other functional areas, the business marketing manager is better equipped to forge effective cross-unit working relationships.

The Business Marketing Planning Process

The business marketing planning process is inextricably linked to planning in other functional areas and to overall corporate strategy. It takes place within the larger strategic marketing management process of the corporation. To survive and prosper, the business marketer must properly balance the firm's resources with the objectives and opportunities of the environment. Marketing planning is a continuous process that involves the active participation of other functional areas.

THE MARKETING PLAN

Responsive to both corporate and business unit strategy, the marketing plan formally describes all the components of the marketing strategy—markets to be served, products or services to be marketed, price schedules, distribution methods, and so on. The key components of the marketing planning process are highlighted in Figure 8.8. Note that the planning process format centers on clearly defined market segments, a thorough assessment of internal and external problems and opportunities, specific goals, and courses of action. Business marketing intelligence (Chapter 5), market segmentation (Chapter 6), and market potential and sales forecasting (Chapter 7) are fundamental in the planning process.

At a fundamental level, the marketing plan establishes specific objectives by market segment, defines marketing strategy and action programs required to accomplish these objectives, and pinpoints responsibility for the implementation of these programs. Ultimately, the marketing plan translates objectives and strategies into forecasts and budgets that provide a basis for planning by other functional areas of the firm.

Summary

Guided by a deep understanding of the needs of customers and the capabilities of competitors, market-driven organizations are committed to a set of processes, beliefs, and values that promote the achievement of superior performance by satisfying customers

Figure 8.8 The Marketing Planning Process

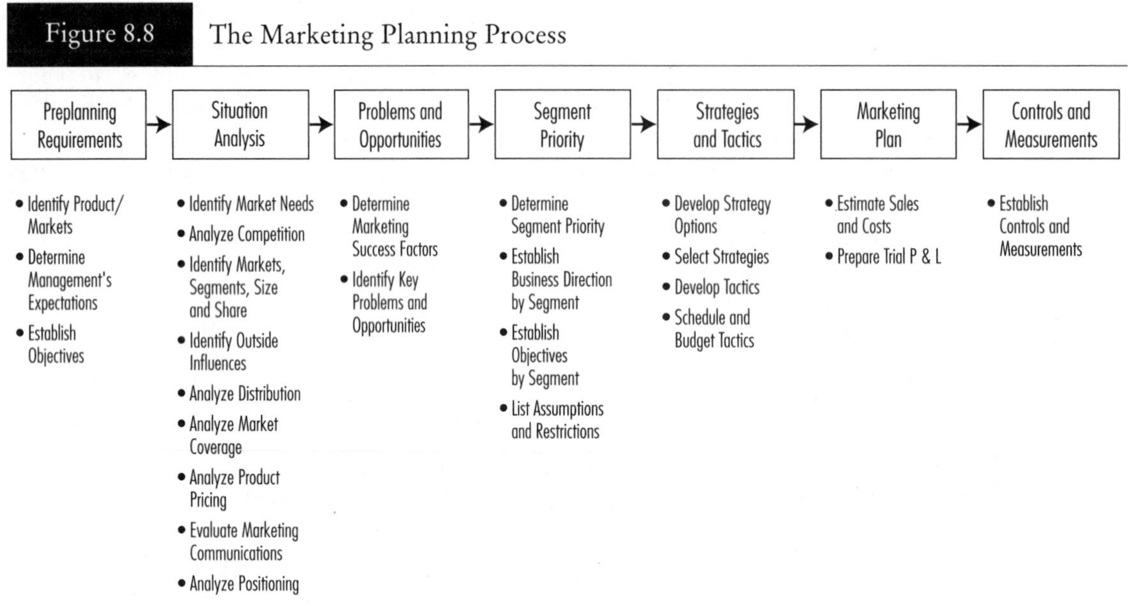

Source: Howard Sutton, *The Marketing Plan in the 1990s,* report no. 951 (New York: The Conference Board, 1990), p. 10. Reprinted by permission of The Conference Board.

better than competitors do. What sets market-driven firms apart is their ability to continuously sense and act on events and trends in their markets. A business marketing firm gains a competitive advantage through its superior skills and resources. To isolate core competencies, benchmarking provides a valuable tool that goes beyond a mere analysis of competitors. Benchmarking involves identifying the best practices employed by organizations around the world, learning about them, and implementing them in the firm. Positions of advantage—providing the lowest delivered cost or superior customer value—can be secured by effectively managing and deploying the skills and resources of the organization.

Because many industrial firms have numerous divisions, product lines, and brands, three major levels of strategy exist in most large organizations: (1) corporate, (2) business level, and (3) functional. Moving down the strategy hierarchy, the focus shifts from strategy formulation to strategy implementation. Firms that operate in high-technology industries must be alert to the rigors that may signal a strategic inflection point—a fundamental change in the basis of competition in the industry. To successfully cope with such change, top management must assess the firm's strategic goals and competencies in light of the new competitive reality. Companies that prosper in high-technology markets demonstrate an ability to transform themselves by adjusting strategic goals, building new competencies, and adapting strategies to the new industry conditions.

Business marketing planning must be coordinated and synchronized with corresponding planning efforts in other functional areas. Strategic plans emerge out of a bargaining process among functional areas. Managing conflict, promoting cooperation, and developing coordinated strategies are all fundamental to the business marketer's role in the firm. A continuous process, marketing planning involves several stages: (1) situation analysis, (2) evaluation of problems and opportunities, (3) formulation of marketing strategy, (4) development of an integrated marketing plan, and (5) measurement and evaluation of results. The result of the planning process is the marketing plan—the formal written description of the marketing strategy. The succeeding chapters will analyze each marketing mix variable.

Discussion Questions

1. Describe the major elements that characterize a market-driven organization and outline the steps a firm might follow in becoming more market driven.

2. Michael Porter proposes that the drivers of positional advantage are those particular skills and resources that have the greatest impact on reducing costs or creating value to customers. Explain.

3. Select a firm such as Federal Express, Apple Computer, IBM, Boeing, G.E., or Caterpillar and assess its competitive advantage. Develop a list of particular skills and resources that are especially important to the selected firm's position of advantage. Give particular attention to those skills and resources that competitors would have the most difficulty in matching.

4. Critique this statement: Positions of advantage tend to erode quickly in high-tech markets. Next, trace the changing fortunes of Apple Computer, Inc. during the past decade.

5. Does the introduction of relatively inexpensive, easy-to-use information appliances by Sony and others signal a strategic inflection point for personal computer makers such as Compaq and key suppliers, like Intel? Explain.

6. Commenting on the decision-making process of his organization, a senior executive noted: "Sometimes the process is bloody, ugly, just like sausage meat being made. It's not pretty to watch but the end results are not too bad." Why do various functional interest groups often embrace conflicting positions during the strategic decision process? How are decisions ever made?

7. Since corporate planners are often consumed with financial and operating details, instead of competitive positioning and the creation of future markets, corporations are moving responsibility for strategy down to the division or business unit level. Describe the advantages of this shift toward a business unit focus.

8. Xerox shifted its goal from being a manufacturer of copier, printer, and facsimile products to becoming a provider of document tools and services

that enhance a customer's productivity. Describe how this new strategic intent may call for new strategies and the development of new core competencies.

9. John F. Welch, G.E.'s aggressive chairman and chief executive officer, has stated that he only wants to stay in businesses where G.E. is number 1 or number 2. How will this clear statement of corporate objectives influence marketing objectives and, in turn, marketing strategy?

10. A day in the life of a business marketing manager will involve interactions with managers from other functions in the firm. First, identify the role that the R&D, manufacturing, and logistics functions assume in the creation and implementation of marketing strategy. Next, describe some of the common sources of conflict that can emerge in cross-functional relationships.

Chapter 9

Business Marketing Strategies for Global Markets

Business marketing firms that restrict their attention to the domestic market are overlooking enormous international market opportunities and a challenging field of competitors. After reading this chapter, you will understand

1. the factors that shape the competitive advantage of a country.
2. the forces that drive the globalization of a particular industry.
3. the spectrum of international market-entry options and the strategic significance of different forms of global market participation.
4. the key strategic marketing issues that emerge as a firm's level of participation in international markets expands.

Motorola is helping the People's Republic of China leapfrog one stage of industrial evolution for which Western nations have invested billions of dollars—the need to tie every home and business together with copper wire. Motorola's pagers and cell phones provide valuable solutions to customers in an unwired world and the firm's sales in China and Hong Kong exceed $3 billion annually. Going forward, the market potential is huge but the competition will be fierce from rivals such as Sweden's Ericsson and Finland's Nokia.[1]

Many large business marketing firms—such as General Electric (G.E.), IBM, Intel, Dow Chemical, Alcoa, Otis Elevator, Boeing, Caterpillar, and Motorola—derive a significant portion of their sales and profits from international markets. These firms also have extensive operating facilities dispersed around the world. For example, in China alone, Motorola employs more than 6,000 people. Likewise,

[1]Melanie Warner, "Motorola Bets Big on China," *Fortune,* 27 May 1996, pp. 116–124.

countless small firms with less familiar names enjoy strong ties with international customers. In addition to extending a firm's base of operations and thereby enhancing sales and profits, participation in global markets can provide an important pathway to a competitive advantage. Meeting the needs of diverse international customers may speed learning in the firm and spawn improvements in product features and quality.

The discussion in this chapter is divided into four parts. First, a foundation for understanding global markets is established by examining the forces that shape the competitive advantage of a nation. Second, attention centers on the factors that are reshaping the way managers think about markets and competitors: the drivers of globalization in an industry. Third, international market-entry options are isolated and described, and, fourth, linked to the central strategy questions that must be addressed by firms as their international operations evolve.

The Competitive Advantage of Nations[2]

As global competition intensifies, national competitiveness has become a major preoccupation of government and business in every nation. Some see the competitiveness of a country as an outgrowth of plentiful national resources. Others argue that competitiveness is driven by cheap and abundant labor or is a macroeconomic phenomenon shaped by exchange rates, interest rates, or government budgeting policies. But Japan has prospered with limited national resources; Germany has been successful despite high wage rates and labor shortages in critical areas; Switzerland, despite appreciating currency; Italy, despite high interest rates; and South Korea, despite government budget deficits. Clearly, none of these factors fully explains the competitive position of industries within a particular country.

Michael Porter suggests that to understand national competitiveness, attention should center on specific industries and industry segments rather than the economy as a whole. Supported by a large research team, he conducted a five-year study of ten important trading nations and focused on this question: *What are the decisive characteristics of a nation that allow its companies to create and sustain competitive advantage in particular industries?* Thus, the study examined those industries in which a nation's companies were internationally successful—that is, possessed a competitive advantage relative to the best worldwide competitors. The findings provide rich insights into the patterns of competition and strategy in the global market.

[2]This section is based on Michael E. Porter, "The Competitive Advantage of Nations," *Harvard Business Review* 68 (March/April 1990): pp. 73–93. See also Andreas F. Graein and C. Samuel Craig, "Economic Performance over Time: Does Porter's Diamond Hold at the National Level?" *International Executive,* 1 May 1996, p. 303.

DETERMINANTS OF NATIONAL COMPETITIVE ADVANTAGE

Firms achieve competitive advantage through acts of innovation. Such innovation can be reflected in a new product design, a new production process, a new marketing approach, or a new method for training employees. Porter asserts that

> *Much innovation is mundane and incremental, depending more on an accumulation of small insights and advances than on a single, major technological breakthrough.... In international markets, innovations that yield competitive advantage anticipate both domestic and foreign needs.*[3]

Once achieved, a competitive advantage can only be sustained through relentless improvement.

Why are particular companies, based in certain countries, capable of consistent innovation? Michael Porter contends that four broad attributes of a nation, individually and as a system, constitute the playing field that each nation establishes and operates for its industries (see Figure 9.1).

Factor Conditions

In technology industries, a nation creates the most important factors of production, such as skilled employees or a scientific base. Moreover, the inventory of factors that a country enjoys at a particular time is less important than the rate and efficiency with which it creates, improves, and deploys them in particular industries. Basic factors of production, such as a pool of labor or a local raw-material source of supply, do not constitute an important advantage in knowledge-intensive industries. In fact, factor disadvantages can force companies to innovate—thereby creating competitive advantage. To illustrate, just-in-time production economizes on the prohibitively expensive space in Japan. Factors that support competitive advantage are those that are highly specialized in relation to an industry's particular needs, such as a pool of venture capital to fund software companies or a scientific institute that specializes in a particular technology.

Demand Conditions

By forcing companies to respond to tough challenges, demand conditions also provide advantages. Japanese companies have pioneered compact, quiet, energy-efficient air-conditioning units to meet the needs of Japanese consumers who must cope with small homes and high energy costs. Across several industries, the tightly constrained space requirements of the Japanese market have forced Japanese companies to innovate, yielding products that are lighter, thinner, shorter, and smaller. Often these products become internationally accepted.

---

[3]Michael E. Porter, "The Competitive Advantage of Nations," p. 74.

Figure 9.1 Determinants of National Competitive Advantage

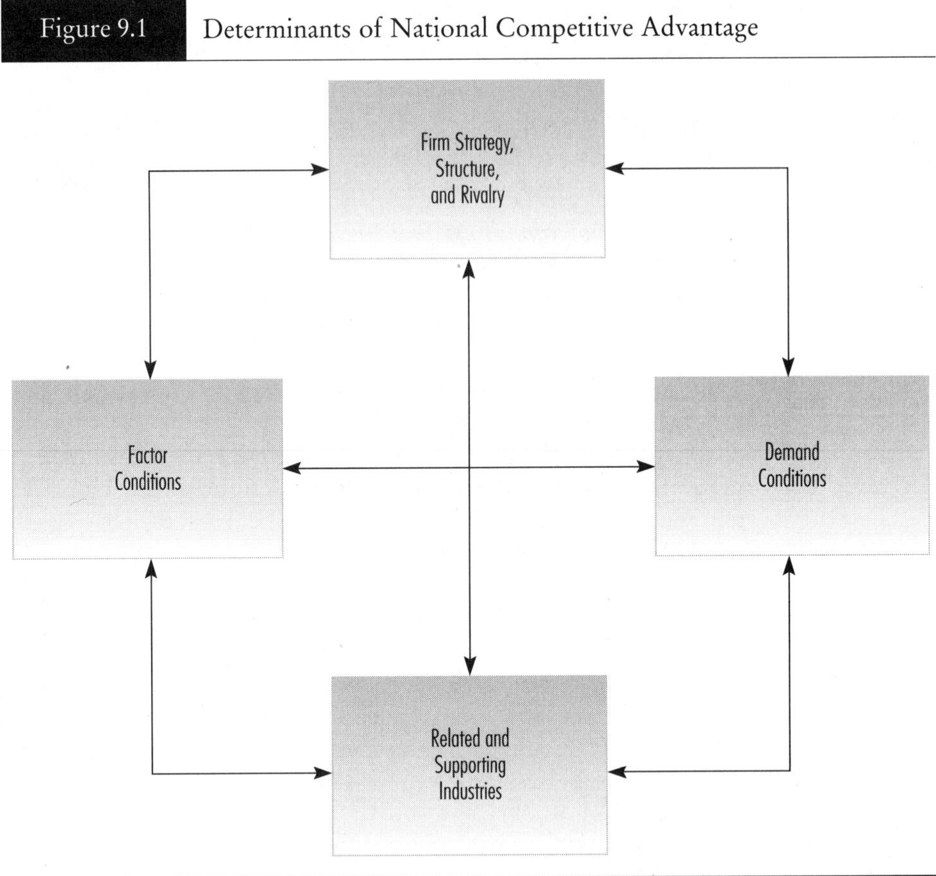

Source: Reprinted by permission of *Harvard Business Review,* from Michael E. Porter, "The Competitive Advantage of Nations," *Harvard Business Review* 68 (March/April 1990): p. 77. Copyright 1990 by the President and Fellows of Harvard College. All rights reserved.

Related and Supporting Industries

A third broad determinant of competitive advantage is the presence in the nation of interconnected industries that are all internationally competitive. In addition to providing cost-efficient inputs on a timely basis, home-based suppliers can provide end users with a steady flow of ideas, information, and innovations. Such advantages are an outgrowth of close working relationships that may be easier to form and sustain in a home market. Although aided by proximity, the parties must actively manage the relationship for it to prosper. The strength of the U.S. computer firms in the global computer market is based on the contributions of several supporting industries that constitute the supply chain: personal computer producers (for example, Compaq Computer); microprocessor suppliers (for example, Intel); producers of semiconductor manufacturing equipment (for example, Applied Materials, Inc.); and leading software developers (for example, Microsoft). Home-based competitiveness in related industries also provides information flow and technical exchanges that speed the rate of innovation. To illustrate, the success of Swiss firms in the pharmaceutical industry grew out of previous international success in the dye industry.

Firm Strategy, Structure, and Rivalry

Michael Porter warns against applying a single management technique across all businesses:

> *No one managerial system is universally appropriate—notwithstanding the current fascination with Japanese management. Competitiveness in a specific industry results from convergence of the management practices and organizational modes favored in the country and the sources of competitive advantage in the industry.*[4]

In industries where Italian companies are global market leaders—such as packaging machines, lighting, and woolen fabrics—a company strategy that emphasizes customized products, niche marketing, speed, and flexibility fits both the dynamics of the industry and the nature of the Italian management system. In contrast, German firms, characterized by a highly disciplined management structure, perform well in technical industries—including optics, chemicals, and machine tools—where complex products require a careful development process and precision manufacturing.

The goals that a country's institutions set for individuals and companies and the prestige it associates with certain industries direct the flow of capital and human resources, thereby affecting the competitive performance and structure of certain industries. Nations tend to be especially competitive in activities from which the country's heroes emerge: banking and pharmaceuticals in Switzerland; agriculture and defense-related industries in Israel.

A final, and extremely powerful, stimulus to the creation and persistence of competitive advantage for a country is the presence of strong local rivals. The United States has secured a leading worldwide position in the computer and software industries, and Japan has a dominant position in machine tools and semiconductors. For each country, vigorous domestic competition goes hand in hand with international success. Such rivalry pressures companies to lower costs, to improve quality and service, and to develop new products and processes. Ultimately, vigorous competition in the home market pressures domestic firms to examine and succeed in global markets.

A Self-Reinforcing System

The four determinants of national competitive advantage discussed above and highlighted in Figure 9.1 constitute a self-reinforcing system. For example, domestic

---

[4]Ibid., p. 81.

rivalry stimulates the formation of unique pools of specialized factors and heightens the expectations of consumers who learn to expect improved products and services. Domestic rivalry also spawns the formation of related and supporting industries, as is evident in the personal computer and software industries in the United States. Moreover, countries are rarely home to just one industry that enjoys a national competitive advantage. One competitive industry aids in the development of another.

Drivers of Globalization

Several forces are driving companies around the world to globalize by expanding their participation in foreign markets. Trade barriers are falling and nearly every product market —computers, fast food, electronic components, nuts and bolts—includes foreign competitors. Maturity in domestic markets is also driving firms to seek global expansion. For example, U.S. companies, nourished by the large home market, have typically lagged behind their European and Japanese rivals in internationalization. Many of these firms are now finding that strong foreign demand can propel future growth.

Business marketers who wish to pursue international market opportunities must first assess the extent of globalization in their particular industry. Some industries are global in character (for example, computers and automobiles), others are moving in this direction (for example, food), while still others remain resolutely national in character (for example, cement). An industry's potential for globalization is driven by market, economic, environmental, and competitive factors (see Figure 9.2).[5] Market factors determine the customers' receptivity to and acceptance of a global product; economic forces determine whether pursuing a global strategy can provide significant cost advantages; environmental forces address the question of whether the necessary supporting infrastructure is in place; and competitive factors can require firms to match the moves of competing firms in other countries.

MARKET FACTORS

Singled out most frequently as a major force driving the globalization of markets is the assertion that customer needs are becoming increasingly homogeneous worldwide.[6] When customers in different countries around the world want essentially the same type of product or service, the opportunity exists to market a global product or brand. Whereas global segments with similar interests and response tendencies may be identified

[5]The discussion of these factors draws on George S. Yip, *Total Global Strategy: Managing for Worldwide Competitive Advantage* (Englewood Cliffs, N.J.: Prentice-Hall, 1992), chaps. 1 and 2. See also Yip, "Global Strategy in a World of Nations," *Sloan Management Review* 31 (fall 1989): pp. 29–41; and Christopher H. Lovelock and George S. Yip, "Developing Global Strategies for Services Businesses," *California Management Review* 38 (winter 1996): pp. 64–86.

[6]Theodore Levitt, "The Globalization of Markets," *Harvard Business Review* 61 (May/ June 1983): pp. 92–102.

Figure 9.2 External Drivers of Industry Potential for Globalization

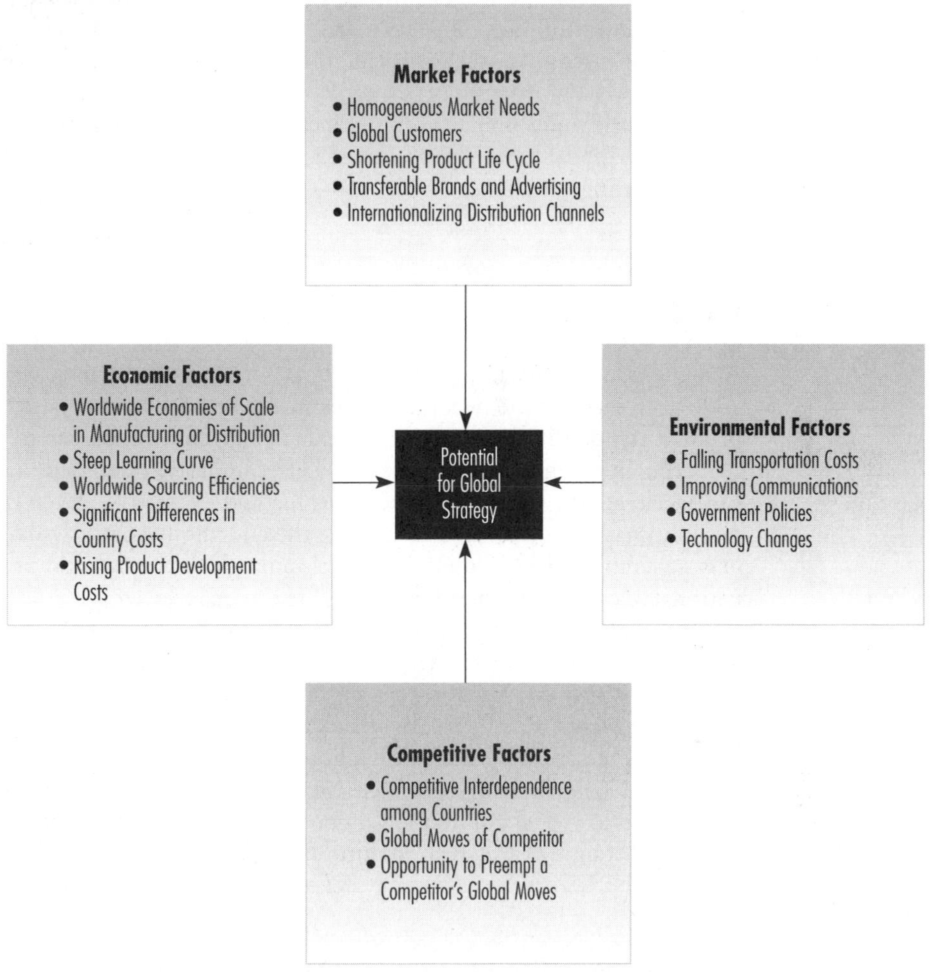

Source: George S. Yip, Pierre M. Loewe, and Michael Y. Yoshino, "How to Take Your Company to the Global Market," *Columbia Journal of World Business* 23 (winter 1988): p. 40. Reprinted with permission.

in some product markets, considerable debate surrounds the issue of whether this is a universal trend.[7] Some research suggests, however, that compared to consumer goods, industrial and high-technology products (for example, computers and machine tools) may be more appropriate for global brand strategies.[8]

[7]See, for example, Susan P. Douglas and Yoram Wind, "The Myth of Globalization," *Columbia Journal of World Business* 22 (winter 1987): pp. 19–29.

[8]Subhash C. Jain, "Standardization of International Marketing Strategy: Some Research Hypotheses," *Journal of Marketing* 53 (January 1989): pp. 70–79.

In the business-to-business market, firms with multinational operations are particularly likely to have common needs and requirements worldwide. Such **global customers** search the world for suppliers, but use the purchased product or service in many countries. G.E. expects many of its suppliers to provide uniform products to its businesses around the world. The presence of global customers both allows and demands a uniform marketing program—common brand name and corporate image—worldwide. Similarly, some channels of distribution may buy on a global or at least on a regional basis, thereby increasing the viability and importance of standardized marketing programs.

ECONOMIC FACTORS

A single-country market may not be large enough for a firm to realize economies of scale or to warrant the necessary investments in R&D and production equipment. If product standardization is feasible, scale at a given location can be increased by participating in a number of national markets. Similarly, expanded market participation can accelerate the accumulation of learning and experience. Even the largest national markets may be too small to amortize the enormous costs involved in developing a new generation of computers. By developing global or regional products rather than national ones, product development costs can be reduced.

Cost advantages can also be secured by seeking suppliers for components and materials on a worldwide basis. Firms such as Xerox, Ford, and Westinghouse have reduced costs by coordinating the purchase of raw materials across their global manufacturing plants. Finally, global firms can exploit differences in the factor costs and skills across countries. To illustrate, hourly labor costs are twice as high in West Germany as in Spain. A firm might increase productivity or reduce costs by concentrating activities in low-cost countries. Of course, the benefits must be weighed against the dangers of training foreign competitors.

ENVIRONMENTAL FACTORS

Host governments affect globalization potential through trade policies, restrictions, and incentives. The liberalization of trade policies can provide a supportive environment for expanded market participation. The harmonization of trade policies in the European Community (EC); the North American Free Trade Agreement involving the United States, Canada, and Mexico; and the formation of a trading zone in the Pacific Rim are all favorable signs. Christopher Lovelock and George Yip suggest that "with the rise of non-Japan Asia, Latin America, and Eastern Europe, operating in just the 'Triad' of North America, Western Europe, and Japan is no longer sufficient" for a truly global company.[9]

---

[9]Lovelock and Yip, "Developing Global Strategies," p. 65.

Outside the Triad, however, government and trade restrictions can hamper the standardization of marketing programs—for example, through import tariffs and quotas, local content requirements, and constraints on technology transfer. To illustrate, local content requirements, which specify that products contain a certain proportion of component parts manufactured locally, can affect production costs, hamper uniform pricing, and require changes in product design.[10]

Improvements in telecommunications and in logistical systems have markedly increased a firm's capacity to manage operations on a global scale. The spread of fax systems as well as international computer networks facilitates highly coordinated global strategies. Likewise, more responsive transportation systems, coupled with computerized inventory systems, reduce the time and cost required to move goods to distant markets. For example, the harmonization of trade policies in the European Community speeds the flow of goods across the borders of members, thereby lowering logistics costs.

Protecting the Environment

Through increased regulation and legal action, governments around the world have taken a tough stand against firms that follow environmentally irresponsible practices. In turn, consumers are increasingly demanding environmentally friendly products. Leading global companies understand that environmental soundness provides a form of value to customers and other important stakeholders. (See the ad in Figure 9.3, in which Canon describes its Clean Earth Campaign.)

COMPETITIVE FACTORS

Competitors can raise the globalization potential of their industry by creating competitive interdependence among countries. George Yip contends that this is achieved through the sharing of activities:

> *When activities such as production are shared among countries, a competitor's market share in one country affects its scale and overall cost position in the shared activities. Changes in that scale and cost will affect its competitive position in all countries dependent on the shared activities.*[11]

A global orientation can prompt firms to make moves to match or preempt individual competitors. As Ford has become more cost efficient by concentrating production and by sharing activities, Japanese manufacturers are pressured to enter more markets so that increased production volume will cover costs. Moreover, as

---

[10]Douglas and Wind, "Myth of Globalization." pp. 28–29.
[11]Yip, "Global Strategy in a World of Nations," p. 38.

Figure 9.3 An Ad Describing Canon's Clean Earth Campaign

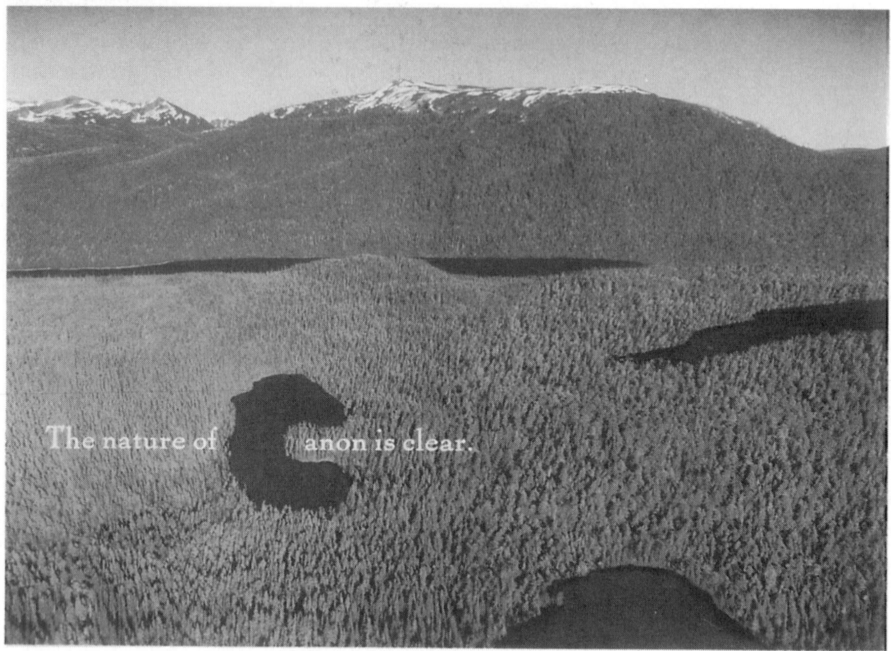
The nature of Canon is clear.

Our name is known around the world as a pioneer in technology. And our commitment to developing innovative and reliable products in this country has been clear for over 40 years. But concern for the environment is also a big part of our nature.

Our Clean Earth Campaign, for example, started as a program to recycle used toner cartridges from Canon products. Today, it has grown to include partnerships with such leading environmental organizations as the National Parks Foundation, the Nature Conservancy and the National Wildlife Federation. Within each organization, we're sponsoring programs to preserve the health and well being of our great wilderness.

Of course, Canon is also hard at work in the corporate environment. From our National Office Paper Recycling Program, to our ozone-free and ENERGY STAR℠ compliant copiers, we're helping to conserve and protect our natural resources for generations to come.

Imagine. A world where technology and nature exist in harmony. Clearly, it's the vision you'd expect from a leader like Canon.

energy

Canon

Source: Courtesy of Canon U.S.A., Inc.

INNOVATIVE SOLUTIONS FOR THE ENVIRONMENT

Leading strategists suggest that companies that adopt innovative approaches to meet rising environmental standards around the world can gain a competitive edge in the global marketplace.

- **Cummins Engine Company** developed a low-emission diesel engine for trucks and buses—an innovation that U.S. environmental regulations spurred—and gained a strong position in international markets where similar needs are growing.
- To comply with new regulations to reduce solvent emissions, **3M** discovered a way to avoid the use of solvents altogether by coating products with safer, water-based solutions. The company gained an important early-mover advantage over its competitors.
- In response to Japanese law that set standards to make products easier to recycle, **Hitachi** redesigned its appliances to reduce disassembly time. In the process, the number of parts in a washing machine was reduced by 16 percent and the number of parts in a vacuum cleaner was reduced by 30 percent. Fewer parts make the products not only easier to disassemble, but also to produce in the first place.

Source: Michael E. Porter and Claas van der Linde, "Green and Competitive: Ending the Stalemate," *Harvard Business Review* 73 (September/October 1995): pp. 120–134.

Motorola's communication business was threatened in the United States by Japanese competitors, the firm sought to defend its home market while launching a sustained effort to secure markets in Japan. While preserving its market leadership at home, Motorola has also logged some successes in Japan. For example, the Japanese government selected a Motorola design for a cellular telephone component as a national standard.

International Market-Entry Options[12]

A first step in developing effective international marketing strategy centers on understanding the alternative ways that a firm can participate in international markets. The particular mode of entry selected should take into consideration the level of a firm's experience overseas and the stage in the evolution of its international involvement. Figure 9.4 illustrates a spectrum of options for participating

[12]The following discussion is based on Franklin R. Root, *Entry Strategy for International Markets* (Lexington, Mass.: D. C. Heath, 1987); and Michael R. Czinkota and Ilka A. Ronkainen, *International Marketing,* 2d ed. (Hinsdale, Ill.: The Dryden Press, 1990).

in international markets. They range from low-commitment choices, such as exporting, to highly complex levels of participation, such as global strategies. Each is examined in this section.

EXPORTING

An industrial firm's first encounter with an overseas market usually involves **exporting** because it requires the least commitment and risk. Goods are produced at one or two home plants and sales are made through distributors or importing agencies in each country. Exporting is a viable entry strategy when the firm lacks the resources to make a significant commitment to the market, wants to minimize political and economic risk, or is unfamiliar with the market requirements and cultural norms of the country.

While preserving flexibility and reducing risk, exporting also limits the future prospects for growth in the country. First, exporting involves giving up direct control of the marketing program, which makes it difficult to coordinate activities, implement strategies, and resolve conflicts with customers and channel members. George Day explains why customers may sense a lack of commitment on the part of the exporter:

> *In many international markets customers are loath to form long-run relationships with a company through its agents because they are unsure whether the business will continue to service the market, or will withdraw at the first sign of adversity. This problem has bedeviled U.S. firms in many countries, and only now are they living down a reputation for opportunistically participating in many countries and then withdrawing abruptly to protect short-run profits.*[13]

[13]George S. Day, *Market Driven Strategy: Processes for Creating Value* (New York: The Free Press, 1990), p. 272.

CONTRACTING

A somewhat more involved and complex form of international market entry is **contracting.** Included among contractual entry modes are (1) licensing, (2) franchising, and (3) management contracts.

Licensing

Under a **licensing** agreement, one firm permits another to use its intellectual property in exchange for royalties or some other form of payment. The property might include trademarks, patents, technology, know-how, or company name. In short, licensing involves exporting intangible assets.

As an entry strategy, licensing requires neither capital investment nor marketing strength in foreign markets. This provides a means for a firm to test foreign markets without a major commitment of management time or capital. Because the licensee is typically a local company that can serve as a buffer against government action, licensing also reduces the risk of exposure to government action. With increasing host country regulation, licensing may enable the business marketer to enter a foreign market that is closed to either imports or direct foreign investment.

Licensing agreements do pose some limitations. First, some companies are hesitant to enter license agreements because the licensee may become an important competitor in the future. Second, licensing agreements typically include a time limit. Although terms may be extended once after the initial agreement, additional extensions are not readily permitted by a number of foreign governments. Third, a firm has less control over a licensee than over its own exporting or manufacturing abroad.

Franchising

Franchising is a form of licensing in which a parent company (the franchisor) grants another independent entity (the franchisee) the right to conduct business in a specified manner. This right can include selling the franchisor's product or using its name, production and marketing methods, or a general business approach. Franchising has provided an attractive means for U.S. firms, especially service organizations, to penetrate foreign markets at a low cost and to leverage their skills with local knowledge and entrepreneurial spirit. Foreign government intervention represents a major problem for franchise systems in the international arena. For example, government restrictions on franchising and royalties hindered ComputerLand's Manila store from offering a complete range of services, leading to an eventual split between the company and its franchisee.

Despite such problems, franchising provides a viable foreign market entry alternative for business marketing firms—large and small. To illustrate, Automation Papers Company, a New Jersey-based supplier of high-technology paper products, used franchising to gain exclusive representation by a highly motivated sales force in selected foreign markets. The franchisees receive rights to the firm's trademarks, extensive training for local employees, and the benefit of Automation Papers' experience, credit lines, and advertising program.[14]

Other contractual modes of entry have grown in prominence in recent years. **Contract manufacturing** involves sourcing a product from a producer located in a foreign country for sale there or in other countries. Here assistance might be required to ensure that the product meets the desired quality standards. Contract manufacturing is most appropriate when the local market lacks sufficient potential to justify a direct investment, export entry is blocked, and a quality licensee is not available.

Management Contracts

To expand their overseas operations, many firms have turned to management contracts. In a **management contract** the industrial firm assembles a package of skills that will provide an integrated service to the client. When equity participation, either in the form of full ownership or a joint venture, is not feasible or is not permitted by a foreign government, a management contract provides a means for participating in a venture. Management contracts have been employed effectively in the service sector in areas such as computer services, hotel management, and food services. Michael Czinkota and Ilka Ronkainen point out that management contracts can "provide organizational skills not available locally, expertise that is immediately available rather than built up, and management assistance in the form of support services that would be difficult and costly to replicate locally."[15]

One specialized form of a management contract is a **turnkey operation.** This arrangement permits a client to acquire a complete operational system, together with the skills sufficient to allow the unassisted maintenance and operation of the system. Once the package agreement is on line, the system is owned, controlled, and operated by the client. Management contracts provide a means for firms to commercialize their superior skills (know-how) by participating in the international market.

STRATEGIC ALLIANCES

Strategic alliances (treated in Chapter 4) are assuming an increasingly prominent role in the global strategy of many business marketing firms. Frederick Webster Jr. defines strategic alliances as "collaborations among partners involving the commitment of capital and management resources with the objective of enhancing the partners' competitive

[14]Czinkota and Ronkainen, *International Marketing,* pp. 392–396. See also Gianni Lorenzoni and Charles Baden-Fuller, "Creating a Strategic Center to Manage a Web of Partners," *California Management Review* 37 (spring 1995): pp. 146–163.

[15]Czinkota and Ronkainen, *International Marketing,* p. 493.

positions."[16] Strategic alliances offer a number of benefits, such as access to markets or to technology, economies of scale in manufacturing and marketing activities, and the sharing of risk among partners.

Although offering potential, global strategic alliances pose a special management challenge. Among the stumbling blocks that have been isolated are these:[17]

- Partners are organized quite differently for making marketing and product design decisions, creating *problems in coordination and trust.*
- Partners that combine the best set of skills in one country may be poorly equipped to support each other in other countries, leading to *problems in implementing alliances on a global scale.*
- The quick pace of technological change often guarantees that the most attractive partner today may not be the most attractive partner tomorrow, leading to *problems in maintaining alliances over time.*

Firms that are adept at managing global alliances choose partners carefully. Observe in Figure 9.5 that potential partners can be evaluated on the basis of their strengths and/or fit across five areas: resources, relationships, reputation, capabilities, and chemistry/culture. This provides a framework for assessing the strengths and weaknesses of a proposed partnership in different-country markets. Once established, effective relationship management skills are needed to coordinate activities, control conflict, and keep alliance strategy centered on the ever-changing customer in the global marketplace.

JOINT VENTURES

In pursuing international-entry options, a corporation confronts a wide variety of ownership choices, ranging from 100 percent ownership to a minority interest. Frequently, full ownership may be a desirable, but not essential, prerequisite for success in the international market arena. Thus a joint venture becomes a feasible option. The **joint venture** involves a joint-ownership arrangement (between, for example, a U.S. firm and one in the host country) to produce and/or market goods in a foreign market. In contrast to a strategic alliance, a joint venture involves the creation of a new firm. Some joint ventures are structured so that each partner holds an equal share; in others, one partner has a majority stake. The contributions that the partners bring to the joint venture can also vary widely and may include financial resources, technology, sales organizations, know-how, or plant and equipment.

---

[16]Frederick E. Webster Jr., "The Changing Role of Marketing in the Corporation," *Journal of Marketing* 56 (October 1992): p. 8.

[17]Thomas J. Kosnik, "Stumbling Blocks to Global Strategic Alliances," *Systems Integration Age,* October 1988, pp. 31–39. See also Michael Y. Yoshino, and Srinivasa Rangan, *Strategic Alliances: An Entrepreneurial Approach to Globalization* (Boston: Harvard Business School Press, 1995).

Figure 9.5 What Does Each Partner Bring to the Party? A Framework for Evaluating Strategic Alliances

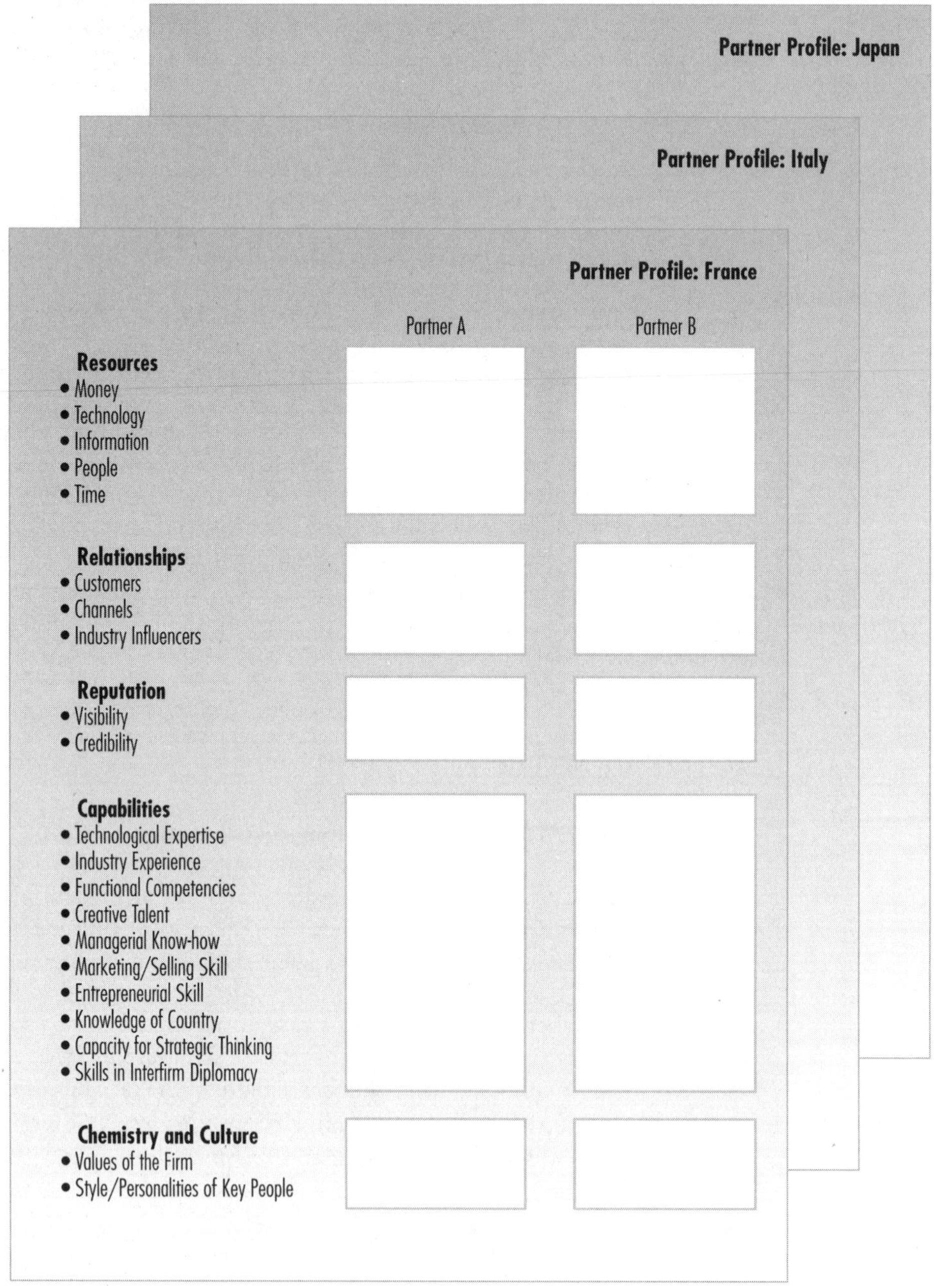

Source: Rowland T. Moriarty and Thomas J. Kosnik, "High-Tech Marketing Concepts, Continuity, and Change," *Sloan Management Review* 31 (summer 1989): p. 15 by permission of the publisher.

Representing a successful relationship is the 50–50 joint venture between Xerox Corporation and Tokyo-based Fuji Photo Film Company. Through the joint venture, Xerox gained a presence in the Japanese market, learned valuable quality management skills that improved its products, and developed a keen understanding of important Japanese rivals such as Canon, Inc. and Ricoh Company. This joint venture has thrived for over three decades.[18]

Advantages

Joint ventures offer a number of advantages. First, joint ventures provide the only path of entry into many foreign markets. In most developing countries and even in some developed countries, the governments require firms to either form or accept joint ventures in order to participate in the local market. Second, joint ventures may open up market opportunities that neither partner to the venture could pursue alone. Kenichi Ohmae explains the logic:

> *If you run a pharmaceutical company with a good drug to distribute in Japan but have no sales force to do it, find someone in Japan who also has a good product but no sales force in your country. You get double the profit by putting two strong drugs through your fixed cost sales network, and so does your new ally. Why duplicate such high expenses all down the line? . . . Why not join forces to maximize contribution to each other's fixed costs?*[19]

Third, joint ventures may provide for better relationships with local organizations (for example, local authorities) and with customers. By being attuned to the local culture and environment of the host country, the local partner may enable the joint venture to respond to changing market needs and to be more aware of cultural sensitivities.

The Downside

Problems can arise in maintaining joint venture relationships. A study suggests that perhaps 70 percent of joint ventures are disbanded or fall short of expectations.[20] The reasons involve problems with the disclosure of sensitive information, disagreements over how profits are to be shared, clashes over management style, and differing perceptions on the course that strategy should follow. Some experts point to another risk that must be evaluated in considering venture partners. What would happen in the event of a breakup? Michael R. Czinkota and Jon Woronoff warn that companies "must decide whether they really do want to tie up with a knowledgeable partner that could become a troublesome rival at a later date, or

---

[18]David P. Hamilton, "United It Stands—Fuji Xerox Is a Rarity in World Business: A Joint Venture That Works," *The Wall Street Journal,* 26 September 1996, p. R19.

[19]Kenichi Ohmae, "The Global Logic of Strategic Alliances," *Harvard Business Review* 67 (March/April 1989): p. 147.

[20]Based on studies by Coopers and Lybrand and by McKinsey and Company, reported in "Corporate Odd Couples," *Business Week,* 21 July 1986, pp. 100–106.

Ethical Business Marketing

BRIBERY AND DIFFERING BUSINESS PRACTICES

International marketing managers often face a dilemma when home country regulations clash with foreign business practices. To illustrate, the Foreign Corrupt Practices Act makes it a crime for U.S. firms to bribe a foreign official for business purposes. A number of U.S. firms have complained about the law, arguing that it hinders their efforts to compete in the international market against those competitors who operate under no such antibribery laws. Likewise, many managers argue that the United States should not apply its moral principles to other cultures in which bribery and corruption are common. In their view, firms should be free to use the most common methods of competition in the host country. Others counter, however, that if bribes are permitted, a host of unethical business practices will follow.

Jack Welch, General Electric's CEO, insists that G.E.'s policy prohibiting bribes doesn't make it less competitive:

> *In a global business, you can win without bribes. But you better have technology. That's why we win in businesses like turbines, because we have the best gas turbine. You've got to be the low-priced supplier, but in almost all cases, if you have quality, price, technology, you win—and nobody can sleazeball you.*

Instead of offering a long list of rules, or debating the fine points of ethical issues, Welch uses one simple question to address the conscience of every individual G.E. employee directly: "Can you look in the mirror every day and feel proud of what you are doing?"

Source: Michael R. Czinkota and Ilka A. Ronkainen, *International Marketing,* 2d ed. (Hinsdale, Ill.: The Dryden Press, 1990), pp. 112–121; and Noel M. Tichy and Stratford Sherman, *Control Your Destiny or Someone Else Will* (New York: Doubleday, 1993), pp. 111–114.

whether they would not prefer one that is just a distributor or maybe a manufacturer in a different sector."[21]

MULTIDOMESTIC VERSUS GLOBAL STRATEGIES

The most complex forms of participation in the global arena are multidomestic and global strategies. Multinational firms have traditionally managed operations outside their home country with **multidomestic strategies** that permit individual subsidiaries to compete independently in different-country markets. The multinational headquarters coordinates marketing policies and financial controls and may centralize R&D and some support activities. Each subsidiary, however, resembles a strategic

[21]Michael R. Czinkota and Jon Woronoff, *Unlocking Japan's Markets: Seizing Marketing and Distribution Opportunities in Today's Japan* (Chicago: Probus, 1991), p. 157.

business unit that is expected to contribute earnings and growth to the organization. The firm can manage its international activities like a portfolio.

In contrast, a **global strategy** seeks competitive advantage with strategic choices that are highly integrated across countries.[22] For example, features of a global strategy might include a standardized core product that requires minimal local adaptation and that is targeted on foreign-country markets chosen on the basis of their contribution to globalization benefits. Major volume and market share advantages might be sought by directing attention to the United States, Europe, and Japan. The value chain concept illuminates the chief differences between a multidomestic and a global strategy.

INTERNATIONAL STRATEGY AND THE VALUE CHAIN[23]

To diagnose the sources of competitive advantage, domestic or international, Michael Porter divides the activities performed by a firm into distinct groups. The value chain, displayed in Figure 9.6, provides a framework for categorizing these activities. Primary activities are those involved in the physical creation of the product, the marketing and logistical program, and the service after the sale. Support activities provide the infrastructure and inputs that allow the primary activities to occur. Every activity employs purchased inputs, human resources, and a combination of technologies. Likewise, the firm's infrastructure, including such functions as general management, supports the entire value chain. Porter asserts that "A firm may possess two types of competitive advantage: low relative cost or differentiation—its ability to perform the activities in its value chain either at a lower cost or in a unique way relative to its competitors."[24] A firm that competes in the international market must decide how to spread the activities among countries. Central to this decision is the need to distinguish upstream from downstream activities (see Figure 9.6).

Downstream activities involve those primary activities that are closely tied to the location of the buyer. For example, a business marketer wishing to serve the Japanese market must ensure that a local service network is in place. By contrast, upstream activities (for example, manufacturing and operations) and support activities (for example, procurement) are not tied directly to the buyer's location. Caterpillar, for example, uses a few large-scale manufacturing facilities to produce components to meet worldwide demands.

This assessment provides a foundation for valuable strategic insights. Competitive advantage created by downstream activities is largely country-specific: A firm's reputation, brand name, and service network grow out of the firm's activities

---

[22]Yip, "Global Strategy in a World of Nations," pp. 33–35.

[23]Michael E. Porter, "Changing Patterns of International Competition," *California Management Review* 28 (winter 1986): pp. 9–40; see also Porter, *Competitive Advantage: Creating and Sustaining Superior Performance* (New York: The Free Press, 1985).

[24]Porter, "Changing Patterns," p. 13.

Figure 9.6 The Value Chain: Upstream and Downstream Activities

Firm Infrastructure					
Human Resource Management					Margin
Technology Development					
Procurement					
Inbound Logistics	Operations	Outbound Logistics	Marketing and Sales	Service	Margin

Upstream Value Activities ⟷ **Downstream Value Activities**

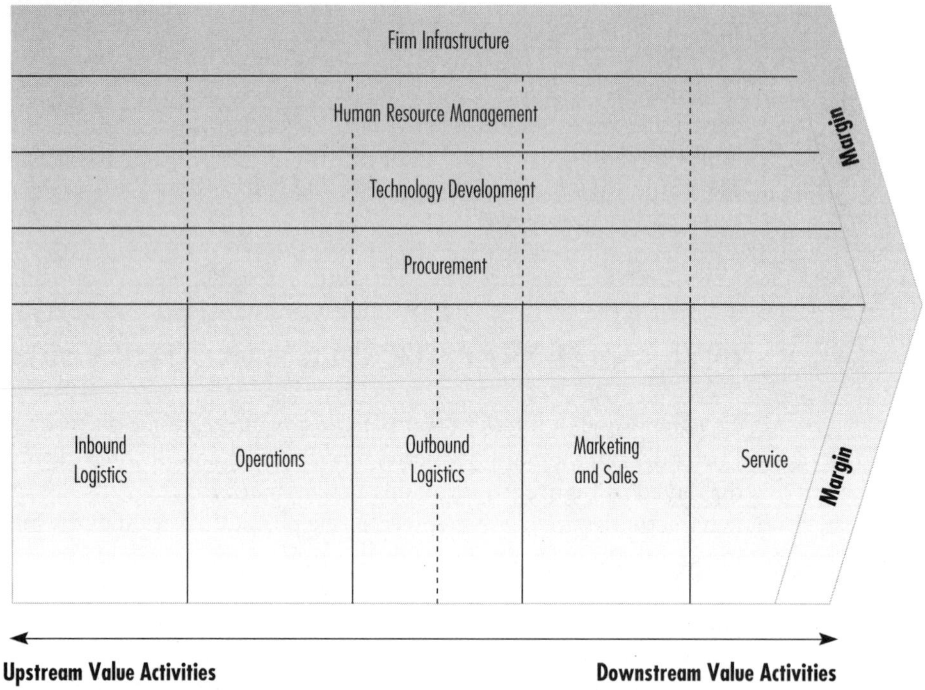

Source: Reprinted from Michael E. Porter, "Changing Patterns of International Competition," *California Management Review* 28 (winter 1986): p. 16. Copyright 1986 by the Regents of the University of California, reprinted by permission of the Regents.

in a particular country. Competitive advantage in upstream and support activities stems more from the entire network of countries in which a firm competes than from its position in any one country.

Source of Advantage: Multidomestic versus Global

When downstream activities (those tied directly to the buyer) are important to competitive advantage, a multidomestic pattern of international competition is common. In **multidomestic industries,** firms pursue separate strategies in each of their foreign markets—competition in each country is essentially independent of competition in other countries (for example, Alcoa in the aluminum industry, Honeywell in the controls industry).

Global competition is more common in industries in which upstream and support activities (such as technology development and operations) are vital to competitive advantage. A **global industry** is one in which a firm's competitive position in one country is significantly influenced by its position in other countries (for example, Motorola in the semiconductor industry, Boeing in the commercial aircraft industry).

Coordination and Configuration

Further insights into international strategy can be gained by examining two dimensions of competition in the global market: configuration and coordination. **Configuration** centers on where each activity is performed, including the number of locations. Options range from concentrated (for example, one production plant serving the world) to dispersed (for example, a plant in each country—each with a complete value chain).

Coordination refers to how similar activities performed in various countries are coordinated or coupled with each other. If, for example, a firm has three plants—one in the United States, one in England, and one in Japan—how do the activities in these plants relate to one another? Numerous coordination options exist because of the many possible levels of coordination and the many ways an activity can be performed. For example, a firm operating three plants could, at one extreme, allow each plant to operate autonomously (unique production processes, unique products). At the other extreme, the three plants could be closely coordinated, utilizing a common information system and producing products with identical features.

Types of International Strategy

Some of the possible variations in international strategy are portrayed in Figure 9.7. Observe that the purest global strategy concentrates as many activities as possible in one country, serves the world market from this home base, and closely coordinates those activities that must be performed near the buyer (for example, service). Caterpillar, for example, views its battle with the formidable Japanese competitor, Komatsu, in global terms. As well as employing automated manufacturing systems that allow it to fully exploit the economies of scale from its worldwide sales volume, Caterpillar also carefully coordinates activities in its global dealer network. This integrated global strategy gives Caterpillar a competitive advantage in cost and effectiveness.[25] By serving the world market from its home base in Seattle, Washington, and by closely coordinating sales and service activities with customers around the world, Boeing also aptly illustrates a pure global strategy.[26]

Figure 9.7 can be used to illustrate other international strategy patterns. Canon, for example, concentrates manufacturing and support activities in Japan but gives local marketing subsidiaries significant latitude in each region of the world. Thus, Canon pursues an export-based strategy. In contrast, Xerox concentrates some activities and disperses others. Coordination, however, is extremely high: The Xerox brand, marketing approach, and servicing strategy are standardized worldwide.

---

[25]Donald V. Fites, "Make Your Dealers Your Partners," *Harvard Business Review* 74 (March/April 1996): pp. 84–95.

[26]Andy Reinhardt and Seanna Browder, "Booming Boeing," *Business Week,* (28 September 1996), pp. 118–125.

Figure 9.7 Types of International Strategy

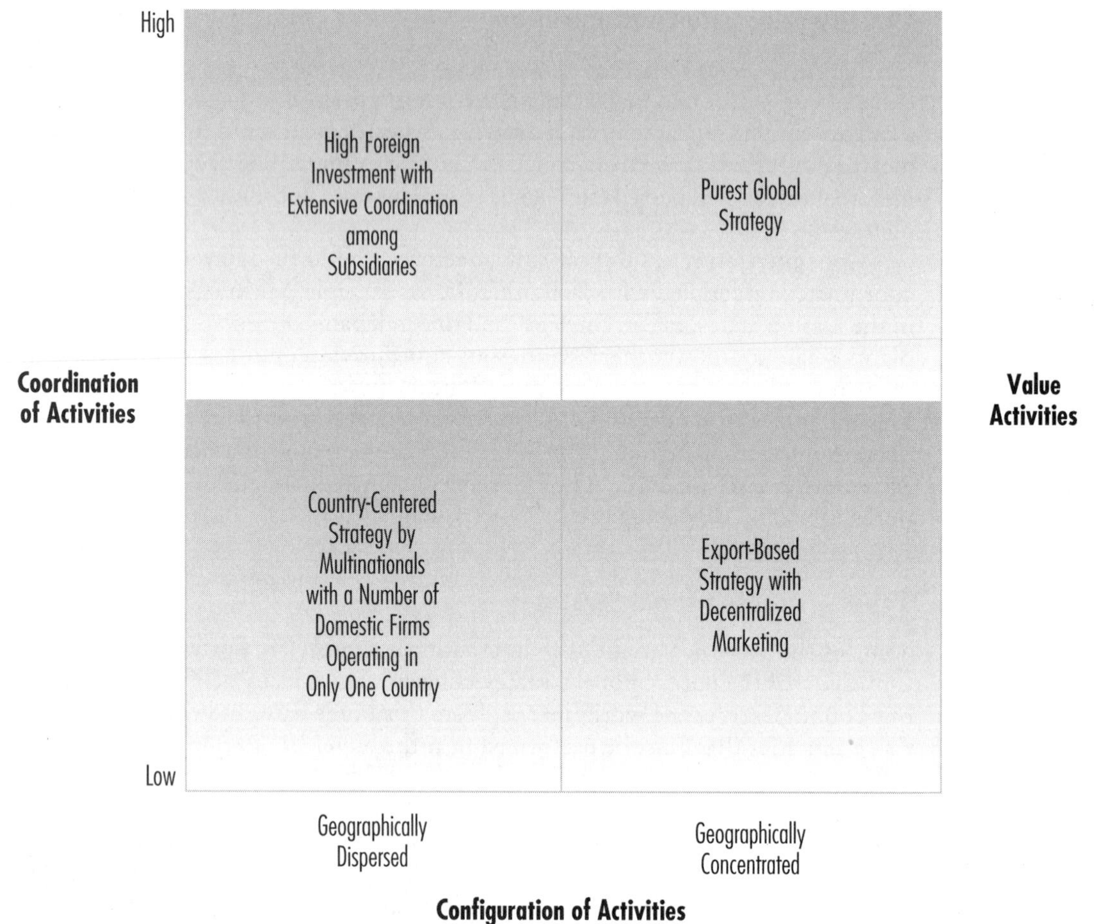

Source: Reprinted from Michael E. Porter, "Changing Patterns of International Competition," *California Management Review* 28 (winter 1986): p. 19. Copyright 1986 by the Regents of the University of California, reprinted by permission of the Regents.

Michael Porter notes that

> *International strategy has often been characterized as a choice between worldwide standardization and local tailoring, or as the tension between the economic imperative (large-scale efficient facilities) and the political imperative (local content, local production)… A firm's choice of international strategy involves a search for competitive advantage from configuration/coordination throughout the value chain.*[27]

[27]Porter, "Changing Patterns," p. 25.

BOEING'S CLOSE TIES IN ASIA

For its long-haul 777, Boeing has received multibillion-dollar orders from leading air carriers in Hong Kong, Singapore, Indonesia, Malaysia, Thailand, the Philippines, South Korea, and Japan. Boeing also has a strong record of success with China—a country that expects to spend $100 billion on aircraft during the next 15 years. Boeing will be engaged in a fierce battle with Europe's Airbus Industrie to dominate the Asian market.

Consider Boeing's presence in China. Since selling a 707 airliner to China in the early 1970s, Boeing's salespersons have maintained close ties with aviation officials, pilots, and mechanics throughout the country. Recently, Boeing has invested more than $150 million to expand sales, maintenance, and training operations across China. It has established a headquarters in Beijing's Capital Airport. It has also assisted China in developing a modern air-traffic control network and has worked closely with numerous airlines in establishing maintenance programs and flight training programs. While Boeing has established long-lasting ties with Chinese customers, Airbus is increasing its presence in the market and predicting that it will win a sizable share of new orders.

An intense competitive battle has begun.

Source: Pete Engardio and Dexter Roberts, "The Relentless Pursuit of Guanxi," *Business Week,* (30 September 1996), pp. 124–125.

Evolution of International Marketing Strategy[28]

International marketing strategy should be formulated in light of the firm's current position overseas and geared to its vision of growth and future position in worldwide markets. To this point, the chapter has laid a foundation for understanding the forces that shape the competitive advantage of countries and that drive the globalization of markets. In turn, consideration has been given to the array of international market-entry options available to the business marketing firm. For the individual firm, strategy formulation in international markets is an evolutionary process in which the central direction of strategy and the key decisions vary at each successive phase of involvement in international operations.

Figure 9.8 traces the phases in global marketing evolution from the preliminary phase of pre-internationalization through (1) initial entry, (2) local or national market expansion, and (3) globalization. At each phase a number of triggers may prompt movement into a new phase, thereby stimulating a new strategic direction. Those triggers that prompt a company to reassess its current strategy

[28]This section draws on Susan P. Douglas and C. Samuel Craig, "Evolution of Global Marketing Strategy: Scale, Scope, and Synergy," *Columbia Journal of World Business* 24 (fall 1989): pp. 47–59; and Craig and Douglas, "Developing Strategies for Global Markets: An Evolutionary Perspective," *Columbia Journal of World Business* 31 (spring 1996): pp. 70–81.

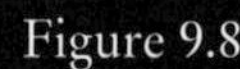

Figure 9.8 Phases in Global Marketing Evolution

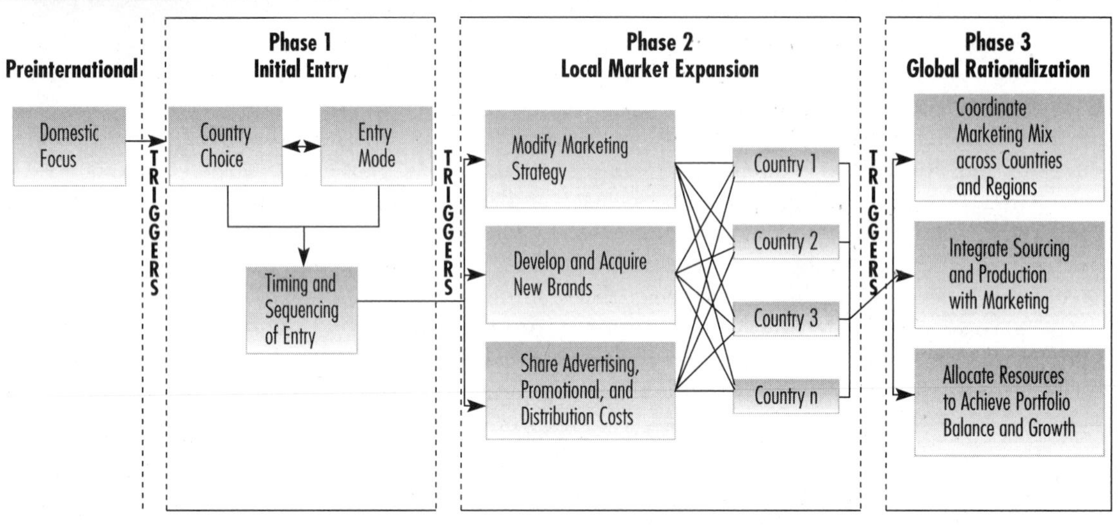

Source: Susan P. Douglas and C. Samuel Craig, "Evolution of Global Marketing Strategy: Scale, Scope, and Synergy," *Columbia Journal of World Business* 24 (fall 1989): p. 50. Reprinted with permission.

may be external (for example, competitive pressures or industry trends) or internal (for example, management initiative).

PRE-INTERNATIONALIZATION

A strong domestic orientation may cause a firm to overlook changes that are occurring in target segments and market forces worldwide and to be vulnerable to aggressive foreign competitors. A variety of factors may prompt the domestically oriented firm to reexamine its position, triggering initial entry into international markets. For example, the domestic market may have become saturated or the firm may wish to diversify risk across a range of countries and product markets.

PHASE ONE: INITIAL INTERNATIONAL MARKET ENTRY

Given the industrial firm's lack of experience and knowledge in international markets, attention centers on identifying the most attractive market opportunities overseas for its existing (i.e., domestic) products and services. The guiding principle is to extend the geographic base of operations to those international markets that provide the closest match to the firm's current offerings and market conditions. By leveraging its domestic competitive position and core competency internationally, the firm seeks to

GLOBAL ACCOUNT MANAGEMENT AT IBM

Large computer customers, like General Electric, are demanding more consistent service and support on a worldwide basis. These customers seek suppliers who will provide compatible equipment across international locations, deal with them in a coordinated fashion, and offer consistent and seamless service across countries. To meet the special needs of these important global customers, IBM developed its selected international accounts (SIA) program. Customers are chosen for this program on the basis of revenue potential, the installed base of IBM products across international locations, and the anticipated demand for IBM products and services.

Each SIA is supported by an IBM account manager who is stationed near the customer's headquarters and is responsible for the entire account on a worldwide basis. "SIAs are provided discounts on global purchases based on customer commitment to purchase a particular product volume worldwide (an international volume purchase agreement). The client is allowed to accrue purchases of one product around the world for a volume percentage discount."

Source: George S. Yip and Tammy L. Madsen, "Global Account Management: The Next Frontier in Relationship Marketing," *International Marketing Review,* 13 (no. 3, 1996), p. 32.

extend economies of scale by establishing a presence in multiple markets. The key decisions in this phase of initial international market entry are (1) the choice of countries to enter, (2) the timing of entry, and (3) how operations are to be performed in these countries. In addition to selecting an entry strategy, the firm must develop mechanisms for **learning** about international markets and how to operate successfully in specific foreign-country markets.

Choice of Countries

Both risk and opportunities need to be evaluated in choosing which countries to enter. Here the political, financial, and legal risks of entry need to be weighed in relation to the stability and rate of economic growth of a country. Similarly, the size and growth of market potential must be gauged relative to the level of competition and costs of market entry. Difficult trade-offs are common (for example, high growth potential and high country risks or entry costs). Managers are often prone to choose countries where they have had prior contact or experience. To illustrate, Swedish firms tend to enter neighboring countries such as Denmark, Norway, and Finland first and more distant markets such as Brazil, Argentina, and Australia last.[29]

[29]Jan Johanson and Finn Wiedershein-Paul, "The Internationalization of the Firm—Four Swedish Cases," *Journal of Management Studies* (October 1975): pp. 305–322.

Timing of Entry

Should the firm enter a number of country markets simultaneously or, alternatively, should the firm enter one country first to develop a base of experience and then fan out to other countries sequentially? Simultaneous entry might allow the firm to preempt competition by establishing a beachhead in key markets, thereby reducing opportunities for imitation. Multiple market entry may also provide potential scale economies to the firm. Often the determining factor in the decision is the level of resource commitment required to enter a given international market. If, for example, an overseas sales organization must be developed and/or a production facility established, a significant resource commitment is needed.

Mode of Entry

Closely intertwined with the evaluation of market potential and country risk is the decision concerning how to operate in a foreign market. The full range of entry modes, presented earlier in the chapter, may be adopted—from exporting, licensing, and contract manufacturing to joint ventures and wholly owned subsidiaries. In high-risk markets, firms can reduce their equity exposure by adopting low-commitment modes such as licensing, contract manufacturing, or joint ventures with a minority share. Although nonequity modes of entry—such as licensing or contract manufacturing—involve minimal risk and commitment, they may not provide the desired level of control or financial performance. Joint ventures and wholly owned subsidiaries provide a greater degree of control over operations and greater potential returns.

The choice of a particular entry mode will also depend on the size of the market and its growth potential. Susan Douglas and Samuel Craig note that

> *Markets of limited size surrounded by tariff barriers may be supplied most cost effectively via licensing or contract manufacturing. Where there are potential economies of scale, exporting may, however, be preferred. Then, as local market potential builds up . . . a local production and marketing subsidiary may be established.*[30]

Once operations are established in a number of foreign markets, the focus often shifts away from foreign opportunity assessment to local market development in each country. This shift might be prompted by the need to respond to local competitors or the desire to more effectively penetrate the local market. Planning and strategy assume a country-by-country focus.

PHASE TWO: LOCAL MARKET EXPANSION

The expansion effort is generally directed by local management in each country rather than from corporate headquarters. The major objective in this phase is to build strategy

---

[30]Douglas and Craig, "Evolution of Global Marketing Strategy," p. 53.

Managing in the 21st Century

Caterpillar's Close Connections with Global Customers

Caterpillar is putting an information system in place that will enable it to deliver a part **before** customers even realize they need it! The system will monitor the firm's construction equipment or heavy-duty engines after purchase and notify the local dealer when a particular part is beginning to show signs of an impending problem.

Consider this scenario: A component part on a Caterpillar machine, operating at a copper mine in Chile, begins to signal impending failure. A district center, which monitors all Caterpillar machines in the region by remotely reading the sensors on each machine, detects a problem in the making and sends an electronic alert to the local dealer's field technician. Through a portable computer, the technician validates the diagnosis, determines the repair or service required, and the parts and tools that will be needed to complete the job. The technician can also access Caterpillar's worldwide information system to determine the closest source and to order the part.

Caterpillar plans to have the system fully operational in several years. Most of the pieces are already in place: sensors in the machines; computers that diagnose problems; and an information system that connects Caterpillar's factories distribution centers, dealers, and large customers. Two pieces are missing: the remote monitoring system and the open sharing of inventories by Caterpillar and its dealers and suppliers. However, a prototype of the monitoring system is already being tested by Caterpillar.

Source: Donald V. Fites, "Make Your Dealers Your Partners," *Harvard Business Review* 74 (March/April 1996): pp. 88–89.

on the organizational structure developed in each country in order to leverage assets and to more fully utilize core competencies to foster local market growth. Attention centers on capitalizing on R&D and market knowledge, on sharing production and distribution facilities across product lines, and on identifying opportunities for shared marketing expenditures. While continuing to learn, central attention is given to **building** a presence in each market.

Decisions

Economies of scope are provided if the addition of new products or product variants within a country permit a more effective and efficient utilization of an existing operational structure, such as the distribution network or the sales force. Thus, priority is given to making product and strategy modifications in each country in order to broaden the local market base and reach new segments. Extensions to the product line and new product research may be explored to more precisely meet local preferences. In developing countries, machine tool manufacturers, for example, may consider streamlining and simplifying their products to reach less sophisticated market segments. The costs of initial entry into a country can be substantial, including the costs of establishing relations with distributors, agents, or local authorities and of gaining familiarity with market conditions and competition. The goal in the local market expansion phase is to capitalize on this resource base by pursuing market development and by realizing economies of scope.

Triggers to a Global Perspective

The country-by-country orientation can yield a patchwork of domestic national businesses. Different marketing strategies are pursued in each country with little or no coordination of operations between countries. The inefficiencies generated by this fragmented system, coupled with external forces that are integrating markets on a global scale, create pressures toward increased coordination across countries. The following factors can trigger this move:

- cost inefficiencies and duplication of effort between the various country operations of the firm
- opportunities to transfer products, strategies, and experience from one country to another
- emergence of global customers (for example, customers such as G.E. or Citibank that search the world for suppliers and use the purchased product or service in many countries)
- emergence of global competitors that derive strength from highly coordinated operations worldwide
- improved linkages between the firm's marketing infrastructure units operating in different countries

PHASE THREE: GLOBAL ORIENTATION

In the final phase of internationalization, Douglas and Craig maintain that the country-by-country orientation disappears as "markets are viewed as a set of interrelated, interdependent entities which are becoming increasingly integrated and interlinked worldwide."[31] The firm seeks to capitalize on possible synergies and to take maximum advantage of its worldwide operations. Management attention centers on allocating resources and measuring performance on a global scale, guided by this question: What is the optimal allocation of resources across countries, across product markets, and across target segments to maximize global profits? In this phase, learning and building continue but the central focus is on consolidating the firm's market position to establish a global **leadership** position.

Key Decisions

A dual thrust is utilized as a firm adopts a global orientation: (1) improving the efficiency of operations worldwide and (2) formulating a global strategy for expansion and growth.

[31]Ibid., pp. 55–56.

Efficiency

By coordinating operations across countries and between different functional areas, a firm can reduce worldwide costs in several ways.[32] First, economies of scale can be secured by pooling production, R&D, or other activities for two or more countries. Second, a global firm can reduce costs by moving manufacturing or other activities to low-cost countries. For example, the Mexican side of the U.S.–Mexican border is the site of numerous manufacturing plants established and operated by U.S. companies, but employing Mexican labor. Third, a global firm can reduce costs by exploiting flexibility. A company with manufacturing capability in several countries can move production from one location to another to take advantage of the lowest costs at a particular time. Dow Chemical uses this strategy and examines international differences in exchange rates, tax rates, and transportation and labor costs; production volume for the planning period is then set for each Dow plant. Fourth, efficiency can be enhanced through the coordination across countries of marketing strategies such as brand names, advertising themes, and the standardization of product lines.

Strategy Development

A global strategy should define the needs of target segments and determine the geographic configurations of segments. As markets become increasingly international, opportunities for identifying segments that are regional or global in scope, rather than country-specific, are on the increase. In support, expert Kenichi Ohmae notes that

> *The market for IBM computers or Toshiba laptops is not defined by geographic borders but by the inherent appeal of the product to users, regardless of where they live. And with the proliferation of trade journals, trade shows, and electronic databases, users have regular access to the same sources of product information.*[33]

In fact, IBM has consolidated worldwide advertising with one advertising agency.

The global strategy should also include marketing programs tailored to the needs of the regional and global target segments. Often, the organizational structure must be reshaped to successfully implement strategy on a global scale. For example, some companies—such as Citibank—that serve multinational corporations have developed a global account management system whereby an executive is given responsibility for ensuring that the needs of a given client are satisfied worldwide. Importantly, the successful implementation of a global strategy requires the establishment of mechanisms to coordinate and control activities and the flows of information and resources across country boundaries and product markets. Firms such as Citibank and IBM have begun to develop organizational structures that will enable them to compete effectively in the twenty-first century.

---

[32] Yip, "Global Strategy in a World of Nations," pp. 33–35.
[33] Ohmae, "Global Logic of Strategic Alliances," p. 144.

Thus, strategy formulation in international markets is an evolutionary process in which the key strategic decisions vary at each phase of involvement in international operations. After initial entry and as experience in the international market builds, the firm can often effectively pursue growth opportunities in selected international markets. This forms a foundation for advancing to the next stage and pursuing the more complex challenges of strategy integration and coordination across country markets.

Summary

Initial insights into the dynamic character of international competition can be secured by addressing this question: Why are certain firms based in certain nations capable of consistent innovations that yield competitive advantage? Research suggests that four broad national attributes, working individually and as a system, determine the competitive advantage of a nation: (1) factor conditions (for example, skilled labor), (2) demand conditions (for example, the nature of the home market demand), (3) related and supporting industries (for example, an excellent supply network), and (4) firm strategy, structure, and rivalry.

In developing international strategy, the business marketer must first assess the globalization potential of the industry. It is driven by market, economic, environmental, and competitive conditions. For example, market forces determine the customers' receptivity to a standardized global product, whereas economic forces dictate whether a global strategy will yield a cost advantage.

Once a business marketing firm decides to sell its products in a particular country, an entry strategy must then be selected. A range of options are available, including exporting, contractual entry modes (for example, licensing), strategic alliances, and joint ventures. A more elaborate form of participation is represented by multinational firms that employ multidomestic strategies. Here a separate strategy might be pursued in each country served. The most advanced level of participation in international markets is provided by firms that employ a global strategy. Such firms seek competitive advantage by pursuing strategies that are highly interdependent across countries.

Strategy in the international arena should be tailored to the firm's degree of experience in overseas markets and its vision of growth and future position in markets worldwide. Strategy formulation in international markets is an evolutionary process, in which a firm's involvement in overseas operations may advance through three phases: (1) initial foreign market entry, (2) local or national market expansion, and (3) globalization.

Discussion Questions

1. Boeing represents one of the premier global competitors based in the United States. The firm's backlog of orders for new planes extends well into the next century. Using the determinants of national competitive advantage as a guide, examine the U.S. aerospace industry.

2. Michael Porter notes that "It is vigorous domestic competition that ultimately pressures domestic companies to look at global markets and it toughens them to succeed in them."[34] Explain.
3. A key premise of the philosophy of global products is that customers' needs are becoming increasingly homogeneous worldwide. Does this trend fit consumer goods more than industrial goods? Does this signal the end of market segmentation strategies?
4. Describe the *competitive* and *economic* factors that are driving the globalization of some industries.
5. A small Michigan-based firm that produces and sells component parts to General Motors, Ford, and Chrysler wishes to extend market coverage to Europe and Japan. What type of market entry strategy would provide the best fit?
6. Global companies must be more than just a bunch of overseas subsidiaries that execute decisions made at headquarters. Using the value chain concept as a guide, compare a global strategy to a multidomestic strategy.
7. Downstream activities in a firm's value chain create competitive advantages that are largely country-specific. Why?
8. The development of effective international marketing strategy should consider the extent of a firm's experience overseas and the stage in the evolution of its international development. Describe the key strategic issues that must be examined as a firm moves from initial market entry to a more extensive level of involvement in global markets.
9. Hewlett-Packard has scored a major success in the Mexican computer market. Discuss the changes (if any) a firm would have to make in its marketing strategy if it extended its reach beyond the U.S. border into Mexico.

[34]Porter, "The Competitive Advantage of Nations," p. 83.

Chapter 10

Managing Products for Business Markets

The industrial product constitutes the central force in marketing strategy. The ability of the firm to put together a line of products and services that provides superior value to customers is the heart of business marketing management. After reading this chapter, you will understand

1. core products—the tangible link between core competencies and end products.
2. the strategic importance of providing competitively superior value to customers.
3. the various types of industrial product lines and the value of product positioning.
4. a strategic approach for managing products across the stages of the technology adoption life cycle.

Gary Hamel asserts that "In every industry, there is a ratio that relates price to performance: *X* units of cash buys *Y* units of value. The challenge is to improve that ratio and to do so radically. . . ." [1] Smart marketing means thinking of your company and your product in a fresh way and choosing the way in which you can lead.[2] A business marketer's identity in the marketplace is established through the products and services offered. Without careful product planning and control, marketers are often guilty of introducing products that are inconsistent with market needs, arbitrarily adding items that contribute little to existing product lines, and maintaining weak products that could be profitably eliminated.

Product management is directly linked to market analysis and market selection. Products are developed to fit the needs of the market and are modified as those needs change. Drawing upon such tools of demand analysis as business market segmentation and market potential forecasting, the marketer evaluates opportunities and selects

[1]Gary Hamel, "Strategy as Revolution," *Harvard Business Review* 74 (July/August 1996): p. 72.
[2]Regis McKenna, *Relationship Marketing* (Reading, Mass.: Addison-Wesley, 1991), p. 7.

viable market segments, which in turn determines the direction of product policy. Product policy cannot be separated from market selection decisions. In evaluating potential product/market fits, a firm must evaluate market opportunities, determine the number and aggressiveness of competitors, and gauge its own strengths and weaknesses. The marketing function assumes a lead role in transforming the distinctive skills and resources of an organization into products and services that enjoy positional advantages in the market.[3]

This chapter first explores the strategic importance of core competencies—the roots of successful industrial products—and isolates the distinctive skills of leading-edge companies. Second, product quality and value are examined from the customer's perspective and directly linked to business marketing strategy. Third, because industrial products can assume several forms, industrial product line options are described while offering an approach for positioning products and for managing products in high-technology markets.

Core Competencies: The Roots of Industrial Products[4]

You can miss the strength of competitors in the business market by looking only at their product line, in the same way that you can underestimate the strength of a tree if you look only at its leaves. C. K. Prahalad and Gary Hamel offer this analogy: "The diversified corporation is a large tree. The trunk and major limbs are core products, the smaller branches are business units; the leaves, flowers, and fruit are end products. The root system that provides nourishment, sustenance, and stability is the core competence."[5] The success of firms such as 3M, Honda, Canon, Motorola, and others can be traced to a particular set of competencies that each has developed and enriched.

Core competencies are embodied in the superior skills of employees—the technologies they have mastered, the unique ways in which these technologies are combined, and the market knowledge that has been accumulated.[6] Thus, core competencies constitute the collective learning of the organization (see Chapter 8). They focus on the basics of what creates value from the customer's perspective and include both technical and organizational skills. For example, a core competence of Honda is in the design and development of small motors. To apply this competence to one of its products, Honda must ensure that R&D scientists, engineers, and marketers have a shared understanding of consumer needs and of the technological possibilities.

---

[3]P. Rajan Varadarajan, "Marketing's Contribution to Strategy: The View from a Different Looking Glass," *Journal of the Academy of Marketing Science* 20 (fall 1992): pp. 335–343.

[4]This discussion is based on C. K. Prahalad and Gary Hamel, "The Core Competence of the Organization," *Harvard Business Review* 68 (May/June 1990): pp. 79–91. See also James M. Higgins, "Achieving the Core Competence—It's As Easy As 1, 2, 3 . . . 47, 48, 49," *Business Horizons* 39 (March/April 1996): pp. 27–32.

[5]Prahalad and Hamel, "The Core Competence," p. 82.

[6]George S. Day, "Marketing's Contribution to the Strategic Dialogue," *Journal of the Academy of Marketing Science* 20 (fall 1992): p. 326.

IDENTIFYING CORE COMPETENCIES

Three tests can be applied to identify the core competencies of a firm. First, a core competence provides potential access to an array of markets. Capitalizing on its core competencies in precision mechanics, fine optics, and micro-electronics, Canon is a strong competitor in markets as diverse as cameras, laser printers, fax equipment, and image scanners (see Figure 10.1). Canon appeared to be merely a camera producer at the point it was preparing to become a world leader in copiers.

Second, a core competence should make an important contribution to the perceived customer benefits of the firm's end products. To illustrate, Honda's core competency in

Figure 10.1 Core Competencies and Selected Products at Canon

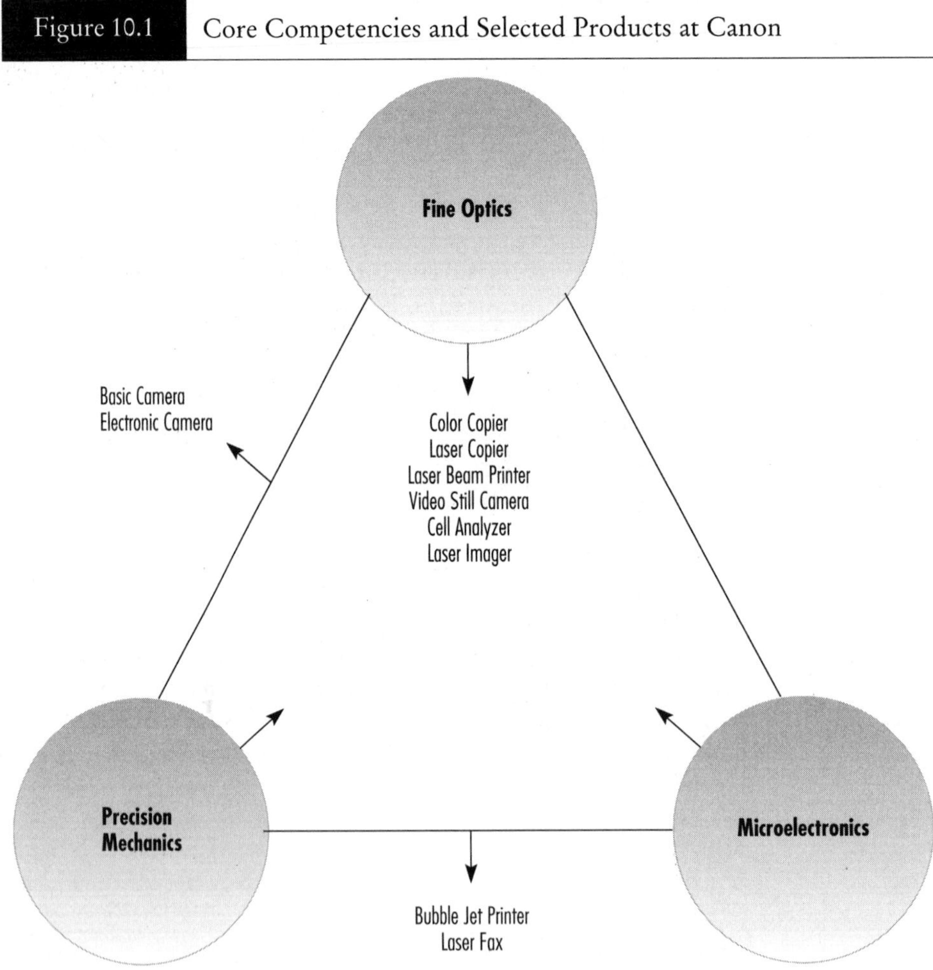

Source: Adapted from C. K. Prahalad and Gary Hamel, "The Core Competence of the Corporation," *Harvard Business Review* 68 (May/June 1990): pp. 75–84.

small engines is tied directly to important benefits sought by customers: product reliability and fuel efficiency. Honda emphasizes these benefits in its marketing strategy across product lines: motorcycles, automobiles, lawn mowers, snow blowers, and lawn tools.

Third, Prahalad and Hamel point out that "a core competence should be difficult for competitors to imitate. And it will be difficult if it is a complex harmonization of individual technologies and production skills."[7] Even though rivals might acquire the same production equipment or some of the technologies that contribute to a core competence of Motorola, they may encounter severe difficulty in duplicating its internal pattern of coordination and learning. For example, Motorola can produce one of several million different electronic pagers to the exact specifications of an individual customer within two hours of receiving the order.[8]

Table 10.1 isolates several successful companies and the core competencies that support their success. Three common characteristics make a core competence difficult for a competitor to easily imitate:[9]

- ***Complexity.*** Core competencies tend to be developed in business processes that are extremely complex and are further strengthened through patient organizational learning over time.

Example: *Continuous quality improvement program at Motorola.*

- ***Organizational Diffuseness.*** Core competencies involve processes that generally cut across the functional areas of a firm and frequently involve external groups, such as important suppliers and leading edge customers.

Example: *Rapid product development process at Sun Microsystems.*

- ***Well-Developed Interfaces.*** Core competencies "depend as much on the way that individuals/organizations have learned to work with each other as they do on the particular expertise of the individuals/organizations themselves."

Example: *The rich, informal communication networks that guide strategy at 3M.*

FROM CORE PRODUCTS TO END PRODUCTS

Core products—the tangible link between core competencies and end products—are the components or subassemblies that significantly contribute to the value of end products. Although Canon's brand has a small share of the laser printer market (end

---

[7]Prahalad and Hamel, "The Core Competence," p. 84.

[8]James Brian Quinn, *Intelligent Enterprise* (New York: The Free Press, 1992), p. 185.

[9]Andrew Bartmess and Keith Cerny, "Building Competitive Advantage through a Global Network of Capabilities," *California Management Review* 35 (winter 1993): pp. 78–103.

Table 10.1 Illustrative Core Competencies

Company/Industry	Nature of Competition in Industry	Competencies
Applied Materials/Semiconductor equipment	Technology driven with high requirements for customization and service	Rapid, high-technology product development and rollout
		Rapid production/delivery of highly customized product
Cooper Tire/Replacement auto and truck tries	Near commodity market	Low-cost product design and manufacturing
	Difficult for buyer to discern differences in products	Continual cost control reduction
	Buying decision based on price and dealer recommendation	Constantly improving customer service
Analog Devices/Analog and digital semiconductors	Analog circuits bought on technical performance	Attracting, developing, and retaining talented employees
	Talented analog designers create most of the customer value and are a scarce resource	
Sun Microsystems/Workstations	Easily copied products	Rapid, high-technology product development and rollout
	Competition based on latest available technology	Operational flexibility
Motorola/Semiconductors and electrical equipment	Technology, cost, and quality	Continuous quality improvement
		Rapid, high-technology product development and rollout
		Operational flexibility

Source: Andrew Bartmess and Keith Cerny, "Building Competitive Advantage through a Global Network of Capabilities," *California Management Review* 35 (winter 1993): p. 82.

product), the firm is reputed to hold more than 80 percent world manufacturing share in desktop laser printer "engines" (core product). Similarly, Matsushita has 20 percent of the VCR market, but enjoys a world manufacturing share more than twice as large in key VCR components. Strategy experts suggest that core product share may be a better predictor of profitability than traditional measures of end product market share.[10] By providing core products for a variety of markets, a firm secures the resources and market knowledge to enhance and extend its chosen core competence

[10]C. K. Prahalad, "Weak Signals versus Strong Paradigms," *Journal of Marketing Research* 32 (August 1995): pp. iii–vi.

areas. In turn, the firm can assume a leading role in shaping new applications and developing new end markets.

EXPLOITING SELECTED CORE COMPETENCIES

Realizing that they cannot dominate in every activity, leading business marketers concentrate their talent and resources on those selected core competencies that will be crucial in serving customers in the future. Canon emphasizes its core competencies directly in its advertising (see Figure 10.2). The 3M company also provides a classic example.[11] The firm's growth for the past several decades has been spawned to a significant extent by its R&D skills in three critical related technologies: adhesives, abrasives, and coating–bonding. In each of these areas, 3M has developed a knowledge base and a depth of skills surpassing those of its major competitors. These historic competencies, coupled with the firm's unique innovation system and entrepreneurial values, have given 3M a continuing stream of successful products: From a producer of sandpaper in the 1920s, historic core competencies have combined to produce Post-it notes, magnetic tape, pressure sensitive tapes, coated abrasives, photographic film, and a wealth of other products.

Product Quality

Increasing global competition and rising customer expectations make product quality and customer value important strategic priorities for marketers. All sectors of the business market are affected. To illustrate, a survey of 700 purchasing managers at the largest U.S. manufacturing companies revealed that more than 70 percent are pressuring suppliers to increase product quality.[12] In turn, the Department of Defense and other governmental units are giving quality an unprecedented level of emphasis in their procurement activities. On a global scale, many international companies insist that suppliers, as a prerequisite for negotiations, meet quality standards set out by the Geneva-based International Standards Organization (ISO). These quality requirements, referred to as **ISO-9000 standards,** were developed for the European Community, but have gained a global following[13] (see Chapter 3). Certification requires a supplier to thoroughly document its quality-assurance program. The certification program is becoming a seal of approval to compete for business not only overseas but also in the United States. For instance, the Department of Defense is employing ISO standards in its contract guidelines. Although Japanese firms continue to set the pace in the application of sophisticated quality-

[11]Quinn, *Intelligent Enterprise*, pp. 216–219.

[12]James Morgan, "The New Look of Quality," *Purchasing* 119 (11 January 1996): pp. 49–98.

[13]Wade Ferguson, "Impact of ISO 9000 Series Standards on Industrial Marketing," *Industrial Marketing Management* 25 (July 1996): pp. 325–310.

Figure 10.2 A Canon Ad That Emphasizes the Firm's Core Competencies

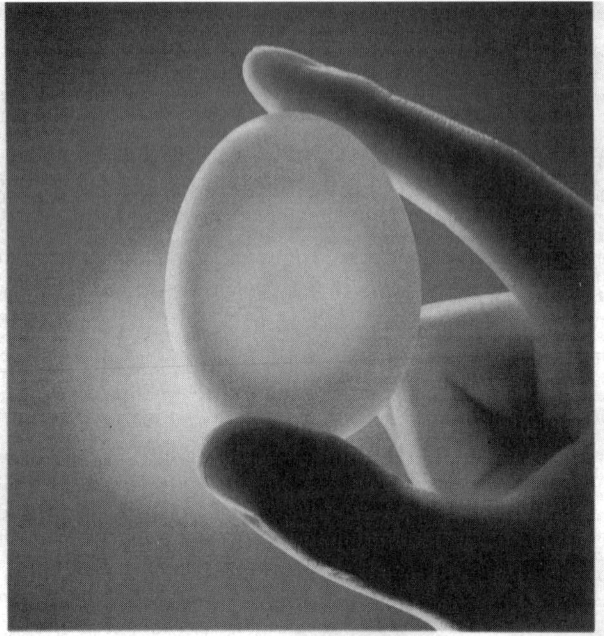

Think about it.
What's waiting inside?
What's inside your laser beam printer, plain paper fax or personal copier? In genuine Canon cartridges, we've not only included all of the imaging system's core components in one user-replaceable unit. We've also improved the design in numerous ways. We've made the toner finer, for higher resolution and beautiful halftones. We've reduced the number of parts for greater reliability. And we've simplified the construction making the cartridge smaller and easier to use. For the best possible output, we do, of course, recommend that you choose a Canon printer, fax or copier. But this, at least, we do ask. Is the cartridge you're using designed and made with Canon quality built in at every step? Before you choose another cartridge, ask yourself what's missing inside.

EP-A
The all-in-one Canon cartridge.
The genuine choice.

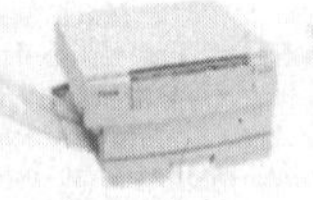

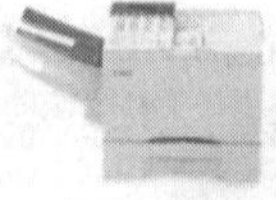

As part of our Clean Earth Campaign, Canon supports leading environmental organizations. Used cartridges are returned under the Clean Earth Campaign via UPS or MBE in the U.S. and Canada Post in Canada. Shipping costs are paid by Canon, so there's no charge to our end users. Easy shipping instructions can be found in the cartridge box. Pack two or more used cartridges in one box for efficiency.
For details, call 1-800-962-2708 (in U.S.A.) or 1-800-667-2666 (in Canada).
Cartridges returned via:

MAIL BOXES ETC.®
All registered trademarks belong to their respective holders.
Canon
CANON INC. 30-2, Shimomaruko 3-chome, Ohta-ku, Tokyo 146, Japan. ©1996 Canon Inc.

Source: Courtesy Canon Inc.

Managing in the 21st Century

THE MEANING OF MARKET INFLUENCE

C. K. Prahalad, a well-recognized strategy expert, argues that existing measures of market influence, such as market share, center primarily on short-term performance and profitability in an existing market. In his view, strategists must ask this question: What is the appropriate measure of a firm's capacity both to create new businesses—thereby satisfying new customer needs and creating new sources of profit—and to influence the evolution of new industries?

He persuasively argues that core competence share and core product share may provide the best indication of a firm's ability to manage long-term profitable growth. First, the competencies of a firm provide a measure of its capacity to create new business opportunities. Second, core product share provides a measure of market influence.

Prahalad points to the competencies and core product share of Intel and its influence on the personal computer industry. "Intel is not in the personal computer (PC) assembly business (for example, IBM, Compaq) or purely PC marketing business (for example, Dell, Packard Bell). Intel manufactures a key module. However, Intel's influence in the PC industry is significantly greater than any single PC manufacturer."

C. K. Prahalad, "Weak Signals versus Strong Paradigms," *Journal of Marketing Research* 32 (August 1995): p. iv.

control procedures in manufacturing, significant strides have been made by companies such as Kodak, AT&T, Xerox, Ford, Hewlett-Packard, Intel, General Electric, and others. The quest for improved product quality touches the entire supply chain as these and other companies demand improved product quality from their suppliers, large and small.

MEANING OF QUALITY

The quality movement has passed through several stages.[14] **Stage one** centered on conformance to standards or success in meeting specifications. But conformance quality or zero defects will not satisfy a customer if the wrong features are embodied in a product. **Stage two** emphasized that quality was more than a technical specialty and that the pursuit of quality should drive the core processes of the entire business. Particular emphasis was given to total quality management and to measuring customer satisfaction. However, customers choose a particular product over competing offerings

[14]Bradley T. Gale, *Managing Customer Value: Creating Quality and Service That Customers Can See* (New York: The Free Press, 1994), pp. 25–30.

Figure 10.3 What Value Means to Customers

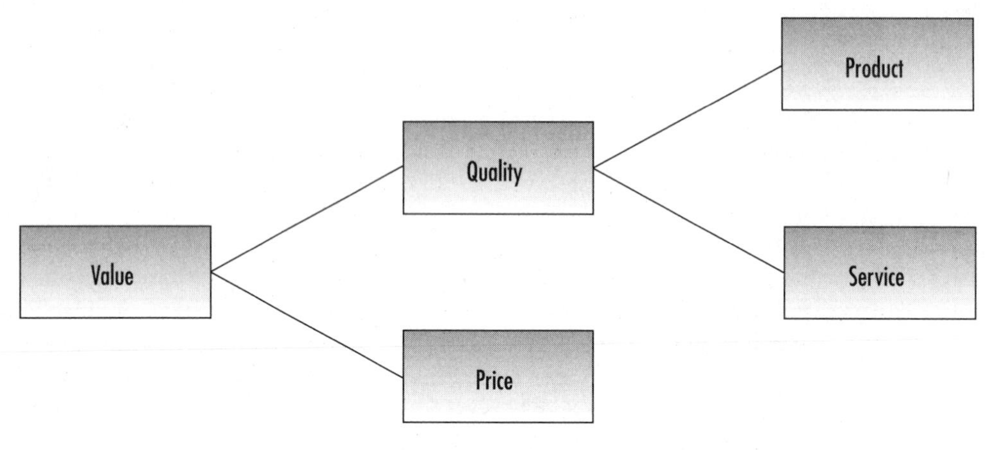

Source: Adapted from Bradley T. Gale, *Managing Customer Value* (New York: The Free Press, 1994), p. 29.

because they perceive it as providing superior *value*—the product's price, performance, and service render it the most attractive alternative. **Stage three,** then, examines a firm's quality performance relative to competitors and examines customer perceptions of the value of competing products. The focus here is on market-perceived quality and value versus that of competitors.

MEANING OF VALUE

Strategy experts Dwight Gertz and João Baptista suggest that "a company's product or service is competitively superior if, at price equality with competing products, target segments always choose it. Thus, value is defined in terms of consumer choice in a competitive context."[15] To Bradley T. Gale, "value is simply quality, however the *customer* defines it, offered at the right price."[16] In essence, value equals quality relative to price. Observe in Figure 10.3 that value has two components: quality and price. In turn, quality includes a customer service component.

[15]Dwight L. Gertz and João P. A. Baptista, *Grow to Be Great: Breaking the Downsizing Cycle* (New York: The Free Press, 1995), p. 128.
[16]Bradley T. Gale, *Managing Customer Value*, p. 26.

VALUE IN USE

An industrial product represents the total package of benefits that customers receive when they purchase and use it.[17] This includes the physical and performance attributes of the product; technical assistance provided before the sale; training, maintenance, or repair services provided after the sale; assurance of reliable and timely delivery support; and benefits that the customer derives from the reputation of the seller. Benefits might also include the buyer-seller relationship itself when close interpersonal relationships develop among personnel in the buying and selling organizations. A product is all of the value satisfactions that a customer derives at both an organizational and personal level.[18]

Big Q

Thomas Hogue, vice president of materials and services at Intel Corporation, aptly describes the link between quality and value:

> *What I call Big Q (or what others might call "total quality") involves more than product quality. Quality has come to include level of service to the customer, responsiveness to the customer, delivery performance, competitive pricing, comprehension or anticipation of where the customer is going in the marketplace—all of the things that define your worth in the mind of the customer.*[19]

PRODUCT SUPPORT STRATEGY: THE SERVICE CONNECTION

The marketing function must ensure that every part of the organization focuses on delivering superior value to customers. Business marketing programs involve a number of critical components that are carefully evaluated by customers: tangible products, service support, and ongoing information services both before and after the sale. To provide value to customers and to successfully implement these programs, the business marketing firm must carefully coordinate activities among personnel in product management, sales, and service.[20] For example, to customize a product and delivery schedule for an important customer requires close coordination among product, logistics, and sales personnel. Moreover, some customer accounts might

---

[17]Frank V. Cespedes, "Once More: How Do You Improve Customer Service?" *Business Horizons* 35 (March/April 1992): pp. 58–67.

[18]Theodore Levitt, *The Marketing Imagination,* new expanded ed. (New York: The Free Press, 1986), pp. 81–85.

[19]Anne Millen Porter, "Intel Corp. Takes on Big Q," *Purchasing* 119 (11 January 1996): p. 54.

[20]Frank V. Cespedes, *Concurrent Marketing: Integrating Product, Sales, and Service* (Boston, Mass.: Harvard Business School Press, 1995), pp. 58–85.

CANDID OBSERVATIONS FROM A QUALITY JUDGE

George S. Eaton, an examiner for the Malcolm Baldrige National Quality Award, provides a candid appraisal of the procedures that candidate firms employ in achieving "customer focus and satisfaction." He has observed the following strengths and areas for improvement in his field visits.

Strengths

- Many companies are using survey-type instruments to assess customer satisfaction and customer needs and expectations.
- Customer service representatives are gaining increased authority to satisfy the customer.
- Formal customer complaint resolution is an area of rising importance to management.

Areas for Improvement

- Customer satisfaction surveys center on the company's current customers, and neglect lost customers and the customers of competitors.
- Customers continue to have difficulty reaching an employee with real authority to resolve their problems.
- Many managers still believe that customers should be completely satisfied with replacement guarantees.

Source: George S. Eaton, "The 1993 State of U.S. Total Quality Management: A Baldrige Examiner's Perspective," *California Management Review* 35 (spring 1993): pp. 44–46.

---

require special field-engineering, installation, or equipment support, thereby increasing the required coordination between sales and service units.

Post-purchase service is especially important to buyers in many industrial product categories ranging from computers and machine tools to custom-designed component parts. Responsibility for service support, however, is often diffused throughout various departments, such as applications engineering, customer relations, or service administration. Significant benefits accrue to the business marketer who carefully manages and coordinates product, sales, and service connections to maximize customer value.

Product Policy

Product policy involves the set of all decisions concerning the products and services that the company offers. Through product policy, a business marketing firm attempts to satisfy customer needs and to build a sustainable competitive advantage by capitalizing on its core competencies. This section explores the types of industrial product lines and the importance of anchoring product management decisions on an accurate definition of the product market. A framework is also provided for assessing product opportunities on a global scale.

TYPES OF PRODUCT LINES DEFINED

Because product lines of industrial firms differ from those of consumer firms, classification is useful. Industrial product lines can be categorized into four types:[21]

1. *Proprietary or catalog products.* These items are offered only in certain configurations and produced in anticipation of orders. Product line decisions concern the addition, deletion, or repositioning of products within the line.
2. *Custom-built products.* These items are offered as a set of basic units, with numerous accessories and options. A lathe manufacturer may offer several basic sizes, with a range of options (such as various motor sizes) and accessories for various applications. The marketer offers the organizational buyer a set of building blocks. Product line decisions center on offering the proper mix of options and accessories.
3. *Custom-designed products.* These items are created to meet the needs of one or a small group of customers. Sometimes the product is a unique unit, such as a power plant or a specific machine tool. In addition, some items produced in relatively large quantities, such as an aircraft model, may fall into this category. The product line is described in terms of the company's capability, and the consumer buys that capability. Ultimately, this capability is transformed into a finished good.
4. *Industrial services.* Rather than an actual product, the buyer is purchasing a company's capability in an area such as maintenance, technical service, or management consulting. (Special attention is given to services marketing in Chapter 12.)

All types of business marketing firms confront product policy decisions, whether they offer physical products, pure services (no physical product), or a product-service combination.[22] Each product situation presents unique problems and opportunities for the business marketer; each draws upon a unique type of capability. Product strategy rests on the intelligent utilization of corporate capability.

---

[21]Benson P. Shapiro, *Industrial Product Policy: Managing the Existing Product Line* (Cambridge, Mass.: Marketing Science Institute, 1977), pp. 37–39.

[22]Albert L. Page and Michael Siemplenski, "Product-Systems Marketing," *Industrial Marketing Management* 12 (April 1983): pp. 89–99.

DEFINING THE PRODUCT MARKET

An accurate definition of the product market is fundamental to sound product policy decisions.[23] Careful attention must be given to the alternative ways customer needs can be satisfied. For example, many different products could provide competition for personal computers. Application-specific products, such as pocket pagers and stock-quotation devices, are potential competitors. A wide array of information appliances that provide easy access to the Internet also pose a threat. In turn, many firms have developed information networks that enable users to easily access information through inexpensive terminals. This provides users with the option of buying a simple terminal or information appliance, rather than a personal computer. In such an environment, Regis McKenna maintains, managers "must look for opportunities in—and expect competition from—every possible direction. A company with a narrow product concept will move through the market with blinders on, and it is sure to run into trouble."[24] By excluding products and technology that compete for the same end-user needs, the product strategist can quickly become out of touch with the market. Both customer needs and the ways of satisfying those needs change.

A **product market** establishes the distinct arena in which the business marketer competes. Four dimensions of a market definition are strategically relevant:

1. *Customer function dimension.* The related benefits are provided to satisfy the needs of organizational buyers.
2. *Technological dimension.* There are alternative ways a particular function can be performed.
3. *Customer segment dimension.* Customer groups have needs that must be served.
4. *Value-added system dimension.* There is a sequence of stages along which competitors serving the market can operate.[25]

Consider the case of a purchasing manager for a stereo manufacturer who is evaluating alternative suppliers of channel display units (a component part). Observe in Figure 10.4 that this need can potentially be satisfied by three different technologies, with perhaps multiple suppliers of each technology. Likewise, some of the suppliers may have the capability to move forward in the value chain and manufacture the complete stereo unit. Competition to satisfy this customer's need exists at the technology level as well as at the supplier or brand level.

By establishing accurate product-market boundaries, the product strategist is better equipped to identify customer needs, the benefits sought by the market segment,

---

[23]For a complete discussion on market definition, see David W. Cravens, *Strategic Marketing*, 5th ed. (Chicago: Richard D. Irwin, 1997), pp. 89–98.
[24]Regis McKenna, *Relationship Marketing*, p. 184.
[25]George S. Day, *Strategic Market Planning: The Pursuit of Competitive Advantage* (St. Paul, Minn.: West, 1984), p. 73.

Figure 10.4 Illustration of a Market Need

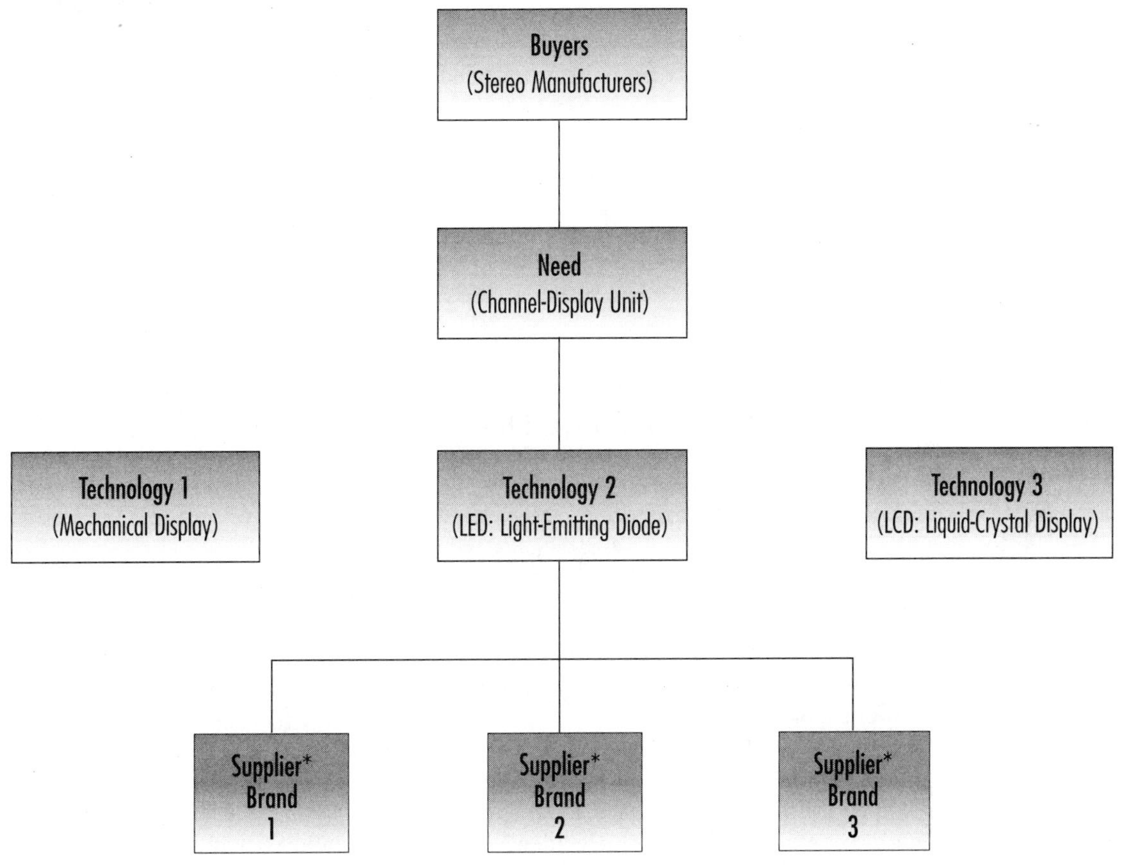

*Suppliers consist of electronic component manufacturers
Source: Adapted from Gary L. Lilien, "New Product Success in Business/Industrial Markets: Progress, Problems, and a Research Program," report no. 2-1985 (Pennsylvania State University College of Business Administration, Institute for the Study of Business Markets, 1985), p. 8.

and the nature of competition at both the technology and supplier or brand levels. George Day notes that

> *The strategist seeking to understand a particular market is dealing with a moving target, for change is continuous along each of the key market dimensions of function, technology, customer segmentation, and degree of integration."*[26]

[26]Ibid., p. 100.

Table 10.2 Assessment of Global Product-Market Opportunities

Product Configuration	Market Needs: Same	Market Needs: Different
Same	Universal or global product	Market segmentation
Different	Product segmentation (modified product)	Specialty segmentation (country-tailored product)

Source: Adapted from Jagdish N. Sheth, "Global Markets or Global Competition," *Journal of Consumer Marketing* 3 (spring 1986): p. 10.

ASSESSING GLOBAL PRODUCT-MARKET OPPORTUNITIES

Because an increasing number of business market sectors—such as the aerospace, telecommunications, computer, agricultural equipment, and automobile industries—include firms that compete on a worldwide basis, an assessment of global product-market opportunities is required. Observe in Table 10.2 that the business marketer has several options in developing an international product strategy. The horizontal dimension represents the similarity in or the difference between market needs across countries, whereas the vertical dimension represents the nature of the product configuration.

A **universal** or **global** product assumes that the needs of organizational customers are the same across countries. This assumption may be valid for some classes of industrial products and for some world markets (for example, Japan, North America, and Western Europe). In fact, some evidence suggests that industrial and high-technology products (for example, computer hardware, airliners, photographic equipment, machine tools, and heavy equipment) may be most appropriate for global product strategies.[27] Customers with multinational operations are particularly likely to have similar requirements worldwide.[28] For example, where the operations are integrated or coordinated across national boundaries, as in the case of financial institutions, compatibility of operation systems and equipment may be essential. Consequently, such firms may seek business marketers who can supply their global operations.

Global strategy experts provide three important guidelines for designing successful global products.[29]

---

[27]Subhash C. Jain, "Standardization of International Marketing Strategy: Some Research Hypotheses," *Journal of Marketing* 53 (January 1989): pp. 70–74.

[28]Susan P. Douglas and Yoram Wind, "The Myth of Globalization," *Columbia Journal of World Business* 22 (winter 1987): pp. 19–30.

[29]George S. Yip, *Total Global Strategy* (Englewood Cliffs, N.J.: Prentice-Hall, 1992), pp. 85–102. See also Jean-Phillippe Deschamps and P. Ranganath Nayak, *Product Juggernauts: How Companies Mobilize to Generate a Stream of Market Winners* (Boston: Harvard Business School Press, 1995), pp. 161–162.

1. In examining customer needs around the world, business marketers should search for similarities as well as differences.
2. Global product designers should try to maximize the size of the common global core of the product while also providing for local tailoring around the core.
3. Rather than being adapted from national products later, the best global products are designed with the global market in mind from the start.

Canon's successful entry into the photocopier business emphasized a strategy that exploited the similarities in buyers' needs across country markets. Because of cost considerations, early models could not accommodate all sizes of Japanese paper. Designed as a global product, Canon was willing to give up the ability to precisely meet all needs in its *domestic* market in order to maximize its position in the *global* market.[30]

A **product segmentation** strategy is appropriate when the market needs across countries are the same, but the products must be adapted to fit the local market. Note also from Table 10.2 that a **market segmentation** strategy fits when consumer needs across countries differ, but the product is standardized; other elements of the marketing mix are adapted to reach various target segments. To illustrate, Apple Computer sells a standardized product line worldwide but employs different positioning, promotional, and distribution strategies in each country. Finally, a **specialty segmentation** strategy involves developing tailor-made products for each country. This represents the most extreme form of specialization as market needs vary from country to country.

Susan P. Douglas and Yoram Wind provide this assessment of global product-market strategies:

> *A firm's international operations are likely to be characterized by a mix of strategies, including not only global products and brands, but also some regional products and brands and some national products and brands. Similarly, some target segments may be global, others regional and others national. Hybrid strategies of this nature thus enable a company to take advantage of the benefits of standardization, and potential synergies from operating on an international scale, while at the same time not losing those afforded by adaptation to specific country characteristics and consumer preferences.*[31]

Planning Industrial Product Strategy

Formulating a strategic marketing plan for an existing product line is the most vital part of a company's marketing planning efforts. Having identified a product market,

[30]Michael E. Porter, "Changing Patterns of International Competition," *California Management Review* 28 (winter 1986): pp. 33–34.

[31]Douglas and Wind, "The Myth of Globalization," p. 28.

HIGH-GROWTH MARKET BLUES

The conventional wisdom that marketers should invest in growth markets is based upon this line of reasoning: In the early phase of a growth market, shares gains are easier and worth more, the experience curve will lead to cost advantages, price pressures will be low, early involvement will provide a technological advantage, and early aggressive entry will deter later entrants. David Aaker and George Day argue that these premises are often shaky. "Numerous firms have entered growth situations only to endure years of painful losses and ultimately an embarrassing, costly, and sometimes fatal exit during a traumatic shakeout phase."

Why do risks often outweigh the rewards of high-growth markets? The authors isolate several factors:

- The number and aggressiveness of competitors is greater than can be supported by the market.
- Adequate distribution may not be available.
- Resources are lacking to maintain a high rate of growth.
- Important success factors change (for example, from product technology to process or production technology) and the firm cannot adapt.
- Technology changes.
- A competitor enters with a superior product or with a low-cost advantage.
- The market growth fails to materialize.

The effective business marketer must challenge the fundamental strategy premises. Aaker and Day point out that "A market is neither inherently attractive nor unattractive because it is experiencing high growth. The real question is whether the firm can exploit the opportunities presented by market growth to gain a competitive advantage.

Source: David A. Aaker and George S. Day, "The Perils of High-Growth Markets," *Strategic Management Journal* 7 (September 1986): pp. 409–421.

attention now turns to planning product strategy. Product positioning analysis provides a useful tool for charting the strategy course.

PRODUCT POSITIONING[32]

Once the product market is defined, a strong competitive position for the product must be secured. **Product positioning** represents the place that a product occupies in a particular market; it is found by measuring organizational buyers' perceptions and

[32]This section is based largely on Behram J. Hansotia, Muzaffar A. Shaikh, and Jagdish N. Sheth, "The Strategic Determinancy Approach to Brand Management," *Business Marketing* 70 (fall 1985): pp. 66–69.

preferences for a product in relation to its competitors. Because organizational buyers perceive products as bundles of attributes (for example, quality, service), the product strategist should examine the attributes that assume a central role in buying decisions.

DETERMINANT ATTRIBUTES

Particular attention should be given to defining those attributes that are **determinant**—attributes that are both important and differentiating. Figure 10.5 displays the possible types of determinant and nondeterminant attributes. A product manager may

Figure 10.5 Determinant and Nondeterminant Attributes

		Attribute					
		Determinant		Nondeterminant			
		D_1	D_2	ND_1	ND_2	ND_3	ND_4
	Important	x	x	x			
	Not Important				x	x	x
Nondifferentiating	(SB=COMP)			x	x		
Differentiating	(SB>COMP)	x				x	
	(SB<COMP)		x				x

SB: Sponsor Brand COMP: Competing Brand

Possible Attribute Types
Determinant:
D_1—Attribute is important as well as differentiating, but sponsor brand is superior to competing brand (SB>COMP).
D_2—Attribute is important as well as differentiating, but sponsor brand is inferior to competing brand (SB<COMP).
Nondeterminant:
ND_1—Attribute is important but not differentiating. Statistically, SB and COMP are perceived to be equal (SB=COMP).
ND_2—Attribute is neither important nor differentiating.
ND_3—Attribute is differentiating (SB>COMP), but not important.
ND_4—Attribute is differentiating (SB<COMP), but not important.

Source: Reprinted with permission from Behran J. Hansotia, Muzaffar A. Shaikh, and Jagdish N. Sheth, "The Strategic Determinancy Approach to Brand Management," *Business Marketing* 70 (February 1985): p. 66. Copyright Crain Communications, Inc.

find the attributes of his or her brand (see sponsor brand [SB]) in any one of several mutually exclusive categories. In this illustration, only two attributes are determinant; each is considered by organizational buyers to be both important and differentiating. Observe also that another attribute is important but is not differentiating. For example, safety might constitute an attribute that would fit this category in the heavy-duty truck market. Business market customers view safety as being important but may consider the competing products offered by Navistar, Volvo, and Mack Trucks as quite comparable on this dimension. Durability, reliability, and fuel economy might constitute the determinant attributes.

STRATEGY MATRIX

After defining the key attributes and assessing the firm's competitive standing, particular strategy options can be evaluated by the product manager. Figure 10.6 suggests how the attributes portrayed in Figure 10.5 might be changed. Thus, each cell of the strategy matrix provides possible generic strategies that the product manager could pursue to improve the brand's competitive standing. For example, the upper left cell (increase importance and brand differentiation) is a strategy requiring measures to (1) increase the attribute importance to customers, and (2) increase the difference between the competition and the sponsor brand. Of the attributes displayed in Figure 10.5, D_1 is the attribute most preferred by a product manager—the attribute is important and differentiating, and the sponsor brand is superior to competing brands.

Figure 10.6 Strategy Matrix

Importance	Brand Difference* Increase	Brand Difference* Decrease	Brand Difference* Maintain
Increase	$ND_2 \rightarrow D_1$		$ND_3 \rightarrow D_1$
Decrease			$D_2 \rightarrow ND_4$
Maintain	$ND_1 \rightarrow D_1$	$D_2 \rightarrow ND_1$	$ND_4 \rightarrow ND_4$ $D_1 \rightarrow D_1$

*Note: The brand difference may be positive or negative, depending on whether the sponsor brand or the competing brand is perceived as being superior.

Source: Reprinted with permission from Behran J. Hansotia, Muzaffar A. Shaikh, and Jagdish N. Sheth, "The Strategic Determinancy Approach to Brand Management," *Business Marketing* 70 (February 1985): p. 68. Copyright Crain Communications, Inc.

Ideally then, the product manager would like to convert attributes wherever possible into the D_1 attribute category. This would require either increasing brand difference (ND_1) or attribute importance (ND_3). Converting ND_2 into D_1 requires increasing both importance and brand difference.

The least-preferred attribute type for the product manager is D_2—attribute is important and differentiating, but the sponsor brand is inferior to competing brands. Here the product manager attempts to convert it into a nondeterminant attribute.

Illustration: Determinancy Analysis

The preceding strategic determinancy approach was successfully applied to a capital equipment product at a major corporation. The product that provided the focus of the analysis is sold in three sizes to two market segments: end users and consulting engineers. Through marketing research, fifteen attributes were identified, including such dimensions as reliability, service support, company reputation, and ease of maintenance.

The research found that the firm's brand enjoyed an outstanding rating on product reliability and service support, both attributes generally being determinant for the company against most competitors. To reinforce the importance of both attributes, management decided to offer an enhanced warranty program. Both end users and consulting engineers view warranties as important but not a point of differentiation across competing brands. Management surmised, however, that by establishing a new warranty standard for the industry, the attribute could become determinant, adding to the brand's leverage over competitors. In addition, management felt that the new warranty program might also benefit the brand's reputation on other attributes such as reliability and company reputation.

The study also provided some surprises. Price was not nearly as important to organizational buyers as management had initially believed. This suggested that there were opportunities to increase revenue through product differentiation and service support. Likewise, the research found that the firm's brand dominated all competitors in the large- and medium-sized products, but not in the small-sized products. This particular product had an especially weak competitive position in the consulting engineer segment. Special service support strategies were developed to strengthen the product's standing in this segment. Clearly, determinancy analysis provides a valuable tool for managing products for business markets.

Managing Products in High-Technology Markets[33]

Enticing opportunities and special challenges confront the product strategist in high-technology markets. This section explores the technology adoption life cycle and provides a blueprint for designing marketing strategy during the turbulent life of a high-technology product.

[33]This section is based on Geoffrey A. Moore, *Inside the Tornado: Marketing Strategies from Silicon Valley's Cutting Edge* (New York: HarperCollins, 1995).

ABOUT THOSE EXTRA BUTTONS ON THE TV REMOTE CONTROL

"Consider all the menu items on your favorite software program, all the buttons on the remote control for your TV, or the ones on the front of your telephone. Do you know what every one of them does?" Few do. What does this suggest? Geoffrey A. Moore argues that until a product feature is used by a customer, it has no value. Hidden inside every popular high-tech product is a wealth of R&D investment that remains untapped. Often the features were suppressed in promotion because company strategists feared that consumers would become confused and view the product as needlessly complex. Once a new technology product gains a foothold in the marketplace, Moore suggests that these product attributes can be leveraged by isolating unused features, matching them up with target segments who would benefit the most from them, and celebrating them in promotional campaigns.

Source: Geoffrey A. Moore, *Inside the Tornado: Marketing Strategies from Silicon Valley's Cutting Edge* (New York: HarperCollins, 1995), p. 119.

After decades of being content with letters, telegrams, and telephones, consumers have embraced fax machines, voice mail, e-mail, and Internet browsers. In each case, the conversion of the market came slowly. Once a particular threshold of consumer acceptance was achieved, there was a stampede. Geoffrey Moore defines **discontinuous innovations** as "new products or services that require the end-user and the marketplace to dramatically change their past behavior, with the promise of gaining equally-dramatic new benefits."[34] During the past quarter-century, discontinuous innovations have been common in the computer and electronics industry, creating massive new influxes of spending, fierce competition, and a whole host of firms that are redrawing the boundaries of the high technology marketplace.

ISOLATING TECHNOLOGY ADOPTERS

A popular tool with strategists at high technology firms is the technology adoption life cycle—a framework developed by Geoffrey Moore, a leading consultant to Sun Microsystems, Silicon Graphics, Hewlett-Packard, and others.

Types of Technology Customers

Fundamental to Moore's framework are five classes of customers who constitute the potential market for a discontinuous innovation (see Table 10.3). Business marketers

[34]Ibid., p. 13.

Table 10.3 The Technology Adoption Life Cycle: Classes of Customers

Customer	Profile
Technology enthusiasts (innovators)	Interested in exploring the latest innovation, these consumers possess significant influence over how products are perceived by others in the organization but lack control over resource commitments.
Visionaries (early adopters)	Desiring to exploit the innovation for a competitive advantage, these consumers are the true revolutionaries in business and government who have access to organizational resources but frequently demand special modifications to the product that are difficult for the innovator to provide.
Pragmatists (early majority)	Making the bulk of technology purchases in organizations, these individuals believe in technology evolution, not revolution, and seek products from a market leader with a proven track record of providing useful productivity improvements.
Conservatives (late majority)	Pessimistic about their ability to derive any value from technology investments, these individuals represent a sizable group of customers who are price sensitive and reluctantly purchase high-tech products to avoid being left behind.
Skeptics (laggards)	Rather than potential customers, these individuals are ever-present critics of the hype surrounding high-technology products.

Source: Adapted from Geoffrey A. Moore, *Inside the Tornado: Marketing Strategies from Silicon Valley's Cutting Edge* (New York: HarperCollins, 1995), pp. 14–18.

can benefit by putting innovative products in the hands of **technology enthusiasts.** They serve as a gatekeeper to the rest of the technology life cycle and their endorsement is needed for an innovation to get a fair hearing in the organization. Whereas technology enthusiasts possess influence, they do not have ready access to the resources needed to move an organization toward a large-scale commitment to the new technology. By contrast, **visionaries** have resource control and can often assume an influential role in publicizing the benefits of an innovation and giving it a boost during the early stages of market development. However, visionaries are difficult for a marketer to serve because each demands special and unique product modifications. Their demands can quickly tax the R&D resources of the technology firm and stall the market penetration of the innovation.

The Chasm

Truly innovative products often enjoy a warm welcome in an early market comprising technology enthusiasts and visionaries, but then sales falter and often even plummet. Frequently, a chasm develops between visionaries who are intuitive and support revolution and the **pragmatists** who are analytical, support evolution, and provide the pathway to the mainstream market. If the business marketer can successfully guide a product across the chasm, an opportunity is created to gain acceptance with the mainstream market comprising pragmatists and conservatives. As Table 10.3 relates, **pragmatists** make the bulk of technology purchases in organizations and **conservatives** include a sizable group of customers who are hesitant to buy high-tech products but do so to avoid being left behind.

THE TECHNOLOGY ADOPTION LIFE CYCLE

The fundamental strategy for crossing the chasm and moving from the early market to the mainstream market is to provide pragmatists with a 100-percent solution to their problems (see Figure 10.7). Many high-technology firms err by attempting to provide something for everyone while never meeting the complete requirements of any particular market segment. What pragmatists seek is the whole product—the minimum set of products and services necessary to support a compelling reason to buy. Geoffrey Moore notes that "the key to a winning strategy is to identify a simple beachhead of pragmatist customers in a mainstream market segment and to accelerate the formation of 100 percent of their whole product. The goal is to win a niche foothold in the mainstream as quickly as possible—that is what is meant by *crossing the chasm*."[35]

The Bowling Alley

In technology markets, each market segment is like a bowling pin and the momentum achieved from hitting one segment successfully carries over into surrounding segments. The bowling alley represents a stage in the adoption life cycle where a product gains acceptance from segments within the mainstream market but has yet to achieve widespread adoption.

Consider the evolution of strategy for Lotus Notes.[36] When first introduced, Notes was offered as a new paradigm for corporatewide communication. To cross into the mainstream market, the Lotus team shifted the product's focus from an enterprisewide vision of corporate communication to specific solutions for particular business functions. The first niche served was the global account management function of worldwide accounting and consulting firms. The solution offered to the customer was enhanced account activity coordination for highly visible products. This led to a second niche—global account management for sales teams where enhanced coordination and information sharing spur productivity.

A Focused Strategy. A logical next step for Lotus was movement into the customer service function where an open sharing of information can support creative solutions to

---

[35]Ibid., p. 22.
[36]Ibid., pp. 35–37.

customer problems. Successful penetration of these segments created another opportunity—incorporating the customer into the Notes loop. Note the key lesson here: A customer-based, application-focused strategy provides leverage so that a victory in one market segment cascades into victories in adjacent market segments.

The Tornado

While economic buyers who seek particular solutions are the key to success in the bowling alley, technical or infrastructure buyers in organizations can spawn a tornado (see Figure 10.7). Information technology (IT) managers are responsible for providing efficient and reliable infrastructures—the systems through which organizational members communicate and perform their jobs. They are pragmatists and they prefer to buy from an established market leader.

IT professionals interact freely across company and industry boundaries and discuss the ramifications of the latest technology. IT managers watch each other closely—they do not want to be too early or too late. Often, they move together and create a tornado. Because a massive number of new customers are entering the market at the same time and because they all want the same product, demand dramatically outstrips supply and a large backlog of customers can appear overnight. At a critical stage, such market forces have surrounded Hewlett-Packard's laser and inkjet printers, Microsoft's Windows products, and Intel's Pentium microprocessors.

Figure 10.7 The Landscape of the Technology Adoption Life Cycle

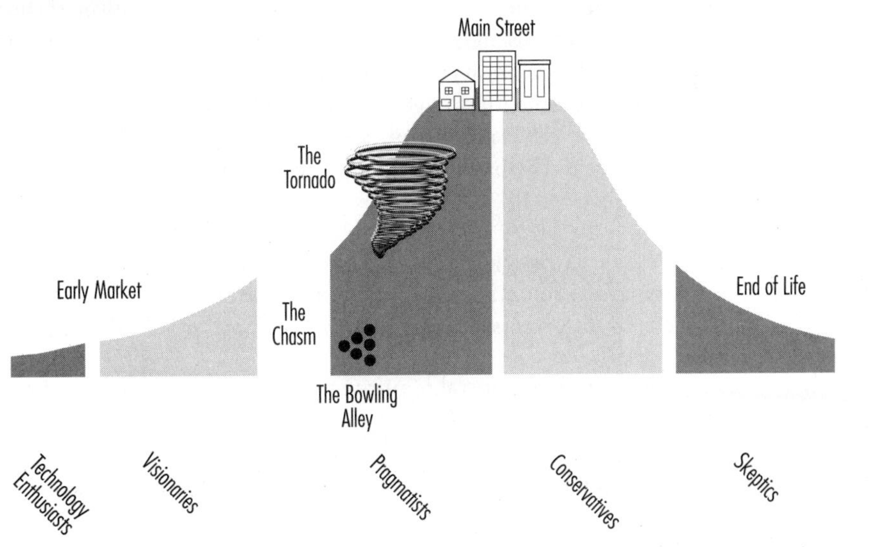

Source: Adapted from Geoffrey A. Moore, *Inside the Tornado: Marketing Strategies from Silicon Valley's Cutting Edge* (New York: HarperCollins, 1995), pp. 19 and 25. Copyright 1995 by Geoffrey A. Moore Consulting Inc. Reprinted by permission of HarperCollins Publishers Inc.

Tornado Strategy. The central success factors for the tornado phase of the adoption life cycle differ from those that are appropriate for the bowling alley. Rather than emphasizing market segmentation, the central goal is to gear up production to capitalize on the opportunity that the broad market presents. In its printer business, Hewlett-Packard (H-P) demonstrated the three critical priorities to emphasize during a tornado:[37]

1. "Just ship"
2. Extend distribution channels
3. Drive to the next lower price point

First, H-P's quality improvement process allowed it to significantly increase production—first with laser printers, and later with inkjet printers—with few interruptions. Second, to extend market coverage, H-P began to sell its laser printers through PC dealer channels and extended its distribution channels for inkjet printers to computer superstores, office superstores, mail order, and, more recently, to price clubs and other consumer outlets. Third, H-P drove down the price points for its printers—moving inkjet printers below $1,000, then below $500, and then well below that. As this example demonstrates, tornado strategy emphasizes product leadership and operational excellence in manufacturing and distribution.

Main Street

This stage of the technology adoption life cycle represents a period of aftermarket development. The frantic waves of mass-market adoption of the product begin to subside. Competitors in the industry have increased production and supply now exceeds demand. Moore points out that "The defining characteristic of Main Street is that continued profitable market growth can no longer come from selling the basic commodity to new customers and must come instead from developing niche-specific extensions to the basic platform for existing customers."[38]

Main Street Strategy. The goal here is to develop value-based strategies targeted on particular segments of end users. H-P, for example, matches its printers to the special needs of different segments of home office users by offering:

- a compact portable printer for those users who are space-constrained
- the OfficeJet printer-fax for those who do not yet own a fax
- a high-performance color printer for those who create commercial flyers

---

[37]Ibid., p. 81. See also Stephen Kreider Yoder, "Shaving Back: How H-P Used Tactics of the Japanese to Beat Them at Their Game," *The Wall Street Journal,* 8 September 1994, pp. A1, A6.
[38]Geoffrey A. Moore, *Inside the Tornado*, p. 111.

Main Street strategy emphasizes operational excellence in production and distribution as well as finely tuned market segmentation strategies. What signals the end of the life for the technology adoption life cycle? A discontinuous innovation appears that incorporates breakthrough technology and promises new solutions for customers.

Summary

The stream of successful products introduced by leading business marketing firms can be traced to a particular set of unique core competencies that each has developed and continually enriched. Core competencies provide access to an array of markets, make an important contribution to the value that customers perceive in a product, and are difficult for competitors to imitate. Conceptualizing a product must go beyond mere physical description to include all the benefits and services that provide value to customers. The unifying goal for the business marketer: *Provide superior market-perceived quality and value versus competitors.* A carefully coordinated product strategy recognizes the role that various functional areas assume in providing value to organizational customers. Special attention should be given to synchronizing the activities among the product management, sales, and service units.

Industrial product lines can be broadly classified into (1) proprietary or catalog items, (2) custom-built items, (3) custom-designed items, and (4) industrial services. Industrial product management can best be described as the management of capability. In monitoring product performance and in formulating marketing strategy, the business marketer can profitably use product positioning analysis. By isolating a product's competitive standing in a market, positioning analysis provides strategy insights to the planner. A product attribute is determinant if it is both important and differentiating.

Rapidly changing high-technology markets present special opportunities and challenges for the product strategist. The technology adoption life cycle includes five categories of customers: technology enthusiasts, visionaries, pragmatists, conservatives, and skeptics. New products gain acceptance from niches within the mainstream market, progress from segment to segment like one bowling pin knocking over another, and, if successful, experience the tornado of general, widespread adoption by pragmatists. Importantly, the technology adoption life cycle calls for different marketing strategies at different stages.

Discussion Questions

1. Microsoft has enjoyed rapid growth and a dominant market position in the software industry. First, develop a list of what you believe to be the core competencies of Microsoft. Next, identify which of these core competencies appear to be especially hard for competitors to duplicate.

2. To enhance the value of an industrial product for a customer, the business marketing strategist must carefully manage and coordinate linkages among product management, sales, and service units. Explain.
3. Regis McKenna notes that "No company in a technology-based industry is safe from unanticipated bumps in the night." In recent years, many industries have been jolted by technological change. In such an environment, what steps can a product strategist take?
4. Bradley Gale, managing director of The Strategic Planning Institute, says: "People systematically knock out income statements and balance sheets, but they often don't monitor the nonfinancial factors that ultimately drive their financial performance. These nonfinancial factors include 'relative customer-perceived quality': how customers view the marketer's offering versus how they perceive competitive offerings." Explain.
5. Distinguish between catalog items, custom-built items, custom-designed items, and services. Explain how marketing requirements vary across these classifications.
6. Describe how a product manager might structure a study to identify the determinant attributes for fax equipment in the university market.
7. A particular product strategy will stimulate a response from the market, and a corresponding response from competitors. Which specific features of the competitive environment should be evaluated by the industrial product strategist?
8. Some industrial product managers argue that their prime function is to market the "capability" of their firm, rather than physical products. Do you agree or disagree? Explain.
9. Moving across the technology adoption life cycle, compare and contrast technology enthusiasts with pragmatists. Give special attention to the strategy guidelines that the marketing strategist should follow in reaching customers that fall into these two adoption categories.
10. Firms like Microsoft, Sony, and Intel have experienced a burst of demand for some of their products. During the "tornado" for a high-tech product, the guiding principle of operations for a market leader is "Just ship." Explain and discuss the changes in marketing strategy that the firm must follow *after* the tornado.

Chapter 11

Managing Innovation and New Industrial Product Development

The long-term competitive position of most organizations is tied to their ability to innovate—to provide existing and new customers with a continuing stream of new products and services. Innovation is a high-risk and potentially rewarding process. After reading this chapter, you will understand

1. the strategic processes through which product innovations take shape.
2. the role of the technology portfolio in new product planning.
3. the factors that drive a firm's new product performance.
4. the determinants of new product success and timeliness.

Product innovation is important in the history of many prominent firms and in the careers of many successful managers. Take Scott Shamlin, who served as project team leader in the development of Motorola's successful "Bandit" pager. Described by team members as a "crusader," a "renegade," and a "workaholic," Shamlin championed the Bandit effort. Kim Clark and Steven Wheelwright describe Shamlin as "a hands-on manager with several years of experience in operations, and [who] played a major role in stimulating and facilitating communication across functions. Moreover, he helped to articulate a vision of the Bandit line, and to infuse it into the detailed work of the project team."[1] The glowing success of the project was extremely satisfying to Motorola and to the team.

The long-term health of industrial companies is tied to their ability to provide existing and new customers with a continuing stream of attractive new products.

[1]Kim B. Clark and Steven C. Wheelwright, *Managing New Product and Process Development* (New York: The Free Press, 1993), p. 534.

Many firms derive a significant portion of their sales and profits from products introduced in the recent past. But the risks associated with product innovation are high; significant investments are involved and the likelihood of failure is high. With shortening product life cycles and accelerating technological change, speed is the new battleground in the innovation battle.[2]

This chapter examines product innovation in the business marketing environment. The first section provides a perspective on the management of innovation in the firm. Second, product innovation is positioned within an overall technological strategy for the firm. Third, key dimensions of the new product development process are examined. Attention centers on the forces that drive successful new product performance in the firm. The final section of the chapter explores the determinants of new product success and timeliness.

The Management of Innovation

Management practices in successful industrial firms reflect the realities of the innovation process itself. James Quinn asserts that "Innovation tends to be individually motivated, opportunistic, customer responsive, tumultuous, nonlinear, and interactive in its development. Managers can plan overall directions and goals, but surprises are likely to abound."[3] Clearly, some new product development efforts are the outgrowth of **deliberate** strategies (intended strategies that become realized), while others result from **emergent** strategies (realized strategies that, at least initially, were never intended).[4] Bearing little resemblance to a rational, analytical process, many strategic decisions involving new products are rather messy, disorderly, and disjointed processes around which competing organizational factions contend. In studying successful innovative companies such as Sony, AT&T, and Hewlett-Packard, Quinn characterized the innovation process as controlled chaos:

> *Many of the best concepts and solutions come from projects partly hidden or "bootlegged" by the organization. Most successful managers try to build some slack or buffers into their plans to hedge their bets. . . . They permit chaos and replications in early investigations, but insist on much more formal planning and controls as expensive development and scale-up proceed. But even at these later stages, these managers have learned to maintain flexibility and to avoid the tyranny of paper plans.*[5]

---

[2]Jean-Phillippe Deschamps and P. Ranganath Nayak, *Product Juggernauts: How Companies Mobilize to Generate a Stream of Market Winners* (Boston, Mass.: Harvard Business School Press, 1995), pp. 54–66; see also Abbie Griffin and Albert L. Page, "An Interim Report on Measuring Product Development Success and Failure," *Journal of Product Innovation Management* 10 (September 1993): pp. 291–309.

[3]James B. Quinn, "Managing Innovation: Controlled Chaos," *Harvard Business Review* 63 (May/June 1985) p. 83.

[4]Henry Mintzberg and James A. Walton, "Of Strategies, Deliberate and Emergent," *Strategic Management Journal* 6 (July/August 1985): pp. 257–272.

[5]Quinn, "Managing Innovation," p. 82.

PATTERNS OF STRATEGIC BEHAVIOR[6]

A planned, deliberate process characterizes the development of some new products whereas a circuitous and chaotic process typifies others. Why? Research suggests that strategic activity within a large organization falls into two broad categories: induced and autonomous strategic behavior.[7]

Induced Strategic Behavior

Induced strategic behavior is consistent with the firm's traditional concept of strategy and takes place in relationship to its familiar external environment (for example, its customary markets). By manipulating various administrative mechanisms, top management can influence the perceived interests of managers at the middle and operational levels of the organization and keep strategic behavior in line with the current strategy course. For example, the existing reward and measurement systems may direct the attention of managers to some market opportunities and not to others. Examples of induced strategic behavior might emerge around product development efforts for existing markets.

Autonomous Strategic Behavior

During any period, the bulk of strategic activity in large, complex firms is likely to fit into the induced behavior category. However, large, resource-rich firms are likely to possess a pool of entrepreneurial potential at operational levels, which will express itself in autonomous strategic initiatives. The 3M Company encourages its technical employees to devote 15 percent of their work time to developing their own ideas. Through the personal efforts of employees, new products are born. For example,

- Art Fry championed Post-it Notes at 3M.
- P. D. Estridge promoted the personal computer at IBM.
- Stephenie L. Kwolck advanced the bulletproof material Kevlar at Du Pont.[8]

Autonomous strategic behavior is conceptually equivalent to entrepreneurial activity and introduces new categories of opportunity into the firm's planning process. Managers at the product-market level conceive of market opportunities that depart from the current strategy course, then engage in product championing activities to mobilize resources and create momentum for further development of the product.

---

[6]This section is based on Michael D. Hutt, Peter H. Reingen, and John R. Ronchetto Jr., "Tracing Emergent Processes in Marketing Strategy Formation," *Journal of Marketing* 52 (January 1988): pp. 4–19.
[7]Robert A. Burgelman, "A Process Model of Internal Corporate Venturing in the Diversified Major Firm," *Administrative Science Quarterly* 28 (April 1983): pp. 223–244.
[8]Timothy D. Schellhardt, "David and Goliath," *The Wall Street Journal*, (23 May 1996), p. R14.

Table 11.1 Induced versus Autonomous Strategic Behavior: Selected Characteristics of the Marketing Strategy Forumlation Process

	Induced	Autonomous
Activation of the strategic decision process	An individual manager defines a market need that converges on the organization's concept of strategy.	An individual manager defines a market need that diverges from the organization's concept of strategy.
Nature of the screening process	A formal screening of technical and market merit is made using established administrative procedures.	An informal network assesses technical and market merit.
Type of innovation	Incremental (e.g., new product development for existing markets uses existing organizational resources).	Major (e.g., new product development projects require new combinations of organizational resources).
Nature of communication	Consistent with organizational work flow.	Departs from organizational work flow in early phase of decision process.
Major actors	Prescribed by the regular channel of hierarchical decision making.	An informal network emerges based on mobilization efforts of the product champion.
Decision roles	Roles and responsibilities for participants in the strategy formulation process are well defined.	Roles and responsibilities of participants are poorly defined in the initial phases but become more formalized as the strategy formulation process evolves.
Implications for strategy formulation	Strategic alternatives are considered and commitment to a particular strategic course evolves.	Commitment to a particular strategic course emerges in the early phases through the sponsorship efforts of the product champion.

Source: Adapted from Michael D. Hutt, Peter H. Reingen, and John R. Ronchetto Jr., "Tracing Emergent Processes in Marketing, Strategy Formation," *Journal of Marketing* 52 (January 1988): pp. 4–19.

Emphasizing political rather than administrative channels, product champions question the firm's current concept of strategy and, states Robert Burgelman, "provide top management with the opportunity to rationalize, retroactively, successful autonomous strategic behavior."[9] Through these political mechanisms, successful autonomous strategic initiatives can become integrated into the firm's concept of strategy.

Product Championing and the Informal Network

Several characteristics that may distinguish induced from autonomous strategic behavior are highlighted in Table 11.1. Observe that autonomous strategic initiatives involve a set of actors and evoke a form of strategic dialogue different from

[9]Robert A. Burgelman, "Corporate Entrepreneurship and Strategic Management: Insights from a Process Study," *Management Science* 29 (December 1983): p. 1352.

GET INNOVATIVE OR GET DEAD

In his provocative style, Tom Peters issues a call: "Survival anywhere now depends upon perpetual innovation and improvement. That is: no renegades means no success." In this challenging, chaotic, competitive environment, Peters urges innovation leaders to

- implement a performance culture and give everyone a piece of the action.
- tell stories that celebrate the renegades, the small wins, and the useful failures.
- preach "failure-as-a-part-of-life" and reduce employee fear of making miscues in the innovation process.
- proclaim "life-is-at-bats"/"try it now."

Peters summarizes, "When it comes to innovation we seem almost to have a death wish. . . . We ignore that final Catch 22—the better you do something, the more open you are . . . to anybody and everybody with a new idea. If innovation is as important as I say, . . . then I contend that you'd better look to radical strategies."

Source: Tom Peters, "Get Innovative or Get Dead," *California Management Review* 33 (winter 1991): pp. 9–23.

those found in induced initiatives. An individual manager, the product champion, assumes a central role in sensing an opportunity and in mobilizing an informal network to explore the technical feasibility and market potential of the idea. A **product champion** is an organization member who creates, defines, or adopts an idea for an innovation and who is willing to assume significant risk (for example, position or prestige) to make possible the successful implementation of the innovation.[10] Senior managers at 3M Company will not commit to a project unless a champion emerges and will not abandon the effort unless the champion "gets tired."

Compared to induced strategic behavior, autonomous initiatives are more likely to involve a communication process that departs from the regular work flow and the hierarchical decision-making channels. The decision roles and responsibilities of managers in this informal network are poorly defined in the early phases of the strategy formulation process but become more formalized as the process evolves. Note in Table 11.1 that autonomous strategic behavior entails a creeping commitment toward a particular strategy course. By contrast, induced strategic initiatives are more likely to involve administrative mechanisms that encourage a more formal and comprehensive assessment of strategic alternatives at various levels in the firm's planning hierarchy.

[10]Modesto A. Maidique, "Entrepreneurs, Champions, and Technological Innovations," Sloan Management Review 21 (spring 1980): pp. 59–70; see also Jane M. Howell, "Champions of Technological Innvation," *Administrative Science Quarterly* 35 (June 1990): pp. 317–341.

MANAGING INNOVATION: IMPLICATIONS

The opposing tendencies toward either stability or change in the new product planning process raise a challenging set of implications for business marketing managers. First, entrepreneurial initiatives cannot be precisely planned, but they can be nurtured and encouraged. Some recommend that the planning and budgeting process should shift away from the primary role of rationing resources toward a role that emphasizes seeking opportunities and taking risks.[11] Robert Burgelman (among others) argues that top management ". . . need not encourage entrepreneurship; it need only make sure not to suppress it."[12]

Second, autonomous strategic initiatives could be encouraged by facilitating the exchange of information between the organization's functional areas and business units. For example, distributing an inventory of the R&D projects that are under way throughout the corporation, and indicating the names of the project leaders, would enhance the flow of technical information in both the formal and the informal networks. Nurturing communications among marketing personnel (including field salespersons) and R&D managers would also be profitable. Clearly, the marketing function can assume a pivotal role in the acquisition and dissemination of information crucial to entrepreneurial initiatives.

By gathering critical environmental information concerning threats and opportunities, by serving as an advocate for desired strategic options, and by channeling organizational attention to these options, business marketing managers assume a critical role in the management of innovation within the firm. Crucial to this process in many firms is the development of a technology strategy.

The Technology Portfolio

Eastman Kodak, Lockheed, IBM, and the management teams of other corporations failed to recognize the major technological opportunity that xerographic copying presented. These firms were among the many that turned down the chance to participate with the small and unknown Haloid Company in refining and commercializing this technology. In the end, Haloid pursued it alone and transformed this one technological opportunity into the Xerox Corporation. Among the "tales of high tech," this will remain a classic. Technological change, Michael Porter asserts, is "a great equalizer, eroding the competitive advantage of even well-entrenched firms and propelling others to the forefront. Many of today's great firms grew out of technological changes that they were able to exploit."[13] Clearly, the long-run competitive position of most

[11]James B. Quinn, *Strategies for Change: Logical Incrementalism* (Homewood, Ill: Richard D. Irwin, 1980).

[12]Burgelman, "Corporate Entrepreneurship and Strategic Management," p. 1361; and Rosabeth Moss Kanter, "Swimming in Newstreams: Mastering Innovation Dilemmas," *California Management Review* 31 (summer 1989): pp. 45–69.

[13]Michael E. Porter, "Technology and Competitive Advantage," *Journal of Business Strategy* 6 (winter 1985) p. 60; and Tamara J. Erickson, John F. Magee, Philip A. Roussel, and Komol N. Saad, "Managing Technology as Business Strategy," *Sloan Management Review* 31 (spring 1990): pp. 73–83.

industrial firms depends on their ability to manage, increase, and exploit their technology base (see Figure 11.1).

CLASSIFYING DEVELOPMENT PROJECTS

A first step in exploring the technology portfolio of a firm is to understand the different forms that development projects can take. Some development projects center on improving the manufacturing *process*, some on improving *products*, and others on both process and product improvements. All of these represent commercial development projects. By contrast, research and development is the precursor to commercial development. Four types of development projects may be included in a firm's portfolio.[14]

1. **Derivative projects** center on incremental product enhancements (for example, a new feature), incremental process improvements (for example, a lower-cost manufacturing process), or incremental changes on both dimensions.

   Illustration: A feature-enhanced or cost-reduced Canon fax machine.

2. **Platform projects** create the design and components that are shared by a set of products. These projects often involve a number of changes both in the product and in the manufacturing process.

   Illustrations: A common motor in all Black & Decker hand tools; multiple applications of Intel's microprocessor.

3. **Breakthrough projects** establish new core products and new core processes that differ fundamentally from previous generations.

   Illustrations: Computer disks and fiber-optics cable each created a new product category.

4. **Research and development** is the creation of knowledge concerning new materials and technologies that eventually leads to commercial development.[15]

   Illustrations: Lucent Technologies' development of communications technology that underlies its telecommunications sytems used by diverse customers like banks and hotel chains.

---

[14]This discussion is based on Steven C. Wheelwright and Kim B. Clark, "Creating Product Plans to Focus Product Development," *Harvard Business Review* 70 (March/April 1992): pp. 70–82.

[15]Ibid., p. 74.

Figure 11.1 Lucent Technologies Emphasizes Its Rich Bell Labs Heritage

Life discovered on Mars.

(got work to do)

Already busy here on Earth.
Plenty more to do. Half of world's
population has never made a phone call.
Most have never used cellular.
Even fewer have surfed Internet.
Now this.
Should keep us canceling vacations into
next millennium.

Lucent Technologies
Bell Labs Innovations
600 Mountain Avenue
Murray Hill, NJ 07974-0636
http://www.lucent.com
1-888-4-Lucent

We make the things that make communications work.™

Source: Courtesy Lucent Technologies.

IDENTIFYING THE PROJECT MIX

The technology portfolio provides a tool that the business marketer can use to evaluate the set of technologies in the firm's asset base, how various technologies complement one another, and how they might be better exploited to gain a competitive advantage.[16] Observe in Figure 11.2 (upper portion) that the entries in the technology portfolio are technologies rather than products. The vertical axis reflects a time dimension and is divided into two intervals reflecting the premarket and postmarket phases of technology exploitation. Each of these phases is further subdivided. The premarket phase is split into the research and the development stages of technology generation, and the postmarket phase is split into the familiar high- and low-growth stages of the product life cycle. Thus, the vertical axis traces the flow of a particular technology through its life cycle, from its conception as a basic research idea through its high growth to its ultimate decline in the low-growth stage of market exploitation.

COMPETITIVE POSITION

The horizontal axis of the technology portfolio (see Figure 11.2) captures the relative strength or competitive position of the firm. In the postmarket phase, attention centers on the relative market share that a particular technology enjoys in the firm's portfolio: high versus low. By contrast, the premarket phase (upper portion) applies to relative technology strength and indicates the extent to which the firm is a leader or follower in the research and/or development of a given technology.

The technology portfolio provides a portrait of how a firm is distributing its resources across its mix of technologies and of where these technologies stand in development, market exploitation, and competitive strength. To ensure both current and future returns, a well-managed set of technologies should be balanced in the matrix in terms of both distribution and size. In particular, heavy concentration of large circles in any part of the portfolio implies that the firm's total flow of resources will be difficult to sustain.

TECHNOLOGY STRATEGY AND COMPETITIVE ADVANTAGE

Each entry in the technology portfolio may provide the foundation or platform for several products. For example, Honda applies its multivalve cylinder technology to

[16]Noel Capon and Rashi Glazer, "Marketing and Technology: A Strategic Coalignment," *Journal of Marketing* 51 (July 1987): pp. 1–14.

Figure 11.2 Relationship between Technology and Product Portfolios

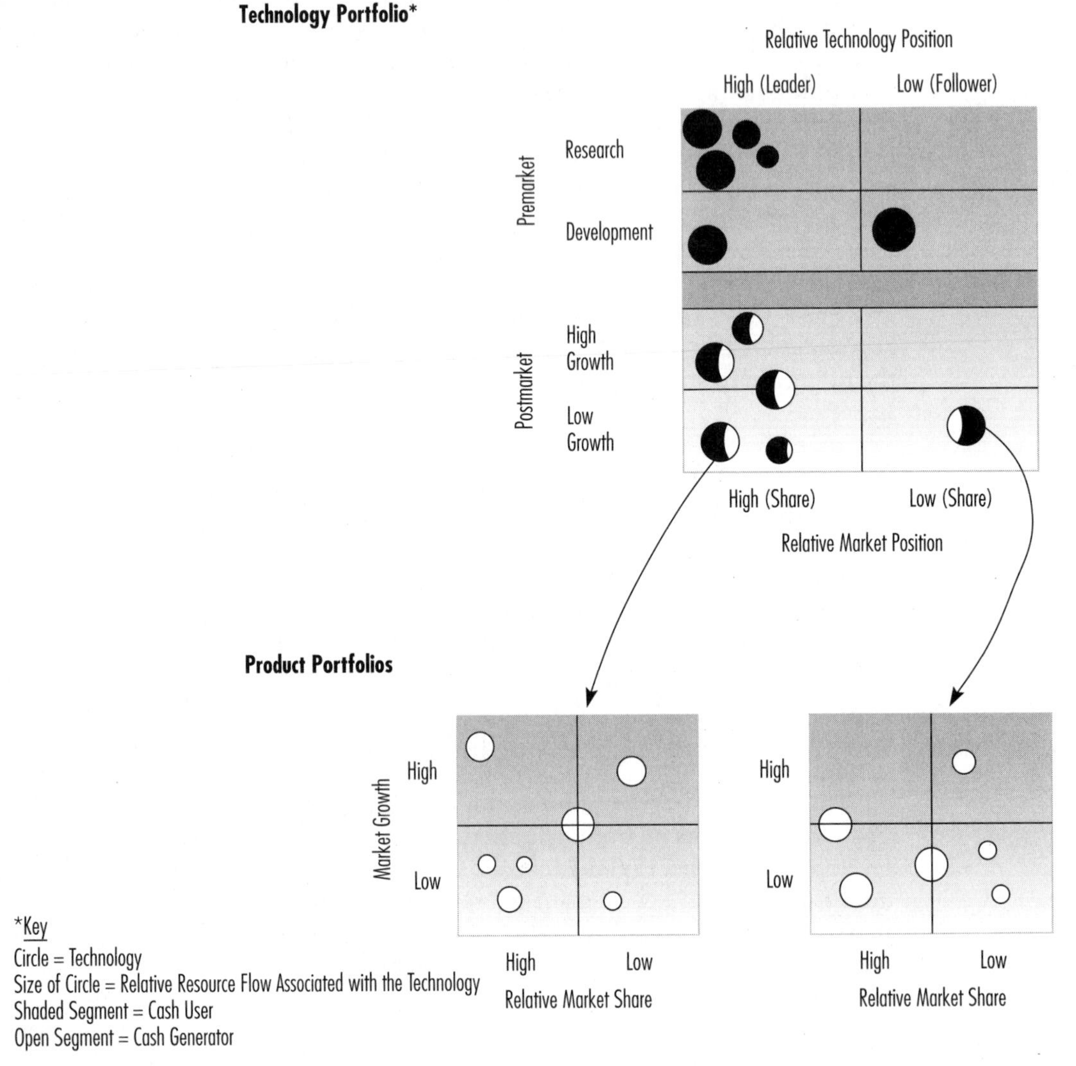

Source: Noel Capon and Rashi Glazer, "Marketing and Technology: A Strategic Coalignment," *Journal of Marketing* 51 (July 1987): p. 11. Published by the American Marketing Association.

power-generation equipment, cars, motorcycles, and lawn mowers.[17] Similarly, Canon drew on its copier and facsimile machine platforms to create laser printer and scanner businesses. Because the products derived from a single technology are likely

[17]T. Michael Nevens, Gregory L. Summe, and Bro Uttal, "Commercializing Technology: What the Best Companies Do," *Harvard Business Review* 60 (May/June 1990): pp. 154–163; see also C. K. Prahalad, "Weak Signals versus Strong Paradigms," *Journal of Marketing Research* 32 (August 1995): pp. iii–vi.

to differ in terms of competitive position and market-segment growth, a single position in the technology portfolio gives rise to multiple entries in the product portfolio (the two lower grids of Figure 11.2). Thus, the single entry in the technology portfolio represents a composite measure (or weighted average) of the associated product portfolio.

PLATFORMS FOR PRODUCT FAMILIES[18]

The technology portfolio highlights the importance of carefully defining the core competencies of a firm and examining how these competencies can be translated into a stream of successful products. Figure 11.3 portrays a set of products and their relationships over time. Products that share a common platform but have different specific features and enhancements that are required for different sets of consumers constitute a **product family.** Each generation of a product family has a platform that provides the foundation for specific products targeted to different or complementary market applications (for example, platform development family A, products 1 through 4). Successive generations refresh older platforms (for example, the 1997 Toyota Camry line) with improved design, technologies, and derivative products (new generation platform family A, products 1^1 through 6). By expanding on technical skills, market knowledge, and manufacturing competencies, entirely new product families may be formed, thereby creating new business opportunities for the business marketing firm (product development family B).

Beyond a Single Product Focus

Strategists argue that a firm should move away from a planning emphasis that centers on single products and focus, instead, on families of products that can grow from a common platform. To illustrate, Sony introduced 160 variations of the Walkman in a decade. These products were based on a platform that Sony continually enriched throughout this period.[19] The move toward a product family perspective requires close interfunctional working relationships, a long-term view of technology strategy, and a multiple-year commitment of resources. While this approach offers significant competitive leverage, Steven Wheelwright and Kim Clark note that companies often fail to make an adequate investment in platforms: "The reasons vary, but the most common is that management lacks an awareness of the strategic value of platforms and fails to create well-thought-out platform projects."[20]

---

[18]The discussion in this section is based on Marc H. Meyer and James M. Utterback, "The Product Family and the Dynamics of Core Capability," *Sloan Management Review* 34 (spring 1993): pp. 29–47; see also Dwight L. Gertz and João P. A. Baptista, *Grow to Be Great: Breaking the Downsizing Cycle* (New York: The Free Press, 1995), pp. 92–103.

[19]Meyer and Utterback, "The Product Family," p. 30.

[20]Wheelwright and Clark, "Creating Project Plans," p. 74.

Figure 11.3 The Product Family Approach to New Product Development

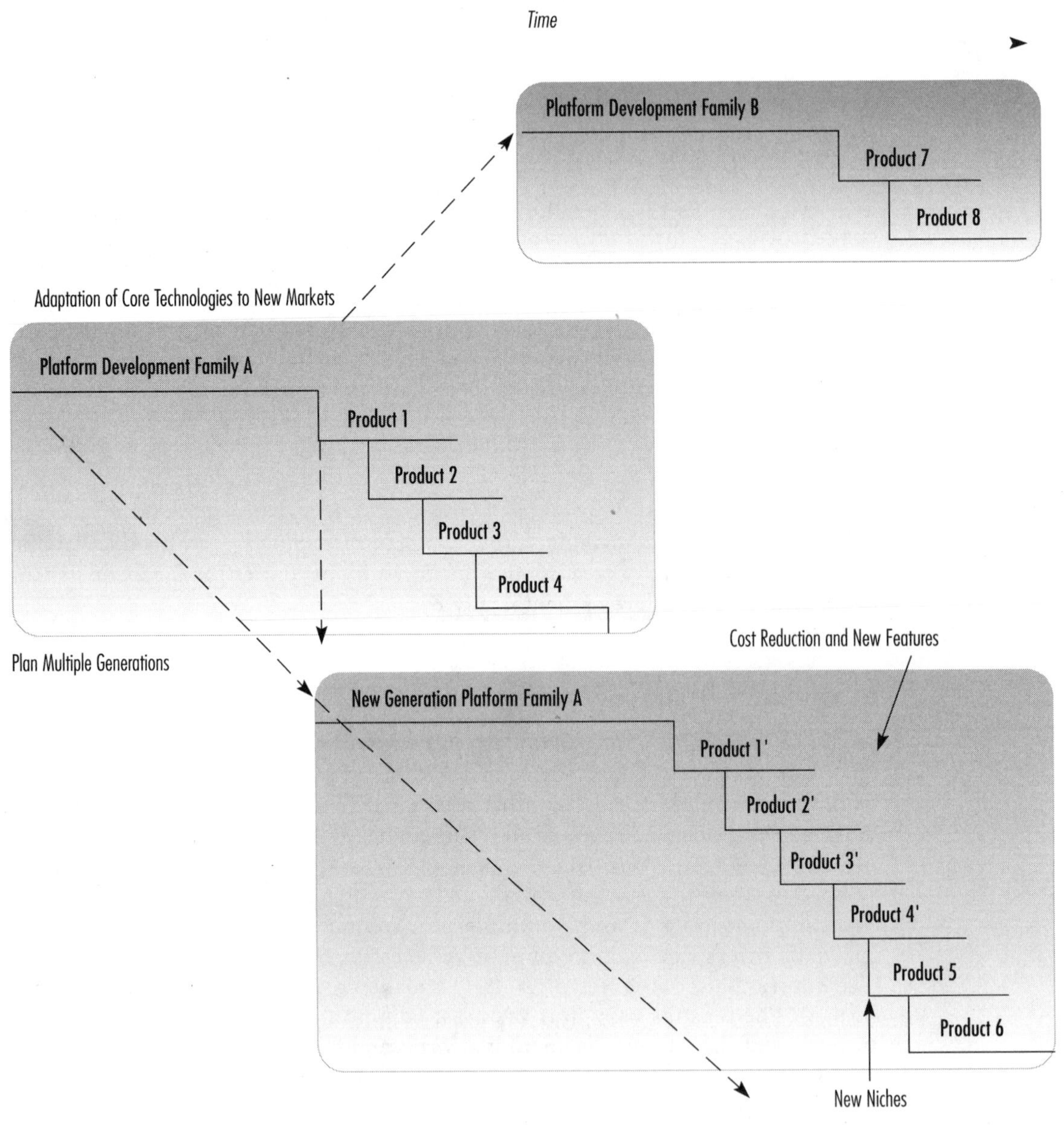

Source: Reprinted from Marc H. Meyer and James M. Utterback, "The Product Family and the Dynamics of Core Capability," *Sloan Management Review* 34 (spring 1993): p. 32.

The New Product Development Process

To sustain their competitive advantage, leading-edge firms such as Canon, Microsoft, Hewlett-Packard, and Boeing make new product development a top management priority. They directly involve managers and employees from across the organization to speed actions and decisions. Because new product ventures can represent a significant risk as well as an important opportunity, new product development requires systematic thought. The high expectations ascribed to new products are often not fulfilled. Worse, many new industrial products fail. Although the definitions of failure are somewhat elusive, research suggests that 30 to 40 percent of industrial products fail.[21] While there may be some debate over the number of failures, there is no debate over the fact that a new product rejected by the market constitutes a substantial waste to the firm and to society.

This section will center on (1) the forces that drive a firm's new product performance, (2) the sources of new product ideas, (3) cross-functional barriers to successful innovation, and (4) team-based processes employed in new product development. A promising method for bringing the "voice of the consumer" directly into the development process is also explored.

WHAT DRIVES A FIRM'S NEW PRODUCT PERFORMANCE?

A benchmarking study sought to uncover the critical success factors that drive a firm's new product performance.[22] Three factors were identified (see Figure 11.4): (1) the quality of a firm's new product development process, (2) the resource commitments made to new product development, and (3) the new product strategy.

Process

Successful companies employ a high-quality new product development process—careful attention is given to the execution of the activities and decision points that new products follow from the idea stage to launch and beyond. The benchmarking study identified the following characteristics among high-performing firms:

- The firms emphasized upfront market and technical assessments before projects moved into the development phase.
- The process featured complete descriptions of the product concept, product benefits, positioning, and target markets before development work was initiated.

[21]Albert L. Page, "Assessing New Product Development Practices and Performances: Establishing Crucial Norms," *Journal of Product Innovation Management* 10 (September 1993): pp. 273–290.

[22]Robert G. Cooper and Elko J. Kleinschmidt, "Benchmarking Firms' New Product Performance and Practices," *Engineering Management Review* 23 (fall 1995): pp. 112–120.

Figure 11.4 The Major Drivers of a Firm's New Product Performance

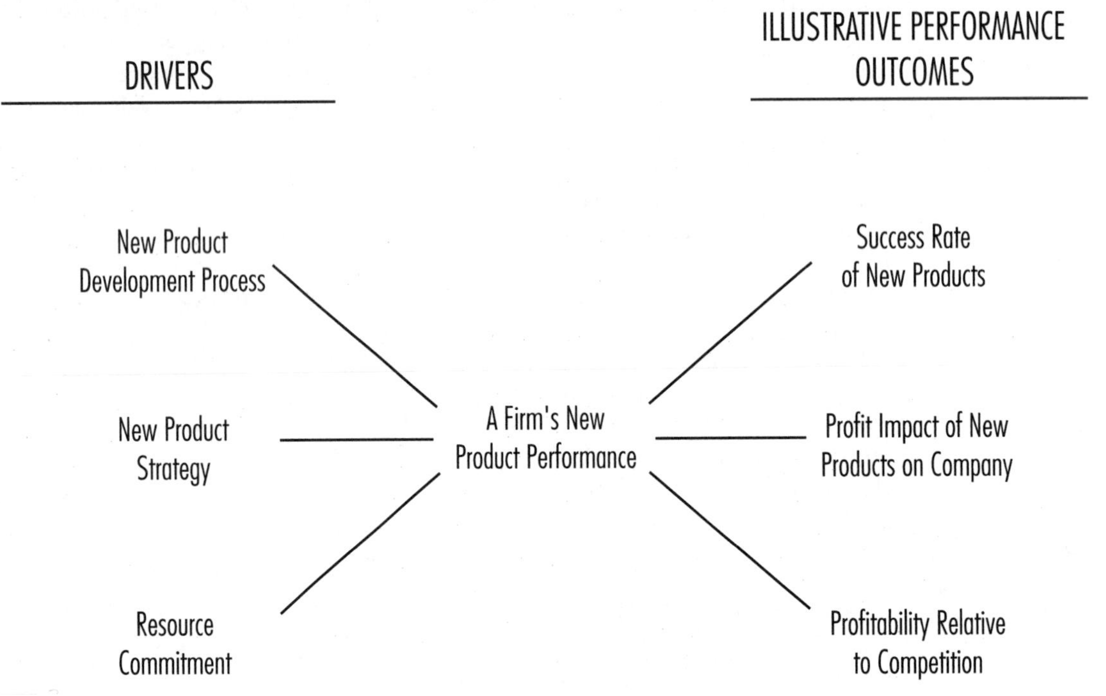

Source: Adapted from Robert G. Cooper and Elko J. Kleinschmidt, "Benchmarking Firms' New Product Performance and Practices," *Engineering Management Review* 23 (fall 1995): pp. 112–120.

- Tough project *go/kill* decision points were included in the process and the kill option was actually used.
- The new product process was flexible—certain stages could be skipped in line with the nature and risk of a particular project.

Detailed upfront homework on the product concept, the likely market response, and the technical feasibility of the product, along with a thorough business and financial assessment, are important dimensions of the process that successful product creators follow.

Resource Commitments

Adequate resources were invested in new product development in top-performing firms. Three ingredients were important here:

1. Top management committed the resources necessary to meet the firm's objectives for the total product effort in the firm.

2. R&D budgets were adequate and aligned with the stated new product objectives.
3. The necessary personnel were assigned and were relieved from other duties so that they could give full attention to new product development.

New Product Strategy

A clear and visible new product strategy was another driver of a firm's new product performance (see Figure 11.4). Successful firms, like 3M, set aggressive new product performance goals (for example, *x* percent of company sales and profit from new products) as a basic corporate goal and communicate it to all employees. In turn, Robert Cooper and Elko Kleinschmidt report that successful firms centered development efforts on clearly defined arenas—particular product, market, and technology domains—to direct the new product program:

> *The new product strategy specifies "the arenas where we'll play the game," or perhaps more important, where we won't play . . . what's in bounds and out of bounds. Without arenas defined, the search for new product ideas or opportunities is unfocused. . . .*[23]

SOURCES OF NEW PRODUCT IDEAS

The business marketer should be alert to new product ideas and to their sources, both inside and outside the company. Internally, the new product ideas may flow from salespersons who are close to customer needs, from R&D specialists who are close to new technological developments, and from top management who know the company's strengths and weaknesses. Externally, ideas may come from channel members, such as distributors or customers, or from an assessment of competitive moves.

Eric von Hippel challenges the traditional view that marketers typically introduce new products to a passive market.[24] His research suggests that the customers in the business market often develop the idea for a new product and even select the supplier to make that product. The customer is responding to the perceived *capability* of the business marketer, rather than to a specific physical product. This points up the need for involving the customers in new product development, and for promoting corporate capability to consumers (idea generators).

---

[23]Ibid., p. 117; see also Jean-Marie Choffray and Gary L. Lilien, "Assessing Response to Industrial Marketing Strategy," *Journal of Marketing* 42 (April 1978): pp. 20–31; and Eunsang Yoon and Gary L. Lilien, "New Industrial Product Performance: The Effects of Market Characteristics and Strategy," *Journal of Product Innovation Management* 3 (September 1985): pp. 134–144.

[24]Eric von Hippel, "Get New Products from Customers," *Harvard Business Review* 60 (March/April 1982): pp. 117–122; see also von Hippel, *The Sources of Innovation* (New York: Oxford University Press, 1988).

Managing in the 21st Century

MANAGING THE IDEA FLOW FOR SUCCESSFUL PRODUCT INNOVATION

While many firms concentrate attention on improving the development and launch stages of the new product development process, the real gains will come from enhancing the front end of the process: idea management. George Day notes that "Seldom is idea generation, screening, and monitoring considered as a formal ongoing process to be carefully managed. We are more likely to find a haphazard system for collecting unsolicited suggestions from random sources, with a priority given to 'catch up' ideas that are a derivative of prior moves by competitors."

He argues that idea management can be nurtured and developed as a distinctive capability of a firm. The following actions can enhance this capability:

1. mapping the current sequence of activities in the idea management process and benchmarking it against the best practices of firms in similar industries;
2. assigning ownership of the process to a manager, providing the necessary coordination of inputs and follow-up research, and synthesis and dissemination of findings; and
3. creation of a formal idea bank with full documentation of all ideas.

One firm that instituted such a process received 150 ideas in the first six months. Innovative firms believe that a large pool of creative ideas is an essential ingredient for future success.

Source: George S. Day, "Significant Issues for the Future of Product Innovation," *Engineering Management* 22 (winter 1994): pp. 2–4. See also Jean-Phillippe Deschamps and P. Ranganath Nayak, *Product Juggernauts: How Companies Mobilize to Generate a Stream of Market Winners* (Boston, Mass.: Harvard Business School Press, 1995), pp. 54–66.

Because many industrial product markets for high-technology and, in particular, capital equipment consist of a small number of high-volume buying firms, special attention must be given to the needs of **lead users,** which include a small number of highly influential buying organizations who are consistent early adopters of new technologies.[25] Lead users face needs that will be general in the marketplace, but they confront these needs months or years before the bulk of that marketplace encounters them. In addition, they are positioned to benefit significantly by obtaining a solution that satisfies those needs. For example, Intel is a lead user of production equipment tailored to the delicate task of forming advanced microchips.

Staying Ahead of Customers

Rather than merely asking customers what they want, some firms succeed by leading customers where they want to go before the customers actually know it themselves.[26]

---

[25]Ibid. von Hippel, "Get New Products from Customers," pp. 120–121.

[26]Gary Hamel and C. K. Prahalad, "Corporate Imagination and Expeditionary Marketing," *Harvard Business Review* 69 (July/August 1991): pp. 81–92.

To illustrate, Motorola envisions a global communication environment where telephone numbers are attached to people rather than to places, and where a personal communicator allows millions of business travelers to be reached anywhere, anytime. Deep insights into the needs and aspirations of today's and tomorrow's customers is needed to plan the course for innovation. In addition to providing critical customer feedback to technical personnel, procedures are needed to inform those closest to the customer (marketers) about the coming technological possibilities. Motorola succeeds by educating customers to *what is possible*.

CROSS-FUNCTIONAL BARRIERS

Successful new product creation is a collective achievement that requires the energy and commitment of multiple functions (for example, R&D and manufacturing) and stakeholders (for example, suppliers). Three obstacles can damage new product development efforts: turf barriers, interpretive barriers, and communication barriers.[27]

Turf Barriers

New product decisions engage and arouse members who may gain or lose. **Turf** includes an area of expertise, or authority, a particular task, or access to resources. Functional units are strongly motivated to defend against loss of status or power. By signaling a new direction for the firm, new product development projects often ignite turf battles among functional units as each competes for resources, information, and support.

Consider the Techno project story: An R&D team at a telecommunications company developed technology that would enable it to fully automate the sales function and introduce a range of new services. In turn, the R&D team wanted to assume the lead role in developing the new products and services. Fearing a declining budget and a loss of control, the marketing unit strongly resisted and a turf battle ensued. Ultimately, the marketing function embraced the technology and introduced a whole host of successful products and services. But months were lost in the development process as the turf squabbles were being settled. Thus, constructive debate and tension across organizational units can speed learning while destructive turf wars stifle it.

Interpretive Barriers

In an organization, asserts Deborah Dougherty, "departments are like 'thought worlds': each focusing on different aspects of technology–market knowledge and making different sense of the total."[28] Collaboration across functions is necessary for

---

[27]This discussion is based on Michael D. Hutt, Beth A. Walker, and Gary L. Frankwick, "Hurdle the Cross-Functional Barriers to Strategic Change," *Sloan Management Review* 36 (spring 1995): pp. 22–30.

[28]Deborah Dougherty, "Interpretive Barriers to Successful Product Innovation in Large Firms," *Organization Science* 3 (May 1992): p. 179.

successful innovation, and differing interpretations are major barriers. Each department has common judgments and procedures that produce a qualitatively different understanding of product innovation.

Figure 11.5 graphs the contrasting views of the Techno project that marketing and R&D managers held at a key milestone in the development process. Recall that the technology would enable customers of a telecommunications firm to order products and services without a salesperson's intervention. Marketing managers had negative opinions of Techno's impact on customer service and selling efficacy. Marketers also

Figure 11.5 Managers' Opinions about the Techno Project at Milestone One

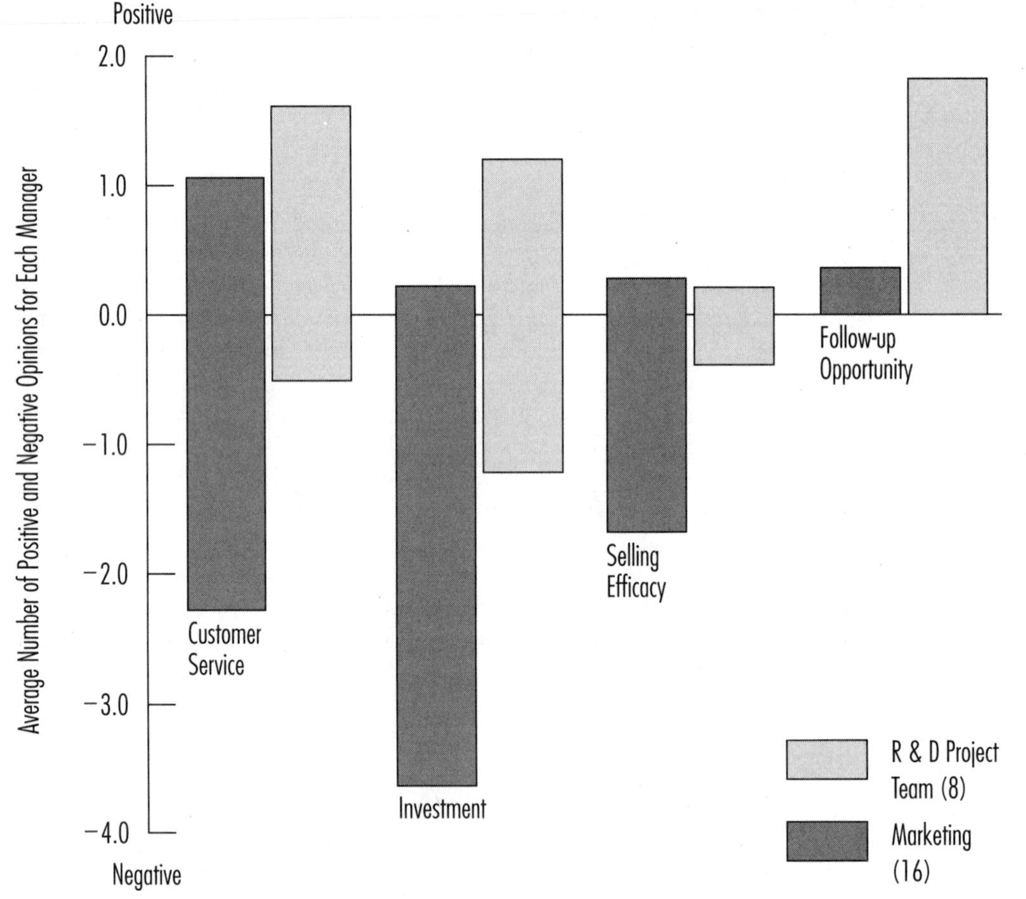

Source: Reprinted from Michael D. Hutt, Beth A. Walker, and Gary L. Frankwick, "Hurdle the Cross-Functional Barriers to Strategic Change," *Sloan Management Review* 36 (spring 1995): p. 25, by permission of the publisher.

saw the sizable investment in Techno as significantly negative and were less enthusiastic than R&D managers about its follow-up opportunities. R&D managers were positive about customer service, the investment, and follow-up opportunities, and less negative about selling efficacy.

Communication Barriers

Departments or functional areas develop a shared language that reflects similarities in the way in which members interpret, understand, and respond to information. This language or coding enhances communication within the department. However, organizational members who are unfamiliar with it may find communication with the departmental members difficult.

The new product development process involves a growing network of participants. Research clearly indicates that cooperation and frequent communication among participants is critical to new product success. In particular, interfunctional harmony between marketing and R&D strongly correlates with project success.

Successful Collaboration

Underlying an innovative organization's strength is the ability to harmonize technology with a clear understanding of customers' present and future needs.[29] A shared appreciation of each function's distinctive skills contributes to creating competitive advantage. R&D can articulate the technological possibilities, while marketing thoughtfully assesses the possibilities in light of market opportunities and competitive realities. Collaboration creates new, sharper conceptualizations of how technology can profitably serve customers and strengthen competitive advantage.

A TEAM-BASED PROCESS

Jon Katzenbach and Douglas Smith offer the following insight regarding teams and performance:

> *A **team** is a small number of people with complementary skills who are committed to a common purpose, set of performance goals, an approach for which they hold themselves mutually accountable. The essence of a team is common commitment. Without it, groups perform as individuals; with it, they become a powerful unit of collective performance.*[30]

---

[29]For a comprehensive review, see Abbie Griffin and John R. Hauser, "Integrating R&D and Marketing: A Review and Analysis of the Literature," *Journal of Product Innovation Management* 13 (May 1996): pp. 191–215.

[30]Jon R. Katzenbach and Douglas K. Smith, "The Discipline of Teams," *Harvard Business Review* 71 (March/April 1993): p. 112.

To an unprecedented degree, multidisciplinary teams are the preferred structure for organizing the new product development process in business marketing firms.[31] In turn, firms are increasingly turning to *concurrent engineering* to speed new product development and to tighten cross-functional connections (see Chapter 8).

With concurrent engineering, the entire development process is characterized by the constant interaction of a hand-picked interfunctional team whose members work together from start to finish. The team includes experts from marketing, design, manufacturing, R&D, purchasing, and other functional areas. Importantly, key suppliers are involved in the process from the outset to capitalize on their specialized knowledge. The core idea is that the team is responsible for conceptualizing the product correctly up front.[32] Rather than proceeding through highly structured stages, the cross-functional team manages the development process in an integrated manner—it moves as a unit toward a singular objective.

Choosing a Team Structure

A business marketing firm should ensure that the structure of its new product development effort matches its strategic priorities and its environment. Research evidence suggests that a firm should match the innovativeness of a new product to the type of organization used to manage its development.[33] Cross-functional teams appear to work best for *new to the world products*—products that are new to the company developing them and to customers using them. Traditional organizational structures can be used when the products are familiar such as *product modifications*—existing products that have been slightly modified.

QUALITY FUNCTION DEPLOYMENT[34]

Cooperation and communication among marketing, manufacturing, engineering, and R&D are fundamental to greater new-product success and more profitable products. **Quality function deployment,** or **QFD,** is a method used to identify critical customer attributes and to establish a specific link between customer attributes and product design attributes. Cross-functional communication is improved by linking the voice of the customer directly to engineering, manufacturing, and R&D decisions. The approach has been adopted widely by Japanese, U.S., and European firms.

The organizing framework for the QFD process is a planning approach termed the **house of quality.** Figure 11.6 portrays a house of quality for the gear design for a new

---

[31]Page, "Assessing New Product Development Projects," p. 276.

[32]See, for example, Willard I. Zangwill, *Lightning Strategies for Innovation* (New York: Lexington Books, 1993), pp. 231–265.

[33]Erik M. Olson, Orville C. Walker, and Robert W. Ruekert, "Organizing for Effective New Product Development: The Moderating Role of Product Innovativeness," *Journal of Marketing* 59 (January 1995): pp. 48–62.

[34]This section is based on John R. Hauser, "How Puritan-Bennett Used the House of Quality," *Sloan Management Review* 34 (spring 1993): pp. 61–70.

Figure 11.6 Quality Function Deployment in the "House of Quality": A Gear Design Problem at New West Photo

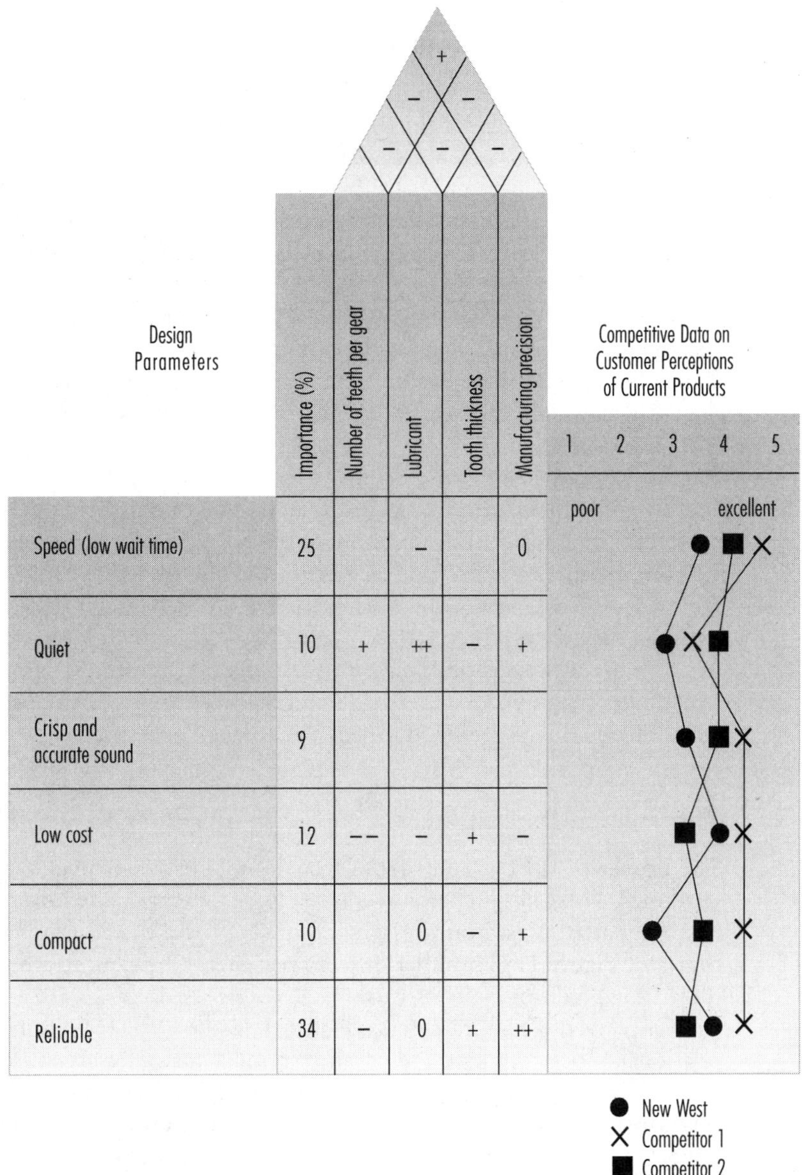

Note: The "house of quality" relates primary customer requirements to the major design parameters about which the development team will make design choices. The right-hand side shows customer perceptions of existing competitive products, while the top portion shows the interrelationship of the design parameters.

Source: Kim B. Clark and Steven C. Wheelwright, *Managing New Product and Process Development* (New York: The Free Press, 1993), p. 609. Reprinted by permission of The Free Press, Division of Simon & Schuster. Copyright © 1993 by Kim B. Clark and Steven C. Wheelwright.

camera at New West Photo. The new product development team uses the approach to understand the voice of the consumer and to translate it into the voice of the engineer.

The Voice of the Customer

The first task of QFD is to identify customer needs, which are expressions in the customers' own words of the benefits they want the product to deliver. Discussions with customers will often create a lengthy list of needs. Particular attention, however, is given to the five to ten top-level needs or primary needs that set the strategic direction for the product. Recent research suggests that interviews with 20 to 30 customers should identify 90 percent or more of the customer needs in a relatively homogeneous market segment.[35]

In Figure 11.6, note that six critical customer attributes are included in our gear design illustration: speed, quiet operation, crisp and accurate sound, cost, size, and reliability. Since some of the customer attributes have more importance to some customers than others, weights are assigned to represent the relative importance of the attributes from the customer's perspective. Such weighting or prioritizing enables the QFD team to balance the cost of meeting a need with the benefit sought by the customer.

To guide product design, competitive data on customer perceptions of current products also constitutes a component of QFD (see the right side of Figure 11.6). As Abbie Griffin and John Hauser point out, "Knowledge of which products fulfill which needs best, how well those needs are fulfilled, and whether there are any gaps between the best product and 'our' existing product provide further input into product development decisions being made by the QFD team."[36] Note in Figure 11.6 that consumers perceive Competitor 1 to have an edge in both cost and performance. Such information is obtained through surveys of customers.

The Voice of the Engineer

The power of QFD comes from translating customer needs into product design attributes. These design parameters should be measurable requirements that are tied to customer attributes. Four design parameters form the columns of the matrix in the center of Figure 11.6: number of teeth per gear, lubricant, tooth thickness, and manufacturing precision.

Once the design parameters are identified, the QFD team can begin to examine the relationship between a design parameter and a customer attribute. Simple pluses and minuses are used in the gear design illustration to indicate the nature and strength of the relationships. For example, increasing the number of teeth per gear has a positive impact on the customer attribute "quiet" but, because machinery costs will increase, may have a negative impact on the customer attribute "low cost." An evaluation of the relationship between design parameters and customer attributes draws on information from customers, engineering experience, and data from designed experiments.

---

[35] Abbie Griffin and John R. Hauser, "The Voice of the Customer," *Marketing Science* 12 (winter 1993): pp. 1–25.

[36] Ibid., p. 5.

The matrix, symbolized in Figure 11.6 as the cross-hatched roof, quantifies the interrelationships between design parameters. Here the strength and direction of the interrelationships between design parameters are isolated. Note, for example, the minus sign in the cell connecting lubricants and number of teeth per gear. Clark and Wheelwright conclude that increasing "the value of one (for example, using lubricants to reduce noise) tends to decrease the value of the others (for example, with a better lubricant, the design engineer can tolerate fewer teeth per gear) in engineering design."[37] The roof matrix clarifies the important trade-offs that may exist in selecting design parameters and identifies design opportunities that closely fit customer needs.

Using Quality Function Development

QFD provides an important framework for bringing critical information on customer needs together with appropriate engineering data on fulfilling those needs. Rather than yielding design solutions, QFD provides a mechanism for exposing and tackling difficult design trade-offs that inevitably appear in the new product development process. The approach enables the interfunctional product team to develop a common understanding of the design issues. In a head-to-head comparison with a traditional product development process, research indicates that QFD enhances communication among team members.[38] In some applications, QFD has reduced design time by 40 percent and design costs by 60 percent, while maintaining or enhancing design quality.[39]

Determinants of New Product Performance and Timeliness

What factors are most important in determining the success or failure of the new product? Why are some firms faster than others in moving projects through the development process? Let's review the available evidence.

THE DETERMINANTS OF SUCCESS

Both strategic factors as well as a firm's proficiency in carrying out the new product development process determine new product success.[40]

[37]Clark and Wheelwright, *Managing New Product and Process Development*, p. 610.

[38]Abbie Griffin and John R. Hauser, "Patterns of Communication among Marketing, Engineering and Manufacturing: A Comparison between Two New Product Teams," *Management Science* 38 (March 1992): pp. 360–373.

[39]John R. Hauser and Don P. Clausing, "The House of Quality," *Harvard Business Review* 66 (May/June 1988): pp. 63–73.

[40]Mitzi M. Montoya-Weiss and Roger Calantone, "Determinants of New Product Performance: A Review and Meta-Analysis," *Journal of Product Innovation Management* 11 (November 1994): pp. 397–417; see also Robert G. Cooper, *Winning at New Products: Accelerating the Process from Idea to Launch* (Reading, Mass.: Addison-Wesley, 1993).

Strategic Factors

Research suggests that four strategic factors appear to be crucial to new product success. The level of **product advantage** is the most important. Product advantage refers to customer perceptions of product superiority with respect to quality, cost-performance ratio, or function relative to competitors. Successful products offer clear benefits, such as reduced customer costs, and are of higher quality (for example, more durable) than the products of competitors. A study of more than 100 new product projects in the chemical industry illustrates the point. Here, Robert Cooper and Elko Kleinschmidt assert, "the winners are new products that offer high relative product quality, have superior price/performance characteristics, provide good value for the money to the customer, are superior to competing products in meeting customer needs, [and] have unique attributes and highly visible benefits that are easily seen by the customer."[41]

Marketing synergy and technical synergy are also pivotal in new product outcomes. **Marketing synergy** represents the degree of fit between the needs of the project and the firm's resources and skills in marketing (for example, personal selling or market research). By contrast, **technical synergy** concerns the fit between the needs of the project and the firm's R&D resources and competencies. New products that match the skills of the firm are likely to succeed.

In addition to the preceding three factors, an **international orientation** also contributes to the success of product innovation.[42] New products that are designed and developed to meet foreign requirements, and that are targeted at world or nearest-neighbor export markets, outperform domestic products on almost every measure, including success rate, profitability, and domestic and foreign market shares. Underlying this success is a strong international focus in market research, product testing with customers, trial selling, and launch efforts.

Development Process Factors

New product success is also associated with particular characteristics of the development process. **Predevelopment proficiency** provides the foundation for a successful product. Predevelopment involves several important tasks such as initial screening, preliminary market and technical assessment, detailed market research study, and preliminary business/financial analysis. Firms that are skilled in completing these upfront tasks are likely to experience new product success.

Market knowledge and **marketing proficiency** are also pivotal in new product outcomes. As might be expected, business marketers with a solid understanding of market needs are likely to succeed. Robert Cooper describes the market planning for a successful product he examined: "Market information was very complete: there was a solid understanding of the customer's needs, wants, and preferences; of the

[41]Robert G. Cooper and Elko J. Kleinschmidt, "Major New Products: What Distinguishes the Winners in the Chemical Industry?" *Journal of Product Innovation Management* 10 (March 1993): p. 108.

[42]Elko J. Kleinschmidt and Robert G. Cooper, "The Performance Impact of an International Orientation on Product Innovation," *European Journal of Marketing* 22, no. 9 (1988): pp. 56–71.

customer's buying behavior and price sensitivity; of the size and trends of the market; and of the competitive situation. Finally, the market launch was well planned, well targeted, proficiently executed, and backed by appropriate resources."[43]

Technical knowledge and **technical proficiency** constitute other important dimensions of the new product development process. When technical developers possess a strong base of knowledge concerning the technical aspects of a potential new product, and when they can proficiently pass through the stages of the new product development process (for example, product development, prototype testing, pilot production, and production start-up), these products succeed.

DETERMINANTS OF PRODUCT SUCCESS FOR JAPANESE COMPANIES

What factors separate the new product winners from the losers in Japanese companies? X. Michael Song and Mark Parry addressed this intriguing question in a study of nearly 800 new product introductions by Japanese firms.[44] They found that Japanese new product managers view the keys to new product success in much the same way as their North American counterparts. Product advantage was identified as the most important success factor by Japanese managers. Other important success factors include technical and marketing synergy as well as predevelopment proficiency.

Assessing Product Advantage

The Japanese study also provides some useful guidelines for assessing potential product advantage. In making this assessment, warn Song and Parry, "managers should consider whether the product offers potential for reducing consumer costs and expanding consumer capabilities, as well as the likelihood that the product offers improved quality, superior technical performance, and a superior benefit-to-cost ratio."[45]

FAST-PACED PRODUCT DEVELOPMENT

Rapid product development offers a number of competitive advantages. To illustrate, speed enables a firm to respond to rapidly changing markets and technologies. Moreover, fast product development is usually more efficient because lengthy development

---

[43]Cooper, *Winning at New Products*, p. 27.

[44]X. Michael Song and Mark E. Parry, "What Separates Japanese New Product Winners from Losers," *Journal of Product Innovation Management* 13 (September 1996): pp. 422–436.

[45]Ibid., p. 422.

processes tend to waste resources on peripheral activities and changes.[46] Of course, while an overemphasis on speed may create other pitfalls, it is becoming an important strategic weapon, particularly in high-technology markets.

Matching the Process to the Development Task

How can a firm accelerate product development? A major study of the global computer industry provides some important benchmarks.[47] Researchers examined 72 product development projects of leading U. S., European, and Asian computer firms. The findings suggest that multiple approaches are used to increase speed in product development. Speed comes from properly matching the approach to the product development task at hand.

Compressed Strategy for Predictable Projects

For well-known markets and technologies, a **compression strategy** speeds development. This strategy views product development as a predictable series of steps that can be compressed. Speed comes from carefully planning these steps and shortening the time it takes to complete each step. This research indicates that the compressed strategy increased the speed of product development for products that had predictable designs and that were targeted for stable and mature markets. Mainframe computers fit into this category—they rely on proprietary hardware, have more predictable designs from project to project, and compete in a mature market.

Experiential Strategy for Unpredictable Projects

For uncertain markets and technologies, an **experiential strategy** accelerates product development. The underlying assumption of this strategy, explain Kathleen Eisenhardt and Behnam Tabrizi, is that "product development is a highly uncertain path through foggy and shifting markets and technologies. The key to fast product development is, then, rapidly building intuition and flexible options in order to learn quickly about and shift with uncertain environments."[48]

Under these conditions, speed comes from multiple design iterations, extensive testing, frequent milestones, and a powerful leader who can keep the product team focused. Here real-time interactions, experimentation, and flexibility are essential. The research found that the experiential strategy increased the speed of product development for unpredictable projects such as personal computers—a market characterized by rapidly evolving technology and unpredictable patterns of competition.

---

[46]See, for example, Robert G. Cooper and Elko J. Kleinschmidt, "Determinants of Timeliness in Product Development," *Journal of Product Innovation Management* 11 (November 1994): pp. 381–417.

[47]Kathleen M. Eisenhardt and Behnam N. Tabrizi, "Accelerating Adaptive Processes: Product Innovation in the Global Computer Industry," *Administrative Science Quarterly* 40 (March 1995): pp. 84–110.

[48]Ibid., p. 91.

Summary

Product innovation is a high-risk and potentially rewarding process. Sustained growth is dependent on innovative products that respond to existing or emerging consumer needs. Effective managers of innovation channel and control its main directions, but have learned to maintain flexibility and expect surprises. Within the firm, marketing managers pursue strategic activity that falls into two broad categories: induced and autonomous strategic behavior.

New product development efforts for existing businesses or market development projects for the firm's present products are the outgrowth of induced strategic initiatives. In contrast, autonomous strategic efforts take shape outside the firm's current concept of strategy, depart from the current course, and center on new categories of business opportunity; middle managers initiate the project, champion its development, and, if successful, see the project integrated into the firm's concept of strategy.

The long-run competitive position of most business marketing firms depends on their ability to manage and increase their technological base. The technology portfolio provides the business marketer with a tool for evaluating the particular mix of technologies in the firm's asset base, analyzing the associated products that issue from each technology, and planning resource allocation for future technology scenarios. Core competencies provide the basis for products and product families. Each generation of a product family has a platform that serves as the foundation for specific products targeted at different or complementary market applications.

Effective new product development requires a thorough knowledge of customer needs and a clear grasp of the technological possibilities. Top-performing firms are proficient in executing the new product development process, provide adequate resources to support new product objectives, and develop clear new product strategy. Business marketing firms are emphasizing concurrent engineering and multidisciplinary teams to speed product development, reduce cost, and improve quality. Quality function deployment provides a useful method that the development team can use to link the needs of the customer directly to specific design decisions.

Both strategic factors as well as the firm's proficiency in executing the new product development process are critical to the success of industrial products. Fast-paced product development can provide an important source of competitive advantage for a firm. Speed comes from adapting the process to the new product development task at hand.

Discussion Questions

1. Research by James Quinn suggests that few major innovations result from highly structured planning systems. What does this imply for the business marketer?

2. Compare and contrast induced and autonomous strategic behavior. Describe the role that the product champion assumes in the new product development process.

3. Some firms have a better record in developing new products than others. Describe the critical factors that drive the new product performance of firms.
4. Explore the significance of a product platform to new product strategy and to the speed with which successive new products can be introduced to a market segment.
5. Critique this position: "How many of us were asking for cellular telephones and home fax machines? It's important to listen to customers, but you can't be a market leader if you do no more than that."
6. Hewlett-Packard is working on a health monitoring system. The product features sensors and devices that measure a patient's vital signs in a hospital—or home—and relay data directly to a doctor's computer. What steps can the firm take to ensure that the new product is responsive to customer needs and will be adopted?
7. Getting managers from marketing and R&D "on the same page" is a major challenge during the new product development process. Describe the barriers that often divide functional areas and hamper the new product development process.
8. Describe the process that you would follow in defining the customer needs component of quality function deployment. Assume that the new product in development is an interactive notepad that, when plugged into a telephone, enables people to talk and exchange notes and diagrams.
9. New industrial products that succeed in the marketplace provide clear-cut advantages to customers. Define product advantage and provide an example of a recent new product introduction that fits this definition.
10. Evaluate this statement: "To increase the speed of the new product development process, a firm might follow one strategy for unpredictable projects and an entirely different one for more predictable ones."

Managing Services for Business Markets

Chapter 12

The important and growing market for business services poses special challenges and meaningful opportunities for the marketing manager. This chapter explains the unique aspects of business services and explores the special role they play in the business market environment. After reading this chapter, you will understand

1. the unique role and distinguishing characteristics of business services.
2. the role that service quality, customer satisfaction, and loyalty assume in service market success.
3. the significant factors that must be considered in formulating a service marketing strategy.
4. the determinants of new service success and failure.
5. the nature and scope of global opportunities for service businesses.

As General Electric Company faces slow domestic growth and cutthroat price competition abroad for its manufactured items, chairman and CEO Jack Welch is again transforming the global giant.[1] Across G.E.'s business units, Welch sees huge growth by providing specialized services that spring from the firm's core competencies. Take the Medical Equipment Systems unit at G.E. and its expanding relationship with Columbia/HCA Healthcare Corporation—an operator of a chain of more than 300 hospitals. G.E. sells medical imaging equipment to Columbia and now services all of the chain's imaging equipment, including that made by G.E.'s competitors. Recently, Columbia turned over the management of all medical supplies to G.E.—most of these supply items represent products that G.E. does not produce. As the contract evolved, Columbia executives asked a team of G.E. managers to help them improve the way

[1]Tim Smart, "Jack Welch's Encore: How G.E.'s Chariman Is Remaking His Company—Again," *Business Week*, 28 October 1996, pp. 155–160.

Columbia runs hospitals. The consulting and employee training services provided by G.E. significantly boosted Columbia's productivity and yielded millions of dollars of cost savings.

Similar service initiatives are being launched throughout G.E.: The aircraft engine unit landed a $2.3 billion, 10-year contract with British Airways to perform engine maintenance; G.E.'s power equipment unit foresees $1 billion dollars in annual new business by operating and maintaining power plants for utilities in the United States and Europe; G.E. Capital is responding to the growing interest of firms in outsourcing and is competing head-on with IBM and EDS for multimillion-dollar contracts that involve operating computer networks for others.

Given his stunning record of profitable growth at G.E., some believe that Jack Welch's aggressive services strategy provides a blueprint for refashioning an industrial company in a post-industrial economy. For example, reengineering expert Michael Hammer sees G.E.'s strategic move as a bellwether: "This is the next big wave in American industry. The product you sell is only one component of your business."[2]

This example demonstrates the important role that services play in the business marketing environment. Many original equipment manufacturers are now using effective service and support as a core marketing strategy for creating sales growth; moreover, a vast array of "pure service" firms exist to supply businesses and organizations with everything from office cleaning to management consulting and just-in-time delivery service to key customers.

Importantly, the marketing of business services has many unique aspects that set it apart from product marketing. James Heskett, W. Earl Sasser Jr., and Christopher Hart succinctly capture the magnitude of these differences in their well-respected book, *Service Breakthroughs: Changing the Rules of the Game*:

> *Outstanding service organizations are managed differently from their merely "good" competitors. Missions are stated differently. Managers act differently. Actions are based on totally different assumptions about the way success is achieved. And the results show it, in terms of both conventional measures of performance and the impact these services have on their competitors.*[3]

This chapter will examine the nature of business services, the key buying behavior dimensions associated with their purchase, the major strategic elements related to services marketing, and the international environment for business services.

Business Services: Role and Importance

The importance of services marketing is easy to demonstrate: The United States has become a service economy. In fact, fully 80 percent of the employment and 76

---

[2]Ibid., p. 157.

[3]James L. Heskett, W. Earl Sasser Jr., and Christopher W. L. Hart, *Service Breakthroughs: Changing the Rules of the Game* (New York: The Free Press, 1990), p. 1.

percent of the gross domestic product (GDP) in the United States is accounted for by the service sector.[4] The significance of services to the U. S. economy is underscored by the fact that in 1995, the U. S. *trade surplus in services* reached a record $63.1 billion, compared to a *merchandise trade deficit* of $174 billion. The total employment in the service-producing sectors of the economy is projected to reach 108.1 million by 2005, an increase of 17.7 million from 1994 levels.[5] The dramatic growth in the service sector is occurring in both consumer and business markets.

Business services are growing even in regions where manufacturing is in decline. Three factors account for the growth of business services:[6]

1. *Manufacturing growth.* Manufacturing output is still growing despite the decline in the number of manufacturing employees. With this growth, the demand for services like logistics, advertising, and information processing continues its upward trend.
2. *Outsourcing.* Manufacturers of products are buying more services than in the past. The trend is to outsource functions and services that are not the company's core expertise (like the cafeteria, payroll processing, warehousing, and computer support services).
3. *Innovations.* New services, never considered ten years ago, are stimulating increasing services demand. Security systems, waste-management firms, and benefit specialists are examples of service innovations stimulating the rising service demand.

PRODUCT SUPPORT SERVICES

Services in the business-to-business market can be categorized in two distinct groups. The first category is **products supported by services.** In this situation, the wide range of service elements that accompany the physical product are frequently as important as the technical solutions offered by the product itself[7] (see Chapter 10). Some examples of product-service linkages include equipment repair and maintenance, consultation services associated with the sale of computers and other technical products, training programs on the use and application of equipment or customized software, distribution and delivery service, and spare parts. At Otis Elevator, for example, more than 65 percent of its $5 billion in annual sales now comes from service and maintenance. Services also play a key part in the core business of industrial distributors, where up to 25 percent of their revenues come from value-added services.[8]

---

[4] "The Service Economy," *Coalition of Service Industries Reports* 10 (June 1996): pp. 1–20.

[5] "Charting the Projections, 1994–2005—Industrial Employment," *Occupational Outlook Quarterly* 39 (fall 1995): p. 18.

[6] John Case, "The Invisible Powerhouse," *INC.* 11 (September 1989): p. 25.

[7] Lauren K. Wright, "Characterizing Successful New Services: Background and Literature Review," Report #9-1985, Institute for the Study of Business Markets, Pennsylvania State University, 25 April 1985, p. 37.

[8] "Value-Added Services Equal Greater Revenues," *Industrial Distribution* 85 (January 1996): p. 19.

The business marketing manager must recognize that service activities augment the physical product and can create a differential advantage for the firm in the eyes of organizational buyers. Observe that the ad by Oracle Corporation in Figure 12.1 features the adoption of its software by a key customer—Silicon Graphics—and the diverse business functions that its software can serve. Here a customer is purchasing a solution to a business problem provided by the software (product) *and* the accompanying application services.

PURE SERVICES

The second category is **pure services,** those that are marketed in their own right without necessarily being associated with a physical product. The list of such business services is vast, including insurance, consulting, banking, maintenance services, transportation, market research, information technology management, temporary personnel, security and protection services, and travel booking services. Revenue from business services was estimated to reach the level of $806 billion by the end of 1996 as a result of the continuing global trend by businesses to outsource numerous functions. [9] The variety of business services provided and the quantity of services purchased by businesses and organizations is expanding, and services make up a significant percentage of total corporate purchases. A number of factors have contributed to the growth of business services:

1. Companies and other organizations increasingly rely on the services of specialists because of the complexity of economic organization and the costs involved in the division and specialization of labor.
2. Technology, particularly in the data collection, manufacturing, and computer information transmission systems, requires the use of outside, specialized services to remain current. Companies need advice concerning what equipment to buy and continuing guidance on how to use it. For instance, the Arthur Andersen ad in Figure 12.2 emphasizes the firm's knowledge of global best practices and its expertise in providing leading-edge management solutions to clients.
3. Organizations can remain flexible and better control their capital commitment by hiring services that provide "use" without "ownership."
4. Time pressures (long lead time to develop in-house expertise) and lack of available internal resources encourage organizations to use outside services rather than providing services internally.[10]

---

[9]"Who Says You Can't Find Good Help?" *Business Week*, 8 January 1996, p. 107.

[10]Based on Donald Cowell, *The Marketing of Services* (London: William Heinemann, 1984), p. 13.

Figure 12.1 Ad Highlighting the Application Skills of Oracle Corporation

"Silicon Graphics chose and implemented Oracle Applications in just 15 months."

Ed McCracken, Chairman and Chief Executive Officer
Silicon Graphics, Inc.

Over the last decade Silicon Graphics, the leading manufacturer of high-performance visual and enterprise computing systems, has been one of the fastest growing companies in the world. They needed new business applications with the flexibility, scalability and technical architecture to support their phenomenal growth. Silicon Graphics chose and implemented Oracle Applications on SGI's high-performance CHALLENGE server in just 15 months.

Market Management
Supply Chain Management
Human Resources
Manufacturing
Projects
Finance
Applied Technology

Oracle Applications are the only applications designed for rapid business change and built on Oracle's integrated stack of database, tools, workflow, data warehousing and Web technologies.

Oracle Applications automate your entire enterprise with over 30 integrated software modules for finance, supply chain management, manufacturing, projects, human resources and market management.

Do your business applications enable rapid growth? If not, **call Oracle** at **1-800-633-1061**, ext. 10072 today. Or find us on the Web at **http://www.oracle.com/applications**

Source: Courtesy Oracle Corporation.

Figure 12.2 Ad Emphasizing Arthur Andersen's Consulting Capabilities

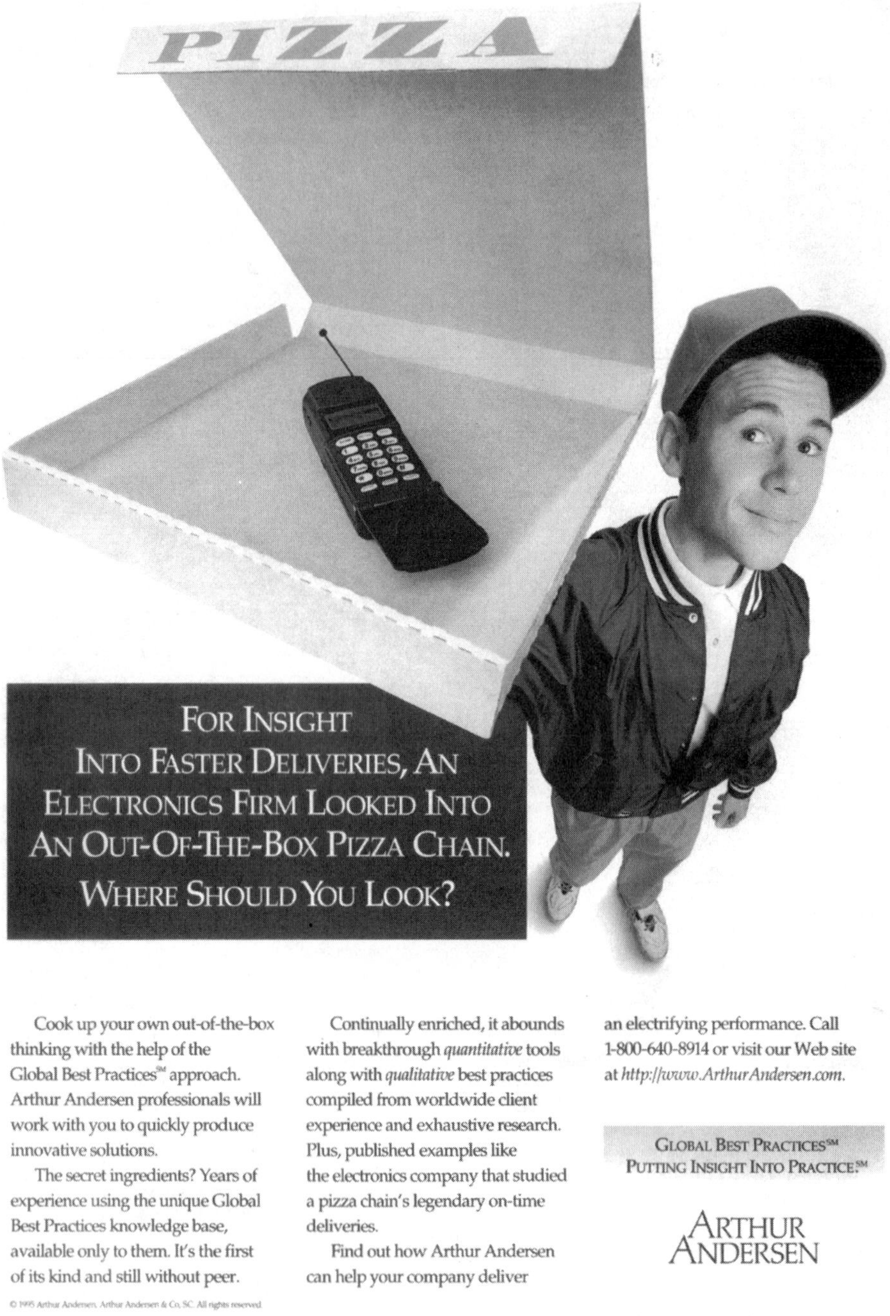

PIZZA
FOR INSIGHT
INTO FASTER DELIVERIES, AN
ELECTRONICS FIRM LOOKED INTO
AN OUT-OF-THE-BOX PIZZA CHAIN.
WHERE SHOULD YOU LOOK?
Cook up your own out-of-the-box thinking with the help of the Global Best Practices℠ approach. Arthur Andersen professionals will work with you to quickly produce innovative solutions.
The secret ingredients? Years of experience using the unique Global Best Practices knowledge base, available only to them. It's the first of its kind and still without peer.
Continually enriched, it abounds with breakthrough *quantitative* tools along with *qualitative* best practices compiled from worldwide client experience and exhaustive research. Plus, published examples like the electronics company that studied a pizza chain's legendary on-time deliveries.
Find out how Arthur Andersen can help your company deliver an electrifying performance. Call 1-800-640-8914 or visit our Web site at *http://www.ArthurAndersen.com.*
GLOBAL BEST PRACTICES℠
PUTTING INSIGHT INTO PRACTICE℠
ARTHUR ANDERSEN
© 1995 Arthur Andersen, Arthur Andersen & Co, SC. All rights reserved.

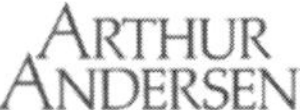

Source: Courtesy Arthur Andersen & Co.

Current and projected trends in the business environment suggest that these forces will further expand the demand for services and create significant opportunities in the business market.

BUSINESS SERVICE MARKETING: SPECIAL CHALLENGES

The development of marketing programs for both products and services can be approached from a common perspective, yet the relative importance and form of various strategic elements will differ between products and services. The underlying explanation for these strategic differences, asserts Henry Assael, lies in the distinctions between a product and a service:

> *Services are intangible; products are tangible. Services are consumed at the time of production, but there is a time lag between the production and consumption of products. Services cannot be stored; products can. Services are highly variable; most products are highly standardized. These differences produce differences in strategic applications that often stand many product marketing principles on their head.*[11]

Thus, success in the business service marketplace begins with an understanding of the meaning of *service*.

DEFINING BUSINESS SERVICES

Given the diversity of services, special insights can be secured by considering a product-service continuum where the basic underlying variable is *tangibility*. As Donald Cowell suggests, "What is significant about services, where they are objects being marketed, is the relative dominance of intangible attributes in the make-up of the 'service product.' Services are a special kind of product. They may require special understanding and special marketing efforts."[12]

TANGIBLE OR INTANGIBLE?

Figure 12.3 provides a useful tool for understanding the product-service definitional problem. The continuum suggests that there are very few *pure products* or *pure services*. For example, industrial grease is a physical object made up of tangible elements

---

[11]Henry Assael, *Marketing Management: Strategy and Action* (Boston, Mass.: Kent Publishing Company, 1985), p. 693.

[12]Donald Cowell, *The Marketing of Services*, p. 35.

Figure 12.3 Business Product-Service Classification Based on Tangibility

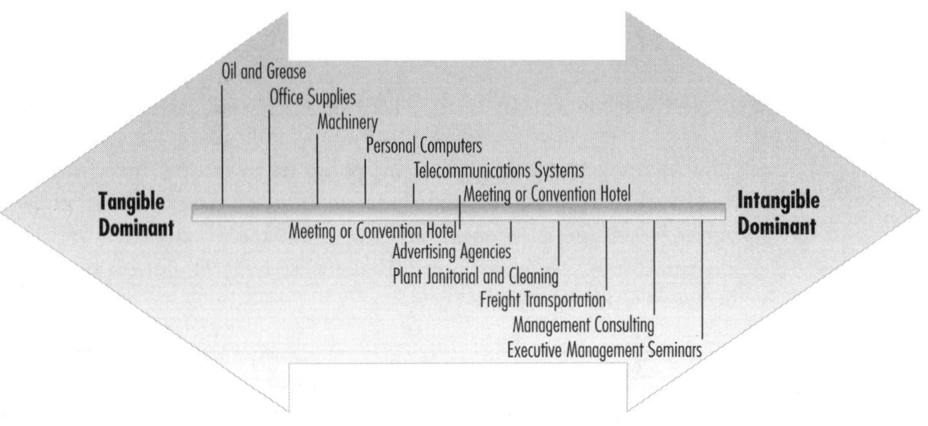

Source: Adapted from G. Lynn Shostack, "Breaking Free from Product Marketing," *Journal of Marketing* 41 (April 1977): p. 77. Published by the American Marketing Association.

(petroleum, chemicals, and so forth). However, it does provide a service (lubrication). In addition, delivery service may be an important aspect in marketing the product. Thus, most market offerings comprise a combination of tangible and intangible elements.

Whether an offering is classified as a good or as a service depends on how the organizational buyer views what is being bought—whether the tangible or the intangible elements dominate. On one end of the spectrum, grease and oil are tangible-dominant, and the essence of what is being bought is the physical product. Management seminars, on the other hand, are intangible-dominant because what is being bought—professional development, education, learning—has few, if any, tangible properties. A convention hotel is in the middle of the continuum because the buyer will receive an array of both tangible elements (meals, beverages, notepads, and so on) and intangible benefits (courteous personnel, fast check-ins, meeting room ambiance, and so forth).

The concept of tangibility is especially useful to the business marketer because many business offerings are composed of product and service combinations. The key management task is to evaluate carefully (from the buyer's standpoint) which elements of the offering dominate. The more the market offering is characterized by intangible elements, the more difficult it is to apply the standard marketing tools that were developed for products. The business marketer must focus on specialized marketing approaches appropriate for services.

The concept also helps the manager to focus clearly on the firm's *total market offering.* In addition, it helps the manager recognize that a change in one of the elements of the market offering may completely change the offering in the view of the customer. For example, a business marketer who decides to hold spare parts inventory at a central location and use overnight delivery to meet customer requirements must refocus marketing strategy. The offering has moved toward the intangible end of the continuum because of the intangible benefits associated with reduced customer inventory and fast transportation. This new "service," which is less tangible, must be carefully explained and the intangible results of lower inventory costs must be made more concrete to the buyer through an effective promotion program.

In summary, business services are those market offerings that are intangible-dominant. However, few services are totally intangible—they often contain elements with tangible properties. In addition to the tangibility criterion, business services have other important distinguishing characteristics that influence how they are marketed. Table 12.1 provides a summary of the core characteristics that further delineate the nature of business services.

SIMULTANEOUS PRODUCTION AND CONSUMPTION

Because services are generally *consumed as they are produced,* a critical element in the buyer-seller relationship is the effectiveness of the individual (repair technician, truck driver, consultant) who actually provides the service. From the service firm's

Table 12.1 Unique Service Characteristics

Characteristics	Examples	Marketing Implications
Simultaneous production and consumption	Telephone conference call; management seminar; equipment repair	Direct-seller interaction requires that service be done "right"; requires high-level training for personnel; requires effective screening and recruitment
Nonstandardized output	Management advice varies with the individual consultant; merchandise damages vary from shipment to shipment	Emphasizes strict quality control standards; develop systems that minimize deviation and human error; prepackage the service; look for ways to automate
Perishability: inability to store or stockpile	Unfilled airline seats; an idle computer technician; unrented warehouse space	Plan capacity around peak demand; use pricing and promotion to even out demand peaks and valleys; use overlapping shifts for personnel
Lack of ownership	Use of railroad car; use of consultant's know-how; use of mailing list	Focus promotion on the advantages of nonownership: reduced labor, overhead, and capital; emphasize flexibility

perspective, the entire marketing strategy may rest on how effectively the individual service provider interacts with the customer. The recruiting, hiring, and training of personnel assume special importance in business service firms.

SERVICE VARIABILITY

Observe in Table 12.1 that the service offering is *nonstandardized,* meaning that the quality of the service output may vary each time it is provided.[13] Services vary in the amount of equipment and labor that are utilized to provide the service. For example, a significant human element is involved in teaching an executive seminar compared to providing overnight airfreight service. Generally, the more labor involved in a service, the less uniform the output. In these labor-intensive cases, the user may also find it difficult to judge the quality before the service is provided. Because of uniformity problems, business service providers must focus on finely tuned quality-control programs, invest in "systems" to minimize human error, and seek approaches for automating the service.

SERVICE PERISHABILITY

Generally, services *cannot be stored;* that is, if they are not provided at the time they are available, the lost revenue cannot be recaptured. Tied to this characteristic is the fact that demand for services is often unpredictable and widely fluctuating. The service marketer must carefully evaluate capacity—in a service business, **capacity** is a substitute for inventory. If capacity is set for peak demand, a "service inventory" must exist to supply the highest level of demand. As an example, some airlines that provide air shuttle service between New York, Washington, and Boston offer flights that leave every hour. If, on any flight, the plane is full, another plane is brought to the terminal—even for one passenger. An infinite capacity is set so that no single business traveler will be dissatisfied. Obviously, setting high capacity levels is costly, and the marketer must analyze the cost versus the lost revenue and customer goodwill that might result from maintaining lower capacity.

NON-OWNERSHIP

The final dimension of services shown in Table 12.1 is the fact that the service buyer uses, but *does not own,* the service purchased. Essentially, payment for a service is a

---

[13]Valarie A. Zeithaml, A. Parasuraman, and Leonard R. Berry, "Problems and Strategies in Services Marketing," *Journal of Marketing* 49 (spring 1985): p. 34; see also Zeithaml, Berry, and Parasuraman, "Communication and Control Processes in the Delivery of Service Quality," *Journal of Marketing* 52 (April 1988): pp. 35–48.

Table 12.2 The Components of Service Quality

Component	Description	Examples
Corporate image	The overall image of the organization and its overall attractiveness	United Airlines: friendly; Hertz: market leader
Technical quality	Whether the service provides the appropriate technical attributes, *what* the user receives—the material content of the service	A clean building; a new marketing strategy from a consultant; goods transported from point A to point B
Functional quality	How the service is rendered; the way in which the service is provided	Appearance and behavior of a flight attendant; presentation of a consultant's report; how rapidly an office machine is repaired

Source: Adapted from Christian Gronroos, *Strategic Management and Marketing in the Service Sector* (Cambridge, Mass.: Marketing Science Institute, 1983), p. 25.

payment for the use of, access to, or hire of items. The service marketer must feature the advantages of non-ownership in its communications to the marketplace. The key benefits to emphasize are reductions in staff, overhead, and capital associated with a third party providing the service.

Although there may be exceptions to the general prescriptions, these characteristics provide a useful framework for understanding the nature of business services and for isolating special marketing strategy requirements.

Service Quality

Christian Gronroos suggested that the total quality of a service is a function of three components: **corporate image, technical quality,** and **functional quality.**[14] (Each is described in Table 12.2.) It is difficult to evaluate which aspect of quality is the most important from the customer's view. However, all three aspects must be given attention by management. From the marketing manager's perspective, corporate image is the most remote and the most difficult to control, even though it can be important in "excusing" minor deficiencies in the other quality components.

Technical and functional quality are the most readily managed and most easily controlled. It is important to note that these dimensions are very different in nature. Technical quality—*what* the customer receives—is more amenable to measurement

[14]Christian Gronroos, *Strategic Management and Marketing in the Service Sector* (Cambridge, Mass.: Marketing Science Institute, 1983), p. 25. For a related discussion, see Christian Gronroos, "Relationship Marketing: Strategic and Tactical Implications," *Management Decision* 34, no. 3 (1996): pp. 5–14.

and to the application of systems, procedures, and techniques intended to assure its quality. For example, a freight company can employ new trucks, purchase computer programs to route shipments, and use effective driver-training programs in order to improve delivery performance.

Functional quality—*how* the customer is served—is more difficult to measure objectively and may be more difficult to standardize and systematize. For the freight company, controlling how truck drivers interact with customers is difficult because each driver is performing in a remote location without direct supervision. In addition, the functional quality of the transport service will depend on the customer's perceptions, biases, and prejudices.

EVALUATING SERVICE QUALITY

Because business services are intangible and nonstandardized, buyers tend to have greater difficulty in evaluating services than in evaluating goods. The inability to depend on consistent service performance and quality may lead service buyers to experience more perceived risk.[15] As a result, buyers utilize a variety of prepurchase information sources to reduce risk. Information from current users (word of mouth) is particularly important. In addition, the evaluation process for services tends to be more abstract, more random, and more heavily based on symbology rather than on concrete decision variables.[16] Thus the business service marketer must consider procedures for facilitating the evaluation process. For example, some freight companies provide detailed evaluation models to prospective clients. These models help potential buyers specify the full range of key decision variables and compare competing carriers on the basis of these variables. An important part of services marketing is helping potential buyers make comparisons, thereby reducing the risk associated with the evaluation and selection process.

Perceived Quality

Quality standards are ultimately defined by the business customer. Actual performance by the service provider or the provider's perception of quality are of little relevance compared to the customer's perception of the service. "Good" service results when the service provider meets or exceeds the customer's expectations.[17] As a result, many management experts argue that service companies should carefully position themselves so that customers expect a little less than the firm can actually deliver. The strategy: underpromise and overdeliver.

---

[15]Valarie A. Zeithaml, "How Consumer Evaluation Processes Differ between Goods and Services," in *Marketing of Services,* ed. James H. Donnelly and William R. George (Chicago: American Marketing Association, 1981), pp.200–204.

[16]Ibid.

[17]"William H. Davidow and Bro Uttal, "Service Companies: Focus or Falter," *Harvard Business Review* 67 (July/August 1989): p. 84.

IMPORTANCE OF EMPLOYEES

High-quality service performance will result from a combination of technical and functional effectiveness. A vital question, from the service marketer's standpoint, is: Which dimension is most important? Research by Christian Gronroos provides some useful insights.[18] His study suggests that the performance of employees who are in contact with the customer may compensate for temporary problems with technical quality. In some cases, performance of these employees may even compensate for a lower level of technical quality. The survey provides strong evidence that functional quality, of which employee performance is a major element, is of utmost importance. Other studies have shown that customers receiving acceptable technical service without adequate functional quality tend to be generally dissatisfied, irrespective of the degree of satisfaction with the technical performance.[19]

Empowering Contact Employees

Some service firms have chosen to create "focus" in their business by entrusting the job of how to respond to each individual customer's need to the **customer contact employee.**[20] For example, a hotel chain may provide a wide range of services to business travelers, but it is the receptionist's or concierge's job to offer a specific set of services to each customer. Considerable skill and training of each customer contact person is required and these individuals will need to be empowered to adapt the services offered to the needs of the individual customer.

CUSTOMER SATISFACTION AND LOYALTY

Four components of a firm's offering and its customer-linking processes affect customer satisfaction:

1. the basic elements of the product or service that customers expect all competitors to provide,
2. basic support services, such as technical assistance or training, that make the product or service more effective or easier to use,
3. a recovery process for quickly fixing product or service problems, and

[18]Gronroos, *Strategic Management and Marketing in the Service Sector*, p. 29.

[19]J. E. Swan and L. J. Comb, "Product Performance and Consumer Satisfaction: A New Concept," *Journal of Marketing* 40 (April 1976): p. 42.

[20]Robert Johnston, "Achieving Focus in Service Organizations," *Service Industries Journal* 16 (January 1996): pp. 10–20.

4. extraordinary services that so excel in solving customers' unique problems or in meeting their needs that they make the product or service seem customized.[21]

Leading service firms carefully measure and monitor customer satisfaction because it is linked to customer loyalty and, in turn, to long-term profitability.[22] Xerox, for example, regularly surveys more than 400,000 customers regarding product and service satisfaction using a five-point scale from 5 (high) to 1 (low). In analyzing the data, Xerox executives made a remarkable discovery: *very* satisfied customers (a 5 rating) were far more loyal than satisfied customers. Very satisfied customers, in fact, were *six times* more likely to repurchase Xerox products than satisfied customers.

Customers as Apostles

Based on this analysis, Xerox now places a high priority on creating **apostles**—a term describing customers so satisfied that they convert others to a firm's product or service. To create totally satisfied customers, firms like Xerox are upgrading service levels and *guaranteeing* customer satisfaction. These firms, assert Thomas Jones and W. Earl Sasser Jr., also have well-established recovery processes to respond to unhappy customers when service falters. "If a company excels in making amends—that is, in recovering—when failures occur, customers' faith in the company is not just restored, it is deepened, and they become apostles, spreading the good word about the company to potential customers."[23]

Customers as Terrorists

While seeking to create apostles, business marketers should strive to avoid creating **terrorists,** a term describing customers so dissatisfied that they speak out against a firm and its product and service. Often, these customers spoke to representatives of the service firm first, but no one responded. They now recount their unhappy experiences to others.[24]

ZERO DEFECTIONS

The quality of service provided to business customers has a major effect on customer "defections"—customers who will not come back. Service strategists point out that

---

[21]Thomas O. Jones and W. Earl Sasser Jr., "Why Satisfied Customers Defect," *Harvard Business Review* 73 (November/December 1995): p. 90.

[22]The Xerox illustration is based on James L. Heskett, Thomas O. Jones, Gary W. Loveman, W. Earl Sasser Jr., and Leonard A. Schlesinger, "Putting the Service-Profit Chain to Work," *Harvard Business Review* 72 (March/April 1994): pp. 164–174.

[23]Jones and Sasser, "Why Satisfied Customers Defect," p. 96.

[24]Ibid.

customer defections have a powerful impact on the bottom line.[25] As a company's relationship with a customer lengthens, profits rise—and generally rise considerably. For example, one service firm found that profit from a fourth-year customer is triple that from a first-year customer. Many additional benefits accrue to service companies that retain their customers: They can charge more, the cost of doing business is reduced, and the long-standing customer provides "free" advertising. The implications are clear: Service providers should carefully track customer defections and recognize that continuous improvement in service quality is not a cost, but, say Frederick Reichheld and W. Earl Sasser, "an investment in a customer who generates more profit than the margin on a one-time sale."[26]

RETURN ON QUALITY

A difficult decision for the business services marketing manager is to determine how much to spend on improving service quality. Clearly, expenditures on quality have diminishing returns—at some point, additional expenditures on service quality do not increase profitability. To make good decisions on the level of expenditures on quality, managers must justify quality efforts on a financial basis, knowing where to spend on quality improvement, how much to spend, and when to reduce or stop the expenditures. Roland Rust, Anthony Zahorik, and Timothy Keiningham have developed a technique for calculating the "return on investing in quality."[27] Under this approach, service quality benefits are successively linked to customer satisfaction, customer retention, market share, and, finally, to profitability. The relationship between expenditure level and customer satisfaction change is first measured by managerial judgment and then through market testing. When the relationship has been estimated, the return on quality can be measured statistically. The significant conclusion is that quality improvements should be treated as investments: They must pay off, and spending should not be wasted on efforts that do not produce a return.

Marketing Mix for Business Service Firms

To meet the needs of service buyers effectively, an integrated marketing strategy is required. First, target segments must be selected, and then a marketing mix must be tailored to the expectations of each segment. The key elements of the service marketing mix include the development of service packages, pricing, promotion, and distribution. Each requires special consideration by the business marketing manager.

---

[25]Frederick F. Reichheld and W. Earl Sasser, "Zero Defections: Quality Comes to Services," *Harvard Business Review* 68 (September/October 1990): p. 105.

[26]Ibid., p. 107.

[27]Roland T. Rust, Anthony J. Zahorik, and Timothy L. Keiningham, "Return on Quality (ROQ): Making Service Quality Financially Accountable," *Journal of Marketing* 59 (April 1995): pp. 58–70.

SEGMENTATION

As with any marketing situation, development of the marketing mix will be contingent upon the customer segment to be served. Every facet of the service to be offered, as well as the methods for promoting, pricing, and delivering the service, will hinge upon the needs of a reasonably homogeneous group of customers. The process for segmenting business markets described in Chapter 6 will find application in the services market. However, William Davidow and Bro Uttal suggest that customer service segments differ from usual market segments in significant ways.[28]

First, service segments are often narrower. This situation reflects the fact that many service customers expect services to be customized. Expectations may not be met if the service received is standardized and routine. Second, service segmentation focuses on what the business buyers expect as opposed to what they need. The assessment of buyer expectations will play a very large role in selecting a target market and developing the appropriate service package. This assessment is critical because so many studies have shown large differences between the ways that customers define and rank different service activities and the ways suppliers define and rank them.[29]

Because expectations play such an important role in determining ultimate satisfaction with a service, it has been suggested that service quality expectations be utilized to segment business-to-business markets. One study in the mainframe software industry revealed significant differences between "software specialists" (software experts) and "applications developers" (users of software) in the same firm regarding their expectations of new software. The developers (users) had higher expectations regarding the quality of the supplier's equipment, the responsiveness of their employees, and the amount of personal attention provided.[30] The study concluded that different buying center members may well have different perspectives and different expectations of service quality. The business marketer should carefully evaluate the possibility of using service quality expectations as a guide for creating marketing strategy.

Finally, segmenting service markets helps the firm to adjust service capacity more effectively. Segmentation will usually reveal that total demand is made up of numerous smaller, yet more predictable, demand patterns. For a hotel, the demand patterns of a convention visitor, business traveler, foreign tourist, or vacationer can all be forecast individually and capacities adjusted for each segment's demand pattern.

---

[28]Davidow and Uttal, "Service Companies: Focus or Falter," p. 79.

[29]Ibid., p. 83.

[30]Leyland Pitt, Michael H. Morris, and Pierre Oosthuizen, "Expectations of Service Quality As an Industrial Market Segmentation Variable," *The Service Industries Journal* 16 (January 1996): pp. 1–9. See also Ralph W. Jackson, Lester A. Neidell, and Dale A. Lunsford, "An Empirical Investigation of the Differences in Goods and Services As Perceived by Organizational Buyers," *Industrial Marketing Management* 24 (March 1995): pp. 99–108.

SERVICE PACKAGES

The service package can be thought of as the product dimension of service, including decisions involving the essential concept of the service, the range of services provided, and the quality and level of service. In addition, the service package must consider some factors that are unique to services—the personnel who perform the service, the physical product that accompanies the service, and the process of providing the service.[31] A useful way to conceptualize the service product is shown in Figure 12.4.

Figure 12.4 Conceptualizing the Service Product

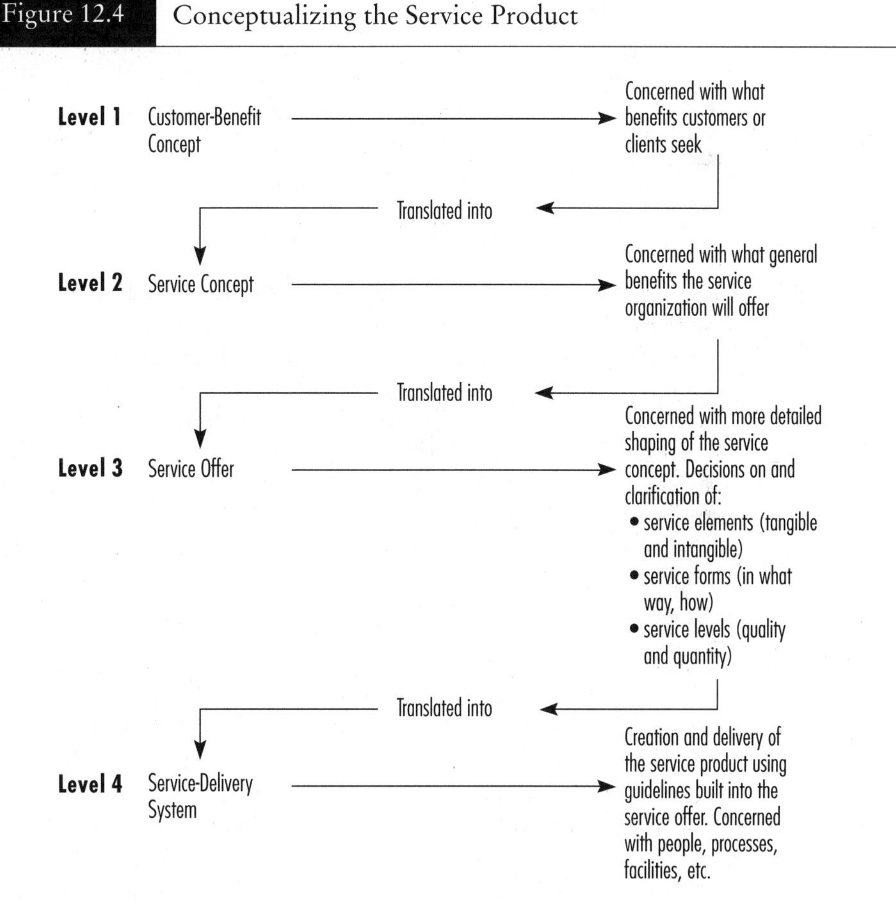

Source: Adapted from Donald Cowell, *The Marketing of Services* (London: William Heinemann, Ltd., 1984), p. 100. Published by Heinemann Professional Publishing, Ltd.

[31]Cowell, *The Marketing of Services*, p 73.

Customer-Benefit Concept

Services are purchased because of the benefits they offer, and a first step in either creating a service or evaluating an existing one is to define the **customer-benefit concept**—that is, evaluate the core benefit that the customer will derive from the service. An understanding of the customer-benefit concept will focus the business marketer's attention on those attributes—functional, effectual, and psychological—that must be not only offered but also tightly monitored from a quality-control standpoint. For example, a sales manager selecting a resort hotel for an annual sales meeting is purchasing a core benefit that could be stated as "a successful meeting." The hotel marketer must then assess the full range of service attributes and components necessary to provide a successful meeting. Obviously, a wide variety of service elements will come into play: (1) meeting room size, layout, environment, acoustics; (2) meals; (3) comfortable and quiet sleeping rooms; (4) audiovisual equipment; and (5) staff responsiveness.

As another example, Dun & Bradstreet does not provide its customers with "financial services." Its customer-benefit concept focuses on objective and accurate credit information, security, and even "peace of mind."[32]

Service Concept

Once the customer-benefit concept is understood, the next step is to articulate the **service concept**, which defines the general benefits the service company will provide in terms of the bundle of goods and services sold to the customer. The service concept translates the customer-benefit concept into the range of benefits the service marketer will *provide*. For a hotel, the service concept might specify the benefits that it will develop: flexibility, responsiveness, and courteousness in providing meeting rooms; a full range of audiovisual equipment; flexible meal schedules; message services; professional personnel; climate-controlled meeting rooms; and the like.

Service Offer

Intimately linked with the service concept is the **service offer**, which spells out in more detail those services to be offered; when, where, and to whom they will be provided; and how they will be presented. The service elements that make up the total service package, including both tangibles and intangibles, must be determined. The service offer of the hotel includes a multitude of tangible elements (soundproof meeting rooms, overhead projectors, video players, slide projectors, flip charts, refreshments, heating and air-conditioning, meals) and intangible elements (attitude of meeting room set-up personnel, warmth of greetings from desk clerks and bellhops, response to unique requests, meeting room ambiance). Generally, management will find it easier to manage the tangible (equipment and physical) elements of the service than to control the intangible elements.

---

[32]James L. Heskett, *Managing in the Service Economy* (Boston: Harvard Business School Press, 1986), p. 17.

EXPANDING THE SERVICE PACKAGE

With an ever-increasing pressure to lower costs and to streamline the supplier base, buyers are asking express carriers like Federal Express, UPS, and Airborne Express to do more than just deliver a package. Not surprisingly, the express industry has answered the call. Carriers are continually improving their tracking and tracing, customs clearance, electronic data interchange, and bar-coding systems. The real payoff—for both shippers and carriers—has come when carriers provide value-added services not traditionally associated with the package express industry.

Today, buyers rely on carriers to handle inventory, pick and pack parts, and even answer customer inquiries. Thanks to a big push by carriers to establish sites on the Internet and commercial on-line services, buyers equipped with a PC, modem, printer, and the proper software can do everything from checking a carrier's capabilities to tracking a shipment with a few simple keystrokes.

Source: Adapted from Tim Minahan, "Value-Added Takes on a New Meaning," *Purchasing* 120 (15 February 1996): pp. 68–69.

Service Delivery System

The final dimension of the service product is the **service delivery system**—how the service is provided to the customer. The delivery system includes carefully conceived jobs for people; personnel with capabilities and attitudes necessary for successful performance; equipment, facilities, and layouts for effective customer work flow; and carefully developed procedures aimed at a common set of objectives.[33] Thus, the service delivery system should provide a carefully designed blueprint that describes how the service is rendered for the customer.

For physical products, manufacturing and marketing are generally separate and distinct activities; for services, these two activities are often inseparable.[34] The service performance and the delivery system both create the product and deliver it to the customers. This feature of services underscores the important role that people, particularly service providers, play in the marketing process. Technicians, repair personnel, and maintenance engineers are intimately involved in customer contact, and they decidedly influence the customer's perception of service quality. The business service marketer must pay close attention to both people and physical evidence (tangible elements such as uniforms) when designing the service package.

Service Personnel

A first step in creating an effective service package is to ensure that the customer-benefit concept is known, understood, and accepted by all personnel. As Donald

[33]Ibid., p. 20.
[34]Cowell, *The Marketing of Services*, p. 110.

Cowell states, "So important are people and their quality to organizations and . . . services that 'internal marketing' is considered to be an important management role to ensure that all staff are customer conscious."[35] In short, the attitudes, skills, knowledge, and behavior of service personnel have a critical impact on the levels of satisfaction that the user derives from the service. Because service production and consumption are inseparable, a variety of operating personnel have direct contact with the customer and help shape customer perceptions of the service performance.

Two successful service marketers, Marriott Corporation and Delta Airlines, pay particular attention to employee training, involvement, incentives, and, in some cases, ownership. Managers are often on a first-name basis with employees, and employees are regularly featured in their ads. Marketing communications directed to employees are as important as those targeted for potential customers. Such internal communications emphasize the company's purpose, its high standards of service, and the role that each employee assumes in creating satisfied customers.[36]

Physical Evidence

The many tangible objects used to create and deliver a service—buildings, computers, equipment, tools, plants, documents—are what Christian Gronroos refers to as the physical/technical resources. "The customer experiences such resources when its personnel come to the service company or when the service employee comes to the customer's location to deliver the service."[37] Physical evidence plays an important role in creating the atmosphere and environment in which a service is bought or performed, and it influences the customer's perception of the service. Physical evidence is the tangible aspect of the service package, which the business service marketer can control to a significant degree.

For business service marketers, uniforms, logos, written contracts and guarantees, building appearance, and color schemes are some of the many ways to make their services tangible. An equipment maintenance firm that provides free, written, quarterly inspections helps make its service more tangible. Xerox offers a Total Satisfaction Guarantee that allows customers to return copiers for any reason. The credit card created by car rental companies is another example of an attempt to make a service more tangible. A key concern for the service marketer is to develop a well-defined strategy for managing physical evidence—to enhance and differentiate service evidence through the creation of tangible clues.

PRICING BUSINESS SERVICES

Although product and service pricing policies and strategies share many common threads, the unique characteristics of services create some special pricing problems and opportunities.

---

[35]Ibid.

[36]This example is based on Heskett, *Managing in the Service Economy*, p. 40.

[37]Christian Gronroos, "An Applied Service Marketing Theory," working paper no. 57, Swedish School of Economics and Business Administration, Helsinki, 1980.

Perishability and Managing Demand/Capacity

The demand for services is rarely steady or predictable enough to avoid service perishability. An extremely difficult decision for the business service marketer is to determine the capacity (inventory) of the system: Should it meet peak demand, average demand, or somewhere in between? Pricing can be used to manage the timing of demand and align it with capacity levels.

To manage demand, the marketer may offer off-peak pricing schemes and price incentives for service orders that are placed in advance. For example, resort hotels, crowded with pleasure travelers during school vacations and holidays, develop special packages for business groups during the off-season. Similarly, various utilities may offer significant rate reductions for off-peak usage. It may also be possible, depending on demand elasticity and competition, to charge premium rates for services provided at peak demand periods. It is interesting to note, however, that a recent study of strategies utilized by service firms showed that many service firms do not reduce prices to increase business during slow periods.[38]

Service Bundling

Many business services include a core service as well as a variety of peripheral services. How should the services be priced—as an entity, as a service bundle, or individually? **Bundling** is the practice of marketing two or more services in a package for a special price.[39] Bundling makes sense in the business service environment because most service businesses have a high ratio of fixed costs to variable costs and a high degree of cost sharing among their many related services. Hence the marginal cost of providing additional services to the core service customer is generally low.

A key decision for the service provider is whether to provide pure or mixed bundling.[40] In **pure bundling,** the services are only available in bundled form—they cannot be purchased separately. In **mixed bundling,** the customer can purchase one or more services individually or purchase the bundle. For example, a public warehouse firm can provide its services—storage, product handling, and clerical activities—in a price-bundled form by charging a single rate (8 cents) for each case received by the warehouse from its manufacturer-client. Or the firm may market each service separately and provide a rate for each service individually (3 cents per case for storage, 4 cents per case for handling, and 1 cent per case for clerical). Additionally, a multitude of peripheral services can be quoted on an individual basis: physical inventory count, freight company selection and routing, merchandise return and repair, and so on. In this way, the customer can choose the services desired and pay for each separately.

Attracting New Business

Various bundling strategies can be used to expand sales either by **cross-selling**—selling a new service to customers who buy an existing service—or by attracting

---

[38]Zeithaml, Parasuraman, and Berry, "Problems and Strategies in Services Marketing," p. 41.

[39]Joseph P. Guiltinan, "The Price Bundling of Services: A Normative Framework," *Journal of Marketing* 51 (April 1987): p. 74.

[40]Ibid., p. 75.

entirely new customers. In the cross-selling situation for a public warehouse, current customers (utilizing storage services) may be attracted to a new product-labeling service by the offer of a bundled price that results in a discount on the total cost of the two services. Bundling services in order to attract new customers can be efficient when the service attributes can be evaluated before purchase and when the core service is demand elastic.[41] Thus, noncustomized services, where significant competition exists, would seem to be a fertile environment. Bundling insurance coverage with the rental of an automobile may be effective in attracting new business customers for a car rental firm.

In the computer service industry, manufacturers are finding that services formerly sold on an ad hoc basis can be sold more effectively if bundled together. Hewlett-Packard is testing a variety of service bundles with customers in order to determine how customers want to buy the services.[42] Clearly, the services, how they are combined, and how the bundle is priced have critical effects on the service firm's success.

SERVICES PROMOTION

The promotional strategies for services follow many of the same prescriptions as do those for products. However, the unique characteristics of business services pose special challenges for the business marketer.

Communication with Employees

Personnel are vital to many people-based service businesses, and they can have a profound effect on the customer's satisfaction with the service. Internal advertising to employees accomplishes the following:

- Promotes an understanding of the firm's mission and customer service benefit
- Influences them regarding how the service is to be provided
- Motivates them to perform
- Defines management's expectations of them

A Federal Express ad campaign emphasizes the responsiveness of its employees. The copy includes employees and shows situations in which employees take extra steps to assist customers. Even though the ad is ostensibly meant for the customer, it is clearly also aimed at Federal Express personnel. The ad helps define management's perceptions and expectations of employees.

---

[41]Ibid., p. 81.

[42]Diane Lynn Kastiel, "Service and Support: High-Tech's New Battleground," *Business Marketing* 73 (June 1987): p. 66.

Keith Murray presents evidence suggesting that "managers should not only train and equip service employees to carry out their service functions per se, but also ensure their knowledgeability and understanding of the service product and process. Managers' ability to influence contact employees' knowledge and understanding of the service encounter—and hence their ability and willingness to communicate that to customers—may directly enhance customer satisfaction or mitigate dissatisfaction."[43] Service personnel play a critical role in reducing the risk that customers associate with purchasing services, and that role can be enhanced by preparing personnel to offer information that anticipates customer concerns with the service.

Word of Mouth

Service purchases are frequently considered to be riskier than product purchases because it is more difficult for buyers to evaluate quality and value. As a result, buyers are more apt to be influenced by colleagues, peers, and other professionals who have had experience in purchasing and using the service. Promotion must concentrate on the dominant role of personal influence in the buying process and build on word-of-mouth communication. This can be done by[44]

- Persuading satisfied customers to inform others of their satisfaction
- Developing materials that customers can pass on to noncustomers
- Targeting opinion leaders in ad campaigns
- Encouraging potential customers to talk to existing customers

Service marketers can capitalize on the satisfaction of current customers and word-of-mouth promotion by featuring customers (and their comments) in nonpersonal advertising. The promotional brochures for many management development seminars feature pictures of customers and statements of satisfaction by these prior attendees.

Developing Tangible Clues

As indicated earlier in this chapter, service marketers must concentrate either on featuring the physical evidence elements of their service or on making the intangible elements more tangible. Attempts should be made to translate the image of intangible attributes of a service into something more concrete. In business service marketing, this is typically accomplished by showing pictures of buildings, equipment, and personnel. Federal Express, through a series of highly creative television commercials, helped make their overnight delivery service more tangible by showing situations where shippers did not use their service. The foul-ups that were displayed showed

[43]Keith B. Murray, "A Test of Services Marketing Theory: Consumer Information Acquisition Activities," *Journal of Marketing* 55, no. 1 (January 1991): p. 21.
[44]Cowell, *The Marketing of Services*, p. 171.

the viewer the results of using a firm other than Federal Express: unhappy superiors, embarrassment, and delayed meetings were tangible results to be avoided.

Operating Personnel as Salespeople

Marketing and operations are generally inseparable in the service business. This means that service personnel also play key selling and marketing roles. The operating personnel must be equipped and ready to deal effectively with the customer; they must also be motivated to do so. At Marriott Corporation, according to G. M. Hostage, "bellmen are often looked at subconsciously by guests as being 'Mr. Marriott' himself because many times a guest will speak to and deal with the bellman more often during a visit than with any other employees of the hotel. The bellman represents the all-important first and last impression for many guests. . . .They are coached to smile often and do all they can to make the guest feel welcome and special."[45] Many successful business service companies put considerable effort into ensuring that their operating personnel communicate effectively with the customer.

SERVICES DISTRIBUTION

Distribution decisions in the service industry are focused on how to make the service package available and accessible to the user. Direct sale may be accomplished by the user going to the provider (for example, a manufacturer using a public warehouse for storing its product) or, more often, by the provider going to the buyer (for example, photocopier repair). In some instances, service intermediaries can be used.

Service Intermediaries

Financial services, insurance, lodging, warehousing, and transportation are some of the many services sold through intermediaries. For example, in the freight transportation business, selling agents, brokers, and freight forwarders are some of the typical intermediaries used, generally because they can cost-effectively cover the entire freight service market. In addition, some of these channel members may develop bundles of services from a variety of transportation companies. Thus, a freight forwarder may arrange for a shipment to be moved by three separate modes of transportation—air, rail, and truckline. The forwarder takes care of all arrangements and invoices the customer only once for a single fee.

Franchising

As an alternative channel of distribution, franchising has experienced considerable growth in recent years. Such services as office and factory cleaning, car rental, temporary help, employment agencies, uniform rental, and equipment maintenance are now

---

[45]G. M. Hostage, "Quality Control in the Service Business, *Harvard Business Review* 53 (July/August 1975): p. 102.

distributed through franchised dealerships. Franchising works best when the service can be standardized (for example, office cleaning). Franchising enables the service provider to expand its market coverage rapidly and to minimize capital investment.

The design of the marketing strategy for a business service must be tailored to those unique factors that are associated with an intangible product. In similar fashion, the marketer developing new service packages must also recognize these important elements. The next section will briefly examine the development of new service packages.

Developing New Services

The conventional process for developing new physical products—exploration, screening, business analysis, development, testing, and commercialization—appears to apply equally well to services[46] (see Chapter 11). However, the design and introduction of new service offerings has been cited as one of the more difficult challenges for managers in the service sector:

> *New product development is inherently more difficult, messier and less successful in the service sector. If a service company perceives a new need and develops a new service, there is less confidence in the result because the service is not subject to the same rigor and predictable outcomes that new products are subject to in the R&D lab. Most service companies focus on geographic extensions of their service or on minor modifications rather than on truly innovative approaches. Innovation in the service sector is the result of trial and error. . . . Service firms have difficulty in linking innovations and imagination to execution of a new offer.*[47]

A major stumbling block to creating and launching a new service is the difficulty in "tangibilizing" the service concept. Traditional approaches, such as product prototyping, do not work effectively with services because it is hard to prototype services that are often customized for individual buyers. However, the business service firm can overcome these difficulties by taking steps to improve the new service development process and resulting marketing success. James Heskett offers five steps that a firm can take to improve the new service development process (see Table 12.3). Consistent with the discussion of product innovation, it is important to create the proper organizational climate (for example, entrepreneurial culture, championing, taking risks).

SCENARIOS FOR SUCCESS AND FAILURE[48]

Services depend on the skills and expertise of the people that deliver them; if a new service lies outside the knowledge base of company personnel (no synergy), the quality and

---

[46]Cowell, *The Marketing of Services,* p. 133.

[47]"Service Management: The Toughest Game in Town," *Management Practice,* 7 (fall 1984): p. 8.

[48]This section is based on Ulrike de Brentani, "New Industrial Service Development: Scenarios for Success and Failure," *Journal of Business Research* (February 1995): pp. 93–103.

Table 12.3 Steps for Enhancing the New Service Development Process

Step	Description
1. Establish a culture for entrepreneurship	Facilitate risk taking and new ideas by creating the proper climate: providing R&D funds, doing customer-need research, allowing employees to voice contrary opinions
2. Create an organization to foster new service development	Assemble a "cast": **senior sponsor,** who has authority; **product champion,** who provides continuity and enthusiasm; **integrator,** who brings the functions together and coordinates them; and **referee,** who establishes rules for the process and then administers them
3. Test ideas in the marketplace	New ideas must weather the acid test of the marketplace because the service concept is intangible
4. Monitor results	Establish success measures and evaluate against these; track customer reaction
5. Reward risk-takers	Reward those taking good risks, even when they are not consistently successful

Source: Adapted from James L. Heskett, *Managing in the Service Economy* (Boston: Harvard Business School Press, 1986), pp. 86–90.

delivery of the service may be deficient, resulting in a less than effective experience for the customer. Therefore, when managers screen and select new service ideas, those proposals that score highest on marketing, technical, and operations synergy should be favored.

A recent study tackled these issues: What new service development scenarios do managers in industrial service companies typically pursue, and what factors explain why some are likely to succeed while others fail? Observe in Table 12.4 that three scenarios describe the characteristics of successful situations, while two others characterize failed attempts at developing and launching new business services.

New Service Projects That Succeed.

The three successful scenarios differ in terms of the nature of the service initiative, the extent of service innovativeness, and the approach followed in developing and marketing the new service offering. The following profiles highlight key differences.

- **The Customized, Expert Service:** These new services are relatively straightforward and inexpensive but are customized to fit the needs and operating systems of client firms. To respond to a customer's unique requirements, expert personnel are crucial to successful strategy execution. Examples include a customized learning center offered by management consultants and a media planning model developed by a marketing communication firm.
- **The Planned, Pioneering Venture:** These are first-to-market services that are unique, complex, and expensive. A formal and carefully

Table 12.4 New Industrial Service Development: Scenarios for Success and Failure

Successes

Customized expert service — New services that fully leverage the firm's expert capabilities and resources—in particular, its expert personnel—in providing clients with a customized and high quality service outcome. Success at new service development depends on a high-involvement and innovation-oriented corporate environment.

Planned "pioneering" venture — Pioneering new service ventures aimed at attractive, high volume markets. Key descriptive factors include companies first to market, excellent fit with customer/market segment needs—as well as with the company expertise and resources, tangible evidence used to promote the service, and a detailed and high quality execution of the stages of the new service development (NSD) process.

Improved service experience — Enhanced speed and reliability are essential features of these equipment-based new service offerings. Developers have a good understanding of client needs, they have a reputation for service quality, and they use a fairly planned approach for researching, designing, and marketing the new service product.

Failures

Peripheral, low market potential service — The service offers few real benefits and has only low market potential. It is peripheral to the firm's core line of services and appears to lack any real commitment on the part of the firm. The NSD process is haphazard and companies misuse tangible evidence to feign service quality.

Poorly planned, "industrialized" clone — These are failed "me-too" attempts at "industrializing" complex, equipment-based services. Entering the market long after competitors, the new service projects are deficient in terms of customer orientation, service quality and innovativeness, their fit with corporate capabilities and resources, and the quality of execution of new service development activities.

Source: Ulrike de Brentani, "New Industrial Service Development: Scenarios for Success and Failure," *Journal of Business Research* 32 (February 1995): p. 96. Copyright © 1995. Reprinted by permission of the publisher, Elsevier–Science, Inc.

planned new service development process is a distinguishing feature of these service projects. Special attention is given to providing potential customers with tangible evidence that illuminates the benefits of the new service offering for them. Examples of these services include a terminal device linking stockbrokers to multiple information origins developed by a telecommunications firm and a computer-based remote access system developed by a bank to simplify payroll processing by organizations.

- **The Improved Service Experience:** Represented here are equipment-based improvements made to a current service offering that increase the speed and reliability of the service process. Examples include an information systems–based expert production system provided by a computer systems organization and a mutual fund order network developed by a large financial services organization.

All three of these scenarios share certain critical elements that appear to be crucial to the success of new service offerings. Whereas industrial services can take many forms, new service success is closely associated with offerings that respond to market needs; that capitalize on a firm's reputation, skills, and resources; and that issue from a well-managed new service development process.

New Service Projects That Fail

What are the characteristics of new service initiatives that fail in the business market and what can we learn from them? The following two common scenarios for failure are also described in Table 12.4.

- **The Peripheral, Low Market Potential Service:** These new services tend to be peripheral to the firm's core offerings, fail to provide added value to the customer, and enter a market with very limited potential. Failures of this type are common across service sectors in the business market.
- **The Poorly Planned "Industrialized" Clone:** These are complex new services that rely on "hard" technology (that is, equipment) for their production and delivery. Often, these are "me-too" services that offer no real customer benefits or improvements over those of well-entrenched competitors. While many of the new industrial service initiatives fitting this profile were developed by well-established banks and insurance firms, inadequate planning by managers was the key feature distinguishing these failed services from other more successful projects.

Clearly, efforts to improve the efficiency and reliability of services by reducing customer contact and introducing equipment-intensive processes have succeeded in certain sectors of the business market. But, states Ulrike de Brentani, "such development efforts must be accompanied by apparent customer benefits—that is, greater efficiencies and/or superior solutions to problems; a good fit with the capabilities of the developing firm; some competitive advantage in terms of service competitiveness; as well as a set of activities for researching, designing, and launching the new service offerings."[49] Overall, then, the determinants of success for new services closely resemble those found for successful new products (see Chapter 11).

Global Dimensions of Business Services

Many U.S. service businesses realize a considerable portion of their total revenue from sales outside the United States. The United States is the world's leading exporter of services, led by the aerospace, telecommunications, financial software, and entertainment industries.[50] U.S. service exports to the European Community alone total more than $50 billion annually, representing more than 25 percent of worldwide service exports.[51] Importantly, the United States continues to show a net surplus in service trade,[52] and services represent an estimated 25 to 30 percent of total world trade. Advances in information technology have vastly expanded the range of services that

[49]Ibid., p. 101.

[50]Reginald Biddle and Toni Dick, "Selling Services to Canada," *Business America* 114 (31 May 1993): p. 2.

[51]Josephine Ludolph, "The EC's Accomplishments in and Prospects for a Single Market in Services," *Business America* 114 (8 March 1993): p. 6.

[52]"The Service Economy," *Coalition of Service Industries Reports*, p. 2.

Managing in the 21st Century

OUTSOURCING SPURS GROWTH OF BUSINESS SERVICES

Most companies are carefully evaluating every task and function that they perform in house to isolate tasks that can be outsourced to third-party specialists. Everything from computer operations, clerical services, warehousing, and cafeteria operations to providing employees with financial advice is being examined to assess its potential for outsourcing. As firms handle fewer of their own accounting, janitorial, trucking, and other services, the service sector is experiencing dramatic growth.

Outsourcing has spread to almost every phase of private and public sector operations. Hewlett-Packard (H-P) recently signed a $200 million contract covering temporary professional and technical support for services ranging from secretarial to engineering work, sparing H-P the cost and obligation of hiring regular employees. Municipal governments have moved to outsource one of their long-standing operations—water purification. Resistance to tax hikes and bond issues limit municipalities' ability to improve their water systems, so they are increasingly turning to outside contractors. Some experts predict that as many as 8 percent of the more than 15,500 municipal water-treatment facilities in the United States will be outsourced by the year 2000. Outsourcing has penetrated the Pentagon as well. One firm recently signed two five-year contracts with the Defense Department to provide a $100 million computerized battlefield simulator and a system to track Air Force reconnaissance missions.

Strong growth of business services is forecasted to continue well into the 21st century as businesses and governments continue to position themselves for the maximum flexibility provided by outsourcing.

Source: Based on Kate Boliner Lewis, "Business Services and Supplies," *Forbes*, 1 January 1996, pp. 84–86; and Michael V. Maciosek, "Behind the Growth of Services," *Illinois Business Review* 52 (fall 1995): pp. 3–6.

can be traded internationally.[53] In particular, developing countries stand to benefit by the fact that they can increase their export of services as well as gain access to services unavailable domestically. Although representing significant opportunity, international service markets pose special challenges for the marketing manager.

KEY CONSIDERATIONS IN GLOBAL SERVICES MARKETING

The principles of marketing services apply in any context, yet marketing efforts must adjust to the environment in which the firm operates. This section high-

[53]Carlos Primo Braga, "The Impact of Internationalization of Services on Developing Countries," *Finance and Development* 33 (March 1996): pp. 34–37.

lights selected factors that business marketers should explore as they contemplate global service offerings.[54]

Global Marketing Risks

Some experts suggest that the global expansion of service sales is more risky than expansion of product sales. The increased risk results because products can be introduced gradually to international markets, whereas services, because of their inherent characteristics, must be introduced in totality. This places a heavy burden on service strategy implementation. The service provider must immediately produce on foreign soil, deal directly with customers, and respond to their needs. Immediate on-site procedures, controls, and processes must be established. As a consequence, the business service marketer wishing to reach international markets must give special attention to customer research, service design, and quality control.

Adaptation of Operations to Foreign Markets

Service firms must adjust to the business norms and laws of the host government. Often, service firms are not highly regarded by foreign governments because they provide little capital or technology to the country. Professional accounting, consulting, and law service firms have experienced considerable difficulty in demonstrating quality to potential foreign customers and adopting a professional style that fits the local culture.[55] Strategies for overcoming such hurdles include intensive advertising and public relations as well as hiring host country nationals who have obtained education and work experience in other countries.

One way to reduce the problem of adapting to foreign markets is to focus initially on markets with the greatest similarity to the home market. A study of 180 service firms operating in foreign markets showed that firms with less international experience prefer entering markets that are similar to those in their home country.[56] However, as their experience increases and becomes more diversified, these firms increasingly seek out markets that are geographically and culturally distant. It appears that an effective approach to reducing risks and adapting to foreign markets is to follow a gradual spread of international operations, beginning in the country with whose language and culture the firm is most familiar. Entry into familiar markets facilitates the transfer of technology and managerial resources and helps reduce uncertainty.[57]

Success Profiles

International markets represent a significant growth opportunity for many business service marketers. Firms seeking to offer their services in overseas markets must carefully evaluate the risks, market setting, and barriers that may restrict their operations and eventual success.

---

[54]Parts of this section are based on Cowell, *The Marketing of Services*, pp. 265–267.
[55]Christopher Lovelock and George S. Yip, "Developing Global Strategies for Service Businesses," *California Management Review* 38 (winter 1996): p. 79.
[56]M. Krishna Erramilli, "The Experience Factor in Foreign Market Entry Behavior of Service Firms," *Journal of International Business Studies* 23, no. 3 (third quarter, 1991): p. 481.
[57]Ibid., p. 496.

Many firms, however, are succeeding: Citibank has positioned itself as a "uniquely global consumer bank" with its automated teller machines that are linked across 28 countries; Hewlett-Packard provides a globally standardized set of services for customers around the world through its global network of 30 Response Centers; McKinsey & Company, the management consulting firm, serves customers on a global scale and improves efficiency and effectiveness by shifting some of its work for clients from high-cost countries to its offices in low-cost countries like India; and Arthur Andersen is pursuing a lead role in offering globally standardized accounting services.[58]

Summary

Business services can be categorized into two segments: pure services, marketed in their own right, and support services, marketed along with goods and equipment. Both segments of the business service market are large, expanding as the world moves toward a service economy. Given the diversity of services, special insights can be secured by classifying business services on a product-service continuum for which the basic underlying factor is tangibility.

Business services are distinguished by their intangibility, linked production and consumption, lack of standardization, perishability, and use as opposed to ownership. Together, these characteristics have profound effects on how services should be marketed. Buyers of business services focus their choice processes on the perceived quality of the service as well as technical and functional quality. Because of intangibility and lack of uniformity, service buyers have significant difficulty in the comparison and selection of service vendors. Service providers must address this issue in the development of their marketing mix.

The marketing mix for business services centers on the traditional elements—service package, pricing, promotion, and distribution—as well as on service personnel, service delivery system, and physical evidence. The goal of the services marketing program is to create satisfied customers. A key first step in creating strategies is to define the customer-benefit concept and the related service concept and offer. Pricing concentrates on influencing demand and capacity as well as on the bundling of service elements. The promotion arena emphasizes developing employee communication, enhancing word-of-mouth promotion, providing tangible clues, and developing interpersonal skills of operating personnel. Distribution is accomplished through direct means, through intermediaries, or by franchising.

New service marketing can improve effectiveness by creating an organizational culture that fosters risk taking and innovation. Successful new services respond to carefully defined market needs, capitalize on the strengths and reputation of the firm, and issue from a well-planned new service development process.

A large and growing international market exists for business service. Transferring services to overseas markets is complex and studded with a variety of challenges.

[58]Lovelock and Yip, "Developing Global Strategies," pp. 78–79.

Unique risks, adaptation to foreign settings, and trade barriers are the significant hurdles to be crossed in the international arena.

Discussion Questions

1. Critique this statement: "The effective business marketer of technical equipment is the one who successfully develops high-quality services to support the product; the less effective firm focuses on technical solutions offered by the product."
2. The Norris Company markets mainframe computers, whereas the Neeb Company markets computer maintenance and repair services. What key characteristics distinguish the Neeb product from the Norris product?
3. Distinguish between the technical and the functional quality of a business service. Which is most important in terms of customer satisfaction with a service?
4. Leading service companies, such as AT&T and Federal Express, measure customer satisfaction on a quarterly basis across the global market. Discuss the relationship between customer satisfaction and loyalty.
5. Many firms have a recovery process in place for those situations when their products or services fail to deliver what has been promised to the customer. Illustrate how such a process might work.
6. A new firm has recently been created to provide waste removal for industrial plants. Describe the essential elements to be included in its service product.
7. What is the role of physical evidence in the marketing of a business service?
8. As a luxury resort hotel manager, what approaches might you utilize to manage business demand for hotel space?
9. Critique this statement: "A key dimension of success in services marketing, as opposed to products marketing, is that operating personnel in the service firm play a critical selling and marketing role."
10. What steps could a manager take to enhance the chances of success for a new business service?

Chapter 13

Managing Business Marketing Channels

The channel of distribution is the marketing manager's bridge to the market. Designing and managing the business marketing channel is a challenging and ongoing task. The business marketer must ensure that the firm's channel is properly aligned to the needs of important market segments. At the same time, the marketer must also satisfy the needs of channel members, whose support is crucial to the success of business marketing strategy. After reading this chapter, you will understand

1. the central components of channel design.
2. the alternative forms of business marketing channels.
3. managerial aids that can be used to evaluate alternative channel structures.
4. the nature and function of industrial distributors and manufacturers' representatives.
5. requirements for managing the existing channel.

Going to Market, a book by E. Raymond Corey, Frank Cespedes, and V. Kasturi Rangan, provides an excellent analysis of industrial distribution channels. A rich description brings the industrial channel to life:

> *Channels of distribution, those networks through which industrial products flow from point of manufacture to point of use, are basic to an industrial economy. If farms and factories are the heart of industrial America, distribution networks are its circulatory system. Composed of many thousands of manufacturers' sales branches, wholesalers, agents, and brokers, industrial distribution systems generate and fulfill demand; they buy and sell, store and transport goods, provide sales financing, often fill the need for after-sale repair and maintenance services, and make markets for used and reconditioned*

equipment. These distribution networks are loosely organized federations of independent enterprises that are held together by contractual arrangements, information understandings, and mutual expectations.[1]

As suggested in this statement, the marketing channel is the primary means through which the industrial firm finds new prospects for its products, communicates with existing customers, and physically delivers the product. Louis Stern and Frederick Sturdivant indicate the channel's strategic importance: "Of all marketing decisions, the ones regarding distribution are the most far-reaching. A company can easily change its prices or its advertising. It can hire or fire a market research agency, revamp its sales promotion program, even modify its product line. But once a company sets up its distribution channels, it will generally find changing them to be difficult."[2] The selection of the best channel to accomplish objectives is challenging because (1) the alternatives are numerous, (2) marketing goals differ, and (3) the variety of business market segments often requires that separate channels must be employed concurrently.

The channel component of business marketing strategy has two important and related dimensions. First, the channel structure must be designed to accomplish desired marketing objectives. The ever-changing business environment requires that the channel structure be periodically reevaluated. Just-in-time (JIT) requirements and greater demands for buying assistance are but a few of the marketplace factors that signal the need for channel redefinition.[3] Among the challenges in the design of a distribution channel are specifying channel goals, evaluating constraints on the design, analyzing channel activities, specifying channel alternatives, and selecting channel members. Each requires evaluation.

Second, once the channel structure has been specified, the business marketer must manage the channel to achieve prescribed goals. To administer channel activities effectively, the manager must develop procedures for selecting intermediaries, for motivating them to achieve desired performance, for mediating conflict among channel members, and for evaluating performance.

Channels are pivotal in the overall scheme of business marketing. The purpose of this chapter is to provide a structure for designing and administering the business marketing channel. Chapter 14 will concentrate on the logistic aspects of the channel, which focus on making the product physically available on a timely basis.

The Business Marketing Channel

The link between manufacturers and customers is the channel of distribution. The channel accomplishes all the tasks necessary to effect a sale and to deliver products to the customer. These tasks include making contact with potential buyers, negotiating,

---

[1] E. Raymond Corey, Frank V. Cespedes, and V. Kasturi Rangan, *Going to Market: Distribution Systems for Industrial Products* (Boston: Harvard University Press, 1989), p. xxvii.

[2] Louis W. Stern and Frederick D. Sturdivant, "Customer-Driven Distribution Systems," *Harvard Business Review* 65 (July/August 1987): p. 34.

[3] Harold J. Novick, "The Ideal Salesforce for the 21st Century: Part I," *Agency Sales Magazine*, June 1996, pp. 4–7.

contracting, transferring title, communicating, arranging financing, servicing the product, and providing local inventory, transportation, and storage. These tasks may be performed entirely by the manufacturer or entirely by intermediaries, or may be shared between them. The customer may even undertake some of these functions; for example, customers granted certain discounts may agree to accept larger inventories and the associated storage costs.

THE SUPPLY CHAIN MANAGEMENT CONCEPT

The concepts of the *supply chain* and *supply chain management,* introduced in Chapters 1 and 2 respectively, come to fruition in the discussion of business marketing channels. The channel of distribution, which may include different marketing intermediaries, is one segment of the overall supply chain for a particular industrial product or service. The intermediaries—distributors, manufacturer's reps, and other outlets that make up the channel of distribution—are vital links in the overall supply chain. These channel links focus on the marketing processes—selling, advertising, transportation, and so on—that result in the successful sale and service of industrial products and services.

Recall from Chapter 2 that supply chain management is a strategic integration initiative that links a manufacturer's operations with those of all its strategic suppliers and its key intermediaries and customers. The supply chain management approach, with its focus on integration of operations and fostering effective relationships among parties in the supply chain, will be the approach that successful business marketing firms will take when formulating a strategy for managing the relationships with the intermediaries in their channel of distribution. A key element of that approach is the *relationship* emphasis described in Chapter 4, whereby the primary focus of the manufacturer is on establishing a long-term interaction with channel members that benefits both parties and still accomplishes the long-term sales and profit goals of the manufacturer. Michael S. Gaffney, chairman and CEO of Motion Industries, one of the largest industrial distributors in the world, recently highlighted the critical importance of the supply chain view when he observed that "Old paradigms for manufacturers, distributors and industrial customers are shifting. Where once each operated as independent, almost isolated units, the pressures of cost control, competition, and productivity demand that these three elements integrate more fully, almost seamlessly today."[4]

One of the most challenging aspects of business marketing is to allocate the channel tasks so as to ensure effective performance. The tasks must always be performed as the product moves from the manufacturer to the customer. Figure 13.1 shows the various ways industrial channels can be structured. Some channel structures are **indirect;** that is, some type of intermediary (such as a distributor or dealer) is involved in selling or handling the products. Other channels are **direct;** the manufacturer must accomplish all the marketing functions necessary to create a sale and

---

[4]Susan Avery, "Motion Industries Works to Improve Supply Chain," *Purchasing* 119 (25 April 1996): p. 92.

Figure 13.1 Channel Alternatives in the Business Market

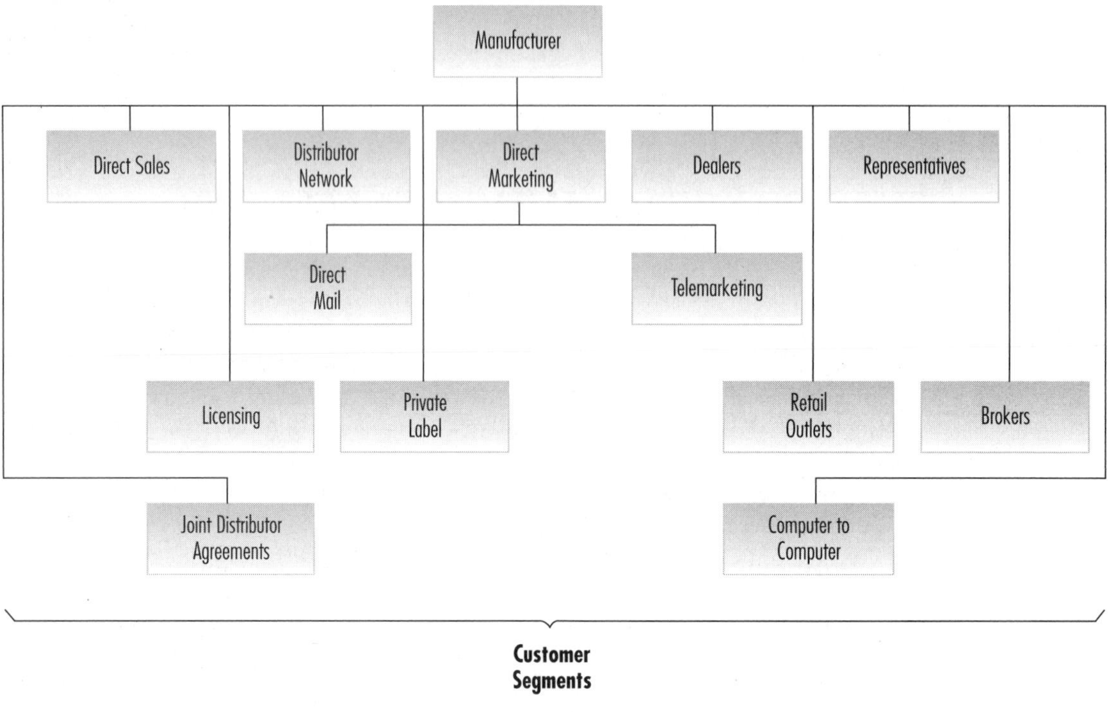

Source: Adapted from David Perry, "How You'll Manage Your 1990s Distribution Portfolio," *Business Marketing* 74 (June 1989), p. 54.

to deliver products to the customer. The manufacturer's direct sales force and the direct marketing channels are examples.

A basic issue in channel management, then, is how to structure the channel so that the tasks are performed optimally. One alternative is for the manufacturer to do it all.

DIRECT DISTRIBUTION

Direct distribution, common in business marketing, is a channel strategy that does not use intermediaries. The manufacturer's own sales force deals directly with the customer, and the manufacturer has full responsibility for performing all the necessary channel tasks. Direct distribution is often required in business marketing because of the nature of the selling situation. The direct sales approach is viable when (1) the customers are large and well defined, (2) the customers insist on direct sales, (3) sales involve extensive negotiations with upper management, and (4) control of the selling job is necessary to ensure proper implementation of the total product package and to guarantee a quick response to market conditions. One recent study found that direct channels result when the end user has a strong need for information service (that is, to explain product use and features for a product like an airplane or a bottling machine) and very minimal needs for logistics services (like lot size, delivery time, assortments, and so on).[5]

Pitney Bowes attributes success in the highly competitive facsimile market to its direct sales efforts. The company only sells direct and only to the top U.S. firms, offering them extra service and the products they require. The firm's strategy is to "concentrate on and service the largest companies in the world with large and growing fax networks."[6] It may take months to make a sale, but deals rarely number less than 10 units; one sale involved 7,000 units to a single customer! Large, complex fax systems require significant amounts of telecommunications expertise, which the Pitney Bowes direct sales force is able to provide.

A direct sales force may include both generalists and specialists. **Generalists** sell the entire product line to all customers; **specialists** concentrate on certain products, certain customers, or certain industries.

INDIRECT DISTRIBUTION

Indirect distribution uses one or more types of intermediaries. Business marketing channels typically include fewer types of intermediaries than do consumer-goods channels. Manufacturers' representatives and industrial distributors account for most of the business handled through indirect industrial channels. Indirect distribution is generally found where (1) markets are fragmented and widely dispersed, (2) low transaction amounts prevail, and (3) buyers typically purchase a number of items, often different brands, in one transaction.[7]

Xerox phased out its direct sales force for general markets (businesses making fewer than 30,000 copies per month) and replaced it with manufacturer's representatives.[8] This changeover doubled Xerox's general market's sales force, enabling the firm to more effectively cover the large number of small accounts. The company makes a sale on 40 percent of the small business accounts to whom a sales pitch is made.

MANY CHANNELS ARE OFTEN REQUIRED

Various combinations of intermediaries and direct selling may be employed in the business marketing channel. In fact, one manufacturer could use several of the avenues

---

[5]Louis P. Bucklin, Venkatram Ramaswamy, and Sumit K. Majumdar, "Analyzing Channel Structures of Business Markets Via the Structure-Output Paradigm," *International Journal of Research in Marketing* 13, no. 1 (1996): p. 84.

[6]"Fax Channels Shift as Market Shrinks," *Purchasing* 114 (18 February 1993): p. 77.

[7]Corey, Cespedes, and Rangan, *Going to Market*, p. 26.

[8]Joe Mullich, "Xerox Counts on Big Bucks from Small Businesses," *Business Marketing* 78 (April 1993): p. 10.

shown in Figure 13.1. The wide array of options reflects the many marketing tasks to be performed and the fact that many business marketers are creating unique channel systems to appeal to a wide variety of customer niches. As business markets evolve, new channel arrangements have been formed to reach every one of the identifiable segments. For example, direct mail and telemarketing have become important channel systems for many products because they can penetrate the low-sales, low-profit customer segments efficiently and effectively. In the PC industry, numerous channels are available—from mail order to direct sales—each of which offers variations on service, delivery, and price.[9] For PC products no one channel can be all things to all buyers; thus, big corporate buyers will often prefer to purchase from a large reseller that offers overnight delivery, outstanding service, and a wide variety of products. Each channel used by a business marketer will address specific market segments or perform specific types of marketing tasks.

Use of indirect channels of distribution is common for a wide variety of business products. The quality and performance of the intermediaries have a critical impact on whether the business marketer achieves his or her goals. A channel management strategy begins with an understanding of the various intermediaries that may be utilized in a business marketing channel.

Participants in the Business Marketing Channel

The types of business marketing intermediaries are distributors, manufacturers' representatives (reps), jobbers, brokers, and commission merchants. Distributors and reps handle the vast preponderance of business-to-business sales made through intermediaries. This section of the chapter will emphasize the role of each intermediary in the business marketing channel and the nature of each operation.

DISTRIBUTORS

Industrial distributors are the most pervasive and important single force in distribution channels. U.S. distributors number more than 10,000, with sales exceeding $50 billion. Distributors are heavily used for MRO (maintenance, repair, and operations) supplies, with many industrial buyers reporting that they buy as much as 75 percent of their MRO supplies from distributors. In one study, McGraw-Hill found that only 24 percent of all business marketers sell their products directly to end users exclusively; the remaining 76 percent use some type of intermediary, of which industrial distributors are the most prominent.[10] What accounts for the unparalleled position of the distributor in the industrial market? What role do distributors play in the industrial distribution process?

---

[9]Kate Evans-Correia, "PC Distribution Channels Shift," *Purchasing* 112 (20 February 1992): p. 61.

[10]"Industry Markets Goods through Dual Channels, Says McGraw-Hill Study," *Industrial Distribution* 75 (April 1985): p. 15.

Managing in the 21st Century

DISTRIBUTOR ALLIANCES RESPOND TO CHANGING CUSTOMER NEEDS

A major initiative by many U.S. manufacturers has been to simplify the buying process and reduce the costs involved with acquiring MRO (maintenance, repair, and operating) supplies. To accomplish these objectives, manufacturers are entering into integrated supply agreements with limited numbers of MRO distributors. The integrated supply agreement typically states that the buyer will purchase all of a given commodity or group of commodities from the distributor in exchange for a certain level of service and price. It may also specify that activities like anticipating needs and scheduling and disbursing of MRO products be handled by the distributor. This approach usually results in reducing the number of suppliers and holding the remaining distributors responsible for driving costs out of the acquisition process through efficiencies in delivery, invoicing, and selling.

One way that industrial distributors are responding to these important customer demands is through the formation of unique alliances *among themselves.* Distributors that carry dissimilar product lines are banding together to offer customers single-source access to an extremely large array of products along with simplification in the purchasing process, consolidated deliveries, and a single invoice. The alliances function in the following way: Each distributor serves as a preferred supplier for the other distributors in the alliance when an "integrated supply customer" requires access to products not included in the alliance companies' core offerings. The alliances can take many forms and several different arrangements have been created to deal with specific issues in individual industries.

One significant alliance comprises three of the largest industrial distributors in the United States: Motion Industries, W.W. Grainger, and Ferguson Enterprises. Customers dealing with this alliance have access to more than 1.8 million products carried by the three distributors. Ferguson is one of the largest distributors of pipe, valves, and fittings, carrying over 200,000 items at 228 stocking locations across the country. Motion Industries is the largest U.S. distributor of bearings and power transmission equipment, with 370 locations nationwide and a product line that exceeds one million items. Grainger is a leading nationwide distributor of MRO items whose product line totals almost 100,000 products sold through 342 branches located in all 50 states.

Companies buying MRO supplies can now deal with a distribution alliance able to service a multitude of plant locations with ready access to hundreds of thousands of MRO products not typically found in one distributor's core inventory—and the acquisition process is customer-friendly.

Source: Adapted from "Good May Not Be Good Enough," *Purchasing* 119 (9 May 1996): pp. 38–52; and "Distributor Alliances Continue to Form, Strengthen," *Purchasing* 119 (15 February 1996): p.80.

Distributors are generally small, independent businesses serving narrow geographic markets. Sales average almost $2 million, although some top $3 billion. Net profits are relatively low as a percentage of sales (4 percent); return on investment averages 11 percent. The typical order is small, and the distributors sell to a multitude of customers in many industries. The typical distributor is able to spread its costs

DISTRIBUTORS TAKE TO THE INTERNET

The Duncan Bolt Company uses the Internet to provide customers with product information and to promote special prices and selected product lines. The home page costs Duncan about $20 per month and the revenues generated through the Web site make it a very effective way to communicate with the marketplace. The material shown below is an excerpt from the Duncan Bolt home page.

Source: http://www.duncanbolt.com/index.html

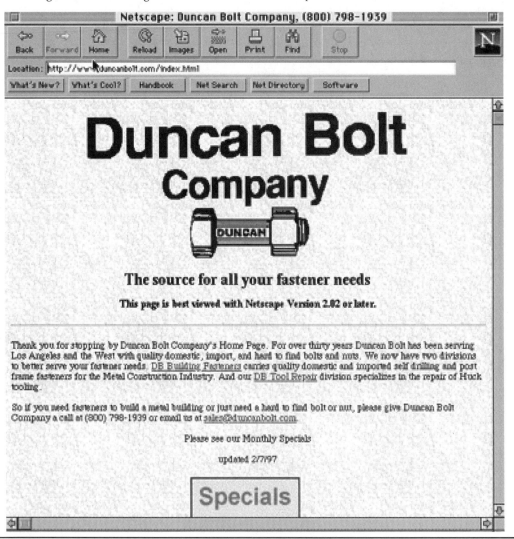

Netscape: Duncan Bolt Company, (800) 798-1939

Location: http://www.duncanbolt.com/index.html

Duncan Bolt
Company

DUNCAN

The source for all your fastener needs

This page is best viewed with Netscape Version 2.02 or later.

Thank you for stopping by Duncan Bolt Company's Home Page. For over thirty years Duncan Bolt has been serving Los Angeles and the West with quality domestic, import, and hard to find bolts and nuts. We now have two divisions to better serve your fastener needs. DB Building Fasteners carries quality domestic and imported self drilling and post frame fasteners for the Metal Construction Industry. And our DB Tool Repair division specializes in the repair of Huck tooling.

So if you need fasteners to build a metal building or just need a hard to find bolt or nut, please give Duncan Bolt Company a call at (800) 798-1939 or email us at sales@duncanbolt.com.

Please see our Monthly Specials

updated 2/7/97

Specials

Table 13.1 Key Distribution Responsibilities

Responsibility	Activity
Contact	Reach all customers in a defined territory through an outside sales force that calls on customers or through an inside group that receives telephone orders
Product availability	Provide a local inventory and include all supporting activities: credit, delivery, order processing, and advice
Repair	Provide easy access to local repair facilities (unavailable from a distant manufacturer)
Assembly and light manufacturing	Purchase material in bulk, then shape, form, or assemble to user requirements

over a sizable group of vendors—it stocks goods from between 200 and 300 manufacturers. Orders are generated by a sales force of outside and inside salespersons. **Outside salespersons** make regular calls on customers and handle normal account servicing and technical assistance. **Inside salespersons** complement these efforts, processing orders and scheduling delivery; their primary duty is to take telephone orders. Most distributors operate from a single location, but some approach the "supermarket" status with as many as 130 branches.

Compared to their smaller rivals, large distributors seem to have significant advantages. Small distributors are typically unable to achieve the operating economies enjoyed by larger firms.[11] The ability of large firms to automate much of their operations enables them to significantly reduce their sales and general administrative expenses, often to levels approaching 10 percent of sales.

Distributor Responsibilities

An industrial distributor's primary responsibilities are shown in Table 13.1. The products that distributors sell—cutting tools, abrasives, electronic components, ball bearings, handling equipment, pipe, maintenance equipment, and hundreds more—are generally those that buyers need quickly to avoid production disruptions. Thus, the critical elements of the distributor's function are to have these products readily available and to serve as the selling arm of the manufacturer.

Distributors are full-service intermediaries; that is, they take title to the products they sell, and they perform the full range of marketing functions. Some of the more important functions are providing credit, offering wide product assortments, delivering goods, offering technical advice, and meeting emergency requirements. Distributors are valuable not only to their manufacturer-suppliers, but also are generally

[11]Heidi Elliott, "Distributors, Make Way for the Little Guys," *Electronic Business Today* 22 (September 1996): p. 19.

viewed favorably by their customers. Some purchasing agents view the distributor as an extension of their "buying arms" because of the service, technical advice, and product application suggestions they provide.

Today, many firms have adopted the just-in-time (JIT) concept—the buyer demands that the supplies and components it purchases be delivered on a specified day, at a specific time. The effect of the JIT trend is to move the distributor into a position of prominence in many channel situations because few manufacturers are organized to make JIT deliveries all over the country.

Classification of Distributors

To select the most appropriate distributor for a particular channel, the marketing manager must understand the diversity of distributor operations. Industrial distributors vary according to product lines handled and user markets served. Firms may be ultraspecialized (for example, selling only to municipal water works), or they may carry a broad line of generalized industrial products. However, three primary distributor classifications are usually recognized.

General-Line Distributors. **General-line** distributors cater to a broad array of industrial needs. They stock an extensive variety of products and could be likened to the supermarket in consumer-goods markets.

Specialists. **Specialists** focus on one line or on a few related lines. Such a distributor may handle only power transmission equipment—belts, pulleys, and bearings. The most common specialty is fasteners, although specialization also occurs in cutting tools, power transmission equipment, pipes, valves, and fittings. There is a trend toward increased specialization as a result of increasing technical complexity of products and the need for higher levels of precision and quality control.

Combination House. A **combination house** operates in two markets: industrial and consumer. Such a distributor might carry electric motors for industrial customers and hardware and automotive parts to be sold through retailers to final consumers.

The selection of a distributor will depend upon the manufacturer's requirements. The general-line distributor offers the advantage of one-stop purchasing to the manufacturer's potential customers. If a high level of service and technical expertise is not required, the general-line distributor is a good choice. The specialist, on the other hand, provides the manufacturer with a high level of technical capability and a well-developed understanding of complex user requirements. Fasteners, for instance, are handled by specialists because of the strict quality-control standards that users impose.

The Distributor as a Valuable Asset

The quality of a firm's distributors is often the difference between a highly successful marketing strategy and an ineffective one. Good distributors are prized by customers, making it all the more necessary to strive continually to engage the best in any given market. Distributors often provide the only economically feasible way of obtaining comprehensive market coverage.

In summary, the industrial distributor is a full-service intermediary who takes title to the products sold; maintains inventories; provides credit, delivery, wide product assortment, and technical assistance; and may even do light assembly and manufacturing. Although the distributor is primarily responsible for contacting and supplying present customers, industrial distributors also solicit new accounts and work to expand the market. Products handled by industrial distributors are generally established products—typically used in manufacturing operations, repair, and maintenance—with a broad and large demand.

Industrial distributors are a powerful force in business marketing channels, and all indications point to an expanded role for them. The manufacturer's representative is an equally viable force in the business marketing channel.

MANUFACTURERS' REPRESENTATIVES

For many business marketers who need a strong selling job with a technically complex product, manufacturers' representatives, or reps, are the only cost-effective answer. **Reps** are salespeople who work independently (or for a rep company), represent several companies in the same geographic area, and sell noncompeting but complementary products. Table 13.2 provides a concise sketch of a typical rep.

The Rep's Responsibilities

A rep neither takes title to nor holds inventory of the products handled. (Some reps do, however, keep a limited inventory of repair and maintenance parts.) The rep's forte is expert product knowledge coupled with a keen understanding of the markets and customer needs. Reps are usually limited to defined geographical areas;

Table 13.2 Profile of a Manufacturers' Representative

Company	Alcon Company
Location	Middle Village, New York
End-user market	Bottling and brewery industry
Estimated average commission	10 to 14 percent
Geographic market coverage	New England states, New York, New Jersey, Pennsylvania, Maryland, Delaware, eastern Virginia.
Products handled	Bottle filler replacement parts (conveyors, case packers, uncasers, warmers and reusers, empty bottle inspectors, plastic cases, decappers)
Companies represented	P. T. Barkmann & Sons, Hamrich Manufacturing, McQueen Technology, Bacmis Volckening, Kyowa American Corp.

thus, a manufacturer seeking nationwide distribution will usually work with several rep companies.

The Rep-Customer Relationship

Reps are the selling arm for manufacturers—making contact with customers, writing orders, following up on orders, and linking the manufacturer with the industrial end users. Although paid by the manufacturer, the rep is also important to the customers served. Often, the efforts of a rep during a customer emergency (for example, an equipment failure) means the difference between continuing or stopping production. Most reps are thoroughly experienced in the industries they serve; they can offer technical advice while enhancing the customer's leverage with suppliers in securing parts, repair, and delivery. The rep also provides customers with a continuing flow of information on innovations and trends in equipment, as well as on the industry as a whole.

Commission Basis

Reps are paid a commission on sales; the commission varies by industry and by the nature of the selling job. Commissions typically range from a low of 4 percent to a high of 18 percent for selected high-tech products. Percentage commission compensation is attractive to manufacturers because they have few fixed sales costs. Reps are paid only when orders are generated. Because reps are paid on commission, they are motivated to generate high levels of sales—another fact appreciated by the manufacturer.

Experience

Reps possess sophisticated product knowledge and typically have extensive experience in the markets they serve. Most reps develop their field experience while working as a salesperson for a manufacturer. They are motivated to become reps by the desire to be independent and to reap the substantial monetary rewards possible on commission.

When Reps Are Used

- *Large and Small Firms:* Small- and medium-sized firms generally have the greatest need for a rep, although many large firms—for example, Dow Chemical and W. R. Grace—use them. The reason is primarily economic: smaller firms cannot justify the expense of maintaining their own sales forces. The rep provides an efficient means to obtaining total market coverage, with costs incurred only as sales are made. The quality of the selling job is often very good as a result of the rep's prior experience and market knowledge.
- *Limited Market Potential:* The rep also plays a vital role when the manufacturer's market potential is limited. A manufacturer may use a direct sales force in heavily concentrated industrial markets where the demand is sufficient to support the expense and use reps to cover less dense markets.

Because the rep carries several lines, expenses can be allocated over a much larger sales volume.

- *Servicing Distributors:* Reps may also be employed by a firm that markets through distributors. When a manufacturer sells through hundreds of distributors across the United States, reps may sell to and service those distributors.
- *Reducing Overhead Costs:* Sometimes the commission rate paid to reps exceeds the cost of a direct sales force, yet the supplier continues to use reps. This policy is not as irrational as it appears. Assume, for example, that costs for a direct sales force approximate 8 percent of sales and that a rep's commission rate is 11 percent. The use of reps in this case is often justified because of the hidden costs associated with a sales force. First, the manufacturer does not provide fringe benefits or a fixed salary to reps. Second, the costs of training a rep are usually limited to those required to provide product information. Thus, the use of reps eliminates significant overhead costs.

Channel Design

Channel design is the dynamic process of developing new channels where none existed and modifying existing channels. The business marketer usually deals with modification of existing channels, although new products and customer segments may require entirely new channels. Regardless of whether the manager is dealing with a new channel or modifying an existing one, channel design is an active rather than a passive task. Effective distribution channels do not simply evolve; they are developed by management, which takes action on the basis of a well-conceived plan that reflects overall marketing goals.

Channel design is best conceptualized as a series of stages that must be completed so that the business marketing manager can be sure that all important channel dimensions have been evaluated (Figure 13.2). The result of the channel design process is to specify the structure that provides the highest probability of achieving the firm's objectives. Note that the process focuses on channel structure and not on channel participants. **Channel structure** refers to the underlying framework: the number of channel levels, the number and types of intermediaries, and the linkages among channel members. Selection of individual intermediaries is indeed important; it will be examined later in the chapter.

STAGE 1: CHANNEL OBJECTIVES

Business firms formulate their marketing strategies to appeal to selected market segments, to earn targeted levels of profits, to maintain or increase sales and market share growth rates, and to achieve all this within specified resource constraints. Each element of the marketing strategy has a specific purpose. Thus, whether the business marketer is designing a totally new channel or redesigning an existing one, the first

Ethical Business Marketing

WHAT DOES A MANUFACTURER OWE ITS REPS?

The Milton Boiler and Compressor Company, a market leader in its industry, has focused all its marketing attention on markets in the East and Southeast. The company, with a very aggressive and professional sales force, was the clear market share leader in its territories. In 1982, the company's strategic planning task force recommended that the firm expand marketing efforts to the West Coast. The firm carefully evaluated its channel options and made the decision to utilize manufacturers' reps in the new market. Although Milton's sales expertise was widely heralded, it opted for reps because of their vast market knowledge and the fact that the firm had no sales volume at all west of the Mississippi.

George Borne and Associates was selected as the rep firm. Borne was located in Los Angeles, and the firm has sold boiler and compressor equipment in the Southwest and West for almost 30 years. Sales of Milton products were slow at first, but Borne nevertheless worked diligently to establish Milton's line in its territory. Over the first five years of the relationship Borne "invested heavily" in the Milton business: (1) They hired three new salespeople to sell the Milton line, (2) the salespeople were sent to at least four training sessions each year, (3) Borne contracted with a service firm to handle repair and maintenance of Milton equipment, (4) at least $20,000 was invested in sales aids, promotional material, and catalogs for the Milton line each year, and (5) Borne agreed to a lower-than-normal commission for the first three years until sales reached an "acceptable level."

By 1989, sales of Milton original equipment and repair and maintenance parts exceeded $9 million in the western area, and sales appeared to be growing at an annual rate of 12 percent. Although such estimates are difficult to make, trade publications forecast Milton's western share of market to exceed 13 percent in late 1989. Milton's sales and profit goals were exceeded every year except the first one.

On February 4, 1990, Milton management notified the Borne company that within 90 days Borne would no longer represent Milton in the western territory. Beginning June 1, 1990, Milton would sell product through its own sales force (one individual, it was rumored, was to be hired away from Borne).

Borne management was stunned. They felt cheated and believed they had been used. They felt that Milton had intended all along to sack them as soon as sales volume reached a predetermined level. Most employees believed that Milton management had no ethical standards.

What are the ethical issues underlying this controversial decision by Milton? Does Borne have a right to feel "cheated"? Has Milton breached a faith or violated an ethical standard?

---

phase of channel design is to comprehend fully the marketing goals and to formulate corresponding channel objectives.

Structure Based on Profits and Strategy Integration

Profit considerations and asset utilization must be reflected in channel objectives and design. For example, the cost of maintaining a salesperson in the field—including lodging,

Figure 13.2 The Channel Design Process

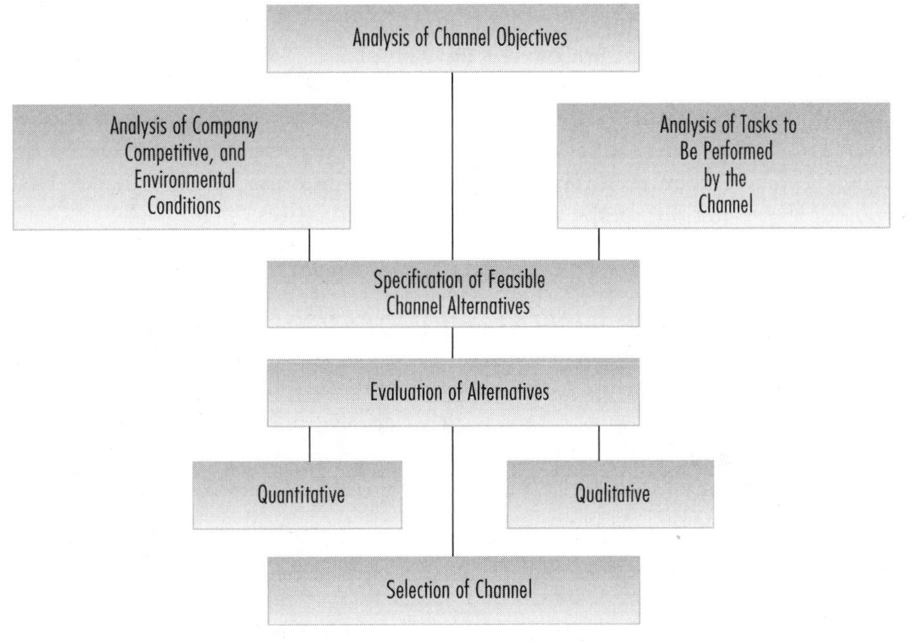

Source: Michael D. Hutt and Thomas W. Speh, "Realigning Industrial Marketing Channels," *Industrial Marketing Management* 12 (July 1983): pp. 171–177.

meals, and auto rental—is substantial: the total cost-per-call figure is between $225 and $275.[12] For the manufacturer, these costs are somewhat fixed in the short run. The need to commit working capital to these costs might be eliminated by switching from a direct sales force to manufacturers' reps, whose compensation, as a percentage of sales, is totally variable. Of course, many other factors, such as the quality of the selling job, must also be evaluated. Channel structure must be compatible with all marketing strategy elements.

Channel Objectives Reflect Marketing Goals

Specific distribution objectives are established on the basis of broad marketing objectives. Distribution objectives force the manager to relate channel design decisions to broader marketing goals. A manufacturer of industrial cleaning products might have a distribution objective of providing product availability in every county in the Midwest with more than $5 million in market potential. The distribution objective of a supplier of air-conditioning units might be to make contact with industrial plant architects once every month and with industrial contractors once every two months.

[12]Mary Welch, "Database Marketing Begins to Register," *Business Marketing* 78 (March 1993): p. 48.

Marketing and distribution objectives guide the channel design process and actually limit the range of feasible channel structures. Channel structures need to be developed to reflect both strategic goals (for example, to achieve market share) and efficiency goals (for example, to reduce administrative costs). Generally, management decision models have emphasized effectiveness criteria (strategic issues) and evaluated channel arrangements on the basis of their ability to accomplish certain functions.[13] Both efficiency and effectiveness criteria need to be evaluated when alternative channel arrangements are under investigation. Before the alternative channel structures can be evaluated, the business marketing manager must examine other limitations on the choice of channel structures.

STAGE 2: CHANNEL DESIGN CONSTRAINTS

Frequently, the manager has little flexibility in the selection of channel structures because of trade, competitive, company, and environmental factors. In fact, the decision on channel design may be imposed on the manager. The variety of constraining factors is almost limitless.[14] Figure 13.3 summarizes those factors most relevant to the business marketer.

STAGE 3: PERVASIVE CHANNEL TASKS

Each channel structure will be evaluated on its ability to perform the required channel activities effectively and efficiently. The concept of a channel as a sequence of activities to be performed, rather than as a set of channel institutions, is essential to channel design. The business marketing manager must creatively structure the tasks necessary to meet customer requirements and company goals rather than merely accepting existing channel structures or traditional distribution patterns.

How the channel tasks will be assigned among the channel participants will be affected by changes in the technological and business environments. Research by Mini Hahn and Dae Chang suggests that advances in telecommunications systems generally have increased the "power" of manufacturers:

> *These systems enable the companies, among other things, to selectively reach a large number of end users, qualify leads and develop prospects, take orders, check inventory, disseminate information, and dispatch customer service. The relative power of producers with respect to both end users and intermediaries is increased because they are able to influence end users directly and to take over many functions of the intermediaries. Distributors in these channels,*

---

[13]Jan B. Heide, "Interorganizational Governance in Marketing Channels," *Journal of Marketing* 58 (January 1994): p. 83.

[14]For example, see Louis W. Stern and Frederick D. Sturdivant, "Customer-Driven Distribution Systems," *Harvard Business Review* 65 (July/August 1987): pp. 34–41; and Louis Stern and Adel I. El-Ansary, *Marketing Channels*, 4th ed. (Englewood Cliffs, N.J.: Prentice-Hall, 1992), pp. 202–223.

Figure 13.3 Factors Limiting Choice of Industrial Channel

1. **Availability of Good Intermediaries**

   Competitors often "lock up" the better intermediaries.

   Established intermediaries are not always receptive to new products.

2. **Traditional Channel Patterns**

   Established patterns of distribution are difficult to violate.

   Large customers may demand direct sales.

3. **Product Characteristics**

   Technical complexity dictates direct distribution.

   Extensive repair requirements may call for local distributors to service the product line.

4. **Company Financial Resources**

   Capital requirements often preclude direct distribution.

5. **Competitive Strategies**

   Direct service by competitors may force all firms to sell direct.

6. **Geographic Dispersion of Customers**

   A widely dispersed market of small customers often requires low-cost representation afforded by intermediaries.

therefore, fulfill ancillary functions to producers such as following-up the sales call, providing feedback on leads, inventory status, delivery arrangements and other relevant information.[15]

Increasing manufacturer power may diminish the distributor's role in the channel as the manufacturer assumes more channel activities; the distributor's share of profits and revenues could be reduced accordingly.

Manufacturers' reps typically carry no inventory of their suppliers' products. A manufacturer of semiconductors and microcircuits, upon a careful analysis of required channel activities, may decide that although reps can provide the level of sales service needed, large accounts need emergency local inventories of a few selected microcircuits. In this case the solution would not be to abandon the rep as a viable channel, but to compensate the rep for carrying a limited inventory of emergency circuits. Analysis of required tasks and a view of the channel as a sequence of activities would lead the firm to a creative solution to the inventory problem.

The backbone of channel design is the analysis of objectives, constraints, and channel activities. Once these are understood, channel alternatives can be evaluated.

[15]Mini Hahn and Dae R. Chang, "An Extended Framework for Adjusting Channel Strategies in Industrial Markets," *Journal of Business and Industrial Marketing* 7 (spring 1992): p. 36.

STAGE 4: CHANNEL ALTERNATIVES

Specification of channel alternatives involves four primary issues:

1. The number of levels to be included in the channel (that is, the degree of "directness")
2. The types of intermediaries to employ
3. The number of channel intermediaries at each level of the channel
4. The number of channels to employ

The decisions made for each are predicated upon the objectives, constraints, and activities previously analyzed.

Degree of Directness

The issue of directness concerns whether products will be marketed directly to customers or through intermediaries. The critical aspects of this decision were presented earlier in the chapter.

Assessing Product/Market Factors

The number of channel levels depends on a host of company, product, and market variables. A study involving 300 industrial firms suggested that business marketing channel length is influenced by availability of capable intermediaries, market factors, and customer characteristics. Market factors include the number of customers, the geographic concentration of customers, and the industry concentration. Customer characteristics include the significance of the purchase as perceived by the customer and the volume potential of a customer. Channel length increases with greater availability of effective intermediaries and with the number of customers; it decreases when the purchase becomes more significant, when customer potential increases, and when market or industry concentration increases.

There is a greater tendency in business than in consumer-goods marketing to sell directly to the customer. However, direct selling is often not feasible. For such products as tools, abrasives, fasteners, pipes, valves, materials-handling equipment, and wire rope, as much as 97 percent of the annual volume moves only through industrial distributors. These products are typically bought frequently, repetitively (straight rebuy), and in small quantities. Instantaneous availability is fundamental; industrial distributors handle such products efficiently.

Type of Intermediary

A wide array of factors influences the choice of intermediaries, with the tasks they perform being of prime importance. These tasks were carefully detailed for both reps and distributors earlier in the chapter.

A host of product and market conditions also appear to play a role in indicating which type of intermediary will be used. A study by Donald Jackson and

Michael d'Amico evaluated the product and market conditions that differed between manufacturer-rep channels and manufacturer-distributor channels.[16] Their findings showed that the manufacturer-rep channel is generally used when:

- the product is not standard but is closer to made-to-order
- the product tends toward technical complexity
- the gross margin is not large
- the market comprises a relatively few number of customers that are concentrated geographically and concentrated in a few industries
- these customers order relatively infrequently and allow fairly long lead times

Use of distributors is associated with the opposite conditions. A review of market and product situations should be made when making the rep versus distributor decision.

A second question concerns whether more than one type of intermediary will be needed to satisfy all target markets. The primary reason for using more than one type of intermediary for the same product is that different market segments require different channel structures. Some firms use three distinct approaches. Large accounts are called on by the firm's own sales force, distributors handle small repeat orders, and manufacturers' reps develop the market that comprises medium-sized firms.

Like size of accounts, differences in purchase behavior may also dictate using more than one type of intermediary. If a firm produces a wide line of industrial products, some may require high-caliber selling to a multitude of buying influences within a single buyer's firm. When this occurs, the firm's own sales force would focus on the more complex buying situations, whereas the distributors would sell standardized products from local stocks.

The Number of Intermediaries

How many intermediaries of each type are required to cover a particular market effectively? The answer is sometimes easy—for example, when a firm distributes through reps. Since reps act as the firm's sales force, it would be pointless for more than one rep to call on a specific customer (unless, of course, each rep specialized in a unique part of the company's product line). The business marketer would select the single best rep organization in each of the geographical areas to be covered.

In the case of distribution through industrial distributors, the company may require two, three, or even more carefully selected distributors in a geographic market to ensure adequate market coverage. The policy of carefully choosing channel members in a particular geographical area is referred to as **selective distribution.** The nature of the product and the purchasing process usually dictate a selective policy.

---

[16]Donald M. Jackson and Michael F. d'Amico, "Products and Markets Served by Distributors and Agents," *Industrial Marketing Management* 18 (February 1989): p. 33.

Materials-handling equipment, electric motors, power-transmission equipment, and tools typically fall into the category of straight or modified rebuy situations. The time spent in evaluating sources for these products is not great, yet the purchase is not always simple and repetitive. The buyer needs advice about applications, maintenance, and repair, and usually demands rapid product delivery, repair, and service. The manufacturer wants to be represented by a distributor that can satisfy these customer requirements. To ensure that distributors will perform the job required and provide proper emphasis to the manufacturer's line, the number of distributors will be limited to a few in a given market.

Generally, the more standardized the products, the more frequently they are purchased, and the smaller their unit value, the greater the number of distributors in a given market. The abrasives manufacturer who requires up to 1,000 general-line distributors is following an intensive rather than a selective distribution policy. An **intensive distribution** policy is especially appropriate when availability is a requirement. Customers must have a product source near their plants.

The Number of Channels

More than one channel will be required when various market segments are served and when the characteristics of the segment dictate a fundamentally unique approach to distribution.

Channels need to change to match the life cycle position of the product. For example, small office copiers were first sold directly through manufacturers' direct sales forces. The Japanese then began marketing copiers through office equipment dealers, and today these machines are available through a variety of channels—direct, dealers, mass merchandisers, and mail order. When a product reaches the maturity stage, it may be necessary to find low-cost distributors that offer minimal services and broader market reach.[17] Once in decline, the channel may be contracted to the point of selling through electronic ordering systems and telemarketing. Often the goal in the maturity and decline stages is to create channels that will provide cost-effective market coverage.

MagneTek, Inc., a marketer of electronic ballasts, supplements its traditional method of selling through distributors and advertising in trade magazines with a direct sales force designed to reach larger retail chains.[18] Wal-Mart and Toys "R" Us, Inc., for example, are both heavy users of fluorescent lighting systems that use electronic ballasts, and their size justifies the direct sales force. MagneTek still relies heavily on its 4,000-strong distributor network to market most of its other products. However, using multiple channels is not without its problems because of the potential competition that exists between the channels. Direct selling activities of manufacturers, sales by nondealer resellers, and compensation splits on joint sales are some of the sources of friction. Managing conflicts of this nature is discussed later in this chapter.

Legal Issues

When a firm maintains more than one channel, some accounts may be double-covered, or various channel members may find themselves competing for business. Business marketers

---

[17]"Distribution and the Product Life Cycle," *Sales and Marketing Management* 148 (July 1996): p. 36.
[18]Russell Shaw, "MagneTek Turns on Direct Sales Effort," *Business Marketing* 78 (October 1993): p. 9.

often want to reserve large accounts for their own sales force or restrict certain territories for "selected" distributors. There are complex legal issues associated with such restrictions. Channel experts Corey, Cespedes, and Rangan highlight these legal issues:

> *The terms and conditions of channel member agreements may require that the reseller do the following:*
>
> - *Carry the producer's full line*
> - *Either not stock competing brands or treat them strategically as secondary lines*
> - *Not solicit business from certain "reserved" accounts, specified classes of trade, and/or beyond the territory in which the reseller is franchised to sell*
> - *Observe resale price schedules set by the producer*
> - *Maintain specified inventory levels*
> - *Meet specified sales quotas*
>
> *The supplier may secure adherence to these conditions by withholding producer support from nonconforming distributors and by rewarding those that do conform, with resellers resisting such methods of control and sometimes taking legal action against offending suppliers.*
>
> *In general, the kinds of terms and conditions outlined above and their enforcement are not illegal per se unless they are construed as being "in restraint of trade or commerce." If franchise conditions serve to build and preserve monopoly power as defined by the Sherman Act, and/or if franchise enforcement is carried out through conspiratorial arrangements, both the conditions and the actions to secure adherence are likely to be judged illegal.*[19]

The final task facing the business marketing manager is to select the most effective channel structure from among the feasible alternatives.

STAGE 5: CHANNEL SELECTION

Most channel design decisions are only slight modifications of the channel structure in response to changing markets, expanding geographic coverage, new customer requirements, or new products. Selection of the appropriate modification in channel structure may be fairly straightforward; in fact, the range of choices may be quite limited.

Evaluating Alternative Channels

A useful approach to evaluating channel options is provided by Louis Stern and Frederick Sturdivant.[20] The approach, as depicted in Table 13.3, takes into account all the elements

---

[19]Corey, Cespedes, and Rangan, *Going to Market*, p. 146.
[20]Stern and Sturdivant, "Customer-Driven Distribution Systems," pp. 34–41.

Table 13.3 Procedure for Evaluating Channel Alternatives

Process	Key Analytical Activities
Step 1: Determine customer requirements	Assess desire for sales assistance, locational convenience, one-stop buying, depth of assortment, and the whole range of possible services.
Step 2: Evaluate potential intermediaries	Assess which type of intermediaries are possible, including direct sale.
Step 3: Analyze costs	Involves three dimensions: (1) Is it feasible for the company to satisfy all customer requirements? (2) What types of supplier support are required? (3) What are the costs of the support systems for each type of channel alternative?
Step 4: Specify constraints—create the "bounded" system	Develop management input on key constraints and company long-term objectives. Specify the channel system structure based on these constraints.
Step 5: Compare options	Compare the "ideal system" specified by customers to the "feasible" system specified by constraints and objectives. If an existing channel is being reviewed, compare it to the ideal and feasible systems.
Step 6: Review constraints and assumptions	Use experts—consultants, lawyers, accountants—to evaluate assumptions.
Step 7: Evaluate gaps	If gaps exist between the existing, ideal, and feasible systems, analyze the underlying reasons.
Step 8: Implementation	Modify the ideal system according to objectives and constraints.

Source: Adapted from Louis W. Stern and Frederick Sturdivant, "Customer-Driven Distribution Systems," *Harvard Business Review* 65 (July/August 1987): pp. 34–41.

of the channel design process as well as important customer requirements. The focus of their approach is to create an "ideal" channel system that fully addresses customer needs; once this system is specified, it is compared to the "feasible" channel system created on the basis of management objectives and constraints. The critical element is to compare both systems on the basis of customer service performance, structure, and costs.

Channel selection is facilitated by looking at "gaps" that may exist between the systems—existing, ideal, and feasible. One of three conclusions could emerge:

1. *All three systems resemble each other.* In this case, the existing system is about as good as it can be. If customer satisfaction is low, the fault is not with the channel design, it is with poor management.
2. *Existing and feasible systems are similar, but differ from the ideal.* Management constraints and objectives may be causing the gap. A careful review is required as specified in step 6 of Table 13.3.
3. *All three systems are different.* If the feasible system lies between the ideal and existing system, the existing system can be changed without sacrificing

management goals. Relaxing management constraints might produce even greater benefits.

Made-to-Order and Delivered

Michael Dell, the founder of Dell Computer, saw a market opportunity and responded with a channel innovation. He reasoned that a large number of savvy personal computer customers did not need the hand-holding of dealer salespeople. His company created a direct sales channel to customers through phone ordering. Guided by information systems that provide extensive product information, Dell customer service personnel function as computer consultants to all types of customers—from novices to experts, from individuals to large corporate accounts.[21] Capitalizing on its agile production process, customer service personnel at Dell can precisely define a customer's needs, trigger an order to assemble a machine to match those needs, and put the product in the hands of that U.S. customer in less than one week. The company has increased its revenue from $100 million to well over $3 billion during the past several years through direct marketing, bypassing well-established dealer channels.

Qualitative Dimensions

The channel decision maker must consider qualitative as well as quantitative factors. Given two channels with nearly similar economic performance, the critical factor may be the degree of *control* that the business marketer can exercise over the channels. Compared to a distributor channel, a rep generally gives the manager more control because the manufacturer maintains title and possession of the goods. The manufacturer may be willing to trade off short-run economic benefits in order to gain long-term control over channel activities.

Adaptation by channel members may be important in the long run. Small, undercapitalized distributors may not be able to respond effectively to new competitive thrusts or to problems caused by economic downturns. The viable alternatives, then, will be to sell direct or to use reps and make products available through a system of public warehouses.

Such factors as intermediary image, financial capacity, sales, and merchandising ability must also be analyzed. And once the channel is designed, it must be administered.

Channel Administration

Once a particular industrial channel structure is chosen, channel participants must be selected, and arrangements must be made to ensure that all obligations are assigned. Next, channel members must be motivated to perform the tasks necessary to achieve channel objectives. Third, conflict within the channel must be properly controlled. Last, performance must be controlled and evaluated.

---

[21]Dwight L. Gertz and João P. A. Baptista, *Grow To Be Great: Breaking the Downsizing Cycle* (New York: The Free Press, 1995), pp. 107–109.

SELECTION OF INTERMEDIARIES

Why is the selection of channel members (specific companies, rather than *type*, which is specified in the design process) part of channel management rather than an aspect of channel design? The primary reason is that intermediary selection is an ongoing process; some intermediaries choose to leave the channel, and others are terminated by the supplier. Thus, selection of intermediaries is more or less continuous. Performance of individual channel members must be evaluated continuously. The manufacturer should be prepared to move quickly, replacing poor performers with potentially better ones. Including the selection process in ongoing channel management puts the process in its proper perspective.

Selection Criteria

Because all firms do not share the same channel objectives or perform the same activities, no single set of criteria universally applies. Some firms find it impossible to reduce the selection of intermediaries to a rigid procedure, but some means for objectively comparing potential channel members is vital. Ideally, the business marketing manager should examine objective factors concerning the channel situation and sensibly temper these evaluations with personal impressions, opinions, and judgment.

Each business marketer must develop criteria that are relevant to the firm's own product/market situation. Many companies use checklists to compare prospective distributors or reps. The McGraw-Edison Company uses an intensive checklist, and the criteria it considers important are market coverage, product lines, personnel, growth, and financial standing.

Securing Good Intermediaries

The marketer can identify prospective intermediaries through discussions with company salespeople and existing or potential customers, or through trade sources, such as *Industrial Distribution* magazine or the *Verified Directory of Manufacturers' Representatives*. Once the list of potential intermediaries is reduced to a few names, the manufacturer will use the selection criteria to evaluate them.

The formation of the channel is not at all a one-way street. The manufacturer must now persuade the intermediaries to become part of the channel system. Some distributors evaluate potential suppliers just as rigorously as the manufacturers rate them—using many of the same considerations. Manufacturers must often demonstrate the sales and profit potential of their product and be willing to grant the intermediaries some territorial exclusivity.

Firms that effectively use independent reps (manufacturers' representatives and agents) often view the rep as a customer; controlling relationships usually do not work well with reps.[22] Business marketing managers must recognize that reps are not employees; rather, they are autonomous entities who are under contract with several companies and answer to several managers. Special efforts will be required to convince

[22]Sally J. Silberman, "Best Supporting Role," *Sales and Marketing Management* 147 (December 1995): p. 22.

the very best rep in a particular market to represent a particular manufacturer's product. Those efforts will often focus on showing the potential rep that the company will be treated as a partner and supported by the manufacturer.

MOTIVATING CHANNEL MEMBERS

Distributors and reps are independent and profit oriented. They are oriented toward their customers and toward whatever means are necessary to satisfy customer needs for industrial products and services. Their perceptions and outlook may vary substantially from those of the manufacturers they represent. As a consequence, marketing strategies can fail when managers at the manufacturers' level do not tailor their programs to the capabilities and orientations of their intermediaries. To manage the business marketing channel effectively, the marketer must understand the intermediaries' perspective and devise methods for motivating these intermediaries to perform in a way that will enhance the manufacturer's long-term success. The manufacturer must continually seek support from intermediaries, and the quality of that support will depend on the motivational techniques employed.

The degree to which an intermediary will comply with manufacturer directives appears to be influenced by the intermediary's dependence on the manufacturer.[23] Manufacturers who wish to enhance their ability to affect the decisions and behavior of their channel members should consider strategies that increase the channel member's dependence on them. Such tactics as increasing commissions, encouraging full-line representation, new product introduction, and increased promotion may be effective at increasing the percentage of sales and profits an intermediary earns from a given manufacturer, and, as a consequence, strengthening its dependence on the manufacturer.[24]

A Partnership

Channel member motivation begins with the understanding that the channel relationship is a *partnership*. Manufacturers and intermediaries are in business together; whatever expertise and assistance the manufacturer can provide to the intermediaries will improve total channel effectiveness. Some business firms recognize the partnership concept by preparing formal contracts to be signed by both parties. Columbus McKinnon Corporation, a large industrial manufacturer, makes the following agreement with its distributors: "The distributor will maintain an inventory that gives four turns based on last year's sales, will purchase at least $15,000 a year from the supplier, [and] will actively promote the sale of the supplier's products. The supplier (Columbus McKinnon), in turn, extends the latest discount service and freight, contributes a specific amount to joint advertising, works a specified length of time with each distributor sales[person], and helps develop annual sales targets."[25] Both manufacturers and distributors agree that

[23]Janet E. Keith, Donald W. Jackson, and Lawrence A. Crosby, "Effects of Alternative Types of Influence Strategies Under Different Channel Dependence Structures," *Journal of Marketing* 54 (July 1990): p. 37.
[24]Ibid., p. 38.
[25]Duffy Marks, "Post Carborundum: Distributors Evaluate Their Vendor Relations," *Industrial Distribution* 7 (June 1983): p. 35.

a formal contract is the only effective way to operationalize the partnership idea and avoid potential misunderstandings.

One study of channel relationships suggested that manufacturers may be able to increase the level of resources directed to their products by developing a trusting relationship with their reps; by improving communication through recognition programs, product training, and consultation with the reps; and by informing the reps of plans, explicitly detailing objectives, and providing positive feedback.[26] Another study of distributor-manufacturer working partnerships recommended similar approaches and also suggested that manufacturers and their distributors engage in joint annual planning that focuses on specifying the cooperative efforts each firm requires of its partner to reach its objectives as well as periodic reviews of progress toward objectives.[27] The net result will be trust and satisfaction with the working partnership as the cooperative relationship leads to meeting performance goals.

Knowing When to Invest

In some situations it may not be prudent to expend significant effort and commit large sums of money to create relationship commitment among the parties in the channel of distribution. Commitment in the channel context refers to the "extent to which two organizations are closely tied to each other on a stable basis."[28] Keysuk Kim and Gary Frazier suggest that developing high levels of interfirm commitment is an effective strategy for managing interfirm relationships only under certain channel contexts; in other contexts, it makes little sense.[29] Developing and maintaining high levels of commitment is effective in situations where (1) distributors or reps contribute significantly to the value added as the product moves through the distribution process and (2) changing suppliers is difficult. An uncertain business environment also suggests the need for commitment because of the benefits derived by the channel members from jointly coping with such difficult situations. When intermediaries contribute little to the value added by the channel, when it is relatively easy to replace suppliers, and when the business environment is stable, strong channel ties may not be necessary: An arms-length relationship will suffice. Evaluating channel context is particularly important for firms entering new markets: They need to examine the context of the channel and assess how much effort should be allocated to building commitment in the relationship.

Management Aids

Manufacturers often have the size and skill to develop sophisticated management techniques for areas of purchasing, inventory, order processing, and the like, which can

---

[26]Erin Anderson, Leonard M. Lodish, and Barton A. Weitz, "Resource Allocation in Conventional Channels," *Journal of Marketing Research* 24 (February 1987): p. 95. See also Jan B. Heide and George John, "The Role of Dependence Balancing in Safeguarding Transaction-Specific Assets in Conventional Channels," *Journal of Marketing* 52 (January 1988): pp. 20–35.

[27]James C. Anderson and James A. Narus, "A Model of Distribution Firm and Manufacturing Firm Working Partnerships," *Journal of Marketing* 54 (January 1990): p. 56.

[28]Keysuk Kim and Gary L. Frazier, "A Typology of Distribution Channel Systems: A Contextual Approach," *International Marketing Review* 13, no. 1 (1996): p. 23.

[29]Ibid., p. 29.

INSIDE BUSINESS MARKETING

DISTRIBUTION CHANNEL SETS CAT APART

During the mid-1980s, many business experts predicted the demise of Caterpillar, the large, U.S.–based manufacturer of construction and mining equipment. The predictions were not unfounded—from 1982 to 1992, CAT suffered huge losses in five of those years while their major rival, Komatsu, was enjoying cost advantages of 40 percent in some product lines. Yet, by the mid-1990s, CAT's share of the world market for construction and mining equipment was the highest in the firm's history and the firm's return on equity exceeded 30 percent.

Although several factors played a part in the firm's rebound and strong performance, Donald Fites, Caterpillar chairman and CEO, credits the firm's system of distribution and product support as the biggest reason for the firm's success: "We think we are better engineers and manufacturers than our competitors, but we are convinced our single greatest advantage over our competition is our system of distribution and product support. The backbone of that system is our 186 independent dealers around the world who sell and service our machines and diesel engines. They have played a pivotal role in helping us build and maintain close relationships with customers and gain insights into how we can improve our products and services to better fill customer needs."

Several lessons can be learned from Caterpillar's successful distribution strategy and organization. Firms selling high-ticket, relatively standardized products, requiring significant after-sale service and support on a global basis, can enhance their marketing effectiveness by following CAT's lessons:

1. A large global firm must rely on local dealers, who are long-established members of their communities, to get closer to customers than the global company could on its own. However, to tap the full potential of such dealers, the company must forge extremely close ties with them and integrate them into its critical business systems.
2. Dealers should do more than provide local product availability to customers. Dealers should offer a wide array of services before and after the sale, including advice on the selection and application of a product, financing, insurance, maintenance and repair, training, and advice on product replacement.
3. Creating an effective distributor network requires more than the usual elements of money and assets. Both parties must invest in the softer assets such as training and developing a common understanding of what it takes to provide superior customer service.
4. The best relationships between a company and its dealers are formed on the basis of the quality of the relationship rather than on the formal contractual agreement. Trust, sharing gains and "pains," consistency of policies, and open communication are all critical elements of relationship quality.
5. Dealers should be carefully considered when new products are being evaluated. Two factors are important. First, which new product contenders best fit the current distribution system, and, second, will the distribution system add value to the product in the eyes of the end user?

Source: Adapted from: Donald V. Fites, "Make Your Dealers Your Partners," *Harvard Business Review* 74 (March/April 1996): pp. 84-95.

be passed on to channel members. Some firms may provide elaborate cost accounting and profitability measurement systems for their distributors in order to assist them in tracking product performance.

Experts Allan Magrath and Kenneth Hardy suggest that a manufacturer should "design a full menu of supports, with sufficient variety to appeal to all its key distributors—small, medium, and large—recognizing that participation in some offerings will vary depending upon the relevance to the particular distributor's size and level of sophistication."[30] The key element is to allow the distributor executives to choose which programs fit their situation.

Information Sharing

One way to enhance the performance of all channel members is to facilitate the sharing of information among them. Okuma America Corporation, a large machine tool producer, developed a dynamic shared information technology system. All of its distributors are informed about the location and availability of machine tools and parts in Okuma warehouses in the United States and Japan, as well as the inventories maintained at each distributor's warehouse.[31] This system enables distributors to locate products anywhere in the system, order them from another location, if necessary, and expedite shipment to their customer via an express delivery company. The distributors can offer excellent customer service while reducing their own inventory levels. The information system allows Okuma's distributor to offer this guarantee: *If the parts are not shipped within 24 hours, the customer gets them for free.*

Dealer Advisory Councils

Distributors or reps may be brought together periodically with the manufacturer's management personnel to review distribution policies, provide advice on marketing strategy, and supply industry intelligence.[32] Intermediaries can voice their opinions on policy matters and are brought directly into the decision-making process for channel operations. Dayco Corporation uses a dealer council to keep abreast of distributors' changing needs.[33] One month after their meeting, council members receive a written report of suggestions they made and of the programs to be implemented as a result. Generally, Dayco enacts 75 percent of distributor proposals. For dealer councils to be effective, the input of channel members must have a meaningful effect on channel policy decisions.

---

[30]Allan J. Magrath and Kenneth G. Hardy, "Gearing Manufacturer Support Programs to Distributors," *Industrial Marketing Management* 18 (November 1989): p. 244.

[31]James A. Narus and James C. Anderson, "Rethinking Distribution: Adaptive Channels," *Harvard Business Review* 74 (July/August 1996): p. 115.

[32]Doug Harper, "Councils Launch Sales Ammo," *Industrial Distribution* 80 (September 1990): pp. 27–30.

[33]James A. Narus and James C. Anderson, "Turn Your Distributors into Partners," *Harvard Business Review* 64 (March/April 1986): p. 68. See also Gul Butaney and Lawrence H. Wortzel, "Distributor Power versus Manufacturer Power: The Customer Role," *Journal of Marketing* 52 (January 1988): pp. 52–63.

Margins and Commission

In the final analysis, the primary motivating device will be compensation. The surest way to lose intermediary support is to use compensation policies that do not meet industry and competitive standards. Reps or distributors who feel cheated on commissions or margins will shift their selling attention to products generating a higher profit. The manufacturer must pay the prevailing compensation rates in the industry and must adjust the rates as conditions change. Inflation in travel, lodging, and entertainment expenses forces many reps and distributors to seek higher commissions and margins. Although such increases are painful to the manufacturer, rates that are not adjusted fairly usually cause a marked reduction in sales effort.

The compensation provided to intermediaries should reflect the marketing tasks performed. If the manufacturer seeks special attention for a new industrial product, most reps will require higher commissions. The 3M Corporation has an enlightened attitude regarding compensation of distributors. According to the firm, "We're studying all the distributors' costs—inventory, sales, and so on—and then we're looking at our costs. Maybe we will want to pay the distributor to assume more of the functions we now do. Or maybe we can absorb some activities back here and reduce the distributors' margin. But somebody has to pay for it. We're trying to come up with a classification system so divisions can have different levels of distributor margins, depending on what services the distributor provides."[34]

CONFLICT: THE NEED FOR RELATIONSHIP MANAGEMENT

The very nature of a distribution channel—with each member dependent on another for success—can invite conflict among the members. Although realizing the need for cooperation, individual members seek to maximize their autonomy and, hence, their profitability. **Channel conflict** occurs when one channel member *A* perceives another channel member *B* to be preventing or impeding member *A* from achieving important goals.[35]

The opportunities for conflict in business marketing channels are limitless—for example, a manufacturer's refusal to increase reps' commissions, a distributor's refusal to maintain required inventory levels, a manufacturer's insistence on a nonexclusive distribution policy. Thus, because channel participants have varying goals, varying perceptions of their roles in the channel, and varying evaluations of their spheres of influence, tensions develop that may cause them to perform in ways that damage channel performance.[36] The business marketer must manage conflict through interorganizational and

---

[34] Howard Sutton, "Rethinking the Company's Selling and Distribution Channels," The Conference Board, Report #885, 1986, p. 6.

[35] Stern and El-Ansary, *Marketing Channels*, pp. 202–223, 283.

[36] Louis W. Stern and James L. Heskett, "Conflict Management in Interorganizational Relations: A Conceptual Framework," in *Distribution Channels: Behavioral Dimensions*, ed. Louis Stern (Boston: Houghton-Mifflin, 1969), pp. 293–294.

relationship management approaches.[37] Such approaches improve overall channel performance by coordinating relationships among the organizations that make up the channel and by focusing on the creation of long-term, mutually beneficial interactions.

Building Trust

Conflict can be controlled through a variety of means, including channel-wide committees, joint goal setting, and cooperative programs involving a number of marketing strategy elements. To compete, business marketers need to be effective at cooperating within a network of organizations—the channel. Successful cooperation results from relationships in which the parties have a strong sense of communication and trust.[38] Robert M. Morgan and Shelby D. Hunt suggest that relationship commitment and trust develop when (1) firms offer benefits and resources that are superior to what other partners could offer; (2) firms align themselves with other firms that have similar corporate values; (3) firms share valuable information on expectations, markets, and performance; and (4) firms avoid taking advantage of their partners.[39] By following these relationship prescriptions, business marketers and their channel networks should be able to enjoy sustainable competitive advantages over their rivals and their networks.

International Business Marketing Channels

A variety of channel options are available to a foreign business-to-business marketer. Typically, U.S. business marketers distribute their goods to international markets through three distinct channels (or through some combination of them):[40]

1. *American-based export intermediaries:* Domestic export intermediaries are utilized by smaller companies that lack experience in foreign sales or by firms that are not deeply involved in international marketing.
2. *Foreign-based intermediaries:* Firms that are deeply committed to foreign sales will often use foreign-based intermediaries. This decision depends on the availability of good intermediaries, financial requirements, local customs, desired control, and the nature of the product.

---

[37]For example, see Larriane Segil, *Intelligent Business Alliances* (New York: Random House, 1996); James C. Anderson and James A. Narus, "A Model of Distributor Firm and Manufacturing Firm Working Partnerships," *Journal of Marketing* 54 (January 1990): pp. 42–58; Louis W. Stern and Adel I. El-Ansary, *Marketing Channels*, 4th ed.(Englewood Cliffs, N.J.: Prentice-Hall, 1992); Robert F. Lusch, "Sources of Power: Their Impact on Intrachannel Conflict," *Journal of Marketing Research* 13 (November 1976): p. 384; Stern and Heskett, "Conflict Management in Interorganizational Relations," p. 293; Larry J. Rosenberg and Louis Stern, "Conflict Measurement in the Distribution Channel," *Journal of Marketing Research* 8 (November 1971): pp. 437–442; Louis Stern and Ronald H. Gorman, "Conflict in Distribution Channels: An Exploration," in *Distribution Channels: Behavioral Dimensions*, p. 156; Larry J. Rosenberg, "A New Approach to Distribution Conflict Management," *Business Horizons* 16 (October 1974): pp. 67–74; and Louis P. Bucklin, "A Theory of Channel Control," *Journal of Marketing* 37 (January 1973): pp. 39–47.

[38]Robert M. Morgan and Shelby D. Hunt, "The Commitment-Trust Theory of Relationship Marketing," *Journal of Marketing* 58 (July 1994): pp. 20–38.

[39]Ibid., p. 36.

[40]Phillip R. Cateora, *International Marketing*, 5th. ed. (Homewood, Ill.: Richard D. Irwin, 1983), p. 442.

3. *Company-managed and company-organized sales force:* This alternative is pursued by firms heavily involved in international sales. For this approach to be effective, the firm must be strong when providing after-sales service, maintaining delivery reliability, supplying spare parts, and providing many other support services.

It is important to recognize that international channels of distribution are not clear-cut, precise, or easily defined entities.[41] A necessary step in developing international channels is to understand the functions of intermediaries; international intermediaries are referred to by a multitude of misleading titles. The final section of the chapter will briefly examine these intermediaries and their roles.

To be effective, international business marketers may have to develop a truly global, integrated channel strategy and be willing to invest considerable resources. James Bolt suggests that successful global competitors are companies that, among other things, "develop an integrated and innovative strategy, aggressively implement it and back it with large investments."[42] In the channels realm, a well-conceived distribution structure, utilizing the best intermediaries and backed by the required financial resources, may be a critical element that acts as a barrier to competitors.

DOMESTIC INTERMEDIARIES

As the name implies, **domestic intermediaries** are located in the country of the producer. They are convenient to use, but their critical drawback is the lack of proximity to the foreign marketplace. The quality of representation and the access to market information available through domestic intermediaries is limited.

Domestic intermediaries can be broadly distinguished by whether they take title to the goods or not. Nontitle, or agent, intermediaries include **export management companies (EMCs), manufacturer's export agents (MEAs),** and **brokers,** who are primarily engaged in the selling function, making contact with foreign buyers and negotiating sales. Playing a pivotal role for many small firms, EMCs take over much of the marketing job necessary to reach foreign markets, including responsibility for advertising, credit, and product handling. Agent intermediaries are paid on a commission basis.

The other broad groups of domestic intermediaries are similar to wholesalers—they take title to the products they sell and perform a broad array of marketing functions. **Export merchants** are wholesalers operating in a foreign market. Intermediaries dealing in bulky commodities in foreign markets are referred to as **export jobbers. Trading companies** accumulate, transport, and distribute goods from many countries.[43] Recent legislation in the United States has paved the way for the

---

[41]Ibid., p. 581.

[42]James F. Bolt, "Global Competitors: Some Criteria for Success," *Business Horizons* (January/February 1988): pp. 35, 36.

[43]Cateora, *International Marketing*, p. 590.

development of American trading companies (ATCs).[44] Although early success of the ATCs has been limited, they are expected to eventually provide effective one-stop export service.

FOREIGN-BASED INTERMEDIARIES

Foreign-based intermediaries offer the advantage of close and constant contact with the marketplace and generally provide a more direct channel to the customer. As with domestic intermediaries, foreign intermediaries are distinguished by whether they take title.

Title-holding intermediaries include distributors, dealers, and import jobbers. The tasks they perform are similar to those with the same name in domestic settings. In similar fashion, nontitle foreign intermediaries include brokers, reps, and factors. **Factors** are similar to brokers, but are also involved in financing the sale, which is complex and cumbersome in many foreign transactions. Essentially, they eliminate the credit risk for both the buyer and the seller.

Selection of a particular type of foreign-based intermediary is dictated by the type of product, margins, and the market conditions.[45] For example, brokers have no inventory and take no risk, whereas importers take title, bear the risk, and guarantee distribution. Consequently, distribution of product through importers will mean a higher landed price for the product because their margins have to be higher to accommodate these risks and additional activities. Whichever type of foreign-based intermediary is used, it may be necessary to creatively structure the initial contract. An importer, for example, may be given a 90-day exclusive contract and agree to buy only 5,000 items. This initial order enables the importer to "test the market." If sales go as expected, large volume commitments can be written into a long-term contract.

Selecting Effective Foreign Distributors

Finding effective foreign distributors is a challenging task that requires considerable planning and effort. Because the consequences of selecting the wrong distributor are significant—either because large severance payments may be required or because of missed market opportunities—the business marketing manager should pursue a systematic approach to the selection process. The evaluation of foreign distributors involves identifying both where to go for information and what to look for.[46] The U.S. Department of Commerce provides two information services:

---

[44]Daniel C. Bello and Nicholas C. Williamson, "The American Export Trading Company: Designing a New International Marketing Institution," *Journal of Marketing* 49 (fall 1985): p. 60.

[45]Jack Nadel, "Distribution, the Key to Success Overseas," *Management Review* (September 1987): p. 41.

[46]S. Tamer Cavusgil, Poh-lin Yeoh, and Michel Mitri, "Selecting Foreign Distributors," *Industrial Marketing Management* 24 (August 1995): p. 299.

the Agent/Distributor Service and the World Traders Data Report. In addition, private sources like Dun and Bradstreet provide trade directories that list foreign representatives both geographically and by product line. Banks and shipping companies also may be excellent sources of distributor information.

S. Tamer Cavusgil, Poh-lin Yeoh, and Michel Mitri interviewed a large number of international executives to assess the decisive criteria for assessing foreign distributors.[47] Their criteria include 35 dimensions that can be grouped into five categories:

1. *Financial and company strength* (for example, management quality, capitalization)
2. *Product factors* (for example, complimentary lines, familiarity with the new line)
3. *Marketing skills* (for example, experience with target customers, logistics capability)
4. *Commitment* (for example, investments in sales training, available advertising dollars)
5. *Facilitating factors* (for example, "political" connections, language skills)

The researchers created an expert model (DISTEVAL) that weights the criteria to systematically evaluate potential distributors. They suggest carefully investigating distributors on these dimensions and then supplementing that analysis with actual site visits, a review of the marketing plans of potential distributors, and an evaluation of the distributor's assessment of their own local competition.

COMPANY-ORGANIZED SALES FORCE

The difference between using intermediaries for foreign sales and using a company-organized sales force is complex. The decision, however, is a very important one because managing buyer-seller relationships in the global marketplace is often the key to corporate success in foreign markets.[48] Deeper, more effective relationships with customers are critical as global competition intensifies, product life cycles shorten, quality standards rise, and technological change accelerates. The company sales force gives the company control over the international marketing process but also poses serious challenges and risks due to the foreign environment. Erin Anderson and Anne Coughlan suggest that a company-organized sales force is more likely to be used when one or more of the following exist:

---

[47]Ibid., p. 300.

[48]John S. Hill and Arthur W. Allaway, "How U.S.–Based Companies Manage Sales in Foreign Countries," *Industrial Marketing Management* 22 (February 1993): p. 7.

1. The product requires a high service level
2. Competing products are differentiated
3. There are fewer legal constraints to direct foreign investment
4. The product is closely related to the firm's core product
5. The country's culture is similar to U.S. culture
6. Competitors utilize a company-organized sales force[49]

Anderson and Coughlan also indicate that the decision-making process in international channels is often nonsystematic and often based on little information. One reason for this is that managers operating outside familiar domestic settings have few guidelines to use.

In some foreign markets, business marketers may need a local presence—a plant, a distribution facility, an R&D facility, or a joint venture with a domestic partner in order to participate in the market without substantial penalties (import duties). Many U.S. manufacturers are concerned that the European Community (EC) market may be difficult to penetrate because of possible protectionist initiatives by the members. Investment in manufacturing, channel, and physical distribution operations within the EC may prove effective in guarding against these barriers to EC outsiders.

Consequently, channel strategy may enhance a company's ability to compete in the EC through joint ventures or licensing agreements with existing EC channel intermediaries. These partnerships with local firms would be viewed favorably and may allow the firm to avoid any duties imposed on imported, non-EC goods.

The channel decision in the international arena is a difficult one—made complex by the nature of the unfamiliar setting. However, global competition and worldwide marketing are realities of today's business environment, and the business marketing manager must be prepared to accept the challenge of making an informed and thoroughly deliberated choice.

Summary

Channel strategy is an exciting and challenging aspect of business marketing. The challenge derives from the number of alternatives available to the manufacturer in distributing business products. The excitement results from the ever-changing nature of markets, user needs, and competitors.

Channel strategy involves two primary management tasks: designing the overall structure and managing the operation of the channel. Channel design

---

[49]Erin Anderson and Anne T. Coughlan, "International Market Entry and Expansion via Independent or Integrated Channels of Distribution," *Journal of Marketing* 51 (January 1987): p. 74.

includes the evaluation of distribution goals, activities, and potential intermediaries. Channel structure includes the number, types, and levels of intermediaries to be used in the channel. The primary participants in business marketing channels are distributors and reps. Distributors provide the full range of marketing services for their suppliers, although customer contact and product availability are their most essential functions. Manufacturers' representatives specialize in the selling side of marketing, providing their suppliers with quality representation in the market and with extensive product and market knowledge. The rep is not involved with physical distribution, leaving that burden to the manufacturers.

Channel management is the ongoing task of administering the channel structure in order to achieve distribution objectives. Maintaining effective relationships through sound supply chain management approaches is a key ingredient for success in channel management. Selection and motivation of intermediaries are two management tasks vital to channel success. The industrial marketing manager may need to apply interorganizational management techniques in order to resolve channel conflict. The choice of channels for business marketers competing in overseas markets is both vast and confusing. The manager must choose among domestic and foreign intermediaries and a company sales force.

Discussion Questions

1. Explain how the supply chain management concept affects a firm's approach to managing its channels of distribution.
2. Explain how a direct channel of distribution may be the lowest-cost alternative for one business marketer and the highest-cost alternative for another competing in the same industry.
3. Describe specific product, market, and competitive conditions that lend themselves to (a) a direct channel of distribution, and (b) an indirect channel of distribution.
4. Compare and contrast the functions performed by industrial distributors and manufacturers' representatives.
5. What product/market factors lend themselves to the use of manufacturers' representatives?
6. Often, the business marketer may have very little latitude in selecting the number of channel *levels*. Explain.
7. Explain how a change in segmentation policy (that is, entering new markets) may trigger the need for drastic changes in the industrial channel of distribution.
8. Explain, using examples, when business marketers would be well advised to maintain an arms-length relationship with their channel intermediaries.

9. Both industrial marketers and distributors are interested in achieving profit goals. Why, then, are manufacturer-distributor relationships characterized by conflict? What steps can the marketer take to reduce the level of conflict and thus improve channel performance?

10. For many years, critics have charged that intermediaries contribute strongly to the rising prices of goods in the American economy. Would business marketers improve the level of efficiency and effectiveness in the channel by reducing as far as possible the number of intermediate links in the channel? Support your position.

Chapter 14

Business Marketing Channels: The Logistical Interface

When promised delivery performance is not provided, buyers will search for a new supplier. Organizational buyers assign great importance to responsive physical distribution, or logistical, systems. Therefore, substantial resources are invested to service demand through the logistical system. After reading this chapter, you will understand

1. the role of logistical management in business marketing strategy.
2. the importance of achieving the desired interface between logistics and the distribution channel.
3. the importance of cost and service trade-offs in creating effective and efficient logistical systems.

Business marketers frequently delegate selling and other demand stimulation to intermediaries. Other functions of equal importance, however, must be performed to implement marketing strategies successfully and to satisfy customer needs. Products must be delivered *when* they are required, *where* they are required, and in *usable condition*. Unfortunately, a business marketer cannot shift the total burden of these functions to intermediaries. Even if distributors are employed in the channel, manufacturers must be able to deliver products to the distributor efficiently. The business marketer's effectiveness in delivery will dramatically influence the distributor's ability to satisfy delivery requirements of the end user. Direct channels place even greater logistical burdens on the manufacturer. The overall significance of logistics to marketing performance is underscored by the conclusion drawn by Edward Morash, Cornelia Droge, and Shawnee Vickery in their recent research study on the strategic impact of logistics:

> *Demand-oriented logistics capabilities—delivery speed and reliability, and responsiveness, for example—have substantial and pervasive influences on company performance. Logistics capabilities, like super fast delivery time, can*

be major pillars of corporate strategy and even provide the core competencies of company strategy.[1]

This chapter will describe the role of logistical management in business marketing strategy, both in general and in channel performance.[2] The discussion will be directed by such questions as: How do logistical activities interface with the distribution channel? What are the logistical variables that must be managed to create an effective interface with the channel? What role does logistical service play in the organizational purchase decision? What types of logistical services are sought by buyers? How can these services be designed and implemented most effectively and efficiently? The nature of logistical management is the first topic examined.

Elements of Logistical Management

Logistics is an imposing and sometimes mysterious term that originated in the military. In business usage, **logistics** refers to the design and management of all activities (primarily transportation, inventory, warehousing, and communications) necessary to make materials available for manufacturing and to offer finished products to customers when and in the condition they are needed. Logistics thus embodies two primary product flows: (1) **physical supply,** or those flows that provide raw materials, components, and supplies to the production process, and (2) **physical distribution,** or those flows that deliver the completed product to customers and channel intermediaries. The flows of physical supply and physical distribution must be coordinated to meet delivery requirements of business customers successfully. The physical supply aspect of logistics requires a business supplier's logistical system to interact with the customer's logistics and manufacturing process. A repair part delivered a few hours late may cost a manufacturer thousands of dollars in lost production time. Although the physical supply dimension of logistics is important, this chapter will concentrate on the physical distribution component because it is the key element of a business marketer's strategy.

Good business marketing demands efficient, systematic delivery of finished products to intermediaries and industrial users. The importance of this capability to efficiently deliver products has elevated the logistics function to a place of prominence in the marketing strategy of many business marketers. In a recent article, Joseph Fuller, James O'Connor, and Richard Rawlinson effectively capture the essence of the strategic significance of logistics:

[1]Edward A. Morash, Cornelia L. M. Droge, and Shawnee K. Vickery, "Strategic Logistics Capabilities for Competitive Advantage and Firm Success," *Journal of Business Logistics* 17, no. 1 (1996): p. 19.

[2]For a comprehensive discussion of all facets of businesses logistics, see James R. Stock and Douglas M. Lambert, *Strategic Logistics Management*, 4th ed. (Homewood, Ill.: Richard D. Irwin, 1996); James E. Johnson and Donald F. Wood, *Contemporary Logistics*, 6th ed. (New York: Macmillan, 1996); and John J. Coyle, Edward J. Bardi, and C. John Langley Jr., *The Management of Business Logistics*, 6th ed. (St. Paul, Minn.: West, 1996).

Figure 14.1 Supply Chain for Electric Motors

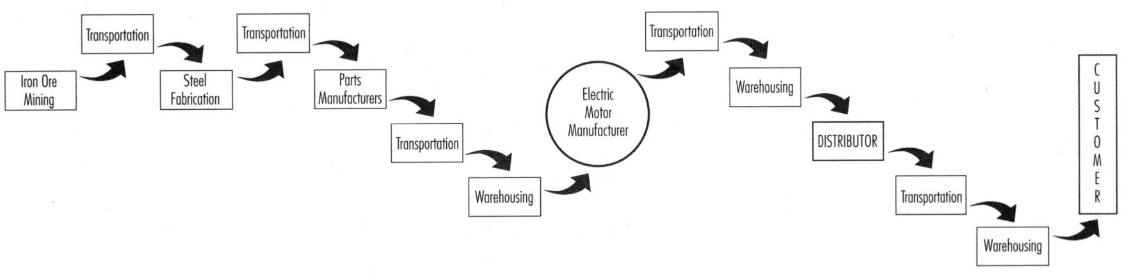

Logistics has the potential to become the next governing element of strategy as an inventive way of creating value for customers, an immediate source of savings, an important discipline on marketing, and a critical extension of production flexibility. Customer needs vary, and companies can tailor logistics systems to serve them better and more profitably.[3]

SUPPLY CHAIN MANAGEMENT PERSPECTIVE

Nowhere in business marketing strategy is the supply chain management approach more important than in the logistics realm. During the 1980s and 1990s, the rising importance of time-based competition, rapidly improving information technology, expanding globalization, increasing attention to quality, and the changing face of interfirm relationships combined to cause companies to expand their perspective on the logistics process to include all the firms involved in creating a finished product and delivering it to the ultimate buyer/user on time and in perfect condition. For example, the supply chain for electric motors would include raw material suppliers, steel fabricators, component parts manufacturers, transportation companies, the electric motor manufacturer, the distributor of electric motors, the warehouse companies involved in storing and shipping components and finished products, and the ultimate buyer of the electric motor. Figure 14.1 graphically depicts such a supply chain. The supply chain management concept is an integrating philosophy for coordinating the total flow of a supply channel from supplier to ultimate user.[4]

[3]Joseph B. Fuller, James O'Connor, and Richard Rawlinson, "Tailored Logistics: The Next Advantage," *Harvard Business Review* 71 (May/June 1993): p. 87.

[4]Lisa M. Ellram and Martha C. Cooper, "Characteristics of Supply Chain Management and the Implications for Purchasing and Logistics Strategy," *International Journal of Logistics Management* 4, no. 1 (1993): pp. 1–10.

Managing Flows

The significance of the supply chain perspective in logistical management is that the business marketing manager focuses attention on the performance of *all participants* in the supply chain and works to coordinate their efforts to enhance the timely delivery of the finished product to the ultimate user at the lowest possible total logistics cost. Inherent in the supply chain approach is the need to form close *relationships* with the supply chain participants, including vendors, transportation suppliers, warehousing companies, and distributors. The focus of supply chain management in logistics for business marketers is the *flow of product* through the supply chain, with *timely information* driving the entire process.

Successful logistics supply chain management is based upon the integration and management of three basic flows or processes—information, product, and cash as shown in Figure 14.2.[5] Typically, information and cash flow in both directions in an industrial supply chain, with product usually flowing from suppliers to the ultimate user. However, many business marketing firms are seeing an increasing volume of product flowing in the *reverse* direction. **Reverse logistics systems** are becoming significant to many business marketers as a result of increased emphasis on remanufacturing, recycling, and concern with the environment. A number of specialist third-party logistics firms have evolved to handle the reverse logistics process for firms like Xerox that must bring back machines for retrofitting with new components.

Creating Value

The supply chain management approach promises customers reduced cost and enhanced value through timely delivery of damage-free product. The approach involves the broadening of a company's perspective on logistics management to include a larger set of supply chain participants (for example, suppliers several tiers removed or intermediaries and customers several tiers forward in the supply chain) and an emphasis on effectively managing the variety of supply chain relationships. The goal is to integrate the flow of product, information, and cash in a way that adds the most value for the ultimate customer. An effective supply chain is one that operates seamlessly, where information and risk are shared easily among the supply chain participants. These are lofty goals that, as a result of the significant barriers that often exist in complex relationships among a wide array of organizations, are not always achieved. However, supply chain management is just one aspect of the critical role that logistics assumes in business marketing strategy.

TIMELY LOGISTICAL SUPPORT

Owens-Illinois, a major supplier of glass containers, shows how precisely a supplier must tailor its logistics system to customer needs. Owens-Illinois is a primary supplier to the J. M. Smucker Company, the jam and jelly manufacturer. Because of its vast

[5]John J. Coyle, Edward J. Bardi, and C. John Langley Jr., *The Management of Business Logistics*, 6th ed. (St. Paul, Minn.: West, 1996), p. 9.

Figure 14.2 The Integrated Supply Chain

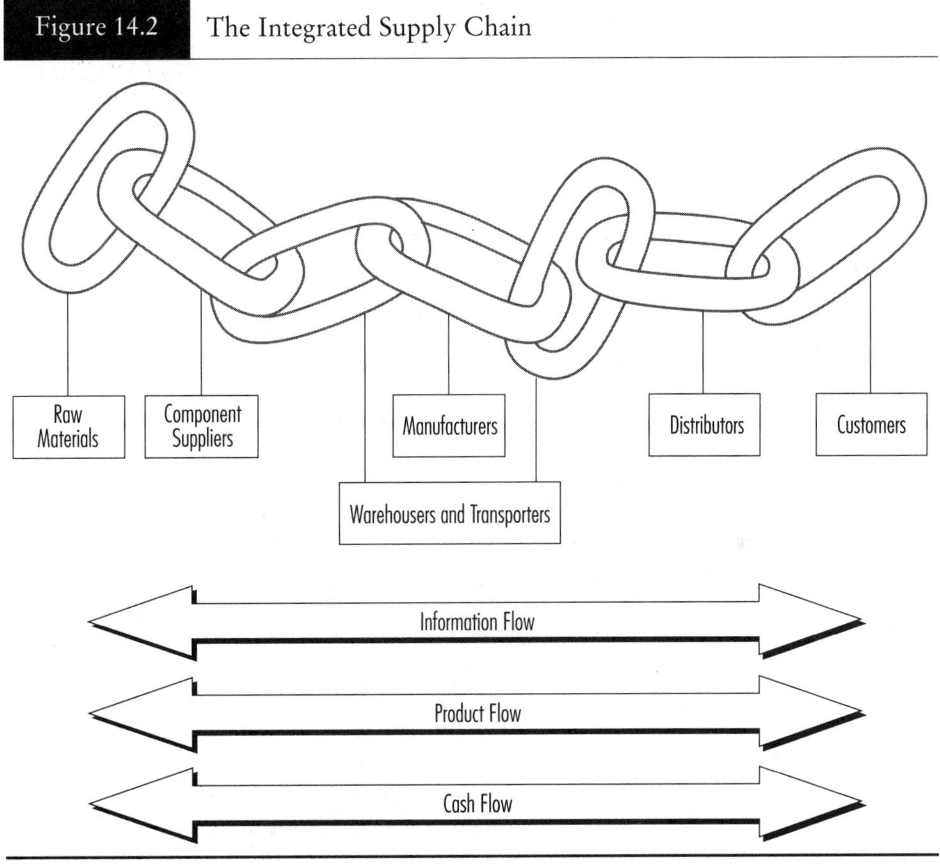

container requirements, Smucker must carefully manage inventory and delivery of glass containers. To reduce container inventory, Smucker maintains only enough glass containers to run the production line for a few hours. The burden of this policy falls directly on Owens-Illinois. First, Owens-Illinois must schedule the production process at its Toledo plant to provide all the inventories Smucker requires. Then, warehouse systems and reliable motor carriers assure that deliveries match Smucker's inventory policy and avoid production interruptions. Consistent delivery performance to Smucker standards is surely an essential ingredient in this long-term supplier-customer relationship. For Owens-Illinois, logistical service may have created the differential advantage.

A Source of Competitive Advantage

In the past, logistics was viewed simply as a cost of doing business and a function whose only goal was higher productivity.[6] Today, logistics is viewed by many

[6]Robert Horne, "Charting a Course for Integrated Logistics," *Transportation & Distribution* 30 (October 1989): p. 46.

companies as a critical strategic weapon because of its tremendous impact on a customer's operation. For many business marketers, logistics is their *primary* marketing tool for gaining and maintaining competitive superiority. Donald Bowersox reports that after studying more than 1,000 companies, "it became clear that some companies stand head and shoulders above their competitors in logistics performance and they use this superiority to gain and keep customer loyalty."[7] These firms typically recognize that logistics performance is an important part of marketing strategy, and they exploit their logistics competencies.

Compaq Computer, the world's leading producer of PCs, estimates it lost almost $1 billion in sales over the course of a year because its laptop and desktop computers weren't available when and where customers were ready to buy them. Compaq has now revamped its logistics system in an effort to make it the "next source of competitive advantage."[8]

Sales-Marketing-Logistics Integration[9]

The rising value of logistics as a strategic marketing weapon has fostered the integration of the sales, marketing, and logistics functions of many business marketers. In progressive firms, unified teams of sales, production, logistics, information systems, and marketing personnel develop integrated logistics programs to offer to potential customers. Sales calls are made by teams of specialists from each area and the teams create tailored logistics solutions to customer problems. United Stationers, the largest distributor of office products in the United States, brings operations and sales people together to meet with the company's resellers in an effort to create customer-responsive logistics service. As a result of its efforts, United guarantees customers that orders placed by 7:00 P.M. will be received before noon on the following day. Customers can dial into United's mainframe computer and place orders electronically.[10] The company considers all of its logistics people to be part of the sales function. Some firms have taken the integration even further. Baxter Healthcare warehouse workers team up with warehouse personnel at the hospitals Baxter serves. During visits to the customer warehouse, the Baxter warehouser evaluates the operation, looking for ways to improve packing so shipments will be easier for the customer to unload and unpack. As a result, Baxter warehousers have become salespeople.

Just-in-Time Systems

Many business marketers have realized they have no choice other than to provide almost immediate delivery of their products. The reason is the widespread adoption

[7]Donald J. Bowersox, "The Strategic Benefits of Logistics Alliances," *Harvard Business Review* 68 (July/August 1990): p. 40.
[8]Ronald Henkoff, "Delivering the Goods," *Fortune,* 28 November 1994, p. 64.
[9]E. J. Mueller, "Selling the Process, Not Just the Product," *Distribution* 90 (January 1991): p. 50.
[10]Bruce Caldwell, "United Stationers' Combination Shot," *Informationweek* (September 1996) p. 48.

by U.S. manufacturing firms of the just-in-time (JIT) inventory principle.[11] Under this principle, all suppliers must carefully coordinate delivery of parts and supplies with the manufacturer's production schedule—often delivering products just hours before they are used (see Chapter 2). The objective of a JIT system is to eliminate waste of all kinds from the production process. It requires the delivery of the specified product at the precise time, and in the exact quantity needed. Importantly, the quality must be perfect—there is no opportunity to inspect products in the JIT process. Because JIT attempts to relate purchases to production requirements, the typical order size shrinks, and more frequent deliveries are required. Increased delivery frequency presents a challenge to the business marketing production and logistics system.

JIT Relationship

A significant effect of JIT purchasing has been the drastic reduction in the number of suppliers utilized by manufacturers.[12] Suppliers who are able to meet customers' JIT requirements will find their share of business growing with the JIT-oriented customer.[13] Meeting the JIT requirements often represents a marketing edge, and may mean survival for some suppliers. The relationship that emerges between JIT suppliers and manufacturers is unique and often requires extensive integration of their operations.[14] As a result, suppliers find that the relationships are longer lasting and are usually formalized with a written contract that may span up to five years. Charles O'Neal summarizes the important JIT impacts on the buyer-seller relationship: "The JIT concept introduces a new philosophy of supplier-customer interorganizational linkage which has significant implications for marketing management. The linkage has many of the attributes of a (positive) marriage relationship, including careful choice of marriage partner, extended time horizon, partner interdependence, intimacy of partners, openness of communications, and provision of support activities to maintain the positive relationship."[15]

Speed and Hewlett-Packard's Success

Some business marketers effectively capitalize on their ability to deliver product quickly to customers. The success of Hewlett-Packard's (H-P) in high-margin laser printers is attributed not only to product features and marketing, but also to savvy

---

[11]Charles R. O'Neal, "The Buyer-Seller Linkage in a Just-in-Time Environment," *Journal of Purchasing and Materials Management* 23 (spring 1987): p. 7; and Tom Murray, "Just-in Time Isn't Just for Show—It Sells," *Sales and Marketing Management* 142 (May 1990): pp. 62–67.

[12]O. Felix Offodile and David Arrington, "Support of Successful Just-in-Time Implementation, the Changing Role of Purchasing," *International Journal of Physical Distribution and Logistics Management* 22, no. 5 (1992): p. 42.

[13]Peter Bradley, "Just-in-Time Works, but . . ." *Purchasing* 118 (September 1995): p. 36.

[14]Gary L. Frazier, Robert E. Spekman, and Charles R. O'Neal, "Just-in-Time Exchange Relationships in Industrial Markets," *Journal of Marketing* 52 (October 1988): p. 53.

[15]Charles R. O'Neal, "JIT Procurement and Relationship Marketing," *Industrial Marketing Management* 18 (February 1989): p. 60.

distribution that has entrenched the company in computer superstores, computer electronic outlets, and office suppliers.[16] Speed is a major element of H-P's distribution success. Large retailers like CompUSA and Price Club refuse to keep large inventories and demand immediate fulfillment of their orders from vendors. Because H-P can meet these stringent requirements, it has solidified a leading position with its key customers. As such delivery requirements become industry standards, those business firms with effective and efficient logistical systems already in place will enjoy significant marketing advantages.

ELEMENTS OF A LOGISTICAL SYSTEM

Table 14.1 presents the controllable variables of a logistical system. Almost no decision on a particular logistical activity can be made without evaluating its impact on the other areas.

The system of warehouse facilities, inventory commitments, order-processing methods, and transportation linkages will determine the supplier's ability to provide timely product availability to industrial users. As a result of poor supplier performance, customers may have to bear the extra cost of higher inventories, institute expensive priority-order-expediting systems, develop secondary supply sources, or, worst of all, turn to another supplier.

TOTAL-COST APPROACH

In the management of logistical activities, two performance variables must be considered: (1) total distribution costs and (2) the level of logistical service provided to customers. The logistical system must be designed and administered to achieve that combination of cost and service levels that yields maximum profits.

Logistical costs vary widely for business marketers, depending on the nature of the product and on the importance of logistical service to the buyer. Logistical costs can consume 16 to 36 percent of each sales dollar at the manufacturing level, and assets required by logistical activities can exceed 40 percent of total assets. Thus logistics can have a significant impact on corporate profitability.[17] Many believe that opportunities for productivity gains in production, selling, and promotion have been exploited, and Wendell Stewart states that logistics can be considered "the last frontier of cost reduction in American business."[18] How, then, can the marketer manage logistical costs?

---

[16]Joe Mullich, "H-P Conquers Channels with Speed," *Business Marketing* 78 (July 1993): p.44.

[17]Horne, "Charting a Course for Integrated Logistics," p. 46.

[18]Wendell M. Stewart, "Physical Distribution: Key to Improved Volume and Profits," *Journal of Marketing* 39 (January 1965): pp. 65–70; see also Thomas W. Speh and Michael D. Hutt, "The Other Half of Marketing: Lost or Found," in *Proceedings: Southern Marketing Association,* ed. Robert S. Franz, Robert M. Hopkins, and Al Toma (University of Southwestern Louisiana: Southern Marketing Association, 1978), pp. 332–335.

Table 14.1 Controllable Elements in a Logistics System

Elements	Key Aspects
Customer service	The "product" of logistics activities, *customer service* relates to the effectiveness in creating time and place utility. The level of customer service provided by the supplier has a direct impact on total cost, market share, and profitability.
Order processing	Order processing triggers the logistics process and directs activities necessary to deliver products to customers. Speed and accuracy of order processing affect costs and customer service levels.
Logistics communications	Information exchanged in the distribution process guides the activities of the system. It is the vital link between the firm's logistics system and its customers.
Transportation	The physical movement of products from source of supply through production to customers is the most significant cost area in logistics, and it involves selecting modes and specific carriers as well as routing.
Warehousing	Providing storage space serves as a buffer between production and use. Warehousing may be used to enhance service and to lower transportation costs.
Inventory control	Inventory is used to make products available to customers and to ensure the correct mix of products is at the proper location at the right time.
Packaging	The role of packaging is to provide protection to the product, to maintain product identity throughout the logistics process, and to create effective product density.
Materials handling	Materials handling increases the speed of, and reduces the cost of, picking orders in the warehouse and moving products between storage and the transportation carriers. It is a cost-generating activity that must be controlled.
Production planning	Utilized in conjunction with logistics planning, production planning ensures that products are available for inventory in the correct assortment and quantity.
Plant and warehouse location	Strategic placement of plants and warehouses increases customer service and reduces the cost of transportation.

Source: Adapted from James R. Stack and Douglas M. Lambert, *Strategic Logistics Management*, 4th ed. (Homewood, Ill.: Richard D. Irwin, 1996).

The **total-cost** or **trade-off approach** to logistical management offers a guarantee that total logistical costs in the firm and within the channel are minimized. The assumption is that costs associated with individual logistical activities are interactive; that is, a decision about one logistical variable affects all or some of the other variables. Management is thus concerned with the efficiency of the entire system rather than with minimizing the cost of any single logistical activity. The interactions among logistical activities (that is, transportation, inventory, warehousing) are described as **cost trade-offs,** because a cost increase in one activity is traded for a large cost decrease in another activity, the net result being an overall cost reduction.

Figure 14.3 Cost Trade-Offs

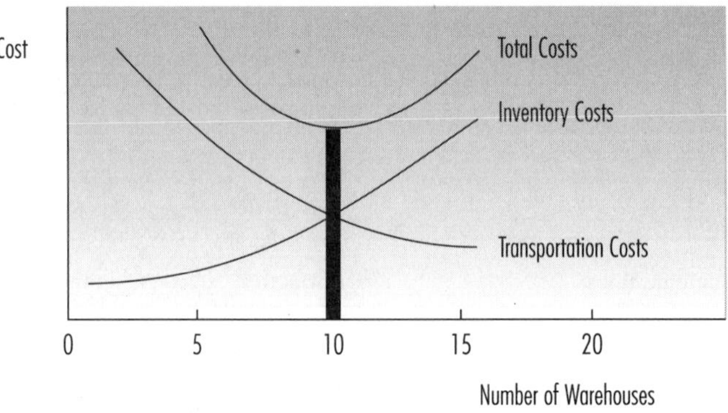

Evaluating Cost Patterns

Figure 14.3 shows costs associated with a change in the number of warehouses maintained by an industrial firm. As additional warehouses are added, transportation costs decline as a result of high-volume low-cost shipments entering the warehouses and small-volume high-cost shipments moving only short distances to the customers. Total transportation costs decline with more warehouses because the high-cost small-volume shipments are moved over shorter and shorter distances. Conversely, inventory costs rise as more warehouses are added because more stock is required to maintain the same level of product availability. Combining inventory and transportation costs, the least-cost solution—in which the trade-off of inventory for transportation is optimized—is to maintain ten warehouses. A warehouse decision solely based either on inventory costs or on transportation costs would not result in the most cost-effective total system.

Cost trade-offs occur among all logistical activities. Union Carbide makes numerous gases (nitrogen, oxygen, and so forth) and delivers them through regional branch operations around the country. In this industry, control of logistics cost is a major competitive advantage. In an attempt to prune total logistics cost, Carbide introduced the "storefront" approach to product distribution. Its many distribution points were transformed to "storefronts," only taking orders and maintaining small inventories of a few products.[19] Originating most deliveries from fewer, centralized plants and distribution points resulted in important cost trade-offs: Storefront branches dramatically lowered inventory and warehousing costs, transportation cost from plants to the branches was eliminated, and double handling of products was reduced. Still, overall transportation costs rose because of longer distances from plant

[19]Donald B. Rosenfield, "Storefront Distribution for Industrial Products," *Harvard Business Review* 67 (July/August 1989): p. 45.

to customer and the need for more drivers. In total, however, overall logistics costs were reduced, service was unaffected, and the firm's competitive position improved.

The widespread application of JIT concepts and the increasing emphasis on total quality programs suggest that business marketers should carefully consider the "quality costs" generated by their logistics systems.[20] Quality costs, which include costs associated with defective products (higher inventory, additional transport costs for product return), product appraisal (inspection and evaluation expenses), and prevention (training, data analysis, and planning expenses) should be explicitly considered in conjunction with the set of traditional total costs of logistics. The goal is to create a logistics system that delivers a given quality level at the lowest cost.

CALCULATING LOGISTICS COSTS

Activity-Based Costing

The **activity-based costing (ABC)** technique is used to precisely measure the costs associated with performing specific activities, and then trace those costs to the products, customers, and channels that consumed the activities.[21] It is a powerful tool to use in managing the logistics operations within a supply chain. ABC provides a mechanism to trace the cost of performing logistics services to the customers that use the services, thereby making it easier to assess the appropriate level of customer service to offer. Firms using ABC analysis can obtain more accurate information concerning how a particular customer or a specific product contributes to overall profitability.[22]

Total Cost of Ownership (TCO)

TCO is applied to determine the total costs associated with the acquisition and subsequent use of a given item from a particular supplier. The approach identifies costs—often buried in overhead or general expenses—that relate to the cost of holding inventory, poor quality, and delivery failure.[23] A buyer using TCO would explicitly consider the costs that the supplier's logistics system either added to, or eliminated from, the purchase price. Thus, a supplier particularly efficient at logistics might be able to reduce the buyer's inventory costs and the buyer's expenses of inspecting inbound merchandise for damage. As a result, the total cost of ownership from that supplier would be lower than the cost from other suppliers that were not able to

[20]James M. Kenderdine and Paul D. Larson, "Quality and Logistics: A Framework for Strategic Integration," *International Journal of Physical Distribution and Materials Management* 18, no. 6 (1988): p. 5.

[21]Bernard J. LaLonde and Terrance L. Pohlen, "Issues in Supply Chain Costing," *The International Journal of Logistics Management* 7, no. 1 (1996): p. 3.

[22]Joseph B. Fuller, James O'Connor, and Richard Rawlinson, "Tailored Logistics: The Next Advantage," *Harvard Business Review* 71 (May/June 1993): pp. 87–97.

[23]Lisa M. Ellram, "Activity-Based Costing and Total Cost of Ownership: A Critical Linkage," *Journal of Cost Management* 8 (winter 1995): pp. 22–30.

rapidly deliver undamaged products. Increasing acceptance of the TCO approach will cause efficiency in logistics operations to become an even more critical element of a business marketer's strategy.

Customized Solutions

As firms learn how to assess the true costs associated with customizing logistics services to the customer and the product, they will be positioned to offer a "cafeteria" of logistics services from which each customer can choose. In this way, logistics services can be tailored to the unique requirements of individual customers. With this approach, a customer requesting one-day delivery service can determine whether the cost of such rapid service is worth the price charged by the supplier.

Business-to-Business Logistical Service

Many studies have shown that the importance of logistics service often equals that of product quality as a measure of supplier performance.[24] In many industries a quality product at a competitive price is recognized as a given, and customer service is the key differentiator among competitors.[25] In one industry, for example, purchasing agents begin the buying process by calling suppliers with the best delivery service to see whether they are willing to negotiate prices. Similar approaches to vendor selection are evidenced in other situations. Because it is so important to customers, logistics service can lead to higher market share and higher profits. A study by Bain and Company showed that companies with superior logistics service grow 8 percent faster, realize a 7 percent price premium, and are 12 times as profitable as firms with inferior service levels.[26] These facts, together with the extensive implementation of just-in-time manufacturing systems, makes it clear that logistical service is important to the organizational buyer.

DEFINITION OF CUSTOMER SERVICE

Logistical service relates to the availability and delivery of products to the customer and can be conceptualized as the series of sales-satisfying activities that begin when the customer places the order and that end with the delivery of the product to that customer. Responsive logistical service advances customer satisfaction and creates the

---

[24]Mary Collins Holcomb, "Customer Service Measurement: A Methodology for Increasing Customer Value through Utilization of the Taguchi Strategy," *Journal of Business Logistics* 15, no. 1 (1994): p. 29.

[25]"Customer Service: The Great Differentiator," *Traffic Management* 31 (November 1992): p. 40.

[26]Neil S. Novich, "How to Sell Customer Service," *Transportation and Distribution* 33 (January 1992): p. 46.

Table 14.2 Common Elements of Logistics Service

Elements	Description
Delivery time	The time from the creation of an order to the fulfillment and delivery of that order includes both order-processing time and delivery or transportation time.
Delivery reliability	The most frequently used measure of logistics service, delivery reliability focuses on the capability of having products available to meet customer demand.
Order accuracy	The degree to which items received conform to the specification of the order. The key dimension is the incidence of orders shipped complete and without error.
Information access	The firm's ability to respond to inquiries about order status and product availability.
Damage	A measure of the physical conditions of the product when received by the buyer.
Ease of doing business	A range of factors including the ease with which orders, returns, credits, billing, and adjustments are handled.
Value-added services	Such features as packaging, which facilitates customer handling, or other services such as prepricing and drop shipments.

Source: Reprinted with permission from Jonathon L. S. Byrnes, William C. Copacino, and Peter Metz, "Forge Service into a Weapon with Logistics," *Transportation & Distribution, Presidential Issue* 28 (September 1987): p. 46.

opportunity for closer and more profitable buyer–seller relationships.[27] Logistical service includes whatever aspects of performance are important to the business customer (see Table 14.2). These service elements range from delivery time to value-added services, and each of these elements has the potential to affect production processes, final product output, costs, or all three.

IMPACTS OF SUPPLIER LOGISTICAL SERVICE ON BUSINESS CUSTOMERS

Supplier logistical service translates into product availability. For a manufacturer to produce or for a distributor to resell, industrial products must be available at the right time, at the right place, and in usable condition. The longer the supplier's delivery time, the less available the product; the more inconsistent the delivery time, the less available the product.

For example, a reduction in the supplier's delivery time permits a buyer to hold less inventory because needs can be met rapidly. The customer reduces the risk of interruption in the production process. Consistent delivery performance enables the buyer to program more effectively—or routinize—the purchasing process, thus lowering buyer costs. The dramatic impact of consistent delivery cycle performance

[27] Arun Sharma, Dhruv Grewal, and Michael Levy, "The Customer Satisfaction/Logistics Interface," *Journal of Business Logistics* 16, no. 2 (1995): p. 1.

presents an opportunity for the buyer to cut the level of buffer or safety stock maintained, thereby reducing the inventory cost. However, for many business products, such as those that are low in unit value and relatively standardized, the overriding concern is not inventory cost, but simply having the products. A malfunctioning 95-cent bearing could shut down a whole production line.

THE ROLE OF LOGISTICAL SERVICE IN THE BUYING DECISION

Because the impacts of logistical service are so dramatic, it is not surprising that buyers rank logistical service above many other important supplier characteristics.[28] A recent publication reviewed a multitude of research studies that investigated the importance of logistics service on purchasing decisions. The authors concluded that:

> *Across multiple products and industries logistics service remains an important element in supplier evaluation, customer perception and satisfaction, and the resulting purchasing decision. It would be tempting to make a definite statement as to the exact importance of logistics service relative to other purchase criteria but it is much more reasonable to state that there is an indication that logistics service stands out as a major factor.*[29]

In a number of these studies, logistics service ranked right behind "quality" as a criterion for selecting a vendor.

It is equally important to evaluate logistics service from the standpoint of the cost of poor customer service. Good service can attract and hold customers; ineffective logistics service can harm customer relationships or drive customers away. A study conducted at Ohio State University found that a variety of punitive actions will be taken in response to poor logistics service.[30] For example, chemical companies expect to lose market share in about 50 percent of the situations in which their logistics service is unpredictable. In the pharmaceutical and electronics industries, between 16 and 20 percent of the customers would be expected to stop all purchases from the vendor as a result of repeated instances of erratic logistics service. Clearly, the business marketer must develop an effective logistics strategy or risk the loss of substantial business. This key impact of logistics services provides a strong argument for integrating logistics strategy into the overall marketing strategy.

DETERMINING THE LEVEL OF SERVICE

Obviously, not all products nor all customers require the same level of logistical service. Many business products that are made to order—such as heavy machinery—

---

[28]Holcomb, "Customer Service Measurement," p. 29.

[29]John T. Mentzer, Roger Gomes, and Robert E. Krapfel Jr., "Physical Distribution Service: A Fundamental Marketing Concept," *Journal of the Academy of Marketing Science* 17 (winter 1989): p. 59.

[30]Bernard J. LaLonde, Martha Cooper, and Thomas G. Noordewier, *Customer Service: A Management Perspective*, (Oak Brook, Ill.: Council of Logistics Management, 1988), p. 133.

have relatively low logistical service requirements. Others, such as replacement parts, components, and subassemblies, require extremely demanding logistical performance. Similarly, customers may be more or less responsive to varying levels of logistical service.

Some business buyers are far more sensitive to poor service than the majority of buyers. Market segments must be identified on the basis of logistical service sensitivity.[31] For example, buyers of scientific instruments were classified into groups—private firms, government, secondary schools, and so forth. Private firms ranked delivery time more highly than did other groups, and secondary schools ranked ordering convenience more highly than did others. Business marketing managers should attempt to isolate segments and to adjust the logistical service offerings accordingly.

Business purchasers may also vary in terms of their sensitivity to the various elements of logistics service. One study found that consistency of delivery was most important for materials and components; in-stock performance and consistent deliveries were central for supplies; and in-stock performance was most important for small capital items and was perceived to be more important than delivery time.[32] Managers must target their logistics service mix to the requirements of their product type and customer.

Profitability is the major criterion for evaluating the appropriate customer service levels. Information on alternative service levels and their associated sales results must be evaluated in relation to their costs.[33] Figure 14.4 demonstrates the cost/service relationship, showing that profit contribution varies with the service level. In this case, the current service level is 73 percent of orders filled completely. The chart indicates that higher service levels would generate higher levels of profits. The optimal service level is 85 percent because, at service levels below 85 percent, revenue gains exceed the additional costs. At service levels greater than 85 percent, the marginal costs to produce that level of service exceed the additional revenue that would be gained.

To recap, service levels are developed by assessing customer service requirements. The sales and cost effects of various service levels are analyzed to find the service level generating the highest profits. The needs of various customer segments will dictate various logistical system configurations. For example, when logistical service is critical, industrial distributors can provide the vital product availability, whereas customers with less rigorous service demands can be served from factory inventories.

The Interface of Channel Logistics

Logistical activities, whether by manufacturer or intermediary, touch every phase of channel performance and are inherent in the success or failure of most industrial channel systems. The task of the business marketer is, first, to understand the

---

[31]Fuller, O'Connor, and Rawlinson, "Tailored Logistics: The Next Advantage," p. 93.

[32]Donald W. Jackson Jr., Janet E. Keith, and Richard K. Burdick, "Examining the Relative Importance of Physical Distribution Service Elements," *Journal of Business Logistics* 7, no. 9 (1986): p. 25.

[33]For example, see David P. Herron, "Managing Physical Distribution for Profit," *Harvard Business Review* 57 (May/June 1979): pp. 121–132; and Harvey N. Shycon and Christopher Sprague, "Put a Price Tag on Your Customer Servicing Levels," *Harvard Business Review* 53 (July/August 1975): pp. 71–78.

Figure 14.4 Cost/Service Relationship

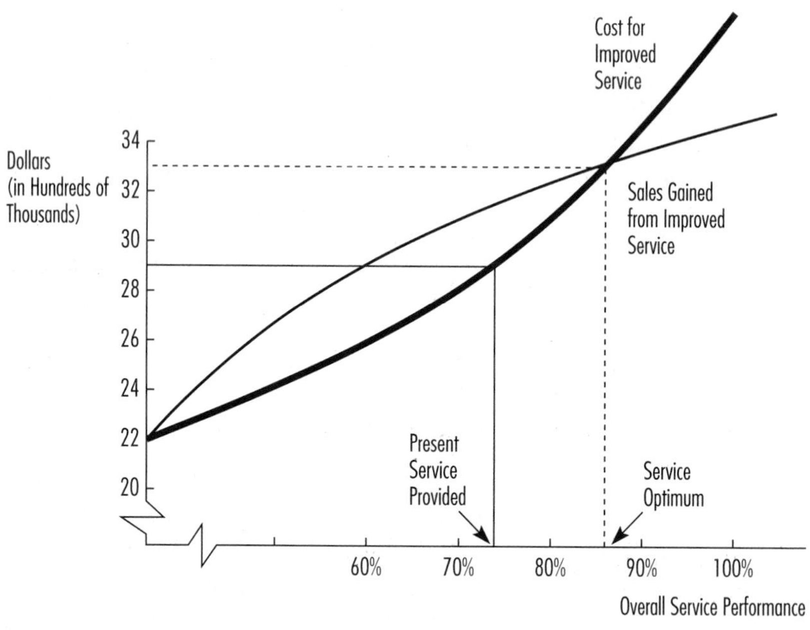

Note: How much should a firm spend on customer-service in order to gain extra sales? Graph shows how much a typical firm can improve its share of market for each $100,000 spent. Indicated too is the point of diminishing returns at which additional expenditures will exceed the value of increased sales. Though the graph suggests a breakpoint of about 85 percent, a company can determine its own figure only by studying specific conditions in its field. The nature of the product, geographic circumstances, transport characteristics, and other factors all affect the optimum service point.

Source: "Does Your Customer Service Program Stack Up?" *Traffic Management,* September 1982, p. 55.

impact of supplier logistical performance on the intermediary's operations, and, next, to effect programs that will enhance the intermediary's performance and overall channel coordination.

LOGISTICAL IMPACTS ON INDUSTRIAL INTERMEDIARIES

A supplier's logistical system directly affects an intermediary's ability to control cost and service to end users. Delivery time not only influences the customer's inventory requirements but also the operations of channel members. If a supplier provides erratic delivery service to distributors, the distributor is forced to carry higher inventory in order to provide a satisfactory level of product availability to end users. Observe in Figure 14.5 that Ryder Systems, Inc. emphasizes the benefits of its Integrated Logistics system in reducing inventory investment.

Inefficient logistics service to the distributors either increases distributor costs (larger inventories) or creates shortages of the supplier's products at the distributor level. Neither result is good. In the first instance, distributor loyalty and marketing efforts will suffer; in the second, end users will eventually change suppliers. In some industries, distributors are expanding the role they play in the logistics process, which makes them even more valuable to their suppliers and customers. In the chemical industry, for example, the role of distributors is completely transforming as they offer logistics solutions—JIT delivery, repackaging, inventory management—to their customers.[34] The logistics expertise provided by distributors enables their vendors to focus on their own core competencies of manufacturing and marketing.

IMPACT ON CUSTOMER SERVICE

Poor logistical performance is a double-edged sword. It constricts sales possibilities and antagonizes intermediaries. A 5 percent reduction in customer service can result in a sales decrease of 20 percent.[35] An industrial distributor will not long remain loyal to a manufacturer whose logistical performance reduces service levels to end users. Because inventories typically represent the single largest item among distributor assets, and also the largest distribution expense, distributors are increasingly aware of the impact of supplier logistical service. Also, poor logistics may necessitate the use of faster-than-usual freight methods—at premium prices—to get products to customers on time. Because distributors often pass freight charges along to their customers, abnormally high transportation costs can place the manufacturer's product at a price disadvantage in the marketplace.

IMPROVING LOGISTICAL PERFORMANCE IN THE CHANNEL

The business marketer can do much to improve channelwide logistical performance. First, information systems can be developed to provide realistic sales forecasts for individual channel members, and their inventory control systems can be linked to the manufacturer's information system. Second, coordination of logistical activities can be facilitated, perhaps by standardizing packaging, handling, and palletization systems. Third, the manufacturer may perform certain functions (for example, warehousing) that contribute to improved efficiency for the entire channel. Finally, shipment consolidation is often effective in reducing channelwide transportation

[34]Daniel J. McConville, "More Work for Chemical Distributors," *Distribution* 95 (August 1996): p. 63.
[35]LaLonde, Cooper, and Noordewier, *Customer Service*, p. 133.

Figure 14.5 An Ad Emphasizing that an Integrated Logistics System Can Reduce Inventory Costs

Source: Courtesy of Ryder Systems, Inc.

costs. Distributors in a particular area might be encouraged to "pool" shipments into a truckload quantity, or to place all of their orders on the same day. In summary, logistics must be integrated channelwide to implement marketing strategy effectively.

Business-to-Business Logistical Management

The elements of logistics strategy are part of a system, and, as such, each affects every other element. The proper focus is the total-cost view. Although this section treats the decisions on facilities, transportation, and inventory separately, it must be remembered that they are so intertwined it is impossible to evaluate one without considering the other two.

LOGISTICAL FACILITIES

The strategic development of a warehouse provides the business marketer with the opportunity to increase the level of delivery service to buyers, to reduce transportation costs, or both. Business firms distributing repair, maintenance, and operating supplies often find that the only way to achieve desired levels of delivery service is to locate warehouses in key markets. The warehouse circumvents the need for premium transportation (air freight) and costly order processing by keeping products readily available in local markets.

Servicing Channel Members

The nature of the business-to-business channel affects the warehousing requirements of a supplier. When manufacturers' reps are utilized, the supplier will often require a significant number of strategically located warehouses. On the other hand, a channel system using distributors will offset the need for warehousing. Obviously, local warehousing by the distributor is a real service to the supplier. A few well-located supplier warehouses may be all that is required to service the distributors effectively.

Renting or Leasing

Operating costs, service levels, and investment requirements are essential considerations regarding the type of warehouse to use. The business firm may either own, rent, or lease warehouse space. At a **third-party warehouse,** space may be rented by the month or leased for a longer time. Short-term arrangements involve **public** warehousing firms, while longer term agreements, including the provision of special services, are provided by **contract** warehousers. The advantage is flexibility—the firm can increase or decrease its use of space in a given market or move into or out of any market quickly. Public warehousing involves no fixed investment; user costs are totally variable. When sales volume is seasonal, erratic, or generally low in a given market, the public warehouse is an economical means of providing excellent product availability. Contract warehousing is effective when the firm requires unique service and special equipment in the warehousing function.

Public or contract warehousing may sometimes supplement or replace distributors in a market. Many public and contract warehouses provide a variety of logistical services for their clients, including packaging, labeling, order processing, and some light assembly. GATX Logistics, a public/contract warehouse company based in Jacksonville, Florida, maintains warehouse facilities in a number of major markets. Clients can position inventories in all these markets while dealing with only one firm. Also, GATX can link its computer with the suppliers' computers to facilitate order processing and inventory updating. The GATX warehouse will also repackage products to the end user's order, label, and arrange for local delivery. A business marketer could ship standard products in bulk to the GATX warehouse, gaining transportation economies, and still enjoy excellent customer delivery service. The public or contract warehouse is a feasible alternative to the distributor channel when the sales function can be economically executed either with a direct sales force or with reps.[36]

Owning

The alternative to renting or leasing warehouse space is the **private warehouse,** in which the manufacturer makes a capital investment. Although the investment is substantial, private facilities can provide operating cost advantages when they are regularly used at close to capacity. Often more important than the cost and investment aspects is the enhancement of customer service. The private warehouse offers more control over the warehousing operation, permitting efficient levels of operation and delivery service.

TRANSPORTATION

Transportation is usually the largest single logistical expense, and with the impact of continually rising fuel costs, its importance will probably increase. Typically, the transportation decision involves the evaluation and selection both of a mode of transportation and of the individual carrier(s) that will ensure the best performance at the lowest cost. **Mode** refers to the type of carrier—rail, truck, water, air, or some combination of the four. **Individual carriers** are evaluated on rates and delivery performance.[37] The supply chain view is important when considering the selection of individual carriers. Carriers become an integral part of the supply chain process and close relationships are important. One study found evidence that carriers' operating performance improved when they were more involved in the relationship between buyer and seller.[38] By further integrating carriers into the supply chain, the entire supply can

[36]Michael D. Hutt and Thomas W. Speh, "Realigning Industrial Marketing Channels," *Industrial Marketing Management* 12 (July 1983): pp. 171–177.

[37]For example, see Roy J. Sampson, Martin T. Farris, and David L. Schrock, *Domestic Transportation: Practice, Theory and Policy* (Boston, Mass.: Houghton Mifflin, 1990).

[38]Julie Gentry, "The Role of Carriers in Buyer-Supplier Strategic Partnerships: A Supply Chain Management Approach," *Journal of Business Logistics* 17, no. 2 (1996): p. 52.

improve its competitive position. In this section we will consider (1) the role of transportation in industrial channels, (2) the criteria for evaluating transportation options, and (3) the private carrier alternative.

Transportation and Logistical Service

A business marketer must be able to effectively move finished inventory between facilities, to channel intermediaries, and to customers. The transportation system is the link that binds the logistical network together and ultimately results in timely delivery of products. Efficient warehousing will not enhance customer service levels if transportation is inconsistent or inadequate.

Effective transportation service may be used in combination with warehouse facilities and inventory levels to generate the required customer service level, or it may be used in place of them. Inventory maintained in a variety of market-positioned warehouses can be consigned to one centralized warehouse when rapid transportation services exist to deliver products from the central location to business customers. Xerox is one company that uses premium air freight service to offset the need for high inventories and extensive warehouse locations. The decision on transportation modes and particular carriers will depend on the cost trade-offs and service capabilities of each.

Transportation Performance Criteria

Cost of service is the variable cost associated with moving products from origin to destination, including any terminal or accessory charges. The cost of service may range from as little as 0.25 cents per ton-mile via water to as high as 50 cents per ton-mile via air freight. The important aspect of selecting the mode of transportation is not cost per se but cost relative to the objective to be achieved. Bulk raw materials generally do not require prepaid delivery service, so the cost of anything other than rail or water transportation could not be justified. On the other hand, although air freight may be almost ten times more expensive than motor freight, the cost is inconsequential to a customer who needs an emergency shipment of spare parts. The cost of premium (faster) transportation modes may be justified by the resulting inventory reductions.

Speed of service refers to the elapsed time to move products from one facility (plant or warehouse) to another facility (warehouse or customer plant). Again, speed of service often overrides the cost of service. Rail, a relatively slow mode used for bulk shipments, requires inventory buildups at the supplier's factory and at the destination warehouse. The longer the delivery time, the more inventory customers must maintain to service their needs while the shipment is in transit. The slower modes involve lower variable costs for product movement, yet they result in lower service levels and higher investments in inventory. The faster modes produce just the opposite effect. Not only must a comparison be made between modes in terms of service, but various carriers within a mode must be evaluated on their "door-to-door" delivery time.

Service consistency is usually more important than average delivery time, and all modes of transportation are not equally consistent. Although air provides the lowest

REDUCING HEALTHCARE COST THROUGH EFFICIENT LOGISTICS

In the years before the nationwide squeeze on health-care costs, St. Luke's Episcopal Hospital in Houston kept a hoard of expensive medical supplies in its 20,000-square-foot warehouse. Like all hospitals, St. Luke's cannot afford to run short of vital items—least of all in the operating rooms. At St. Luke's, Dr. Denton A. Cooley's teams perform open-heart surgery on 3,000 patients each year, using prodigious quantities of supplies.

But to achieve economies as the pressure to control costs intensified, St. Luke's shut its warehouse and sold the inventory to Baxter International, a major hospital supplier. Baxter is becoming a full-time partner with this 950-bed hospital in managing, ordering, and delivering Baxter's wares as well as the products of 400 other companies. Baxter's daily just-in-time deliveries to the hospital loading dock were only the first step. In an innovative system that hospitals call stockless inventory, Baxter fills orders in exact, sometimes small, quantities and delivers directly to departments, including the operating rooms and nursing floors, inside St. Luke's.

Stockless systems lower hospitals' holding and handling costs. "We think we've saved $1.5 million a year since 1988 from just-in-time deliveries alone," said Randy Jackson, a St. Luke's vice president, with another $500,000 likely once the stockless system is fully implemented. Annual savings already have included $350,000 from reducing staff and $162,500 from eliminating inventory. The hospital has converted storerooms to patient care and other money-generating uses.

Hospital distributors like Baxter profit from stockless services because they impose extra charges, raise prices more readily, and often become a hospital's sole source of medical supplies. They typically add 3 to 5 percent service fees.

The stockless systems work like this:

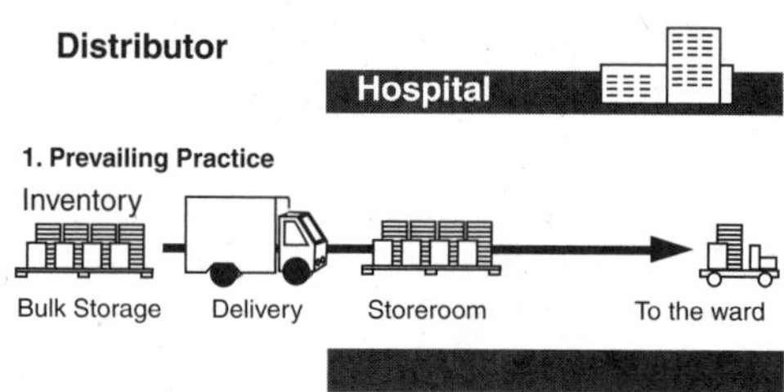

Most hospitals keep a large inventory of supplies that are replenished regularly by suppliers, but require a large amount of space and staff.

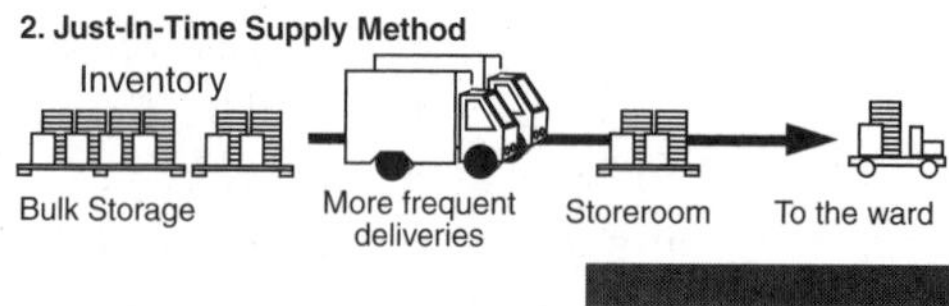

If a hospital implements a just-in-time plan in coordination with a distributor, it can give up some of its inventory space in return for more frequent deliveries.

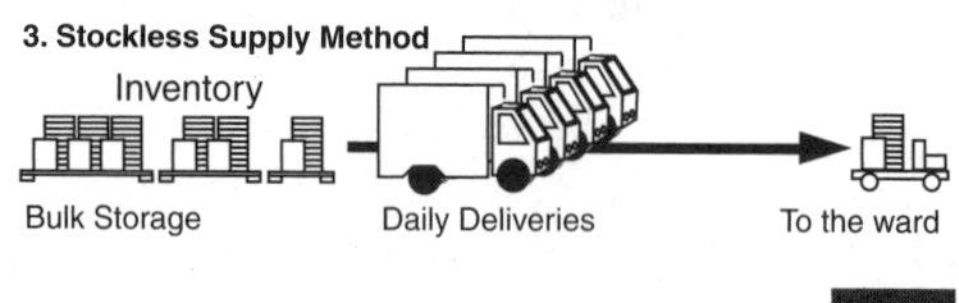

A stockless supply plan shifts all inventory responsibilities on the distributor. Deliveries are made daily, sometimes directly to departments that need supplies.

Source: Milt Freudenheim, "Removing the Warehouse from Cost-Conscious Hospitals," *The New York Times,* 3 March 1991, p. 5.

average delivery time, generally it has the highest variability in delivery time relative to the average. The wide variations in modal service consistency are particularly critical in business marketing planning. The choice of transportation mode must be made on the basis of cost, average transit time, and consistency if effective customer service is to be achieved.

In summary, because business buyers often place a premium on effective and consistent delivery service, the choice of transportation mode is an important one—one in which the cost of service is often secondary. However, the best decision on transportation carriers will result from a balancing of service, variable costs, and investment requirements. The manager must also consider the transportation requirements of ordinary versus expedited, or rush-order, shipments.

Private Carriers

Sometimes the only way for a supplier to achieve the consistent delivery performance required by customers is with its own trucks. Service improvement is the primary justification for a company fleet, because the private fleet may be more expensive than hired transportation. The investment requirements are significant—vehicles, maintenance facilities, and the like—though they can sometimes be reduced by leasing equipment. The decision to operate a private fleet is a complex one.[39] However, the advantages of private ownership and management of transportation service may effectively balance the cost, investment, and service aspects of transportation. Inventory, the third leg of logistical management, is interrelated with the transportation decision.

INVENTORY MANAGEMENT

Inventory management is the buffer in the logistical system. Inventories are needed in business channels because (1) production and demand are not perfectly matched, (2) operating deficiencies in the logistical system often result in product unavailability (for example, delayed shipments, inconsistent carrier performance), and (3) industrial customers cannot predict their product needs with certainty (for example, because a machine may break down or there may be a sudden need to expand production). Inventory may be viewed in the same light as warehouse facilities and transportation: It is an alternative method for providing the level of service required by customers, and the level of inventory is determined on the basis of cost, investment, service required, and anticipated revenue.

Quality Focus: Eliminate Inventories

Today's prevalent total quality management techniques and just-in-time management principles emphasize the reduction or outright elimination of inventories. Current thinking suggests that inventories exist because of inefficiencies in the system: Erratic delivery, poor forecasting, and ineffective quality control systems all force companies to hold excessive stocks to protect themselves from delivery, forecasting,

---

[39]For example, see Johnson and Wood, *Contemporary Logistics*, pp. 240–244.

and product failure. Instead, improved delivery, forecasting, and manufacturing processes should prevent the need to buffer against failures and uncertainty. Information technology involving bar coding, scanner data, total quality processes, better transportation management, and more effective information flow among firms in the supply chain have made it possible to more carefully control inventories and reduce them to the lowest possible levels.[40] Successful business marketing managers must develop quality processes that in themselves reduce or eliminate the need to carry large inventories, while coordinating and integrating a system that can function effectively with almost no inventory.

Inventory Costs

Inventory costs are subtle and difficult to comprehend because often they are not segregated but found throughout a firm's system of accounts. Inventory costs include four basic cost categories: (1) capital costs, (2) inventory service costs (for example, cases and insurance), (3) storage space costs, and (4) inventory risk costs (for example, damage and pilferage).[41]

Together these four cost categories are known as **inventory carrying costs,** typically stated as a percentage of the value of the products held in inventory. (A carrying charge of 20 percent means that the cost of holding one unit in inventory for one year is 20 percent of the value of the product.) Inventory carrying costs usually range from 12 to 35 percent, yet these percentages may be much higher when all relevant inventory-related costs are considered. One company that had historically used a 19 percent carrying charge figure for making inventory decisions was found to have a true carrying charge of 38 percent.[42]

The implications are clear: To make sound inventory decisions, business managers must be able to determine the real cost of holding inventories. Only after the true inventory costs are known can management evaluate the cost/service and the inventory/transportation trade-offs. Effective inventory policy also demands a product-by-product analysis.

The 80/20 Rule

Most business marketers with extensive product lines know that the great bulk of their products do not turn over very rapidly. This is the **80/20 principle:** 80 percent of the sales are generated by 20 percent of the product line.

The major implication of the 80/20 principle is that business marketers must manage their inventory selectively, treating fast- and slow-moving items differently. If a company has half its inventory committed to products that produce only 20 percent

---

[40]Tim Loar, "Patterns of Inventory Management and Policy: A Study of Four Industries," *Journal of Business Logistics* 13, no. 2 (1992): p. 70.

[41]Bernard J. LaLonde and Douglas M. Lambert, "A Methodology for Determining Inventory Carrying Costs: Two Case Studies," in *Proceedings of the Fifth Annual Transportation and Logistics Educators Conference,* ed. James Robeson and John Grabner (October 1975), p. 47.

[42]Ibid., pp. 39, 47.

of the unit sales volume, significant gains can be made by reducing inventories of the slow sellers to the point at which their turnover rate approximates that of the fast sellers.[43] This rule applies regardless of how the inventory function is handled in the channel. Thus, suppliers can develop more efficient channels and substantially reduce distributor inventory costs by allowing the distributor to cut back inventory on slow-turnover items. Not only will distributor cost performance improve, but enhanced channel goodwill should result.

Selective Inventory Strategies

The evaluation of selective inventory strategies depends on the cost and service trade-offs involved. First, inventory of slow movers can be reduced at all locations; the result, however, may be a marked reduction in customer service. As with transportation, one workable alternative is to centralize the slow-moving items at a single location, thereby reducing total inventories. The result is a higher sales volume per unit of product at a given location. In turn, inventories of fast-moving items can be expanded, enhancing their service levels.

A selective inventory policy must be applied cautiously. Typically, fast-moving items are standardized items that customers expect to be readily available; slow movers are often nonstandardized, and customers expect to wait to receive them.[44] However, there is no rule that all slow-moving items require low service levels. If a slow-moving item is critical in the production process or is needed to repair a machine, an extremely high level of service is required. Thus, a selective inventory policy mandates that both turnover rates and the criticalness of the product to the customer be evaluated in determining the inventory/transportation system.

LOGISTICS INFORMATION SYSTEMS

Computer-based information systems play a crucial role in the management of the logistics process. The development of logistics information systems has paralleled the increased awareness among top firms of logistics' potential for providing competitive advantage through value enhancement.[45] The types of information technology that are important in today's environment—for managing sophisticated logistics systems—are electronic data interchange (EDI), order management systems, transportation control systems, and process automation such as bar coding and radio frequency (RF) capabilities.

Information systems control and direct everything that happens in a logistics system, from order placement to measuring customers' satisfaction with service. For example, many firms now place orders electronically through EDI systems that

---

[43]James L. Heskett, "Logistics—Essential to Strategy," *Harvard Business Review* 56 (November/December 1977): p. 89.

[44]Ibid., p. 29.

[45]Craig M. Gustin, Patricia J. Dougherty, and Theodore P. Stank, "The Effects of Information Availability on Logistics Integration," *Journal of Business Logistics* 16, no. 1 (1995): p. 3.

directly link the vendor and customer. Once the vendor receives the order, the computer system will direct a warehouse worker where to find the requested product in the warehouse. When the order filler arrives at the proper location, he or she scans the product with a hand-held scanner, which transmits the information to a host computer through a radio frequency (RF) linkup in the warehouse. Inventory records are updated and a computer communication notifies the customer that the order was packed and shipped. An Advance Shipping Notice (ASN) is also transmitted to the customer, specifying exactly what is on the shipment, the transportation carrier, and when it will arrive. This enables the customer to plan production or warehouse schedules before receiving the shipment. These types of information systems help to ensure that a firm meets the logistical needs of its customers and provide the necessary data to manage each element of the logistics process.

THIRD-PARTY LOGISTICS

An emerging development in performing the logistics process is the utilization of *third-party logistics firms*. These external firms perform a wide range of logistics functions traditionally performed within the organization. A study of *Fortune* 500 firms revealed that 60 percent of the responding companies use third-party logistics services.[46] In more than half of the firms using third-party logistics services, the strategic decision to outsource logistics was made by top management. The functions performed by the third-party company can encompass the entire logistics process or selected activities within that process.[47] Third parties can perform the warehousing function (for example, public or contract warehousing, as discussed earlier) or they may perform the transportation function (a truck line like Schneider National) or they may perform the entire logistics process from production scheduling to delivery of finished products to the customer (for example, Ryder Dedicated Logistics). The use of third parties enables a manufacturer or distributor to concentrate on its core business while enjoying the expertise and specialization of a professional logistics company. The results are often lower costs, better service, improved asset utilization, increased flexibility, and access to leading-edge technology.[48]

Despite the advantages offered by third-party logistics firms, some firms are weary of their use because of a reduction in control over the logistics process,

---

[46]Robert C. Lieb and Hugh L. Randall, "A Comparison of the Use of Third-Party Logistics Services by Large American Manufacturers, 1991, 1994, and 1995," *Journal of Business Logistics* 17, no. 1 (1996): pp. 306, 307.

[47]Robert C. Lieb, "The Use of Third-Party Logistics Services by Large American Manufacturers," *Journal of Business Logistics* 13, no. 2 (1992): p. 29.

[48]Lisa Harrington, "Third-Party Logistics: Solving Problems and Saving Many," *Inbound Logistics* 11 (October 1991): pp. 19–24; Helen L. Richardson, "Explore Outsourcing," *Transportation and Distribution* 31 (July 1990): pp. 17–19; and Perry A. Trunick, "Outsourcing: A Single Source for Many Talents," *Transportation and Distribution* 30 (July 1989): pp. 20–23.

Managing in the 21st Century

CASE CORPORATION CONSTRUCTS A LOGISTICS MODEL FOR THE FUTURE

Case Corporation, an agricultural and construction equipment manufacturer, provides a wonderful example of the types of partnerships that many predict will be the wave of the future in terms of logistics outsourcing. In an effort to speed delivery to customers, improve customer satisfaction, and reduce operating costs and working capital requirements, Case Corporation globally integrated its logistics network and outsourced it to a strategic partnership of three logistics providers. Although Case still controls the strategic direction of its logistics system, the alliance of third-party logistics firms will manage all facets of Case's logistics operations.

Managing the flow of raw materials, parts, and finished goods through Case's supply chain is a complex and expensive task. Case products are sold through a network of 4,100 dealers in more than 150 countries. The supply chain includes more than 750 suppliers and 16 warehousing facilities, with eight manufacturing plants, nine parts depots, and 1,700 dealers in North America. Annually, Case makes more than 800,000 shipments that weigh over 1.6 billion pounds. According to the company's vice president of supply chain management, "Our supply chain management vision is focused on delighting our customers, and covers everything from the order to the delivery of the final product. We believe we are the first in our industry to make significant progress toward that goal. A lot of companies are reengineering their processes, but very few are reengineering their total supply chain."

The strategic alliance to which the logistics operations were outsourced includes: Fritz Companies, Inc., which serves as global integrator of the alliance; GATX Logistics, which will manage off-site warehousing; and Schneider Logistics, Inc., which will have responsibility for transportation and material flow management. The alliance will also provide global data management and logistics support. Case has signed a long-term agreement with each firm in the alliance and all four firms are linked electronically so they can operate "as one" in a virtual response mode. The alliance allows each firm to focus on its unique competencies while Case reaps the benefits of the synergies among the three alliance partners. Case management designed interdependent measures for the alliance that are geared to the success of the supply chain: the partners are dependent on one another to achieve goals and, when goals are reached, all three parties benefit.

Source: Adapted from Leslie Hansen Harps, "Case Corporation Constructs Logistics Model of the Future," *Inbound Logistics*, 16 (October 1996), pp. 24–32.

diminished direct contact with customers, and the problems associated with terminating internal operations. In analyzing the most effective and efficient way to accomplish logistics cost and service objectives, the business marketing manager should carefully consider the benefits and drawbacks to outsourcing part or all of the logistics function to third-party providers. Only recently have business marketers begun to use logistics strategy as a variable for creating competitive advantage.

Summary

The systems perspective in logistical management cannot be stressed enough—it is the only way that management can be assured that the logistical function will meet prescribed goals. Not only must each logistical variable be analyzed in terms of its impact on every other variable, but the sum of the variables must be evaluated in light of the service level provided to customers. Logistics elements throughout the supply chain must be integrated to assure smooth product flow.

Logistical service is critical in buyer evaluation of industrial suppliers. Logistical service seems to rank second only to product quality as a desired supplier characteristic. Business marketing managers are faced with a stern challenge to develop cost-effective logistical systems that provide the necessary service levels.

Decisions in the logistical area must be based on cost trade-offs among the logistical variables and on comparisons of the costs and revenues associated with alternative levels of service. The optimal system produces the highest profitability relative to the capital investment required.

Three major variables—facilities, transportation, and inventory—form the basis of logistical decisions regarding the number of warehouses, whether they are to be owned or rented, the transportation mode and the specific carrier, the level and deployment of inventory, and the selectivity of inventory levels. The systems approach can structure these three variables effectively. The business supplier must monitor the impact of logistics on channel members and on overall channel performance. Finally, the strategic role of logistics should be carefully evaluated: Logistics can often provide a strong competitive advantage.

Discussion Questions

1. Adopting the perspective of an organizational buyer, carefully illustrate how the most economical source of supply might be the firm that offers the highest price but also the fastest and most reliable delivery system.

2. Why is the logistical function often singled out as "the last frontier of cost reduction in American business"?

3. When a firm adopts a supply chain management approach to logistics, on what key elements will it focus attention in order to serve the final user at the lowest cost? Discuss.

4. Describe a situation in which total logistical costs might be reduced by doubling transportation costs.

5. A key goal in logistical management is to find the optimum balance of logistical cost and customer service that yields optimal profits. Explain.

6. Explain how consistent delivery performance gives the organizational buyer the opportunity to cut the level of inventory maintained.

7. Explain how the use of reps versus distributors influences the number of warehouses that the industrial marketer must maintain in the logistical system.
8. Inventory decisions for the business marketer are based on cost/service and inventory/transportation trade-offs. Illustrate the nature of these trade-offs.
9. Excessive premium freight charges and slow inventory turnover are two signs of maldistribution. If these danger signals appear, what steps should the business marketer take?
10. An increasing number of manufacturers are adopting a materials management philosophy (see Chapter 2) and more sophisticated inventory control systems. What are the strategic implications of these developments for business marketers wishing to serve these customers?

Chapter 15

Pricing Strategy for Business Markets

The price that a business marketer assigns to a product or service is one of many factors scrutinized by the organizational buyer. Pricing decisions complement the firm's overall marketing strategy. The diverse nature of the business market presents unique problems and opportunities for the price setter. After reading this chapter, you will understand

1. the role of price in the cost/benefit calculations of organizational buyers.
2. the central elements of the industrial pricing process.
3. how effective new product prices are established and the need for periodic adjustment of the prices of existing products.
4. strategic approaches to competitive bidding.

According to Richard D'Aveni, "While the average competitor fights for niches along a common ratio of price and value ('You get what you pay for'), innovative firms can enter the market by providing better value to the customer ('You can get more than what you pay for'). These companies offer lower cost *and* higher quality. This shift in value is like lowering the stick while dancing the limbo. All the competitors have to do the same dance with tighter constraints on both cost and quality."[1] The business marketer must remember this unifying strategic principle: Be better than your very best competitors in providing customer value.[2]

The business marketing manager must blend the various components of the marketing mix into a total offering that responds to the needs of the market and that provides a return consistent with the firm's objectives. Price must be carefully meshed with the product, distribution, and communication strategies of the firm. Thomas Nagle points out that "If effective product development, promotion, and distribution sow the seeds of business

[1]Richard A. D'Aveni, *Hypercompetitive Rivalries* (New York: The Free Press, 1995), p. 27.
[2]Bradley T. Gale, *Managing Customer Value: Creating Quality and Service that Customers Can See* (New York: The Free Press, 1994), pp. 73–75.

success, effective pricing is the harvest. While effective pricing can never compensate for poor execution of the first three elements, ineffective pricing can surely prevent these efforts from resulting in financial success. Regrettably, this is a common occurrence."[3]

The interdependence of price and other strategy components must be recognized before the pricing function can be isolated for analysis. Clearly, there is no single best way to establish the price of a new industrial product or to modify the price of existing products. The price setter must know the firm's objectives, markets, costs, competition, and customer demand patterns—not easy when time is short, information is incomplete, and the competitive and business climate is changing rapidly.

This chapter is divided into five parts. First, the special meaning of price is defined in a business marketing context. Second, key determinants of the industrial pricing process are analyzed, and an operational approach to pricing decisions is provided. Third, pricing policies for new and existing products are examined, emphasizing the need to actively manage a product throughout its life cycle. Fourth, price administration (that is, types of price adjustments) is considered, before finally turning to an area of particular importance to the business marketer: competitive bidding.

The Meaning of Price in Business Markets

When members of a buying center select a particular product, they are buying a given level of product quality, technical service, and delivery reliability. Other elements may be important—the reputation of the supplier, a feeling of security, friendship, and other personal benefits flowing from the buyer-seller relationship. Observe in Figure 15.1 that the attribute bundles sought by the buying center may fall into three categories: **product-specific** attributes (for example, product quality), **company-related** attributes (for example, reputation for technological excellence), and **salesperson-related** attributes (for example, dependability).[4]

Thus, the total product (as discussed in Chapter 10) is much more than its physical attributes. Likewise, the *cost* of an industrial good includes much more than the seller's *price*. Pricing decisions and product policy decisions are inseparable and must be balanced within the firm's market segmentation plan.[5]

BENEFITS

Various market segments, each with unique needs, base their evaluation of a product on dimensions of particular value to them. The benefits of a particular product can be functional, operational, financial, or personal.[6] These benefits are of varying degrees of importance to different market segments and to different individuals within

[3]Thomas T. Nagle, *The Strategy and Tactics of Pricing: A Guide to Profitable Decision Making* (Englewood Cliffs, N.J.: Prentice-Hall, 1987), p. 1.

[4]David T. Wilson, "Pricing Industrial Products and Services," Report #9-1986, Institute for the Study of Business Markets, College of Business Administration, The Pennsylvania State University.

[5]Benson P. Shapiro and Barbara B. Jackson, "Industrial Pricing to Meet Customer Needs," *Harvard Business Review* 56 (November/December 1978): p. 125.

[6]Ibid., pp. 119–127.

Figure 15.1 Pricing Environment: The Relationship between Buyer, Seller, and Competitor

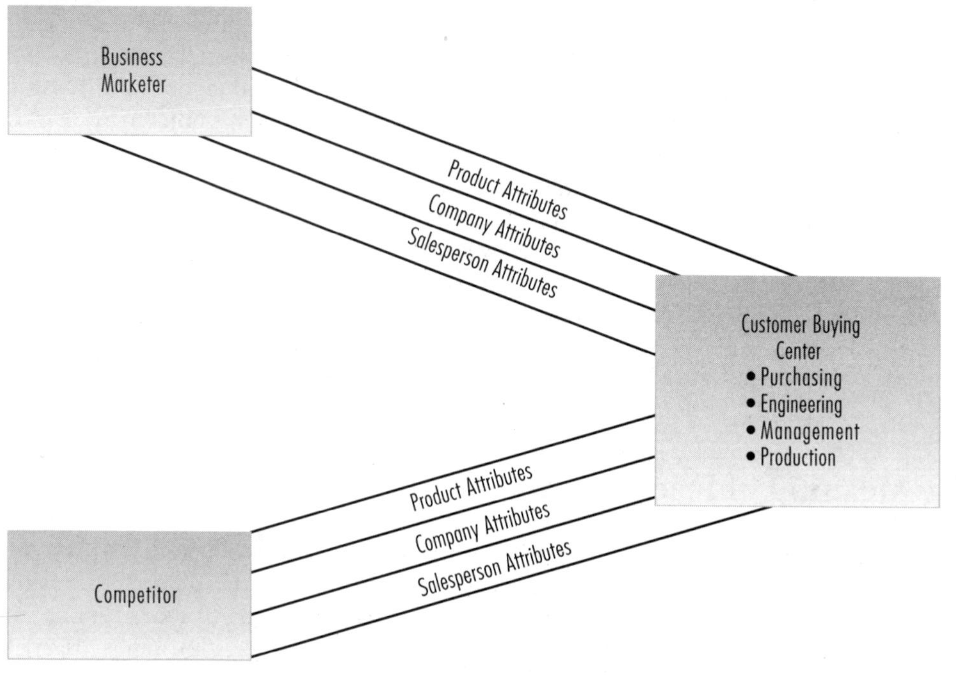

Source: Adapted with modifications from David T. Wilson, "Pricing Industrial Products and Services," Report #9-1986, Institute for the Study of Business Markets, The Pennsylvania State University.

the buying center. **Functional benefits** are the design characteristics that might be attractive to technical personnel. **Operational benefits** are durability and reliability, qualities desirable to production managers. **Financial benefits** are favorable terms and opportunities for cost savings, important to purchasing managers and controllers. Organizational status, reduced risk, and personal satisfaction are among the **personal benefits** that might accrue to an individual from a particular supplier choice.

COSTS

A broad perspective is likewise needed in examining the costs a particular alternative may present for the buyer. When purchasing a product or service, an organizational customer always assumes various costs above and beyond the actual purchase price. Rather than making a decision on the basis of price alone, organizational buyers emphasize the **total cost in use** of a particular product or service.[7] Observe in Table 15.1 that

[7]Frank V. Cespedes, "Industrial Marketing: Managing New Requirements," *Sloan Management Review* 35 (spring 1994): pp. 45–60.

Table 15.1 Customers' Cost-in-Use Components

Acquisition Costs	+	Possession Costs	+	Usage Costs	=	Total Cost in Use
Price Paperwork cost Transportation costs Expediting cost Cost of mistakes in order Prepurchase product evaluation costs		Interest cost Storage cost Quality control Taxes and insurance Shrinkage and obsolescence General internal handling costs		Installation costs Training cost User labor cost Product longevity Replacement costs Disposal costs		

Source: Adapted from Frank V. Cespedes, "Industrial Marketing: Managing New Requirements," *Sloan Management Review* 35 (spring 1994): p. 46.

three different types of costs are considered in a total cost-in-use calculation by an organizational customer:

1. **acquisition costs** include not only the selling price and transportation costs, but also the administrative costs of evaluating suppliers, expediting orders, and correcting errors in shipments or delivery.
2. **possession costs** include financing, storage, inspection, relevant taxes and insurance, and other internal handling costs.
3. **usage costs** involve costs associated with the ongoing utilization of the purchased product such as installation, employee training, user labor, field repair, as well as product replacement and disposal costs.

Value-Based Strategies[8]

Aided by sophisticated supplier evaluation systems (see Chapter 3), buyers can measure and track the total cost/value of dealing with alternative suppliers. In turn, astute business marketers can pursue value-based strategies that provide customers with a lower cost-in-use solution. For example, the logistical expenses associated with health-care supplies typically account for 10–15 percent of a hospital's operating costs. Medical products firms, like Becton, Dickinson and Company, develop innovative product/service packages that respond to each component of the cost-in-use equation. Such firms can reduce a hospital's acquisition costs by offering an electronic ordering system, its possession costs by emphasizing just-in-time service, and its usage costs by creating an efficient system for disposing of medical supplies after use.

[8]Frank V. Cespedes, *Concurrent Marketing: Integrating Product, Sales, and Service* (Boston: Harvard Business School Press, 1995), pp. 152–160.

THE COST IN USE OF A BOEING PASSENGER JET

American Airlines recently signed an agreement to purchase 103 jets from the Boeing Company valued at $6.5 billion at list prices. The agreement also incorporates a unique feature: American can buy an additional 527 airplanes at guaranteed prices. These purchase rights were granted by Boeing at no cost in exchange for American's agreement to buy Boeing planes exclusively until 2018. The agreement also gives American price protection in the event that Boeing later gives better terms to competing airlines than those specified in the contract. Throughout the contract period, American can buy jets at present prices with as little as 18 months' notice for large, widebody jets.

Over the next two decades, American's fleet will become an all-Boeing air force. To secure the exclusive contract, Boeing provided price concessions that it expects to more than recover through the expanded volume. By relying on a single manufacturer, American will reduce the total cost in use of each plane through reduced spare parts inventory, maintenance staff training, and flight crew training costs.

Source: Scott McCartney and Jeff Cole, "American Airlines Signs Exclusive Pact to Buy Boeing Jets for Two Decades," *The Wall Street Journal,* 22 November 1996, pp. A3, A6.

Value-based strategies seek to move the selling proposition from one that centers on current prices and individual transactions to a longer-term relationship built around value and lower total cost in use. The successful implementation of value-based strategies requires close coordination between the product, sales, and service units in the firm (see Chapter 10). Each unit performs activities that ultimately determine the customer's cost in use.

The Industrial Pricing Process

There is no easy formula for pricing an industrial product or service. The decision is multidimensional: The interactive variables of demand, cost, competition, profit relationships, and customer usage patterns each assume significance as the marketer formulates the role that price will play in the firm's marketing strategy. Pertinent considerations, illustrated in Figure 15.2, include (1) pricing objectives, (2) demand determinants, (3) cost determinants, and (4) competition. The additional considerations in the figure—effect on product line and legal implications of a particular pricing decision—are treated later in this chapter.

PRICE OBJECTIVES

The pricing decision must be based on objectives congruent with marketing and overall corporate objectives. The marketer starts with principal objectives and adds collateral

Figure 15.2 Key Components of the Industrial Pricing Process

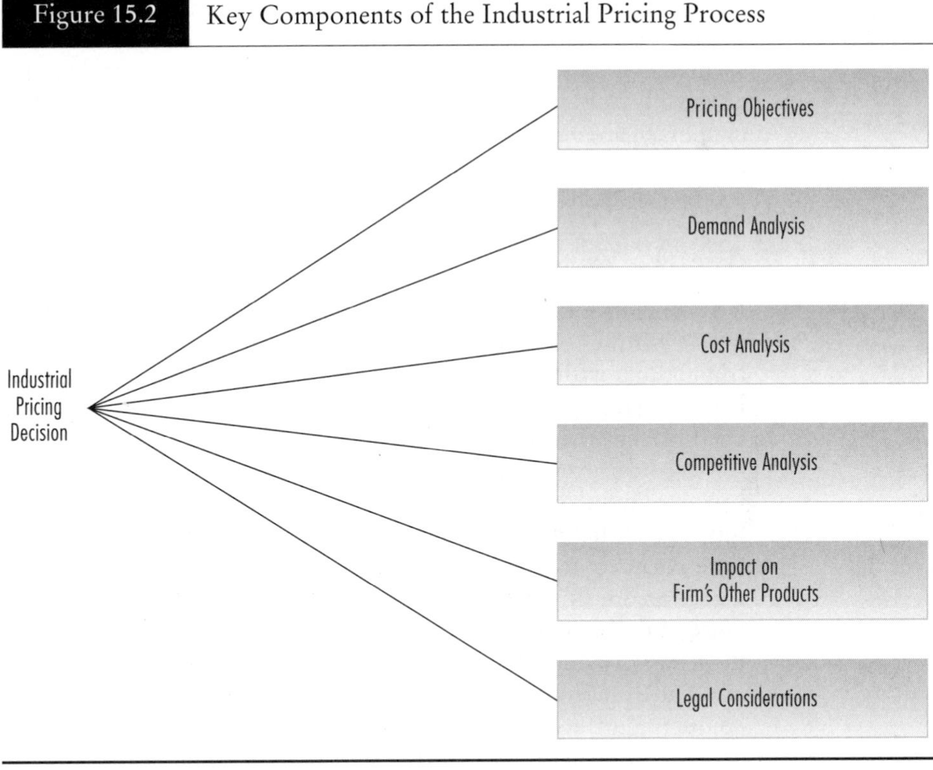

pricing goals: (1) achieving a target return on investment, (2) achieving a market-share goal, or (3) meeting competition. There are many other potential pricing objectives that extend beyond profit and market-share goals, taking into account competition, channel relationships, and product line considerations.

Because of their far-reaching effects, pricing objectives must be established with care. Each firm faces unique internal and external environmental forces. Contrasting the strategies of Du Pont and Dow Chemical Company illustrates the importance of a unified corporate direction. Dow's strategy focuses first on pricing low-margin commodity goods *low* to build a dominant market share and then on maintaining that dominant share. Du Pont's strategy, on the other hand, emphasizes specialty products that carry a higher margin. Initially, these products are priced at a *high* level, and prices are reduced as the market expands and competition intensifies. Each firm requires explicit pricing objectives that are consistent with its corporate mission.

DEMAND DETERMINANTS

A strong market perspective is fundamental in pricing. The business market is diverse and complex. A single industrial product can be used in many ways; each market segment may represent a unique application for the product and a separate usage level. The degree of importance of the industrial good in the buyer's end product also varies by market segment. Therefore, potential demand, sensitivity to price, and potential profitability can vary markedly across market segments. To establish an effective pricing policy, attention should center first on the value a customer will place on a product or service. This reverses the typical process that gives immediate attention to the product cost and the desired markup.[9]

Assessing Value[10]

How organizational buyers will evaluate the cost/benefit trade-offs of the total offering determines the appropriateness of a particular industrial pricing strategy. Two competitors with similar products may ask differing prices because their total offerings are perceived as being unique by buyers. In the eyes of the organizational buyer, one firm may provide more value than another.

A core pricing issue concerns which attributes of the offering contribute most to its perceived value. Table 15.2 identifies total product offering attributes that have value to buyers and that differ among competitors. Two levels of performance are provided for each attribute. Since higher costs are incurred in providing higher levels of performance on one or more of the attributes, the strategist should assess the relative importance of the attributes to different market segments and should assess the strength of the firm's offering on each of the important attributes vis-à-vis competitors.

The equation in Figure 15.3 highlights how the relative perceived values of two competing offerings are compared. Irv Gross contends that the relative perceived value of offering *A* versus offering *B* "can be thought of as the price differential at which the buyer would be indifferent between the alternatives."[11] As in Figure 15.3, the premium price differential, or perceived relative value, can be broken down into components based on each important attribute: (1) the value of the attribute to the buyer, and (2) the perception of how competing offerings perform on that attribute. By summing all of the component values, we reach the total relative perceived value of an offering. Thus, product offering *A* may have a total perceived value of $24 per unit, compared to $20 per unit for offering *B*. The $4 premium might be derived from the value that buyers assign to a high level of product quality and a responsive delivery system, and the perceived advantage of offering *A* over others on these attributes.

Strategy Implications of the Cost/Benefit Analysis

By isolating the important attributes and the perceptions that enter into the cost/benefit calculations of organizational buyers, the business marketer is better

---

[9]Robert J. Dolan, "How Do You Know When the Price Is Right?" *Harvard Business Review* 73 (September/October 1995): pp. 174–183.

[10]Irwin Gross, "Insights from Pricing Research," in *Pricing Practices and Strategies,* ed. Earl L. Bailey (New York: The Conference Board, 1978), pp. 34–39. See also Valerie Kijewski and Eunsang Yoon, "Market-Based Pricing: Beyond Price-Performance Curves," *Industrial Marketing Management* 19 (February 1990): pp. 11–19; and G. Dean Kortge and Patrick A. Okonkwo, "Perceived Value Approach to Pricing," *Industrial Marketing Management* 22 (May 1993): pp. 133–140.

[11]Gross, "Insights from Pricing Research," p. 35.

Table 15.2 Attributes of a Total Product Offering: Some Trade-Offs

Attribute	High Level	Low Level
Quality	Impurities less than one part per million	Impurities less than ten parts per million
Delivery	Within one week	Within two weeks
System	Supply total system	Supply chemical only
Innovation	High level of R&D support	Little R&D support
Retraining	Retrain on request	Train on initial purchase
Service	Locally available	Through home office

Source: Irwin Gross, "Insights from Pricing Research," in *Pricing Practices and Strategies,* ed. Earl L. Bailey (New York: The Conference Board, 1978), p. 37. Reprinted by permission of the Conference Board.

equipped to establish a price and to shape other elements of the marketing strategy. First, if the firm's performance on a highly valued product attribute is truly higher than that offered by competitors, but the market perceives no differences, marketing communications can be developed to bring perceptions into line with reality. Second, marketing communications may also alter the values that organizational buyers assign to a particular attribute. The importance of an attribute such as customer training might be elevated through marketing communications emphasizing the improved efficiency and safety that training affords the potential buying organization.

Third, the perceived value of the total product offering can be changed by improving the firm's level of performance on attributes that are assigned special importance by organizational buyers. Fourth, knowledge of the cost/benefit perceptions of potential customers presents market segmentation opportunities. For example, good strategy might target those market segments that value the particular product attributes where the firm has a clear competitive advantage.

Figure 15.3 Relative Perceived Value of Two Product Offerings

Source: Irwin Gross, "Insights from Pricing Research," in *Pricing Practices and Strategies,* ed. Earl L. Bailey (New York: The Conference Board, 1978), p. 38. Reprinted by permission.

Elasticity Varies by Market Segment

Price elasticity of demand is a measure of the degree to which customers are sensitive to price changes. Specifically, **price elasticity of demand** refers to the rate of percentage change in quantity demanded attributable to the percentage change in price. Price elasticity of demand is not the same at all prices. A business marketer contemplating an alteration in price policy must understand the elasticity of demand. For example, total revenue (price × quantity) will *increase* if price is decreased and demand is price elastic, whereas revenues will *fall* if the price is decreased and demand is price inelastic. Many factors influence the price elasticity of demand—the ease with which customers can compare alternatives and switch suppliers, the importance of the product in the cost structure of the customer's product, and the value that the product represents to a customer.

Search Behavior and Switching Costs

The price sensitivity of buyers increases—and a firm's pricing latitude decreases—to the degree that:[12]

- organizational buyers can easily shop around and assess the relative performance and price of alternatives. Purchasing managers in many firms use information technology to track supplier prices on a global basis.
- the product represents one for which it is easy to make price comparisons. For example, it is easier to compare alternative photocopiers than it is to compare specialized manufacturing equipment options.
- buyers can switch from one supplier to another without incurring additional costs. As highlighted in Chapter 3, low switching costs allow a buyer to focus on minimizing the cost of a particular transaction.

End Use

Important insights can be secured by answering this question: How important is the business marketer's product as an input into the total cost of the end product? If the business marketer's product has an insignificant effect on cost, demand is likely inelastic. Consider this example:

> *A manufacturer of precision electronic components was contemplating an across-the-board price decrease to increase sales. However, an item analysis of the product line revealed that some of its low-volume components had exotic applications. A technical customer used the component in an ultrasonic testing apparatus which was sold for $8,000 a unit. This fact prompted the electronics manufacturer to raise the price of the item. Ironically, the firm then*

[12]Dolan, "How Do You Know When the Price Is Right?" pp. 178–179.

experienced a temporary surge of demand for the item as purchasing agents stocked up in anticipation of future price increases.[13]

Of course, the marketer must temper this estimate with an analysis of the costs, availability, and suitability of substitutes. Generally, when the industrial product constitutes an important but low-cost input into the end product, price is less important than quality and delivery reliability.

When the industrial product input assumes a more substantial portion of the final product's total cost, changes in price may have an important effect on the demand for both the final product and the industrial product input. When demand in the final consumer market is price elastic, a reduction in the price of the end item (for example, a personal computer) that is caused by a price reduction of an industrial component (for example, a microprocessor) generates an increase in demand for the final product (personal computer) and, in turn, for the industrial product (microprocessor).

End Market Focus

Because the demand for many industrial products is derived from the demand for the product of which they are a part, a strong end-user focus is needed. The marketer can benefit by examining the trends and changing fortunes of important final consumer markets. Different sectors of the market grow at differing rates, confront differing levels of competition, and face differing short-run and long-run challenges. A downturn in the economy does not fall equally on all sectors. Pricing decisions demand a two-tiered market focus—on organizational customers and on final product customers. "All things being equal," comment Reed Moyer and Robert Boewadt, "an industrial supplier will have more success in passing on a price increase to customers who are prospering than to customers who are hard pressed."[14]

Value-Based Segmentation

The value that customers assign to a firm's offering can vary by market segment because the same industrial product may serve differing purposes for various customers. This underscores the important role of market segmentation in the development of profitable pricing strategies. Take Sealed Air Corporation, the innovative supplier of protective packaging materials including coated air bubbles.[15] The company recognized that for some applications of the product, viable substitutes were readily available to buyers. But for other applications, Sealed Air had an enormous advantage—for example, its packaging materials offered superior cushioning for heavy items with long shipping cycles. By identifying those applications where the firm

---

[13]Reed Moyer and Robert J. Boewadt, "The Pricing of Industrial Goods," *Business Horizons* 14 (June 1971): pp. 27–34; see also George Rostky, "Unveiling Market Segments with Technical Focus Research," *Business Marketing* 71 (October 1986): pp. 66–69.

[14]Moyer and Boewadt, "The Pricing of Industrial Goods," p. 30.

[15]Dolan, "How Do You Know When the Price Is Right?" pp. 176–177.

had a clear advantage and understanding the unique value differential in each setting, marketing managers were ideally equipped to tackle product line expansion and pricing decisions and to ignite the remarkable revenue growth that Sealed Air has experienced for nearly two decades.

Methods of Estimating Demand

How can the business marketer measure the price elasticity of demand? Some techniques rely on objective statistical data, others on the intuition and judgment of managers.

Test marketing, as a rule, is considered appropriate only for consumer-goods manufacturers. However, this technique should not be eliminated from the business marketer's repertoire. Industrial products that are sold to a large number of potential users, that have short usage cycles (permitting analysis of repurchase patterns), and that have feasible test market sites lend themselves to test marketing. Most high-priced capital items do not fit this profile; products like industrial paints and maintenance items do.

The **survey approach** examined in Chapter 5 can also be used to measure price elasticity, testing for willingness to buy at various prices or price ranges. On occasion, joint research with a consumer-goods customer could be conducted to survey final consumer demand. Because price is only one variable, the survey instrument must also probe for product and service perceptions. It would be useful to ascertain how organizational buyers view price in fundamental cost/benefit trade-offs. This broader perspective is particularly useful in isolating market segments.

When, as often happens, the price setter lacks time and resources, a more informal, subjective approach becomes practical. This technique, drawing upon executive experience, judgment, and customer knowledge, analyzes the relationship of price to other marketing mix variables such as product, promotion, and distribution strategies and a particular competitive setting.

Knowledge of the market is the cornerstone of industrial pricing. A strong market focus, which examines how consumers trade off benefits and costs in their decision making, establishes a base for assigning prices. In this precarious task, the goal is to estimate as precisely as possible the probable demand curve for the firm's product. Knowledge of demand patterns must be augmented by knowledge of costs.

COST DETERMINANTS

Business marketers often pursue a strong internal orientation; they base prices on their own costs, reaching the selling price by calculating unit costs and adding a percentage profit. A strict cost-plus philosophy of pricing overlooks customer perceptions of value, competition, and the interaction of volume and profit. Many progressive firms, such as Canon, Toyota, and Hewlett-Packard (H-P), use target costing to capture a significant competitive advantage in the marketplace (see Chapter 4).

Target Costing

Target costing features a design-to-cost philosophy that begins by examining the marketplace: The firm identifies and targets the most attractive market segments.[16] It then determines what level of quality and types of product attributes will be required to succeed in each segment, given a predetermined target price and volume level. The firm then breaks down the target cost of a new product into a cascade of target costs for each subassembly, component, or part. Organizational members then design the product, plan the production process, and select the suppliers that will enable the firm to achieve its desired cost target and profit goals.

A Profit-Management Tool

Toyota used target costing to reduce the price of its 1997 Camry model and did so while offering as standard equipment certain features that were expensive options on the model it replaced. Similarly, Canon used target costing to develop its breakthrough personal copier that transformed the photocopier industry.[17] Rather than a cost-control technique, Japanese managers who pioneered the approach view target costing as a profit-management tool. As Robin Cooper and W. Bruce Chew assert, "The task is to compute the costs that must not be exceeded if acceptable margins from specific products at specific price points are to be guaranteed."[18]

Classifying Costs[19]

The target costing approach stresses why the marketer must know which costs are relevant to the pricing decision and how these costs will fluctuate with volume and over time; they must be considered in relation to demand, competition, and pricing objectives.. Product costs are crucial in projecting the profitability of individual products as well as of the entire product line. Proper classification of costs is essential.

The goals of a cost classification system are to (1) properly classify cost data into their fixed and variable components and (2) properly link them to the activity causing them. The manager can then analyze the effects of volume and, more important, identify sources of profit. The following cost concepts are instrumental in the analysis:

1. *Direct traceable or attributable costs:* Costs, fixed or variable, are incurred by and solely for a particular product, customer, or sales territory (for example, raw materials).

---

[16]Robin Cooper and W. Bruce Chew, "Control Tomorrow's Costs through Today's Designs," *Harvard Business Review* 74 (January/February 1996): pp. 88–97.
[17]Jean-Phillippe Deschamps and P. Ranganath Nayak, *Product Juggernauts: How Companies Mobilize to Generate a Stream of Market Winners* (Boston: Harvard Business School Press, 1995), pp. 119–149.
[18]Cooper and Chew, p. 95.
[19]Kent B. Monroe, *Pricing: Making Profitable Decisions* (New York: McGraw-Hill, 1979), pp. 52–57. See also Nagle, *The Strategy and Tactics of Pricing*, pp. 14–43.

2. *Indirect traceable costs:* Costs, fixed or variable, can be traced to a product, customer, or sales territory (for example, general plant overhead may be indirectly assigned to a product).

3. *General costs:* Costs support a number of activities that cannot be objectively assigned to a product on the basis of a direct physical relationship (for example, the administrative costs of a sales district).

General costs will rarely change because an item is added or deleted from the product line. Marketing, production, and distribution costs must all be classified. When developing a new line or when deleting an item or adding an item to an existing line, the marketer must grasp the cost implications:

- What proportion of the product cost is accounted for by purchases of raw materials and components from suppliers?
- How will costs vary at differing levels of production?
- Based on the forecasted level of demand, can economies of scale be expected?
- Does our firm enjoy cost advantages over competitors?
- How does the experience effect impact our cost projections?

Experience Effect

The marketing strategist must also consider the behavior of costs over time. The experience effect is a concept of strategic importance in forecasting costs and, in turn, prices. The experience curve reflects the theory that costs (measured in constant dollars) decline by a predictable and constant percentage each time accumulated production experience (volume) is doubled. Thus, each time accumulated volume is doubled, the unit costs of many products fall, usually by 20 to 30 percent.[20] The experience curve effect encompasses a broad range of manufacturing, marketing, distribution, and administrative costs.

The three major sources of the experience effect are (1) learning by doing, (2) technological improvements, and (3) economies of scale.[21] Figure 15.4 traces the cost experience for steam turbine generators. The cost per megawatt of output of steam generators followed a 70 percent slope (alternatively, a 30 percent reduction in costs for every doubling in production). The sources of the decline in costs resulted from (1) practice in producing units of each size, which followed an 87 percent slope; (2) scale economies derived from building larger (600-megawatt rather than 200-megawatt)

[20]William J. Abernathy and Kenneth Wayne, "Limits of the Learning Curve," *Harvard Business Review* 52 (September/October 1974): pp. 109–119. See also Staff of the Boston Consulting Group, *Perspectives on Experience* (Boston: Boston Consulting Group, 1972).

[21]George S. Day and David B. Montgomery, "Diagnosing the Experience Curve," *Journal of Marketing* 47 (spring 1983): pp. 44–58. See also George S. Day, *Analysis for Strategic Market Decisions* (St. Paul, Minn: West Publishing Company, 1986), pp. 25–56.

Figure 15.4 Cost Experience for Steam Turbine Generators

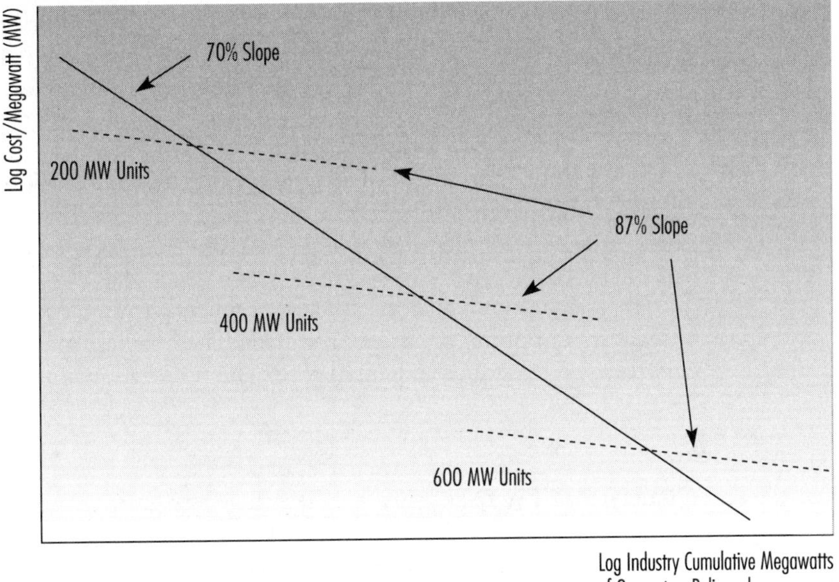

Source: George S. Day and David B. Montgomery, "Diagnosing the Experience Curve," *Journal of Marketing* 47 (spring 1983): p. 47. Reprinted by permission of the American Marketing Association.

units; and (3) technological improvements in such areas as bearings and high-strength steels, which permitted the design of larger units.[22]

Strategic Relevance of Experience

Unfortunately, as experience is gained, costs do not automatically decline. In fact, costs that are not carefully managed will inevitably rise. Experience merely gives management the opportunity to seek cost reductions and efficiency improvements. A thorough effort is needed to exploit the benefits of experience. Product standardization, new production processes, labor efficiency, and work specialization are only a few of the many areas that must be examined to capitalize on the experience effect.

The experience effect can raise a strategic dilemma for the business marketer. Often, the aggressive pursuit of a cost minimization strategy leads to a reduced ability to make innovative product changes in the face of competition.[23] Clearly, any firm following an efficiency strategy must ensure that its product remains in line

[22]Ralph Sultan, *Pricing in the Electrical Oligopoly*, vols. I and II (Cambridge, Mass.: Harvard Graduate School of Business Administration, 1974), cited in Day and Montgomery, "Diagnosing the Experience Curve."

[23]Abernathy and Wayne, "Limits of the Learning Curve," pp. 109–119.

with the needs of the market. A product that is efficiently produced and carries a low price can survive only if significant market segments emphasize low price as a choice criterion.

The experience effect can be used to project costs and prices. The concept is also valuable when product line modifications are being considered. Often, two or more products in the firm's line share a common resource or involve the same production or distribution activity. With such shared experience, the costs of one item in the product line are reduced even more because of the accumulated experience with the other product-line item. For example, the same production operations may be used to produce high-torque motors for oil exploration and low-torque motors for conveyor belts.[24] The marketer that has carefully classified costs is best equipped to take advantage of shared experience opportunities.

Experience curve analysis is relevant when learning, technology, and economies of scale are important in the environment. The business marketer can use experience curve analysis to project potential cost reduction opportunities.

COMPETITION

Competition establishes an upper limit on price. An individual industrial firm's degree of latitude in its pricing decision depends heavily on the product's level of differentiation in the perceptions of organizational buyers. Price is only one component of the cost/benefit equation of buyers; the marketer can gain a differential advantage over competitors on many dimensions other than physical product characteristics—dimensions such as reputation, technical expertise, delivery reliability, and related factors. Regis McKenna contends that "Even if a company manufactures commodity-like products, it can differentiate the products through the service and support it offers, or by target marketing. It can leave its commodity mentality in the factory, and bring a mentality of diversity to the marketplace."[25] In addition to assessing the product's degree of differentiation in various market segments, one must ask how competitors will respond to particular pricing decisions.

Hypercompetitive Rivalries

Some strategy experts emphasize that traditional patterns of competition in stable environments is being replaced by hypercompetitive rivalries in a rapidly changing environment.[26] In a stable environment, a company could create a fairly rigid strategy designed to accommodate long-term conditions. The firm's strategy focuses on sustaining its own strategic advantage and to establish equilibrium where less dominant firms in the industry accepted a secondary status.

---

[24]Day and Montgomery, "Diagnosing the Experience Curve," p. 54.

[25]Regis McKenna, *Relationship Marketing* (Reading, Mass.: Addison-Wesley, 1991), pp. 178–179.

[26]D'Aveni, *Hypercompetitive Rivalries*, pp. 149–170.

Managing in the 21st Century

THE PRICE/PERFORMANCE ENGINE IN HIGH-TECHNOLOGY MARKETING

The driver behind the rapidly escalating price/performance equation in high-tech products is the semiconductor integrated circuit. Price/performance increased by a power of ten during the decade of the 1970s; it sped to a tenfold increase in seven years during the 1980s; and it has experienced a tenfold increase every 3–5 years in the 1990s. In other words, ten times the performance has been provided at the same price three different times in the 1990s, and the rate of progress is still accelerating.

Firms that compete in this intensely competitive environment cannot rest on past successes—they must prepare for the next tornado. Geoffrey Moore maintains that infinite improvements in the price/performance of high-tech products generate a rapid series of paradigm shifts. "Each time the underlying constructs that shape the current paradigm are removed, the design trade-offs that characterize its strategy become obsolete, and a new generation of capabilities are enabled." Business marketers who built a position of strength under the old paradigm must switch to the new—or else leave themselves open to attack from new competitors that enter on each new technology wave.

Source: Geoffrey A. Moore, *Inside the Tornado: Marketing Strategies from Silicon Valley's Cutting Edge* (New York: HarperCollins, 1995), p. 104.

In hypercompetitive environments, successful companies pursue strategies that create temporary advantage and destroy the advantages of rivals by constantly disrupting the equilibrium of the market. For example, Intel continually disrupts the equilibrium of the microprocessor industry sector and H-P stirs up the computer printer business by its consistent drives to lower price points. Leading firms in hypercompetitive environments constantly seek out new sources of advantage, further escalating competition and contributing to hypercompetition.

Consider the hypercompetitive rivalries in high-technology markets. Firms that sustain quality and that are the first to hit the next lower strategic price point enjoy a burst of volume and an expansion of market share. However, as Geoffrey A. Moore observes, some firms hold off matching the price reduction to sustain profitability:

> *Fat margins are a habit that is hard to kick. IBM couldn't kick it when Compaq underpriced them, nor could Compaq when Dell underpriced them. Both companies have since reversed their courses, but not before institutionalizing a permanent rival to their core business. H-P, by contrast, has ruthlessly pursued the next lower price point, even as it cannibalized its own sales and margins. As Lew Platt, H-P's CEO, likes to put it, "If we don't eat our own lunch, somebody else will."*[27]

(See Figure 15.5 for an example of Hewlett-Packard's aggressive pricing strategy.)

[27] Geoffrey A. Moore, *Inside the Tornado: Marketing Strategies from Silicon Valley's Cutting Edge* (New York: HarperCollins, 1995), pp. 84–85.

Figure 15.5 Hewlett-Packard Ad Emphasizing the Firm's Aggressive Pricing Strategy

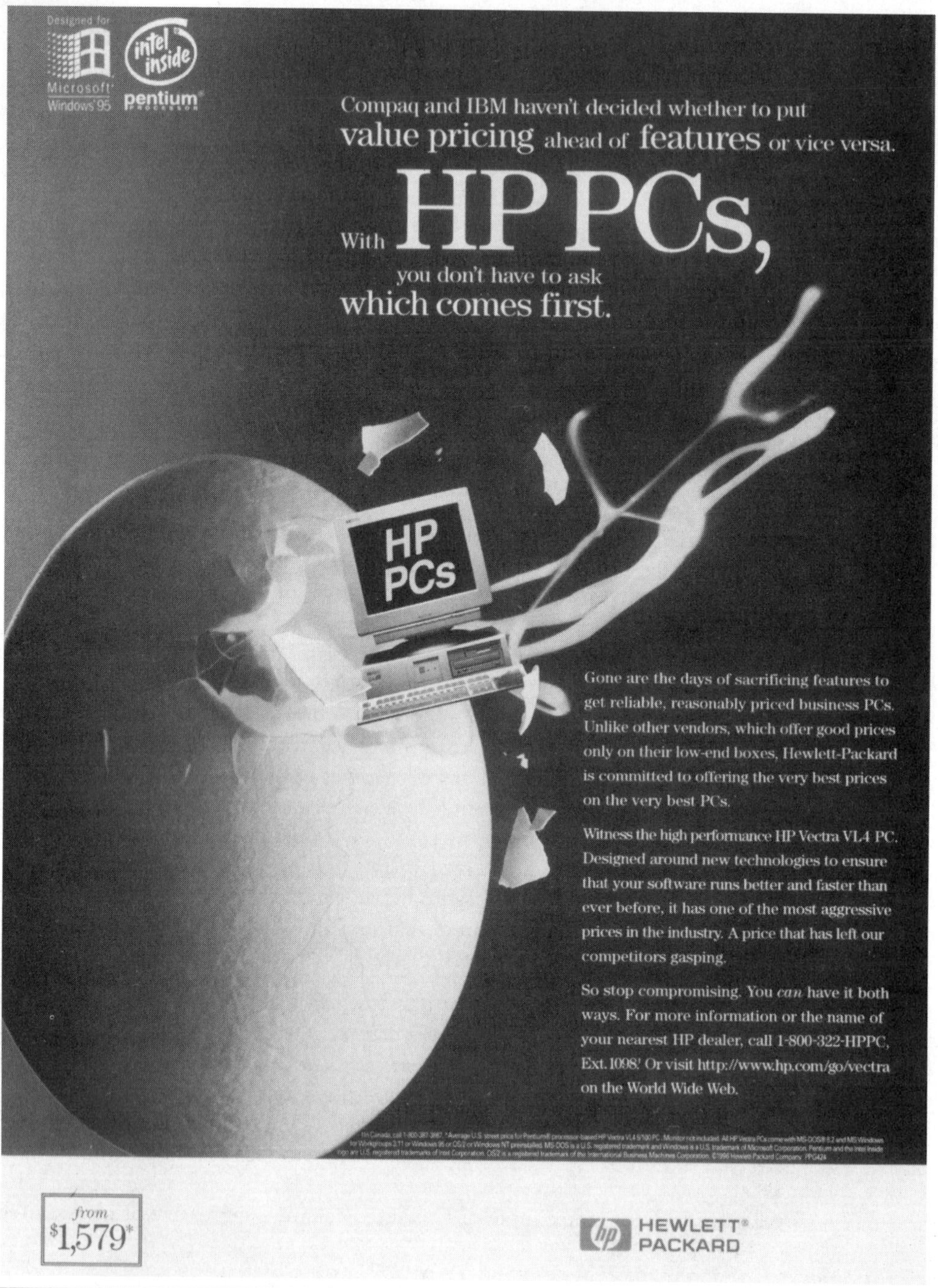

Source: Courtesy Hewlett-Packard Company.

Table 15.3 Selected Cost Comparison Issues: Followers versus the Pioneer

Technology/economies of scale	Followers may benefit by using more current production technology than the pioneer or by building a plant with a larger scale of operations.
Product/market knowledge	Followers may learn from the pioneer's mistakes by analyzing the competitor's product, hiring key personnel, or identifying through market research the problems and unfulfilled expectations of customers and channel members.
Shared experience	Compared to the pioneer, followers may be able to gain advantages on certain cost elements by sharing operations with other parts of the company.
Experience of suppliers	Followers, together with the pioneer, benefit from cost reductions achieved by outside suppliers of components or production equipment.

Source: Adapted from George S. Day and David B. Montgomery, "Diagnosing the Experience Curve," *Journal of Marketing* 47 (spring 1983): pp. 48–49.

Gauging Competitive Response

To predict the response of competitors, the marketer can first benefit by examining the cost structure and strategy of both direct competitors and producers of potential substitutes. The marketer can draw upon public statements and records (for example, annual reports) to form rough estimates. The experience effect can also be used to assess the cost structure of competition. Competitors that have ascended the learning curve may have lower costs than those just entering the industry and beginning the climb. An estimate of the cost structure is valuable when gauging how well competitors can respond to price reductions and when projecting the pattern of prices in the future.

Under certain conditions, however, followers into a market may confront lower initial costs than did the pioneer. Why? Some of the reasons are highlighted in Table 15.3. By failing to recognize potential cost advantages of late entrants, the business marketer can dramatically overstate cost differences.

The market strategy employed by competing sellers is also important here. Competitors will be more sensitive toward price reductions that threaten those market segments they deem important. They learn of price reductions earlier when their market segments overlap. Of course, competitors may choose not to follow a price decrease, especially if their products enjoy a differentiated position. Rather than matching the price cuts of competitors, one successful medical supplies firm promptly reacts to the competitive challenge by enhancing service benefits such as speed of delivery.[28]

The manager requires a grasp of objectives, demand, cost, competition, and legal factors (discussed later) to approach the multidimensional pricing decision. Price setting is not an act but an ongoing process.

[28]Robert A. Garda, "How to Avoid a Price War," *The Wall Street Journal*, 10 May 1993, p. A12.

Pricing Across the Product Life Cycle

What price should be assigned to a distinctly new industrial product or service? When an item is added to an existing product line, how should it be priced in relation to products already in the line?

PRICING NEW PRODUCTS

The strategic decision of pricing new products can be best understood by examining the policies at the boundaries of the continuum—from **skimming** (high initial price) to **penetration** (low initial price). Consider again the pricing strategies of Du Pont and Dow Chemical. Whereas Du Pont assigns an initial high price to new products in order to generate immediate profits or to recover R&D expenditures, Dow Chemical follows a low price strategy with the objective of gaining market share.

In evaluating the merits of skimming compared to penetration, the marketer must again examine price from the buyer's perspective. This approach, asserts Joel Dean, "recognizes that the upper limit is the price that will produce the minimum acceptable rate of return on the investment of a sufficiently large number of prospects."[29] This is especially important in pricing new products, because the potential profits accruing to buyers of a new machine tool, for example, will vary by market segment, and these market segments may differ in the minimum rate of return that will induce them to invest in the machine tool.

Skimming

A skimming approach, appropriate for a distinctly new product, provides the firm with an opportunity to profitably reach market segments that are not sensitive to the high initial price. As a product ages, as competitors enter the market, and as organizational buyers become accustomed to evaluating and purchasing the product, demand becomes more price elastic. The policy of using skimming at the outset, followed by penetration pricing as the product matures, is referred to by Joel Dean as **time segmentation.**[30] A skimming policy enables the marketer to capture early profits, then reduce the price to reach segments that are more price sensitive. It also enables the innovator to recover high developmental costs more quickly.

Robert Dolan and Abel Jeuland demonstrate that during the innovative firm's monopoly period, a skimming policy is optimal if the demand curve is stable over time (no diffusion) and if production costs decline with accumulated volume, whereas a penetration policy is optimal if there is a relatively high repeat purchase rate for nondurable goods or if a durable good's demand is characterized by diffusion.[31]

---

[29]Joel Dean, "Pricing Policies for New Products," *Harvard Business Review* 54 (November/December 1976): p. 151.

[30]Ibid., p. 152.

[31]Robert J. Dolan and Abel P. Jeuland, "Experience Curves and Dynamic Demand Models: Implications for Optimal Pricing Strategies," *Journal of Marketing* 45 (winter 1981): pp. 52–62.

Ethical Business Marketing

ON ETHICS AND PRICING AT RAYTHEON

Because price negotiations present the opportunity for unfair, unethical, and even illegal behavior, most firms have established a set of business conduct guidelines. The following excerpts from Raytheon's standards of conduct for buying emphasize the importance of fairness in business relationships.

- Raytheon expects its procurement personnel to be fair, do no favors, and *accept no favors.* Accepting kickbacks is a crime—both morally and legally. It is the fastest way for procurement personnel to find the way out the door and for sellers to cease doing business with us.
- The rules apply to all Raytheon employees who influence the buying process.
- Gifts, services, or consideration other than an advertising novelty such as a paperweight, key chain, or coffee cup will be returned to the supplier.
- Luncheons with suppliers should not be encouraged. Under some circumstances they are necessary if there is a legitimate business purpose for the get-together. But they should not be a habit. Company facilities should be used wherever possible.
- Raytheon's goal has been to establish a reputation in the marketplace that meets the highest standards of ethical conduct. We want to protect this reputation for both Raytheon and our suppliers.

Source: Robert L. Janson, Linda A. Grass, Arnold J. Lovering, and Robert C. Parker, "Ethics and Responsibility," in *The Purchasing Handbook,* ed. Harold E. Fearon, Donald W. Dobler, and Kenneth H. Killen (New York: McGraw-Hill, 1993), pp. 360–361.

Penetration

A penetration policy is appropriate when there is (1) high price elasticity of demand, (2) strong threat of imminent competition, and (3) opportunity for a substantial reduction in production costs as volume expands. Drawing upon the experience effect, a firm that can quickly gain substantial market share and experience can gain a strategic advantage over competitors. The viability of this strategy increases with the potential size of the future market. By taking a large share of new sales, experience can be gained when there is a large market growth rate. Of course, the value of additional market share differs markedly between industries and often among products, markets, and competitors within a particular industry.[32] Factors to be assessed in determining the value of additional market share include the investment requirements, potential benefits of experience, expected market trends, likely competitive reaction, and short- and long-term profit implications.

[32]Robert Jacobsen and David A Aaker, "Is Market Share All that It's Cracked Up to Be?" *Journal of Marketing* 49 (fall 1985): pp. 11–22; and Yoram Wind and Vijay Mahajan, "Market Share: Concepts, Findings, and Directions for Future Research," in *Review of Marketing 1981,* ed. Ben M. Enis and Kenneth J. Roering (Chicago: American Marketing Association, 1981), pp. 31–42.

Product Line Considerations

The contemporary industrial firm with a long product line faces the complex problem of achieving balance in pricing the product mix. Firms extend their product lines because the demands for various products are interdependent, because the costs of producing and marketing those items are interdependent, or both.[33] A firm may add to its product line—or even develop a new product line—to fit more precisely the needs of a particular market segment. If both the demand and the costs of individual product line items are interrelated, production and marketing decisions about one product line item inevitably influence both the revenues and costs of the others.

Are specific product line items substitutes or complements? Will a change in the price of one item enhance or retard the usage rate of this or other products in key market segments? Should a new product be priced high at the outset in order to protect other product line items (for example, potential substitutes) and in order to give the firm time to revamp other items in the line? Such decisions require a knowledge of demand, costs, competition, and strategic marketing objectives.

TACTICAL PRICING[34]

Tactical pricing constitutes an important component of price administration and considers the unique customer and order-specific costs of each transaction. Such a customer-specific focus is fundamental in developing and managing successful relationship strategies in the business market. The goal of tactical pricing, asserts Robert Garda, is "to optimize the frequently competing selling objectives of winning orders, maximizing order profitability, building long-term account value, and assuring competitive positioning in the marketplace."[35] Sound tactical pricing issues from a well-developed marketing intelligence system (see Chapter 5) that can provide detailed information by customer. Figure 15.6 provides the information that might be assembled to support a tactical pricing decision for an important customer account. This system aids the price setter in forecasting competitive pricing and in establishing the firm's pricing strategy in line with vivid price/probability trade-offs.

Win/Loss

An especially valuable tool for gauging the behavior of competitors and customers is **win/loss analysis.** What factors did a salesperson feel were decisive in winning a particular account? In a head-to-head battle with a new competitor, how well did our strategy hold

---

[33]Monroe, *Pricing*, p. 143; see also Robert J. Dolan, "The Same Make, Many Models Problem: Managing the Product Line," in *A Strategic Approach to Business Marketing*, ed. Robert E. Spekman and David T. Wilson (Chicago: American Marketing Association, 1985), pp. 151–159.

[34]Robert A. Garda, "Use of Tactical Pricing to Uncover Hidden Profits," *Journal of Business Strategy* 12 (September/October 1991): pp. 17–23.

[35]Ibid., p. 19.

Figure 15.6 Tactical Pricing: The Supporting Information System

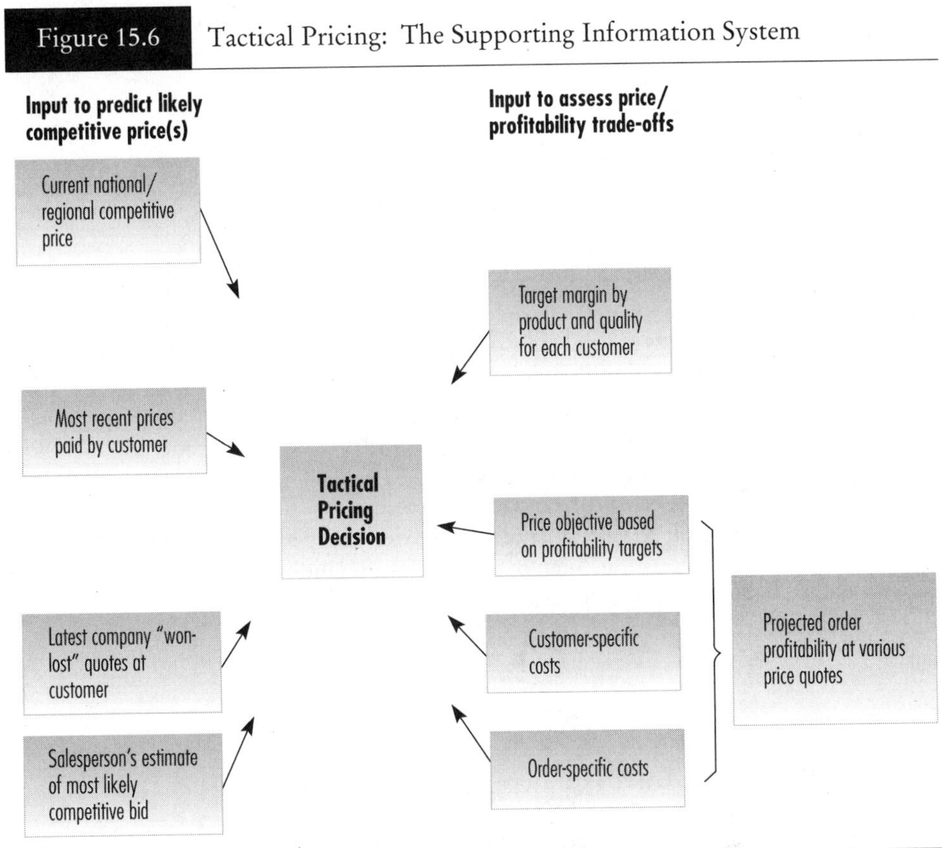

Source: Adapted with modifications from Robert A. Garda, "Use of Tactical Pricing to Uncover Hidden Profits," *Journal of Business Strategy* 12 (September/October 1991): p. 22. Reprinted with permission by Faulkner and Gray, Inc., 11 Penn Plaza, New York, N.Y. 10001.

up? Which factors prompt some of our accounts to switch to a competitor? What strategy did a particular salesperson follow who won back a major account? Win/loss analysis also provides insight into how customers define value. Often, contends Bradley Gale, "when the competition wins a battle on price, either the competition has learned to deliver at lower cost than you or the potential customer didn't believe your salespeople when they discussed the quality attributes that *should* have made your product worth more."[36]

The business marketer cannot leave price administration to chance. Discounts must be aligned with the firm's pricing policies and related to the requirements of key market segments. Pricing policies are often based on a defensive, or risk-aversive, perspective rather than on a positive one.[37] For example, industrial firms might offer larger

[36]Bradley T. Gale, *Managing Customer Value: Creating Quality and Service that Customers Can See* (New York: The Free Press, 1994), p. 222.

[37]Joseph P. Guiltinan, "Risk-Aversive Pricing Policies: Problems and Alternatives," *Journal of Marketing* 40 (January 1976): pp. 10–15.

quantity discounts in order to partially offset price increases; opportunities for revising discount schedules may emerge as costs change. Tradition-bound firms can easily overlook creative uses of pricing policies.

LEGAL CONSIDERATIONS

Since the business marketer deals with various classifications of customers and intermediaries as well as various types of discounts (for example, quantity discounts), an awareness of legal considerations in price administration is vital. The Robinson-Patman Act holds that it is unlawful to "discriminate in price between different purchasers of commodities of like grade and quality . . . where the effect of such discrimination may be substantially to lessen competition or tend to create a monopoly, or to injure, destroy, or prevent competition. . . ." Price differentials are permitted, but they must be based on cost differences or the need to "meet competition."[38] Cost differentials are difficult to justify, and clearly defined policies and procedures are needed in price administration. Such cost justification guidelines are useful not only when making pricing decisions, but also when providing a legal defense against price discrimination charges.

Competitive Bidding

A significant volume of business in the business market is transacted through competitive bidding. Rather than relying on a specific list price, the business marketer must develop a price, or a bid, to meet particular product or service requirements of a customer.

Buying by government and other public agencies is done almost exclusively by competitive bidding. Competitive bidding in private industry is less frequent and is usually applied to the purchase of nonstandard materials, complex fabricated products where design and manufacturing methods vary, and products made to the buyer's specifications. The types of items procured through competitive bidding are those for which there is no generally established market level. Competitive bids enable the purchaser to evaluate the appropriateness of the prices.[39] Competitive bidding may be either closed or open.

---

[38]For a comprehensive discussion of the Robinson-Patman Act, see Monroe, *Pricing*, pp. 249–267; see also James J. Ritterskamp Jr. and William A. Hancock, "Legal Aspects of Purchasing," in *The Purchasing Handbook*, ed. Harold E. Fearon, Donald W. Dobler, and Kenneth H. Killen (New York: McGraw-Hill, 1993), pp. 529–544.

[39]Stuart St. P. Slatter, "Strategic Marketing Variables under Conditions of Competitive Bidding," *Strategic Management Journal* 11 (May/June 1990): pp. 309–317; see also Arthur H. Mendel and Roger Poueymirou, "Pricing," in *The Purchasing Handbook*, ed. Harold E. Fearon, Donald W. Dobler, and Kenneth H. Killen (New York: McGraw-Hill, 1993), pp. 201–227.

CLOSED BIDDING

Closed bidding, often used by industrial and governmental buyers, involves a formal invitation to potential suppliers to submit written, sealed bids for a particular business opportunity. All bids are opened and reviewed at the same time, and the contract is generally awarded to the lowest bidder who meets desired specifications. The low bidder is not guaranteed the contract—buyers often make awards to the lowest responsible bidder; the ability of alternative buyers to perform remains part of the bidding process.

OPEN BIDDING

Open bidding is more informal and allows suppliers to make offers (oral and written) up to a certain date. The buyer may deliberate with several suppliers throughout the bidding process. Open bidding may be particularly appropriate when specific requirements are hard to define rigidly or when the products and services of competing suppliers vary substantially.

In selected buying situations, negotiated pricing may be employed. Complex technical requirements or uncertain product specifications may lead buying organizations first to evaluate the capabilities of competing industrial firms and then to negotiate the price and the form of the product-service offering. Negotiated pricing is appropriate for procurement decisions in both the commercial and the governmental sectors of the business market (see Chapter 2).

STRATEGIES FOR COMPETITIVE BIDDING

Careful planning is fundamental to success in competitive bidding. Planning has three important steps: (1) precise definition of objectives, (2) a screening procedure for evaluating alternative bid opportunities, and (3) a method for assessing the probability of success for a particular bidding strategy.

Objectives

Before preparing a bid for any potential contract, the industrial firm must carefully define its objectives. This helps the firm to decide what types of business to pursue, when to bid, and how much to bid. The objectives may range from profit maximization to company survival. Other objectives might be to keep the plant operating and the labor force intact or to enter a new type of business. The marketer can also benefit by analyzing the objectives of likely bidding rivals.

Screening Bid Opportunities

Because developing bids is costly and time-consuming, contracts to bid on should be chosen with care. Contracts offer differing levels of profitability according to the related technical expertise, past experience, and objectives of the bidding firm. Thus, a screening procedure[40] is required to isolate the contracts that offer the most promise (see Table 15.4).

The use of a screening procedure to evaluate contracts has improved the bidding success of business marketers.[41] The procedure has three steps: First, the firm identifies criteria for evaluating contracts. Although the number and nature of the criteria vary by firm and industry, five prebid factors are common:

1. The impact of the contract on plant capacity
2. The degree of experience the firm has had with similar projects
3. Follow-up bid opportunities
4. Expected competition
5. Delivery requirements

Second, once identified, the prebid factors are assigned weights based on their relative importance to the firm (for example, a weight of 25 out of the total of 100 is assigned to plant capacity). The third step is to evaluate each factor, giving it a high (10), medium (5), or low (0) value. In Table 15.4, the contract is evaluated favorably on all factors except follow-up bid opportunities. Summing the product of each factor's weight and rating provides a total score. The business marketer can use this procedure to evaluate alternative potential contracts. The firm may wish to establish a minimum acceptable score before effort will be invested in preparing a bid. Since the bid opportunity evaluated in Table 15.4 yields a score above the cutoff point, a bid would be prepared.

Bidding Strategy

Having isolated a project opportunity, the marketer must now estimate the probabilities of winning the contract at various prices. Assuming that the contract is awarded to the lowest bidder, the chances of the firm winning the contract decline as the bid price increases. How will competitors bid?

In many industries, business marketers confront situations in which the supplier winning the initial contract has the advantage in securing long-term follow-up business. To illustrate, suppliers bidding on contracts to meet 3M's worldwide office equipment needs often provide attractive bids in order to secure an initial relationship with the centralized purchasing unit.[42] Although some immediate profit may be sacrificed, the low bid is seen as an investment that will lead to a continuing stream of profitable follow-up business.

---

[40]This method is adapted from Stephen Paranka, "Competitive Bidding Strategy," *Business Horizons* 14 (June 1971): pp. 39–43; see also Stephen Paranka, "Question: To Bid or Not to Bid? Answer: Strategic Prebid Analysis," *Marketing News,* 4 April 1980, p. 16.

[41]For example, see Paul D. Boughton, "The Competitive Bidding Process: Beyond Probability Models," *Industrial Marketing Management* 16 (May 1987): pp. 87–94.

[42]Margaret Nelson, "3M Centralizes Its Office Buy," *Purchasing* 101 (25 June 1987): pp. 62–65.

Table 15.4 Evaluation of a Bid Opportunity

Prebid Factors	Weight	Rating: High (10)	Rating: Medium (5)	Rating: Low (0)	Score
Plant capacity	25	10			250
Degree of experience	20	10			200
Follow-up bid opportunities	15			0	0
Competition	25	10			250
Delivery requirements	15	10			150
Total	100				850

Note: Ideal bid score is 1,000; minimum acceptable score is 750.

In pursuing this type of bidding strategy, the business marketer must carefully assess the strength of the association between the initial contract and the follow-up business opportunities. For example, the purchase of an office automation system may bond the buyer to a particular seller, thus providing the potential for future business. The costs of switching to another supplier are high because the buyer has made investments in employee training and in new business procedures, as well as in the equipment itself.[43] Such investments create inertia against change. By contrast, for more standardized purchases, such bonding does not occur because the costs of switching to another supplier are quite low for the buyer. In determining the initial bid strategy, the business marketer should examine the strength of the buyer-seller relationship, the probability of securing additional business, and the expected return from that business.

Summary

At the outset, the business marketer must assign pricing its role in the firm's overall marketing strategy. Giving a particular industrial product or service, an "incorrect" price can trigger a chain of events that undermines the firm's market position, channel relationships, and product and personal selling strategies. Price is but one of the costs that buyers examine in the buying process. Thus, the marketer can profit by adopting a strong end-user focus that gives special attention to the way buyers trade off the costs and benefits of various products. Responsive pricing strategies can be developed by understanding the total cost in use of a product for a customer. Value-based strategies can then be designed for particular business market segments.

---

[43] Barbara Bund Jackson, "Build Customer Relationships That Last," *Harvard Business Review* 63 (November/December 1985): pp. 120–128.

Price setting is a multidimensional decision. To establish a price, the manager must identify the firm's objectives and analyze the behavior of demand, costs, and competition. Hypercompetitive rivalries characterize the nature of competition in many high-technology industry sectors. Although this task is clouded with uncertainty, the industrial pricing decision must be approached actively rather than passively. For example, many business marketing firms use target costing to capture a competitive advantage in the business market. Likewise, by isolating demand, cost, or competitive patterns, the manager can gain insights into market behavior and opportunities that have been neglected. Tactical tools, such as win/loss analysis, can be used to refine pricing decisions.

Competitive bidding, a unique feature of the industrial market, calls for a unique strategy. Again, carefully defined objectives are the cornerstone of strategy. These objectives, combined with a meticulous screening procedure, help the firm to identify projects that mesh with company capability.

Discussion Questions

1. A Pac-10 university library recently purchased 60 personal computers from Dell Computer. Illustrate how a purchasing specialist at the university could employ a total cost-in-use approach in evaluating the value of the Dell offering in relation to the value provided by its rivals.

2. Explain why it is often necessary for the business marketer to develop a separate demand curve for various segments of the market. Would one total demand curve be better for making the industrial pricing decision? Explain.

3. Evaluate this statement: To move away from the commodity mentality, companies must view their products as problem solvers, and then sell the product on that basis.

4. Illustrate the process that a firm would follow in using target costing while developing a fax machine for the home office user.

5. The XYZ Manufacturing Corporation has experienced a rather large decline in sales for its component parts. Mary Vantage, vice president of marketing, believes that a 10 percent price cut may get things going again. What factors should Mary consider before reducing the price of the components?

6. Define the *experience effect* (behavior of costs) and explain why it occurs. How does the experience effect relate to strategic pricing decisions?

7. A business marketing manager often has great difficulty in arriving at the optimum price level for a product. First, describe the factors that complicate the pricing decision. Second, outline the approach that you would follow in pricing an industrial product. Be as specific as possible.

8. Rather than time to market, Intel refers to the product development cycle for a new chip as "time to money." Intel's CEO Andrew Grove says that "Speed is the only weapon we have." What pricing advantages issue from a rapid product development process?
9. Describe win/loss analysis and explore the role that it can assume in tactical strategy decisions.
10. Identify a particular industry—like software—that you would describe as hypercompetitive. Who are the key competitors in that industry? What forces are contributing to its rapid rate of change?

Chapter 16

Business Marketing Communications: Advertising and Sales Promotion

Advertising supports and supplements personal selling efforts. The share of the marketing budget devoted to advertising is smaller in business than it is in consumer-goods marketing. A well-tailored business-to-business advertising campaign together with a carefully planned promotion program can, however, contribute to the increased efficiency and effectiveness of the overall marketing strategy. After reading this chapter, you will understand

1. the specific role of advertising in business marketing strategy.
2. the decisions that must be made when forming a business advertising program.
3. the business media options.
4. the methods for measuring business advertising effectiveness.
5. the role of trade shows in the business communications mix and how trade show effectiveness can be measured.

Communication with existing and potential customers is vital to business marketing success. Experience has taught marketing managers that not even the best products sell themselves: The benefits, problem solutions, and cost efficiencies of those products must be effectively communicated to all the individuals who influence the purchase decision. As a result of the technical complexity of business products, the relatively small number of potential buyers, and the extensive negotiation process, the primary communication vehicle in business-to-business marketing is the salesperson. However, nonpersonal methods of communication, including advertising, catalogs, and trade shows, have a unique and often crucial role in the communication process.

Consider the valuable role advertising assumes in Xerox's marketing strategy. After tracking photocopier sales, Xerox found that its salespeople met with actual corporate decision makers on only about 4 percent of their sales calls. Clearly, it is challenging to find who is involved in a purchase decision and, once identified, to be able to make contact with them. However, it is possible that numerous specialists will be involved in the decision, and advertisements can be placed in selected business trade publications to reach these influentials. An important role for business-to-business advertising is to reach those buying influentials inaccessible to the salesperson. Business-to-business advertising and promotion, of course, serve many other functions in the communication strategy as well.

The focus of this chapter is fourfold: (1) to provide a clear understanding of the role of advertising in business marketing strategy; (2) to present a framework for structuring advertising decisions—a framework that integrates the decisions related to objectives, budgets, messages, media, and evaluation; (3) to develop an understanding of each business-to-business advertising decision area; and (4) to evaluate the valuable role that trade shows can assume in the promotional mix of the business marketer.

The Role of Advertising

INTEGRATED COMMUNICATION PROGRAMS

Advertising and sales promotion are rarely employed alone in the business-to-business setting, but are intertwined with the total communications strategy—particularly personal selling. Personal and nonpersonal forms of communication interact to inform key buying influencers. The challenge for the business marketer is to create an advertising and sales promotion strategy that effectively blends with personal selling efforts in order to achieve sales and profit objectives. In addition, the advertising and sales promotion tools must be integrated; that is, a comprehensive program of media and sales promotion methods must be coordinated to achieve the desired results.

NATURE OF ORGANIZATIONAL BUYING AFFECTS BUSINESS ADVERTISING

To understand the role of advertising, we must recognize the forces that shape and influence organizational buying decisions, which are typically joint decisions. The intricacies of the buying center were well documented in Chapter 3. Recall that a business marketer must focus on the full range of individuals involved in the buying center for a particular purchase. The size of the buying center varies, sometimes including as many as 25 people. In most cases, it is not feasible for salespeople to make contact with everyone in the buying center.

Hewlett-Packard's advertising strategy for their laptop computer, Omnibook 300, involved a campaign directed at target customers through ads in the business press and inflight airline magazines.[1] A key second component of the strategy included ads in PC industry publications. Research showed that the target buyer is heavily influenced by business associates and friends whom the buyer considers to be "computer literate." These computer literate friends refer to PC industry publications for their knowledge of new computer technology, and Hewlett-Packard believes it is necessary to reach these influencers as they will be consulted by the target buyer when a laptop computer decision is made.

The point is clear: Business-to-business advertising fills the void.[2] Carefully targeted advertising extends beyond the salesperson's reach to unidentified buying influentials. Advertising is often the *only* means of communicating the existence of a product to potential buyers. Advertising also increases recognition of the company's name and reputation, enhancing the salesperson's opportunity to create a sale (see Figure 16.1).

ADVERTISING: ENHANCING SALES EFFECTIVENESS

Effective advertising can make personal selling more productive. John Morrill examined nearly 100,000 interviews on 26 product lines at 30,000 buying locations in order to study the impact of business-to-business advertising on salesperson effectiveness.[3] He concluded that dollar sales per salesperson call were significantly higher when customers had been exposed to advertising. In addition to increasing company and product awareness, research indicates that buyers who had been exposed to a supplier's advertisement rated the supplier's sales personnel substantially higher on product knowledge, service, and enthusiasm.[4] For example, Oracle Corporation used advertising to focus attention on its software's ability to run on large parallel processing computers. This approach helped Oracle's sales force to make significant sales inroads against its major database software competitor, Sybase, Inc.[5] A primary role of business-to-business advertising is to enhance the reputation of the supplier.

Business-to-business advertising also contributes to increased sales efficiency. Increased expenditures on advertising lead to greater brand awareness for industrial

---

[1]Tim Clark, "Four H-P Success Story Strategies," *Business Marketing* 78 (July 1993): p. 18. See also B. G. Yovovich, *New Marketing Imperatives: Innovative Strategies for Today's Marketing Challenges* (Englewood Cliffs, N.J.: Prentice-Hall, 1995), pp. 190–192.

[2]A number of studies have documented the ability of advertising to reach industrial buying influentials not accessible to the salesperson. Two of the most frequently cited are *The U.S. Steel/Harnischfeger Study: Industrial Advertising Effectively Reaches Buying Influences at Low Cost* (New York: American Business Press, 1969); and *The Evolution of a Purchase Study* (Bloomfield Hills, Mich.: Bromsom Publishing Company, 1967).

[3]John E. Morrill, "Industrial Advertising Pays Off," *Harvard Business Review*, 48 (March/April 1970): pp. 4–14.

[4]Ibid., p. 6. For a comprehensive study of the relationship between brand awareness and brand preference, see Eunsang Yoon and Valerie Kijewski, "The Brand Awareness-to-Preference Link in Business Markets: A Study of the Semiconductor Manufacturing Industry," *Journal of Business-to-Business Marketing* 2, (no. 4 1995): pp. 7–36.

[5]Al Ries, "One and the Same?" *Sales and Marketing Management*, 148 (February 1996): p. 22.

Figure 16.1 An Ad Emphasizing How Advertising and Personal Selling Work Together

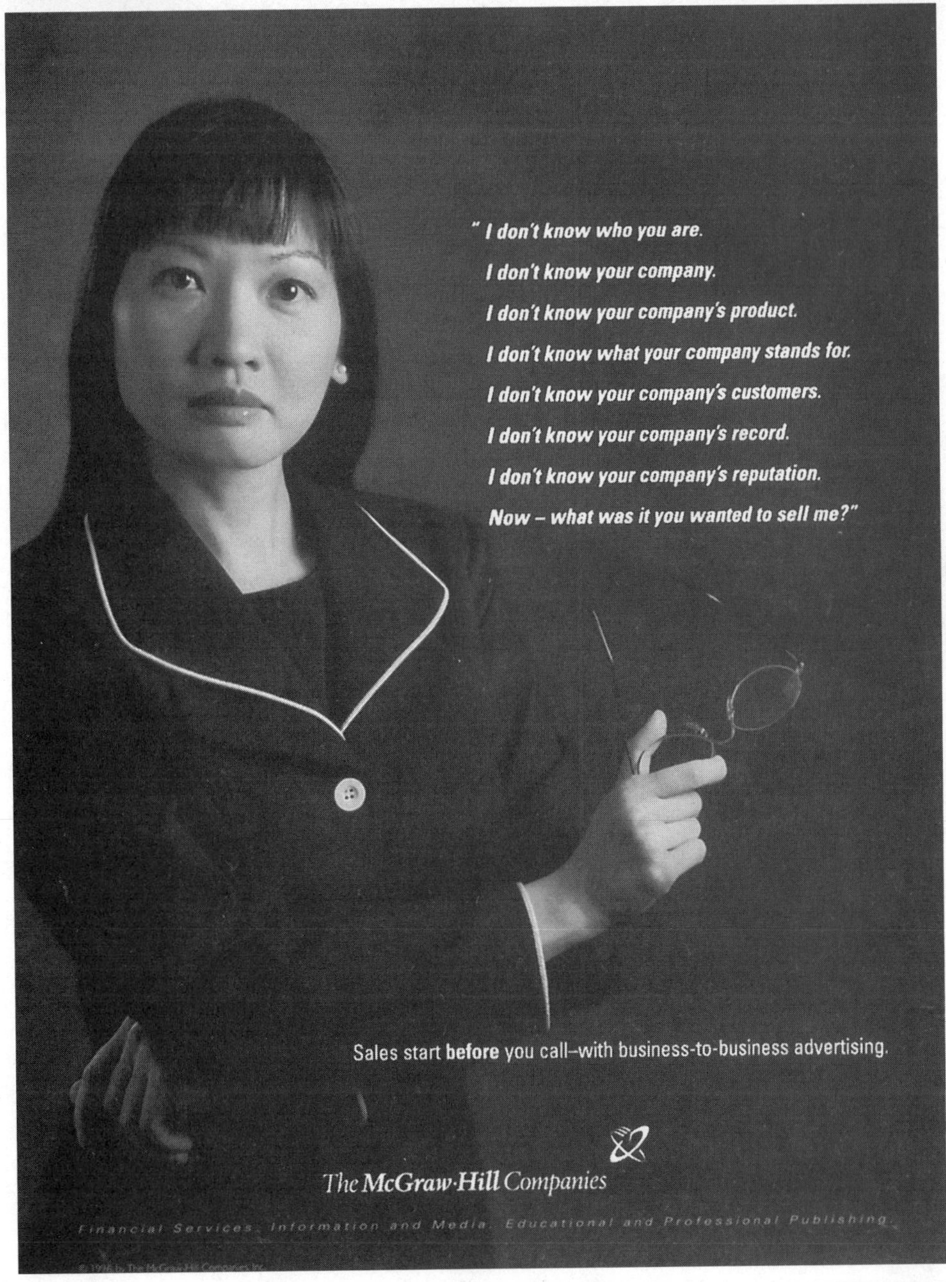

Source: Courtesy of the McGraw-Hill Companies, Inc.

products, which translates into larger market shares and higher profits.[6] In one study, a tightly controlled experimental design was used to measure the impact of business-to-business advertising on sales and profits. For one product in the study, sales, gross margin, and net profit were significantly higher with advertising, compared to the pretest period with no advertising.[7] In fact, gross margins ranged from four to six times higher with advertising, compared to the nonadvertising period.

ADVERTISING: INCREASED SALES EFFICIENCY

The impact of advertising on the overall efficiency of the business marketing program is evidenced in two ways. First, business suppliers frequently need to remind actual and potential buyers of their products or need to make them aware of new products or services. Although these objectives could be partially accomplished through personal selling, the costs of reaching a vast group of buyers would be prohibitive. A properly placed advertisement can reach hundreds of buying influentials for only a few cents each; the average cost of a business sales call is currently approaching $300. Sales call costs are determined by the salesperson's wages, travel and entertainment costs, and fringe benefits costs. If these costs total $1,200 per day and a salesperson can make four calls per day, then each call costs $300. Second, advertising appears to make all selling activities more effective. Advertising interacts effectively with all communication and selling activities, and it can result in higher levels of efficiency for the entire marketing expenditure.

ADVERTISING: CREATING AWARENESS

From a communications standpoint, the buying process can be viewed as taking potential buyers sequentially from unawareness of a product or supplier to awareness, to brand preference, to conviction that a particular purchase will fulfill their requirements, and, ultimately, to actual purchase. Business advertising often creates awareness of the supplier and the supplier's products. Sixty-one percent of the design engineers returning an inquiry card from a magazine ad indicated that they were unaware of the company that advertised before seeing the ad.[8] Business advertising may also make some contribution to creating preference for the product—all very cost effectively. In addition, advertising can create a corporate identity or image. Hewlett-Packard uses ads in general business publications such as *Business Week* and even television advertising to trumpet the value of its brand and to develop desired perceptions in a broad audience.[9]

---

[6]"New Proof of Industrial Ad Values," *Marketing and Media Decisions*, February 1981, p. 64.
[7]"ARF/ABP Release Final Study Findings," *Business Marketing*, 72 (May 1987): p. 55.
[8]Raymond E. Herzog, "How Design Engineering Activity Affects Supplies," *Business Marketing*, 70 (November 1985): p. 143.
[9]B. G. Yovovich, *New Marketing Imperatives*, p. 190.

WHAT BUSINESS-TO-BUSINESS ADVERTISING CANNOT DO

To develop an effective communications program, the business marketing manager must blend all communication tools into an integrated program, using each tool where it is most effective. Business advertising quite obviously has limitations. Advertising cannot substitute for effective personal selling; it must supplement, support, and complement that effort. In the same way, personal selling is constrained by its costs and should not be used to create awareness or to disseminate information—tasks quite capably performed by advertising.

Generally, advertising alone cannot create product preference; this requires demonstration, explanation, and operational testing. Similarly, conviction and actual purchase can be ensured only by personal selling. Advertising has a supporting role in creating awareness, providing information, and uncovering important leads for salespeople; that is how the marketing manager must use it in order to be effective.

Managing Business-to-Business Advertising

The advertising decision model in Figure 16.2 shows the structural elements involved in the management of business-to-business advertising. First, advertising is only one aspect of the entire marketing strategy and must be integrated with other components in order to achieve strategic goals. The advertising decision process begins with the formulation of advertising objectives, which are derived from marketing goals. From this formulation follows a determination of expenditures necessary to achieve those goals. Then, specific communication messages are formulated to achieve the market behavior specified by the objectives. Equally important is the evaluation and selection of the media used to reach the desired audience. The result is an integrated advertising campaign aimed at eliciting a specific attitude or behavior from the target group. The final, and critical, step is to evaluate the effectiveness of the campaign.

DEFINING ADVERTISING OBJECTIVES

Knowing what advertising must accomplish enables the manager to determine an advertising budget more accurately and provides a yardstick against which advertising can be evaluated. In specifying advertising goals, the marketing manager must realize that (1) the advertising mission flows directly from the overall marketing strategy: advertising must fulfill a marketing strategy objective, and the goal set for advertising must reflect the general aim and purpose of the entire strategy; and (2) the objectives of the advertising program must be responsive to the roles for which advertising is suited: creating awareness, providing information, influencing attitudes, and reminding buyers of company and product existence.

Figure 16.2 The Decision Stages for Developing the Business-to-Business Advertising Program

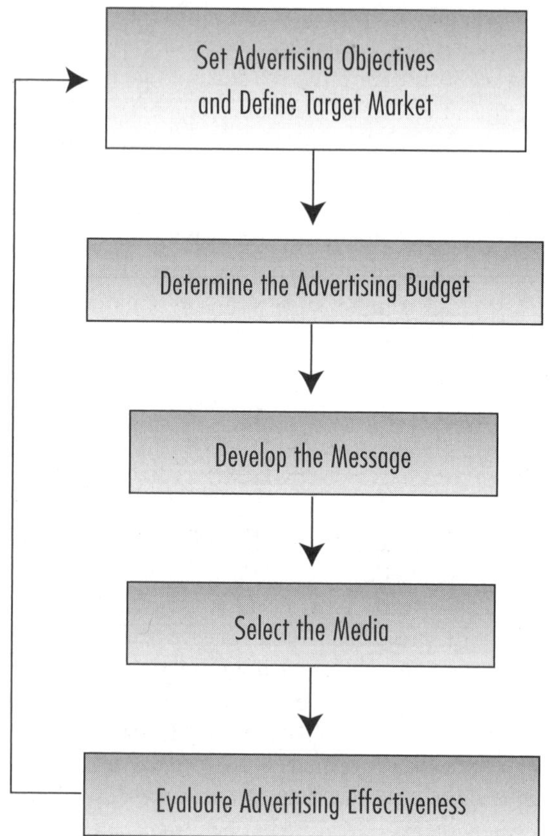

WRITTEN OBJECTIVES

An advertising objective must specify what is to be achieved and when, must be measurable, and must be realistic.[10] The objective must speak in unambiguous terms of a specific outcome. The purpose is to establish a single working direction for everyone involved in creating, coordinating, and evaluating the advertising program. Correctly conceived objectives set standards against which the advertising effort can be evaluated. A specific objective might be: "to increase from 15 percent (as measured in June

[10]Jack Edmonston, "Practical Tips to Measure Advertising's Performance," *Business Marketing*, 81 (April 1996): p. 26.

1998) to 30 percent (by June 1999) the proportion of design engineers associating 'lubrication for life' feature with our brand of hydraulic pumps." The objective directs the manager to create a message related to the major product benefit, using media that will reach design engineers. The objective also provides a way to measure accomplishment (awareness among 30 percent of the target audience).

Business advertising objectives frequently bear no direct relationship to specific dollar sales targets. Although dollar sales results would provide a "hard" measure of advertising accomplishment, it is often impossible to link advertising directly to sales. Personal selling, price, product performance, and competitive actions have a more direct relationship to sales levels, and it is almost impossible to sort out the impact of advertising. Thus, advertising goals are typically stated in terms of *communication goals* such as brand awareness, recognition, and buyer attitudes. These goals can be measured; it is presumed that achieving them will stimulate sales volume.

Target Audience

A significant task is the specification of target audiences. Because a primary role of advertising is to reach buying influentials inaccessible to the salesperson, the business marketing manager must define the buying influential groups to be reached. Generally, each group of buying influentials is concerned with distinct product and service attributes and criteria, and the advertising must focus on these. Thus, the objectives must specify the intended audience and its relevant decision criteria.

Creative Strategy Statement

A final consideration is the specification of the creative strategy statement. Once objectives and targets are established, the **creative strategy statement** provides guidelines for company and advertising agency personnel on how the product is to be positioned in the marketplace. **Product position** relates to how the target market perceives the product.

For example, if the hydraulic pumps cited earlier currently have an unfavorable product position in regard to lubrication, the firm might use the following creative strategy statement: "Our basic creative strategy is to support a repositioning of the product from that of a reliable pump to a high-performance, reliable self-lubrication pump."

All creative efforts—copy, theme, color, and so forth—as well as media and tactics should be developed to support the creative strategy statement. Effective advertising campaign planning requires objectives upon which to structure media decisions and measure results.

DETERMINING ADVERTISING EXPENDITURES

Collectively, business marketers spend nearly $3 billion on media advertising annually. The leading advertisers are shown in Table 16.1. Note the preponderance of high-tech firms in the top-ten list. Typically, business marketers use a blend of intuition,

Table 16.1 1996 Top Business-to-Business Advertisers

Company	Total Advertising Expenditures (millions)
AT&T	$248.3
IBM	228.0
Microsoft	124.2
MCI	108.2
Hewlett-Packard	84.2
Sprint	77.3
United Parcel Service	66.8
Compaq Computer	59.2
American Express	58.4
Canon	55.0

Source: Charmain Kosek, "B-to-B Advertising Tops $2.72 Billion," *Business Marketing*, 81 (September 1996): pp. 10, 11.

judgment, experience, and, only occasionally, more advanced decision-oriented techniques to determine advertising budgets. Some of the techniques most commonly utilized by business marketers are rules of thumb (for example, percentage of past years' sales) and the objective-task method.

Rules of Thumb

Often, because advertising is a relatively small part of the total marketing budget for business firms, the value of using sophisticated methods for advertising budgeting is not great. In these cases, managers tend to follow simple **rules of thumb** (for example, allocate 1 percent of sales to advertising or match competition spending). Unfortunately, percentage-of-sales rules are all too pervasive throughout business marketing, even where advertising is an important element.

The fundamental problem with percentage-of-sales rules is that they implicitly make advertising a consequence rather than a determinant of sales and profits and can easily give rise to dysfunctional policies. Percentage-of-sales rules suggest that the business advertiser reduce advertising when sales volume declines, just when increased advertising may be more appropriate. Nevertheless, simple rules of thumb will continue to be applied in budget decisions because they are easy to use, and familiar to management.

Objective-Task Method

The task method for budgeting advertising expenditures is an attempt to relate advertising costs to the objective it is to accomplish. Because the sales dollar results of

BUSINESS-TO-BUSINESS ADVERTISING EXPENDITURES: THE INCREASING ROLE OF CONSUMER MEDIA

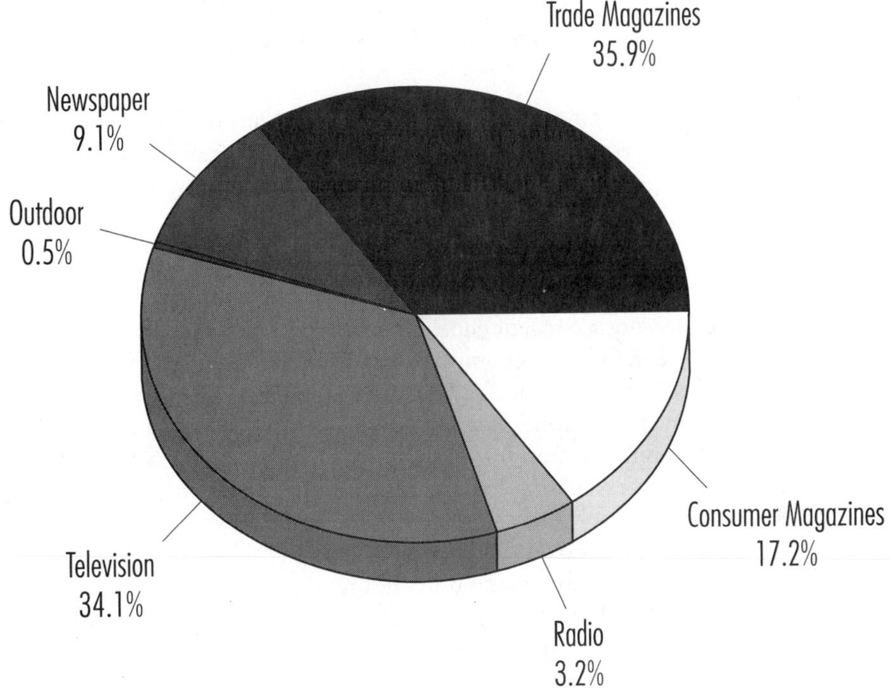

Business marketers spent almost $1 billion in trade magazine advertising in 1995. However, ad spending in consumer magazines by business-to-business marketers increased 52 percent in 1995, which accounted for almost half the total increase in business-to-business advertising. Cable TV moved ahead of local newspapers as an advertising media for business-to-business firms. Spending on national radio surged 91 percent to $32 million, offsetting a drop in spot radio spending. Outdoor advertising, although a minor element in business-to-business advertising, did increase 46 percent to $13 million in 1995. In all, business marketers are increasingly using consumer-focused advertising media as a way to reach key buying influencers.

Source: Charmain Kosek, "B-to-B Advertising Tops $2.72 Billion," *Business Marketing* 81 (September 1996): p. 11.

advertising are almost impossible to measure, the task method focuses on the communications effects of advertising, not on the sales effects.

The task method is applied by evaluating the tasks to be performed by advertising, analyzing the costs associated with each task, and summing up the total costs in order to arrive at a final budget. The process can be divided into four steps:

1. Establish specific marketing objectives for the product in terms of such factors as sales volume, market share, profit contribution, and market segments.
2. Assess the communication functions that must be performed in order to realize the marketing objectives and then determine the role of advertising and other elements of the communications mix in performing these functions.
3. Define specific goals for advertising in terms of the measurable communication response required to achieve marketing objectives.
4. Estimate the budget needed to accomplish the advertising goals.

The task method addresses the major problem of the rules-of-thumb methods—funds are applied to accomplish a specific goal so that advertising is a *determinant* of those results, not a consequence. Using the task approach, managers will allocate all the funds necessary to accomplish a specific objective, rather than allocating some arbitrary percentage of sales. The most troubling problem of the method is that management must have some instinct for the proper relationship between expenditure level and communication response. It is difficult to know what will produce a certain level of awareness among business marketing buying influentials. Will 12 two-page insertions in *Iron Age* over the next six months create the desired recognition level, or will 24 insertions over one year be necessary?

Budgeting for advertising must not ignore the political and behavioral aspects of the process. Nigel Piercy's research suggests that attention to budgeting technique is insufficient because organizations operate through structures and processes that are often political in nature.[11] Piercy suggests that what actually determines advertising budgets are the power "interests" in the company and the political behavior of various parties in the budgeting process. An implication of this research is that the manager may be well-served by focusing considerable attention on the budgetary process as a political activity, and not simply as a technique-driven process.

Passing the Threshold

Several communications are often needed to capture the attention of buyers, which complicates the budgeting decision. Research suggests that a brand must surpass a

[11]Nigel Piercy, "Advertising Budgeting: Process and Structure as Explanatory Variables," *Journal of Advertising*, 16, no. 2 (1987): p. 34.

threshold level of awareness in the market before meaningful additions can be made in its brand preference share. A small advertising budget may not allow the marketer to move the firm's brand beyond a threshold level of awareness and on to preference. Eunsang Yoon and Valerie Kijewski warn that "The communications manager having limited marketing resources will then be in danger of making the mistake of stopping the program prematurely, thus wasting past investment, rather than pressing on to pass the threshold awareness level." [12]

Because the budgeting process is so important to advertising effectiveness, managers must not blindly follow rules of thumb. Instead, they should evaluate the tasks required and their associated costs against industry norms. With clear objectives and proper budgetary allocations, the next step is to design effective advertising messages.

DEVELOPING THE ADVERTISING MESSAGE

Message development is a complex, critical task in industrial advertising. Highlighting a product attribute that is unimportant to a particular buying group is not only a waste of advertising dollars but also a lost opportunity. Both the appeal and the way that appeal is conveyed are vital to successful communication. Thus, creating business-to-business advertising messages involves determining advertising objectives, evaluating the buying criteria of the target audience, and analyzing the most appropriate language, format, and style for presenting the message.

Perception

For an advertising message to be successful, an individual must first be exposed to it and pay attention to it. Thus, a business advertisement must catch the decision maker's attention. Then, once the individual has noticed the message, he or she must interpret it as the advertiser intended. Perceptual barriers often prevent the intended message from being perceived by a receiver. A business advertisement must be successful at catching the decision maker's attention. Yet, even though the individual is exposed to an advertisement, there is no guarantee that the message will be processed. In fact, the industrial buyer may read every word of the copy and find a meaning in it opposite to that intended by the advertiser.

The business advertiser must thus contend with two important elements of perception: attention and interpretation. Buyers tend to screen out messages that are inconsistent with their own attitudes, needs, and beliefs, and they tend to interpret information in the light of those beliefs (see Chapter 3). Unless advertising messages

[12]Eunsang Yoon and Valerie Kijewski, "The Brand Awareness-to-Preferences Link," p. 32.

are carefully designed and targeted, they may be disregarded or interpreted improperly. Advertisers must put themselves in the position of the receivers in order to evaluate how the message will appear to them.

Whether an ad uses technical wording appears to have some effect on readers' perceptions of both the industrial product and the ad. [13] Technical ads were shown to create less desire in some readers to seek information because such ads suggest "more difficulty in operation." Therefore, it is important to remember that technical readers (engineers, architects, and so on) respond more favorably to the technical ads, and nontechnical readers respond more favorably to nontechnical ads. From a message development viewpoint, the business advertiser must carefully tailor the technical aspects of promotional messages to the appropriate audience.

Humor

Humor finds its way into business-to-business advertising, according to a study conducted by Lynette McCullough and Ronald Taylor. [14] Their study of more than 600 ads from a wide sample of American, British, and German trade publications found that 23 percent of the ads contained humor and that the incidence of humor varied by industry. Basic industries like paper, fishing, and mining used humor less often. It appears that humor may be effective in facilitating the processing of advertising information because it commands audience attention and it also can create a positive emotional response—which is then generalized onto the product. Some managers question whether humor might have a detrimental effect on comprehension or have a negative effect if inappropriate for the product.

Focus on Benefits

An industrial buyer purchases benefits—a better way to accomplish some task, a less expensive way to produce a final product, a solution to a problem, or a faster delivery time. Advertising messages need to focus on the benefits sought by the target customer and to persuade the reader that the advertiser can deliver the benefit. Messages that have direct appeals or calls to action are viewed to be "stronger" than those with diffuse or indirect appeals to action.

Advertisers often tend to concentrate on a physical product, forgetting that the physical product is useless to an industrial buyer unless it solves some problem. Note that the ad for SAS software displayed in Figure 16.3 is clearly focused on user benefits: The software is user-friendly, can be custom-tailored to you and your business, and will improve your decision-making capabilities. Concrete benefits are

---

[13]Joseph A. Bellizzi and Jacqueline J. Mohr, "Technical Versus Nontechnical Wording in Industrial Print Advertising," in *AMA Educators' Proceedings,* ed. Russell W. Belk et al. (Chicago: American Marketing Association, 1984), p. 174.

[14]Lynette S. McCullough and Ronald K. Taylor, "Humor in American, British, and German Ads," *Industrial Marketing Management*, 22 (February 1993): pp. 17–28.

Figure 16.3 An Ad Focusing on the Benefits Provided to Users

Free for a Limited Time... A Guide to

The Top New Data Warehousing Software

When 200,000 IS managers were asked to choose the top software for data warehousing, their answer had a familiar ring:

SAS® software from SAS Institute.

With SAS software, you can integrate your company's vast data resources with proven data discovery capabilities that can be custom tailored to you and your business: **multi-dimensional analysis, data mining, database marketing, data visualization, data query and reporting,** and much more.

PRODUCT
YEAR 1996
IS MANAGERS CHOICE

It's never been easier to access your data...or to arrive at informed decisions. No wonder more than 3.5 million decision makers already rely on SAS software. Or why it's now at work in the Fortune 100.

SAS® **SAS Institute**

Software for Successful Decision Making

Phone 919.677.8200 Fax 919.677.4444

Get the facts for yourself in our free data warehousing guide. Just give us a call or visit SAS Institute on the World Wide Web at http://www.sas.com/

E-mail: bw@sas.com

SAS is a registered trademark of SAS Institute Inc. Copyright © 1996 by SAS Institute Inc.

SAS Institute. Software for Successful Decision Making.

Source: Courtesy of SAS Institute Inc.

communicated in a clear and simple fashion and the ad positions SAS Institute as a leader in data warehousing software.

Understanding Buyer Motivations

Which product benefits are important to each group of buying influentials? The business advertiser cannot assume that a standard set of "classical buying motives" applies in every purchase situation. Many business advertisers often do not understand the buying motives of important market segments. The development of effective advertising messages often requires extensive marketing research in order to fully delineate the key buying criteria of each buying influencer in each of the firm's different target markets.

Physical Characteristics of an Advertisement

Once the perception process has been evaluated and the user benefits identified, the business advertiser must decide how the advertisement should be structured.[15] A wide variety of factors must be considered, including size of the ad, use of color and illustrations, and media placement; readership and recall of business advertisements are strongly related to mechanical and format characteristics (size, color, placement, and so on) of the advertisement.[16]

McGraw-Hill analyzed five years of ad readership scores for nearly 3,600 individual business advertisements in order to evaluate the impact of various elements on the effectiveness of industrial advertisements.[17] The findings indicate that "the copy factor of an advertised proposition contributes perhaps 80 percent of an ad's success or failure."[18] Although certain mechanical aspects may help create awareness and interest in the advertisement, its ultimate success will depend on how well the message is targeted to the benefits sought by the buying influential.

Some evidence exists that business marketers have difficulty creating advertisements that capture the reader's attention. [19] Roper Starch Worldwide, a New York copy testing firm, interviewed more than 10,000 regular readers of transportation, architecture, and office-product journals. Overall, the ads in these publications attracted much less attention than typical ads in consumer magazines. The research suggests that business marketers need to reevaluate the basic principles of message development: focus on single benefits, illustrating them with a single, dramatic image;

---

[15]For an excellent discussion of how to improve business advertising copy, see Joseph A. Bellizzi and Robert E. Hite, "Improving Industrial Advertising Copy," *Industrial Marketing Management*, 15 (May 1986): pp. 117–122.

[16]Dominique Hanssens and Barton A. Weitz, "The Effectiveness of Industrial Print Advertisements across Product Categories," *Journal of Marketing Research*, 17 (August 1980): p. 304.

[17]Bob Donath, "Q: What Makes the Perfect Ad? A: It Depends," *Industrial Marketing*, 67 (August 1982): pp. 89–92.

[18]Ibid., p. 90.

[19]Laura Bird, "Business-to-Business Ads Need More Pizazz in Pitch, Study Says," *The Wall Street Journal*, 1 October 1993, p. B8.

focus ads on the reader's needs rather than the advertiser's needs; and do not mistakenly assume that readers are as interested in the topic as the creators of the ad are.

SELECTING ADVERTISING MEDIA FOR BUSINESS MARKETS

Although the message is vital to advertising success, an equally important factor is the medium through which it is presented. Business-to-business media are selected by target audience—the particular purchase decision participants to be reached. Generally, the first decision is whether to use trade publications, direct mail, or both. Selection of particular media also involves budgetary considerations: Where are dollars best spent to generate the customer contacts desired?

Business Publications

More than 2,700 business publications carry business-to-business advertising, for a total exceeding $2 billion. For those specializing in distribution, *Inbound Logistics*, *Distribution*, *Logistics Management*, and *Modern Materials Handling* are a few of the publications available. *Iron Age* and *Steel* are aimed at individuals in the steel industry. Business publications are either horizontal or vertical. **Horizontal publications** are directed at a specific task, technology, or function whatever the industry. *Advertising Age*, *Purchasing*, and *Materials Handling Engineering* are horizontal. **Vertical publications**, on the other hand, may be read by everyone from floor supervisor to president within a specific industry. Typical vertical publications are *Glass Industry* or *Manufacturing Confectioner.*

If a business marketer's product has applications only within a few industries, vertical publications are a logical media choice. When many industries are potential users and well-defined functions are the principal buying influencers, a horizontal publication is effective.

Another important aspect of trade publications is **controlled circulation,** which involves free (as opposed to paid) subscriptions, and which is distributed to selected readers in a position to influence buying decisions. Subscribers must provide their title, function, and buying responsibilities, among other information. Thus, the advertiser can tell whether each publication reaches the desired audience.

Obviously, publication choice is predicated on a complete understanding of the range of purchase decision participants and of the industries where the product will be used. Only then can the target audience be matched to the circulation statements of alternative business publications.

Characteristics of an Effective Print Ad

Recent research on the effectiveness of business-to-business print ads provides strong evidence that the marketing strategist should emphasize a "rational approach" in print ads and provide a clear description of the product and the benefits it offers to customers.[20] The effectiveness of ads is also enhanced by detailing product quality and performance information in a concrete and logical manner.

Advertising Cost

Circulation is an important criterion in the selection of publications, but circulation must be tempered by coşt. First, the total advertising budget must be allocated among the various advertising tools. Most studies indicate that the breakdown of expenditures is approximately as follows:

- Trade publications: 40%
- Sales promotion: 25%
- Direct mail: 25%
- Trade shows: 10%

Of course, these allocations vary with company situation and advertising mission. However, the 40 percent allocation to trade publications appears fairly consistent from company to company.Allocation of the trade publication budget among various journals will depend on their relative effectiveness and efficiency, usually measured in cost per thousand using the following formula:

$$\text{Cost per thousand} = \frac{\text{Cost per page}}{\text{Circulation in thousands}}$$

To compare two publications by their actual page rates would be misleading, because the publication with the lower circulation will usually be less expensive. The cost-per-thousand calculation should be based on circulation to the *target* audience, not the total audience. Although some publications may appear high on a cost-per-thousand basis, they may in fact be cost-effective, with little wasted circulation.

Frequency and Scheduling

Even the most successful business publication advertisements are seen by only a small percentage of the people who read the magazine; therefore, one-time ads are generally ineffective. Because a number of exposures are required before a message "sinks in," and because the reading audience varies from month to month, a schedule of advertising insertions is required. To build continuity and repetitive value, at least 6

---

[20]Ritu Lohtia, Wesley J. Johnston, and Linda Rab, "Business-to-Business Advertising: What Are the Dimensions of an Effective Print Ad?" *Industrial Marketing Management*, 24 (October 1995): pp. 369–378.

INSIDE BUSINESS MARKETING

DOES BUSINESS-TO-BUSINESS ADVERTISING HAVE TO BE BLAND?

Conventional wisdom might suggest that business-to-business advertising is pretty straightforward—factual presentations with rational appeals that are long on copy and short on pictures and pizzazz.

Today, many challenge the conventional wisdom and argue that business-to-business advertising does and should use emotion, color, and all the tools that are used in consumer advertising—as long as the *situation* is right for such approaches. A new steam boiler for an electric utility plant is a multimillion-dollar purchase and suppliers submit proposals totaling hundreds of pages. So what role can advertising play here? It can shift the focus of what's important about the product. To persuade utility companies to try a new type of boiler, Babcock & Wilcox placed a full-page ad in *The Wall Street Journal* every time they sold one of the new units. The impact of the ad was to pressure a major competitor, Combustion Engineering, to shift its marketing program to the new type of boiler!

Some business-to-business firms have been successful by following a strategy that is opposite of what their competitors are doing. This approach enhances the chance that a message will be remembered due to the contrast with the message from the competition. Thus, a factual, rational approach used by the competitor might invite a highly graphic, impassioned appeal from another firm. By saying or showing something the viewer or listener doesn't expect, the business-to-business advertiser increases the chance of gaining attention.

Emotion is also not out of place in business-to-business advertising. One of the most successful ads of all time was the IBM "pillow" ad. The copy showed a very large white pillow with the well-known IBM logo printed across it in the standard IBM light blue. A headline read: "*What most people want from a computer service company is a good night's sleep.*" The obvious reference is to the peace of mind the buyer gets when they do business with IBM. The ad emphasized the important benefits of doing business with the industry leader—in a way that touched the reader emotionally.

Source: Adapted from Al Ries, "One and the Same?" *Business Marketing* 148 (February 1996): pp. 22–23.

---

insertions per year may be required in a monthly publication, and 26 to 52 insertions (with a minimum of 13) in a weekly publication.[21]

Direct Mail Advertising

Direct mail delivers the advertising message firsthand to selected individuals. Possible mailing pieces range from a sales letter introducing a new product to a lengthy

[21]See Stanton G. Cort, David R. Lambert, and Paula L. Garrett, "Effective Business-to-Business Frequency: New Management Perspectives from the Research Literature," *Advertising Research Foundation Literature Review* (October 1983).

brochure or even a product sample. Direct mail can accomplish all of the major advertising functions, but its real contribution is in delivering the message to a precisely defined prospect.

Direct mail is commonly used for corporate image promotion, product and service promotion, sales force support, distribution channel communication, and special marketing problems. In promoting corporate image, direct mail may help to establish a firm's reputation of technological leadership. On the other hand, product advertising by direct mail can be used to put specific product information in the hands of buying influentials. Booklets from Kaiser Aluminum explain aluminum's advantages to industrial buyers and specifiers, whereas messages on how to work with aluminum and a quantity/weight calculator are sent to machine operators and shop supervisors.

Direct Mail: Benefits and Requirements

Direct mail also supports the salespeople—providing leads from returned inquiry cards and paving the way for a first sales call. Direct mail can be used effectively to notify potential customers of the location of local distributors. John Deere and Company sent a series of three mailings, by name, to 20,000 farmers who had never purchased their brand, to persuade them to simply visit a John Deere dealer. More than 5,800 farmers did visit a dealer, and purchased more than $35 million worth of Deere equipment over the next three months.[22] In terms of response performance, a typical direct mail package will approximately equal 10 to 50 print or broadcast exposures.[23] Finally, direct mail applies to a host of special situations such as identifying new customers and markets, meeting competitor claims, and promoting items that are not receiving enough sales support.

From a cost standpoint, direct mail is efficient when compared to other media. However, direct mail can be a wasteful medium if the prospect lists are so general in nature that it is difficult or impossible to find a common denominator among the prospects. It is a viable advertising medium when potential buyers can be clearly identified and easily reached through the mail. When buying center members have been identified, direct mail is a cost-effective device for making contact with the buying center members. When combined with telemarketing follow-up, even "inaccessible" buying center members can be exposed to promotional efforts.[24]

A direct mail advertisement typically gains the full attention of the reader and therefore provides greater impact than a trade publication advertisement. Industrial buyers usually will at least scan the direct mail promotions sent to them. However, reaching top executives with direct mail may be more difficult. A survey of secretaries of top executives at *Fortune* 500 companies showed that the average executive receives 175 pieces of unsolicited mail each week, and less than 10 percent of this

---

[22]John D. Yeck, "Direct Marketing Means Accountability," *Business Marketing*, 78 (July 1993): p. A4.

[23]Shell R. Alpert, "Testing the 'TOO-Frequent' Assumption," *Business Marketing*, 73 (March 1988): p. 14.

[24]Robert D. McWilliams, Earl Naumann and Stan Scott, "Determining Buyer Center Size," *Industrial Marketing Management*, 21 (February 1992): p. 48.

mail is passed on to the executive, [25] who then spends only five minutes a day looking at the 17 or so pieces of mail. Clearly, the direct mail piece must have effective copy and headlines to grab the attention of both the secretary and the executive.

Timing of direct mail advertising is also flexible; a new price schedule or new service innovation can be communicated to the buyer as needed. Finally, direct mail makes it easy for the buyer to respond—usually a reply postcard is included or the name, address, and phone number of the local salesperson or distributor are provided.

A Planned Response Package

Most direct mail programs seek some type of response. Often, the potential buyer is asked to return a reply card in order to receive additional information such as a sample or a brochure explaining the benefits and applications of a product. Only 1 out of every 40 raw leads developed from a direct mail campaign may be actually worth a salesperson's attention.[26] As a result, there is often a tendency to adopt a casual approach toward responding to sales leads. However, to realize the potential of direct mail, there must be a formal program to "qualify" each inquiry and respond promptly. Qualification may be accomplished by telephoning the respondent and assessing his or her authority and readiness to purchase. Once the respondent has been qualified, the response program might involve mailing literature to the prospect, referring the prospect to a salesperson, or calling to explain product details. A planned response "package" aims to generate a sale and should include a motivating cover letter, a descriptive brochure, and a reply card that makes it easy to respond.

The Mailing List

The critical ingredient of a direct mail advertising campaign is the list of buying influentials—thus selectivity, although direct mail's primary advantage, is also its greatest challenge. Literally hundreds of mailing lists are available. Mailing lists for business marketing advertising purposes may be (1) circulation lists provided by trade publications, (2) lists provided by industrial directories, (3) lists provided by mailing-list houses (for example, firms specifically engaged in renting industrial mailing lists), and (4) self-generated lists of previous customers and prospects. Information systems are playing an increasing role in maintaining mailing lists. These systems enable the advertiser to supplement the list with sales data and NAISC codes. A catalog published by Standard Rate and Data Service both inventories and describes most of the industrial mailing lists available, often including names of individual executives. However, if the lists are even slightly out of date only company and functional titles (rather than actual names) should be used.

---

[25]Tom Eisenhart, "Breakthrough Direct Marketing," *Business Marketing*, 75 (August 1990): p. 20.
[26]John L. DeFazio, "An Inquiry-Based MIS," *Business Marketing*, 68 (August 1983): p. 54.

Database Marketing

Effective direct marketing requires application of a concept known as *database marketing*. In essence, database marketing involves knowing a wealth of information about customers and prospects so that the business marketer can direct the appropriate marketing efforts with the correct appeal to the selected target market. Thus, a computer database is built and maintained in the computer that includes a wide range of information on the customer/prospect that can be used to tailor the seller's presentation to that customer/prospect. Based on the success of its database marketing program, IBM has streamlined its sales force, reduced the cost of sales as a percentage of revenue by 50 percent, and seen its sales increase by 12 percent annually.[27] Maintaining and upgrading the database is an ongoing task requiring considerable effort; however, this effort is crucial to effective direct marketing because the information enables the seller to focus on needs and desires relevant to the buyer.

Communication Programs on the Internet[28]

The Internet provides a powerful channel for enhanced communication with present and potential customers. Some forecasters predict that the global sales of goods and services through the Internet will grow from $1 billion in 1996 to $395 billion by the year 2000.[29] In considering this strategic path, the business marketer should assess the added value that Internet communications and transactions would provide over existing alternatives. At a fundamental level, state John Quelch and Lisa Klein, a "company must also assess who its diverse Web audiences are, what specific customer needs the medium will satisfy, and how its Internet presence will respond to a changing customer base, evolving customer needs, competitor actions, and technological developments." [30]

Internet Strategy Benefits

Some business marketers are pursuing creative Internet strategies to forge closer working relationships with their customers. For example:

- Sun Microsystems provides product support, software updates, and hardware services to its customers on a worldwide basis.
- Federal Express's tracking service enables customers to track packages and estimate delivery times anywhere in the world.

---

[27]Shari Caudron, "Right on Target," *Industry Week*, 245 (2 September 1996): p. 45.
[28]This section is based on John A. Quelch and Lisa R. Klein, "The Internet and International Marketing," *Sloan Management Review*, 37 (spring 1996): pp. 60–75.
[29]*A Guide to Business on the Internet* (New York: IBM Corporation, 1996), p. 6.
[30]Quelch and Klein, "The Internet and International Marketing," p. 74.

- Digital Equipment Corporation's home page enable "demonstrations" of its systems and software.[31]

The Internet provides the opportunity for truly interact customers. Business marketers can test advertising copy over instant feedback. They can conduct marketing research survey can generate E-mail mailing lists by asking visitors to their home page to voluntarily sign up for company news updates.

A Proactive Internet Response

Many firms have adopted a defensive stance or merely a "banner" presence on the Internet. However, innovative firms are inventing new ways of using the Internet to serve customer needs and also to connect their worldwide operations. Here the Internet strategy is tightly integrated with the firm's overall marketing communications and distribution strategy. In turn, a specialized customer service staff is often formed to provide the quick response that Internet users demand. The ad shown in Figure 16.4 highlights software solutions for firms that wish to do business on the Internet.

MEASURING ADVERTISING EFFECTIVENESS

The business advertiser rarely expects orders to result immediately from advertising. Advertising is designed to create awareness, stimulate loyalty to the company, or create a favorable attitude toward a product. Even though advertising may not directly precipitate a purchase decision, advertising programs must be held accountable. Thus, the business advertiser must be able to measure the results of current advertising in order to improve future advertising and must be able to evaluate the effectiveness of advertising expenditures against expenditures on other elements of marketing strategy.

Measuring Impacts on the Purchase Decision

Measuring advertising effectiveness means assessing advertising's impact on what "intervenes" between the stimulus (advertising) and the resulting behavior (purchase decision). The theory is that advertising can affect awareness, knowledge, and other dimensions that more readily lend themselves to measurement. In essence, the advertiser attempts to gauge advertising's ability to move an individual through the purchase decision process. This approach assumes, correctly or not, that enhancement of any one phase of the decision process or movement from one step to the next increases the ultimate probability of purchase.

---

[31]Jeffrey F. Ruyport and John J. Sviokla, "Exploiting the Virtual Value Chain," *Harvard Business Review*, 73 (November/December 1995): p. 80. See also Mary J. Cronin, ed., *The Internet Strategy Handbook: Lessons from the New Frontiers of Business* (Boston: Harvard Business School Press, 1996).

ure 16.4 An Ad Highlighting Software Solutions for Firms Interested in Internet Commerce

Source: Courtesy of Open Market, Inc.

A study completed at Rockwell International Corporation suggests that business marketers should also measure the **indirect communication effects** of advertising.[32] This study revealed that advertising affects word-of-mouth communications (indirect effect), and such communications play an important role in buyer decision making. Similarly, advertising was shown to indirectly affect buyers on the basis of its impact on overall company reputation and on the sales force's belief that advertising facilitates their selling tasks. The study suggested that advertising effectiveness measurement include a procedure for tracking and measuring the impact of advertising on the indirect communication effects.

In summary, advertising effectiveness will be evaluated against objectives formulated in terms of the elements of the buyer's decision process as well as some of the indirect communication effects. Advertising efforts will also be judged, in the final analysis, on cost per level of achievement (for example, dollars spent to achieve a certain level of awareness or recognition).

[32]C. Whan Park, Martin S. Roth, and Philip F. Jacques, "Evaluating the Effects of Advertising and Sales Promotion Campaigns," *Industrial Marketing Management*, 17 (May 1988): p. 130.

Figure 16.5 The Primary Areas for Advertising Evaluation

AREA		FOCUS OF MEASUREMENT
Target Market Coverage	→	Degree to which advertising succeeded in reaching defined target markets
Key Buying Motives	→	Factors that triggered purchase decision
Effectiveness of Messages	→	Degree to which the message registered with key buying influentials in defined market segments
Media Effectiveness	→	Degree to which various media were successful in reaching defined target markets with message
Overall Results	→	Degree to which advertising accomplished its defined objectives

The Measurement Program

A sound measurement program entails substantial advanced planning. Figure 16.5 shows the basic areas of advertising evaluation. The advertising strategist must determine in advance what is to be measured, how, and in what sequence. A pre-evaluation phase is required to establish a benchmark for a new advertising campaign. For example, a pre-evaluation study would be conducted to capture the existing level of awareness a firm's product enjoys in a defined target market. After the advertising campaign, the postevaluation study will examine changes in awareness against this benchmark. Five primary areas for advertising evaluation include (1) markets, (2) motives, (3) messages, (4) media, and (5) results.

The evaluation of business-to-business advertising is demanding and complex, but absolutely essential. Budgetary constraints are generally the limiting factors. However, professional research companies can be called on to develop field research studies. When determining the impact of advertising on moving a decision participant from an awareness of the product or company to a readiness to buy, the evaluations will usually measure knowledge, recognition, recall, awareness, preference, and motivation. Measurements of effects on actual sales are unfortunately not often possible.

Managing Trade Show Strategy

Media and direct mail advertising constitute the cornerstone of most nonpersonal, business-to-business promotional programs. Business advertising funds are designated primarily for trade publication and direct mail, but these are reinforced by other promotional activities such as exhibits and trade shows, catalogs, and trade promotion. Special attention is given here to trade shows—an important promotional vehicle for business markets.

TRADE SHOWS: STRATEGY BENEFITS

Most industries stage a business show or exhibition annually to display new advances and technological developments in the industry. The Trade Show Bureau indicates that some 600,000 U.S. firms place displays at trade shows each year and that 80 percent of trade show visitors are classified as "buying influencers." [33] Generally, sellers present their products and services in booths visited by interested industry members. The typical exhibitor will contact four to five potential purchasers per hour on the show floor.

A trade-show exhibit offers a unique opportunity to publicize a significant contribution to technology or to demonstrate new and old products. According to Thomas Bonoma, "For many companies, trade-show expenditures are the major—and for more than a few, the only—form of organized marketing communication activity other than efforts by sales force and distributors." [34] Through the trade show,

- an effective selling message can be delivered to a relatively large and interested audience at one time (for example, more than 30,000 people attend the annual Plant Engineering Show).
- new products can be introduced to a mass audience.

---

[33]"Trade Shows Make More Sense than Ever," *Business Marketing*, 77 (November 1992): pp. A7, A8.
[34]Thomas V. Bonoma, "Get More Out of Your Trade Shows," *Harvard Business Review*, 61 (January/February 1983): p. 76.

- customers can get hands-on experience with the product in a one-on-one selling situation.
- potential customers can be identified, providing sales personnel with qualified leads.
- general goodwill can be enhanced.
- free publicity is often generated for the company.

The cost of reaching a prospect at a trade show is approximately $185, whereas the cost of making an industrial sales call approaches $290. [35] Further, trade shows offer an excellent and cost-effective short-term method for introducing a product in new foreign markets.[36] An international trade fair enables a manufacturer to meet buyers directly, observe competition, and gather market research data. The entry time for exporting can easily be cut from six years to six months by attending foreign trade fairs.

TRADE SHOWS EFFECTIVENESS

A study by Exhibit Surveys, Inc., found that an average of 61 percent of the attendees of surveyed trade shows planned to purchase products displayed at the show in the next year. [37] According to the same firm, about 75 percent of the visitors to a sponsor's booth were able to recall the visit and the sponsor eight to ten weeks after the exhibit closed.[38] Trade show visitors usually have some buying authority—88 percent of trade show attendees have a role in buying and 40 percent have the final say, according to one study.[39] Among business marketing promotion tools for influencing the purchase decision process, trade shows have been ranked third behind peer recommendations and personal selling.[40] Both print advertising and direct mail followed trade shows in the rankings.

A recent study evaluated the impact of a trade show on the sales and profitability of a new laboratory testing device.[41] In a controlled experiment where new product sales could be traced to customers both attending and not attending the show, sales levels were higher among attendees. In turn, the proportion of customers buying the

---

[35] Trade Show Bureau, research publication SM20 (1992).

[36] Brad O'Hara, Fred Palumbo, and Paul Herbig, "Industrial Trade Shows Abroad," *Industrial Marketing Management*, 22 (August 1993): p. 235.

[37] Richard K. Swandby, Jonathan M. Cox, and Ian K. Sequeira, "Trade Shows Poised for 1990's Growth," *Business Marketing*, 75 (May 1990): p. 48.

[38] John M. Browning and Ronald J. Adams, "Trade Shows: An Effective Promotional Tool for the Small Industrial Business," *Journal of Small Business Management*, 26 (October 1988): p. 33.

[39] Jonathon Cox, "Making a Case for Trade Shows," *Business Marketing*, 81 (June 1996): p. T4.

[40] "Trade Shows Make More Sense Than Ever," p. A18; and A. Parasuraman, "The Relative Importance of Industrial Promotion Tools," *Industrial Marketing Management*, 10 (October 1981): pp. 277–281.

[41] Srinath Gopalakrishna, Gary L. Lilien, Jerome D. Williams, and Ian K. Sequeira, "Do Trade Shows Pay Off?" *Journal of Marketing*, 59 (July 1995): pp. 75–83.

product was higher among those who had visited the booth during the show. Importantly, there was a positive return on trade show investment (23 percent) based on incremental profits related to the cost of the trade show. This research is one of the first studies to show that the returns from trade show investments can indeed be measured. Although dramatically enhancing sales effectiveness, trade shows can be extremely costly, and must be carefully planned.

PLANNING TRADE SHOW STRATEGY

To develop an effective trade-show communications strategy, managers must address four questions:

1. What functions should the trade show perform in the total marketing communications program?
2. To whom should the marketing effort at trade shows be directed?
3. What is the appropriate show mix for the company?
4. What should the trade show investment–audit policy be? How should audits be carried out?[42]

Answering these questions helps managers crystallize their thinking about target audiences, about results to be expected, and about how funds should be allocated.

ROLE OF TRADE SHOWS

Trade shows play an important role in both the buying and selling processes. For example, based on the buygrid framework discussed in Chapter 3, trade shows can help a buyer recognize the need for a product, help develop product specifications, and assist in the search for a potential supplier. Trade shows can also be a useful medium for the buyer to provide feedback on product/service performance to current suppliers. Similarly, from the seller's perspective, the selling process may be considered as a sequence of six stages—prospecting, opening the relationship, qualifying the prospect, presenting the sales message, closing the sale, and servicing the account.[43] Except for actually closing the sale, trade shows can be very effective for the seller in almost every stage in the sales process. Trade shows also provide an excellent environment for nonselling activities such as information exchange, relationship building, and channel partner assessment. [44]

---

[42]Thomas V. Bonoma, "Get More Out of Your Trade Shows," p. 79.

[43]Gilbert A. Churchill Jr., Neil M. Ford, and Orville C. Walker, Jr., *Sales Force Management,* 4th ed. (Boston: Irwin, 1993): p. 42.

[44]Alex Sharland and Peter Balogh, "The Value of Nonselling Activities at International Trade Shows," *Industrial Marketing Management*, 25 (January 1996): pp. 59–66.

TRADE SHOW OBJECTIVES

Some of the functions of trade shows in generating sales include identifying decision influencers; identifying potential customers; providing product, service, and company information; learning of potential application problems; creating actual sales; and handling current customer problems. In addition to these selling-related functions, the trade show can be a valuable activity for building corporate image, gathering competitive intelligence, and enhancing sales force morale. Specific objectives are needed to guide the development of trade-show strategy and to specify the activities of company personnel while there. Given the importance of establishing clear objectives, it is surprising that the National Trade Show Bureau indicates that only 56 percent of firms that participate in trade shows have specific objectives.[45] Once specific objectives are formulated, however, the exhibitor must evaluate alternative trade shows in light of the target market.

SELECTING THE SHOWS

The challenge is to decide which trade shows to attend and how much of the promotional budget to expend.[46] Clearly, the firm will want to be represented at those shows frequented by its most important customer segments. A useful service is the *Exposition Audit* provided by the Business Publication Audit of Circulation. The audit reports registered attendance at trade shows and a complete profile of each registrant's business, job title, and function. Trade Show Central is an Internet site (http://www.tscentral.com) that provides access to 8,000 trade shows in a searchable database. A wealth of information on each show is provided and exhibitors can promote their presence at the show on the site.

Some firms will use the reports published by Exhibit Surveys, Inc., a company that surveys trade show audiences. Two of the important measures developed by Exhibit Surveys are the **Net Buying Influences** and the **Total Buying Plans.** The first measures the percentage of the show audience that has decision authority for the types of products being exhibited; the second measures the percentage of the audience planning to buy the products being exhibited within the next 12 months. These measures are very useful to the business marketing manager when selecting the most effective shows to attend.

Many firms make a preshow survey of their target prospects in order to learn which trade shows they will attend and what they hope to gain from attending. In this way the exhibitor can prepare its trade show strategy to fit the needs of its potential customers.

---

[45]Trade Show Bureau, "The Exhibitor: Their Trade Show Practices," The Trade Show Bureau study no. 19 (1983).

[46]See Aviv Shoham, "Selecting and Evaluating Trade Shows," *Industrial Marketing Management*, 21 (November 1992): pp. 335–341.

Others suggest that a firm rank order various shows based on expected profitability.[47] The expected profitability is computed by calibrating a model of "lead efficiency" using the firm's historical sales lead and lead conversion-to-sale data, gross margin information, and total attendance at past shows. **Lead efficiency** is defined as the number of sales leads obtained at the show divided by the total number of show visitors with definite plans to buy the exhibitor's product or one similar to it.

MANAGING THE TRADE SHOW EXHIBIT

In an effort to generate interest in an exhibit, Nippon Electric runs advertisements in trade publications profiling new projects to be exhibited at the show. This enables many exhibitors to schedule appointments with prospects and customers during the show.

Sales personnel must be trained to perform in the trade-show environment. The selling job differs from the typical sales call in that the salesperson may have only five to ten minutes to make a presentation. On a typical sales call, salespersons usually sell themselves first, then the company, and finally the product. At the trade show, the process is reversed.

There must be a system for responding effectively to inquiries generated at the show. Some business marketers find it effective to use a computer at the show to transmit information to corporate headquarters electronically. Headquarters staff then generate a letter and mailing label and send out the required information. When prospects return to their offices after a show, the material is already on their desks.

EVALUATING TRADE SHOW PERFORMANCE

The measurement of trade show performance is very important in assessing the success of a firm's trade show strategy. Srinath Gopalakrishna and Gary Lilien present a useful framework to assess performance by considering traffic flow through the firm's booth as a sequence of three stages.[48] Figure 16.6 illustrates the process and the development of three different indices of performance—attraction, contact, and conversion efficiency for the three respective stages.

An important contribution of this framework is the link between performance indices and key decision variables under the control of the firm. Attraction efficiency

---

[47]Srinath Gopalakrishna and Jerome D. Williams, "Planning and Performance Assessment of Industrial Trade Shows: An Exploratory Study," *International Journal of Research in Marketing*, 9 (September 1992): pp. 207–224.

[48]Srinath Gopalakrishna and Gary L. Lilien, "A Three-Stage Model of Industrial Trade Show Performance," *Marketing Science*, 14 (winter 1995): pp. 22–42.

Figure 16.6 Representation of Traffic Flow Model at Trade Shows as a Sequence of Stages

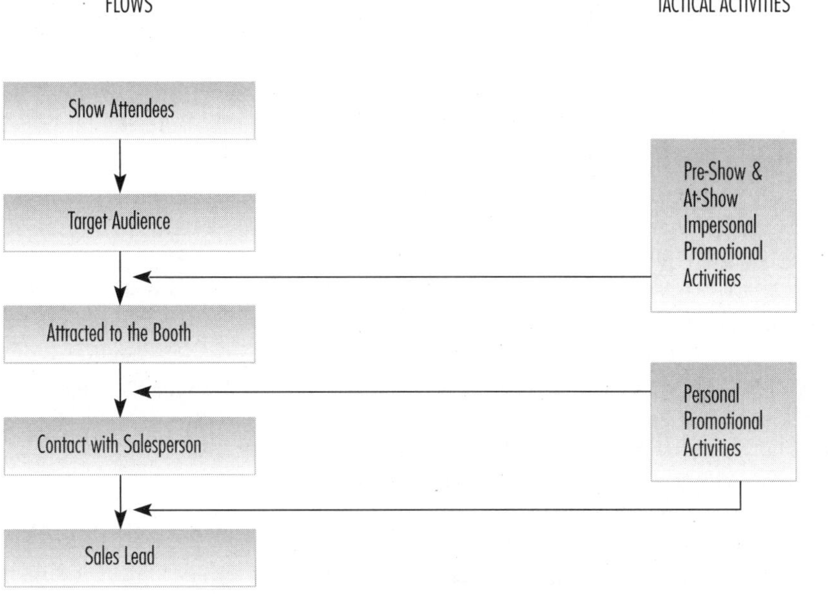

Source: Srinath Gopalakrishna and Gary L. Lilien, "A Three-Stage Model of Industrial Trade Show Performance," working paper #20-1992, Institute for the Study of Business Markets, Pennsylvania State University.

is the proportion of *interested* visitors that the booth is able to attract. Notice that the firm's target audience is the pool of visitors at the show who are interested in the firm's products, which is usually smaller than the total number of attendees at the show. The booth's attraction power is a function of booth space (square feet), show promotion, use of attention-getting techniques, and so on. Similarly, contact and conversion efficiencies are modeled as a function of the number of booth personnel and their level of training.

Firms spend more than $16 billion annually on trade shows.[49] For an individual firm, trade show expenditures should be tied to concrete marketing communication goals to secure an adequate return on investment. To this end, business marketing managers must carefully evaluate each trade show and its associated expenses in terms of the likely sales, profit, and corporate image impacts. As with all other promotional vehicles, the planning and budgeting for trade shows must focus on specific objectives. Once these objectives have been determined, the rational approach will then identify the tasks that must be accomplished and the levels of expenditure required.

[49]Gianna Jacobson, "Excellent Expos," *Success*, 43 (September 1996): p. 27.

Managing in the 21st Century

USING HIGH TECH TO PURSUE TRADE SHOW LEADS

Marketers fail to follow up on roughly 70 percent of leads from all sources, including trade shows. Electronic solutions are now being explored in the trade show arena to dramatically improve the lead management process.

Integrated Leads Management Systems, Inc. (ILMS) is a leader in the application of technology to follow up on leads generated at trade shows. ILMS places touch-screen monitors in an exhibitor's booth to enter data about an attendee's buying authority, buying intentions, budget, and other relevant data. This information is linked with data from the attendee's business card—name, company, address, and phone number—that is fed into the computer via a business card scanner.

Once data has been captured, the exhibitor can distribute the electronic leads via the Internet, fax, or proprietary E-mail. The ILMS system includes a wireless modem that allows for immediate distribution of the leads to the sales force. Use of this technology permits trade show exhibitors to determine if sales materialize, as well as estimate the cost per sales lead. Capturing information in real time and delivery through the Internet is predicted to be the "wave of the future" in lead management strategies.

Source: Adapted from Kate Bertrand, "High Tech Enhancements Fortify Trade Show Leads," *Business Marketing*, 81 (February 1996): pp. 1, 4.

Summary

Because of the nature of the business-to-business buying process, personal selling is the primary technique for creating sales; advertising supports and supplements personal selling. Yet advertising does perform some tasks that personal selling simply cannot perform. Advertising is able to reach buying influentials to whom sales personnel often do not have access.

Advertising supports personal selling by making the company and product known to potential buyers. The result is greater overall selling success. Effective advertising makes the entire marketing strategy more efficient, often lowering total marketing and selling costs. Finally, advertising can provide information and company or product awareness more efficiently than can personal selling.

Managing the advertising program begins with the determination of advertising objectives, which must be written and which must be directed to a specific audience. Once objectives are specified, funds must be allocated to advertising efforts. Rules of thumb, though common, are not the ideal methods for specifying advertising budgets. The objective-task method is more effective.

Advertising messages are created with the understanding that the potential buyer's perceptual process will influence receptivity to the message. The most effective appeal is one that projects product benefits sought by the targeted buying influential.

Advertising media are selected on the basis of their circulation; that is, how well their audience matches the desired audience of buying influentials. As business use of the Internet expands, business marketers will increasingly employ this media to communicate with target customers. Direct mail places advertisements in the hands of precisely defined audiences.

Finally, advertising effectiveness must be evaluated against the communication objectives established for the advertising campaign. Readership, recognition, awareness, attitudes, and intention to buy are typical measures of business-to-business advertising performance.

Trade show visitors tend to be buying influentials and the cost of reaching a prospect here is far lower than through the personal selling vehicle. A carefully planned and executed strategy is needed to secure promising returns on trade show investments. Trade shows are an effective way to reach large audiences with a single presentation, but funds must be allocated carefully.

Discussion Questions

1. Although the bulk of the promotional budget of the business marketing firm is allocated to personal selling, advertising can play an important role in business marketing strategy. Explain.

2. The Hamilton Compressor Company increased advertising expenditures 15 percent in the Chicago market last year, and sales increased 4 percent. Upon seeing the results, Mr. White, the president, turns to you and asks, "Was that increase in advertising worth it?" Outline your reply. (Feel free to include questions that you would ask Mr. White.)

3. Breck Machine Tool would like you to develop a series of ads for a new industrial product. Upon request, Breck's marketing research department will provide you with any data that they have concerning the new product and the market. Outline the approach that you would follow in selecting media and developing messages for the campaign. Specify the types of data that you would draw on to improve the quality of your decisions.

4. Outline how you would evaluate the effectiveness and efficiency of a business firm's advertising function. Focus on budgeting practices and performance results.

5. Explain how a message presented in an industrial advertisement may be favorably evaluated by the production manager, unfavorably evaluated by the purchasing manager, and fail even to trigger the attention of the quality control engineer.

6. Given the rapid rise in the cost of making industrial sales calls, should the business marketer attempt to substitute direct mail advertising for personal selling whenever possible? Support your position.

7. Describe the role that an Internet strategy might assume in the promotional mix of the business marketer.

8. It is argued that business advertising is not expected to precipitate sales directly. If business advertising does not persuade organizational buyers to buy brand *A* versus brand *B*, what does it do, and how can we measure its impact against expenditures on other marketing strategy elements?

Business Marketing Communications: Managing the Personal Selling Function

Chapter 17

Business marketing communications consist of advertising, sales promotion, and personal selling. As explored in the last chapter, advertising and related sales promotion tools supplement and reinforce personal selling. Personal selling is the most important demand-stimulating force in the business marketer's promotional mix. Through the sales force, the marketer links the firm's total product and service offering to the needs of organizational customers. After reading this chapter, you will understand

1. the role of personal selling in business marketing strategy.
2. the importance of viewing business marketing management as a buyer-seller interaction process.
3. the nature of the industrial sales management function.
4. the selected managerial tools that can be applied to major sales force decision areas.

The president and CEO of Motorola, Inc., aptly describes the strategic role that the salesperson assumes in the business market:

> *Members of our sales force are surrogates for customers. They should be able to reach back into Motorola and pull out technologists and other people that they need to solve problems and anticipate customer needs. We want to put the salesperson at the top of the organization. The rest of us then serve the salesperson. If we could get that mentality ingrained throughout Motorola, . . . I think we could move a long way toward where we need to be.*[1]

[1]Bernard Avishai and William Taylor, "Customers Drive a Technology-Driven Company: An Interview with George Fisher," *Harvard Business Review* 67 (November/December 1989): pp. 107–114.

In the marketing operations of the typical industrial firm, selling has been a dominant component, as well as a major determinant, of overall company success.[2] Personal selling is dominant in business markets because the number of potential customers is relatively small, compared to consumer markets, and the dollar purchases are large. The importance of personal selling in the marketing mix depends on such factors as the nature and composition of the market, the nature of the product line, and the company's objectives and financial capabilities. Business marketers have many potential links to the market. Some may rely on manufacturers' representatives and distributors, others rely exclusively on a direct sales force. Similarly, each firm must determine the relative importance of the various components of the promotional mix—advertising versus sales promotion versus personal selling.

Across all industries, the cost of an industrial sales call is nearly $300.[3] Computer firms report much higher costs, whereas chemical producers experience much lower ones. Of course, these figures vary, depending upon a host of company, product, and market conditions. They do indicate, however, that significant resources are invested in personal selling in the business market. To maximize effectiveness and efficiency, the personal selling function must be carefully managed and integrated into the firm's marketing mix. To enhance productivity and to respond to intense competition, sales strategists are employing a host of new approaches and technologies. Table 17.1 explores the changing face of the personal selling function.

Regardless of how a firm implements its sales strategy, the salesperson is the initial link to the marketplace and specific customers. The task of the salesperson is both complex and challenging. To meet all their customer's expectations, salespeople are required to have broad knowledge that extends beyond their own products.[4] They must be able to talk intelligently about competitors' products and about trends in the customer's industry. They must know not only their customer's business but also the business of their customer's customers. This chapter first considers how relevant aspects of organizational buying behavior (Chapter 3) are related to the personal selling process. The chapter then turns to sales force management and the need for defining personal selling objectives, structuring the sales organization, allocating the sales force, and evaluating and controlling sales force operations.

Foundations of Personal Selling: An Organizational Customer Focus

Personal selling is the means through which business marketing strategy is executed. Once the marketer defines target market segments on the basis of organizational characteristics (macrolevel) or the characteristics of decision-making units (microlevel), the sales force is deployed to meet the needs of these segments. The

[2]Thomas R. Wotruba, "The Transformation of Industrial Selling: Causes and Consequences," *Industrial Marketing Management* 25 (September 1996): p. 328.

[3]"1993 Sales Manager's Budget Planner," *Sales and Marketing Management* 143 (June 1993): p. 65.

[4]Martin Fojt, "Becoming a Customer-Driven Organization," *Journal of Services Marketing* 9, no. 3 (1995): pp. 7–8.

Table 17.1 The Evolution of Personal Selling: New Approaches and Technologies

Change	Sales Management Response
Intensified competition	More emphasis on developing and maintaining trust-based, long-term customer relationships
Greater emphasis on productivity	Increased use of technology (for example, portable computers, electronic mail, cellular phones, fax machines, telemarketing, and sales support systems)
Fragmentation of traditional customer bases	Sales specialists or support staff for specific customer types Multiple selling approaches (such as national accounts programs, traditional territory sales force, manufacturers' reps, and telemarketing) Globalization of sales effort
Customers dictating vendor quality and delivery standards	Team selling Compensation based on team performance and customer satisfaction
Demand for specialized knowledge as an input to purchase decisions	Team selling More emphasis on customer-oriented sales training More highly educated sales recruits

Source: From Thomas N. Ingram and Raymond W. LaForge, *Sales Management: Analysis and Decision Making*, 2d ed., (Fort Worth, Texas: 1992). Copyright © 1992 by The Dryden Press; reproduced by permission of the publisher.

salesperson augments the total product offering and serves as a representative for both seller and buyer. The image, reputation, and need-satisfying ability of the seller firm is conveyed, to an important degree, by the sales force. By helping procurement decision makers to define requirements and match the firm's product or service to requirements, the salesperson is offering not just a physical product but also ideas, recommendations, technical assistance, experience, confidence, and friendship. A large toy manufacturer, for example, evaluates suppliers on the basis of product quality, delivery reliability, price, *and* the value of ideas and suggestions provided by the sales personnel. This buying organization, in fact, openly solicits ideas, and evaluates suppliers formally on the number and quality of these recommendations.

As a representative for the buyer, the salesperson often articulates the specific needs of a customer to R&D or production personnel in the industrial firm. Product specifications, delivery, and technical service are often negotiated through the salesperson. The salesperson serves as an uncertainty absorption point, reducing conflict in the buyer-seller relationship. John Knopp, a regional sales manager at Hewlett-Packard, identifies this trait in high-performing salespersons: "They know how to get special things done for the customer inside or outside the system. When something has to be done outside of normal policies and practices, they find a way to get it done smoothly."[5]

[5]Thayer C. Taylor, "Anatomy of a Star Salesperson," *Sales and Marketing Management* 136 (May 1986): pp. 49–51.

ORGANIZATIONAL BUYING BEHAVIOR

Successful personal selling relies heavily on a recognition of the unique requirements of each organizational customer. Industrial products may have numerous applications; organizational buyers have varying levels of experience and information in purchasing certain products. A sensitivity to how buying organizations vary, coupled with a knowledge of organizational buying behavior, is the foundation for successful personal selling.

A salesperson can benefit by examining a potential buyer organization from several perspectives. First, how would the organization view this specific buying situation—new task, modified rebuy, or straight rebuy? As emphasized in Chapter 3, each buying situation calls for a unique personal selling strategy—the exact form depending on whether the marketer is an "in" or an "out" supplier. Second, what are the environmental, organizational, group, and individual influences on the organizational buying process?

The following considerations contribute to the personal selling task:[6]

1. *Environmental factor identification:* How do business conditions (for example, growth, inflation) or political and legal trends (for example, governmental regulation) affect the industry within which this firm operates?
2. *Organizational factor identification:* Is procurement in this buying organization centralized or decentralized? What are the strategic priorities of this firm? What role can our products and services assume in creating a competitive advantage for this firm?
3. *Buying center identification:* Which organization members are included in the buying center?
4. *Influence pattern identification:* Which buying center members exert the most power in the buying decision? What are the selection criteria of each?

Knowledge of the special competitive challenges that the buying firm faces, how the proposed product/service offering will be applied, how it will influence the cost structure and performance of various departments—these are the insights that enable the marketer to sharply focus personal selling strategy. Empathy with the buyer is the core of a mutually beneficial buyer-seller relationship.

Understanding the Customer's Business

Knowledge of customers' customers has been shown to be an effective way to create differentiation for a business marketer.[7] By developing a keen understanding of the

---

[6]Richard E. Plank and William Dempsey, "A Framework for Personal Selling to Organizations," *Industrial Marketing Management* 9 (April 1980): pp. 143–149; see also Barton A. Weitz, Harish Sujan, and Mita Sujan, "Knowledge, Motivation, and Adaptive Behavior: A Framework for Improving Selling Effectiveness," *Journal of Marketing* 50 (October 1986): pp. 174–191; and David M. Szymanski, "Determinants of Selling Effectiveness: The Importance of Declarative Knowledge to the Personal Selling Concept," *Journal of Marketing* 52 (January 1988): pp. 64–77.

[7]Daniel C. Smith, "Knowledge of Customers' Customers as a Basis for Sales Force Differentiation," *Journal of Personal Selling and Sales Management* 15 (summer 1995): pp. 1–15.

customer's business and using end-user market research, the salesperson can assist the buying company in creating value-adding services for the buyer's target customers. One study in the machine tool industry showed that successful firms in the industry demonstrated a clear understanding of the changing needs of machine tool buyers.[8] Less successful firms lacked an appreciation of their customers' requirements and did not understand the necessity of developing machine tools that focus on their customers' changing needs.

It appears that many firms are not very effective in understanding their customers' business. A study by *Sales and Marketing Management* revealed that only 20 percent of a sample of more than 400 purchasing managers were satisfied with the salesperson's knowledge about their business.[9] These findings suggest that salespeople should focus more attention on what a customer *really* needs: They should invest sufficient time to develop an in-depth knowledge of the key elements of the customer's business.

RELATIONSHIP MARKETING

The trend toward close relationships, or even strategic partnerships, between manufacturers and their suppliers is accelerating in many sectors of the business market. Several forces, highlighted throughout this textbook, support the movement toward closer buyer-seller relationships and away from distant, or even adversarial, relations: rising global competition, the quest for improved quality, rapidly changing technology, and the increased adoption of a just-in-time operations philosophy.[10]Assuming a key role in the relationship marketing program of the firm (see Chapter 3) is the industrial salesperson.

Selling Center

The members of the selling organization who are involved in initiating and maintaining exchange relationships with industrial customers constitute the **organizational selling center**[11] (see Figure 17.1). The needs of a particular selling situation, especially the information requirements, significantly influence the composition of the selling center. Its primary objectives are the acquisition and processing of pertinent marketing-related information and the execution of selling strategies. In many industries, teamwork has emerged as a necessary prerequisite for sales success—often requiring a formal selling team approach that is more structured than the loose

---

[8]Vivienne Shaw, "Successful Marketing Strategies: A Study of British and German Companies in the Machine Tool Industry," *Industrial Marketing Management* 24 (August 1995): pp. 329–339.
[9]Andy Cohen, "No Deal," *Sales and Marketing Management* 148 (August 1996): p. 51.
[10]See, for example, Charles O'Neal, "Concurrent Engineering with Early Supplier Involvement: A Cross Functional Approach," *International Journal of Purchasing & Materials Management* 29 (winter 1993): pp. 3–9.
[11]Michael D. Hutt, Wesley J. Johnston, and John R. Ronchetto Jr., "Selling Centers and Buying Centers: Formulating Strategic Exchange Patterns," *Journal of Personal Selling & Sales Management* 5 (May 1985): pp. 33–40; see also J. Brock Smith and Donald W. Barclay, "Team Selling Effectiveness: A Small Group Perspective," *Journal of Business-to-Business Marketing* 1, no. 2 (1993): pp. 3–32.

Figure 17.1 Relationship Management Processes in Business Marketing

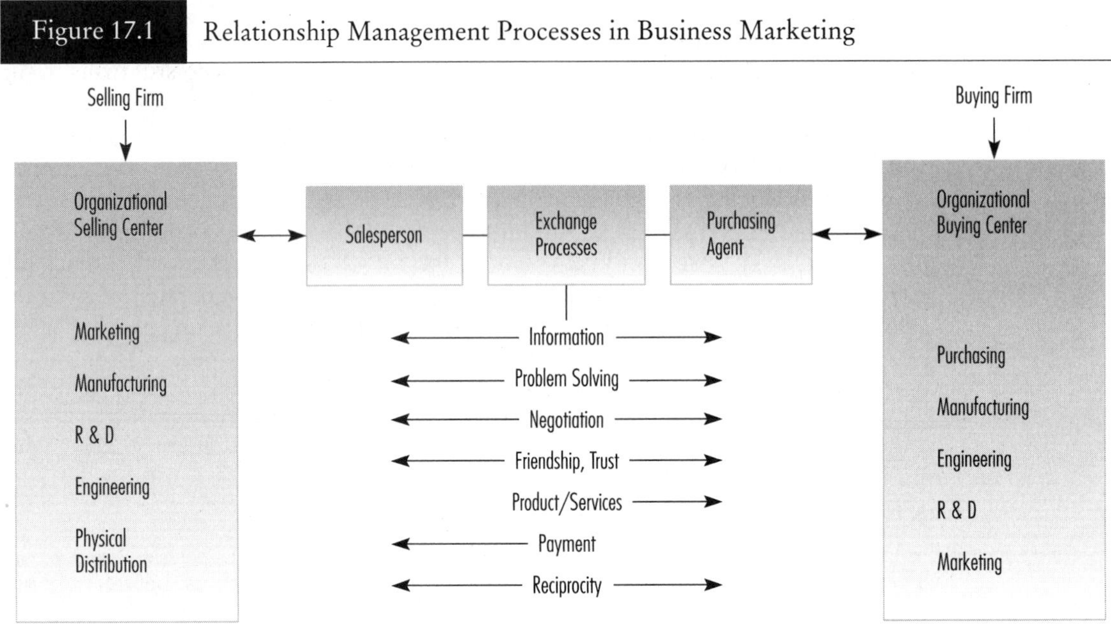

coalition of individuals in the selling center. [12] Some firms such as Xerox, Hewlett-Packard, and Du Pont have adopted formal selling teams.

The **organizational buying center** includes those individuals who participate in the purchasing decision and who share the goals and risks arising from that decision. The needs of a particular buying situation dictate the composition of the buying center (see Chapter 3). To illustrate, a new complex buying situation may include several participants representing different functional areas.

Assuming visible roles in this exchange process are the salesperson (selling-center representative) and the purchasing agent (buying-center representative). The salesperson and the buyer each begin the interaction with particular plans, goals, and intentions. The salesperson exchanges information and assistance in solving a purchasing problem for the reward of a sale given by the buyer or by members of the buying center.

In addition to external negotiations with members of the buying center, the industrial salesperson, acting on behalf of the potential customer, is often involved in internal negotiations with other members of the selling center, such as manufacturing or R&D, to ensure a successful exchange relationship with a particular customer. Internal negotiations also occur within the buying center because various members represent the interests of their functional areas in the selection of suppliers. Complex flows

[12]Dawn R. Deeter-Schmelz and Rosemary Ramsey, "A Conceptualization of the Functions and Roles of Formalized Selling and Buying Teams," *Journal of Personal Selling & Sales Management* 15 (spring 1995): pp. 47–60.

of influence characterize buyer-seller interactions in the business market.[13] To ensure maximum customer satisfaction and the desired market response, business marketers must effectively manage the complex web of influences that intersect in buyer-seller relationships.[14]

RELATIONSHIP QUALITY

By occupying a position close to the customer and drawing upon the collective strength of the organization, the industrial salesperson is often best suited to perform the role of "relationship manager." For many complex purchase decisions, industrial buyers face considerable uncertainty. From the customer's perspective, relationship quality is achieved through the salesperson's ability to reduce this uncertainty. **Relationship quality** comprises at least two dimensions: (1) trust in the salesperson and (2) satisfaction with the salesperson.[15] Confronting the uncertainty often present in complex industrial exchange settings, relationship quality contributes to a lasting bond by offering assurance that the salesperson will continue to meet the customer's expectations (satisfaction), and not knowingly distort information or otherwise damage the customer's interests (trust).[16] As Lawrence Crosby, Kenneth Evans, and Deborah Cowles conclude, "The continuity of interaction that relationship quality provides then creates ongoing opportunities for the seller to identify the customer's unmet needs and propose new business." [17]

Managing the Sales Force

Effective management of the industrial sales force is fundamental to the firm's success. Sales management refers to the planning, organizing, directing, and controlling of personal selling efforts.[18] Sales force decisions are tempered by overall marketing objectives

---

[13]Thomas V. Bonoma and Wesley J. Johnston, "The Social Psychology of Industrial Buying and Selling," *Industrial Marketing Management* 7 (July 1978): pp. 213–224; see also Nigel C. G. Campbell, John L. Graham, Alain Jolibert, and Hans Gunther Meissner, "Marketing Negotiations in France, Germany, the United Kingdom, and the United States," *Journal of Marketing* 52 (April 1988): pp. 49–62.

[14]John F. Tanner Jr., "Buyer Perspectives of the Purchase Process and Its Effect on Customer Satisfaction," *Industrial Marketing Management* 25 (March 1996): pp. 125–133.

[15]Lawrence A. Crosby, Kenneth R. Evans, and Deborah Cowles, "Relationship Quality in Services Selling: An Interpersonal Influence Perspective," *Journal of Marketing* 54 (July 1990): pp. 68–81. See also Jon M. Hawes, Kenneth E. Mast, and John E. Swan, "Trust Earning Perceptions of Sellers and Buyers," *Journal of Personal Selling & Sales Management* 9 (September 1989): pp. 1–8.

[16]Jon M. Hawes, James T. Strong, and Bernard S. Winick, "Do Closing Techniques Diminish Prospect Trust?" *Industrial Marketing Management* 25 (September 1996): pp. 349–360.

[17]Crosby, Evans, and Cowles, "Relationship Quality in Services Selling," p. 76. For a discussion of specific strategies, see James C. Anderson and James A. Narus, "Partnering as a Focused Market Strategy," *California Management Review* 33 (spring 1991): pp. 91–99.

[18]A comprehensive treatment of all aspects of sales management is beyond the scope of this volume. For more extensive discussion, see Gilbert A. Churchill Jr., Neil M. Ford, and Orville C. Walker Jr., *Sales Force Management*, 4th ed. (Homewood, Ill: Richard D. Irwin, 1993).

Managing in the 21st Century

THE 21ST CENTURY SALESPERSON

In an insightful article about the transformation of industrial selling, Thomas Wotruba suggests that dramatic changes are in store for business-to-business selling in the next century. He offers the following scenarios to describe how three aspects of selling will be altered in the coming years—the sales *position*, the selling *process*, and the *salesperson*.

THE SALES POSITION

- The salesperson becomes the manager of customer value and assumes direct responsibility for defining all components of the total package of value sought by each customer.
- The salesperson becomes a customer advocate, communicating to others inside the salesperson's firm what customers need and truly value.
- The salesperson becomes an important resource to policy and strategy makers inside the firm regarding product development, pricing, competitor behavior, and other customer-related information.

THE SALES PROCESS

- The salesperson must establish a relationship of trust and mutual benefit and compatibility with each key buying influence in the customer firm.
- The salesperson must actively obtain information from the customer as the basis for devising and revising the supplier's offerings.
- The salesperson must be the coordinator responsible to the customer for all exchanges in the relationship with that customer.

THE SALESPERSON

- The new salesperson will have eminent responsibility for sensing and diagnosing what must be offered to customers to make them happy. Additionally, the salesperson will need to relate to a wide variety of organizational members who represent various specialties within both vendor and customer companies.
- The new salesperson will require knowledge of the customer and customer operations, coordination skills, an ability to work in groups, analytical abilities, a top management perspective on what drives profitability of the company, broadened cultural perspectives, multiple language skills, ethical sensitivity, and a firm understanding of the legal and competitive environment.
- The new salesperson will require initiative moderated by discipline, and a desire to excel personally but with an orientation to company success. Importantly, the new salesperson will be self-managed, self-directed, and self-motivated.

Source: Thomas R. Wotruba, "The Transformation of Industrial Selling: Causes and Consequences," *Industrial Marketing Management* 25 (September 1996): pp. 335–337.

and must be integrated with the other elements of the marketing mix. Forecasts of the expected sales response guide the firm in determining the total selling effort required (sales force size) and in organizing and allocating the sales force (perhaps to sales territories). The techniques for estimating market potential and for forecasting sales (discussed in Part III, Assessing Market Opportunities) are particularly valuable in sales planning. Sales management also involves the ongoing activities of selecting, training, deploying, supervising, and motivating sales personnel. Finally, sales operations must be monitored to identify problem areas and to assess the efficiency, effectiveness, and profitability of personal selling units.

This section will consider three strategic components of sales force management: (1) methods for organizing the sales force, (2) the requirements for successful sales force administration, and (3) models that can be employed in deploying the industrial sales force.

ORGANIZING THE PERSONAL SELLING EFFORT

How should the sales force be organized? The appropriate form depends on many factors, including the nature and length of the product line, the role of intermediaries in the marketing program, the diversity of the market segments served, the nature of the buying behavior in each market segment, and the structure of competitive selling. The size and financial strength of the manufacturer often dictate, to an important degree, the feasibility of particular organizational forms. The business marketer can organize the sales force by geography, product, or market. Large industrial enterprises that market diverse product lines may employ all three at various points throughout the organizational structure.

Geographical Organization

The most common form of sales organization in business marketing is geographical. Each salesperson sells all the firm's products in a defined geographical area. By reducing travel distance and time between customers, this method usually minimizes costs. Likewise, sales personnel know exactly which customers and prospects fall within their area of responsibility.

The major disadvantage of the geographical sales organization is that each salesperson must be able to perform all of the selling tasks for all of the firm's products and for all customers in a particular territory. If the products have diverse applications, this can be very difficult. A second disadvantage is that the salesperson has substantial flexibility in choosing which products and customers to emphasize. Sales personnel may emphasize those products and end-use applications with which they are most familiar. Of course, this problem can be remedied through training and through capable first-line supervision. Because the salesperson is crucial in implementing the firm's segmentation strategy, careful coordination and control are required to align personal selling effort with marketing objectives.

Product Organization

A product-oriented sales organization is one in which salespersons specialize in relatively narrow components of the total product line. This is especially appropriate when the product line is large, diverse, or technically complex and when a salesperson needs a high degree of application knowledge in order to meet customer needs.

Furthermore, various products often elicit various patterns of buying behavior. The salesperson concentrating on a particular product becomes more adept at identifying and communicating with members of buying centers.

A prime benefit of this approach is that it enables the sales force to develop a level of product knowledge that enhances the value of the firm's total offering to customers. The product-oriented sales organization may also facilitate the identification of new market segments.

One drawback is the cost of developing and deploying a specialized sales force. A product must have the potential for generating a level of sales and profit that justifies individual selling attention. Thus, a "critical mass" of demand is required to offset the costs. In turn, several salespersons may be required to meet the diverse product requirements of a single customer. To reduce selling costs and improve productivity, some firms have launched programs to convert product specialists into general line specialists who are knowledgeable about all the firm's products and account strategies. Often, as customers learn to use technology, they outgrow the need for product specialists and prefer working with a single salesperson for all products.

Market-Centered Organization

The business marketer may prefer to organize personal selling effort by customer type. Owens-Corning Fiberglass Corporation recently switched from a geographical-based sales structure to one that is organized by customer type. Similarly, Hewlett-Packard successfully employed this structure to strengthen its market position in retailing, financial services, and oil and gas exploration.[19] Sales executives at *Fortune* 500 companies that utilize sales teams believe that they are better able to secure customers and improve business results by adopting a more customer-focused sales structure.[20]

By learning the specific requirements of a particular industry or customer type, the salesperson is better prepared to identify and respond to buying influentials. Also, key market segments become more accessible, thus providing the opportunity for differentiated personal selling strategies. The market segments must, of course, be sufficiently large to warrant specialized treatment.

ORGANIZING TO SERVE NATIONAL ACCOUNTS

To serve large and important customers, an increasing number of business marketers are establishing a national accounts program. The activities of several functional areas in the selling firm, such as design engineering, manufacturing, and logistics, can be carefully integrated to meet special customer needs.

National account management programs have been established by such corporations as Hewlett-Packard, AT&T, Dow Chemical, Union Carbide, Xerox, 3M, and Westinghouse. Why? The concentration of the business market, the trend toward centralized procurement, the rising importance of materials management and the ensu-

---

[19]Thayer C. Taylor, "Hewlett-Packard," *Sales and Marketing Management* 145 (January 1993): p. 59.
[20]Vincent Alonzo, *Incentive* 170 (September 1996): p. 46.

ing need for close buyer-seller coordination of inventory and logistical support, the increasing complexity of industrial products—these are among the forces that encourage the development of national account management programs.[21]

National Account Management[22]

A distinction can be made between major accounts and national accounts. A **major account** represents a significant amount of potential business. Major accounts are often served through multilevel selling with participation by salespersons, sales and marketing managers, and general managers from the selling organization. Major accounts typically are given separate attention because of their size, rather than because of the complexities of their requirements or organization. **National accounts** are both large and complex, requiring an even more elaborate selling process.

For example, Pitney Bowes' U.S. Business System Division, a producer of mailing, shipping, and copying products, serves more than one million business market customers.[23] The sales force has the following configuration:

- 50 national account managers serve its 400 largest customers.
- 100 major account managers reach the 1,500 multilocation customers who have centralized procurement.
- 3,500 area sales representatives cover all of its other existing and potential customers (approximately one million).

The complexity that requires a national accounts response can involve three customer dimensions: Customer buying points may be geographically dispersed; several functions (for example, engineering, purchasing, and procurement) are involved in the buying decision; and several autonomous divisions exist within the buying company.

National account management provides a mechanism for responding to these three dimensions of customer complexity. For example, rather than reaching the geographically dispersed plants of the Mead Corporation through geographically dispersed sales offices, a national account management program might be devised to deal with Mead centrally.

Characteristics of National Account Programs

National account management programs vary depending on the company and the industry environment, but they do have some features in common:[24]

1. National accounts are large, relative to other accounts served by the company, sometimes generating more than $50 million in sales revenue each.

---

[21]Benson P. Shapiro and Rowland T. Moriarty, *National Account Management: Emerging Insights*, Report No. 82-100 (Cambridge, Mass.: Marketing Science Institute, 1982), see also Andy Cohen, "A National Footing," *Sales and Marketing Management* 148 (April 1996): pp. 76–80.

[22]This section is largely based on Shapiro and Moriarty, *National Account Management*.

[23]Howard Sutton, *Rethinking the Company's Selling and Distribution Channels* (New York: The Conference Board, 1986), pp. 10–11.

[24]Benson P. Shapiro and John Wyman, "New Ways to Reach Your Customers," *Harvard Business Review* 59 (July/August 1981): p. 106.

2. The national account manager's responsibility often spans multiple divisions in the selling company.
3. The national account manager's team frequently includes support and operations personnel.
4. The selling activities of the national account manager span several functional areas in the buying company and may involve highly conceptual, financially oriented, systems sales.

Although the organizational structure can vary by company, Benson Shapiro and Rowland Moriarty assert that the common objective of national account management programs is "to provide incremental profits from large or potentially large complex accounts by being the preferred or sole supplier. To accomplish this goal, a supplier seeks to establish, over an extended period of time, an 'institutional' relationship, which cuts across multiple levels, functions, and operating units in both the buying and selling organization."[25] In other situations, a national accounts program is instituted to improve service, reduce sales costs, and reduce channel conflict.[26] Digital Equipment directly serves 2,000 corporate accounts. Several sales personnel are assigned to the 1,000 top-tier accounts in an effort to increase service and reduce selling expenses.

National Account Success

Research suggests that successful national account units enjoy senior management support; have well-defined objectives, assignments, and implementation procedures; and are staffed by experienced individuals who have a solid grasp of the resources and capabilities of the entire company.[27] Successful national account programs also adopt a strong relationship marketing perspective and consistently demonstrate their ability to meet the customer's immediate and future needs. Barbara Bund Jackson asserts that "Customers making long-term commitments care about longer-term issues: a vendor's general technological capabilities and direction, its financial ability to survive, the staying power of a particular technology, and so on."[28]

SALES ADMINISTRATION

Successful administration of the sales force involves recruiting and selecting salespersons and training, motivating, supervising, evaluating, and controlling the sales force. The industrial firm should foster an organizational climate that encourages the development of a successful sales force.

---

[25]Shapiro and Moriarty, *National Account Management*, p. 8.

[26]Jaikumar Vijayan, "Digital Sales Revamp Speeds Channels Push," *Computerworld* 30 (17 June 1996), p. 12.

[27]Linda Cardillo Platzer, *Managing National Accounts* (New York: The Conference Board, 1984), pp. 13–19; see also Thomas R. Wotruba and Stephen B. Castleberry, "Job Analysis and Hiring Practices for National Account Marketing Positions," *Journal of Personal Selling & Sales Management* 13 (summer 1993): pp. 49–65; and Andy Cohen, "A National Footing," pp. 76–80.

[28]Barbara Bund Jackson, *Winning and Keeping Industrial Customers* (Lexington, Mass.: Lexington Books, 1985), p. 105.

INSIDE BUSINESS MARKETING

FROM NATIONAL TO GLOBAL ACCOUNT MANAGEMENT AT HEWLETT-PACKARD

A global account management program was developed by Hewlett-Packard (H-P) to provide important customers with consistent worldwide service and support. Global accounts are chosen carefully. These customers must generate product and service revenue greater than $10 million, have significant computer purchases across two or three field operations, and be in a global industry segment of importance to H-P.

Once chosen, these customers are served by a global account manager (GAM). GAMs are located near the customer's headquarters and assume full responsibility for directly managing H-P's relationship with the global account. Specifically, GAMs are responsible for:

- worldwide customer sales, support and satisfaction;
- assuring that H-P is perceived as a single company at all customer locations;
- ensuring that adequate resources and personnel are provided to realize the potential identified in the global account;
- building a close working relationship with the senior corporate executives at H-P who are assigned to support the account.

A central feature of H-P's program involves measuring performance on a global account basis rather than on a product or geographic basis. Clear cost and revenue objectives are established for each global account. Moreover, through the program, customers receive globally-standardized products and services. Overall, senior executives and H-P customers believe that the program is extremely successful. Hewlett-Packard is strengthening its relationships with its best customers, increasing revenue per account, reducing costs, and sharing best practices with leading-edge global customers.

Source: George S. Yip and Tammy L. Madsen, "Global Account Management: The Next Frontier in Relationship Marketing," *International Marketing Review* 13 (No. 3, 1996), pp. 33- 38.

Recruitment and Selection of Salespersons

Today more emphasis is being placed on the recruiting process and on reducing salesperson turnover because, say Ben Enis and Lawrence Chonko, "today's salesperson must have many talents: knowledge of business, current affairs, and organizational politics; social graces to mingle with company presidents and workers on the shop floor; patience, persistence, and so forth."[29] In high-technology markets, the training costs per recruit may exceed $100,000.

The recruiting process presents numerous trade-offs for the business marketer. Should experienced salespersons be sought or should inexperienced individuals be hired and trained by the company? The answer is situation-specific; it varies with the

[29]Ben M. Enis and Lawrence B. Chonko, "A Review of Personal Selling: Implications for Managers and Researchers," in *Review of Marketing 1978,* ed. Gerald Zaltman and Thomas V. Bonoma (Chicago: American Marketing Association, 1978), p. 291.

size of the firm, the nature of the selling task, the firm's training capability, and its market experience. Smaller firms often reduce training costs by hiring experienced and more expensive salespersons. In contrast, large organizations with a more complete training function can hire less experienced personnel and support them with a carefully developed training program.

A second trade-off is the quantity-versus-quality question.[30] Often, sales managers screen as many recruits as possible when selecting new salespersons. However, this can overload the selection process, thus hampering the firm's ability to identify quality candidates. Recruiting, like selling, is an exchange process between two parties. Sales managers are realizing that for prospective salespersons, they need to demonstrate the personal development and career opportunities that a career with the firm offers. [31] A poorly organized recruiting effort that lacks closure leaves candidates with a negative impression. A well-organized recruiting effort ensures that candidates fitting the position requirements are given the proper level of attention in the screening process. Thus, procedures must be established to ensure that inappropriate candidates are screened out early, so that the pool of candidates is reduced to a manageable size.[32]

Responsibility for recruiting and selecting salespersons may lie with the first-line supervisor (who often receives assistance from an immediate superior), or with the human resources department, or with other executives at the headquarters level. The latter group tends to be more involved when the sales force is viewed as the training ground for marketing or general managers.

Training

To prepare new industrial salespersons adequately, the training program must be carefully designed. Periodic training is required to sharpen the skills of experienced salespersons, especially when the firm's environment is changing rapidly. Changes in business marketing strategy (for example, new products, new market segments) require corresponding changes in personal selling styles. One important trait for successful salespeople is adaptability. A recent study found that adaptable salespeople are effective at identifying cues that signify differences in purchase behavior across differing customer groups.[33]

The salesperson needs a wealth of knowledge about the company, the product line, customer segments, competition, organizational buying behavior, and effective communication skills. All these must be part of industrial sales training programs. Compared to their counterparts, top performing sales organizations train new salespeople in a broader range of areas: market knowledge, communication skills, listening techniques, complaint-handling skills, and industry knowledge.[34]

---

[30]Benson P. Shapiro, *Sales Management: Formulation and Implementation* (New York: McGraw-Hill, 1977), p. 457.

[31]Charles Butler, "Why the Bad Rap?" *Sales and Marketing Management* 148 (June 1996): pp. 58–66.

[32]Wesley J. Johnston and Martha C. Cooper, "Industrial Sales Force Selection: Current Knowledge and Needed Research," *Journal of Personal Selling & Sales Management* 1 (spring/summer 1981): pp. 49–53.

[33]John J. Withey and Eric Panitz, "Face-to-Face Selling: Making It More Effective," *Industrial Marketing Management* 24 (August 1995): pp. 239–246.

[34]Adel I. El-Ansary, "Selling and Sales Management in Action: Sales Force Effectiveness Research Reveals New Insights and Reward-Penalty Patterns in Sales Force Training," *Journal of Personal Selling & Sales Management* 13 (spring 1993): pp. 83–90.

With the expansion in global marketing, firms need to include a sales training module that examines how to approach and respond to customers of different cultures. The focus of such training would be on the role of intercultural communication in developing global buyer-seller relationships.[35] Effective training builds confidence and motivation in the salesperson, thereby increasing the probability of successful performance. In turn, training helps the business marketer by keeping personal selling in line with marketing program objectives. A successful training effort can reduce the costs of recruiting; many industrial firms have found that salesperson turnover declines as training improves. Clearly, a salesperson who is inadequately prepared to meet the demands of selling can quickly become discouraged, frustrated, and envious of friends who chose other career options. Much of this anxiety—which is especially prevalent in the early stages of many careers—can be alleviated by effective training and capable first-line supervision.[36]

Supervision and Motivation

The sales force must be directed in a way that is consistent with the company's policies and marketing objectives. Critical supervisory tasks are continued training, counseling, assistance (for example, time management), and activities that help sales personnel plan and execute their work. Supervision also sets sales performance standards, fulfills company policy, and integrates the sales force with higher organizational levels.

Orville Walker Jr., Gilbert Churchill Jr., and Neil Ford define motivation as the amount of effort the salesperson "desires to expend on each of the activities or tasks associated with his (her) job, such as calling on potential new accounts, planning sales presentations, and filling out reports."[37] The model presented in Figure 17.2 hypothesizes that a salesperson's job performance is a function of three factors: (1) level of motivation, (2) aptitude or ability, and (3) perceptions about how his or her role should be performed. Each is influenced by personal variables (for example, personality), organizational variables (for example, training programs), and environmental variables (for example, economic conditions). Sales managers can influence some of the personal and organizational variables through selection, training, and supervision.

Motivation to perform is thought to be related strongly to (1) the individual's perceptions of the types and amounts of rewards that will accrue from various degrees of job performance and (2) the value the salesperson places on these rewards. For a given level of performance, two types of rewards might be offered:

---

[35]Victoria D. Bush and Thomas Ingram, "Adapting to Diverse Customers: A Training Matrix for International Marketers," *Industrial Marketing Management* 25 (September 1996): pp. 373–383.

[36]For a discussion of salesperson turnover, see George H. Lucas Jr., A. Parasuraman, Robert A. Davis, and Ben M. Enis, "An Empirical Study of Salesforce Turnover," *Journal of Marketing* 51 (July 1987): pp. 34–59; and Charles M. Futrell and A. Parasuraman, "The Relationship of Satisfaction and Performance to Salesforce Turnover," *Journal of Marketing* 48 (fall 1984): pp. 33–40.

[37]Orville C. Walker Jr., Gilbert A. Churchill Jr., and Neil M. Ford, "Motivation and Performance in Industrial Selling: Present Knowledge and Needed Research," *Journal of Marketing Research* 14 (May 1977): pp. 156–168. See also Steven P. Brown, William L. Cron, and Thomas W. Leigh, "Do Feelings of Success Mediate Sales Performance-Work Attitude Relationships?" *Journal of the Academy of Marketing Science* 21 (spring 1993): pp. 91–100.

Figure 17.2 Determinants of a Salesperson's Performance

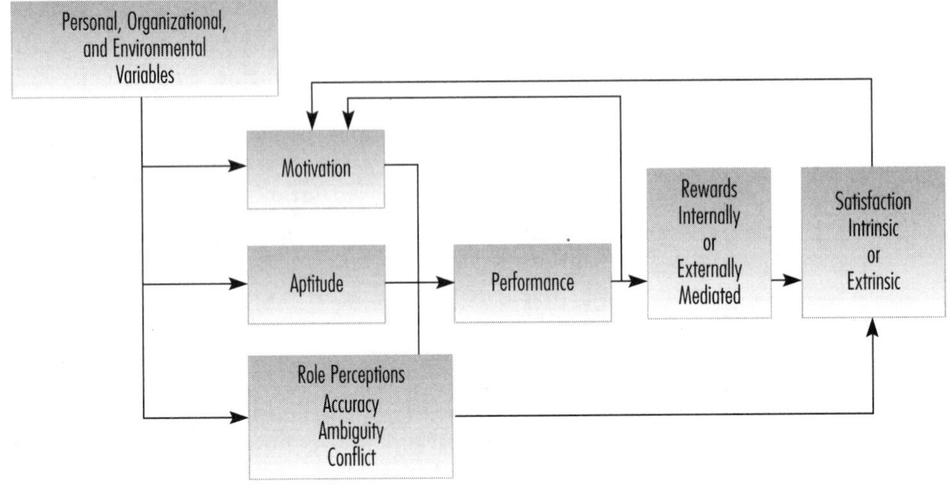

Source Orville C. Walker Jr., Gilbert A. Churchill Jr., and Neil M. Ford, "Motivation and Performance in Industrial Selling: Present Knowledge and Needed Research," *Journal of Marketing Research* 14 (May 1977): p. 158. Reprinted by permission of the American Marketing Association.

1. *Internally mediated rewards:* The salesperson attains rewards on a personal basis, such as feelings of accomplishment or self-worth.
2. *Externally mediated rewards:* Rewards are controlled and offered by managers or customers, such as financial incentives, pay, or recognition.

The rewards strongly influence salesperson satisfaction with the job and the work environment, which is also influenced by the individual's role perceptions. Job satisfaction is theorized to decline when the salesperson's perception of the role is (1) *inaccurate* in terms of the expectations of superiors, (2) characterized by *conflicting* demands among role partners (company and customer) that the salesperson cannot possibly resolve, or (3) surrounded by *uncertainty* due to a lack of information about the expectations and evaluation criteria of superiors and customers.

Business marketers often utilize formal incentive programs to achieve specified customer service, sales, and profit results. Typically, an incentive program offers rewards for achieving a well-defined goal during a specified time frame. The rewards used in such programs must be well conceived, based on what salespeople value, tied to achieving desired behavior, and recognize both individual and team behavior.[38] Frequently, recognition is a key ingredient in sales incentive programs and may run the

[38]Katherine Morrall, "Motivating Sales Staff with Rewards," *Bank Marketing* 28 (July 1996): pp. 32–38.

gamut from Hewlett-Packard's quarterly award for a salesperson who was particularly astute in converting an objection into an order to the elaborate sales award presentations at IBM.

Organizational Climate and Job Satisfaction[39]

Gilbert Churchill Jr., Neil Ford, and Orville Walker Jr., who contributed the model presented in Figure 17.2, also provide empirical support for some propositions that flow from the model. In examining job satisfaction in a cross section of industrial salespersons, the authors found that role ambiguity and role conflict have a detrimental influence on job satisfaction. Salespersons are likely to experience anxiety and dissatisfaction when they are uncertain about the expectations of role partners or when they feel that role partners (for example, customers, superiors) are making demands that are incompatible and impossible to satisfy.

An effective approach for reducing role ambiguity among new salespeople is a program of training and socialization that offers sufficient information about role expectations and minimizes potential confusion concerning performance requirements. Strategies that reduce role ambiguity are likely to have positive effects on sales performance as well as on job satisfaction.[40] Moreover, a socialization program that provides newly hired salespersons with a realistic picture of their job will strengthen their organizational commitment.[41]

Job Satisfaction: Managerial Implications

Salespersons tend to have a higher level of job satisfaction when (1) they perceive that their first-line supervisor closely directs and monitors their activities, (2) management provides them with the assistance and support needed to meet unusual and nonroutine problems, and (3) they perceive themselves to have an active part in determining company policies and standards that affect them. Job satisfaction also appears to be related more to the substance of the contact between sales managers and salespersons than to its frequency. Also, salespersons appear to be able to accept direction from a number of departments in the organization without a significant negative impact on job satisfaction; unity of command does not appear to be a prerequisite for high morale.

---

[39]This section is based on Gilbert A. Churchill Jr., Neil M. Ford, and Orville C. Walker Jr., "Organizational Climate and Job Satisfaction in the Salesforce," *Journal of Marketing Research* 13 (November 1976): pp. 323–332. For related discussions, see R. Kenneth Teas and James C. McElroy, "Causal Attributions and Expectancy Estimates: A Framework for Understanding the Dynamics of Salesforce Motivation," *Journal of Marketing* 50 (January 1986): pp. 75–86; William L. Cron, Alan J. Dubinsky, and Ronald E. Michaels, "The Influence of Career Stages on Components of Salesperson Motivation," *Journal of Marketing* 52 (January 1988): pp. 78–92; and Jeffrey K. Sager, Charles M. Futrell, and Rajan Varadarajan, "Exploring Salesperson Turnover: A Causal Model," *Journal of Business Research* 18 (June 1989): pp. 303–326.

[40]Steven P. Brown and Robert A. Peterson, "Antecedents and Consequences of Salesperson Job Satisfaction: Meta-Analysis and Assessment of Causal Effects," *Journal of Marketing Research* 30 (February 1993): pp. 63–77.

[41]Mark W. Johnston, A. Parasuraman, Charles M. Futrell, and William C. Black, "A Longitudinal Assessment of the Impact of Selected Organizational Influences on Salespeople's Organizational Commitment during Early Employment," *Journal of Marketing Research* 27 (August 1990): pp. 333–343.

Turnover

Performance and individual differences in achievement motivation, self-esteem, and verbal intelligence may also affect job satisfaction. Richard Bagozzi notes that "Salespeople tend to be more satisfied as they perform better, but the relationship is particularly sensitive to the level of motivation and positive self-image of the person. Although management may have no direct control over the performance achieved by salespeople, they can influence the level of motivation and self-esteem through effective incentive and sensitive supervisor-employee programs and thereby indirectly affect both performance and job satisfaction."[42] Research suggests that the leadership behavior of sales managers directly and indirectly influences salespersons' job satisfaction, which in turn affects sales force turnover.[43] In addition, another study indicates that salespeople who are managed by "high performing" sales managers exhibit less role stress and are more satisfied than their colleagues.[44] Although there are some factors that influence job satisfaction and performance beyond the control of sales managers, this line of research points up the importance of responsive training, supportive supervision, and clearly defined company policies that are congruent with the needs of the sales force.

Evaluation and Control

An ongoing sales management responsibility is the monitoring and control of the industrial sales force at all levels—national, regional, and district—in order to determine whether objectives are being attained and to identify problems, recommend corrective action, and keep the sales organization in tune with changing competitive and market conditions.

Performance Measures[45]

Sales managers use both behavior-based and outcome measures of salesperson performance. When a sales force control system is more **behavior-based,** the sales manager monitors and directs the activities of salespeople, uses subjective measures of salesperson behavior to evaluate performance, and emphasizes a compensation system with a large fixed component. Behavior-based selling measures include the salesperson's knowledge of product applications, knowledge of the company's

---

[42]Richard P. Bagozzi, "Performance and Satisfaction in an Industrial Sales Force: A Causal Modeling Approach," in *Sales Management: New Developments from Behavioral and Decision Model Research,* (Cambridge, Mass.: Marketing Science Institute, 1979), pp. 70–91; see also Bagozzi, "Performance and Satisfaction in an Industrial Sales Force: An Examination of Their Antecedents and Simultaneity," *Journal of Marketing* 44 (spring 1980): pp. 65–77.

[43]Eli Jones, "Leader Behavior, Work Attitudes, and Turnover of Salespeople: An Integrative Study," *Journal of Personal Selling & Sales Management* 16 (spring 1996): pp. 13–23.

[44]Frederick A. Russ, Kevin M. McNeilly, and James M. Comer, "Leadership, Decision-Making, and Performance of Sales Managers," *Journal of Personal Selling & Sales Management* 16 (summer 1996): pp. 1–15.

[45]This section is based on David W. Cravens, Thomas N. Ingram, Raymond W. LaForge, and Clifford E. Young, "Behavior-Based and Outcome-Based Salesforce Control Systems," *Journal of Marketing* 57 (October 1993): pp. 47–59.

technology, and the clarity of the salesperson's presentations to customers. By contrast, an **outcome-based** sales force control system involves less direct field supervision of salesperson activities, and employs objective measures to evaluate performance and a compensation system with a large incentive component. Sales force outcome measures include sales results, market-share gains, new-product sales, and profit contributions.

Setting Performance Standards

The standards by which salespersons are evaluated offer the means for comparing the performance of various salespersons or sales units (for example, districts), as well as for gauging the overall productivity of the sales organization. Managerial experience and judgment are important in developing appropriate standards. Importantly, the standards must relate to overall marketing objectives, and they must take into account differences in sales territories, for which the number and aggressiveness of competitors, the level of market potential, and the workload can vary markedly.

Recent evidence suggests that a strict reliance on outcome measures and incentive compensation plans may not produce the desired sales or marketing performance results: "The alleged automatic supervisory power of incentive pay plans has lulled some sales executives into thinking that important sales outcomes could be reasonably accomplished without intense management reinforcement in noncompensation areas."[46] Often, a more balanced approach that assigns a more prominent role to field sales managers and emphasizes behavior-based measures is more effective.[47]

Behavior-based measures also fit relationship selling—an important strategy in the business market. Relationship selling requires salespeople who can relate to a team orientation and who can focus on activities such as sales planning and sales support, as well as on goals such as customer satisfaction.

Models for Industrial Sales Force Management

To this point, our discussion has been concerned with (1) recruiting and selection, (2) training, (3) motivation and supervision, and (4) evaluation and control. Poor decisions in one area can create a backlash in other areas. One critical sales management task remains: deploying the sales force. The objective is to form the most profitable sales territories, deploy salespersons to serve potential customers in those territories, and effectively allocate sales force time among those customers.

---

[46]Ibid., p. 56.

[47]Richard L. Oliver, "Behavior- and Outcome-Based Sales Control Systems: Evidence and Consequences of Price-Form and Hybrid Governance," *Journal of Personal Selling & Sales Management* 15 (fall 1995): pp. 1–15.

Ethical Business Marketing

ETHICS IN SELLING

Here are some common scenarios that a sales person confronts. Consider how you would handle each.

Scenario 1: In an attempt to negotiate the best price, sales rep Bill Smith tries to communicate to purchasing agents that plant capacity is at a very high level because of the popularity of this product. Bill does this even when plant capacity is low.

Scenario 2: Occasionally customers of Bill Smith ask which of his products he recommends for their company. Regardless of real customer need, Bill recommends one of the more expensive items in his product line.

Scenario 3: Industrial sales representative Mary Johnson needs to make a yearly quota of $500,000. During the last month of the year, Mary is $10,000 below quota. Toward the end of the month, Mary is still about $5,000 below quota when she receives an order for $3,000. To make quota, Mary doubles the order without telling the customer. Mary turns in a $6,000 order and makes quota. Mary decides to tell the customer that the order processing department made the mistake. She figures there is a good chance the customer will accept the double order rather than go to the inconvenience of returning the goods.

As links between their organizations and the customers, salespersons encounter situations that may lead to ethical conflicts. Consider the personal, organizational, and societal stakes that underlie each of these vignettes.

Source: Joseph A. Bellizzi and Robert E. Hite, "Supervising Unethical Salesforce Behavior," *Journal of Marketing* 53 (April 1989): pp. 36–47; see also Shelby D. Hunt and Arturo Z. Vasquez-Parraga, "Organizational Consequences, Marketing Ethics, and Salesforce Supervision," *Journal of Marketing Research* 30 (February 1993): pp. 78–90.

DEPLOYMENT ANALYSIS: A STRATEGIC APPROACH

The size of the sales force establishes the level of selling effort that can be employed by the business marketer. The selling effort is then organized by designating sales districts and sales territories. Allocation decisions determine how the selling effort is to be assigned to customers, prospects, and products. All these are illustrated in Table 17.2.

Proper deployment requires a multistage approach to find the most effective and efficient means of assigning sales resources (for example, sales calls, number of salespersons, percentage of salesperson's time) across all of the **planning and control units (PCUs)** served by the firm (for example, prospects, customers, territories, districts, products).[48] Thus, effective deployment means understanding the factors that influence sales in a particular PCU, such as a territory.

[48]David W. Cravens and Raymond W. LaForge, "Sales Force Deployment," in *Advances in Business Marketing*, vol. 1, ed. Arch G. Woodside (Greenwich, Conn.: JAI Press, 1986), pp. 67–112; and LaForge and Cravens, "Steps in Selling Effort Deployment," *Industrial Marketing Management* 11 (July 1982): pp. 183–194.

Table 17.2 Deployment Decisions Facing Sales Organizations

Type of Decision	Specific Deployment Decisions
Set total level of selling effort	Determine sales force size
Organize selling effort	Design sales districts Design sales territories
Allocate selling effort	Allocate effort to trading areas Allocate sales calls to accounts Allocate sales calls to prospects Allocate sales call time to products Determine length of sales call

Source Reprinted by permission of the publisher from "Steps in Selling Effort Deployment," by Raymond LaForge and David W. Cravens, *Industrial Marketing Management* 11 (July 1982): p. 184. Copyright © 1982 by Elsevier Science Publishing Co., Inc.

Territory Sales Response

What influences the level of sales that a salesperson might achieve in a particular territory? Eight classes of variables are outlined in Table 17.3. This list shows the complexity of estimating sales response functions. Such estimates are needed, however, to make meaningful sales allocations.

Three territory traits deserve particular attention in sales response studies: potential, concentration, and dispersion.[49] **Potential** (as discussed in Chapter 7) is a measure of the total business opportunity for all sellers in a particular market. **Concentration** is the degree to which potential is confined to a few larger accounts in that territory. If potential is concentrated, the salesperson can cover with a few calls a large proportion of the potential. Finally, if the territory is geographically **dispersed,** sales will probably be lower due to time wasted in travel. Past research often centered on **territory workload**—the number of accounts. However, Adrian Ryans and Charles Weinberg report that workload is of questionable value in estimating sales response: "From a managerial standpoint, the recurrent finding of an association between potential and sales results suggests that sales managers should stress territory potential when making sales force decisions."[50]

Sales Resource Opportunity Grid

Deployment analysis matches sales resources to market opportunities. Planning and control units such as sales territories or districts are part of an overall portfolio, with

[49]Adrian B. Ryans and Charles B. Weinberg, "Territory Sales Response," *Journal of Marketing Research* 16 (November 1979): pp. 453–465; see also Ryans and Weinberg, "Territory Sales Response Models: Stability over Time," *Journal of Marketing Research* 24 (May 1987): pp. 229–233.

[50]Ryans and Weinberg, "Territory Sales Response," p. 464.

Table 17.3 Selected Determinants of Territory Sales Response

1. Environmental factors (e.g., health of economy)
2. Competition (e.g., number of competitive salespersons)
3. Company marketing strategy and tactics
4. Sales force organization, policies, and procedures
5. Field sales manager characteristics
6. Salesperson characteristics
7. Territory characteristics (e.g., potential)
8. Individual customer factors

Source Adapted from Adrian B. Ryans and Charles B. Weinberg, "Territory Sales Response," *Journal of Marketing Research* 16 (November 1979): pp. 453–465.

various units offering various levels of opportunity and requiring various levels of sales resources. A sales resource opportunity grid can be used to classify the industrial firm's portfolio of PCUs.[51] In Figure 17.3, each PCU is classified on the basis of PCU opportunity and sales organization strength.

PCU opportunity is the total potential that the PCU represents for all sellers, whereas **sales organization strength** includes the competitive advantages or distinctive competencies that the firm enjoys within the PCU. By positioning all PCUs on the grid, the sales manager can assign sales resources to those PCUs that have the greatest level of opportunity and that also capitalize on the particular strengths of the sales organization.

At various points in deployment decision making, the sales resource opportunity grid is important for screening the size of the sales force, the territory design, and the allocation of sales calls to customer segments. This method can isolate deployment problems or deployment opportunities worthy of sales management attention and further data analysis.

THE AUTOMATED SALES FORCE

Business marketing firms, large and small, have equipped their salespersons with personal computers and have created automated sales systems that integrate the sales, telemarketing, marketing, and customer service functions. A laptop computer provides an important tool for the salesperson in account management, time management, call planning, sales forecasting, and other activities. Users report that the productivity gains derived from the automation of the sales force often exceed 20 percent.[52]

---

[51] LaForge and Cravens, "Steps in Selling Effort Deployment," pp. 183–194.

[52] Thayer C. Taylor, "Computers Bring Quick Return," *Sales and Marketing Management* 145 (September 1993): pp. 22–25.

Figure 17.3 Sales Resource Opportunity Grid

PCU Opportunity	Sales Organization Strength: High	Sales Organization Strength: Low
High	**Opportunity Analysis** PCU offers good opportunity because it has high potential and because sales organization has strong position **Sales Resource Assignment** High level of sales resources to take advantage of opportunity	**Opportunity Analysis** PCU may offer good opportunity if sales organization can strengthen its position **Sales Resource Assignment** Either direct a high level of sales resources to improve position and take advantage of opportunity or shift resources to other PCUs
Low	**Opportunity Analysis** PCU offers stable opportunity because sales organization has strong position **Sales Resource Assignment** Moderate level of sales resources to keep current position strength	**Opportunity Analysis** PCU offers little opportunity **Sales Resource Assignment** Minimal level of sales resources; selectively eliminate resource coverage; possible elimination of PCU

Source Reprinted by permission of the publisher from "Steps in Selling Effort Deployment," by Raymond LaForge and David W. Cravens, *Industrial Marketing Management* 11 (July 1982): p. 187. Copyright © 1982 by Elsevier Science Publishing Co., Inc.

Applying Sales Technology

Many of the software systems used for sales force automation provide more informational power for a salesperson than most desktop PCs offered just a short time ago.[53] The typical system connects to large database servers that draw information from existing business systems, management reports, outside sources, and data provided by sales staff. Often, Web-based intranets are used to manage and track the sales process and these systems provide accessibility to document databases from any Web

[53]Mindy Blodget, "Sales Force Automation Tools: You Just Gotta Have 'Em," *Computerworld,* 29 July 1996, p. 78.

client.[54] Kodak salespeople are equipped with IBM Thinkpads, which give them easy access to product catalogs, price lists, and competitive information. The Kodak reps are able to create a sales proposal in one day and transmit it electronically.[55]

Although sales force automation has become a competitive necessity, many salespersons are slow to apply the technology to the selling task. In some cases, the benefits do not meet the sales rep's expectations. Some salespeople find that the greatest help is with nonselling activities like forecasting, billing, and account management—activities that support, but are ancillary to, the main selling mission. Analyzing needs, diagnosing problems, and communicating—the core of the selling process—are often felt to be more "art" than science and, therefore, less amenable to automation.[56] Importantly, the business marketing manager must carefully direct the introduction of technology to the sales force, provide the required training and support, and ensure that the technology is being applied to improve the efficiency and effectiveness of the selling process.

Compaq Computer's Electronic Sales Force

By automating its 225-member sales force in North America, Compaq Computer has recorded impressive gains in revenues per sales rep and other productivity measures. Compaq's CEO, Eckard Pfeifer, describes the system:

> *Every workday our reps log into our client/server network with a billion bytes on-line. The database includes a centralized account listing where Compaq people from different departments record their contact with each present and prospective customer. All customers have market segment codes. The system also contains marketing material, technical reports, application stories, and electronic mail. Sales managers and engineering, customer service, and other staffers can scan the network for updates. Reps typically download the material they need for their current day's meetings into a notebook computer or what they call their tool box. . . . They don't have to carry around overhead projectors and transparencies. If they want to leave a brochure or schematic with a client, they just produce one on the laptop computer. . .*[57]

A MODEL FOR ALLOCATING SALES EFFORT

Several models are available to support the decision maker in allocating sales effort.[58] These models can be used in conjunction with the sales resource opportunity grid.

---

[54]Jim Rosenberg, "Mobile Ad Sales Systems Multiply," *Editor and Publisher,* 6 July 1996, p. 26.

[55]Tom Field, "Covering New Territory," *CIO* 9 (September 1996): p. 66.

[56]Kim Harris, "Issues Concerning Adoption and Use of Sales Force Automation in the Agricultural Input Supply Sector," *Agribusiness* 12 (July/August 1996): pp. 317–326.

[57]B. Charles Ames and James D. Hlavacek, *Market-Driven Management: Creating Profitable Top-Line Growth* (Chicago: Irwin Professional Publishing, 1997), pp. 138–139.

[58]For example, see Leonard M. Lodish, "CALLPLAN: An Interactive Salesman's Call Planning System," *Management Science* 18 (December 1971): pp. 25–40; see also Lodish, "Sales Territory Alignment to Maximize Profit," *Journal of Marketing Research* 12 (February 1975): pp. 30–36; and James M. Comer, "The Computer, Personal Selling and Sales Management," *Journal of Marketing* 39 (July 1975): pp. 27–33.

To illustrate the workings of these models, the Purchase Attitudes and Interactive Response to Sales[people] (PAIRS) model will be discussed. Developed by A. Parasuraman and Ralph Day, this model draws on the relevant features of earlier models—most notably CALLPLAN—and incorporates some new features.[59] Key components, or building blocks, of this model are discussed in sequence.

1. Customers in a territory who are similar in their response to selling efforts are classified into mutually exclusive and collectively exhaustive groups of approximately equal potential.
2. Salesperson characteristics that management deems useful to the selling job are employed. Selling ability is dependent on characteristics such as education, knowledge of the company's products, and personal traits.
3. The impact of selling effort on a customer in any period depends on the selling ability of sales personnel as well as on the number of sales calls made.
4. The planning horizon is divided into periods of time based on the average length of the purchase cycle or a similar criterion.
5. Variations in the time per sales call for various customers are included.
6. The expected total volume of sales from each type of customer is specified in terms of potential dollar revenue.
7. The model's output consists of an estimate of the sales revenue for each customer or customer group for each period in the planning horizon.

Using the PAIRS Model

The PAIRS model draws upon the experience and judgment of sales managers as well as on that of salespersons. Sales managers participate in the development of a salesperson's **effectiveness index** by defining the selling skills viewed as important in dealing with the company's customers. Each salesperson is rated on each characteristic on a scale of 0 (extremely poor) to 10 (excellent). These skills or characteristics are then weighted for each customer category that the firm serves. This approach recognizes that various skills or qualities may be required to reach various market segments or customer types.

Sales personnel also participate in the implementation of the model. They provide three estimates of the potential sales revenues for each customer in each district—a most likely estimate, a pessimistic estimate, and an optimistic estimate. Likewise, sales personnel provide subjective estimates of the sales response at each of four different call levels for each customer, which are used in developing a sales response function for each customer.

---

[59] A. Parasuraman and Ralph L. Day, "A Management-Oriented Model for Allocating Sales Effort," *Journal of Marketing Research* 14 (February 1977): pp. 22–33. For a comprehensive review and analysis of sales management models, see Gary L. Lilien and Philip Kotler, *Marketing Decision Making: A Model-Building Approach* (New York: Harper & Row, 1983), pp. 558–602.

Note that the model does not replace the seasoned judgment of sales managers or the field experience of sales personnel, but instead relies heavily on the experience and judgment of both for key inputs. Such an approach forces all parties involved to ask the right questions and think creatively about the factors that influence territory sales response.

Territory Promotional Mix

The PAIRS model, by identifying the most promising accounts in a territory, provides a valuable tool for the sales manager in deploying the sales force. Often, however, resource constraints prevent the firm from reaching many other customers in the territory. Here telemarketing can fill the gap.

To illustrate, the customers for 3M's Medical-Surgical Division comprise the more than 6,000 hospitals in the United States.[60] These hospitals are divided into three groups—A, B, and C—based on potential sales volume. Nearly half of the hospitals fall into the low-volume (C) group. The 3M Corporation developed a successful telephone sales program to serve this customer group. The program has significantly reduced selling costs and improved sales penetration, and it enables field salespersons to concentrate on the high-volume A and B hospitals.

Benson Shapiro and John Wyman point out that telemarketing can also be used to supplement personal sales calls: "Often the cost of the required call frequency is greater than the sales volume justifies and, in these cases, telephone calls can supplement personal visits. The visits might be made two to four times per year and the telephone calls eight to ten times per year for a total frequency of one per month—but at a cost substantially lower than twelve visits."[61]

Driven by new technology and the search for increased efficiency and effectiveness, business marketers are formulating integrated marketing communication programs to reach target segments.

Summary

Personal selling is a significant demand-stimulating force in the business market. Given the rapidly escalating cost of industrial sales calls and the massive resources invested in personal selling, the business marketer must carefully manage this function and take full advantage of available technology to enhance sales force productivity. Recognition of both the needs of organizational customers and the rudiments of organizational buying behavior is fundamental to effective personal selling. Exchange processes often involve multiple parties on both the buying and selling sides—the buying center and the selling center. Likewise, important insights emerge when the industrial salesperson is viewed as a relationship manager. From the consumer's perspective, relationship quality consists of trust in and satisfaction with the salesperson. Developing and sustaining profitable long-term customer relationships is a central goal of the business marketing firm.

[60]Sutton, *Rethinking the Company's Selling and Distribution Channels*, pp. 23–25.
[61]Shapiro and Wyman, "New Ways to Reach Your Customers," p. 106.

Managing the industrial sales force is a multifaceted task. First, the marketer must clearly define the role of personal selling in overall marketing strategy. Second, the sales organization must be appropriately structured—by geography, product, market, or some combination of all three. Regardless of the method used to organize the sales force, an increasing number of business-to-business firms are also establishing a national account sales force so they can profitably serve large customers with complex purchasing requirements. Third, the ongoing process of sales force administration includes recruitment and selection, training, supervision and motivation, and evaluation and control.

A particularly challenging sales management task is the deployment of sales effort across products, customer types, and territories. The sales resource opportunity grid is a useful organizing framework for sales deployment decisions. Likewise, the business marketer can benefit by examining management-oriented models that address sales allocation problems. Such tools can aid the sales manager in pinpointing attractive accounts, deploying the selling effort, and implementing an integrated marketing communications program in a territory. By capitalizing on advanced information technology and automating the sales force, the sales manager is better equipped to plan, organize, and control selling strategies for the business market and to provide enhanced product-service solutions for customers.

Discussion Questions

1. Relationships in the business market may involve more than the salesperson and a purchasing agent. Often, both a selling team and a buying team are involved. Describe the role that the other team members assume on the selling side.

2. When planning a sales call on a particular account in the business market, what information would you require concerning the buying center, the purchasing requirements, and the competition?

3. Some business marketers organize their sales force around products; others are market-centered. What factors must be considered in selecting the most appropriate organizational arrangement for the sales force?

4. Christine Lojacono started as a Xerox sales rep several years ago and is now a national accounts manager, directing activities for five national accounts. Compared to the field sales representative, describe how the nature of the job and the nature of the selling task differ for a national accounts manager.

5. Explain how a successful sales training program can reduce the costs associated with recruiting.

6. An emerging body of research suggests that role ambiguity and role conflict have a detrimental impact on the job satisfaction of industrial salespersons. What steps can sales managers take to deal with these problems? What role might a management-by-objectives system play in these efforts?

7. To make effective and efficient sales force allocation decisions, the sales manager must analyze sales territories. Describe how the sales manager can profit by examining (a) the potential, (b) the concentration, and (c) the dispersion of territories.

8. Hewlett-Packard Corporation has outfitted all of its 2,000 sales representatives with portable personal computers and printers. Early results with the new program suggest that sales force productivity has improved—in some cases, rather significantly. First, describe some specific dimensions of the salesperson's job that lend themselves to such computer support. Second, describe the type of information that Hewlett-Packard should try to capture about each customer account.

Part V

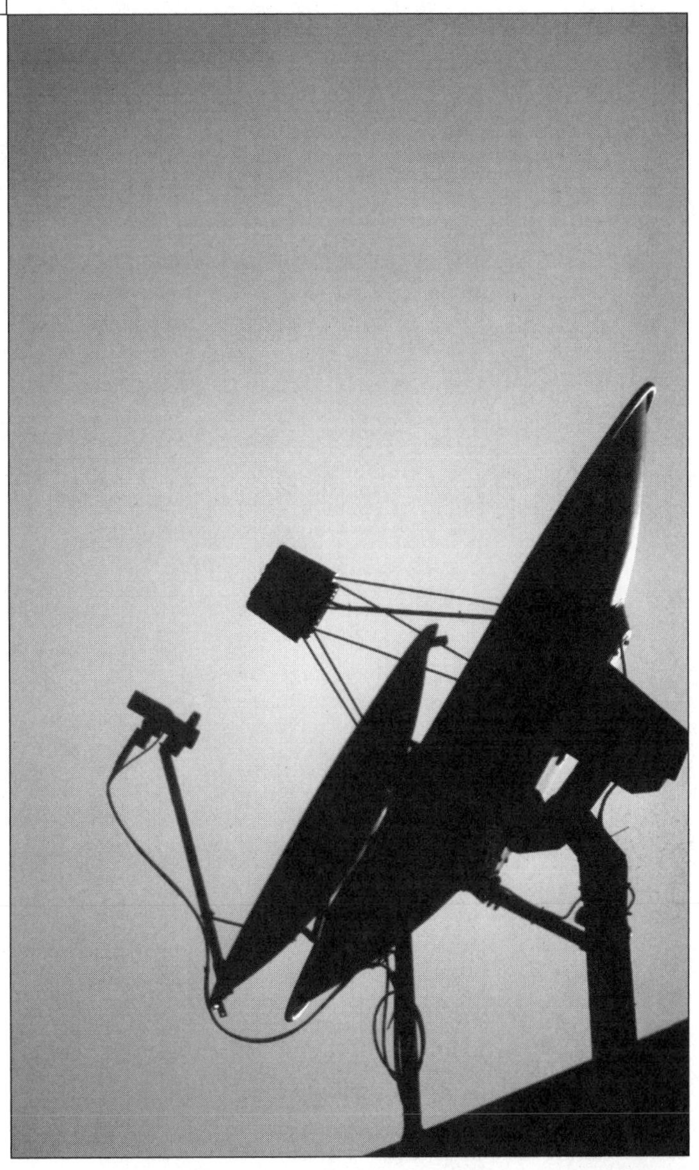

Evaluating Business Marketing Strategy and Performance

Chapter 18

Controlling Business Marketing Strategies

Two business marketing managers facing identical market conditions and possessing equal resources to invest in marketing strategy could generate dramatically different performance results. Why? One manager could carefully monitor and control the performance of marketing strategy, while the other could not. The astute marketer evaluates the profitability of alternative segments and examines the effectiveness and efficiency of the components of the marketing mix so that he or she can isolate problems and opportunities and alter the marketing strategy as market or competitive conditions dictate. After reading this chapter, you will understand

1. a system for converting a strategic vision into a concrete set of performance measures.
2. the function and significance of marketing control in business marketing management.
3. the components of the control process.
4. the specific methods for evaluating marketing strategy performance.
5. the importance of execution or implementation to the success of business marketing strategy.

Managing a firm's marketing strategy is similar to coaching a football team: The excitement and challenge rests in the formulation of strategy. Shall we focus on running or passing? What weaknesses of the opposition can we exploit? How shall we vary our standard plays? So too, the business marketer applies managerial talent creatively when developing and implementing unique marketing strategies that not only respond to customer needs but also capitalize on competitive weaknesses.

However, formulating effective strategy is only half of coaching, or management. A truly great coach devotes significant energy to evaluating team performance during the previous week's game in order to set strategy for the following week. Did our strategy work? Why? Where did it break down? Similarly, a successful marketing strategy depends on evaluations of marketing performance. The other half of strategy planning is **marketing control,** the system by which a firm checks actual against planned performance, evaluating the profitability of products, customer segments, and territories. An effective control system should measure those elements of the business that are key drivers of success in the business environment.[1]

Information generated by the marketing control system is essential for revising current marketing strategies, formulating new strategies, and allocating funds. The requirements for an effective control system are strict—data must be gathered continuously on the appropriate performance measures. Thus, an effective marketing strategy is rooted in a carefully designed and well-applied control system. Such a system must also monitor the quality of strategy implementation. Gary Hamel asserts that "Implementation is often more difficult than it need be because only a handful of people have been involved in the creation of strategy and only a few key executives share a conviction about the way forward."[2]

This chapter presents the rudiments of a marketing control system, beginning with a framework that converts strategy goals into concrete performance measures. Next, the components of the control process are examined. Finally, attention centers on the particular implementation skills that ultimately shape successful business marketing strategies.

The Balanced Scorecard

Measurement is a central element in the strategy process. As new strategies and innovative operating systems are developed to achieve breakthrough results, new performance measures are needed to monitor new goals and new processes. The **balanced scorecard** provides managers with a comprehensive system for converting a company's vision and strategy into a tightly-connected set of performance measures.[3] The balanced scorecard combines financial measures of *past* performance with measures of the drivers of performance. Observe in Figure 18.1 that the scorecard measures the performance of a business unit from four perspectives: (1) financial, (2) customer, (3) internal business processes, and (4) learning and growth.

The architects of the approach, Robert Kaplan and David Norton, emphasize that "the scorecard should tell the story of the strategy, starting with the long-run financial objectives, and then linking them to the sequence of actions that must be taken with financial processes, customers, and finally employees and systems to deliver the desired long-run economic performance."[4]

---

[1]Robert S. Kaplan and David P. Norton, "Using the Balanced Scorecard as a Strategic Management System," *Harvard Business Review* 74 (January/February 1996): pp. 75–85.
[2]Gary Hamel, "Strategy as Revolution," *Harvard Business Review* 74 (July/August 1996): p. 82.
[3]The discussion in this section is based on Robert S. Kaplan and David P. Norton, *The Balanced Scorecard: Translating Strategy into Action* (Boston: Harvard Business School Press, 1996), chaps. 1–3. See also Kaplan and Norton, "Using the Balanced Scorecard as a Strategic Management System," pp. 75–85.
[4]Kaplan and Norton, *The Balanced Scorecard*, p. 47.

Figure 18.1 The Balanced Scorecard Provides a Framework to Translate a Strategy into Operational Terms

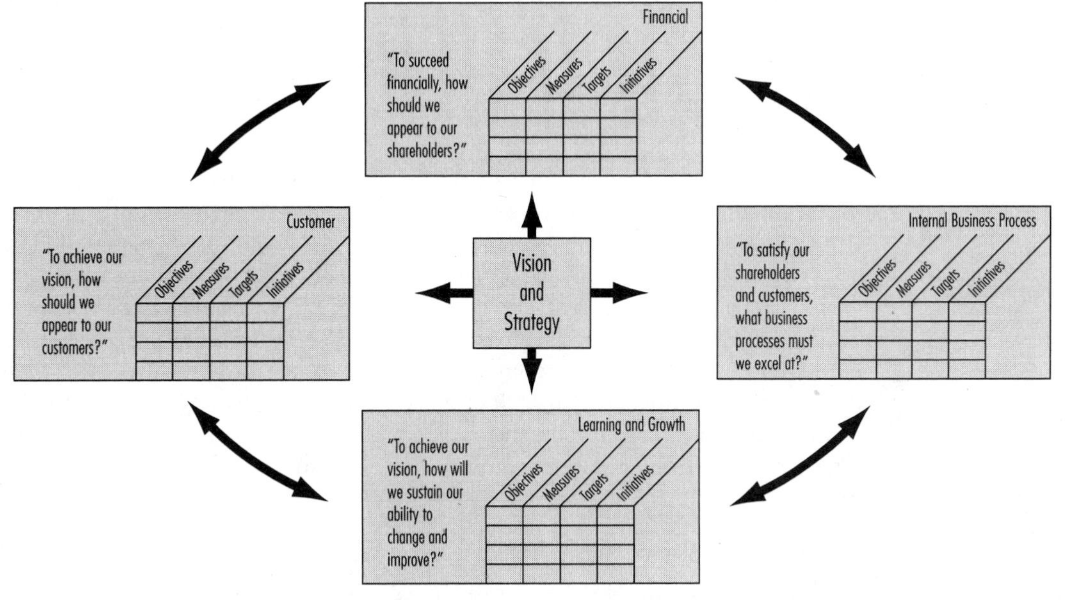

Source: Robert S. Kaplan and David P. Norton, "Using the Balanced Scorecard as a Strategic Management System," *Harvard Business Review* 74 (January/February 1996): p. 76. Reprinted by permission of *Harvard Business Review.* Copyright © 1996 by the President and Fellows of Harvard College; all rights reserved.

FINANCIAL PERSPECTIVE

Financial performance measures allow business marketing managers to monitor the degree to which the firm's strategy, implementation, and execution are contributing to improvements in profitability. The balanced scorecard seeks to match financial objectives to the particular growth and life cycle stages of a business unit. Three stages of a business are isolated and linked to appropriate financial objectives:

1. **Growth:** business units that have products and services with significant growth potential and that must commit considerable resources (for example, production facilities and distribution networks) to capitalize on the market opportunity
   Financial Objectives: Sales growth rate by segment; percentage of revenue from new product, services, and customers

2. **Sustain:** business units, likely representing the majority of businesses within a firm, that expect to maintain or to perhaps moderately increase market share from year to year
   Financial Objectives: Share of target customers and accounts; customer and product line profitability

3. **Harvest:** mature business units that warrant only enough investment to maintain production equipment and capabilities
   Financial Objectives: Payback; customer and product line profitability

CUSTOMER PERSPECTIVE

In the customer component of the balanced scorecard, the business unit identifies the market segments that it will target (see Chapter 6). Those segments supply the revenue stream that will support critical financial objectives. Marketing managers must also identify the value proposition—how the firm proposes to deliver competitively superior value to the target customers and market segments.[5] Customers derive value from the total offering—the product, supporting services, and the reputation of the supplier (see Chapter 10). Figure 18.2 presents the core customer outcome measures that are used to monitor performance in each target segment. The customer perspective complements traditional market share analysis by tracking customer acquisition, customer retention, customer satisfaction, and customer profitability.

A Customer Profitability Focus

In addition to measuring the share of business a firm does with a particular customer, attention should also center on the profitability of that business. Activity-based accounting systems (discussed later in this chapter) provide a valuable tool for managers in measuring individual customer profitability. As Kaplan and Norton affirm, "A financial measure, like customer profitability, helps keep customer-focused organizations from being customer-obsessed."[6] When customer profitability is examined, managers may be surprised by the results. For example, one industrial firm found that 225 percent of its net income was derived from less than 20 percent of its customer accounts. Seventy percent of its customers provided break-even returns, and 10 percent were significant money losers.[7]

When the customer profitability measures indicate that certain targeted customers are unprofitable, further analysis is required in order to choose an appropriate response. Importantly, new customer accounts may differ from long-standing ones. Newly acquired customers, who are unprofitable now but represent future growth prospects, may be valuable on the basis of **lifetime profitability.** However, unprofitable long-standing customers require action. Profitability might be restored for these customers by developing more efficient processes for producing and delivering these products and services. If infeasible, then price increases may be required for the products and services that these customers use extensively.

---

[5]Frederick E. Webster Jr., *Market-Driven Management: Using the New Marketing Concept to Create a Customer-Oriented Company* (New York: John Wiley & Sons, 1994), p. 60.

[6]Kaplan and Norton, *The Balanced Scorecard*, p. 71.

[7]Robert S. Kaplan, "Kanthal (A)," Case No. 9-190-002 (Boston: Harvard Business School Press, 1990), cited by Frank V. Cespedes, *Concurrent Marketing Marketing: Integrating Product, Sales, and Service* (Boston: Harvard Business School Press, 1995), p. 192.

Figure 18.2 The Customer Perspective—Core Measures

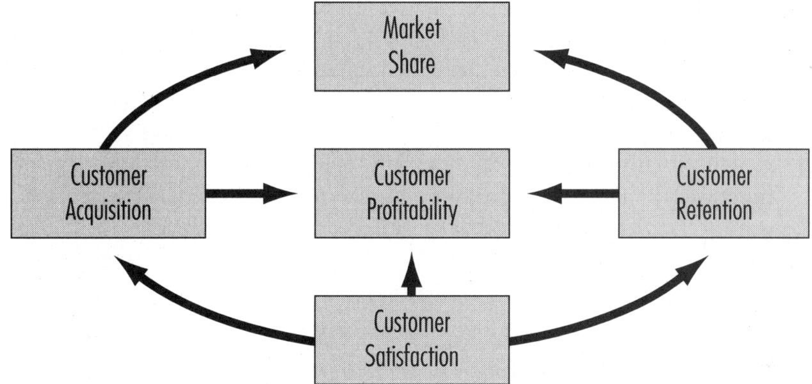

Market Share	Reflects the proportion of business in a given market (in terms of number of customers, dollars spent, or unit volume sold) that a business unit sells.
Customer Aquisition	Measures in absolute or relative terms, the rate at which a business unit attracts or wins new customers or business.
Customer Retention	Tracks, in absolute or relative terms, the rate at which a business unit retains or maintains ongoing relationships with its customers.
Customer Satisfaction	Assesses the satisfaction level of customers along specific performance criteria within the value proposition.
Customer Profitability	Measures the net profit of a customer, or segment, after allowing for the unique expenses required to support that customer.

Source: Robert S. Kaplan and David P. Norton, *The Balanced Scorecard: Translating Strategy into Action* (Boston: Harvard Business School Press, 1996), p. 68. Reprinted by permission of Harvard Business School Press.

INTERNAL BUSINESS PROCESS PERSPECTIVE

To develop the value proposition that will reach and satisfy targeted customer segments and to achieve the desired financial objectives, critical internal processes must be developed and continually enriched. This constitutes the focus of the internal business process perspective. Processes that are critical to the creation of customer value include the innovation process (Chapter 11), operations processes involved in delivering products and services (Chapters 13 and 14), and postsale service processes (Chapters 10 and 12). Leading firms seek the best global practices for managing the control processes of their businesses (see Figure 18.3).

Market-Driven Capabilities

Market-driven organizations develop superior processes in two areas: market sensing and customer linking[8] (see Chapters 1 and 8). **Market sensing** involves the processes for gathering, interpreting, and using market information. These well-developed processes enable market-driven firms to sense market trends and to act on information in a more comprehensive and proactive manner than their rivals. By contrast, **customer-linking** processes include the well-defined procedures and systems that a firm uses to achieve collaborative customer relationships. Customer-linking processes are cross-functional in nature, difficult for competitors to imitate, and are designed to provide the product-service solutions that targeted customers desire.

Building Blocks

George S. Day argues that market-sensing and customer-linking capabilities provide the foundation for building a market-driven organization:

> *The overall objective is to demonstrate a pervasive commitment to a set of processes, beliefs, and values, reflecting the philosophy that all decisions start with the customer and are guided by a deep and shared understanding of the customer's needs and behavior and competitors' capabilities and intentions, for the purpose of realizing superior performance by satisfying customers better than competitors.*[9]

LEARNING AND GROWTH PERSPECTIVE

The fourth component of the balanced scorecard, **learning and growth,** isolates the infrastructure that the organization must develop to achieve long-term goals. The three principal drivers of organizational learning and growth are employee capabilities, information system capabilities, and the organizational climate for employee motivation and initiative. To achieve desired performance goals in the other areas of the scorecard, key objectives must be achieved on measures of employee satisfaction, retention, and productivity. Likewise, front-line employees, like sales or technical service representatives, must have ready access to timely and accurate customer information. However, skilled employees who are supported by a carefully designed information system will not contribute to organizational goals if they are not motivated or not empowered to do so. Many firms, such as Federal Express and Southwest Airlines, have demonstrated the vital role that motivated and empowered employees assume in securing a strong customer franchise.

A Market-Driven, Entrepreneurial Culture

Stanley Slater suggests that a well-developed learning capability is required to develop and sustain a competitive advantage.[10] Firms such as Johnson & Johnson, Hewlett-Packard,

---

[8]George S. Day, "The Capabilities of Market-Driven Organizations," *Journal of Marketing* 58 (October 1994): pp. 37–52.

[9]Ibid., p. 45.

[10]Stanley F. Slater, "Learning to Change," *Business Horizons* 38 (November/December 1995): pp. 13–20. See also Stanley F. Slater and John C. Narver, "Market Orientation and the Learning Organization," *Journal of Marketing* 59 (July 1995): pp. 63–74.

Figure 18.3 Compare Your Business Processes to Those of the Best Firms in the World: An Illustrative Business Marketing Ad

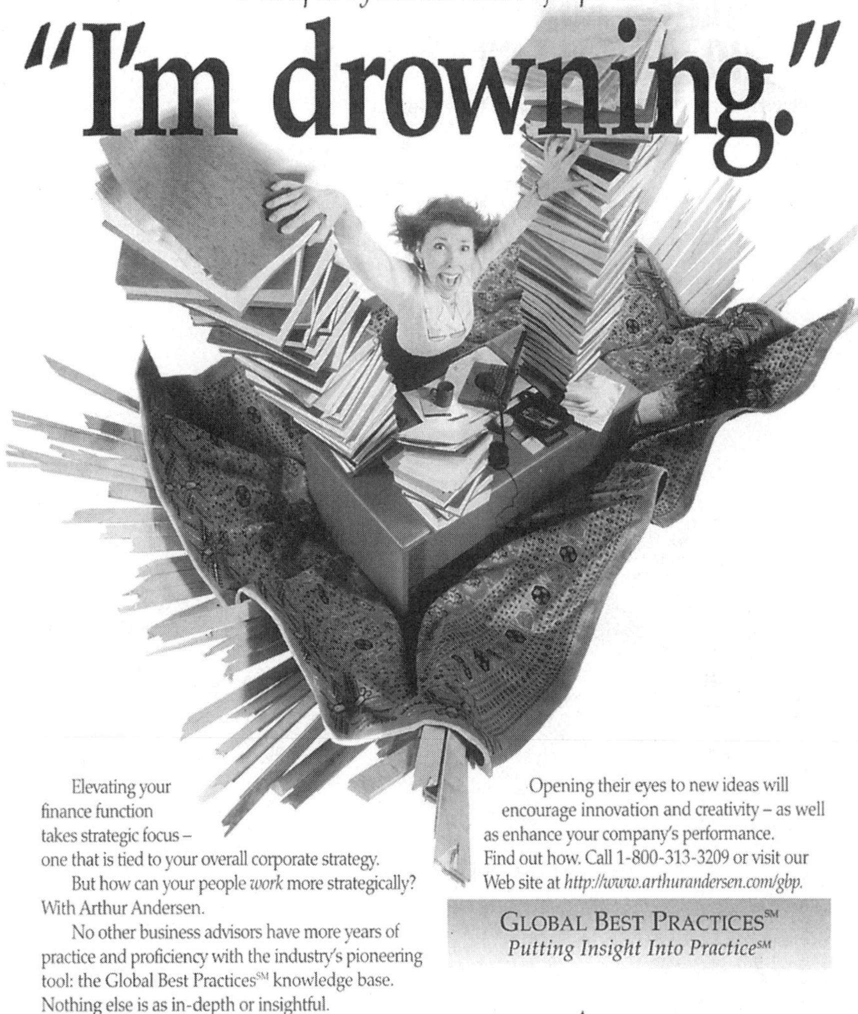

Pam Voth. Your top controller. Financial genius. Great analyst.
Swamped by endless stacks of reports.
"I'm drowning."
Elevating your finance function takes strategic focus – one that is tied to your overall corporate strategy.
But how can your people *work* more strategically? With Arthur Andersen.
No other business advisors have more years of practice and proficiency with the industry's pioneering tool: the Global Best Practices℠ knowledge base. Nothing else is as in-depth or insightful.
Using it, Arthur Andersen business advisors will help your people redefine and refocus the finance function, giving it more relevance and a new vitality.
Opening their eyes to new ideas will encourage innovation and creativity – as well as enhance your company's performance.
Find out how. Call 1-800-313-3209 or visit our Web site at *http://www.arthurandersen.com/gbp.*
GLOBAL BEST PRACTICES℠
Putting Insight Into Practice℠
ARTHUR ANDERSEN
©1996 Arthur Andersen, Andersen Worldwide SC. All rights reserved.

Source: Courtesy of Arthur Andersen. Andersen Worldwide, S.C.

and 3M aptly demonstrate this capability—each has displayed an ability to reinvent itself in order to close performance gaps and seize new and exciting market opportunities (see Figure 18.4). Slater argues that

Figure 18.4 3M Emphasizes Its Culture for Innovation

1

Sometimes the best laid plans need a little help.

2 We help deliver.

Scotch™ Magic™ Tape from 3M has been helping people for years. When we learned that farmers were taping cracked eggs so they could hatch, we knew yet another great use had been born. From insulating electrical splices, to pin-striping cars, people trust Scotch™ brand tapes for strength, consistency and value. It all comes from our unique corporate spirit – which lets us make the leap

from need to...

3M *Innovation*

For more information, call 1-800-3M-HELPS, or Internet: http://www.mmm.com

Source: Courtesy of 3M Corporation.

> *Continuous, innovative learning is most likely to occur in firms characterized by a facilitative, empowering style of leadership; a market-driven, entrepreneurial culture in which challenging the status quo is encouraged; and a structure that has flexible processes for communication, coordination, and conflict resolution among its own members and with its learning partners. Companies that possess all three characteristics achieve superior new product success, sales growth, and profitability.*[11]

To recap, the balanced scorecard provides a series of measures and objectives across four perspectives: financial, customer, internal-business-process, and learning and growth. By developing mutually reinforcing objectives across these four areas, the scorecard tells the story of a business unit's strategy. Attention now turns to the central role that the control process assumes in business marketing management.

Marketing Strategy: Allocating Resources

The purpose of any marketing strategy is to yield the best possible results to the company. Resources are allocated to marketing in general and to individual strategy elements in particular in order to achieve prescribed objectives. Profit contribution, market share percentage, number of new customers, and level of expenses and sales are typical performance criteria; but regardless of the criteria chosen, four interrelated evaluations are required to design a marketing strategy:

1. How much should be spent on marketing in the planning period? (This is the budget for achieving marketing objectives.)
2. How are marketing dollars to be allocated? (For example, how much should be spent on advertising? On personal selling?)
3. Within each element of the marketing strategy, how should dollars be allocated to best achieve marketing objectives? (For example, which advertising media should be selected? How should sales personnel be deployed among customers and prospects?)
4. Which market segments, products, and geographic areas will be most profitable? (Each market segment may require a different amount of effort as a result of competitive intensity or market potential.)

GUIDING STRATEGY FORMULATION

Evaluation outcomes provide the foundation for the integration of the market strategy formulation and the marketing control system. Results in the most recent operating

[11]Slater, "Learning to Change," p. 18.

period will show how successful past marketing efforts were in obtaining desired objectives. Performance below or above expectations will then signal where funds should be reallocated. If the firm expected to reach 20 percent of the OEM market and actually realized only a 12 percent market share, a change in strategy may be required. Performance information provided by the control system might demonstrate that sales personnel in the OEM market were reaching only 45 percent of potential buyers; additional funds could be allocated to expand either the sales force or the advertising budget.

Marketing managers must weigh the interactions among the strategy elements and allocate resources in order to create effective and efficient marketing strategies. In order to develop successful strategies, a system for monitoring past performance is an absolute necessity. In effect, the control system enables management to keep abreast of all facets of performance.

THE MARKETING CONTROL PROCESS

Marketing control is a process whereby management generates information on marketing performance. Two major forms of control are (1) control over efficient allocation of marketing effort and (2) comparison of planned and actual performance. In the first case, the business marketer may use past profitability data as a standard against which to evaluate future marketing expenditures. The second form of control alerts management to any differences between planned and actual performance and may also reveal reasons for performance discrepancies.

INFORMAL CONTROL AFFECTS BEHAVIOR

It is important to recognize that in every organization, systems of informal controls—unwritten, typically worker-initiated mechanisms designed to influence the behavior of marketing personnel—are in operation, and have the potential to affect how the organization operates.[12] Informal controls include shared values and beliefs that guide behavior norms in the organization (for example, the belief that the customer is always right) as well as standards that might be set by the marketing department, which are monitored and have sanctions applied for noncompliance (for example, sales personnel writing reports during evening hours because the typical 8 to 5 work day is reserved for sales calls). The informal control mechanisms combine with formal control devices (the written, management-initiated mechanisms that influence behavior to support organizational goals) in affecting behavior and the resulting achievement or nonachievement of goals. It has been shown that managers often overemphasize formal control and either misread or ignore the impact of informal controls.

---

[12]Bernard J. Jaworski, "Toward a Theory of Marketing Control: Environmental Context Control Types, and Consequences," *Journal of Marketing* 52 (July 1988): pp. 23–39.

Research by Bernard Jaworski, Vlasis Stathakopoulus, and H. Shanker Krishnan stresses the importance of using combinations of control mechanisms, and suggests that some informal control mechanisms be "managed" to ensure high morale and group cohesiveness.[13] The researchers conclude that managers need to be more aware of the effects of informal controls and their role in shaping them. Clearly, the business marketing manager must recognize that guiding the organization to achieve its goals cannot be accomplished through the use of formal controls alone; the informal control mechanisms must be recognized and managed simultaneously. In either case, management must have an information system that will provide timely and meaningful data.

Control at Various Levels

The control process is universal in that it can be applied to any level of marketing analysis. For example, business marketers must frequently evaluate whether their general strategies are appropriate and effective. However, it is equally important to know whether the individual elements in the marketing strategy are effectively integrated for a given market. Further, management must evaluate resource allocation within a particular element; for example, the effectiveness of direct selling versus the effectiveness of industrial distributors. The control system should work in any of these situations. The four primary levels of marketing control are delineated in Table 18.1.

STRATEGIC CONTROL

Strategic control is based on a comprehensive evaluation of whether the firm is headed in the right direction. Strategic control focuses on assessing whether the strategy is being implemented as planned and whether it produces the intended results.[14] Because the business marketing environment is subject to rapid change, existing product/market situations may lose their potential, whereas new product/market matchups provide important opportunities. Philip Kotler suggests that the firm periodically conduct a **marketing audit**—a comprehensive, periodic, and systematic evaluation of the firm's marketing operation that specifically analyzes the market environment and the firm's internal marketing activities.[15] An analysis of the environment assesses company image, customer characteristics, competitive activities, regulatory constraints, and economic trends. Evaluation of this information may uncover threats that the firm can counter and future opportunities that it can exploit.

---

[13]Bernard J. Jaworski, Vlasis Stathakopoulus, and H. Shanker Kirshnan, "Control Combinations in Marketing: Conceptual Framework and Empirical Evidence," *Journal of Marketing* 57 (January 1993): pp. 57–69.

[14]E. Frank Harrison, "Strategic Control at the CEO Level," *Long Range Planning* 24, no. 6 (1991): p. 78.

[15]Philip Kotler, *Marketing Management: Analysis, Planning, Implementation, and Control*, 9th ed. (Englewood Cliffs, N.J.: Prentice-Hall, 1997), pp. 779–781; and Michael P. Mokwa, "The Strategic Marketing Audit: An Adoption/Utilization Perspective," *Journal of Business Strategy* 7 (winter 1986): pp. 88–95.

Table 18.1 Levels of Marketing Control

Type of Control	Primary Responsibility	Purpose of Control	Tools
Strategic control	Top management	To examine whether the company is pursuing its best opportunities with respect to markets, products, and channels	Marketing audit
Annual plan control	Top management, middle management	To examine whether the planned results are being achieved	Sales analysis; market-share analysis; expense-to-sales ratios; other ratios; attitude tracking
Efficiency and effectiveness control	Middle management	To examine how well resources have been utilized in each element of the marketing strategy to accomplish a specific goal	Expense ratios; advertising effectiveness measures; market potential; contribution margin analysis
Profitability control	Marketing controller	To examine where the company is making and losing money	Profitability by product territory, market segment, trade channel, order size

Source: Adapted from Philip Kotler, *Marketing Management: Analysis, Planning, Implementation, and Control*, 9th ed. (Englewood Cliffs, N.J.: Prentice-Hall, 1997), p. 765.

An internal evaluation of the marketing system scrutinizes marketing objectives, organization, and implementation. In this way, management may be able to spot situations in which existing products could be adapted to new markets or new products could be developed for existing markets. The regular, systematic marketing audit is a valuable technique for evaluating the direction of marketing strategies.[16]

Strategic Dialogue: Ask Tough Questions!

To offer promise, George Day asserts, a strategic option must meet several tests. "Effective business strategies are formed in a crucible of debate and dialogue between and within many levels of management. The challenge is to encourage realism in the dialogue—so critical decisions are not distorted by wishful thinking and myopic analysis—while not suppressing creativity and risk taking."[17] Day suggests that many strategies fail because the right questions are not asked at the right time during the strategy formulation process. He offers insightful questions (listed in Table 18.2) to guide the analysis of strategy options. These tough questions are fundamental to the strategic control process.

---

[16]For example, see Philip Kotler, William T. Gregor, and William Rogers III, "SMR Classic Reprint: The Marketing Audit Comes of Age," *Sloan Management Review* 20 (winter 1989): pp. 49–62; and Mokwa, "The Strategic Marketing Audit," pp. 88–95.

[17]George S. Day, "Tough Questions for Developing Strategies," *Journal of Business Strategy* 7 (winter 1986): p. 68.

Table 18.2 Reviewing Strategic Options: Seven Tough Questions

1. **Suitability: Is there a sustainable advantage?**
   (For example, assess each strategy option in light of the capabilities of the business and the likely responses of key competitors.)
2. **Validity: Are the assumptions realistic?**
   (For example, are assumptions concerning sales, profits, and competitions based on fact?)
3. **Flexibility: Do we have the skills, resources, and commitments?**
   (For example, is there an adequate sales force, advertising budget, and commitment of key personnel?)
4. **Consistency: Does the strategy hang together?**
   (For example, is it internally consistent across the functional areas in the firm?)
5. **Vulnerability: What are the risks and contingencies?**
   (For example, if important assumptions are wrong, what are the risks inherent in each strategy alternative?)
6. **Adaptability: Can we retain our flexibility?**
   (For example, if a major contingency occurs, could the strategy be reversed in the future?)
7. **Financial desirability: How much economic value is created?**
   (For example, relate the attractiveness of expected performance to the probable risk of each option.)

Source: Adapted from George S. Day, "Tough Questions for Developing Strategies," *Journal of Business Strategy* 7 (winter 1986): pp. 60–68.

ANNUAL PLAN CONTROL

In annual plan control, the objectives specified in the plan become the performance standards against which actual results are compared. Sales volume, profits, and market share are the typical performance standards for business marketers. **Sales analysis** is an attempt to determine why actual sales varied from planned sales. Expected sales may not be realized because of price reductions, inadequate volume, or both. A sales analysis separates the effects of these variables so that corrective action can be taken.

Market share analysis is an assessment of how the firm is doing relative to competition. A machine-tool manufacturer may experience a 10 percent sales gain that, on the surface, appears favorable. However, if total machine-tool industry sales are up 25 percent, an analysis of market share would show that the firm has not fared well relative to competitors.

Finally, expense-to-sales ratios are analyses of the efficiency of marketing operations. In this regard, management is concerned with overspending or underspending. Frequently, industry standards or past company ratios are used for standards of comparison. Total marketing expenses and expenses of each strategic marketing element are evaluated in relation to sales. Recall the discussion in Chapter 16 on advertising expenditures, which provided a range of advertising expense-to-sales ratios for industrial firms. These figures provide management with a basis for evaluating the company's performance.

A Framework for Marketing Control

James Hulbert and Norman Toy suggest a comprehensive framework for integrating such measures into a marketing control system.[18] Table 18.3 describes how the

[18]James M. Hulbert and Norman E. Toy, "A Strategic Framework for Marketing Control," *Journal of Marketing* 41 (April 1977): pp. 12–19; see also Nigel F. Piercy, "The Marketing Budgeting Process: Marketing Management Implications," *Journal of Marketing* 51 (October 1987): pp. 45–59.

Table 18.3 Operating Results for a Sample Product

Item	Planned	Actual	Variance
Revenues			
Sales (units)	20,000,000	22,000,000	+2,000,000
Price per unit ($)	0.50	0.4773	-0.0227
Total market (units)	40,000,000	50,000,000	-10,000,000
Share of market	50%	44%	-6%
Revenues ($)	10,000,000	10,500,000	+500,000
Variable costs ($0.30 unit) ($)	6,000,000	6,600,000	-600,000
Profit contribution ($)	4,000,000	3,900,000	-100,000

Source: Adapted from James M. Hulbert and Norman E. Toy, "A Strategic Framework for Marketing Control," *Journal of Marketing* 41 (April 1977): p. 13.

framework can identify the factors that caused a variance of actual product profitability from planned profitability. The objective is to isolate the reasons for the differences between planned and actual results (the variances displayed in the last column)—specifically the profit contribution variance.

In this case, management seeks to understand why actual profit contribution was $100,000 less than planned profits. A detailed analysis of the data shows that although total sales were larger than expected (22 million versus 20 million units), the firm failed to achieve its targeted market share. In addition, the firm was unable to maintain its price policy. Management must review its forecasting, considering that the market size was underestimated by 25 percent (40 million versus 50 million). To the extent that marketing strategy allocations are predicated on estimated market size, the firm may have failed to allocate sufficient effort to this market. The variances point to some real weaknesses in the forecasting process.

Because the firm did not share proportionately with its competitors in the market growth, the entire marketing strategy must be reevaluated. Management apparently underestimated the magnitude of price reductions necessary to expand volume. Clearly, annual plan control provides valuable insights into where the plan faltered and suggests the type of remedial action that should be taken.

EFFICIENCY AND EFFECTIVENESS CONTROL

Efficiency control examines the efficiency with which resources are being used in each element of marketing strategy (for example, sales force, advertising); effectiveness control evaluates whether the strategic component is accomplishing its objective. A good control system will provide continuing data on which to evaluate the efficiency of resources used for a given element of marketing strategy to accomplish a given objective. Table 18.4 provides a representative sample of the types of data required. Performance measures and standards will vary by company and situation, according to the goals and objectives delineated in the marketing plan.

Table 18.4 Illustrative Measures for Efficiency and Effectiveness Control

Product
Sales by market segments
Sales relative to potential
Sales growth rates
Market share
Contribution margin
Percentage of total profits
Return on investment

Distribution
Sales, expenses, and contribution by channel type
Sales and contribution margin by intermediary type and individual intermediaries
Sales relative to market potential by channel, intermediary type, and specific intermediaries
Expense-to-sales ratio by channel, etc.
Logistics cost by logistics activity by channel

Communication
Advertising effectiveness by type of media
Actual audience/target audience ratio
Cost per contact
Number of calls, inquiries, and information requests by type of media
Dollar sales per sales call
Sales per territory relative to potential
Selling expenses to sales ratios
New accounts per time period

Pricing
Price changes relative to sales volume
Discount structure related to sales volume
Bid strategy related to new contracts
Margin structure related to marketing expenses
General price policy related to sales volume
Margins related to channel member performance

Recall the extensive discussion in Chapter 7 of techniques and procedures for calculating market potential. Because potential represents the opportunity to sell, it provides an excellent benchmark against which to measure performance. Analysis of performance relative to potential can be made for distribution channels, channel members, and products. The results are sometimes combined with profitability control, the last area of a comprehensive control system.

PROFITABILITY CONTROL

The essence of profitability control is to describe where the firm is making or losing money in terms of the important segments of its business. A **segment** is the unit of analysis used by management for control purposes; it may be customer segments, product lines, territories, or channel structures. Suppose an industrial firm focuses on three customer segments:

machine tools, aircraft parts, and electronics manufacturers. To allocate the marketing budget among the three segments, management must consider the profit contribution associated with each segment and its expected potential. Profitability control, then, provides a methodology for associating marketing costs and revenues to specific segments of the business.

Profitability by Market Segment

Relating sales revenues and marketing costs to market segments improves decision making. More specifically, say Leland Beik and Stephen Buzby,

> *For both strategic and tactical decisions, marketing managers may profit by knowing the impact of the marketing mix upon the target segment at which marketing efforts are aimed. If the programs are to be responsive to environmental change, a monitoring system is needed to locate problems and guide adjustments in marketing decisions. Tracing the profitability of segments permits improved pricing, selling, advertising, channel, and product management decisions. The success of marketing policies and programs may be appraised by a dollar-and-cents measure of profitability by segment.*[19]

Profitability control, a prerequisite to strategy planning and implementation, has stringent information requirements. To be effective, the firm needs a marketing-accounting information system.

An Activity-Based Cost System

The accounting system must first be able to associate costs with the various marketing activities and must then attach these "activity" costs to the important segments to be analyzed. The critical element in the process of determining the appropriate marketing costs associated with a product or customer segment is to trace all costs to the activities (warehousing, advertising, and so on) for which the resources are used and then to the products or segments that consume them.[20] Such an **activity-based cost (ABC) system** reveals the links between performing particular activities and the demands those activities make on the organization's resources. As a result, it can give managers a clear picture of how products, brands, customers, facilities, regions, or distribution channels both generate revenues and consume resources.[21] An ABC analysis focuses attention on improving those activities that will have the greatest effect on profits.

Robin Cooper and Robert Kaplan capture the essence of ABC in the following statement:

> *ABC analysis enables managers to slice into the business many different ways—by product or group of similar products, by individual customer or client group,*

---

[19]Leland L. Beik and Stephen L. Buzby, "Profitability Analysis by Market Segments," *Journal of Marketing* 37 (July 1973): p. 49.

[20]Robin Cooper and Robert S. Kaplan, "Measure Costs Right: Make the Right Decisions," *Harvard Business Review* 66 (September/October 1988): p. 96. For a related discussion, see Robin Cooper and W. Bruce Chew, "Control Tomorrow's Costs through Today's Designs," *Harvard Business Review* 74 (January/February 1996): pp. 88–97.

[21]Robin Cooper and Robert S. Kaplan, "Profit Priorities from Activity-Based Costing," *Harvard Business Review* 69 (May/June 1993): p. 130.

or by distribution channel—and gives them a close-up view of whatever slice they are considering. ABC analysis also illuminates exactly what activities are associated with that part of the business and how those activities are linked to the generation of revenues and the consumption of resources. By highlighting those relationships, ABC helps managers understand precisely where to take actions that will drive profits. In contrast to traditional accounting, activity-based costing segregates the expenses of indirect and support resources by activities. It then assigns those expenses based on the drivers of the activities, rather than by some arbitrary percentage allocation.[22]

ABC System Illustrated

For example, a building supply company used six different channels to reach its industrial customers.[23] Using conventional methods, selling, general, and administrative expenses were assigned to each channel on the basis of the company average (each channel was allocated about 16 percent of sales for SG&A expenses). The original equipment manufacturer (OEM) channel, under this process, was determined to be the worst of the six channel systems with 27 percent gross margin and 2 percent operating margin. Application of activity-based systems for developing SG&A costs showed the OEM channel did not use many SG&A activities—the OEMs required no advertising, catalog, or sales promotion expenses. As a result, the OEMs' actual SG&A expenses were only 9 percent of sales, well below the 16 percent average for the six channels. The operating profit, under the new analysis, turned out to be 9 percent, not 2 percent. Clearly, an activity-based costing system provides more accurate information on which to make important marketing decisions and guides management attention to those factors that have the biggest impact on the bottom line.

Hewlett-Packard has also changed its accounting system to an activity-based cost system.[24] The costs of producing a printed circuit board are determined by first evaluating the activities required to produce the board and then costing out each of the activities. For example, because each printed circuit board has diodes inserted into it, the firm analyzes the cost of each insertion. If one insertion costs 6 cents, then the diode insertion activity can be determined by multiplying $0.06 times the number of diodes. The remaining costs are built up in the same fashion. This costing process creates more accurate costs because the system measures the factors that truly drive costs.

Using the ABC System

An ABC system requires the firm to break from traditional accounting concepts. Managers must refrain from allocating all expenses to individual units and instead separate the expenses and match them to the level of activity that consumes the resources.[25] Once resource expenditures are related to the activities they produce, management can explore

---

[22]Ibid., p. 131.
[23]Cooper and Kaplan, "Measure Costs Right" pp. 100, 101.
[24]Debbie Berlont, Reese Browning, and George Foster, "How Hewlett-Packard Gets Numbers It Can Trust," *Harvard Business Review* 68 (January/February 1990): pp. 178–183.
[25]Cooper and Kaplan, "Profit Priorities from Activity-Based Costing," p. 130.

different strategies for reducing the resource commitments. To enhance profitability, the business marketing managers will need to figure out how to reduce expenditures on those resources or increase the output those resources produce. For example, a sales manager would search for ways to reduce the number of sales calls on unprofitable customers or find ways to make the salesperson more effective with the unprofitable accounts. In summary, ABC systems enable the business marketing manager to focus on increasing profitability by understanding the sources of cost variability and developing strategies to reduce resource commitment or enhance resource productivity.

FEEDFORWARD CONTROL

Much of the information provided by the firm's marketing control system offers feedback on what has been accomplished in both financial (profits) and nonfinancial (customer satisfaction, market share) terms. As such, the control process is remedial in its outlook. Raghu Tadepalli argues that the control system should be forward-looking and preventative, and the control process should start at the same time as the planning process, checking the validity of planning assumptions at each stage.[26] Such a form of control is referred to as *feedforward control.*

Feedforward control involves continuous evaluation of plans, monitoring the environment to detect changes that would support the revision of objectives and strategies. Feedforward control monitors variables other than performance—variables that may change before performance itself changes. The result is that deviations can be controlled before their full impact has been felt. For example, a manufacturer would want to monitor events that are correlated to sales and that would provide early warnings. Thus, continuous evaluation of late delivery complaints by distributors would cause an adjustment in logistics service if the level of complaints showed an increasing trend. In this way a possible loss of sales precipitated by slow deliveries could be avoided. Feedforward control focuses on information that is prognostic: It tries to discover problems waiting to occur. Formal processes of feedforward control can be incorporated into the business marketer's total control program to considerably enhance its effectiveness. Utilization of a feedforward approach would help ensure that planning and control are treated as concurrent activities.

Implementation of Business Marketing Strategy

Many marketing plans fail because they are poorly implemented. **Marketing implementation** is the process that translates marketing plans into action assignments and ensures that such assignments are executed in a manner that will accomplish a plan's defined objectives.[27] Special implementation challenges emerge for the marketing manager because diverse functional areas participate in both the development and the execution of business marketing strategy.

---

[26]Raghu Tadepalli, "Marketing Control: Reconceptualization and Implementation Using the Feedforward Method," *European Journal of Marketing* 26, no. 1 (1992): pp. 24–40.

[27]Kotler, *Marketing Management: Analysis, Planning, Implementation, and Control*, p. 763.

ABC ANALYSIS SAYS, "CHANGE THE 80-20 RULE TO 20-225"

Activity-based cost (ABC) analysis highlights for managers where their actions will likely have the greatest impact on profits. The ABC system at Kanthal Corporation led to a review of profitability by size of customer.

Kanthal, a manufacturer of heating wire, used activity-based costing to analyze its customer profitability and discovered that the well-known 80-20 rule (80 percent of sales generated by 20 percent of customers) was in need of revision. A 20-225 rule was actually operating: 20 percent of customers were generating 225 percent of profits. The middle 70 percent of customers were hovering around the break-even point, and Kanthal was losing 125 percent of its profits on 10 percent of its customers!

The Kanthal customers generating the greatest losses were among those with the largest sales volume. Initially, this finding surprised managers, but it soon began to make sense. You can't lose large amounts of money on a small customer. The large, unprofitable customers demanded lower prices, frequent deliveries of small lots, extensive sales and technical resources, and product changes. The newly revealed economics enabled management to change the way it did business with these customers—through price changes, minimum order sizes, and information technology—transforming the customers into strong profit contributors.

Source: Robin Cooper and Robert S. Kaplan, "Profit Priorities from Activity-Based Costing," *Harvard Business Review* 69 (May/June 1993): p. 130.

THE STRATEGY-IMPLEMENTATION FIT

Thomas Bonoma asserts that "Marketing strategy and implementation affect each other. While strategy obviously affects actions, execution also affects marketing strategies, especially over time."[28] Although the dividing line between strategy and execution is a bit fuzzy, it is often not difficult to diagnose implementation problems and to distinguish them from strategy deficiencies. Bonoma presents the following scenario:

> *A firm introduced a new portable microcomputer that incorporated a number of features that the target market valued. The new product appeared to be well positioned in a rapidly growing market, but initial sales results were miserable. Why? The 50-person sales force had little incentive to grapple with a new unfamiliar product and continued to emphasize the older models. Given the significant market potential, management had decided to set the sales incentive compensation level lower on the new machines than on the older ones. The older models had a selling cycle one-half as long as the new product and required no software knowledge or support.*

In this case, poor execution damaged good strategy.[29]

[28]Thomas V. Bonoma, "Making Your Marketing Strategy Work," *Harvard Business Review* 62 (March/April 1984): pp. 69–76.
[29]Ibid., p. 70.

Marketing strategy and implementation affect each other. When both strategy and implementation are appropriate, the firm is likely to be successful in achieving its objectives. Diagnosis becomes more difficult in other cases. For example, the cause of a marketing problem may be hard to detect when the strategy is on the mark but the implementation is poor. The business marketer may never become aware of the soundness of the strategy. Alternatively, excellent implementation of a poor strategy may give managers time to see the problem and correct it.

IMPLEMENTATION SKILLS

Thomas Bonoma identifies four implementation skills that are particularly important to the marketing manager: (1) interacting, (2) allocating, (3) monitoring, and (4) organizing.[30] Each assumes special significance in the business marketing environment.

Marketing managers are continually *interacting* with others both within and outside the corporation. Inside, a number of peers (for example, R&D personnel) over whom the marketer has little power often assume a crucial role in strategy development and implementation. Outside, the marketer deals with important customers, channel members, advertising agencies, and the like. The best implementers have good bargaining skills and the ability to understand how others feel.[31]

The implementer must also *allocate* time, assignments, people, dollars, and other resources among the marketing tasks at hand. Astute marketing managers, says Bonoma, are "tough and fair in putting people and dollars where they will be most effective. The less able ones routinely allocate too many dollars and people to mature programs and too few to richer ones."[32]

Bonoma asserts that marketing managers with good *monitoring* skills exhibit flexibility and intelligence in dealing with the firm's information and control systems: "Good implementers struggle and wrestle with their markets and businesses until they can simply and powerfully express the 'back of the envelope' ratios necessary to run the business, regardless of formal control system inadequacies."[33]

Finally, the best implementers are effective at *organizing*. Sound execution often hinges on the marketer's ability to work with both the formal and the informal networks within the organization. The manager customizes an informal organization in order to solve problems and to facilitate good execution.

THE MARKETING STRATEGY CENTER: AN IMPLEMENTATION GUIDE[34]

Diverse functional areas participate to differing degrees in the development and implementation of business marketing strategy. Research and development, manufacturing,

[30]Ibid.

[31]Michael D. Hutt, "Cross-Functional Working Relationships in Marketing," *Journal of the Academy of Marketing Science* 23 (fall 1995): pp. 351–357.

[32]Bonoma, "Making Your Marketing Strategy Work," p. 75.

[33]Ibid.

[34]Michael D. Hutt and Thomas W. Speh, "The Marketing Strategy Center: Diagnosing the Industrial Marketer's Interdisciplinary Role," *Journal of Marketing* 48 (fall 1984): pp. 53–61; and Michael D. Hutt, Beth A. Walker, and Gary L. Frankwick, "Hurdle the Cross-Functional Barriers to Strategic Change," *Sloan Management Review* 36 (spring 1995): pp. 22–30.

technical service, physical distribution, and other functional areas play fundamental roles. Ronald McTavish points out that "marketing specialists understand markets, but know a good deal less about the nuts and bolts of the company's operations—its internal terrain. This is the domain of the operating specialist. We need to bring these different specialists together in a 'synergistic pooling' of knowledge and viewpoint to achieve the best fit of the company's skills with the market and the company's approach to it."[35] This suggests a challenging and pivotal interdisciplinary role for the marketing manager in the industrial firm.

The marketing strategy center (discussed in Chapter 8) provides a framework for highlighting this interdisciplinary role and for exploring key implementation requirements. Table 18.5 highlights important strategic topics examined throughout this textbook. In each case, nonmarketing personnel play active implementation roles. For example, product quality is directly or indirectly affected by several departments: manufacturing, research and development, technical service, and others. In turn, successful product innovation reflects the collective efforts of individuals drawn from several functional areas. Clearly, effective strategy implementation requires well-defined decision roles, responsibilities, timetables, and coordination mechanisms.

On a global market scale, special coordination challenges emerge when selected activities such as R&D are concentrated in one country and other strategy center activities such as manufacturing are dispersed across countries. Xerox, however, has been successful in maintaining a high level of coordination across such dispersed activities. The Xerox brand, marketing approach, and servicing procedures are standardized worldwide.[36]

The Marketer's Role

To ensure maximum customer satisfaction and the desired market response, the business marketer must assume an active role in the strategy center by negotiating market-sensitive agreements and by developing coordinated strategies with other members. While being influenced by other functional areas to varying degrees in the marketing decision-making process, the marketer can potentially serve as an influencer in key areas such as the design of the logistical system, the selection of manufacturing technology, or the structure of a materials management system. Such negotiation with other functional areas is fundamental to the business marketer's strategic interdisciplinary role. Thus, the successful business marketing manager performs as an integrator by drawing on the collective strengths of the enterprise to satisfy customer needs profitably.

Looking Back

Figure 18.5 synthesizes the central components of business marketing management and highlights the material presented in this textbook. Part I introduced the major classes of customers that constitute the business market: commercial enterprises,

[35]Ronald McTavish, "Implementing Marketing Strategy," *Industrial Marketing Management* 26 (5 November 1988): p. 10. See also Deborah Dougherty and Edward H. Bowman, "The Effects of Organizational Downsizing on Product Innovation," *California Management Review* 37 (summer 1995): pp. 28–44.

[36]Michael E. Porter, "Changing Patterns of International Competition," *California Management Review* 28 (winter 1986): pp. 9–40.

Table 18.5 Interfunctional Involvement in Marketing Strategy Implementation: An Illustrative Responsibility Chart

Decision Area	Marketing	Sales	Manufacturing	R&D	Purchasing	Physical Distribution	Technical Service	Strategic Business Unit Manager	Corporate-Level Planner
Product/ service quality									
Technical service support									
Physical distribution service									
National accounts management									
Channel relations									
Sales support									
Product/ service innovation									

Note: Use the following abbreviations to indicate decision roles: R = responsible; A = approve; C = consult; M = implement; I = inform; X = no role in decision.

governmental units, and institutions. The buying behavior of these consumers was considered in Part II, with particular attention to the myriad forces that act upon organizational decision makers and decision influencers. Part III discussed the business marketing intelligence system and the tools for assessing market opportunities; it explored techniques for measuring market potential, identifying market segments, and forecasting sales. Functionally integrated marketing planning provides a framework for dealing with each component of the business marketing mix, as detailed in Part IV.

Once business marketing strategy is formulated, the manager must evaluate the response of target market segments in order to ensure that any discrepancy between planned and actual results is minimized. This chapter, which constitutes Part V, explored the critical dimensions of the marketing control process, which is the final loop in the model presented in Figure 18.5: planning for and acquiring marketing information. Such information forms the core of the firm's management information system; it is derived internally through the marketing-accounting system and externally through the marketing research function. The evaluation and control process enables the marketer to reassess business market opportunities and to make adjustments as needed in business marketing strategy.

Figure 18.5 A Framework for Business Marketing Management

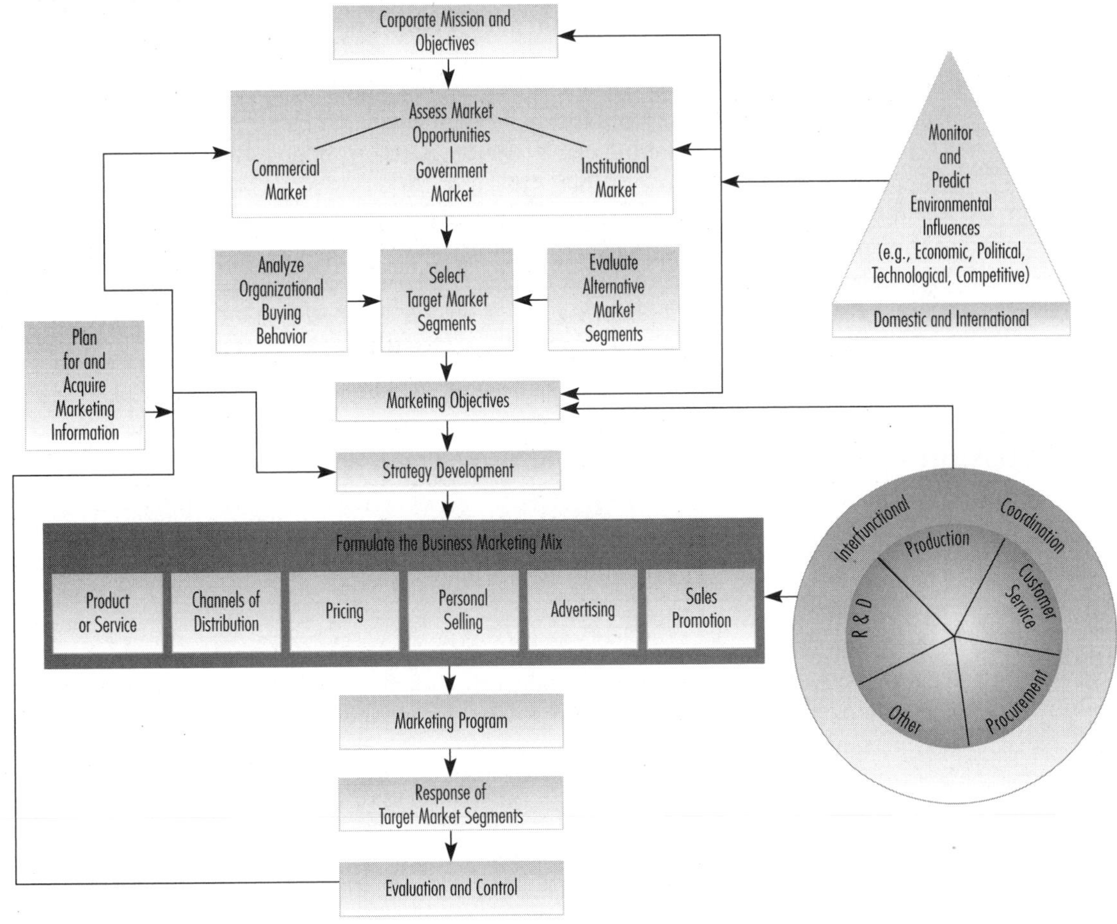

Summary

Central to market strategy is the allocation of resources to each strategy element and the application of marketing efforts to segments. The marketing control system is the process by which the industrial firm generates information to make these decisions. Moreover, the marketing control system is the means by which current performance can be evaluated and steps can be taken to correct deficiencies. The balanced scorecard converts a strategy vision into concrete objectives and measures, organized into four different perspectives: financial, customer, internal business process, and learning and growth. The approach involves identifying target market segments, isolating the critical internal processes that the firm must develop to deliver value to customers in these segments, and selecting the organizational capabilities that will be required to achieve customer and financial objectives.

An effective control system has four distinct components. Strategic control, which is operationalized through the marketing audit, provides valuative information on the present and future course of the firm's basic product/market mission. Annual plan control compares annual to planned results in order to provide input for future planning. Efficiency and effectiveness control evaluates whether marketing strategy elements achieve their goals in a cost-effective manner. Finally, profitability control seeks to evaluate profitability by segment.

Many business marketing plans fail because they are poorly executed. Marketing implementation is the process that translates marketing plans into action assignments and ensures that such assignments are executed in a timely and effective manner. Four implementation skills are particularly important to the business marketing manager: (1) interacting, (2) allocating, (3) monitoring, and (4) organizing. Nonmarketing personnel play active roles in the implementation of business marketing strategy. This suggests a challenging and pivotal interdisciplinary role for the marketing manager.

Discussion Questions

1. Discuss why a firm that plans to enter a new market segment may have to develop new internal business processes to serve customers in this segment.

2. Not all customer demands can be satisfied in ways that are profitable to a firm. What steps should be taken by a marketing manager who learns that particular customer accounts—including some long-standing ones—are unprofitable?

3. Describe the relationships between and among the four central perspectives represented in the balanced scorecard: financial, customer, internal business process, and learning and growth.

4. Last December, Lisa Schmitt, vice president of marketing at Bock Machine Tool, identified four market segments that her firm would attempt to penetrate this year. As this year comes to an end, Lisa would like to evaluate the firm's performance in each of these segments. Of course, Lisa turns to you for assistance. First, what information would you seek from the firm's marketing information system in order to perform the analysis? Second, how would you know whether the firm's performance in a particular market segment was good or bad?

5. Susan Breck, president of Breck Chemical Corporation, added three new products to the firm's line two years ago in order to serve the needs of five SIC groups. Each of the products has a separate advertising budget, although they are sold by the same salespersons. Susan requests your assistance in determining what type of information the firm should gather in order to monitor and control the performance of these products. Outline your reply.

6. Assume that the information you requested in question 5 has been gathered for you. How would you determine whether advertising and personal selling funds should be shifted from one product to another?

7. Hamilton Tucker, president of Tucker Manufacturing Company, is concerned about the seat-of-the-pants approach used by managers in allocating the marketing budget. He cites the Midwest and the East as examples. The firm increased its demand-stimulating expenditures (for example, advertising, personal selling) in the Midwest by 20 percent, but sales climbed only 6 percent last year. In contrast, demand-stimulating expenditures were cut by 17 percent in the East, and sales dropped by 22 percent. Hamilton would like you to assist the midwestern and eastern regional managers in allocating their funds next year. Carefully outline the approach you would follow.

8. Delineate the central components of the marketing control process. Describe the role of the control system in formal marketing planning.

9. Using the marketing strategy center concept as a guide, describe how a strategy that is entirely appropriate for a particular target market might fail due to poor implementation in the logistics and technical service areas.

10. Describe how the strategy implementation challenges for a marketing manager working at Du Pont (an industrial firm) might be different from those for a marketing manager working at Pillsbury (a consumer-goods firm).

Part VI

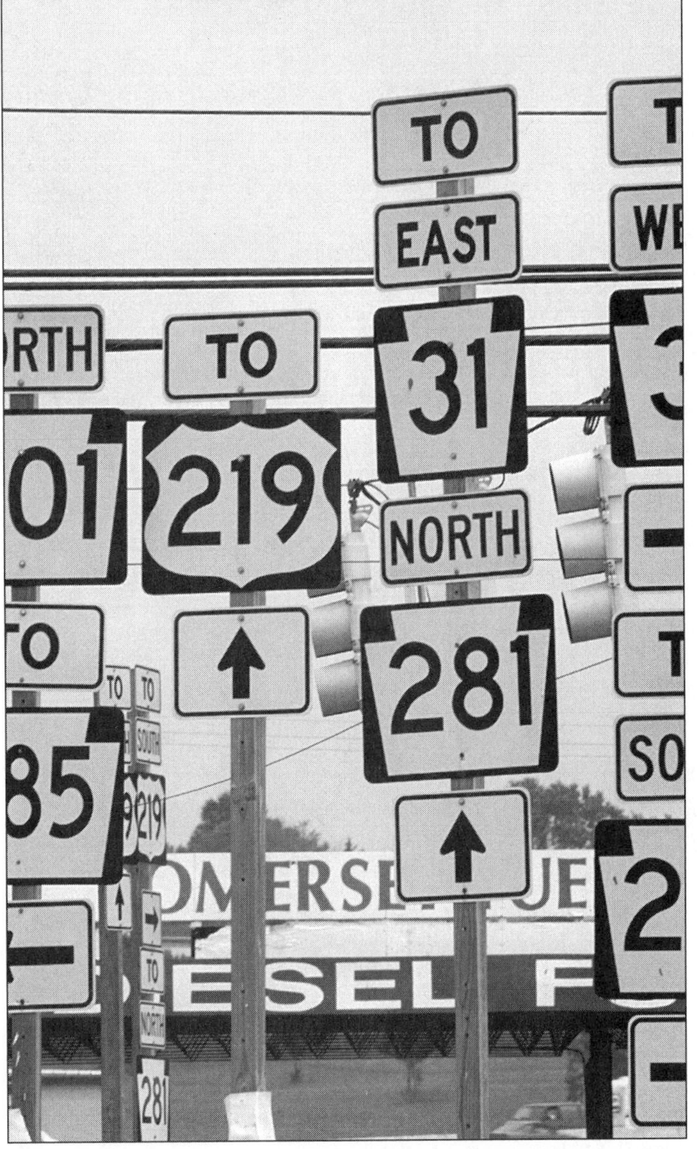

Cases

Case Planning Guide

PAGE	CASE #	CASE TITLE	1	2	3	4	5	6	7	8	9	10	11	12	13	14	15	16	17	18
			Relevant Chapters																	
559	1	The Brownie Factory	★	★	★	★											★			
569	2	MacTec Control AB			★	★	★	★	★	★	★									
577	3	Data General and New York's Division of Substance Abuse Services		★	★	★											★		★	
593	4	Cross-Functional Strategy Decision Making: The Techno Project								★			★							★
600	5	Roscoe Nondestructive Testing			★	★		★						★					★	
608	6	Barro Stickney, Inc.													★				★	
614	7	W.L. Gore & Associates, Inc.—1996: A Case Study								★		★	★							
639	8	Beta Pharmaceuticals: Pennsylvania Distribution System													★	★				
645	9	Calox Machinery Corporation (A)									★				★					
654	10	Calox Machinery Corporation (B)									★				★					
657	11	Hewlett-Packard Company: Developing & Packaging Marketing-Friendly Serivces										★		★	★	★		★		
676	12	PeopleSoft Corporation: Delivering Outrageous Customer Service										★		★					★	
687	13	Augustine Medical, Inc.: The Bair Hugger® Patient Warming System										★	★		★		★			
709	14	Brand Pipe Company			★	★		★		★		★			★	★	★	★	★	
720	15	Ohmeda Monitoring Systems			★	★	★	★	★	★	★	★	★	★					★	
736	16	BWI Kartridge Pak						★		★	★	★	★							★
756	17	Ethical Dilemmas in Business Marketing	★	★	★															

Case 1

The Brownie Factory

John Pollock hung up the phone and walked out of the office and into the prep area of the small Charlotte, North Carolina, wholesale bakery. He smiled at his wife Terri and exclaimed, "It looks like we have a chance to become The Brownie Factory!" The call, from an airline supplier, brought back to life a proposal that John and Terri had all but dismissed. The only catch was that the firm wanted John to indicate his level of interest in the alternative by July 18, 1988, and that was only 48 hours away. "It's really a blessing," thought John. "We've needed to make a decision on the brownie and this will force us to do just that."

In the last two months, the goal of transforming the small, wholesale bakery operation from one of producing limited quantities of a relatively large number of products to the exclusive production of a gourmet brownie had become a passion of the couple. As a result, John had gathered information on several marketing options for the brownie. John and Terri were both extremely excited about the product. In fact, they had tentatively decided to change the name of their wholesale bakery to The Brownie Factory. Their excitement notwithstanding, the couple had been hesitant to take any action because they were not totally comfortable with any of the alternatives.

When John finished telling Terri about the call, she suggested that they take the information on all their options home that night and reconsider them at the same time that they were evaluating the latest alternative. "That's a good idea," agreed John. "It could be that the best strategy would be a combination of options." Regardless of the result, John wanted to be certain they considered every angle—particularly since this new option would commit the bakery under a production contract.

Source: This case was prepared by D. Michael Fields and Neil C. Herndon Jr., both of Southwest Missouri State University.

The Pollock's Bakery

In the 20 months that the bakery had been in operation, the business had enjoyed a steady, if unspectacular, increase in business. "We started with no commercial baking experience, but with a commitment to quality. I approached a number of restaurants and specialty shops in Charlotte and convinced them to add some of our dessert items to their product line on a trial basis. Almost every one turned into a regular customer," noted John. The couple attributed this success to the consistently high quality of their products. "If we're not completely satisfied with a product, then it will never be delivered to a customer," explained John. "Yes," added Terri, "we've given a lot of 'rejected' products to our family and friends."

The couple felt that a key to the success of their products was the quality of the ingredients that they used. Terri's most important contribution to the operation was development of the recipes that the bakery used. She insisted on using only the highest-quality ingredients and on mixing by hand rather than using the commercial mixer when possible, as well as limiting or eliminating the use of preservatives. While these decisions almost certainly contributed to the products' quality, they also increased costs. John justified their approach by saying, "I couldn't look my customers in the eye if I left them a shoddy product."

Making bakery products with all natural ingredients generally carries with it two disadvantages. In addition to the higher cost of ingredients, products with all natural ingredients are usually higher in calories. "None of our customers have raised either of these concerns," noted John. "The quality of our products has seemed to justify the higher price. And as far as buying a premium dessert goes, it appears that people either don't care how many calories a product has or they just don't want to know."

Another indication of the couple's level of personal pride was the manner in which they maintained the bakery. Even with the powdery nature of many of the ingredients, the bakery was consistently in spotless condition. This was particularly significant, since few of their customers ever saw the wholesale bakery and they really didn't have to maintain such high standards. "Both our products and our place of business are reflections of the kind of people we are," noted Terri.

Both John and Terri were comfortable with the bakery's manufacturing/supplier role. Neither desired their business to become a retail operation. "We're working enough as it is now. We just don't have the time to handle single-item sales," explained Terri. "And besides," she added, "our bakery's main entrance is from an alley—it just wouldn't work." "It also opens another can of worms," interjected John, "when you produce for retail, the sale of your production run is no longer guaranteed."

The present product line had grown to eighteen items in five different categories (see Exhibit 1.1). Although not all products were produced daily, all were being produced at least once a week and some were being baked several times each week. "We spend a lot of time shifting from product to product," admitted Terri.

Some of the growth in the product line had been the result of the couple's effort to be responsive to the requests of their customers. On several occasions, customers had asked the bakery to develop new items for them. Typically, these requested items found their way into the regular product line. Unfortunately, many of them were

Exhibit 1.1 Bakery Product Line, May 1988

Item	Unit Price	Ingredient Cost	Margin	Quantity Sold 1/1/88–4/1/88
Cheesecake (14.5%)*				
Plain	$12.00	$4.35	$7.65	95
Chocolate	13.00	6.47	6.53	60
New York	15.50	8.75	6.75	65
Amaretto	13.00	6.72	6.28	9
Coffee cake (1.0%)				
Plain	11.00	5.24	5.76	15
Chocolate Chip	6.50	3.99	2.51	2
Other Cakes (8.3%)				
Spice	6.50	3.74	2.76	4
Carrot	12.00	7.35	4.65	12
Truffle	8.25	4.93	3.32	36
Pound	10.00	5.13	4.87	80
Muffins (20.1%)				
Bran	6.00 (doz)	2.68	3.32	275
Blueberry	6.60 (doz)	3.25	3.35	80
Pumpkin	6.60 (doz)	3.25	3.35	80
Applenut	6.60 (doz)	3.25	3.35	40
Miscellaneous snacks (56.1%)				
Chocolate Oatmeal Bars	7.20 (pan)	4.01	3.19	300
Lemon Bars	6.00 (doz)	3.68	2.32	35
Blond Brownies	10.00 (pan)	5.13	4.87	120
Cupcakes	4.80 (pan)	2.94	1.86	40

* The numbers in parentheses indicate the estimated percentage of actual production time spent on each category.

low-volume items (see Exhibit 1.1), and John admitted that they were unprofitable to produce. "Some of these were bad business decisions," explained John, "but it's hard to say 'no' to the requests of regular customers."

John and Terri were the only two employees of the bakery, and the demands of the broad product line had lengthened both total production time and their work week. "Most weeks, we work at least 55 hours over 5 ½ days," noted Terri. "On an average day we will be involved in production of the various products for 8 hours. It usually takes John about 2 hours to make deliveries and while he's doing that, I clean the bakery up. It can get tiring. There are some friends we could call on in case of emergency, but we just can't allow ourselves to get sick." In fact, in the last fiscal year, the couple had only used 25 to 30 hours of additional labor.

As is the case with most new businesses, the bakery did not make a profit in its first year of operation (see the firm's income statement for fiscal 1987 in Exhibit 1.2). Although the loss was not unexpected, John was concerned about the prospects for reaching profitability in the near term. "I know it's normal, but it's still awfully frustrating to put in the kind of hours we are working and still lose money," explained John. John felt that increased volume would help the bakery achieve profitability.

Exhibit 1.2 Income Statement, 1987

Sales		**$35,710.66**
Cost of goods sold		
Ingredients	$13,352.48	
Bakery Supplies	770.90	
Labor	123.00	
Samples	16.00	
Total cost of goods sold		14,262.38
Gross margin		**$21,448.28**
Operating expenses		
Kitchen equipment	$1,968.39	
Delivery expense	1,917.52	
Salaries—officers	9,450.00	
Rent	3,250.00	
Utilities	2,091.00	
Interest expense	2,267.62	
Depreciation expense	2,978.35	
Amortization expense	857.94	
Insurance	1,384.13	
Advertising	291.50	
Bank charges	113.06	
Maintenance and repairs	308.03	
Office supplies	300.72	
Payroll taxes	878.86	
Taxes and licenses	240.00	
Telephone	799.99	
Miscellaneous	52.98	
Total operating expenses		29,150.09
Net income (loss)		($7,701.81)

Both John and Terri were apprehensive about the potential impact on product quality if another production shift was added. Their decisions on the product line had been complicated by the fact that the bakery had continued to increase sales in the first quarter of 1988 with its present product line. Although sales for many retailers are traditionally slowest in the first quarter, John had noticed in the bakery's first full year of operation that demand from the firm's customers had remained relatively constant, making the first quarter proportionally representative for the year.

John felt that the key to long-term profitability was trimming the product line. Clearly, the optimal solution in terms of efficiency would be to dedicate the entire production to a single product that would support an acceptable contribution margin. "I think our brownie holds the key to the future success of our business," noted John. "But the problem is figuring out how to transform 'the bakery' into The Brownie Factory."

The Brownie

The present brownie was the result of several months of hard work by Terri. She had started with what she considered to be an excellent family recipe and incorporated the bakery's philosophy of using all-natural ingredients. Terri enlisted the help of a series of the couple's friends to evaluate the results as she varied the brownie recipe. The present, and what John and Terri considered to be the final, recipe had drawn the most enthusiastic support of the testers. Terri had made two changes which the couple felt significantly differentiated their product from anything on the market. Terri explained, "The first thing I did was to give our brownie a more cake-like texture—rather than making it soft and gooey. The second difference was the use of pure chocolate instead of cocoa, which gives it a distinctive flavor."

John had decided that the most appropriate unit size for the brownie would be a 2 × 3 × ¾ inch serving. The cost of the ingredients for a brownie of these dimensions would be $0.20 per unit. Individual packaging would add an additional 3 cents to the cost. The bakery had traditionally targeted a markup of 50 percent (twice the cost) to reach a selling price for each of the categories of products (see Exhibit 1.1) and John saw no reason to alter the pricing philosophy. Given these price parameters, John had set the bakery's selling price for the brownie at $0.40 each in the tray or $0.46 each if they were individually wrapped.

With the present equipment, John estimated that the small bakery's production potential was 5,000 brownies per week. The capacity could be doubled with the addition of another oven. John felt that a used oven could be purchased for $2,000.

■ The Local Brownie Market

The Charlotte market, like most, offered consumers a wide range of choices in their selection of brownies. John felt the overall market could be broken down into two major segments, based on how the brownies were sold. The "tray" market consisted of retailers who offered full-service counters for bakery products. These were typically limited to retail bakery operations, supermarkets that had a bakery department, and a few convenience stores that sold individual products from a display case. John did not consider the traymarket to be a lucrative segment, since most of these outlets had facilities on hand to produce their own brownies. However, four of the bakery's present customers had expressed interest in selling John and Terri's brownie from the tray (see Exhibit 1.3), and the projected quantities were substantial.

The market for individually wrapped brownies appeared to John to hold the greatest promise. It also attracted a large number of established competitors. A list of the major companies selling individually wrapped brownies to supermarkets and convenience stores in the Charlotte market can be found in Exhibit 1.4. As shown, the per-brownie prices ranged from a low of $0.99 for a dozen 1-ounce Little Debbie brownies to a high of $0.79 for a 3-ounce Sara Lee brownie.

To give him a better idea of how the new brownies stacked up against the competition, John had dimensioned the brownies on the familiar basis of texture and sweetness. John was pleased with the results (see Figure 1). The couple's brownie had a position that distinguished it from the existing competitors' offerings. John was also encouraged by the interest expressed in the projected new brownie by the bakery's present customers. John had mentioned that the couple was considering

Exhibit 1.3 Brownie Purchase Estimates of Existing Customers

Customer	Brownies per Week (Dozens)	Trays of 6 Dozen Brownies per Week
1. Out to Lunch (3 locations)	30	
2. Treats	8	
3. Reed's Supermarket	6	12
4. Wine Shop	2	
5. Eat Out	5	
6. Phil's Deli	9	
7. Berry Brook	2	
8. The Home Economist	4	
9. The Mill	3	12
10. Selwyn's	2	24
11. People's	3	12
12. The Fresh Market	8	
Totals	82 dozen	60 trays

Exhibit 1.4 Sample of Individually Wrapped Brownies Sold in Area Stores

Brownie Name	Weight (Oz.)	Price
Bebo	3.00	$0.49
Claey's	1.75	0.49
Hostess	3.00	0.69
Little Debbie*	12.00	0.99
Moore's	1.60	0.49
Sara Lee	3.00	0.79

* Packaged and sold in boxes with 12 1-oz. brownies.

adding a gourmet brownie to their product line and, in some cases, had left a sample of their brownie. Customers had estimated that they could sell 82 dozen of the individually wrapped new brownies each week (see Exhibit 1.3).

The possibility of an additional competitor in the Charlotte market had gained John's attention. Two months before, John had heard a rumor that Rachel's Brownies was close to signing an agreement with a local distributor to begin selling Rachel's own gourmet brownie in the Charlotte market. Rachel's was a firm that started selling its brownies in a produce shop and in an ice cream store in Philadelphia in 1975. In less than 10 years the firm had grown to the point that they were producing more than five million brownies annually. They typically marketed brownies in one-pound tins to supermarkets (retailing at $3.79) and individually wrapped units to convenience stores (retailing at $0.75).

Figure 1 Local Brownie Market Dimensioned by Sweetness and Texture

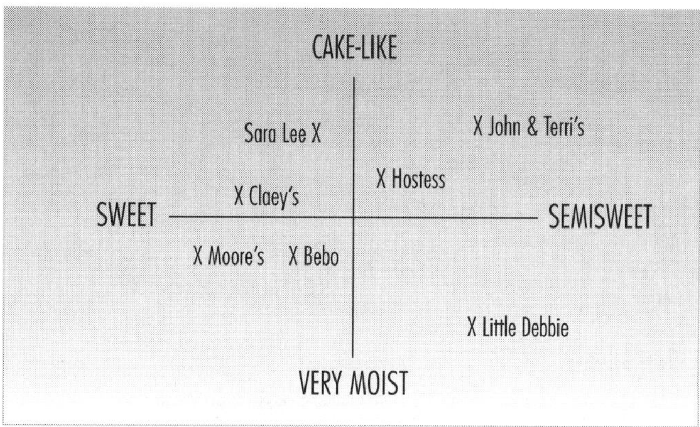

John was clearly concerned. "If they do enter the market," noted John, "they'll be difficult to compete with. Their gourmet brownie and ours will be competing for the same customers, and I am sure distributors would prefer to handle Rachel's product because of their proven history." Although John had heard nothing more about Rachel's entering the market, he felt there was a 75 percent likelihood that they would be in the Charlotte market in the next six months.

The Options

John had initially considered four alternative ways to market the brownie: selling to distributors, retailing from carts on the street, selling to existing customers, and selling to airline food suppliers. His listing of the advantages and disadvantages of each is shown in Exhibit 1.5.

Selling the brownie to distributors had initially been John's first choice. This method would allow the brownie to quickly be exposed to a wide range of customers through the distributors' established networks of retailers. John had made presentations to two local distributors and had received a cool reception in both instances. "I was surprised," noted John. "The volume that both required was much larger than I had anticipated. One distributor said that he would not touch a new product that wouldn't produce $6,000 per week in sales. The other, although less specific, indicated that any new product he added to his product line would have to be accompanied with 'substantial' advertising to the ultimate consumer to help assure product movement. Also, both indicated their markup would be in the 15 to 20 percent range because of the risk of adding a product which had not previously been on the market."

Exhibit 1.5 Advantages and Disadvantages of Options to Market Brownies

Advantages	Disadvantages
Distributors	
Wide distribution Maximum consumer exposure Opportunity to establish brand name Guaranteed sales	Prohibitively high sales minimums Accompanying advertising expected Pushes retail price higher
Retail on street	
Active downtown area Accepted mode of sale Begin to establish brand name	Startup costs of $1,200 Widely fluctuating (weather-dependent) sales Must find, train, and retain salespersons
Sell to existing customers	
Little resistance Brownie would receive favorable placement	Limited market exposure Lengthening of product line Cannibalization of blond brownies
Sell to airline food supplier	
Guaranteed sales Known quantities Exposure to consumers Begin to establish brand name	Cost exceeds stated maximum price Limited contract time

Another option that John had pursued was selling brownies from a vending cart in the downtown section of Charlotte. Charlotte had become a regional banking center, and it was estimated that over 40,000 people worked in the immediate downtown area. The city had approved and encouraged organized street vending. Presently ten vendors had licenses and were selling their products from carts on downtown streets (see Exhibit 1.6). John estimated that it would take approximately $1,200 to put a cart on the street. As John explained it:

> *I know that the downtown area is filled with upscale customers, but the thing that bothers me here is that I've just never been involved with retail. Also, I don't know how difficult it will be to find and keep a salesperson. Are we going to be able to find someone who will be willing to work only when the weather's good? What are we going to do if the product is already baked and the person doesn't show up? These uncertainties concern me.*

An additional option which John had considered was the addition of the brownie to the bakery's existing product line. Periodically, customers asked John if he had started baking the gourmet brownie yet. As could be expected, the customers that were particularly interested were those who had projected the highest level of sales for the brownie (see Exhibit 1.3). John admitted:

Exhibit 1.6 Presently Licensed Street Vendors, Charlotte, North Carolina

Vendor	Products Sold
1. Halfpenny	Nachos, baked potatoes
2. TCBY	Frozen yogurt
3. Zackebobs	Shish kebob
4. LaLamas	Hot dogs, drinks
5. Purple Shop	Sundry items
6. John C's	German hot dogs
7. Kwik Way	Hot dogs
8. Larry's	Ice cream
9. Lemon Quench	Drink products
10. Jerry's	Ice cream

This would clearly be the easiest way to introduce our brownie, but the exposure to the total Charlotte market would be limited and I have so little time to go out and try to find new accounts. Our customers are excited about it, but I think our new brownie would cannibalize about half of the sales of our blond brownie. Besides, if we add the brownie, where is the time to produce it going to come from? Does it mean we will need to get to the bakery at 4 A.M. instead of 5 A.M.? We want the brownie to shorten our product line, not to lengthen it.

The final option was the sale of the brownie to Food Service Professionals (FSP), an airline food supplier. John had made the proposal about three months earlier. At that time, he had taken samples of the brownie in its standard 2 × 3 × ¾ inch serving and had suggested that the individually wrapped brownie be the dessert portion of the in-flight meal. John described the negotiation this way:

It seemed that this might be a good way to get some brand recognition. That's why I suggested the individually wrapped brownie. I remember that the first Eagle snacks I ever had were on an airplane. Then when I later saw them in the store, I had already sampled them and knew how good they were. I wanted to do this on a smaller scale with our brownie. If we sold the brownies by the tray (unwrapped), then I can't see any long-term benefits for us. FSP didn't think long-term, either; their standard supply contract was for about 90 days. Anyway, the proposal died when we talked about the price. When I gave them our $0.46 unit price, Ms. Abrams, the FSP rep, indicated that they targeted their dessert cost at $0.30 and that their absolute cost ceiling for dessert portions was $0.35. That essentially ended the discussion; they clearly weren't going to budge from that figure and I didn't feel we could come down that much on our price either.

The couple realized that most options for the brownies would require at least some additional capital to implement. "We've got a family member who has indicated a willingness to invest $10,000 to help us. If that's not enough, then I'll go to the bank and take out a loan for more. I'll do whatever is necessary," explained John.

The Call

The call that July morning had been from Jan Abrams at Food Service Professionals. After summarizing the results of their previous meeting, she indicated that the firm had a counterproposal for John to consider. Rather than the 2 × 3 × ¾ inch portion that had been initially presented, she proposed that the size of the individually wrapped brownies be reduced to 2 × 2 × ¾ inch and, since the size of the brownie was being reduced by one-third, that the price be reduced to $0.30 per unit. Jan also indicated that FSP needed to determine in the next two days whether John had any interest in the alternative proposal. "I apologize for our sense of urgency, but we are going to make a change in our dessert offerings and we want to get our fourth quarter menus resolved. Using a reduced portion of your brownie was a last minute suggestion from a member of my staff," explained Jan. She concluded the call by indicating that she felt that acceptance of her counterproposal would likely lead to a contract for a guaranteed order for at least 4,000 units per week for a period of 13 weeks—beginning October 1. FSP would also require an option to renew the contract. Jan indicated that in instances where firms maintained expected quality, the renewal option was usually exercised.

As John reflected on the call, he was excited, but realized that he would have to weigh the decision carefully. He had to make sure that every issue was considered. The option could contractually bind the small bakery for as long as six months. Still, he was smiling as he walked out of the office to tell Terri.

Case 2

MacTec Control AB

Georg Carlsson is president of MacTec Control AB, a Swedish firm located in Kristianstad. Georg began MacTec in 1980 with his wife, Jessie. MacTec grew rapidly and now boasts of 30 employees and annual revenues of about $2.8 million. Since 1985, MacTec has been partly owned by the Perstorp Corporation whose headquarters are located nearby. Perstorp is a large manufacturer of chemicals and chemical products, with operations in 18 countries and annual revenues of about $600 million. Perstorp has provided MacTec with capital and managerial advice, as well as chemical analysis technology.

MacTec's Aqualex System

MacTec's product line centers around its Aqualex system: computer hardware and software designed to monitor and control pressurized water flow. The water flow consists mostly of potable water or sewage effluent as these liquids are stored, moved, or treated by municipal water departments.

The system employs MacTec's MPDII microcomputer (see Exhibit 2.1) installed at individual pumping stations where liquids are stored and moved. Often these stations are located quite far apart, linking geographically dispersed water users (households, businesses, etc.) to water and sewer systems. The microcomputer performs a number of important functions. It controls the starts, stops, and alarms of up to four pumps, monitors levels and available capacities of storage reservoirs, checks pump capacities and power consumptions, and records pump flows. It even measures the amount of rainfall entering reservoirs and adjusts pump operations or activates an alarm as needed. Each microcomputer can also easily be connected to a main computer

---

Source: This case was written by Professor James E. Nelson, University of Colorado. This case is intended for use as a basis for class discussion rather than to illustrate either effective or ineffective administrative decision making. Some data are disguised.

Exhibit 2.1

The Aqualex System is based on the MPDII which controls and monitors the pumping stations

An MPDII microcomputer is installed at a pumping station and works as an independent, intelligent computer. When required, it can go online with the central computer and report its readings there.

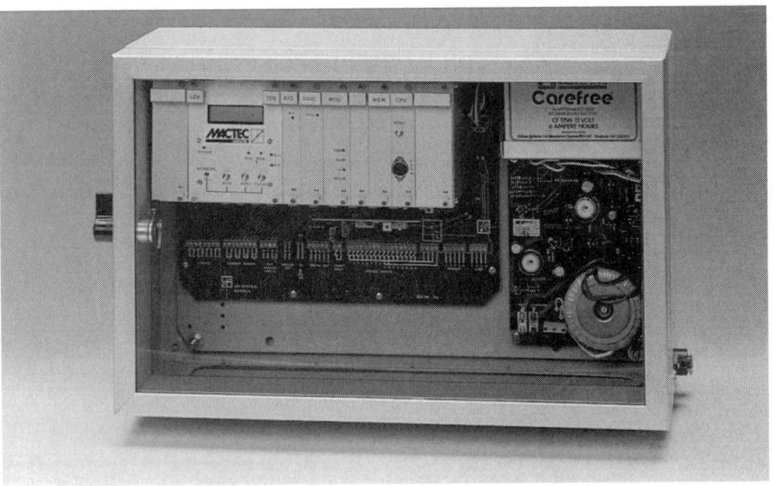

Here are some of the functions of the MPDII:

- *It governs the starts, stops, and alarms of up to four pumps, controlled by an integrated piezo-resistive pressure-level sensor.*
- *It checks the sump level.*
- *It checks pump capacity and changes in pump capacity.*
- *It activates an alarm when readings reach preset deviation limits.*
- *It registers precipitation and activates an alarm in case of heavy rain.*
- *It constantly monitors pump power consumption and activates an alarm in case of unacceptable deviation.*
- *It registers current pump flow by means of advanced calculations of inflow and outfeed from the sump.*
- *It can register accumulated time for overflow.*
- *It switches to forward or reverse action, even by remote command.*
- *It stores locally the last nine alarm instances with time indications. These may be read directly on an LCD display.*
- *It can be remotely programmed from the central computer.*

An MPDII does a great job, day after day, year after year.

to allow remote control of pumping stations and produce a variety of charts and graphs useful in evaluating pump performance and scheduling needed maintenance.

The Aqualex system provides a monitoring function that human operators cannot match in terms of sophistication, immediacy, and cost. The system permits each individual substation to control its own pumping operations; collect, analyze, and store data; forecast trends; transmit data and alarms to a central computer; and receive remote commands. Alarms can also be transmitted directly to a pocket-size receiver carried by one or more operators on call. A supervisor can continually monitor pumping operations in a large system entirely via a computer terminal at a central location and send commands to individual pumps, thereby saving costly service calls and time. The system also reduces the possibility of overflows that could produce disastrous flooding in nearby communities.

MacTec personnel work with water and sewage engineers to design and install the Aqualex system. Personnel also train engineers and operators to work with the system and are available 24 hours a day for consultation. If needed, a MacTac engineer can personally assist engineers and operators if major problems arise. MacTac also offers its clients the option of purchasing a complete service contract whereby MacTac personnel provide periodic testing and maintenance of installed systems.

An Aqualex system has several versions. In its most basic form, the system is little more than a small "black box" that monitors two or three lift station activities and, when necessary, transmits an alarm to one or more remote receivers. An intermediate system monitors additional activities, sends data to a central computer via telephone lines and receives remote commands. An advanced system provides the same monitoring capabilities but has forecasting features, maintenance management, auxiliary power back-up, and data transmission and reception via radio. Prices for the three different types in early 1989 are $1,200, $2,400, and $4,200.

Aqualex Customers

Aqualex customers can be divided into two groups—governmental units and industrial companies. The typical application in the first group is a sewage treatment plant having 4 to 12 pumping stations, each station containing one or more pumps. Pumps operate intermittently and, unless an Aqualex or similar system is in place, are monitored by one or more operators who visit each station once or twice each day for about half an hour. Operators take reservoir measurements, record running times of pumps, and sometimes perform limited maintenance and repairs. The sewage plant and stations are typically located in flat or rolling terrain, where gravity cannot be used in lieu of pumping. If any monitoring equipment is present at all, it typically consists of a crude, on-site alarm that activates when fluid levels rise or fall beyond a preset level. Sometimes the alarm activates a telephone dialing function that alerts an operator away from the station.

Numerous industrial companies also store, move, and process large quantities of water or sewage. These applications usually differ very little from those in governmental plants except for their smaller size. On the other hand, there are considerably more industrial companies with pumping stations and so, Georg thinks, the two markets often offer close to identical market potentials in many countries.

The two markets desire essentially the same products, although industrial applications often use smaller, simpler equipment. Both markets want their monitoring equipment to be accurate and reliable, the two dominant concerns. Equipment should also be easy to use, economical to operate, and require little regular service or maintenance. Purchase price often is not a major consideration. As long as the price is in an appropriate range, customers seem more interested in actual product performance than in initial cost outlays.

Georg thinks worldwide demand for Aqualex systems and competing products will continue to be strong for at least the next 10 years. While some of this demand represents construction of new pumping stations, many applications are replacements of crude monitoring and alarm systems at existing sites. These existing systems depend greatly on regular visits by operators, visits that often continue even after new equipment is installed. Most such trips are probably not necessary. However, many managers find it difficult to dismiss or reassign monitoring personnel that are no longer needed; many are also quite cautious and conservative, desiring some human monitoring of the new equipment "just in case." Once replacement of existing systems is complete, market growth is limited to new construction and, of course, replacements with more sophisticated systems.

Most customers (and noncustomers) consider the Aqualex system the best on the market. Those knowledgeable in the industry feel that competing products seldom match Aqualex's reliability and accuracy. Experts also believe that many competing products lack the sophistication and flexibility present in Aqualex's design. Beyond these product features, customers also appreciate MacTec's knowledge about water and sanitation engineering. Competing firms often lack this expertise, offering products somewhat as a sideline and considering the market too small for an intensive marketing effort.

The market is clearly not too small for MacTec. While Georg has no hard data on market potential for Western Europe, he thinks annual demand could be as much as $9 million. About 40 percent of this figure represents potential, the rest is demand for replacing existing systems. Industry sales in the latter category could be increased by more aggressive marketing efforts on the part of MacTec and its competitors. Eastern European economies represent additional potential. However, the water and sewer industries in these countries seem less interested in high-technology equipment to monitor pumping operations than do their Western counterparts. Additionally, business is often more difficult to conduct in these countries. In contrast, the U.S. market looks very attractive.

MacTec Strategy

MacTec currently markets its Aqualex system primarily to sewage treatment plants in Scandinavia and other countries in northern and central Europe. The company's strategy could be described as providing technologically superior equipment to monitor pumping operations at these plants. The strategy stresses frequent contacts with customers and potential customers to design, supply, and service Aqualex systems. Superior knowledge of water and sanitation engineering with up-to-date electronics and computer technology is also important. The result is a line of highly specialized sensors, computers, and methods for process controls in water treatment plants.

The essence of MacTec's strategy is demonstrating a special competence that no firm in the world can easily match. MacTec also prides itself on being a young, creative company, without an entrenched bureaucracy. Company employees generally work with enthusiasm and dedication; they talk with each other regularly and openly. Most importantly, customers—as well as technology—seem to drive all areas of the company.

MacTec's strategy in its European markets seems fairly well-decided. That is, Georg thinks that a continuation of present strategies and tactics should continue to produce good results. However, one change is the planned creation of a branch office conducting sales and manufacturing activities somewhere in the European Community (EC), most likely the Netherlands. The plan was to have such an office in operation well before 12 countries in the EC (Belgium, Denmark, France, Greece, Ireland, Italy, Luxembourg, the Netherlands, Portugal, Spain, United Kingdom, and West Germany) would mutually eliminate national barriers to the flow of capital, goods, and services. Having a MacTec office located in the EC would greatly simplify sales to these member countries. Moreover, MacTec's presence should also avoid problems with any protective barriers the EC itself might raise to limit or discourage market access by outsiders.

Notwithstanding activities related to this branch office, Georg is considering a major strategic decision to enter the U.S. market. His two recent visits to the United States have led him to conclude that the market represents potential beyond that for Western Europe and that the United States seems perfect for expansion. Industry experts in the United States agree with Georg that the Aqualex system outperforms anything used in the U.S. market. Experts think many water and sewage engineers would welcome MacTec's products and knowledge. Moreover, Georg thinks U.S. transportation systems and payment arrangements would present few problems. The system would be imported under U.S. Tariff Regulation 71249 and pay a duty of 4.9 percent.

Entry would most likely occur in the form of a sales and service office located in Philadelphia. The Pennsylvania and New York state markets seem representative of the United States and appear to offer a good test of the Aqualex system. The two states together probably represent about 18 percent of total U.S. market potential for the system. The office would require an investment of $200,000 for inventory and other balance sheet items. Annual fixed costs would total close to $250,000 for salaries and other operating expenses; Georg plans to employ only a general manager, two sales technicians, and a secretary for at least the first year or two. Each Aqualex system sold in the United States would be priced to provide a contribution of about 30 percent. Georg wants a 35 percent annual return before taxes on any MacTec investment, beginning no later than the second year. The issue is whether Georg can realistically expect to achieve this goal in the United States.

Marketing Research

Georg had commissioned the Browning Group in Philadelphia to conduct some limited marketing research with selected personnel in the water and sewage industries in the city and surrounding areas. The research had two purposes: to obtain a sense of market needs and market reactions to MacTec's products, and to calculate a rough estimate of market potential in Pennsylvania and New York. Results were intended to help Georg interpret his earlier conversations with industry experts and perhaps facilitate a decision on market entry.

The research design employed two phases of data collection. The first consisted of five one-hour, tape-recorded interviews with water and sewage engineers employed by local city and municipal governments. Questions included:

1. What procedures do you use to monitor your pumping stations?
2. Is your current monitoring system effective? Costly?
3. What are the costs of a monitoring malfunction?
4. What features would you like to see in a monitoring system?
5. Who decides on the selection of a monitoring system?
6. What is your reaction to the Aqualex system?

Interviewers listened closely to the engineers' responses and probed for additional detail and clarification.

Tapes of the personal interviews were transcribed and then analyzed by the project manager at Browning. The report noted that these results described typical industry practices and viewpoints. A partial summary from the report appears below:

> *The picture that emerges is one of fairly sophisticated personnel making decisions about monitoring equipment that is relatively simple in design. Still, some engineers would appear distrustful of this equipment because they persist in sending operators to pumping stations on a daily basis. The distrust may be justified because potential costs of a malfunction were identified as expensive repairs and cleanups, fines of $10,000 per day of violation, lawsuits, harassment by the Health department, and public embarrassment. The five engineers identified themselves as key individuals in the decision to purchase new equipment. Without exception, they considered MacTec features innovative, highly desirable, and worth the price.*

The summary also noted that the primary purpose of the interview results was for construction of a questionnaire to be administered by telephone.

The questionnaire was used in the second phase of data collection, as part of a telephone survey that contacted 65 utility managers, water and sewage engineers, and pumping station operators in Philadelphia and surrounding areas. All respondents were employed by governmental units. Each interview took about 10 minutes to complete, covering topics identified in questions 1, 2, and 4 above. The Browning Group's research report stated that most respondents were quite cooperative, although 15 people refused to participate at all.

The telephone interviews produced results that could be considered more representative of the market because of the larger sample size. The report organized these results under the topics of monitoring procedures, system effectiveness and costs, and features desired in a monitoring system:

> *All monitoring systems under the responsibility of the 50 respondents were considered to require manual checking. The frequency of operator visits to pumping stations ranged from monthly to twice daily, depending on flow rates, pumping station history, proximity of nearby communities, monitoring equipment in operation, and other factors. Even the most sophisticated automatic systems were checked because respondents "just don't trust the machine." Each operator was responsible for some 10 to 20 stations.*
>
> *Despite the perceived need for double-checking, all respondents considered their current monitoring system to be quite effective. Not one reported a serious pumping malfunction in the past three years that had escaped detection. However, this reliability came at considerable cost—the annual wages and other expenses associated with each monitoring operator averaged about $40,000.*
>
> *Respondents were about evenly divided between those wishing a simple alarm system and those desiring a sophisticated, versatile microprocessor. Managers and engineers in the former category often said that the only feature they really needed was an emergency signal such as a siren, horn, or light. Sometimes they would add a telephone dialer that would be automatically activated at the same time as the signal. Most agreed that a price of around $2,000 would be reasonable for such a system. The latter category of individuals contained engineers desiring many of the Aqualex System's features, once they knew such equipment was available. A price of $4,000 per system seemed acceptable. Some of these respondents were quite knowledgeable about computers and computer programming while others were not. Only four respondents voiced any strong concerns about the cost to purchase and install more sophisticated monitoring equipment. Everyone demanded that the equipment be reliable and accurate.*

Georg found the report quite helpful. Much of the information, of course, simply confirmed his own view of the U.S. market. However, it was good to have this knowledge from an independent, objective organization. In addition, to learn that the market consisted of two, apparently equal-size segments—of simple and sophisticated applications—was quite worthwhile. In particular, knowledge of system prices considered acceptable by each segment would make the entry decision easier. Meeting these prices would not be a major problem.

An important section of the report contained an estimate of market potential for Pennsylvania and New York. The estimate was based on an analysis of discharge permits on file in governmental offices in the two states. These permits are required before any city, municipality, water or sewage district, or industrial company can release sewage or other contaminated water to another system or to a lake or river. Each permit showed the number of pumping stations in operation. Based on a 10 percent sample of permits, the report estimated that governmental units in Pennsylvania and New York contain approximately 3,000 and 5,000 pumping stations for waste water, respectively. Industrial companies in the two states were estimated to add 3,000 and 9,000 more pumping stations, respectively. The total number of pumping stations in the two states (20,000) seemed to be growing at about 2 percent per year.

Finally, a brief section of the report dealt with the study's limitations. Georg agreed that the sample was quite small, that it contained no utility managers or engineers from New York, and that it probably concentrated too heavily on individuals in larger urban areas. In addition, the research told him nothing about competitors and their marketing strategies and tactics. Nor did he learn anything about any state regulations for monitoring equipment, if indeed any existed. However, these shortcomings came as no surprise, representing a consequence of the research design proposed to Georg by the Browning Group six weeks ago, before the study began.

The Decision

Georg's decision seems difficult. The most risky option is to enter the U.S. market as soon as possible; the most conservative is to stay in Europe. The option also exists of conducting additional marketing research.

Case 3

Data General and New York's Division of Substance Abuse Services

On June 28, 1991, Data General Corporation was informed that it had been successful in winning a major contract with New York State's Division of Substance Abuse Services (DSAS).

For sales representative Daniel Snell it was no doubt a satisfying win. Both he and his manager, Kenneth Canastar, had worked hard over recent months to build a close relationship with DSAS and to put together a proposal for its computer requirements. Canastar and Snell had managed to win over both the state agency's staff and consultants at Diversified Business Enterprises of America, Inc., a third-party consulting firm hired to assist with vendor selection.

But celebrations were short-lived. On September 6, 1991, before the computer equipment had been installed, Snell received an appearance subpoena from New York's Office of the State Inspector General for an investigation of events surrounding the Data General order. Data General management had to determine quickly whether there was a problem with this particular transaction, how it should respond to the Inspector General's request, and whether to proceed with the equipment installation, scheduled for late September.

Data General

In 1990, Data General's business was the design, manufacture, and sale of multiuser computer systems and associated products and services. Based in Westboro, Massachusetts,

Source: This case was written by Andrew D. Dyer, Georgetown University, under the supervision of Professor N. Craig Smith. The assistance of Edward T. Dominelli of the New York Office of State Inspector General and funding from the John F. Connelly Program in Business Ethics at Georgetown University School of Business are gratefully acknowledged. This case was written from public sources, solely for the purpose of stimulating student discussion.

the corporation did business in over 70 countries around the world, through 26 subsidiaries and 300 sales and service offices. Total sales were $1.22 billion, on which the firm incurred a loss of $140 million. It employed 10,600 people, down from 15,400 in 1988, and operated manufacturing plants in the United States, Canada, Mexico, and the Philippines. Exhibit 3.1 provides a five-year summary of Data General's financial performance.

The modern computer had its origins in the late 1940s, meeting the needs of the military, large corporations, and university research laboratories. At that time, computers were used for repetitive applications such as bookkeeping and solving mathematical problems. They were large and required controlled environments for their operation. As a result, computers were expensive to buy and operate, and most organizations opted for a single large machine (a mainframe) to serve their needs. Over time, it became clear that individual user needs were not being met by this centralized approach. Difficulties arose for two major reasons: (1) users resented the monopoly-like control exercised by computer departments and (2) mainframe computer technology had severe limitations in the area of user-defined applications. Users, especially scientists and engineers, called for a relatively inexpensive computer that they could operate themselves. Their demands led to the birth of the minicomputer and, with it, manufacturers such a Digital Equipment Corporation (DEC), Hewlett-Packard, and Data General.

Data General was founded in 1968 by a small team of engineers led by Edson de Castro. De Castro had been part of the design team for the DEC PDP-8, a highly successful minicomputer. After leaving DEC, de Castro and his team incorporated Data General and began producing their own minicomputers. Data General's first product, the NOVA, was unveiled at the 1969 National Computer Conference and was an immediate success in the fast-growing minicomputer marketplace. Over the next ten years, Data General grew at a phenomenal rate. By 1978, it was ranked third in sales of minicomputers; in the same year it made the *Fortune* 500 list for the first time.

CHANGES IN STRATEGY

Minicomputer vendors such as Data General, Digital Equipment Corporation (DEC), and Hewlett-Packard originally produced products that used proprietary architectures. That meant that the operating system software (the software that directs all the computer's functions) was unique to the manufacturer, and therefore all applications had to be specifically designed to run on the manufacturer's equipment under the manufacturer's operating system. Thus, for example, an application running on a DEC computer could not run on a Data General computer without extensive modification (or "rewrite"). Hence, when an organization selected a particular computer vendor, they were locked in to that vendor for future equipment purchases unless they decided to modify their applications, or implement new applications, which would run on a machine from a different vendor. Within organizations, individual departments using different vendors were often unable to communicate via computer or share data, and each department would set up its own computer support group to manage and administer its own system.

Exhibit 3.1 Data General Corporation:
Five Year Summary of Selected Financial Data (Dollar Amounts in Thousands)

	Year Ended				
	Sept. 28, 1991	Sept. 29, 1990	Sept. 30, 1989	Sept. 24, 1988	Sept. 26, 1987
Total revenues	$1,228,854	$1,216,401	$1,314,395	$1,364,734	$1,274,348
Total cost of revenues	659,559	692,015	722,084	694,869	685,778
Research and development	101,986	140,743	149,023	156,421	157,499
Selling, general, and administrative	384,317	444,583	490,653	470,616	437,675
Restructuring charge	—	71,700	80,000	48,700	53,800
Total costs and expenses	1,145,862	1,349,041	1,441,760	1,370,606	1,334,752
Income (loss) from operations	82,992	(132,640)	(127,365)	(5,872)	(60,404)
Gain on sale of subsidiary and facilities	13,000	—	14,857	5,889	—
Interest expense, net	4,451	3,905	1,422	6,754	9,545
Income (loss) before income taxes, net loss from unconsolidated affiliate, and extraordinary items	91,541	(136,545)	(113,930)	(6,737)	(69,949)
Income tax provision (benefit)	5,900	3,230	5,800	8,800	(10,400)
Income (loss) before net loss from unconsolidated affiliate and extraordinary items	85,641	(139,775)	(119,730)	(15,537)	(59,549)
Net loss from unconsolidated affiliate	—	—	—	—	19,958
Income (loss) before extraordinary items	85,641	(139,775)	(119,730)	(15,537)	(79,507)
Extraordinary losses	—	—	—	—	44,158
Net income (loss)	$ 85,641	$(139,775)	$(119,730)	$ (15,537)	$(123,665)
Primary net income (loss) per share					
Before extraordinary items	$ 2.62	$ (4.65)	$ (4.10)	$ (.55)	$ (2.95)
Including extraordinary items	$ 2.62	$ (4.65)	$ (4.10)	$ (.55)	$ (4.59)
Net income (loss) per share assuming full dilution					
Before extraordinary items	$ 2.45	$ (4.65)	$ (4.10)	$ (.55)	$ (2.95)
Including extraordinary items	$ 2.45	$ (4.65)	$ (4.10)	$ (.55)	$ (4.59)

	As of				
	Sept. 28, 1991	Sept. 29, 1990	Sept. 30, 1989	Sept. 24, 1988	Sept. 26, 1987
Current assets	$ 690,537	$ 595,602	$ 709,988	$ 669,803	$ 641,609
Current liabilities	284,694	447,027	442,491	390,417	383,287
Working capital	405,843	148,575	267,497	279,386	258,322
Total assets	$ 944,046	$ 909,437	$1,040,165	$1,077,713	$1,068,311
Annual expenditures for property, plant, and equipment	$ 82,766	$ 85,066	$ 91,467	$ 96,592	$ 142,918
Long-term debt	$ 164,911	$ 56,918	$ 70,748	$ 65,945	$ 79,990
Stockholder's equity	$ 494,441	$ 405,492	$ 522,126	$ 611,921	$ 591,656
Cumulative computers shipped	326,200	297,600	276,800	253,600	226,400
Employees	8,500	10,600	13,700	15,400	15,700

Notes: Results of operations are for 52-week periods except for 1989, which is a 53-week period. The company has not declared or paid cash dividends since inception.
Source: Data General *Annual Report,* 1991.

Toward the end of the 1980s, the growing popularity of UNIX (an operating system developed by AT&T and the University of California at Berkeley) changed the minicomputer market dramatically. UNIX was an "open" system, defined by a set of public domain standards; all interested manufacturers could design their computers to operate under UNIX. Applications then became portable between the different computers that supported UNIX, allowing a customer to be totally vendor-independent. Data General, DEC, Hewlett-Packard, and a number of other major vendors began introducing UNIX products to meet this new demand. Price competition increased on minicomputers as vendors positioned themselves to maintain or acquire market share in this new environment.

As a result, Data General's strategy changed from being a supplier of proprietary systems, developing long-term customers with a stable installed base, to being a supplier of low-cost, generic computers that could be sold to virtually any organization (regardless of the incumbent computer vendor) as well as to other equipment manufacturers, including its traditional competitors, such as IBM and Unisys. Key to Data General's success in the 1990s was to aggressively pursue the fast-growing open systems marketplace while profitably providing support and solutions to its extensive base of proprietary systems customers.

In 1991, Data General offered to the marketplace a mix of open and proprietary solutions: AViiON and Eclipse MV.

Introduced in 1989, the AViiON open system product line comprised 17 models of servers and 7 workstations, designed using RISC (reduced instruction set computing) processors. AViiON operated under Data General's UNIX operating system software, and over 3,000 software programs were available from suppliers of database products, languages, compilers, and word processing and other applications packages. (A *server* is a computer shared by one or more users through a local area network. The server can provide sharing of data and applications among local users as well as acting as a communications gateway to other computers or networks. The term *workstation* generally refers to high-powered desktop computer that can be used for processor-intensive applications, such as computer-aided design and drawing, mapping, and complex problem solving, as well as general commercial applications.)

The Eclipse MV was a proprietary system product line that had been introduced in 1980. The MV product ranged from desktop models to models with mainframe power. Over 45,000 systems had been installed, and users had access to a range of industry-specific applications.

Data General also provided systems integration and professional, education, and maintenance services to complement its products and meet customer needs.

Data General products and services were sold through a variety of distribution channels. Direct sales were handled by over 700 salespeople, supported by approximately 600 sales engineers. The sales force was located around the world and marketed the full Data General product line to large organizations. Data General also used third-party distribution channels including original equipment manufacturers, value-added resellers, system suppliers, and independent hardware and software vendors. Data General's international sales were conducted through foreign subsidiaries, independent representatives, and distributors, with the majority of its international revenues coming from Western Europe, Canada, Japan, and Australia.

Data General customers represented a diverse range of industries, including health care, manufacturing, finance, business administration, retail, telecommunications, utilities, and government. With its AViiON products, Data General was also penetrating new growth markets such as geographic information systems and financial services. Data General's customer base was diverse. No single customer represented more than 8 percent of the firm's revenues, and total sales made directly to various agencies of the United States federal government represented only 2 percent of Data General's revenues.

The Computer Industry in 1991

THE BUYING PROCESS

The computer industry in 1991 consisted of thousands of organizations worldwide that provided equipment, software, facilities installation and management, and a wide variety of professional and advice services. There were many different types of vendors in the industry, as well as many types of buyers and buying criteria. Computer buyers ranged from technical staff, making purchase decisions based on the equipment's price and capabilities, to executives, making purchase decisions based on application requirements and/or strategic issues, with equipment as a secondary consideration. Equipment vendors like Data General tended to focus on the technical decision maker, often the actual end user. Service providers, such as consultants, and system integrators, tended to focus on executives and marketed top-down to the customer organization.

Equipment vendors generally concentrated their direct sales force on large customers, where there were opportunities for high revenues and multiple sales. A sales representative was assigned a territory on either an industry or geographic basis and was responsible for generating sales from that territory as well as maintaining overall customer satisfaction. The representative would be part of a sales unit or branch, located within or close to the territory. The sales unit could also contain product or technical specialists who would assist the sales representative.

Computer equipment sales representatives were generally compensated through revenue commissions and product bonuses. A representative would be allocated a quota (which could be a monthly, quarterly, or annual target) of sales to make, and paid a base salary plus commission (in proportion to his or her achievement against quota). Quota targets were based on a number of measurements, but the most common were revenue, profit, or points. (*Points,* a measure used by some companies, including IBM until 1990, were a numerical value placed on a product that reflected a combination of the revenue, profit, and strategic significance of the product. The point score was fixed and did not take into account any discount offered on the product.) In addition to quota achievement compensation, sales representatives could receive bonuses for strategic product sales, displacing a competitor's system, or selling multiple units of a particular product to a single customer. In 1991, computer industry sales representatives could earn from as little as $25,000 to over $250,000 per annum.

Although computer systems and services were bought by organizations, quite often the purchase decision or recommendation came down to a single individual within an organization. A competent sales representative would normally determine who that individual was and then attempt to build a strong relationship with the customer. The nature of these relationships varied widely. Some were strictly business, where the sales representative developed a strong relationship by providing excellent service and support. Others involved more personal elements, where the sales representative developed a strong relationship through hosting external activities for the customer, including lunches, dinners, attendance at sporting activities, and other events. Some customers expected the latter type of relationship, just as some sales representatives expected customers to be more likely to buy if they had been appropriately entertained. As the value of computer contracts was significant (typically ranging from $1 million to $40 million), the relative expense of such entertainment was small. A sales representative would typically have an expense budget of $2,000 to $10,000 for a sales quota of around $5 million (i.e., 0.04 to 0.20 percent of sales). Government agencies, however, often limited the amount of entertainment that could be received from vendors by its employees, requiring both sales representatives and customer employees to be cautious in their activities. For example, New York State officers and employees were required to abide by the guidelines set forth in the state publication A *Guide to the Ethics Law*. An extract from the *Guide* is provided in Exhibit 3.2.

To assist organizations with these complex and significant purchase decisions, external consultants were often called in to provide an independent assessment. The consultants would either manage the entire procurement process under contract or provide specialist advice to the customer, usually on technical matters. Consultants were used to assist with buying equipment, software, and services and, depending on their contract and relationship with the client, could have a significant influence on a purchase decision. Competent sales representatives were aware of the involvement of external consultants and tailored their marketing plans accordingly.

Sometimes, individual departments in an organization used the proprietary nature of different computer brands to "protect" the department's role. For example, if Department A used Brand X computer and Department B used Brand Y, the incompatibility of the two brands meant that Department A could not use B's computer or applications. As long as the two departments continued to run different types of systems, they could not be easily merged and neither department could "take over" the other department's computer operations. Sales representatives were aware that the political advantage of having a unique system would often be a factor in a computer purchase decision.

DECLINING PROFITABILITY

The computer industry was intensely competitive in 1991, particularly for equipment sellers. IBM-compatible personal computers and UNIX-based minicomputers had become "commodity" products, with less and less differentiation available to vendors (such as value-added support and services) that would be valued by buyers. The industry's overall profitability had fallen sharply, with return on sales dropping from

Exhibit 3.2 The New York State Ethics Code

New York State has an official Code of Ethics that was created by Section 74 of the Public Officers Law. It is contained in the *Public Officers Law* booklet that all State employees receive when they join state service.

While many private companies and professional associations have their own codes of ethics, there is a major difference between their codes and the state's code: The state code is also the law. The following material summarizes some of the applicable provisions of the *Public Officers Law*.

General Summary

You are prohibited from engaging in any activity that is in substantial conflict with the proper discharge of your duties in the public interest, accepting other employment that would impair your judgment in the exercise of your official duties, and disclosing confidential information which you gain from your State position.

You cannot use your official position to secure unwarranted privileges for yourself or others. If you have a financial interest in a business entity, you should not engage in any transaction between the State and that entity which might be in conflict with the proper discharge of your official duties. You also must avoid making personal investments in enterprises that you might reasonably believe may be directly involved in decisions you make or that might create a conflict of interest.

You cannot, by your conduct, leave the impression that anyone can influence you based on their family relationship, rank, position or influence. Nor should you act in a way that raises a suspicion among the public that you are likely to be engaged in acts that are in violation of your public trust.

If you are a full-time employee, neither you nor any firm or association of which you are a member—or a corporation which you own or control—can sell goods or services to any person, firm or association which either is licensed or has its rates set by the State agency in which you are employed.

Extract from the *Public Officers Law*—Section 74(3)
f. An officer or employee of a state agency, member of the legislature or legislative employee should not by his conduct give reasonable basis for the impression that any person can improperly influence him or unduly enjoy his favor in the performance of his official duties, or that he is affected by the kinship, rank, position or influence of any party or person.

h. An officer or employee of a state agency, member of the legislature or legislative employee should endeavor to pursue a course of conduct which will not raise suspicion among the public that he is likely to be engaged in acts that are in violation of his trust.

Gifts

The following is from *New York Ethics: A Guide to the Ethics Law,* The New York State Ethics Commission, New York, 1991.

Gifts may come in many forms and from many people: a keychain from the company that delivers overnight mail; tickets to the ballgame from a vendor who deals with your agency; even flowers from a satisfied taxpayer. Some companies consider the distribution of such "freebies" to be part of an effective marketing plan, while others consider it good public relations.

Under the law, covered individuals may not accept any gifts valued at more than $75, in whatever form, under circumstances in which it could be inferred that the gift was intended to influence or reward the recipient in performing official duties, or was offered in anticipation of some action. Gifts under $75 may also be suspect, under Section 74 of the law, if they were intended to influence or reward the recipient.

Example: A complaint has been filed with the Department of Health regarding the facilities at a local health club. Rita, a state investigator, screens the complaint and decides that no action should be taken The grateful club owner offers Rita a club membership valued at $300. She cannot accept the membership.

Example: Denyce, an auditor for the Department of Taxation and Finance, audits the returns of a local automobile dealership. She may not accept money for a favorable report and may not take delivery on a car from the dealership at a special discount—normally unavailable to the public—during or after the audit.

---

around 9.5 percent in 1984 to –1.0 percent in 1991 (profits as a percent of sales for 92 computer companies, according to McKinsey and Company). New competitors were entering all sectors of the industry, and unprecedented numbers of new products were introduced in 1991. Purchase decisions were being driven more by price and machine performance. With the large number of suppliers competing in the marketplace, sales representatives such as Data General's Kenneth Canastar and Daniel Snell worked under enormous pressure to continually win business and meet sales targets.

Procurement Policies in the Public Sector

Public sector organizations such as DSAS required formal procedures to be followed for the procurement of goods and services. These procedures were to ensure that the department or agency was getting the lowest price possible and that there was clear accountability and an audit trail for the spending of public funds.

Typically, purchases over a prescribed value—say $50,000—required the agency to go out to the marketplace with a formal quotation request, often referred to as a request for proposal (RFP). Vendors then had a fixed time period to respond with a written quotation and proposal, usually agreeing to the buyer's terms. The agency then evaluated the proposals against a set of criteria (such as price, functionality, service, support, etc.) and made a recommendation to management. The level of expenditure dictated how high within the organization a recommendation needed to go for approval.

Certain types of purchases also required the approval of departments other than the department originating the order. For example, it might be mandatory for a computer purchase to be approved by a central information systems group with companywide responsibility for systems applications. If a central or statewide computer procurement contract was in place, a financial group might have to sign off on a purchase. Although there were advantages in involving these groups, and usually their involvement was mandatory, the procurement process could become more complex and take longer to complete.

Despite the controls and accountability guidelines, there was generally enough flexibility for the buyer to ensure that his or her choice would be the successful tenderer. For example, the specifications issued could be based upon a particular vendor's product or solution, or the evaluation criteria could deliberately emphasize a particular vendor's (or product's) strengths. The individual buyer thus had substantial influence on the outcome of the procurement process and was a logical target of vendors' marketing plans.

Division of Substance Abuse Services

DSAS was one of a number of divisions of the state of New York that managed substance abuse programs. New York's programs were aimed at both prevention of drug trafficking and related criminal activities and at treatment of the growing number of substance abuse victims in the state. DSAS administered funds for programs to support the prevention of drug abuse and the treatment of drug abusers. The division did not actually operate any of the programs directly; instead it used a variety of external organizations to administer or operate each program. These programs included school- and community-based prevention efforts; expanding drug-free treatment by making more beds and ambulatory service slots available; maintaining a statewide registry of eligible methadone recipients; and doing substance abuse research, focusing on the culture of drug use and how and where drugs were obtained. All program operators (i.e., contractors) were monitored by the division through its Quality Assurance department. DSAS also played a regulatory role in ensuring that the quality of service given by treatment providers met state standards. The DSAS budget in 1990–1991 was $400 million. (The total budget for New York State at the time was $55 billion.) The organization of the division is shown in Exhibit 3.3.

Discussions had been under way for a number of years regarding merging DSAS with the Division of Alcoholism and Alcohol Abuse, an agency that performed a similar function in the areas of alcohol abuse. The merger could eliminate duplication of functions and expenditure incurred by the two separate divisions. Merger discussions had intensified during 1991 and were expected to be completed within 12 months.

In 1990, in an effort to streamline the management of some of its programs, DSAS decided to upgrade its computer facilities and implement new applications. Management commissioned an Information Resource Management (IRM) Plan as a starting point for the project. In February 1991, Peter Pezzolla, a senior DSAS director, hired Robert Quick to develop the IRM Plan. Quick was appointed to the position of Assistant

Exhibit 3.3 New York State Division of Substance Abuse Services

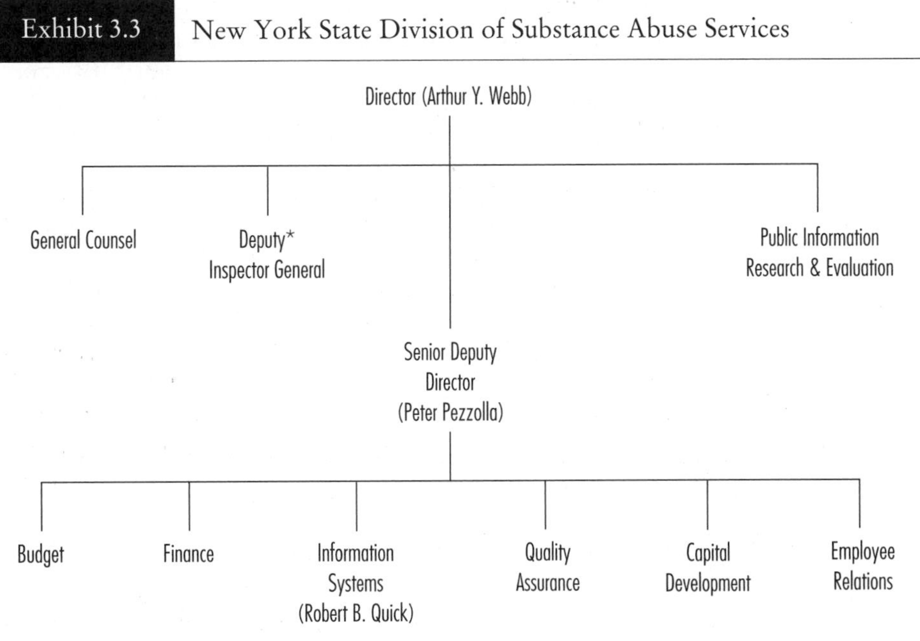

*The Deputy Inspector General reports to the State's Inspector General and is assigned to DSAS to audit its activities, with a dotted-line reporting to Webb.

Director of Management Information and Analysis. Prior to joining the division, Quick had worked for another New York State department, the Office of Mental Retardation and Developmental Disabilities, where he worked on computer-related contracting matters as an Assistant Director in the office's Information Services Group. Pezzolla, who joined DSAS in February 1990, had previously been Assistant Deputy Commissioner at the Office of Mental Retardation and Developmental Disabilities, where he was Quick's second line manager. Quick had limited information systems education. He had been hired primarily for his administrative skills.

The purpose of the IRM Plan was to document current DSAS information systems and hardware components, define systems requirements for future computer applications, and define the requirements for future hardware and software. The plan would form the basis for selecting a new computer system for the division, to be implemented later that year. DSAS had engaged a consultant, Diversified Business Enterprises of America, to assist with producing the plan and selecting a computer vendor. Diversified, headed by Glenn Mazula, quoted the division a fixed price fee of $169,500 for these services. The primary application for the new system was an upgraded Client Tracking System to better match clients with available services. The system was being funded under the Target Cities Program, a federal program designed to assist certain United States cities with economic and social difficulties. DSAS had a large office in New York City, one of the cities targeted under this program.

Working with three computer vendors that had been selected by Robert Quick and Diversified Business Enterprises, a generic set of computer specifications was developed for the new computer system, which was to replace the department's antiquated system. The three vendors were Data General, DEC, and Hewlett-Packard. After completing the IRM Plan and the system specification, DSAS invited all three vendors to submit design and cost proposals for the new system. Data General proposed one of its AViiON products (i.e., an open system), together with a Database Manager to be supplied directly by ORACLE (a database software vendor).

Dan Snell had been assigned by Data General to win the DSAS contract. An experienced sales representative with over ten years in the computer industry, Snell worked closely with Ken Canastar, his manager, on the sale. He dealt primarily with the technical people, while Canastar worked more with Mazula and Quick. Canastar was the firm's senior salesperson at Albany. He reported to a regional manager, located in Pittsburgh. Canastar was also a seasoned sales representative and understood the significance of winning this deal and the potential future business for his sales territory. He also understood that losing the sale could jeopardize the future of the firm's Albany office.

After receiving the vendor bids, Diversified and the division's staff analyzed the proposals and determined that Hewlett-Packard had the lowest bid. After reviewing the bid results, Quick informed his staff that the bids were too high and there were insufficient funds to cover costs. As a result, the vendors were asked to resubmit their bids and propose a less costly system. During the interim period, Quick advised Canastar and Snell that he was looking favorably on awarding the contract to Data General. Diversified reviewed and analyzed the second vendor proposals and submitted the results to Quick, who, along with his staff, found Data General was the lowest bidder. Peter Pezzolla approved Quick's selection and on June 28, 1991, Data

General was notified in writing of its success. The initial DSAS order was for computer equipment at a cost of $536,000.

The sale by Canastar and Snell was a significant achievement for Data General, especially as sister departments to DSAS (such as the Division of Alcoholism and Alcohol Abuse and the Office of Mental Retardation and Developmental Disabilities) were strong DEC users and there was substantial pressure on DSAS by the Division of Alcoholism and Alcohol Abuse to implement a DEC-based solution. Because Data General's annual sales to New York State were currently only $2 million, this particular sale had the attention and involvement of Data General's president and CEO, Ronald Skates. Skates, who had viewed DSAS as a strategic opportunity, met with Quick in Albany during the selling phase and subsequently called Quick to demonstrate his support for the deal.

Robert Quick and Vendor Relationships

During his time at the Office of Mental Retardation and Developmental Disabilities, Quick had dealt regularly with computer vendors. The vendors, keen to maintain their relationships and business with the department, had made regular donations to events and funds that Quick was associated with. These included the Information Systems Group Christmas parties and summer picnics, and the Kevin Quick Memorial Scholarship Fund. The Fund was established in January 1990 by friends of Robert Quick in honor of his deceased son. It was designed to award a $1,000 scholarship to a graduating senior of Amsterdam High School in Albany. Quick's friends were designated as trustees of the fund.

It was in April 1990, when Quick was still at the Office of Mental Retardation and Developmental Disabilities, that Pezzolla had asked him for suggestions for the request for proposal to select consultants for the DSAS IRM Plan development. Quick had nominated CMA, General Electric Consulting Services, and Diversified Business Enterprises. (Diversified Business Enterprises at the time was co-owned by Glenn Mazula. Mazula sold his interest in this firm in early 1991 and formed Diversified Business Enterprises of America; the latter firm was hired by DSAS to assist with implementing its IRM Plan, Mazula was the sole proprietor of the new firm.) All three companies had made donations to the Information Systems Group functions and/or the scholarship fund. Typical donations ranged between $500 and $1,000 per vendor, per event. Quick chose not to disclose information about these donations to Pezzolla. However, they were apparently common knowledge within the computer industry.

Quick and Mazula had first met in the late 1970s when both were employed at the New York State Department of Social Services. Quick had a passion for sports, and Mazula had the potential to assist Quick with financing and with access to sporting venues. In April 1990, Quick approached Mazula, by then a well-known sports entrepreneur in the Albany area, about financial sponsorship of a softball team that Quick managed on his own time. Mazula agreed to Quick' suggestions and provided over $60,000 between June 1990 and August 1991 for the softball team's salaries and expenses. Meanwhile, Pezzolla, using the information supplied by Quick, chose Diversified Business Enterprises to produce the request for proposal to select the IRM consultants.

Glenn Mazula, then head of Diversified Business Enterprises, had worked at the Department of Social Services for three years and the state Medicaid payment unit for another year before becoming a data administrator back at Social Services. Using his acquired knowledge in the administration of nursing homes and acute health care, Mazula then started a consulting business in 1980, specializing in the health and human services field. Mazula was also co-owner of the Albany Patroons (basketball) and Albany Firebirds (arena football) teams.

Diversified Business Enterprises, Mazula's original consulting firm, completed the request for proposal for the Information Resource Management consultants in August 1990, billing DSAS for $19,500 in fees. However, in its haste to expedite the project's start date, the division had never signed a formal contract for the work, so payment of the $19,500 was delayed until a contract was finally issued, in June 1991.

The 1990 RFP was never used to select a consultant, however. Instead, Quick, arriving at his new $70,000 a year job at DSAS in February 1991, hired Mazula's new firm, Diversified Business Enterprises of America, to produce the IRM Plan without soliciting competitive bids. To establish a contract directly between the division and Diversified would have required a number of approvals and a competitive bidding process. Instead, Quick used NDRI-State, a nonprofit corporation largely supported by DSAS funding, as the vehicle to establish a contract with Diversified, bypassing the normal state contracting procedures. The division's funding to NDRI-State was approximately $7.4 million in 1991.

Diversified was given an initial payment of $20,000 in April 1991 for IRM Plan services. Later that month, some $17,000 was transferred from Diversified's corporate bank account to the Albany Professional Baseball Inc. account, which had been opened by Mazula. These funds were then used to cover expenses incurred by Quick's team.

Quick also hired Diversified for a related project—assisting the division with the takeover of the methadone registry from Creative Socio-Medics, another DSAS vendor. The registry was a database service accessed by methadone providers so that they could ensure recipient eligibility. The database contained a confidential roster of methadone recipients across the state. Creative Socio-Medics was paid $200,000 per year for providing the methadone registry service. Creative Socio-Medics also generated revenues of some $3.5 million per annum for providing related services that used information from the database. Diversified negotiated a fee of $85,000 with Quick for initial work on the registry takeover. The project would include software development and programming, and also opened up the opportunity for Diversified to sell the software to agencies of other states. Diversified commenced this work without a formal contract, leaving the ownership of software rights in question.

On May 18 and 19, 1991, the second annual memorial softball tournament was held to benefit the Kevin Quick Memorial Scholarship Fund. (The first softball tournament had been held May 19 and 20, 1990. A Kevin Quick Memorial Golf Tournament had taken place in August 1990. Detailed figures were not publicly available for the softball tournament; however, the golf tournament had yielded a net contribution of $127 to the Fund while $1,200 worth of prizes had been awarded.) Quick solicited donations to fund the tournament from a number of vendors, including those bidding for the division's computer contract. DEC's sales representative made a $500 donation on May third, and Canastar and Snell made a $1,000 personal donation at a breakfast meeting with Quick on May 10. Canastar and Snell planned to claim back the $1,000 from Data General by submitting, under the guise of legitimate expenses, receipts for personal expenditures, such as restaurant meals unrelated to business.

Prior to the breakfast meeting, Canastar and Snell had held discussions with Mazula to explore the possibility of Diversified becoming a Data General subcontractor and software supplier should Data General be successful at DSAS. Mazula had told the Data General representatives during the discussion that the scholarship fund was important to Quick. These discussions between Data General and Diversified did not result in any formal business relationship. In fact, Canastar's proposal to pay Diversified a 5 percent commission bonus if it won the DSAS deal was rejected by Stan Driban, Data General's Director of Contract Negotiations, in late May 1991. He said, "This smacks of a bribe." Mazula continued discussions with Canastar and Snell beyond Data General's initial rejection in the first round of bidding. Mazula also had discussions with Hewlett-Packard, and suggested that Hewlett-Packard entertain Quick during a trip to New York City. Exhibit 3.4 provides a chronology of events leading up to the award of the contract to Data General.

The New York State Office of State Inspector General

The Office of the New York State Inspector General was established by Governor Mario M. Cuomo in 1986 under an Executive Order. (An extract from the Executive Order establishing the Office of State Inspector General is provided as Exhibit 3.5.) As Governor Cuomo explained, "The public has every right to demand integrity in its government. This new mechanism, the Office of the State Inspector General, will ensure that New York State's government remains as free as possible from activities that reduce public confidence." The Office was established primarily to prevent fraud, abuse, and corruption in New York State government and was one of six such offices in the United States. It had a budget of around $1.5 million and a staff of 27 people. Investigations were often initiated by complaints by vendors or members of the public. A complaint by a vendor had prompted the DSAS investigation.

When Dan Snell received the appearance subpoena from the Inspector General, on September 6, 1991, Data General senior management realized it had some important decisions to make.

- How should the company respond to Snell and (shortly after) Canastar's subpoenas by the New York State Inspector General?
- Was there genuine cause for concern over how Data General's representatives had made the sale to DSAS, and, if so, should Data General take internal action?
- Should Data General delay delivery of the equipment, scheduled for September 13?

Exhibit 3.4 Chronology of Events

1990

January: Kevin Quick Memorial Scholarship Fund was established by friends of Quick. Quick solicited and accepted both Fund donations and contributions to Fund-related activities during the year, in excess of $4000. (Quick is employed by the Office of Mental Retardation and Developmental Diseases.)

April: Quick asked by Pezzolla to identify a consultant to produce an RFP for soliciting vendors to develop an Information Resources Management (IRM) Plan for DSAS. Quick recommends CMA, GECON, and Diversified Business Enterprises; all three firms have previously made donations to Information Systems Group Christmas parties and/or to the Fund. Quick approaches Mazula (co-owner of Diversified Business Enterprises) regarding the possibility of Mazula becoming the financial sponsor of Quick's softball team.

May: Pezzolla approves Diversified Business Enterprises to begin work on the request for proposal for a fee of $19,500. No contract is put in place.

June 13: Mazula provides $4650 in "seed" money to cover expenses for Quick's softball team. Over the next 12 months, Mazula provides in excess of $60,000 to Quick's softball team for expenses and salaries.

August: Diversified Business Enterprises completes the request for proposal and submits it to DSAS. Payment cannot be made by DSAS due to absence of formal contract. DSAS announces the contract in the NYS Contract Reporter in October, awards the contract to Diversified Business Enterprises in April 1991, and finally disburses payment of $19,500 on June 24, 1991.

1991

January: Quick prepares and submits to Mazula a final 1991 budget for a new softball team Quick is to manage, showing a budget deficit of $18,000. Mazula incorporates Diversified Business Enterprises of America, Inc.

February: Quick transfers to DSAS from the Office of Mental Retardation and Developmental Disabilities, to direct the development of the division's IRM Plan. The request for proposal is not used to select a vendor to develop the plan. Diversified is hired, without competitive bids, to perform the work by Pezzolla based on Quick's recommendation.

April: Diversified signs a contract with NDRI-State for the IRM Plan services. It is paid an initial amount of $20,000 on the $169,500 contract.

April 18: $17,000 transferred from Diversified's corporate bank account to another account, opened by Mazula in the name of Albany Professional Baseball, Inc. These funds are used to pay for Quick's team expenses.

April: Diversified is hired by Quick to assist DSAS in taking over the methadone registry from another DSAS vendor, Creative Socio-Medics. Diversified's fee for initial work is $85,000. Pezzolla is aware of discussions with Diversified but unaware of this verbal agreement between the firm and Quick.

May: Data General, Hewlett-Packard, and DEC are presented with an information package prepared by DSAS and Diversified, specifying the proposed computer system resulting from the IRM plan. Quick solicits these firms for donations to a memorial softball tournament to benefit the Fund. DEC's sales represented, Peter Link, makes a $500 donation to the fund in the form of a check.

Mazula informs Data General representatives Canastar and Snell that the Fund is important to Quick. The three also discuss establishing a business relationship between Diversified and Data General, including subcontracting to Data General for the forthcoming DSAS contract and becoming a Data General software supplier.

Quick meets with Canastar and Snell and receives a $1000 personal donation to the fund, in the form of a check.

June 4: Data General, Hewlett-Packard and DEC submit their proposals to DSAS.

June 5–10: DSAS and Diversified review and evaluate the proposals and deem that Hewlett-Packard has the lowest bid.

Quick informs DSAS and Diversified staff that the bids were too high and there are insufficient funds to cover costs. Quick directs the vendors to resubmit proposals for a less costly centralized system.

June 10–11: Quick advises Snell and Canastar that he is looking favorably on awarding the contract to Data General.

June 11: Mazula suggests to Hewlett-Packard that a relationship with Quick should include dinners and a trip to New York City.

June 12: Diversified presents its analysis of the revised bids to DSAS. Data General is now the lowest bidder, with Hewlett-Packard second and DEC third.

June 28: Quick formally notifies Data General in writing of the award.

September 6: Subpoena issued to Snell.

September 19: Subpoena issued to Canastar.

Exhibit 3.5 Extract from Executive Order Establishing the Office of State Inspector General

III. Authority of the State Inspector General

1. Pursuant to section 6 of the Executive Law, the State Inspector General is authorized to examine and investigate the management and affairs of the covered agencies concerning fraud, abuse or corruption and, if there exist reasonable grounds that justify further inquiry, may specifically:
   (a) subpoena and enforce the attendance of witnesses;
   (b) administer oaths and examine witnesses under oath; and
   (c) require the production of any books or papers deemed relevant and material.
2. The State Inspector General is further authorized to perform any other functions necessary to fulfill the duties and responsibilities of the office.

IV. Duties and Responsibilities of the State Inspector General

1. The State Inspector General shall receive complaints of fraud, abuse or corruption in covered agencies and determine whether they warrant investigation.
2. The State Inspector General shall investigate complaints of fraud, abuse or corruption when appropriate, determine whether disciplinary action, civil or criminal prosecution or further investigation by relevant Federal, State or local agencies is warranted and take further action as appropriate.
3. The State Inspector General shall report complaints of fraud, abuse or corruption to such Federal, State or local agencies when there is evidence that non-state agency personnel have engaged in what may be criminal activity and when otherwise appropriate, and shall otherwise cooperate with them in any further action.
4. The State Inspector General shall help prevent fraud, abuse or corruption in covered agencies by periodically reviewing policies and procedures and monitoring day-to-day operations and making recommendations for improvement.
5. In performing his duties and responsibilities, the State Inspector General shall keep the Director of Criminal Justice informed of allegations and evidence of fraud, abuse or corruption in covered agencies and of the progress of any investigation, and shall keep the appropriate agency commissioner or director so informed unless, in the judgment of the State Inspector General, special circumstances require full confidentiality.
6. The State Inspector General shall prepare written reports of investigations as appropriate and such reports shall be released to the public, subject to any reductions needed to protect witnesses, unless the Director of Criminal Justice determines that release of all or portions of the report should be deferred so as not to compromise an ongoing investigation.

V. Responsibilities of Covered Agencies

1. All officers and employees in covered agencies shall extend full cooperation and all reasonable assistance to the State Inspector General and his designees. No provision of this order shall be construed to diminish the responsibility of said officers and employees to be vigilant in preventing and reporting fraud, abuse or corruption.
2. Complaints of fraud, abuse or corruption shall be made to the agency inspector general, agency commissioner or director, Deputy Inspector General or the State Inspector General as appropriate. The agency inspector general and agency commissioner or director shall report all complaints of fraud, abuse or corruption to the State Inspector General.

IV. Covered Agencies

The following agencies shall be subject to the provisions of the order and the authority of the State Inspector General: Department of Environmental Conservation; Office of General Services; Division of Housing and Community Renewal; Insurance Department; State Liquor Authority; New York State Lottery; Department of Transportation; Division for Youth; and such other agencies as may from time to time be determined by the State Inspector General.

REFERENCES

"Albany Drug Agency Is Accused of Sidestepping Bidding Rules." *The New York Times,* 30 July 1992, p. B4.

"Arenaball Could Be Right for Glory-Seeking Businessmen." Gannet News Service, 21 August 1991.

Data General Annual Reports, 1991 and 1992.

Data General Corporation 1992 Securities and Exchange Commission Form 10k.

Data General Prospectus $110,000,000 7&3/4% Convertible Subordinated Debentures Due 2001. 13 June 1991. Prepared by Morgan Stanley & Co. and Kidder Peabody & Co.

"Foreclosure by Bank Will Pave Way for New Owners at Adult Care Home," *Capital District Business Review,* 25 November 1991, sec. 1, p. 1.

"An Introduction to Data General Systems." Data General Brochure, 1990.

Kidder, Tracy. *The Soul of a New Machine.* New York: Avon, 1990.

New York Ethics: A Guide to the Ethics Law. The New York State Ethics Commission, New York, 1991.

"No-Bid Contractor Sponsors Team Run by Agency Manager." *The Times Union,* 31 October 1991, p. B11.

"Patroons Want Business to Provide Season-Ticket Boost." *Capital District Business Review,* 28 September 1992, sec. 1, p. 1.

Public Officers Law, The New York State Ethics Commission, New York, 1990.

Report of Investigation Concerning Awarding of No-Bid Contracts and Related Contracting Matters. New York State Office of Inspector General, 28 July 1992. File #009-029.

"Survey: The Computer Industry," *The Economist,* 27 February 1993.

The Wall Street Journal, 8 October 1992.

"Washington County Town Becoming Host to Fourth Private Adult Home." *Capital District Business Review,* 6 January 1992, sec. 1, p. 2.

Case 4

Cross-Functional Strategy Decision Making: The Techno Project

Strategic decisions involve complex and unique situations where simple decision rules or policies will not provide solutions. Decisions of this type entail large commitments of resources with potentially large gains or losses, and are collective in that solutions include inputs and decisions from various interest groups. Thus, strategic decisions are consequential, producing profound internal and external ramifications for the organization.

The Techno project deals with the development of new technologies that will provide the interface between the Alpha company and its markets. In addition, the Techno project has the potential to spawn many products and services for the company. Decisions regarding the Techno project require input and analysis from functional units throughout the organization. Each functional unit advocates a different strategy and interprets the significance of the technology in a different light. The case presents the perspectives of several managers from various functional units and hierarchical levels in the company. The major details in the case are factual, though names have been changed to maintain the anonymity of the company and its managers.

After reading the case, you should select one of the offered solutions and write a short defense of your position.

The Communications Industry

Seven large companies comprise this regulated, high-tech communications industry. Each company is the major competitor in a geographically distinct territory competing against only a few mid-sized competitors within that territory. However, since the inception of this industry structure in the mid 1980s, many small companies have entered the industry by selling access to their corporate systems. Other small companies have entered the industry by selling private systems to institutional

Source: This case was prepared by Gary L. Frankwick, Oklahoma State University, and Michael D. Hutt, Arizona State University. From Arch G. Woodside, ed., *Advances in Business Marketing and Purchasing*, Volume 7, pp. 33-41.

buyers, both corporate and government. Selling prices for these new small companies are not regulated to the same degree as are prices for the original large and mid-sized companies.

CUSTOMERS

The market for the communications industry consists of individual homeowners and renters, small businesses, large businesses, and government–institutional buyers. In addition, many of the large and mid-sized companies have international units involved in joint ventures to produce and supply communication services outside the United States.

PRODUCTS/SERVICES

Until the early 1980s the communication industry was very stable. Products and services had changed little in decades. However, with advances in computer technology and software, the industry began a metamorphosis that even industry experts had not foreseen. Fiber optics, digital signals, voice recognition, and the emerging televideo technologies were spawning competition within and across industries faster than management could collect, distill, and evaluate data on the many options facing them.

The Techno Project

Currently the Alpha company provides its service with an amalgam of technology developed primarily since World War II. The eclectic array of technology sometimes causes compatibility problems when repairing and replacing equipment and software. Much of this equipment also lacks the capability to handle the higher speed and more dense information that the market will demand in the near future. These problems, along with cost, were the primary forces pushing large corporate customers, who already need some of these features, to develop or purchase their own systems. In addition, several of the other large competitors, in other geographic areas, were beginning to update their technologies. The eventual availability of greater capabilities in other geographic areas could cause problems for Alpha if they could not provide those services to customers who operate across geographic boundaries. Having identified these factors, top management at Alpha determined that a major initiative to update the company was required to compete into the next century.

The Techno project is an attempt at this update and top management has a great deal of confidence in the technology. According to Cid Levey, head of strategic planning, "We cannot afford not to do it. It's a way to make ourselves more competitive. We have demonstrated to our own satisfaction that we can manage through any of the technical problems involved." However, implementing the project will require cooperation from each of the functional units.

R&D'S PERSPECTIVE OF TECHNO

Jack English, the Techno project manager, was assigned the responsibility of putting together a research team and conducting experiments to develop the technology required to achieve the Techno directives. He explains the project as a formidable task involving many sensitive issues resulting in "opposition coming out of probably every single organizational unit because what we're doing is changing the fundamental structure of the business. Everybody who is organized to operate the business the way it operates today is going to be affected by it." Nevertheless, the R&D team was quite enthusiastic about the promise of the Techno project. From the team's perspective, one potential use of the technology would allow customers, including new ones, to order products and services via computer interface without contacting a salesperson, thus providing the services much faster and efficiently than the current system. If the technology (now untested) indeed proved to be feasible, Techno offered potential applications beyond the automation of the sales function, including a whole host of promising new services for customers. However, full implementation of the technology across Alpha's market areas would require an investment of $1 billion or more.

Top management may not support some of the drastic changes that Techno may spawn because of the perceived reaction of stockholders. Norma Lin, an R&D manager, explains that "we are going to discover some things that are the right things to do but that the corporation may not want to do. Top management may feel that maybe the shareholder would be not too anxious for us to make a lot of these changes."

Since market units are rewarded for generating revenue, spending money to cut costs does not support their goals. As a regulated industry, prices charged to customers are based on the cost of producing services: as costs decrease, revenue also decreases. Norma explains that "If we prove some of these [concepts], they are in direct conflict with some of the long-range strategies of some of the market units. They are revenue driven. If it is counter to their long-range strategy, and it is not going to do anything for their bottom line in the short term, they are going to react 'Why do that?'." Using the same logic, she proposes that managers in the operations unit "are going to be pretty positive about it because their major thrust is keeping costs down and a lot of the things that we are talking about doing would certainly allow them to do that. I think they will go ahead and support the project with the resources required."

One of the major objectives of the Techno project is to cut operating costs so the company can compete with the new small providers, thereby increasing returns to its stockholders. However, most of the cost reduction would occur by reducing labor costs. Achieving this objective would mean the eventual loss of jobs. Most of the initial positions to be replaced by the technology would be lower-level market interface positions, primarily in sales and customer service. However, most middle managers could see the long-term potential of the currently described project. John Erlickman, an R&D manager, summarizes the concern and need to reduce positions, noting that "We are very top heavy from a staff perspective. Large numbers of people right off the bat you don't need." Sara Johnson, an R&D manager, concurs that "with costs being driven out, and changes that simplify the structure of the business, people get very upset and nervous about their job. If you have an organizational structure that has 15 people reporting to a manager, and all of a sudden instead of 15 people you have 5, that has a real dramatic effect on the number of management positions. If we had any barrier to achieving what we want to do, that is probably the biggest barrier. If there really is a loss of their jobs or power, and they are the ones that are making the decisions as to whether or not the project is a 'go', you can see that it is a real uphill battle. By causing resistance or by questioning, they possibly can delay the decision or change the decision so it has less impact, and they can protect themselves."

The decision process itself can facilitate resistance to change if the change means reducing the size of a manager's staff. John explains that "the problem is that the decision makers in the current environment rely upon their staffs to provide them with the important input. How objective are those folks going to be in reviewing, evaluating, and sending the information back? There are at least three layers of management that would be eliminated out of the corporation—middle managers—and those people are fundamentally obstructionists."

Worried that the marketing unit and the operations unit were focused on objectives that conflicted with those of the Techno project, many R&D managers were concerned that those units might attempt to take control of the project in order to reduce its impact on the organization. John Erlickman explains: "The market units haven't cared enough about cost. They only care about product and service, and they are anxious to get things out without being able to support them effectively. Operations, maybe they don't care enough and aren't aware enough of the actual market needs. I believe that the control of this, because of the culture associated with this, can't be given to any one of those units." However, Norma Lin, an R&D manager, claims "the only way that this project gets funds is actually from the market units. The market units have the purse strings. So you have to do things that are going to help the market units in the short term, and in the long term, do what is best for the corporation as a whole." So control is shared with marketing to the extent that the unit must be convinced each fiscal year to (at least partially) fund the project. In reality, about half of the Techno project funds come from the corporate level.

OPERATIONS' PERSPECTIVE OF TECHNO

Operations was enthusiastic about the possibilities of Techno. Don Brock, an operations manager, notes that "It has a potential to provide us an edge in the marketplace . . . to significantly reduce cost and improve service." However, he was cautious regarding a potential revolution in the way the firm provides service: "I am rather conservative regarding this. I think that the effort is worthwhile to this point, the risks are minimal, but I'm not totally sold. There are a number of people, staff directors, who work for me in the daily operation who are still, to a degree, skeptics." For example, Marvin Jerritt, an operations engineer, says that he supports the idea of testing new concepts but "they [R&D] have not bothered to pursue what we already have available." According to Marvin, the company can already do what the Techno project is supposed to create. Thus, the large cost reductions, that are supposed to pay for implementation of Techno, will not materialize. "The only way cost reductions will arise is from the elimination of the service rep and from reduced funding for the development of our current system. I'm very concerned that they're going to underfund what we need [for the current system] to the point that we can't be successful in the existing environment, and we're going to end up without either system."

Funding the project was a major concern mentioned by many managers. According to Ron Winston, "This is going to take longer and more money to realize your gain, so it is a long-term effort. We need the quicker hitters. Who can support long-range projects that are going to take an investment over a continuing period of time before you get any payback? The shorter-term issues are probably going to prevail." Don Brock also wondered, "Can we afford to do it?"

Don was also concerned that R&D might become too independent. Though the Techno project director technically worked for him, top management gave the project team great latitude that included only annual budget approval. Don notes that "the basic development and the capability to be able to do things should be the effort that I am leading." He also notes that "the selection of applications and prioritization of them once we get to that point ought to be driven by the marketplace." Notice, he says that the marketplace should drive applications, not that the market units should control product development.

MARKETING'S PERSPECTIVE OF TECHNO

One of the primary concerns voiced by the marketing unit involved the tradeoff between investments and returns. John Jefferson, a top marketing manager, noted: "If I don't know how I am going to make my 1992 budget and meet my expense commitment to generate the revenue I have to with the resources I have, it's hard for me to get enthusiastic about a gee-whiz item." An equally influential marketing manager, Laura Anderson, declares that "This is not a short-term project. I think there is likely, and should be, considerable discussion on what kind of money we spend there in the next 24 months, and what are we going to gain. I support a short-term focus. I don't think I would agree with an aggressive approach at this point in time because there are several other ways that I think our money can be better spent." Just as emphatically, Andy Reissner asserts, "The cost of deploying it would be, if not a billion, pretty damn close to it. We are not going to do a billion dollar project just because it is neat." Harry Porter agrees that Techno "is a technology demonstration competing with probably twenty other related projects for money. Every system we implement has to have the appropriate payback period and is competing with other projects for funding."

Because the market-interface personnel acted as both sales and customer service representatives, the Techno tradeoff involved increasing automation on one hand, versus customer service levels and new sales on the other. By automating the sales function, marketing managers were concerned that service levels would decline and key sales opportunities would be lost. Andy Reissner summarizes the thoughts of the unit, saying "my thinking is that at [the Techno project site] they can do anything they want to as long as it doesn't impact the customer. If it impacts the customer, they should come visit with me. From a technical standpoint, you know, behind the scenes, I don't care what they do. They ought to have free reign. Since most of our products are intangible kinds of things, . . . I don't want to take the human contact out of our sales calls. I don't want to totally automate the sales contacts. The techies, they want to do it. I don't think the chance of implementing it is very strong. I am open, however, to putting people into a telemarketing job. Then we have people that are on incentives to sell, and do it more efficiently." Laura Anderson supports a hybrid approach, saying, "Some of the technology will simply be unacceptable. Even though we may see tremendous cost improvements, we may be risking customer relationships as well as revenue."

Laura, who is highly involved with the sales force, describes the situation in terms of customer satisfaction from a market segment perspective. "Our research tells us that having service faster does not drive [customer] satisfaction, having their service when it is promised, being flexible in how we arrange their services, and doing it right the first time" drives satisfaction. This of course varies by segment. "The applications need to reflect what we know about the segments of our market. We need to focus on the pieces of our business where the human interface isn't making a big difference in our revenue or service results [i.e. behind the scenes]."

Most of the marketing managers agreed that the Techno project had promise for reducing costs through labor reduction. However, they wanted to see large reductions to offset the risks. Andy Reissner notes that "we need to take about a third of our people off the payroll," and that should be the single most important aspect of the project. "I want them to focus on dragging the cost out of the business. If it can't take hundreds of millions of dollars out of the cost of doing business, then shut it down. I'm not interested in doing a little [project]."

Some marketing managers questioned the technical feasibility and projected cost savings of Techno. For example, John Jefferson observed: "If there is a perception that this can be done on a very large scale with just machine interface, there is naivete about how we serve our customers. We have over 156 different functions that must be covered by a service rep for us to provide service to a customer—very complex. Understanding of that complexity is a must. I have some concerns about whether or not that has occurred." However, if the technology did work and costs were to be driven out of the business, they would come primarily from reduced labor from selling efforts, customer service contact, and error corrections. The benefit of reduced labor costs could cause a problem with morale because people would have to be eliminated from the process to realize the expected savings. Paul Tredlow agrees: "If we can move into an environment where you take a lot of people-handling out of the process, that means that you are going to displace a lot of people, and that is an issue that we have to deal with." On the other hand, Laura Anderson notes that "it will free up our people to do the more creative, problem-solving, aspects of the business."

Who would control new product development was an issue noted by many marketing managers, but one that the top marketing executives felt they could handle. Andy Reissner explains: "I am not that concerned [about new product development]. [Techno] won't get very far, they don't have the talent to do product development. We will do new product development and we will do it in a way that won't bog down the project." Paul Tredlow concurs, saying, "In my opinion it clearly should be market driven. So the market units should drive what applications they want tested."

Alternatives

Select one of the three solutions, write a brief statement supporting your position, and include a discussion of the tradeoffs.

1. R&D solution. Move forward full speed with the Techno project. Realize the cost savings, error reduction, and competitive advantage of a whole new set of possible services. R&D control.
2. Operations solution. Move slowly. Check all of the current technology to see if the company already has or could update to what the Techno project intends to do. Operations control.
3. Marketing solution. Conduct more market research to see exactly what the market wants. Implement a hybrid project in selected areas where the technology is combined with a sales/customer service rep. Marketing control.

Case 5

Roscoe Nondestructive Testing

After nine months, Grover Porter, president of Roscoe Nondestructive Testing, Inc. (Roscoe) was beginning to question the success of his new quality improvement program (QIP). Initiated in March 1991, the QIP had produced substantial increases in recent customer satisfaction surveys; however, none of that satisfaction seemed to be fueling a return to growth in either revenue or number of clients. Porter anticipated Roscoe's second down year in a row as the company continued to lose major customers, and he was eager to re-establish the growth that had preceded the last two years of decline.

It was hard to believe that the cyclical downturn in the pulp and paper industry had pushed the boiler inspection business to competing solely on price. Porter still felt that there was room in the industry for a quality service at a fair price, but the ineffectiveness of the QIP had prompted Porter to reconsider adjusting Roscoe's pricing structure.

The Nondestructive Testing Industry

Nondestructive testing (NDT) involves the examination of materials to discover microscopic cracks, corrosion, or malformation, using inspection techniques that do not damage the material under scrutiny. Common inspection techniques include the use of X-rays, ultrasonics, and electrical eddy currents.

NDT is used in a wide variety of applications, including the examination of aircraft parts, tanks and vessels of various shapes and sizes, and welds of all kinds. Roscoe primarily uses ultrasonic thickness measuring devices to determine the thickness of metal plating.

Source: This case was prepared by Brian Wansink, The Wharton School, University of Pennsylvania, and Eric Cannell, University of Illinois, Champaign-Urbana as the basis for class discussion rather than to illustrate either effective or ineffective handling of an administrative situation.

NDT technicians are certified by area of expertise (e.g., ultrasonic) and accumulated skill and experience (Levels I–III). Technicians certified in more than one inspection technique are a treasured resource in most firms. They were generally employed by four types of companies:

1. *Mom and pop* labs usually employ fewer than 25 people and provide a single type of inspection service to a small number of customers. These firms are the low-cost providers and are quite willing to bid at cost, simply to keep busy. Many are often tied to a single client who wields considerable control over pricing and delivery.
2. *Nation-wide* companies have labs around the country and a high degree of name recognition. These firms also provide inspection services to a large number of different industries; however, individual offices usually serve a narrow segment of the market.
3. *Specialty* firms target very narrow market segments that have specific needs. These firms make large capital investments in the latest inspection equipment and employ the highest skilled technicians. Barriers to entry into these specialized markets are high, so specialty firms have traditionally achieved high levels of profitability.
4. While much larger than the mom and pop labs, *regional* firms lack the name recognition and market strength of the nation-wide companies. These firms employ up to 150 technicians and have the resources to tackle the largest inspection jobs. Roscoe is a regional firm, operating primarily in the central southern part of the United States.

All in all, management of NDT firms has been historically uninspired, driven mainly by owner-operators who managed to survive the lean years.

History of Roscoe

Roscoe was founded in 1973 by Hans Norregaard, in Roscoe, Louisiana. After 30 years as an NDT technician, Norregaard decided to set up shop for himself amidst many of the pulp and paper mills located in western Louisiana. Roscoe focused on the inspection of large boilers, a service designed to monitor the corrosion of the boiler walls. Inspections conducted every two to three years provided mills with sufficient warning to replace weakened, corroded plates in boiler walls before a catastrophic accident occurred.

In 1980, Norregaard sold the company to National Inspection Services (NIS) for \$1.75 million. NIS was a subsidiary of Swanson Industries, a large diversified holding company. At that time, NIS brought in Chad Huerlmann (a Harvard MBA) to manage the company. Huerlmann was eager to own a small business and viewed the Roscoe acquisition as a great opportunity.

The company continued well for four years, until the pulp and paper industry bottomed out again. Hampered by misguided directives and burdened by corporate overhead, Roscoe's low cost position no longer protected it from the growing price pressure facing NDT companies in the pulp and paper industry. Also, Huerlmann failed to establish an effective relationship with the technicians in the company and many resigned or left the NDT industry altogether. By 1984, Swanson Industries decided to divest of NIS completely and Roscoe was once again up for sale.

At that time, Hans Norregaard and a long-time business associate, Grover Porter, decided to get back into the NDT business. Together they bought back Roscoe for about 35 cents on the dollar. They were convinced that by offering an improved inspection service for a fair price, they could rebuild the company's reputation and good fortunes.

After dismissing Huerlmann, Hans and Grover began building a new management team for Roscoe. A new controller, Jane Bottensak, was hired away from MQS Inspection. Ted Witkowski, a staff Professional Engineer (PE) out of Texas A&M, who had previously worked for Exxon, was also taken on. Both men thought Ted would bring some much-needed technical backbone to the company. Also, long-time technician, Ed Brown, was promoted to operations manager. Finally, Roscoe began recruiting technicians from the best vocational tech schools in the country.

In 1987, Hans Norregaard retired and Grover Porter became president. Roscoe was back on track.

In 1990, Roscoe encountered a downturn in both revenues and customers. Many mills simply decided not to release bids as often as they used to. While Roscoe always lost some contracts to lower bidders, Porter felt the recent slowdown in the pulp and paper industry exacerbated Roscoe's situation by forcing mills to be more cost conscious. Still, Porter felt that there must be room for the services that Roscoe offered:

> *Hans and I have put together a great management team over the last three years and our technicians are some of the best in the industry. Roscoe offers an efficient, quality inspection service and we feel that we can price accordingly.*

However, the recent loss of established customers caused Grover Porter to question the validity of Roscoe's purported "high quality" service.

Customer Profiles

Although boiler inspections in pulp and paper mills have been standard practice for many years, mills differed widely on the representative who interacted with Roscoe's inspection team. This contact could be almost anyone from the plant manager down to a purchasing agent. The following descriptions illustrate many of the problems that have plagued Roscoe recently.

George McDonald at the Franklin Paper Company was a typical plant manager who reigned over his plant like a king over his castle. Like any other plant manager, McDonald was primarily concerned about controlling costs and was hostile to the idea of boiler inspections in general. Since inspections could only be conducted during plant shutdowns, McDonald was unhappy about the lost production time:

> *Besides the $85,000 inspection fee, my plant is idle during the two days it takes your team to complete the job. At 750 tons per day, I pay an additional opportunity cost of over $330,000 every day you are in my plant. A boiler will last 20 years without exploding and if it wasn't for corporate HQ, I would never bother with the inspections. Besides, the only thing that I ever get out of it is an "OK" and a pile of figures that I can't make head nor tail of.*

International Paper's plant in Longview, Texas, was one of the few clients that maintained their own NDT department. As with other mills, the department consisted of only one retired NDT technician who interacted with service providers like Roscoe. Bob Kapala typified the kind of NDT person often found in paper mills. He was friendly and eager to help, but was actually often more of a hindrance. The last thing a technician wanted was someone looking over his [or her] shoulder all the time.

After the inspection was completed, Bob would combine the recent inspection data with a pile of past data and attempt to find trends in corrosion patterns. The fact that different inspection firms provided data in different formats complicated Bob's task.

Jim Bulgrin at the Rockton Paper Mill in Texarkana, Texas, presented a different problem. Bulgrin, a recent graduate of Georgia Tech, had been hired into the mill's engineering services department seven months ago. As one of Roscoe's team supervisors described him, Bulgrin was "as wet behind the ears as a new-born calf." But he was eager to learn and was on top of every detail.

Problems arose when Jim noticed that thickness readings on one section of a boiler were considerably greater than when inspected two years before. After confronting the technicians, who ended up getting very angry, Jim eagerly reported the discrepancy to his boss. It was later discovered that a new plate had been welded onto the boiler in that area, but Roscoe lost the contract with Rockton.

Pulp mill supervisors, like Billy Dunlap at the Lufkin Pulp Mill, were Roscoe's most common contact inside a mill. Dunlap has been cajoling his boiler along for the last 15 years and did not take easily to anyone mistreating his "baby."

Finally, the inevitable contact is the purchasing representative who files the paperwork with accounting. Lucy Boyle in purchasing at Lufkin was never happy about processing paperwork relating to inspection services:

> *Corporate headquarters requires us to file additional paperwork for one-time expenses greater than $50,000. With inspection fees well over $75,000, I end up processing over three times more paperwork than normal. My life doesn't return to normal until the mill goes back on-line.*

A Prelude to Action

In January 1991, while attending the Nondestructive Testing Managers Association meeting in Las Vegas, Grover Porter was still struggling with the question of what defined a quality service. As it turned out, one of the speakers in the New Business

Segment of the conference presented a talk on the components of service quality. And in that same month, a number of articles describing quality improvement programs at major aerospace inspection firms ran in both the ASNT and AWS Journals.[1]

At the monthly staff meeting in February, Porter discussed his concerns regarding the level of service provided by Roscoe:

> *As you all know, we've lost a bunch of accounts in the last few months. I suspect our service quality is not what it should be, and I've been thinking about a quality improvement program. If we don't do something soon, we may be forced to reduce our fees.*

Bottensak, the controller, nodded her head in agreement and commented that something had to be done:

> *Let's go for it! None of us needs reminding that 1990 was a bad year, but it looks like this year will be even worse. That's not great for our bonuses!*

Ted Witkowski, the staff PE, and Ed Brown, the operations manager, were extremely skeptical. Ted explained:

> *Look, we have the best trained technicians out there with top of the line equipment. They make some mistakes now and then, but when a boiler inspection requires 20,000 readings, that will happen. Besides, the mill has to look at the readings over an entire area and not just a single point. It's not reasonable to inspect every point twice. The mills couldn't afford the cost or the downtime.*

After further discussion , Porter suggested that they first conduct a short customer survey to determine if there were any areas for improvement. No one resisted the idea so Porter spent the weekend composing the survey, and Bottensak pulled together a mailing list of Roscoe customers from the last five years. On Monday morning 357 surveys were dropped in the mail.

The Survey Results

By the first week of March, Porter had collected 82 responses. With only three responses returned in the last four days, Porter felt his sample was as big as it was going to get and asked Jane Bottensak to aggregate the results into a single report (Exhibit 5.1). The next morning, Jane walked into Porter's office with a grin:

> *Grover, look's like we got something here. I ignored 11 of the responses since they obviously knew nothing about our work. I reckon those surveys didn't even reach the right contact in the mills. Anyway, that left 71 responses. I pulled all the results together to determine the frequency distributions and from what I can see it seems our people skills need work. Even our office staff could use some improvement.*

[1]Trade journals of the American Society of Nondestructive Testing and the American Welding Society.

Exhibit 5.1 Roscoe Customer Satisfaction Survey (March 1991)*

Dear Roscoe Customer,

In an effort to provide you with the best inspection service possible, we would like your opinion of Roscoe and the people who work for us. Simply check the appropriate column on the survey and drop it in the mail within the enclosed stamped envelope. Your cooperation is truly appreciated.

Grover Porter
President

Questions	Poor	Below Average	Average	Above Average	Excellent
On-Site inspection team					
Accuracy of inspection data	1.3%	5.9%	15.3%	34.7%	42.8%
Time to complete inspection	2.9	4.8	8.4	45.6	38.3
Knowledge of technicians	1.5	11.5	25.6	33.3	28.1
Willingness to make an extra effort	24.6	26.0	23.6	13.5	12.3
Courtesy of technicians	26.1	30.3	18.7	16.2	8.7
Degree of individualized attention	17.6	29.6	38.2	9.9	4.7
Conveys trust and confidence	9.2	28.3	34.7	23.8	4.0
Organization of team supervisor	4.2	25.6	37.2	29.9	3.1
Accounting department					
Accuracy of billing	3.4	8.3	16.1	55.8	16.4
Promptness of billing	9.8	43.9	21.7	16.5	8.1
Courtesy of staff	6.9	24.7	38.6	13.5	16.3
Willingness to help	22.7	25.6	38.1	8.9	4.7
Overall performance of Roscoe					
Ability to deliver the promised service	2.7	15.6	18.5	39.4	23.8
Variety of services that meet your needs	2.3	13.2	48.8	26.5	9.2
Overall service value for your money	12.7	34.1	43.2	7.8	2.2

*Recorded percentages are the frequency distribution of 71 responses compiled by Jan Bottensak, RNDT's controller. An average was taken for respondents who checked adjacent ratings (i.e., poor and below average).

Porter was surprised that the accuracy of inspection data and time to completion rated so highly, considering that business was so tough these last months. But then he recalled that the speaker at the NDTMA Conference last month emphasized the importance of the people aspect in service quality.

Unfortunately, Roscoe did not attract the type of people blessed with an abundance of social grace. The environment around a boiler is not pleasant. There is constant noise, grime, and heat. And if there was a reason to climb inside the boiler, the technician . . . [must] struggl[e] through cramped areas with . . . equipment and [a] flashlight. Once out, [the technician's] clothing and equipment were coated with a black muck that not even *Ultra Tide* could remove. Thus, while technicians survived the conditions on-site, they did not necessarily do so quietly.

At the March staff meeting, Porter announced his plans for Roscoe's Quality Improvement Program.

The Quality Improvement Program

The three elements that Porter decided to include in the QIP were initial training, a bonus reward system, and customer surveys at the conclusion of every job. He recognized that the QIP had to be more than a one shot deal to be successful and felt that the proposed combination of training, surveys, and bonuses would establish the lasting, fundamental changes Roscoe needed.

Training was provided by ABS Consultants of Madison, Wisconsin, who specialized in teaching customer contact skills for industrial service companies. Training consisted of guided round table discussions and role playing, through which technicians and office staff explored not only customers' perceptions of Roscoe, but also their perceptions of the customers as well.

ABS also had Ed Brown put together some service guidelines that went beyond the traditional level of service. Brown explained one aspect of the guidelines:

> *For example, while on-site, we need to emphasize constant visual inspection of the customer's plant and equipment. If a technician sees some insulation hanging off a section of piping, we expect that person to make a note in [the] report to the client. It doesn't take much time and our customers appreciate the extra effort.*

Technicians also earned bonus points that were cashed out at the end of the year for $25 per point. Every time a client requested a particular technician to be part of the on-site inspection team, that person received a bonus point. Also, after each job, the client filled out a customer satisfaction survey. At the end of the year, the surveys were ranked and for each instance that a technician's team was in the top 5 percent, that technician received a bonus point.

Porter also gave a cash bonus to technicians who passed their certification tests and advanced a level. Achieving Level II earned a $150 cash bonus, while reaching Level III earned $500, as this was the most difficult level to achieve. Finally, the customer satisfaction surveys were compiled monthly and the statistics displayed in the shop area.

Another Disappointing Year

Jane Bottensak wrapped up her part of the December staff meeting:

> *Well, as I predicted, 1991 is going to be a disappointing year. Revenues were down again and profits were negligible. However, our performance wasn't as bad as I expected, so maybe the quality improvement program was more successful than I thought. But, I think we will still need to re-evaluate our fee structure for the coming year.*

Ted Witkowski agreed that the program was a success and commented that Roscoe had a record number of technicians certified at Levels II and III.

Even Ed Brown conceded that customer satisfaction ratings had improved dramatically over the second half of 1991 (Exhibit 5.2):

Exhibit 5.2 Roscoe Customer Satisfaction Surveys (November 1991)*

Questions	Poor	Below Average	Average	Above Average	Excellent
On-Site inspection team					
Accuracy of inspection data	1.0%	4.2%	2.1%	24.8%	55.9%
Time to complete inspection	1.4	6.3	7.1	60.0	25.2
Knowledge of technicians	0.9	12.1	20.5	37.4	29.1
Willingness to make an extra effort	11.9	18.2	36.5	27.8	5.6
Courtesy of technicians	9.3	8.9	55.3	16.3	10.2
Degree of individualized attention	2.1	16.7	45.9	30.1	5.2
Conveys trust and confidence	3.8	22.7	39.8	30.6	3.1
Organization of team supervisor	0.0	11.9	31.8	44.7	11.6
Accounting department					
Accuracy of billing	1.5	10.4	19.6	44.2	24.3
Promptness of billing	13.5	33.4	25.6	18.5	9.0
Courtesy of staff	7.9	17.8	33.4	35.1	5.8
Willingness to help	8.6	29.4	30.3	24.6	7.1
Overall performance of Roscoe					
Ability to deliver the promised service	0.0	13.2	23.1	44.2	19.5
Variety of services that meet your needs	7.4	13.5	56.1	15.3	7.7
Overall service value for your money	10.2	31.2	47.1	11.5	0.0

*Compilation of 17 customer satisfaction surveys for inspections completed during November 1991. An average was taken for those respondents who checked adjacent ratings.

Most of the experienced technicians are excited about the program. They have been around Roscoe a number of years and have established their families in the area. On the other hand, some of the younger folks have not committed as easily. Part of that is the fact that less experienced workers get smaller bonuses, on average. But, also, the younger technicians are more mobile and easily move from company to company. Overall, our work force is providing a better service to the customer.

However, regardless of how well the quality improvement program increased customer satisfaction, unless it could support new growth in the company, Grover Porter could only deem the program a failure.

In light of the continued downturn in the pulp and paper industry, Porter felt resigned to restructure the company's pricing policies. And that would mean big changes for Roscoe.

Case 6

Barro Stickney, Inc.

Introduction

With four people and sales of $5.5 million, Barro Stickney, Inc. (BSI) had become a successful and profitable manufacturers' representative firm. It enjoyed a reputation for outstanding sales results and friendly, thorough service to both its customers and principals. In addition, BSI was considered a great place to work. The office was comfortable and the atmosphere relaxed but professional. All members of the group had come to value the close, friendly working relationships that had grown with the organization.

Success had brought with it increased profits as well as the inevitable decision regarding further growth. Recent requests from two principals, Franklin Key Electronics and R. D. Ocean, had forced BSI to focus its attention on the question of expansion. It was not to be an easy decision, for expansion offered both risk and opportunity.

Company Background

John Barro and Bill Stickney established their small manufacturers' representative agency, Barro Stickney, Inc., 10 years ago. Both men were close friends who left different manufacturers' representative firms to join as partners in their own "rep" agency. The two worked very well together, and their talents complemented each other.

John Barro was energetic and gregarious. He enjoyed meeting new people and taking on new challenges. It was mainly through John's efforts that many of BSI's

Source: This case was written by Tony Langan, B. Jane Stewart, and Lawrence M. Stratton Jr., under the supervision of Professor Erin Anderson of the Wharton School, University of Pennsylvania. The writing of the case was sponsored by the Manufacturers' Representatives Educational Research Foundation. The cooperation of the Mid-Atlantic Chapter of the Electronic Representatives Association (ERA) is greatly appreciated.

eight principals had signed on with BSI. Even after producing $1.75 million in sales this past year, John still made an effort to contribute much of his free time to community organizations in addition to perfecting his golf score.

Bill Stickney liked to think of himself as someone a person could count on. He was thoughtful and thorough. He liked to figure how things could get done, and how they could be better. Much of the administrative work of the agency, such as resource allocation and territory assignments, was handled by Bill. In addition to his contribution of $1.5 million to total company sales, Bill also had a Boy Scout troop and was interested in gourmet cooking. In fact, he often prepared specialties to share with his fellow workers.

A few years later, as the business grew, J. Todd Smith (J.T.) joined as an additional salesperson. J.T. had worked for a nationally known corporation, and he brought his experience dealing with large customers with him. He and his family loved the Harrisburg area, and J.T. was very happy when he was asked to join BSI just as his firm was ready to transfer him to Chicago. John and Bill had worked with J.T. in connection with a hospital fund-raising project, and they were impressed with his tenacity and enthusiasm. Because he had produced sales of over $2 million this past year, J.T. was now considered eligible to buy a partnership share of BSI.

Soon after J.T. joined BSI, Elizabeth Lee, a school friend of John's older sister, was hired as office manager. She was cheerful and put as much effort into her work as she did coaching the local swim team. The three salespeople knew they could rely on her to keep track of orders and schedules, and she was very helpful when customers and principals called in with requests or problems.

Most principals in the industry assigned their reps exclusive territories, and BSI's ranged over the Pennsylvania, New Jersey, and Delaware area. The partners purchased a small house and converted it into their present office located in Camp Hill, a suburb of Harrisburg, the state capital of Pennsylvania. The converted home contributed to the familylike atmosphere and attitude that was promoted and prevalent throughout the agency.

Over the years, in addition to local interests, BSI and its people had made an effort to participate in and support the efforts of the Electronics Representative Association (ERA). A wall of the company library was covered with awards and letters of appreciation. BSI had made many friends and important contacts through the organization. Just last year BSI received a recommendation from Chuck Goodman, a Chicago manufacturers' rep who knew a principal in need of representation in the Philadelphia area. The principal's line worked well with BSI's existing portfolio, and customer response had been quite favorable. BSI planned to continue active participation in the ERA.

Each week BSI held a five o'clock meeting in the office library where all members of the company shared their experiences of the week. It was a time when new ideas were encouraged and everyone was brought up to date. For example, many customer problems were solved here, and principals' and members' suggestions were discussed. An established agenda enabled members to prepare. Most meetings took about 60 to 90 minutes, with emphasis placed on group consensus. It was during this group meeting that BSI would discuss the future of the company.

Opportunities for Expansion

R. D. Ocean was BSI's largest principal, and it accounted for 32 percent of BSI's revenues. Ocean had just promoted James Innve as new sales manager, and he felt an additional salesperson was needed in order for BSI to achieve the new sales projections. Innve expressed the opinion that BSI's large commission checks justified the additional effort, and he further commented that J.T.'s expensive new car was proof that BSI could afford it.

BSI was not sure an additional salesperson was necessary, but it did not want to lose the goodwill of R. D. Ocean or [its] business. Also, while it was customary for all principals to meet and tacitly approve new representatives, BSI wanted to be very sure that any new salesperson would fit into the close-knit BSI organization.

Franklin Key Electronics was BSI's initial principal and had remained a consistent contributor of approximately 15 percent of BSI's revenues. BSI felt its customer base was well suited to the Franklin line, and it had worked hard to establish the Franklin Key name with these customers. As a consequence, BSI now considered Franklin Key relatively easy to sell.

A few days previously, Mark Heil, Franklin's representative from Virginia, perished when his private plane crashed, leaving Franklin Key without representation in its D.C./Virginia territory. Franklin did not want to jeopardize its sales of over $800,000 and was desperate to replace Heil before its customers found other sources. Franklin offered the territory to BSI and was anxious to hear the decision within one week.

BSI was not familiar with the territory, but it did understand that there were a great number of military accounts. This meant there was a potential for sizable orders, although a different and specialized sales approach would be required. Military customers are known to have their own unique approach to purchase decisions.

Because of the distance and the size of the territory, serious consideration was needed as to whether a branch office would be necessary. A branch office would mean less interaction with and a greater independence from the main BSI office. None of the current BSI members seemed anxious to move there, but it might be possible to hire someone who was familiar with the territory. There was, of course, always the risk that any successful salesperson might leave and start his or her own rep firm.

In addition to possibilities of expanding its territory and its sales force, BSI also wanted to consider whether it should increase or maintain its number of principals. BSI's established customer base and its valued reputation put them in a strong position to approach potential principals. If, however, BSI had too many principals, it might not be able to offer them all the attention and service they might require.

Preparation for the Meeting

Each member received an agenda and supporting data for the upcoming meeting asking them to consider the issue of expansion. They would be asked whether BSI should or should not expand its territory, its sales force, and/or its number of principals. In preparation, they were each asked to take a good hard look at the current BSI portfolio and to consider all possibilities for growth, including the effect any changes would have on the company's profits, its reputation, and its work environment.

It was an ambitious agenda: one that would determine the future of the company. It would take even more time than usual to discuss everything and reach consensus. Consequently, this week's meeting was set to take place over the weekend at Bill Stickney's vacation lodge in the Pocanos starting with a gourmet dinner served at 7 P.M. sharp.

Before the meeting, Bill Stickney examined the sources of BSI's revenue and the firm's income for the previous year. He also estimated the future prospects for each of BSI's lines, considering each line's market potential and BSI's level of saturation in each market. Finally, he estimated the costs of hiring a new employee both in the current sales territory and in the Washington/Virginia area. Immediately before the meeting, Elizabeth finished compiling Bill's data into four exhibits.

Exhibit 6.1 evaluates the amount of sales effort (difficulty in selling) necessary to achieve a certain percentage of sales in BSI's portfolio (return). Difficulty in selling is measured by the level of marketing investment required for growth. Stickney's estimates are shown on the vertical axis. Return for this investment is measured

Exhibit 6.1 Return versus Difficulty in Selling

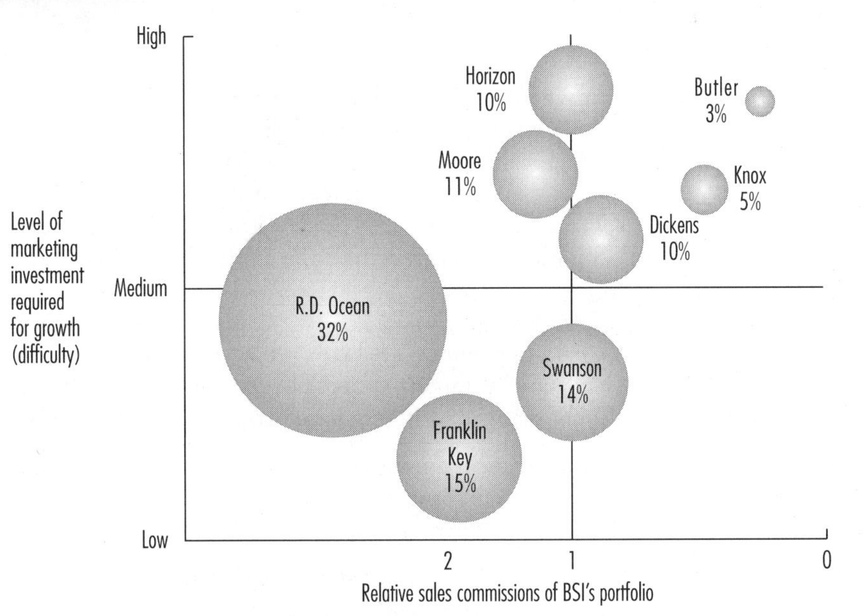

Exhibit 6.2 Barro Stickney, Inc., Estimation of Cost of Additional Sales Representative

Compensation Costs for New Sales Representative

Depending on the new sales representative's level of experience, BSI would pay a base salary of $15,000–$25,000 with the following bonus schedule:

0% firm's commission revenue up to $500,000 in sales
20% firm's commission revenue first $0.5 million in sales over $500,000
25% firm's commission revenue for the next $0.5 million in sales
30% firm's commission for the next $0.5 million in sales
40% firm's commission sales above $2 million

Estimate of Support Costs[1] for New Representative.[2]

Search applicant pool, psychological testing, hiring, training,[3] flying final choice to principals for approval[4]	$28,000
Automobile expenses, telephone costs, business cards, entertainment promotion	22,000
Insurance, payroll taxes (social security, unemployment compensation)	16,000
Total expenses	$66,000

Incremental Expenses for New Territory

Transportation (additional mileage from Camp Hill to Virginia)	$ 2,000
Office equipment and rent (same regardless of headquarter's location)	4,000
Cost of hiring office manager[5]	18,000
Total increment expenses	$24,000

[1]Rounded to the nearest thousand.
[2]In current territory.
[3]Excludes the lost revenue from selling instead of engaging in this activity (opportunity cost).
[4]Although rep agencies are not legally required to show prospective employees to principals, it is generally held to be good business practice.
[5]Discretionary.

by the relative sales commissions as a percent of BSI's portfolio shown on the horizontal axis. If BSI's time were evenly divided among its eight principals, each would receive 12.5 percent of the agency's time. The x-axis shows each principal's time allocation as a proportion of 12.5 percent of the "par" time allocation. The area of each ellipse reflects each principal's share of BSI's commission revenue.

Bill Stickney presented the following additional comments as a result of his research:

1. Swanson's products are being replaced by the competition's computerized electronic equipment, a product category the firm has ignored. As a result, the company is losing its once prominent market position.

2. Although small amounts of effort are required to promote Ocean's product line to customers in the current sales territory, Ocean is extremely demanding of both BSI and other manufacturer's representative firms.

3. According to a seminar at the last ERA meeting, the maximum safe proportion of a rep firm's commissions from a single principal should be

Exhibit 6.3 Barro Stickney, Inc., Statement of Revenue (Total Sales Revenue 1988, $5.5 Million)

Principal	Estimated Market Saturation	Product Type	Sales/ Commission Rate	Share of BSI's Portfolio	Commission Revenue
R. D. Ocean	High	Components	5.00%	32%	$96,756
Franklin Key	High	Components	5.00	15	45,354
Butler	Low	Technical/computer	12.00	3	9,070
Dickens	Low	Components	5.00	10	30,236
Horizon	Medium	Components	5.50	10	30,237
Swanson	High	Components	5.25	14	42,331
Moore	Medium	Consumer/electronics	5.25	11	33,260
Knox	Low	Technical/communications	8.50	5	15,118

25–30 percent. Also, at the meeting, one speaker indicated that if a firm commands 80 percent of a market, it should focus on another product or expand its territory rather than attempt to obtain the remainder of the market.

4. The revenue for investment for the manufacturer's representative firm comes from one or more of several sources. These sources include reduced forthcoming commission income, retained previous income, and borrowed money from a financial institution. Most successful firms expand their sales force or sales territory when they experience income growth and use the investment as a tax write-off.

Exhibit 6.4 Barro Stickney, Inc., Statement of Income (for the Year Ending December 31, 1988)

Revenue		
Commission income	$302,362	
Expenses		
Salaries for sales and bonuses (includes Barro Stickney)	130,250	
Office manager's salary	20,000	
Total nonpersonnel expenses[1]	128,279	
Total expenses	$278,529	
Net Income[2]	**$ 23,833**	**(7.9% of revenue)**

[1]Includes travel, advertising, taxes, office supplies, retirement, automobile expenses, communications, office equipment, and miscellaneous expenses.
[2]Currently held in negotiable certificates of deposit in a Harrisburg bank.

Case 7

W. L. Gore & Associates, Inc.—1996: A Case Study

"To make money and have fun."
—W. L. Gore

The First Day on the Job

Bursting with resolve, Jack Dougherty, a newly minted M.B.A. from the College of William and Mary, reported to his first day at W. L. Gore & Associates on July 26, 1976. He presented himself to Bill Gore, shook hands firmly, looked him in the eye, and said he was ready for anything.

Jack was not ready, however, for what happened next. Gore replied, "That's fine, Jack, fine. Why don't you look around and find something you'd like to do?" Three frustrating weeks later he found that something: trading in his dark blue suit for jeans, he loaded fabric into the mouth of a machine that laminated the company's patented GORE-TEX®[1] membrane to fabric. By 1982, Jack had become responsible for all advertising and marketing in the fabrics group. This story is part of the folklore of W. L. Gore & Associates.

Today the process is more structured. Regardless of the job for which they are hired, new Associates[2] take a journey through the business before settling into their own positions. A new sales Associate in the fabrics division may spend six weeks rotating through different areas before beginning to concentrate on sales and marketing. Among other things the newcomer learns is how GORE-TEX fabric is made,

---

Source: This case was written by Frank Shipper, Department of Management and Marketing, Franklin P. Perdue School of Business, Salisbury State University, Salisbury, Maryland; and Charles C. Manz, Department of Management, College of Business, Arizona State University, Tempe, Arizona.

[1]GORE-TEX is a registered trademark of W. L. Gore & Associates.

[2]In this case the word "Associate" is used and capitalized because in W. L. Gore & Associates' literature the word is always used instead of employees and is capitalized. In fact, case writers were told that Gore "never had 'employees'—always 'Associates.'"

what it can and cannot do, how Gore handles customer complaints, and how it makes its investment decisions.

Anita McBride related her early experience at W. L. Gore & Associates this way:

Before I came to Gore, I had worked for a structured organization, and for the first month it was fairly structured because I was going through training and this is what we do and this is how Gore is and all of that. I went to Flagstaff for that training. After a month I came down to Phoenix and my sponsor said, "Well, here's your office; it's a wonderful office" and "Here's your desk," and walked away. And I thought, "Now what do I do?" You know, I was waiting for a memo or something, or a job description. Finally after another month I was so frustrated, I felt, "What have I gotten myself into?" And so I went to my sponsor and I said, "What the heck do you want from me? I need something from you." And he said, "If you don't know what you're supposed to do, examine your commitment, and opportunities."

Background

W. L. Gore & Associates evolved from the late Wilbert L. Gore's experiences personally, organizationally, and technically. He was born in Meridian, Idaho, near Boise, in 1912. By age six, according to his own account, he was an avid hiker in the Wasatch Mountain Range in Utah. In those mountains, at a church camp, he met Genevieve, his future wife. In 1935, they got married—in their eyes, a partnership. He would make breakfast and Vieve, as everyone called her, would make lunch. The partnership lasted a lifetime.

He received both a bachelor of science in chemical engineering in 1933 and a master of science in physical chemistry in 1935 from the University of Utah. He began his professional career at American Smelting and Refining in 1936. He moved to Remington Arms Company in 1941 and then to E. I. Du Pont de Nemours in 1945. He held positions as research supervisor and head of operations research. While at Du Pont, he worked on a team to develop applications for polytetrafluoroethylene, referred to as PTFE in the scientific community and known as "Teflon" by Du Pont's consumers. (Consumers know it under other names from other companies.) On this team Wilbert Gore, called Bill by everyone, felt a sense of excited commitment, personal fulfillment, and self-direction. He followed the development of computers and transistors and felt that PTFE had the ideal insulating characteristics for use with such equipment.

He tried many ways to make a PTFE coated ribbon cable without success. A breakthrough came in his home basement laboratory while he was explaining the problem to his 19-year-old son Bob. The young Gore saw some PTFE sealant tape made by 3M and asked his father, "Why don't you try this tape?" Bill then explained that everyone knew that you cannot bond PTFE to itself. Bob went on to bed.

Bill Gore remained in his basement lab and proceeded to try what everyone knew would not work. At about 4:00 A.M. he woke up his son, waving a small piece of cable around and saying excitedly, "It works, it works." The following night father and son returned to the basement lab to make ribbon cable coated with PTFE. Because the breakthrough idea came from Bob, the patent for the cable was issued in Bob's name.

For the next four months Bill Gore tried to persuade Du Pont to make a new product—PTFE coated ribbon cable. By this time in his career Bill Gore knew some of the decision makers at Du Pont. After talking to a number of them, he came to realize that Du Pont wanted to remain a supplier of raw materials and not a fabricator.

Bill and his wife, Vieve, began discussing the possibility of starting their own insulated wire and cable business. On January 1, 1958 their wedding anniversary, they founded W. L. Gore & Associates. The basement of their home served as their first facility. After finishing dinner that night, Vieve turned to her husband of 23 years and said, "Well, let's clear up the dishes, go downstairs, and get to work."

Bill Gore was 45 years old with five children to support when he left Du Pont. He put aside a career of 17 years, and a good, secure salary. To finance the first two years of the business, he and Vieve mortgaged their house and took $4,000 from savings. All their friends told them not to do it.

The first few years were rough. In lieu of salary, some of their employees accepted room and board in the Gore home. At one point 11 Associates were living and working under one roof. One afternoon, while sifting PTFE powder, Vieve received a call from the City of Denver's water department. The caller indicated that he was interested in the ribbon cable, but wanted to ask some technical questions. Bill was out running some errands. The caller asked for the product manager. Vieve explained that he was out at the moment. Next he asked for the sales manager and finally, the president. Vieve explained that they were also out. The caller became outraged and hollered, "What kind of company is this anyway?" With a little diplomacy the Gores were able eventually to secure an order for $100,000. This order put the company on a profitable footing and it began to take off.

W. L. Gore & Associates continued to grow and develop new products, primarily derived from PTFE. Its best known product would become GORE-TEX fabric. In 1986, Bill Gore died while backpacking in the Wind River Mountains of Wyoming. He was then Chairman of the Board. His son Bob continued to occupy the position of president. Vieve remained as the only other officer, secretary-treasurer.

The Operating Company

W. L. Gore & Associates has never had titles, hierarchy, or any of the conventional structures associated with enterprises of its size. The titles of president and secretary-treasurer continue to be used only because they are required by the laws of incorporation. In addition , Gore has never had a corporate-wide mission or code of ethics statement; nor has Gore ever required or prohibited business units from developing such statements for themselves. Thus, the Associates of some business units who have felt a need for such statements have developed them on their own. When questioned about this issue, one Associate stated, "The company belief is that (1) its four basic operating principles cover ethical practices required of people in business; (2) it will not tolerate illegal practices." Gore's management style has been referred to as unmanagement. The organization has been guided by Bill's experiences on teams at Du Pont and has evolved as needed.

For example, in 1965 W. L. Gore & Associates was a thriving company with a facility on Paper Mill Road in Newark, Delaware. One Monday morning in the summer, Bill Gore was taking his usual walk through the plant. All of a sudden he realized that he did not know everyone in the plant. The team had become too big. As a result, he established the practice of limiting plant size to approximately 200 Associates. Thus was born the expansion policy of "Get big by staying small." The purpose of maintaining small plants was to accentuate a close-knit atmosphere and encourage communication among associates in a facility.

In 1995, W. L. Gore & Associates consisted of over 44 plants worldwide with approximately 6,000 Associates. In some cases, the plants are grouped together on the same site (as in Flagstaff, Arizona, with ten plants). Overseas Gore's facilities are located in Scotland, Germany, France, and Italy, and the company has two joint ventures in Japan (see Figure 7.1). Gore manufactures electronic, medical, industrial, and fabric products. In addition, it has numerous sales offices worldwide including Eastern Europe and Russia.

Gore electronic products have been found in unconventional places where conventional products will not do—in space shuttles, for example, where Gore wire and cable assemblies withstand the heat of ignition and the cold of space. In addition, they have been found in fast computers, transmitting signals at up to 93 percent of the speed of light. Gore cables have even gone underground, in oil drilling operations,

Figure 7.1 International Locations of W.L. Gore & Associates

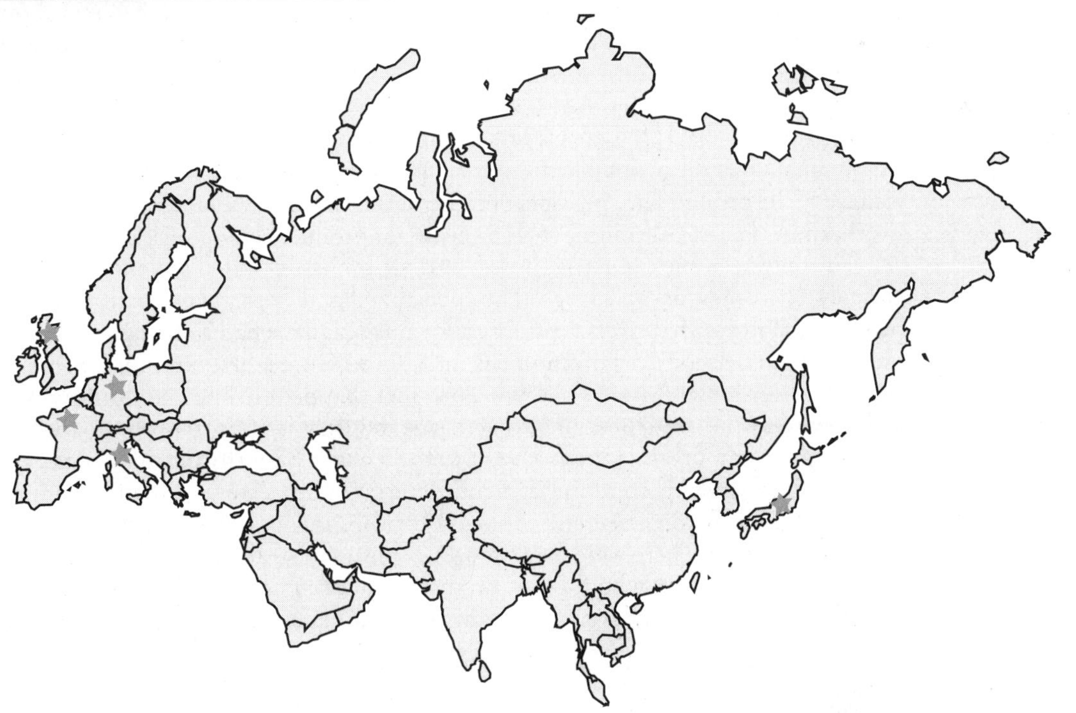

and underseas, on submarines that require superior microwave signal equipment and no-fail cables that can survive high pressure. The Gore electronic products division has a history of anticipating future customer needs with innovative products. Gore electronic products have been well received in industry for their ability to last under adverse conditions. For example, Gore has become, according to Sally Gore, leader in Human Resources and Communications, "... one of the largest manufacturers of ultrasound cable in the world, the reason being that Gore's electronic cables' signal transmission is very, very accurate and it's very thin and extremely flexible and has a very, very long flex life. That makes it ideal for things like ultrasound and many medical electronic applications."

In the medical arena, GORE-TEX–expanded PTFE has been considered an ideal replacement for human tissue in many situations. In patients suffering from cardiovascular disease the diseased portion of arteries has been replaced by tubes of expanded PTFE—strong, biocompatible structures capable of carrying blood at arterial pressures. Gore has a strong position in this product segment. Other Gore medical products have included patches that can literally mend broken hearts by sealing holes, and sutures that allow for tissue attachment and offer the surgeon silk-like handling coupled with extreme strength. In 1985, W. L. Gore & Associates won Britain's Prince Philip Award for Polymers in the Service of Mankind. The award recognized especially the life-saving achievements of the Gore medical products team.

Two recently developed products by this division are a new patch material that is intended to incorporate more tissue into the graft more quickly and GORE™ RideOn®[3] Cable System for bicycles. According to Amy LeGere of the medical division, "All the top pro riders in the world are using it. It was introduced just about a year ago and it has become an industry standard." This product had a positive cash flow very soon after its introduction. Some Associates who were also outdoor sports enthusiasts developed the product and realized that Gore could make a great bicycle cable that would have 70 percent less friction and need no lubrication. The Associates maintain that the profitable development, production, and marketing of such specialized niche products are possible because of the lack of bureaucracy and associated overhead, Associate commitment, and the use of product champions.

The output of the industrial products division has included sealants, filter bags, cartridges, clothes, and coatings. The specialized and critical applications of these products, along with Gore's reputation for quality, have had a strong influence on industrial purchasers. This division has introduced Gore's first consumer product—GLIDE®[4]—a dental floss. "That was a product that people knew about for a while and they went the route of trying to persuade industry leaders to promote the product, but they didn't really pursue it very well. So out of basically default almost, Gore decided, Okay they're not doing it right. Let's go in ourselves. We had a champion, John Spencer, who took that and pushed it forward through the dentist's offices and it just skyrocketed. There were many more people on the team but it was basically getting that one champion who focused on that product and got it out. They told him it 'Couldn't be done,' 'It's never going to work,' and I guess that's all he needed. It was

[3]GORE RideOn is a registered trademark of W. L. Gore & Associates.
[4]GLIDE is a registered trademark of W. L. Gore & Associates.

done and it worked," said Ray Wnenchak of the industrial products division. Amy LeGere added, "The champion worked very closely with the medical people to understand the medical market like claims and labeling so that when the product came out on the market it would be consistent with our medical products. And that's where, when we cross divisions, we know whom to work with and with whom we combine forces so that the end result takes the strengths of all of our different teams." Bob Winterling of the Fabrics Division explained,

> *The product champion is probably the most important resource we have at Gore for the introduction of new products. You look at that bicycle cable. That could have come out of many different divisions of Gore, but it really happened because one or two individuals said, "Look, this can work. I believe in it; I'm passionate about it; and I want it to happen." And the same thing with GLIDE floss. I think John Spencer in this case—although there was a team that supported John, let's never forget that—John sought the experts out throughout the organization. But without John making it happen on his own, GLIDE floss would never have come to fruition. He started with a little chain of drug stores here, Happy Harry's I think, and we put a few cases in and we just tracked the sales and that's how it all started. Who would have ever believed that you could take what we would have considered a commodity product like that, sell it direct for $3–5 apiece. That is so unGorelike it's incredible. So it comes down to people and it comes down to the product champion to make things happen.*

The Gore fabrics division has supplied laminates to manufacturers of foul weather gear, ski wear, running suits, footwear, gloves, and hunting and fishing garments. Firefighters and U.S. Navy pilots have worn GORE-TEX fabric gear, as have some Olympic athletes. The U.S. Army adopted a total garment system built around a GORE-TEX fabric component.

GORE-TEX membrane has nine billion pores randomly dotting each square inch and is feather light. Each pore is 700 times larger than a water vapor molecule, yet thousands of times smaller than a water droplet. Wind and water cannot penetrate the pores, but perspiration can escape. As a result, fabrics bonded with GORE-TEX membrane are waterproof, windproof, and breathable. The laminated fabrics bring protection from the elements to a variety of products—from survival gear to high-fashion rainwear. Other manufacturers, including 3M, have brought out products to compete with GORE-TEX fabrics. The toughest competition came from firms that violated the patents on GORE-TEX. Gore successfully challenged them in court. In 1993, the basic patent on the process for manufacturing ran out. Nevertheless, as Sally Gore explained,

> *What happens is you get an initial process patent and then as you begin to create things with this process you get additional patents. For instance, we have patents protecting our vascular graft, different patents for protecting GORE-TEX patches, and still other patents protecting GORE-TEX industrial sealants and filtration material. One of our patent attorneys did a talk recently, a year or so ago, when the patent expired and a lot of people who were saying, Oh, golly,*

Table 7.1 Gore's Family of Fabrics

Brand Name	Activity/ Conditions	Breathability	Water Protection	Wind Protection
GORE-TEX®	Rain; snow; cold; windy	Very breathable	Waterproof	Windproof
Immersion™ Technology	For fishing and paddle sports	Very breathable	Waterproof	Windproof
Ocean Technology	For offshore and coastal sailing	Very breathable	Waterproof	Windproof
Windstopper®	Cool/cold; windy	Very breathable	No water resistance	Windproof
GORE DRYLOFT™	Cold; windy; light precipitation	Extremely breathable	Water resistant	Windproof
Activent™	Cool/cold; windy; light precipitation	Extremely breathable	Water resistant	Windproof

are we going to be in trouble! We would be in trouble if we didn't have any patents. Our attorney had this picture with a great big umbrella, sort of a parachute, with Gore under it. Next he showed us lots of little umbrellas scattered all over the sky. So you protect certain niche markets and niche areas, but indeed competition increases as your initial patents expire.

Gore, however, has continued to have a commanding position in the active wear market.

To meet the needs of a variety of customer needs, Gore introduced a new family of fabrics in the 1990s. (Table 7.1). The introduction posed new challenges. According to Bob Winterling,

We did such a great job with the brand GORE-TEX that we actually have hurt ourselves in many ways. By that I mean it has been very difficult for us to come up with other new brands, because many people didn't even know Gore. We are the GORE-TEX company. One thing we decided to change about Gore four or five years ago was instead of being the GORE-TEX company we wanted to become the Gore company and that underneath the Gore company we had an umbrella of products that fall out of being the great Gore company. So it was a shift in how we positioned GORE-TEX. Today GORE-TEX is stronger than ever as it's turned out, but now we've ventured into such things as WindStopper®[5] fabric that is very big in the golf market. It could be a sweater or a fleece piece or even a knit shirt with the WindStopper behind it or closer to your skin and what it does is it stops the wind. It's not waterproof;

[5]WindStopper is a registered trademark of W. L. Gore & Associates.

it's water resistant. What we've tried to do is position the Gore name and beneath that all of the great products of the company.

Bill Gore knew that products alone did not a company make. He wanted to avoid smothering the company in thick layers of formal "management." He felt that hierarchy stifled individual creativity. As the company grew, he knew that he had to find a way to assist new people and to follow their progress. This was particularly important when it came to compensation. W. L. Gore & Associates developed its "sponsor" program to meet these needs. When people apply to Gore, they are initially screened by personnel specialists. Those who meet the basic criteria are given interviews with other Associates. Before anyone is hired, an Associate must agree to be his or her sponsor. The sponsor is to take a personal interest in the new Associate's contributions, problems, and goals, acting as both a coach and an advocate. The sponsor tracks the new Associate's progress, helping and encouraging, dealing with weaknesses, and concentrating on strengths. Sponsoring is not a short-term commitment. All Associates have sponsors and many have more than one. When individuals are hired initially, they are likely to have a sponsor in their immediate work area. If they move to another area, they may have a sponsor in that work area. As Associates' commitments change or grow, they may acquire additional sponsors.

Because the hiring process looks beyond conventional views of what makes a good Associate, some anomalies have occurred. Bill Gore proudly told the story of "a very young man" of 84 who walked in, applied, and spent 5 very good years with the company. The individual had 30 years of experience in the industry before joining Gore. His other Associates had no problems accepting him, but the personnel computer did. It insisted his age was 48. The individual success stories at Gore have come from diverse backgrounds.

An internal memo by Bill Gore described three roles of sponsors: helping a new Associate get started on a job, seeing that an Associate's accomplishments are recognized, and ensuring that an Associate is fairly paid. A single person can perform any one or all three kinds of sponsorship.

In addition to the sponsor program, Bill Gore articulated four guiding principles:

1. Try to be fair.
2. Encourage, help and allow other Associates to grow in knowledge, skill, and scope of activity and responsibility.
3. Make your own commitments, and keep them.
4. Consult with other Associates before taking actions that may be "below the water line."

The four principles have been referred to as Fairness, Freedom, Commitment, and Waterline. The waterline terminology is drawn from an analogy to ships. If someone pokes a hole in a boat above the waterline, the boat will be in relatively little real danger. If someone, however, pokes a hole below the waterline, the boat is in immediate danger of sinking.

The operating principles were put to a test in 1978. By this time word about the qualities of GORE-TEX fabric was being spread throughout the recreational and outdoor markets. Production and shipment had begun in volume. At first a few complaints were heard. Next some of the clothing started coming back. Finally, much of the clothing was being returned. The trouble was that the GORE-TEX fabric was leaking. Waterproofing was one of the major properties responsible for GORE-TEX fabric's success. The company's reputation and credibility were on the line.

Peter W. Gilson, who led Gore's fabrics division, recalled: "It was an incredible crisis for us at that point. We were really starting to attract attention; we were taking off—and then this." In the next few months, Gilson and a number of his Associates made a number of those below-the-waterline decisions.

First, the researchers determined that oils in human sweat were responsible for clogging the pores in the GORE-TEX fabric and altering the surface tension of the membrane. Thus, water could pass through. They also discovered that a good washing could restore the waterproof property. At first this solution, known as the "Ivory Snow solution," was accepted.

A single letter from "Butch," a mountain guide in the Sierras, changed the company's position. Butch described what happened while he was leading a group: "My parka leaked and my life was in danger." As Gilson noted, "That scared the hell out of us. Clearly our solution was no solution at all to someone on a mountain top." All the products were recalled. Gilson remembered: "We bought back, at our own expense, a fortune in pipeline material—anything that was in the stores, at the manufacturers, or anywhere else in the pipeline."

In the meantime, Bob Gore and other Associates set out to develop a permanent fix. One month later, a second generation GORE-TEX fabric had been developed. Gilson, furthermore, told dealers that if a customer ever returned a leaky parka, they should replace it and bill the company. The replacement program alone cost Gore roughly $4 million.

The popularity of GORE-TEX outerwear took off. Many manufacturers now make numerous pieces of apparel such as parkas, gloves, boots, jogging outfits, and wind shirts from GORE-TEX laminate. Sometimes when customers are dissatisfied with a garment, they return them directly to Gore. Gore has always stood behind any product made of GORE-TEX fabric. Analysis of the returned garments found that the problem was often not the GORE-TEX fabric. The manufacturer "had created a design flaw so that the water could get in here or get in over the zipper and we found that when there was something negative about it, everyone knew it was GORE-TEX. So we had to make good on products that we were not manufacturing. We now license the manufacturers of all our GORE-TEX fabric products. They pay a fee to obtain a license to manufacture GORE-TEX products. In return we oversee the manufacture and we let them manufacture only designs that we are sure are guaranteed to keep you dry, that really will work. Then it works for them and for us—it's a win-win for them as well as for us," according to Sally Gore.

Organizational Structure

W. L. Gore & Associates has been described not only as unmanaged, but also as unstructured. Bill Gore referred to the structure as a lattice organization (see Figure 7.2). The characteristics of this structure are:

Figure 7.2 The Lattice Structure

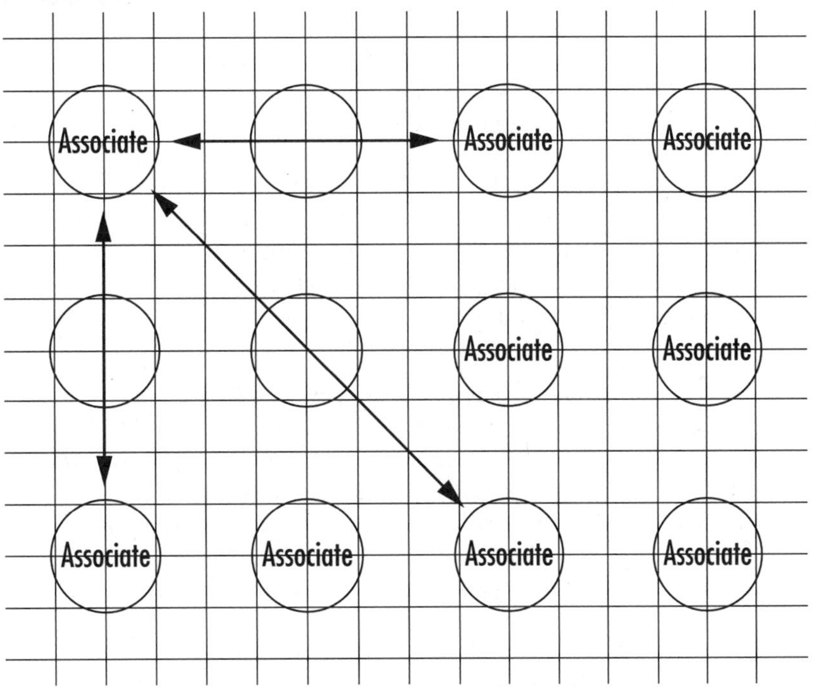

1. Direct lines of communication—person to person—with no intermediary.
2. No fixed or assigned authority.
3. Sponsors, not bosses.
4. Natural leadership defined by followership.
5. Objectives set by those who must "make them happen."
6. Tasks and functions organized through commitments.

The structure within the lattice is complex and evolves from interpersonal interactions, self-commitment to group-known responsibilities, natural leadership, and group-imposed discipline.

Bill Gore once explained the structure this way: "Every successful organization has an underground lattice. It's where the news spreads like lightning, where people can go around the organization to get things done." An analogy might be drawn to a structure of constant cross-area teams—the equivalent of quality circles going on all the time. When a puzzled interviewer told Bill that he was having trouble understanding how planning and accountability worked, Bill replied with a grin: "So am I. You ask me how it works? Every which way."

Outsiders have been struck by the degree of informality and humor in the Gore organization. Meetings tend to be only as long as necessary. As Trish Hearn, an Associate in Newark, Delaware, said, "No one feels a need to pontificate." Words such as "responsibilities" and "commitments" are commonly heard, whereas words such as "employees," "subordinates," and "managers" are taboo in the Gore culture. This is an organization that has always taken what it does very seriously, without its members taking themselves too seriously.

For a company of its size, Gore has always had a very short organizational pyramid. As of 1995 the pyramid consists of Bob Gore, the late Bill Gore's son, as president and Vieve, Bill Gore's widow, as secretary-treasurer. All the other members of the Gore organization were, and continue to be, referred to as Associates.

Gore has never had any managers, but it has always had many leaders. Bill Gore described in an internal memo the kinds of leadership and the role of leadership as follows:

1. *The Associate who is recognized by a team as having a special knowledge, or experience (for example, this could be a chemist, computer expert, machine operator, salesman, engineer, lawyer). This kind of leader gives the team guidance in a special area.*
2. *The Associate the team looks to for coordination of individual activities in order to achieve the agreed upon objectives of the team. The role of this leader is to persuade team members to make the commitments necessary for success (commitment seeker).*
3. *The Associate who proposes necessary objectives and activities and seeks agreement and team consensus on objectives. This leader is perceived by the team members as having a good grasp of how the objectives of the team fit in with the broad objective of the enterprise. This kind of leader is often also the "commitment seeking" leader in 2 above.*
4. *The leader who evaluates relative contribution of team members (in consultation with other sponsors), and reports these contribution evaluations to a compensation committee. This leader may also participate in the compensation committee on relative contribution and pay and reports changes in compensation to individual Associates. This leader is then also a compensation sponsor.*
5. *The leader who coordinates the research, manufacturing, and marketing of one product type within a business, interacting with team leaders and individual Associates who have commitments regarding the product type. These leaders are usually called product specialists. They are respected for their knowledge and dedication to their products.*
6. *Plant leaders who help coordinate activities of people within a plant.*
7. *Business leaders who help coordinate activities of people in a business.*
8. *Functional leaders who help coordinate activities of people in a "functional" area.*
9. *Corporate leaders who help coordinate activities of people in different businesses and functions and who try to promote communication and cooperation among all Associates.*

10. *Entrepreneuring Associates who organize new teams for new businesses, new products, new processes, new devices, new marketing efforts, new or better methods of all kinds. These leaders invite the other Associates to "sign up" for their project.*

It is clear that leadership is widespread in our lattice organization and that it is continually changing and evolving. The situation that leaders are frequently also sponsors should not confuse that these are different activities and responsibilities.

Leaders are not authoritarians, managers of people, or supervisors who tell us what to do or forbid us doing things; nor are they "parents" to whom we transfer our own self-responsibility. However, they do often advise us of the consequences of actions we have done or propose to do. Our actions result in contributions, or lack of contribution, to the success of our enterprise. Our pay depends on the magnitude of our contributions. This is the basic discipline of our lattice organization.

Many other aspects of the Gore culture have been arranged along egalitarian lines: parking lots with no reserved parking spaces except for customers and disabled workers or visitors; dining areas—only one in each plant—set up as focal points for Associate interaction. As Dave McCarter of Phoenix explained: "The design is no accident. The lunchroom in Flagstaff has a fireplace in the middle. We want people to like to be here." The location of a plant is also no accident. Sites have been selected on the basis of transportation access, a nearby university, beautiful surroundings, and climate appeal. Land cost has never been a primary consideration. McCarter justified the selection by stating: "Expanding is not costly in the long run. The loss of money is what you make happen by stymieing people into a box."

Bob Gore is a champion of Gore culture. As Sally Gore related,

We have managed surprisingly to maintain our sense of freedom and our entrepreneurial spirit. I think what we've found is that we had to develop new ways to communicate with Associates because you can't communicate with 6,000 people the way that you can communicate with 500 people. It just can't be done. So we have developed a newsletter that we didn't have before. One of the most important communication mediums that we developed, and this was Bob Gore's idea, is a digital voice exchange which we call our Gorecom. Basically everyone has a mailbox and a password. Lots of companies have gone to E-mail, and we use E-mail, but Bob feels very strongly that we're very much an oral culture and there's a big difference between cultures that are predominantly oral and predominantly written. Oral cultures encourage direct communication, which is, of course, something that we encourage.

Not all people function well under such a system, especially initially. For those accustomed to a more structured work environment, there can be adjustment problems. As Bill Gore said: "All our lives most of us have been told what to do, and some people don't know how to respond when asked to do something—and have the very real option of saying no—on their job. It's the new Associate's responsibility to find out what he or she can do for the good of the operation." The vast majority of the new Associates, after some initial floundering, have adapted quickly.

Others, especially those who require more structured working conditions, have found that Gore's flexible workplace is not for them. According to Bill for those few, "It's an unhappy situation, both for the Associate and the sponsor. If there is no contribution, there is no paycheck."

As Anita McBride, an Associate in Phoenix, noted: "It's not for everybody. People ask me do we have turnover, and yes we do have turnover. What you're seeing looks like utopia, but it also looks extreme. If you finally figure the system, it can be real exciting. If you can't handle it, you gotta go. Probably by your own choice, because you're going to be so frustrated."

In rare cases an Associate "is trying to be unfair," in Bill's own words. In one case the problem was chronic absenteeism and in another, an individual was caught stealing. "When that happens, all hell breaks loose," said Bill Gore. "We can get damned authoritarian when we have to."

Over the years, Gore & Associates has faced a number of unionization drives. The company has neither tried to dissuade Associates form attending an organizational meeting nor retaliated when flyers were passed out. As of 1995, none of the plants has been organized. Bill believed that no need existed for third-party representation under the lattice structure. He asked the question, "Why would Associates join a union when they own the company? It seems rather absurd."

Overall, the Associates appear to have responded positively to the Gore system of unmanagement and unstructure. Bill estimated the year before he died that "the profit per Associate is double" that of Du Pont.

The lattice structure has not been without its critics. As Bill Gore stated, "I'm told from time to time that a lattice organization can't meet a crisis well because it takes too long to reach a consensus when there are no bosses. But this isn't true. Actually, a lattice by its very nature works particularly well in a crisis. A lot of useless effort is avoided because there is no rigid management hierarchy to conquer before you can attack a problem."

The lattice has been put to the test on a number of occasions. For example, in 1975, Dr. Charles Campbell of the University of Pittsburgh reported that a GORE-TEX arterial graft had developed an aneurysm. If the bubble-like protrusion continued to expand, it would explode. Obviously, this life-threatening situation had to be resolved quickly and permanently.

Within only a few days of Dr. Campbell's first report, he flew to Newark to present his findings to Bill and Bob Gore and a few other Associates. The meeting lasted two hours. Dan Hubis, a former policeman who had joined Gore to develop new production methods, had an idea before the meeting was over. He returned to his work area to try some different production techniques. After only three hours and 12 tries, he had developed a permanent solution. In other words, in three hours a potentially damaging problem to both patients and the company was resolved. Furthermore, Hubis's redesigned graft went on to win widespread acceptance in the medical community.

Some outsiders have had problems with the idea of no titles. Sarah Clifton, an Associate at the Flagstaff facility, was being pressed by some outsiders as to what her title was. She made one up and had it printed on some business cards: SUPREME COMMANDER (see Figure 7.3). When Bill Gore learned what she did, he loved it and recounted the story to others.

Eric Reynolds, founder of Marmot Mountain Works Ltd. of Grand Junction, Colorado, and a major Gore customer, raised another issue: "I think the lattice has its problems with the day-to-day nitty-gritty of getting things done on time and out the door. I don't think Bill realizes how the lattice system affects customers. I mean after you've established a relationship with someone about product quality, you can call up one day and suddenly find that someone new to you is handling your problem. It's frustrating to find a lack of continuity." He went on to say: "But I have to admit that I've personally seen at Gore remarkable examples of people coming out of nowhere and excelling."

When Bill Gore was asked if the lattice structure could be used by other companies, he answered: "No. For example, established companies would find it very difficult to use the lattice. Too many hierarchies would be destroyed. When you remove titles and positions and allow people to follow who they want, it may very well be someone other than the person who has been in charge. The lattice works for us, but it's always evolving. You have to expect problems." He maintained that the lattice system worked best when it was put in place in start-up companies by dynamic entrepreneurs.

Research and Development

Like everything else at Gore, research and development has always been unstructured. Even without a formal R&D department, the company has been issued many patents, although most inventions have been held as proprietary or trade secrets. Any Associate could ask for a piece of raw PTFE (known as silly worm) with which to experiment. Bill Gore believed that all people had it within themselves to be creative.

Figure 7.3

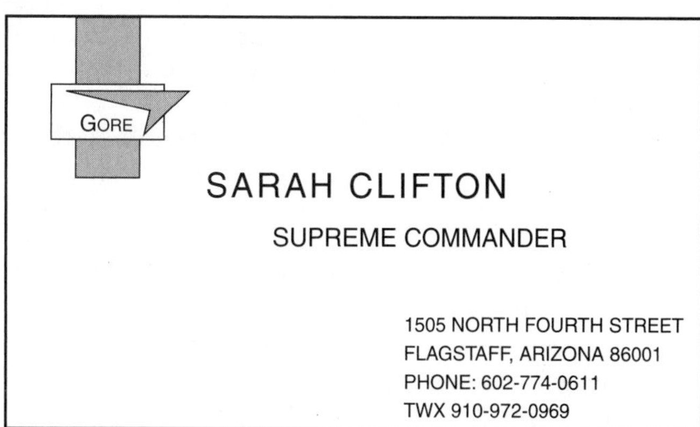

One of the best examples of Gore inventiveness occurred in 1969. At the time, the wire and cable division was facing increased competition. Bill Gore began to look for a way to straighten out the PTFE molecules. As he said, "I figured out that if we ever unfold those molecules, get them to stretch out straight, we'd have a tremendous new kind of material." He thought that if PTFE could be stretched, air could be introduced into its molecular structure. The result would be greater volume per pound of raw material with no effect on performance. Thus, fabricating costs would be reduced and profit margins would be increased. Going about this search in a scientific manner, Bob Gore heated rods of PTFE to various temperatures and then slowly stretched them. Regardless of the temperature or how carefully he stretched them, the rods broke.

Working alone late one night after countless failures, Bob in frustration stretched one of the rods violently. To his surprise, it did not break. He tried it again and again with the same results. The next morning Bob demonstrated his breakthrough to his father, but not without some drama. As Bill Gore recalled: "Bob wanted to surprise me so he took a rod and stretched it slowly. Naturally, it broke. Then he pretended to get mad. He grabbed another rod and said, 'Oh the hell with this,' and gave it a pull. It didn't break—he'd done it." The new arrangement of molecules not only changed the wire and cable division, but led to the development of GORE-TEX fabric.

Bill and Vieve did the initial field-testing of GORE-TEX fabric the summer of 1970. Vieve made a hand-sewn tent out of patches of GORE-TEX fabric. They took it on their annual camping trip to the Wind River Mountains in Wyoming. The very first night in the wilderness, they encountered a hail storm. The hail tore holes in the top of the tent, and the bottom filled up like a bathtub from the rain. Undaunted, Bill Gore stated: "At least we knew from all the water that the tent was waterproof. We just needed to make it stronger, so it could withstand hail."

The largest medical division began on the ski slopes of Colorado. Bill was skiing with a friend, Dr. Ben Eiseman of Denver General Hospital. As Bill Gore told the story: "We were ready to start a run when I absentmindedly pulled a small tubular section of GORE-TEX out of my pocket and looked at it. 'What is that stuff?' Ben asked. So I told him about its properties. 'Feels great,' he said. 'What do you use it for?' 'Got no idea,' I said. 'Well give it to me,' he said, 'and I'll try it in a vascular graft on a pig.' Two weeks later, he called me up. Ben was pretty excited. 'Bill,' he said, 'I put it in a pig and it works. What do I do now?' I told him to get together with Pete Cooper in our Flagstaff plant, and let them figure it out." Not long after, hundreds of thousands of people throughout the world began walking around with GORE-TEX vascular grafts.

Gore Associates have always been encouraged to think, experiment, and follow a potentially profitable idea to its conclusion. At a plant in Newark, Delaware, Fred L. Eldreth, an Associate with a third grade education, designed a machine that could wrap thousands of feet of wire a day. The design was completed over a weekend. Many other Associates have contributed their ideas through both products and process breakthroughs.

Even without an R&D department, innovations and creativity continued to work very well at Gore & Associates. The year before he died, Bill Gore claimed that "the creativity, the number of patent applications and innovative products is triple" that of Du Pont.

Associate Development

Ron Hill, an Associate in Newark, noted that Gore "will work with Associates who want to advance themselves." Associates have been offered many in-house training opportunities, not only in technical and engineering areas but also in leadership development. In addition, the company has established cooperative education programs with universities and other outside providers, picking up most of the costs for the Gore Associates. The emphasis in Associate development, as in many parts of Gore, has always been that the Associate must take the initiative.

Products

Gore's electronic products division has produced wire and cable for various demanding applications in aerospace, defense, computers, and telecommunications. The wire and cable products have earned a reputation for unequaled reliability. Most of the wire and cable has been used where conventional cables cannot operate. For example, Gore wire and cable assemblies were used in the space shuttle *Columbia* because they could stand the heat of ignition and the cold of space. Gore wire was used in the moon vehicle shuttle that scooped up samples of moon rocks, and Gore's microwave coaxial assemblies opened new horizons in microwave technology. Back on earth, Gore's electrical wire products helped make the world's fastest computers possible because electrical signals could travel through them at up to 93 percent of the speed of light. Because of the physical properties of the GORE-TEX material used in their construction, the electronic products have been used extensively in defense systems, electronic switching for telephone systems, scientific and industrial instrumentation, microwave communications, and industrial robotics. Reliability has always been a watchword for Gore products.

In medical products, reliability is literally a matter of life and death. GORE-TEX expanded PTFE proved to be an ideal material for combating cardiovascular disease. When human arteries have been seriously damaged or plugged with deposits that interrupt the flow of blood, the diseased portions can often be replaced with GORE-TEX artificial arteries. Because the patient's own tissues grow into the graft's open porous spaces, the artificial portions are not rejected by the body. GORE-TEX vascular grafts, produced in many sizes to restore circulation to all areas of the body, have saved limbs from amputation, and saved lives. Some of the tiniest grafts have relieved pulmonary problems in newborns. GORE-TEX–expanded PTFE has been used to help people with kidney disease. Associates have also developed a variety of surgical reinforcing membranes, known as GORE-TEX cardiovascular patches, which can literally mend broken hearts by patching holes and repairing aneurysms.

Through the waterproof fabrics division, Gore technology has traveled to the roof of the world on the backs of renowned mountaineers and adventurers facing extremely harsh environments. Because the PTFE membrane blocks wind and water but allows sweat to escape, GORE-TEX fabric has proved ideal for those who work or play hard in foul weather. Backpackers have discovered that a single lightweight GORE-TEX fabric shell will replace a poplin jacket and a rain suit, and dramatically outperform both. Skiers, sailors, runners, bicyclists, hunters, fisher[s], and other outdoor enthusiasts have also become big customers of garments made of GORE-TEX fabric. GORE-TEX sportswear, as well as women's fashion footwear and handwear, have proved to be functional as well as attractive. Boots and gloves, for both work and recreation, became waterproof thanks to GORE-TEX liners. GORE-TEX garments have even become standard items issued to military personnel. Wet suits, parkas, pants, headgear, gloves, and boots have kept the troops warm and dry in foul weather missions. Other demanding jobs have also received the protection of GORE-TEX fabric, with its unique combination of chemical and physical properties.

The GORE-TEX fibers, like the fabrics, have ended up in some pretty tough places, including outer protective layer of a NASA spacesuit. In many ways, GORE-TEX fibers have proved to be the ultimate synthetic. They have been impervious to sunlight, chemicals, heat, and cold. They are strong and uniquely resistant to abrasion.

Industrial filtration products, such as GORE-TEX filter bags, have reduced air pollution and recovered valuable solids from gases and liquids more completely than alternatives—and they have done so economically. In the future they may make coal-burning plants completely smoke free, contributing to a cleaner environment.

Gore's industrial products division has developed a unique joint sealant—a flexible cord of porous PTFE—that can be applied as a gasket to the most complex shapes, sealing them to prevent leakage of corrosive chemicals, even at extreme temperature and pressure. Steam valves packed with GORE-TEX have been sold with a lifetime guarantee, provided the valve is used properly.

Compensation

Traditionally, compensation at W. L. Gore & Associates has taken three forms: salary, profit sharing, and an Associate's Stock Ownership Program (ASOP).[6] Entry level salary has been in the middle for comparable jobs. According to Sally Gore: "We do not feel we need to be the highest paid. We never try to steal people away from other companies with salary. We want them to come here because of the opportunities for growth and the unique work environment." In the past, Associates' salaries have been reviewed at least once a year and more commonly twice a year. The reviews are conducted by a compensation team at each facility, with sponsors for the Associates acting as their advocates during the review process. Prior to meeting with the compensation committee, the sponsor checks with customers or Associates familiar with the person's work to find out what contribution the Associate has made. In addition, the evaluation team considers the Associate's leadership ability and willingness to help others develop to their fullest.

Profit sharing follows a formula based on economic value added (EVA). Sally Gore had the following to say about the adoption of a formula:

---

[6]Similar legally to an ESOP (Employee Stock Ownership Plan). Again, Gore simply has never allowed the word "employee" in any of its documentation.

It's become more formalized and, in a way, I think that's unfortunate because it used to be a complete surprise to receive a profit share. The thinking of the people like Bob Gore and other leaders was that maybe we weren't using it in the right way and we could encourage people by helping them know more about it and how we made profit share decisions. The fun of it before was people didn't know when it was coming and all of a sudden you could do something creative about passing out checks. It was great fun and people would have a wonderful time with it. The disadvantage was that Associates then did not focus much on, "What am I doing to create another profit share?" By using EVA as a method of evaluation for our profit share, we know at the end of every month how much EVA was created that month. When we've created a certain EVA, we then get another profit share. So everybody knows and everyone says, "We'll do it in January," so it is done. Now Associates feel more part of the happening to make it work. What have you done? Go make some more sales calls, please! There are lots of things we can do to improve our EVA and everybody has a responsibility to do that.

Every month EVA is calculated and every Associate is informed. John Mosko of electronic products commented, ". . . (EVA) lets us know where we are on the path to getting one [a profit share]. It's very critical—every Associate knows."

Annually, Gore also buys company stock equivalent to a fixed percent of the Associates' annual income, placing it in the ASOP retirement fund. Thus, an Associate can become a stockholder after being at Gore for a year. Gore's ASOP ensures Associates participate in the growth of the company by acquiring ownership in it. Bill Gore wanted Associates to feel that they themselves are owners. One Associate stated, "This is much more important than profit sharing."

Commitment has long been considered a two-way street. W. L. Gore & Associates has tried to avoid layoffs. Instead of cutting pay, which in the Gore culture would be disastrous to morale, the company has used a system of temporary transfers within a plant or cluster of plants and voluntary layoffs.

Marketing Strategy

Gore's marketing strategy has focused on three assumptions: that it can offer the best-valued products to a marketplace, that people in that marketplace appreciate what it manufactures, and that Gore can become a leader in that area of expertise. The operating procedures used to implement the strategy have followed the same principles as other functions at Gore.

1. Marketing a product requires a leader, or *product champion.* According to Dave McCarter: "You marry your technology with the interests of your champions, since you've got to have champions for all these things no matter what. And that's the key element within our company. Without a product champion, you can't do much anyway, so it is individually driven. If you get people interested in a particular market or a particular product for the marketplace, then there is no stopping them.

2. *A product champion is responsible for marketing the product through commitments with sales representatives.* Again, according to Dave McCarter: "We have no quota system. Our marketing and our sales people make their own commitments as to what their forecasts have been. There is no person sitting around telling them that is not high enough, you have to increase it by 10 percent, or whatever somebody feels is necessary. You are expected to meet your commitment, which is your forecast, but nobody is going to tell you to change it. . . . There is no order of command, no chain involved. These are groups of independent people who come together to make unified commitments to do something and sometimes when they can't make those agreements . . . you may pass up a marketplace, . . . but that's OK, because there's much more advantage when the team decides to do something."
3. *Sales Associates are on salary, not commission.* They participate in the profit sharing and ASOP plans in which all other Associates participate.

As in other areas of Gore, individual success stories have come from diverse backgrounds. Dave McCarter related one of these successes:

I interviewed Sam one day. I didn't even know why I was interviewing him actually. Sam was retired from AT&T. After 25 years, he took the golden parachute and went down to Sun Lakes to play golf. He played golf a few months and got tired of that. He was selling life insurance.

I sat reading the application; his technical background interested me. . . . He had managed an engineering department with 600 people. He'd managed manufacturing plants for AT&T and had a great wealth of experience at AT&T. He said, "I'm retired. I like to play golf but I just can't do it every day so I want to do something else. Do you have something around here I can do?" I was thinking to myself, "This is one of these guys I would sure like to hire but I don't know what I would do with him." The thing that triggered me was the fact that he said he sold insurance and here is a guy with a high degree of technical background selling insurance. He had marketing experience, international marketing experience. So, the bell went off in my head that we were trying to introduce a new product into the marketplace that was a hydrocarbon leak protection cable. You can bury it in the ground and in a matter of seconds it could detect a hydrocarbon like gasoline. I had a couple of other guys working on the product who hadn't been very successful with marketing it. We were having a hard time finding a customer. Well, I thought that kind of product would be like selling insurance. If you think about it, why should you protect your tanks? It's an insurance policy that things are not leaking into the environment. That has implications, big time monetary. So, actually, I said, "Why don't you come back Monday? I have just the thing for you." He did. We hired him; he went to work, a very energetic guy. Certainly a champion of the product, he picked right up on it, ran with it single handed. . . . Now it's a growing business. It certainly is a valuable one too for the environment.

In the implementation of its marketing strategy, Gore has relied on cooperative and word-of-mouth advertising. Cooperative advertising has been especially used to promote GORE-TEX fabric products. Those products are sold through a number of clothing manufacturers and distributors, including Apparel Technologies, Lands End, Austin Reed, Timberland, Woolrich, North Face, Grandoe, and Michelle Jaffe. Gore has stressed cooperative advertising because the Associates believe positive experiences with any one product will carry over to purchases of other and more GORE-TEX fabric products. Apparently, this strategy has paid off. When the Grandoe Corporation introduced GORE-TEX gloves, its president, Richard Zuckerwar, noted: "Sports activists have had the benefit of GORE-TEX gloves to protect their hands from the elements. . . . With this handsome collection of gloves . . . you can have warm, dry hands without sacrificing style."

The power of informal marketing techniques extends beyond consumer products. According to Dave McCarter: "In the technical end of the business, company reputation probably is most important. You have to have a good reputation with your company." He went on to say that without a good reputation, a company's products would not be considered seriously by many industrial customers. In other words, the sale is often made before the representative calls. Using its marketing strategies Gore has been very successful in securing a market leadership position in a number of areas, ranging from waterproof outdoor clothing to vascular grafts.

Environmental Forces

Each of Gore's divisions have faced some environmental forces. The fabric division was hit hard when the fad for jogging suits collapsed in the mid-1980s. The fabric division took another hit from the recession of 1989. People simply reduced their purchases of high-end athletic apparel. By 1995, the fabric division was the fastest growing division of Gore again. The electronic division was hit hard when the mainframe computer business declined in the early 1990s. By 1995, that division was seeing a resurgence for its products partially because that division had developed some electronic products for the medical industry. As can be seen, not all the forces have been negative. The aging population of America has increased the need for health care. As a result, Gore has invested in the development of additional medical products and the medical division is growing.

Financial Information

As a closely held private corporation, W. L. Gore has kept its financial information as closely guarded as proprietary information on products and processes. It has been estimated that Associates who work at Gore own 90 percent of the stock. According to Shanti Mehta, an Associate, Gore's returns on assets and sales have consistently ranked it among the top 10 percent of the Fortune 500 companies. According to another source, W. L. Gore & Associates has been doing just fine by any financial measure. For 35 straight years (from 1961 to 1995) the company has enjoyed profitability and positive return on equity. The compounded growth rate for revenues at W. L. Gore & Associates from 1969 to 1989 was more than 18 percent discounted for inflation.[7] In 1969, total sales were about $6 million; by 1989, the figure was $600 million. As should be expected with the increase in size, the percentage increase in sales has slowed over the last five years (Figure 7.4). Gore

[7]In comparison, only 11 of the 200 largest companies in the *Fortune* 500 had positive ROE each year from 1970 to 1988 and only 2 other companies missed a year. The revenue growth rate for these 13 companies was 5.4 percent compared with 2.5 percent for the entire *Fortune* 500.

Figure 7.4 Growth of Gores Sales vs. Gross Domestic Product

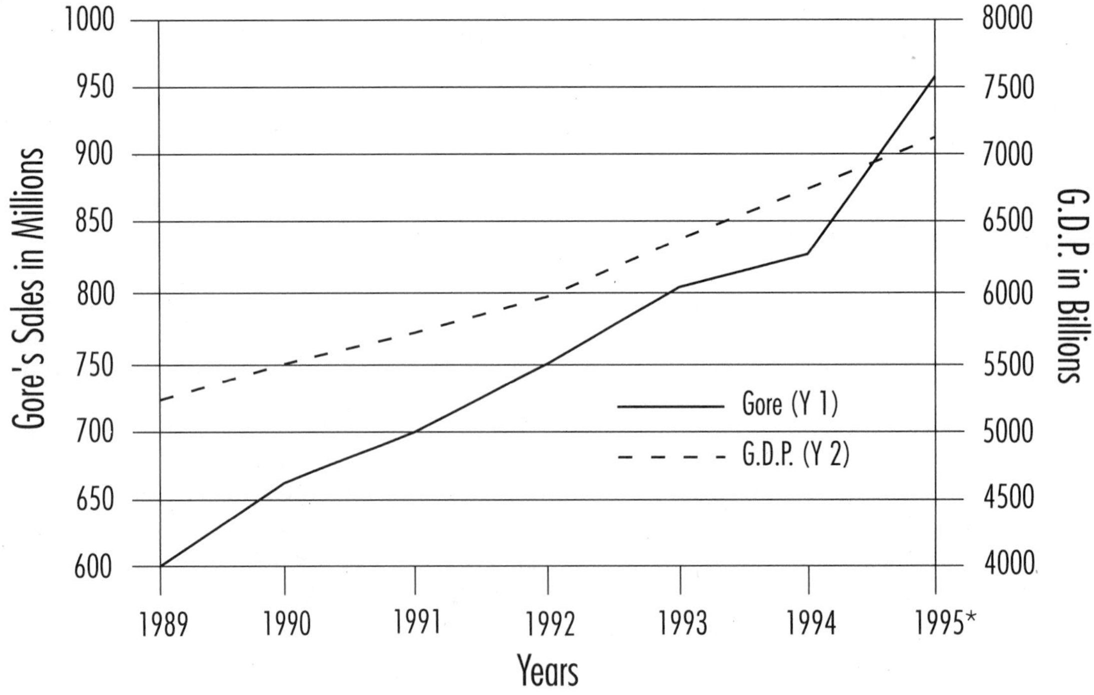

Gore's Sales in Millions (Y 1, 600–1000); G.D.P. in Billions (Y 2, 4000–8000); Years 1989–1995*

Gore (Y 1) — G.D.P. (Y 2)

	1989	1990	1991	1992	1993	1994	1995*
Gore	600	660	700	750	804	828	958
G.D.P.	5244	5514	5673	5951	6343.3	6738.4	7110

Note: *Estimated G.D.P. for 1995

financed this growth without long-term debt unless it made sense. For example, "We used to have some industrial revenue bonds where, in essence, to build facilities the government allows banks to lend you money tax free. Up to a couple of years ago we were borrowing money through industrial revenue bonds. Other than that, we are totally debt free. Our money is generated out of the operations of the business, and frankly we're looking for new things to invest in. I know that's a challenge for all of us today," said Bob Winterling. *Forbes* magazine estimates Gore's operating profits for 1993, 1994, and 1995 to be \$120, \$140, and \$192 million, respectively (Figure 7.5).

Figure 7.5 Operating and Net Profits of W.L. Gore & Associates

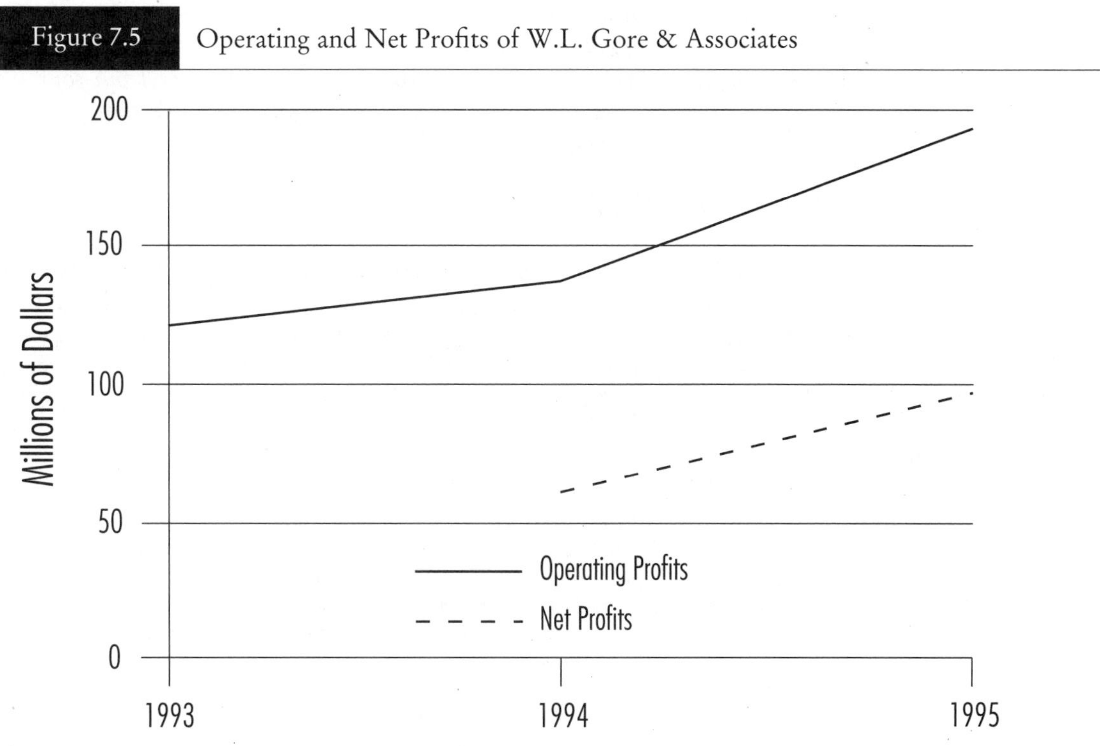

Operating Profits	120	140	192
Net Profits	N.A.	60	96

Data from Forbes Magazine's Annual Report on the 500 Largest Private Companies in the U.S.

When asked about cost control, Sally Gore had the following to say:

You have to pay attention to cost or you're not an effective steward of anyone's money, your own or anyone else's. It's kind of interesting, we started manufacturing medical products in 1974 with the vascular graft and it built from there. The Gore vascular graft is the Cadillac or BMW or Rolls Royce of the business. There is absolutely no contest, and our medical products division became very successful. People thought this was Mecca. Nothing had ever been manufactured that was so wonderful. Our business expanded enormously, rapidly out there [Flagstaff, Arizona] and we had a lot of young, young leadership. They spent some time thinking they could do no wrong and that everything they touched was going to turn to gold. They have had some hard knocks along the way and discovered it wasn't as easy as they initially thought it was. And that's probably good learning for everyone somewhere along the way. That's not how business works. There's a lot of truth in that old saying that you learn more from your failures than you do from your successes. One failure goes a long way toward making you say, Oh, wow!

ACKNOWLEDGMENTS

Many sources were helpful in providing background material for this case. The most important sources of all were the W. L. Gore Associates, who generously shared their time and viewpoints about the company. They provided many resources, including internal documents, and added much to this case through sharing their personal experiences as well as ensuring that the case accurately reflected the Gore company and culture.

BIBLIOGRAPHY

Aburdene, Patricia, and John Nasbit. *Re-inventing the Corporation.* New York: Warner Books, 1985.
Angrist, S. W. "Classless Capitalists." *Forbes,* 9 May 1983, pp. 123–124.
Franlesca, L. "Dry and Cool." *Forbes,* 27 August 1984, p. 126.
Hoerr, J. "A Company Where Everybody Is the Boss." *Business Week,* 15 April 1985, p. 98.
Levering, Robert. *The 100 Best Companies to Work for in America.* (See the chapter on W. L. Gore & Associates, Inc.) New York: Signet, 1985.
McKendrick, Joseph. "The Employees as Entrepreneur." *Management World,* January 1985, pp. 12–13.
Milne, M. J. "The Gorey Details." *Management Review,* March 1985, pp. 16–17.
Price, Kathy. "Firm Thrives without Boss." *Arizona Republic,* 2 February 1986.
Posner, B. G. "The First Day on the Job." *Inc.,* June 1986, pp. 73–75.
Rhodes, Lucien. "The Un-manager." *Inc.,* August 1982, p. 34.
Simmons, J. "People Managing Themselves: Un-management at W. L. Gore Inc." *The Journal for Quality and Participation* (December 1987): pp. 14–19.
"The Future Workplace." *Management Review,* July 1986, pp. 22–23.
Trachtenberg, J. A. "Give Them Stormy Weather." *Forbes,* 24 March 1986, pp. 172–174.
Ward, Alex. "An All-Weather Idea." *The New York Times Magazine,* 10 November 1985, sec. 6.
Weber, Joseph. "No Bosses, and Even 'Leaders' Can't Give Orders." *Business Week,* 10 December 1990, pp. 196–197.
"Wilbert L. Gore." *Industry Week,* 17 October 1983, pp. 48–49.

Excerpts from Interviews with Associates

The first excerpt is from an Associate that was formerly with IBM and has been with Gore for two years:

Q. *What is the difference between being with IBM and Gore?*

A. *I spent 24 years working for IBM and there's a big difference. I can go ten times faster here at Gore because of the simplicity of the lattice organization. Let me give you an example. If I wanted to purchase chemicals at IBM (I am an industrial chemist), the first thing I would need to do is get accounting approval, then I would need at least two levels of managers' approval, then a secretary to log in my purchase and the purchase order would go to Purchasing where it would be assigned a buyer. Some time could be saved if you were willing to "walk" the paperwork through the approval process, but even after computerizing the process, it typically would take one month from the time you initiated the purchase requisition till the time the material actually arrived. Here they have one simple form. Usually, I get the chemicals the next day and a copy of the purchase order will arrive a day or two after that. It happens so fast. I wasn't used to that.*

Q. *Do you find that a lot more pleasant?*

A. *Yeah, you're unshackled here. There's a lot less bureaucracy that allows you to be a lot more productive. Take Lab Safety for example. In my Lab at IBM, we were cited for not having my eyewash taped properly. The first time, we were cited for not having a big enough area taped off. So we taped off a bigger area. The next week the same eyewash was cited again, because the area we taped off was 3 inches too short in one direction. We retaped it and the following week, it got cited again for having the wrong color tape. Keep in mind that the violation was viewed as serious as a pail of gasoline next to a lit Bunsen burner. Another time I had the dubious honor of being selected the functional safety representative in charge of getting the function's labs ready for a Corporate Safety Audit. (The function was a third level in the pyramidal organization: (1) department, (2) project, and (3) function.) At the same time I was working on developing a new surface mount package. As it turned out, I had no time to work on development, and the function spent a lot of time and money getting ready for the Corporate Auditors who in the end never showed. I'm not belittling the importance of Safety, but you really don't need all that bureaucracy to be safe.*

The second interview is with an Associate who is a recent engineering graduate:

Q. *How did you find the transition coming here?*

A. *Although I never would have expected it to be, I found my transition coming to Gore to be rather challenging. What attracted me to the company was the opportunity to "be my own boss" and determine my own commitments. I am very goal oriented, and enjoy taking a project and running with it—all things that you are able to do, and encouraged to do within the Gore culture. Thus, I thought, a perfect fit!*

However, as a new Associate, I really struggled with where to focus my efforts—I was ready to make my own commitments, but to what?! I felt a strong need to be sure that I was working on something that had value, something that truly needed to be done. While I didn't expect to have the "hottest" project, I did want to make sure that I was helping the company to "make money" in some way.

At the same time, though, I was working for a plant that was pretty typical of what Gore was like when it was originally founded—after my first project (which was designed to be a "quick win"—a project with meaning, but one that had a definite end point), I was told "Go find something to work on." While I could have found something, I wanted to find something with at least a small degree of priority! Thus, the whole process of finding a project was very frustrating for me—I didn't feel that I had the perspective to make such a choice, and ended up in many conversations with my sponsor about what would be valuable. . . .

In the end, of course, I did find that project—and it did actually turn out to be a good investment for Gore. The process to get there, though, was definitely trying for someone as inexperienced as I was—so much ground would have been gained by suggesting a few projects to me and then letting me choose from that smaller pool.

What's really neat about the whole thing, though, is that my experience has truly made a difference. Due in part to my frustrations, my plant now provides college grads with more guidance on their first several projects. (This guidance obviously becomes less and less critical as each Associate grows within Gore.) Associates still are choosing their own commitments, but they're doing so with additional perspective, and the knowledge that they are making a contribution to Gore—which is an important thing within our culture. As I said, though, it was definitely rewarding to see that the company was so responsive, and to feel that I had helped to shape someone else's transition!

Beta Pharmaceuticals: Pennsylvania Distribution System

Case 8

Jack Sexton, manager of logistics planning, walked out of his boss's office with a frown on his face. He had just learned that the top management of his company, Beta Pharmaceutical, had been taking a closer look at cost levels in the company's distribution system. In particular, high transportation costs resulting from frequent minimum-size LTL (less than truckload) shipments to customers and low-volume resupply shipments to the smaller warehouses were beginning to raise eyebrows. Total warehousing and material-handling costs had also been questioned.

When he got back to his office, Mr. Sexton sat back and thought the problem over. He recalled that the present plant, warehouse, and customer configuration had evolved during a period of high-growth years, without the systematic development of a master distribution plan. Warehouse location and customer service decisions were based mainly on marketing-centered recommendations, competitive pressures, and customer desires. Customer order frequency and shipment size had been largely in the control of the customer. Basically, Beta believed that to achieve and maintain industry leadership, it was necessary to meet customer demand 100 percent of the time. Thus the cost of customer service, inclusive of distribution, had historically been very high.

Several days later Mr. Sexton settled on a course of action. Calling in a logistics consulting firm, HLW and Associates, he asked that a pilot study be conducted to evaluate a portion of the present product logistics system for cost-service effectiveness. The state of Pennsylvania was determined to be a "typical" subsystem within the national distribution network and was designated by Mr. Sexton as the focal point for the study.[1] An outline of the study proposal is shown in Exhibit 8.1.

Source: This case was prepared by Harvey Boatman, Paul Liguori, and Gary Wiser under the direction of Professor Alan J. Stenger, The Pennsylvania State University.

[1]Pennsylvania represents a "mini model" of the total system in that it contains a three-warehouse configuration, two customer service areas, a customer service representative, and a dollar demand pattern consistent with the rest of the national system.

Exhibit 8.1 Project Description

Project: How should Beta Pharmaceuticals distribute products to customers in the state of Pennsylvania?

Background: Beta currently distributes products to customers from public warehouses in Pittsburgh, Harrisburg, and Philadelphia.

- Cartage carriers are used in the three metropolitan areas.
- Common carriers are used in the balance of the state.
- Customers (hospitals) order both in patterns and randomly.
- Shipments are made within 24 to 48 hours of order receipt.
- Shipment sizes are small, from under 100 pounds to a few thousand pounds.
- The full product line is stocked in Philadelphia and Pittsburgh, but only a partial line is stocked in Harrisburg.
- Distribution costs are a significant element of total costs.

Objective: Determine the best method to distribute products to customers, considering the effects on:

- Distribution costs (freight and handling).
- Levels of customer service.
- Inventory levels.

Scope: The scope of the project should be restricted to the state of Pennsylvania to keep it manageable.

- Inventory policies and methods of replenishing warehouses should be ignored. However, the relationship between aggregate inventory levels and warehouse volume must be recognized.
- Customer order patterns can be assumed to be controllable within certain limits, to be defined. Customer contact will not be allowed.
- The number and location of warehouses should be determined.
- Methods of delivery should be determined, including such alternatives as (1) direct shipment or (2) scheduling of customer orders for pooled delivery, including contact with carriers for rates and feasibility.

Background

THE COMPANY

Beta Pharmaceuticals is a multidivisional manufacturer and distributor of a diversified line of medical care products. Manufacturing, sales, and distribution facilities are located throughout the world, with major operations existing in Europe, Africa, South America, Australia, Asia, Canada, and the United States. Products include intravenous solutions, artificial organs, disposable medical devices, clinical testing and diagnostic supplies and equipment, blood collecting and storage equipment, prescription drugs, and industrial and medical enzymes.

Beta has 12 production or research facilities in the United States, and markets its products through five customer-service or distribution-center regions. The company employs 13,600 persons throughout its worldwide system.

The backbone of Beta's strong marketing position in the hospital supply industry is a well-funded R&D program. New products, as well as improvements to existing products, are constantly being developed and exploited as a key element in market strategy and industry leadership. As a result of this philosophy, Beta increased the

1994 expenditures for research and development by 25.7 percent over 1993 for a total dollar investment of $46.7 million.

The aggressive competitive stance, supported by resourceful research and development, effective quality control, and customer-oriented distribution, has enabled the company to build a 16-year compound growth rate in sales and earnings per share of 20 percent. Its 1994 sales were $855.9 million, which represented a 27.7 percent increase over 1993. Earnings per share for 1994 were $1.95, a 23.4 percent increase over 1993.

THE DISTRIBUTION SYSTEM

The current distribution system used by Beta within the state of Pennsylvania makes use of three public warehouses: Philadelphia, Pittsburgh, and Harrisburg. From these three warehouses, Beta is able to serve most of its customers in 49 of the 67 counties in Pennsylvania: this service is supplemented by shipments from nearby out-of-state warehouses or by carload shipments direct from a Beta plant. The distribution responsibilities of the three Pennsylvania warehouses include shipments to out-of-state customers as well as to the Pennsylvania customers.

Beta maintains either a company-salaried customer service representative or a warehouse employee at each warehouse to handle orders and customer inquiries. Whenever an order is received, company policy dictates that it be filled and tendered to a carrier within 48 hours. Orders are received either electronically or by phone, direct at the warehouse or at company headquarters in Chicago. The 48-hour service goal starts at the point the order is received within the Beta system.

Once the warehouse receives the order, two possibilities exist. If the items are in stock, a bill of lading is cut and the freight is tendered to a common carrier or a cartage carrier. Of those shipments tendered to common carriers, 95 percent are delivered by the second morning. This means a maximum order filling time—including transportation—of four days 95 percent of the time. If the customer is located within the commercial zone of the city and a cartage carrier can be used, total time from order receipt by Beta to delivery to the customer is reduced to two days 95 percent of the time.

When sufficient stock is not available, the warehouse representative will contact the regional distribution center to which the warehouse is assigned. The regional distribution center will review the inventory levels of the surrounding warehouses and assign the order to one of these warehouses. Transportation cost is used as the basis for which warehouse should receive the order. If the item is not available in any of the surrounding warehouses, it will be back-ordered and expedited from a production facility. Since Beta wants to maintain high customer service levels, every attempt is made to maintain inventories high enough to avoid the need of back ordering to Chicago.

The majority of Beta's customers are hospitals. As such, they have limited storage space. They also cannot afford to wait very long after ordering items because their inventory averages approximately one week's demand. Since Beta is the major supplier of medical products in the Pennsylvania area, it falls upon them to provide hospitals with the required service. Traditional performance and marketing pressure have forced Beta into the position of maintaining inventory for its customers. However, very few of the shipments made by Beta are on a life-or-death basis for a patient.

Preliminary Findings and Plans of the Consultants

Beta's present distribution system is structured around basic customer service objectives. Competitive stress and rapid growth contributed to the piecemeal development of the present structure, wherein the customer sets the rules. This resulted in a number of marginal, close-to-the-customer warehouses. Warehouse-to-customer shipments are made without consideration of economic order quantities or potential savings to be recognized by shipping in consolidated lots. Many customers avoid assuming inventory responsibility and cost by ordering frequently, often at random intervals and in varying order quantities. Beta provides 24-hour delivery to all customers within the commercial zone of each warehouse, and 48-hour delivery to other customers. This situation has necessitated the establishment of safety stock of nearly 100 percent at most warehouses.

The piecemeal pattern of development has presented coordination problems at the corporate level. Many problems common to several areas are still handled on an individual basis at the local level. Rarely is the experience and information gained at one point generalized for the benefit of other areas of the system. The nearly exclusive use of public warehouses compounds this situation, particularly when quality control, damage, or liability become the question. The use of public warehouses also complicates the information-gathering process as well as making the control aspects of inventory more difficult to handle.

Even though growth potential remains high for Beta, a plateau has been reached in many areas. For example, the climb to leadership in the medical products industry has been achieved; a reputation for high standards, effective quality control, and an understanding for the specialized problems experienced by hospitals has been established; an impressive record of innovation and responsible research and development has been compiled. In essence, Beta has created a "pull" situation, in the marketing sense, for the products bearing the Beta trademark.

Beta presently has good information potential. Most operations-related facts are collected in the present system, but unfortunately those items not lost due to pure volume are presented in a manner that makes their usefulness limited and suspect. Feedback and information update is slow and complicated under the present system of hand tallies, verbal order placement at each warehouse, and conflicting loyalties (due to the nearly exclusive use of public warehouses). Control at the warehouse level is shaky at best.

The Pennsylvania Subsystem

The following information is available for the Pennsylvania subsystem:

1. *Monthly demand for Pennsylvania customers.* A computer printout for March 1995 gives demand by customers for each of Beta's major product

lines. It shows how many bills of lading were cut and the number of cases per product line on each bill. Every order shipped within the state of Pennsylvania is included, with coded identification of which warehouse filled the order. There is a considerable amount of overlap in the territory served by various warehouses. Out-of-state warehouses appear throughout the printout, indicating service to cities also serviced by the Pennsylvania warehouses. The monthly demand information gives no indication of the timing throughout the month for the orders. It is easy to identify how many shipments a customer received but not when they were received. Finally, there is no indication that March 1995 was a typical month in terms of demand level. A quarterly demand schedule was requested but not provided. As a result, the assumption that March 1995 is a typical month had to be made.

2. *Quarterly transportation cost.* This is a summary of the air and truck costs incurred by each of Beta's warehouses on an outbound basis by product line only. It does show total pieces and weight of each product line shipped by air and truck, but it does not break total cost down past a total for air and truck. Since the total cost is a three-month figure for all shipments out of a warehouse, an average cost would not truly reflect the intrastate rate levels.

3. *March payments to carriers.* Beta provided a list of the total billings for transportation charges paid to carriers in March 1995. The charges are broken down by product line pieces and weight. The list is not very useful because it is for bills paid in March, not for shipments made during March. Also, no information was provided concerning the number of shipments each carrier handled or the destination of these shipments.

4. *Warehouse throughput.* Beta was able to provide estimates of the average monthly throughput in terms of total cases for the three Pennsylvania warehouses, as follows:

Philadelphia:	50,000 cases
Pittsburgh:	35,000 cases
Harrisburg:	9,000 cases

   Warehouse capacity in both Philadelphia and Pittsburgh is large enough to handle the entire throughput of Harrisburg should that location be eliminated. Average monthly throughput would be useful in evaluating the methods of warehouse replenishment.

5. *Warehouse cost.* The three Pennsylvania facilities are public warehouses. Under the contract agreements with Philadelphia and Harrisburg, a single charge is assessed for each carton that comes into the warehouse. There is no annual rental fee, no quantity discount, and no penalty for falling below a minimum level. The single rate per carton includes storage, handling, stenciling, and anything else the warehouse people might have to do to the case. The charge in Philadelphia is 44 cents per case, while the

Harrisburg charge is 43 cents per case. Pittsburgh, which does not have the same type of arrangements, pays an average of 46 cents per case. There is no indication of how this figure would vary with different inventory levels. An additional 10 cents per case is assigned by Beta to each case handled through the Pittsburgh warehouse due to the presence of a Beta customer service representative in that city.

6. *Warehouse replenishment policy.* Beta will not retain a warehouse unless it can be replenished at least once a month in carload quantity. The information provided by Beta concerning actual replenishment schedules is very sketchy. Philadelphia and Pittsburgh are replenished on a carload basis once a week. However, no information was available as to how many cars per week were used, whether they get the 40,000-pound or the 60,000-pound carload rate, or whether additional demand would also move at carload rates. If Harrisburg is eliminated, inbound freight costs to Philadelphia and Pittsburgh will change. The Harrisburg replenishment schedule was stated to be once every two to three weeks and once a month.
7. *Average inventory level.* Both Philadelphia and Pittsburgh hold six weeks' demand in inventory, whereas Harrisburg holds eight weeks' demand in inventory. These figures were unfortunately subject to some uncertainty.
8. *Truck rates.* Evaluating configuration changes in the current system requires a comparison of total cost for both the present and proposed systems. Costing out a system requires a close estimate of the transportation costs generated by that system. In light of the restrictions of a linear programming algorithm in terms of homogeneous product and potential system requirement of over 2,000 rates, weighted rate per county was used. Since the three Pennsylvania warehouses service 49 counties in Pennsylvania, 40 weighted rates were obtained. A weighted rate assumes that all freight destined to a specific county is going to the one city where the major customers' demand is located. By selecting the city having the maximum flow of freight, variation from the actual rates is minimized. The weight break to that city is computed in terms of the average weekly tonnage coming into the entire county. This requires that a maximum of four shipments per month be allowed for any county. After one rate for each commodity group was established, the four rates were combined into one weighted rate, based on the percentage of the total weekly tonnage that the product line accounted for.

Propose several ways in which the Pennsylvania distribution system *might* be improved.

Case 9

Calox Machinery Corporation (A)

Mike Brown, international sales manager, tapped his pencil on the notepad and contemplated his upcoming discussion with Calox's executive committee concerning the distributor situation in New Zealand. The Labor Day weekend break had not been especially conducive to his sorting out the conflicting information and varied opinions concerning the New Zealand predicament. After only three months on the job Mike had not expected to be involved in a decision that would have such far-reaching consequences.

On paper the decision looked simple: whether or not to adhere to his earlier decision to replace the original New Zealand distributor, Glade Industries, with a newly formed company, Calox New Zealand, Ltd. Despite his newness to the company, Mike was confident that Calox's executive committee would agree with whatever recommendations he made in this situation, since he had been charged with "solidifying" the International Sales Division. If he decided to reverse his decision to terminate Glade Industries, could he "undo" any damage done so far?

Three previous faxes were spread on his desk along with the brief notes that he had jotted down during Thursday's conference call between Calox's executives and the company's legal counsel. Mike swung back to the PC behind his desk and began to draft what he hoped would be the definitive Calox policy for New Zealand.

The Company

Calox Machinery Company began in 1946 as a partnership between John Caliguri and William Oxley. The two engineers met during World War II and discovered mutual interests in mechanical engineering and construction. Both were natives of Kansas City, and at the end of the war they established a partnership with the expressed purpose of developing high-quality excavation equipment and accessories. Their first

Source: This case was prepared by Lester A. Neidell, Professor of Marketing, University of Tulsa.

product was an innovative hydraulically-operated replacement blade for a light-duty scraper.

Calox's principal customers were independent contractors engaged in excavation of building sites, and airport and highway construction and maintenance. Calox's products were primarily replacement items for OEM (original equipment manufacturer) parts and accessories. Some OEM sales were achieved; that is, contractors could order new equipment from OEMs with Calox blades and accessories already installed. Growth over the years was slow, but steady.

The product line expanded to include payloader buckets, a number of dozer and scraper blades, and parts for aerial equipment including construction forklifts and snorkels. A key to the company's success was their specialty status; their products were used to enhance the performance of expensive equipment produced by Caterpillar, Eaton, International Harvester, Case, and other OEMs. Calox's strategy was simply to provide a better part, often at a premium price, and to have it readily available in the field through a network of strong distributors. Direct competitors in the United States included small specialty producers such as Bobcat, Dresser, and Gradall, as well as the parts divisions of the large OEM manufacturers. Primary competitors in international markets included Terex, Deutsch, Takeuchi, and Hitachi. William Oxley compared Calox to the Cummins Engine Company, which had achieved a superior position in the diesel engine market through a similar strategy.

The partnership was replaced by an incorporated structure in 1970, when Bill Oxley Jr., became CEO. Despite slow growth of the U.S. economy, both 1990 and 1991 were very good years for Calox; annual sales increases of 12 percent were achieved, and the company set profit records each year. Sales for the 1991 fiscal year broke the $70 million barrier for the first time in the company's history. That year, approximately 280 people were employed at the single location in Kansas City, of which three-fourths were hourly workers engaged in fabrication.

International Sales

Calox's first international sale occurred in 1971, when the company responded to an unsolicited inquiry and shipped a small order to Canada. International sales languished throughout the 1970s, when a great deal of construction was put on hold due to the "energy crisis." Channels of distribution for international sales were much the same as for domestic sales. Independent distributors were given nonexclusive rights, although in practice most countries had only one distributor. Forty of Calox's 110 distributors were located outside the United States. In 1991 almost 25 percent of Calox's sales were generated internationally. In the 1988 to 1991 period, aided by the relative decline of the U.S. dollar against most other currencies, international sales grew at an annual rate of 16 percent.

Prior to Mike's arrival, there was no uniform procedure by which Calox investigated foreign markets and appointed distributors outside the United States. Bill Lawrence, Mike Brown's predecessor, essentially ran export sales as a one-man operation. Since Calox had very limited international experience, and most international markets were relatively small compared to the United States, primary market research was considered to be an unnecessary expense. In those countries guesstimated to have large enough markets, Bill obtained a list of potential distributors by advertising in that country's construction journal(s) (if available) and principal newspapers. He then made a personal visit to interview and select distributors. In smaller markets, distributors were appointed through one of two methods. Most commonly, Bill appointed a distributor after receiving an unsolicited request. In a very few cases, distributor applications were solicited via advertisements as in "large" markets, which were then reviewed in Kansas City. In all cases in which personal visits were not made, distributor applicants had to submit financial statements. Efforts to interview distributor applicants by telephone were not always successful, due to time constraints and the lack of a suitable translation service.

THE NEW ZEALAND DISTRIBUTORSHIP

In 1986 Calox appointed G.W. Diggers, Ltd., as its agent for New Zealand. This arrangement was a novel one, for G.W. Diggers was also a producer of excavating equipment. Because of some earlier poor experiences in certain foreign markets, Calox had instituted a policy of not distributing through any company that also manufactured excavating equipment. This policy was not followed in New Zealand because of the limited distributorship options available. At the time of the appointment, the owner of G.W. Diggers, Geoff Wiggins, assured Calox that the two lines were complementary rather than competitive, and that he intended to keep it that way. During 1989, G.W. Diggers purchased $800,000 of equipment and supplies from Calox.

In 1990 an abrupt change occurred in what had been a very successful, if short, relationship. G.W. Diggers was purchased by a large New Zealand conglomerate, Excel Ltd., which gave a new name, Glade Industries, to its excavating facility. The former owner of G.W. Diggers, Geoff Wiggins, was not associated with Glade Industries. Mike Brown's predecessor felt that the acquisition by Glade could only help Calox's position in New Zealand, because the resources available through Excel, Glade's parent company, were so much greater than what had been available to G.W. Diggers.

However, it soon became apparent that working with Glade was going to be very challenging. Glade raised prices on all Calox products in stock. Then they complained that Calox products were not selling well and that a "rebate" was needed to make Calox's products competitive in the New Zealand market. Simultaneously, Glade began production of a line of products competitive with Calox, but of a substantially poorer quality. During 1991 sales to Glade were virtually zero, and market information obtained by Calox indicated that Calox's former position in the New Zealand market was being occupied by Wescot Industries, with products imported from Great Britain. Table 1 gives annual sales of Calox products to G.W. Diggers and to its successor, Glade Industries.

Mike Brown began his new job as international sales manager for Calox in June 1992. A few weeks after arriving at Calox, Mike received a long letter from Geoff Wiggins. Geoff suggested that the situation in New Zealand was critical, and that he would

Table 1 Annual Sales to G.W. Diggers and Glade Industries (in Thousands of U.S. Dollars)

Sales to G. W. Diggers				Sales to Glade		
1986	1987	1988	1989	1990	1991	1992 (6 months)
21	310	535	801	105	70	10

be willing and able to establish a new distributorship, Calox New Zealand, Ltd., to be exclusive distributors of the Calox product line. Mike then invited Geoff to come to Kansas City the last week of July to discuss the proposal. Mike found Geoff to be very affable, technically knowledgeable, and an excellent marketing person. In the time period since selling his business to Excel Ltd., Geoff had been working as a general contractor. The 24-month "no-compete" clause Geoff had signed when he sold G.W. Diggers had expired. Geoff provided figures that indicated New Zealand's 1991 imports of excavating equipment were roughly NZ$2 million, out of a total domestic market of nearly NZ$3 million. (In 1991, US$1 = NZ$0.62.) He claimed that G.W. Diggers had achieved, at the height of its success, almost a 50 percent share of the New Zealand market. Geoff argued persuasively that with his personal knowledge of New Zealand's needs, Calox could once again achieve a dominant market position. With the blessing of the vice president of marketing, Mike and Geoff shook hands on a deal, with the exact details to be worked out by mail and faxed over the next few weeks. Geoff urged that time was of the essence if Wescot's market advances were to be slowed, and left a $100,000 order for 75 units to be shipped in 120 days, but not later than November 15, 1992.

COMMUNICATIONS WITH GLADE

Mike began to prepare a letter of termination to Glade. However, before this was completed, Calox received three mailed orders from Glade, totaling $81,000. This was the first contact Mike had with Glade and the first order received from Glade in five months. Because the standard distributor's agreement required a 60-day termination notice, Mike felt the Glade orders had to be honored.

A short time later Calox received a letter in the mail from Glade stating that they had heard rumors that another company was going to supply Calox products to Glade's customers and that delivery had been promised within 150 days. The letter continued by saying that this information could not possibly be true because Glade had an exclusive distributor agreement. This was news to Mike as well as to others at Calox headquarters because it was against company policy to grant exclusive distributorships. A search of Bill Lawrence's files turned up a copy of the initial correspondence to Geoff Wiggins, in which Geoff was thanked for his hospitality and a sole distributorship arrangement was mentioned. However, the distributorship agreement signed with Wiggins was the standard one, giving either party the ability to cancel the agreement with 60 days' notice.

Mike and the other senior Calox executives assessed the situation at length. The letter mentioning the "sole distributor agreement" was in a file separate from all other New Zealand correspondence. It was nothing more than a statement of intent and probably not legally binding in the United States. However, New Zealand courts might not agree. Further, the distributorship agreement should have been renegotiated when Excel purchased G.W. Diggers, but this had not happened. Glade could make a case that the distributorship had endured for two years under the existing agreements, which included the letter in which exclusivity was mentioned.

Mike determined that the "sole distributorship" letter also contained "extenuating circumstances" language which Calox could use to justify supplying the new New Zealand distributorship:

> *[T]here may be occasions in the future, when, due to unforeseen circumstances, some entity in your nation refuses to purchase any other way than direct from our factory. We do not want to lose any potential sales, however we pledge our best efforts to cooperate with you for any such possible sales should they present themselves and provided there is a reasonable profit to be made on such sales by us and cooperation can be worked out.*

The letter also specifically stated that all agreements between Calox and G.W. Diggers were subject to the laws of Missouri. Furthermore, Mike felt that Glade had not lived up to the actual signed distributorship agreement in that Glade had not promoted Calox products, had not maintained adequate inventory, and had engaged in activities and trade practices that were injurious to Calox's good name.

Armed with this information, Mike sought legal counsel, both in the United States and New Zealand. After a week, Calox's U.S. attorney, based on their own investigations and those of a law firm in Christchurch, New Zealand, offered four "unofficial" observations:

1. New Zealand is a "common law" nation, whose commercial law is similar to that of the United States.
2. It was possible to argue that because G.W. Diggers had changed ownership, previous agreements might not be binding. However, the most likely court finding would be that there was an implied contract between Calox and Glade on the same terms as with G.W. Diggers, because numerous business dealings between Calox and Glade had occurred after the takeover.
3. Calox was required to give Glade 60 days' termination notice.
4. There was a possibility that a New Zealand court would agree to assume jurisdiction of the case.

After reviewing the above issues Mike suggested to Calox senior management that Glade be terminated. Mike reasoned that Glade would react in one of two ways. One possibility was that they would accept termination, perhaps suggesting some minor compensation. A second scenario was that Glade would attempt to renegotiate the distributorship agreement. Mike was instructed to draft and fax a termination letter to Glade. This letter, sent by fax on August 20, is reproduced in Exhibit 9.1. The next day the first order for the new distributorship was shipped; the expected arrival date in New Zealand was October 10, 1992.

Exhibit 9.1 Fax from Calox to Glade, August 20, 1992

Calox Company, Inc.
P.O. Box 21110
Kansas City, MO 64002
U.S.A.

August 20, 1992

Mr. Ian Wells
Group General Manager
Glade Industries
39 Ames Road
Christchurch, New Zealand 2221

Dear Mr. Wells:

This letter is to inform you that Calox Company terminates any International Distributor's Sales Agreement or other Distribution Agreement that you may have or be a party to as Distributor expressly or impliedly with Calox Co. as Manufacturer. Said termination is effective 60 days from the date of this letter.

During the past year the following have gravely concerned us and effectively shut off our sales to the New Zealand market.

Reorganization of G.W. Diggers under Glade leading to continuous loss of personnel knowledgeable of the excavation business and difficulty for Calox's understanding with whom we are doing business. In June 1990, we were advised by telex that we were dealing with Excel Ltd., not G.W. Diggers or Glade.

Only $10,000 purchases for an eight-month long period from us, which we clearly found led to major loss of Calox sales to the marketplace and a complete domination of the excavation business by Wescot Industries, a major competitor.

Lack of effort on the part of Glade in promoting our product and maintaining effective selling facilities.

Numerous complaints to us from customers in New Zealand about Glade continually changing policies, lack of stock, and wildly increasing prices have clearly pointed out that our reputation, as well as G.W. Diggers, has been badly hurt and will impair sales for some time to come.

No progress has been made in introducing our heavy industrial line to the New Zealand market despite assurances from Glade personnel that progress would be made.

We have thoroughly investigated the New Zealand market and now have firmly decided that it is time for Calox to make a change in its distribution of products.

For the long term, this will allow us to best carve out a full niche in a market we and you have allowed competitors to dominate for too long. We must guarantee ourselves a consistent, aggressive sales effort in the market, which will not be subject to the effects of major policy changes such as those we have seen from Glade.

While two shipments are already en route to you, order number 52557 has not yet been completed for shipment. Since it will be ready imminently, please let us know immediately whether you wish, under the circumstances, to receive shipment or to cancel this order.

Sincerely,

Michael Brown
International Sales Manager

Exhibit 9.2 Fax from Glade to Calox, August 24, 1992

Glade Industries
39 Ames Road
Christchurch, New Zealand 2221

24 August 1992

Mr. Michael Brown
International Sales Manager
Calox Company, Inc.
P.O. Box 21110
Kansas City, MO 64002
U.S.A.

Dear Sir:

We acknowledge receipt of your letter dated 20 August 1992.

We are currently discussing its contents with our solicitors. They are also reviewing the distribution agreement.

Please proceed with the shipment of order #52557.

Yours faithfully,

GLADE INDUSTRIES LTD.
Ian Wells
Group General Manager

Glade's faxed reply, dated August 24, was not encouraging (see Exhibit 9.2). It appeared that Mike and the rest of the Calox management team had miscalculated. Despite the tone of the Glade letter, and the expressed request to ship order #52557, Mike suggested to the executive committee that no additional product be shipped to Glade.

While Mike and the rest of Calox management was deciding how to respond to Glade's initial rejection of the termination letter, a longer fax, one with a more conciliatory tone, dated August 31, was received from Glade (see Exhibit 9.3). In this letter Glade argued that Calox's best interests were served by working with Glade and mentioned an order for approximately ten times the "normal" amount of product. However, the order was not transmitted with the fax letter. Glade offered (for the first time) to come to Kansas City for a visit.

Glade's conciliatory letter created a great deal of consternation at Calox headquarters. Its arrival the week before Labor Day meant that holiday plans would have to be placed on the back burner while a suitable response was formulated. Two distinct camps developed within Calox.

One set of managers, whose position was supported by Mike Brown, felt strongly that despite potential legal risks, retaining Glade as a distributor would be a bad business decision. Although Glade had made promises and was offering to renegotiate, it was still producing a competitive line. Also, Glade's historical performance did not augur well for Calox's long-term competitive situation in New Zealand. The "extraordinary" order was viewed as a ploy to entice Calox into continuing the relationship. It was likely to take upwards of two years for all that machinery to clear the New Zealand market. Cognizant of Glade's earlier price manipulations, many of this group

Exhibit 9.3 Fax from Glade to Calox, August 31, 1992

Glade Industries
39 Ames Road
Christchurch, New Zealand 2221

31 August 1992

Mr. Michael Brown
International Sales Manager
Calox Company, Inc.
P. O. Box 21110
Kansas City, MO 64002
U.S.A.

Dear Sir:

I refer to your letter dated 20 August 1992, terminating our agreement which was executed on 28 February 1986.

In accordance with this agreement and attached to this letter is our order #A1036, for 600 products and parts. We would be pleased if you would confirm this order in due course.

We respectfully ask that you reconsider your termination decision as we believe that it is not in your best interests for the following reasons:

1. G.W. Diggers/Glade were not achieving an adequate return on investment until June 1991. An unprofitable distributor certainly is not in your best interests as principal.

2. The individuals that contributed to that unprofitable performance are no longer working for our company. Incidentally I understand that you have appointed Mr. Geoffrey Wiggins to a position as distributor in New Zealand. How can you justify appointing the person responsible for your market share decline over the past three years?

3. Our purchases certainly have been reduced the last nine months due to our need to get inventory down to lift overall return on investment. That situation has now been corrected with the order attached to this letter.

4. We now have a young aggressive marketing team, all highly experienced in marketing products of a similar nature to yours. When Bill Lawrence was in New Zealand, I advised him that I was restructuring our marketing group. A resume on our three senior marketing men is attached. These men have all commenced in the last four months. I am confident that this team will achieve market leadership in New Zealand and selected export markets with or without Calox's involvement. We have already commenced targeting Wescot's customers. Our recommendation is that you renegotiate your distribution agreement with us, with the inclusion of mutually agreed performance targets which will satisfy your objectives in terms of profitability and market share from the New Zealand market. I would like you to advise me a time which is convenient to you, for me to meet with you in Kansas City to commence negotiation of this distributor agreement.

Yours faithfully,

GLADE INDUSTRIES LTD
Ian Wells
Group General Manager

These are the three new men who have commenced to work for us:

Sean Cox, Sales Manager

35 years old. Formerly CEO of Sean Cox Industries of Christchurch. SCI was the chief contractor for the Auckland airport, but sold its business to Midland Industries. Mr. Cox has fifteen years' experience in the construction industry.

Joshua Dunn, Sales Representative, North Island

46 years old. Formerly an independent sales representative for various equipment manufacturers, including Hitachi and Ford New Holland.

Brian Muldoon, Sales Representative, South Island

23 years old. Construction engineering degree from New South Wales Institute of Technology (Sydney, Australia). Formerly a management trainee with our parent company, Excel Ltd.

felt that Glade might resort to "fire sale" prices when confronted with a large inventory, further damaging Calox's reputation as a premier supplier.

This camp considered that Calox's long-term interests would best be served by terminating the Glade distributorship and completing a formal agreement with Geoff Wiggins. However, there was concern that outright rejection of the Glade order would add to potential legal problems.

These managers also suggested that any further correspondence with Glade should emphasize that Calox could and would exercise a unique product repurchase option upon termination of the distributorship. This provision in the distributorship contract provided that Calox, upon proper termination of the distributorship by either party, could repurchase all remaining Calox inventory from the distributor at 80 percent of its net sales price to the distributor. Thus, if Calox did produce and ship the large Glade order, Calox would, if the order were shipped normally via sea freight, be able to buy it back for 80 percent of the price paid by Glade before it ever reached New Zealand.

The alternative camp wanted to forestall any legal battles. Headed by the U.S. sales manager and the comptroller, they argued that Glade had finally "gotten its act together" and that the new Glade team of three sales executives would provide greater market coverage than Geoff Wiggins's "one man show." This group introduced the possibility of reopening negotiations with Glade, supplying Glade by diverting the order already shipped to Geoff Wiggins, and producing the (yet unreceived) large Glade order.

By Wednesday, September 2, the two sides had hardened their positions. Mike was determined to break with Glade and begin anew in New Zealand. However, he was concerned about legal ramifications, and, on Thursday, September 3, Calox's executive committee and Mike conferred with their Kansas City attorneys via a conference call.

The lawyers agreed that any further business conducted with Glade would be detrimental to a termination decision. They warned that despite the termination letter (Exhibit 9.1) any further shipments to Glade would likely yield a court ruling that the distributorship was still in effect and, furthermore, that the buyback provision could not be enacted. They also said that if all business with Glade were terminated, and Glade did come to the United States to file, the most they would be likely to receive if they won the court case were the profits on the new sales to Geoff Wiggins, which amounted to $10,000. This sum was probably not large enough to warrant legal action by Glade, especially considering the apparently poor financial situation at Glade and the expense of initiating legal action in the United States.

At the end of this conference call, which lasted about 30 minutes, Bill Oxley Jr. turned to Mike and said, "Mike, I'm off to the lake now for the holiday. I'd like your recommendation Tuesday morning on this Glade thing."

Case 10

Calox Machinery Corporation (B)

Mike Brown decided that, despite the potential legal risks, sound business practice dictated that he follow through with the termination of Glade's distributorship, and his recommendation to that effect was accepted by the Calox executive committee. Mike's letter fax of September 9 (Exhibit 10.1) was very specific. First, he restated that it was in the best interests of both parties to terminate the distributorship. Second, since there was no prospect that the Glade order could be completed and delivered prior to the termination date of October 20, 1992 (60 days from the first letter; see Case A, Exhibit 9.1), he made it known that Calox would exercise its buyback option if Glade did indeed forward the missing order. Following legal advice, Mike added the caveat, "We are open to your comments, of course." The legal reasoning behind this was that if Calox did begin producing the large Glade order, and then bought it back while it was on the open seas, it could be interpreted by the courts that Calox was deliberately attempting to damage Glade financially.

Glade's "hardball" reply (Exhibit 10.2) was discouraging. In it Glade requested an accounting of sales to other distributors, claiming that they (Glade) were legally entitled to recover all Calox profits from these sales. Several Glade executives began to waffle, and proposed again the solution of diverting the order already shipped to Geoff Wiggins, producing the (still unreceived) large Glade order, and renegotiating with Glade (see Case A.)

Before an acceptable response could be agreed upon, another fax (Exhibit 10.3) was received from Glade. In this conciliatory letter, Glade offered to forgo any claims if their large order was completed and if Calox agreed not to exercise their buyback right.

Calox management breathed a huge sigh of relief and instructed Mike to inquire about the specifics of the order, complete it, ship it to Glade, and be done with them! Mike, however, felt it was necessary to obtain additional legal counsel before doing this.

Source: This case was prepared by Lester A. Neidell, Professor of Marketing, University of Tulsa.

The lawyers were emphatically negative. They felt quite strongly that if Calox shipped the large order, the courts would rule the original agreement binding, despite all the communication about termination. The courts would interpret the correspondence as a ploy by Calox designed to coerce Glade into placing a large order. They reiterated their previous advice that at the current time, Glade could only obtain minimal damages in U.S. courts; it would hardly be worth Glade's time and energy.

Mike and the company's legal counsel agreed that a final letter had to be written to Glade that would summarize the communications between Calox and Glade and make perfectly clear Calox's position. This letter had to clearly impart that Calox, with the advice of legal counsel, did not recognize as valid Glade's claim that any agreement had been breached. Glade, in fact, had violated the previous distributorship agreement by failing to market Calox's products. Due to Glade's negligence, Calox had sustained damage to their reputation and good name, so that any legal recompense would be forthcoming to Calox. Calox's intent in the New Zealand market was to repair the damage that Glade had done to Calox's reputation by forging ahead with an aggressive new distributor.

Exhibit 10.1 Fax from Calox to Glade, September 9, 1992

Calox Company, Inc.
P. O. 21110
Kansas City, MO 64002
U. S. A.

September 9, 1992

Mr. Ian Wells
Group General Manager
Glade Industries
39 Ames Road
Christchurch, New Zealand 2221

Dear Mr. Wells:

Reference your 31 August letter, we must regretfully advise that we feel it is in our best interest to continue with our termination of sales to Glade Ltd. as we explained. We appreciate the points you made in your letter, but nevertheless remain convinced that working with Glade Industries Ltd. is not the best way for Calox to achieve its goals in New Zealand.

While we have not yet received your order number A1036 for 600 items referenced in your letter, I should point out that first, Calox is not able to complete an order for all 600 items prior to the termination date, and second, we would want to exercise our option to purchase back all good outstanding products at 80% of our net selling price.

In consideration of these factors, we do not believe it advisable to accept your offer. We feel that this would only affect your situation and we do not seek to take advantage of you in this regard. We are open to your comments, of course.

Sincerely,

Michael Brown
International Sales Manager

Exhibit 10.2 Fax from Glade to Calox, September 14, 1992

Glade Industries
39 Ames Road
Christchurch, New Zealand 2221

14 September 1992

Mr. Michael Brown
International Sales Manager
Calox Company, Inc
P. O. Box 21110
Kansas City, MO 64002
U. S. A.

Dear Sir:

I acknowledge receipt of your letter of 9 September 1992.

I am very concerned at the position in which Calox Co. has been selling direct into New Zealand to Glade's customers. This is in direct contravention of your obligations and undertakings under the Distributor Agreement between us and in particular in breach of the undertaking contained in your letter of 27th January 1986.

We have clearly suffered loss and damage as a result of these actions on your part in breach of the Distributor Agreement which we would be entitled to recover in legal proceedings.

We therefore seek from you a full account of all sales made by you direct into New Zealand in breach of the agreement and payment to us of all profits made by you in respect of those sales.

Yours faithfully,

Glade Industries, Ltd.
Ian Wells
Group General Manager

Exhibit 10.3 Fax from Glade to Calox, September 17, 1992

Glade Industries
39 Ames Road
Christchurch, New Zealand 2221

17 September 1992

Mr. Michael Brown
International Sales Manager
Calox Company, Inc.
P. O. Box 21110
Kansas City, MO 64002
U. S. A.

Dear Sir:

I refer to my open letter of 14 September 1992.

As indicated in that letter we are most concerned at the loss and damage we have suffered by your acting contrary to the terms of the existing Distributor Agreement.

We are, however, prepared to forgo our rights in relation to those breaches in return for your agreeing to supply the 600 items referred to in our order #A1036 and not to seek to exercise any rights of repurchase in relation to those items upon termination of the agreement.

Yours faithfully,

Glade Industries Ltd.
Ian Wells
Group General Manager

Hewlett-Packard Company: Developing and Packaging Marketing-Friendly Services

Case 11

Hewlett-Packard is a leading global information technology firm; in 1994, the company's revenue was more than $25 billion. HP has been widely recognized for its excellence in quality and support. Its service and support organization, with 17,500 service professionals, accounted for revenue of $3.6 billion in 1994. In the late 1980s and early 1990s, HP experienced a dramatic shift in its mix of product sales from its direct sales force to indirect channels. This shift in sales mix, in turn, required a substantial change in HP's service strategies. Although the company was successful in selling products through independent resellers, the sale of services was a completely different matter. Channel partners viewed services as complex, difficult to understand, difficult to sell, and burdensome to contract. This Best Practice Case Study describes how HP responded to this challenge by developing a creative service packaging concept designed specifically for channel firms and their customers that purchase low-end products. In the process, HP found a means of generating more sales of services via indirect channels than it did in the past.

HP SupportPack

The HP SupportPack is basically a "packaged" service—that is, a service in a box—that simplifies the sales administration purchasing processes for both the customer and the indirect channel firm selling HP products and services. Pricing, which is typically for a three-year period, of HP SupportPack is based on an "insurance model," that is, the average price (per "pool" of devices) based on an expected probability that only a certain (small) number of devices will actually require service. Designed with dual value propositions, HP SupportPack provides:

Source: This case was written by Richard C. Munn. Best Practice Case Studies provide analysis of a particular company's service marketing strategies and practices, and are presented as educational cases for service marketing professionals. The information in this case study is believed to be reliable but cannot be guaranteed to be correct or complete. The analysis and commentary are the opinions of the author.

- **Customers** with a simple means of contracting for services, delivered by HP, for their printers, personal computers, fax devices, plotters, and so on (that is, HP's low-end, high-volume product line).
- **Indirect channel firms** with a marketing-friendly service package that can be purchased, inventoried, and sold like a product by itself that also offers attractive profit potential.

An Idea Is Spawned

Although the HP SupportPack was first introduced in the United States in 1993, its origins go back to 1990 when Hewlett-Packard in the United Kingdom started thinking about a way to simplify, or "package," services for the dealer channel. Unlike the market in the United States, where many channel firms had developed their own in-house service capability, the vast majority of computer resellers relied on manufacturers or third-party firms for a service solution. HP believed that it should be able to capture more of the potential service business on its products but was frustrated by using the same service sales approach (with indirect channel firms) that had been so successful with its direct sales force.

In the United Kingdom, as in the United States and most other parts of the world, computer resellers are normally led by sales-oriented management, and the business mentality is characterized by "let's move boxes." "You can touch them, buy them, hold them in inventory, show and demonstrate them if need be. You know what they cost and given some experience, you can forecast their sales. Not so with services. Services are intangible, they're more vague, more complex, usually a number of people are involved in getting a service contract signed, and all in all services are much more complicated to deal with."

Hewlett-Packard's European service marketing group, led by Alois Hauk, worked on the U.K. concept further and decided to pilot a service product that could be packaged and sold much like a "box" of software. The product concept was to provide an enhancement to the basic product warranty, which would provide service coverage for three years. Unlike the version that was introduced in the United States in 1993, the European version provided for on-site service the following day (the first version of HP SupportPack in the United States provided for product exchange and did not offer an on-site service option).

Customers could buy this service coverage at the time of product purchase and count on Hewlett-Packard for a quality service response. The "box" was nicely packaged to be displayed beside the HP product at the computer reseller store. The "box" contained a registration card, a label to affix to the HP product showing product serial number, the HP SupportPack serial number, instructions to call a specific HP telephone number for support, procedures to follow, and basic but fairly simple terms and conditions. The computer resellers could buy and stock these HP support "boxes" much like they buy and stock hardware products.

With a recommended selling price (U.S. price range for product exchange version) aimed at 10 percent to 20 percent of the street price of the hardware product, the HP SupportPack would normally provide greater margin to the channel partner than those realized on hardware sales.

HP decided to conduct its first market test of HP SupportPack in the United Kingdom in September 1991 and a second market test in France in February 1992. Based on successful experiences with both market tests, HP rolled out the product throughout Europe a year later and expanded the original concept to cover 150 different HP products with 15 different SupportPacks ranging over 15 different pricing "bands."

A Word about Channel Partners

There has been a great deal of research and study of the computer and peripheral distribution channel over the past few years. Probably some of the best research has been done by Merrin Information Services, Inc. of Palo Alto, California.

Merrin believes that there are, in general, four distinct types of customers that purchase personal computers and related peripherals and software:

- **Vertical-market customers** that are buying industry- or application-specific systems and related support and services.
- **Large corporate customers** that try to standardize on an approved list—for example, a few vendors of PCs, peripherals, or software—and frequently have their own support staff or have outsourced end-user support.
- **Medium-size companies and organizations** that normally have in-house support resources for end users.
- **Small office/home office (SOHO) customers** that rely on an in-house "expert" or turn to some outside source for support and service.

Merrin has segmented the various resellers and channel firms into the following categories:

- **Direct vendors,** such as Dell and Gateway 2000, that sell directly to customers. These vendors take "first" service calls and try to resolve as many problems as possible over the phone. On-site and some depot-type services are usually outsourced to a few large nation/worldwide service organizations.
- **Computer (outbound) dealers,** such as CompuCom, Dataflex, ENTEX, ComputerLand, MicroAge, Inacom, and so on. These dealers focus primarily on the large corporate and medium-size company customers. The parent company usually has a sizable corporate service capability; but many times franchisees may have their own in-house service department or have an established service relationship with some independent service organization.
- **Direct dealers,** such as MicroWarehouse, PCs Compleat, PC (or Macintosh) Connection. These dealers rely on catalogs, direct-mail pieces, and telemarketing, and will sell to a variety of customers. Although these firms

typically provide excellent software and product installation/configuration assistance via the phone, hardware services are not featured in their marketing strategies.

- **VARs/systems integrators** that primarily sell industry or application-specific systems and provide ongoing application support. These firms will frequently provide some of the services required (especially application support, installation assistance, and so on) directly and contract out other parts of the total service requirements.
- **Computer superstores,** such as CompUSA, Computer City, Micro Center. These are very large stores, anywhere from 12,000 to 20,000 square feet, and have wide breadth and depth of product selection and somewhat to reasonably knowledgeable sales staff. These stores have highly visible in-store service departments and, for the most part, market their own service contracts.
- **Office product superstores,** such as Office Depot and Staples. These stores normally sell general office products and supplies but frequently offer a limited selection of PC products, peripherals, and software.
- **Consumer electronic stores,** such as Circuit City, Best Buy, Lechmere, and The Good Guys! These stores are now offering a moderate selection of PC products, peripherals, and shrinkwrapped software. Service is normally performed by their own staff at in-store service depots, although there are also "back-end" service arrangements with independent firms.
- **Software stores,** such as Babbage's, Electronic Boutique, and Egghead. These stores focus primarily on software but will occasionally offer a limited selection of peripherals, supply items, and so on.
- **Warehouse membership clubs,** such as PriceCostco (the result of the merger between Price Club and Costco) and Sam's Club. These stores sell a wide variety of consumer and business products in a warehouse format.
- **Mass merchants,** such a Kmart, Target, and Wal-Mart. These stores do very well with lower-priced PC peripherals, accessories, and supply items, but PC buyers typically would go to some other source.

In a series of Channelmarker™ newsletters in late 1993 and early 1994, Merrin Information Services presented its analysis of the psychographic profiles of various PC product shoppers and the value propositions that these channel firms provide. Psychographic variables that tend to influence where computers are purchased include:

- Price sensitivity
- Comfort level with PC technology
- PC product experience level

- Convenience of and familiarity with the source
- Availability of technical support

Although this may be somewhat self-evident, Merrin concludes that the best or easiest prospect to sell to is an experienced buyer—that is, someone who has already purchased and has had experience with a personal computer, and is reasonably self-confident in his or her ability to install software, add peripherals, and use a personal computer.

Merrin points out that computer buyers come in all shapes and sizes but tend to differentiate on two dimensions: price sensitivity and comfort level with technology.

What Does All This Have to Do with HP SupportPack?

First, no matter what type of channel firm, the salesperson has very, very little capacity to understand complex service offerings or to spend more than a minimal amount of time explaining service and support options to a prospective buyer. Point-of-sale materials and packaging that explains the service product are very important. Second, the majority of these channel firms, other than VARs and systems integrators, are geared to holding inventory, displaying, and selling physical units (stock-keeping units or SKUs) and the HP SupportPack fits this model. In Merrin's analysis, the following types of channel firms "attract" the more price-sensitive and low-comfort-level-with-technology buyers, *not* HP's target buyer:

- Classic consumer electronic stores
- Office product superstores
- Hybrid consumer electronic stores
- Warehouse membership clubs

A seasoned PC user who has experienced a service incident in particular, that is, product malfunction and requirement for break-fix service, has a reference point for considering whether or not to purchase the HP SupportPack with the corresponding HP product. A first-time buyer with an appreciation for the cost and problems of downtime who is looking for a simple "what happens if it breaks?" answer would also find the HP SupportPack of value. In both cases, however, there *must* be a discussion (sales dialogue) between a service-knowledgeable sales person and a prospective buyer.

The ideal buyer for Hewlett-Packard would tend to have these characteristics:

- Reasonable comfort level with PC technology.
- Prior PC product experience (especially when there is a history of a break/fix experience)
- SOHO user where the PC or peripheral is used in a critical, high-availability application.

- Not overly price sensitive

Merrin, in its psychographic analysis of buyers going to different classes of channel firm, would probably say that the "best" firms for HP to focus on would be:

- **Computer (outbound) dealers** with a knowledgeable and competent sales staff
- **Computer stores** (not necessarily superstores with their in-house service centers)
- **Direct dealers,** especially if they will "advertise" the HP SupportPack in their catalogs

Avoiding Channel Conflict

HP has been very careful to avoid channel conflict. The HP SupportPack is a service product designed specifically for channel partners to be sold at or very near the time—that is, within 30 days—of product purchase. HP SupportPack is not sold by HP's direct sales force. Larger customers that purchase a substantial amount of HP technology products, even though they deal with a direct HP salesperson, are normally directed to a channel firm to actually purchase their products and HP SupportPacks.

The HP SupportPack Model

The basic HP SupportPack model is fairly simple but quite elegant in its simplicity. Someone who purchases low-end HP products—ranging from peripheral devices to PCs—can, within 30 days of purchase of the product, elect to purchase an HP SupportPack. HP SupportPack provides Baseline Technical Telephone Support, which provides technical assistance for installation and normal operation of the HP product, including assistance with product configuration and setup, and hardware problem resolution. Depending on the particular HP product, the customer may opt to have HP On-Site Support (either priority or next day) or HP Express Exchange Service.

Under the Express Exchange Service option, HP will send a permanent replacement unit, freight prepaid, via premium air freight carrier, typically to arrive the next day (not including weekends or HP holidays). The customer is expected to return the defective unit within three working days of receipt of the shipment of the product replacement.

Originally, customers could expect that HP SupportPack would have a retail list price of between 10–20 percent of the "street price" of the associated product for HP Express Exchange Service. However, with the introduction of On-Site SupportPacks,

HP has moved to a value pricing model which reflects the various service levels. Each HP SupportPack is now priced to provide the most competitive three-year cost of ownership within that particular product class. HP SupportPack provides service coverage starting with the date of purchase of the HP hardware product and terminates three years later. In effect, this is prepaid service for a three year period.

The customer must return a registration card to Hewlett-Packard within ten days of purchasing HP SupportPack and may transfer HP SupportPack coverage to a subsequent owner. The customer affixes an HP SupportPack label, showing product model number and serial number, to the HP product and refers to the information on this label if service is needed. Customers may call Hewlett-Packard from 8 A.M. to 5 P.M. local time, Monday through Friday, state that they are an HP SupportPack customer, and describe any problem they might be having. If HP is unable to resolve the problem over the phone, it will either dispatch a service person or arrange for a product exchange, depending on the type of contract.

Although these elements [constitute] the generic HP SupportPack model for the most part, it is also important to consider the packaging of the basic generic product. Exhibit 1 provides an example of how HP SupportPack is packaged for both the buyer and the seller.

The slick 5-by-10-inch HP SupportPack packet contains:

- A "Dear Customer" letter with simple instructions describing the steps to register as an HP SupportPack customer and how to obtain service
- A self-mailing registration card, HP SupportPack label, and a repeat of many of the simple instructions in the "Dear Customer" letter
- A card providing HP SupportPack information—for example, HP SupportPack model number, products covered, and type of service (Express Exchange or On-Site Service)—and some brief questions and answers about HP SupportPack
- A small pamphlet with a description of the service and terms and conditions

It is also important to note that in this HP SupportPack architecture, HP has substantially reduced the costs of billing, collection, and administration. Consider the following:

- HP SupportPacks purchased in quantity by channel firms are already "credit checked."
- Customers prepay for three years of service.
- Customers maintain the service administration "database" (date of purchase, service contract length, serial numbers of products and HP SupportPack, "what to do" procedures, and so on)—not HP and not the channel partner.
- Service "files" are only opened when there is an actual incident and service request.

Exhibit 1 H-P SupportPack Packaging

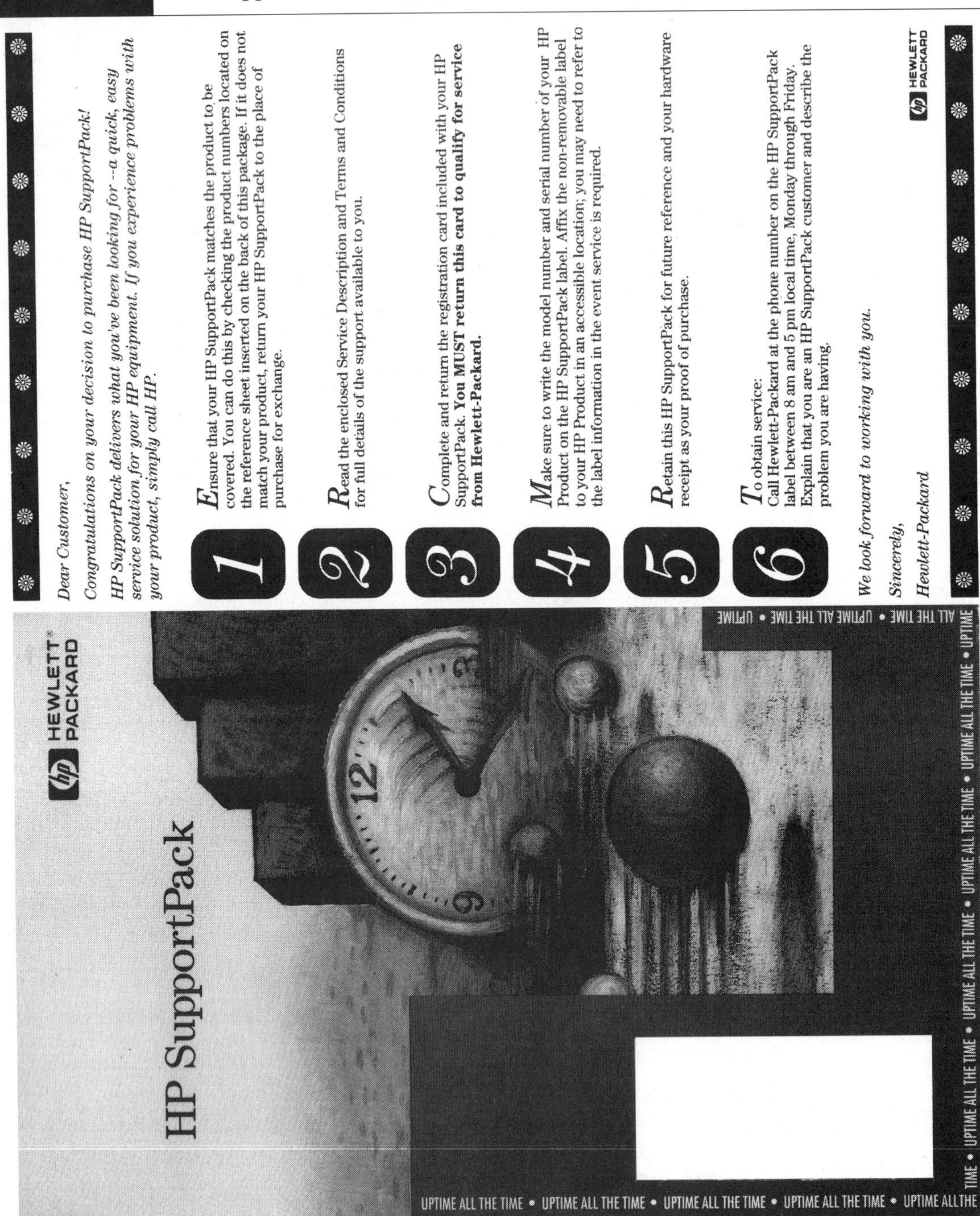

HEWLETT® PACKARD
HP SupportPack
UPTIME ALL THE TIME • UPTIME ALL THE TIME • UPTIME ALL THE TIME • UPTIME ALL THE TIME • UPTIME ALL THE TIME • UPTIME
Dear Customer,
Congratulations on your decision to purchase HP SupportPack!
HP SupportPack delivers what you've been looking for --a quick, easy service solution for your HP equipment. If you experience problems with your product, simply call HP.
1 Ensure that your HP SupportPack matches the product to be covered. You can do this by checking the product numbers located on the reference sheet inserted on the back of this package. If it does not match your product, return your HP SupportPack to the place of purchase for exchange.
2 Read the enclosed Service Description and Terms and Conditions for full details of the support available to you.
3 Complete and return the registration card included with your HP SupportPack. You MUST return this card to qualify for service from Hewlett-Packard.
4 Make sure to write the model number and serial number of your HP Product on the HP SupportPack label. Affix the non-removable label to your HP Product in an accessible location; you may need to refer to the label information in the event service is required.
5 Retain this HP SupportPack for future reference and your hardware receipt as your proof of purchase.
6 To obtain service:
Call Hewlett-Packard at the phone number on the HP SupportPack label between 8 am and 5 pm local time, Monday through Friday. Explain that you are an HP SupportPack customer and describe the problem you are having.
We look forward to working with you.
Sincerely,
Hewlett-Packard
HEWLETT PACKARD

Source: Hewlett-Packard Company.

(continued)

Exhibit 1 *continued*

Important...

To activate your HP SupportPack service, follow these simple instructions.

1 Complete and return the registration card included in your HP SupportPack.

- You must complete the registration card in its entirety and return it to Hewlett-Packard to qualify for service.

2 Write the model and serial number of your HP product to be covered on the HP SupportPack label.

3 Peel off the above HP SupportPack label and affix it to your HP product.

- Place label in an accessible location. Do not place on any moving parts or product accessories. If service is required, the information on this label will be needed.

4 Retain the HP SupportPack box for reference and your receipt as your proof of purchase.

- We suggest that you place all the contents of your HP SupportPack, including both the receipt of your hardware product covered and that of your HP SupportPack, in this box.

HP SupportPack Registration Card HEWLETT® PACKARD

Note: you must return this card to Hewlett-Packard to be eligible for service.

Customer Information

Name Position Department

Company Name Street Address

City, State, County Zip Code

Telephone Number Fax number

Product Information **HP SupportPack information**

Product covered under HP SupportPack Place of purchase

Model number Purchase price of HP SupportPack

Serial number Purchase date of HP SupportPack

Purchase date of hardware product Today's date

Priority (4-Hour) On-Site Support SP 02A994

HP SupportPack

H5487A

Priority (4-Hour) On-Site Support

Exhibit 1 *continued*

HP SupportPack Information

HP SupportPack No.: **H5461A**

Service Level: **Express Exchange**

DeskJet 320
DeskJet 320 w/Sheet feeder
DeskWriter 320
DeskJet 320 w/Sheet feeder
DeskJet 540
DeskWriter 540

Questions and Answers about HP SupportPack

Q. How does HP SupportPack work?
Once you've purchased your HP SupportPack, if your HP product malfunctions for any reason (except abuse, negligence or accident), simply call the HP SupportPack phone line. If our customer support technicians can't resolve the problem over the phone, we'll send out a permanent replacement product to you immediately.

Q. How do I activate HP SupportPack?
Simply send in the registration card and place the HP SupportPack label on your product. You're then covered for a full 3 years from the date of hardware product purchase.

Q. Who provides the HP SupportPack Service?
The service is provided directly by Hewlett-Packard, so you are assured of the highest level of quality and support.

Q. How fast will I get the replacement?
If you call before 6:00 pm eastern time, a replacement unit will be sent out the same day via a premium air carrier. You'll receive your replacement unit the following business day.

Q. What is the replacement like?
All HP replacement products are completely remanufactured, then thoroughly tested and approved to meet the same quality standards as new HP products.

Q. Is there anything else I should know?
Yes. HP SupportPack is only available for new HP products purchased within the last 30 days. HP SupportPack only covers products in good working condition and products for which it is registered.

This product is printed on recyclable paper.

Exhibit 1 *continued*

HEWLETT® PACKARD

HP SupportPack

Service Description and Terms and Conditions

HP SupportPack Service Descriptions

As indicated on your HP SupportPack box and label, you will receive one of the following services:

A. HP On-Site Support

Priority On-Site Service Level: Provides HP's best possible response time during coverage hours of 8:00 am to 5:00 pm, Monday through Friday. HP will arrive at your site to begin hardware maintenance service within four hours of calls received between 8:00 am and 5:00 pm local time, for sites located within one hundred miles of a primary HP Support Responsible Office.

Next Day On-Site Service Level: HP will arrive at your site to begin hardware maintenance service between 8:00 am and 5:00 pm local time, Monday through Friday, during the next working day after the day a call is received. This applies to sites within one hundred miles of a primary HP Support Responsible Office.

Table 1. HP's Response Time for Travel
If on-site assistance is required, an HP engineer arrives at your site as quickly as possible, within the response times shown below:

Distance from customer-designated site to primary HP Service Responsible Office	**Response Time**	
	Priority Support	**Next Day Support**
0 - 100 miles	4 hours	Next working day
101 - 200 miles	8 hours	1 additional coverage day
201 - 300 miles	*	2 additional coverage days
over 300 miles	*	*

* Established at time of service call and subject to resource availability

Baseline Technical Telephone Support: Provides technical assistance for installation and normal operation of standard configuration for selected HP products; including assistance with product configuration and set-up, and hardware problem resolution. Assistance is available 8:00 am to 5:00 pm, Monday through Friday, local time.

B. HP Express Exchange Service

HP will send a permanent replacement unit, freight prepaid, via premium airfreight carrier to the customer who calls the HP Customer Support Center between 9:00 am and 6:00 pm eastern time, Monday through Friday, except for HP holidays. The replacement unit will be free of major cosmetic defects. The customer must return the defective unit within 3 working days of receipt of the shipment to HP. If the failed product is not received by HP within 10 days of the customer's receipt of the replacement product, the customer will be billed the product's list price less any applicable discounts. Service is limited to the continental U.S., as well as restricted areas of Alaska, Hawaii, and Puerto Rico.

HP Support Specifications
HP will provide all labor, parts, and materials necessary to maintain in good operating condition products covered by this Agreement. At the time of repair, HP may install engineering improvements and modifications and will perform preventive maintenance services such as cleaning and inspecting. Replacement parts will be new or their equivalent; replaced parts will become the property of HP. For on-site services, Customer is responsible for providing access to HP products and for ensuring that a representative is present while service is being performed. HP performs all services during HP's normal business hours, excluding HP holidays.

HP SupportPack Service Agreement

Terms and Conditions

1. Support Services: HP will provide the support services described in this Agreement for hardware products purchased in the United States.

2. Charges: Customer will prepay for HP SupportPack at the time of purchase. Customer will pay all applicable taxes. Refunds for prepaid services are available from the place of purchase only if customer cancels within thirty days of purchase of HP SupportPack.

3. Eligible Products: Only those hardware products purchased within the last thirty days, in good operating condition at time of purchase of HP SupportPack, and at current specified revision levels are eligible for support. HP reserves the right to inspect registered product to ensure product is in good operating condition. Work performed by HP to meet these requirements is subject to HP's standard service rates. Services available through HP SupportPack apply to the hardware product for the term of the HP SupportPack, regardless of change in hardware product ownership. Customer's relocation of products may result in additional support charges and modification of response times.

4. HP warrants replacement parts provided to maintain hardware products serviced hereunder are warranted against defects in materials and workmanship. If HP receives notice of defective replacement parts during the term of this Agreement, HP will, at its option, repair or replace the replacement parts that prove to be defective.

THE ABOVE WARRANTY IS EXCLUSIVE AND NO OTHER WARRANTY, WHETHER WRITTEN OR ORAL, IS EXPRESSED OR IMPLIED. HP SPECIFICALLY DISCLAIMS THE IMPLIED WARRANTIES OF MERCHANTABILITY AND FITNESS FOR A PARTICULAR PURPOSE.

5. Remedies and Liability: For any material breach of this Agreement by HP, Customer's remedy and HP's liability will be limited to a refund of price paid for the HP SupportPack for hardware products at issue. HP will not be liable for performance delays or for nonperformance due to causes beyond its reasonable control. HP will be liable for bodily injury or death to the extent that any HP service sold hereunder is determined by a court of competent jurisdiction to be defective and to have directly caused such bodily injury or death. HP will be liable for damage to tangible property per incident up to the greater of 300,000 dollars in damage to tangible property or the purchase price of the specific hardware product being serviced in the event that any HP service sold hereunder is determined by a court of competent jurisdiction to be defective and to have been directly caused by such damage to tangible property.

THE REMEDIES PROVIDED IN THIS AGREEMENT ARE CUSTOMER'S SOLE AND EXCLUSIVE REMEDIES. EXCEPT AS INDICATED ABOVE, IN NO EVENT WILL HP OR ITS SUBCONTRACTORS BE LIABLE FOR LOSS OF DATA OR FOR DIRECT, SPECIAL, INCIDENTAL, CONSEQUENTIAL (INCLUDING LOST PROFIT), OR OTHER DAMAGE WHETHER BASED IN CONTRACT, TORT, OR OTHERWISE.

6. Limitations of Service: HP does not provide support for nonqualified products. "Nonqualified" products are hardware and software not supplied or approved by HP and hardware products for which Customer does not allow HP to incorporate modifications. Customer is responsible for removing nonqualified hardware products to allow HP to perform support services. If support services are made more difficult because of a nonqualified product, HP will charge Customer for the extra work at HP's standard rates.

Services do not cover any damage or failure caused by:

a. use of non-HP media and supplies or use of items not designed for use with products; or

b. site conditions that do not conform to HP's site specifications; or

c. fire or water damage, neglect, improper use, including burned monitor screens, electrical disturbances, transportation by Customer, work or modification by people other than HP employees or subcontractors, or other causes beyond HP's control.

7. Customer is responsible for registering hardware product to be supported by mailing the registration card to HP within ten days of purchase of HP SupportPack, or, in the case of a used hardware product, within ten days of purchase from previous owner. HP is not obligated to provide support services if Customer does not register hardware product as stated herein. Customer will immediately place adhesive HP SupportPack label on support hardware product, in position indicated by HP. If Express Exchange service is purchased and service is requested, Customer will provide credit card number or purchase order number to HP and return defective unit within three days of receipt of replacement unit. Customer will provide HP service personnel with operating supplies used during normal operation. Customer is responsible for the security of its proprietary and confidential information and for maintaining a procedure external to the hardware products for reconstruction of lost or altered files, data, or programs. Customer must notify HP if any hardware product serviced are being used in an environment that poses a potential health hazard to HP employees or subcontractors (HP may require Customer to maintain such products under HP supervision.). Customer must have a representative present when services are being performed by HP on site or by telephone. If remote support is available, allow HP to keep system and network diagnostic programs resident on Customer's system for the exclusive purpose of performing diagnostics. Customer acknowledges that Customer has no ownership interest in diagnostic software provided by HP and that HP will remove these diagnostic programs and any HP loaned modems upon termination of this Agreement. Customer's system must be configured to permit access to one voice-grade telephone line and one data-quality telephone line; both must have terminations located near Customer's system. Upon HP's request, Customer will run HP-supplied diagnostic programs before having a hardware product serviced under this Agreement.

8. Term: This Agreement will begin on the date of purchase of the HP hardware product to be supported and terminate three years thereafter.

9. Termination: Customer may terminate this Agreement by returning the HP SupportPack and label to place of purchase at any time within 30 days of purchase of HP SupportPack. HP may terminate at any time after the effective date of this Agreement if Customer fails to perform or observe any other condition of this Agreement with HP.

10. Governing Laws: Any disputes arising in connection with this Agreement will be governed by the laws of the State of California. The courts of the State of California shall have jurisdiction.

11. Entire Agreement. The terms and conditions of this Agreement constitute the entire understanding between the parties relating to the provision of services listed on the preceding page and will supersede any previous communication, representation or agreement whether oral or written. Customer's additional or different terms and conditions will not apply. Customer's acceptance of this Agreement is deemed to occur upon Customer's registration for service, or failure to return HP SupportPack product to place of purchase within 30 days, or HP's provision of any support services. No change of any of the terms and conditions will be valid unless in writing signed by an authorized representative of each party.

Exhibit 1 *continued*

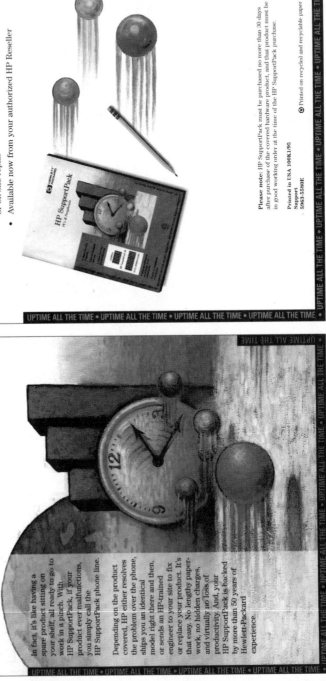

HP SupportPack

HEWLETT® PACKARD

It's a great way to keep you going

Want the peace of mind that comes from knowing your HP PC or peripheral will stay up and running? Then choose HP SupportPack. It's a support solution that covers your HP product *for a full 3 years.* That's right. With this smart and affordable solution, your investment in your Hewlett-Packard products is safe and secure.

In fact, it's like having a spare product sitting on your shelf, all ready to go to work in a pinch. With HP SupportPack, if your product ever malfunctions, you simply call the HP SupportPack phone line.

Depending on the product covered, HP either resolves the problem over the phone, ships you an identical model right there and then, or sends an HP-trained engineer to your site to fix or replace your product. It's that easy. No lengthy paperwork, no hidden charges, and virtually no loss of productivity. And, your HP SupportPack is backed by more than 50 years of Hewlett-Packard experience.

UPTIME ALL THE TIME • UPTIME ALL THE TIME • UPTIME ALL THE TIME • UPTIME ALL THE TIME •

HEWLETT® PACKARD

HP SupportPack

Maximize your productivity

- Affordable price, 3-year hardware support
- Coverage of all parts and labor–no hidden costs
- Simple registration
- Direct phone number for prompt service
- Prompt service by phone, next-day exchange, or on-site repair
- Available now from your authorized HP Reseller

Please note: HP SupportPack must be purchased no more than 30 days after purchase of the covered hardware product, and that product must be in good working order at the time of the HP SupportPack purchase.

Printed in USA 100K1/95
Support
5963-5580E

Printed on recycled and recyclable paper

UPTIME ALL THE TIME • UPTIME ALL THE TIME • UPTIME ALL THE TIME • UPTIME ALL THE TIME •

Value Proposition for Channel Partners

We mentioned at the beginning of this case study that HP SupportPack offers dual value propositions—one for customers and one for indirect channel firms. Let's focus on the value proposition for channel partners.

One of the major issues for channel firms has been and continues to be the severe pressure on margins. Many firms are dealing with razor-thin margins on products, frequently because of their own inclination to compete on price. Any business proposition that offers greater margins is carefully listened to. One HP executive said, "The value proposition for channel partners has to be margin, margin, margin. Everything else is a 'nice-to-have.'"

The characteristics of HP SupportPack that are most attractive to channel partners include the following:

- It is a means of increasing margins when sold at time of product purchase (see analysis later in this section).
- The product is easy to sell with attractive point-of-sale marketing materials, and HP provides co-op incentives.
- It can be bought like a product, stocked like a product, and sold as a product, which fits the way channel firms are geared to do business.
- Administration costs are much lower than typical service contracts.
- The product is exclusive for channel partners.
- The product comes from a firm with an excellent quality and service reputation.
- It provides an answer to those customers that want service, and reduces the need for investment and operating costs for their own service infrastructure.

Although we don't have exact pricing information, we can make some educated estimates and construct a financial model for a channel firm (see Exhibit 2).

Our basic assumption is that the actual margin available from hardware products (because of "special" sales and a competing-on-price mentality) is around 10 percent. We estimate that the margin available to the channel partner on HP SupportPack is more like 25 percent.

Assuming that the street price for an HP LaserPrinter or similar device is $1,200 and the HP SupportPack sells at a price of 15 percent of the product street price or $180, then the following financial scenario could exist:

- The total price to a customer for the hardware product and HP SupportPack would be $1,380, that is, 15 percent higher than a product-only sale.
- At the same time, the margin to the channel partner would be a combination of $120 (the margin on the hardware product and $45 for the margin on HP SupportPack.

Under this scenario, a channel partner firm would be increasing its margin by 38 percent while only increasing the sale price by 15 percent.

Given the channel partners need for margin, margin, margin, HP SupportPack can be a very attractive product to sell.

Exhibit 2 Estimate of SupportPack Impact on Channel Firm Margins

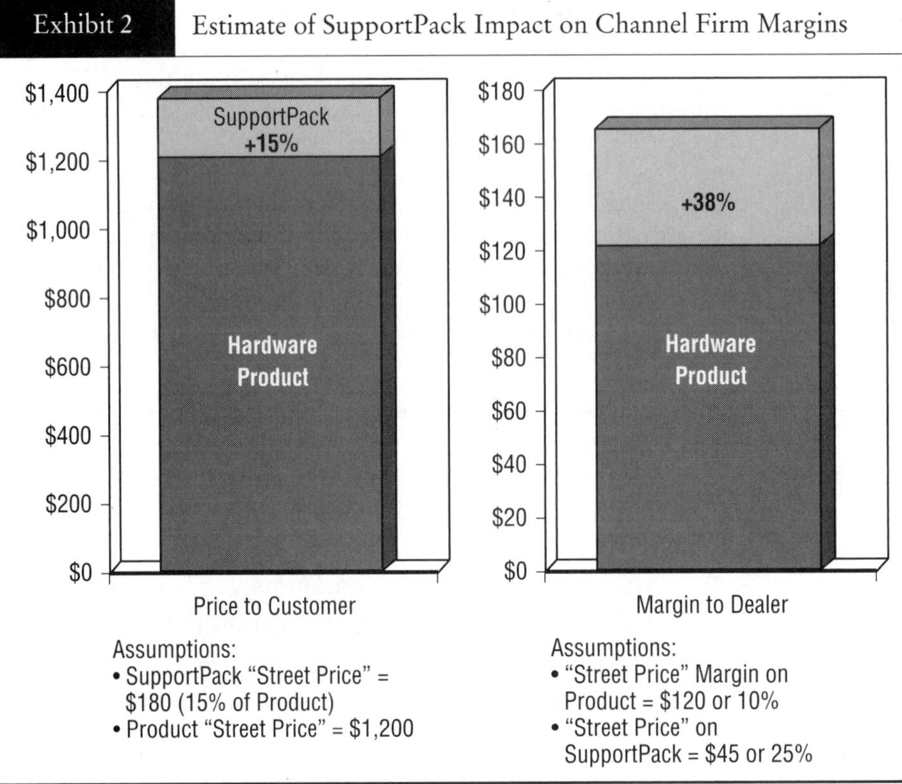

Source: ITSMA

Figure 1 illustrates the benefits, that is, value propositions to both customers and channel partners.

A Third Value Proposition

Years ago a very wise advertising executive came to the conclusion that many companies spend a lot of effort developing marketing propositions and communicating with a target (prospects) customer population, and educating and supporting a sales force to sell a particular product. Although many companies do that fairly well, many fall down on communicating, or selling, with another important constituency—other company employees.

This wise advertising executive pointed out that this third constituency had a great deal of influence over a product's success. Some of this influence came from informal conversations between employees and customers, employees and suppliers, employees and analysts, employees and the media, and so on. And some of it came from the enthusiasm and interest that employees developed for a new product that in turn infected others in the organization.

Gary Khederian, program manager, Channels Support Marketing, Worldwide Customer Support Operations (WCSO), says that although he mostly worries

Figure 1 Dual Value Propositions - HP SupportPack

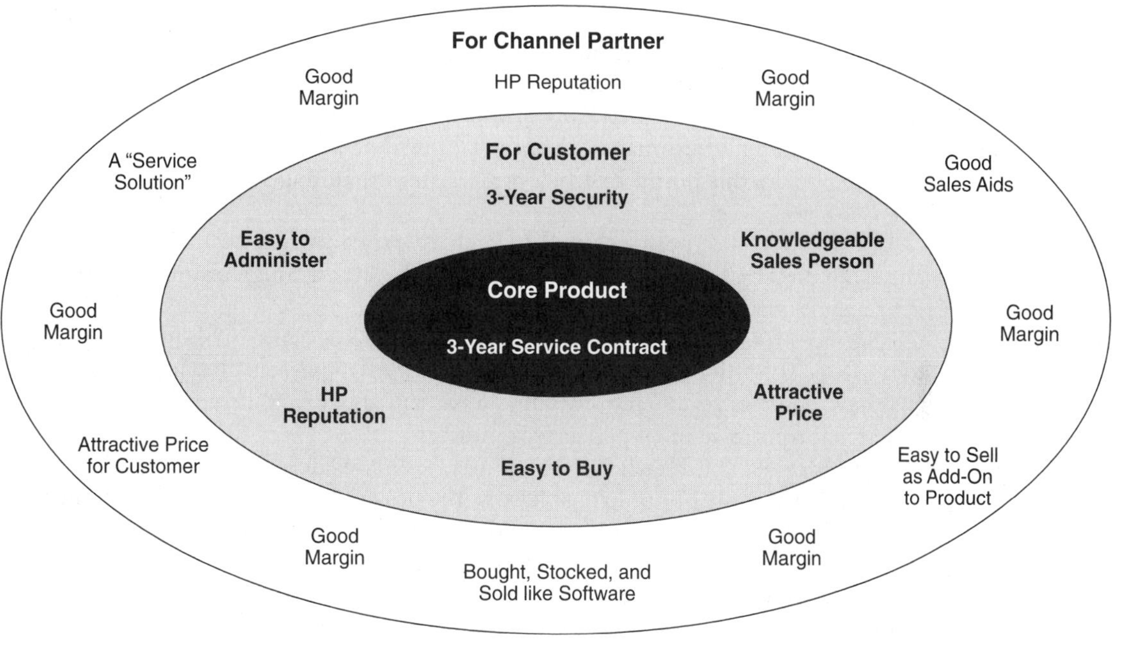

Source: ITSMA

about the marketing/selling messages for channel firms and the ultimate customer, he also spends a fair amount of effort "selling" the product marketers on including HP SupportPack in *their* selling material, for example, packaging, sales collateral, in-store promotions, price lists, and so on. Mr. Khederian believes that the product marketers have come to realize that HP SupportPack enhances their products and adds to the overall value proposition for each product.

Necessity is the Mother of Invention—Another Stimulus

The HP SupportPack came about as a result of trying to find a technique for selling more services through alternate channels and providing customers with a simple-to-buy and cost-effective service solution. But there was another important motivator for HP.

Starting in the late 1980s and continuing into the early 1990s, HP experienced a fairly significant shift in the mix of product sales sold directly compared with those sold through channels. The good news was that the low end of HP's product line—that is, laser printers, ink jet printers, personal computers, and so on—was enjoying tremendous market success, and HP's channel strategy was viewed as being more and more successful. There were, however, two growing concerns on the part of HP's (service) management. First, at that time, HP was finding that a much smaller percentage of these low-end products were sold with service contracts, and as a consequence, the strong leverage HP's service organization played in creating and maintaining loyalty was not being brought into play with smaller customers. Second, overall services revenue (including services revenue from accounts sold and serviced directly by Hewlett-Packard *and* services that somehow came about through channel firms) was flattening and could conceivably decline given this changing mix in direct versus indirect product sales.

I'll use some "guestimates" about what Hewlett-Packard may have been looking at to help make this point. Exhibit 3 represents a planning scenario summary to use as an exercise.

In the 1990 time period, Hewlett-Packard probably had a 50-50 mix of product sales sold directly by its own sales force and indirectly through channels. Total product revenue was around $11 billion.

Services revenue of $2 billion was split with 90 percent attributable to the customer base sold by Hewlett-Packard directly and 10 percent that came via indirect channels. Services revenue expressed as a percentage of total revenue by channel was 25 percent for direct and 4 percent for indirect.

The forecast that Hewlett-Packard may have considered for the 1995 time period showed that the mix of product or hardware sales might swing as much as going from 50-50 percent to 25 percent direct and 75 percent indirect, reflecting the growing success of Hewlett-Packard's low end product line.

Now comes the problem or challenge for customer service. As Ross Perot was fond of saying during the 1992 presidential campaign, "Stay with me on this one."

Assume that Hewlett-Packard felt that the same service percentage rate that held in 1990—that is, 25 percent and 4 percent—would also hold in 1995. If that were the case, total service revenue in five years would have grown only 25 percent—that is, from $2 billion to $2.5 billion —while product revenue was doubling, and total revenue would go from $13 billion to $24.5 billion, an 88 percent increase.

Exhibit 3 Planning Scenario for Changing Mix of Sales (Circa 1990*)

	1990			1995		
	Direct	Indirect	Total	Direct	Indirect	Total
Product ($B)	$5.5	$5.5	$11.0	$5.5	$16.5	$22.0
Mix (%)	50%	50%		25%	75%	
Service ($B)	$1.8	$0.2	$2.0	$1.8	$0.7	$2.5
Mix (%)	90%	10%		72%	28%	
Total Revenues	$7.3	$5.7	$13.0	$7.3	$17.2	$24.5
Service % of Total	25%	4%	15%	25%	4%	10%

*Forecast was made in 1990. In actuality, total revenues exceeded this earlier forcast.
Source: ITSMA.

Again, let me say that this is only an exercise with our "guestimates," but it portrays the potential magnitude of a significant flattening of total services revenue, unless Hewlett-Packard did something differently.

The problem for Hewlett-Packard under this scenario was that future plans for investment in new service technology, service infrastructure, and so on, would probably be severely constrained given the very low growth revenue scenario portrayed in this example. Another significant problem or challenge for service management was that the culture of the company and top corporate management had much higher expectations for continued rapid growth (for example, 15 percent or more per year) that they had been experiencing and most likely expected in the future.

Side Note: As most people who have tracked Hewlett-Packard know, HP's services revenue has continued to grow. And in 1994, net services revenue for the entire company reached $3.6 billion, largely as a consequence of HP's success at deriving more services revenue from indirect channels and, more important, from launching a range of multivendor and professional services that have achieved excellent market acceptance.

Where Does the SupportPack Model Go from Here?

At the time of writing this Best Practice Case Study, HP had yet to announce two new SupportPacks: one offering 24x7 on-site coverage for HP NetServers and one for a range of PC LAN software products. In the first case, HP will extend the service delivery period to any day, anytime. In the second case, HP will expand service coverage to include other vendors' software.

When HP SupportPack was first introduced in the United States in 1993, it was limited to a handful or so of products and provided overnight product exchange. On-site service coverage was added later. Other products with higher price points and more demanding service requirements (for example, color laser jet printers) were also added.

Today, there are more than 20 different HP SupportPacks covering multiple-price bands in the United States and comparable numbers for other major geographic areas (HP markets in 92 countries).

Adding to the complexity of a growing product line is the dimension of having a physical product with its attendant requirements for inventory, serial numbers, packaging for display, and so on. There are a lot of things to plan for, manage, and so on.

Madge Whistler, product marketing manager, Multivendor Services Division, estimates that there are now about 5 to 6 full-time people and another 15 to 20 people on a global basis spending part of their time on HP SupportPack issues. This dedication of headcount speaks to the growing importance and complexity of the HP SupportPack product.

HP recognizes that the HP SupportPack model fits a certain set of products and clearly does not fit others. At some pricing level people will balk at prepaying for three years of service. At some degree of complexity—for example, application software with periodic updates, large multivendor installations, system integration projects, and so on—the HP SupportPack model does not work. Or, if the complexity of selling gets too great or the buying-stocking-administering process for dealers gets too complex, then there will be "push back," and HP will have crossed a line that will lead to problems. But for now, things are running smoothly.

The Role of Service Marketing at HP

As a longtime industry analyst who has observed HP over the years and has gotten to know a number of the company's service executives fairly well, I have come to hold HP's service marketing organization in very high regard. What stands out is the quality of its services marketing professionals; the stability of that organization; and the recognition by the entire company of the importance of the service marketing function. HP named its first service marketing manager in 1980, and since that time there have been only four individuals that have held the top service marketing position. Careful selection and continuity of (service marketing) management have helped to produce excellent results. As you will see in Figure 2, Ann Livermore (like her predecessors) has worldwide service sales and marketing responsibility, and reports directly to the senior vice president of WCSO, who in turn reports to the president and CEO of Hewlett-Packard.

HP is also known for its ability to "package" services; HP SupportPack is just one example. The company also manages service delivery very well and seems to be able to meet or exceed customer expectations consistently. And finally, service marketing works in a synergistic way with all the other elements of the organization.

Figure 2 Worldwide Customer Support Operations Organization

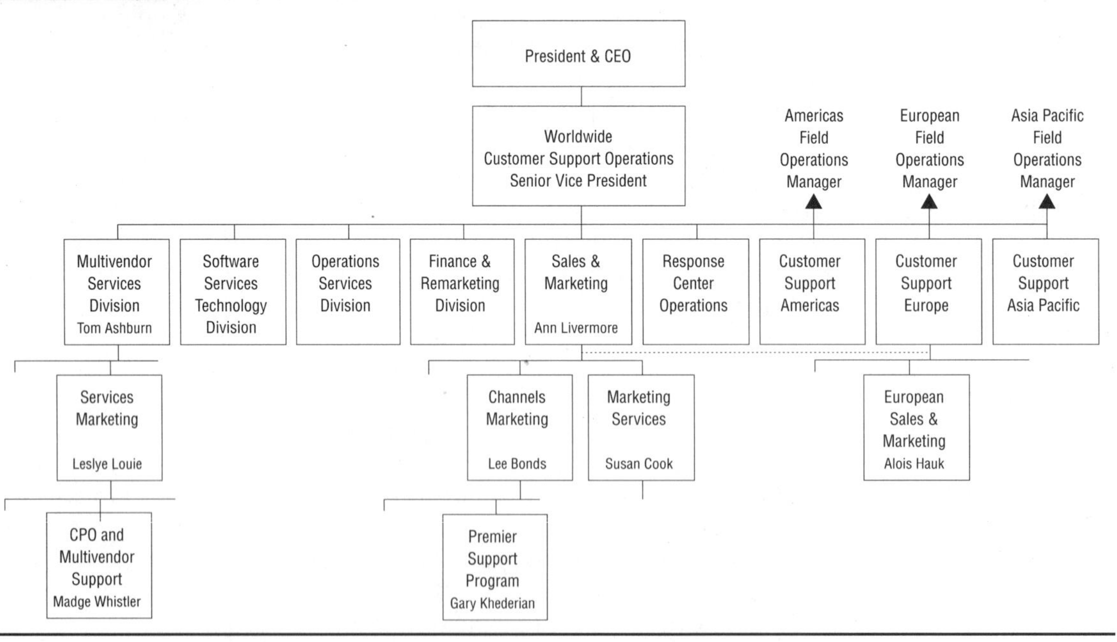

Issue Questions for Discussions

1. HP chose to conduct a limited pilot test in the United Kingdom and then a second test in France before rolling out the product throughout Europe. What are some of the *benefits* of following this type of strategy rather than "going for broke" and making the product available in all markets at the same time? What are some of the *risks*?
2. What could have happened if all of the leading vendors offered three year warranties—some with overnight exchange provisions? Would SupportPack still be as viable under that scenario?
3. Channel firms are notorious for adopting a compete-on-price strategy on products. Was HP smart by initially establishing a price protection provision in its distributor contracts that stated prices for HP SupportPack had to be a certain minimum? (Note: This provision has since been eliminated.) What might have happened if there had not been such a clause when HP SupportPack was first introduced?
4. There have been some other vendors (notably Compaq and Digital Equipment Corporation) that are now offering service-in-a-box products similar to HP SupportPack. What are the implications for HP if many other vendors adopt similar service packaging and SupportPack-like products become generic? How can HP continue to offer a differentiated product?
5. HP SupportPack started simple (low-end peripherals, straightforward services, and so on). Is there a risk in trying to stretch a simple packaging concept to cover products and environments that are more complex—for example, network servers, multivendor software, extended-hour service coverage, and so on? What are those risks, and how can HP avoid or lessen some of those risks?
6. How should "success" be measured/determined for HP SupportPack? Is it just growth in HP SupportPack revenue or are there other important measurements?

Acknowledgments

I would like to thank Susan Cook, marketing services manager; Grant Bentley, consultant relations manager; Madge Whistler, product marketing manager, Multivendor Services Division; and Gary Khederian, program manager, Channels Support Marketing, WCSO; for their assistance in preparing this study. I would also like to acknowledge some earlier research published by Dataquest and International Institute for Management Development (IMD) of Lausanne, Switzerland.

Case 12

PeopleSoft Corporation: Delivering Outrageous Customer Service

This best practice case explores how PeopleSoft has established itself as one of the leading providers of client/server software solutions in a market teeming with competition. The company's success can be attributed to competitive technology, a commitment to what it calls outrageous customer service, a fanatical service culture, good timing, and highly loyal customers. From a customer service perspective, PeopleSoft firmly believes that service is a strategic differentiator in the applications marketplace and will become even more important as other new companies enter the client/server applications segment. In keeping with this belief, PeopleSoft bundles a number of new and traditional services with its software at no additional cost. This is particularly valuable for first-time customers to ensure that they become successful. By bundling software installation services, numerous training credits, the first year of maintenance support, and by assigning a service-focused Account Manager (AM) to be the customer's ongoing advocate, PeopleSoft has differentiated itself from its competitors, receiving high marks from customers in the process. This strategy has helped propel customer loyalty to almost 100 percent, has taken the service business to a position where it now generates 41 percent of corporate revenues, and has led to a 200 percent growth in professional services.

Background

PeopleSoft develops and markets a range of innovative client/server software applications, productivity tools, and services to business customers, universities, and the public sector. The company's growing application family includes: PeopleSoft

---

Source: This case was written by David C. Munn. Best Practice Case Studies provide analysis of a particular company's service marketing strategies and practices, and are presented as educational cases for service marketing professionals. The information in this case study is believed to be reliable but cannot be guaranteed to be correct or complete. The analysis and commentary are the opinions of the author. This profile is the property of ITSMA. Reproduction or disclosure in whole or in part to other parties shall be made only upon the express written consent of ITSMA. ©May 1996 ITSMA.

Human Resources (HRMS), PeopleSoft Financials, PeopleSoft Distribution, PeopleSoft Manufacturing (available by the end of 1996), and PeopleSoft Student Administration Systems (available in 1997). In 1995, PeopleSoft doubled revenues for the fifth year in a row, increasing revenues to $228 million from $113 million in 1994. *Fortune* magazine listed PeopleSoft as one of the fastest growing companies in America during 1994 and 1995. In 1995 alone, PeopleSoft stock almost tripled in value.

The company was founded in 1987 by Dave Duffield and Ken Morris, both computer industry veterans who saw the need for applications based on the emerging paradigm of client/server computing, which promised to empower users and provide greater flexibility than existing applications in the market. In 1989 the company introduced its first product, PeopleSoft Human Resources, targeted at the non-mission-critical function of Human Resources. By doing so, it helped customers get comfortable with this new client/server technology in a low-risk setting. By 1993 PeopleSoft had captured over 50 percent of the client/server Human Resource Management Systems (HRMS) market, helping to give the company an entree into more mission-critical areas, such as financial management and distribution applications, where the projects are larger and have higher visibility.

A key reason for PeopleSoft's market success is the founders' commitment to offer customers what they call outrageous customer service, an intense level of service they felt was lacking in the market. The outrageous attitude translates into a service culture and service mindset at People Soft that radiates throughout the entire organization, now more than ever. Starting with a CEO who still surprises customers when he calls them to ask how they are doing, the customer service commitment ripples all the way out to a field organization where consultants have been known to climb through ceiling tiles at a customer site to finish a weekend PeopleSoft software upgrade. The belief that service was critical to success during the company's early years has clearly influenced the company's service strategy today.

Service Is a Strategic Differentiator

"I firmly believe that service is a strategic differentiator, and as client/server applications become more mature in the future, companies will be measured based on their ability to deliver good service," asserts Peggy Taylor, PeopleSoft's Senior Vice President of Customer Service and Development. Since software acquisition represents a smaller percentage of the overall cost of a system implementation compared to the services required to implement and support the system over time, she continues, "companies will have to get service right to remain competitive—that's why we dedicate over 40 percent of our employees to providing service to our customers."

Eight major components go into PeopleSoft's service strategy of providing customers with a complete solution. Each component alone could benefit an organization; all of them together make for a powerful differentiating service strategy. PeopleSoft's eight service components are:

- The commitment to service as a priority starting at the top of the company. CEO Dave Duffield talks about it in presentations and interviews with the media and spends considerable time with customers.
- A fun culture that ingrains customer service and rewards employees for doing outrageous acts for customers.
- Customer service is an integral part of the corporate marketing message.
- Regional service executives responsible for managing customer service issues are located in the field, close to customers.
- The assignment to every customer of a "free" Account Manager (AM), who acts as the customer's advocate within PeopleSoft, representing the customer across all functions and units within the company.
- Bundling ample product installation assistance, training credits, and one year of maintenance support with the price of software to ensure a successful implementation from the start.
- A professional services organization that leverages a substantial partnership program to deliver whatever in-depth service is required to support the customers' needs.
- Automated tools to enable AMs and customer service representatives to better serve their customers, such as the Lotus Notes Customer Status Database and the Vantive support center call tracking system.

In the following pages, we will examine these eight components, as well as other components such as training.

Service Is a Key Part of the Corporate Marketing Message

"We're in the solutions business, and the services that we provide to customers are a critical component of the overall PeopleSoft solution," declares Ray Gadbois, Vice President of Marketing. Therefore, "when we do any kind of marketing, service is a key part of our message," he continues. And, since PeopleSoft is in a referral business, meaning that it relies on good word-of-mouth for new business, excellent service is critical to its continued growth. "That's why we put so many people and corporate resources into customer service. You can have the best marketing in the world, but it won't do you any good if you don't have happy customers using your products and talking about it," Gadbois concludes.

PeopleSoft's brand of outrageous service pays direct benefits to the customer. In a mainframe applications market, customers typically spend six to seven times more money on implementation than on software. PeopleSoft's client/server customers, however, report spending only two times the price of the software on implementation. "The reason we bundle services with the cost of a license isn't necessarily because we want to give it away for free, but we feel there is a minimum amount of service (in the form of training, installation assistance, account management, and such) a customer needs to be successful with a complex client/server system," Gadbois explains.

PeopleSoft positions itself in the applications market as a client/server technology leader that dedicates significant resources to customer service, and whose development efforts are customer-driven. While corporate marketing's role is to spread the service message to new prospects, it is the field's responsibility to differentiate PeopleSoft by delivering specific product and service benefits.

Competitors may offer similar services, but their service bundling practices vary by company, and are highly negotiable. Some offer an AM, but such positions typically are part of the quota-driven sales organization. At PeopleSoft, the AM is not compensated on the basis of sales, but is a salaried employee responsible for acting as the customer's advocate, facilitator, communicator, and liaison all wrapped up into one. The AM's main objective is to help customers be successful with their long-term investment in PeopleSoft. This account management strategy has led to the perception in the market that PeopleSoft, indeed, is different and better.

Choosing application software is a very complex decision. First, customers have to find the specific functionality that supports their business needs. Second, people are influenced by enabling technology features, such as toolset flexibility, decision support capabilities, query tools, and emerging workflow functionality. Third, customers look at a range of non-technical criteria, such as references and the customer service orientation. Don't underestimate the importance of such non-technical considerations. In some cases, a PeopleSoft application had less functionality than a competitor's but the prospect liked PeopleSoft's people and attitude better. "This is a 5–10 year commitment, so many customers prefer to team up with a vendor that they like, and one that they have an affinity with," observes Gadbois.

PeopleSoft's marketing strategy is tied to its business objectives. That strategy outlines aggressive growth through expansion into new markets, and the addition of new products to PeopleSoft's Enterprise Products Portfolio, a complete suite of business software solutions for the enterprise that includes distribution and manufacturing applications. The company plans to expand geographically, particularly into markets overseas. It also intends to seek growth through tailored solutions and sales/support efforts to new and existing vertical markets, including public sector/government, higher education, healthcare, manufacturing (horizontal focus), and financial services. In this expansion process, service resources such as trainers, professional services consultants, hotline staff, and AMs will be increased substantially to ensure that the company can continue to offer what marketing consultants refer to as the total product.

Applying the Total Product Concept

PeopleSoft is a prime example of a company applying the total product concept described by Ted Levitt in his book, *The Marketing Imagination*, (The Free Press/Macmillan, 1982). According to Levitt, there are two basic aspects to any product: the generic product that seldom has competitive viability by itself, and the expected product, which represents the customer's minimum expectations from the product. The generic product can only be sold if the customer's basic expectations (for the product) are met, in short, if the generic product matches the expected product.

Sustained success in the market, however, requires more than meeting minimum expectations. Levitt goes on to identify an augmented product that comprises additions to the expected product as a means of product differentiation, and a potential product that consists of everything potentially feasible to attract and hold customers. "Nearly everybody employs augmentations, though they are seldom developed as part of a conscious or systematic program of product differentiation," Levitt notes. Only a few marketers push their augmentations to the point where they approach the potential product.

In PeopleSoft's case, it consciously developed a strategy to provide augmentations (bundled services) that deliver significantly more than the expected product (basic application software). As a result, they have differentiated themselves in the client/server applications market.

While PeopleSoft's applications are innovative and technology rich, customers expect certain features and functionality from the generic application as the price of entry into the market. Companies must compare well with competitors on those features just to be viable, but they must go beyond the generic and expected products to create real differentiation via product augmentations. Levitt cautions that augmentations today can become expectations tomorrow, and that companies have to develop new augmentations, rather than cut price to remain differentiated in the future. PeopleSoft, in its drive to deliver Levitt's potential product, has aggressively pursued an augmentation strategy in regards to customer service that raises the bar for the entire software industry. (See Figure 1.)

Figure 1 The Total Product Concept

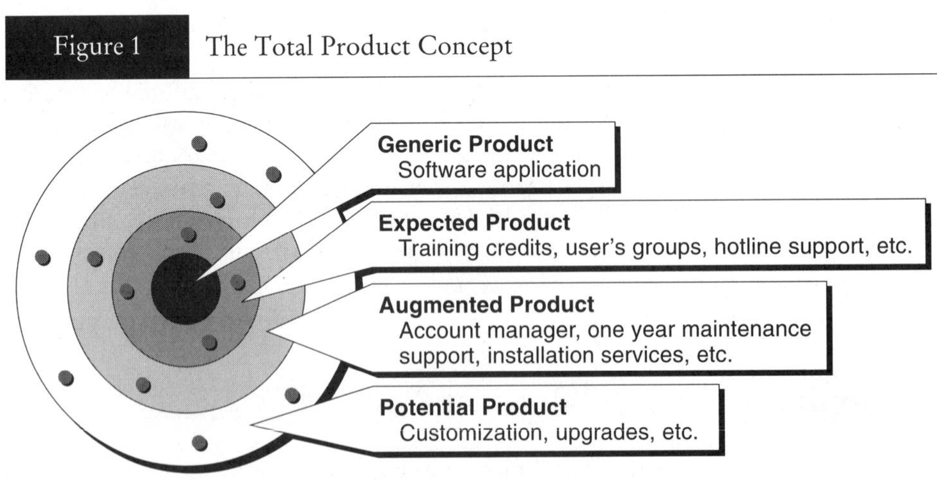

Source: Ted Levitt, *The Marketing Imagination*

Combining Customer Services and Applications Development

A key phase in PeopleSoft's "total product" evolution occurred in 1994, when the company combined customer services and applications development under one senior vice president, Peggy Taylor. Its objective was to bring development closer to the customer by consolidating ownership of products and services in one organization. Since then, both product quality and product feedback have improved as a result of the closer link with customer services. In the same year, PeopleSoft received Sentry Publishing's 1994 Customer Service and Support Award recognizing PeopleSoft as the software vendor providing the best service and support for HRMS applications in the UNIX environment.

The combined services-development organizational structure produces effective checks and balances between development and customer service and has led to vastly improved communication—all benefiting the customer. During regular meetings between the two groups, for instance, you might see a customer service manager advocating a new feature for a customer and a developer outlining reasonable expectations to set and communicate with the customer. The old adage to under-commit and over-deliver clearly applies here.

In addition, Taylor initiated a program where developers visit customers on a regular basis. When the developers return, they readily talk about customer issues and how these issues relate to development plans. As a result, service and development groups now work together more productively as a single entity:

"We've gained a lot of credibility with this structure," observes Taylor. "Customers know that developers get their feedback when it is funneled through the customer service organization."

The PeopleSoft Customer Services Organization

The customer services organization itself has over 600 people, approximately 40 percent of PeopleSoft's employee population of 1,500 individuals worldwide. The company's total employee breakout is as follows: 42 percent in service, 10 percent in general and administrative, 28 percent in sales/marketing, and 20 percent in research and development. The service division is profitable, but it is not tracked as a profit center, although the professional services and education units are tracked as such.

Account management and professional services have the largest groups within the service organization, totaling 170 and 200 people respectively. The hotline group comprises close to 100 employees, education services has 80 people and rising, installation services adds another 30 employees, and management/service analysts account for approximately 20 people. PeopleSoft does not have a formal service marketing group, or anyone with service marketing in their title, but instead has approximately five individuals who manage responsibilities typically handled by service marketers/product managers.

PeopleSoft generated almost $93 million in service revenue during 1995, which constitutes 41 percent of total company revenue (Table 1). The $93 million in service

Table 1 Breakout of PeopleSoft Service Revenue

	1994(SM)	1995(SM)	Growth(%)
Maintenance contracts	22.6	43.9	94
Education services	14.8	28.5	92
Professional services	6.9	20.5	197
Total service revenue	44.3	92.9	110
Percent of total revenue	39%	41%	

Source: ITSMA.

revenue is all that more significant given that the company bundles a significant amount of services with the price of software for first-time buyers. As a result, PeopleSoft derives a lower percentage of total revenue from services than most application providers. By comparison, it generates substantially less than Oracle, which sees close to 60 percent of applications revenue from services (approximately $284 million in 1995), and SAP, which makes close to 56 percent of it applications revenue from services (approximately $333 million in fiscal year 1995). We attribute the lower contribution to revenue from services to PeopleSoft's bundling of services for first-year customers, and the utilization of outside partners for a substantial part of the total professional services delivered to their customers. However, it pays dividends in other ways.

A Culture That Encourages Outrageous Customer Service

At a 1996 ITSMA workshop, author and management professor, Dr. David Bowen noted: "In a recent research study, we discovered that customer satisfaction is directly correlated to employee satisfaction—the happier your service employees are the happier your customers will be. People should be considered a company's number one asset."

Talk to anyone at PeopleSoft and you will hear that the company's success is directly attributable to its people and its culture. The 1994 PeopleSoft Corporate Report devotes 11 pages to a section entitled Our People, which includes a tribute to the value and contributions of its people, a list of every employee's name, and a sampling of their own stories. The company boasts a 3 percent turnover rate, considered highly unusual in the fast-paced information technology market where employees change companies faster than the weather changes in New England.

The company enthusiastically cultivates an environment where people want to work and excel. "Besides encouraging innovation and creativity, we have a corporate policy in place where people are authorized and encouraged to do anything outrageous for the customer," says Sebastian Grady, Vice President of Customer Services. Grady is responsible for customer service strategy, vision, and consistency. He is one of the company's biggest proponents of performing "positively outrageous customer service" for PeopleSoft customers.

Inspired by T. Scott Gross, author of "Positively Outrageous Service," (Warner Books, 1991), who writes about how doing something amazing for a customer at random creates lifetime customers, PeopleSoft continually sparks outrageous incidents. In one case, a consultant worked late at a customer site on a Friday night performing a back-up in preparation for a system conversion. Later that night she found she didn't have access to the locked data center housing the company's computers. Determined to finish the back-up for the customer, she climbed through the ceiling tiles, over a wall, and into the data center, successfully performing the operation.

Another outrageous service story recounts the experience of a consultant who was on his way to a customer site when his car flipped over and slid off the highway. Taken to a nearby hospital for treatment, he called the customer to report where he was and accepted the customer's offer to pick him up. He insisted on helping the customer finish the application installation into the night before leaving.

To call attention to employees' outrageous contributions, PeopleSoft rewards those who perform the most outrageous acts and publicizes a range of team and individual awards that are always announced at company meetings. For example, the recipient of the Outstanding Contributor Award can choose $500 or options for 100 shares of PeopleSoft stock. (The stock is almost always chosen.) Team Awards, given out quarterly, are voted on by peers. The Professional Services Group (PSG) offers a Most Valuable Consultant, voted on by peers as well. Then there's the "Goodwilla Gorilla" award, and even an Honorary PeoplePerson of the Month Award that goes to non-PeopleSoft contributors. One PeoplePerson Award went to a woman at the local sub shop, who enthusiastically served developers and employees at all hours. She was invited to a company meeting and given the award to a standing ovation.

The Benefits of Regionalization

In an effort to get closer to its customers, PeopleSoft moved from a centralized structure to a regional management model in early 1995. The company established four regions in the U.S.: East (headquartered in Teaneck, NJ), South (Atlanta, GA), Midwest (Westchester, IL), West (Walnut Creek, CA), and non-U.S. regions in Canada, Europe, Asia/Pacific, and Latin America, all reporting to Al Duffield, Sr. Vice President of Regional Operations (Figure 2). Distributors handle Spain, South Africa, India and areas in Latin America. Each region has a General Manager who is responsible for all business aspects of the region, including overall profit and loss, and vice presidents of sales, and services, who report in to the regional General Manager.

Each Regional Vice President of Customer Services has overall responsibility for the ongoing service and support needs of local customers. He or she manages AMs, Trainers, Installers, infrastructure people, and the working relationships with PeopleSoft's many local service partners. The Regional Vice Presidents of Customer Services work

Figure 2 PeopleSoft Organization

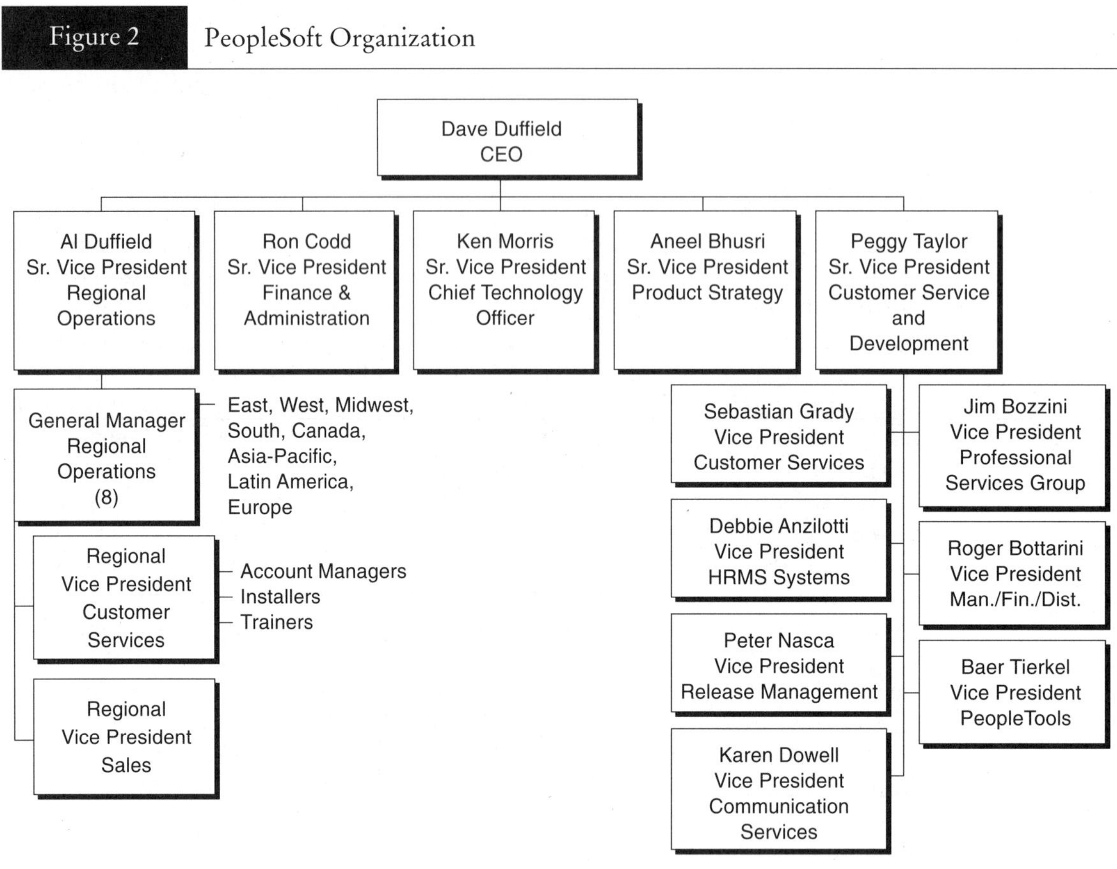

Source: PeopleSoft Corporation.

very closely with the Vice President of Customer Services (Sebastian Grady), who directs the rollout and introduction of service programs and strategies to the field. Grady considers the Regional service VP's his customers, holding weekly meetings with them to stay abreast of their service issues, needs, and priorities. This structure and close working relationship allows Grady's team to focus on planning and implementing service strategies while the regions can focus on day to day customer issues.

One of PeopleSoft's well-respected and more animated regional vice presidents of customer services, Christel Devlin observes that "the key to growing a region's service business is hiring good people who are engaged in their work and who really care about a customer's success." To find good people, the company starts close to home. Almost two-thirds of PeopleSoft's new field hires come through internal referrals, friends of employees and other personal contacts.

"The second key to growing the region's service business involves perpetuating the PeopleSoft culture of fun and outrageous customer service on a daily basis," Devlin continues. During a recent videoconference with the west coast, Devlin spent

$100 on masks and costumes for her team to wear. On Halloween, she rented a full gorilla suit, and surprised customers who were attending training sessions.

Beyond the fun and games, however, is the solid value that first-time buyers find when PeopleSoft bundles a suite of services with the purchase of its product. "Providing lots of services to every customer up front, including a non-sales-oriented Account Manager, helps us win new business. It's a differentiator when prospects make reference calls to existing accounts," Devlin explains. "Customers give us good references because they feel we're easier to do business with than competitors." How else can PeopleSoft boast the fact that a number of their customers have happily taken close to 100 reference calls in a given year, under their own free will?

A Unique Service Account Management Program

Another key differentiator is PeopleSoft's Account Management program, which is available to new and existing customers at no charge. Not to be confused with commissioned sales Account Managers employed by many companies, PeopleSoft AMs are non-commissioned service employees who manage the customer relationship, and provide customers with a single point of contact into PeopleSoft. PeopleSoft considers the Account Management Program so important, it invests close to one-third of its ongoing maintenance revenues in it.

"Account Managers are PeopleSoft ambassadors to our customers. They, more than any group at PeopleSoft, are instrumental to a customer's success," says Duncan Hsia, Corporate Manager of the Account Management Program. The company has approximately 170 AMs, who typically handle 8–12 customers, usually in geographic proximity. They have many responsibilities, including occasional pre-sales involvement, kick-off meetings to discuss working with PeopleSoft, project planning and implementation support, scheduling software installations, facilitating feedback and enhancement requests, communicating all ongoing product and service issues, maintaining accurate on-line records of the account, and managing reference activities. The program has been so successful that a number of customers have even negotiated for a PeopleSoft AM to be dedicated to their account, on a full-time basis.

In the early days of the program, AMs handled all post-sales issues for an account, from installation to implementation and training. Now, the program and the company have matured to the point where AMs can focus on relationship management and on acting as the customer's champion within PeopleSoft.

AMs report to the regional Vice President of Customer Service, and funnel customer needs to sales for follow-on product concerns, to the Professional Services Group (PSG) for special services, to the installation group for installation issues, to business partners for high-end service needs, and to the training organization for regional or in-house training. AMs are also the customer's voice when providing feedback to various development groups. "It's a wonderful program," says Helene Jacobs, Assistant Vice President of HR Administrative Services at The New England (a leading Massachusetts-based insurance company). "They are truly our advocate to the company."

AMs are not compensated based on the sale of services. PeopleSoft AMs receive salaries and bonuses based on customer satisfaction and regional performance. In fact, at this time, no one in the company receives a commission for selling services.

With the growth of the Account Management program, PeopleSoft has developed a distinct career path for AMs. An AM can be promoted to a Senior Account Manager position for Global and Vertical Accounts. A Regional Manager of Account management has also been created. This position reports to the Regional Vice President of Customer Service.

The Account Management program is moving towards handling unique support needs of vertical markets (Federal HRMS, universities, and others), multinational companies, and horizontal markets, such as manufacturing. Hsia has also planned specific meetings in early 1996 to discuss top issues, share best practices, and develop ongoing programs for Global Account Managers, Public Sector Vertical Market Account Managers, and Regional Account Managers.

The Quintessential Customer Database

The AM's primary tool to help manage the customer relationship is the Customer Status Database, a Lotus Notes application that tracks a wealth of information about customers. Once a customer signs a PeopleSoft contract, an Account Manager begins entering data and information about that customer in the Customer Master Profile (Exhibit 1). The AM would then enter in-depth information based on the customer site where a particular application is to be installed, including: customer demographics, application type, release number, database vendor, hardware platform, implementation schedule, production dates (planned and actual), upgrade plans, referenceability, and much more (Exhibit 2). The AM could then proceed to a PSG Work Order screen (Exhibit 3) where he/she would enter information about services needed, work description, start/end dates, application specialist required, systems environment, travel requirements, even dress code at the customer site. Lastly, AMs or other PeopleSoft employees can enter satisfaction level and issue information into a Site Status Report after every contact with a customer, and forward or save the information as needed (Exhibit 4).

Customer Status is also accessed by others in the company to track anything and everything about a particular customer. For example, PeopleSoft's entire management team will access existing information and enter new information into the Customer Status Database as part of their quarterly Call-Ten-Customers program. Chief Executive Officer Dave Duffield has been known to compose some of the most detailed status reports in the system. This dynamic repository of customer information allows PeopleSoft management the ability to stay close to its customers, incorporating their needs into all decision making.

From a historical standpoint, PeopleSoft's focus on customer service required that the company track all sorts of information about their customers. AMs needed information about the customers they managed, as did others. The Customer Status Database was deployed on Lotus Notes due to the ease with which it could be replicated to the field offices for use by various employees.

Exhibit 1 PeopleSoft Customer Master Profile

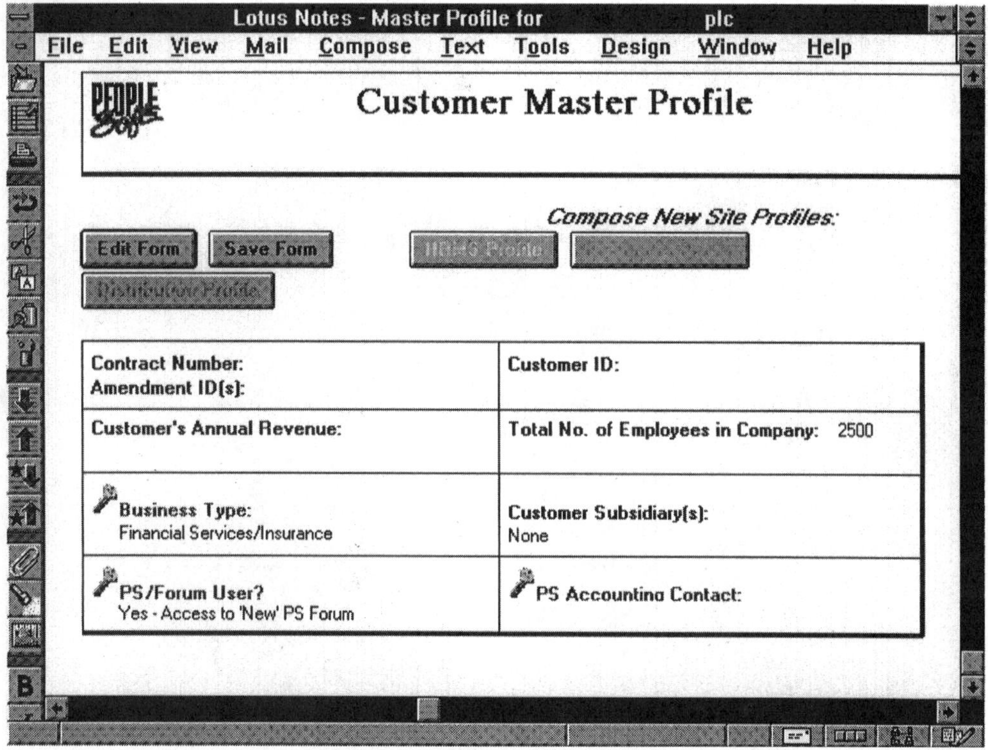

Source: PeopleSoft Corporation.

In 1995, the Customer Status Database was reengineered completely. The new design allows AMs to gain a complete customer-centric perspective by giving them access to information managed from other PeopleSoft groups. For instance, AMs can review installation requests, PSG requests, and account inquiries, and they can query other customer accounts with similar issues. Customers, however, cannot access or input data to the Customer Status Database presently.

The Customer Status Database was used recently in a successful campaign to target and upgrade older PeopleSoft sites (HRMS 3.22 and earlier) to version 5.0 of the PeopleSoft HRMS product suite. Without upgrading, these sites would not have been eligible for PeopleSoft product support because their versions were long outdated. PeopleSoft officially supports customers who install an application product release for 18 months after the general availability of the next major release of a product. This usually equates to 2.5 years of support for a specific release.

In 1996, PeopleSoft is extending its customer-centric initiative by rolling the Customer Status Database into Vantive, an integrated customer interaction application, which will consolidate multiple Lotus Notes databases. Both PeopleSoft employees

Exhibit 2 PeopleSoft HRMS Site Profile

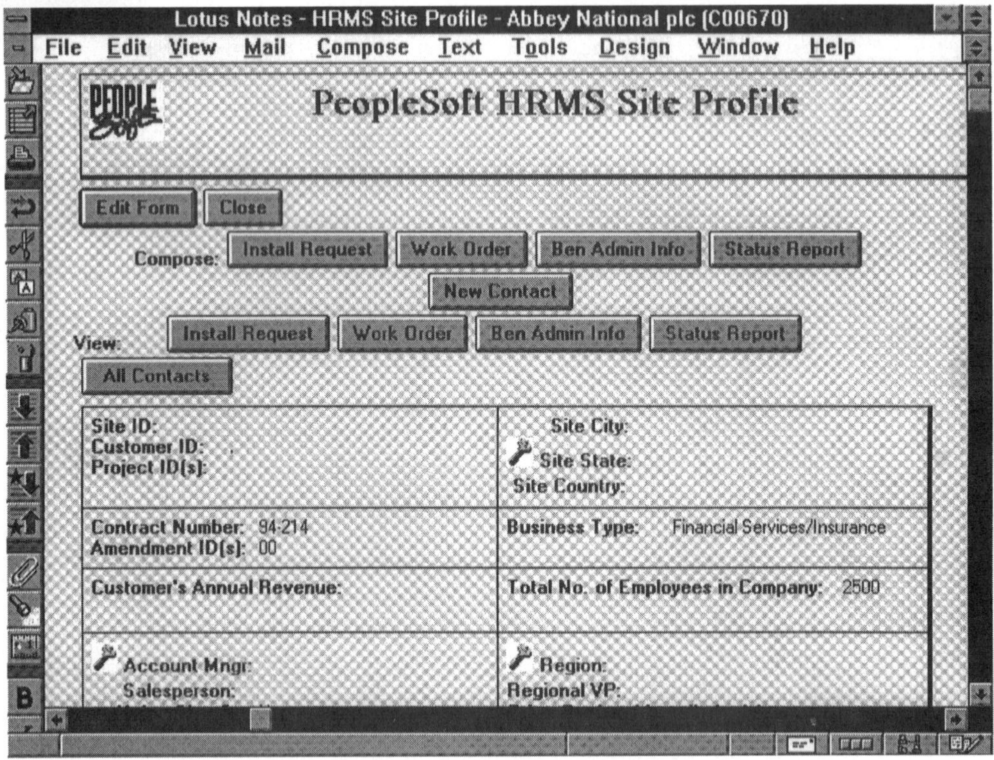

Source: PeopleSoft Corporation.

and customers will have access to status reports, demographic reports, or can submit requests for PSG, installation services education classes, and user group events, all via the Internet.

As mentioned earlier, the Customer Status database has been a key tool for AMs to direct upgrade programs, but the process has been manual with no escalation or automatic notification capabilities. To find out which customers are overdue for an upgrade, AMs must query the database, searching for customers with certain versions of the product. In the new Vantive-based system, pre-defined business rules and conditions will trigger an electronic notification to the appropriate AM. The notification may alert the AM of the need to upgrade certain customers to a new release. Or, AMs could be notified if a customer had placed a certain number of calls into the hotline. Down the road, PeopleSoft will have customers update some of their own information in the Customer Status database, such as satisfaction survey responses or site profile data.

Other major technology initiatives in the customer service area will include a partnership with Inference, a provider of Case Based Retrieval software, to develop knowledgebase or self-help capabilities within PeopleSoft applications. By including

Exhibit 3 PeopleSoft PSG Work Order

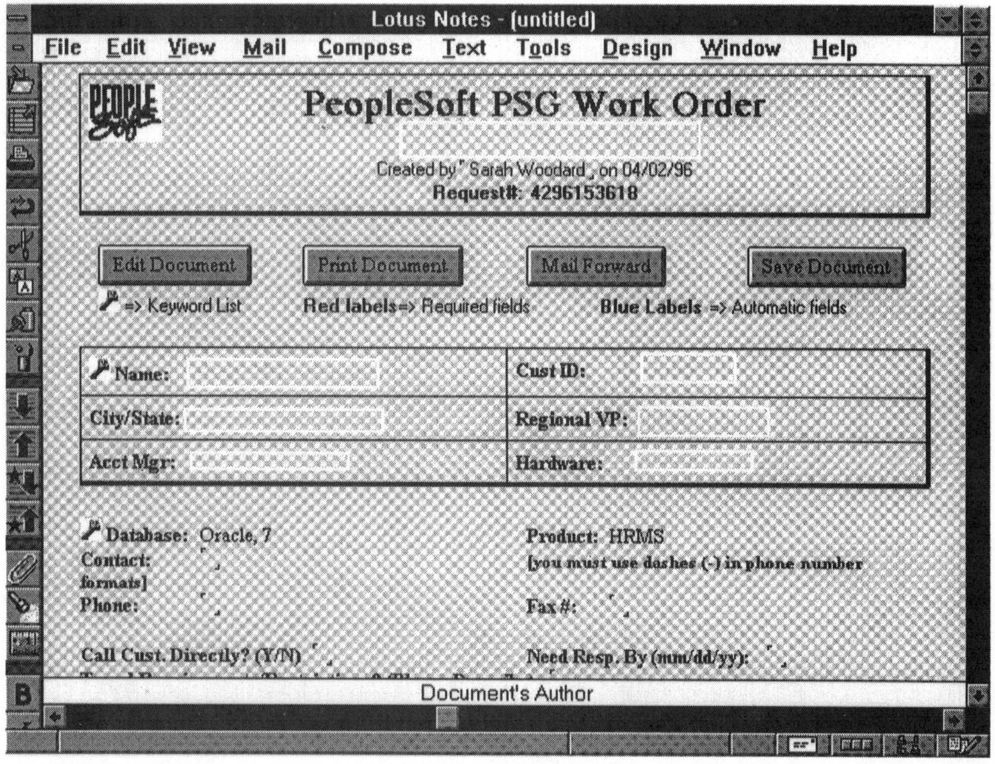

Source: PeopleSoft Corporation.

Inference capabilities in their applications, PeopleSoft customers should be able to solve more problems themselves, thus reducing calls to the hotline. Another major technology initiative will involve upgrading and enhancing PeopleSoft's PS/Forum electronic support area. About 95 percent of maintenance customers use PS/Forum today, with half accessing it through CompuServe, the other half via the World Wide Web. The company expects to see a steady shift of customers accessing PS/Forum via the Web. This will also allow for new features.

Service Marketing Communications Efforts

Marketing communications plays an important role in the service story. AMs rely heavily on the corporate communications group to help relay service news and announcements to customers. Service marketing communication efforts at PeopleSoft are spearheaded by Patty Pasley, Manager of Corporate Communications. Pasley is responsible for a wide range of activities relating to communications with PeopleSoft customers and employees,

Exhibit 4 PeopleSoft HRMS Site Status Report

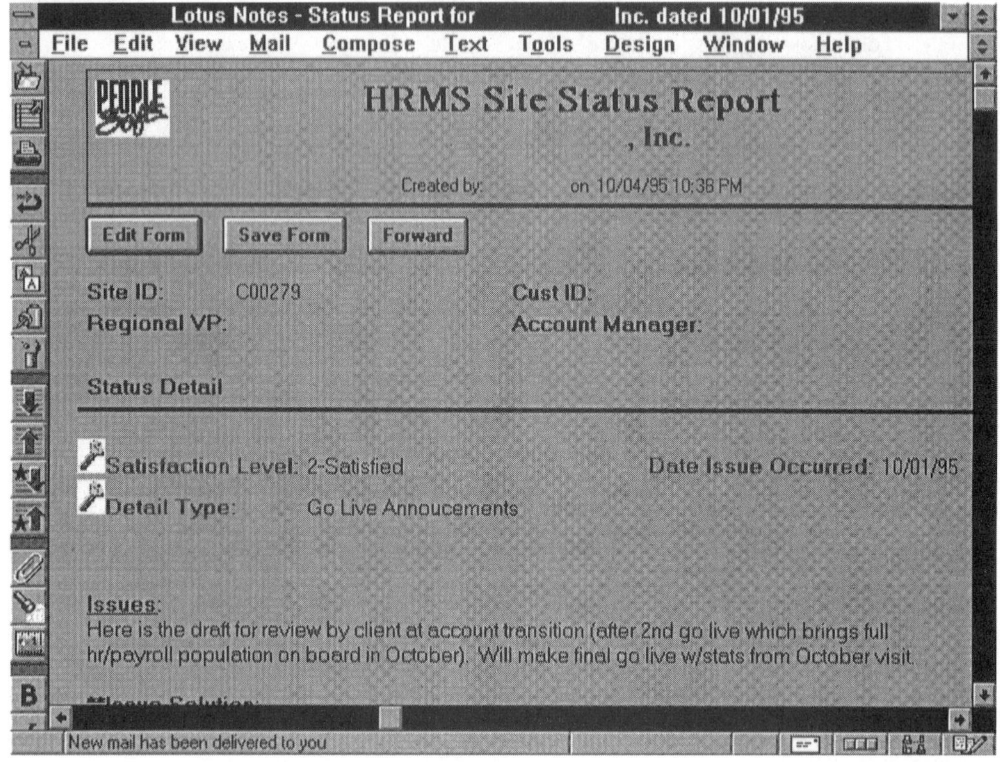

Source: PeopleSoft Corporation.

especially AMs. She also handles a number of traditional service marketing activities, such as helping to design and draft service collateral, data sheets, brochures, and success stories, and she is very active in planning PeopleSoft's well attended, annual user's group conference (which had over 4,000 customers and business partners attend in 1995).

One of the most important tasks of a service marketing communication manager is to help set customer expectations as they relate to services, and to set appropriate expectations with internal employees as to what is being promised to customers. In that light, Pasley orchestrated the recent expansion and publication of an 80-page document entitled *PeopleSoft Customer Services,* which is the complete guide to PeopleSoft's services. "We feel communicating this much information to our customers will help them realize the full potential of their PeopleSoft system," she explains.

The guide discusses:

- Benefits of an annual software maintenance program
- The reasons for regionalization and the names and addresses of all the regional General Managers and Customer Service Vice Presidents

- Release support policies and standards
- Performance engineering services
- AM responsibilities
- Installation services
- Training courses, policies, CBT options, EdFacts voice response system
- The value of survey measurement data to improving service
- Application and technical hotline support guidelines and coverage
- Professional Services Group
- Partner and alliance programs
- On-line support and electronic CD tools (PeopleBooks)
- Newsletters and communications
- Customer and staff involvement
- User group contacts

The document differs from typical vendor service documents in that it is packed with comprehensive information about the services provided, rather than a service sales pitch with little substantive information. It goes to the extent of detailing how PeopleSoft allocates maintenance dollars, how much training PeopleSoft trainers and Professional Services employees receive, and how customers can leverage the PeopleSoft Forum on-line bulletin board service.

In the section entitled "Your Involvement," PeopleSoft outlines customers' responsibilities in making the PeopleSoft system work best for them. It details the ways customers can increase their involvement with PeopleSoft and improve the likelihood of success with a PeopleSoft implementation. "Your Involvement" includes discussions about the successful traits of a strong implementation team, ways to influence development directions, and the value of attending local user's groups and the annual PeopleSoft Users Conference, among other topics.

Lastly, the services document explains a creative program called PeopleDollars. PeopleDollars represent votes that PeopleSoft customers can cast in favor of various product enhancements. Each year, customers receive 100 PeopleDollars per product they've licensed, which they can use to vote (spend) on the product enhancements of their choice. The product enhancement choices are then tallied to help determine PeopleSoft's development plans for the coming year.

PeopleSoft's Partner Program

The PeopleSoft Partnership Program harnesses the capabilities of industry-leading hardware, database, implementation, application, workflow, and systems integration vendors to help customers maximize their use of PeopleSoft applications. In many instances, partners are already working with a prospect, making component recommendations. Partners also are brought in when a quantity of people and skills are needed to supplement PeopleSoft PSG personnel, for such things as implementation or integration assistance. Regional service vice presidents spend a fair amount of time working with PeopleSoft's family of partners (Figure 3 shows all the PeopleSoft partner names and categories).

"Having service partnerships with a number of well-respected organizations has allowed PeopleSoft to focus on its core competency of developing flexible, easy to use, client/server software, rather than trying to become a consulting company," explains Grady, who led the expansion of the partner program in 1993 and 1994. Partners are considered an extension of PeopleSoft's service groups. Most PeopleSoft partners embrace the company's approach because they are not competing with the company for services.

PeopleSoft's biggest challenge in this area is to attract the participation of all the Big Six accounting and consulting firms as partners since the typical PeopleSoft project size is smaller, less complex, and shorter in duration (approximately ten months) than the typical SAP or Oracle project that a Big Six firm might undertake. However, the Big Six firms have begun to see the potential benefits of doing more PeopleSoft projects in a shorter amount of time. In this way a number of them have built more customer references in less time with less people.

Recently PeopleSoft partnered with Andersen Consulting in a joint development effort to create Public Sector HR and Financial applications. The project took one year to complete, with Andersen receiving royalties from application sales over a five-year period. PeopleSoft is presently working with Price Waterhouse on a relationship in the Financial Services (Banking, Insurance, and Brokerage Firms) sector.

The partner program includes a special category of consulting companies that have supported PeopleSoft from the beginning. Referred to as implementation partners, these companies range in size from 30 to 200 consultants and generate 80–90 percent of their business from PeopleSoft implementations. PeopleSoft implementation services business has increased over 100 percent a year at a number of the partners. Companies such as The Application Group, Business Information Technology, Noblestar, The Pinnacle Group, Ramos & Associates, and The Hunter Group are examples of successful implementation partners that have helped fuel PeopleSoft's growth over the past few years.

A recent partner category, Global Solutions Providers, includes companies such as Andersen Consulting, Price Waterhouse, Ernst & Young, and IBM's ISSC. These companies specialize in large, complex, multinational customer implementations.

The last partner category includes PeopleFriends, independent consultants, or small companies, that are used as subcontractors through the professional services organization. These independent contractors are highly skilled, and help reduce the risk to PeopleSoft of carrying a large professional services staff.

Growth of the Professional Services Business

Due to increasing customer demand. PSG at PeopleSoft has grown faster than any other service group, both in terms of revenues and the number of consultants. Staffing has increased from 40 PSG consultants in 1994 to 175 at the end of 1995 to

Figure 3 PeopleSoft Partnerships

Technology Partners

Digital Equipment Corp.
PRC, Inc.
Sequent Computer Systems
SHL
Stream International
Technology Solutions Company
The Gateway Group
The Registry

Application Partners

AVP
BMC Software
Braintree Technology
Business Objects
Citrix Systems
Crystal Services
Ernst & Young
Federal Liaison Services
Frontec
InCap
Intermec
Mercer
Microsoft
MITI
Open Horizon
Premenos
Restrac
SigForms
Skillset Software
Sterling Software
Success Factor Systems
Vertex

Implementation Partners

Andersen Consulting
Beacon Application Services
Business Information Technology
Cap Gemini SOGETI
CITEC
Computer Sciences Corporation
Coopers & Lybrand
CPI Resources, Ltd.
D&M Consultancy
DataStudy, Inc.
Deloitte & Touche
Dimension Systems
Foundation Software
IBM
KPMG Peat Marwick
KYAT - Bilbao, S.A.
Multisystemas
Noblestar
Philippine Computer Solutions
Price Waterhouse
Ramos & Associates
RSA Mexico
SG2 (France)
Siemens Nixdorf IS
Sierra Systems
SYCMA
TSC Mexico
Technology Solutions Company
The Application Group
The Hunter Group
The Pinnacle Group
User Technology Services

Platform Partners

Apple Computer
Data General
Digital Equipment Corp.
Gupta
Hewlett-Packard
IBM
Informix
Intel Corporation
Microsoft
NCR Corporation
Novell
Oracle
Pyramid Technology
Sequent Computer Systems
Siemens Nixdorf IS
Sun Microsystems
Sybase
Unisys

Workflow Partners

Action Technologies
Computer Communication Specialists
Delrina
Edify Corp.
Essense Systems
IBM
JetForm Corp.
Lotus Development Corp.
TALX

Global Solution Providers

Andersen Consulting
Ernst & Young
IBM (ISSC)
Price Waterhouse

Source: PeopleSoft Corporation.

approximately 200 consultants today. During that same period, PSG revenues have almost tripled, jumping from $6.9 million in 1994 to $20.5 million in 1995. In comparison, most of PeopleSoft's competitors generate greater professional services revenues and have more consultants.

Despite the growth of PSG, PeopleSoft still handles less than 10 percent of the professional services called for on PeopleSoft implementations. "We've always emphasized a comprehensive partner program, and have had a great working relationship with most of them, " notes Mike O'Toole, Manager of Business Development, PSG. "Rarely do we compete with our partners, because they typically already have a relationship with the customer." Where PSG gets involved, the customer usually has come directly to PeopleSoft to handle a point solution.

PeopleSoft attributes the rapid growth of the professional services business to customers looking for help when upgrading their software, and to those attempting to maximize their use of PeopleSoft's feature-rich applications, such as workflow capabilities. To give customers a choice of how much help they may need, PeopleSoft packages three upgrade services for customers. Upgrade Planning and Compare, Analysis and Merge, and Migration to Production. The average upgrade project generates about $30,000 in revenues and takes approximately 20 days to complete. Customers consider this a valuable service, as it is done faster and better than they could do themselves. Overall, upgrade services have become a significant source of repeat business for PSG.

As an example of PeopleSoft's nimbleness, it took the company only four weeks to develop, package, and price the upgrade services and publicize them to customers and the field. PSG already had the expertise but had not formally packaged or priced the upgrade services to make it easy for the field to communicate and for customers to buy.

Similarly, PeopleSoft recently introduced a Retroactive Pay modification for existing Payroll customers. The development of this software add-on demonstrates PeopleSoft's responsiveness to its customers' needs, and illustrates how PeopleSoft turned a problem into a new opportunity. It began when a developer was sent to the field for 16 weeks to develop the Retroactive Pay functionality in response to a specific customer who couldn't wait for release 6. Once completed, the details of the upgrade functionality and customer benefits were put on-line in Lotus Notes for internal access, messages were sent to AMs, Sales Representatives, and field management, The Retroactive Pay modification, the company discovered, also solved a technical feature objection that prevented a number of new prospects from adopting PeopleSoft. A future version of Payroll will include the Retroactive Pay functionality, as a standard product feature.

Once the upgrade was packaged and ready to release, regional vice presidents with the help of AMs, used the Customer Status Database to identify and contact customers who could benefit from having Retroactive Pay capability (release 4.x and 5.x customers). Customers were charged a one time fee, plus an hourly consulting fee, to install, implement, and train users on the upgrade, which averaged from 4 to 6 weeks.

While the revenue the Retroactive Pay upgrade generates has been modest and is not the primary objective, the upgrade is considered a success because it resolves a customer problem and overcomes an objection to a PeopleSoft product. The process to introduce, communicate, and roll out this service took just two weeks.

Along with being responsive to customer needs, PeopleSoft's PSG focuses closely on quality. As part of a quarterly, company-wide customer satisfaction survey, PeopleSoft asks specific questions about the quality of services delivered by

PSG. Overall quality of PSG services has risen steadily, increasing to 4.2 out of possible 5.0, between May 1994 and September 1995.

At the individual consultant level, PSG asks customers to fill out a one-page questionnaire for each consultant on a project. Customers rate consultants in ten areas, such as preparedness, demonstrated skills, and timeliness, and they are asked if they would request the consultant again. Since a significant portion of PSG consultants' compensation is tied to customer satisfaction rather than just billable hours (which is the case at many other firms), consultants are focused on delivering a quality job and ensuring that the customer is satisfied.

A range of new professional services are planned for 1996. These will revolve around services targeted to customers implementing the workflow features that exist in PeopleSoft's applications. PSG will also package services for General Ledger customers in need of chartfield customizations. For marketing purposes, the company plans to publish a number of PSG success stories that highlight the benefits of working with PSG, such as a recently published profile, "Teamwork at Texas Instruments."

Education Services a Priority

Education Services has also experienced substantial growth, albeit at a slower rate than other PeopleSoft business units. Education services generated $28.5 million in revenue in 1995, representing an increase of almost 93 percent over 1994. While a 93 percent increase looks impressive, PeopleSoft believes it can do better in this area. "One of our priorities this year is training availability," declares Grady. He plans to rapidly increase the amount of certified training resources to meet growing demand for both on-site and off-site customer training.

In early 1995, the customer service organization forecasted that 88 certified Instructors would be needed by January 1996 to fill the anticipated demand for education and training. These forecasts were shared with the field offices, along with target goals based on customer demands, revenue growth, and other factors. But by January 1, 1996, PeopleSoft had only 72 instructors on board, with just 55 of them certified. The shortfall of certified trainers would translate into a loss to PeopleSoft of 13,000 days of classes.

As a stopgap measure, the training organization worked with PSG to provide on-site training to cover the shortage. In the process, the company realized that many customers preferred on-site training, and now plans to provide 25 percent of its training on-site. Not all the training demand, however, was satisfied through the stopgap measures, and efforts to catch up continue. Through a combined effort of focused recruiting and working with PSG to fill the short term gaps, PeopleSoft expects to be able to fully meet training demands beginning the third quarter of 1996.

PeopleSoft's Customer Service Directions

PeopleSoft plans to expand its service marketing and communications efforts during 1996 to include publishing more service success stories, increasing awareness of on-site training options, monitoring field service activities closer (such as the hiring of trainers), packaging more PSG services, shifting customer access to its PS/Forum electronic (bulletin board) services via the Internet, and publishing results of the company's first major customer profile survey mailed to all customers of record in October 1995.

It was this Customer Profile Questionnaire that confirmed PeopleSoft customers' high level of loyalty. The survey found that 100% of PeopleSoft's Financials customers would choose PeopleSoft again, and 99 percent of PeopleSoft's HRMS customers would also do so. In addition, the survey compiled comprehensive information on customer demographics, database and platform environments, application selection processes and criteria, reasons for choosing PeopleSoft, whether or not the customer's implementation was on time and on budget, repeat purchase plans, an eye opening "hindsight is always 20/20" open-ended question section, along with other information that will be helpful for service planning purposes. PeopleSoft plans to make all the customer responses, both good and bad, on the hindsight is 20/20 section available verbatim to new and existing customers to help them benefit from the experiences of existing customers. This is another example of PeopleSoft's long-term, relationship-focused service philosophy that has contributed to its outrageous customer service reputation.

Issue Questions

1. Utilizing terminology and concepts from the discussion on Ted Levitt's Total Product Concept, develop a service augmentation strategy that will help continue PeopleSoft's differentiation in the client/server applications market for the remainder of the decade.
2. Could PeopleSoft benefit from an advertising and PR campaign that focused on its outrageous customer service stories, and if so, how? Outline an effective service marketing communications strategy based on the examples in the case, along with others.
3. PeopleSoft has relied heavily on its Partners to provide customers a significant amount of professional and implementation services—should PeopleSoft go beyond its "niche" strategy in PSG? If yes, develop a positioning statement and plan, to expand PSG services.
4. If PeopleSoft established a formal service marketing group, what should its responsibilities be, and what are the advantages and disadvantages over the informal or nontraditional structure that is in place?

Acknowledgments

We want to thank Sebastian Grady for his cooperation and assistance in providing information and contacts for this case. We also want to thank Peggy Taylor, Ray Gadbois, Christel Devlin, Patty Pasley, Michael O'Toole, Duncan Hsia, and Sarah Woodard, for their comments, insight, and input into the PeopleSoft service story.

Augustine Medical, Inc.: The Bair Hugger® Patient Warming System

Case 13

In July 1987, Augustine Medical, Inc. was incorporated as a Minnesota corporation to develop and market products for hospital operating rooms and postoperative recovery rooms. The first two products the company planned to produce and sell were a patented patient warming system designed to treat postoperative hypothermia in the recovery room and a tracheal intubation guide for use in the operating room and in emergency medicine.

By early 1988, company executives were actively engaged in finalizing the marketing program for the patient warming system named Bair Hugger® Patient Warming System. The principal question yet to be resolved was how to price this system.

The Bair Hugger® Patient Warming System

The Bair Hugger® Patient Warming System is a device designed to control the body temperature of postoperative patients. Specifically, the device is designed to treat the hypothermia (a condition defined as a body temperature of less than 36 degrees Centigrade or 96 degrees Fahrenheit) experienced by patients after operations.

Medical research indicates that 60 to 80 percent of all postoperative recovery room patients are clinically hypothermic. Several factors contribute to postoperative hypothermia. They are (1) a patient's exposure to cold operating room temperatures (which are maintained for the surgeons' comfort and for infection control), (2) heat loss due to evaporation of the fluids used to scrub patients, (3) evaporation from the exposed bowel, and (4) breathing of dry anesthetic gases.

Source: This case was prepared by Professor Roger A. Kerin, Edwin L. Cox School of Business, Southern Methodist University, Michael Gilbertson, Augustine Medical, Inc. and Professor William Rudelius, University of Minnesota, as a basis for class discussion and is not designed to illustrate effective or ineffective handling of administrative situations. Certain names and data have been disguised. The assistance of graduate students Ann Christensen, Joanne Perty, and Laurel Wichman of the University of Minnesota is appreciated. The cooperation of Augustine Medical, Inc. in the preparation of the case is gratefully acknowledged.

The Bair Hugger® system consists of a heater/blower unit and a separate inflatable plastic/paper cover, or blanket. A photo of the system is shown in Exhibit 1. The heater/blower unit is a large, square, box-like structure that heats, filters, and blows air through a plastic cover. An electric cord wraps around the back of the unit for storage, and the unit is mounted on wheels for easy transport. The blower tubing attaches to the warming cover through a simple cardboard connector strap and can be retracted into the top of the unit for storage. Temperature is set by a dial with four settings on the top of the unit. A top lid opens to a storage bin that holds 12 warming covers for easy access. The disposable warming covers come packaged in 18-inch-long tubes. When unrolled, the plastic/paper cover is flat and covers an average-sized patient from shoulders to ankles. The blanket consists of a layer of thin plastic and a layer of plastic/paper material laminated into full-length channels. Small holes punctuate the inner surface of the cover. When inflated through a connection at the feet of the patient, the tubular structure arcs over the patient's body, creating an individual patient environment. The warm air exits through the slits on the inner surface of the blanket, creating a gentle flow of warm air over the patient. The warming time per patient is about two hours.

The plastic cover was patented in 1986; there is no patent protection for the heater/blower unit.

Competing Technologies

Many competing technologies are available for the prevention and treatment of hypothermia. These technologies generally fall into one of two broad types of patient warming: surface warming or internal warming.

SURFACE-WARMING TECHNOLOGIES

Warmed hospital blankets are the most commonly used treatment for hypothermia in recovery rooms and elsewhere. An application of warmed hospital blankets consists of placing six to eight warmed blankets in succession on top of a patient. Almost all patients receive at least one application; it is estimated that 50 percent of the postoperative patients require more than one application. The advantages of warmed hospital blankets are that they are simple, safe, and relatively inexpensive. The main disadvantage is that they cool quickly, provide only insulation, and require the patient's own body heat for regenerating warmth.

Water-circulating blankets are the second most popular postoperative hypothermic treatment. Water-circulating blankets can be placed under a patient, over a patient, or both. If a blanket is placed just under the patient, only 15 percent of the body's surface area is affected. However, hospitals typically place water-circulating blankets either just over the patient or over and under the patient, forming an insulated environment that encloses 85 to 90 percent of the body's surface area. The disadvantages of water-circulating blankets are that they are heavy and expensive and can cause

Exhibit 1 Bair Hugger® Patient Warming System

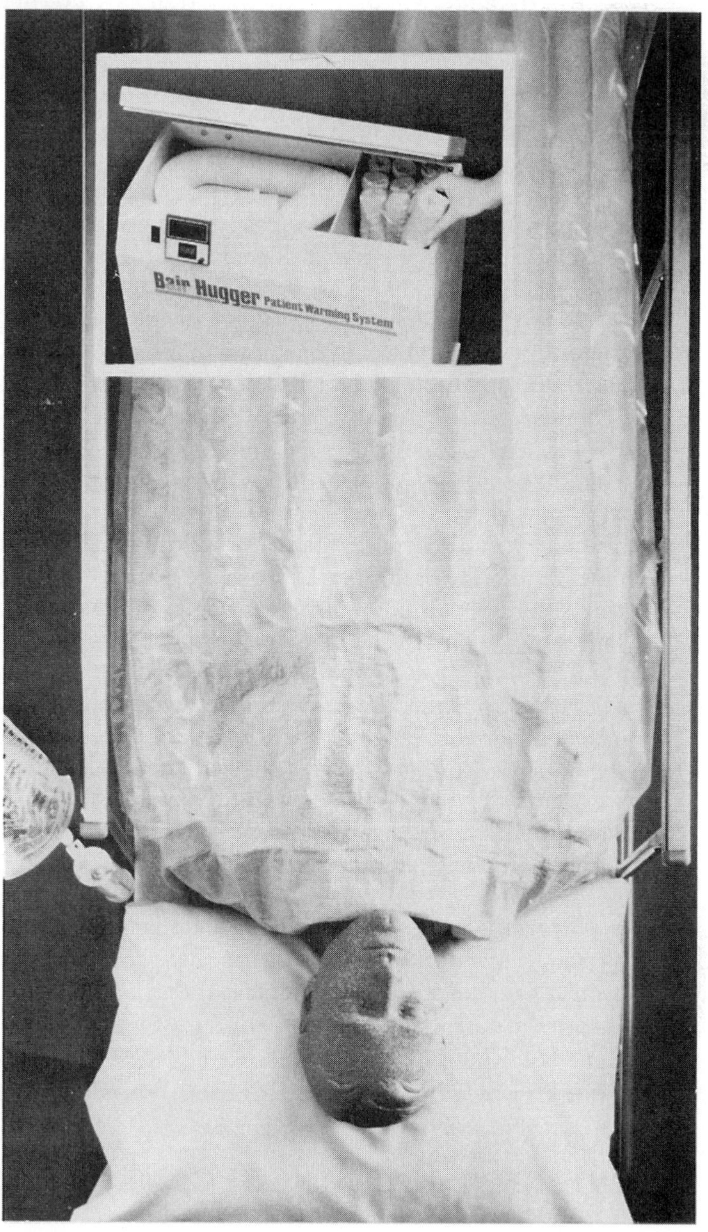

burns on pressure points. Moreover, although a widely used and accepted method of warming, especially for more severe cases of hypothermia, water-circulating blankets are considered only slightly to moderately effective.

Electric blankets are generally unacceptable as a hypothermic treatment because of the risk of burns to the patient and of explosion in areas where oxygen is in use.

Air-circulating blankets and mattresses are not in common use in the United States, although variations on this technology have been used in the past. This technology relies on warmed air flowing over the body to transfer heat to the patient. The advantages of warmed-air technology are that it is safe, lightweight, and theoretically more effective than warmed hospital blankets or water-circulating blankets. Products using this technology are not widely found in the U.S. market, however.

Thermal drapes, also known as reflective blankets, have recently been introduced and are gaining acceptance as a preventive measure used in the operating room. They consist of head covers, blankets, and leggings placed on the uninvolved portions of the patient's body. Their use is recommended when 60 percent of a patient's body surface can be covered. The advantages of this technology are that it is simple, safe, and inexpensive and has been shown to reduce heat loss. The disadvantage is that it merely insulates the patient and does not transfer heat to someone who is already hypothermic.

Infrared heating lamps are popular for infant use. When placed a safe distance from the body and shined on the skin, they radiate warmth to the patient. The advantages of heat lamps are that they are effective and illuminate the patient for observation or therapy. A disadvantage is that since the skin needs to be exposed, modesty prevents widespread use among adults. (They are, however, used in adult skin-graft operations.) Nurses dislike radiant heat lamps and panels because they tend to heat the entire recovery room and are uncomfortable to work under.

Partial warm-water immersion has been used in the past, especially in cases where a patient was deliberately cooled to slow down metabolism. With this method, the patient is placed in a bath of warm water and watched carefully. The advantages of this technology are that it transfers heat very effectively and it is simple. The disadvantages are that the system is inconvenient to set up and requires close monitoring of the patient, which increases labor costs. In addition, water baths must be carefully watched for bacterial growth, and they are very expensive to purchase and use.

Increasing room temperature is the most obvious way to prevent and treat hypothermia, but it is seldom used. The advantages of this method are that it is simple and relatively inexpensive and has been proven effective at temperatures of over 70 degrees Fahrenheit. The disadvantage is that warm room temperatures are not acceptable to the nurses and surgeons who must work in the environment. Furthermore, warm temperatures increase the risk of infection.

INTERNAL-WARMING TECHNOLOGIES

Inspiring *heated and humidified air* is a fairly effective internal-warming technique currently being used with intubated patients (those having a breathing tube in the trachea). However, delivery of heated and humidified air by mask or tent to nonintubated patients is not acceptable in postoperative situations, because mask or tent delivery would interfere with observation and communication and, in the case of a tent, might increase the chance of infection. The fact that the patient must be intubated is a disadvantage, since the vast majority of postoperative patients are not intubated.

Warmed intravenous (I.V.) fluids are used in more severe hypothermic cases to directly transfer heat to the circulatory system. Warmed I.V. fluids are very effective because they introduce warmth directly into the circulatory system. The disadvantages of this technology are that it requires very close monitoring of the patient's core temperature and high physician involvement.

Drug therapy diminishes the sensation of cold and reduces shivering but does not actually increase body temperature. Although drug therapy is convenient and makes patients feel more comfortable, it does not warm them and in fact slows their recovery from anesthesia and surgery.

Competitive Products

A variety of competitive products that use the above-mentioned technologies are available (see Exhibit 2). A review of competitors' sales materials and interviews with hospital personnel provided the following breakdown of competitive products.

Exhibit 2 Representative Competitive Products and Prices

Product	List Price	Company	Estimated Size of Company (sales; employees)	Comments
Blanketrol 200	$2,995/manual unit; $4,895/automatic unit; $165-$305/reusable blanket; $20/disposable blanket	Cincinnati Sub-Zero	$10 million; 90 people	Hypothermia equipment is a small part of its overall business.
MTA 4700	$4,735/unit; $139/reusable blanket; $24/disposable blanket	Gaymar Industries	$17 million; 150 people	Hypothermia equipment seems to be a major part of its business.
Aquamatic	$4,479/unit	American Hamilton (division of American Hospital Supply)	$3.3 billion; 31,300 people	Hypothermia equipment is a very minor part of American Hospital Supply's business.
Climator	$4,000/unit	Hosworth Air Engineering Ltd.	Not available	The company would begin distribution of hypothermia equipment in the United States in 1988.

WARMED HOSPITAL BLANKETS

For treating adult hypothermia, hospitals use their own blankets, which they warm in large heating units. Many manufacturers produce heating units for hospital use. The cost of laundering six to eight two-pound hospital blankets averages $0.13 per pound. Laundering and heating costs are absorbed in hospital overhead.

WATER-CIRCULATING BLANKETS

Several manufacturers produce water-circulating mattresses and blankets, but Cincinnati Sub-Zero, Gaymar Industries, and Pharmaseal are the major suppliers. Prices of automatic control units that measure both blanket and patient temperatures range from $4,850 to $5,295. Manual control units are priced at about $3,000, although they appear to be discounted by as much as 40 percent in actual practice.

The average life of water-circulating control units is 15 years. Reusable blankets list at from $168 to $375, depending on quality. Disposable blankets list at from $20 to $26. Volume discounts for blankets can reduce the list price by almost 50 percent.

Water-circulating blankets technology has changed little over the past 20 years except for the addition of solid state controls. There is little differentiation among the products of different firms.

REFLECTIVE THERMAL DRAPES

O. R. Concepts sells a product named the Thermadrape, which comes in both adult and pediatric sizes. Adult head covers list for $0.49 each: adult drapes list for $2.50 to $3.98, depending on size; leggings are priced at $1.50.

AIR-CIRCULATING BLANKETS AND MATTRESSES

Two competitors are known to provide an air-circulating product like the Bair Hugger® Patient Warming system; however, neither is currently sold in the United States. The Sweetland Bed Warmer and Cast Dryer was in use 25 years ago but is no longer manufactured. This product consisted of a heater/blower unit that directed warm air through a hose placed under a patient's blanket. The Hosworth-Climator is an English-made product that provides a controlled-temperature microclimate by means of air flow from a mattress. The Climator comes in a variety of models for use in recovery rooms, intensive care units, burn units, general wards, and patients' homes. The model most suitable for postoperative recovery rooms is priced at $4,000. This product could be distributed in the United States sometime in 1988. A summary of representative competitor products and list prices is shown in Exhibit 2.

The Hospital Market

Approximately 21 million surgical operations are performed annually in the United States, or 84,000 operations per average eight-hour work day. Approximately 5,500 hospitals have operating rooms and postoperative recovery rooms.

Research commissioned by Augustine Medical, Inc. indicated that there are 31,365 postoperative recovery beds and 28,514 operating rooms in hospitals in the United States. An estimated breakdown of the number of postoperative hospital beds and the percentage of surgical operations is shown below:

Number of Postoperative Beds	*Number of Hospitals*	*Estimated Percentage of Surgical Operations*
0	1,608	0%
1–6	3,602	20
7–11	1,281	40
12–17	391	20
18–22	135	10
23–28	47	6
29–33	17	2
>33	17	2

Given the demand for postoperative recovery room beds, the research firm estimated that hospitals with fewer than seven beds would not be highly receptive to the Bair Hugger® Patient Warming System. The firm also projected that one system would be sold for every eight postoperative recovery room beds.

Interviews with physicians and nurses, followed by a demonstration of the system, yielded a variety of responses:

1. Respondents believed that the humanitarian ethic "to make the patient feel more comfortable" is important.
2. Respondents felt that the Bair Hugger® Patient Warming System would speed recovery for postop patients.
3. Respondents wanted to test the units under actual conditions in postoperative recovery rooms. They were reluctant to make any purchase commitments without testing. A typical comment was, "No one today in this market ever buys a pig in a poke."
4. Respondents felt that the product was price-sensitive to alternative methods. If the product performed as claimed and demonstrated, purchase was probable by at least one-half of the individuals interviewed. Respondents were very receptive to the notion of using the heater/blower free of charge and only paying for the disposable blankets. Physicians wanted to confer with others who would be responsible for using the product to administer the warming treatment, however, such as the head nurse in postoperative recovery rooms and the chief anesthesiologist.

5. Respondents believed that the pressure to move patients through the operating room and out of postop is greater than in the past. Efficiency is the byword.
6. Capital expenditures in hospitals were subject to budget committee approval. Although the amounts varied, expenditures for equipment over $1.500 were typically subject to a formal review and decision process.

Augustine Medical, Inc.

Augustine Medical, Inc. was founded in 1987 by Dr. Scott Augustine, an anesthesiologist. His experience had convinced him that hospitals needed and desired a new approach to warming patients after surgery. His medical knowledge, coupled with a technical flair, prompted the development of the Bair Hugger® Patient Warming System.

The Bair Hugger® Patient Warming System has several advantages over water-circulating blankets. First, warm air makes patients feel warm and stop shivering. Second, the system cannot cause burns, and water leaks around electrical equipment are not a problem, as they are with water-circulating blankets. Third, the disposable blankets eliminate the potential for cross-contamination among patients. Finally, the system does not require that the patient be lifted or rolled. Augustine's personal experience indicated that all of these features would be welcome by nurses and patients alike. Features and benefits of the Bair Hugger® Patient Warming System are detailed in the company's sales literature, shown in Exhibit 3.

Investor interest in Augustine Medical and the medical technology it provided produced an initial capitalization of $500,000. These funds were to be used for further research and development, staff support, facilities, and marketing. It was believed that this initial investment would cover the fixed costs (including salaries, leased space, and promotional literature) of the company during its first year of operation. The company would subcontract the production of the heater/blower unit and would manufacture warming covers in-house using a proprietary machine. Only minor assembly would be performed by the company.

The Bair Hugger® Patient Warming System would be sold by and through medical products distributor organizations in various regions around the country. These distributor organizations would call on hospitals, demonstrate the system, and maintain an inventory of blankets. The margin paid to the distributors would be competitively set at 30 percent of the delivered (that is, less discounts) selling price on the heater/blower unit and 40 percent of the delivered (discounted if necessary) price on the blankets.

Preliminary estimates from subcontractors and a time-and-motion study on assembly indicated that the direct cost of the heater/blower unit would be $380. The cost of materials, manufacturing, and packaging of the plastic disposable blankets was estimated to be $0.85 per blanket.

The central issue at this time was the determination of the list price to hospitals for the heater/blower unit and the plastic blanket, given the widespread incidence of price discounting. Immediate attention to the price question was important for at least three reasons. First, it was felt that the price set for the Bair Hugger® Patient Warming System would influence the rate at which prospective buyers would purchase the

Exhibit 3 Sales Literature for the Bair Hugger® Patient Warming System

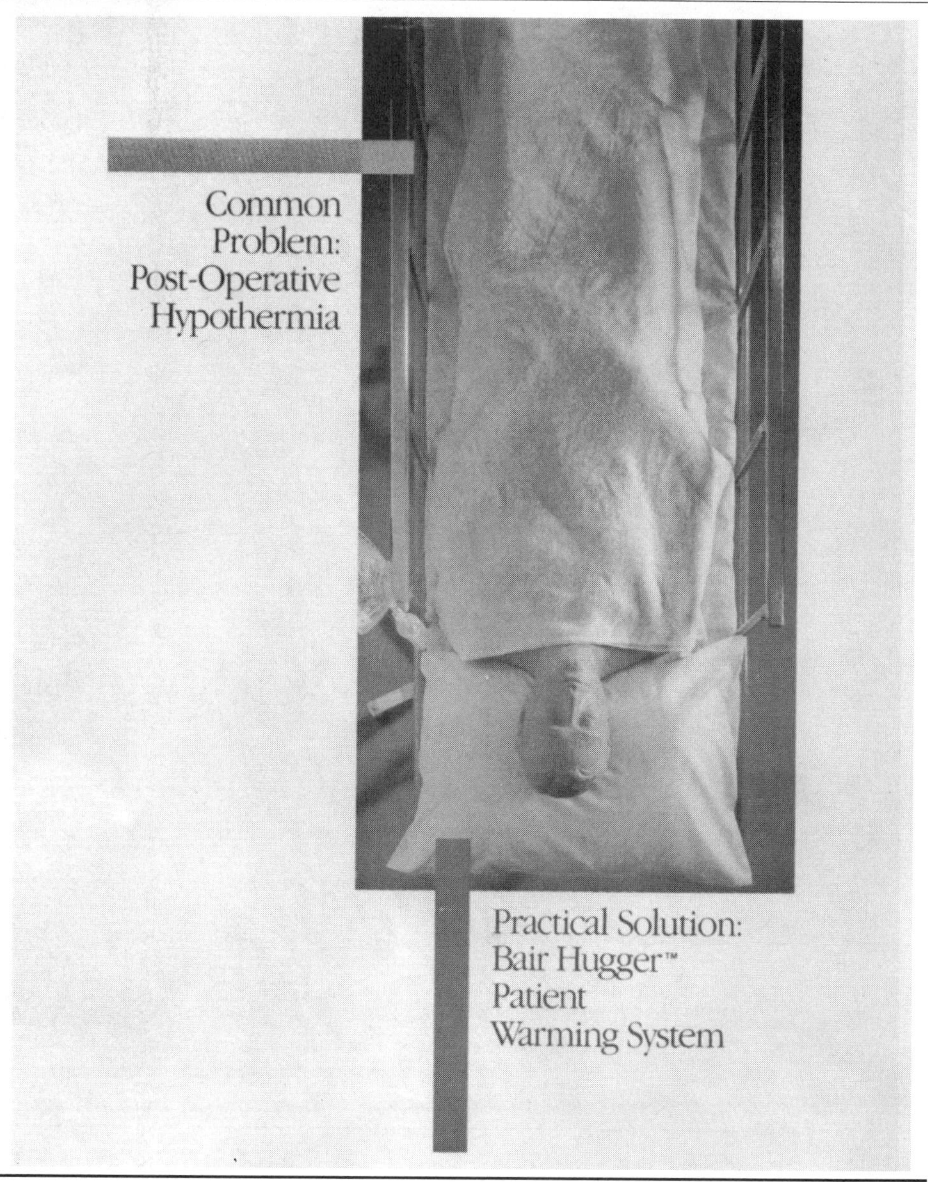

(continued)

system. Second, price and volume together would influence the cash flow position of the company. Third, the company would soon have to prepare price literature for its distributor organizations and for a scheduled medical trade show, where the system would be shown for the first time.

Exhibit 3 *(continued)*

A Warm Welcome for Your Recovery Room Patients

Augustine Medical, Inc.'s new Bair Hugger™ Patient Warming System is the most practical and comforting solution for post-operative hypothermia available today.

Every year more than 10,000,000 hospital patients experience the severe discomfort and vital signs instability associated with post-operative hypothermia. Years later, patients can still vividly recall this discomfort. Augustine Medical's new Patient Warming System is a warm and reliable solution to post-operative hypothermia.

1. PATENTED SELF SUPPORTING DESIGN
   As the tubes fill with air, the Warming Cover naturally arches over the patient's body.
2. TISSUE PAPER UNDERLAYER
   The tissue paper underlayer of the Warming Cover is soft and comfortable against the patient's skin.
3. AIR SLITS
   Tiny slits in the underlayer allow warm air from the Heat Source to gently fill the space around the patient.
4. SHOULDER DRAPE
   The shoulder drape is designed to tuck under the chin and shoulders, trapping warm air under the cover and preventing air flow by the patient's face.
5. DISPOSABLE COVERS
   The disposable Covers prevent cross contamination and reduce laundry requirements.

A Practical Solution to Post-Operative Hypothermia

The Bair Hugger™ Patient Warming System consists of a Heat Source and a separate disposable Warming Cover that directs a gentle flow of warm air across the body and provides for safe and comfortable rewarming.

The Bair Hugger Heat Source uses a reliable, high efficiency blower, a sealed 400W heating element, and a microprocessor-based temperature control to create a continuous flow of warm air. There are no pumps, valves or compressors to maintain. Special features include built-in storage space for the air hose, power cord and a convenient supply of disposable Warming Covers. The Heat Source complies with all safety requirements for hospital equipment.

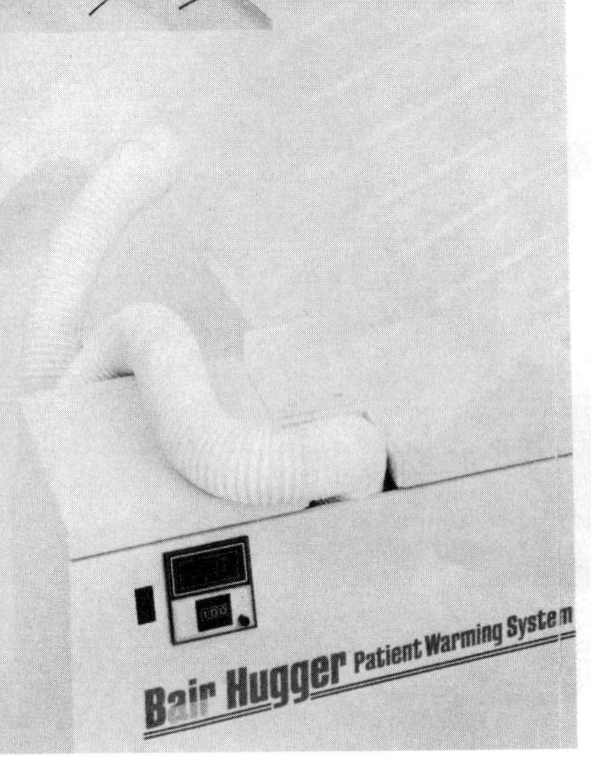

Exhibit 3 *(continued)*

THE BAIR HUGGER™ PATIENT WARMING SYSTEM IS SO EASY TO USE.

Remove a new Warming Cover from the storage compartment and unroll over the patient.

Connect the heater hose to the inlet of the Warming Cover and turn on the heater.

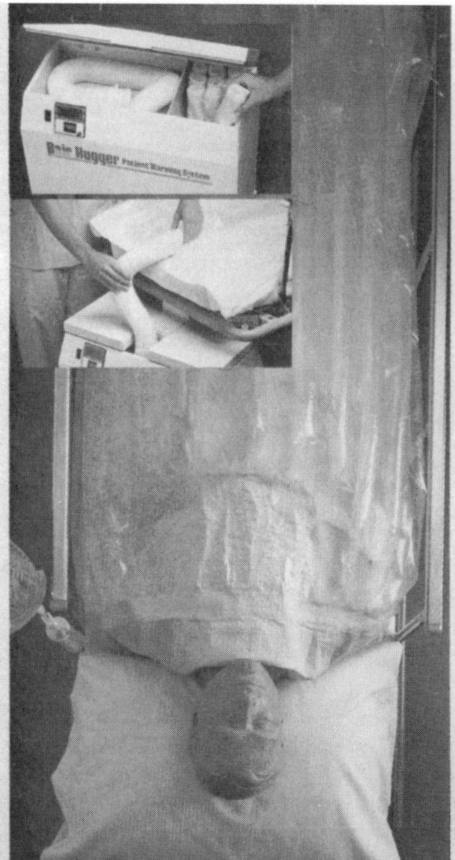

6. SIMPLE CONTROLS
   A preprogrammed temperature range and a preset high temperature limit of 110°F make the Bair Hugger safe and simple to use.
7. INTERNAL WARMING COVER STORAGE
   The storage compartment provides a convenient supply of Warming Covers ready for immediate use.
8. INTERNAL HOSE STORAGE
   The hose retracts into its own compartment for ready access.
9. LIGHTWEIGHT, COMPACT DESIGN
   The Heat Source is designed for convenience and portability. While in use, it tucks under the foot of the gurney. The unit's light weight and small size make it simple to move and store.
10. BUILT-IN POWER CORD STORAGE
    The power cord storage holds up to 12 feet of cord, making the Heat Source portable and easy to store.
11. 5μ AIR FILTER
    The air filter assures dust-free air circulation through the Bair Hugger Warming Cover. The filter is simple to change when necessary.

The Bair Hugger™ Warming Cover:

The Warming Cover consists of a layer of plastic and a layer of tissue paper laminate bonded together into long tubular channels. The self-supporting Warming Cover is designed to arch over the patient's body creating a warm, comfortable environment.

The Warming Cover is convenient to use because no straps, tapes or other fasteners are required to stabilize the cover and the patient does not have to be disturbed or moved.

When the Warming Cover is completely inflated, warm air from the Heat Source exits the tubular channels through slits in the Cover's soft underlayer, surrounding the patient with a gentle flow of warm air.

Exhibit 3 *(continued)*

A Warm and Practical Discovery: Bair Hugger™ Patient Warming System

Post-Operative Hypothermia–A Common Problem

As a practicing anesthesiologist, Dr. Scott D. Augustine observed that there was no practical treatment for the common problem of post-operative hypothermia. An extensive review of post-operative hypothermia revealed several important facts:

- Post-operative hypothermia (T<36°C or <96.7°F) occurs in 60-80% of all post-operative patients (1). This extremely common problem affects more than 10,000,000 surgical patients every year.
- Several factors contribute to post-operative hypothermia including the patient's exposure to cold operating room temperatures, heat loss due to evaporation of fluids used to scrub the patient, evaporation of moisture from exposed bowels, and the breathing of dry anesthetic gases.
- Unlike environmental hypothermia, post operative hypothermia is not usually life threatening. However, it can have serious side effects for older or unstable patients. Negative effects include a decrease in cardiovascular stability and an increase in oxygen consumption of up to 400% during unaided rewarming, as well as severe shivering and significant patient discomfort (2).
- Patients with unstable body temperatures require intensive nursing care, which means higher costs. Recovery room time may also be prolonged due to the instability caused by post-operative hypothermia.

Variety of Treatments–Only One Practical Solution

Many methods have been used to try to warm patients after surgery including warmed hospital blankets, water mattresses and heat lamps (3). Studies have shown, though, that these methods are ineffective.

The most common method of treating hypothermia–heated hospital blankets–does not actively heat the patient. The small amount of heat retained by a cotton blanket quickly dissipates, thereby requiring patients to rewarm themselves. Because multiple blankets are typically used, this method is both inconvenient and time-consuming for nursing staff and produces large amounts of laundry.

Another common method used to try to rewarm post-operative hypothermia patients is the use of a water circulating mattress. Water circulating equipment is heavy, complex, expensive and prone to leakage. While water mattresses have been used for many years, there is no clinical evidence that documents their effectiveness (4, 5). This lack of effectiveness can be explained by the minimal body surface area in contact with the mattress, (only 15%) and the lack of blood flow to this area. The weight of the patient creates a pressure which prevents normal cutaneous blood flow. The heat in the mattress cannot be transported away from the skin and the contact surface becomes an insulator effectively minimizing potential heat transfer to the patient.

New Approach Needed

As Dr. Augustine discussed the problem of post-operative hypothermia with doctors, nurses, and industry experts he became convinced that a new approach to warming patients was needed. A survey of anesthesiologists showed that most were dissatisfied with the current technology available for treating hypothermia. A new technology was definitely needed.

As a result of his research, Dr. Augustine developed the Bair Hugger™ Patient Warming System. Numerous studies and reports have shown that increased ambient room temperatures will prevent hypothermia (6-10). Indeed, before the advent of air conditioning, the average ambient temperature of the OR was higher and hyperthermia in the peri-operative period was not uncommon. Surgical patients will predictably lose or gain heat depending on the ambient temperature of the surrounding environment. The Bair Hugger™ System simulates a warm room by surrounding the patient in a gentle flow of warm air–A Focused Thermal Environment™.

The Bair Hugger™ Patient Warming System combines the convenience and effectiveness of warm air to safely rewarm hypothermic patients. The Warming System's minimal cost is rapidly recovered in saved nursing time, reduced linen expenses and lower overall recovery room costs. There is now a practical and cost-effective solution to post-operative hypothermia.

Two-week Free Trial

To arrange for a free two-week trial of the Bair Hugger™ Patient Warming System, fill out the enclosed reply card or call us collect at (612) 941-8866.

SPECIFICATIONS HEATER/BLOWER UNIT	
Size	26" high x 14" deep x 22" wide
Weight	65 lbs.
Power Requirements	110VAC
Temperature Range	Ambient to 110°F Max
Enclosure	Enameled steel
Displayed Variables	Temperature °F
Power Cable	12 Feet long
Display	.5 inch (1.2 cm) Character LCD
COVERS	
Size	54" x 36"
Weight	8 ounces
Material	Polyethylene and tissue paper laminate.

AUGUSTINE MEDICAL INC.

PRACTICAL SOLUTIONS TO COMMON PROBLEMS IN ACUTE CARE™

10393 West 70th St., Suite 100 Eden Prairie, Minnesota 55344

References: (1) Vaughan MS, Vaughan RW, Cork RC: Anesthesia and Analgesia 60:746-751, 1981. (2) Bay J, Nunn JG, Prys-Roberts C: British Journal of Anaesthesia 40: 398-406, 1968. (3) Kucha DH, Nichols GH, Christ NM, Bynum JW: Military Medicine 139:388-390, 1974. (4) Morris RH, Kumar A: Anesthesiology 36:408-411, 1972. (5) Goundsouzian NG, Morris RH, Ryan JF: Anesthesiology 39:351-353, 1973. (6) Morris, RH: Annals of Surgery 173:230-233, 1971. (7) Morris RH, Wilkey BR: Anesthesiology 32:102-107, 1970. (8) Clark RE, Orkin LR, Rovenstine EA: JAMA 154:311-319, 1954. (9) Bigler JA, McQuistow WO: JAMA 146:551, 1951. (10) Harrison GG, Bull AB, Schmidt HJ: British Journal of Anaesthesia 40:398-406, 1960.

Case 14

Brand Pipe Company

Mr. Alan Buford, manager of the Brand Pipe Company, a division of the Arnol Corporation, was considering a directive he had just received from top management of the parent organization. He was told by Arnol management that he was to come up with a specific marketing strategy and plan to stop the losses of the division as soon as possible and to provide a base for continued growth in the future.

Company Background

Brand Pipe, located in the Puget Sound area of the state of Washington, was a plastic extruder serving the Pacific Northwest. The company began operations in the early 1950s and subsequently was acquired by Arnol Corporation, a large company in an unrelated field. Company sales were $1.8 million, making it the second-largest extruder in the Pacific Northwest. Profits, however, had declined and the company had operated at a loss for the past year and a half.

The management staff at Brand Pipe consisted of Mr. Buford, who acted as both general manager and sales manager; Mr. George Timkin, the plant manager; Mr. Alan Britt, the plant engineer; and a plant foreman.

Industry Background

Thermoplastic pipe was made from four types of plastic resins: polyvinyl chloride (PVC), rubber-modified styrene (styrene), acrylonitrile butadiene styrene (ABS), and polyethylene (poly). The resins differ in chemical and physical characteristics, such as resistance to acids and bases, strength, melting point, and ease of extrusion. These plastic resins were bought from the large national petrochemical suppliers.

Source: This case is produced with the permission of Dr. Stuart U. Rich, Professor of Marketing, and Director Emeritus, Forest Industries Management Center, College of Business Administration, University of Oregon, Eugene, Oregon.

Plastic pipe competed with iron, aluminum, and asbestos-cement pipe in the Northwest market. In comparison with the other materials, plastic pipe was considered superior in terms of cost, ease of installation and maintenance, and deterioration from environmental influences. Plastic pipe was considered inferior to the other materials in terms of crushability, strength, and melting temperature. Plastic pipe could not be extruded in sizes greater than ten inches in diameter and also had a high degree of thermal expansion that restricted its use in some applications.

A machine called an extruder was used to form plastic pipe by heating the resin to near its melting point, forcing the fluid mass through a die, and then cooling the formed pipe in a water bath. A relatively unsophisticated plant to manufacture plastic pipe could be built for approximately $150,000. In fact, one of the successful competitors in the ABS market in the Northwest, the PJ&J Company, had what was called a "backyard operation" and operated out of a converted garage.

The different resins could all be satisfactorily extruded on the same machine, with the possible exception of PVC, which required a stainless steel die instead of the usual mild steel die. All that is required to change resin type is to change the resin fed into the machine. A die change to make different-sized pipe is even simpler. The extruder can be left hot and the pressure relieved so that the die can be changed.

Brand Pipe Company Extruded Pipe

All four thermoplastic resins were being converted by Brand Pipe into plastic pipe ranging from one-half inch to eight inches in diameter. The final product has pressure ratings from 80 psi (pounds per square inch) to 600 psi. The company's pipe was of standard quality and was comparable to that produced by competing pipe extruders.

Brand Pipe Company had just completed capital expenditures for new resin-blending and pipe-extrusion equipment that executives described as "the most technically advanced in the industry." The company had a plant investment of over $2 million. In view of Brand Pipe's unprofitable operating performance, it was considered doubtful that the Arnol Corporation would agree to additional capital expenditure appropriations. Brand Pipe owned and operated four modern pipe-extruding machines as well as three older machines. Despite the modern production setup, a production problem arose from the firm's inability to maintain adequate control over pipe-wall thickness. Pipe production used 7 percent more resin material than was theoretically required to ensure a minimum pipe-wall thickness. The plant engineer was in charge of quality control, but, because of substantial workload, he had spent little time on the costly material waste problem.

Since corporate management imposed tight limits on finished goods inventories, Brand Pipe had aimed at minimizing inventories. Rush orders, which frequently could not be filled from inventory, necessitated daily extrusion machine changeovers. However, a relative cost study conducted by the plant engineer showed that Brand Pipe could conceivably hold a much larger finished goods inventory and still not reach the point where costs of holding inventory would exceed machine changeover costs. Brand Pipe averaged seven machine changeovers per day, at an average loss to contribution to fixed overhead of $25 per changeover.

Plastic Pipe Market Segments

Brand Pipe Company produced some 200 separate pipe products of varying sizes and resin types to supply 11 market segments. Mr. Buford felt that, in order to use plant capacity to the utmost, Brand Pipe had to reach all of these end-use segments. Brand Pipe's sales volume was highest in water transportation markets for PVC and styrene pipe. The company's total pipe production by resin type (in pounds) was as follows:

Poly	450,000
PVC	3,871,000
ABS	769,000
Styrene	1,032,000
Total	6,122,000

Arnol Corporation market researchers had concluded that demand for plastic pipe would increase during the next five years in all market segments in the states served by Brand Pipe—that is, in Oregon, Washington, Idaho, and northern California. A summary analysis of each market segment follows, including current consumption estimates and five-year growth projections for Washington alone and for the four-state region including Washington.

AGRICULTURAL IRRIGATION

The agricultural irrigation segment was the largest-volume plastic pipe market in the Pacific Northwest. Plastic pipe, however, accounted for only 11 percent of all pipe used for agricultural irrigation. Newly developed plastic component systems, particularly plastic-component sprinkler irrigation systems, were replacing many open-ditch and metal pipe water transportation systems. Arnol market researchers, in describing growth potential for this plastic pipe market, stated that the "pendulum is swinging from metal to plastic pipe as the primary water transportation method." PVC resin pipe was used almost exclusively to supply this segment. Total plastic pipe consumption in Washington was 8.25 million pounds. Total for the four-state market area (Washington, Oregon, Idaho, and northern California) was 16.5 million pounds. Estimated growth for the next five years for Washington, as well as for the whole region, was 17 percent.[1]

PRIVATE POTABLE WATER SYSTEM MARKET

Building codes continued to favor copper and aluminum and to exclude plastic pipe from use for home water-supply systems. Although public utilities were utilizing PVC plastic pipe for public water systems, plumbing contractors shied away from

[1] Growth figures are for the five-year period. They are *not* annual growth rates. Therefore, a five-year growth figure of 61 percent is equivalent to a 10 percent average annual growth rate.

using polyethylene pipe in private systems. Total plastic pipe consumption for Washington was 145,000 pounds. For the Northwest region it was 350,000 pounds. No growth was forecast for the next five years.

MOBILE HOME MARKET

Most ABS plastic pipe sold to the mobile home market segment was used in plumbing fixtures. Most mobile home manufacturers sought to buy plastic fixtures on a national contract basis. It was a rare occasion when one of these national concerns purchased pipe from a local or regional extruder. Washington plastic pipe consumption was 130,000 pounds; regional consumption was 1.4 million pounds. A 90 percent growth figure was forecast for Washington, and 75 percent for the region.

PUBLIC POTABLE WATER

Some public water utilities were using PVC plastic pipe for water service lines that connect households to main water distribution lines. Styrene pipe had given way in recent years to the stronger, less brittle, more inert PVC pipe. Washington consumption was slightly over 2 million pounds, and regional consumption over 5 million pounds. A 100 percent growth figure was projected for both the state and the region.

INDUSTRIAL MARKET

Plastic pipe applications in processing, material supply, transfer, and waste disposal were severely limited in the industrial market segment. According to Mr. Buford, this was due to thermoplastic pipe's sensitivity to steam, sparks, and hot fluids. The most prominent industrial application was in copper mining, with minor applications in pulp and paper manufacturing, food processing, and seawater transfer. Total consumption in Washington was 600,000 pounds; for the region, slightly over 1 million pounds. Growth was projected at 45 percent for both the state and the region.

TURF IRRIGATION MARKET

Turf irrigation included applications such as public and private lawn-watering systems. Small-diameter PVC pipe was generally used by this market segment. Consumption in Washington was 3 million pounds; in the region it was 5.9 million. The projected five-year growth was 66 percent for Washington and 57 percent for the region.

DRAIN WASTE AND VENT MARKET

The drain waste and vent market was defined as all plumbing pipe running from and venting sinks, toilets, and drains to the structure drain. ABS pipe accounted for 86-90 percent of the market, with the remaining amount held by PVC. Plumbing unions had opposed the use of plastic pipe in favor of traditional materials, apparently because of the easy installation of plastic pipe with its resultant labor savings. Yet the unions claimed the traditional steel and iron pipes were superior. Consumption in Washington was slightly over 1 million pounds; regional consumption was 1.75 million pounds. Washington growth was projected at 27 percent; regional growth at 35 percent.

CONDUIT

Electric conduit was used primarily to protect and insulate electric power lines and telephone lines, both underground and in buildings. Competitive materials included the traditional aluminum metals. Major users in this market were large contractors and utilities that bought on a competitive bidding system. Consumption in Washington was 465,000 pounds; regional consumption was 1 million pounds. A 75 percent growth figure was projected for Washington, and 50 percent growth was forecast for the region.

SEWER AND OUTSIDE DRAIN

The sewer and outside drain market segment used plastic pipe for connections from house to septic tanks and sewer systems, downspout drainage, water drainage, and septic tank drainage. The primary resins used were styrene and PVC. The major competitive materials were asbestos fibers, cast iron, and vitrified clay; however, they were generally competitive only in the large sizes used in a public sewer system. The FHA had recently approved plastic pipe for rural homes. Washington consumption was 1.4 million pounds, and regional consumption was 2.8 million pounds. A 90 percent growth figure was forecast for Washington, and 78 percent growth was predicted for the region.

GAS TRANSPORTATION MARKET

In the gas transportation segment, plastic pipe was used to distribute low-pressure natural gas from major terminals through distribution mains to residences, businesses, and industrial users. Gas companies, which bought the pipe in large lots or on a yearly basis, had tested the plastic pipe and were not entirely pleased with the results. They favored the traditional steel pipe and the new epoxy-coated steel pipe that combined the inherent advantages of both plastic and steel. Washington consumption was 123,000 pounds; regional consumption, 300,000 pounds. Growth projection was marginal.

WATER WELL SERVICE AND STOCK WATER

Plastic pipe was used in rural areas to bring water from the individual farm wells into the home and to distribute it to outlying farm buildings to water livestock. The primary resins used were PVC and polyethylene. Washington consumption was

400,000 pounds, and regional consumption was 900,000 pounds. Relatively little growth was projected.

The four types of plastic pipe varied in their adaptability to use in the various markets just described. Adaptability depended on the physical attributes of the resin type as well as cost advantages needed for low-grade applications. PVC was the most versatile and was used in all market segments. Poly was suitable for use in all markets except sewer and outside drain, mobile homes, and drain waste and vent. ABS was adaptable for use in six of the eleven markets: public potable water, private potable water, turf irrigation, mobile homes, drain waste and vent, and gas transportation. Styrene was used for the most part in sewer and outside drain, drain waste and vent, and conduit markets.

Promotion and Sales

Brand Pipe used a limited amount of advertising in promoting its plastic pipe, preferring to rely on personal selling as its main promotional device. In the past the company had advertised in trade journals and in agriculturally-oriented magazines such as *Pacific Farmer.* It also sponsored early-morning farm radio programs on local stations, and utilized the usual product information folders and catalogs.

Recently Brand Pipe had used a mailer soliciting inquiries on a "spike sprinkler" coupling for irrigation. The spike sprinkler was a device to position a sprinkler in the field, and it was considered a superior pipe coupling. The company had contracted for exclusive distribution of the coupling to be used with its pipe, but did not itself produce the device. Brand Pipe had mailed 1,000 of the product folders and had received 200 inquiries. Mr. Buford was enthusiastic about the response and planned to increase mailer promotion in the future.

The company salespeople were assigned by geographic area, and they called on pipe distributors and large end-users in each area. They were responsible for sales of all company products in their respective areas. The three main sales areas were the Seattle-Puget Sound area, the Portland and eastern Oregon-eastern Washington area, and the southern Oregon-northern California area. Each of these areas was covered by one salesperson. In addition, Mr. Buford had a number of working contracts and made visits to major accounts. This was relatively simple because most of the major distributors were located within short distances of the division office.

In addition to the field salesperson, there was one in-house salesperson who handled small "drop-in" business, short-notice orders, and customers requiring a quote on an order of pipe. Often, a distributor would phone in an order, asking for a price quote and delivery at the end-user's site the next day. If the company was not capable of meeting a price and delivery schedule, the customer would take that business elsewhere. The company tried its best to provide service on these accounts so that it could maintain plant capacity, even if it meant machine changeovers to produce the order.

Since the salespeople were assigned one to an area, they were responsible for missionary, maintenance, and service selling. They were compensated, according to corporate policy, by straight salary with no commissions paid for different product sales. They called on distributors and large end-users and were expected to educate distributors on product knowledge and use and to handle field complaints. Often these complaints emanated from a do-it-yourself end-user who had not followed the directions for joining pipe sections together correctly. At times the salespeople tried to stimulate sales by going to the end-user and providing technical service such as product specification and pipe-system design.

Distribution

Brand Pipe sold the majority of its plastic pipe through distributors, with 20 percent of the accounts contributing 75 percent of gross revenue. Only in the case of large end-users such as utilities and major contractors did the company try to sell directly. In such cases, the company paid the regular commission to the area distributor only if the distributor managed to learn of the sale and the distributor was of some importance to the company. Marketing terms were 2/10 net 30.

Pipe distributors, who were paid a commission of 5 to 10 percent of sales, performed several major functions: (1) they broke bulk and sold to many retailers in their area; (2) they used the pipe along with many other components in the piping systems that they installed, such as agricultural irrigation systems, plumbing systems, and turf irrigation systems; and (3) they provided financing and inventory service for their customers. Distributors held preparatory inventory in seasonal markets such as agricultural irrigation. In preparation for the seasonal demand, Brand Pipe would deposit "dated" shipments at the distributor's warehouse.

Pipe distributors in most market segments considered price to be the most important factor determining from whom they bought pipe. Most distributors agreed that one pipe was as good as another; they considered delivery service to be the next most important factor. They did not feel that technical service offered by the manufacturer was very important in their choice of suppliers. In fact, some distributors were very ambivalent about the usefulness of manufacturers' salespeople. Some felt that the best thing salespeople could do was stay out of the field. They disliked pipe salespeople's "muddying the water" at the end-user level and making promises to the end-user that the distributor was unable or unwilling to fulfill. Other distributors, however, felt that pipe salespeople could and did help by providing product knowledge to the distributor salespeople. Under no circumstances did any of the distributors favor having pipe salespeople contact the end-user.

Distributors generally viewed the price competition within the industry with disfavor. One reason was the lowered profit margin on sales of the pipe. Since distributors usually made a fixed percentage on sales, their income was reduced by lowered prices. Another reason was the distributors' concern that when they were making a bid on a system including plastic pipe, their competitors might get a more favorable quote on plastic pipe and therefore be able to quote a lower bid. The distributors wanted plastic pipe prices stabilized so that their bids could be based on their own competence and economic situation rather than on the pricing practices of the pipe manufacturers.

Although distributors disliked price competition, they were glad to see that Brand Pipe and other producers had lowered the price to the point where imported pipe was not a major source of market supply. Many were reluctant to handle shipload quantities of imported pipe with its resultant inventory and handling problems. They much preferred a convenient source of supply, which the local producers could provide.

Although some distributors had considered making their own plastic pipe, they did not at the time consider such production attractive. For the time being, they were content to buy pipe from suppliers. Brand Pipe had been a factor in this decision by improving service and by lowering prices.

In view of the continuing poor profit situation of his division, Mr. Buford had considered trying to integrate forward and capture the distributors' margin. One of the salespeople had felt that Brand Pipe salespeople could do as good a job selling plastic pipe to end-users as the distributors did.

Transportation

Approximately 75 percent of Brand Pipe's annual volume was shipped via common carrier, with the remaining 25 percent being delivered by company-leased trucks or through factory "will-call" by customers. Because of competitors' practices, in most cases either Brand Pipe's shipments were prepaid to Northwest destinations or comparable freight allowances were made from gross sales price when pipe orders were picked up at the plant by customers. Because plastic pipe was so bulky, shipping costs averaged about 15 percent of the selling price. This meant that each competitor had a substantial advantage in selling in its own home market.

Pricing Policy

Mr. Buford looked over the profit summary report (see Exhibit 14.1) and wondered whether changes in the present pricing policy might lead to improvements in the profit picture of his division. The present policy of "meeting or beating the price offered by any other supplier" had been initiated earlier when the Japanese began exporting large quantities of plastic pipe to the Pacific Northwest. Because of lower raw material costs and a suspected dumping policy, they were pricing their products below those of local suppliers. Even though there were disadvantages in the sales agreements offered by the Japanese (such as order sizes of shipload quantities only), the Japanese were able to capture a significant portion of the market due to their low price.

The effects of the Japanese entry into the Pacific Northwest market were immediately felt by Brand Pipe, since the Japanese were marketing PVC—the major resin type produced by Brand Pipe. At that time, Mr. Buford reasoned that the size of the Pacific Northwest market could not accommodate another supplier of plastic pipe. He felt that steps must be taken immediately to drive the Japanese out of the Pacific Northwest.

To achieve this goal, Brand Pipe adopted its present pricing policy, thus forcing the Japanese to compete on terms other than price, such as speed of delivery, where the

Exhibit 14.1 Profit Summary Report, per-Pound Basis

	Poly	PVC	ABS	Styrene
Gross sales price	0.3625	0.2760	0.3648	0.2762
Less discounts, freight, and allowances	0.0710	0.0138	0.0378	0.0377
Net sales price	0.2915	0.2622	0.3270	0.2385
Less variable costs (raw materials and conversion)*	0.3050	0.2230	0.3392	0.2110
Direct margin (contribution to fixed costs)	-0.0135	0.0392	-0.0122	0.0275
Less fixed costs	0.0397	0.0375	0.0501	0.0314
Profit	-0.0532	0.0017	-0.0623	-0.0039

For analysis purposes, treat conversion as changeover costs only. Other labor costs are included in the fixed cost figure.

Japanese were at a strict disadvantage. Soon after this, other suppliers followed suit. The average price levels gradually eroded from $0.28 per pound down to $0.26 per pound. With the decreased price, the Japanese left the Pacific Northwest market, and Mr. Buford felt that they would not reenter it until the price came back to $0.28 per pound.

Recently, the Sierra Plastic Pipe plant had burned to the ground. This company had been the major supplier for southern Oregon and northern California. A number of the other suppliers including Brand Pipe increased their plant capacity in anticipation of taking over the accounts that they were sure Sierra would lose. To prevent the loss of its accounts, Sierra bought plastic pipe on the open market and was thus able to maintain its customers while its plant was being rebuilt. Because Sierra was able to remain in business, and because the growth of the Pacific Northwest market was not up to expectations, a considerable overcapacity on the part of all suppliers soon developed in the Pacific Northwest. This overcapacity was estimated at 30–40 percent, but some suppliers were continuing expansion.

Because of the overcapacity and the desire on the part of executives to maintain market share, Brand Pipe had continued its present pricing policy. It was reasoned by Mr. Buford that a reduction in price would increase market share, which would increase production and narrow the gap between plant capacity and the production level, thus minimizing fixed cost per unit.

In evaluating the present pricing policy, Mr. Buford came to two conclusions. First, the profit picture for his division was most likely quite similar to that of the other regional suppliers. Second, although the distributors enjoyed the low price that was resulting from the fierce price competition, they were unhappy with the volatility of the price levels that was also generated.

Competition

Domestic competition in Brand Pipe's marketing area came from six regional manufacturers and five to eight major national producers. The number of national producers varied because some of them moved in and out of the Northwest market, depending on economic conditions. The regional manufacturers had about 75 percent of the market, while the larger national firms and a few import firms controlled the rest. Three of the regional firms controlled 60 percent of the Northwest market. Sierra Plastics was a leader, although Brand Pipe and Tamarack Pipe closely followed. The three companies produced essentially the same products.

Tamarack Pipe was within 50 miles of Brand Pipe's plant and was a strong competitor in the Portland, Oregon, market and the Puget Sound market. Due to its location in southern Oregon, Sierra Plastics had a strong competitive position in the southern Oregon-northern California market, resulting from its lower transportation cost in this area compared with those of Brand Pipe and Tamarack.

Brand Pipe had tried to differentiate its product in the past, but had met with limited success. In an attempt at differentiation, Brand Pipe had changed the color of its PVC pipe from gray to white. Other competitors, especially the nationals, had made some progress in differentiating their products. Babbitt Corporation, a national supplier of pipe and piping systems to industry, had added plastic pipe to its product line and advertised in such national periodicals as *Chemical Engineering*. Babbitt was very strong in the industrial segment of the market. Cable Company had distinguished its pipe by application to sump pump installations and had a virtual monopoly in this specialized application. PJ&J in northern California was the chief supplier of ABS pipe in the Pacific Northwest, primarily through being the least expensive marketer. For example, Brand Pipe was able to buy PJ&J pipe and resell it for less than it would cost to produce comparable pipe.

In recent months, Brand Pipe salespeople had reported that Tamarack had begun to concentrate more on the agricultural irrigation market, while Sierra was concentrating on being the primary supplier of plastic pipe for conduit. Even though this latter market was small, it was anticipated to mushroom when the housing market resumed its growth. The large national firms had concentrated on the mobile home industry and appeared to have the greatest number of manufacturers, since contracts were negotiated on a countrywide basis.

The large national manufacturers were either owned by or affiliated with national petrochemical companies. These companies usually adjusted to the prevailing market conditions and were a stabilizing influence on the market.

The competitive conditions that had prevailed in the Northwest had depressed the financial conditions of some of the smaller independent firms, and it was not known how much longer they would continue operations. The larger independent firms, although experiencing losses, were as well financed as Brand Pipe and were still battling for increased market share.

Conclusion

Mr. Buford realized that a number of changes were needed in many parts of his company's marketing program. He saw that some of these changes were interrelated; for example, decisions on pricing strategy might have an important impact on product policy, and vice versa. Certain decisions had to be made very soon if the company's profit position were to be improved, whereas other decisions could be postponed for a while.

Mr. Buford felt that his planning task was made more difficult by the limited size of the management staff in his division. Although the parent corporation provided help in market research and some coaching in general planning procedures, the actual planning and strategy determination was Mr. Buford's responsibility. Because of the need to keep division overhead expenses down to a minimum, Mr. Buford knew that no additional management staff could be hired at the present time.

As he walked into his office, pondering what to do first in the way of planning, his phone rang and the in-house salesperson asked him to okay a price quote on a drop shipment for the next day. Mr. Buford okayed the quote, and then sat down muttering, "How can I find time to plan for the months and years ahead when daily operating problems demand so much of my time?"

Case 15

Ohmeda Monitoring Systems

Looking out his office window at the magnificent Front Range of the Colorado Rockies, Joseph W. Pepper, general manager of Ohmeda Monitoring Systems, was deep in thought concerning the future of Finapres®, a relatively new Ohmeda product. Introduced in 1987, the product had not lived up to its expectations. Now, in mid-June 1990, Pepper was considering a number of options. His choice, he knew, would have a significant impact on Ohmeda Monitoring Systems.

Background

Finapres (the name was derived from its use of finger arterial pressure) was the product on the market providing *continuous noninvasive blood pressure monitoring* (CNIBP). As such, it was the only unique product that Ohmeda could offer in 1990.

Originally introduced to the market in 1987, initial results had been disappointing. Its introduction in the United States had been generally unsuccessful. Results in Europe, and internationally, had been somewhat better but still had failed to meet the firm's expectations. Concerns about the product had led Ohmeda to stop shipments on May 1, 1990, pending a review of product problems and the overall situation.

At an all-day meeting on May 23, 1990, marketing research, field sales, and R&D had presented information on the status of Finapres. In particular, R&D had given its assessment as to the likelihood that proposed product changes and improvements would solve some of the product's shortcomings.

The specter of the disappointing initial introduction, and the uncertainty that R&D could improve the product sufficiently to satisfy all the concerns, hung over the decision to commit more funds to the product. An unsuccessful reintroduction would further hurt Ohmeda's credibility, both with customers and with the field sales

Source: This case was prepared by Professor H. Michael Hayes and Research Assistant Brice Henderson as a basis for class discussion, rather than to illustrate either effective or ineffective handling of an administrative situation.

force. On the other hand, successful reintroduction of Finapres would ensure a strong, and possibly dominant, position in the noninvasive blood pressure monitoring market, plus the possibility of increased sales of other monitoring products, as Finapres was combined with other Ohmeda products into packaged systems.

Subsequently, Pepper had many discussions with his key managers regarding their views of Finapres. In early June he visited a number of Ohmeda customers and distributors in Japan, many of whom were very interested in Finapres. Although there were several unanswered questions, it was up to Pepper to make the key decisions concerning Finapres.

BOC/Ohmeda

Ohmeda Monitoring Systems was a business unit of The BOC Group, a multinational firm, headquartered in Windlesham, Surrey, England. The Group had an international portfolio of what it described as "world-competitive" businesses, principally industrial gases, health care products and services, and high-vacuum technology. The Group operated in some 60 countries and employed nearly 40,000 people.

Health care products and services were provided by BOC Health Care for critical care in the hospital and in the home. Their equipment, therapies, and pharmaceuticals were used in operating rooms (OR), recovery rooms (PACU), intensive care (ICU), and cardiac care (CCU) units throughout the world. Divisions of BOC Health Care were organized around *pharmaceuticals, home health care, intravascular devices, and equipment and systems.*

Ohmeda Health Care, providing equipment and systems, was an autonomous division of BOC Health Care. It was made up of five major business units, plus a field operations unit. The five business units manufactured products for *suction therapy, infant care, respiratory therapy, anesthesia,* and *monitoring systems.* Field operations provided field sales and sales support, worldwide, on a pooled basis to all the business units. (See Exhibit 15.1 for a partial organization chart of Field Operations.)

A 1985 reorganization had put all business decisions in the hands of the business general managers, and established profit of the business unit as a major performance measure. In 1990, the managers of the business units, and the manager of field operations, reported to the president of Ohmeda Health Care, Richard Leazer, who, in turn, reported to the managing director of BOC Health Care, W. Dekle Rountree.

OHMEDA MONITORING SYSTEMS

Ohmeda Monitoring Systems (headquartered in Louisville, Colorado) designed, manufactured, and sold (through the field operations unit) monitoring equipment for a number of segments of the health care industry. It focused its business activities on three classes of products:

Exhibit 15.1 Ohmeda Monitoring Systems Partial Organization Chart—Field Operations

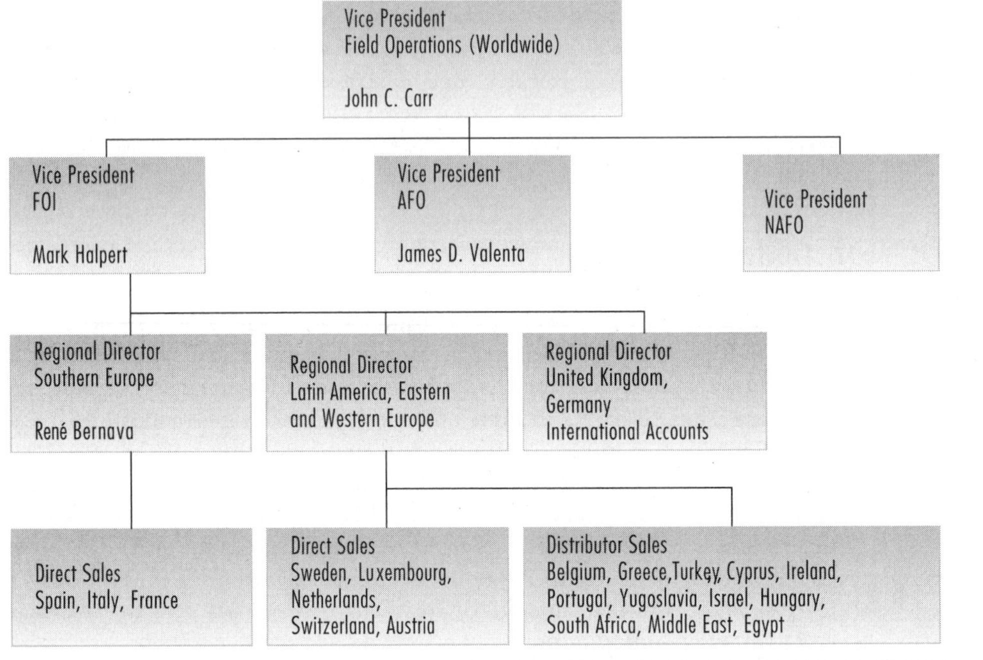

- Oximetry products, used to measure oxygen content in arterial blood.
- Gas analysis products, used to measure a patient's respiratory gas levels.
- Noninvasive blood pressure measurement products.

Applications for these products were found in a wide variety of departments within hospitals and other health care facilities. Products were usually sold to the health care facility, either directly by the field sales force or by a distributor. Some products, however, were also sold to equipment manufacturers (OEMs) for incorporation in a larger measurement package.

Most Ohmeda oximetry and Finapres products consisted of a "box,"containing the hardware, software, and a display unit, and a probe, or cuff, to allow a noninvasive way to measure the parameter of interest. These were of two types, disposable or reusable, and were designed to be attached to the patient's toe, foot, finger, hand, or ear, depending on the application.

Ohmeda had access to Finapres technology by virtue of a worldwide exclusive license, obtained from Research Unit Biomedical Instrumentation TNO (Amsterdam, the Netherlands). Many other technologies had also been acquired, either by license or outright purchase.

Ohmeda estimated the noninvasive monitoring market was $1.2 billion worldwide, with 60 percent of the market in the United States. Overall, its market share was some 15 percent of those segments it served. In selected categories, however, its market share was considerably higher. With considerable variation by country and specific product, Ohmeda estimated the growth rate of its served market at 5–10 percent per year.

The competitive picture for Ohmeda was complex. Its main competitors were U.S.-based firms. Many of its products, however, faced strong competition from European firms. In oximetry there were an estimated 25 competitors, although only 4 had significant shares. Major competitors and estimated market shares were:

Nellcor (U.S.)	50%
Ohmeda (U.S.)	30
Criticare (U.S.)	10
Novametrix (U.S.)	8

In respiratory gases there were an estimated 12 competitors. Major competitors and estimated market shares were:

Datex (Finland)	16%
Ohmeda	15
Siemens (West Germany)	14
Hewlett-Packard (U.S.)	12

In blood pressure measurement only five companies competed. With an 80 percent share, Critikon (U.S.) dominated the noninvasive market with its oscillometric, or noncontinuous, product. Ohmeda's sales of its noninvasive products represented just 2 percent of this market.[1]

Based on pretax operating profits in 1989, Ohmeda's financial situation appeared to be very healthy. There were concerns, however. As Pepper observed:

> *We tend to be more financially driven than market driven. Also, we have not been investing heavily in R&D. As a result, our product line is relatively mature and I don't know how much longer we can count on present products for high contribution margins.*
>
> *Finapres is the only major new product that is close to ready to go. Perfecting Finapres, and successfully reintroducing it, would not only produce direct sales but its uniqueness could also benefit our other monitoring businesses, through integrated packages that included a technology available nowhere else. The sales force in Europe, and also in Asia, is very excited about the product, even with its present deficiencies, and believes that with reasonable improvement it could become a major contributor to sales and profits. In the U.S. there is not the same excitement. There is agreement that if all the product deficiencies could be corrected we would have a real winner, but R&D can't give us any guarantees.*

---

[1]Market shares were for the U.S. market.

FIELD OPERATIONS

Following the 1985 reorganization of Ohmeda Health Care from a functional organization to the five therapy units, the firm had considered how to organize its field sales operations. Given the complexity of the five product lines, and some desire on the part of the therapy unit managers to have more direct control over the sales forces that represented them, there was considerable support to establish specialized sales forces. There was also support for direct sales, as opposed to extensive use of distributors or dealers. Selling anesthesia equipment, it was argued, was very different than selling patient monitors and other Ohmeda products, both because of product differences and customer buying procedures. Many of Ohmeda's competitors (e.g., Siemens and Hewlett-Packard) relied heavily on direct sales, feeling that distributors or dealers could not provide the required level of technical knowledge and service.

Arguing against specialized selling was the belief that it was far more efficient, in terms of time, travel expense, and customer knowledge, to have one salesperson calling on a hospital, rather than three, as was contemplated in one proposed form of organization. Still further, there was great concern about the consequences of terminating distributors or dealers, some of whom had been associated with Ohmeda (or its predecessor companies) for over 70 years. Finally, Ohmeda was aware that Baxter-International, the largest medical supplies and equipment company in the world, had specialized its sales force in 1981 but had subsequently gone back to a general sales organization.

After extensive study, it was decided to continue with a pooled form of sales organization, together with pooled product service, customer service, and finance, all reporting to the vice president of Field Operations. As of early 1990 Field Operations had three principal regional components: NAFO, responsible for sales and service in North America (the United States. and Canada); FOI, responsible for sales and service in Europe, the Middle East, and Latin America; and AFO, responsible for sales and service in Asia, including Japan. Depending on the particular country, sales were all direct, a combination of direct and dealer, or totally through dealers.

Ohmeda recognized the need for making specialized product knowledge, beyond the expertise of the local salesperson, available quickly to the customer. In NAFO it was assumed that such specialized knowledge could be provided by specialists from manufacturing locations. In FOI and AFO it was deemed impractical for specialists to travel from the United States, and product champions were appointed in the major countries. Paid principally on salary (as opposed to the salespeople who were paid on a salary and commission basis), the product champions supported the sales force for their assigned products in a variety of ways. They were available to call on customers with the salespeople. They held product seminars, either for salespeople or for customer groups. In some instances they acted as missionary salespeople, soliciting orders from new customers. In all instances, they provided a focused communication channel between the field and headquarters marketing. It was Ohmeda's view that the product champions had played a major role in assisting the introduction of Finapres in Europe. There was also some concern that not enough manpower was available from headquarters to provide similar support to the field sales force in the United States and Canada.

Health Care Markets

The health care industry was one of the largest, and most rapidly growing, segments of the world economy. While growth was occurring worldwide, the potential for Ohmeda products was greatest in the United States, Europe, Japan, and, generally, in the developed countries of the world. With certain exceptions, the United States tended to lead the world in the development and use of technologically sophisticated health care products. U.S. manufacturers of such products generally felt that the rest of the world followed the U.S. lead in acceptance and use, with countries in Europe following in as little as six months, but with longer delays in other parts of the world.

Hospitals were the principal buyers of Ohmeda products. With some variation, due mainly to government regulations, purchasing practices were very similar in the developed countries of the world. All purchases of medical equipment required budgetary approval of the hospital administration. Their purchasing influence, however, was generally inversely related to the complexity of the item. Purchase decisions of disposable supplies and gases, for instance, were generally made solely by the hospital purchasing agent, based on the lowest price. By contrast, capital equipment was invariably selected by the hospital's medical specialists and clinical area end-users. Because any machine malfunction was potentially life-threatening, medical specialists were especially concerned with precision, reliability, and safety. In addition, both the sophistication of clinical procedures and the technical expertise and interest of medical specialists were increasing. As a result, the product and clinical knowledge required to sell medical equipment was also increasing.

Ohmeda segmented its market by hospital department or application, as follows:

OR/PACU (Operating Room/Post Anesthetic Care Unit, or Recovery Room)

ICU/NICU/CCU (Intensive Care Unit/Neonatal Intensive Care Unit/Coronary Care Unit)

L&D (Labor and Delivery)

Floors (basically patients' rooms in hospital wards)

Nonhospital (the growing nonhospital segment, which included ambulances, surgicenters, physicians' offices, dental and home care, for oximetry and blood pressure products)

Sales potential varied substantially, depending on the particular segment and the product, as shown in Exhibit 15.2. Segments outside the United States generally had lower saturation levels than in the United States. As was pointed out, however, saturation levels were not always the best indicator of sales potential. In many instances the replacement markets offered high potential as well.

In the operating room the physician (generally the anesthetist) was the key buying influence for all products. In all other segments decision making was a shared responsibility, as indicated in Exhibit 15.3. Key buying influences were thought to be influenced by different factors, in order of importance as indicated below:

Exhibit 15.2 Ohmeda Monitoring Systems U.S. Market Size (Sales Potential in Units, 1990–1992)

Segment	Potential Sites*	Oximetry	Gas Analysis	Blood Pressure	Saturation
OR/PACU	60,000	26,000	31,000	15,000	HI
ICU/NICU/CCU	78,000	20,000	15,500	9,750	HI
L&D	57,000	10,000	0	4,000	MED
Floors	800,000	15,000	0	2,000	LO
Nonhospital	65,000	10,500	0	200	MED

*Number of physical locations.

Physician	**Nurse**	**Technician**
Technology	Ergonomics	Serviceability
Ergonomics	Relationship	Technology
Relationship	In-service	
Price/value	Technology	
Administrator	**Financial Officer**	**Materials (Purchasing)**
Company reputation	Leasing options	Price/value
Price/value	Total package cost	Total package cost
Revenue generation	Reimbursement	Serviceability

Personal contact with key buying influences by direct sales representatives or distributors was an essential ingredient to securing an order. Key to success, however, were favorable results from experimental trials, particularly of new products, as reported in medical journals. Manufacturers worked closely with the medical community worldwide to identify opinion leaders interested in equipment who were willing to experiment with it and then publish their results in scholarly journals. Most such experiments were reported in English language journals, but these were widely read in non–English-speaking countries.

Exhibit 15.3 Ohmeda Monitoring Systems Buying Influences

	OR	ICU	NICU	PACU	CCU	Floors	L&D
Probes	P	NTM	NT	NT	NTM	NTM	NT
Blood pressure	P	PNM	PN	PN	PNM	PNM	PN
Gas analysis	P	PTM	PT	PT	—	—	PT
Oximetry	P	NTM	NT	NT	NTM	PNTM	NT

Legend:
P = Physician
N = Nurse
T = Technician
A = Administrator
F = Financial officer
M = Materials (purchasing)

OR = Operating Room
ICU = Intensive Care Unit
NICU = Neonatal Intensive Care Unit
PACU = Post Anesthetic Care Unit
CCU = Coronary Care Unit
L&D = Labor and Delivery

Finapres®

Modern medicine viewed measurement of arterial blood pressure as essential in the monitoring of patients, both during and after surgery. Traditional monitoring techniques have included both invasive and noninvasive methods. Arterial line monitoring provided continuous measurement but invasion (meaning surgical insertion of a long, small-bore catheter into the radial or femoral arteries) involved the risk of thrombosis, embolism, infections, and nerve injuries. These risks were acceptable when arterial blood samples had to be taken regularly but otherwise were to be avoided.

An oscillometric monitor, such as Critikon's Dinamap, was noninvasive. As commonly used, such a device provided readings automatically every three to five minutes, or on demand. It could provide readings more frequently, but this involved considerable patient pain or discomfort. As normally used, therefore, it could miss vital data due to the time lag of the readings. (Ohmeda sold a noninvasive blood pressure monitor of this type, manufactured for them, but had not promoted it heavily.) Manual methods were noninvasive but were highly dependent on the skill of the clinician and the application of the correct size arm cuff and involved even more time lag.

FINAPRES TECHNOLOGY

In 1967 a Czech physiologist, Dr. Jan Peñaz, patented a method with which it was possible to measure finger arterial pressure noninvasively. (See Exhibit 15.4 for a detailed description of the method.) In 1973 the device was demonstrated at the 10th International Conference on Medical and Biological Engineering at Dresden. Subsequently, a group of engineers at the Research Unit Biomedical Instrumentation TNO in the Netherlands became interested in the technology and constructed, first, a laboratory model, and then a model that they felt was clinically and experimentally useful and commercially viable. In 1983 Ohmeda acquired an exclusive license for the Finapres technology.

FINAPRES AND OHMEDA

Although TNO had produced a working model of Finapres, Ohmeda had invested between two and three million dollars in R&D in order to develop a manufacturable box and cuff and to recode the software to conform to Ohmeda protocols. The resultant design could be built largely on existing equipment, although some $100,000 was required for tooling the cuff. Prior to commercial introduction, extensive work was done with opinion leaders to establish the credibility of the product. Favorable test results of clinical studies of Finapres were reported in medical journals, and were widely distributed to the medical profession. Cost of this work, and other market development expenditures, was roughly equivalent to the cost of R&D.

Ohmeda introduced a commercial design of Finapres in 1987 in the United States and in 1988 in Europe and other world markets. The initial offering consisted of a box,

Exhibit 15.4 Ohmeda Monitoring Systems Principles of Operation

Arteries transport blood under high pressure to the tissues. The artery walls are strong and elastic; that is, they stretch during systole (when blood is forced onward by contraction of the heart) and recoil during diastole (dilation of the heart when its chambers are filling with blood). This prevents arterial pressure from rising or falling to extremes during the cardiac cycle, thus maintaining a continuous uninterrupted flow of blood to the tissues. The volume of blood inside the artery increases when it expands and decreases when it contracts. This change in volume is the key phenomenon on which the Peñaz/Finapres technology was based.

In the Finapres system, a cuff with an inflatable bladder was wrapped around the finger (see diagram below). A light source (LED) was directed through the finger and monitored by a detector on the other side. This light was absorbed by the internal structures according to their various densities. The emitted light was an indication of blood volume in the artery. Through a complex servomechanism system, the cuff was inflated, or deflated, to maintain the artery size at a constant level. Thus, cuff pressure constantly equaled arterial pressure and was displayed on the monitor as an arterial waveform and also digitally.

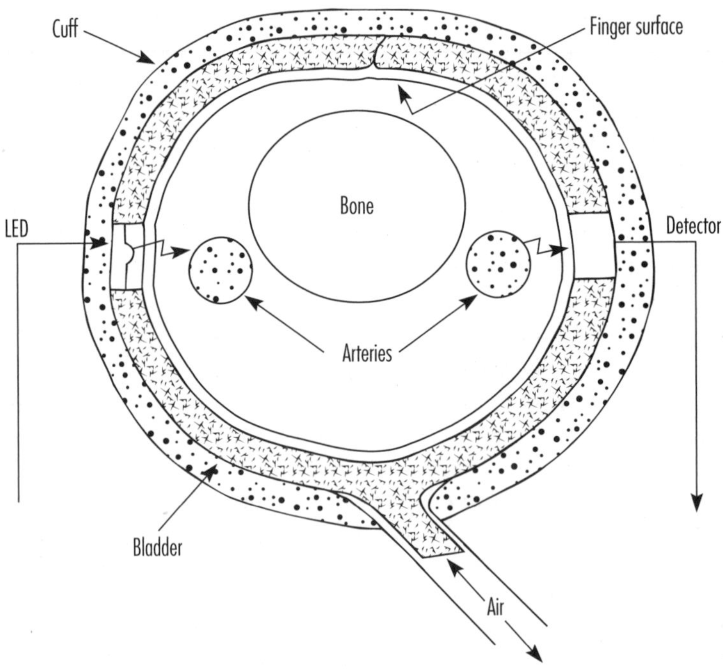

a patient interface module that attached to the patient's hand, and three reusable cuffs. It was positioned to compete against invasive measuring products. Although it was expected it would ultimately be offered to the OEM market it was originally introduced directly to the OR market. Priced at approximately $9,500 it was expected to return a contribution margin in excess of 70 percent (generally typical for new and unique products in the health equipment industry). Some price resistance was experienced and the U.S. price was reduced to $8,500, six months after introduction. Disappointingly, U.S. sales through 1989 totaled only 200 units.

In 1988 the product was introduced internationally, at a U.S. equivalent price of $9,600. In contrast to the U.S. introduction, the product was targeted, for direct sale, at a number of segments in hospitals. As in the United States, price resistance was encountered and by 1989 the price had been reduced to approximately the U.S. equivalent of $5,000.

To some extent low sales in the United States were blamed on tactical marketing errors, such as the positioning and price of the product at introduction. There were also some technical problems with the system. Some were cosmetic in nature and easily fixed. Others were more serious, both for the clinicians using the equipment and for Ohmeda. Major problems were the difficulty in applying the cuff properly in order to get an accurate reading, and drift in readings that occurred after several hours of continuous use, a particularly serious problem in OR. Another problem was the inability of the equipment to accurately monitor patients with poor blood circulation.

Results were more promising in Europe. The European medical community had been anxious to get access to Finapres. Much had been written about the Peñaz methodology and the system developed by TNO in the European medical press. The noninvasive aspect of Finapres was particularly attractive. European doctors were less comfortable with arterial line methodology than were their American counterparts. In addition, they tended to be more willing to invest time and effort to learn new technologies and there was less preoccupation with patient throughput than in the United States.

News of the problems experienced in the ORs in the United States had made penetration of the OR segment in Europe difficult. With its broader contacts, the sales force was able to introduce the product to other segments, particularly in CCU and physiology in teaching hospitals, where stability over long periods of time was either not as critical as in OR or where continuous blood pressure monitoring was of paramount importance. With this approach, supported by the willingness of the sales force to train medical personnel in application of the cuff, the company experienced much greater success, selling a total of 700 units in these markets through 1989.

Commenting on results through 1989, Melvyn Dickinson, international marketing manager observed:

> *There are significant differences between the hospital markets in the United States and Europe, and in how our sales forces sell to them. In the United States, for example, anesthetic machines, made by one of our sister therapy units, are sold by the same field sales force that sells our monitoring equipment. The U.S. machines are made to more stringent requirements and are much more expensive than those sold in Europe. In addition, they tend to be replaced on a 5-year cycle, compared to 10-15 years in, say, Italy. As a result, our sales force in the United States tends to really concentrate on the OR market, whereas in Europe the sales force takes a broader approach.*
>
> *It's also important to recognize that the key influence for OR purchases is an anesthesiologist, for whom blood pressure is just one of many concerns. In other segments of the hospital, the situation is very different. In the CCU, or the cardiac operating theater, blood pressure is of paramount importance. Not all procedures are lengthy, and even when they are, many cardiologists saw value in CNIBP, even though there was drift. For physiological measurements in research hospitals, or in hypertension units, there were even fewer drawbacks, plus the clinicians in these situations were much more inclined to take extra care with application of the cuff.*

> *Beyond these differences, we misread the market in general. It had been our assumption that arterial lines (the term for invasive systems) were the major competitors for Finapres. We priced and positioned Finapres accordingly. Unfortunately, our promotion didn't get this position established in the minds of our customers. As it turned out, many customers viewed the oscillometric machines as our major competitor. For these customers, our original price involved too large a premium, versus the less expensive oscillometric machines. Now there is some real question about going back to the original positioning strategy.*

The two years following the introduction of Finapres were characterized by indecision about its future and lack of significant support for the product. Once introduced, Ohmeda required it to be self-supporting, with product improvements made on an ongoing basis financed out of current revenues. When the sales force began to report complaints from the clinicians in the field, it was felt that the major problems were cosmetic, concerning the size of the box and the readability of the screen. Complaints regarding inaccurate readings were thought to result from misapplication of the cuff. Despite some modifications, complaints continued and sales declined. As 1990 began, it was apparent that decisions as to the future of Finapres needed to be made.

REASSESSMENT

Reassessment of Finapres had started with the development of the five-year plan for Ohmeda Monitoring Systems. Subsequently, concerns on the part of the sales force about the commitment to Finapres indicated the desirability of a meeting involving sales force management, product management, and R&D. On May 23, 1990, Joe Pepper convened a meeting of representatives of all three groups, as well as headquarters marketing. The main points that emerged from the meeting were as follows:

- There was general agreement that the market potential for CNIBP was large. There was, however, considerable disagreement as to its exact size. Some estimates of the U.S. market were as large as 7,740 units per year. International estimates were considerably lower. There was general agreement that the largest market segments for Finapres were OR and ICU/CCU. It was the view of Ohmeda's product managers, however, that the focus of the NAFO sales force on the OR market made selling to the ICU/CCU segment difficult.
- It was emphasized that the diffusion of innovation in many instances took a long time. Acceptance of some currently standard medical equipment came only after a number of years. Oximetry, for example, took 14 years, echocardiography took 10 years, and, as it was emphasized, capnometry

(CO_2 gas analysis) took 40 years to become accepted. However, if Finapres was to ultimately succeed, investment was necessary not only in technological development, but in market development as well.

- The following reasons for lack of success to date were identified:
  - — *Drift in readings over time.*
  - — *Not accurate for average clinician.*
  - — *Not easy to use.*
  - — *Inadequate alert for misapplied cuff.*
  - — *No alerts for problems with poor circulation.*
  - — *No toe/pediatric/neonatal thumb cuffs.*

- Concerns were expressed about:
  - — *Lack of a research culture.*
  - — *Bottom line/short-term focus.*
  - — *R&D research shortage.*

- R&D gave its assessment of time and cost to develop fixes and their likelihood of success:
  - — *The cause of drift was not certain, but there was a high probability that the problem could be fixed with changes in software, probably in 1990. If this fix worked the cost would be relatively modest.*
  - — *Assessing the present cuff as offering 30 percent of ideal requirements, currently contemplated modifications could be expected to improve performance to 40 percent by January 1991, again with relatively modest cost. With a more substantial effort it was expected performance could be improved to 80 percent in two years.*

- Noninvasive oscillometric blood pressure machines were not likely to be "thrown out" in favor of Finapres. It was more likely they would be replaced on a normal schedule.

- On the positive side a number of strengths were identified:
  - — *Patents lasting past the year 2000 (except the U.K. and Germany).*
  - — *Strong distribution, particularly in OR.*
  - — *Technical expertise.*
  - — *Head start over competition.*

Following extensive discussion, four options were presented:

1. Stay on the present course. Make sufficient modifications to make it possible to carefully reintroduce the product in selected markets. This approach was estimated to cost $307,000 in R&D expense, generate sales of 820 units through 1994, and have a net present value of $30,000.
2. Stop the project. Taking into account writing off current inventory costs and possible return costs, this approach was estimated to have a negative NPV of $160,000.
3. Make a significant investment in R&D and marketing (including going forward with a mini-Fini, a much smaller version of Finapres that would be targeted at the OEM market). This contemplated a 50 percent penetration of the OR market by 1995, a 50 percent penetration of the ICU market by 1998, and significant penetration of the OEM market. Cumulative sales estimates for this approach were 7,700 units in the United States and 4,000 internationally (through 1995). With projected revenues of $40 million, investment in R&D of $2 million, investment in marketing of $1.2 million, the net present value of this approach through 1995 was estimated to be $2,200,000.
4. Sell the business. There was considerable discussion of this option but the general view was that it was not likely Ohmeda could find a buyer willing to pay any significant amount for the business. In any event, it was unlikely that top management at BOC would approve such a step.

MANAGEMENT VIEWS

Subsequent to the May 23 meeting a number of views were expressed by Ohmeda managers. As John Carr, vice president of Field Operations, saw it:

> *The international experience with Finapres was more successful for a variety of reasons. The original technology was developed by a European company (TNO) so the European medical community was familiar with the concept. The sales force is more balanced in its approach to the market. Hence, it was able to exploit niche markets where the device worked very well. The initial sales built confidence. The real key was the use of product champions. The product was given support and attention that it did not receive in the States.*
>
> *Finapres represented a once-in-5-to-10-years type of opportunity. It was a significant new technology which didn't seem to fit Ohmeda's culture or annual financial cycle. If the initial effort had been followed by product enhancements, Finapres would have been successful. From here, the only two decisions I see are sell or go.*

Similar views were expressed by James Valenta, vice president for Asia (AFO):

Finapres is a great product, which, from my view in the Asian markets, has significant customer appeal. It seems that things were stacked against the product from the beginning. Soon after Finapres was purchased, Ohmeda reorganized. The individual who had pushed to buy the technology moved on to other assignments, which resulted in some lost momentum. Finapres never really had a home, which compounded the problems with the system itself. Had there been a quicker response to feedback from the international sales force, most of what was discussed at the meeting today, the drift issue and the cuff, could have been resolved some time ago. Ohmeda had trouble accepting the fact that there was a problem. The feedback domestically was focused more on cosmetic rather than substantive issues. Changes were made without knowledge of the impact to other parts of the system.

Japan is more technologically oriented, they grasped the idea of the system quickly and easily. Maybe it's just that invasive technology isn't as advanced overseas as in the United States. The doctors in Japan seem more interested in learning about new technology than in the States.

If Ohmeda doesn't want to continue with Finapres, I'll buy it and produce it. I believe in the product that much.

A somewhat different perspective was given by René Bernava, regional director for Southern Europe:

Europe was ready for Finapres. The medical community, especially in Germany, was excited about the studies and papers written about the product. As a whole, European doctors were much less comfortable with arterial monitoring than their American counterparts. Finapres should have been a dazzling success in Europe, but there were problems, both with the product and the way it was marketed.

The technology for Finapres was purchased but not improved. The early version did not work. The project had software problems and lacked leadership. The original plan was to make an inexpensive disposable cuff. With this focus, a cuff that really worked regardless of cost was never developed. Also, the product was introduced at a premium price. That philosophy did not work.

The international sales force felt we had the top technology and wanted to go ahead. The meeting today occurred because we were the most vocal. I went to Dekle (President Dekle Rountree) some time ago and asked him to investigate the product, renew agreements with TNO, and put some money into the project. Some money was forthcoming but it wasn't a continuing process.

As Mark Halpert, vice president for FOI, saw the situation:

There are several reasons Finapres was more successful in Europe and overseas than in the United States. The sales force in Europe sells many products whereas in the United States the sales force only sells Ohmeda products. With the large product line, we developed customer expertise. We know what the customer wants, and we use technical support to help conclude the transactions.

The organization or the medical community in Europe is different also. Anesthesia and monitoring are the same customer. In the United States there are more specialists. The sales force, with its broader coverage and experience, went after other niches rather than anesthesia, where the product had failed in the United States.

The key difference internationally was the product champion. Internationally, the product champion was part of the sales force, thus closer to the customers. In the United States, management served this role. Europe is still enthusiastic about the product. In Germany, just with the 1991 cuff, the product will be a success.

Bonnie Queram was manager of Sales Programs and Administration in NAFO and reported to the vice president of Sales. As she recalled:

Everyone was enthusiastic when Finapres was introduced. It looked easy to sell, although the box was big and clunky. Initially there was a high level of sales activity and orders. Unfortunately, when problems surfaced we tended to focus on cosmetic fixes and sales tapered off in the United States. In contrast, sales held up well in Europe. I developed a questionnaire to find out why. The responses indicated there is a major difference in clinical practice between the United States and Europe. The physicians, for instance, are more down-to-earth there. In contrast to the United States, they are very patient and want to work with the manufacturer, particularly on a new product. The anesthesiologists will spend lots of time in pre-op making sure things like the cuff are OK, whereas in the United States they are very impatient. For these reasons, and a number of others, I concluded that the European experience wouldn't transfer to the United States. Our normal assumption is that we can develop our products for the U.S. market, and then go abroad with the same strategy. This is the one case in a hundred where this assumption doesn't apply.

Bill Belew, a senior product manager in Louisville, had a somewhat different view. According to Belew:

The product problems in Europe and the United States are identical. The only difference is the sales approach. What we need is a complete fix. That will cost in the neighborhood of $2 million, but once we have it we can go after the OR/ICU markets anywhere in the world.

He went on to say:

The May 23 meeting was both good and bad. The potential for the product was reiterated, and we heard the product would not be killed. On the other hand, it didn't sound as if we were going to make the kind of commitment the potential justified. And this was despite information that Nellcor might introduce a CNIBP product in September.

The enthusiasm for Finapres was shared by Lloyd Fishman, director of marketing. He had a number of concerns, however:

I've been watching Finapres evolve since joining Ohmeda 2 ½ years ago. I think the product has potential to represent as much as 10% of our sales, but I was concerned that there was no sense of purpose, no vision, about the product. We were doing lots of little "fixits" without any real sense of our markets or what the product should be. I called the May 23 meeting to see if we couldn't develop such a sense of purpose or vision.

There's no question that we face a complex situation. The markets in the United States and international are very different. The financial orientation of the doctors in the United States rubs off on our sales force and they're much less inclined to sell concept products than in Europe, where the doctors like to work with us on new developments.

Ray Jones had recently joined Ohmeda as R&D group manager and was responsible for the Finapres R&D effort. As he put it:

I think Finapres has lots of potential, but we need to resolve a number of critical issues. For instance, we use finger pressure as a measure of central blood pressure, but we're not sure how closely finger pressure simulates central pressure or how accurately we're measuring finger pressure.

Management would like us to give some performance guarantees, but that's not the nature of R&D. We can, however, identify the key technical and physiological issues and identify milestones with the expectation that we can get data to indicate if the issue is resolvable.

One of the things that would really help would be for marketing to give us some better performance criteria.

Finally, Joe Pepper reflected on his thoughts subsequent to the May 23 meeting, his various discussions with his managers, and his visit to Japan:

I know the people in the organization feel we don't spend enough on R&D. But its a question of balance. We have been spending over 6 percent of sales on R&D, plus the corporation has a major research facility at Murray Hill, New Jersey, where we do the riskier, blue sky, R&D. In the past our competitors have spent a higher percent of sales on R&D. We estimate that Nellcor, for instance, spent over 10 percent during the last four years. However, we also estimate that they will reduce this in the next four years.

The May 23 meeting was valuable and we got a lot of opinions on the table. One option that was not looked at, however, was to go exclusively with OEMs.

In Japan the product is selling well. The physicians appear more willing to fiddle with the product to make it work. Based on what's going on in Japan, and what is going on in Europe, I wonder if we might not be able to bootstrap their experience back into the U.S. market.

Part of our problem is our whole development process. We've hired some new people, Ray Jones as product development manager and Nick Jensen as a research scientist, but it's going to take them some time to sort out the problems and establish better procedures.

I know John Carr wants us to go with a product that will sell in the United States. Part of the question, though, is how much faith do I put in the numbers?

Case 16

BWI Kartridg Pak

Kartridg Pak (KP) was a mid-sized manufacturer of food processing and packaging equipment located in the Midwest. The firm was a subsidiary of BWI, a British firm which consisted of three divisions comprised of a total of six subsidiaries, all of which manufactured packaging equipment. Kartridg Pak was one of the larger firms in the food packaging machinery industry, with sales between $25 and 30 million in 1992.[1]

Although Kartridg Pak was an established food packaging machinery firm, with four product lines, sales had not been growing as fast as the company would have liked. To continue its own growth, and to keep up with some of its larger competitors, the firm felt it must consider several options, including entry into a new market. Thus, in early 1993, KP was considering entry into the growing vertical form-filled-seal (VFFS) segment of the packaging machinery market. If the firm decided to enter the market it would also have to decide what subsegments to enter, whether to enter de novo or by acquiring an existing firm, and how such a market would fit into its existing organization.

Packaging Machinery

Starting in the middle to late 1980s several important trends began to have a serious impact on consumer packaged goods industries, especially those producing food products: a rising demand for packages which offered the consumer convenience, an increased demand for bulk packaging, and a rising level of environmental consciousness

Source: This case was prepared by Peter G. Goulet of the University of Northern Iowa and Bryan R. Hoyt and Carol D. Willenbring of Teikyo Marycrest University. It is intended as the basis for class discussion rather than to illustrate either effective or ineffective handling of an administrative situation.

[1]The actual sales of this firm are unknown because it is a subsidiary of a larger firm. Dun and Bradstreet estimates 1992 sales at $30 million; although parent company financial statements indicate that actual sales may be up to $32 million; although it is possible that some of KP's sales are included in another of the three BWI divisions. Please refer to the financial statements in Exhibit 4.

about the role of packaging in reducing resource use and increasing recycling options. Firms selling consumer packaged goods, and facing increased pressure on profits, also adopted new packaging techniques to control costs and product quality.

The consumer packaged goods industry consisted of firms producing a wide variety of products with two essential components: the product itself and the package. A package not only contains and protects a product, but also supports shipping and distribution needs. Finally, and perhaps most importantly, a package conveys important information about the product it contains. For these reasons, an important supplier to the packaged goods industry was the industry producing packaging machinery and equipment.

The packaging machinery industry was a fragmented industry serving a variety of market segments. The total value of the U.S. packaging machinery industry shipments, including services and import/export activity, was estimated to be $3.171 billion in 1993, up 6.0 percent from 1992, and it was expected to grow to $3.394 billion in 1994. Industry growth reached an average annual compound rate of 6.4 percent per year bewteen 1987 and 1992. The total value of 1993 shipments included services of $92 million, 4 percent of the total, leaving $3.079 billion of final products. Of the total shipments recorded by the industry in 1993, $670 million were exported. In addition to U.S. production there were imports estimated at $758 million in 1993. The chief export markets are Canada, Mexico, Great Britain, and various European countries. The major countries supplying imports were Germany and Italy. Roughly 23 percent of the value of imports was composed of parts for U.S. affiliates of foreign companies.[2]

Major segments of the packaging machinery industry included strapping machines, bottling and canning equipment, thermoforming equipment, blister packaging machines, code marking equipment, machinery for collating, sorting, and filling, aerosol filling machines, shrink-wrap packagers, testing and quality control equipment, and form-fill-seal machines. Major buyers of equipment in the early 1990s included the food, cosmetics, drug, and chemical industries, as well as producers of liquids. The industry also contained a hybrid segment which included producers of equipment used to package food during its production. (For example, products such as commercially available sandwich spread were packaged, during processing, in flexible tubes.)

The largest single firm in the package machinery industry was the Signode division of Illinois Tool Works (ITW). Signode was a leading supplier of strapping equipment which, by itself, accounted for roughly one-quarter of all industry shipments in 1992. After Signode, only one other U.S. firm, Figgie International, Inc., had sales in excess of $100 million. At least 50 firms had sales of $10 million or less in 1992.

FORM-FILL-SEAL SEGMENT

The form-fill-seal segment of the packaging machinery industry involved the manufacture of machines that create packages, fill them, and seal them, all in one continuous operation. The package was essentially a bag which could be sealed on four sides

[2]Data for this section were taken from "Industrial Machinery," *U.S. Industrial Outlook 1994.* Washington, D.C.: U.S. Department of Commerce, 1994, p.17-10.

or on three sides (top, bottom, and back), or a pillow pouch which was sealed at the top and bottom. These packages were made of various films which ranged from simple cellophane, plastic, or paper to complex, high-barrier films combining paper, various plastics, and/or foil, for example, paper on the outside and foil or plastic on the inside. These barrier films were used for chemicals, liquid and perishable food, or other products which must be protected against leakage or spoilage. In addition, form-fill-seal packages could be injected with air or gas to protect products such as salty snacks from spoilage or damage. Form-fill-seal machines could be designed to operate horizontally (candy bars) or vertically (potato chips, liquid brick packs).

Although the total value of shipments was not known precisely for the various segments of the packaging machinery industry, some estimates placed the market for all types of form-fill-seal equipment at roughly $165 million in 1992 ("Meeting of Minds" 1990). This market was subdivided into horizontal machines, which were used primarily to package dry products, and vertical machines (VFFS) which could be used for both liquid and dry products. The breakdown of sales in these two subsegments was not known exactly. However, given the high percentage of total sales resulting from VFFS machines for the dominant firms in the VFFS market segments, it is likely that the VFFS market was the larger of the two subsegments (see Exhibit 1). Those firms for which sales could be estimated collectively had VFFS sales in excess of $120 million in 1992. In addition, there were other firms for which sales could not be estimated, making the $120 million figure conservative.

The form-fill-seal packaging machinery industry supplied two major customer groups. The first consisted of large producers of food products such as snacks, candy, and frozen foods, as well as certain industrial products producers, that purchased packaging machines and materials and filled their own packages. The second customer group consisted of contract packaging firms hired by food, candy, and other firms not

Exhibit 1 Large Packaging Machinery Firms Including Firms Selling VFFS Packaging Machinery (Dollar Figures in Millions)

Firm	Estimated Firm Sales	Percent of Sales in VFFS	Estimated VFFS Sales
Package Machinery	$63	NA	NA
Woodman/Kliklok	56	<70%	$ 35–40
Hayssen	50	90%	45
Paxall	37	<20%	7
Triangle	18	100%	18
W. A. Lane	7	95%	7
Prodo Pak	5	95%	5
Approximate total VFFS sales			$117-122

Source: This data was estimated from firm sales supplied by *Ward's Business Directory*, and through informed sources in the industry.

able to afford the machines themselves. The contract firms not only packaged the goods, but also often shipped them to the customers of their clients directly. The industry structure is summarized in Figure 1.

The Packaging Industry Environment

Packaging is perhaps the major common feature which characterizes all the major players in the sophisticated world of consumer goods in the United States and other developed economies. The top 100 packaged brands in the U.S. consumed $12 billion in containers and packaging materials in 1993 (*Packaging* 1994). The demand for specific types of packaging machinery was derived demand which depends on the demand for the products to be packaged. In addition, machinery demand was also affected by various economic, social, and technological factors.

CONSUMER TRENDS

Consumers want packages to perform several functions. According to a survey conducted in 1993, the most important of those functions were keeping the product in good condition up to the time of purchase (95.8 percent) and keeping the remaining product in good condition after it was opened (78.2 percent) (Baum 1994: 40-43). Packages were also expected to inform the customer, make the product more appealing, and dispense the product to the user.

Figure 1 Packaging Machinery Industry

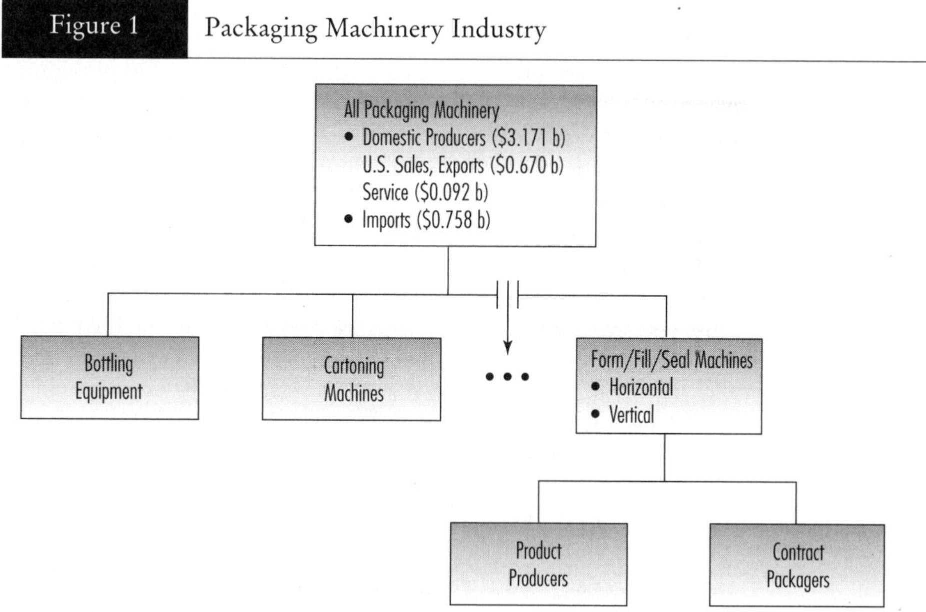

Starting in the 1980s, consumers began to demand increasing convenience in their purchases. There was a sharp growth in the number of products offered in single-serving and convenience packages suitable for microwave cooking, carrying to work, or eating "on the run." Products such as General Foods Lunchables, General Mills Incredibites granola snacks, and single-serving brick packs of Hi C and other fruit drinks were representative of this trend. However, in the 1990s, consumer attitudes concerning the need for convenient packages changed somewhat. The number of consumers desiring single-serving packages fell by nearly 50 percent. The proportion of consumers who wished to prepare a product in its package or consume it from the package similarly fell from 26 percent of the population to roughly 15 percent (Baum 1994: 41).

While the demand for convenience had abated somewhat, there was evidence of increasing demand for resealable packages. General Foods Post cereals division won an award for its resealable cereal package. Sixty percent of the consumers responding to a 1992 survey reported that they would switch brands to get a resealable package ("Studying the Form" 1992). This trend represented the addition of value to the concept of convenience. Resealable packages reduced spoilage, while permitting consumers to use only what they needed.

In the early 1990s many consumers began to look for the cost savings associated with large bulk packages. Distributors such as Sam's Club and many supermarket chains began to stock an increasing variety of family-size and bulk packaged goods. In addition to value, bulk packaging could reduce package waste, and about one-third of consumers said they would buy bulk packages to achieve waste reduction (Baum 1994: 42).

ECONOMIC FACTORS

The consumer packaged goods segments involving form-fill-seal packages included items such as candy, snack foods, convenience foods in single-serving boil-in-bags, microwave products such as popcorn, single-serving fruit drinks, and premium side dish products. Although convenience foods clearly became a part of everyday life in the 1990s, they were relatively expensive compared to cooking "from scratch." In times of economic weakness, the demand for these foods could decline. Similarly, snack foods, while consumed widely, could not only stress the family budget, but might also be viewed as undesirable by health-conscious families, resulting in reduced sales growth for these foods. These economic factors may have contributed to a rise in bulk size packages. However, while bulk packages were made on form-fill-seal equipment, the number of packaging units was smaller with bulk packages, reducing unit sales growth. Further, after 1989, the number of people who felt packaging was contributing increasingly to product costs rose. By the mid-1990s, more than 80 percent felt they were paying more for packaging in the 1990s than they had been in the past (Baum 1994: 43).

SOCIAL FACTORS

In the late 1980s and through the early and mid-1990s, a growing concern for the state of the natural environment began to exert a strong influence on the packaging industry. A major component of the trash deposited into landfills across the country was packaging material. As landfills began to fill, there was increasing concern over how to dispose of package materials. In one survey, more than half of all consumers felt that foods, cosmetics, and pharmaceuticals were overpackaged (Baum 1994: 42). This led to several critical trends. Consumers wanted packages that could be recycled. A 1990 consumer survey reported that 75 percent of respondents said they were trying to buy products with recyclable packages and recycle the waste material ("Environmental Concern" 1991). In addition, between one-third and one-half of all consumers would buy bulk packages and/or concentrated products, and reject products that appeared to be "overpackaged" to reduce waste (referred to as "source reduction") (Baum 1994: 42).

TECHNOLOGICAL FACTORS

The demand for waste reduction, coupled with rising energy costs, encouraged the development of new packaging technologies. In the past many products were packaged in two or three layers of packaging. Many snack foods, for example, often used a simple (form-fill-seal) bag inside a box. However, increasingly, the box and bag were being replaced by a stand-alone bag product with form-fill-seal equipment. Not only did such packages reduce waste by as much as 70 to 80 percent, but they also lowered the use of energy and of natural resources such as trees, the cost of materials, and inventory. Further, stand-alone bags could be shipped in less space than rigid containers which contained more air. This lowered shipping costs and the use of energy resources. Flexible, stand-alone form-fill-seal packages were used for chemicals, household liquids, and other similar products, as well as for food products.

A critical factor affecting expansion in the use of flexible film-based packaging was the development of appropriate films. Although flexible packages provided many benefits, their use could result in reduced shelf life, increased product damage, and other undesirable consequences. These problems were reduced by improvements in film technology. Glass barrier films, complex multilayer laminates, polyolefin, and other materials were emerging as solutions to such problems. However, the new materials were more costly and, because they were difficult to recycle and not readily biodegradable, posed new environmental problems In spite of these drawbacks, the demand for these films was still expected to rise 12 percent per year through 1996, when total film demand was expected to be 11 billion pounds ("Researcher Sees the Demand" 1991).

While some products can be packaged and used without rigid boxes or outer packages, some types of liquids cannot. For these packaging problems, the industry developed the "exchange pouch." This system consisted of a rigid, reusable container which held a pouch of liquid. As the liquid was consumed, only the pouch had to be discarded. It was then replaced with an exchange pouch pierced by a spout inside the rigid container. This system could reduce material costs by as much as 30 percent over more conventional designs.

Important components of the packaging process other than the packaging itself included sterilizing, weighing, measuring, and checking the contents of packages.

These additional functions were especially critical for controlling costs, enhancing quality, and reducing contamination, and began to require increasingly sophisticated computer controls and sensor devices.

PRODUCT DEMAND

In general, the packaging of liquid products, especially household cleaning preparations, was expected to create the most demand for flexible packaging through the mid-1990s. Drackett adopted flexible pouch packages for Windex, and firms like Du Pont, S. C. Johnson, Colgate, and Procter & Gamble introduced products in that type of packaging, especially in Canada. It was estimated that North America used 270 billion containers for liquid in 1991 in the dairy, beverage, chemical, food, and personal care markets. Pouches were expected to take as much as 10 percent of this market over the long term ("Pouch Packaging" 1992).

Snack food growth also influenced the demand for flexible packaging. Snack food volume grew at an increasing rate from 1987 to 1991, achieving 6.3 percent growth in dollars and 4.7 percent in volume in 1991, in spite of the onset of a recession. Frozen foods were a mainstay for flexible package demand for some years. However, in 1991 demand fell 3.2 percent, although long-run demand by institutions and bulk purchasers was expected to raise frozen vegetable output later in the decade. Health concerns and other factors also began to slow the growth in candy demand. A survey in *Candy Industry* noted that demand for new candy packaging equipment in 1992 had fallen from 46 percent of the firms surveyed to 20 percent ("Confectioners Bear Out Bulldog Economy" 1992). Pharmaceuticals were also an important source of packaging machinery demand. Their demand grew at just about 6 percent in 1991. Other users of flexible packaging saw their demand rise at roughly 4 percent during the same period.

While the basic product demand for most users of flexible packaging achieved a growth rate only slightly higher than that of the GNP in the early 1990s, the demand for flexible packaging for liquids pushed the overall industry growth rate to 7 percent. Environmental problems with rigid plastic containers caused them to be replaced with flexible packages for many liquids. By some estimates this trend was expected to cause global demand for pouch packages for liquids to rise 25 percent annually through 1996 ("Design May Be the Key" 1992).

INTERNATIONAL TRENDS

Consumer packaged goods demand was largely centered in the world's developed economies. However, as the developing world became increasingly integrated with the developed world, consumers in large markets such as the former Eastern Bloc countries and China, for example, were expected to demand more packaged goods, and manufacturers of packaging machinery were expected to see demand for their products rise. In China, the largest untapped market in the world, the demand for food and packaging machinery increased by 250 percent between 1990 and 1991. This type of growth was expected to increase as the Chinese government emphasized food production in its 1991-1995 five-year plan ("China" 1991).

It was expected that many less developed countries, in addition to servicing their domestic markets, would attempt to enhance their stock of hard currency by increasing exports. Lower labor costs gave developing nations a natural price advantage, but to succeed in export markets, these countries needed to raise the quality of their packaging to meet the expectations of their prospective customers. One source estimated that shoddy packaging practices cost China roughly $3.7 billion in lost export earnings in 1989 (Saenz 1990: 12-19). The low quality of packaging in China was attributed to the use of largely obsolete machines and poor materials. Quality control was also often poor, giving further impetus to the demand for sophisticated equipment and technical assistance. While government support for equipment imports was limited in the early 1990s, increasing export activity was expected to force the government to enhance their purchasing levels (Saenz 1990: 18).

Exports of U.S. packaging machinery benefited from the increase in the international demand for packaged goods. Exports by industry firms, reported as $486 million in 1989, were expected to rise to $723 million in 1994, representing growth of more than 8.2 percent per year, compounded. However, United States firms were not the only ones who could satisfy this international demand. In fact, imports of packaging machinery by the United States exceeded exports every year from 1989 through 1994, growing at 4.9 percent per year from $597 million in 1989 to an estimated $795 million in 1994 ("Industrial Machinery" 1994).

The VFFS Equipment Segment

The VFFS segment of the packaging machinery industry was generally competitive. Three of the existing firms were relatively large players in the industry, with total sales of at least $50 million (Exhibit 1). Although the size of packaging machinery producers covered a wide range, in 1991, the average producer had sales of just over $6 million and employed just over 60 workers ("Packaging Machinery" 1992: 1313).

PRODUCTS AND PROCESSES

Packaging machines were generally complex, multifunction products. Because customer needs differed, producers, especially smaller producers, often built machines to customer specifications or modified stock designs to meet special needs. Packaging was critical to customer perceptions of product differentiation, causing *innovation* to be critical to package machine design. In addition to providing the user the ability to improve products, innovative machines could provide enhanced quality control or lower the cost of operations, providing the user with competitive advantages. Equipment makers could enhance their own research and development efforts to meet customer needs by forming relationships and alliances with suppliers of machine components or packaging materials, including package films.

In addition to being innovative, it was important that packaging machinery be *flexible,* providing the user with the ability to use the equipment for more than one product or package size. While the ability to change the equipment quickly from one use to another was critical, it was more important to firms trying to control costs than it was for providing product differentiation for the user, so this factor was not as important as innovation. Flexibility was especially important to contract market customers who provided packaging services to many firms.

The materials used in packaging machinery were similar to those used in other complex machine tools, consisting of various kinds of metal stock, castings, motors, hydraulic cylinders, computer control devices, and related parts. While some of these parts were fairly standard and could be obtained from a variety of suppliers, many critical components were highly sophisticated and could only be obtained from a few key suppliers. In 1988, materials comprised 40 percent of sales. Although some of the equipment required to manufacture packaging machinery was complex, the industry was not, generally speaking, capital-intensive, requiring only 32 percent of the capital equipment employed by the average of all manufacturing firms.

The production processes in much of the packaging equipment industry could be characterized as *job shop* or *batch* processes, rather than mass production.[3] Skilled labor was a key component of the production process, making up roughly 31 percent of sales in 1988. Average wages in the industry were relatively high, exceeding the average for all manufacturing by about 20 percent. This premium was partially offset by productivity, however, as the value added per worker exceeded the average of all manufacturing by 8 percent and the cost per employee was only 53 percent of the manufacturing average.

Since the manufacture of machinery did not require a large capital investment, capital was not really a significant entry barrier in this industry, especially for a larger firm in a related industry. The small size of the typical packaging machinery firm made them popular takeover targets, and many were subsidiaries of larger firms. Although such subsidiaries were not large by themselves, there were substantial resources available to many of them. Much of the equipment used in the manufacture of packaging equipment was fairly standard and could be used by other machinery manufacturers. Thus, exit from this business, like entry, was relatively easy.

CUSTOMERS AND MARKETS

Because of changing technology and the relatively small size of most packaging equipment producers, successful packaging machinery firms generally tried to focus on one or more market niches, concentrating on product *differentiation,* rather than cost leadership, as a generic strategy. This factor, which was as important as innovation, required a firm to have a thorough understanding of its customers and a strong research and product development effort to satisfy the needs of those customers.

[3]Data in this section is taken from "Packaging Machinery," *Manufacturing U.S.A.,* 2d ed., ed. A. J. Dalway (Detroit: Gale Research, Inc., 1992), pp. 1313-1316.

These strategies gave package machinery firms increased pricing flexibility, which was critical to small firms, which experienced lower volumes and had more difficulty covering fixed costs than larger firms. When the number of machinery firms in a given niche was small, customers had fewer choices to satisfy their equipment needs. The market for snack food packaging machines, on the other hand, was very competitive because of the relatively small number of customers in a large, attractive market.

Another critical factor, *customer base,* was as important as flexibility for every producer. A firm which could capture one or more large customers who were leaders in their product markets could expect growing demand for its equipment, as well as the prospect of maintenance, parts, and technical service business. Postpurchase activities were critical not only for the equipment maker's reputation, but also to support sales, especially since the machines had a relatively long life. Moreover, having leading firms as customers further enhanced the product reputation of the equipment firm, encouraging other customers to buy. While having large customers was important, many producers tried to satisfy specific market niches. Therefore, the growth of these specific market subsegments was also critical.

There were few substitutes for having the appropriate mix of packaging machinery. However, there were alternative ways to package some products, and this could close some niche producers out of markets for substitute types of equipment. Some products could even be packaged by manual labor, although this was rare even for small regional producers. The primary complementary product for the packaging industry was the film used in the packages, and technological changes in film production had a great influence on technological improvements in packaging as a whole. For this reason, long-term relationships between form-fill-seal equipment firms and film producers were relatively common. Each needed the other for success.

Overall, the segmented nature of the package machinery industry, the relatively low barriers to both entry and exit, and the number of small competitors who must fight to stay in business made the rivalry in this industry moderate overall. Rivalry was intensified in certain segments, such as snack foods, where the customer bargaining power was relatively strong. In general, the high proportion of variable cost, the relatively low levels of operating leverage, the need for R&D spending, and the lack of pricing flexibility in some markets combined to create stress on the profits of equipment producers.

ATTRACTIVENESS OF THE VFFS MARKET

Exhibit 2 shows the results of an analysis of the overall attractiveness of the VFFS market done by a consultant to the management at Kartridg Pak. A five-point rating scale was used for each factor, with all factors receiving equal weight.

The Competition

As noted in Exhibit 1, there were a number of competitors supplying the VFFS machinery market segment in 1992. Six of these competitors are described below.[4]

[4]This competitive analysis was developed by the company's consultant based on public information, interviews with industry insiders, and the results of an extensive market survey conducted by Kartridg Pak.

Exhibit 2 Evaluation of Attractiveness of VFFS Market Segment

Attractiveness Factors	Rating	Comments
Market factors		
Size	4.0	Relatively large segment
Growth	4.0	Faster than GNP
Customer bargaining power	3.0	Snacks a problem
Overseas sales potential	4.0	Europe
Price elasticity	3.0	
Environmental factors		
Speed of change	3.0	
Experience curve effects	4.0	Demand high enough
Rapid product innovation	4.0	
Social factors	5.0	High support for VFFS
Regulatory climate	4.0	
Substitutability	3.0	
Competitive factors		
Industry structure	2.0	3 big competitors
Potential for differentiation	5.0	Function of R&D
Competitive stability	3.0	
Average rating	**3.6+**	

To clarify Kartridg Pak's evaluation of the prospects in the VFFS market, the firm's consultant suggested that management might enhance its understanding of these competitors by evaluating each in relation to the critical success factors influencing the industry.

HAYSSEN

Hayssen, a subsidiary of Bemis Company, a major packaging producer, had total sales of about $50 million, with an estimated $45 million in VFFS sales, the highest in the industry. This translated into a market share in excess of 35 percent. The firm served a variety of markets, with 30 percent of its sales overseas. Hayssen's growth was expected to follow the industry, although the percentage of overseas sales was expected to rise to 35 percent by 1994. Approximately 20 percent of its output was for liquid packaging machines, with the other 80 percent composed of machines for packaging dry products. Hayssen was a major innovator, employing over 100 R&D personnel in its headquarters. The firm also prided itself on the flexibility of its machines, a major factor influencing customer purchases. Hayssen's machines could even be adapted for use in both wet and dry packaging. Hayssen had roughly 2,000 customers, including such major producers as Eagle Snacks (Anheuser Busch) and General Mills. The firm had a strong reputation for quality and engineering, although some felt its start-up training was not always up to expectations. Its prices were in line with the industry average base price of $100,000 per machine. It had strengthened its reputation through an exclusive agreement with a leading Japanese scale manufacturer.

WOODMAN

Woodman was a subsidiary of Kliklok, which also produced packaging machinery. Together, they had sales of $56 million, of which roughly $35 to $40 million was VFFS equipment, giving them a VFFS market share of about 30 percent. They employed about 500 people. Although Woodman produced a variety of packaging machines, including cartoning systems, it had a strong commitment to VFFS machines, especially for the snack market. All of its systems were for the packaging of dry products. Growth was expected to roughly parallel the growth in snack food demand. Woodman was known as an innovative company, with 35 people employed in R&D. Its innovative focus was on whole systems—for example, systems that not only packaged the product, but could also put the packages into cases. Although Woodman's machines were not quite as flexible as those of industry leader Hayssen, they did have the latest computerized controls and their machines could be quickly adjusted for a variety of packaging situations. Woodman's major customers included Frito-Lay. Roughly 65 to 70 percent of sales were overseas, although this proportion was expected to decline to about 50 percent by 1994. Woodman's prices, which were a bit higher than the industry average, were supported by product quality and excellent postpurchase training and service. The firm also permitted customers to try a machine before they bought it, adjusting the machine to meet the customer's specific needs.

TRIANGLE

Triangle was an independent firm with $18 million in overall sales, all of which was in the VFFS market. This gave the firm about a 15 percent market share. Triangle focused on the dry segment of the market, concentrating on pouches for convenience foods and other bag-in-a-box applications such as frozen vegetables, cereals, and pastas. Innovation at Triangle concentrated on two areas: making faster machines and developing improved scales for weighing the material to be packaged. Triangle's developments in scale technology enabled it to sell weighing equipment to other package machinery producers. Triangle approached the question of flexibility by supplying a base machine for which options were available to meet customers' specific needs. This flexibility was increased by Triangle's ability to manufacture its own scales. Triangle served over 5,000 customers, the largest of which was General Mills. Only 10 to 15 percent of Triangle's sales were exported, chiefly to Canada and Mexico. The firm enjoyed only modest growth, including growth in exports. Triangle machines were rated as durable and reliable. It differentiated itself through its scale systems and its start-up services.

PAXALL

Paxall was a subsidiary of a larger machine manufacturer, Sasib Corporation of America. Although Paxall had overall sales of $37 million, its VFFS sales were only about $7 million, giving the firm a market share of slightly less than 6 percent. Paxall produced VFFS machines for both wet and dry applications, with 60 percent of its sales in the former. Its chief markets were for household products and pharmaceutical applications. Paxall supplied a complete line of equipment, scales, and cartoners. Expectations were that Paxall's strong presence in the liquids markets would permit it to achieve higher than average growth. Paxall's focus in innovation was in the extensive use of sophisticated servomotors and user-friendly computer control systems. These systems were considered superior to older technologies based on air and hydraulic cylinders. However, Paxall was not committing R&D resources to the development of improved VFFS machines. Rather, it was concentrating its efforts on other types of packaging equipment. Paxall produced a considerable number of custom machines. In general, its machines were not as flexible as those of its competitors. Paxall had a large number of accounts, although they did not have any very large customers. Their foreign sales were limited to 5 to 10 percent of the total, and growth was expected to be at about the industry average. Paxall's biggest source of differentiation was its ability to customize its machines for specific customer needs. Although they appeared to have a good reputation among their existing customers, they were not widely known outside this group.

W. A. LANE

W. A. Lane had total sales of $7 million, most of which was in the VFFS segment. It employed only about 60 people. In spite of its size, the firm was the leader in machines for liquid applications, with 100 percent of its business in that area. Because of its concentration in the liquid segment, Lane expected growth to be considerably above average in the next few years. In the last two years Lane had concentrated its R&D on the development of highly flexible machines. Its basic line included machines which could package liquid pouches ranging in size from 1 ounce to 5 gallons. This success in innovation greatly improved the firm's reputation for flexibility. Lane had a small customer base with only about 100 customers, several of which were large institutional market packagers. Lane had concentrated primarily on the domestic market, although it expected exports, chiefly to the U.K., to increase to 20 percent of sales by 1994. Lane's chief source of differentiation was found in its expertise for liquid pouch machines, where it was able to command a strong price premium. Its reputation for postpurchase service was also excellent.

PRODO-PAK

Prodo-Pak was the smallest and weakest of the competitors in the VFFS packaging market. It had a market share of only about 5 to 6 percent, with 85 percent of its sales concentrated in the market for liquid applications. Prodo-Pak was not known for innovation, although it had developed machines which provided intermittent motion, allowing more time for sealing the package. This added some flexibility to its machines, along with some ability to make easy changeovers from one application to another. Although it was a small company, Prodo-Pak had numerous customers, mostly small. The firm differentiated itself by having lower prices than its competitors, thereby providing a "bargain" for the small customer who required a relatively unsophisticated machine. Prodo-Pak sold about 20 percent of its output overseas, and sales growth was modest, although future growth might be aided by the firm's concentration on liquid applications. Postpurchase parts service was strong.

KARTRIDG PAK

As one of the largest subsidiaries of BWI, Kartridg Pak (KP) played a key role in the overall firm's sales, growth, and profitability. With sales of $25 to $30 million (depending on how the sales of Aerofill were allocated between KP and KP Aerofill), KP made up the bulk of the Food Machinery Division of BWI. KP had four main product lines divided into two groups, food equipment and filling equipment. KP's largest product line was the Chub machine. This machine was a highly versatile system for packaging viscous food or industrial products in flexible film. Two major customer groups for this product were meat processors and explosives manufacturers. Available with capacities to 30,000 pounds per hour, KP's chub machines were able to produce packages ranging in weight from 1 ounce to 30 pounds and ranging in length from 2 to 72 inches.

In addition to the Chub machine, the food equipment line included the Anal-Ray line of fat analyzers. These machines were able to determine, almost instantaneously, the percent of fat in processed meat products. A microprocessor accessory for this machine also calculated the protein and moisture content of meat products. KP's Yieldmaster mechanical deboning systems were designed to remove trimmed or untrimmed meat from the bones of beef, pork, goat, mutton, lamb, poultry, or fish. The fourth product in KP's food equipment line was a smoke generator. This machine produced wood smoke to finish processed meat products. The KP smoke generator allowed precise control of smoking time, color, and flavor.

The filling equipment product line included two major product groups, aerosol packing equipment and liquid filling equipment. The Aerosol packing equipment included a complete line of machines offering capacities of more than 450 containers per minute. The liquid filling product group included a variety of piston-driven filling machines which filled containers with liquid products in precise amounts. The base machine handled self-supporting containers of up to 32 ounces at rates up to 25 containers per filling head per minute. A filling machine could be fitted with from 3 to 24 heads, giving a total capacity of over 600 containers per minute. A rotary, gravity-driven machine with an available pressurized loading bowl provided an alternative to the piston-driven line.

In addition to these major product lines, KP also supplied testing and other accessory machines and tortilla folders. Exhibit 3 presents the analysis provided by the company's consultant of the market attractiveness of the four major product lines produced by Kartridg Pak. For this analysis each attractiveness factor was given equal weight, and "5" represented a "Very Attractive" rating.

Exhibit 3 Evaluation of Attractiveness of Kartridg Pak Product Lines

Attractiveness Factor	Chub Machine	Anal-Ray	Yieldmaster	Aerosol Products
Market factors				
Size	2.0	4.0	2.0	4.0
Growth	2.0	2.0	2.0	4.0
Customer bargaining power	4.0	3.0	3.0	3.0
Overseas sales potential	4.0	4.0	2.0	3.0
Price elasticity	3.0	4.0	2.0	4.0
Environmental factors				
Speed of change	4.0	3.0	3.0	3.0
Experience curve effects	3.0	3.0	3.0	4.0
Rapid product innovation	3.0	3.0	3.0	3.0
Social factors	2.0	3.0	3.0	2.0
Regulatory climate	2.0	2.0	2.0	1.0
Substitutability	3.0	3.0	3.0	2.0
Competitive factors				
Industry structure	5.0	4.0	4.0	4.0
Potential for differentiation	4.0	4.0	2.0	4.0
Competitive stability	2.0	3.0	3.0	3.0
Average rating	**3.1**	**3.2**	**2.6**	**3.1**
Estimated ranking in sales contribution to KP	**1**	**3–4**	**3–4**	**2**

The biggest product line for KP in 1992 was the Chub machine. The strongest aspect of the industry for this product was the relatively small number of competitors. The lack of competition had reduced price sensitivity, compared to the firm's other markets. A slowdown in growth in the 1990s was largely offset by replacement and overseas sales. The company entered the Chinese market and, as a result, KP's overseas sales rose from 30 to 60 percent of the firm's total sales in 1992.

The strongest market served by KP was the market for fat analyzers. Although this market was large, its growth potential was not strong. This slow growth reduced the rate of technological change, permitting the firm to allocate R&D resources elsewhere. However, the reduced risk of obsolescence for customers also served to depress growth in demand.

The weakest market for KP was the market for deboning equipment. This market had low growth and restricted overseas potential. It also offered little opportunity to differentiate or innovate. This reduced technological threats, but also limited the advantage for competitive opportunities.

KP's aerosol line was strong, with good market prospects. The problem in this market was the need to overcome environmental problems associated with traditional propellants. The competitive structure of the aerosol market was favorable, and this market had the potential to become much more attractive if new, safe propellants could be developed. If not, potential users were likely to turn away from traditional pressurized aerosol containers.

STRATEGIES AND ISSUES[5]

Kartridg Pak employed several strategies to enhance its performance and reputation. First and foremost, KP focused on the production of high-quality packaging machines. KP also tried to design products that were relatively easy to use, flexible, and relatively fast. These characteristics were intended to increase customer productivity and allow the customer to reduce costs.

KP's products were distributed through a strong dealer network based on long-term relationships. In addition to its U.S. dealers, KP worked through 23 dealers in all parts of the world to distribute its products in Japan and the Far East, South Africa, Europe, Israel, Egypt, and South and Central America. This overseas dealer network, coupled with the firm's recent presence in China and its British parent, had the potential to make the firm a strong international player. The firm's dealer network, coupled with quality replacement parts, had helped it develop a strong reputation for postpurchase service. The firm's service reputation was also supported by a strong technical staff which provided customers with quality installation and a quick startup for new equipment. KP's market success and the resources of BWI provided the firm with a potentially strong financial base.

KP was historically a strong player in its current market niche, the meat segment of the food industry. However, packaging equipment had a relatively long life (some machines lasted 20 years or more). Further, if a machine was not obsolete, or did not reduce its user's competitiveness, its life could often be prolonged through maintenance and repair, especially when quality, factory-built spare parts were available. Both theses factors had resulted in market saturation in this niche, and growth had slowed, reducing the demand for KP's products.

Although KP's dealer network was strong, its sales force was relatively small and all sales personnel were stationed in the home office in Davenport, Iowa. One of the most important considerations in the competitive strength of packaging machine producers was product development and innovation. Because it concentrated on the meat industry, KP tended to focus on accessories and features, rather than significant innovations. Further, some industry insiders felt the firm's strength in its primary market tended to dampen its competitive drive.

BWI GROUP

Kartridg Pak's parent firm of BWI Group was Barry Wehmiller International PLC (BWI) located in Altrincham, Cheshire, England. BWI was a multiunit packaging machinery company which consisted of six subsidiary companies, divided into three divisions: the Vision Division, the Food Equipment Division, and the General Packaging Division. BWI reported total sales of slightly less than £74,000,000 in 1992 (see the financial statements in Exhibit 4).

---

[5]The information for this section was based largely on a customer survey commissioned by the firm.

Exhibit 4 Selected Financial Information for BWI and Kartridg Pak for Fiscal Years July 31, 1991, to July 31, 1992

BWI AND KARTRIDG PAK
Income Statement
July 31, 1991–July 31, 1992
(Amounts in Thousands of Pounds)

		1992		1991
Sales		73,699		75,358
Vision division	18,154		17,415	
Food equipment	16,949		17,403	
General packaging	38,596		40,540	
	73,699		75,358	
By origin				
United Kingdom	39,081		44,375	
North America	34,618		30,983	
	73,699		75,358	
By destination				
U.K.	22,485		28,434	
Europe	14,269		17,074	
North America	21,683		17,046	
Central and South America	3,560		1,931	
Middle East	2,822		1,569	
Africa	2,529		2,918	
Asia	5,463		5,014	
Australia	888		1,372	
	73,699		75,358	
Cost of sales		49,162		49,139
Gross profit		24,537		26,219
Operating Expenses		18,122		20,091
Distribution costs	5,141		6,950	
Administration				
Depreciation	1,219		1,295	
R&D	2,235		2,531	
Other	9,527		9,315	
	18,122		20,091	
Operating income		6,415		6,128
Vision division	670		(1,633)	
Food equipment	3,489		4,221	
General packaging	2,256		3,540	
	6,415		6,128	
Other (expense)		133		(1,099)
Income before taxes	6,548	5,029		
Taxes		1,594		1,191
Net income		4,954		3,838

Note: To convert these statements to dollars use the following assumptions:

	Year End	*Average Last 12 Months*
7/31/1991	£1 = $1.66	£1 = $1.73
7/31/1992	£1 = $1.90	£1 = $1.78

Exhibit 4 *(continued)*

BWI AND KARTRIDG PAK
Income Statement
July 31, 1991–July 31, 1992
(Amounts in Thousands of Pounds)

		1992		1991
Current assets	49,332		41,364	
Fixed assets	8,990		10,262	
		58,322		51,626
Current debt	23,764		29,182	
Long-term debt	6,373		5,820	
Equity	28,185		16,624	
		58,322		51,626

Note: To convert these statements to dollars use the following assumptions:

	Year End	*Average Last 12 Months*
7/31/1991	**£1 = $1.66**	**£1 = $1.73**
7/31/1992	**£1 = $1.90**	**£1 = $1.78**

The Vision Division consisted of BWI Index which produced vision, inspection, and process control machines for glass and plastic container manufacturers; food, beverage, and pharmaceutical companies; and other producers of consumer goods. These products were used to inspect both the containers and their contents during the packaging process.

The Food Machinery Division of BWI consisted of two subsidiaries: Kartridg Pak and Fords. Fords manufactured filling, sealing, and end-of-line packaging machines for the food, dairy, pharmaceutical, cosmetics, household, and automotive care industries. The product line included cup and tray filling/sealing machines, heat sealing machinery, capping/lidding equipment, and container handling equipment. Kartridg Pak manufactured a range of packaging and process equipment for the food and meat industries. Products included fat analyzers, deboning equipment, Chub packaging machines, smoke generators, and tortilla folders.

The General Packaging Division was BWI's largest division, contributing just over half of the firm's sales and about 35 percent of its profits in 1992. The division consisted of three subsidiaries: Manesty, Dawson, and KP Aerofill. Manesty produced machinery to make tablets and similar products for the pharmaceutical, household products, and confectionery industries. Dawson produced machinery for container handling and bottling for the dairy, brewing, soft drink, food, pharmaceutical, and other industries. KP Aerofill manufactured machines to fill aerosol containers for the cosmetic, pharmaceutical, and health care industries. The product lines included liquid fillers, propellant fillers, testing equipment, and valve assembly and related machines. General Packaging was relatively new and combined existing resources of Kartridg Pak and what was formerly BWI Aerofill.

The Future

As the financial statements in Exhibit 4 illustrate, BWI experienced a number of changes from 1991 to 1992. Growth in Kartridg Pak's primary market, meat processing, slowed dramatically, and both sales and profits for BWI's Food Equipment Division declined in 1992. In late 1992 and early 1993, management began to consider various options to enhance performance.

One strategy considered by KP was entry into new markets. Because of its relative attractiveness, one market considered for entry was the VFFS machinery market. KP felt it had three options:

- *Develop a base machine for the VFFS market in-house.* This option would enable the firm to establish its own name in the market. KP felt it could develop such a machine and seek a competitive advantage based on quality, speed, support, and flexibility. Management felt the new product could be designed and introduced in 18 to 24 months, although some of the company's lower-level personnel felt development time might be significantly less.
- *Acquire an existing liquid-focus manufacturer.* Liquid pouch packaging was the hottest area in the VFFS market. By acquiring an existing liquid-focus firm, entry into this market could be accomplished very quickly. The size of the market, coupled with its projected high growth rates, might reduce potential competitive pressures, at least for the time required to assimilate the acquisition. If KP made such an acquisition, divisional resource limitations might limit the size of the acquisition. Regardless of which firm KP chose to acquire, it was likely some key personnel would have to move to KP's headquarters in Davenport. Failure to attract these people could cause problems with any prospective merger.
- *Acquire an existing dry-focus manufacturer.* This option was attractive because, although expected growth in the dry packaging market was slower than for liquids, the market was bigger, and the immediate gains for KP could be larger.

In addition to the factors noted above, several other considerations might influence the decision to enter the VFFS market. If this market were, in fact, larger than some of the more conservative estimates, other competitors might choose to enter the market. Early in 1993, President Clinton had just been inaugurated and his impact on economic conditions was unknown. Because the companies KP might choose to acquire were privately held or divisions of other companies, they might not be available for acquisition. Furthermore, the cost of such an acquisition might be difficult to estimate. Profits of such firms might range from 2 to 3 percent of sales to 6 to 7 percent after tax. Mature manufacturing firms might command prices ranging from as little as 8 times earnings to as much as 15 times earnings or more.

Another issue faced by KP and its industry competitors was an increasing emphasis on quality. The advent of ISO 9000 (an international process standard related to quality) as a de facto quality standard was forcing firms to make a choice about whether or not to seek conformity with this standard, especially if they wanted to do significant business with major firms in the United States and firms overseas. Seeking ISO 9000 certification was an expensive, time-consuming process. KP and Paxall had started to seek ISO certification by early 1992, although Hayssen had not.

KP had alternatives to entering the VFFS market. It could leave the entry decision to the managers of BWI and concentrate on its existing business. KP's recent gains in sales to China, and the expansion of its overseas markets, especially with the need for development in Eastern Europe, might offer all the opportunities the firm could handle at this point. After all, the effort required to develop a new VFFS machine, or assimilate an acquisition, could be expended to develop the firm's existing markets. Many manufacturing businesses were expanding sales by reengineering their manufacturing and sales organizations and developing strategies based on an increased customer orientation. These firms realized that they could increase their own sales by helping their customers to develop an enhanced competitive position. These options, too, would require resources and KP would have to determine whether it could afford to do any of this. KP had many choices. The firm knew it would probably have to do something. What it should do and when was the question.

References

C. Baum. "Consumers Want It All—and Now." *Packaging,* August 1994, pp. 40-43.

"China to Hold International Food Machine Exposition." Xinhua General News Service, November 21, 1991.

"Confectioners Bear Out Bulldog Economy in Poll." *Candy Industry,* November 1992. pp. 32-38.

"Design May Be the Key to U.S. Business for the Flexible Pouch." *Modern Plastics International,* February 1992, pp. 20-23.

"Environmental Concern: Consumers Say They'll Buy Recyclables, Concentrates." *Packaging,* August 1991, p. 1.

"Industrial Machinery." *U.S. Industrial Outlook 1994,* Washington, D.C.: U.S. Department of Commerce 1994, p. 17-10.

"Meeting of Minds by Leading Analysts Leads to Realistic Composite Outlook." *Packaging,* April 1990, pp. 32-43.

Packaging. Special Report, January 1994, p. 37.

"Packaging Machinery." In *Manufacturing U.S.A.,* 2d ed., ed. A. J. Dalway. Detroit: Gale Research, Inc., 1992, p. 1314.

"Pouch Packaging." *Modern Plastics International,* June 1992, pp. 30-31.

"Researcher Sees the Demand for Film Hitting 11 Billion Pounds by '96." *Packaging,* August 1991, p. 1.

H. Saenz. "Overwrapped and Underprotected." *The China Business Review,* September/October, 1990.

"Studying the Form." *Packaging Today,* October 1992, pp. 53-58.

Case 17

Ethical Dilemmas in Business Marketing

Individuals in marketing and sales positions are frequently confronted by ethical problems and dilemmas. The scenarios presented below were real situations faced by individuals during their first year on the job after graduation from college. After reading each scenario you should decide what action you would have taken.

1. I presently sell a line of industrial compressors to customers and the standard sales pitch indicates that they are the best for the money available in the market. Unfortunately, I also know that this isn't true. However, they make up 40 percent of my line and I cannot successfully make my quota without selling at least $85,000 worth per month. It's probably okay, because all salespersons say theirs are the best.
Would you take the same selling approach?

2. My field sales manager drinks excessively and has accompanied me on sales calls hung over and smelling of alcohol. This behavior does not enhance my professional reputation with my customers or the company. I have decided not to say anything, as the field sales manager writes my review and can dramatically influence my success or failure in this, my first selling assignment.
Would you report the sales manager to upper level management?

3. I am working for a large company which is heavily involved in defense contracts. I have recently been transferred to a new division that builds nuclear weapons. These are weapons of which the public is not aware and of which I do not personally approve. However, our work is entirely legal and classified top secret. I have decided to stay with the company because I find my work challenging and I am not directly involved with any phase of the actual nuclear component of the project.
If you had similar attitudes, would you stay with the company?

Source: These scenarios were developed by Professor John B. Gifford and Jan Willem Bol, Miami University. They were part of a study of the ethical problems recent business school graduates faced on their first job.

4. I recently had the opportunity to buy a new ... computer, printer, and software for $1000 from our MIS Director. He apparently received these items "free" with a large computer order for the company. I would be doing mostly work for the company at home on the computer. I decided to accept his offer and paid him $1000 cash.
What action would you have taken?

5. After a business dinner with an important client in California, he implied that he wanted to go out and "do the town" plus.... Although I wasn't sure what the "plus" might involve, there was a 50/50 chance he wanted an affair on the side. I said I was tired, and retired alone for the evening. I also lost the account which had been a 90 percent sure thing.
What action would you have taken?

6. By coincidence, your salesperson and your distributor are both pitching your product to the same prospect. The distributor, however, does not know this yet. You know that when he finds out he will offer a competitor's product that will most certainly undercut your price. Your salesperson is totally dependent on commission.
Should you ask your salesperson to back off?

7. A buyer for a large government institution (a good prospect with potentially high volume) offers you information about the sealed bids of competitors. You know the practice is questionable, but he is a good friend and no one is likely to find out. Besides, you are below quota, and need the commission badly.
Will you accept his offer?

8. An industrial customer has indicated that our lubricants were priced about 5 percent higher than those being offered by our competition. He indicated that if I would drop my price 7 ½ percent, he would cancel his order with our competition and buy from me. This will mean a $1,400 commission for me personally. I agreed.
What action would you have taken?

9. As an industrial salesperson, you are in the office of a prospect to provide a verbal price on a project. You and your sales manager have determined that a specific price is the right price for your organization and you believe you will win the contract. However, as the prospect walks out of his office you see a copy of your competitor's proposal on his desk with a substantially lower price. You will need to give him your price now, as he walks back into the room.
Will you change your price?

10. I have a set quota of goods that I must sell every month. Sometimes it becomes necessary to overstock my customers in order to meet my quota. Most of the customers are not very sophisticated, and don't even know how much inventory they should carry.
Is this an appropriate sales tactic?

NAME INDEX

SUBJECT INDEX

Bold indicates key terms